The Thomas Guide®

Pacific Northwest
road atlas

Contents

Cover photo: Deer on hillside at Ecola State Park. © Craig Tuttle/CORBIS.
Interior Photo Credits: Page D Ann Manner/Getty Images. Page E Michael
Masters/Columbia River Maritime Museum (mb); Page F Lincoln City Visitor and
Convention Bureau (l); remaining photos Oregon Tourism Commission.

PageFinder™ Map   U.S. Patent No. 5,419,586
                   Canadian Patent No. 2,116,425
                   Patente Mexicana No. 188186

⬥ RAND McNALLY

Rand McNally Consumer Affairs
P.O. Box 7600
Chicago, IL 60680-9915

randmcnally.com

For comments or suggestions
please call (800) 777-MAPS (-6277)
or email us at:
consumeraffairs@randmcnally.com

General Information

HIGHWAY PATROL

British Columbia	In case of emergency, call 911
Washington State	In case of emergency, call 911
Oregon State	In case of emergency, call 911
Idaho State	In case of emergency, call 911

ROAD CONDITIONS

British Columbia	British Columbia Ministry of Transportation and Highways: (800) 550-4997 www.drivebc.ca
Washington State	Washington State Department of Transportation: (800) 695-7623 www.wsdot.wa.gov
Oregon State	Salem Online: (503) 588-6161 www.oregonlink.com
Idaho State	itd.idaho.gov

DEPARTMENT OF TRANSPORTATION

British Columbia	BC Ministry of Transportation & Highways: (800) 550-4997 www.drivebc.ca
Washington State	Washington State Department of Transportation: (800) 695-7623 www.wsdot.wa.gov
Oregon State	Oregon Department of Transportation: (888) 275-6368 www.odot.state.or.us
Idaho State	Idaho State Department of Transportation: (208) 334-8000 www.state.id.us

FERRY CROSSING

British Columbia	BC Ferries' Corporate Marketing Group: (888) 223-3779 www.bcferries.bc
Washington State	Washington State Department of Transportation: (206) 464-6400 Toll free in state: (888) 808-7977 or (800) 843-3779 www.wsdot.wa.gov/ferries

CROSSING THE BORDER

British Columbia	Revenue Canada: (800) 461-9999 www.cbsa-asfc.gc.ca
Washington State	U.S. Customs: (206) 553-0770 www.customs.ustreas.gov

WEATHER CONDITIONS

British Columbia	www.cnn.com/WEATHER
Washington State	www.weather.com
Oregon State	www.weather.com
Idaho State	www.weather.com

VISITOR'S INFORMATION

Tourism British Columbia	British Columbia Visitor's Information: (800) 435-5622 www.tourismvancouver.com
Washington State Tourism	(800) 544-1800 www.experiencewashington.com
Oregon Tourism Commission	(800) 547-7842 www.traveloregon.com
Idaho Tourism	(800) 847-4843 www.visitid.org

A Pacific Northwest *passage*

A Best of the Road™ trip

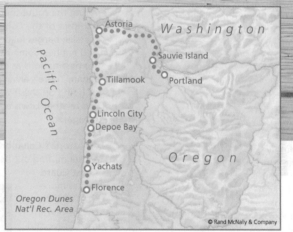

Twilight at Cannon Beach

Curvy roads along Oregon's Columbia River and coast cut through mountain tunnels and snake from deep woods to scenic overlooks. Ocean waves crash at the base of jagged cliffs, and dense forests loom over nearly every bend in the highway. There's no doubt this route from Portland to Astoria to Florence is breathtaking, but it's also just plain fun to drive. Car commercial fantasies aside, this road trip promises herbal wonders, whale-watching spots, fiery furnace art, and haunted tales, too.

The Portland skyline is dwarfed by the majesty of Mt. Hood.

The trip begins in Portland's trendy **Pearl District**, where shopping reigns. Countless turn-of-the-century warehouses have been converted into home décor shops, loft apartments, brewpubs, and art galleries. Head toward NW Glisan and 12th streets on the first Thursday night of each month, when neighborhood galleries host open houses. On rainy days, the magical and whimsical **Lux Lighting store** offers a healthy dose of light. Thousands of decorative lamps are on display, including a four-bug set of dragonflies, a yellow tractor, and a $9,000 magic carpet made of hand-blown Italian glass.

Not too many tourists make their way into the laid-back bohemian **Belmont District** on the city's west side. But it's absolutely worth the trip. Here, residents hang out in coffeehouses or pick up loose tea leaves at **The Leaf Room**,

Portland and its neighborhoods are walkable.

whose owners also run the tea room in Portland's popular **Classical Chinese Garden**. Copper and silver jars behind the counter hold 120 varieties of tea, their competing aromas filling the air.

Just outside city limits, the road leads to **Sauvie Island**. There's so much farmland here, nearly every stretch of the old road is marked with some sort of muddy tractor tread. The island is home to the **Blue Heron Herbary**. More than 300 types of herbs grow in these lush aromatic gardens open March through October. The owner actually invites visitors to pinch, sniff, or graze anything he grows, and that includes the chocolate mint and lavender. Near the play area and kids' garden, doves coo and laugh, cats play hide-and-seek, and bunnies nuzzle into petting hands.

The beautifully desolate road that leads to Oregon's coast is wedged between the Columbia River to the north and a woodsy mountain range to the south. One minute the sun may shine brightly, then in a flash it's lost somewhere behind a torrential downpour. Depending on the day, the sky's dramatic changes can be the most noteworthy highlight along Highway 30, which is sparsely populated with mom-and-pop grocery stores and motor inns.

There are a number of marinas along the Columbia River.

Along the route there are a few good glimpses of the **Columbia River**. Tugs pull massive barges loaded with wheat, corn, and lumber. Some cargo ships are bound for destinations as distant as Pakistan or Japan. There's always river traffic coming or going on these waters that explorers Meriwether Lewis and William Clark once navigated.

At Astoria's **Columbia River Maritime Museum**, find out how and why the Coast Guard makes more than 400 rescues a year in the "Graveyard of the Pacific" just downriver from the museum. One surround-sound exhibit depicts a treacherous rescue scene, with a 44-foot lifeboat working its way through a 20-foot swell.

The night sky accents the architecture of Astoria's Columbia River Maritime Museum.

Docked outside is the **Lightship Columbia**, a National Historic Landmark. The ship was once an anchored beacon at the mouth of the Columbia.

On the outskirts of town is the **Fort Clatsop National Memorial**, part of Lewis and Clark National Historical Park. It is where Lewis and Clark spent the winter of 1805-1806. Costumed interpreters demonstrate candle making and gun

Fort Clatsop National Memorial includes many early 19th-century reconstructions..

firing each summer and tell stories of events that occurred there. Year-round, visitors can tour the fort or museum and see an original dugout canoe. Eagles occasionally make an appearance at the canoe landing.

Drive south on **coastal Highway 101** to **Cannon Beach**, an oceanside resort town. Even before you reach the quaint shopping village, you'll see an unmistakable bullet-shaped seastack pointing up through the ocean mist: **Haystack Rock**. In town, gift shops and specialty stores abound. Extra special: ExploraStore, a one-of-a-kind toy and gadget store for kids and adults. Bubblegum-making kits, Noah's Ark origami, and fun glowing things are part of the unique assortment.

Small, weathered towns dot the highway. Some are so tiny you can hold your breath as you pass through – even at a 30 mph speed limit. In Tillamook County, cows actually outnumber people. But expect long lines at the **Tillamook County Creamery Association**, where throngs of visitors press against the glass and watch cheese being made. Cheese samples are free and the deliciously rich ice cream cones are $1.35. It's recommended to finish your scoops of root beer or banana-split flavored ice cream before walking outside to the parking lot, which is often downwind from the cows.

For lighthouses, state parks with rain forests, and spectacular views, follow the signs to **Three Capes Scenic Drive**. This bumpy detour hugs the coastline while Highway 101 cuts through pastures. At seaside, pelicans, herons, and other shore birds swoop and mingle on the tidal flats. Ambitious hikers will find panoramic vistas atop secluded rocky bluffs.

A kite festival on the beach near Lincoln City.

In **Lincoln City**, colorful kites and windsocks are everywhere, and whirling wildly. They sail high on beaches and whip along busy thoroughfares here on the windy 45th parallel. Choose from nearly 8,000 different types of wind catchers at **Catch the Wind**. The kite store's mélange of hues and choices is dizzying. Lucky for novices, small drawings and descriptions that hang on store walls explain each type of kite and its history, along with the kind of wind and flying line that are needed.

Visitors take a seat on a well-worn church pew by the fiery 2,150° F furnace at the **Alder House III** in Lincoln City to watch glassblowers at work. As the artisans blow, twirl, and shape pieces in the smoldering "glory hole," they explain each step of the process. The gallery's top-selling items include Japanese fishing net floats ($28-$65 each), replicas

Fishing net floats are favorite keepsakes from the Glass Festival in Lincoln City.

of the ones that would wash ashore years ago. During the annual **Glass Festival**, which stretches from October through May, multicolored floats are hidden for beachcombers to discover. Although much of Oregon's shoreline butts sheer rock faces, the central coast boasts long sandy beaches and tidepools. But the **Yaquina Head** Outstanding Natural Area tidepools in **Quarry Cove** near Newport are unique; they're fully accessible for wheelchairs and strollers. Paved pathways slope right into the water filled with green anemones, spiky purple sea urchins, and hermit crabs. Those in search of drier pursuits can try Yaquina Head's interpretive center or lighthouse, which sit atop the basaltic rock that was once quarried here.

Oregon's central coast is more sandy than rocky.

The view from **Heceta Head**, or any overlook around Yachats for that matter, is what Oregon guidebooks are made of. Many visitors trek up the stairs to the top of **Heceta Head Lighthouse**, the state's most famous lighthouse. But a fascinating alternative is a tour in summer of the Heceta Head Light Keeper's House, the historic and reportedly haunted home where lighthouse keepers and their

Heceta Head Lighthouse is the state's most famous.

families once lived. Guides tell captivating stories about the daily lives of the families and of their spirits that some say still roam the cliffside home, now a beautifully restored bed and breakfast (with amazing views out every window).

The Oregon Dunes National Recreation Area in nearby Florence is no stranger to view-seekers either. **Sandland Adventures** rents single-seat dune buggies for a speedy delivery to the summit, and the more relaxed group tour is in a giant buggy. No promises on covering all 40 miles of this grainy paradise, but at least you'll make a dent.

It pays to plan sunsets wisely while on the coast, especially at the dunes. That way a slow-motion sprint to the top of a sandy ridge won't be for nothing. After all, few spots rival this for the best place to eke out the last moments of an Oregon vacation.

For additional information

Alder House III
611 Immonen Rd
Lincoln City, OR 97637
(541) 996-2483
www.alderhouse.com

Blue Heron Herbary
27731 NW Reeder Rd
Sauvie Island, OR 97231
(503) 621-1457
www.blueheronherbary.com

Catch the Wind
240 SE Hwy 101
Lincoln City, OR 97367
(541) 994-9500 or
(800) 227-7878
www.catchthewind.com

Columbia River Maritime Museum
1792 Marine Dr
Astoria, OR 97103
(503) 325-2323
www.crmm.org

ExploraStore
164 North Hemlock
Cannon Beach, OR 97110
(503) 436-1844
www.explorastore.com

Fort Clatsop National Memorial
92343 Fort Clatsop Rd
Astoria, OR 97103
(503) 861-2471
www.nps.gov/focl

Haystack Rock
Cannon Beach Info Center
Cannon Beach, OR 97110
(503) 436-2623
www.cannonbeach.org/main/haystackrock.html

Heceta Head Light Keeper's House
92072 Hwy 101 South
Yachats, OR 97498
(541) 547-3696 or
(866) 547-3696
www.hecetalighthouse.com

The Leaf Room
3430 SE Belmont St
Portland, OR 97214
(503) 736-0119
www.teamuse.com

Lux Lighting
1333 NW Glisan
Portland, OR 97209-2716
(503) 299-6754
www.luxlights.com

Oregon Dunes National Recreation Area
855 Hwy Ave
Reedsport, OR 97467
(503) 271-3611 (Visitor Center, Oregon Dunes)
(541) 750-7000 (Siuslaw National Forest)
www.fs.fed.us/r6/siuslaw

Sandland Adventures
85366 Highway 101 South
Florence, OR 97439
(541) 997-8087
www.sandland.com

Tillamook County Creamery Association
4175 Hwy 101 North
Tillamook, OR 97141
Phone: (503) 815-1300
www.tillamookcheese.com

Yaquina Head Outstanding Natural Area
750 NW Lighthouse Dr
Newport, OR 97365
(541) 574-3100
www.yaquinalights.org

Plus:

Oregon Tourism Commission
(800) 547-7842
www.traveloregon.com

Visit the Oregon Coast
(541) 574-2679
www.VisitTheOregonCoast.com

Using Your Road Atlas

City Listings

- The Cities and Communities Index on page J includes all communities large or small. County, page number, and grid location for each are listed.

- Find the community you're looking for in the list, then turn to the page number indicated.

Index

- Street listings are separate from points of interest.

- In the street listings, read across for city, state, page number, and grid reference.

- Points of interest include campgrounds, ski areas, and more.

- The grid reference, a letter-number combination such as D6, tells where on the map to find a listing.

STREET		
City	State	Page-Grid
DAVENPORT CREEK RD		
SAN LUIS OBISPO CO CA		. . . 271-D6
DAVID AV		
MONTEREY CO CA		. . . . 337-E4
PACIFIC GROVE CA		. . . . .337-D5

FEATURE NAME		
City	State	Page-Grid
1000 STEPS CO BCH		
PACIFIC COAST HWY, LAGUNA BEACH CA		365-G10
ALISO BEACH		
S COAST HWY, LAGUNA BEACH CA		365-F9
ANCHOR MARINA		
1970 TAYLOR RD, CONTRA COSTA CO CA		174-C2

Working with the Maps

- The grid is created by combining letters running along the top of the map with numbers running along the side.

- To use a grid reference, follow the numbered row until it crosses the lettered column.

- To find an adjacent map, turn to the map number indicated on map edges.

- The Legend on page A explains symbols and colors.

Using Four Types of Maps

PageFinder™ Map

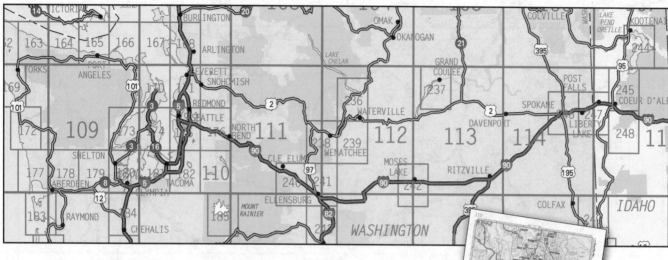

You will find red boxes on many different types of maps in this atlas. Each box indicates an area covered in greater detail on a subsequent page. If your area of interest falls within one of these boxes, turn to the indicated page to view in greater detail.

PageFinder™ Map

- The PageFinder™ map provides an overview of the entire area covered in this atlas.

- Use the PageFinder™ map to guide you to the page(s) showing your general area of interest.

Highway Maps

- Highway maps offer a general view of your area of interest.

- Use Highway maps for long distance planning and navigation.

Metro Maps

- Metro maps offer greater detail than Highway maps and cover major cities and areas of special interest.

- Use Metro maps for navigation within cities and for locating points of interest.

Detail Maps

- Detail maps offer street detail as well as multiple points of interest.

- Use Detail maps for local planning and navigation and for locating many points of interest.

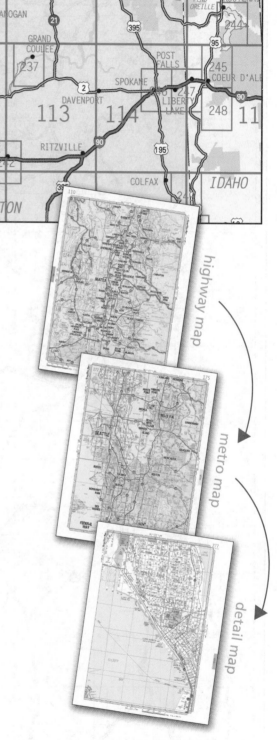

highway map

metro map

detail map

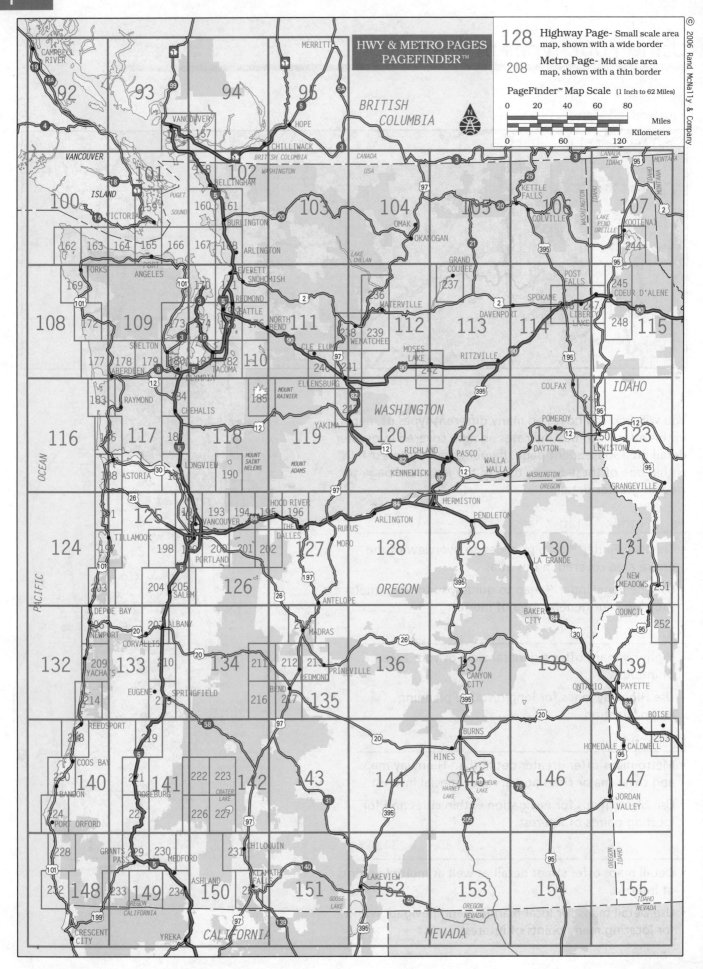

Cities and Communities

Community	State	Page	Grid	Community	State	Page	Grid	Community	State	Page	Grid	Community	State	Page	Grid
A				Appleyard	WA	239	A5	Bayshore	WA	180	B2	Blue River	OR	134	A2
*ABBOTSFORD	BC	102	B1	Arago	OR	220	D6	Bayside Gardens	OR	191	B4	Bluestem	WA	114	A2
Aberdeen	BC	102	B1	Arbor Heights	WA	284	D4	Bayview	ID	245	C1	Bly	OR	151	B1
*ABERDEEN	WA	178	A7	Arbor Lodge	OR	308	D5	Bayview	OR	328	C2	Blyn	WA	109	C1
Aberdeen Gardens	WA	178	B5	Arbutus	BC	254	D14	Bay View	WA	160	D6	*BOARDMAN	OR	128	C1
Abernethy	OR	317	H1	Arcadia	WA	180	C3	Bayview	WA	170	D1	Boardman Junction	OR	128	C1
Abrams	OR	141	C1	Archabal	ID	251	C6	Bay View	WA	181	C2	Bodie	OR	129	C2
Acme	WA	161	C2	Arch Cape	OR	191	A2	Bazan Bay	BC	159	B3	Bogachiel	WA	169	D3
Acton	WA	120	C2	Arden	WA	171	A6	Beach Grove	BC	101	C1	Boise	OR	313	F1
Ada	OR	214	B5	Ardenvoir	WA	112	A1	Beach Haven	BC	101	C2	Boise	WA	110	C3
*ADAIR VILLAGE	OR	207	B4	Ardenwald	OR	318	A6	Beacon Hill	WA	282	C2	*BOISE	ID	253	D3
*ADAMS	OR	129	C1	Argay	OR	193	A7	Beacon Hill	WA	303	C3	Boise Hills Village	ID	253	D2
Addy	WA	106	A3	Ariel	OR	118	A3	Bear	ID	131	B3	Boistfort	WA	187	A2
Adel	WA	152	B2	Arletta	WA	181	B1	Beatty	OR	151	A1	Bolton	OR	199	D4
Adelaide	WA	175	D1	*ARLINGTON	OR	128	A1	Beaumont Wilshire	OR	314	B1	*BONANZA	OR	151	A2
Adelaide	WA	182	A1	*ARLINGTON	WA	168	D5	*BEAUX ARTS VLG	WA	175	C3	Bonifer	OR	129	C1
Adna	WA	184	A7	Arlington Heights	OR	312	B7	Beaver	OR	197	C5	Bonita	OR	199	B3
Advance	OR	199	C5	Arlington Heights	WA	102	C3	Beaver	WA	163	A6	Bonlow	WA	243	A4
Agassiz	BC	94	C3	Arnold Creek	OR	320	C2	Beavercreek	OR	200	A6	*BONNERS FERRY	ID	107	B2
Agate Beach	OR	206	B3	Arock	OR	146	C3	Beaver Homes	OR	189	C6	Bonnerville	OR	194	B7
Agness	OR	148	B1	Arrow Head Beach	WA	167	D3	Beaver Marsh	OR	142	C2	*BONNEY LAKE	WA	182	C4
Agnew	WA	165	D6	Artondale	WA	181	B1	Beaver Springs	OR	189	B5	Bonny Slope	OR	199	B1
Ahsahka	ID	123	C2	Asert	OR	200	B1	*BEAVERTON	OR	199	B2	Bordeaux	WA	184	A2
Ahtanum	WA	243	A7	Ashdale	OR	199	D4	Bedford	WA	117	B1	Boring	OR	200	B3
Ainsworth Corner	CA	150	C3	Ashford	WA	118	B1	Beebe	WA	236	D3	Boston Bar	BC	95	A1
Ainsworth Corner	OR	151	A2	*ASHLAND	OR	337	D9	Beech Creek	OR	137	A1	Boston Harbor	WA	180	C4
Airlie	OR	207	A2	Ashwood	OR	135	C1	Bel Air	OR	199	B2	*BOTHELL	WA	171	C6
*AIRWAY HEIGHTS	WA	246	A4	*ASOTIN	WA	250	B6	*BELCARRA	BC	157	A3	Boulevard Park	WA	285	J6
Ajlune	OR	118	A2	Aspen Grove	BC	95	C1	Belfair	WA	173	D5	Boundary	WA	106	B1
Alameda	OR	314	A1	*ASTORIA	OR	300	F5	Belknap Springs	OR	134	B2	Bourne	OR	138	A1
*ALBANY	OR	326	A12	*ATHENA	OR	129	C1	Bellevue	OR	204	A2	*BOVILL	ID	123	B1
Albee	OR	129	B2	*ATHOL	ID	245	B2	*BELLEVUE	WA	175	C2	Bow	WA	161	A4
*ALBION	WA	249	A4	Atkinson	WA	176	A6	Bellfountain	OR	133	B2	Bowen Island	BC	93	B3
Alder	OR	130	C2	*AUBURN	WA	182	C2	*BELLINGHAM	WA	258	G4	Bowers Junction	OR	192	A7
Alder	OR	133	A1	*AUMSVILLE	OR	205	B7	Bells Beach	WA	167	D7	Bowmont	WA	147	C1
Alder	WA	118	B1	*AURORA	OR	199	B7	*BEND	OR	332	E7	Bowser	BC	92	B2
Alder Creek	OR	201	A4	Aurora Village	WA	171	A6	Bendemeer	OR	192	A7	Boyd	OR	127	B2
Aldergate	WA	128	B1	Austa	OR	133	A2	Benewah	ID	115	A3	Brackendale	BC	93	C1
Alderton	WA	182	C4	Austin	OR	137	C1	Benge	WA	122	A1	Bradwood	OR	117	B3
Alderwood Manor	WA	171	B5	Austin	WA	170	D2	*BENTON CITY	WA	120	C3	Brady	WA	179	A7
Alexander Beach	WA	259	D6	Austin Junction	OR	137	C1	Berkeley	WA	182	A6	Brandstrom	WA	168	B3
Alfalfa	OR	135	B3	Avon	WA	161	A7	Berne	WA	111	B1	Braymill	OR	150	C1
Alger	WA	161	B3	Avondale	WA	171	D7	Berrydale	WA	182	D1	Breakers	WA	186	A5
Algoma	OR	235	C1	Ayer	WA	121	C2	Berteleda	CA	148	B3	Breidablick	WA	170	B5
*ALGONA	WA	182	B2	Azalea	OR	225	C6	Bertsche Terrace	CA	148	B3	Breitenbush Hot Spgs	OR	134	B1
Alicel	OR	130	A2	Azwell	WA	112	B1	Bethany	OR	192	A7	*BREMERTON	WA	270	G10
Alkali Lake	OR	144	B3					Bethel	OR	329	F4	Bremerton Junction	WA	174	A4
Alki	WA	280	A5	**B**				Bethel	WA	174	B4	Brentwood Bay	BC	159	C4
Allegany	OR	218	D7	Baby Island Heights	WA	167	D7	Bethel Gospel Park	OR	205	A3	Brentwd-Darlington	OR	318	D6
Allentown	WA	286	D7	Bade	OR	129	C1	Beulah	OR	138	A3	*BREWSTER	WA	104	B3
Allison	WA	182	A4	Badger Corner	OR	323	E12	Beverly	WA	120	B1	Briarwood	OR	321	G4
Allyn	WA	173	D6	Bagdad Junction	WA	237	D4	Beverly Beach	OR	206	B2	Brickerville	OR	214	D1
Allyn-Grapeview	WA	173	D7	Bagley Junction	WA	176	C6	Beverly Beach	WA	167	D7	Bridal Veil	OR	201	A1
*ALMIRA	WA	237	D7	*BAINBRIDGE ISLND	WA	174	D2	Beverly Park	WA	268	D4	Bridesville	BC	105	A1
Almota	WA	122	B1	*BAKER CITY	OR	138	B1	Bickleton	WA	120	A3	Bridge	OR	140	C3
Aloha	OR	199	A2	Baker-Langdon	WA	345	E13	Biggam	WA	120	C3	Bridgeport	OR	138	B1
Aloha	WA	177	B2	Balch	WA	117	B1	Biggs	OR	127	C1	*BRIDGEPORT	WA	112	C1
Alpha	WA	118	A1	Balder	WA	114	C3	Biggs Junction	OR	127	C1	Bridgton	OR	309	G2
Alpine	OR	128	C1	Ballard	WA	272	D4	Biloxi	WA	174	D4	Bridgeview	OR	233	B5
Alpine	OR	133	B2	Ballston	OR	204	A3	*BINGEN	WA	195	D5	Bridlemile	OR	316	A2
Alsea	OR	133	A2	Bamberton	BC	159	B3	Bingham Springs	OR	130	A1	*BRIER	WA	171	B6
Alston	OR	189	A4	Bamfield	BC	100	A1	Birch	WA	110	C3	Brighouse	BC	156	B6
Altamont	OR	338	H11	Bancroft	OR	140	C3	Birch Bay	WA	158	B4	Brighton	OR	191	B5
Alta Vista	WA	118	B2	*BANDON	OR	220	B6	Birchfield	WA	120	A2	Brightwood	OR	201	B4
Alto	WA	122	A2	Bangor	WA	170	A7	Birchfield	WA	243	C7	Brinnon	WA	109	C1
Altoona	WA	117	A2	Barber	ID	253	D3	Birkenfeld	OR	117	B3	Bristol	WA	196	A4
Alvadore	OR	133	B2	Barberton	WA	192	D5	Bissell	OR	200	D6	Britannia Beach	BC	93	C2
Amanda Park	WA	109	A2	Baring	WA	111	A1	Bitter Lake	WA	171	A7	Broadacres	OR	205	B1
Amber	WA	114	B2	Barnesdale	OR	191	B5	Blachly	OR	133	A2	Broadbent	OR	140	B3
Amboy	WA	193	B1	Barneston	WA	176	B7	Black Butte Ranch	OR	211	C3	Broadmoor	BC	156	B7
American	OR	210	A3	Barnett	OR	128	A2	Black Creek	BC	92	A1	Brogan	OR	138	C2
American Lk Gdns	WA	181	C4	Barnhart	OR	129	B1	*BLACK DIAMOND	WA	110	C3	Bromart	WA	171	D3
*AMITY	OR	204	B2	Barton	OR	200	B4	Black River Jct	WA	289	H2	Brookdale	WA	182	A5
*ANACORTES	WA	259	D4	Barton Heights	OR	131	B2	Blaine	OR	197	D6	Brookfield	WA	117	A2
Anatone	WA	122	C3	Barview	OR	191	A7	*BLAINE	WA	158	A3	*BROOKINGS	OR	232	C6
Anderson	OR	200	B3	Barview	OR	220	C1	Blakeley	OR	129	C1	Brooklyn	OR	317	H2
Andrews	OR	153	C1	Basin City	WA	121	A2	Blalock	OR	128	A1	Brooks	OR	205	A3
Angle Lake	WA	290	D2	Basque	WA	154	B1	Blanchard	ID	107	A3	Brookwild	OR	318	D7
Anlauf	OR	219	B2	Bassett Junction	WA	113	A3	Blanchard	WA	161	A4	Brothers	OR	135	C3
*ANMORE	BC	157	A3	Bates	OR	137	C1	Blewett	WA	238	A5	Brownsboro	OR	149	C1
Annapolis	WA	271	A13	Batterson	OR	191	D4	Bliss Landing	BC	92	B1	Brownsmead	OR	117	A3
Annex	WA	139	A2	Battin	OR	319	G7	Blitzen	OR	153	B1	Browns Point	WA	181	D1
Annieville	BC	156	D6	*BATTLE GROUND	WA	192	D3	Blockhouse	WA	127	B1	Brownstown	WA	119	C2
*ANTELOPE	OR	127	C3	Bay Center	WA	183	C7	Blodgett	OR	133	A1	*BROWNSVILLE	OR	210	C2
Antone	OR	136	B2	*BAY CITY	OR	191	B7	Blooming	OR	198	C2	Brush Prairie	WA	193	A4
Apex	OR	129	B1	Bay City	WA	183	B2	Blubber Bay	BC	92	B1	Bryant	WA	168	D4
Apiary	OR	189	B5	Bayne	WA	110	C3	Bluecreek	WA	106	A3	Bryn Mawr	WA	175	C4
Applegate	OR	149	B2	Bayocean	OR	191	A7	Blue Mountain	WA	129	C1	Buchanan	OR	145	C1
Appleton	WA	196	B3	Bay Park	OR	333	J13	Blue Ridge	WA	171	A7	Buck Fork	OR	141	B2

*Indicates incorporated city

Cities and Communities

Community	State	Page	Grid	Community	State	Page	Grid	Community	State	Page	Grid	Community	State	Page	Grid
*BUCKLEY	WA	182	D4	Cascade Summit	OR	142	B1	Cinebar	WA	118	A2	Concordia	OR	310	A6
Buckman	OR	313	H6	Cascade Valley	WA	242	C3	City Center	WA	181	C4	*CONCRETE	WA	102	C2
Bucks Corners	OR	129	A1	Cascadia	OR	134	A2	*CITY OF CHILLIWCK	BC	94	C3	*CONDON	OR	128	A2
*BUCODA	WA	184	D4	*CASHMERE	WA	238	C2	*CITY OF COLWOOD	BC	159	B7	Conkling Park	ID	248	A5
Buell	OR	125	B3	Casino	BC	106	B1	*CTY OF N VANCVR	BC	254	J4	Conley	OR	130	A2
Buena	WA	120	A2	Casino Corner	WA	268	B5	*CITY OF SURREY	BC	157	B7	*CONNELL	WA	121	B1
Buena Vista	OR	207	C2	Casland	WA	111	C3	*CITY OF VICTORIA	BC	256	H7	Conway	WA	168	B2
Buenna	WA	175	A7	*CASTLE ROCK	WA	187	C7	*CITY OF WHT ROCK	BC	158	A2	Cook	WA	195	B5
Bull Run	OR	200	D3	Cataldo	ID	115	B2	Clackamas	OR	199	D3	Coolin	ID	107	A2
Bunker Hill	OR	333	J11	Cathcart	WA	171	D5	Clackamas Heights	OR	199	D4	Coombs	BC	92	C3
Burbank	WA	121	B3	Cathedral Park	WA	192	B6	Clallam Bay	WA	163	B3	*COOS BAY	OR	333	D10
Burbank Heights	WA	121	A3	*CATHLAMET	WA	117	B3	Claquato	WA	184	B6	Cooston	OR	218	B7
*BURIEN	WA	285	F7	Caufield	BC	156	A3	Clarkes	OR	200	A7	Copalis Beach	WA	177	B4
Burley	WA	174	B6	Cavalero Corner	WA	171	D1	*CLARK FORK	ID	107	C3	Copalis Crossing	WA	177	C4
Burlington	OR	192	A6	*CAVE JUNCTION	OR	233	A5	Clarkia	ID	115	C3	Copco	CA	150	A3
*BURLINGTON	WA	260	D7	Cavelero Beach	WA	167	D5	*CLARKSTON	WA	250	B4	Copeland	ID	107	B1
*BURNABY	BC	255	H10	Caycuse	BC	100	C1	Clarkston Heights	WA	250	B4	Coppei	WA	122	A3
Burnett	WA	182	D5	Cayuse	OR	129	C1	Clarksville	ID	245	B5	Copperfield	OR	131	A3
*BURNS	OR	145	A1	Cecil	OR	128	B1	Clarno	OR	128	A3	Copperville	ID	131	C1
Burns Junction	OR	146	B3	Cecil	WA	106	C2	*CLATSKANIE	OR	117	B3	*COQUILLE	OR	220	D4
Burnt Woods	OR	133	A1	Cedar	BC	93	A3	Clatsop Station	OR	188	B3	*COQUITLAM	BC	157	A3
Buroker	WA	122	A3	Cedardale	BC	254	G4	Clay City	WA	118	B1	Corbett	OR	200	C1
Burop	WA	111	A3	Cedardale	OR	126	A3	Clayton	WA	114	B1	Corbt-Trwlgr-Lair Hl	OR	317	F4
Burr Canyon	WA	121	B2	Cedar Falls	WA	176	C6	Clearbrook	BC	102	B1	Cordova Bay	BC	159	C5
Burrows	WA	177	C5	Cedar Hills	OR	199	B1	Clear Creek	CA	149	A3	*CORNELIUS	OR	198	C1
Burton	WA	174	D6	Cedarhome	WA	168	B3	Clear Creek	OR	125	B1	Cornelius Pass	OR	192	A6
Busby	WA	249	B6	Cedarhurst	WA	174	D5	Clear Lake	OR	204	D4	Cornell	WA	168	A6
*BUTTE FALLS	OR	150	A1	Cedar Mill	OR	199	B1	Clear Lake	WA	161	C6	Cornell Place	OR	129	A1
Butter Creek Jct	OR	128	C1	Cedar Mountain	WA	175	D6	Clearview	WA	171	D5	Corner	WA	168	B3
Butteville	OR	199	A6	Cedar Point	OR	220	D4	Clearwater	OR	222	D4	Cornucopia	OR	130	C3
Buxton	OR	125	B1	Cedar Valley	WA	171	B5	Clem	OR	128	A2	Coronado Shores	OR	203	A6
B Z Corner	WA	195	D2	Cedarville	WA	117	B1	Cleo	OR	220	D2	Cortes Bay	BC	92	B1
				Celilo Village	OR	127	B1	Cleveland	OR	221	A3	*CORVALLIS	OR	327	F7
C				Centennial	OR	200	A1	Cleveland	WA	120	A3	*COSMOPOLIS	WA	178	B7
Cabell City	OR	129	C3	Center	OR	314	D5	Clifton	OR	117	B3	*COTTAGE GROVE	OR	215	B7
Cadboro Bay	BC	257	E4	Center	WA	170	A2	Clifton	OR	195	C5	*COTTONWOOD	ID	123	C3
Calder	ID	115	C2	Centerville	WA	127	B1	Clinton	WA	171	A2	Cottonwood Bay	WA	158	B4
*CALDWELL	ID	147	B1	Central Area	WA	278	C5	Clo-oose	BC	100	B2	Cottrell	OR	200	C3
Calhounville	WA	121	C3	Central Ferry	WA	122	B1	Cloquallum	WA	179	C4	Cougar	WA	190	A5
Callahan	OR	141	A2	*CENTRALIA	WA	299	E4	Cloverdale	BC	158	B1	*COULEE CITY	WA	113	A2
Cama Beach	WA	167	D6	Central Park	WA	178	C7	Cloverdale	ID	253	B3	*COULEE DAM	WA	237	C2
Camano	WA	167	D5	Central Point	OR	199	C6	Cloverdale	OR	197	B7	*COUNCIL	ID	139	C1
*CAMAS	WA	193	B7	*CENTRAL POINT	OR	336	A6	Cloverdale	OR	212	D4	Country Homes	WA	347	B11
Camas Valley	OR	141	A3	Central Valley	WA	174	B1	Cloverdale	WA	189	D6	County Line	BC	158	D1
*CAMBRIDGE	ID	139	B1	Ceres	WA	117	B2	Cloverland	WA	122	C2	*COUPEVILLE	WA	167	B4
Camden	WA	106	C3	Chaffee	WA	120	C3	Clow Corner	OR	204	B6	*COURTENAY	BC	92	A2
Cameron	ID	123	B1	Chain Hill	WA	184	D2	Clyde	WA	121	C2	Courtrock	OR	137	A1
Cameron	WA	106	C3	Chamber	WA	249	B7	*CLYDE HILL	WA	175	C2	*COVE	OR	130	B2
*CAMPBELL RIVER	BC	92	A1	Chapman	OR	125	C1	Coal Canyon	WA	118	B2	Cove	WA	174	D5
Camp Discover	WA	170	A5	Chard	WA	122	B2	Coal Creek	WA	175	D4	Covello	WA	122	B2
Camp Elkanah	OR	129	C2	Charleston	OR	220	C1	Coal Creek	WA	189	B2	Cove Orchard	OR	198	B4
Camp Grande	WA	167	D4	Charleston	WA	270	G11	Coaledo	OR	220	D3	*COVINGTON	WA	175	D7
Camp Lagoon	WA	167	D4	Charlestown	OR	129	A1	Coalfield	WA	175	D4	Cowichan Bay	BC	101	B1
Camp Sealth	WA	174	C7	Chattaroy	WA	114	C1	Coalmont	BC	95	C2	Cowiche	WA	119	C1
Camp Sherman	OR	211	C1	*CHATCOLET	ID	248	A6	Cobble Hill	BC	159	A1	Cowlitz	WA	118	A2
Camp Twelve	OR	206	C3	*CHEHALIS	WA	299	C10	*COBURG	OR	210	B7	Crabtree	OR	133	C1
Camp Union	WA	173	D2	Chehalis Junction	WA	299	B14	Cocolalla	ID	107	A3	Crab Tree	WA	114	C3
Canaan	OR	189	C7	Chehalis Village	WA	117	B1	*COEUR D'ALENE	ID	355	E11	*CRAIGMONT	ID	123	B2
Canary	OR	214	B4	*CHELAN	WA	236	D3	Cohassett	WA	183	B2	Crane	OR	145	C2
*CANBY	OR	199	C6	Chelan Falls	WA	236	D4	Cokedale	WA	161	D5	Crates	WA	196	C6
Canby	WA	114	A2	Chelatchie	WA	118	A3	Colbert	WA	114	C1	Crawfordville	OR	133	C2
Canemah	OR	199	D5	Chemainus	BC	101	A1	Colburn	ID	107	B2	Creosote	WA	174	D2
*CANNON BEACH	OR	188	A7	Chemawa	OR	323	D5	Colby	WA	271	H13	Crescent	OR	142	C1
Cannon Beach Jct	OR	188	B6	Chemult	OR	142	C2	Colchester	WA	271	H14	Crescent Beach	BC	158	A1
*CANYON CITY	OR	137	B2	*CHENEY	WA	246	A7	Cold Springs	OR	129	A1	*CRESCENT CITY	CA	148	B3
Canyon Park	WA	171	C6	Chenois Creek	WA	177	D6	Cold Springs Jct	OR	129	A1	Crescent Lake	OR	142	B1
*CANYONVILLE	OR	225	C3	Chenoweth	OR	196	C6	Coles Corner	WA	111	C1	Crescent Lake Jct	OR	142	B1
Cape Meares	OR	197	A1	Cherry Grove	OR	198	A2	Colestin	OR	234	D7	*CRESTON	WA	113	C1
Capitol Hill	WA	278	C3	Cherry Heights	OR	196	C7	*COLFAX	WA	122	C1	Creston Kenilworth	OR	318	B2
*CARBONADO	WA	182	D6	Cherry Valley	WA	110	C1	College Hill	OR	329	J9	Crestwood	OR	316	A7
Carlsborg	WA	166	A6	Cherryville	OR	201	A4	*COLLEGE PLACE	WA	344	G11	*CRESWELL	OR	215	C5
Carlson	WA	118	B1	Chesaw	WA	105	A1	Collins	WA	195	A5	Creswell Heights	WA	193	C5
*CARLTON	OR	198	B5	Cheshire	OR	133	B2	Collins View	OR	320	D2	Criterion	OR	127	B3
Carlton	WA	104	A3	Chester	WA	350	H14	Colton	OR	126	A3	Crocker	WA	182	C5
Carnahan	OR	188	B3	*CHEWELAH	WA	106	B3	*COLTON	WA	250	A1	Crofton	BC	101	B1
Carnation	OR	198	B1	Chico	WA	270	B4	Columbia	WA	283	E5	Cromwell	WA	181	B2
*CARNATION	WA	176	B1	Chilco	ID	245	A3	Columbia Beach	WA	171	A2	Crosby	WA	173	D3
Carpenterville	OR	232	C2	*CHILLIWACK	BC	102	C1	*COLUMBIA CITY	OR	192	B1	Croskey	WA	114	A2
Carrolls	WA	189	C4	*CHILOQUIN	OR	231	D4	Columbia Gardens	BC	106	B1	Cross	WA	174	C6
Carson	OR	131	A3	Chimacum	WA	170	A1	Columbia Heights	WA	302	G2	Crossing	WA	168	C6
*CARSON	WA	194	D4	Chinook	WA	186	B7	Columbia Vly Gdns	WA	302	G6	Crow	OR	133	B3
Carson River Valley	WA	194	D4	Chiwaukum	WA	111	C2	*COLVILLE	WA	106	A2	Crowfoot	OR	133	C1
Carus	OR	199	D6	*CHRISTINA LAKE	BC	105	C1	Colvos	WA	174	D5	Crown Hill	WA	273	E1
Carver	OR	200	A4	Christmas Valley	OR	143	C2	*COMOX	BC	92	A2	Crown Point	OR	220	C2
Cascade	BC	105	C1	Christopher	WA	182	C1	Comstock	OR	219	C1	Cruzatt	WA	194	A7
*CASCADE	ID	252	D6	Chrome	OR	220	D4	Concomly	OR	205	A2	Crystal Springs	WA	271	D5
Cascade Gorge	OR	150	A1	Chuckanut Village	WA	258	B13	*CONCONULLY	WA	104	B2	*CULDESAC	ID	123	B2
Cascade Heights	BC	156	C5	Chumstick	WA	111	C2	Concord	WA	321	J7	Cully	OR	310	D7
*CASCADE LOCKS	OR	194	D5	Cicero	WA	102	C3					Culp Creek	OR	141	C1

*Indicates incorporated city

Community	State	Page	Grid	Community	State	Page	Grid	Community	State	Page	Grid	Community	State	Page	Grid
Cultus Lake	BC	102	C1	Diablo	WA	103	B2	*EAGLE	ID	253	B1	Empire	OR	333	C6
*CULVER	OR	208	B7	Diamond	OR	145	C3	Eagle Creek	OR	200	B4	Enaville	ID	115	C2
Cumberland	BC	92	A2	Diamond	WA	122	B1	Eagledale	WA	174	D2	*ENDICOTT	WA	122	B1
Cumberland	WA	110	C3	Diamond Lake	OR	223	C6	Eagle Harbour	BC	156	A2	Enetai	WA	271	C9
Cunningham	WA	121	B1	Diamond Lake	WA	106	C3	*EAGLE POINT	OR	230	D5	Englewood	OR	333	F12
Cuprum	ID	131	B3	Diamond Lake Jct	OR	142	C3	Eakin	OR	127	C2	*ENTERPRISE	OR	130	C2
Curlew	WA	105	B1	Dickey Prairie	OR	126	A3	Earl	WA	113	C2	*ENTIAT	WA	236	A6
Currinsville	OR	200	C5	Dieringer	WA	182	C2	Earlington	WA	289	H3	*ENUMCLAW	WA	110	C3
Curtin	OR	219	B1	Dillard	OR	221	B7	Earlmont	WA	175	C1	Eola Village	OR	204	C1
Curtis	WA	187	A1	Dilley	OR	198	B2	Earls Cove	BC	93	A2	*EPHRATA	WA	112	C3
Cushman	OR	214	B3	Dilworth	WA	174	D5	East Aberdeen	WA	17	B7	Erlands Point	WA	270	D6
*CUSICK	WA	106	C3	Disautel	WA	105	A3	East Bremerton	WA	270	H6	Ernies Grove	WA	176	D4
Custer	WA	158	C4	Dishman	WA	350	A9	East Columbia	OR	309	H3	Espanola	WA	114	B2
Cutler City	OR	203	A5	Disque	WA	164	C5	East Farms	WA	352	G7	*ESTACADA	OR	200	C6
				Disston	OR	141	C1	East Gardener	OR	218	D1	Eufaula	WA	189	A2
D				*DIST OF CNTL SNCH	BC	159	C3	Eastgate	WA	175	D3	*EUGENE	OR	330	B6
Dabob	WA	170	A4	*DIST OF DELTA	BC	101	C1	*EAST HOPE	ID	244	D2	Eureka	WA	121	C3
Dahl Pine	OR	127	A3	*DIST OF KENT	BC	94	C3	East Hoquiam	WA	178	A7	Evaline	WA	187	C2
Dahua	WA	117	A2	*DIST OF LANGFORD	BC	159	B6	East Kamiah	ID	123	C2	*EVERETT	WA	267	G3
Dairy	OR	151	A2	*DIST OF MATSQUI	BC	94	B3	East Kittitas	WA	241	D6	Evergreen	ID	131	C3
Dale	OR	129	B3	*DIST OF METCHOSN	BC	159	A7	East Lind	WA	121	C1	Evergreen	OR	321	F6
*DALLAS	OR	204	A6	*DIST OF MISSION	BC	94	B3	Eastman	WA	122	A3	*EVERSON	WA	102	B1
Dallesport	WA	196	C7	*DIST OF N SAANICH	BC	159	C2	East Maupin	OR	127	B3	Ewan	WA	114	B3
*DALTON GARDENS	ID	355	E3	*DIST OF N VANCVR	BC	254	H2	Eastmoreland	OR	318	A5	Excelsior Beach	ID	115	A1
Damascus	OR	200	A3	*DIST OF OAK BAY	BC	257	C7	East Olympia	WA	184	D1				
Danner	OR	146	C3	*DIST OF SAANICH	BC	256	B1	Easton	WA	111	B3	**F**			
Dant	OR	127	B3	*DIST OF W VANCVR	BC	254	C1	Eastport	ID	107	B1	Factoria	WA	175	C3
Danville	WA	105	C1	Divide	OR	219	C1	East Port Orchard	WA	174	C4	Fairbanks	OR	127	B1
Danville	WA	175	D7	Divide	WA	118	B1	East Quilcene	WA	109	C1	Fairchild	WA	114	B2
Darknell	WA	114	C2	Dixie	WA	122	A3	Eastside	OR	220	D1	Fairfax	WA	110	C3
Darlington	WA	267	J1	Dixonville	OR	221	D5	East Sooke	BC	164	D1	Fairfield	OR	204	D2
Darlingtonia	CA	148	C3	Dockton	WA	174	D7	Eastsound	WA	101	C2	*FAIRFIELD	WA	114	C2
*DARRINGTON	WA	103	A3	Dodge	WA	122	B2	East Spokane	WA	350	A9	Fairholm	WA	164	A6
Dartford	WA	346	H5	Dodson	OR	194	B7	*EAST WENATCHEE	WA	239	A4	Fairmont	WA	109	C1
Dash Point	WA	181	D1	Dole	WA	193	C3	East Wntchee Bnch	WA	239	A4	Fairmount	WA	171	A2
Dash Point	WA	182	A1	Dollarton	BC	156	D3	*EATONVILLE	WA	118	B1	Fairoaks	OR	221	D1
*DAVENPORT	WA	114	A2	Dollers Corner	WA	192	D3	Eby	OR	126	A3	Fair Oaks	OR	321	H5
Davidson	ID	131	B1	Dolomite	WA	106	A1	*ECHO	OR	129	A1	Fairview	OR	128	B2
Davis	WA	117	B1	*DONALD	OR	199	A7	Echo Beach	ID	115	A1	Fairview	OR	140	B2
Davis Creek	CA	152	A3	Donald	WA	120	A2	Echo Dell	OR	200	A5	Fairview	OR	197	C2
Davis Terrace	WA	303	F10	*DONNELLY	ID	252	D1	Eckman Lake	OR	328	G7	*FAIRVIEW	OR	200	B1
Dawson	OR	133	B2	Dora	OR	140	C2	Eddyville	ID	248	B1	Fairview	WA	270	E3
Day Island	WA	181	C2	Dorena	OR	141	C1	Eddyville	OR	133	A1	Fairview Sumach	WA	243	C7
Days Creek	OR	225	D2	Dorris	CA	150	B3	Edgecomb	WA	168	D6	Fairwood	WA	175	D5
*DAYTON	OR	198	C7	Dot	WA	128	A1	Edgewater	WA	171	B2	Fairwood	WA	346	H7
*DAYTON	WA	122	A2	Doty	WA	117	B1	Edgewick	WA	176	C6	Falcon Heights	OR	235	C5
Dayton	WA	179	D2	Douglas	WA	236	D7	*EDGEWOOD	WA	182	B3	Fall City	WA	176	B3
*DAYVILLE	OR	136	C2	Douglas Ridge	OR	200	C5	Edison	WA	161	A4	Fall Creek	OR	133	C3
Deadwood	OR	132	C3	*DOVER	ID	244	A1	Edison Station	WA	161	A4	*FALLS CITY	OR	125	A3
Deady	OR	221	C2	Dover	OR	200	D5	*EDMONDS	WA	171	A5	Falls View	OR	200	A7
*DEARY	ID	123	B1	Downing	OR	189	A3	Edwall	WA	114	A2	Fanny Bay	BC	92	B2
Deckerville	WA	179	A2	Downs	OR	205	C4	Eglon	WA	170	D4	Fargher Lake	WA	193	A1
Deep Cove	BC	156	D3	Downs	WA	113	C2	Eightmile	OR	128	B2	Farmington	OR	198	D3
Deep Cove	BC	159	B2	Downtown	OR	313	F6	Elbe	WA	118	B1	*FARMINGTON	WA	115	A3
Deep Creek	ID	107	B2	*DRAIN	OR	219	A3	Elberton	WA	114	C3	Farron	WA	119	C2
Deep Creek	WA	114	B2	Drakes Crossing	OR	205	D6	Eldon	WA	173	B3	Faubion	OR	201	C5
Deep Harbor	WA	101	C2	Draperville	OR	207	D4	*ELECTRIC CITY	WA	237	C3	Fauntleroy	WA	284	D3
Deerhorn	OR	133	C3	Drew	OR	141	C3	Elgarose	OR	221	A3	Fawn	OR	134	A1
Deer Island	OR	189	C7	Drewsey	OR	137	C3	*ELGIN	OR	130	A1	Fayetteville	OR	210	A1
*DEER PARK	WA	114	B1	Drift Creek	OR	209	B1	Elgin	WA	174	B7	*FEDERAL WAY	WA	182	A1
Dehlinger	OR	235	D6	Dryad	WA	117	B1	Eliot	OR	313	G2	Felida	WA	192	C5
Delake	OR	203	A5	Dry Creek	WA	121	C3	Elk	WA	114	C1	Fenn	ID	123	C3
Delaney	WA	122	A2	Dryden	WA	238	B2	Elk City	OR	206	D4	*FERDINAND	ID	123	B3
Delano Heights	WA	237	C3	Dryland	OR	205	D1	Elkhead	OR	219	C5	*FERNAN LAKE VLG	ID	355	J11
Delena	OR	189	A4	Duckabush	WA	173	C1	Elkhorn	OR	134	A1	Ferncliff	WA	174	D1
Delkena	WA	106	C3	Dudley	ID	115	B2	Elk Lake	OR	216	A4	Ferndale	OR	121	C3
Dellwood	OR	140	C2	Dudley	WA	240	D3	*ELK RIVER	ID	123	C1	*FERNDALE	WA	158	C6
Dellwood	OR	198	B3	*DUFUR	OR	127	B2	*ELKTON	OR	141	A1	Fern Heath	WA	175	A6
Delphi	WA	184	B1	Dukes Valley	OR	195	C7	Elk Valley	CA	233	A7	Fern Hill	OR	188	D2
Delta	ID	115	C2	*DUNCAN	BC	101	A1	Ella	OR	128	B1	Fernwood	ID	115	B3
Deming	WA	102	B1	Duncan	WA	246	C7	Ellendale	OR	125	B3	Fernwood	WA	173	A7
Denio	NV	153	C3	Duncan Bay	BC	92	A1	*ELLENSBURG	WA	241	B6	Fernwood	WA	174	B4
Denison	WA	114	B1	Dundarave	BC	254	B2	Elliott Avenue	WA	243	A6	Fields	OR	153	C2
Denman Island	BC	92	B2	*DUNDEE	OR	198	C6	Ellisford	WA	104	C1	*FIFE	WA	182	A3
Denmark	OR	224	B3	Dune	OR	127	B1	Ellisport	WA	174	D6	Finley	WA	121	A3
Denneux	OR	199	B2	*DUNES CITY	OR	214	B4	Ellsworth	WA	311	G2	Finn Rock	OR	134	A3
*DEPOE BAY	OR	203	A7	Dungeness	WA	262	D2	*ELMA	WA	179	B7	*FIRCREST	WA	294	A1
Deroche	BC	94	C3	Dunnean	OR	146	A2	*ELMER CITY	WA	237	C2	Firdale	WA	117	A1
De Smet	ID	115	A3	Dunthorpe	OR	321	G4	Elmira	ID	107	B2	Firdale	WA	171	A6
*DES MOINES	WA	290	B5	*DUPONT	WA	181	B5	Elmira	OR	133	B2	Fir Grove	OR	200	A5
Deschutes Rvr Wds	OR	217	B4	Durham	WA	110	C3	Elmonica	OR	199	A1	Fir Grove	OR	215	A1
Detour	OR	198	B1	Durkee	OR	138	C1	Elsie	OR	125	A1	First Hill	WA	278	C5
*DETROIT	OR	134	B1	Duroc	OR	129	C1	Eltopia	WA	121	A2	Fir Villa	OR	204	A6
Dewatto	WA	173	B5	Dusty	WA	122	B1	Elwood	OR	200	B7	Firwood	OR	200	D4
Dewdney	BC	94	B3	*DUVALL	WA	110	C1	Embro	WA	111	B1	Fischers Mill	OR	200	B5
Dewey	OR	198	C4	Dynamite	WA	246	B7	Emerald Heights	OR	300	H4	Fisher	OR	209	D4
Dewey	WA	259	J14					Emerson	OR	127	B2	Fisher	WA	193	A7
Dexter	OR	133	C3	**E**				Emida	ID	115	B3	Fishers Corner	OR	199	D6
Dexter By The Sea	WA	183	B5	Eagle	ID	115	C1	*EMMETT	ID	139	C3	Five Corners	OR	152	A2

*Indicates incorporated city

Cities and Communities

*Indicates incorporated city

*Indicates incorporated city

Cities and Communities

Community	State	Page	Grid	Community	State	Page	Grid	Community	State	Page	Grid	Community	State	Page	Grid
Littell	WA	184	B7	Manitou Beach	WA	174	D1	Meadow Creek	WA	111	A3	Mist	OR	117	B3
Little Albany	OR	209	C2	Manning	OR	125	B1	Meadowdale	WA	171	B4	Mitchell	OR	136	A1
Little Falls	WA	114	A1	Manning	WA	122	C1	Meadowdale	WA	270	H2	Moclips	WA	177	B2
Little Hoquiam	WA	180	C1	*MANSFIELD	WA	112	C1	Meadows	ID	251	B4	Modoc Point	OR	231	D6
Little Oklahoma	WA	165	D7	Manson	WA	236	B2	Meadows	WA	184	B4	Mohler	OR	191	B4
Little River	BC	92	A2	Manson Landing	BC	92	A1	Meaghersville	WA	238	A7	Mohler	WA	113	C2
Littlerock	WA	184	B2	*MANZANITA	OR	191	B4	*MEDFORD	OR	336	D11	Mohrweis	WA	179	D1
Little Shasta	CA	150	A3	Manzanita	WA	174	C1	*MEDICAL LAKE	WA	114	B2	*MOLALLA	OR	126	A3
Little Valley	OR	138	C3	Manzanita	WA	174	D7	Medical Springs	OR	130	B3	Mondovi	WA	114	A1
Lobert Junction	OR	231	D4	Maple Bay	BC	101	B1	Medimont	ID	248	C4	Monitor	OR	205	C2
Lochdale	BC	156	D4	Maple Grove	WA	164	D6	*MEDINA	WA	279	J4	Monitor	WA	238	C3
Lochsloy	WA	102	C3	*MAPLE RIDGE	BC	157	D6	Mehama	OR	134	A1	Monkland	OR	127	C2
Locoda	OR	117	B3	Mapleton	OR	214	D2	*MELBA	ID	147	C1	*MONMOUTH	OR	204	B7
Lofall	WA	170	B5	*MAPLE VALLEY	WA	176	A6	Melbourne	WA	117	A1	Monohon	WA	175	D3
Logan	OR	200	B5	Maplewood	WA	174	C6	Melmont	ID	147	C1	*MONROE	OR	133	B2
Logan Hill	WA	184	D7	Maplewood	WA	175	C5	Melrose	OR	221	A4	*MONROE	WA	110	C1
Logsden	OR	133	A1	Marble Creek	ID	115	C3	Melville	OR	188	C4	Monson Corner	WA	168	B3
London	OR	219	D3	Marblemount	WA	103	A2	Mendota	WA	184	D5	*MONTAGUE	CA	150	A3
Lone Cemetery	ID	248	D3	Marcellus	WA	113	C3	Menlo	WA	117	A1	Montavilla	OR	315	G6
Lone Elder	OR	199	C7	Marcola	OR	210	D7	Menlo Park	WA	181	C3	Montborne	WA	168	C1
Lone Pine	OR	150	C1	Marcus	WA	106	A2	*MERCER ISLAND	WA	283	J2	Monte Cristo	WA	111	A1
Lone Pine	WA	237	C2	Marengo	WA	122	B2	Merideth	WA	175	B7	*MONTESANO	WA	178	D6
*LONEROCK	OR	128	B3	Marial	OR	140	C3	*MERIDIAN	ID	253	A3	Montlake	WA	278	C1
Lone Tree	OR	130	A2	Marietta	WA	158	C7	Merlin	OR	229	A4	Montour	ID	139	C3
*LONG BEACH	WA	186	A5	Marine Drive	WA	270	D8	*MERRILL	OR	150	C2	*MONTROSE	BC	106	B1
Longbranch	WA	181	A3	Marion	OR	133	C1	Merritt	BC	95	C1	*MONUMENT	OR	136	C1
*LONG CREEK	OR	137	A1	Marion Forks	OR	134	C1	Merritt	WA	111	C1	Moody	OR	127	B1
Long Lake	WA	114	A1	Markham	WA	320	B1	Merville	BC	92	A1	Moores Corner	WA	186	A5
Longmire	WA	185	B5	*MARLIN	WA	113	A2	Mesa	ID	139	C1	Moreland	OR	317	H6
Long Tom Station	OR	133	A2	Marmot	OR	201	A4	*MESA	WA	121	A2	Morgan	OR	128	B2
*LONGVIEW	WA	302	F8	Marquam	OR	205	D3	Meskill	WA	117	B1	Morgan Acres	WA	347	D11
Looking Glass	OR	130	B1	Marshall	WA	246	B6	*METALINE	WA	106	B1	*MORO	OR	127	C2
Lookingglass	OR	221	A5	Marshall Park	OR	320	C1	*METALINE FALLS	WA	106	C1	*MORTON	WA	118	B2
Lookout	OR	142	A1	Marshland	OR	117	B3	Metchosin	BC	165	A1	*MOSCOW	ID	249	C5
Loomis	WA	104	C1	*MARSING	ID	147	B1	Methow	WA	104	B3	*MOSES LAKE	WA	242	C3
Loon Lake	WA	106	B3	Martin	WA	111	A3	*METOLIUS	OR	208	C5	*MOSIER	OR	196	A5
Lopez	WA	101	C2	Martindale	WA	121	B3	Metzger	OR	199	B3	*MOSSYROCK	WA	118	A2
Lorane	OR	133	B3	Maryhill	WA	127	C1	Mica	ID	247	D4	Mountaindale	OR	125	C1
Lorella	OR	151	A2	Marylhurst	OR	199	C4	Mica	WA	247	A5	Mountain Home	OR	198	D4
*LOSTINE	OR	130	C2	Marys Corner	WA	187	D2	Michigan Hill	WA	184	A4	Mountain Home	WA	238	A6
Loveland	WA	182	A6	*MARYSVILLE	WA	168	C7	Middle Grove	OR	323	F9	Mountain Home Pk	WA	122	A3
Lowden	WA	121	C3	Mason	WA	114	B2	*MIDDLETON	ID	147	B1	Mountain View	WA	158	C6
*LOWELL	OR	133	C3	Massinger Corner	OR	200	A7	Middleton	OR	199	A5	Mountain View Bch	WA	168	A6
Lowell	WA	265	F7	Matlock	WA	179	B2	Midland	OR	235	B5	*MOUNT ANGEL	OR	205	C3
Lower Highland	OR	200	B7	Matsqui	BC	102	B1	Midland	WA	182	A4	Mount Baker	WA	282	E2
Lower Nicola	BC	95	C1	*MATTAWA	WA	120	B1	*MIDVALE	ID	139	B1	Mount Hebron	CA	150	B3
Loyal Heights	WA	272	D2	*MAUPIN	OR	127	B3	Midway	BC	105	B1	Mount Hood	OR	200	B1
Lucerne	WA	103	C3	Maury	WA	175	A6	Midway	ID	147	B1	Mount Hood	OR	202	C1
Lucile	ID	131	C1	May Creek	WA	175	C4	Midway	OR	125	A3	Mount Hope	OR	126	A3
Lummi Island	WA	160	B1	Mayfield	WA	118	A2	Midway	OR	129	B1	Mount Hope	WA	114	C2
Lund	BC	92	B1	Mayger	OR	189	A2	Midway	OR	198	D3	Mount Idaho	ID	123	C3
Lunnville	OR	198	B4	Maynard	WA	109	C1	Midway	OR	336	A3	*MOUNTLAKE TER	WA	171	B6
Lyle	WA	196	B5	Mayne	BC	101	B1	Midway	WA	181	C1	Mount Pleasant	WA	193	D7
*LYMAN	WA	102	C2	Maytown	WA	184	C2	Midway	WA	290	D7	Mount Scott-Arleta	OR	318	D3
*LYNDEN	WA	158	D4	Mayview	WA	122	C1	Mikkalo	OR	128	A2	Mount Tabor	OR	314	D6
Lynn Creek	BC	255	F1	Mayville	OR	128	A3	Milan	WA	114	C1	*MOUNT VERNON	OR	137	A2
Lynn Valley	BC	255	C1	Maywood	OR	133	B3	Milburn	WA	184	A7	*MOUNT VERNON	WA	260	H12
*LYNNWOOD	WA	171	B5	*MAYWOOD PARK	OR	315	J2	Miles	WA	113	C1	Mount View	OR	150	A2
Lynwood Center	WA	271	F6	Mazame	OR	142	C3	Miles Crossing	OR	300	C10	Mowich	OR	142	C2
*LYONS	OR	134	A1	McBee	OR	129	B1	Mileta Raeco	WA	175	A7	*MOXEE CITY	WA	243	D7
				*MCCALL	ID	251	D5	Mill A	WA	195	B4	*MOYIE SPRINGS	ID	107	B1
M				*MCCLEARY	WA	179	D6	Mill Bay	BC	159	A2	Mud Springs	WA	112	B1
Mabel	OR	133	C2	McCormac	OR	333	J14	*MILL CITY	OR	134	A1	*MUKILTEO	WA	266	D5
*MABTON	WA	120	B3	McCormick	WA	117	B2	*MILL CREEK	WA	171	C4	Mulino	OR	199	D7
Macdoel	CA	150	B3	McCormmach	OR	129	B1	Miller	OR	192	B6	Mulloy	OR	199	B5
Machias	WA	110	C1	McCoy	OR	204	B3	Miller River	WA	111	A1	Multnomah	OR	316	B6
Mack	WA	122	A1	McCoy	WA	114	C3	*MILLERSBURG	OR	326	G2	Mumby	WA	184	B2
Macksburg	OR	199	C7	McCredie Springs	OR	142	B1	Millican	OR	135	B3	Munra	OR	129	B1
Macleay	OR	205	B6	McDermitt	NV	154	B2	Millington	OR	220	D2	Murdock	WA	196	C6
Madison Park	WA	279	F2	McDermitt	OR	154	B2	Mill Park	OR	200	A1	Murnen	WA	117	B1
Madison South	OR	315	G3	McDonald	WA	242	D4	Mill Plain	WA	193	A6	Murphy	ID	147	C2
*MADRAS	OR	208	C5	McEwan	OR	138	A1	Millwood	OR	141	A2	Murphy	OR	229	A3
Madras Station	OR	208	C5	McGuire	ID	353	D7	*MILLWOOD	WA	350	D5	Murrayhill	OR	199	A3
Madrona Beach	WA	167	D4	McKay	OR	129	C2	Milner	BC	157	C7	Murrayville	BC	158	C1
Madrona Park	WA	278	D4	McKee Bridge	OR	149	B2	Milnes Landing	BC	101	A2	Myrick	WA	129	B1
Magnolia Beach	WA	174	D7	McKenna	WA	118	A1	Milo	OR	141	B3	*MYRTLE CREEK	OR	225	C1
Magnolia Bluff	WA	276	D1	McKenzie Bridge	OR	134	B2	*MILTON	WA	182	B2	*MYRTLE POINT	OR	140	B2
Mahan	OR	198	D1	McKinley	OR	140	C2	*MILTON-FREEWTR	OR	121	C3				
Malahat	BC	159	A4	McLeod	OR	149	C1	*MILWAUKIE	OR	318	A7	**N**			
Malaga	WA	239	B5	McLoughlin Heights	WA	306	D6	Milwaukie Heights	OR	321	J4	*NACHES	WA	243	A4
*MALDEN	WA	114	B3	McMicken Heights	WA	288	D6	Mima	WA	184	B3	Naef	OR	199	D4
*MALIN	OR	151	A3	McMillin	WA	182	C5	Minam	OR	130	B1	Nahcotta	WA	186	A2
Malone	WA	179	C7	*MCMINNVILLE	OR	198	A7	Mineral	ID	139	A1	*NAMPA	ID	147	B1
Malott	WA	104	C3	McMurray	WA	168	C2	Mineral	WA	118	B1	*NANAIMO	BC	93	A3
Maltby	WA	171	D5	McNab	OR	128	B2	Minerva	OR	214	C1	Nanoose Bay	BC	92	C1
Manchester	WA	271	H12	McNary	OR	129	A1	Minnehaha	WA	305	J1	*NAPAVINE	WA	187	B1
Manette	WA	271	B10	Meacham	OR	129	C2	Minnick	WA	122	A3	Naples	ID	107	B2
Manhattan	WA	290	A1	Meacham Corner	OR	125	C1	Mirrormont	WA	176	A5	Napton	OR	147	A1
Manhattan Beach	OR	191	B5	Mead	WA	347	F7	Mission	OR	129	B1	Narrows	OR	133	C2

*Indicates incorporated city

Community	State	Page	Grid	Community	State	Page	Grid	Community	State	Page	Grid	Community	State	Page	Grid
Narrows	OR	145	B2	North Howell	OR	205	B4	Oreana	ID	147	C2	Penn Cove Park	WA	167	B4
Naselle	WA	186	C5	Northilla	WA	174	D7	*OREGON CITY	OR	199	D5	Peola	WA	122	C2
Nashville	OR	133	A1	N Jct (Davidson)	OR	127	B3	Oregon Trunk Jct	OR	127	B1	Peoria	OR	210	A1
Nason Creek	WA	111	C1	North Lewiston	ID	250	C4	Orenco	OR	199	A1	Perrinville	WA	171	B5
Natal	OR	117	B3	North Olympia	WA	180	D5	Oretown	OR	203	B1	Perry	OR	130	A2
National	WA	118	B1	*NORTH PLAINS	OR	125	C1	Orient	OR	200	C1	Perrydale	OR	204	B3
Navy Yard City	WA	270	E11	*NORTHPORT	WA	106	A1	Orient	WA	105	C1	Peshastin	WA	238	A1
Naylor	WA	112	C3	*NORTH POWDER	OR	130	B2	Orilla	WA	289	J7	Petersburg	WA	196	D7
Neah Bay	BC	100	B2	North Prosser	WA	120	C3	*OROFINO	ID	123	C2	Peterson	BC	106	A1
Neahkahnie Beach	OR	191	B3	North Puyallup	WA	182	A3	Orondo	WA	236	A1	Peyton	WA	122	B1
Neawanna Station	OR	301	J6	North Santiam	OR	133	C1	*OROVILLE	WA	104	C1	*PHILOMATH	OR	133	B1
Necanicum Jct	OR	188	D7	North Scholls	OR	198	D3	Orrs Corner	OR	204	B6	Phoenix	BC	105	B1
Nedonna Beach	OR	191	B5	North Springfield	OR	330	G2	*ORTING	WA	182	C5	*PHOENIX	OR	234	B2
Needy	OR	205	D1	Northwest	OR	312	C4	Osborn Corner	WA	171	C4	Piedmont	OR	309	F6
*NEHALEM	OR	191	B4	Northwest Industrl	OR	312	B2	*OSBURN	ID	115	C2	Piedmont	WA	164	C6
Neilton	WA	109	A2	Norway	OR	220	D6	Osceola	WA	182	D3	Pigeon Springs	WA	118	A3
Nelscott	OR	203	A5	Norwood	ID	251	C7	Oso	WA	102	C3	Pilchuck	WA	168	D4
Nelson	WA	240	A2	Norwood	OR	199	B4	*OSOYOOS	BC	104	C1	Pillar Rock	WA	117	A2
Nelway	BC	106	C1	Noti	OR	133	A2	Ostrander	WA	303	F1	*PILOT ROCK	OR	129	B2
Nena	OR	127	B3	*NOTUS	ID	147	B1	*OTHELLO	WA	121	A1	Pinckney	OR	322	G11
Neotsu	OR	203	B4	Novelty	WA	110	C1	Otis	OR	203	B3	Pine	WA	131	A3
Neptune Beach	WA	158	B6	Nulls Crossing	WA	184	D6	Otis Junction	OR	203	B3	Pine City	OR	128	C1
Nesika Beach	OR	228	A4	Nye	OR	129	B2	Otis Orchards	WA	352	B9	Pine City	WA	114	B3
Neskowin	OR	203	B2	Nyland	WA	110	C1	Otter Bay	BC	101	B1	Pine Glen	WA	111	B3
*NESPELEM	WA	105	A3	*NYSSA	OR	139	A3	Otter Point	BC	101	A2	Pine Grove	OR	127	A3
Netarts	OR	197	A2					Otter Rock	OR	206	B2	Pine Grove	OR	195	D6
Newaukum	WA	184	B7	**O**				Outlet Bay	ID	107	A2	*PINEHURST	ID	115	C2
*NEWBERG	OR	198	D5	*OAKESDALE	WA	114	C3	Outlook	OR	200	A4	Pinehurst	ID	131	C2
New Bridge	OR	139	A1	Oak Grove	OR	195	C6	Outlook	WA	120	B2	Pinehurst	OR	150	A2
New Brighton	BC	93	B2	Oak Grove	OR	321	J6	Overland	OR	220	D3	Pinehurst	WA	269	F2
*NEWCASTLE	WA	175	C4	*OAK HARBOR	WA	167	B2	Overlook	OR	308	C6	Pine Ridge	ID	131	C3
New Era	OR	199	C5	Oak Hills	OR	199	A1	Owyhee	ID	253	D6	Pine Ridge	OR	231	D3
Newell	CA	151	A3	*OAKLAND	OR	219	A7	Owyhee	OR	139	A3	Ping	WA	122	B1
Newhalem	WA	103	B2	Oakland	WA	180	B2	Oxman	OR	138	C1	Pirtle	OR	207	C5
New Hope	OR	229	B7	Oak Park	OR	323	E9	Oxyoke	OR	229	B3	Pistol River	OR	232	B1
New Idaho	OR	152	A2	Oak Park	WA	193	B7	Oyhut	WA	177	B6	Pitt	WA	196	C3
New Idanha	OR	134	B1	Oak Point	WA	117	B3	Oyster River	BC	92	A1	*PITT MEADOWS	BC	157	B5
New Kamilche	WA	180	A5	*OAKRIDGE	OR	142	A1	Oysterville	OR	206	B5	Pittsburg	WA	125	B1
New London	WA	178	A5	Oaks	OR	334	E11	Oysterville	WA	186	A1	Placer	OR	229	C2
Newman Lake	WA	352	F6	Oak Springs	OR	127	B3					Plain	WA	111	C1
*NEW MEADOWS	ID	251	A4	*OAKVILLE	WA	117	B1	**P**				Plainview	OR	210	C1
New Pine Creek	CA	152	A3	OBrien	OR	233	A6	*PACIFIC	WA	182	B2	Plainview	OR	212	A6
New Pine Creek	OR	152	A3	OBrien	WA	291	J5	Pacific Beach	WA	177	B2	Plaza	WA	114	C2
*NEW PLYMOUTH	ID	139	B3	Ocasta	WA	183	B2	Pacific Beach	WA	186	A4	Pleasantdale	OR	204	D1
*NEWPORT	OR	206	B4	Ocean City	WA	177	B5	Pacific City	OR	197	A7	Pleasant Hill	OR	215	D4
*NEWPORT	WA	106	C3	Oceanlake	OR	203	A4	Packard	WA	113	C3	Pleasant Hill	WA	189	C1
Newport Heights	OR	206	B4	Ocean Park	BC	158	D1	Packwood	WA	118	C2	Pleasant Home	OR	200	C1
Newport Hills	WA	175	C4	Ocean Park	WA	186	A2	Page	ID	115	C2	Pleasant Valley	OR	197	C4
New Princeton	OR	145	C2	*OCEAN SHORES	WA	298	C2	*PAISLEY	OR	151	C1	Pleasant Valley	OR	200	A1
Newton	BC	157	A7	Oceanside	OR	197	A2	Palmer Junction	OR	130	B1	Pleasant Valley	OR	229	B3
Newton	OR	198	D1	Oceanside	WA	186	A4	*PALOUSE	WA	249	B1	Pleasant View	WA	121	C2
Newton	WA	177	C5	Odell	OR	195	C7	Panakanic	WA	196	B1	*PLUMMER	ID	115	A2
*NEW WESTMNSTR	BC	156	D5	Odell Lake	OR	142	B1	Pandora	WA	114	C3	Plush	OR	152	B1
*NEZ PERCE	ID	123	C2	Odessa	OR	231	B6	Park	WA	161	C2	Pluvius	WA	117	B2
Niagara	OR	134	A1	*ODESSA	WA	113	B3	Parkdale	OR	202	C2	Plymouth	WA	121	A3
Nicola	BC	95	C1	Ohop	WA	118	B1	Parker	WA	120	A2	Pocahontas	OR	138	A1
Nighthawk	WA	104	C1	*OKANOGAN	WA	104	C3	Parkersburg	OR	220	B5	Pocahontas Bay	WA	106	C3
Nile	WA	119	B1	Oklahoma Hill	OR	117	B3	Parkers Mill	WA	128	C3	Pocono	ID	115	C3
Nimrod	OR	134	A3	Olalla	OR	141	A2	Parkland	WA	181	D4	Point Roberts	WA	101	C1
Nine Mile Falls	WA	246	A2	Olalla	WA	174	C6	Park Place	OR	199	D4	Point Terrace	OR	214	D2
Ninety One	OR	205	C1	Old Colton	OR	126	A3	Parkrose	OR	315	J1	Point White	WA	271	F7
Nippon	WA	111	B1	Old Town	OR	219	A7	Parkrose Heights	OR	315	J3	Pollock	ID	131	C2
Nisqually	WA	181	A6	Oldtown	WA	106	C3	*PARKSVILLE	BC	92	C3	*POMEROY	WA	122	B2
Nisson	WA	178	B4	Oldtown-Chinatwn	OR	313	F5	Parkwater	WA	349	H6	Pomona	WA	243	C4
Nitinat	BC	100	B1	Olene	OR	150	C2	Parkwood	WA	174	C4	*PONDERAY	ID	244	A1
Nolin	OR	129	A1	Olex	OR	128	A2	Parliament	OR	131	B1	Ponderosa Estates	WA	182	C4
Nonpareil	OR	141	B2	Olga	WA	160	A3	*PARMA	ID	139	A3	Ponders	WA	181	C4
*NOOKSACK	WA	102	B1	Olney	OR	188	D3	Parvin	WA	122	C1	Pondosa	OR	130	B3
Nksck Slmn Htchry	WA	102	B1	*OLYMPIA	WA	297	C7	Pasadena Park	WA	350	E3	Portage	WA	174	D6
Noon	OR	133	B1	Olympic View	WA	170	A7	*PASCO	WA	343	E4	*PORT ALBERNI	BC	92	B3
Norgate	BC	254	H5	*OMAK	WA	104	C2	Pataha	WA	122	A2	*PORT ANGELES	WA	261	E5
Norma Beach	WA	171	B4	Omens	WA	114	A2	Pataha	WA	122	B2	*PORT COQUITLAM	BC	157	B4
Norman	WA	168	B4	Ona	OR	206	B7	*PATEROS	WA	112	B1	Porter	WA	117	B1
*NORMANDY PARK	WA	175	A6	Onalaska	WA	118	A2	Paterson	WA	120	C3	Port Gamble	WA	170	C4
North Albany	OR	326	B5	*ONAWAY	ID	249	D1	Patrick Creek	CA	148	C3	Port Hammond	BC	157	C6
North Beach	OR	214	B5	ONeil	OR	213	A4	Paulina	OR	136	B3	Porthill	ID	107	B1
North Beach	WA	171	A7	ONeil Corners	OR	199	C6	*PAYETTE	ID	139	A3	Port Kells	BC	157	B6
North Bend	BC	95	A1	*ONTARIO	OR	139	A3	Payette Heights	ID	139	A3	*PORTLAND	OR	316	C3
*NORTH BEND	OR	333	F6	Ontario Heights	OR	139	A3	Pearl District	OR	313	E4	Port Ludlow	WA	170	B3
*NORTH BEND	WA	176	C4	Opal City	OR	212	D2	Pebble Beach	WA	168	A7	Port Madison	WA	170	D7
*NORTH BONNEVLE	WA	194	C6	Ophir	OR	228	A3	Peck	ID	123	B2	Port Mellon	BC	93	B2
North Central	OR	200	B1	Opportunity	WA	350	H12	Pedee	OR	133	B1	*PORT MOODY	BC	157	A4
North City	WA	171	B6	Orcas	WA	101	C2	PE ELL	WA	117	B2	*PORT ORCHARD	WA	270	J14
North Cowichan	BC	101	A1	Orchard	OR	193	A6	Pelican City	OR	338	A3	*PORT ORFORD	OR	224	A6
Northeast	OR	200	B1	Orchard Avenue	WA	350	B5	Penawawa	WA	122	B1	Port Renfrew	BC	100	C2
Northfork	OR	151	B1	Orchard Heights	WA	271	B14	Pendair Heights	OR	129	B1	Portsmouth	OR	308	A3
North Fork	OR	214	C7	Orchard Park	WA	349	J6	Pender Island	BC	101	B1	*PORT TOWNSEND	WA	263	C2
North Gate	WA	171	B7	Orchard View	OR	198	A6	*PENDLETON	OR	129	B2	Port Washington	BC	101	B1
North Gresham	OR	200	A1	Ordnance	OR	128	C1	Pend Oreille Village	WA	106	B1	Port Williams	WA	262	J8

*Indicates incorporated city

Cities and Communities

Community	State	Page	Grid
Possession	WA	171	A3
Post	OR	136	A2
*POST FALLS	ID	353	F5
*POTLATCH	ID	249	D1
Potlatch	WA	173	A6
Potlatch Junction	ID	249	D1
*POULSBO	WA	170	B7
Powell Butte	OR	213	B6
Powellhurst	OR	200	A1
*POWELL RIVER	BC	92	C1
Powell Valley	OR	200	B1
Power City	OR	129	A1
Power House	WA	243	A4
*POWERS	OR	140	B3
Powers	WA	122	A2
Prahl	OR	199	B6
Prairie Center	WA	167	B4
*PRAIRIE CITY	OR	137	B2
Prairie Heights	WA	182	D4
Prairie Ridge	WA	182	C4
Pratum	OR	205	B5
Preachers Slough	WA	117	A1
*PRESCOTT	OR	189	C5
*PRESCOTT	WA	121	C2
Preston	WA	176	B4
Prichard	ID	115	C1
Priest Rapids	WA	120	B2
*PRIEST RIVER	ID	107	A3
*PRINCETON	BC	95	C3
Princeton	ID	123	A1
Prindle	WA	194	A7
*PRINEVILLE	OR	213	C4
Prineville Junction	OR	212	D4
Pringle	OR	324	J1
Proebstel	WA	193	A5
Prospect	OR	226	C7
Prosper	OR	220	B5
*PROSSER	WA	120	B3
Pryor	OR	142	A1
*PULLMAN	WA	249	B5
Purdy	WA	174	C6
Purrington	WA	122	B1
*PUYALLUP	WA	182	B4
Q			
Qualicum Beach	BC	92	C3
Quartz Mountain	OR	151	C2
Quatama	OR	199	A1
Quathiaski Cove	BC	92	A1
Queen Anne Hill	WA	277	G2
Queen Borough	BC	156	D6
Queets	WA	172	B3
Quilcene	WA	109	C1
Quilchena	BC	95	C1
Quinaby	OR	204	D4
Quinault	WA	109	A2
Quincy	OR	117	B3
*QUINCY	WA	112	B3
Quines Creek	OR	225	C6
R			
Rafton	OR	192	A6
Rahms	WA	114	C2
Rainbow	OR	134	B2
*RAINIER	OR	302	F14
*RAINIER	WA	118	A1
Rainier Beach	WA	287	G3
Rainier Valley	WA	282	D6
Rainrock	OR	214	D1
Raleigh Hills	OR	199	B2
Ramapo	WA	164	D6
Ramey	ID	139	A3
Ramsey	ID	245	A3
Rand	OR	149	A1
Randle	WA	118	C2
*RATHDRUM	ID	115	A1
Ravenna	WA	274	D4
Ravensdale	WA	176	A7
*RAYMOND	WA	117	A1
*REARDAN	WA	114	A2
Redd	WA	121	B2
Redland	OR	200	A5
*REDMOND	OR	212	D5
*REDMOND	WA	171	D7
Redondo	WA	175	B7
Redwood	OR	229	B6
Reed	OR	318	A3
Reeds Mill	OR	128	C3
*REEDSPORT	OR	218	C2

Community	State	Page	Grid
Reedville	OR	199	A2
Rees Corner	WA	171	D4
Relief	WA	122	A2
Remac	BC	106	B1
Remote	OR	140	C3
Renfrew Heights	BC	255	E14
*RENTON	WA	289	J4
Renton Junction	WA	289	J6
*REPUBLIC	WA	105	B2
Reser	WA	121	C2
Reston	OR	141	A2
*REUBENS	ID	123	B2
Rex	OR	198	D5
Rhinehart	OR	130	A2
Rhodesia Beach	WA	183	C7
Rhododendron	OR	201	C5
Rhododendron Pk	WA	182	C4
Rice	OR	127	B2
Rice	WA	105	C2
Rice Hill	OR	219	A5
*RICHLAND	OR	139	A1
*RICHLAND	WA	340	E13
*RICHMOND	BC	156	C6
Richmond	OR	136	B1
Richmond	OR	318	B1
Richmond Beach	WA	171	A6
Rickreall	OR	204	B6
*RIDDLE	OR	225	B3
*RIDGEFIELD	WA	192	C3
Rieth	OR	129	B1
Rifton	WA	121	C2
*RIGGINS	ID	131	C2
Riley	OR	144	C1
Riparia	WA	122	A2
Ripplebrook	OR	126	B3
Risbeck	WA	122	C1
Ritter	OR	129	A3
*RITZVILLE	WA	113	C3
Riverdale	OR	321	G2
River Jordan	BC	100	C2
River Junction	OR	192	B6
Riversdale	OR	221	B3
Riverside	ID	123	C2
Riverside	OR	146	A1
Riverside	OR	207	B5
Riverside	WA	102	C3
Riverside	WA	104	C2
Riverton	OR	220	C5
Riverton	WA	289	F1
Riverton Heights	WA	288	D3
Riverwood	OR	321	G3
Roads End	OR	203	A4
Roanoke	WA	283	J1
Roberts	OR	135	C3
Robinette	OR	139	A1
Robinwood	OR	199	C4
Roche Harbor	WA	101	C2
Rochester	WA	184	A3
Rockaway Beach	ID	245	B5
*ROCKAWAY BEACH	OR	191	B6
Rock Creek	BC	105	A1
Rock Creek	OR	128	A2
Rock Creek	OR	130	A3
Rock Creek	OR	192	A7
Rockdale	WA	111	A1
Rockford	OR	195	C5
*ROCKFORD	WA	114	C2
Rockford Bay	ID	247	D4
*ROCK ISLAND	WA	239	B5
Rockport	WA	103	A2
Rockwood	OR	200	A1
Rocky Point	ID	248	B6
Rocky Point	OR	231	B5
Rocky Point	WA	270	E7
Rocky Point	WA	303	E4
Rodena Beach	WA	167	C4
*ROGUE RIVER	OR	229	D6
Rollingbay	WA	174	D1
Rollins	WA	114	C2
Rome	OR	146	C3
Ronald	WA	240	A1
Rony	WA	117	B1
Roosevelt	OR	110	C1
Roosevelt	WA	128	A1
*ROSALIA	WA	114	C3
Rosario	WA	101	C2
Rosario Beach	WA	259	C14
Roseberry	ID	252	D1
*ROSEBURG	OR	334	H4

Community	State	Page	Grid
Rosebush	OR	127	C2
Rose City Park	OR	314	C4
Rosedale	BC	94	C3
Rosedale	OR	324	F11
Rosedale	WA	174	B7
Rosehilla	WA	174	D7
Rose Lake	ID	248	D2
Rose Lodge	OR	203	C4
Rosemont	OR	199	C4
Rose Springs	WA	122	B2
Roseway	OR	315	E2
Rosewood	OR	199	C4
*ROSLYN	WA	240	A1
*ROSSLAND	BC	106	A1
Roswell	ID	139	A3
Rothe	OR	199	D4
Round Prairie	OR	221	B7
Rowena	OR	196	B6
*ROY	WA	181	C7
*ROYAL CITY	WA	120	C1
Royal Oak	BC	159	C5
Royston	BC	92	A2
Roy Vadis	OR	125	C1
Roza	WA	243	C3
Rubicon	ID	131	C3
Ruch	OR	149	B2
Ruff	WA	113	A3
*RUFUS	OR	127	C1
Ruggs	OR	128	C2
Rupple	WA	119	C2
Rural Dell	OR	205	D2
Russell	OR	133	A1
Russell Landing	WA	311	F1
*RUSTON	WA	181	D1
Rutledge	OR	127	C2
Ryderwood	WA	187	B5
Rye Valley	OR	138	C2
Rykerts	BC	107	B1
S			
Saanichton	BC	159	C3
Sabin	OR	313	H1
Safley	OR	219	B2
Saginaw	OR	215	B6
Sagle	ID	244	A3
Sago	OR	130	B3
Sahalee	WA	175	D2
Saint Andrews	WA	112	C2
*SAINT HELENS	OR	192	B2
Saint Joe	ID	115	B2
*SAINT JOHN	WA	114	B3
Saint Johns	OR	192	B6
Saint Joseph	OR	198	B7
Saint Louis	OR	205	A2
*SAINT MARIES	ID	248	D7
St. Martins Hot Spgs	WA	195	A4
*SAINT PAUL	OR	198	D7
Saint Urbans	WA	187	C2
*SALEM	OR	325	D5
Salisbury	OR	138	B1
Salishan	WA	182	A3
Salkum	WA	118	A2
Salmon	OR	201	B4
Salmon Beach	WA	181	C1
Salmonberry	OR	125	A1
Salmon Creek	WA	192	C5
Saltery Bay	BC	92	C1
Samish Island	WA	160	D4
*SAMMAMISH	WA	175	D2
Sams Valley	OR	230	B5
San de Fuca	WA	167	B4
Sanders	ID	115	A3
Sand Hollow	ID	139	B3
Sand Hollow	OR	128	C1
Sandlake	OR	197	B5
*SANDPOINT	ID	244	A1
Sandwick	BC	92	A2
*SANDY	OR	200	C4
San Marine	OR	328	B14
Santa	ID	115	B3
Santa Clara	OR	215	A1
Santa Cruz	OR	200	C7
Santiam Junction	OR	134	C2
Sappho	WA	163	B6
Saratoga	WA	167	D7
Sardis	BC	94	C3
Sardis	ID	115	A3
Satsop	WA	179	A7
Saturna	BC	101	C1
Saunders Lake	OR	218	B5

Community	State	Page	Grid
Savary Island	BC	92	B1
Saxby	WA	247	B7
*SCAPPOOSE	OR	192	A3
Scenic	WA	111	B1
Schaefer	WA	113	C3
Schefflin Corner	OR	125	C1
Schneiders Prairie	WA	180	B5
Scholls	OR	198	D4
Schoonover	WA	113	C3
Schrag	WA	113	B3
Schwana	WA	120	B1
Schwarder	WA	243	B7
*SCIO	OR	133	C1
Scofield	OR	125	B1
Scott Bar	CA	149	B3
*SCOTTS MILLS	OR	205	D4
Scottsburg	OR	140	C1
Scribner	WA	246	B6
Seabeck	WA	173	D1
Seabold	WA	170	C7
Seahurst	WA	175	A5
Seal Rock	OR	206	A7
Seal Rock	OR	109	C1
Searose Beach	OR	209	A5
*SEASIDE	OR	301	E9
*SEATAC	WA	288	C3
*SEATTLE	WA	273	G3
Seattle Heights	WA	171	A5
Seaview	WA	186	A6
Sechelt	BC	93	A2
*SEDRO-WOOLLEY	WA	260	J2
Seekseequa Jct	OR	208	A4
Seiad Valley	CA	149	B3
Sekiu	WA	163	B2
*SELAH	WA	243	B5
Selleck	WA	176	B7
Sellwood	OR	317	H5
Selma	OR	233	B2
*SENECA	OR	137	B3
*SEQUIM	WA	262	D13
Service Creek	OR	136	B1
Seven Mile	WA	246	A2
Seven Oaks	OR	230	C7
Sexton Mountain	OR	199	A2
Seymour	BC	255	J5
Shadowood	OR	199	C4
Shady	OR	334	E13
Shady Brook	OR	125	C1
*SHADY COVE	OR	230	D2
Shady Pine	OR	235	C1
*SHANIKO	OR	127	C3
Shale City	OR	150	A2
Shangri-la Mill	OR	141	C3
Sharps Corner	OR	129	A1
Shawnee	WA	122	C1
Shawnigan Lake	BC	159	A2
Sheaville	OR	147	A2
Shedd	OR	210	B1
Shelburn	OR	133	C1
Shelfler	WA	121	B2
*SHELTON	WA	180	A3
Sherar	WA	127	B2
*SHERIDAN	OR	125	B3
Sheridan Park	WA	270	H8
Sherman	WA	113	B1
*SHERWOOD	OR	199	A4
Sherwood Beach	ID	107	A2
Shine	WA	170	B4
Shirley	BC	101	A2
Shore Acres	WA	181	C1
*SHORELINE	WA	171	A6
Shorewood	OR	218	B6
Shorewood	WA	285	G7
Shorewood Beach	WA	181	B2
Shortys Corner	OR	200	D4
Shrine Beach	WA	236	A1
Shutler	OR	128	A1
Sidley	BC	105	A1
Sidney	OR	207	C2
Sifton	WA	193	A5
Sightly	WA	118	A2
Silcott	WA	250	A4
*SILETZ	OR	206	C2
Silica	BC	106	A1
Siltcoos	OR	214	B5
Silvana	WA	168	C5
Silver Beach	WA	102	B1
Silver Brook	WA	118	C2
Silver City	ID	147	B3

*Indicates incorporated city

Community	State	Page	Grid	Community	State	Page	Grid	Community	State	Page	Grid	Community	State	Page	Grid
Silver Creek	WA	118	A2	*SPRAY	OR	136	B1	Sunset Beach	OR	188	B3	Tiller	OR	141	C3
Silverdale	WA	174	B1	Spring Beach	WA	174	C7	Sunset Beach	WA	167	D4	Tillicum	BC	256	E5
Silver Falls City	OR	205	D7	Springbrook	OR	198	D5	Sunset Beach	WA	173	D6	Tillicum	WA	181	C5
Silver Lake	BC	95	A3	Springbrook	WA	181	D4	Sunset Beach	WA	174	D6	Timber Grove	OR	126	A3
Silver Lake	OR	143	B2	Springdale	OR	200	C1	Sunset Beach	WA	177	B2	Timberlane	WA	175	D7
Silverlake	WA	187	D7	*SPRINGDALE	WA	106	B3	Sunset Beach	WA	181	C3	Tokeland	WA	183	C5
Silver Sands Beach	ID	115	A1	*SPRINGFIELD	OR	331	E6	Suplee	OR	136	C3	Toketee Falls	OR	222	D4
Silverton	ID	115	C2	Springfield Jct	OR	330	F7	Suquamish	WA	170	C7	Tokio	WA	113	C3
*SILVERTON	OR	205	C4	Spring Glen	WA	175	C5	Surrey Centre	BC	157	B7	Tokul	WA	176	C4
Silvies	OR	137	B3	Spring Lake	OR	235	C5	Susanville	OR	137	B1	*TOLEDO	OR	206	C4
Similk Beach	WA	160	C7	Springston	ID	248	B4	*SUTHERLIN	OR	221	C1	*TOLEDO	WA	187	D4
Simnasho	OR	127	A3	Spring Valley	WA	114	C2	Sutico	WA	117	B1	Tolovana Park	OR	191	B1
Sims Corner	WA	112	C1	Spuzzum	BC	95	A2	Sutton	WA	122	A1	Tongue Point Vlg	OR	188	D1
Sisco	WA	168	D6	*SQUAMISH	BC	93	C2	Suver Junction	OR	207	B2	Tono	WA	184	D4
Sisco Heights	WA	168	D6	Squaw Canyon	WA	114	C3	Svensen	OR	117	A3	Top Hat	WA	285	J5
Siskiyou	OR	234	D6	Stabler	WA	194	C3	Svensen Junction	OR	117	A3	*TOPPENISH	WA	120	A2
*SISTERS	OR	211	D5	Stafford	OR	199	C4	Swansonville	WA	170	B3	Torga	WA	111	A2
Sitkum	OR	140	C2	Staley	WA	249	B6	Swedetown	OR	189	A5	Touchet	WA	121	B3
Siuslaw	OR	132	C3	Stampede	WA	111	A3	Sweeney	ID	115	C2	Toutle	WA	118	A2
Six Corners	OR	199	A4	*STANFIELD	OR	129	A1	Sweet	ID	139	C3	Town & Country	WA	346	J14
Sixes	OR	224	B4	Stanfield Junction	OR	129	A1	*SWEET HOME	OR	134	A2	*TWN OF ESQUIMLT	BC	256	C8
Six Prong	WA	128	B1	*STANWOOD	WA	168	B4	Sweetwater	ID	123	A2	*TOWN OF SIDNEY	BC	159	C2
Skamania	WA	194	B7	Star	ID	147	C1	Swem	WA	117	B1	*TWN OF VW ROYAL	BC	256	A4
Skamokawa	WA	117	B2	*STARBUCK	WA	122	A2	Swift	WA	122	B1	*TWP OF LANGLY	BC	157	D7
Skelley	OR	219	A4	Starkey	ID	131	C3	Swinomish Village	WA	160	D7	Tracy	OR	200	C6
*SKYKOMISH	OR	111	A1	Starkey	OR	125	C1	Swisshome	OR	132	C3	Tracyton	WA	270	G4
Skyway	WA	287	J7	Starkey	OR	129	C2	Sylvan	WA	181	B2	Trail	OR	230	D2
Slate Creek	ID	131	C1	Starlake	WA	175	B7	Sylvan Beach	WA	174	D5	Treharne	OR	125	B1
Sliammon	BC	92	B1	Startup	WA	110	C1	Sylvan Highlands	OR	312	A7	Trenholm	OR	125	C1
Smelter Heights	ID	115	C2	Starvation Heights	OR	229	D5	Sylvanite	MT	107	C1	Trent	OR	215	D4
*SMELTERVILLE	ID	115	C2	State Line Village	ID	352	H9					Trentwood	WA	351	A3
Smeltz	OR	129	B1	Stave Falls	BC	94	B3	**T**				Trestle Creek	ID	244	C2
Smith Prairie	WA	167	C4	*STAYTON	OR	133	C1	Table Rock	OR	230	C6	Tri-City	OR	225	C2
Smith River	CA	148	B3	Steelhead	BC	94	B3	*TACOMA	WA	292	D5	Trinity	WA	103	C3
Smithville	WA	196	C6	Stehekin	WA	103	C3	Taft	OR	203	A5	*TROUTDALE	OR	200	B1
Smokey Point	WA	168	C6	*STEILACOOM	WA	181	B4	Tahlequah	WA	181	D1	Trout Lake	WA	119	A3
Snake River	WA	121	B2	Stephens	OR	221	B1	Taholah	WA	172	B6	*TROY	ID	123	A1
Snake River Jct	WA	121	B2	Steptoe	WA	114	C3	Tahuya	WA	173	B7	*TROY	MT	107	C2
Snee Oosh	WA	160	D7	Stevens	ID	131	C3	Takilma	OR	233	B6	Troy	OR	122	C3
*SNOHOMISH	WA	171	D3	*STEVENSON	WA	194	C5	Talache	ID	244	B5	Trude	WA	176	B7
*SNOQUALMIE	WA	176	B4	Steveston	BC	156	B7	Talbot	OR	207	C2	Tsawwassen	BC	101	C1
Snowden	WA	196	A2	Stillwater	BC	92	C2	*TALENT	OR	234	B3	*TUALATIN	OR	199	B4
Snug Harbor	WA	164	D6	Stillwater	WA	176	B1	Tamarack	ID	131	C3	Tucannon	WA	122	A2
*SOAP LAKE	WA	112	C2	Stimson Mill	OR	198	B2	Tampico	WA	119	C2	*TUKWILA	WA	289	F3
Soda Springs	WA	119	B2	Stoddard	ID	147	C2	*TANGENT	OR	207	C6	Tulalip	WA	168	B7
*SODAVILLE	OR	133	C2	Stratford	WA	113	A2	Tanner	WA	176	C5	Tulalip Shores	WA	168	B7
Sokulk	WA	114	C3	Strawberry	OR	128	C2	Tasker	WA	119	C1	Tulameen	BC	95	C2
Somerset West	OR	199	A1	Striebels Corner	WA	170	C5	Taylorville	OR	117	B3	Tulare Beach	WA	168	B6
Sooke	BC	101	A2	Stronghold	CA	151	A3	Teanaway	WA	240	C2	Tulelake	CA	151	A3
Sorrento Ridge	OR	199	B3	Stuck	WA	182	C2	*TEKOA	WA	114	C3	Tulips	WA	177	C5
South Aberdeen	WA	178	B7	Sturdies Bay	BC	101	B1	Telford	WA	113	C1	Tumalo	OR	217	B1
South Arm	BC	156	B6	Sturgeon	ID	115	A1	Telma	WA	111	C1	*TUMWATER	WA	296	F9
South Bay	WA	180	D5	*SUBLIMITY	OR	133	C1	Telocaset	OR	130	B3	Tumtum	WA	114	B1
South Beach	OR	206	B4	Sudden Valley	WA	161	B1	Templeton	OR	218	C4	Turkey	WA	166	D2
South Beach	WA	101	C1	Sullivans Gulch	OR	313	J4	*TENINO	WA	184	D3	*TURNER	OR	325	G12
South Beach	WA	174	D3	Sulphur Springs	OR	214	D7	Tenino Junction	WA	184	D3	Turner	WA	122	B2
South Bellingham	WA	258	C10	*SULTAN	WA	110	C1	Tenmile	OR	141	A2	Turner Corner	WA	171	C5
*SOUTH BEND	WA	183	D6	*SUMAS	WA	102	B1	Tenmile	OR	218	B4	Twickenham	OR	136	A1
South Burlingame	OR	316	D6	Summer Lake	OR	143	C3	*TENSED	ID	115	A3	Twin Beaches	ID	248	A1
South Cheney	WA	114	B2	*SUMMERVILLE	OR	130	A2	Terrace Heights	WA	243	C6	Twin Lakes	WA	182	A1
*SOUTH CLE ELUM	WA	240	B2	Summit	OR	195	C6	Terrebone	OR	212	D4	Twinlow	ID	115	A1
South Colby	WA	174	C4	Summit	WA	176	A7	Terrys Corner	WA	167	D4	Twin Rocks	OR	191	A6
South Elma	WA	179	B7	Summit	WA	182	A4	*THE DALLES	OR	196	C7	*TWISP	WA	104	A3
South Highlands	WA	343	C12	Summits	OR	133	A1	Thomas	WA	175	B7	Twomile	OR	220	B7
South Junction	OR	208	C1	Sumner	OR	140	B2	Thompson	BC	156	A6	Tye	WA	111	B1
South Lk Oswego	OR	320	E7	*SUMNER	WA	182	B3	Thompson Place	WA	181	A6	Tyee	OR	141	A1
*SOUTH PRAIRIE	WA	182	D5	*SUMPTER	OR	138	A1	Thorndyke	WA	289	E4	Tyee Beach	WA	168	A7
South Slope	BC	156	C5	Suncrest	BC	156	C5	Thorn Hollow	OR	129	C1	Tygh Valley	OR	127	B2
South Tabor	OR	318	E1	Sundale	WA	128	A1	Thornton	WA	114	C3	Tyler	WA	114	B2
South Tacoma	WA	294	D5	Sunderland	OR	310	B4	Thorp	WA	241	A4	Tynehead	BC	157	B6
South Union	WA	184	C1	Sunlight Beach	WA	170	D2	Thrall	WA	241	B7				
South Wellington	BC	93	A3	Sunnycrest	OR	198	C5	Thrashers Corner	WA	171	C5	**U**			
Southwest	OR	200	A1	Sunnydale	WA	175	A5	Three Lakes	WA	110	C1	*UKIAH	OR	129	B3
Southwest Hills	OR	316	B1	Sunnydale	WA	184	C3	Three Lynx	OR	126	B3	Umapine	WA	121	C3
South Westminister	BC	156	D6	Sunny Shores	WA	168	B6	Three Pines	OR	229	B3	*UMATILLA	OR	129	A1
Southwick	ID	123	B1	Sunny Shores Acres	WA	168	A6	Three Rivers	OR	217	A7	Umli	OR	142	B1
Southworth	WA	174	D4	Sunnyside	OR	200	A2	Three Rocks	OR	203	A3	Umpqua	OR	221	A1
Spanaway	WA	181	D5	Sunnyside	OR	314	A7	Three Tree Point	WA	175	A5	Umtanum	WA	243	C1
*SPANGLE	WA	114	C2	Sunnyside	OR	324	J12	Thrift	WA	182	B6	Uncas	WA	109	C1
Sparks	OR	129	B1	*SUNNYSIDE	WA	120	B2	Thurston	OR	331	J6	Underwood	WA	195	C4
Sparta	OR	130	C3	Sunnyside	WA	121	C3	Tide	OR	132	C3	Underwood Heights	WA	195	C4
Spee-bi-dah	WA	168	B7	Sunnyslope	OR	174	A4	Tidewater	OR	209	C1	*UNION	OR	130	B2
*SPIRIT LAKE	ID	115	A1	Sunnyslope	WA	238	D3	Tiernan	OR	214	C2	Union	WA	173	A7
Spitzenberg	OR	125	C1	Sunny Valley	OR	229	B2	Tierra Del Mar	OR	197	A6	Union Bay	BC	92	B2
*SPOKANE	WA	346	B13	Sunriver	OR	217	A6	*TIETON	WA	119	C1	Union Creek	OR	141	A3
Spokane Valley	WA	349	G10	Sunset	BC	156	B5	Tietonview Grange	WA	119	C2	Union Creek	OR	226	D4
*SPRAGUE	WA	114	A3	Sunset	OR	131	A3	*TIGARD	OR	199	B3	Union Gap	OR	221	C1
Sprague River	OR	151	A1	Sunset	OR	199	D4	*TILLAMOOK	OR	197	B2	*UNION GAP	WA	243	C7
				Sunset	WA	114	B3	Tillamook Junction	OR	125	C1				

*Indicates incorporated city

Cities and Communities

Community	State	Page	Grid
Union Junction	OR	130	B2
Union Mills	OR	126	A3
Union Mills	WA	181	A6
*UNIONTOWN	WA	250	B2
Unionville	OR	204	C2
United Junction	OR	192	B6
*UNITY	OR	138	A2
University	WA	274	C5
*UNV ENDWMT LDS	BC	156	A4
University Park	OR	308	A5
*UNIVERSITY PLACE	WA	294	A4
Upper Farm	OR	206	D2
Upper Highland	OR	200	B7
Upper Mill	WA	110	C3
Upper Preston	WA	176	B4
Upper Soda	OR	134	B2
Usk	WA	106	C3
Ustick	ID	253	B2
Utsalady	WA	167	D3
V			
*VADER	WA	187	C4
Vadis	OR	125	C1
Vail	WA	118	A1
Valby	OR	128	B2
*VALE	OR	138	C3
Valle Vista	OR	192	A7
Valley	WA	106	B3
Valleycliffe	BC	93	C2
Valley Falls	OR	152	A1
Valleyford	WA	246	D6
Valley Junction	OR	125	A3
Van	OR	137	B3
Vananda	BC	92	B2
Van Asselt	WA	286	D1
*VANCOUVER	BC	254	G13
*VANCOUVER	WA	305	F3
Vancouver Junction	WA	192	C5
Van Horn	OR	195	D6
Vantage	WA	120	B1
Van Zandt	WA	102	B1
Vasa Park	WA	175	D3
Vashon	WA	174	D5
Vashon Center	WA	174	D6
Vashon Heights	WA	174	D4
Vaughn	OR	133	A2
Vaughn	WA	174	A7
Vega	WA	181	A4
Venator	OR	146	A2
Venersborg	WA	193	B3
*VENETA	OR	133	B3
Venice	WA	174	C1
Veradale	WA	351	C8
Verboort	OR	125	B1
Vermon	OR	309	J6
*VERNONIA	OR	125	B1
Vesuvius	BC	101	B1
Victoria	BC	156	C5
Vida	OR	134	A2
View Ridge	WA	275	G3
Village Bay	BC	101	B1
Vineland	WA	250	B4
Vinemaple	OR	125	A1
Vinland	WA	170	B6
Vinson	OR	129	A2
Viola	ID	249	C3
Viola	OR	200	B6
Virden	WA	240	D1
Virginia	WA	170	B7
Vision Acres	WA	189	C4
Voltage	OR	145	B2
Voorhies	OR	234	B2
W			
Wabash	WA	182	D2
Waconda	OR	205	A3
Wagner	WA	110	C1
Wagnersburg	WA	239	A1
Wagontire	OR	144	B2
Wahkiacus	WA	196	D3
*WAITSBURG	WA	122	A2
Waitsburg Junction	WA	122	A2
Wakonda Beach	OR	328	B10
Waldale	WA	241	B5
*WALDPORT	OR	328	C7
Walker	OR	215	B6
*WALLACE	ID	115	C2
Wallace	OR	199	B6
*WALLA WALLA	WA	344	E6
Walla Walla East	WA	345	E9
Wallingford	WA	274	A5
*WALLOWA	OR	130	B1
Wallula	WA	121	B3
Walnut Grove	BC	157	C6
Walnut Grove	WA	192	D5
Walters	WA	114	C3
Walters Ferry	ID	147	B2
Walterville	OR	133	C3
Walton	OR	133	A2
Walville	WA	117	B2
Wamic	OR	127	A2
Wanapum Village	WA	120	B1
Waneta	BC	106	B1
Wankers Corner	OR	199	C4
Wapato	OR	198	B3
*WAPATO	WA	120	A2
Wapinitia	OR	127	A3
*WARDEN	WA	121	A1
*WARDNER	ID	115	C2
Warm Beach	WA	168	A5
Warm Springs	OR	208	A3
Warner	OR	140	B3
Warren	OR	192	A2
Warren	WA	181	B1
*WARRENTON	OR	188	B2
Warwick	WA	127	B1
*WASCO	OR	127	C1
Washington Harbor	WA	166	B7
*WASHOUGAL	WA	193	B7
*WASHTUCNA	WA	121	C1
*WATERLOO	OR	133	C1
Waterman	OR	129	C1
Waterman	OR	136	B1
Waterman	WA	271	E9
Waterman Point	WA	271	F8
*WATERVILLE	WA	236	C7
Watseco	OR	191	A6
Waukon	WA	114	A2
Wauna	OR	117	B3
Wauna	WA	174	B6
Wautauga Beach	WA	271	G8
*WAVERLY	WA	114	C2
Wawawai	WA	122	C1
Wayland	OR	129	C1
Wayside	WA	114	B1
Weaver	OR	225	C1
Webster Corners	BC	157	D5
Wecoma Beach	OR	203	A4
Wedderburn	OR	228	A5
Weikel	WA	243	A6
*WEISER	ID	139	A2
Welches	OR	201	C5
Wellington	BC	93	A3
Wellpinit	WA	114	A1
Wells	WA	114	A3
Wemme	OR	201	C5
*WENATCHEE	WA	238	D4
Wenatchee Heights	WA	239	A6
Wendling	OR	133	C2
Wendson	OR	214	C3
West Beach	WA	101	C2
West Blakely	WA	271	H7
West Fairfield	WA	114	C2
*WESTFIR	OR	142	A1
West Fork	WA	105	B2
West Haven	OR	199	B1
Westhaven	WA	298	F11
West Highlands	WA	342	H10
West Kelso	WA	303	B7
West Klamath	OR	235	B4
West Lake	OR	188	B4
Westlake	OR	214	A5
Westlake	WA	242	C3
Westland	OR	129	A1
*WEST LINN	OR	199	C4
Westma	ID	147	C1
Westmond	ID	244	A5
*WESTON	OR	129	C1
Weston	WA	111	A3
West Park	WA	270	D11
West Pastco	WA	342	E5
Westport	OR	117	B3
*WESTPORT	WA	298	G13
West Portland Park	OR	320	A2
*WEST RICHLAND	WA	341	A3
West Salem	OR	322	F12
West Seattle	WA	280	D4
West Side	OR	152	A2
West Slope	OR	199	B2
Westsound	WA	101	C2
West Spokane	WA	348	F8
West Stayton	OR	133	C1
West Union	OR	192	A7
West Valley	WA	243	A6
West Wenatchee	WA	238	D4
Westwood	WA	285	G2
West Woodbury	OR	205	B1
Wetico	WA	118	A1
Wetmore	OR	128	B3
Wetzels Corner	OR	200	B3
Wheatland	OR	204	D3
*WHEELER	OR	191	B4
Wheeler Heights	OR	191	B4
Whelan	WA	249	B4
Whetstone	WA	122	A2
Whiskey Hill	OR	205	C1
*WHISTLER	BC	93	C1
Whiststran	WA	120	C3
White	WA	171	D7
*WHITE BIRD	ID	131	C1
White Center	WA	285	G4
White City	OR	230	D6
Whites	OR	179	C6
*WHITE SALMON	WA	195	D4
Whiteson	OR	204	B1
White Swan	WA	119	C2
Whitewater	OR	126	B3
Whitlow	WA	249	B5
Whitman	WA	121	A3
Whitney	OR	138	A1
Whitney	WA	344	J12
Whittier	WA	111	A3
Whonnock	BC	94	B3
Wickersham	WA	161	C3
Wilbur	OR	221	C2
*WILBUR	WA	113	B1
Wilburton	WA	175	C2
Wilcox	OR	127	C3
Wildcat Lake	WA	174	A2
*WILDER	ID	147	A1
Wilderness	WA	176	A7
Wilderville	OR	229	A7
Wildwood	OR	187	A4
Wildwood Heights	BC	92	B1
Wiley City	WA	243	A7
Wilhoit Springs	OR	126	A3
Wilkes	OR	200	A1
Wilkes East	OR	200	A1
*WILKESON	WA	182	D5
Wilkins	OR	210	B6
Willada	OR	114	B3
Willamette	OR	199	C5
Willamette City	OR	142	A1
*WILLAMINA	OR	125	A3
Willapa	OR	117	A1
Willard	WA	195	B3
Williams	OR	149	B2
Willow Creek	OR	138	C2
Willow Ranch	CA	152	A3
Willows	WA	263	A8
Wilson	OR	316	D5
Wilson	WA	118	A2
Wilson Corner	OR	200	B3
*WILSON CREEK	WA	113	A2
*WILSONVILLE	OR	199	B5
Wimer	OR	229	D4
Winant	OR	206	B5
Winberry	OR	133	C3
Winchester	ID	123	B2
Winchester	OR	221	C3
Winchester	WA	112	C3
Winchester Bay	OR	218	C2
Windermere	WA	275	F5
Windmaster Corner	OR	195	C5
Winema Beach	OR	203	B1
Wingville	OR	130	B3
Winlock	OR	128	B3
*WINLOCK	WA	187	C3
Winona	OR	229	C3
Winona	OR	322	E13
Winona	WA	122	B1
Winslow	WA	271	H2
*WINSTON	OR	221	B6
Winston	WA	118	A2
Winterville	OR	220	B6
*WINTHROP	WA	104	A2
Winton	WA	111	C1
Wishkah	WA	178	B6
Wishram	WA	127	B1
Wishram Heights	WA	127	B1
Witch Hazel	OR	198	D2
Withrow	WA	112	B2
Wocus	OR	338	B1
Wolf Creek	OR	229	B1
Wolf Lodge	ID	248	C1
Wollochet	WA	181	C2
Wonder	OR	149	A1
*WOODBURN	OR	205	B1
Woodfibre	BC	93	C2
*WOODINVILLE	WA	171	D6
Woodland	ID	131	C3
*WOODLAND	WA	189	D7
Woodland Beach	WA	167	D4
Woodland Park	OR	200	A1
Woodland Park	OR	315	J4
Woodland Park	WA	118	A3
Woodlawn	OR	309	H5
Woodmans	WA	170	A1
Woodmont	WA	175	B7
Woodruff	WA	110	C1
Woodruff Mill	WA	196	D2
Woods	OR	197	A7
Woodson	OR	117	B3
Woodstock	OR	318	B4
*WOOD VILLAGE	OR	200	B1
*WOODWAY	WA	171	A6
Worden	WA	235	B7
*WORLEY	ID	115	A2
Wren	OR	133	A1
Wrentham	OR	127	B2
Wye	BC	256	F4
Wyeth	OR	195	A5
Wymer	WA	243	C2
Wynaco	WA	182	C1
Y			
*YACHATS	OR	209	A3
*YACOLT	WA	193	B1
Yaculta	BC	92	A1
*YAKIMA	WA	243	B6
Yale	BC	95	A2
Yale	WA	118	A3
*YAMHILL	OR	198	B5
Yamsay	OR	142	C3
Yankton	OR	192	A1
Yaquina	OR	206	B5
*YARROW POINT	WA	175	C1
*YELM	WA	118	C1
Yennadon	BC	157	D5
Yeomalt	WA	174	D2
Yoakum	OR	129	A1
Yoder	OR	205	D2
Yokeko Point	WA	160	C7
Yoman	WA	181	A3
Yoman Dock	WA	181	B4
*YONCALLA	OR	219	A4
Youbou	BC	100	C1
Young	OR	133	C1
*YREKA	CA	149	C3
Z			
Zena	OR	204	C4
Zenith	WA	290	A7
Zigzag	OR	201	C5
*ZILLAH	WA	120	A2
Zumwalt	OR	131	A1
Zumwalt	WA	122	B2

*Indicates incorporated city

Mileage Chart

	Astoria, OR	Bellingham, WA	Bend, OR	Boise, ID	Coos Bay, OR	Corvallis, OR	Ellensburg, WA	Eugene, OR	Grants Pass, OR	Hood River, OR	Medford, OR	Moses Lake, WA	Newport, OR	Oak Harbor, WA	Olympia, WA	Pasco, WA	Port Angeles, WA	Portland, OR	Prosser, WA	Salem, OR	Sea-Tac Airport, WA	Seattle, WA	Spokane, WA	The Dalles, OR	Vancouver, BC	Victoria, BC	Yakima, WA
Aberdeen, WA	76	198	303	573	309	224	198	253	388	205	416	266	211	142	50	290	144	143	253	190	94	107	368	226	248	146	203
Albany, OR	158	330	123	437	147	11	293	44	179	131	207	349	65	330	183	287	300	69	268	24	227	241	420	152	382	302	257
Anacortes, WA	251	39	410	559	462	331	179	360	495	312	523	239	364	21	137	286	87	250	261	297	90	78	329	333	92	25	211
Ashland, OR	374	546	200	483	182	222	468	178	41	346	12	534	252	546	399	461	516	285	447	240	443	457	597	331	598	518	432
Astoria, OR		262	255	518	233	151	266	199	334	154	362	338	135	220	114	305	212	95	267	136	163	176	413	175	319	214	217
Baker City, OR	396	451	247	126	466	356	270	356	488	242	459	230	393	469	408	159	454	304	197	350	383	389	296	221	521	456	247
Bellingham, WA	262		421	570	473	342	189	371	506	323	534	249	375	50	148	297	116	261	272	308	101	89	340	344	54	64	222
Bend, OR	255	421		314	237	127	281	128	241	152	212	323	183	421	274	252	391	160	276	131	318	332	423	131	473	393	245
Boise, ID	518	570	314		552	442	384	442	524	366	496	350	478	570	521	279	643	430	313	446	492	491	379	347	623	645	361
Bremerton, WA	150	116	329	533	381	250	110	279	414	231	442	179	283	73	59	218	79	169	193	216	13	1	280	252	142	81	143
Burns, OR	385	547	130	184	367	257	370	259	339	282	311	330	310	551	404	259	554	290	297	261	448	462	395	260	603	556	347
Chehalis, WA	102	175	247	507	299	168	176	197	332	149	360	245	201	171	29	234	145	87	197	154	73	87	343	170	228	147	147
Cheney, WA	396	341	406	370	541	415	161	447	647	279	618	92	448	341	307	123	342	338	158	381	268	267	17	249	395	269	183
Coeur d'Alene, ID	444	371	454	427	589	463	205	495	695	327	667	136	496	371	351	167	385	382	202	429	312	311	31	297	423	313	227
Coos Bay, OR	233	473	237	552		135	431	116	142	273	170	488	98	473	326	444	443	212	407	177	370	384	558	294	558	445	396
Corvallis, OR	151	342	127	442	135		305	40	182	142	210	361	54	342	195	299	312	81	280	35	239	254	432	163	394	314	269
Crater Lake, OR	332	504	98	412	177	173	379	133	86	250	71	421	225	504	357	350	474	243	374	197	401	415	521	229	556	476	343
Ellensburg, WA	266	189	281	384	431	305		330	522	153	493	72	338	188	149	111	187	224	86	271	111	110	174	137	242	112	36
Eugene, OR	199	371	128	442	116	40	330		138	172	166	387	92	371	224	328	341	110	306	64	268	282	464	193	423	343	295
Everett, WA	204	61	360	509	412	281	128	310	445	262	473	188	314	61	87	236	80	200	211	247	40	27	279	283	114	29	161
Florence, OR	184	425	190	504	48	83	391	61	162	224	190	448	50	432	285	389	402	164	367	118	329	343	525	245	484	404	356
Forks, WA	185	93	411	681	418	332	241	361	496	313	524	310	320	122	158	406	56	251	368	298	144	132	408	334	226	58	319
Gold Beach, OR	311	551	316	630	78	213	597	194	134	468	162	639	179	551	404	568	521	290	592	555	448	462	739	373	603	523	561
Grand Coulee, WA	366	262	384	424	547	416	123	446	580	274	596	75	449	265	269	145	286	340	166	382	230	226	87	253	315	228	153
Grants Pass, OR	334	506	241	524	142	182	522	138		307	29	564	212	506	359	493	476	245	517	199	403	417	664	327	558	478	486
Hillsboro, OR	87	278	176	445	206	78	241	117	252	79	280	297	106	278	131	235	248	17	216	50	175	189	368	101	330	250	205
Hood River, OR	154	323	152	366	273	142	153	172	307		335	209	174	323	176	165	293	62	128	108	220	234	296	21	375	295	117
Kennewick, WA	301	295	248	275	440	295	109	324	489	161	460	77	328	293	246	4	293	212	36	261	217	216	142	141	348	295	86
Klamath Falls, OR	364	540	137	419	245	213	418	173	104	289	76	460	265	540	393	389	510	279	413	234	437	451	560	268	592	512	382
La Grande, OR	352	401	271	169	471	340	226	369	504	198	484	186	372	412	363	115	410	259	153	306	334	333	252	177	465	412	203
Lake Oswego, OR	102	269	169	435	216	78	232	108	239	70	271	288	110	269	122	226	239	8	207	41	166	180	359	89	321	241	196
Lewiston, ID	437	391	379	277	557	425	202	455	590	289	591	159	226	390	377	128	389	362	176	492	313	312	102	263	444	314	216
Long Beach, WA	17	260	272	534	250	168	260	216	351	171	379	329	152	214	112	323	206	126	294	153	157	170	431	192	313	208	244
Long View, WA	50	214	210	478	260	131	200	160	295	112	323	265	162	214	67	246	184	48	217	97	112	126	362	133	267	186	167
McMinnville, OR	105	299	158	465	174	46	262	86	224	99	252	318	76	299	152	256	269	38	237	26	196	210	389	120	351	271	226
Medford, OR	362	534	212	496	170	210	493	166	29	335		535	240	534	387	464	504	273	488	227	431	445	635	343	586	506	457
Milton-Freewater, OR	329	350	271	242	449	317	164	347	482	181	483	123	118	350	301	55	350	237	90	284	271	270	166	155	402	352	140
Moses Lakek WA	338	249	323	350	488	361	72	387	564	209	535		394	250	218	71	255	280	106	327	179	178	105	194	302	180	102
Mt. Rainier, WA	142	156	302	431	352	188	106	252	38	187	415	172	254	156	66	158	164	140	120	189	55	68	266	171	209	166	70
Mount St. Helens, WA	107	235	267	535	317	188	222	217	352	169	380	288	219	231	89	274	205	105	236	154	133	147	382	190	288	207	186
Mount Vernon, WA	237	28	392	542	44	313	161	342	477	294	505	221	346	29	120	269	94	232	243	279	73	60	311	315	81	46	193
Newport, OR	135	375	183	478	98	54	338	92	212	174	240	394		375	228	332	345	114	313	83	272	286	465	196	427	347	302
Newport, WA	482	387	435	436	627	482	221	511	676	348	647	153	515	387	367	183	401	439	218	448	328	327	47	313	439	329	243
Oak Harbor, WA	220	50	421	570	473	342	188	371	506	323	534	250	375		148	297	66	261	272	308	101	89	340	324	104	46	222
Okanogan, WA	386	204	445	461	596	469	158	495	686	317	657	112	502	207	271	182	272	377	203	435	231	221	145	301	256	221	190
Olympia, WA	114	148	274	521	326	195	149	224	359	176	387	218	228	148		248	121	114	211	161	46	60	320	195	201	123	161
Ontario, OR	464	508	260	54	498	388	322	388	470	312	442	288	424	508	459	217	581	374	251	392	430	429	317	293	561	583	299
Pasco, WA	305	297	252	279	444	299	111	328	493	165	464	71	332	297	248		295	218	38	265	219	218	136	130	350	297	88
Pendleton, OR	300	349	241	221	419	288	174	318	452	146	454	134	321	360	311	63	358	208	101	254	282	281	200	125	413	360	151
Port Angeles, WA	212	116	391	643	443	312	187	341	476	293	504	255	345	66	121	295		231	257	278	90	77	354	311	168	2	282
Portland, OR	95	261	160	430	212	81	224	110	245	62	273	280	114	261	114	218	231		199	47	158	172	351	83	313	233	188
Portland Airport, OR	98	261	160	430	223	92	213	121	256	51	284	269	125	261	114	207	220	11	188	58	158	172	340	72	313	222	177
Prosser, WA	267	272	276	313	407	280	86	306	517	128	488	106	313	272	211	38	257	199		246	186	182	171	116	324	259	50
Richland, WA	323	285	255	285	447	302	99	331	496	168	467	80	335	285	236	9	286	219	28	268	207	206	145	136	338	288	76
Roseburg, OR	266	438	192	507	85	111	473	71	68	239	96	515	144	438	291	444	408	177	468	132	335	349	615	260	490	410	437
St. Helens, OR	66	236	189	453	240	109	222	139	274	91	302	287	143	236	89	268	206	29	239	76	134	148	384	108	289	208	189
Salem, OR	136	308	131	446	177	35	271	64	199	108	227	327	83	308	161	265	278	47	246		205	219	398	129	360	280	235
Sea-Tac Airport, WA	163	101	318	492	370	239	111	268	403	220	431	179	272	101	46	219	90	158	186	205		13	281	238	154	15	136
Seattle, WA	176	89	332	491	384	254	110	282	417	234	445	178	286	89	60	218	77	172	192	219	13		280	244	141	2	142
Shelton, WA	112	167	292	543	344	113	174	242	377	194	405	240	246	170	22	269	98	132	232	179	68	82	342	215	223	100	182
Spokane, WA	413	340	423	379	558	432	174	464	664	296	635	105	465	340	320	136	354	351	171	398	281	280		266	392	282	196
Tacoma, WA	145	121	303	422	355	224	122	253	388	205	416	190	257	121	30	224	110	143	187	190	18	32	292	226	173	112	137
The Dalles, OR	175	344	131	347	294	163	137	193	327	21	343	194	196	324	195	130	311	83	116	129	238	244	266		376	313	101
Tillamook, OR	66	335	206	502	167	90	502	130	269	136	297	354	69	235	188	292	305	74	273	74	232	246	425	157	387	307	262
Vancouver, BC	319	54	473	623	558	394	242	423	558	375	586	302	427	104	210	350	168	313	324	360	154	141	392	376		69	274
Vancouver, WA	90	253	168	438	220	89	216	118	253	70	281	272	122	253	106	210	222	8	191	55	150	164	343	91	305	224	180
Victoria, BC	214	64	393	645	445	314	112	343	478	295	506	180	347	46	123	297	2	233	259	280	15	2	282	313	43		290
Walla Walla, WA	337	342	279	250	457	325	156	355	490	189	491	115	126	342	293	47	342	262	82	392	263	262	158	163	394	344	132
Wenatchee, WA	304	184	353	407	504	377	75	403	594	225	565	66	410	184	188	134	198	296	126	343	148	138	164	209	236	140	108
Yakima, WA	217	222	245	361	396	269	36	295	486	117	457	102	302	222	161	88	282	188	50	235	136	142	196	101	180	290	

Mileage requires ferry use and does not include ferry miles

National, Provincial & State Park Information

CAMPING & LODGING INFORMATION

British Columbia	Campgrounds of Canada: www.campcanada.com
Washington State	Online Travel Information: www.experiencewashington.com
Oregon State	Oregon State Parks Reservation Center: (800) 547-7842, www.oregon.gov
Idaho State	Idaho Camping and Lodging: (208) 334-4199, www.idahoparks.org

NATIONAL, PROVINCIAL & STATE PARK INFORMATION

British Columbia	British Columbia Ministry of Environment Lands & Parks: (800) 689-9025 www.gov.bc.ca
Washington State	Washington State Parks & Recreation Commission: www.parks.wa.gov
Oregon State	Oregon State Parks: www.oregon.gov
Idaho State	Idaho State Parks: idoc.state.id.us/irti/stateparks

Selected National & State Parks including Recreation Areas, Forests, and National Monuments

PROVINCE	PARK	PAGE & GRID	Camping	Trailer/RV	Picnicking	Swimming	Fishing	Hiking	Boating	Beach
BC	**NATIONAL PARKS**									
	Pacific Rim National Park	100, A1	•	•	•	•	•	•	•	•
	PROVINCIAL PARKS									
	Carmanah Pacific Provincial Park	92, B2	•	•	•			•		
	Cathedral Provincial Park	104, A1	•	•	•		•	•		
	Cultus Lake Provincial Park	102, C1	•		•	•	•	•	•	•
	Desolation Sound Provincial Marine Park	92, B1	•			•	•		•	
	Garibaldi Provincial Park	94, A1	•		•		•	•		•
	Golden Ears Provincial Park	94, B2	•		•	•	•	•	•	•
	Manning Provincial Park	95, C3	•		•	•	•	•	•	•
	Skagit Valley Provincial Park	103, B1	•		•	•	•	•	•	
	Strathcona Provincial Park	92, A2	•	•	•	•	•	•	•	•
STATE	**PARK**									
WA	**NATIONAL PARKS**									
	Mount Rainier National Park	118, C1	•	•	•		•	•	•	
	North Cascades National Park	103, A1	•	•	•		•	•	•	
	Olympic National Park	109, B1	•	•	•		•	•	•	
	NATIONAL/STATE FORESTS									
	Colville National Forest	105, C2	•	•	•	•	•	•	•	•
	Gifford Pinchot National Forest	118, C2	•	•	•	•	•	•	•	•
	Kaniksu National Forest	106, C2	•	•	•	•	•	•	•	•
	Mount Baker National Forest	103, A2	•	•	•	•	•	•	•	•
	Mount Baker-Snoqualmie National Forest	111, A2	•	•	•	•	•	•	•	•
	Okanogan National Forest	104, B2	•	•	•	•	•	•	•	•
	Olympic National Forest	109, B2	•	•	•	•	•	•	•	•
	Wenatchee National Forest	112, A1	•	•	•	•	•	•	•	•
	PARKS/RECREATION AREAS/MONUMENTS									
	Beacon Rock State Park	194, B6	•		•		•		•	•
	Birch Bay State Park	158, B5	•	•	•					•
	Bogachiel State Park	169, D3	•		•		•			•
	Brooks Memorial State Park	119, C3	•	•	•					
	Columbia River Gorge National Scenic Area	200, C1	•	•	•		•	•	•	
	Coulee Dam National Recreation Area	237, D3	•	•	•	•	•		•	•
	Fort Canby State Park	186, A6	•	•	•		•		•	•
	Fort Flagler State Park	167, B6	•	•	•		•		•	•
	Fort Worden State Park	167, A6	•	•	•		•		•	•
	Kanaskat-Palmer State Park	110, C3	•	•	•		•		•	
	Lake Chelan National Recreation Area	103, C3					•	•	•	•
	Larrabee State Park	160, D2	•	•	•		•		•	•
	Millersylvania State Park	184, C2	•		•	•	•			
	Mount Saint Helens National Volcanic Monument	190, B1						•		
	Mount Spokane State Park	114, C1	•		•					
	Ocean City State Park	177, B6	•	•	•		•			•
	Pacific Beach State Park	177, B2	•	•			•			•
	Potholes State Park	242, C6	•	•			•		•	•
	Ross Lake National Recreation Area	103, B1	•	•			•	•	•	
	Schafer State Park	179, A5	•	•	•		•			•
	Seaquest State Park	187, D7	•	•	•		•			
	Sequim Bay State Park	166, C7	•	•	•		•		•	•
	Sun Lakes State Park	112, C2	•	•	•	•	•		•	•
	Twanoh State Park	173, C7	•	•	•		•		•	•
	Wenberg State Park	168, B6	•	•	•		•		•	•
	Yakima Sportsman State Park	243, C7	•	•	•		•			•
OR	**NATIONAL PARKS**									
	Crater Lake National Park	227, C3	•	•	•			•		
	NATIONAL/STATE FORESTS									
	Clatsop State Forest	191, D2	•	•	•		•	•	•	•
	Deschutes National Forest	143, A1	•	•			•	•	•	

STATE	PARK	PAGE & GRID	Camping	Trailer/RV	Picnicking	Swimming	Fishing	Hiking	Boating	Beach
	Elliott State Forest	140, C1	•	•	•	•	•	•	•	•
	Fremont National Forest	151, C2	•	•	•	•	•	•	•	•
	Malheur National Forest	137, B1	•	•	•	•	•	•	•	•
	McDonald State Forest	207, A5	•	•	•	•	•	•	•	•
	Mount Hood National Forest	202, B2	•	•	•	•	•	•	•	•
	Ochoco National Forest	136, B2	•	•	•	•	•	•	•	•
	Rogue River National Forest	149, B3	•	•	•	•	•	•	•	•
	Santiam State Forest	134, A1	•	•	•	•	•	•	•	•
	Siskiyou National Forest	148, B2	•	•	•	•	•	•	•	•
	Siuslaw National Forest	132, C2	•	•	•	•	•	•	•	•
	Tillamook State Forest	125, A1	•	•	•	•	•	•	•	•
	Umatilla National Forest	129, B3	•	•	•	•	•	•	•	•
	Umpqua National Forest	142, A2	•	•	•	•	•	•	•	•
	Wallowa-Whitman National Forest	138, A1	•	•	•	•	•	•	•	•
	Willamette National Forest	134, B1	•	•	•	•	•	•	•	•
	Winema National Forest	142, C2	•	•	•	•	•	•	•	•
	PARKS/RECREATION AREAS/MONUMENTS									
	Beachside State Park	328, A11	•	•	•	•	•			
	Beverly Beach State Park	206, B2	•	•	•		•	•		•
	Bullards Beach State Park	220, B5	•	•	•		•	•		•
	Cape Blanco State Park	224, A4	•	•	•		•	•		•
	Cape Lookout State Park	197, A3	•	•	•		•	•		•
	Champoeg State Park	199, A6	•	•	•		•	•	•	
	Collier Memorial State Park	231, D2	•	•	•		•	•		
	Columbia River Gorge National Scenic Area	200, C1	•	•	•		•	•	•	
	Detroit Lake State Park	134, B1	•	•	•		•	•	•	
	Emigrant Lake County Recreation Area	243, D4								
	Fort Stevens State Park	188, B1	•	•	•	•	•	•	•	•
	Harris Beach State Park	232, C6	•	•	•		•			•
	Hells Canyon National Recreation Area	131, B1	•	•	•	•	•	•		•
	Humbug Mountain State Park	224, B7	•	•	•		•	•		•
	Jessie M Honeyman Memorial State Park	214, B4	•	•	•	•	•	•	•	•
	John Day Fossil Beds National Monument	136, C1			•			•		
	Joseph Stewart State Park	149, C1		•	•		•	•	•	
	Lake Owyhee State Park	147, A1	•	•	•		•		•	
	Lewis & Clark National Historical Park	188, C3	•	•	•	•	•	•	•	•
	Memaloose State Park	196, A5	•	•						
	Milo McIver State Park	200, B6	•	•	•		•	•	•	
	Nehalem Bay State Park	191, B5	•	•	•		•		•	•
	Newberry National Volcanic Monument	143, B1						•		
	Oregon Cascades Recreation Area	142, B1	•	•	•	•	•	•	•	•
	Oregon Caves National Monument	149, D5			•			•		
	Oregon Dunes National Recreation Area	214, A5	•				•	•		•
	Silver Falls State Park	205, D7	•	•	•		•	•		•
	South Beach State Park	206, B5	•	•	•		•	•		
	Sunset Bay State Park	220, B1	•	•	•	•	•	•		
	The Cove Palisades State Park	208, A6	•	•	•		•	•	•	•
	Umpqua Lighthouse State Park	218, B2	•	•	•		•	•	•	
	Valley of the Rogue State Park	229, D6	•	•	•		•	•	•	
	Viento State Park	195, B5	•	•	•					
	Wallowa Lake State Park	130, C2	•	•	•		•	•	•	•
	William M Tugman State Park	218, C3	•	•	•		•	•	•	
ID	**NATIONAL/STATE FORESTS**									
	Coeur d'Alene National Forest	115. B1	•	•	•	•	•	•	•	•
	Kaniksu National Forest	106, C2	•	•	•	•	•	•	•	•
	Nez Perce National Forest	131, C1	•	•	•	•	•	•	•	•
	Payette National Forest	131, B3	•	•	•	•	•	•	•	•
	Saint Joe National Forest	115, B3	•	•	•	•	•	•	•	•
	PARKS/RECREATION AREAS/MONUMENTS									
	Farragut State Park	245, C1	•	•	•	•	•	•	•	
	Heyburn State Park	248, A6	•	•	•	•	•	•	•	
CA	**NATIONAL PARKS**									
	Redwood National Park	148, B3	•	•	•		•	•	•	
	NATIONAL/STATE FORESTS									
	Klamath National Forest	149, B3	•	•	•	•	•	•	•	•
	Modoc National Forest	151, B3	•	•	•	•	•	•	•	•
	Siskiyou National Forest	148, B2	•	•	•	•	•	•	•	•
	Six River National Forest	148, C3	•	•	•	•	•	•	•	•
	PARKS/RECREATION AREAS/MONUMENTS									
	Del Norte Coast Redwoods State Park	148, B3	•	•	•		•	•		
	Lava Beds National Monument	151, A3	•	•	•			•		
	Smith River National Recreation Area	148, C3	•	•	•	•	•	•		•
NV	**NATIONAL/STATE FORESTS**									
	Humboldt National Forest	154, C3	•	•	•		•	•		•
MT	**NATIONAL/STATE FORESTS**									
	Kootenai National Forest	107, C1	•	•	•		•	•		•

A   B   C

© 2006 Rand McNally & Company

HWY

DISCOVERY PASSAGE

Duncan Bay
BLENKIN MEMORIAL PARK
ELK FALLS PARK
Quathiaski Cove
Yacuita
FRANSISCO POINT
CAMPBELL RIVER

MARINA ISLAND
Manson Landing
Cortes Bay

DESOLATION SOUND

POWELL LAKE

GOAT LAKE

SMELT BAY CAMPGROUND
SARAH POINT
Bliss Landing
DESOLATION SOUND PROVINCIAL MARINE PARK
BUNSTER HILLS

GOAT ISLAND

WINDSOR LAKE

WILLOW POINT

SHELTER POINT

OYSTER BAY

HERNANDO ISLAND

MANSON PASSAGE

MITLENATCH ISLAND NATURE PARK

COPELAND ISLANDS MARINE PARK
Lund

OKEOVER ARM CAMPGROUND

MALASPINA PENINSULA

POWELL LAKE

INLAND LAKE

DODD LAKE

1   **1**

101

SLIAMMOA LAKE

SMITH RANGE

HASLAM LAKE

HORSESHOE LAKE

KUHUSHAN POINT

BRITISH COLUMBIA

SAVARY ISLAND
Savary Island

Wildwood Heights
Sliammon

HANWOOD ISLAND

POWELL RIVER HISTORIC MUSEUM

POWELL RIVER

LOIS LAKE

Black Creek

19A
19
WOLF LAKE

MOUNT WASHINGTON

Marville

MOUNT TROUBRIDGE
SALTERY BAY CAMPGROUND
Saltery Bay

LITTLE RIVER - POWELL RIVER FERRY

Blubber Bay
GRILSE POINT
GRIET POINT

MALASPINA STRAIT

Lang Bay

KIN BEACH CAMPGROUND
Little River

Vananda

FAVADA POINT

Stillwater

HARDY ISLAND

NELSON ISLAND

INLAND HWY

Sandwick

KYE BAY

COMOX AIRPORT

COURTENAY
FISH HATCHERY
MUS
COMOX
COMOX HARBOUR
Royston
GARTLEY POINT

2   STRATHCONA PROVINCIAL PARK

WOOD MOUNTAIN SKI PARK

MUS
Cumberland

SANDY ISLAND PARK

Gillies Bay

TEXADA ISLAND

NORTHEAST POINT

MOUNT DAVIES

2

Union Bay

COMOX LAKE

DENMAN ISLAND

HORNBY ISLAND

STRAIT OF GEORGIA

SABINE CHANNEL

MOUNT SHEPHERD

TSABLE LAKE

WILLEMAR LAKE

BEAUFORT RANGE

BAYNES SOUND

Denman Island
FILLONGLEY CAMPGROUND

HELLIWELL CAMPGROUND
St JOHN POINT

Hornby Island
TRIBUNE BAY CAMPGROUND
NORMAN POINT

Lasqueti
LASQUETI ISLAND

UPWOOD POINT

ELSIE LAKE

Fanny Bay
BOYLE POINT

JENKINS ISLAND

YOUNG POINT

Bowser

SANGSTER ISLAND

LOWRY LAKE

19A
INLAND

QUALICUM BAY

PARKSVILLE - LASQUETI FERRY

3
GREAT CENTRAL LAKE

ROBERTSON FISH HATCHERY
STAMP FALLS CAMPGROUND

HORNE LAKE CAVES CAMPGROUND

SPIDER LAKE CAMPGROUND
19

Qualicum Beach

BIG QUALICUM RIVER HATCHERY
CRAIG HERITAGE MUS

PARKSVILLE

RATHTREVOR BEACH CAMPGROUND

BALLENAS ISLAND

SPROAT LAKE
TAYLOR ARM CAMPGROUND
SPROAT LAKE CAMPGROUND

HORNE LAKE

CAMERON LAKE

LITTLE QUALICUM FALLS CAMPGROUND

ISLAND HWY

BUTTERFLY WORLD
Coombs

MUS
4
PORT ALBERNI

MACMILLAN CAMPGROUND

MOUNT ARROWSMITH PARK

ENGLISHMAN RIVER FALLS CAMPGROUND

19
Nanoose Bay

NANOOSE HARBOUR

3

MOUNT ANDERSON

NAHMINT LAKE

MCLAUGHLIN

CHINA CREEK PARK

MOUNT MORIARTY

LABOUR DAY LAKE

MOUNT DE COSMOS

HANNAH MOUNTAIN

ALBERNI INLET

RIDGE

EFFINGHAM INLET
HENDERSON LAKE

NANAIMO LAKES

SEE 93 MAP

SEE 100 MAP

0   2.5   5   7.5   10
miles   1 in. = 7.5 mi.

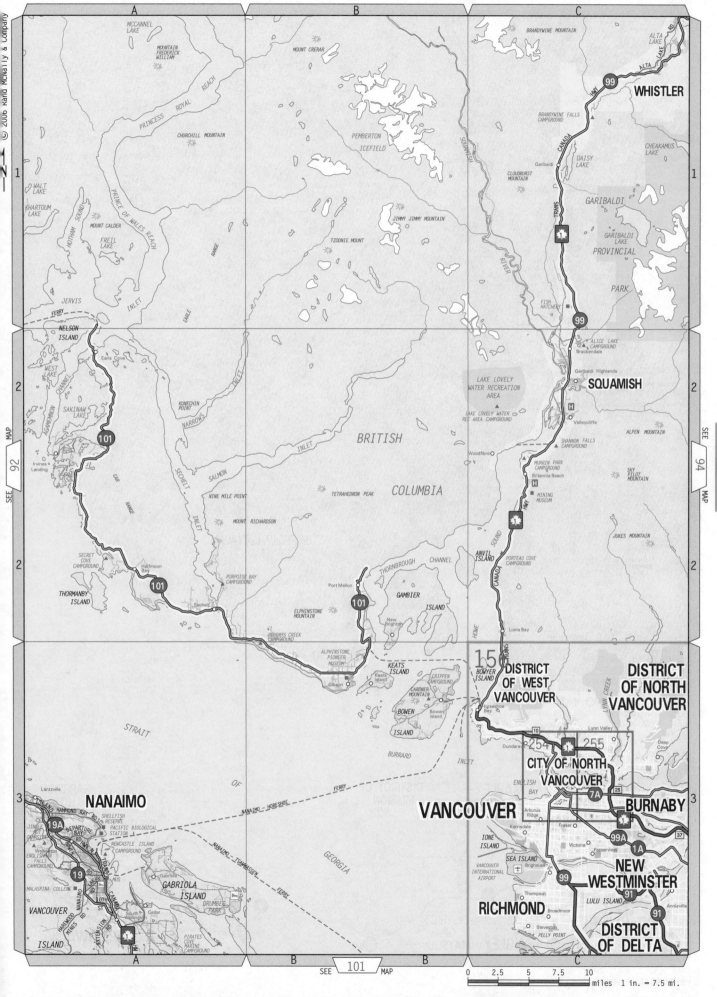

© 2006 Rand McNally & Company

HWY

WHISTLER

BRITISH

COLUMBIA

SQUAMISH

NANAIMO

VANCOUVER

BURNABY

CITY OF NORTH VANCOUVER

DISTRICT OF WEST VANCOUVER

DISTRICT OF NORTH VANCOUVER

NEW WESTMINSTER

RICHMOND

DISTRICT OF DELTA

SEE 92 MAP

SEE 94 MAP

SEE 101 MAP

0   2.5   5   7.5   10
miles   1 in. = 7.5 mi.

A   B   C

© 2006 Rand McNally & Company

N

SUMMER LAKE

WEDGE MOUNTAIN

LILLOOET

CHEAKAMUS MOUNTAIN

COAST

CHEAKAMUS LAKE

MOUNT SIR RICHARD

1

GARIBALDI

LILLOOET LAKE

MOUNTAINS

MOUNT PITT

PROVINCIAL

RIVER

SEE 93 MAP

HWY

2

MAMQUAM MOUNTAIN

MOUNT BREAKENRIDGE

2

PARK

SEE 95 MAP

BRITISH COLUMBIA

HARRISON LAKE

MESLILLOET MOUNTAIN

GOLDEN

THOMAS LAKE

LONG ISLAND

2

MOUNT BONNYCASTLE

PITT

EARS

OSPREY MOUNTAIN

LAKE

MOUNT BREIER

PENEPLAIN PEAK

CHEHALIS LAKE

CROKER ISLAND

COQUITLAM LAKE

WIDGEON LAKE

PROVINCIAL

GOOSE ISLAND

INDIAN

ARM

RAVEN LAKE

MOUNT JASPER

HEMLOCK VALLEY

ECHO ISLAND

COQUITLAM ISLAND

WIDGEON PEAK

PARK

STAVE LAKE

MOUNT CATHERWOOD

WEAVER CREEK PROV PARK

BUNTZEN LAKE

MOUNT BLANSHARD

SIWASH ISLAND

ALOUETTE MOUNTAIN

HEMLOCK SKI AREA

SASQUATCH PROV PARK

BELCARRA

BELCARRA PARK

BURKE MOUNTAIN REGIONAL PARK

EUNICE LAKE

GOLDCREEK CAMPGROUND

ALOUETTE LAKE

SAYRES LAKE

DAVIS LAKE PROVINCIAL PARK

DICKSON LAKE

CHEHALIS HATCHERY

ANMORE

LOON LAKE

ALOUETTE CAMPGROUND

MOUNT CRICKMER

HARRISON HOT SPRINGS

7A

PORT MOODY

COQUITLAM

MAPLE RIDGE

DISTRICT OF MISSION

MOUNT "AGASSIZ"

MCCALLUM RD

DISTRICT OF KENT

7

3

PITT MEADOWS

WINDY POINT

Agassiz

7

PORT COQUITLAM

RIVER

ROLLEY LAKE

CANNELL LAKE

HARTLEY

Harrison Mills

9

FRASER

Haney

DEWDNEY

Yennadon

Webster Corners

ROLLEY LAKE PROVINCIAL PARK

STAVE FALLS

HAYWARD LAKE

Steelhead

Deroche

SKUMALASPH ISLAND

CASTLEMAN

9

48

Port Hammond

Walnut Grove

Fort Langley

TRUNK

BELL ST

KEYSTONE AV

NEVIN RD

YALE RD

Port Kells

7

Whonnock

WILSON ST

Glen Valley

LOUGHEED

MANZER ST

CLAY ST

CEDAR ST

Dewdney

NICOMEN ISLAND

SLOUGH

Rosedale

BRIDAL VEIL FALLS PROV PARK

CITY OF SURREY

TOWNSHIP OF LANGLEY

Forest Knolls

58

DISTRICT OF MATSQUI

7TH AV

HWY

NICOMEN ISLAND

FRASER RIVER

CITY OF CHILLIWACK

McSCHEH

TOMS RD

Newton

99A

15

Milner

10

LANGLEY

Surrey Centre

Matsqui Island

11

PAGE RD

SUMAS MOUNTAIN PARK

TRANS CANADA

Sikdis McGUIRE RD

RD

CHADSEY LAKE

SOUTH SUMAS

LICKMAN

VEDDER

BAILEY RD

SEE 102 MAP

0 2.5 5 7.5 10

miles 1 in. = 7.5 mi.

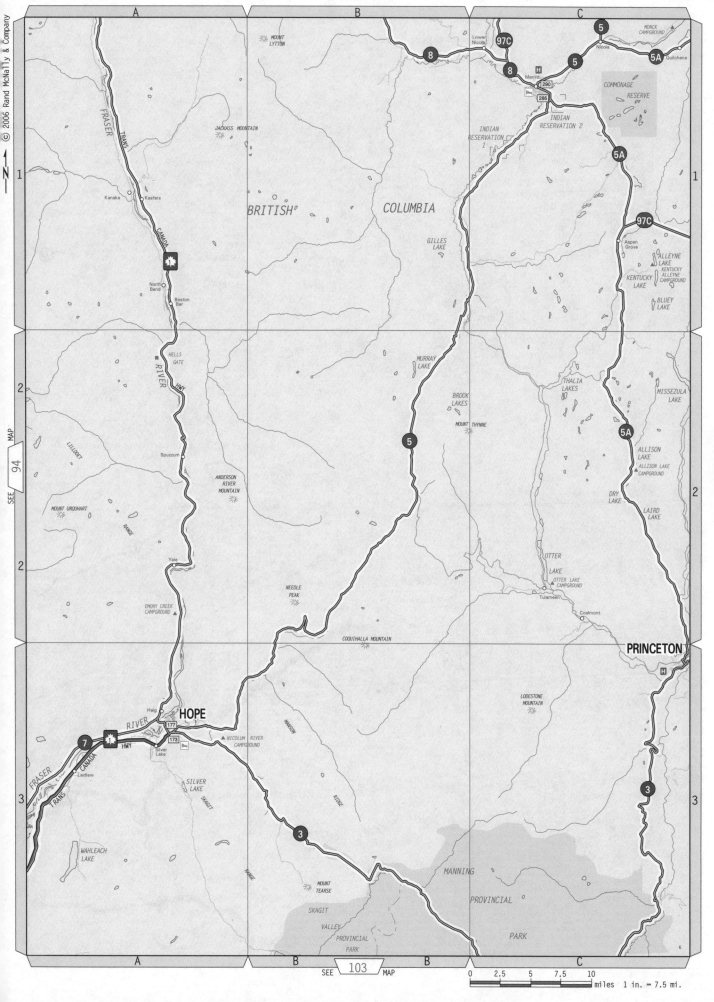

© 2006 Rand McNally & Company

N

HWY

A | B | B | C

CATARACT LAKE

Kildonan

ALMA RUSSELL ISLAND

SEDALT ISLAND

IMPERIAL EAGLE CHANNEL

FERRY

TZARTUS ISLAND

SARITA LAKE

FLEMING ISLAND

FERRY

SANDFORD ISLAND

DIANA ISLAND

Bamfield

H

CAPE BEALE

PACHENA BAY

BLACK LAKE

SOMERSET RANGE

PACHENA POINT

TSUSIAT LAKE

SQUALICUM LAKE

HOBITON LAKE

DOOBAH LAKE

SPRISE LAKE

SMOKEHOUSE MOUNTAIN

NITINAT LAKE

FRANKLIN Camp

MOUNT GREY

TUCK LAKE

HEATHER LAKE

Nitinat

HEATHER MOUNTAIN

BRITISH COLUMBIA

MCCLURE LAKE

FOURTH LAKE

NANAIMO LAKES

RHEINHART LAKE

MOUNT LANDALT

MOUNT WHYMPER

COWICHAN

Caycuse

Youbou

TOWINCUT MOUNTAIN

VANCOUVER ISLAND

GORDON BAY PROVINCIAL PARK

LAKE

GORDON BAY PROVINCIAL CAMPGROUND

LAKEVIEW PARK CAMPGROUND

Honeymoon Bay

Gordon River

HONEYMOON BAY NATURE PARK

18

1

PACIFIC

RIM

NATIONAL

PARK

CHEEWHAT LAKE

Clo-oose

CARMANAH POINT

CARMANAH PACIFIC PROVINCIAL PARK

GLAD LAKE

MOUNT WALBRAN

EDINBURGH MOUNTAIN

2

STRAIT OF JUAN DE FUCA

PORT SAN JUAN

MUSEUM

Port Renfrew

SAN JUAN POINT

LOSS CREEK PROVINCIAL PARK

14

River Jordan

CANADA

USA

BRITISH COLUMBIA

WASHINGTON

2

DUNTZE ROCK

TATOOSH ISLAND

CAPE FLATTERY LIGHTHOUSE

ARCHAWAT PEAK

WAADAH ISLAND

NEAH BAY RD

Neah Bay

CLALLAM CO

MAKAH

WAATCH PEAK

INDIAN

RESERVATION

SHIPWRECK POINT

CLALLAM

COUNTY

Hoko

Sekiu

Clallam Bay

112

112

3

PACIFIC

OCEAN

FLATTERY

ROCKS

NATIONAL

OLYMPIC

NATIONAL

WILDLIFE

REFUGE

WASHBURN HILL

RIVER

SNAG PEAK

SEKIU MOUNTAIN

OZETTE RD

HOKO

KOKO

OLYMPIC

NATIONAL

PARK

OZETTE LAKE

PREACHERS POINT

NELSON HILL

BLUE CANYON

STOLZENBERG MOUNTAIN

BURNT MOUNTAIN RD

113

BURNT MOUNTAIN

OLYMPIC

NATIONAL

FOREST

DICKEY HOKO SUMMIT

Sappho

Beaver

101

BIGLER MOUNTAIN

SCHUTZ PASS

SOL DUC RIVER

CALAWAH RIDGE

QUILLAYUTE NATIONAL WILDLIFE REFUGE

KAYOSTIA BEACH

DICKEY RIVER

WEST FORK DICKEY RIVER

EAST FORK DICKEY RIVER

GUNDERSON MOUNTAIN

A | B | B | C

0 2.5 5 7.5 10 miles   1 in. = 7.5 mi.

SEE 93 MAP

DISTRICT OF DELTA

WESTHAM ISLAND

BOUNDARY BAY AIRPORT

BOUNDARY BAY

BRITISH COLUMBIA

WASHINGTON

Tsawwassen

CANADA
USA WHATCOM CO

Point Roberts
POINT ROBERTS
ROBERTS YOUNG AIRPORT
ROBERTS LIGHTHOUSE
South Beach

MOUNT HALL

BRITISH

COLUMBIA

THETIS ISLAND

Ladysmith

MUSEUM

MOUNT BRENTON

TRANS CANADA HWY

ISLAND HWY

FERRY

Chemainus

KUPER ISLAND

INDES ISLAND

VALDES ISLAND

DIONISIO POINT PROV PARK

GALIANO

ISLAND

SALTSPRING ISLAND

MARYS LAKE CAMPGROUND

MAPLE MOUNTAIN CENTENNIAL CAMPGROUND

Vesuvius

Crofton

MOUNT MAXWELL PROV PARK

BRITTANCOURT HOUSE MUSEUM

North Cowichan

Maple Bay

MONTAGUE HARBOUR CAMPGROUND

Galiano

Sturdies Bay

MAYNE ISLAND

Mayne

WINTER COVE CAMPGROUND

NORTH PENDER ISLAND

SATURNA ISLAND

Saturna

WHATCOM COUNTY

GEORGIA

STRAIT

OF

SAN JUAN CO

WHATCOM CO

CHEMAINUS RIVER PROV PARK

LAKE COWICHAN

18

DUNCAN

MUSEUM

COWICHAN RIVER CAMPGROUND

COWICHAN INDIAN RESERVE

Cowichan Bay

STURAT CHANNEL

BRIGHT ANGEL PARK MUSEUM

159

Cobble Hill

DEEP COVE

DISTRICT OF NORTH SAANICH

VICTORIA INTL AIRPORT

TOWN OF SIDNEY

Sidney

Bazan Bay

STUART ISLAND

ANACORTES

SAN JUAN CO

BRITISH COLUMBIA
WASHINGTON

CANADA
USA

San Juan Co

TURN POINT LIGHTHOUSE

WALDRON ISLAND

Beach Haven

Eastsound

CROW VALLEY

West Beach

SAN JUAN COUNTY

ORCAS

Westsound

ISLAND

MOUNT TODD

KOKSILAH RIVER PROV PARK

WEST SHAWNIGAN LAKE PARK

Mill Bay

Shawnigan Lake

MEMORY ISLAND PARK

Bamberton

TRANS CANADA HWY

ISLAND HWY

Malahat

SQUALLY REACH

Saanichton

17A

Brentwood Bay

DISTRICT OF CENTRAL SAANICH

DISTRICT OF SAANICH

17

Cordova Bay

Royal Oak

CADBORO BAY

Roche Harbor

Deep Harbor

SAN JUAN ISLAND

ENGLISH CAMPSITE

WHALE MUSEUM

BEAVERTON VALLEY

LIME KILN LIGHTHOUSE

BAILER HILL RD

CATTLE POINT RD

FRIDAY HARBOR

SHAW ISLAND

Orcas

Argyle

Lopez

Port Stanley

TURN ROCK LIGHT

LOPEZ HISTORICAL MUSEUM

LOPEZ ISLAND

Richardson

MOUNT SURVEY

SOOKE LAKE

EMPRESS MOUNTAIN

MOUNT MUIR

DISTRICT OF LANGFORD

256

257

VIEW ROYAL

1A

1

ESQUIMALT

COLWOOD

VICTORIA

DIST OF OAK BAY

DISCOVERY ISLAND MARINE PARK

AMERICAN CAMPSITE

CATTLE POINT LIGHT

SOOKE MOUNTAIN PROV PARK

14

Shirley

FRENCH BEACH CAMPGROUND

Otter Point

Milnes Landing

14

Sooke

SOOKE

SOOKE BAY

EAST SOOKE REGIONAL PARK

EAST SOOKE BASIN

DISTRICT OF METCHOSIN

Metchosin

Parry Bay

ROCKY POINT NAVAL ESTABLISHMENT

VICTORIA FERRY

SEATTLE

164

165

166

SAN JUAN CO

JEFFERSON CO

CANADA
USA

BRITISH COLUMBIA
WASHINGTON

STRAIT OF JUAN DE FUCA

CLALLAM

CLALLAM CO

JEFFERSON CO

CLALLAM COUNTY

CLALLAM JEFFERSON CO

JEFFERSON COUNTY

OLYMPIC

112

Disque

Joyce

PIEDMONT RD

Ramapo

PORT ANGELES

261

PORT ANGELES HARBOR

Crane

Agnew

DUNGENESS

Jamestown

26

Port Williams

WASHINGTON

Piedmont

101

Fairholm

LAKE CRESCENT

SOL DUC RIVER

OLYMPIC NATIONAL PARK

Maple Grove

Snug Harbor

OLYMPIC

EDGEWOOD

BLACK DIAMOND RD

LITTLE RIVER RD

MOUNT ANGELES RD

NATIONAL FOREST

DEER PARK RD

Little Oklahoma

BLUE MOUNTAIN RD

101

OLYMPIC HWY

Carlsborg

Port Washington

OLYMPIC

CAYS RD

SEQUIM-DUNGENESS HWY

SEQUIM

HAPPY VALLEY

DUNGENESS RD

MILLER PENINSULA

CAPE GEORGE RD

101

Gardiner

Tuke

SEE 100 MAP

SEE 102 MAP

HWY

SEE 109 MAP

0 2.5 5 7.5 10

miles 1 in. = 7.5 mi.

© 2006 Rand McNally & Company

SURREY

TOWNSHIP OF LANGLEY

DISTRICT OF MATSQUI

CITY OF CHILLIWACK

WHITE ROCK

BRITISH COLUMBIA

ABBOTSFORD

BLAINE

LYNDEN

SUMAS

EVERSON

NOOKSACK

FERNDALE

WHATCOM COUNTY

WASHINGTON

USA

MOUNT BAKER-SNOQUALMIE NATIONAL FOREST

BELLINGHAM

MOUNT BAKER

WILDERNESS

160 161

SEE 101 MAP HWY

SEE 103 MAP

SKAGIT CO

LYMAN HAMILTON CONCRETE

ANACORTES

SEDRO-WOOLLEY

BURLINGTON

MOUNT VERNON

LA CONNER

SAN JUAN COUNTY

MOUNT BAKER-SNOQUALMIE

167 168

OAK HARBOR

COUPEVILLE

WHIDBEY ISLAND NAVAL AIR STATION

ISLAND COUNTY

SKAGIT CO

SNOHOMISH COUNTY

WASHINGTON

NATIONAL FOREST

STANWOOD

ARLINGTON

PORT TOWNSEND

263

GRANITE FALLS

SNOHOMISH COUNTY

SEE 94 MAP

SEE 110 MAP

0 2.5 5 7.5 10

miles 1 in. = 7.5 mi.

N

SEE 95 MAP

SEE 102 MAP

SEE 104 MAP

HWY

SEE 111 MAP

Grid columns: A | B | B | C (top and bottom)
Grid rows: 1, 2, 3

CHILLIWACK
CHILLIWACK LAKE
CHILLIWACK RIVER
MOUNT PIERCE
SLESSE MOUNTAIN
MOUNT LINDEMAN
SLESSE CREEK
BRITISH COLUMBIA
WHITWORTH PEAK
SKAGIT VALLEY PROVINCIAL PARK
SHAWATUM MOUNTAIN
BRITISH COLUMBIA
MANNING PROVINCIAL PARK
ALLISON PASS
CROWNSNEST
3
GIBSON PASS
COLDSPRING CAMPGROUND
SPRUCE BAY CAMPGROUND
LIGHTNING LAKE
STRIKE LAKE
FLASH LAKE
THUNDER LAKE
LONE MOUNTAIN
FROSTY MOUNTAIN
MULE DEER CAMPGROUND
HAMPTON CAMPGROUND
CHUWANTEN MOUNTAIN

AMERICAN BORDER PEAK
WHATCOM CO
MIDDLE PEAK
SILESIA CREEK SHELTER
HIGH PASS
YELLOW ASTER BUTTE
WASHINGTON
LITTLE CHILLIWACK SHELTER
BEAR CREEK SHELTER
CUSTER RIDGE
OKANOGAN CO
WASHINGTON USA
CASTLE PEAK
PASAYTEN RIVER
BLIZZARD PEAK
SMOKY MOUNTAIN
SODA PEAK
THREE FOOLS PEAK

MOUNT BAKER
GOAT MOUNTAIN
SNOQUALMIE
RUTH
HANNEGAN CAMPGROUND
542
COPPER MOUNTAIN
INDIAN CREEK SHELTER
GREYBALL SHELTER
REDOUBT GLACIER
RIDGE OF GENDARMES
PERRY CREEK SHELTER
HOZOMEEN CAMPGROUND
ROSS LAKE NATIONAL RECREATION AREA
LITTLE BEAVER CAMPGROUND
CAT ISLAND CAMPGROUND
MOUNT PASAYTEN
LITTLE FISH SHELTER
HOLMAN PEAK
POWDER MOUNTAIN
PTARMIGAN PEAK
DOT MOUNTAIN
HOLMAN CAMPGROUND

WHATCOM COUNTY
HANNEGAN PEAK
NATIONAL FOREST
NORTH
MOUNT BAKER SKI AREA
WEST NOOKSACK GLACIER
EAST NOOKSACK GLACIER
MOUNT SHUKSAN
RUTH MOUNTAIN
WHATCOM PASS SHELTER
WHATCOM GLACIER
CHALLENGER GLACIER
CROOKED THUMB PEAK
BEAVER PASS
BEAVER PASS SHELTER
LIGHTING CREEK CAMPGROUND
TENMILE ISLAND CAMPGROUND
BEAR SKULL SHELTER
DEVILS DOME
WILDERNESS
OKANOGAN COUNTY
BLACKCAP MOUNTAIN

SULPHIDE GLACIER
PIONEER RIDGE
MOUNT CHALLENGER
CASCADES
BAKER RIVER
NATIONAL
TENMILE SHELTER
ELEPHANT BUTTE
BIG BEAR CAMPGROUND
ROSS LAKE
RAINBOW POINT CAMPGROUND
NOHOKOMEEN GLACIER
JACKITA RIDGE
TAMARACK PEAK
LAKE MOUNTAIN

RAINBOW FALLS
BAKER HOT SPRING
SHANNON CREEK CAMPGROUND
PARK CREEK CAMPGROUND
PANORAMA POINT CAMPGROUND
JASPER PASS
PINNACLE PEAK
HAGAN MOUNTAIN
BAKER LAKE
MAPLE GROVE CAMPGROUND
HORSESHOE COVE CAMPGROUND
TRIUMPH PASS
DAVIS PEAK
GORGE CREEK FALLS VIEW POINT
DIABLO LAKE
RUBY ARM
JERRY GLACIER
ROSS LAKE VIEW POINT
CHANCELLOR CAMPGROUND
CANYON CREEK
WHATCOM CO
HAYSTACK MOUNTAIN
MOUNT BAKER-SNOQUALMIE
ROWLEY CHASM
CADY PASS
ROBINSON MOUNTAIN
MEADOWS CAMPGROUND
LAST CHANCE POINT

BAKER
TRAPPERS PEAK
20
GORGE CREEK FALLS
DIABLO
JOHN PIERCE WATERFALL
DIABLO VISTA
COLONIAL CREEK CAMPGROUND
PARK
EAST BACON CREEK
DAMNATION PEAK
BACON PEAK
GROUP CAMPGROUND
NEWHALEM CAMPGROUND
LADDER CREEK FALLS
GOODELL CAMPGROUND
OAKES PEAK
COLONIAL GLACIER
NEVE GLACIER
ELIJA RIDGE
THUNDER CREEK
MCKAY RIDGE
NATIONAL
TATIE PEAK
RATTLESNAKE CAMPGROUND
BALLARD
NFD RD 5400
METHOW RIVER
RIVERS BEND CAMPGROUND
FLAGGS MOUNTAIN

UPPER BAKER LAKE VIEWPOINT
WELKER PEAK
MOUNT
DIOBSUD BUTTES
WHATCOM CO
SKAGIT CO
SNOWFIELD PEAK
ROSS LAKE NATL REC AREA
BOREALIS GLACIER
RED MOUNTAIN
GABRIEL PEAK
MESAHCHIE GLACIER
FOREST
OKANOGAN
HOLLIWAY MOUNTAIN
TOWER MOUNTAIN
KLIPCHUCK CAMPGROUND
LONE FIR CAMPGROUND

SKAGIT COUNTY
BAKER-SNOQUALMIE
BALD MOUNTAIN
MARBLEMOUNT
NORTH CASCADES NATIONAL PARK
LITTLE DEVIL PEAK
MCALLISTER GLACIER
ELDORADO PEAK
KLAWATTI PEAK
FISHER PEAK
MOUNT LOGAN
BANDED GLACIER
SKAGIT CO
CHELAN CO
BLACK PEAK
SILVER STAR MOUNTAIN
20
OKANOGAN NATIONAL FOREST

20
CONCRETE
BACKPORT
CASCADE RD
NORTH CASCADES HWY
ROCKPORT
CASCADE
SKAGIT RIVER
MARBLE CREEK CAMPGROUND
CASCADE ISLAND CAMPGROUND
INSPIRATION GLACIER
ELDORADO GLACIER
HIDDEN LAKE PEAKS
BOSTON GLACIER
FORBIDDEN GLACIER
MOUNT BUCKNER
NYETH GLACIER
SAHALE GLACIER
LYALL GLACIER
CORTED PEAK
STILETTO PEAK
WENATCHEE NATL FOREST
GIBERT MOUNTAIN
ROADS END CAMPGROUND

SAUK VALLEY RD
RAZORBACK MOUNTAIN
CASCADE RIVER
NATIONAL
MINERAL PARK CAMPGROUND
YAWNING GLACIER
MAGIC MOUNTAIN
HURRY-UP PEAK
S GLACIER
BOOKER MOUNTAIN
GLORY MOUNTAIN
WASHINGTON
LAKE CHELAN
SOUTH CREEK CAMPGROUND

RINKER RIDGE
ILLABOT PEAKS
SUIATTLE MOUNTAIN
SNOWKING MOUNTAIN
MIDDLE CASCADE GLACIER
STEHEKIN
BRIDGE CREEK CAMPGROUND
PARK CREEK CAMPGROUND
SPIDER MOUNTAIN
LE CONTE MOUNTAIN
SHADY CAMPGROUND
DOLLY VARDER CAMPGROUND
STEHEKIN VALLEY
TUMWATER CAMPGROUND
MCALESTER MOUNTAIN
LAKE CHELAN
RENNIE PEAK

DEARINGER CAMPGROUND
GLACIER
530
SKAGIT CO
SNOHOMISH CO
SEGELSEN RIDGE
NORTH MOUNTAIN
TEEPEE FALLS
HURRICANE PEAK
SOUTH CASCADE GLACIER
LE CONTE GLACIER
LIZARD MOUNTAIN
SIXMILE SHELTER
SPIRE GLACIER
DANA GLACIER
AGNES MOUNTAIN
DOME PEAK
GUNSIGHT PEAK
HIGH BRIDGE
NATIONAL RECREATION AREA
RAINBOW MOUNTAIN
RAINBOW FALLS
COMPANY CREEK CAMPGROUND
RAINBOW FALLS CAMPGROUND
PURPLE POINT CAMPGROUND
STEHEKIN
WILDERNESS

DARRINGTON
BENNETT'S STORE RD
530
DARRINGTON
SQUIRE CREEK
PRAIRIE MOUNTAIN
GOLD MOUNTAIN
HUCKLEBERRY MOUNTAIN
BUCK CREEK CAMPGROUND
EAST SIDE BUCK CREEK CAMPGROUND
GIBSON FALLS
PEAK
DOWNEY CREEK CAMPGROUND
SULPHUR HOT SPRINGS
SULPHUR CREEK CAMPGROUND
SUIATTLE RIVER
KAIWHAT PASS
SNOHOMISH CO
CHELAN CO
SADDLE BOW MOUNTAIN
DARK GLACIER
MARY GREEN GLACIER
WEAVER POINT CAMPGROUND
TUPSHIN PEAK
DEVORE PEAK
FLICK CREEK CAMPGROUND
MANLY WHAM CAMPGROUND
BRIDAL VEIL FALLS
CHELAN COUNTY

CLEAR CREEK CAMPGROUND
ASBESTOS FALLS
SQUIRE CREEK PASS
BAKER-SNOQUALMIE
HELENA RIDGE
FOREST
SAUK RIVER
WHITE CHUCK MOUNTAIN
CRYSTAL CREEK CAMPGROUND
WHITE CHUCK CAMPGROUND
WHITE CHUCK RIVER
STUJACK PASS
SNOHOMISH COUNTY
LIME RIDGE
MEADOW MOUNTAIN
FIRE MOUNTAIN
DOLLY VISTA
OWL CREEK CAMPGROUND
MINERS CREEK SHELTER
CANYON CREEK SHELTER
SULPHUR MOUNTAIN
CLOUDY PEAK
CROWN POINT FALLS
DUMBELL MOUNTAIN
LYMAN MOUNTAIN
RED MOUNTAIN
HOLDEN VILLAGE
HOLDEN
LUCERNE
REFRIGERATOR CREEK
MOORE POINT CAMPGROUND
ELEPHANT ROCK CAMPGROUND
LAKE CHELAN
DOMKE LAKE
DOMKE MOUNTAIN
HATCHERY CAMPGROUND
DOMKE FALLS CAMPGROUND

GRANITE PASS
DEER CREEK PASS
COAL LAKE VIEW POINT
STILLAGUAMISH PEAK
NORTH FORK FALLS
SAUK RIVER
KENNEDY HOT SPRING
GAMMA HOT SPRINGS
GLACIER RIDGE
WILDERNESS
BUCK MOUNTAIN
ENTIAT GLACIER
TWIN HARBOR
WENATCHEE NATIONAL FOREST

RIVER BAR CAMPGROUND
DICK SILVERTON
SPERRY CAMPGROUND
MARIEN CREEK
RED BRIDGE CAMPGROUND
MOUNTAIN LOOP HWY
BIG FOUR
BEDAL
BEDAL CAMPGROUND
PERRY CREEK CAMPGROUND
CHOCWICH CAMPGROUND
PAINTED MOUNTAIN
GLACIER PEAK
BUTTERFLY GLACIER
PT GLACIER
TRINITY
CHIWAWA RIVER RD
CARNE MOUNTAIN
ICE CREEK SHELTER
GOPHER MOUNTAIN
PHELPS CREEK CAMPGROUND
LARCH LAKE CAMPGROUND
PYRAMID MOUNTAIN

SEE 111 MAP

0 2.5 5 7.5 10 miles   1 in. = 7.5 mi.

A   B   C

CATHEDRAL PROVINCIAL PARK

QUINISCOE LAKE
PYRAMID LAKE
LAKEVIEW MOUNTAIN
GLACIER LAKE
LADYSLIPPER LAKE

SNOWY MOUNTAIN

BRITISH COLUMBIA

3A
97
3

OSOYOOS

DEADMAN LAKE PROVINCIAL PARK
OSOYOOS LAKE
OKANOGAN INDIAN CAMPING GROUND
ANARCHIST MOUNTAIN
BLUE LAKE
MOUNT KRUGER
OSOYOOS MUSEUM

CUSTOMS POST

BRITISH COLUMBIA — CANADA
USA

BUNKER HILL
SHEEP MOUNTAIN
OKANOGAN CO
CATHEDRAL PEAK
AMPHITHEATER MOUNTAIN
BALD MOUNTAIN
WOLFRAMITE MOUNTAIN
WASHINGTON
APEX MOUNTAIN
ROCK MOUNTAIN
HAIG MOUNTAIN
SNOWSHOE MOUNTAIN
JOE MILLS MOUNTAIN
NIGHTHAWK CUSTOMS
Nighthawk
LOOMIS-OROVILLE
SIMILKAMEEN RIVER
SIMILKAMEEN
OSOYOOS LAKE
COPPER MOUNTAIN
EDER RD
CHESAW RD

PASAYTEN

MIDDLE MOUNTAIN
VAN PEAK
FREDS MOUNTAIN
SADDLE PEAK
TEAPOT DOME
TOPAZ MOUNTAIN
PICK PEAK
WINDY PEAK
HORSESHOE MOUNTAIN
CHOPAKA MOUNTAIN
ELLEMEHAM MOUNTAIN
PALMER LAKE CAMPGROUND
MOLSON SCHOOL MUSEUM

OROVILLE
97
HIGHWAY 7

DOLLAR WATCH MOUNTAIN
TWO POINT MOUNTAIN
PEEPSIGHT MOUNTAIN
CAL PEAK
CHEWACK FALLS
HICKEY HUMP
DAISY CAMPGROUND
CHOPAKA LAKE CAMPGROUND
NORTH FORK NINEMILE CAMPGROUND
GRANDVIEW MOUNTAIN
PALMER MOUNTAIN
SOUTH FORK JUNCTION CAMPGROUND
PALMER LAKE
BLUE LAKE RD
WANNACUT LAKE
WANNACUT

WILDERNESS

NANNY GOAT MOUNTAIN
COLEMAN PEAK
LONG SWAMP CAMPGROUND
TILLMAN MOUNTAIN
RATTLESNAKE MOUNTAIN
GOLD HILL
SPECTACLE LAKE CAMPGROUND
Loomis
LOOMIS-OROVILLE
Ellisford

PASS BUTTE
BILLY GOAT MOUNTAIN
BURCH MOUNTAIN
OBSTRUCTION PEAK
KAY PEAK
THIRTYMILE PEAK
THIRTYMILE CAMPGROUND
ANDREWS CREEK CAMPGROUND
THUNDER MOUNTAIN
DOUGLAS MOUNTAIN

PISTOL PEAKS
EIGHTMILE PEAK
BIG CRAGGY PEAK
SHERMAN PEAK
FAREWELL PEAK
NORTH TWENTYMILE PEAK
OKANOGAN COUNTY
CAYUSE MOUNTAIN
AENEAS MOUNTAIN
BONAPARTE
TWIN PEAKS

TONASKET
20
97

BURGETT PEAK
OKANOGAN
HONEYMOON CAMPGROUND
RUFFED GROUSE CAMPGROUND
TIFFANY SPRING CAMPGROUND
ROCK MOUNTAIN
COUGAR MOUNTAIN
BLUE GOAT MOUNTAIN
PINE CREEK
HAVILLAH RD
CARTER MOUNTAIN
JANIS RAPIDS
MCLOUGHLIN FALLS
CHINCHILLX VALLEY

MCLEOD MOUNTAIN
SWEETGRASS BUTTE
CHEWUCH CAMPGROUND
FALLS CREEK FALLS
TIFFANY MOUNTAIN
SALMON MEADOWS CAMPGROUND
MIDDLE MOUNTAIN
US 97

BALLARD CAMPGROUND
GATE CREEK CAMPGROUND
ISLAND MOUNTAIN
NICE CAMPGROUND
FLAT CAMPGROUND
CLARK PEAK
ALDER CAMPGROUND
KERR CAMPGROUND
ORIOLE CAMPGROUND
SUGARLOAF CAMPGROUNDS
COTTONWOOD CAMPGROUND
FISH LAKE RD
PINE CREEK
20

EARLY WINTERS CAMPGROUND
BUCK LAKE CAMPGROUND
MEMORIAL CAMPGROUND
OLD BALDY
MINERAL HILL
SCHALOW MOUNTAIN
KEYSTONE

RENDEVOUS MOUNTAIN
GRIZZLY MOUNTAIN
LEWIS BUTTE
TRIPOD PEAK
BOULDER CREEK
SALMON FALLS
CONCONULLY
ALBRIGHT CAVE
Riverside

NORTH GARDNER MOUNTAIN
GARDNER MOUNTAIN
MILTON MOUNTAIN
20
SHAFER MUSEUM
BLUE BUCK MOUNTAIN
CONGER CREEK RD
WEST FORK
PEACOCK MOUNTAIN
GRANITE MOUNTAIN
RUBY HILL
OMAK

LAKE CHELAN-OKANOGAN
POPLAR FLAT CAMPGROUND
WINTHROP NATL FISH HATCHERY
PATTERSON LAKE
PATTERSON MOUNTAIN
WINTHROP
FOREST
BOBCAT MOUNTAIN
ROCK LAKES CAMPGROUND
WRIGHT MOUNTAIN
WENATCHEE VALLEY COLLEGE

MYSTERY CAMPGROUND
METHOW VALLEY STATE AIRPORT
KDA CAMPGROUND
BEAVER CAMPGROUND
BEAR MOUNTAIN
LOUP LOUP CAMPGROUND
LOUP LOUP SKI AREA
ROCK CREEK CAMPGROUND
LEADER LAKE CAMPGROUND
SAINT MARYS MISSION
215
155

WAR CREEK CAMPGROUND
TWISP RIVER
TWISP
20
COOK MOUNTAIN
20
OKANOGAN
SAINT MARYS FARM

SAWTOOTH
DUCKBILL MOUNTAIN
BLOCK MOUNTAIN
BLACKPINE LAKE CAMPGROUND
MCCLURE MOUNTAIN
TWISP MUNICIPAL AIRPORT
POLE PICK MOUNTAIN
FINLEY MOUNTAIN

BATTLE MOUNTAIN
OVAL PEAK
GRAY PEAK
SPIRIT MOUNTAIN
NATIONAL
OKANOGAN
CO
Malott
COLVILLE

BALDY MOUNTAIN
CHELAN
HOODOO PEAK
CRATER CREEK CAMPGROUND
LIBBY CREEK RD
Carlton
BENSON CREEK RD
INDIAN
SALT HILL
153

FINNEY PEAK
SKOOKUM PUSS MOUNTAIN
OLD MAID MOUNTAIN
MARTIN PEAK
FOGGY DEW CAMPGROUND
FOGGY DEW FALLS
CRAZY RAPIDS

PRINCE CREEK CAMPGROUND
WENATCHEE
NATIONAL
FERRY PEAK
NORTH NAVARRE PEAK
HUNGRY MOUNTAIN
BUCKHORN MOUNTAIN
PARADISE
RESERVATION

CHELAN COUNTY
UNO PEAK
GRAHAM HARBOR CAMPGROUND
SOUTH NAVARRE CAMPGROUND
SAFETY HARBOR CREEK CAMPGROUND
LAKE CHELAN
SKI PEAK
POISON CREEK CAMPGROUND
END MOUNTAIN
FOREST
Methow
BREWSTER
TENAS MOUNTAIN
LAKE PATEROS
97
17
173
EAGLE RAPIDS
BOX CANYON
LONG RAPIDS
97
CRANES RD

0 2.5 5 7.5 10 miles 1 in. = 7.5 mi.

SEE 103 MAP
SEE 105 MAP
SEE 112 MAP

HWY

© 2006 Rand McNally & Company

A   B   C

GREENWOOD
GRAND FORKS
CHRISTINA LAKE

KETTLE RIVER PROVINCIAL RECREATION AREA
JOHNSTONE CREEK PROVINCIAL PARK
BRITISH COLUMBIA
INGRAM RIDGE
CAMPGROUND
BOUNDARY CREEK PROVINCIAL PARK
PHOENIX SKI HILL
Phoenix
HARDY MOUNTAIN
CHRISTINA LAKE
CHRISTINA LAKE PROVINCIAL PARK
Cascade
Rock Creek
Kettle Valley
CAMPGROUND
MOUNT ATTWOOD
EAGLE MOUNTAIN
STADIUM ARENA
H
Bridesville
RUSTY MOUNTAIN
CUSTOMS POST
Midway
Sidley
BRITISH COLUMBIA
CUSTOMS POST
CANADA
USA
CUSTOMS POST

WASHINGTON
OKANOGAN CO
OKANOGAN
Danville
FERRY CO
AVEY FIELD STATE AIRPORT
STEVENS
MOLSON MUSEUM
GRAPHITE MOUNTAIN
VULCAN MOUNTAIN
COLVILLE NATIONAL FOREST
BOUNDARY MOUNTAIN
OWL MOUNTAIN
McKINLEY
MOLSON HILL
MOLSON
Chesaw
TORODA CREEK RD
SNOW PEAK
TOGO MOUNTAIN
INDEPENDENT MOUNTAIN
PIERRE LAKE CAMPGROUND
ROCK OUT RD
BANGSTON-PIERRE RD
CREEK RD
STRAWBERRY MOUNTAIN
BUCKHORN MOUNTAIN
COLVILLE
GREEN MOUNTAIN
CHESAW
HAVILLAH
HUNGRY HOLLOW RD
NEALEY RD
CHESAW
KETTLE RIVER
CURLEW AIRPORT
DEER CREEK-BOULDER CREEK
DRUMMER MOUNTAIN
MARBLE MOUNTAIN
ROCKY MOUNTAIN
JASPER MOUNTAIN
Orient
TOULOU
OKANOGAN NATIONAL FOREST
HALEY MOUNTAIN
BETH LAKE CAMPGROUND
BEAVER LAKE CAMPGROUND
COLVILLE
Curlew
RIVER RD
FRANSON PEAK
SENTINEL BUTTE
NORTH BOULDER RIDGE
DEER CREEK SUMMIT CAMPGROUND
HEINKEL CANYON
THOMPSON RIDGE
395
ANTOINE
LOST LAKE CAMPGROUND
BONAPARTE RD
BODIE MOUNTAIN
NATIONAL
GRANITE MOUNTAIN
CURLEW
PROFANITY PEAK
RABBIT MOUNTAIN
BURGE MOUNTAIN
HA-VILLAH
CUMBERLAND CAMPGROUND
BUNCH RD
BONAPARTE CAMPGROUND
HARDSCRABBLE MOUNTAIN
FOREST
TONASKET
CREEK
RYAN HILL
OKANOGAN
NATIONAL
HORSESHOE MOUNTAIN
21
LAMBERT RD
STICKPIN HILL
DAVIS LAKE CAMPGROUND
FOREST
BONAPARTE LAKE
CREEK RD
TORODA MOUNTAIN
TORODA
WAUCONDA SUMMIT
STORM KING MOUNTAIN
BALD PEAK
KNOB HILL-TROUT CREEK RD
CURLEW LAKE
CURLEW LAKE CAMPGROUND
BELCHER MOUNTAIN
NATIONAL
ALLIGATOR RIDGE
20
ISLAND MOUNTAIN
SWEAT CREEK CAMPGROUND
FIR MOUNTAIN
FERRY COUNTY AIRPORT
COPPER BUTTE
TWIN SISTERS
C C MOUNTAIN
BARKER MOUNTAIN
OKANOGAN COUNTY
CORNER BUTTE
KLONDIKE
GOLD HILL
TIMBER RIDGE
SCAR MOUNTAIN
HOODOO MOUNTAIN
BISBEE MOUNTAIN
BONAPARTE
AENEAS VALLEY
3010 RD
NFD RD 200
COPPER MOUNTAIN
20
REPUBLIC
FERRY COUNTY
ALBIAN HILL
GRAVES MOUNTAIN
SHERMAN
TROUT LAKE CAMPGROUND
BANNON MOUNTAIN
NFD RD
SHERMAN PASS CAMPGROUND
SHERMAN CREEK FALLS
CANYON CREEK CAMPGROUND
CHEWILIKEN RD
CAMEL BACK
FROSTY CREEK RD
SHEEP MOUNTAIN
SANPOIL LAKE RD
MURPHY HILL
MOUNT WASHINGTON
SHERMAN PEAK
PARADISE PEAK
20
EAGLE ROCK
SCALAWAG RIDGE
HAAG COVE CAMPGROUND
OKANOGAN
BEEHIVE MOUNTAIN
AENEAS MOUNTAIN
FERRY LAKE CAMPGROUND
QUARTZ MOUNTAIN
EDDS MOUNTAIN
SNOW PEAK
BALD MOUNTAIN
CEDAR RIDGE
FOREST
TUNK CREEK RD
NATIONAL
BAILEY MOUNTAIN
SWAN LAKE CAMPGROUND
LONG LAKE CAMPGROUND
BROWN MOUNTAIN
BEAR MOUNTAIN
BARNABY BUTTES
BALD HILL
CRAWFISH LAKE CAMPGROUND
DUGOUT MOUNTAIN
FOREST
COUGAR MOUNTAIN
GRANITE MOUNTAIN
WASHINGTON
LAKE ELLEN CAMPGROUND
SEVENTEENMILE MOUNTAIN
THIRTEENMILE CAMPGROUND
West Fork
ELBOW LAKE CAMPGROUND
ONION RIDGE
25
GRANITE MOUNTAIN
MOSES LAKE
STRAWBERRY MOUNTAIN
HALL CREEK
BUCKSKIN CREEK CAMPGROUND
Rice
OMAK MOUNTAIN
GOLD LAKE
BALD KNOB
PAINT ROCK
LITTLE WHITE MOUNTAIN
LITTLE MOSES MOUNTAIN
21
COLVILLE
SOUTH SEVENTEENMILE MOUNTAIN
VAN BRUNT MOUNTAIN
LYMAN LAKE
TWENTYONE MILE CAMPGROUND
GORDON BUTTE
CENTRAL PEAK
JOHNS MOUNTAIN
LYNX MOUNTAIN
INCHELIUM-KETTLE FALLS RD
Disautel
OMAK CREEK
MOSES MOUNTAIN
CODY BUTTE
CARSON MOUNTAIN
JOHNNYS HILL
RAINY RIDGE
COLVILLE
GOLD LAKE RIVER
OKANOGAN CO
FERRY CO
SANPOIL
ROCKY POINT CAMPGROUND
NORTH TWIN LAKE
Inchelium
155
INDIAN
ARMSTRONG MOUNTAIN
PARK CITY LOOP RD
GOLD LAKE RD
OWHI LAKE
HIDDEN BEACH CAMPGROUND
STRANGER CREEK
SILVER CREEK RD
BOOT MOUNTAIN
OWHI LOOP RD
BRIDGE
MINNEHAHA CREEK
SOUTH TWIN LAKE
RATTLESNAKE MOUNTAIN
STRAY DOG CANYON
STEVENS FERRY CO
WHITMORE MOUNTAIN
INDIAN
CACHE CREEK
GOLD MOUNTAIN RIDGE
BEAR-HIDE GAP
RESERVATION
HAMILTON MOUNTAIN
MULTNOMAH FALLS
SCHOOLHOUSE LOOP RD
NESPELEM RIVER
CACHE CREEK RD
GOLD MOUNTAIN
SEYMOUR HILL
COUGAR CANYON
MIDDLE MOUNTAIN
Hunter
NESPELEM
COLUMBIA
NESPELEM RAPIDS
JOE MOSES RD
BUFFALO LAKE RD
SCLOME MOUNTAIN
COULEE DAM NATIONAL RECREATION AREA RD
25
PARSON RAPIDS
STRAHL RD
CHINA CREEK
DEEP CANYON
SPRAY CANYON RD
OKANOGAN CO
DOUGLAS CO
COLUMBIA RIVER
BUFFALO LAKE
KELLER BUTTE
WATSON RIDGE
SILVER CREEK
SILVER CREEK RD
DODGE POINT
STRAHL CANYON RD
D REX RD
RESERVATION

A   B   B   C

SEE 104 MAP
SEE 106 MAP
SEE 113 MAP
HWY

0   2.5   5   7.5   10   miles   1 in. = 7.5 mi.

© 2006 Rand McNally & Company

A   B   C

BRITISH COLUMBIA

RED MOUNTAIN SKI AREA

NANCY GREENE RECREATIONAL AREA

MOUNT JELONESS

ROSSLAND   Casino   BEAVER CREEK PROV PARK   **MONTROSE**   Columbia Gardens

LOST MOUNTAIN

RIPPLE MOUNTAIN

STAGLEAP PROVINCIAL PARK

BALDY MOUNTAIN   GROUSE RIDGE   LAKE MOUNTAIN   VIOLIN LAKE

Silica   Paterson

FRISCO MOUNTAIN

USA

Remac   Waneta   Nelway

PEWEE FALLS

PEND OREILLE CO   SALMO-PRIEST WILDERNESS

BOUNDARY CO   SNOWY TOP   IDAHO

BRITISH COLUMBIA
WASHINGTON

CRESCENT LAKE CAMPGROUND   SLUMBER PEAK

GYPSY PEAK

HUGHES RIDGE VIEW POINT

1

STEVENS CO   HOPE MOUNTAIN   LEAD PENCIL MOUNTAIN

MITCHELL MOUNTAIN

COLVILLE NATIONAL FOREST

CHURCHILL MOUNTAIN   SHEEP CREEK FALLS   SHEEP CREEK

BELSHAZZAR MOUNTAIN

NORTHPORT

BLUE BIRD RIDGE   CROWELL MOUNTAIN

METALINE FALLS

GREEN MOUNTAIN   THUNDER MOUNTAIN

GOLD PEAK

BILLY GOAT MOUNTAIN

NORTHPORT-FLAT   LITTLE DALLES   BLACK HAWK MOUNTAIN

METALINE

Pend Oreille Village

HELMER MOUNTAIN

JUMBO MOUNTAIN   Dolomite

STONE MOUNTAIN   BLACK CANYON

ELECTRIC POINT

COLVILLE

SULLIVAN CREEK   SULLIVAN LAKE CAMPGROUND   SULLIVAN LAKE

ROUND TOP MOUNTAIN

LASOTA FALLS   GRANITE FALLS   STAGER INN CAMPGROUND

COULEE DAM NATIONAL RECREATION AREA

FREDERICKSON HILL

BALDY MOUNTAIN

DEER MOUNTAIN

NATIONAL

MILL POND CAMPGROUND

NOISY CREEK CAMPGROUND

NATIONAL

HIGH ROCK MOUNTAIN

NORTH GORGE CAMPGROUND

LOOKOUT MOUNTAIN

MEADOW CREEK

HUCKLEBERRY MOUNTAIN

BOX CANYON DAM VIEW POINT

EDGEWATER CAMPGROUND

Maitlen

PEND OREILLE   TILLICUM PEAK

IDAHO

SNAG COVE CAMPGROUND   KETTLE RIVER CAMPGROUND

SPION KOP   BONANZA HILL   EVANS HILL CUTOFF

EVANS CAMPGROUND

395

Marcus

COLVILLE NATIONAL FOREST

STEVENS COUNTY

ONION MOUNTAIN

RABBIT MOUNTAIN

ALADDIN MOUNTAIN

SELDOM SEEN MOUNTAIN

IONE

IONE MUNI AIRPORT

MOLYBDENITE MOUNTAIN

COYOTE HILL

MONUMENTAL MOUNTAIN

COUNTY

KANIKSU

PETIT LAKE CAMPGROUND

NFD RD 302   DUSTY PEAK

FRANKLIN D ROOSEVELT LAKE   ECHO MOUNTAIN

ST PAULS MISSION

DOUGLASS FALLS

NORTH FORK MILL CREEK RD

GREEN MOUNTAIN   LAKE THOMAS CAMPGROUND

LAKE LEO CAMPGROUND

GRANITE PEAK

HANLON MOUNTAIN

DIAMOND PEAK   KALISPELL FALLS

NATIONAL

HUNGRY MOUNTAIN

KETTLE FALLS

OLD KETTLE   LIONS ISLAND

COLVILLE

BONANZA LEAD MILL

DOUGLAS FALLS

COLVILLE MOUNTAIN

OLD DOMINION MOUNTAIN

CLIFF RD

KANIKSU

FOURTH OF JULY PEAK   GLEASON MOUNTAIN

NORTH BALDY

COLVILLE

COLVILLE MUNI AIRPORT

COLVILLE-TIGER

20

LITTLE CRYSTAL FALLS   FLODELLE CAMPGROUND

PEND SCRABBLER MOUNTAIN OREILLE

RUBY MOUNTAIN

PANHANDLE CAMPGROUND

GROUSE KNOB   TOLA POINT

RIVER BEND AIRPORT

PELKE DIVIDE

NATIONAL FOREST

MINGO MOUNTAIN

MILL BUTTE

NATIONAL WILDLIFE REFUGE

BOULDER MOUNTAIN

Cecil

BROWNS LAKE CAMPGROUND

NORTH SKOOKUM CAMPGROUND

SOUTH SKOOKUM LAKE CAMPGROUND

BRADBURY CAMPGROUND

CARTER CANYON   NORTH BASIN

BEAR CANYON

TACOMA PEAK

SULLIVAN POINT

DAY MOUNTAIN   RICE-ORIN

FREEMAN HILL

ROCKY BUTTE

LITTLE CALISPELL PEAK

KINGS MOUNTAIN

MARBLE   SOUTH

ADDY MOUNTAIN

BREWER MOUNTAIN

FOURTH OF JULY MOUNTAIN

DEADMAN HILL

COLVILLE

WILSON MOUNTAIN

CUSICK

COOKS MOUNTAIN

57

MCKERN-SCOTT

GOLD HILL   BECK

DUNN MOUNTAIN

Addy

FORTY NINE DEGREES NORTH SKI AREA

WINCHESTER PEAK

KALISPEL INDIAN RESERVATION

NO NAME PEAK

FOREST

ADDY-GIFFORD

SUMMIT VALLEY   BLUE CREEK   WEST

Bluecreek

GOLD HILL   EAGLE MOUNTAIN

FLOWERY TRAIL

CHEWELAH

QUARTZITE MOUNTAIN

Usk

SKOOKUM PEAK

NO NAME LAKE CAMPGROUND

NEWPORT GEOPHYSICAL OBSERVATORY

STONE JOHNNY

QUARTZ MOUNTAIN

CLOVERLEAF BEACH CAMPGROUND

NATIONAL

PARKER MOUNTAIN

CALISPELL LAKE   CALISPELL PEAK

BARTLETTE RD

Dalkena

CUBAN HILL

COULEE DAM NATIONAL RECREATION AREA

25

CEDONIA-ADDY   LESSIG SOUTH FORK RD

HUCKLEBERRY MOUNTAIN

FRONT TO MARKET LOOP

Newton   SHAFER

ROUNDTOP MOUNTAIN

POWER PEAK

DAVIS LAKE

ROCKY GORGE

SADDLE MOUNTAIN

COOKS MOUNTAIN

20

SAND BUTTE VALLEY

NEWPORT

Priest River

STENSGAR MOUNTAIN

WAITTS LAKE   LANE MOUNTAIN

NELSON PEAK

BOYER MOUNTAIN

SACHEEN LAKE

LITTLE BLUE GROUSE MOUNTAIN

DIAMOND LAKE

Oldtown

2

SPRINGDALE-HUNTERS

LITTLE COYOTE MOUNTAIN   BOUDES HILL

LONG PRAIRIE

BENSON PEAK

GRANITE MOUNTAIN

LITTLE ROUNDTOP

BRUSH MOUNTAIN

211

SCOTIA VALLEY

41

CEDAR CANYON

EMPEY MOUNTAIN

HESSELTINE RD

231

LIMEKILN HILL

JUMPOFF JOE MOUNTAIN

395

DEER CREEK RD   DEER LAKE

DEER LAKE MOUNTAIN

BLUE GROUSE MOUNTAIN

SHADOW VALLEY   FERTILE VALLEY   WEST BRANCH

BARE MOUNTAIN

LONE MOUNTAIN   SCOTIA CANYON

SPRING VALLEY

SPRINGDALE

CAMAS VALLEY

292

Loon Lake   LOON LAKE RD   LOON LAKE MOUNTAIN

Camden

Pocahontas Bay

PEND OREILLE CO

SPOKANE CO

A   B   C

SEE 105 MAP   SEE 107 MAP   SEE 114 MAP

HWY

0   2.5   5   7.5   10

miles   1 in. = 7.5 mi.

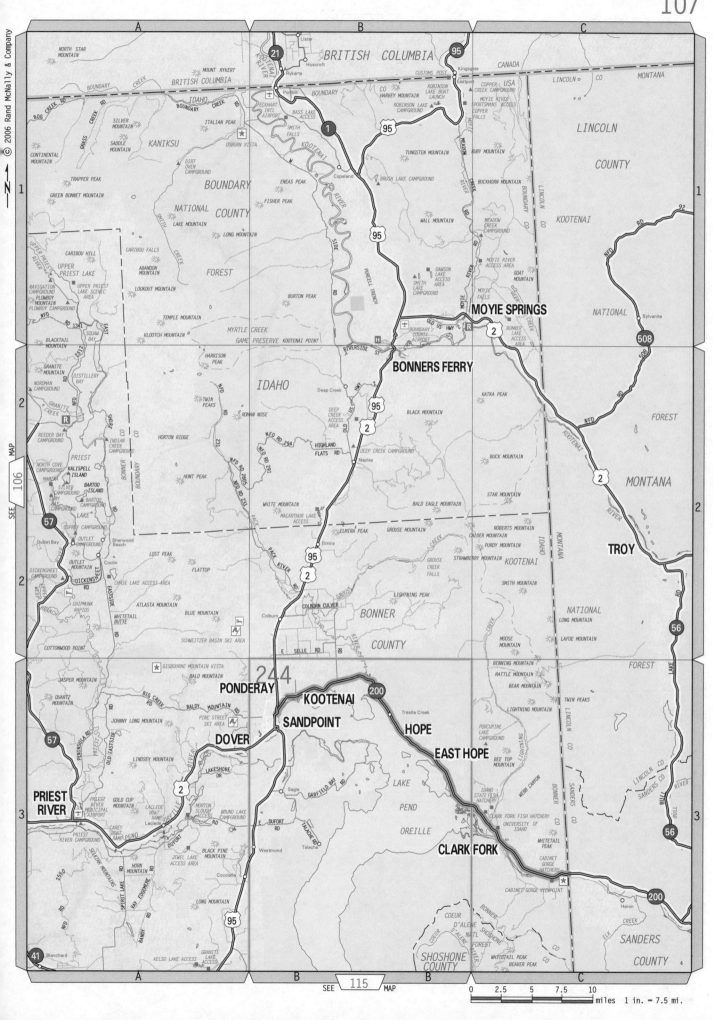

© 2006 Rand McNally & Company

N

SEE 106 MAP

HWY

BRITISH COLUMBIA

LINCOLN COUNTY

BOUNDARY COUNTY

NATIONAL FOREST

KANIKSU

IDAHO

KOOTENAI

MONTANA

MOYIE SPRINGS

BONNERS FERRY

TROY

PRIEST RIVER

PONDERAY

KOOTENAI

SANDPOINT

DOVER

HOPE

EAST HOPE

CLARK FORK

BONNER COUNTY

NATIONAL FOREST

SHOSHONE COUNTY

SANDERS COUNTY

SEE 115 MAP

0   2.5   5   7.5   10
miles   1 in. = 7.5 mi.

A
B
SEE 100 MAP
B
C

169

OLYMPIC
NATIONAL
FOREST
HUNGER MOUNTAIN
RIVER

QUILLAYUTE RIVER
DICKEY RIVER
SOL DUC RD
QUILLAYUTE RD
PUSH
MORA RD
LA
La Push

101
110
FORKS

SITKUM
SHELTER
ELK RIDGE
CALAWAH SHELTER
OLYMPIC
RUGGED RIDGE
FIFTEENMILE SHELTER

CLALLAM
COUNTY

CLALLAM CO
JEFFERSON CO
Bogachiel

BOGACHIEL
SHELTER
NATIONAL
FLAPJACK SHELTER
PARK

OLYMPIC

NATIONAL

PARK

BOGACHIEL RIVER

SPRUCE MOUNTAIN
GEODETIC HILL

UPPER
HOH
OX
BOW
HOH
HOH
RD

MINNIE
PETERSON
CAMPGROUND

RIVER
RD

HUELSDONK
CAMPGROUND
SOUTH
FORK
HOH

WILLOUGHBY
CREEK
CAMPGROUND

HOH
RIVER

HUELSDONK RIDGE

JEFFERSON
COUNTY

CITY
OIL
101

HOH INDIAN
RESERVATION

WASHINGTON

DESTRUCTION
ISLAND

BROWNS POINT

COPPER MINE
BOTTOM
CAMPGROUND

OIL
RD

CLEARWATER
RIVER

UPPER
CLEARWATER
CAMPGROUND

YAHOO
LAKE
CAMPGROUND

OLYMPIC
NATIONAL
FOREST

PACIFIC

1

172

CLEARWATER

OLYMPIC

NATIONAL

OLYMPIC
NATIONAL
PARK

Queets
QUEETS
QUEETS RIVER
RIVER
JEFFERSON
PARK
CO

GRAYS HARBOR
CO

RD

101

GRAYS HARBOR
COUNTY

QUINAULT

THIMBLE MOUNTAIN
LONE MOUNTAIN

2

OCEAN

WILLOUGHBY
ROCK

SPLIT
ROCK

INDIAN

QUINAULT RIVER

RESERVATION

OLYMPIC
NATIONAL
FOREST

Taholah
109

2

177

Moclips
Sunset Beach
Highland Heights
Pacific Beach
Aloha
OCEAN

YELLOW
BLUFF

COPALIS ROCK
Iron Springs
COPALIS HEAD

COPALIS
BEACH
Copalis Beach
Copalis
Crossing

Ocean City

109
115
Illahee
Dyhut

OCEAN
SHORES

298

Humptulips

KIRKPATRICK RD
RIVER

BEACH RD

HUMPTULIPS RD

Newton
Tulips

Burrows
BURROWS
RD
Chenois Creek

Gray Gables

Grays
Harbor
City

BRECKENRIDGE
BLUFF

3

A
B
SEE 116 MAP
B
C

0 2.5 5 7.5 10 miles 1 in. = 7.5 mi.

HWY

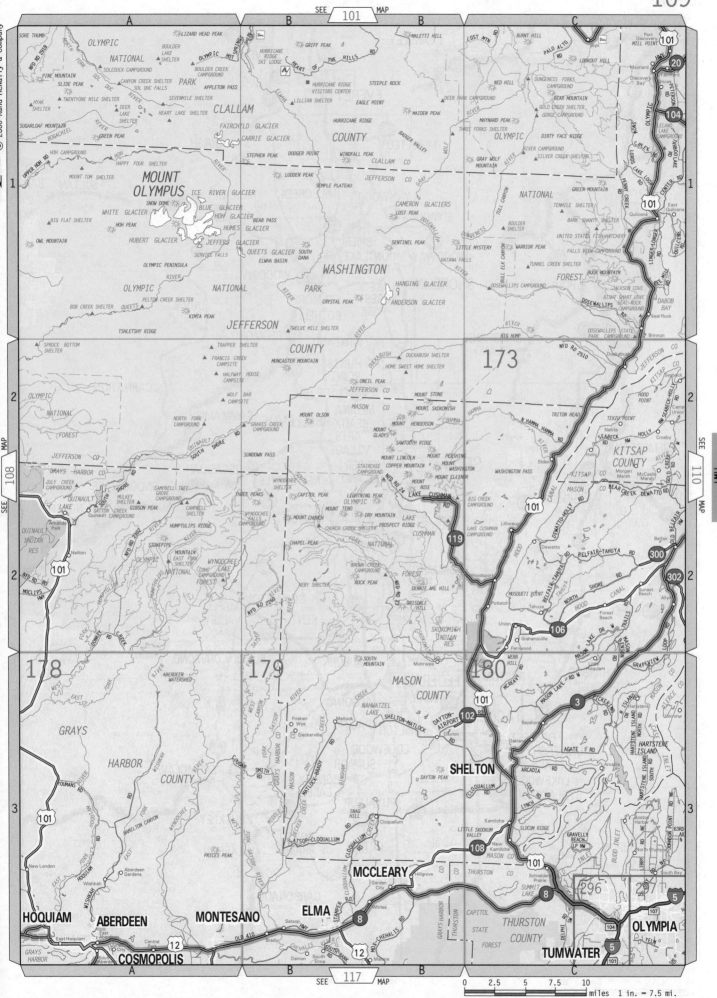

SEE 101 MAP

OLYMPIC NATIONAL PARK

MOUNT OLYMPUS

CLALLAM COUNTY

JEFFERSON COUNTY

WASHINGTON

OLYMPIC NATIONAL PARK

OLYMPIC NATIONAL FOREST

173

KITSAP COUNTY

MASON CO

GRAYS HARBOR COUNTY

178   179   180

GRAYS HARBOR COUNTY

MASON COUNTY

SHELTON

MCCLEARY

ELMA

MONTESANO

ABERDEEN

HOQUIAM

COSMOPOLIS

THURSTON COUNTY

THURSTON STATE FOREST

TUMWATER

OLYMPIA

296   297

SEE 117 MAP

0   2.5   5   7.5   10   miles   1 in. = 7.5 mi.

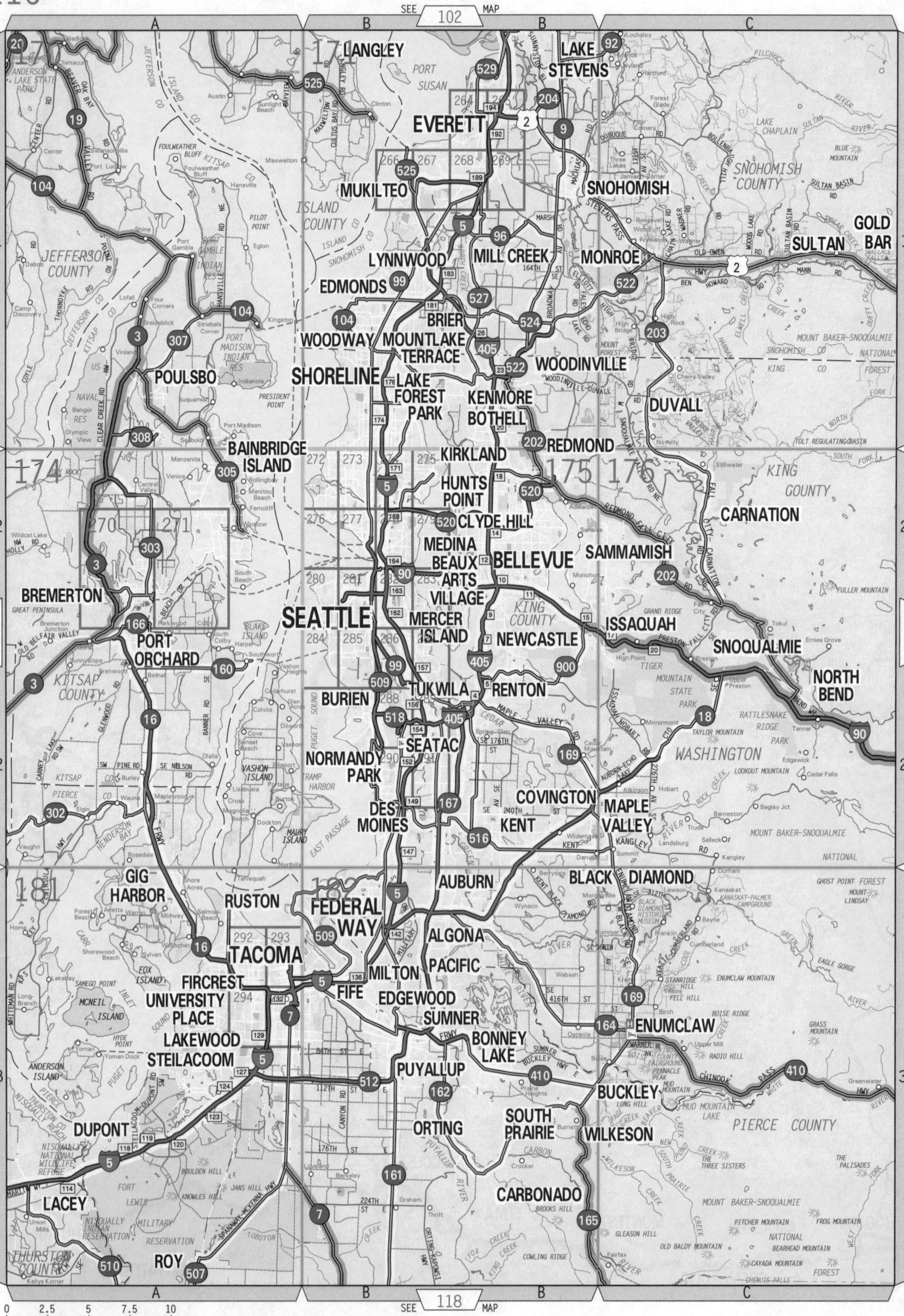

© 2006 Rand McNally & Company

SEE 102 MAP

SEE 118 MAP

SEE 109 MAP

SEE 111 MAP

HWY

Counties and regions:
JEFFERSON COUNTY, ISLAND COUNTY, SNOHOMISH COUNTY, KITSAP COUNTY, KING COUNTY, PIERCE COUNTY, THURSTON CO., WASHINGTON

MOUNT BAKER-SNOQUALMIE NATIONAL FOREST

Cities and towns:
LANGLEY, LAKE STEVENS, EVERETT, MUKILTEO, SNOHOMISH, GOLD BAR, SULTAN, MILL CREEK, MONROE, LYNNWOOD, EDMONDS, BRIER, WOODINVILLE, WOODWAY, MOUNTLAKE TERRACE, SHORELINE, LAKE FOREST PARK, KENMORE, BOTHELL, DUVALL, POULSBO, BAINBRIDGE ISLAND, KIRKLAND, REDMOND, HUNTS POINT, CARNATION, CLYDE HILL, MEDINA, BEAUX ARTS VILLAGE, BELLEVUE, SAMMAMISH, SEATTLE, MERCER ISLAND, ISSAQUAH, SNOQUALMIE, BREMERTON, PORT ORCHARD, NEWCASTLE, NORTH BEND, BURIEN, TUKWILA, RENTON, SEATAC, NORMANDY PARK, DES MOINES, KENT, COVINGTON, MAPLE VALLEY, GIG HARBOR, RUSTON, FEDERAL WAY, AUBURN, BLACK DIAMOND, TACOMA, FIRCREST, ALGONA, PACIFIC, MILTON, FIFE, EDGEWOOD, SUMNER, BONNEY LAKE, ENUMCLAW, UNIVERSITY PLACE, LAKEWOOD, STEILACOOM, PUYALLUP, ORTING, BUCKLEY, DUPONT, SOUTH PRAIRIE, WILKESON, LACEY, ROY, CARBONADO

0 2.5 5 7.5 10 miles   1 in. = 7.5 mi.

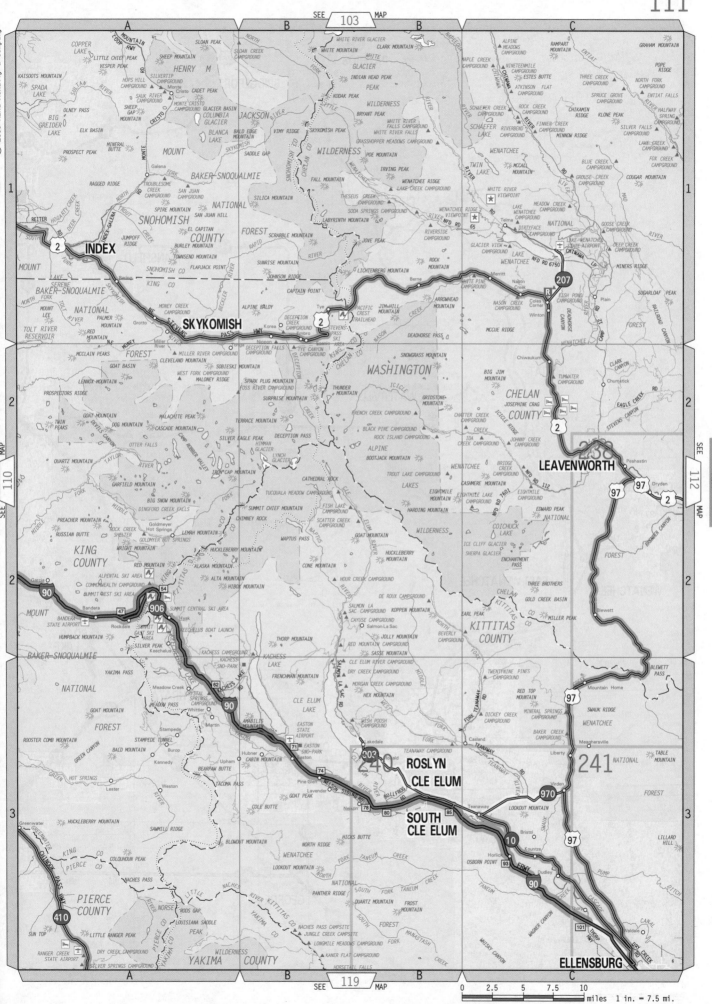

SEE 103 MAP

SEE 110 MAP

SEE 112 MAP

HWY

SEE 119 MAP

0   2.5   5   7.5   10   miles   1 in. = 7.5 mi.

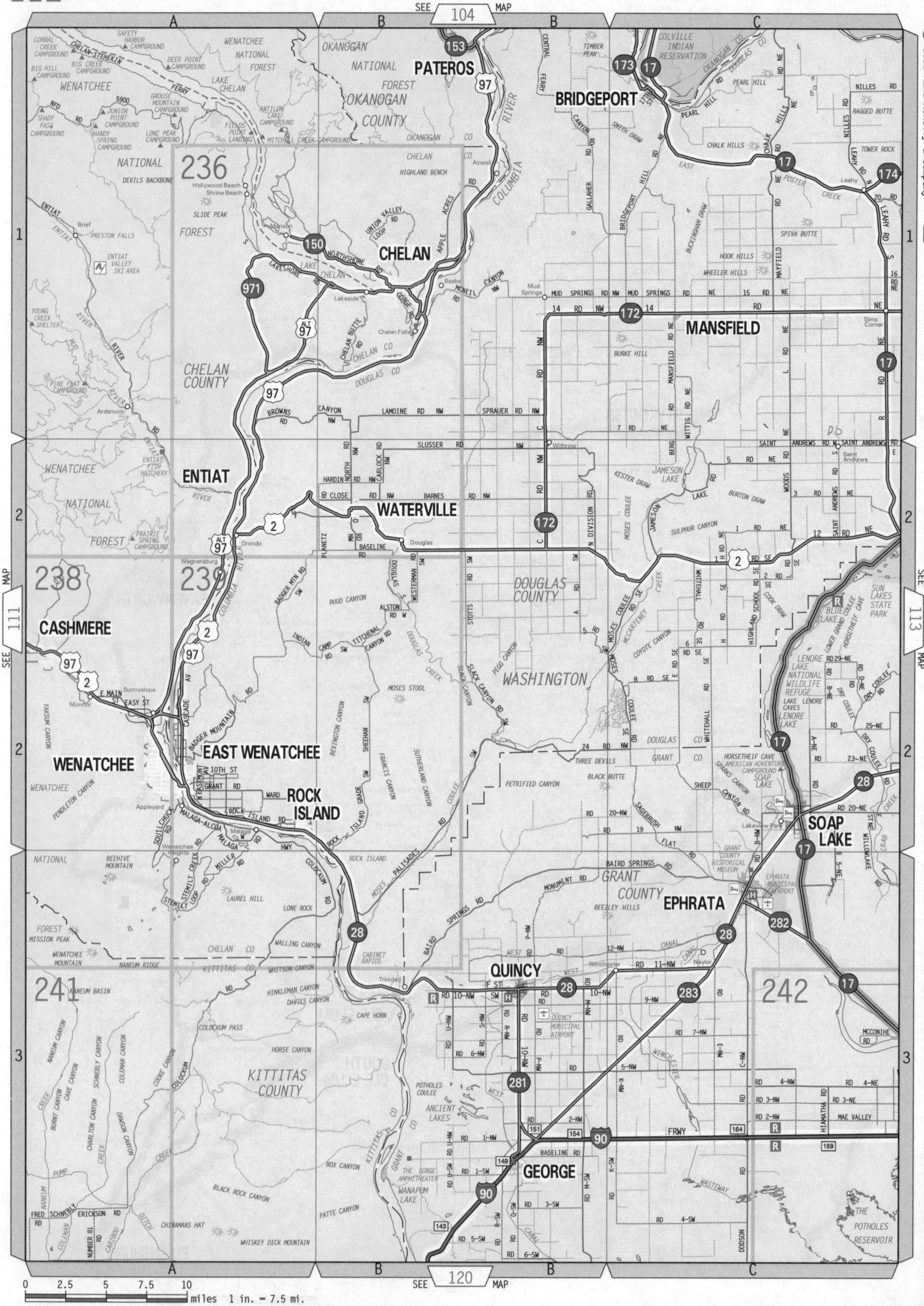

SEE 104 MAP
SEE 111 MAP
SEE 113 MAP
SEE 120 MAP
236
238
239
241
242
PATEROS
BRIDGEPORT
CHELAN
MANSFIELD
ENTIAT
WATERVILLE
CASHMERE
EAST WENATCHEE
WENATCHEE
ROCK ISLAND
SOAP LAKE
EPHRATA
QUINCY
GEORGE
CHELAN COUNTY
OKANOGAN COUNTY
DOUGLAS COUNTY
GRANT COUNTY
KITTITAS COUNTY
WASHINGTON
WENATCHEE NATIONAL FOREST
OKANOGAN NATIONAL FOREST
COLVILLE INDIAN RESERVATION
LAKE CHELAN
COLUMBIA RIVER
ENTIAT RIVER
SUN LAKES STATE PARK
LENORE LAKE NATIONAL WILDLIFE REFUGE
QUINCY MUNICIPAL AIRPORT
EPHRATA MUNICIPAL AIRPORT
THE POTHOLES RESERVOIR
WANAPUM LAKE
ANCIENT LAKES
0 2.5 5 7.5 10
miles 1 in. = 7.5 mi.

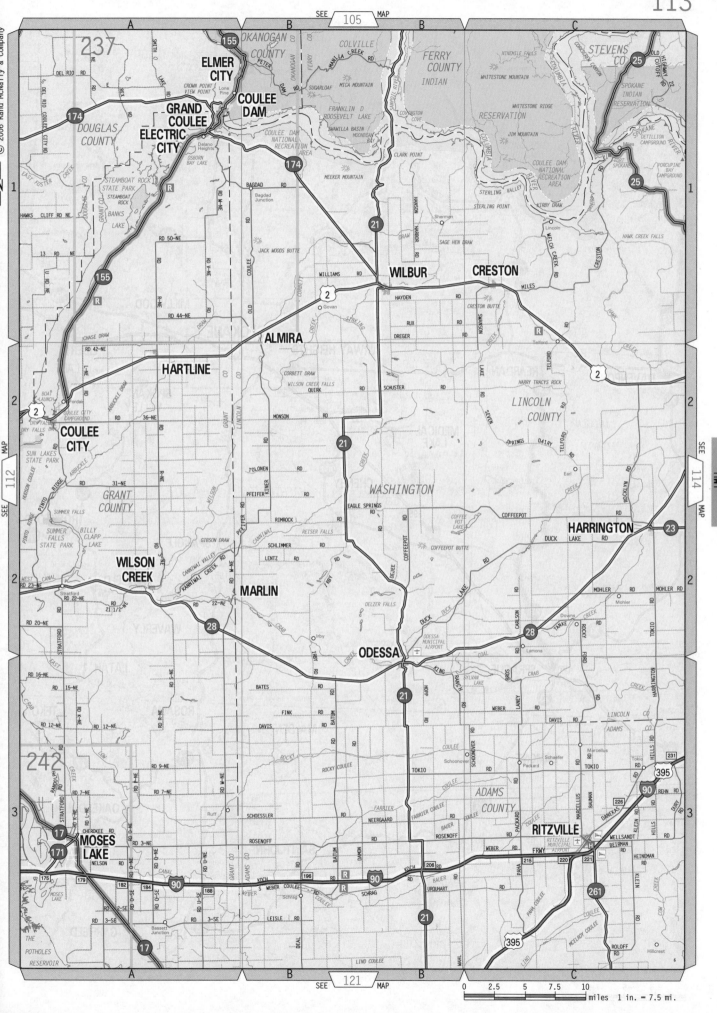

HWY

0   2.5   5   7.5   10
miles 1 in. = 7.5 mi.

© 2006 Rand McNally & Company

SEE 106 MAP

SEE 113 MAP HWY

SEE 115 MAP

SEE 122 MAP

miles 1 in. = 7.5 mi.
0 2.5 5 7.5 10

Counties & Regions

STEVENS COUNTY
SPOKANE INDIAN RESERVATION
COULEE DAM NATIONAL RECREATION AREA
LINCOLN COUNTY
SPOKANE COUNTY
WHITMAN COUNTY
ADAMS COUNTY

Cities & Towns

DEER PARK
SPOKANE
MILLWOOD
LIBERTY LAKE
SPOKANE VALLEY
AIRWAY HEIGHTS
DAVENPORT
REARDAN
MEDICAL LAKE
CHENEY
ROCKFORD
SPANGLE
FAIRFIELD
WAVERLY
LATAH
TEKOA
ROSALIA
MALDEN
OAKSDALE
SPRAGUE
LAMONT
SAINT JOHN
GARFIELD

WASHINGTON

Landmarks & Features

BLUE MOUNTAIN
BOUNDARY BUTTE
SPRINGDALE HUNTERS RD
LYONS HILL
BEAR MOUNTAIN
DEER MOUNTAIN
ROUND MOUNTAIN
SPOKANE MOUNTAIN
WELLPINIT
ELLIAM
WELLPINIT MOUNTAIN
SHERWOOD MOUNTAIN
CAYUSE MOUNTAIN
PITNER BUTTE
PORCUPINE BAY
LITTLE FALLS
DEVILS GAP
EAGLE ROCK
LONG LAKE
FOUR MOUND RD
RIVERSIDE STATE PARK
MCMILLAN MOUNTAIN
LITTLE MOUNTAIN
STONY PEAK
SADDLE MOUNTAIN
MOUNT GODFREY
CORKSCREW CANYON
HAPPY HILL
BECKS HILL
TUMTUM
BALD MOUNTAIN
SPOKANE STATE GAME FARM
DEER PARK MUNICIPAL AIRPORT
MILAN HILL
MOUNT SPOKANE STATE PARK
MOUNT SPOKANE
TRIPPS KNOB
BALD KNOB
SELKIRK MOUNTAIN
DAY MOUNTAIN
ROUND TOP MOUNTAIN
GREEN MOUNTAIN
NEWMAN LAKE
FAIRCHILD AIR FORCE BASE
FOUR LAKES
TURNBULL NATIONAL WILDLIFE REFUGE
BADGER LAKE
BUNKER HILL
PINE SPRINGS
WILLIAMS LAKE
WATERMELON HILL
DOWNS LAKE
ROCK LAKE
CASTLE ROCK
JOHNSONS BEACH
THE ARM SLAUGHTER PEN BAY
ROCK CREEK FALLS
COW LAKE
SPRAGUE LAKE
HARPER ISLAND
STEPTOE BUTTE
MOREFIELD BUTTE
TEKOA MOUNTAIN
GELBERT MOUNTAIN
NAFF RIDGE
GRANITE BUTTE
STEAM SHOVEL HILL
TOWELL FALLS

Routes

2, 25, 27, 28, 90, 195, 206, 231, 245, 246, 247, 257, 264, 270, 271, 272, 276, 278, 290, 291, 346, 347, 348, 349, 352, 395, 902, 904

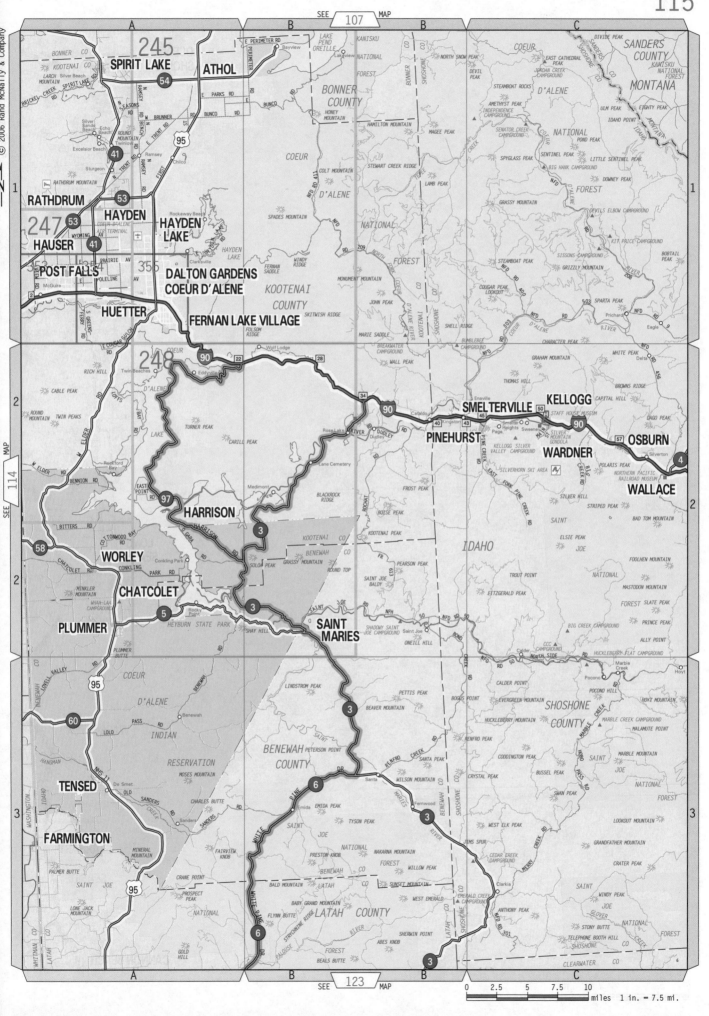

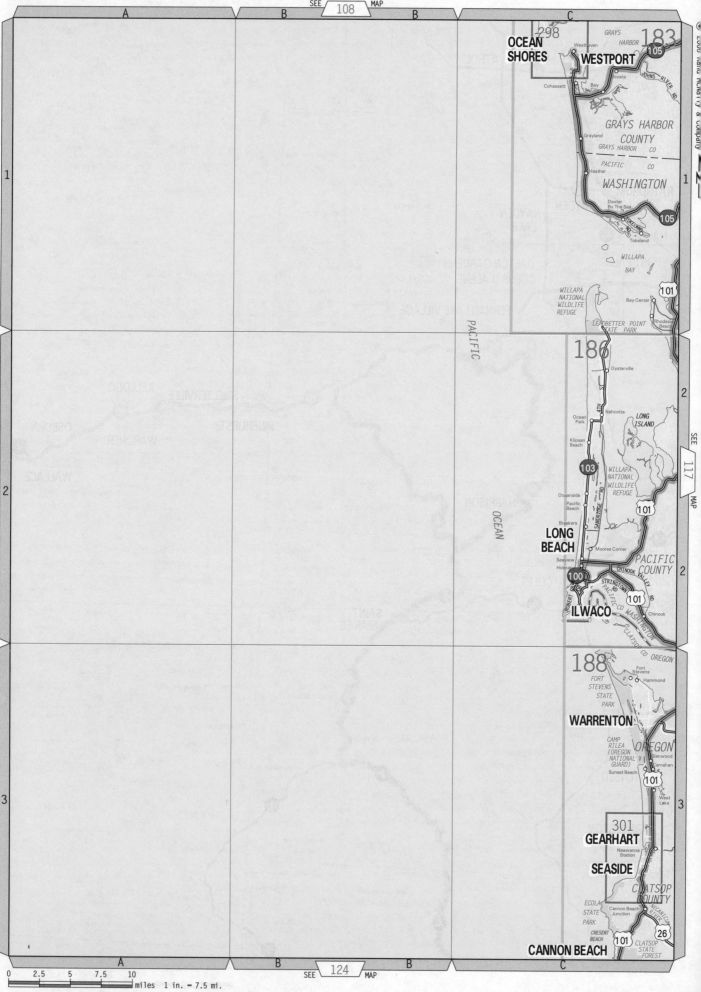

SEE MAP 109

183 105 COSMOPOLIS 107

184

GRAYS HARBOR COUNTY

101

12

CAPITOL STATE FOREST

OAKVILLE

TENINO

BUCODA

507

CENTRALIA

RAYMOND

101

105

SOUTH BEND

6

PACIFIC COUNTY

LEWIS COUNTY

WASHINGTON

29

CHEHALIS

72

508

6

186

PE ELL

187

NAPAVINE

505

WINLOCK

TOLEDO

VADER

506

504

4

401

WAHKIAKUM COUNTY

4

COWLITZ COUNTY

CASTLE ROCK

SEE MAP 116   SEE MAP 118

101

CATHLAMET

409

LONGVIEW

411

189

100 ASTORIA

30

CLATSOP COUNTY

COLUMBIA RIVER

432

KELSO

433   432

WALLACE ISLAND

30

CLATSKANIE

47

RAINIER

PRESCOTT

202

OREGON

202

47

COLUMBIA COUNTY

KALAMA

30

5

26   188   26

SEE MAP 125

0 2.5 5 7.5 10 miles   1 in. = 7.5 mi.

© 2006 Rand McNally & Company

SEE MAP 110

185

MOUNT RAINIER

A B B C

YELM

RAINIER

510 507 702 7 161 165

FORT LEWIS MILITARY RESERVATION

McKenna
Tanwax
Kapowsin
KAPOWSIN LAKE
304TH ST E
336TH ST E
352ND ST E

EATONVILLE

PIERCE COUNTY

Clay City
Ohop
Ohop Valley
Pioneer Farm Museum
La Grande
Lake Alder

THURSTON COUNTY

Wetico
CRAWFORD MOUNTAIN
BAUMGARD HILL
BALD HILL
MILLER HILL
SKOOKUMCHUCK RESERVOIR
CLAM MOUNTAIN
JONAS HILL
CLEAR LAKE
BASS LAKE
GREEN HILL
DESCHUTES FALLS

THURSTON CO
LEWIS CO

WASHINGTON

Independence Ridge
Sluiskin Mountain
Old Desolate
Eagle Cliff
Ptarmigan Ridge
Point Success
Satulick Mountain

MOUNT BAKER-SNOQUALMIE

Junction Park
National
Ashford
Longmire
706 7

MINERAL LAKE
Mineral
Carlson
Divide

NATIONAL FOREST

LEWIS COUNTY

GIFFORD

PINCHOT

Skate Creek
Big Creek Campground

PACKWOOD
Packwood

508 122 12 7

MORTON

MOSSYROCK

CENTRALIA ALPHA
Onalaska
Lacamas
Salkum
Harmony
Cinebar
Coal Canyon
Hopkins Hill View Point
Indian Hole Campground
Tilton
Ike Kinswa Campground
Mossyrock Trout Hatchery
Silver Creek
Cowlitz Trout Hatchery
MAYFIELD LAKE
Mayfield
Winston
Ajlune
Cowlitz
Alta Vista
Glenoma
Kosmos
Randle
Silver Creek Campground
Silver Brook
Maple Leaf Campground

RIFFE LAKE

131

NATIONAL FOREST

GIFFORD PINCHOT NATIONAL FOREST

Toner Rock Campground
North Fork Campground

Knab
Wilson

505 504

SKAMANIA CO
LEWIS CO
BLUE LAKE RIDGE
Blue Lake Creek Campground
SPUD HILL

Tower
BEIGLE MOUNTAIN
FRANK SMITH RD
Signal Peak

Green River Salmon Hatchery
Hoffstadt Mountain
Toutle Mountain
Debris Dam View Point
Elk Rock
Forest Learning Center
Mount Saint Helens

BLACK MOUNTAIN
GOAT MOUNTAIN
MOUNT SAINT HELENS NATIONAL VOLCANIC MONUMENT
Coldwater Lake
Spirit Lake
Ryan Lake View Point
Strawberry Mountain
Bear Pass
Bear Meadow View Point
Mount Saint Helens View Point
Independence Pass View Point

Quartz Creek Big Trees Campground
Iron Creek Campground
Iron Creek Information Center
Greenhorn Buttes
Pole Patch Campground
French Butte
Pinto Rock
Jumbo Peak
Dark Mountain
Adams Fork Campground

COWLITZ COUNTY

190

MOUNT SAINT HELENS

SKAMANIA COUNTY

Kirk Rock
Snagtooth Mountain
Clearwater Overlook
Mount Adams View Point
Quartz Creek Ridge
Quartz Creek Butte
Twin Falls Campground
Island Shelter

LOGGING
HEMLOCK PASS
MERIDIAN MOUNTAIN
WOLF POINT
ROSE VALLEY
BAIRD MOUNTAIN
LITTLE COW PEAK
BIG BULL
ONEIL PEAK
SMITH MOUNTAIN
GOBLE MOUNTAIN
NINETEEN MOUNTAIN
WILD HORSE PEAK
ELK MOUNTAIN
WASHBOARD FALLS
BUTLER BUTTE
GEORGES PEAK
ZILLIG
BALDY MOUNTAIN
MONUMENT PEAK
SHELLEY MOUNTAIN
BEAR PASS
PIGEON SPRINGS
WOOLFORD MOUNTAIN
LOWER KALAMA RIVER FALLS
KALAMA FALLS SALMON HATCHERY
DEVILS PEAK
ROSS PEAK
SCHUMAKER MOUNTAIN
CLOVER VALLEY
BUTTE HILL

SPUD MOUNTAIN
CASTLE PEAK
SPOTTED BUCK MOUNTAIN
Cinnamon Peak
MERRILL LAKE
LAKEVIEW PEAK
WILKINSON SADDLE
Cougar
Yale
YALE LAKE
Woodland Park
N DUBOIS
DAVIS PEAK
REID MOUNTAIN
LAKE MERWIN
Ariel
Chelatchie
TUMTUM MOUNTAIN
MCCLELLAN MOUNTAIN

SWIFT CREEK FLOW
PUMICE BUTTE
SWIFT CREEK RESERVOIR
NFD RD 90

GIFFORD PINCHOT NATIONAL FOREST

SMITH CREEK BUTTE

503 503

CLARK COUNTY

Curly Creek
Lewis River Campground
Breezy Point
Spencer Peak
Big Creek Falls View Point
Bolt Shelter
House Rock
Kum Back Shelter
Sawtooth Mountain
Lone Butte
Curly Creek Campground
Outlaw Ridge Volcanic View Point
Termination Point
Rock Point
Gifford Peak
Berry Mountain
Lava Caves
Paradise Creek Campground
North Butte
Indian View Point

Lower Falls Campground
Steamboat Mountain
Tillicum Campground
Steamboat Lake Campground
Saddle Campground
South Campground
Cold Spring Campground
Indian View Point
Cultus Creek Campground
Smoky Creek Campground
East Crater
Ice Caves
Peterson Butte
Little Goose Campground
Peterson Prairie Campground
Ice Cave Campground
Goose Lake Campground
PACIFIC CREST TR

0 2.5 5 7.5 10 miles   1 in. = 7.5 mi.

HWY

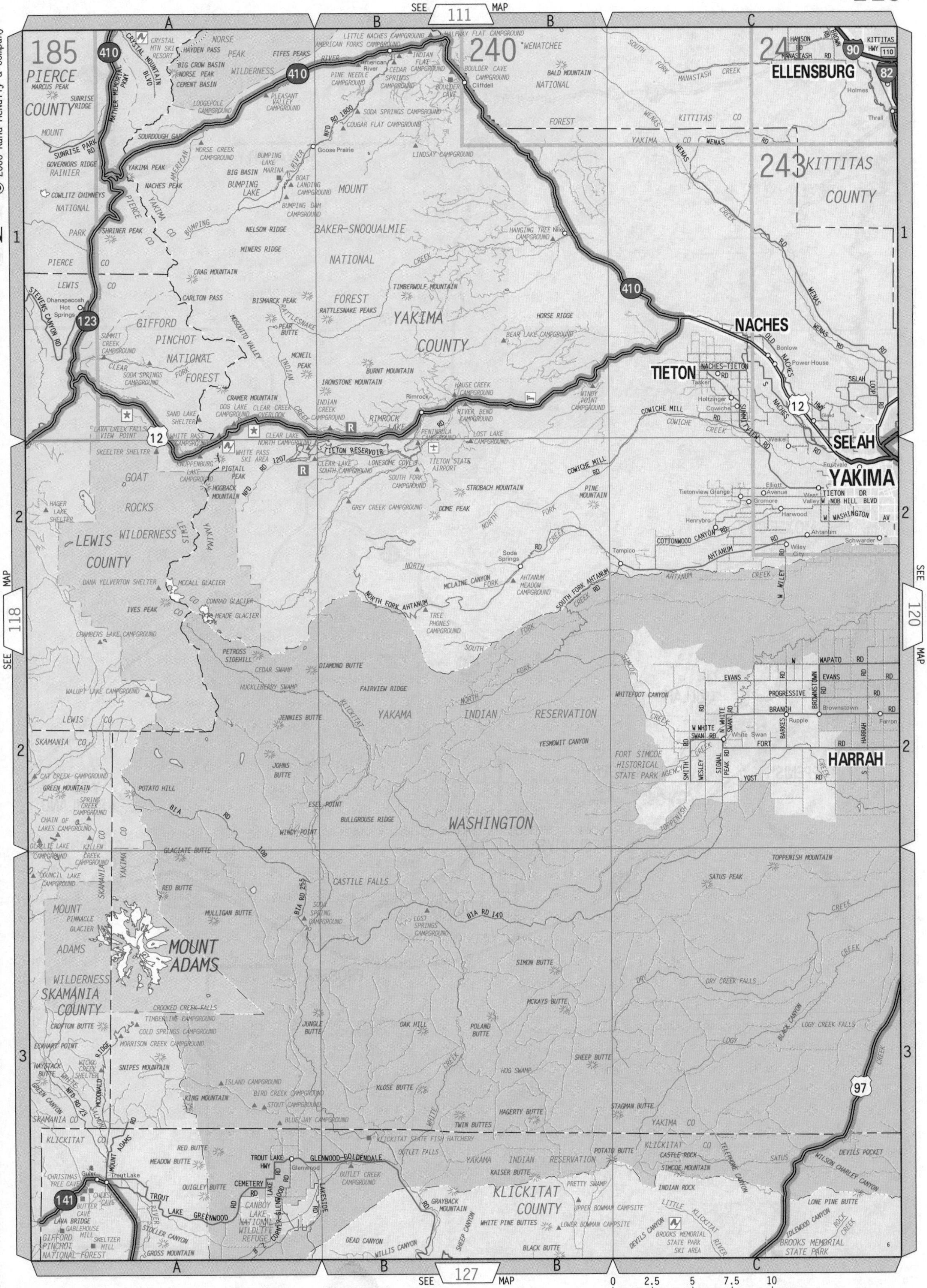

Map

185 PIERCE COUNTY

240

24 ELLENSBURG

243 KITTITAS COUNTY

GIFFORD PINCHOT NATIONAL FOREST

MOUNT BAKER-SNOQUALMIE NATIONAL FOREST

YAKIMA COUNTY

NACHES

TIETON

SELAH

YAKIMA

HARRAH

LEWIS COUNTY

GOAT ROCKS WILDERNESS

SKAMANIA COUNTY

MOUNT ADAMS

ADAMS WILDERNESS

YAKAMA INDIAN RESERVATION

WASHINGTON

FORT SIMCOE HISTORICAL STATE PARK AGENCY

KLICKITAT COUNTY

TROUT LAKE

GLENWOOD-GOLDENDALE HWY

CANBOY LAKE NATIONAL WILDLIFE REFUGE

BROOKS MEMORIAL STATE PARK SKI AREA

SEE 111 MAP

SEE 127 MAP

SEE 118 MAP

SEE 120 MAP — HWY

0 2.5 5 7.5 10 miles   1 in. = 7.5 mi.

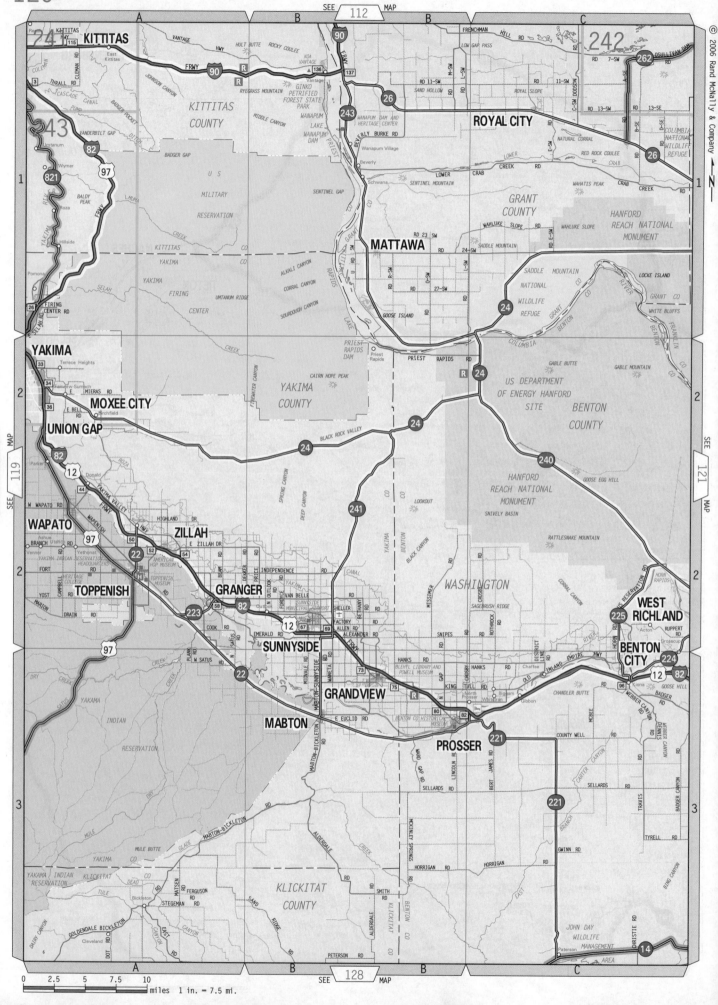

KITTITAS

241

RD 115
East Kittitas
KITTITAS HWY
COLEMAN RD
CLEMAN RD
THRALL RD
BADGER POCKET RD
CASCADE CANAL
PUMP RD
VANDERBILT GAP
243
82
97
821
VANTAGE HWY
HULT BUTTE
ROCKY COULEE
KOA VANTAGE
136
137
Vantage
GINKO PETRIFIED FOREST STATE PARK
RYEGRASS MOUNTAIN
JOHNSON CANYON RD
90
FRWY
R
R

KITTITAS COUNTY

U S MILITARY RESERVATION

FRENCHMAN HILL RD
LOW GAP PASS
RD 7-SW
242
262
OSULLIVAN DAM

90

26
243
WANAPUM DAM AND HERITAGE CENTER
PRIEST RAPIDS LAKE
Wanapum Village
Beverly
Schwana
BEVERLY BURKE RD
SENTINEL GAP
SENTINEL MOUNTAIN

RD 11-SW
SAND HOLLOW
ROYAL SLOPE
RD 13-SW
11-SW
13-SE

ROYAL CITY

26

COLUMBIA NATIONAL WILDLIFE REFUGE

Umtanum
Wymer
Roza
BALDY PEAK
Hillside
Pomona
YAKIMA RIVER
L MONA
SELAH RD
26
FIRING CENTER RD

KITTITAS CO
YAKIMA CO

YAKIMA FIRING CENTER

UMTANUM RIDGE

ALKALI CANYON
CORRAL CANYON
SOURDOUGH CANYON

CREEK RD

PRIEST RAPIDS DAM
CAIRN HOPE PEAK
YAKIMA COUNTY
FORESTER CANYON

LOWER CRAB CREEK RD
LOWER CRAB CREEK RD
WAHATIS PEAK
WAHLUKE SLOPE
WAHLUKE SLOPE
SADDLE MOUNTAIN
RD 23 SW
24-SW
27-SW
GOOSE ISLAND

MATTAWA

GRANT COUNTY

HANFORD REACH NATIONAL MONUMENT

SADDLE MOUNTAIN NATIONAL WILDLIFE REFUGE

GABLE BUTTE
GABLE MOUNTAIN
LOCKE ISLAND
WHITE BLUFFS
COLUMBIA RIVER
GRANT CO
BENTON CO
FRANKLIN CO

YAKIMA
33
34
36
Terrace Heights
FAIRVIEW-SUMACH
E MIERAS RD
E BELL RD
Birchfield
MOXEE CITY
UNION GAP
Parker
82
12
44
Donald
ROZA CANAL
YAKIMA VALLEY HWY
24
BLACK ROCK VALLEY
SPRING CANYON
DEEP CANYON
24
24
PRIEST RAPIDS RD
R
24
US DEPARTMENT OF ENERGY HANFORD SITE
BENTON COUNTY
240
HANFORD REACH NATIONAL MONUMENT
GOOSE EGG HILL
SNIVELY BASIN
LOOKOUT
241
RATTLESNAKE MOUNTAIN

WAPATO
97
Ashue
Utahki
Venner
Yethonat
YAKIMA INDIAN RESERVATION HEADQUARTERS
FORT RD
YOST RD
MARION DRAIN RD
Branch
50
52
54
22
AMERICAN HOP MUSEUM
TOPPENISH
HERITAGE COLLEGE
CAMPBELL RD
ZILLAH
HIGHLAND DR
E ZILLAH DR
BEAM RD
DECKER RD
PRICE RD
INDEPENDENCE RD
GRANGER
223
58
82
Outlook
N SATUS RD
COOK RD
EMERALD RD
SUNNYSIDE
12
67
69
FACTORY RD
ALLEN RD
ALEXANDER RD
SHELLER RD
BETHANY RD
VAN BELLE RD
SUNNYSIDE MUNICIPAL AIRPORT
YAKIMA CANAL
MISSIMER RD
SAGEBRUSH RIDGE
ROTHROCK RD
SNIPES RD
WASHINGTON
CORRAL CANYON
HORN RAPIDS RD
WEST RICHLAND
225
Acton
RUPPERT RD
BENTON CITY
224
12
82
Kiona
GOOSE HILL RD
BADGER CANYON RD
WEBBER CANYON RD
MCBEE RD
DENNIS RD
BADGER CANYON RD

22
MAPENISH RD
97
W SATUS RD
PLANK RD
SATUS CREEK
DRY CREEK RD
SATUS
YAKAMA INDIAN RESERVATION
MABTON
GRANDVIEW
73
75
80
R
82
221
PROSSER
221
MILVALE-SUNNYSIDE RD
MABTON-SUNNYSIDE RD
MANETA RD
E EUCLID RD
HANKS RD
BLEHYL LIBRARY AND POWELL MUSEUM
KING RD
TULL RD
North Prosser
Whitstran
Bigham
Gibbon
Chaffee
DISTRICT LINE RD
OLD INLAND EMPIRE HWY
CROSBY RD
HANKS RD
BENTON CO HISTORICAL MUSEUM
96
CHANDLER BUTTE
MABTON-BICKLETON RD
WARD GAP RD
LINCOLN GAP RD
BERT JAMES RD
COUNTY WELL RD
SELLARDS RD
CARTER CANYON RD
SELLARDS RD
TRAVIS RD
TYRELL RD
BADGER CANYON RD
BIRK CANYON RD

MULE BUTTE
GLADE CREEK
MABTON-BICKLETON RD
ALDERDALE RD
MCKINLEY SPRINGS RD
HORRIGAN RD
HORRIGAN RD
GWINN RD
MILE CREEK RD
WATSON RD
FERGUSON RD
STEGEMAN RD
Bickleton
DRY CANYON
GOLDENDALE BICKLETON RD
Cleveland
6
EAST CANYON RD
DOT RD
SAND RIDGE RD
PETERSON RD
SMITH RD
KLICKITAT COUNTY
YAKAMA INDIAN RESERVATION
KLICKITAT CO
DEAD CANYON RD
TULE CREEK
EAST CANYON RD
JOHN DAY WILDLIFE MANAGEMENT AREA
Paterson
CHRISTIE RD
14
BENTON CO
KLICKITAT CO

SEE MAP 119 HWY
SEE MAP 121

0 2.5 5 7.5 10
miles 1 in. = 7.5 mi.

© 2006 Rand McNally & Company
N

SEE 113 MAP

A   B   B   C

24

262 OSULLIVAN DAM RD

170

WARDEN

WARDEN MUNICIPAL AIRPORT

JACKASS MOUNTAIN

17

OTHELLO

26

24

COLUMBIA NATIONAL WILDLIFE REFUGE

SADDLE MOUNTAINS

LIND

21

21

LIND AIRPORT

RALSTON-BENGE RD

261

ADAMS COUNTY

PROVIDENCE

WASHTUCNA

26

26

HATTON

CONNELL

MESA

260

17

CONNELL CITY AIRPORT

KAHLOTUS

263

260

261

395

FRANKLIN COUNTY

WALLA WALLA COUNTY

WASHINGTON

JUNIPER DUNES WILDERNESS

RICHLAND

340

240

224

2

PRESCOTT

124

124

PASCO

343

182

12

14

WEST RICHLAND

240

82

KENNEWICK

395

397

113

114

BENTON COUNTY

125

82

395

344

34E

WALLA WALLA

12

COLLEGE PLACE

125

UMATILLA COUNTY

OREGON

MILTON-FREEWATER

11

14

131

730

SEE 129 MAP

SEE 120 MAP

SEE 122 MAP

HWY

0 2.5 5 7.5 10

miles 1 in. = 7.5 mi.

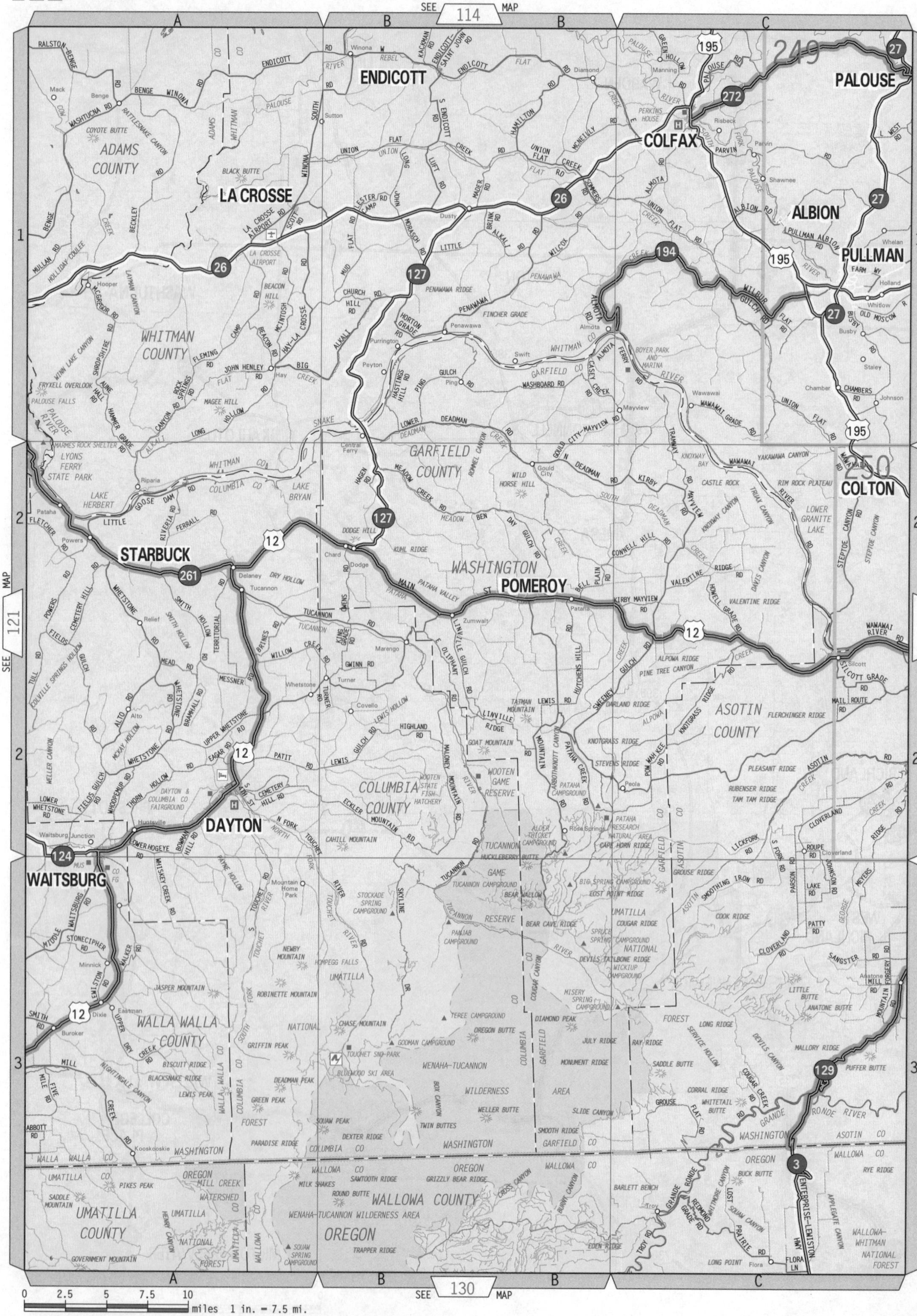

© 2006 Rand McNally & Company

ADAMS COUNTY

ENDICOT

LA CROSSE

WHITMAN COUNTY

COLFAX

PALOUSE

ALBION

PULLMAN

COLTON

GARFIELD COUNTY

STARBUCK

POMEROY

WASHINGTON

ASOTIN COUNTY

DAYTON

COLUMBIA COUNTY

WAITSBURG

WALLA WALLA COUNTY

WENAHA-TUCANNON WILDERNESS AREA

UMATILLA NATIONAL FOREST

UMATILLA COUNTY

OREGON

WALLOWA COUNTY

WALLOWA-WHITMAN NATIONAL FOREST

0 2.5 5 7.5 10 miles 1 in. = 7.5 mi.

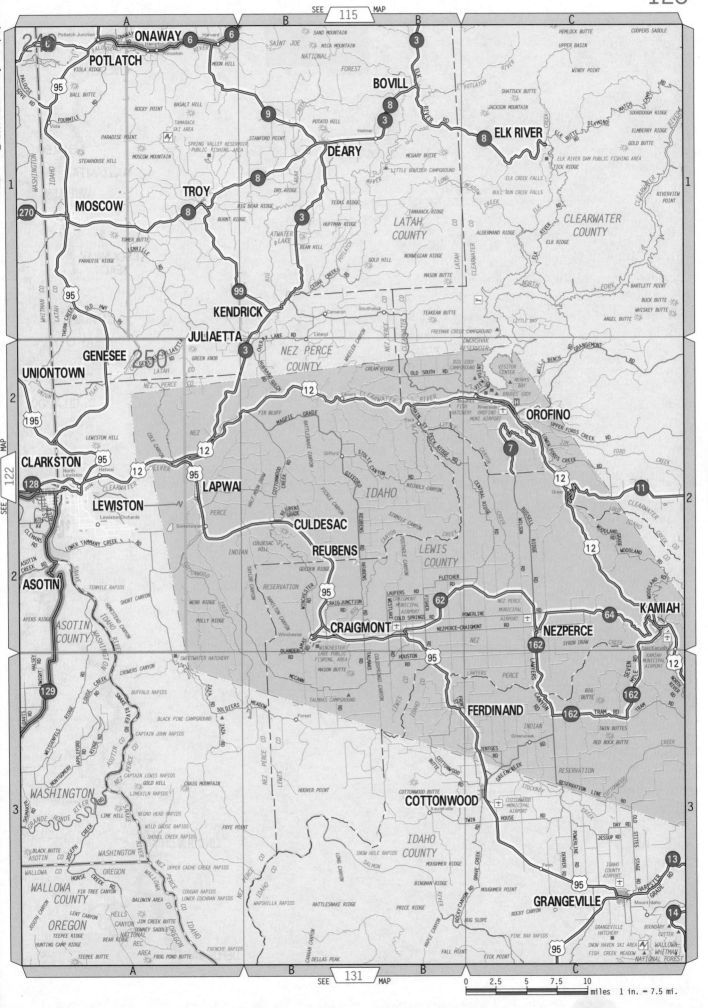

HWY

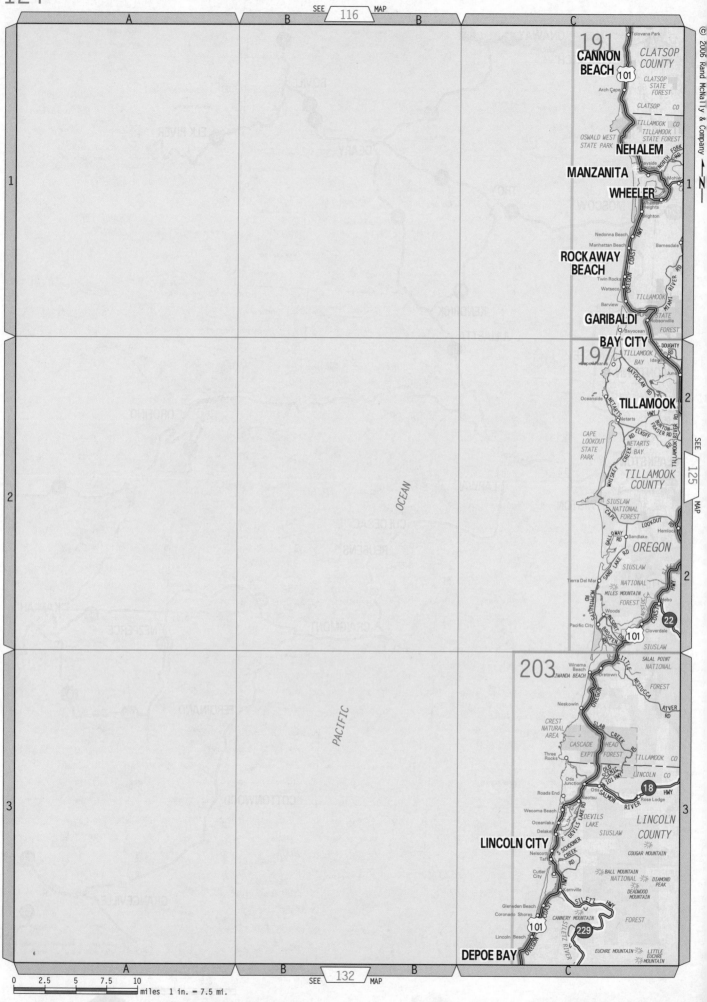

SEE 116 MAP

191

CANNON BEACH
(101)

Tolovana Park

CLATSOP COUNTY

Arch Cape

CLATSOP STATE FOREST

CLATSOP CO

TILLAMOOK CO

OSWALD WEST STATE PARK

TILLAMOOK STATE FOREST

NEHALEM
Bayside Gardens
Mohler
NORTH FORK RD

MANZANITA

WHEELER
Wheeler Heights
Brighton

1

N

Nedonna Beach
Barnesdale
Manhattan Beach

ROCKAWAY BEACH
Twin Rocks
Watseco

MIAMI RIVER RD

TILLAMOOK STATE FOREST

Barview

GARIBALDI
Robsonville
Bayocean

BAY CITY
DOUGHTY RD

197
TILLAMOOK BAY
Idaville
Cape Meares
BAYOCEAN RD
Jun

Oceanside
NETARTS

TILLAMOOK

Netarts
ELKOFF RD
BURTON FRASER RD

CAPE LOOKOUT STATE PARK

WHISKEY CREEK RD

NETARTS BAY

TILLAMOOK COUNTY

SIUSLAW NATIONAL FOREST

CAPE LOOKOUT RD
Sandlake
Hemlock

GALLOWAY RD

OREGON

SAND LAKE RD

OCEAN

SIUSLAW NATIONAL FOREST

Tierra Del Mar
MILES MOUNTAIN

NESTUCCA

Hebo

NORTH RD
Woods

2

(22)

Pacific City
RESORT DR
BROOTEN RD
(101)
Cloverdale

SIUSLAW

SEE 125 MAP

PACIFIC

203
Winema Beach
KIWANDA BEACH
Oretown

SALAL POINT NATIONAL FOREST

LITTLE NESTUCCA

OREGON COAST HWY

Neskowin

RIVER RD

CREST NATURAL AREA

SLAB CREEK RD

CASCADE HEAD EXPT FOREST

Three Rocks

OLD SCENIC 101 HWY

TILLAMOOK CO
LINCOLN CO

Otis Junction
SALMON RIVER
(18) HWY
Rose Lodge

Roads End
Otis

3

Neotsu

Wecoma Beach
DEVILS LAKE

LINCOLN COUNTY

Oceanlake
E DEVILS LAKE RD
Delake
SIUSLAW
Cougar Mountain

LINCOLN CITY
Nelscott
S SCHOONER CREEK RD
Taft

BALL MOUNTAIN NATIONAL
DIAMOND PEAK

Cutler City
DEADWOOD MOUNTAIN

Kernville

SILETZ HWY

FOREST

Gleneden Beach
CANNERY MOUNTAIN
Coronado Shores
(101)
(229)

Lincoln Beach
OREGON
SILETZ RIVER

EUCHRE MOUNTAIN
LITTLE EUCHRE MOUNTAIN

DEPOE BAY

SEE 132 MAP

0 2.5 5 7.5 10 miles   1 in. = 7.5 mi.

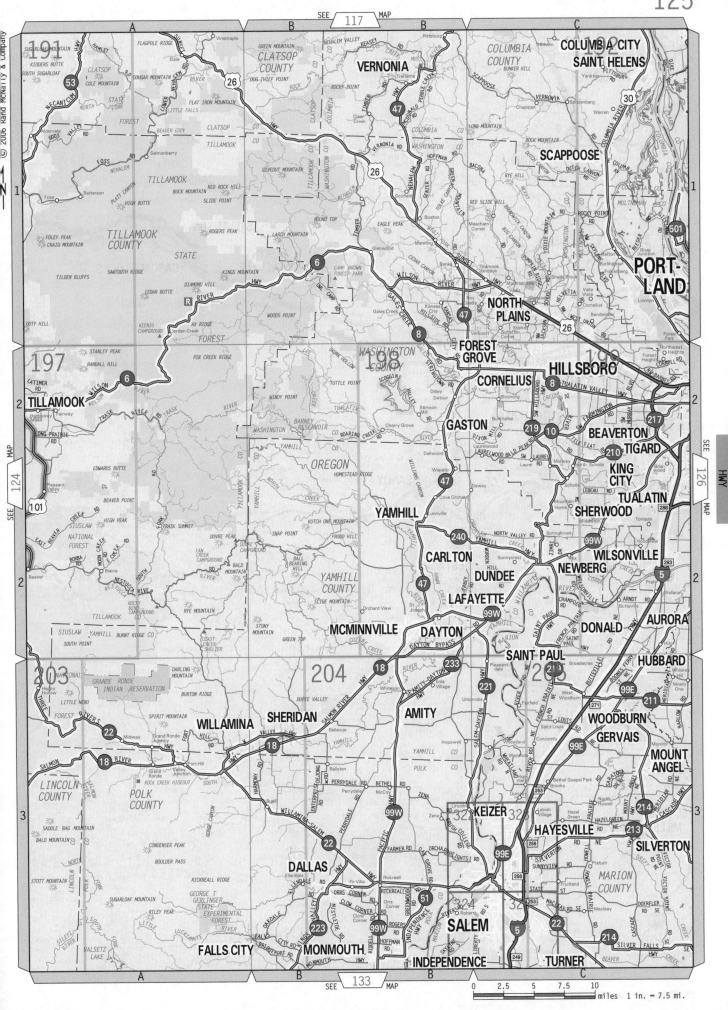

126

SEE 118 MAP

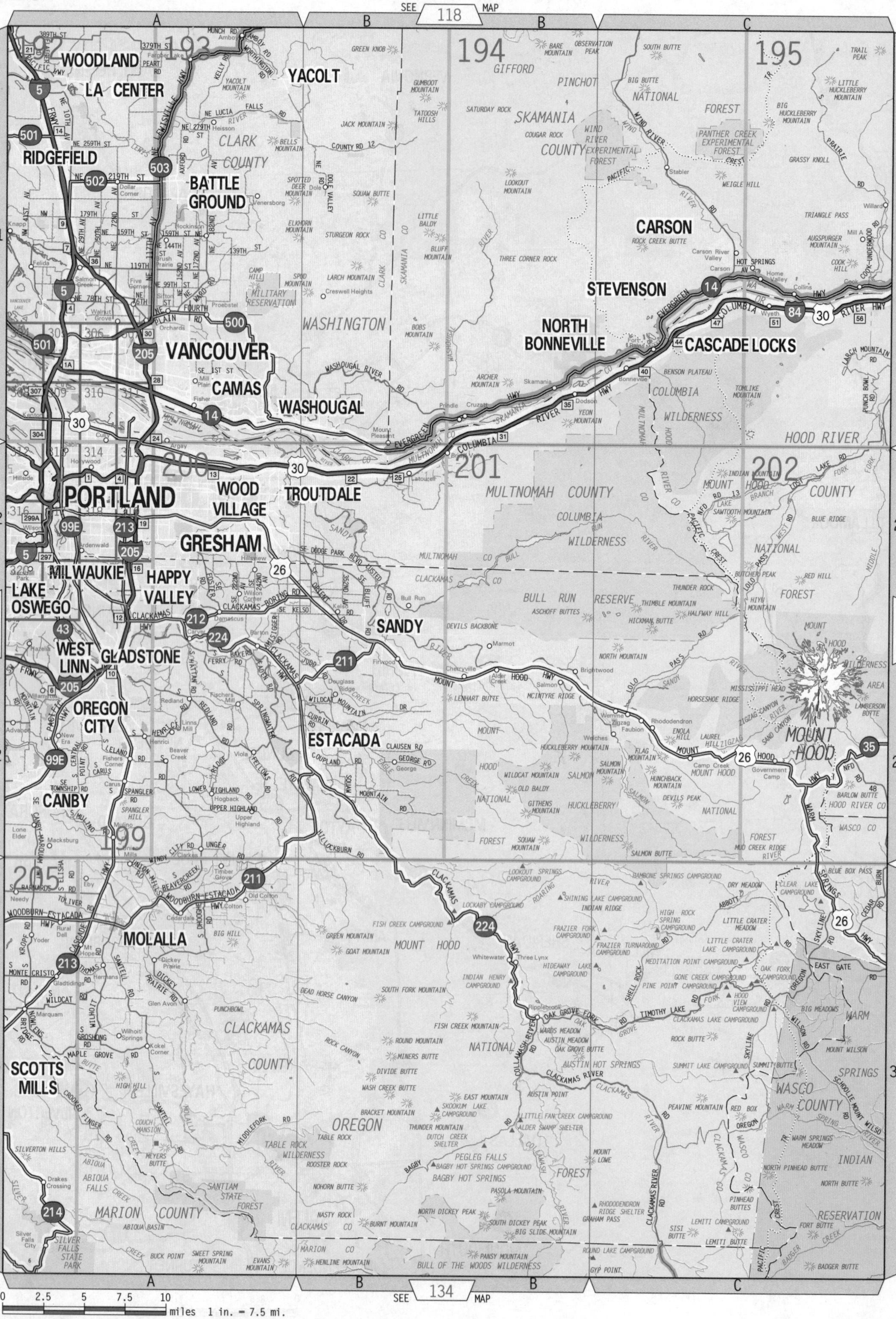

A   B   B   C

192 193   194   195

WOODLAND
LA CENTER
YACOLT

GIFFORD PINCHOT NATIONAL FOREST

RIDGEFIELD

CLARK COUNTY

BATTLE GROUND

SKAMANIA COUNTY

CARSON

STEVENSON

NORTH BONNEVILLE   CASCADE LOCKS

WASHINGTON

VANCOUVER
CAMAS
WASHOUGAL

COLUMBIA WILDERNESS

HOOD RIVER

200   201   202

PORTLAND
WOOD VILLAGE   TROUTDALE

MULTNOMAH COUNTY

MOUNT HOOD

GRESHAM

MILWAUKIE
LAKE OSWEGO   HAPPY VALLEY

SANDY

CLACKAMAS COUNTY

BULL RUN RESERVE

MOUNT HOOD NATIONAL FOREST

WEST LINN   GLADSTONE

OREGON CITY

ESTACADA

MOUNT HOOD

MOUNT HOOD WILDERNESS AREA

CANBY

199

MOUNT HOOD NATIONAL FOREST

WASCO CO

205

MOLALLA

CLACKAMAS COUNTY

MOUNT HOOD NATIONAL FOREST

WARM SPRINGS

SCOTTS MILLS

OREGON

WASCO COUNTY

MARION COUNTY

WARM SPRINGS INDIAN RESERVATION

SILVER FALLS STATE PARK

A   B   B   C

SEE 134 MAP

0 2.5 5 7.5 10 miles   1 in. = 7.5 mi.

© 2006 Rand McNally & Company

SEE 125 MAP HWY

SEE 127 MAP

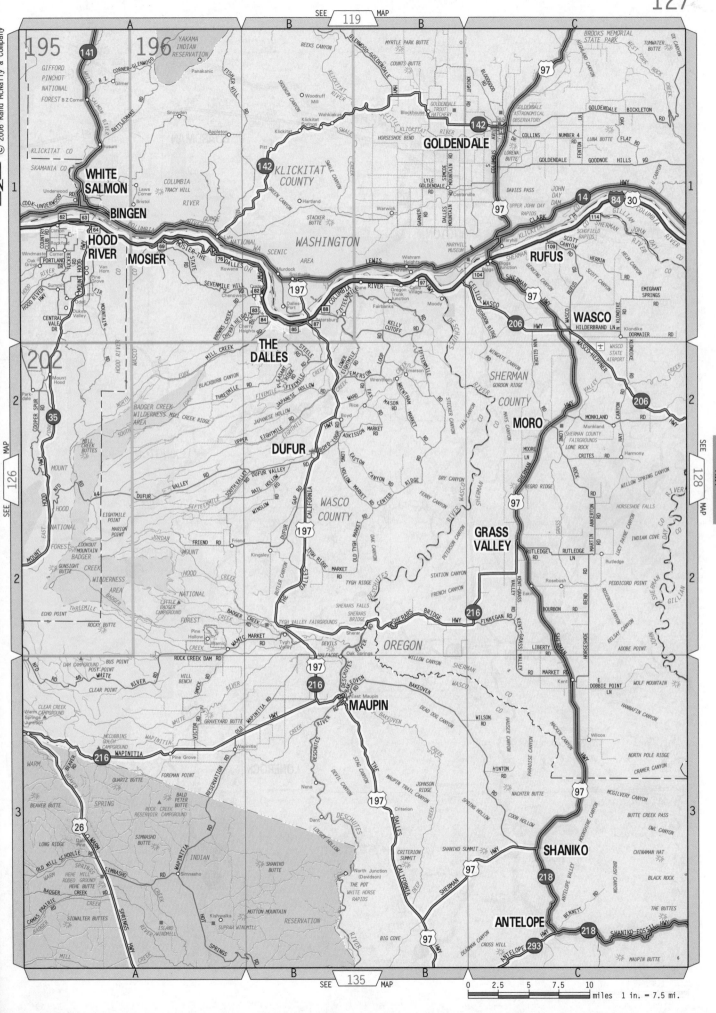

© 2006 Rand McNally & Company

N

WASHINGTON

KLICKITAT COUNTY

COLUMBIA RIVER

BENTON COUNTY

UMATILLA NATIONAL WILDLIFE REFUGE

IRRIGON

BOARDMAN

MORROW COUNTY

OREGON

BOARDMAN BOMBING RANGE

UMATILLA CHEMICAL DEPOT

ARLINGTON

GILLIAM COUNTY

ARLINGTON MUNICIPAL AIRPORT

WEATHERFORD HISTORICAL MONUMENT

OLD OREGON TRAIL MONUMENT

IONE

LEXINGTON

HEPPNER

CONDON

GILLIAM COUNTY FAIRGROUNDS

CONDON STATE AIRPORT

MORROW COUNTY FAIRGROUNDS

LONEROCK

WHEELER COUNTY

WHEELER COUNTY FAIRGROUNDS

FOSSIL

JOHN DAY FOSSIL BEDS NATIONAL MONUMENT

UMATILLA NATIONAL FOREST

GRANT CO

MORROW CO

SPRAY

SHANIKO-FOSSIL

0 2.5 5 7.5 10 miles   1 in. = 7.5 mi.

HWY

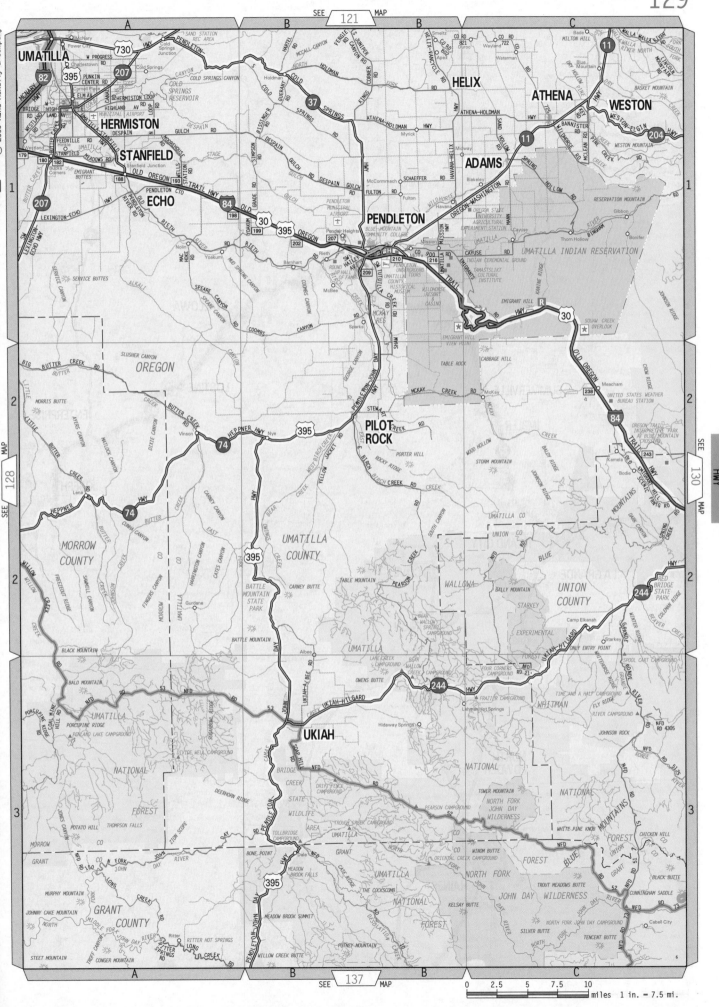

0   2.5   5   7.5   10
miles   1 in. = 7.5 mi.

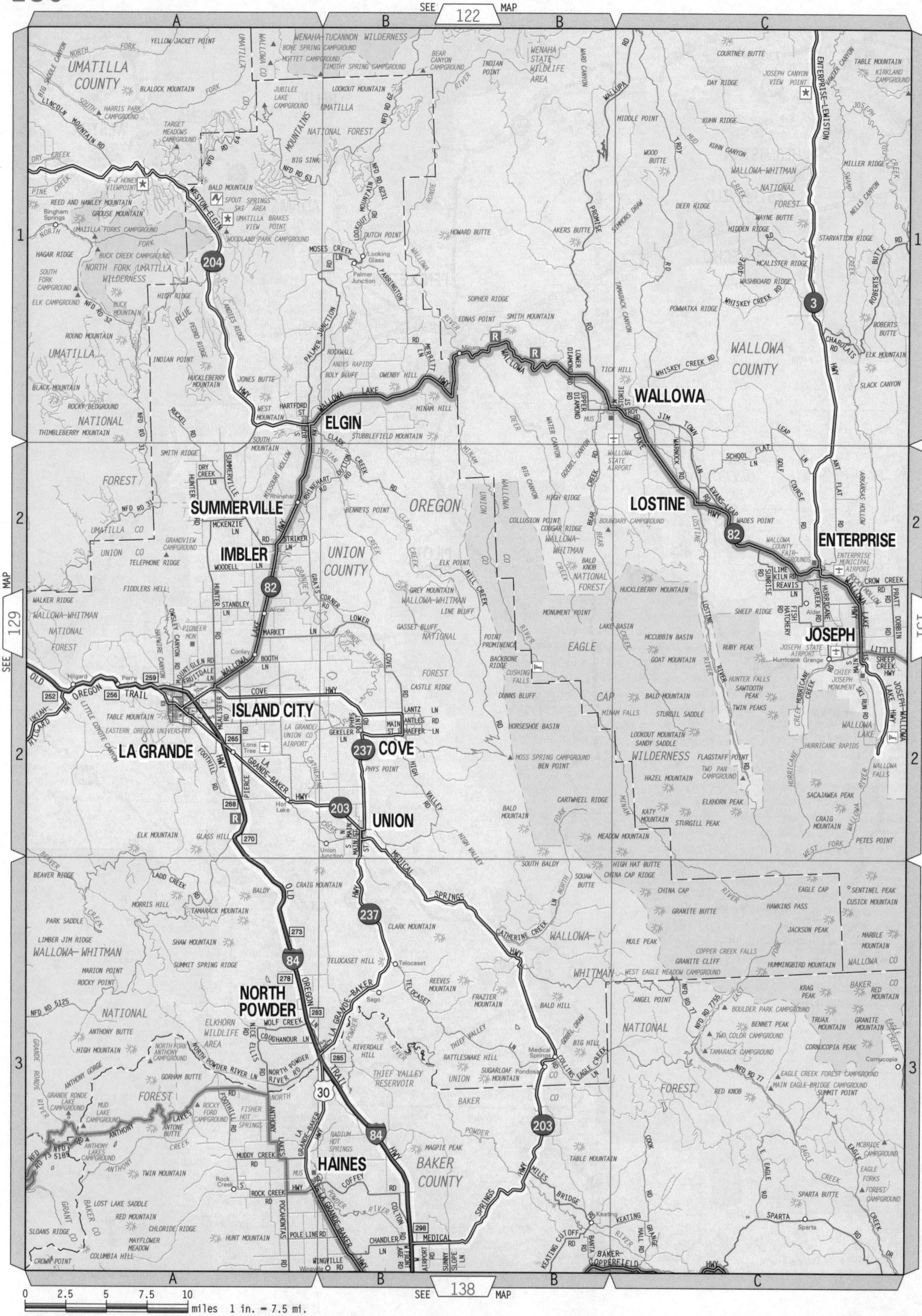

SEE 122 MAP

© 2006 Rand McNally & Company

N

UMATILLA COUNTY

WENAHA-TUCANNON WILDERNESS

WENAHA STATE WILDLIFE AREA

UMATILLA NATIONAL FOREST

NORTH FORK UMATILLA WILDERNESS

BLUE

UMATILLA

NATIONAL

WALLOWA-WHITMAN NATIONAL FOREST

WALLOWA

WALLOWA COUNTY

ELGIN

SUMMERVILLE

IMBLER

LOSTINE

ENTERPRISE

OREGON

UNION COUNTY

WALLOWA-WHITMAN NATIONAL FOREST

JOSEPH

ISLAND CITY

COVE

LA GRANDE

EAGLE

CAP

WILDERNESS

UNION

WALLOWA-WHITMAN NATIONAL FOREST

WALLOWA LAKE

NORTH POWDER

ELKHORN WILDLIFE AREA

UNION CO

BAKER CO

BAKER COUNTY

HAINES

NATIONAL FOREST

Keating

Sparta

SEE 129 MAP   HWY

SEE 131 MAP

SEE 138 MAP

0 2.5 5 7.5 10 miles   1 in. = 7.5 mi.

Highways: 204, 3, 82, 237, 203, 84, 30, 298

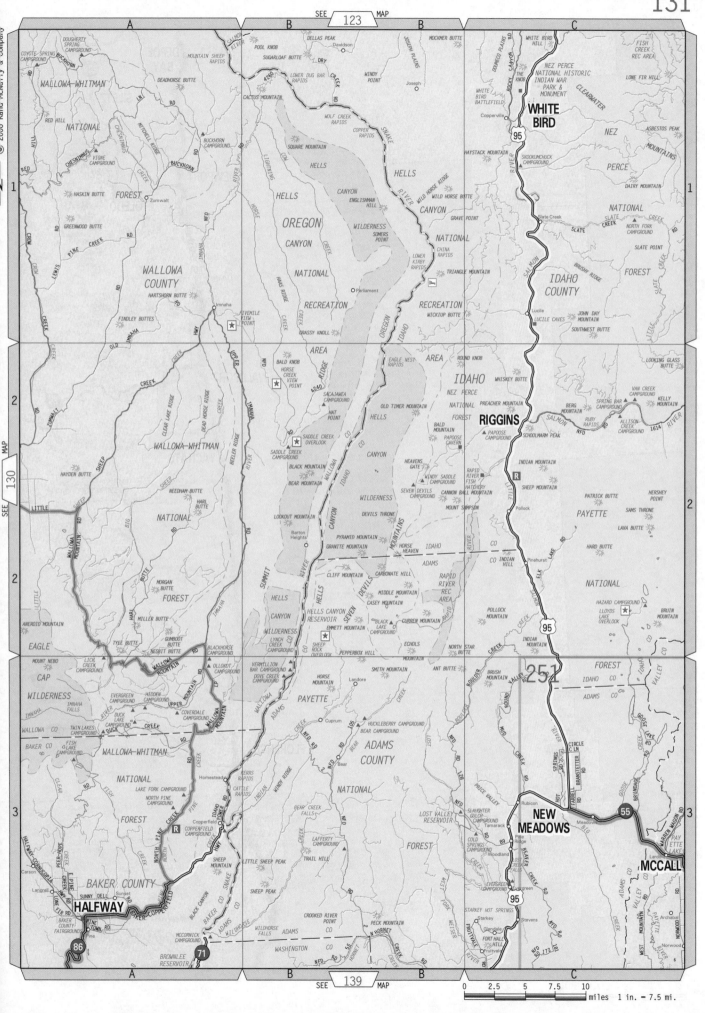

0   2.5   5   7.5   10
miles   1 in. = 7.5 mi.

A   B   SEE 124 MAP   B   C

HMY

206

DEPOE BAY

SILETZ

229

Upper Farm

Otter Rock

LOGSDEN RD

Beverly Beach

MOOLACK BEACH

Camp Twelve

IRON MOUNTAIN

Agate Beach

PIONEER MOUNTAIN

SAMS CREEK RD

20

SILETZ RD

OLALLA

ELK CITY

ELK CITY RD

HARLAN

UPDIKE

NEWPORT

Newport Heights

TOLEDO

Southbeach

Yaquina

Winant

YAQUINA BAY RD

Elk City

ELK

HARLAN

STRAWBERRY MOUNTAIN

Oysterville

Holiday Beach

YAQUINA

PALMER MOUNTAIN

Forfar

1 0 1

ONA BEACH

Ona

S BEAVER CREEK RD

LINCOLN COUNTY

DRIFT CREEK WILDERNESS

Seal Rock

OREGON

SIUSLAW

TABLE MOUNTAIN

208

DRIFT

NATIONAL

209

WALDPORT

Bayview

CRESTLINE DR

ALSEA

Tidewater

ALSEA HWY

SCOTT MOUNTAIN

Eckman Lake

Little Albany

Drift Creek

34

Wakonda Beach

San Marine

PACIFIC

FOREST

YACHATS

CANNIBAL MOUNTAIN

FIVE RIVERS RD

Fisher

SEE 133 MAP

GREEN MOUNTAIN

YACHATS MOUNTAIN

YACHATS

COAST

LINCOLN CO.

LANE CO.

RIVER

CUMMINS CREEK

CUMMINS PEAK

WILDERNESS

Searose Beach

TENMILE

CREEK

RD

INDIAN

FAIRVIEW MOUNTAIN

OCEAN

ROCKY KNOLL

ROCK CREEK WILDERNESS

OREGON

CREEK

BIG

CREEK

OREGON

HECETA HEAD LIGHTHOUSE

CONICAL ROCK

CAPE COVE

SEA LION POINT

THREE BUTTES

SIUSLAW

COX ROCK

214

Deadwood

Minerva

Rainrock

SIUSLAW

36

Heceta Beach

Tide

Siuslaw

Heceta Junction

FORK

NORTH

Brickerville

BALD MOUNTAIN

Swisshome

RIVER

1 0 1

NATIONAL

126

Tiernan

Mapleton

HWY

126

ARCHIE KNOWLES CAMPGROUND

FLORENCE

Wendson

FLORENCE-EUGENE

Point Terrace

LANE COUNTY

SWEET CREEK RD

Cushman

CREEK

FOREST

Glenada

UPPER

CREEK

SUNSET MOUNTAIN

GOODWIN PEAK

RIVER

BALDY MOUNTAIN

OREGON DUNES NATIONAL REC AREA

Canary

DUNES CITY

North Beach

Westlake

Siltcoos

Ada

LANE CO.

DOUGLAS CO.

FORK

NORTH

DOUGLAS COUNTY

1 0 1

OREGON COAST HWY

TAHKENITCH LAKE

FIVEMILE

HENDERSON PEAK

NORTH

North Fork

SMITH

RIVER

Sulphur Springs

SMITH RIVER

WASSON RIDGE

A   B   SEE 140 MAP   B   C

1   2   3

WHITE BIRD

FIGGINS

NEW MEADOWS

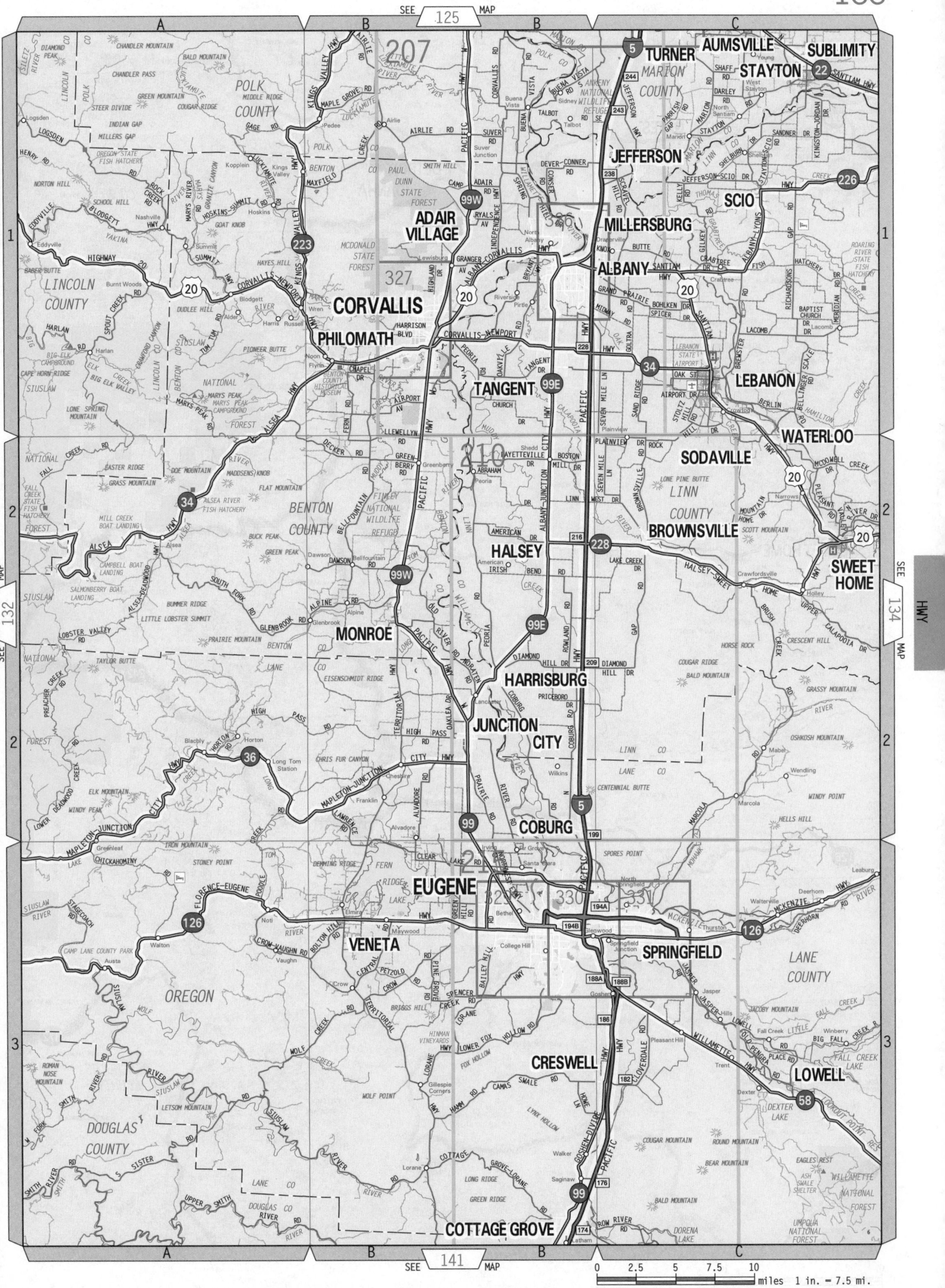

SEE 125 MAP

207

SEE 132 MAP

SEE 134 MAP

HWY

POLK COUNTY

LINCOLN COUNTY

CHANDLER MOUNTAIN
CHANDLER PASS
BALD MOUNTAIN
DIAMOND PEAK
GREEN MOUNTAIN
COUGAR RIDGE
MIDDLE RIDGE
STEER DIVIDE
INDIAN GAP
MILLERS GAP
Logsden
NORTON HILL
SCHOOL HILL
BLODGETT
Nashville
Summit
HAYES HILL
GOAT KNOB
Burnt Woods
Blodgett
Wren
Alder
Harris
Russell
Kopplein
Kings Valley
Pedee
Airlie
Airlie
TURNER
AUMSVILLE
STAYTON
SUBLIMITY
22
MARION COUNTY
JEFFERSON
SCIO
226
Talbot
Buena Vista
ADAIR VILLAGE
327
MILLERSBURG
ALBANY
20
LEBANON
WATERLOO
SODAVILLE
LINN COUNTY
BROWNSVILLE
SWEET HOME
20
CORVALLIS
PHILOMATH
TANGENT
99E
34
HALSEY
228
MONROE
HARRISBURG
JUNCTION CITY
COBURG
5
99
EUGENE
VENETA
SPRINGFIELD
126
CRESWELL
LOWELL
58
COTTAGE GROVE
99
LANE COUNTY
BENTON COUNTY
DOUGLAS COUNTY
OREGON
SIUSLAW NATIONAL FOREST
36
126
223
34

miles 1 in. = 7.5 mi.
0 2.5 5 7.5 10

SEE 141 MAP

HWY SEE 133 MAP

© 2006 Rand McNally & Company

N

A | B | B | C

LYONS
MILL CITY GATES
DETROIT
IDANHA
SWEET HOME

SILVER FALLS STATE PARK
SHELLBURG FALLS
LOWER SHELLBURG FALLS
STOUT CREEK FALLS
LOOKOUT MOUNTAIN
HOUSE MOUNTAIN
Elkhorn
NFD RD 2207
SHADY COVE CAMPGROUND
SALMON FALLS CAMPGROUND
BULL OF THE WOODS WILDERNESS
BATTLE CREEK SHELTER
BATTLE AX
HAWK MOUNTAIN
CORNPATCH MEADOW
CEDAR BUTTE
CINDER CONE
WASCO CO
JEFFERSON CO

SILVER FALLS
BASL HILL
FERN RIDGE RD
LOWER STASEL FALLS
STASEL FALLS
Mehama
LITTLE NORTH SANTIAM
RIVER
MOUNT HOREB SE
BUCK MOUNTAIN
ROCKY TOP
WILLAMETTE
BOULDER PEAK
BYARS PEAK
ELK LAKE CAMPGROUND
GOLD BUTTE
SHORT MOUNTAIN
SCORPION MOUNTAIN
MOUNT HOOD NATIONAL FOREST
TWIN PEAKS
OLALLIE BUTTE
OLALLIE LAKE CAMPGROUND
OLALLIE LAKE
SCENIC AREA
BIA RD 33
TROUT
BOULDER
NORTH CONE

226
22
ALBANY
LYONS
5TH
FOX Valley
LYONS-MILL CITY DR
KINGWOOD AV
HWY Niagara
R
SANTIAM
DETROIT LAKE STATE PARK
HOOVER RIDGE
BOULDER RIDGE
BREITENBUSH
BREITENBUSH RIVER
HUMBUG CAMPGROUND
Breitenbush Hot Springs
NORTH
MARION COUNTY
MOUNT JEFFERSON WILDERNESS AREA
PARK BUTTE
SHITIKE BUTTE
WARM SPRINGS
ROCK CONE
JEFFERSON INDIAN COUNTY RESERVATION
Lionshead
CAMP CREEK BUTTE
WHITEWATER GLACIER

CAMP
JORDAN
BLUE RIVER
CREEK RD
MCCULLY MOUNTAIN
5TH
LYONS THOMAS
MORRISON DR
JORDAN VALLEY
CREEK DR
THOMAS
Fawn
SANTIAM STATE FOREST
Davis Airport
MONUMENT PEAK
DETROIT LAKE
STAHLMAN POINT
New Idanha
COOPERS RIDGE
WHISPERING FALLS CAMPGROUND
LITTLE PIGEON PRAIRIE
BIG SPRINGS CAMPGROUND
MARION CO.
LINN CO.
NORTH SANTIAM
WHITEWATER CAMPGROUND
MOUNT JEFFERSON
PARK BUTTE
WHITEWATER GLACIER
WALDO GLACIER
BALD PETER

THOMAS CAIRN
SNOW PEAK
HARRY MOUNTAIN
SLATE ROCK
LUCKY BUTTE
WILLAMETTE
LINN COUNTY
GREEN MOUNTAIN
WHITE BULL MOUNTAIN
PINNACLE PEAK
BUCK MOUNTAIN
MARION FORKS
MARION FORKS CAMPGROUND
MOUNT JEFFERSON
BINGHAM RIDGE
MAZAMA CREEK CAMPGROUND
FORKED BUTTE
BEAR BUTTE
CANDLE CREEK CAMPGROUND
LOWER BRIDGE CAMPGROUND
ABBOT CREEK CAMPGROUND
NFD 12 PIONEER FORD CAMPGROUND
ALLAN SPRINGS CAMPGROUND
WIZARD FALLS
WIZARD FALLS

CRABTREE
CRABTREE MOUNTAIN
YELLOWSTONE MOUNTAIN
GREEN MOUNTAIN
KEEL MOUNTAIN
QUARTZVILLE DR
CASCADE FALLS
ROCKY TOP
MIDDLE
MCQUADE CREEK SHELTER
SANTIAM
MIDDLE SANTIAM WILDERNESS AREA
MCNABB FALLS
NATIONAL
SCAR MOUNTAIN
OREGON
THREE PYRAMIDS
PINE RIDGE
MARION FALLS
MARION MOUNTAIN
SADDLE MOUNTAIN
RED BUTTE
RIVERSIDE CAMPGROUND
RANGE
MILK CREEK GLACIER

ROUND MOUNTAIN
HAMILTON CREEK
BALD PETER
ROCKY TOP

MCDOWELL CREEK
GREEN PETER
HOGBACK RIDGE
QUARTZVILLE DR
SUNNYSIDE RD
GREEN PETER LAKE
HIGH DECK
COUGAR ROCK
MOOSE MOUNTAIN
MENAGERIE WILDERNESS AREA
HARTER MOUNTAIN
CRESCENT MOUNTAIN
SOUTH PYRAMID
CONE PEAK
SAWYER CAVE
Santiam Junction
LOST LAKE CAMPGROUND
MAXWELL BUTTE
DUFFY BUTTE
BIG MEADOWS CAMPGROUND
211
DESCHUTES
Camp Sherman
METOLIUS RIVER

SWEET HOME
NORTH RIVER
BOAT LAUNCH
Foster
FOSTER LAKE
MEARES BEND CAMPGROUND
Cascadia
CASCADIA CAVE
CASCADIA STATE PARK
SANTIAM
HWY
Upper Soda
SANTIAM
20 HWY
TOMBSTONE PRAIRIE CAMPGROUND
Santiam Junction
SANTIAM JUNCTION STATE AIRPORT
HOODOO SKI BOWL SNO-PARK
BIG LAKE CAMPGROUND
BIG LAKE
SAND MOUNTAIN
CLAYPOOL BUTTE
20
JEFFERSON CO.
DESCHUTES CO.
SUTTLE-SHERMAN
CAMP SHERMAN CO
SUTTLE LAKE
BLACK BUTTE
BLACK CROSSING
126
Black Butte Ranch
SANTIAM

WILES CREEK DR
WHISKEY BUTTE
MOSS BUTTE
DOE MOUNTAIN
CHIMNEY ROCK
WILLAMETTE NATIONAL FOREST
GREEN BUTTE MOUNTAIN
SWAMP MOUNTAIN
NFD RD 2022
NFD RD 2036
SOAPGRASS MOUNTAIN
TWIN BUTTES
WILDCAT MOUNTAIN RESEARCH NATURAL AREA
WILDCAT MOUNTAIN
SMITH RESERVOIR
TAMOLITCH FALLS
126
SCOTT MOUNTAIN
HAND LAKE SHELTER
MOUNT WASHINGTON WILDERNESS AREA
LITTLE CACHE MOUNTAIN
CACHE CREEK
GRAHAM BUTTE
242
DESCHUTES NATIONAL

FARMERS BUTTE
GREEN MOUNTAIN RIDGE
UPPER CALAPOOIA
CALAPOOIA DR
LINN CO
LANE CO
GOLD HILL RD
MONA CAMPGROUND
TIDBITS MOUNTAIN
GATE CREEK
RABBIT CAMP
WOLF ROCK
RIVER
ANDREWS EXPERIMENTAL FOREST
LOOKOUT MOUNTAIN
H J MONUMENT
BELKNAP SPRINGS
SCOTT LAKE CAMPGROUND
TWO BUTTE
SCOTT PASS
SCOTT LAKE
CREST
TROUT CREEK BUTTE
FOREST
SQUAW CREEK LAKE RD

MOHAWK RIVER
NORTH FORK
BLUE RIVER LAKE
McKenzie Bridge
Rainbow
RAINBOW FALLS
Blue River
DELTA CAMPGROUND
MCKENZIE BRIDGE CAMPGROUND
Belknap Springs
McKENZIE
MCKENZIE BRIDGE STATE AIRPORT
Foley Springs
HORSE
SIMS BUTTE
242 HWY
PROXY POINT
216
BROKEN TOP

MCKENZIE TROUT HATCHERY
Vida
ELK MOUNTAIN
126
GREENWOOD LANDING
MCKENZIE SALMON HATCHERY
Finn Rock
MCKENZIE HWY
R
Nimrod
SILVER CREEK LANDING
ECHO CAMPGROUND
COUGAR RESERVOIR
(AUFDERHEIDE)
MACDUFF MOUNTAIN
HARVEY MOUNTAIN
SLIDE CREEK CAMPGROUND
YANKEE MOUNTAIN
LANE COUNTY
OLALLIE MOUNTAIN
THREE SISTERS WILDERNESS AREA
SPHINX BUTTE
BURNT TOP
HORSE MOUNTAIN
CASCADE LAKES HWY
SPARKS LAKE
TUMALO MOUNTAIN
HOSMER LAKE
ELK LAKE
Elk Lake
372
TOT MOUNTAIN
CENTURY DRIVE

PERNOT MOUNTAIN
HERE MOUNTAIN
SCENIC BYWY
SOUTH FORK
PYRAMID MOUNTAIN
TWIN SPRINGS CAMPGROUND
ROARING RIVER CAMPGROUND
PACKSADDLE MOUNTAIN
CLIFF LAKE SHELTER
LITTLE ROUNDTOP MOUNTAIN
LAVA LAKE
DESCHUTES COUNTY
DESCHUTES NATIONAL
SHERIDAN MOUNTAIN
SIAH BUTTE

DEER MOUNTAIN
BIG FALL CREEK
LITTLE FORK
DEER CREEK SHELTER
DELP CREEK SHELTER
LOWELL MOUNTAIN
SINKER MOUNTAIN
GRASSHOPPER MOUNTAIN
KIAHANIE CAMPGROUND
MOOLACK MOUNTAIN
LUCKY BUTTE
CULTUS LAKE
WEST CULTUS LAKE CAMPGROUND
EDISON ICE CAVE RD
WAKE BUTTE

58
Hampton
UPPER END CAMPGROUND
BIG POOL CAMPGROUND
DOLLY VARDEN CAMPGROUND
CHILCHESTER FALLS
BEDROCK CAMPGROUND
BEAR MOUNTAIN
WINBERRY CAMPGROUND
LITTLE BLANKET SHELTER
WINBERRY MOUNTAIN
NATIONAL
SOUTH FORK SHELTER
WILLAMETTE
SCENIC BYWY
HUCKLEBERRY MOUNTAIN
BLAIR LAKE CAMPGROUND
WALDO LAKE
IRISH MOUNTAIN
IRISH AND TAYLOR CAMPGROUND
LITTLE CULTUS LAKE
PILLAR PEAK
CULTUS LAVA LAKE
CRANE PRAIRIE RES
PRINGLE FALLS EXPERIMENTAL FOREST ADDITION
FOREST

LOOKOUT POINT RESERVOIR
WILLAMETTE BOUNDARY
HAMPTON CAMPGROUND
ROCK KNOB
NORTH FORK
CANYON RD
STAG SHELTER
SALMON
CREEK
FORK
LOOKOUT MOUNTAIN
SIAH BUTTE

0 2.5 5 7.5 10 miles   1 in. = 7.5 mi.

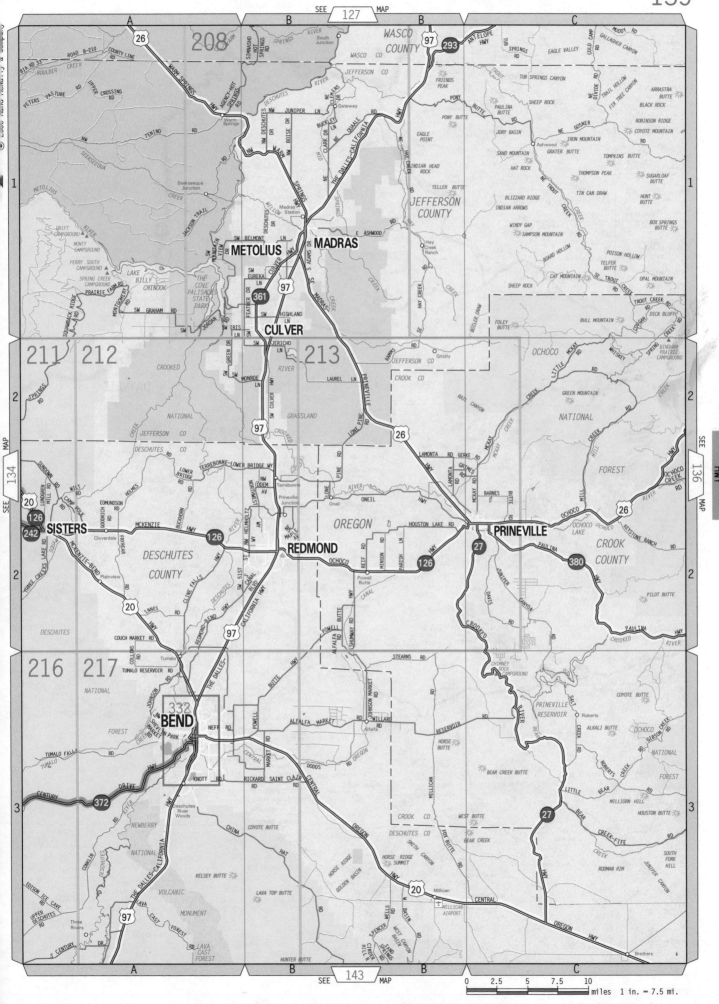

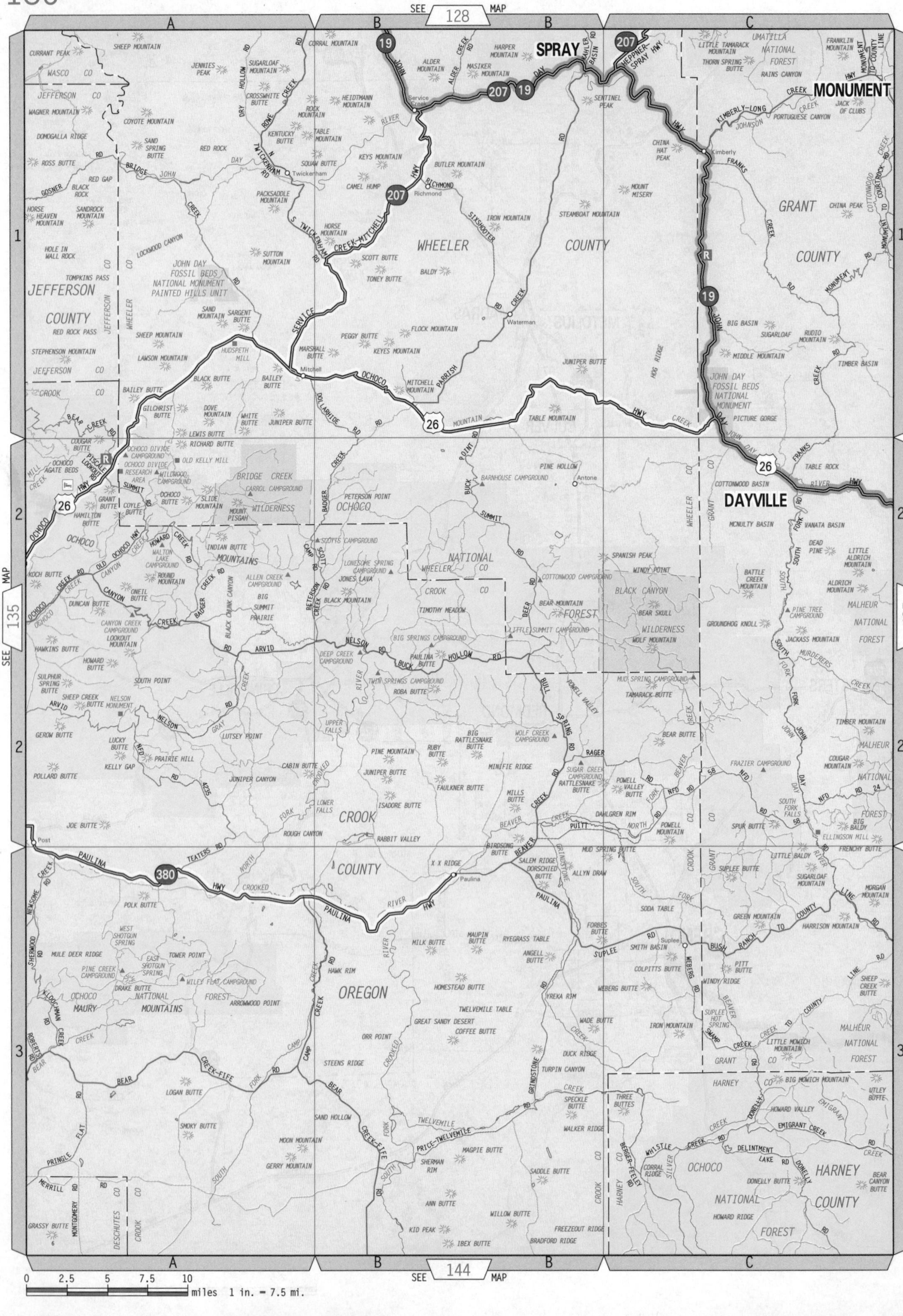

SEE MAP 135

SEE MAP 137

SPRAY

MONUMENT

DAYVILLE

© 2006 Rand McNally & Company

N

HWY

JEFFERSON COUNTY

WHEELER COUNTY

GRANT COUNTY

CROOK COUNTY

OREGON

HARNEY COUNTY

OCHOCO NATIONAL FOREST

MALHEUR NATIONAL FOREST

JOHN DAY FOSSIL BEDS NATIONAL MONUMENT PAINTED HILLS UNIT

JOHN DAY FOSSIL BEDS NATIONAL MONUMENT

OCHOCO MOUNTAINS

MAURY MOUNTAINS

miles 1 in. = 7.5 mi.
0 2.5 5 7.5 10

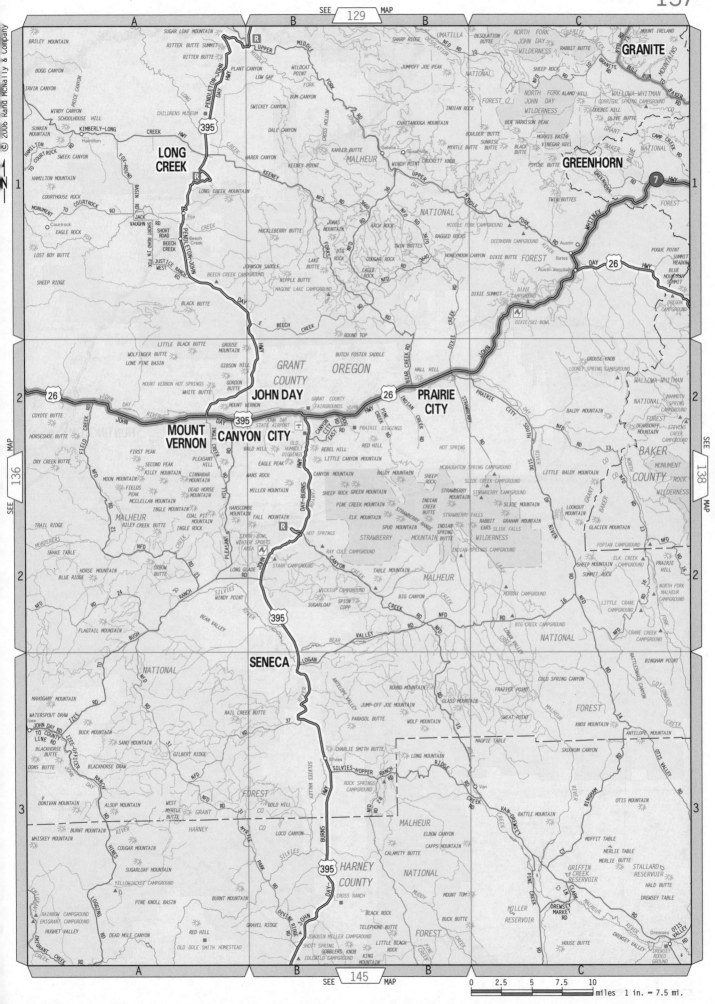

HWY

SUMPTER

BAKER CITY

UNITY

HUNTINGTON

VALE

BAKER COUNTY

WALLOWA-WHITMAN NATIONAL FOREST

WALLOWA-WHITMAN NATIONAL FOREST

MALHEUR COUNTY

GRANT COUNTY

MALHEUR NATIONAL FOREST

HARNEY COUNTY

OREGON

Wind Creek Peak
Elkhorn Ridge
Elkhorn Peak
Bourne
Pocahontas
Wingville
La Grande
Flagstaff Hill
Baker-Copperfield
NATIONAL HISTORIC OREGON TRAIL INTERPRETIVE CENTER
Smith Lake
Coyote Peak
Lone Pine Mountain
Fivemile
Baker-Copperfield
John Whitman
Glasgow Butte
Love Reservoir
Sinclair
Sardine Creek
Little Lookout Mountain
Sheep Mountain
Marble Point
Deer Creek Campground
McCully Forks Campground
Granite Hill
Cracker
McEwen
Mowitch Campground
Union Creek Campground
Mason Dam Campground
Blue Canyon
Salisbury
Big Lookout Mountain
Iron Mountain
Oxman
Durkee
Sugarloaf Mountain
Huckleberry Mountain
Big Huckleberry Butte
Skyline
Black Mountain
Phillips Lake
Southwest Shore Campground
Black Mountain
Sheep Rock
Dooley Mountain
Beaver Mountain
Stump Spring Butte
Dead Horse Canyon
Burnt River Canyon
Lost Basin
Gold Hill
Martins Mill
Beaverdam Buttes
Cottonwood Buttes
Little Bald Mountain
Bald Mountain
Chicken Peak
Baldy Mountain
Fur Mountain
Juniper Mountain
Weatherby Mountain
Morgan Mountain
Yellow Pine Campground
Netmore Campground
King Mountain
Hereford
Bridgeport
Clarks Creek
Rye Valley
Pedro Mountain
Dixie
Durbin
Lime
Shoestring Grade
WHITED RESERVOIR
Higgens Reservoir
Three Pine Butte
MALHEUR RESERVOIR
Bill Neighbor Peak
Sunday Hill
Rye Valley-Mormon
Spirit Hill
California Mountain
Cinder Butte
Tamarack Spring Campground
Buck Mountain
Murray Peak
Rock Creek Butte
Baldy Mountain
Devils Heel
Cave Hollow
Shasta Butte
Mormon Basin
South Fork Burnt Campground
Long Creek Campground
Eldorado Campground
Rastus Mountain
Ironside Valley
Worsham Butte
MALHEUR RESERVOIR
Huntington Junction
Limestone Butte
Lost Tom Mountain
BULLRUN MOUNTAIN
Table Rock
Bullrun Rock
Ironside
Saddle Butte
Cow Valley Butte
Brogan Hill Summit
Striped Mountain
Brosman Mountain
MONUMENT ROCK WILDERNESS
Luther Butte
SHEEPHEAD MOUNTAIN
Squaw Butte
Lone Rock
Ironside Mountain
Cow Valley
Brogan
McDowell Butte
McCarthy-Ridge
Rose
Squaw Butte
Ring Butte
Clevenger Butte
Juniper Mountain
Jamieson
Circle Butte
Scratch Post Butte
Brushy Hollow
Willow Creek
Tin Wagon Canyon
Happy Canyon
Goodwin Tomb
Black Butte
Bonita
Little Poison Butte
Buckbrush Poison Butte
Big Poison Butte
Burnt Stump Butte
Hope Butte
Sugarloaf Butte
Hot Spring
BULLY CREEK RESERVOIR
Bully Creek Campground
Castle Rock
Bendire
Hunter Mountain
Hunter Campground
Bendire Mountain
De Armond Mountain
Westfall Butte
Danger Point
Vale West (Graham Blvd)
West Bench
East Bench
COTTONWOOD RESERVOIR
Agency Mountain
Beulah Reservoir
Kelsay Butte
Beulah
Beede Desert
Beulah Butte
Little Valley
Vines Hill
Hope
Harper
Harper Junction
McClellan Mountain
Petes Mountain
Currey Canyon
South Mountain
Red Rock Canyon
Hog Creek Ridge
Central Oregon Hwy
Drinkwater Pass
Double Mountain

miles 1 in. = 7.5 mi.
0   2.5   5   7.5   10

HMY

218

SEE 132 MAP

A B B C

OREGON DUNES NATIONAL RECREATION AREA

Gardiner
East Gardiner

101

Winchester Bay

REEDSPORT

SIUSLAW NATIONAL FOREST

UMPQUA HWY

Scottsburg

38

CLEAR LAKE

SCHOFIELD RD

NORTH LAKE RD

LAKESIDE

BEAR MOUNTAIN

DOUGLAS COUNTY

OREGON DUNES NATIONAL RECREATION AREA

TEN MILE LAKE

LANDING RD

ELLIOTT

STATE

1

MILLICOMA RIVER

Saunders Lake

SHUTTERS RD

WEST FORK MILLICOMA

STULLS FALLS

GOLDEN & SILVER FALLS STATE PARK

SILVER FALLS

GOLDEN FALLS

MATSON CREEK

Hauser

OCEAN

Shorewood

TRAIL BUTTE RD

WEST FORK

EAST FORK GLEN

HWY

Allegany

TAYLOR BUTTE

EAST FORK MILLICOMA RIVER

Glasgow

NORTH BAY DR

NORTH BEND

338

Empire

EAST BAY DR

Cooston

MCKEEVER MOUNTAIN

COOS RIDGE

CO

220

COOS RIVER RD

COOS RIVER

NORTH FORK

COOS BAY

Barview

LIBBY DR

Englewood

Bay Park

McCormac

Millington

COOS RIVER FISH HATCHERY

Charleston

CAPE ARAGO HWY

Crown Point

CATCHING SLOUGH

LAVERNE PARK NORTH

NORTH FORK COQUILLE RIVER

OREGON

2

DEVILS HILL RD

SEVEN DEVILS RD

SOUTH SLOUGH NATIONAL ESTUARY

COOS CITY SUMNER RD

Sumner

COOS MOUNTAIN

SEE 141 MAP

AGATE BEACH

101 42

Green Acres

SUMNER-FAIRVIEW RD

LAVERNE FALLS

BEAVER HILL RD

Overland

COQUILLE-FAIRVIEW RD

MIDDLE CREEK FALLS

BURNT RIDGE

COX CANYON

Coaledo

MIDDLE CREEK ACCESS RD

BULLARDS BEACH STATE PARK

OREGON COAST HWY

BANK RD

Leneve

Chrome

Fairview

FAIRVIEW

McKinley

FAIRVIEW-MCKINLEY RD

BREWSTER ROCK

MOUNTAIN ACCESS RD

PACIFIC

Cedar

COQUILLE

COQUILLE

SHELLEY RD

RINK PEAK

MARIA C JACKSON STATE PARK

LOST CREEK FALLS

Parkersburg

Prosper

BANK RD

Riverton

BANDON-ROSEBURG HWY

LEE MCKINLEY RD

Dora

Sitkum

SITKUM COUNTY

BREWSTER CANYON

Winter Villa

42S

COQUILLE VALLEY

Johnson

SHUCK MOUNTAIN

NORWAY-LEE-FAIRVIEW RD

FAIRVIEW RD

EAST FORK COQUILLE RIVER

SITKUM-COUNTY LINE RD

BREWSTER VALLEY

BANDON

BEACH LOOP RD

ROSA RD

MYRTLE POINT RD

Arago

Norway

Gravelford

MYRTLE POINT-SITKUM RD

SPLIT MOUNTAIN

2

BANDON STATE PARK

BEAR CREEK RD

MORRISON RD

TWOMILE RANGE

COOS COUNTY FAIRGROUNDS

BRIDGE RD

MYRTLE POINT

COOS COUNTY

SCOTT MOUNTAIN

THOMAS MOUNTAIN

Twomile

Laurel Grove

COOS BAY-ROSEBURG HWY

224

SEE 148 MAP

NEW RIVER PARK

NORTH FOURMILE RD

Fourmile

BUZZARD BUTTE

CATCHING CREEK

WEST SIDE RD

SCHNEIDER BUTTE

Bridge

ANDERSON MOUNTAIN

SOUTH FORK COQUILLE RIVER

Remote

KENYON MOUNTAIN

42

COAST RD

BENNETT BUTTE

COTTON BUTTE

WHITNEY BUTTE

Broadbent

ROBBINS BUTTE

SAMISON MOUNTAIN

MYRTLEWOOD CAMPGROUND

BEAR CREEK CAMPGROUND

ROUND TOP

WATCHES BUTTE

POWERS RD

Warner

WHOOREY MOUNTAIN

MYRTLE ROCK

ELBOW POINT

COOS BAY-ROSEBURG HWY

Langlois

Floras

FLORAS CREEK

MOUNTAIN

WHITE MOUNTAIN

Gaylord

HOOD MOUNTAIN

PYRAMID ROCK

BEN GRANT RIDGE

BONE MOUNTAIN

DOUGLAS COUNTY

FLORAS LAKE RD

Denmark

SUMMIT MOUNTAIN

CALF RANCH MOUNTAIN

Bancroft

SUICIDE ROCK

POWERS

FLORAS LAKE

101

EIGHTMILE PRAIRIE MOUNTAIN

COUNTY LINE CANYON

BINGHAM MOUNTAIN

SISKIYOU NATIONAL FOREST

GOLD MOUNTAIN

3

AIRPORT RD

CURRY

COUNTY

SUGARLOAF MOUNTAIN

POWERS STATE AIRPORT

COQUILLE RD

WOODBY MOUNTAIN

EDEN VALLEY

CAPE BLANCO STATE PARK

CAPE BLANCO HWY

Sixes

SIXES

CURRY CREEK

BOUNDARY CAMPGROUND

COAL CREEK CAMPGROUND

ELK FALLS CREEK

PIONEER CAMPGROUND

ELK RIVER RD

SAND ROCK MOUNTAIN

ELK CREEK FALLS

BIG TREE CAMPGROUND

BLM RD 32

EDEN VALLEY CAMPGROUND

DIAMOND PEAK

DOUGLAS CO

ELK WALLOWS

MOON MOUNTAIN

JOHNSON MOUNTAIN

3348

GRASSY KNOB

CHINA PEAK

RUSTY BUTTE

CHINA FLAT CAMPGROUND

MYRTLE GROVE CAMPGROUND

SOUTH POWERS RD

SADDLE PEAKS

CURRY COUNTY

ELK RIVER

BARKLOW MOUNTAIN CAMPGROUND

BRAY RIDGE

EDEN RIDGE

WILD ROGUE WILDERNESS

ANVIL MOUNTAIN WILDERNESS

SISKIYOU

NATIONAL

DAPHNE GROVE CAMPGROUND

COQUILLE RIVER FALLS

ROCK CREEK CAMPGROUND

SQUAW LAKE CAMPGROUND

KELSEY PEAK

PORT ORFORD

HUMBUG MOUNTAIN STATE PARK

PEARSE PEAK OAK RIDGE

FATHER MOUNTAIN

MILBURY MOUNTAIN

IRON MOUNTAIN

FOREST

ELK RIVER

BALD KNOB

FORT LAMERICK

Marial

ROGUE RIVER

CLAY HILL

JOSEPHINE CO

CURRY CO

A B B C

SEE 148 MAP

0 2.5 5 7.5 10
miles 1 in. = 7.5 mi.

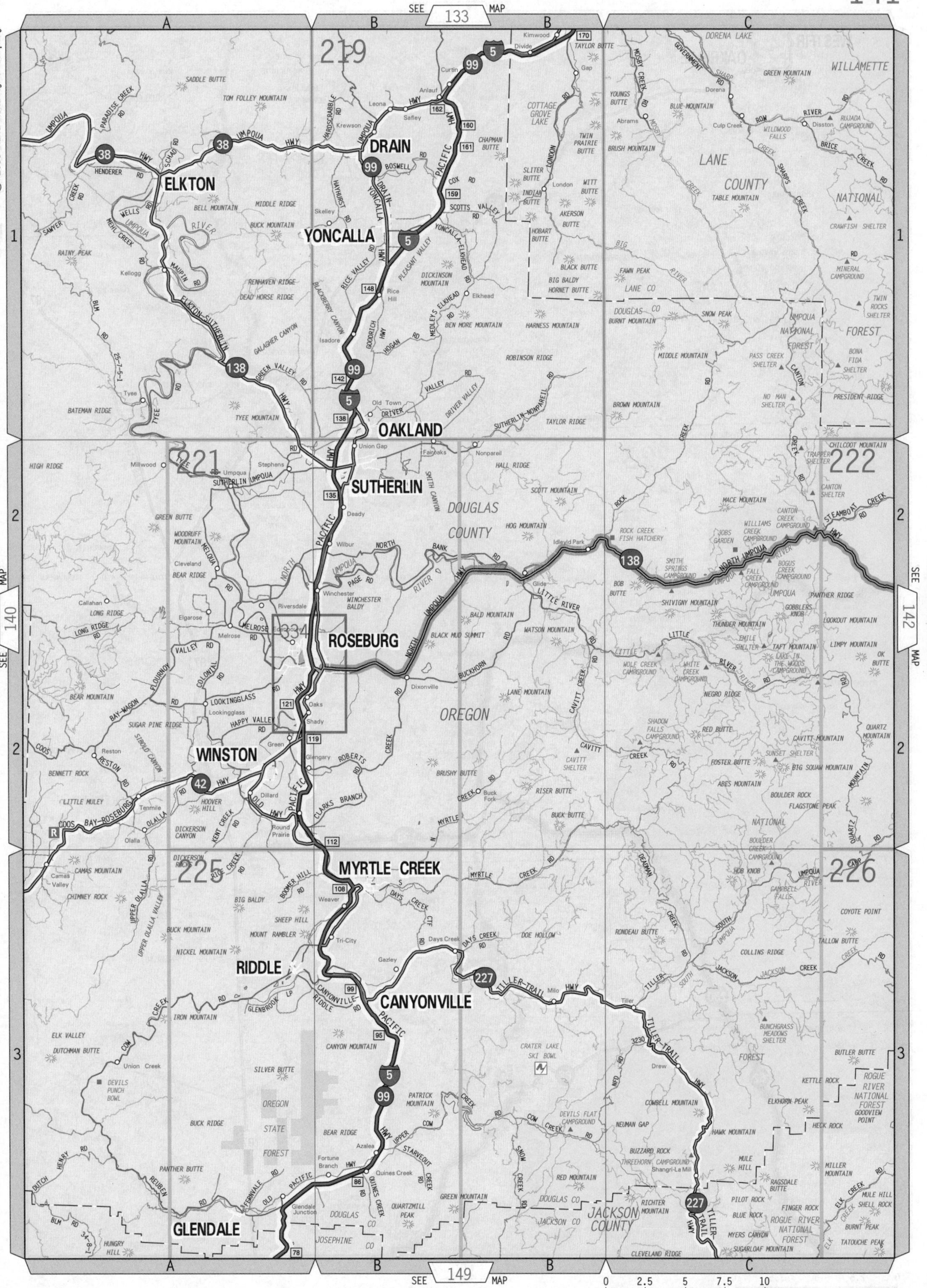

© 2006 Rand McNally & Company

SEE 133 MAP

219   222

ELKTON   **DRAIN**   **YONCALLA**   **OAKLAND**   **SUTHERLIN**

ROSEBURG   **WINSTON**   **MYRTLE CREEK**   **RIDDLE**   **CANYONVILLE**   **GLENDALE**

221   225   226

DOUGLAS COUNTY

OREGON

LANE COUNTY

UMPQUA NATIONAL FOREST

WILLAMETTE

JACKSON COUNTY

ROGUE RIVER NATIONAL FOREST

OREGON STATE FOREST

SEE 140 MAP   SEE 142 MAP

HWY

SEE 149 MAP

0   2.5   5   7.5   10 miles   1 in. = 7.5 mi.

WESTFIR

OAKRIDGE

A B B C

© 2006 Rand McNally & Company

N

WILLAMETTE

NATIONAL

FOREST

WILLAMETTE

DESCHUTES COUNTY

DESCHUTES

LANE COUNTY

KLAMATH CO

PRINGLE FALLS EXPERIMENTAL FOREST ADDITION

WICKIUP RESERVOIR

58

58

97

222 223

WILLAMETTE NATIONAL FOREST

BOULDER CREEK WILDERNESS

UMPQUA NATIONAL FOREST

DOUGLAS COUNTY OREGON

OREGON CASCADES RECREATION AREA

Diamond Lake

THIELSEN WILDERNESS

WINEMA NATIONAL FOREST

KLAMATH COUNTY

138

230

138

DIAMOND LAKE HWY

SEE 141 MAP

SEE 143 MAP

HWY

226 227

CRATER LAKE

CRATER LAKE NATIONAL PARK

ROGUE RIVER NATIONAL FOREST

JACKSON COUNTY

WINEMA NATIONAL FOREST WILDERNESS

KLAMATH FOREST NATIONAL

SILVER WILDLIFE REFUGE

230

62

62

97

THE DALLES-CALIFORNIA

A B B C

SEE 150 MAP

0 2.5 5 7.5 10 miles   1 in. = 7.5 mi.

1

2

2

3

SEE MAP 135

© 2006 Rand McNally & Company

97
20
31

FALL RIVER
LA PINE STATE REC AREA
Three Rivers
DESCHUTES RIVER
PRINGLE FALLS
OGDEN GROUP CAMPGROUND
NORTH COVE CAMPGROUND
WARM SPRINGS CAMPGROUND
PRAIRIE CAMPGROUND
PAULINA CREEK
PAULINA-EAST LAKE
PAULINA LAKE
EAST LAKE
NEWBERRY NATIONAL VOLCANIC MONUMENT
LAVA CAST FOREST
NEWBERRY
KAWAK BUTTE
LOMULLO BUTTE
PILPIL BUTTE
COMPANY BUTTE
CINDER HILL
CINDER HILL CAMPGROUND
HOT SPRINGS CAMPGROUND
EAST LAKE CAMPGROUND
LITTLE CRATER CAMPGROUND
CHIEF PAULINA GROUP CAMPGROUND
SAND BUTTE
NEWBERRY CRATER
SIX MILE SNOWPARK
TEN MILE SNOWPARK
PAULINA LAKE CAMPGROUND
PAULINA MOUNTAINS
DEVILS HORN
SURVEYORS ICE CAVE
TORSO BUTTE
BOX BUTTE
WEASEL BUTTE
KELLY BUTTE
ROGERS BUTTE
CHINA HAT
CHINA HAT CAMPGROUND
GROUND HOG BUTTE
CINDER HILL RD
CHINA HAT RD
SAND SPRINGS RD
PINE MOUNTAIN OBSERVATORY
PINE RIDGE
MAHOGANY BUTTE
FIRESTONE BASIN
SAND SPRING CAMPGROUND
LAVACICLE CAVE
ANTELOPE BUTTE
WHISKEY ROCK
WATKINS BUTTE
SOLDIERS CAP
DOG BUTTE
QUARTZ MOUNTAIN
QUARTER BUTTE
DEVILS HOLE
TRAIL BUTTE
POLY TOP BUTTE
DESCHUTES COUNTY
DESCHUTES CO
LAKE CO
KLAMATH CO
BURGESS
6TH ST
PENN-CALIFORNIA
RIVERVIEW
FINLEY BUTTE
La Pine
SAND FLATS-ICE CAVE RD
DESCHUTES CO
KLAMATH CO
IPSOOT BUTTE
GREEN BUTTE
INDIAN BUTTE
SPRING BUTTE
MOFFITT BUTTE
HOOLIGAN HILL
NATIONAL FOREST
FREMONT
YOUTLKUT BUTTE
WIGTOP BUTTE
SQUAW MOUNTAIN
DERRICK CAVE
CABIN LAKE CAMPGROUND
HOGBACK BUTTE
TWIN BUTTES
BUTTE
MILLICAN RD

KLAMATH COUNTY
FREMONT
MOWICH SPRING BUTTE
STAMS MOUNTAIN
CORRAL BUTTE
LOOKOUT POINT
WICKIUP BUTTE
MCCARTHY BUTTE
BIG HOLE
FORT ROCK CAVE
FORT ROCK STATE MONUMENT
Fort Rock
FORT ROCK RD
DERRICK
CAVES
FRAZEE-FREDERICK
ICE CAVE
COUGAR MOUNTAIN
TABLE MOUNTAIN
GREEN MOUNTAIN
EAST GREEN MOUNTAIN
SOUTH GREEN MOUNTAIN
PUMICE BUTTE
TIMBER BUTTE
SPROATS MEADOW
PARKER BUTTE
BALD MOUNTAIN
NATIONAL
WART PEAK
WINEMA
STIMSON MEADOW
PARKER MEADOW
TEA TABLE MOUNTAIN
FOREST
BEAR FLAT DRAW
SAGEBRUSH DRAW
DAVIS FLAT
HIDDEN MEADOW
NATIONAL
BEAR WALLOW
LOCATION BUTTE
ANTELOPE MOUNTAIN
TIMOTHY BUTTE
SPIKE BUTTE
COYOTE BUTTE
CONNLEY HILLS
FORT ROCK VALLEY
LN
TUFF BUTTE
TABLE ROCK
CHRISTMAS VALLEY-WAGONTIRE
Christmas Valley
OLD LAKE RD
SINK
LAKE RD
LAKE COUNTY
OREGON
SAINT PATRICK MOUNTAIN
JUNIPER CANYON
SQUAW BUTTE
ROCKY BUTTE
SNUFFIELD RD
CARLON RD
ROCK BUTTE
BEAR FLAT
MCCARTY MEADOW
BEAR BUTTE
FOREST
DOESKIN BUTTE
BUCKSKIN BUTTE
FIRE BUTTE
DILLON BUTTE
LITTLE YAMSAY MOUNTAIN
JACKSON CREEK CAMPGROUND
SILVER
WILLIAMSON RIVER
BLOODY POINT
BUCK RIDGE
JACKSON RIDGE
YAMSAY MOUNTAIN
WILDHORSE RIDGE
WINEMA
NATIONAL
WILLIAMSON RIVER
FOREST
HAYSTACK DRAW
HAMBLETON BUTTE
KLAMATH CO
LAKE CO
MCCARTY BUTTE
RODMAN ROCK
BRIDGE CREEK
SILVER CREEK
SILVER CREEK MARSH CAMPGROUND
MAHOGANY MOUNTAIN
HAGER MOUNTAIN
DEAD INDIAN MOUNTAIN
THOMPSON RESERVOIR CAMPGROUND
THOMPSON RESERVOIR
PARTIN BUTTE
WEST
ROUND BUTTE
DEER HEAD
NATIONAL
FREMONT
FORK
SYCAN MARSH
LONG CREEK RD
SYCAN RIVER
SILVER LAKE CO
FOREST
WINTER RIDGE
CAMPBELL HILL
HUNTER HILL
SUMMER LAKE
SUMMER LAKE GAME MANAGEMENT AREA
Summer Lake
DIABLO PEAK
DIABLO MOUNTAINS
FOURMILE POINT
FIVEMILE POINT
SILVER LAKE
Silver Lake
FREMONT HWY
PICTURE ROCK

SEE MAP 142
SEE MAP 144 HWY
SEE MAP 151

miles 1 in. = 7.5 mi.
0 2.5 5 7.5 10

A | B | B | C

© 2006 Rand McNally & Company

MONTGOMERY RD
VAN LAKE
HARMAN RD
20
LIZARD CREEK RD
HAMPTON BUTTE
CREEK-FIFE RD
BEAR
CROOK COUNTY
BUCK CREEK RD
MACKEY BUTTE
BUCK SPRING CAMPGROUND
OCHOCO
NATIONAL FOREST
CHAPIN TABLE
MINERAL CANYON
DONNELLY RD
CENTRAL
CROOK
DESCHUTES
CO
SCHRAEDER RD
RANCH
CROOK CO
HARNEY CO
GIBBONS MILL CANYON
SAMMILL CREEK
MCCANLIES RD
EGYPT CANYON
OREGON
FREDERICK BUTTE
COYOTE ROCK
BRONCO BUTTE
HAMPTON STATE AIRPORT
Hampton
DESCHUTES COUNTY
OCHOCO NATIONAL FOREST
DRY MOUNTAIN
SILVER CREEK VALLEY
MILLER CANYON
EGYPT CANYON
MILLER RD

1

CORRAL BUTTE
FREDERICK BUTTE
YREKA BUTTE
DESCHUTES CO
HWY
20
HAT BUTTE
CHICKAHOMINY RESERVOIR
SILVER CREEK
SILVER
GUM BOOT CANYON
ROCK QUARRY CANYON RESERVOIR

1

INDIAN BUTTE
RD
LAKE CO
FRAZEE-FREDERICK BUTTE
PETERS BUTTE
HARDER BUTTE
GLASS BUTTES
BUCK BUTTE
MIDNIGHT POINT
LITTLE GLASS BUTTE
CENTRAL
20 OREGON
SHIELDS BUTTE
JUNIPER RIDGE
Riley
HWY
CREEK

EAST BUTTE
BENJAMIN CAVES
STUDHORSE BUTTE
WEST BUTTE
ROUND TOP BUTTE
SQUAW BUTTE RANGE EXPERIMENT STATION HQ
SQUAW
SQUAW BUTTE EXPERIMENT STATION
TURPIN CANYON
ROCKY DRAW
395

MOONLIGHT BUTTE
PILOT BUTTE
TIRED HORSE BUTTE
SHEEP MOUNTAIN
RANCH-WAGONTIRE RD
EGLI CANYON
SPRING CANYON
BUTTE RD
COYOTE RIM

2

LOST FOREST RESEARCH NATURAL AREA
WAGONTIRE MOUNTAIN
LAKEVIEW-BURNS
ALEC BUTTE
BIG STICK
BLACK CANYON RD

2

HWY

ELK MOUNTAIN
RAMS BUTTE
GAP
Wagontire
LITTLE TANK CANYON
VALLEY RD
GOOSE EGG BUTTE
IRON MOUNTAIN
BUZZARD CREEK

CHRISTMAS
WAGON DRAW
HAPPY CAMP
DRY

VALLEY-WAGONTIRE
RD
DRY VALLEY HWY
HORSEHEAD MOUNTAIN
WILSON

2

LAKE COUNTY
HORSE MOUNTAIN
LITTLE JUNIPER MOUNTAIN
SMOKE OUT CANYON
WILSON BUTTE

2

HWY
DRY VALLEY

DOUGHNUT MOUNTAIN
ALKALI LAKE STATE AIRPORT
HARNEY COUNTY

ALKALI BUTTES
LAKEVIEW-BURNS
JUNIPER
LAKE CO
HARNEY CO
DRY VALLEY RIM

OREGON
ALKALI LAKE
GRAYS BUTTE
LITTLE
DRY VALLEY
LITTLE VALLEY
ROCK CAMP DRAW

VENATOR BUTTE
JUNIPER MOUNTAIN
BACON
OPEN DRAW
OREJANA CANYON

3

SHARP TOP
TWIN BUTTES
395
BACON CAMP RD
KIT CANYON
MULE TIT
THREE STORY RIM

3

JUG MOUNTAIN
R
LITTLE STEAMBOAT POINT

BISCUIT POINT
NASTY FLAT
HORSESHOE RIM
HARNEY CO
MULE SPRING RD

COGUAN
XL RANCH RD
SHELL ROCK CANYON
BLACK CAP
BLUEJOINT LAKE

SAWED HORN
FLINT HILLS
HARNEY CO
BLACK RIM

A | B | B | C

0 2.5 5 7.5 10 miles 1 in. = 7.5 mi.

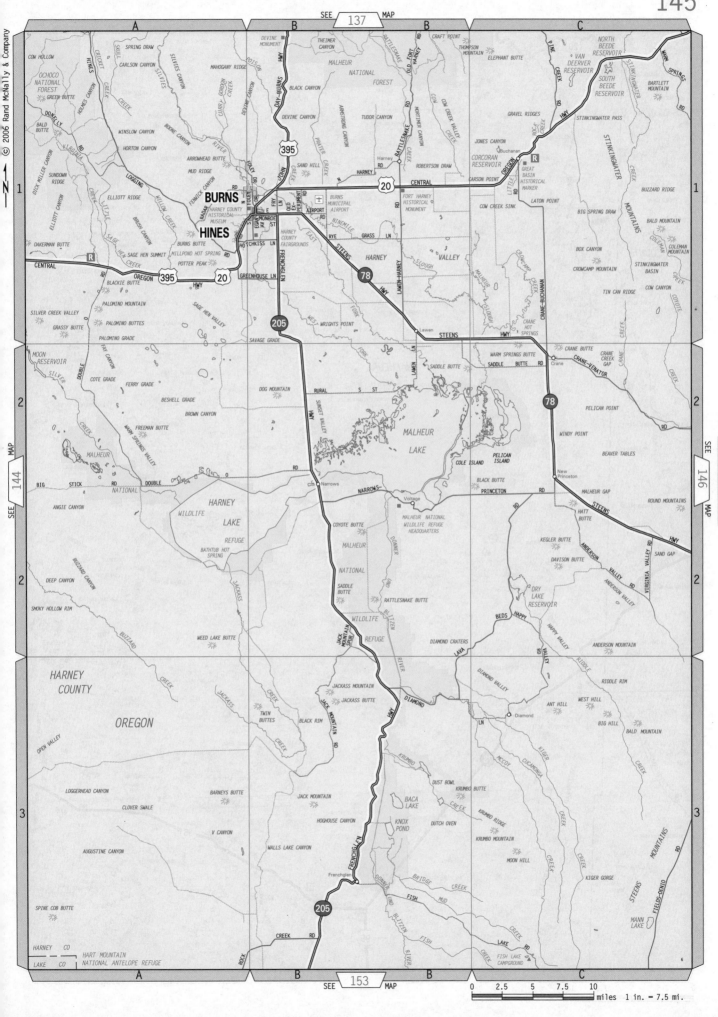

SEE MAP 138

A B B C

20 20

MALHEUR RIVER
CHIMNEY CREEK RD
CENTRAL
BEULAH HWY
OREGON

CLARK CANYON
HARPER BASIN
HOODOO RIDGE
SHELL ROCK BUTTE
MITCHELL BUTTE
HAYSTACK ROCK
MITCHELL ROCK RD

ALTNOW GAP
BLACK BUTTE
HUNTER CREEK RD
Juntura

HUNTER CREEK
HUNTER PEAK
TIMS PEAK
SQUAW CREEK
NEW CREEK
SAND HOLLOW
CANYON
ROCK CANYON
NEGRO ROCK

CAT ROCK
RIVERSIDE RD
TABLE TOP
JONES BUTTE
MONUMENT PEAK
HAT TOP
COTTONWOOD CREEK

UPTON MOUNTAIN
MEEKER MOUNTAIN
PRAVA PEAK
CAMP CREEK
RUFINO BUTTE
SOURDOUGH MOUNTAIN
GRASSY MOUNTAIN

WARM SPRINGS
TWIN KNOLLS
SHUMWAY RANCH RD
FREEZEOUT MOUNTAIN
NEGRO CTO
DRY CREEK
BURNT MOUNTAIN
NIMI RD

RILEY BUTTE
WARM SPRINGS RESERVOIR
MOSQUITO MOUNTAIN
RED BUTTE
CUTOFF
CROWLEY RD
DRY CREEK FARM
DRY CREEK

1 1

TEXACO BASIN
RESERVOIR RD
SHUMWAY
NANNYS NIPPLE
DEER BUTTE
BURNT MOUNTAIN

HARNEY COUNTY
SOUTH FORK
GRANITE CREEK
HAMMOND HILL
DRY CREEK BUTTES
IRON MOUNTAIN

Riverside
LUCE HOT SPRINGS
SKULL SPRING
SAND HILLS
OWYHEE LAKE

COLEMAN
MCEWEN BUTTE
SWAMP CREEK
MONUMENTAL ROCK
COPELAND BUTTE
BUTTE CREEK
QUARTZ MOUNTAIN
SADDLE BUTTE
DEADMAN GULCH RD

CRANE CREEK
COYOTE CREEK
BUCK MOUNTAIN
WHISKEY CREEK
SWAMP
CROWLEY-RIVERSIDE
DRY BUTTES
ANTELOPE FLAT
JUNIPER RD
OWYHEE RESERVOIR STATE AIRPORT
NORTH TABLE MOUNTAIN

Dunnean
MCEWEN RD
CROWLEY STAR RD
PAGE RD
MUD
KNOTTINGHAM BUTTE
BLACK BUTTE

VENATOR
HARNEY CO
MALHEUR CO
SWAMP CREEK BUTTES
MALHEUR COUNTY
RED BUTTE
SOUTH TABLE MOUNTAIN
ROOSTER COMB

2 2
Venator
CRANE RD
SADDLE DRAW
MALHEUR RIVER
STOCKADE MOUNTAIN
STAR MOUNTAIN
TURNBULL MOUNTAIN
CREEK RD
OWYHEE BREAKS
LESLIE GULCH RD
HOT SPRING

CHINA HILL
OREGON
CEDAR MOUNTAIN
RINEHART RD
DIAMOND BUTTE
THE TONGUE

CAVE RD
SOUTH FORK
HAT BUTTE
STOCKADE BUTTES
WHITEHORSE MOUNTAIN
PIUTE LAKE BED
CROWLEY
RINEHART
RANCH

BARREN VALLEY
INDIAN CREEK BUTTES
DRY LAKE
RIVER
MORCOM RD
BIRCH CREEK RD
MAHOGANY RD

MALHEUR CAVE
RED MOUNTAIN
DUCK CREEK BUTTE
DOWELL BUTTE
SACRAMENTO BUTTE
BLOWOUT RESERVOIR

R
STEENS
BIG GULCH
INDIAN CREEK
MUSTANG BUTTE
IRON POINT
OWYHEE
CRATER LAKE RD
COFFEEPOT CRATER
DEER BUTTE
UPPER COW LAKE

78
HWY
CROWLEY-RIVERSIDE
WRANGLE BUTTE
JORDAN CRATERS
BISCUIT BUTTE

REEDS BASIN
SADDLE BUTTE
BISCUIT BUTTE
LOWER COW LAKE
COW CREEK

INDIAN CREEK BUTTE
TURNBULL PEAK
TUB SPRINGS
BOGUS
CLARKS BUTTE
LAVA BUTTE

FOLLY FARM RD
FOLLY FARM CTO
IRON CTO
BOGUS CREEK CAVE
WEST CRATER
SADDLE BUTTE
HAMMOND HILL

TENCENT LAKE
RYEGRASS BUTTE
MOUNTAIN
BURNS CAVE
OWYHEE BUTTE
THREEMILE HILL
DANNER HWY

FIFTEENCENT LAKE
SMALL BUTTE
FARM CTO
TIRE TUBE CAVE
FORTYMILE CAVE
OWYHEE RIVER CAVE
TUCKNESS RD
Danner

SQUAW FLAT
FIELDS-DENIO
78
STEENS
COYOTE TRAP CAVE
KIGER
AIRSTRIP
LITTLE OWYHEE BUTTE
OREGON-NEVADA
RATTLESNAKE CAVE

SHEEPSHEAD
NORTH FORK
Arock
GRAHAMS HILL
THREE FORKS RD

3 3
TUDOR LAKE
STONEHOUSE CANYON
IRON MOUNTAIN
JORDAN CREEK
NEVADA HWY
95
ROUND MOUNTAIN

COFFIN BUTTE
RESERVOIR FORKS RD
PALOMINO
SCOTT BUTTE
ROME
Rome
OREGON OLD HWY
ARRITOLA MOUNTAIN
LITTLE GRASSY MOUNTAIN
LITTLE GRASSY RESERVOIR

TABLE MOUNTAIN
RYEGRASS
PALOMINO HILLS
CREEK
CREEK STATE HISTORIC MONUMENT
ROME STATE AIRPORT
GRASS CREEK
SKULL
OWYHEE CANYON

THREE
WILDCAT
MOUNTAINS
R
95
Burns Junction
IDAHO
INDIAN FORK CREEK
RIVER
DEAD HORSE BUTTE

MICKEY BASIN
WILDCAT CREEK
FLAT TOP MOUNTAIN
CROOKED CREEK
DRY CREEK
OLD IDAHO-OREGON HWY
INDIAN FORT CREEK

A B B B C

SEE MAP 154

SEE MAP 145

SEE MAP 147

HWY

0 2.5 5 7.5 10 miles 1 in. = 7.5 mi.

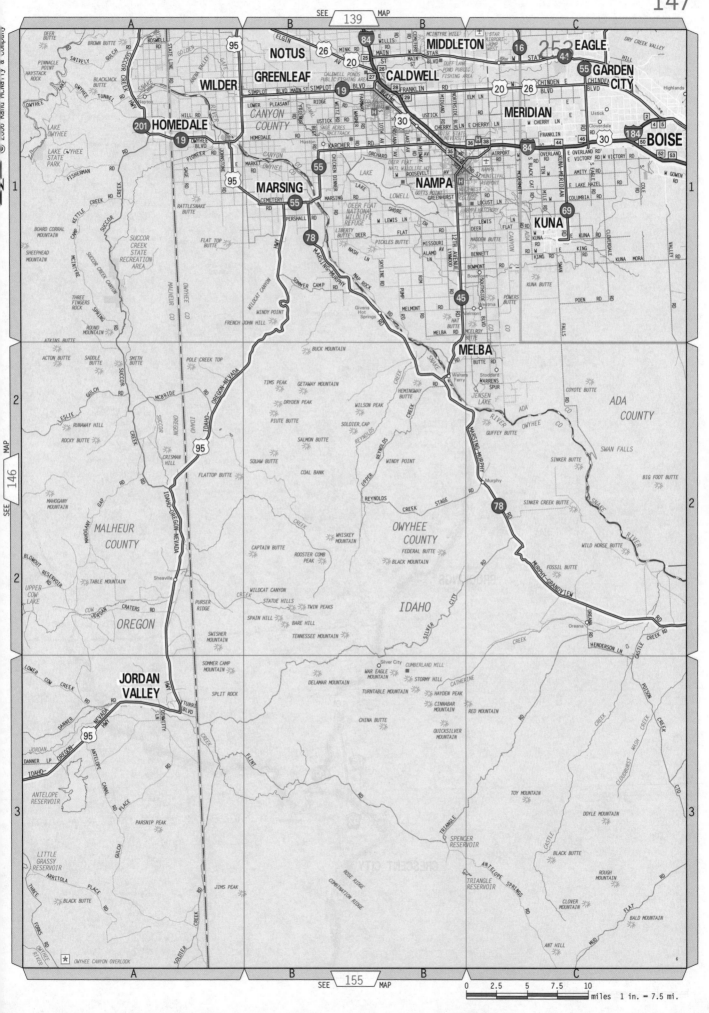

© 2008 Rand McNally & Company

HWY

SEE 146 MAP

SEE 155 MAP

0   2.5   5   7.5   10
miles 1 in. = 7.5 mi.

© 2006 Rand McNally & Company

HWY

228

232

233

SEE 149 MAP

GOLD BEACH

BROOKINGS

CRESCENT CITY

PACIFIC

OCEAN

JOSEPHINE COUNTY

CURRY COUNTY

DEL NORTE COUNTY

SISKIYOU NATIONAL FOREST

KALMIOPSIS WILDERNESS

OREGON

SIX RIVERS NATIONAL FOREST

SIX RIVERS NATIONAL FOREST

SISKIYOU NATIONAL FOREST

OREGON

CALIFORNIA

DEL NORTE CO.

SMITH RIVER NATIONAL REC AREA

CALIFORNIA

Nesika Beach

Ophir

Wedderburn

Agness

Carpenterville

Harbor

O'Brien

Elk Valley

Hunter Rock

Smith River

Fort Dick

Hiouchi

Gasquet

Darlingtonia

Berteleda

Bertsch Terrace

Patrick Creek

PISTOL RIVER STATE PARK

SAMUEL H BOARDMAN STATE PARK

PELICAN BEACH STATE PARK

CAMEL ROCK

TOLOWA DUNES STATE PARK

LAKE TOLOWA

PELICAN BAY

JACK McNAMARA FIELD

COLLEGE OF THE REDWOODS

JEDEDIAH SMITH REDWOODS STATE PARK

J. SMITH REDWOODS STATE PARK CAMPGROUND

REDWOOD NATIONAL PARK

DEL NORTE COAST REDWOODS STATE PARK

CALIFORNIA COASTAL NATIONAL MONUMENT

WILD ROGUE WILDERNESS

ROCKY PEAK

ELK RIVER

OPHIR MOUNTAIN

COLEBROOK BUTTE

CREW CANYON

FALL MOUNTAIN

LAKE OF THE WOODS MOUNTAIN

CEDAR POINT

SECOND PRAIRIE MOUNTAIN

SKOOKUMHOUSE BUTTE

SIGNAL BUTTES

GRIZZLY MOUNTAIN

Hunter Creek

SUGARLOAF MOUNTAIN

QUOSATANA BUTTE

SADDLE MOUNTAIN

FAIRVIEW MOUNTAIN

SNOW CAMP MOUNTAIN

PYRAMID ROCK

WINDY VALLEY

BIG CRAGGIES

GRANITE BUTTE

TINCUP PASS

SOUTH BEND MOUNTAIN

BALD MOUNTAIN

SILVER PEAK

HORSE SIGN BUTTE

PEBBLE HILL

DUNBAR RIFFLE

RASPBERRY MOUNTAIN

SILVER PEAK

FISH HOOK PEAK

SUGARLOAF MOUNTAIN

SQUIRREL PEAK

BRANDY PEAK

BEAR CAMP RIDGE

BOBS GARDEN MOUNTAIN

BRUSHY BAR CAMPGROUND

ILLAHE CAMPGROUND

FOSTER BAR CAMPGROUND

BIG WINDY CREEK CAMPGROUND

PLEASANT VALLEY

SILVER CREEK

CEDAR MOUNTAIN

RIDGE

CHROME RIDGE

BRIGGS VALLEY

DUTCH CK RD

ONION MTN RD

FREELAND SADDLE

HOBSON HORN

DORR CANYON

CHROME RIDGE

FLAT TOP

CHINAMAN HAT

BRIGGS CREEK CAMPGROUND

HORSE MOUNTAIN

SWEDE BASIN

SPALDING MILL CAMPGROUND

GOLD BASIN

PEARSOLL PEAK

WHETSTONE BUTTE

JOHNSON BUTTE

EAGLE GAP

MEADOW CREEK CAMPGROUND

CANYON PEAK

BAILEY MOUNTAIN

RED MOUNTAIN

DOE GAP

BISCUIT HILL

HENRY ROCK

Pistol River

RED ROCK

HOG MOUNTAIN

STACK YARDS

LONG RIDGE CAMPGROUND

LONG RIDGE

MACK POINT

YELLOW ROCK

WINDY POINT

FITZPATRICK RIDGE

INDIAN ROCK

THOMAS HILL

WHALEHEAD ISLAND

SAND HILL

BARNACLE ROCK

HOUSE ROCK

MORTON BUTTE

BASIN BUTTE

LITTLE REDWOOD CAMPGROUND

GARDNER RIDGE

HARRIS BUTTE

DIVER ROCK

BOAR BACKBONE

GARDNER RIDGE

SHORT RIDGE

WHEELER RIDGE

ELK MOUNTAIN

WINCHUCK CAMPGROUND

BEAR RIDGE

PACKSADDLE MOUNTAIN

PRINCE ISLAND

HIGH DOME

COLD SPRING MOUNTAIN

BROKEN RIB MOUNTAIN

SANGER PEAK

WASHINGTON PEAK

WOUNDED KNEE MOUNTAIN

TWIN PEAKS

BEAR BASIN BUTTE

TABLE MOUNTAIN

HURDYGURDY BUTTE

BEAR MOUNTAIN

PRESCOTT MOUNTAIN

KELLY PEAK

UPPER COON CAMPGROUND

GRASSY FLAT CAMPGROUND

CAMP SIX

GORDON MOUNTAIN

SHIP MOUNTAIN

BALDY PEAK

MUSLATT MOUNTAIN

BUCK MOUNTAIN

RATTLESNAKE

WILSON CREEK

ILLINOIS RIVER

ROGUE RIVER

CHETCO RIVER

SMITH RIVER

Illinois Valley

HAZEL VIEW SUMMIT

101

101

101

101

199

199

197

NFD RD

COAST HWY

REDWOOD HWY

OREGON COAST HWY

SMITH RIVER

NORTH FORK SMITH RIVER

MIDDLE FORK SMITH RIVER

SOUTH FORK SMITH RIVER

0 2.5 5 7.5 10 miles 1 in. = 7.5 mi.

A   B   B   C

© 2008 Rand McNally & Company

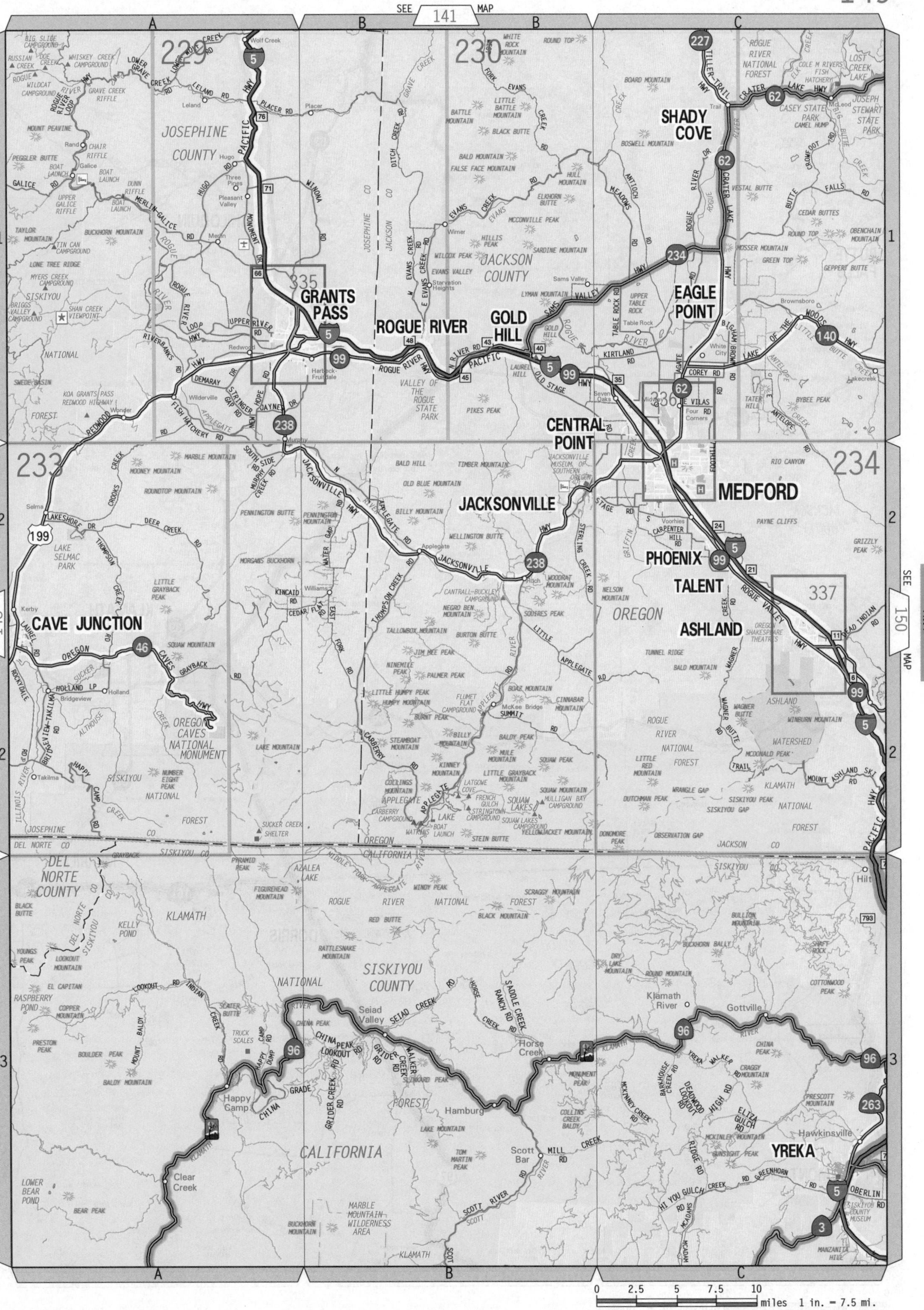

229　230　227

SHADY COVE

ROGUE RIVER NATIONAL FOREST

JOSEPHINE COUNTY

JACKSON COUNTY

335 **GRANTS PASS**

ROGUE RIVER　**GOLD HILL**

EAGLE POINT

CENTRAL POINT

336 **MEDFORD**

233　234

JACKSONVILLE

CAVE JUNCTION

PHOENIX

TALENT

337

ASHLAND

Oregon Shakespeare Theatres

OREGON CAVES NATIONAL MONUMENT

SISKIYOU NATIONAL FOREST

DEL NORTE COUNTY

KLAMATH NATIONAL FOREST

SISKIYOU COUNTY

OREGON
CALIFORNIA

ROGUE RIVER NATIONAL FOREST

MARBLE MOUNTAIN WILDERNESS AREA

YREKA

OBERLIN

Happy Camp

Clear Creek

CALIFORNIA

0　2.5　5　7.5　10 miles　1 in. = 7.5 mi.

SEE 148 MAP
SEE 150 MAP

SEE MAP 142

HWY
SEE MAP 149
SEE MAP 151

© 2000 Rand McNally & Company

A   **B**   **B**   **C**

231

BUTTE FALLS

ROGUE RIVER

NEEDLE ROCK
CASCADE GORGE
SOUTH FORK
LOST CREEK LAKE
BOUNDARY BUTTE
ROUND MOUNTAIN
OLSON MOUNTAIN
DUDLEY MOUNTAIN
RUSTLER PEAK
SANTIAM PEAK
FREDENBURG BUTTE
BUTTE FALLS
MCKEE BASIN
SNOWSHOE BUTTE
BLUE ROCK
CAT HILL
LITTLE BALDY
POVERTY HILL
ESHOND MOUNTAIN
WASSON CANYON
BROPHY HILL
LONG CANYON
MOUNT MCLOUGHLIN
HEPPSIE MOUNTAIN
DOE POINT

SKY LAKES
NATIONAL FOREST
ALTA CAMPGROUND
VIOLET HILL
SOUTH LAKE CAMPGROUND
HEMLOCK LAKE CAMPGROUND
BICKNUP SHELTER
LUTHER MOUNTAIN
GARDNER PEAK
GRASS LAKE CAMPGROUND
CLIFF LAKE CAMPGROUND
IMAGINATION PEAK
RED LAKE CAMPGROUND
ISLAND LAKE CAMPGROUND
SOUTH ISLAND CAMPGROUND
SKY LAKES WILDERNESS
NORTH SQUAW TIP
FOURMILE LAKE CAMPGROUND

CHERRY PEAK
PELICAN BUTTE
ROCKY POINT
HARRIMAN LODGE
ODESSA

WINEMA
FORT KLAMATH
WINEMA NATIONAL FOREST
SEVENMILE
LOOSLEY
SEVENMILE RD
KLAMATH AGENCY
AGENCY LAKE
LOBERT JUNCTION
KLAMATH AGENCY JUNCTION

STATE PARK
SOLOMAN BUTTE
CRAWFORD BUTTE
CAVE MOUNTAIN
BRAYMILL
PINE RIDGE
WILLIAMSON RIVER
SPRAGUE RIVER
SOCHOLIS CAMPGROUND
LONE PINE
SADDLE MOUNTAIN

CHILOQUIN

62
97
140

UPPER KLAMATH LAKE

235

SWAN LAKE MOUNTAIN
EDGEWOOD MOUNTAIN
GRIZZLY BUTTE
ALGOMA
NAYLOX MOUNTAIN
SHADY PINE
BALD HILL
PLUM HILLS
HOPPER HILL
MOYINA HILL
LAKEVIEW HWY
WOCUS

338 **339**
KLAMATH FALLS
39
140

JACKSON COUNTY
SHELL ROCK BUTTE
SHALE CITY
LUCKY CANYON
POOLE HILL
LITTLE FORK BUTTE
OLD BALDY
HOWARD PRAIRIE LAKE
WILLOW POINT CAMPGROUND
DEEP HOLLOW
EDWARDS CANYON
HENRY MOUNTAIN
TOM SPRING MOUNTAIN
TABLE MOUNTAIN
EMIGRANT LAKE
GREEN SPRINGS MOUNTAIN
SUGAR PINE CAMPGROUND
ASPENKAHA CAMPGROUND
LITTLE CHINQUAPIN MOUNTAIN
HYATT LAKE
HYATT PRAIRIE
HYATT LAKE CAMPGROUND

SKY LAKES WILDERNESS
POLE BRIDGE CAMPGROUND
BEAVER DAM CAMPGROUND
CRATER MOUNTAIN
HIGH KNOB
CLOVER
BUCK PEAK
SURVEYOR MOUNTAIN
SPENCER CREEK
BUCK MOUNTAIN

GREYLOCK MOUNTAIN
DOAK MOUNTAIN
SPENCE MOUNTAIN
ASPEN LAKE
ROUND LAKE HILL
GOVERNMENT HILL
WEST KLAMATH

66 **66**
39

MOUNT VIEW
PINEHURST
LINCOLN
KEENE CREEK
PINEHURST STATE AIRPORT
GREEN SPRINGS HWY
KING COLE
GROUSE BUTTE
PARKER MOUNTAIN
MULE HILL
HAYDEN MOUNTAIN
GREEN MOUNTAIN
HOBART PEAK
JOES ROCK
SODA MOUNTAIN
ROSEBUD MOUNTAIN
GRIZZLY MOUNTAIN
PORCUPINE MOUNTAIN
MUD SPRING MOUNTAIN
GRIZZLY BUTTE
CHICKEN HILLS

KLAMATH COUNTY
CHASE MOUNTAIN
BEAR VALLEY NATIONAL WILDLIFE REFUGE
HAMAKER MOUNTAIN
CAPTAIN JACK
KENO
WORDEN
KLAMATH HILLS
STUKEL MOUNTAIN
HOSLEY

HENLEY
SPRING LAKE
FALCON HEIGHTS
MIDLAND
TINGLEY
GEM
DEHLINGER
CROSS
OCONNOR RD
OLENE
CRYSTAL SPRINGS RD
KLAMATH VALLEY

97

MERRILL

JACKSON CO OREGON
BEAVER BASIN

SISKIYOU CO CALIFORNIA
BAILEY HILL
LITTLE PILOT
IRON GATE RESERVOIR
COPCO
COPCO LAKE
DAGGETT HILL
AGER
BESWICK
HORN PEAK
HORNBROOK

SECRET SPRING MOUNTAIN
PICARD
RICHARDSON

DORRIS

INDIAN TOM LAKE
LAKE MILLER
SHEEPY LAKE
LOWER KLAMATH LAKE
STATE LINE
WHITE LAKE
SHEEPY PEAK
DORRIS

161 **161**

LOWER KLAMATH NATIONAL WILDLIFE REFUGE
BROWNELL
MAHOGANY MOUNTAIN
INLOW BUTTE
LOWER

5
786
6
3
766

HENLEY
BLACK MOUNTAIN
PARADISE CRAGGY
SISKIYOU COUNTY AIRPORT

MONTAGUE
GREGORY MOUNTAIN
SNOWDEN
HOVEY GULCH RD
TABLE ROCK
LITTLE SHASTA RD
LITTLE SHASTA
STEAMBOAT MOUNTAIN
OWLS HEAD
RABBIT

SISKIYOU COUNTY
KLAMATH NATIONAL FOREST
EAGLE ROCK
BOGUS MOUNTAIN
BLACK ROCK
IKES MOUNTAIN
WILLOW CREEK MOUNTAIN
BALL MOUNTAIN
MEISS LAKE
SCHONCHIN
TOCHOLS
MEISS LAKE RD
MCGAVIN PEAK
LAKE SAMS NECK RD
MACDOEL
MOUNT HEBRON
GOOSENEST
CEDAR MOUNTAIN
MOUNT HEBRON
HORSETHIEF BUTTE
ORR MOUNTAIN
LITTLE DEER MOUNTAIN
MILLER MOUNTAIN

97

SISKIYOU CO CALIFORNIA
KLAMATH CO OREGON

CEDAR POINT
DORRIS RD
RED ROCK RD
MOUNT DOME
MODOC NATIONAL FOREST
THREE SISTERS
BONITA BUTTE
WHITNEY BUTTE
WILD HORSE MOUNTAIN
LAVA BEDS NATIONAL MONUMENT
EAGLE NEST BUTTE
CINDER
TECHNOR
ROBISON RD
SHARP MOUNTAIN
CALIFORNIA

0   2.5   5   7.5   10   miles   1 in. = 7.5 mi.

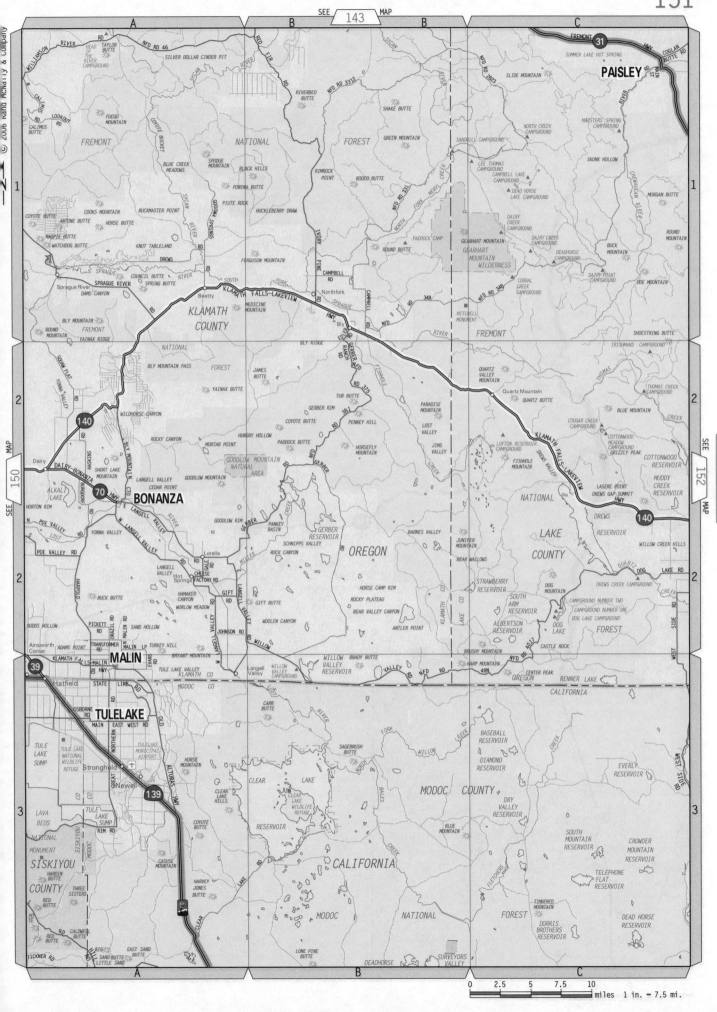

SEE 143 MAP

A | B | B | C

PAISLEY

FREMONT NATIONAL FOREST

BONANZA

MALIN

TULELAKE

OREGON

LAKE COUNTY

KLAMATH COUNTY

MODOC COUNTY

CALIFORNIA

MODOC NATIONAL FOREST

SISKIYOU COUNTY

TULE LAKE SUMP

LAVA BEDS NATIONAL MONUMENT

0   2.5   5   7.5   10 miles   1 in. = 7.5 mi.

A | B | B | C

SEE MAP 144

A | B | B | C

COGLAN BUTTE RED HOUSE RD
COGLAN BUTTES
CHEWAUCAN
LAKE ABERT
FREMONT HWY
31
395
TUCKER HILL

LAKE COUNTY OREGON

BLUEJOINT LAKE
CREEK
SNYDER CANYON
TURPIN LAKE
STONE CORRAL LAKE
ROCK RD
CAMPBELL LAKE
FLAGSTAFF LAKE
MOUNTAIN RD FRENCHGLEN

RABBIT HILLS
HOBACK CREEK
FLAGSTAFF RD
MUGWUMP LAKE
COYOTE HILLS
RABBIT
SWAMP LAKE
ANDERSON LAKE
HART
HART MOUNTAIN NATIONAL ANTELOPE REFUGE STATION
HOT SPRINGS
HOT SPRINGS CAMPGROUND
SOUTH FORK DEGARMO CANYON
WARNER PEAK
GUANO

HART MOUNTAIN NATIONAL ANTELOPE REFUGE

VALLEY FALLS
ABERT RIM HISTORICAL MARKER
ABERT RIM VIEW POINT
★
1
CREEK
HONEY CREEK
CREEK
HART RD
HART CREEK
Plush
HART LAKE
HART MOUNTAIN
61064

FREMONT NATIONAL FOREST
CAMPBELL MILL
395

HWY
NORTH WARNER VIEW POINT
★
FISK HILL
CROOK PEAK
MCDOWELL PEAK
TWELVEMILE PEAK
LIGHT PEAK
DRAKE PEAK
TWELVEMILE CUTOFF
PLUSH
IRISH HILL

PRIDAY RESERVOIR
HOBACK RD
CRUMP LAKE
HOT SPRINGS
FISHER LAKE
CALDERWOOD RESERVOIR
BIG FLAT
CAT BUTTE
MUD LAKE RESERVOIR
SHIRK LAKE
61064

2

THOMAS
GILMORE PEAK
New Idaho
WARNER
CREEK RD
THOMAS
CORNERS RD
FIVE
Five Corners
KLAMATH FALLS–LAKEVIEW
OLD PERPETUAL GEYSER
WARNER CANYON SKI AREA
MUD CREEK CAMPGROUND
SQUAW BUTTE
CAMAS CREEK
FREMONT
HWY

BLACK CAP
CO
STOCK
OAK
140
HWY
ROBERTA
DRIVE RD
AV
9TH ST
SCHMINCK MEMORIAL MUSEUM
LAKEVIEW

CRUMP RESERVOIR
CRUMP GEYSER
PELICAN LAKE
Adel
WARNER
140
COLEMAN
R

LITTLE JUNIPER MOUNTAIN
RD
BLM

SEE MAP 153

FREMONT NATIONAL FOREST
SAGE HEN BUTTE
CAMAS CREEK
DEEP CREEK FALLS
GREASER CANYON
GREASER BASIN
GREASER RESERVOIR
VALLEY
GUANO VALLEY
BARRY RESERVOIR
BEATYS BUTTE
WARNER HWY

WEST SIDE
140
TUNNEL HILL RD
WEST SIDE
DOG LAKE RD
West Side
WEST SIDE
LAKE COUNTY AIRPORT
RED PEAK
WILLOW CREEK CAMPGROUND
WILLOW POINT
BIG VALLEY
DEEP CREEK
TWENTYMILE CREEK
HORSE
COLEMAN VALLEY
RD
PLUTE RESERVOIR
LANGSLET MONUMENT
R

CRANE MOUNTAIN
DEEP CREEK CAMPGROUND
ROUND MOUNTAIN
TWENTYMILE

DIXIE CREEK
SUGAR PEAK
New Pine Creek
GOOSE LAKE REC AREA
BALD HILLS
OREGON
LAKE CO
OREGON
STATE LINE CANYON

LAKE CO
MODOC CO
New Pine Creek
HIGHGRADE
CALIFORNIA
TWIN LAKES
WASHOE CO
NEVADA
ANTELOPE FLAT
MACY FLAT
CHARLES SHELDON REFUGE

395
GOOSE LAKE
Willow Ranch
YELLOW MOUNTAIN
BIDWELL MOUNTAIN
MOUNT VIDA
MODOC COUNTY
BIDWELL CREEK
TWO BUTTES
COW HEAD LAKE
CALIFORNIA
NEVADA
COW HEAD LAKE
ANTELOPE REFUGE
CATNIP RES
RACETRACK RESERVOIR
CHARLES
CALCUTTA LAKE
CHARLES SHELDON

3
WILLOW CREEK
FANDANGO
Lake Annie
LAKE ANNIE MOUNTAIN
CALIFORNIA
Fort Bidwell
BIG MUD LAKE
VALLEY
MOSQUITO LAKE
WASHOE COUNTY
MULE MOUNTAIN
YELLOW PEAK
WILDLIFE
3

WEST SIDE
395
SUGAR HILL
FANDANGO PEAK
FORT BIDWELL INDIAN RESERVATION
LASSEN CREEK
SURPRISE
FORT BIDWELL PASS RD
FEE RESERVOIR
LITTLE MUD LAKE
ROCK FLAT
COW LAKE
WILLOW CREEK
LONG VALLEY
PAINTED POINT RANGE
REFUGE
CHARLES SHELDON ANTELOPE REFUGE
BITNER BUTTE
FISH CREEK
BADGER

WEST SIDE RD
DAVIS CREEK
Davis Creek
BUCK MOUNTAIN
GOOSE CREEK
MODOC NATIONAL FOREST
UPPER ALKALI LAKE
HOLY VALLEY
NEW YEAR LAKE
NEVADA
MIDDLE LAKE
LITTLE BASIN

BENTON MEADOW

A | B | B | C

0 2.5 5 7.5 10 miles 1 in. = 7.5 mi.

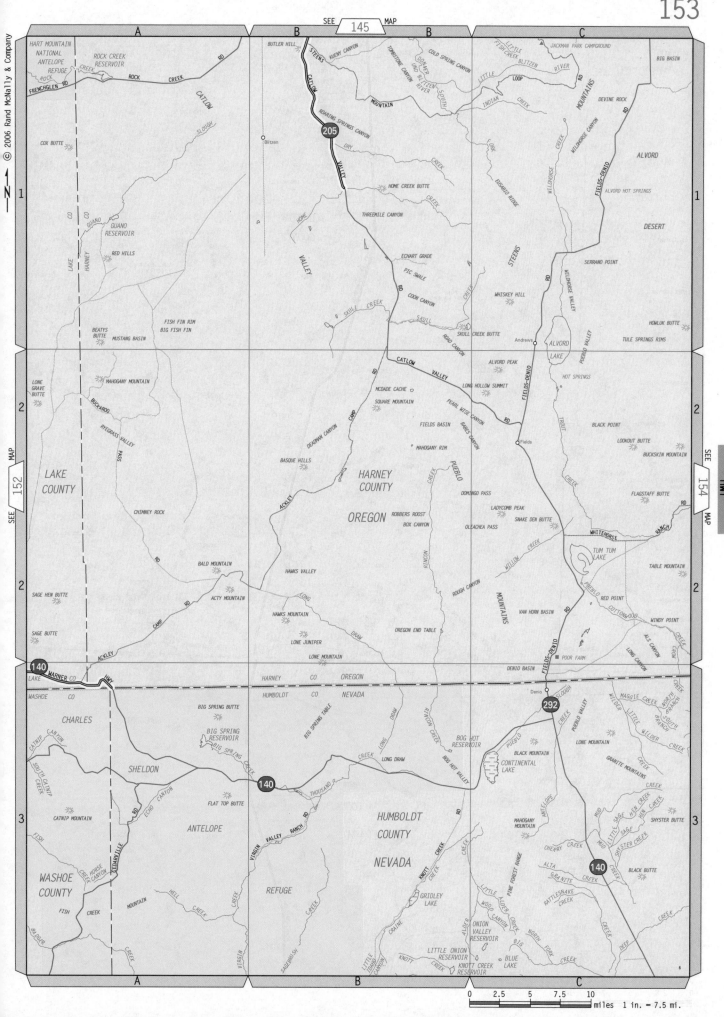

N

SEE 152 MAP

SEE 154 MAP

HWY

HART MOUNTAIN NATIONAL ANTELOPE REFUGE

FRENCHGLEN RD

ROCK CREEK RESERVOIR

ROCK CREEK RD

ROCK CREEK

CATLOW

COX BUTTE

GUANO RESERVOIR

RED HILLS

LAKE CO
HARNEY CO
GUANO CO

SLOUGH

FISH FIN RIM
BIG FISH FIN

BEATYS BUTTE
MUSTANG BASIN

LONE GRAVE BUTTE

MAHOGANY MOUNTAIN

BUCKAROO

RYEGRASS VALLEY PASS

CHIMNEY ROCK

SAGE HEN BUTTE

SAGE BUTTE

BLITZEN

HOME VALLEY

DRY VALLEY

205

BUTLER HILL

STEENS

CATLOW

KUENY CANYON

TORESTINE CANYON

ROARING SPRINGS CANYON

HOME CREEK BUTTE

THREEMILE CANYON

ECHART GRADE
PIC SWALE

COON CANYON

SKULL CREEK

CATLOW VALLEY

RD

MCDADE CACHE

SQUARE MOUNTAIN

DEADMAN CANYON

BASQUE HILLS

ACKLEY

CAMP

BALD MOUNTAIN

ACTY MOUNTAIN

HAWKS VALLEY

HAWKS MOUNTAIN

LONG DRAW RD

LONE JUNIPER

LONE MOUNTAIN

OREGON END TABLE

HARNEY COUNTY

OREGON

ROBBERS ROOST

BOX CANYON

RINCON CREEK

ROUGH CANYON

MOUNTAIN

DOMER AND BLITZEN RIVER
SOUTH

COLD SPRING CANYON

LITTLE BLITZEN RIVER

LITTLE FISH CREEK

INDIAN CREEK

F FORK

BUSARIO RIDGE

WHISKEY HILL

SKULL CREEK

ROAD CANYON

SKULL CREEK BUTTE

LONG HOLLOW SUMMIT

PEARL WISE CANYON

BABES CANYON

FIELDS BASIN

MAHOGANY RIM

CREEK

PUEBLO

DOMINGO PASS

LADYCOMB PEAK

SNAKE DEN BUTTE

OLEACHEA PASS

WILLOW CREEK

MOUNTAINS

VAN HORN BASIN

JACKMAN PARK CAMPGROUND

BIG BASIN

LOOP

DEVINE ROCK

STEENS MOUNTAINS

FIELDS-DENIO RD

ALVORD HOT SPRINGS

ALVORD

DESERT

SERRANO POINT

ALVORD PEAK

Andrews

Fields

WILDHORSE CANYON
WILDHORSE VALLEY

ALVORD LAKE

HOT SPRINGS

PUEBLO VALLEY

TROUT CREEK

HOWLUK BUTTE

TULE SPRINGS RIMS

BLACK POINT

LOOKOUT BUTTE

BUCKSKIN MOUNTAIN

FLAGSTAFF BUTTE

RD

WHITEHORSE RANCH

TUM TUM LAKE

PUEBLO RD

RED POINT

TABLE MOUNTAIN

COTTONWOOD

WINDY POINT

ALS CANYON

LONG CANYON

140

WARNER CO
LAKE HWY

HARNEY CO
OREGON

HUMBOLDT CO
NEVADA

WASHOE CO

CHARLES

CATNIP CANYON

SOUTH CATNIP CREEK

CATNIP MOUNTAIN

SHELDON

ECHO CANYON RD

CEDARVILLE

HORSE CANYON

FISH CREEK

MOUNTAIN

WASHOE COUNTY

FISH CREEK

BALCHER CREEK

VIRGIN CREEK

BIG SPRING BUTTE

BIG SPRING RESERVOIR

BIG SPRING CREEK

FLAT TOP BUTTE

ANTELOPE

REFUGE

VIRGIN VALLEY RANCH RD

THOUSAND R.

SAGEBRUSH CREEK

LITTLE IDAHO CANYON

BIG SPRING TABLE

LONG DRAW

LONG DRAW

140

LONG CREEK

RINCON CREEK

BOG HOT VALLEY

KNOTT CREEK

CRAINE CREEK

GRIDLEY LAKE

LITTLE ONION RESERVOIR

KNOTT CREEK RESERVOIR

HUMBOLDT COUNTY

NEVADA

BOG HOT RESERVOIR

CONTINENTAL LAKE

PUEBLO CREEK

BLACK MOUNTAIN

RD

ALDER CREEK

WOOD CANYON

ONION VALLEY RESERVOIR

BIG CREEK

NORTH FORK

Denio

292

DENIO BASIN

POOR FARM

FIELDS-DENIO RD

SLOUGH

MAGGIE CREEK

WILDER CREEK
NORTH BRANCH
SOUTH BRANCH
LITTLE WILDER CREEK

PUEBLO VALLEY

LONE MOUNTAIN

GRANITE MOUNTAINS

MAHOGANY MOUNTAIN

ANTELOPE CREEK

CHERRY CREEK

MUD CREEK

LITTLE SAGE HEN CREEK
SAGE HEN CREEK

SHYSTER BUTTE

SHYSTER CREEK

PINE FOREST RANGE

ALTA GRANITE CREEK

BATTLESNAKE CREEK

BLACK BUTTE

140

BLUE LAKE

DEEP CREEK

0 2.5 5 7.5 10 miles 1 in. = 7.5 mi.

© 2006 Rand McNally & Company

SEE 146 MAP

A B B C

HARNEY COUNTY

MICKEY BUTTE
MICKEY HOT SPRINGS
BIG SAND GAP
LITTLE SAND GAP
WHITEHORSE VALLEY
TWIN BUTTES
THREE MAN BUTTE

N FORK RYEGRASS CREEK RD
WILDCAT CREEK RD
BLACK HILLS
RATTLESNAKE CREEK
RED HILLS
BOWDEN
BOWDEN HILLS

95

IDAHO-OREGON-NEVADA

MALHEUR COUNTY

CORBIN CREEK
MUSTANG BUTTE
MUSTANG RESERVOIR
GRASSY MOUNTAIN
JACKIES BUTTE
WATER HOLE BUTTE
GARLOW BUTTE
UPPER HORSE CAMP RESERVOIR RD
COYOTE BUTTE
DEADMAN BUTTE
LITTLE GRASSY MOUNTAIN
RATTLESNAKE

OREGON

RED LOOKOUT BUTTE
OLD PONY EXPRESS STATION (RUINS)
RED MOUNTAIN
WHITEHORSE
WHITEHORSE BUTTE
FLAGSTAFF BUTTE
WILLOW BUTTE
HOT SPRING
ANTELOPE SPRING RD
MUD CREEK
BLUE MOUNTAIN
SCHOOLHOUSE HILL
OREGON CANYON
ECHAVE RANCH RD
POLE CREEK RD
TWIN PEAKS
OREGON CANYON
CLETO
MENDI SURI
HOT SPRING

BATTLE MOUNTAIN
JACKSON
POTOMAC RANCH RD
BATTLE CREEK
POLE CREEK
ANTELOPE
FIELD CREEK RD
LUCKY SEVEN COM. CAMP RD
POLE CREEK RD
HIGH PEAK
NOVIQUE
SUGARLOAF
RANCH RD
HORSE HILL
WEST LITTLE OWYHEE RIVER

SEE 155 MAP

SEE 153 MAP

HWY

CHALK CANYON
POLE CANYON
RED MOUNTAIN
WINDY PASS
CATLOW PEAK
GRASSY BASIN
EAST BASIN
TROUT CREEK MOUNTAINS
TROUT CREEK
LITTLE WHITEHORSE CREEK
FIFTEENMILE CREEK
RESERVOIR
MCDERMITT CREEK
TURNER RANCH RD
CHEROKEE CREEK RD
ARCHIE MYERS RANCH
DISASTER PEAK
BRETZ MINE RD
COTTONWOOD
ZIMMERMAN RANCH RD
SHERMAN FIELD
MALHEUR CO
MCDERMITT STATE AIRPORT
TENMILE
MOT SPRINGS
CORRAL CREEK
WILKINSON CREEK
FRENCHMAN CREEK
AIRPLANE RESERVOIR RD
FORT MCDERMITT INDIAN RESERVATION

OREGON
McDERMITT NEVADA

COTTONWOOD CK HARNEY CO
LINE CANYON
CORRAL CANYON
SAGE CK
DISASTER PEAK
LONG RIDGE
WASHBURN CREEK
HUMBOLDT CO
MCDERMITT CREEK
QUINN RIVER
QUINN RIVER
HUMBOLDT COUNTY
McCONNELL PEAK
HUMBOLDT
SOUTH FORK QUINN RIVER
B3
EAST FORK
NATIONAL

SOUTH FORK
HALLOWAY MOUNTAIN
KINGS RIVER
BENGIA
RODEO
HORSE CREEK RD
HOUSE CREEK RD
GRANITE CREEK
WEST FORK
CHIMA CREEK
FRANCES CREEK
RESER CREEK
LITTLE WASHBURN CREEK
WASHBURN
MEADOW CREEK
JORDAN CREEK RD
CROWLEY CREEK
POLE CREEK
ROCK CREEK
MONTANA MOUNTAINS
KINGS RIVER VALLEY
KINGS RIVER RD
QUINN RIVER
WILLOW CREEK
EAGLE CREEK
RIVER VALLEY HWY
BUCKSKIN CANYON RD
THREEMILE CREEK
SKULL CREEK
FLAT CREEK
POLE CREEK
SANTA ROSA RANGE
NORTH FORK LITTLE HUMBOLDT RIVER
BUCKSKIN MOUNTAIN
STOCKS CREEK
CABIN CREEK
MARTIN CREEK
NFD RD 531
NFD RD 96
LONG VALLEY RD
KLONDIKE CANYON
GROUNDHOG RD
NFD 529
SPRING CREEK
NFD RD 84
DEEP CREEK RD
NFD RD 471
ROUND CORRAL
SINGLE TREE STR
NFD RD 87
GRANITE PEAK
SANTA

BILK CREEK MOUNTAINS
DRY CREEK
NINEMILE RD
KINGS RIVER RD
SENTINEL ROCK
COYOTE POINT RD

HUMBOLDT COUNTY NEVADA
FOREST

95

IDAHO-OREGON-NEVADA

A B C

0 2.5 5 7.5 10   miles 1 in. = 7.5 mi.

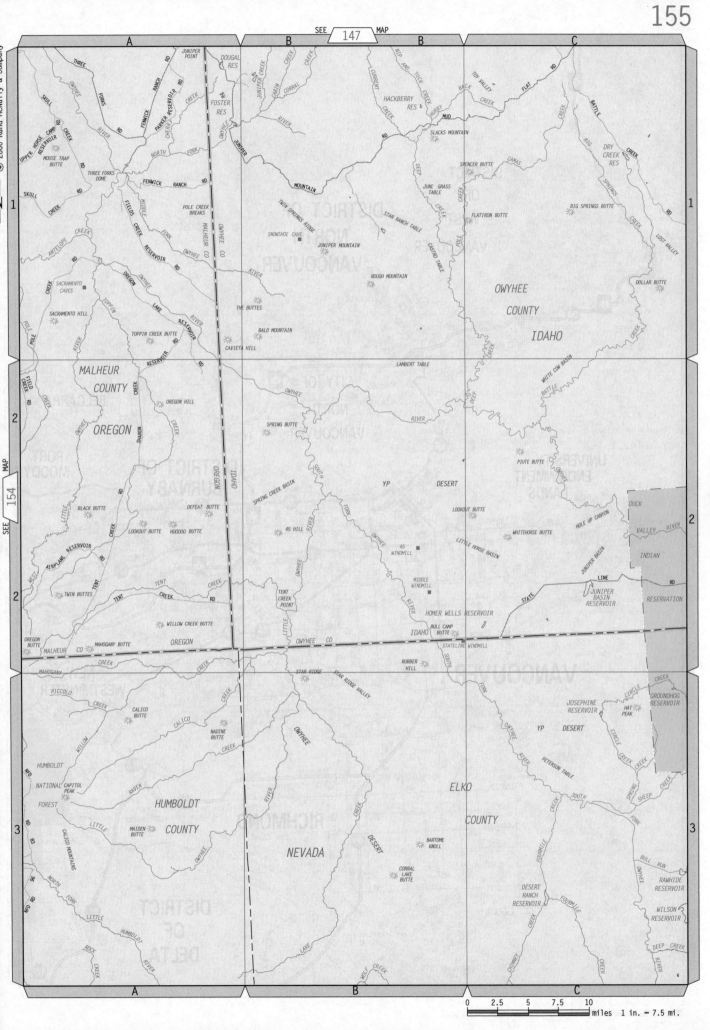

HWY

A | B | B | C

THREE

OWYHEE

SKULL

FORKS RANCH RD

FENWICK RD

JUNIPER POINT

DOUGAL RES

PARKER RESERVOIR

CHERRY RD

FOSTER RES

UPPER HORSE CAMP RESERVOIR

CREEK

MOUSE TRAP BUTTE

RIVER

RD

NORTH FORK

OWYHEE CO

MALHEUR CO

SKULL

THREE FORKS DOME

FENWICK RANCH

RD

OWYHEE RD

JUNIPER CREEK

CABIN CORRAL

NIP AND TUCK CREEK

CURRENT CREEK

TOY VALLEY

FLAT RD

1

CREEK

ANTELOPE CREEK

RD

FIELDS CREEK

MIDDLE FORK

POLE CREEK BREAKS

MALHEUR RESERVOIR

OWYHEE RIVER

JUNIPER RIVER

MOUNTAIN

TWIN SPRINGS RIDGE

HACKBERRY RES

MURRY CREEK

SLACKS MOUNTAIN

MUD

BACK CREEK

SPENCER BUTTE

CAMAS

BATTLE CREEK

BIG CREEK

DRY CREEK RES

RD

1

SACRAMENTO CAVES

OREGON

OWYHEE RD

LAKE RESERVOIR

SNOWSHOE CAVE

JUNIPER MOUNTAIN

ROUGH MOUNTAIN

STAR RANCH TABLE

JUNE GRASS TABLE

CASTRO TABLE

FLATIRON BUTTE

POLE

BIG SPRINGS BUTTE

CREEK

SPRINGS

RD

LOST VALLEY

SACRAMENTO HILL

TOPPIN

TOPPIN CREEK BUTTE

RESERVOIR RD

THE BUTTES

BALD MOUNTAIN

CAVIETA HILL

OWYHEE COUNTY

IDAHO

DOLLAR BUTTE

CREEK

POLE

FIELD CREEK RD

CREEK

MALHEUR COUNTY

OREGON

OWYHEE RD

SHARON CREEK

CREEK

OREGON HILL

SPRING BUTTE

LAMBERT TABLE

OWYHEE

RIVER

SOUTH FORK

DEEP CREEK

WHITE COM BASIN

BATTLE

2

2

LITTLE

BLACK BUTTE

CREEK RD

LOOKOUT BUTTE HOODOO BUTTE

DEFEAT BUTTE

SPRING CREEK BASIN

45 HILL

RIVER

OWYHEE RIVER

YP DESERT

LOOKOUT BUTTE

WHITEHORSE BUTTE

PIUTE BUTTE

LITTLE HORSE BASIN

HOLE UP CANYON

OWYHEE

JUNIPER BASIN

DUCK

VALLEY RIVER

INDIAN

2

AIRPLANE RESERVOIR

RD

WEST

TWIN BUTTES

TENT

TENT CREEK RD

TENT CREEK POINT

45 WINDMILL

MIDDLE WINDMILL

RIVER

HOMER WELLS RESERVOIR

STATE

LINE

JUNIPER BASIN RESERVOIR

RD

RESERVATION

OREGON BUTTE

MALHEUR CO

MAHOGANY BUTTE

OREGON

WILLOW CREEK BUTTE

LITTLE OWYHEE CO

IDAHO

BULL CAMP BUTTE

STATELINE WINDMILL

MAHOGANY

CREEK

CREEK

STAR RIDGE

STAR RIDGE VALLEY

RUBBER HILL

SOUTH

FORK

PICCOLO

WILLOW CREEK

CALICO BUTTE

CALICO CREEK

NADINE BUTTE

CREEK

OWYHEE

OWYHEE RIVER

JOSEPHINE RESERVOIR

CIRCLE CREEK

HAT PEAK

CREEK

GROUNDHOG RESERVOIR

CIRCLE CREEK

YP DESERT

PETERSON TABLE

CREEK

SPRING CREEK

SHEEP

3

HUMBOLDT NATIONAL CAPITOL PEAK

RAVEN CREEK

LITTLE OWYHEE

MAIDEN BUTTE

HUMBOLDT COUNTY

DESERT

ELKO COUNTY

SOUTH FORK

FOURMILE CREEK

FOREST

NFD RD

96 RD

CALICO MOUNTAINS

NORTH FORK

LITTLE HUMBOLDT

NEVADA

DESERT

BARTOME KNOLL

CORRAL LAKE BUTTE

DESERT RANCH RESERVOIR

FOURMILE CREEK

BULL RUN

OWYHEE

RAWHIDE RESERVOIR

WILSON RESERVOIR

3

ROCK CREEK

RIVER

LAKE CREEK

WOLF CREEK

QUINNEY CREEK

CREEK

DEEP CREEK

RIVER

A | B | B | C

0 2.5 5 7.5 10 miles 1 in. = 7.5 mi.

© 2008 Rand McNally & Company

SEE 93 MAP

A | B | C | D

METRO

DISTRICT
OF
WEST
VANCOUVER

DISTRICT OF
NORTH
VANCOUVER

CYPRESS

PROVINCIAL

PARK

LYNN

HEADWATERS

REGIONAL

PARK

PROVINCIAL

PARK

MOUNT
SEYMOUR

FISH
HATCHERY

FERRY

TRANS CANADA HWY

Horseshoe Bay

EAGLE LAKE

NELSON CANYON PARK

LARSEN BAY

Eagle Harbour

BEACON

LIGHTHOUSE PARK

Point Atkinson

CYPRESS BOWL

CAPILANO

CYPRESS FALLS PARK

BALLANTREE PARK

LAKE

CANADA

Caulfield

TRANS

RD

Dundarave

Hollyburn

QUEENS

MATHERS

MARINE DR

21ST ST

15TH ST

11TH ST

KEITH RD

Norgate

WELCH 1ST ST

13TH AV

EYREMOUNT DR

STEVENS DR

SOUTHBOROUGH DR

GREENWOOD

HIGHLAND BLVD

NANCY GREENE WY

CLIFFRIDGE AV

CAPILANO RD

EDGEMONT BLVD

DELBROOK AV

MONTROYAL BLVD

Cedardale

22ND ST

23RD ST

LONSDALE AV

GRAND BLVD

13TH

19TH ST

QUEENS RD

ERACMAR

DEMPSEY

29TH ST

Lynn Valley

LYNN

Lynn Creek

MCNAIR

VALLEY RD

HWY

CITY OF
NORTH
VANCOUVER

Keith Lynn

Lower Lonsdale

SEYMOUR

BERKLEY

Seymour

MOUNT

Deep Cove

INDIAN RIVER DR

INDIAN ARM

BELCARRA

ADMIRALTY PARK

PORT
MOODY

SEYMOUR RIVER

SEYMOUR PKWY

DOLLARTON HWY

Dollarton

CATES PARK

BETWELL BAY RD

UNIVERSITY
ENDOWMENT
LANDS

MUSEUM OF ANTHROPOLOGY

UNIV OF BRITISH COLUMBIA

Point Grey

Wreck Beach

CHANCELLOR BLVD

MARINE DR

NW MARINE DR

WESTBROOK MALL

16TH AV

10TH AV

UNIVERSITY GOLF COURSE

PACIFIC SPIRIT REGIONAL PARK

Ferguson Point

BEAVER LAKE

ENGLISH BAY

Vancouver Harbour

SEA

NELSON ST

DAVIE ST

PACIFIC ST

JERVIS ST

SEYMOUR ST

CORNWALL

4TH AV

BROADWAY

6TH AV

2ND AV

TERMINAL AV

POWELL

PRIOR

12TH AV

16TH AV

BURRARD ST

FIR ST

GRANVILLE ST

OAK ST

CAMBIE ST

MAIN ST

FRASER ST

KNIGHT ST

VICTORIA DR

NANAIMO ST

RENFREW ST

CLARK DR

COMMERCIAL DR

GRANDVIEW HWY

KINGSWAY

VANCOUVER

Shaughnessy Golf Course

IONE ISLAND

BLENHEIM ST

DUNBAR ST

CROWN ST

MARINE DR

QUADRA ST

MACDONALD ST

ARBUTUS ST

Arbutus Ridge

Kerrisdale

33RD AV

41ST AV

49TH AV

57TH AV

70TH AV

KING EDWARD AV

29TH AV

33RD AV

41ST AV

49TH AV

Marpole

57TH AV

Cedar Cottage

TROUT LAKE

Central Park

Fraser

Killarney

Fraserview

54TH AV

KERR ST

ARGYLE ST

Sunset

MARINE DR

Victoria

EARLES ST

JOYCE ST

TYNE ST

45TH AV

BURKE ST

NELSON ST

RUMBLE ST

IMPERIAL ST

PATTERSON AV

BOUNDARY RD

SMITH AV

MCKAY AV

BOND ST

Cascade Heights

MOSCROP ST

DISTRICT OF
BURNABY

Lochdale

CURTIS ST

HASTINGS ST

PARKER ST

GILMORE AV

WILLINGDON AV

DELTA AV

DOUGLAS RD

CANADA WY

DEER LAKE PARK

MUSEUM

BURNABY MTN

SIMON FRASER UNIV

UNIVERSITY DR

GAGLARDI WY

LOUGHEED HWY

BURNABY LAKE REGIONAL PARK

SPERLING AV

DUTHIE AV

BROADWAY

WINSTON ST

CARIBOO RD

GOVERNMENT RD

NEW
WESTMINSTER

10TH AVE

6TH AVE

8TH AVE

COLUMBIA ST

MCBRIDE BLVD

Queen's Park

Queensborough

Douglas College

South Westminster

Annieville

RICHMOND

LULU ISLAND

Brighouse

Thompson

South Arm

Steveston

Broadmoor

MYLORA GOLF COURSE

INTERNATIONAL BUDDHIST TEMPLE

DISTRICT OF
DELTA

GRANVILLE AV

BLUNDELL RD

FRANCIS RD

WILLIAMS RD

STEVESTON HWY

FINN RD

DYKE RD

MONCTON ST

LONDON HERITAGE FARM

GARRY POINT

GULF OF GEORGIA CANNERY NATIONAL HISTORIC SITE

BRITANNIA SHIPYARD NATIONAL HISTORIC SITE

KIRKLAND ISLAND

628

REIFEL WILDLIFE SANCTUARY

WOODWARD ISLAND

FRASER

BAYVIEW

RIVER RD

WESTMINSTER HWY

NO 1 RD

NO 2 RD

NO 3 RD

NO 4 RD

NO 5 RD

NO 6 RD

GARDEN CITY RD

SHELL RD

JACOMBS RD

GILBERT RD

RAILWAY AV

SIDAWAY RD

CITITRON WY

ALDERBRIDGE WY

BRIDGEPORT RD

VULCAN WY

CAMBIE RD

Vancouver International Airport

GRANT MCCONACHIE WY

SWISHWASH ISLAND

SEA ISLAND

STURGEON BANK

STRAIT
OF
GEORGIA

RICHMOND FRWY

WESTMINSTER HWY

FRASER RIVER

ANNACIS ISLAND

ANNACIS CHANNEL

DEAS ISLAND REGIONAL PARK

TILBURY ISLAND

GRAVESEND REACH

DEAS ISLAND

River Road

96TH AV

92ND AV

88TH AV

84TH AV

80TH AV

72ND AV

64TH AV

SUNSHINE HILLS GOLF COURSE

KITTSON PKWY

NORDEL WY

WESTVIEW DR

BOYD ST

CLIVEDEN AV

SCOTT RD

112

116

120

104

miles 1 in. = 2.5 mi.

0 1 2 3 4

SEE 101 MAP

SEE 157 MAP

SEE 93 MAP

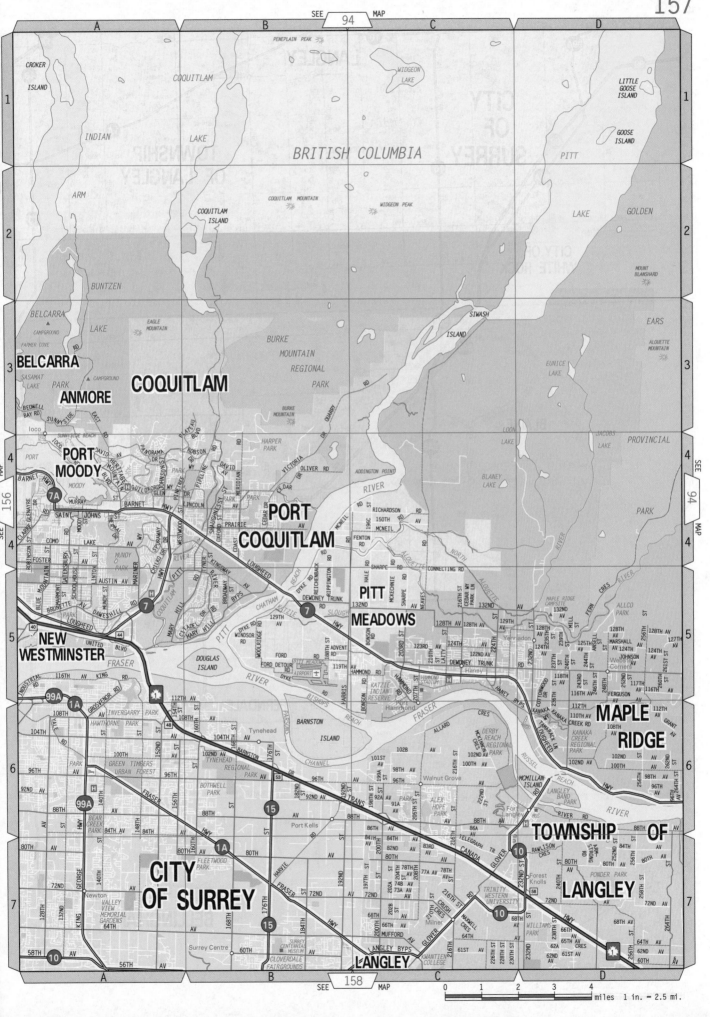

METRO

A B C D

CROKER
ISLAND

LITTLE
GOOSE
ISLAND

COQUITLAM

PENEPLAIN PEAK

WIDGEON
LAKE

CITY
OF
SURREY

GOOSE
ISLAND

INDIAN

LAKE

BRITISH COLUMBIA

PITT

LAKE

GOLDEN

ARM

COQUITLAM MOUNTAIN

WIDGEON PEAK

MOUNT
BLANSHARD

BUNTZEN

SIWASH
ISLAND

EARS

BELCARRA
CAMPGROUND
FARMER COVE

LAKE

EAGLE
MOUNTAIN

BURKE
MOUNTAIN
REGIONAL
PARK

EUNICE
LAKE

ALOUETTE
MOUNTAIN

JACOBS
LAKE

PROVINCIAL

SASAMAT
LAKE
PARK
BEDWELL
BAY RD

CAMPGROUND

BURKE
MOUNTAIN

LOON
LAKE

BELCARRA

ANMORE

COQUITLAM

IOCO

PARK

PORT
MOODY

HARPER
PARK

**PORT
MOODY**

DAVID
HERITAGE

PANORAMA DR

ROBSON DR

DAVID
AV

VICTORIA DR

OLIVER RD

ADDINGTON POINT

RIVER

BLANEY
LAKE

PARK

BARNET HWY

MURRAY ST

BARNET

SAINT JOHNS ST

MOODY ST

GUILDFORD

PINETREE

LINCOLN AV

**PORT
COQUITLAM**

CEDAR
AV

MCNEIL

RICHARDSON
150TH
AV

MCNEIL
196C

COMO

LAKE AV

SPRAYWAY

PRAIRIE

FENTON
RD

132ND

HALE

SHARPE

MCKECHNIE
SHARPE

NEAVES

CONNECTING RD

NORTH

MAPLE RIDGE
CAMPSITE

ALLCO
PARK

ROBINSON ST
FOSTER AV

GATENSBURY

MUNDY
PARK

MARINER

CLARKE DR

PITT

TYNEK

KINGSWAY

CHATHAM ST

**PITT
MEADOWS**
132ND ST

128TH
128TH

129TH

128TH ST

MARSHALL

128TH
127TH ST

124TH ST

FERN
CRES

128TH
AV

**NEW
WESTMINSTER**

BLUE MOUNTAIN

BRUNETTE AV

DAWESHILL

MARY
HILL

CLYADE DR
MARY HILL RD

DYKE RD
WINDSOR
RD

129TH
AV

188TH ST

ADVENT RD

DEWDNEY
TRUNK

203RD
RD

123RD

124TH
AV

237TH
ST

116TH
AV

239TH
ST

235TH ST

125TH ST
ANSELL

JOHNSON

118TH
AV

124TH ST

Webster
Corners

116TH AV

FRASER

MOOLRIDGE
RD

FORD

DOUGLAS
ISLAND

FORD DETOUR
DYKE

119TH

HAMMOND RD

122ND
AV

DEWDNEY
TRUNK

Haney

243RD
ST

117TH
AV

116TH AV

252ND
ST

260TH
ST

261ST ST

Ferguson

**MAPLE
RIDGE**

112TH
AV

INDUSTRIAL
116TH AV

KING

99A

1A

GROSVENOR RD

INVERGARRY
PARK

HAWTHORNE
PARK

112TH AV

154TH ST

48

160TH ST

104TH

112TH AV

PITT
MEADOWS
AIRPORT

HARRIS

BISHOPS

BONSON

HAMMOND RD

KATZIE
INDIAN
RESERVE

Port
Hammond

HAMMOND
STADIUM

207TH ST

H

FRASER

DERBY
REACH
REGIONAL
PARK

MCKINNON
CRES

ALLARD

102ND AV

CRES

KANAKA
CREEK RD

TIMBERLINE
TOUCHEED

KANAKA
CREEK
REGIONAL
PARK

COTTONWOOD
DR

108TH
AV

GRANT

112TH AV

110TH AV

104TH

PARK

FRASER HWY

116TH

152ND ST

140TH

100TH

GREEN TIMBERS
URBAN FOREST

102ND AV
BARNSTON

TYNEHEAD
REGIONAL
PARK

176TH ST

BARNSTON
ISLAND

96TH AV

101ST
ST

98TH AV

100TH AV

96TH

Walnut Grove

222ND

MCMILLAN
ISLAND

RUSSEL

REACH

RIVER

102ND AV
100TH

102B

256TH

98TH AV
96TH AV

264TH ST

6

99A

BEAR
CREEK
PARK

148TH ST

88TH AV

84TH AV

88TH

156TH

FRASER HWY

182ND ST

92ND AV

15

192ND

TRANS

86TH AV

198TH ST

199A

91A

205TH ST

PARK
AV

92A

ALEX
HOPE
PARK

Fort
Langley

216TH
ST

H

LANGLEY
BAND
PARK

Langley
bus

RIVER

88TH AV

TOWNSHIP OF

256TH

88TH AV

92ND

80TH AV

H

140TH

GEORGE

KING

1A

FLEETWOOD
PARK

80TH AV

HARVIE

FRASER HWY

Port Kells

86TH AV

84TH AV
84TH AV

200TH ST

80TH AV
82ND

197TH ST

202A

78TH
204TH ST

83RD
74B

78TH AV

77A
73A

216TH ST

CANADA

GLOVER RD

TELEGRAPH TR

86A

10

RAWLISON
CRES

58

Forest
Knolls

80TH
AV

STRONG
RD

252ND

80TH AV

PONDER PARK

LANGLEY

88TH AV

80TH AV

72ND

**CITY
OF SURREY**

128TH ST

132ND

King

64TH

Newton

VALLEY
VIEW
MEMORIAL
GARDENS

168TH ST

176TH ST

184TH

72ND AV

FRASER HWY

192ND

68TH AV

72ND

202B

197TH ST

204TH ST

211TH CRES

Milner

216TH CRES

MAXWELL
CRES

64TH

TRINITY
WESTERN
UNIVERSITY

10

68TH

226TH ST

230TH ST

232ND

WILLIAMS
PARK

238TH ST

62A

61ST AV

68TH AV

64TH AV

62ND
AV

60TH

58TH AV

10

56TH
AV

LANGLEY

60TH

Surrey Centre

Surrey
Centennial
Museum

CLOVERDALE
FAIRGROUNDS

LANGLEY BYPS

Kwantlen
College

KWANTLEN
COLLEGE

216TH

GLOVER

61ST AV

240TH

256TH

AV

0 1 2 3 4 miles 1 in. = 2.5 mi.

SEE 156 MAP

SEE 94 MAP

SEE MAP 157

LANGLEY

CITY OF SURREY

BRITISH COLUMBIA

TOWNSHIP OF LANGLEY

CITY OF WHITE ROCK

Crescent Beach

South Surrey

Athletic Park

Ocean Park

BOUNDARY BAY

Serpentine Fen Bird Sanctuary

KOA Vancouver

MUD BAY

Murrayville

Kwantien College

Langley Airport

Hopington

County Line

Cloverdale

Peace Arch

US Customs Station

Campbell River Regional Park

BRITISH COLUMBIA — WASHINGTON

WHATCOM CO — CANADA / USA

BLAINE

Blaine Municipal Airport

Semiahmoo Spit

Tongue Point

Drayton Harbor

Semiahmoo Golf & Country Club

WHATCOM COUNTY

LYNDEN

WASHINGTON

Birch Point

Cottonwood Bay

Birch Bay

BIRCH BAY STATE PARK

Point Whitehorn

Cherry Point

Lake Terrell

Holman Hill

Aldergrove

FERNDALE

Willeys Lake

Custer

STRAIT OF GEORGIA

Mountain View

Silver Reef Casino

Northwest Indian College

Neptune Beach

LUMMI INDIAN RESERVATION

LUMMI BAY

Sandy Point

Fish Point

Bellingham International Airport

North Bellingham Golf Course

Marietta

BELLINGHAM

BELLINGHAM BAY

ROSARIO STRAIT

WHATCOM CO / SAN JUAN CO

SEE MAP 101

SEE MAP 102

METRO

SEE MAP 160

© 2006 Rand McNally & Company

miles 1 in. = 2.5 mi.

0 1 2 3 4

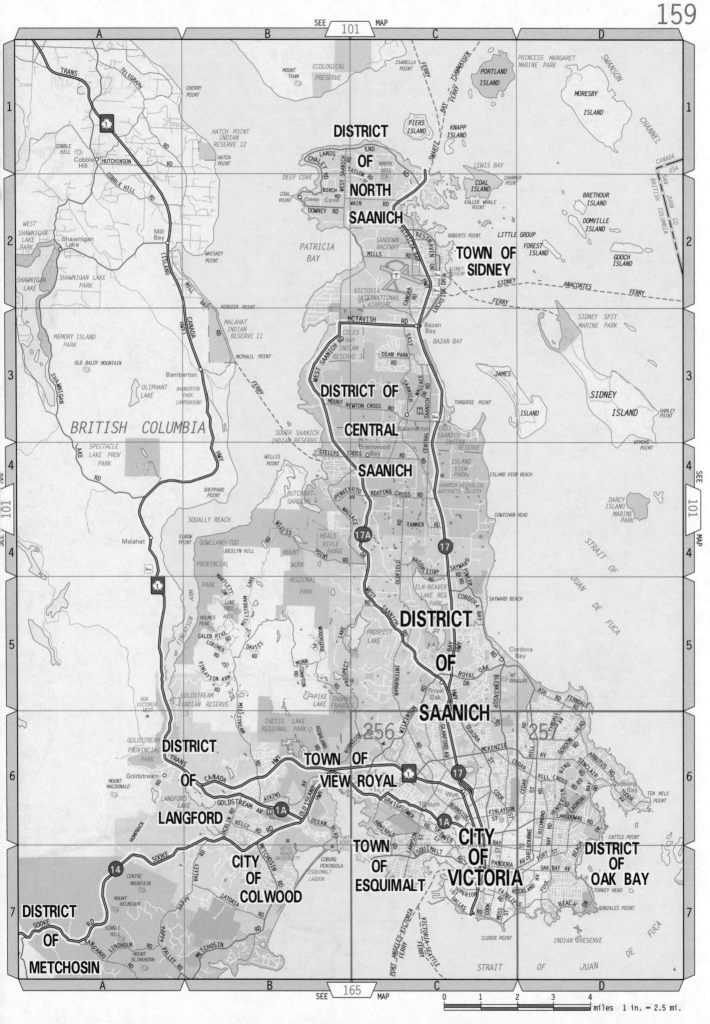

miles 1 in. = 2.5 mi.

SEE MAP 158

A | B | C | D

258

BELLINGHAM

METRO

SEE MAP 101

SEE MAP 161

MATIA ISLAND
MATIA ISLAND STATE PARK
ROLFE COVE
EAGLE POINT

ROSARIO STRAIT

BUCK MOUNTAIN
RACCOON POINT

SAN JUAN COUNTY
MORAN
MOUNT CONSTITUTION
HIDDEN RIDGE
MOUNT PICKETT
STATE
LITTLE SUMMIT
MOUNTAIN LAKE
ORCAS ISLAND
PARK
CASCADE LAKE
ENTRANCE MOUNTAIN
OLGA
OLGA RD
OLGA TO PT
RUSTIC FALLS
OBSTRUCTION PASS RD
BUCK BAY
DIAMOND POINT
EAST SOUND
BROWN ROCK
DEER POINT

LAWRENCE POINT
SEA ACRES RD
KANGAROO POINT
NORTH PEAPOD
PEAPOD ROCKS
SOUTH PEAPOD
DOE BAY
DOE ISLAND
DOE ISLAND STATE MARINE PARK
BOND MILL RD
HOMESTEAD RD

POINT MIGLEY
FERN POINT
SHORE DR
N NUGENT
BLIZZARD RD
TUTTLE LN
LANE SPIT
FISHERMANS COVE
LEGOE
LEGOE BAY
LUMMI ISLAND
BAY RD
LOVERS BLUFF
S NUGENT
SEACREST
SUNRISE RD
HALE
PASSAGE
LUMMI ROCKS
DEVILS SLIDE

WEST BEACH
SMOKEHOUSE RD
HATTON
LUMMI SHORE
LUMMI INDIAN
RESERVATION
LUMMI POINT
LUMMI VIEW DR
PORTAGE POINT
BUNSTEAD SPIT
NEONTAWANTA BEACH
PORTAGE BAY
PORTAGE ISLAND
SUNRISE COVE
ECHO POINT

BRANT ISLAND
HERMOSA BEACH
BRANT POINT
BELLINGHAM

WHATCOM COUNTY
SMUGGLERS COVE
INATI BAY
LUMMI PEAK
REIL HARBOR
LUMMI ISLAND
THREE ROCKS
CARTER POINT
ELIZA ISLAND
WILDCAT COVE
GOVERNORS POINT
PLEASANT BAY
CHUCKANUT BAY
CHUCKANUT ISLAND
LARRABEE STATE PARK
CHUCKANUT
11

BELLINGHAM BAY

SAMISH BAY

WHATCOM CO
SKAGIT CO

CLARK ISLAND
CLARK ISLAND STATE MARINE PARK
BARNES ISLAND
LONE TREE ISLAND
LITTLE SISTER

SAN JUAN CO
SKAGIT CO
STRAIT
ROSARIO STRAIT

SINCLAIR ISLAND
TOWHEAD ISLAND
SINCLAIR ISLAND LIGHT
VENDOVI ISLAND
VITI ROCKS

EAGLE CLIFF
CONE ISLANDS
CONE ISLANDS STATE PARK
EAGLE HARBOR
TIDE POINT
CYPRESS ISLAND
CYPRESS ISLAND LIGHT
STRAWBERRY ISLAND
STRAWBERRY BAY
DEEPWATER BAY
SECRET HARBOR
OLIVINE HILL
REEF POINT
BLACK ROCK

OBSTRUCTION ISLAND
HORSESHOE LAKE
BLAKELY PEAK
BLAKELY
SPENCER LAKE
ISLAND
BALD BLUFF
THATCHER BAY
LEO REEF LIGHT
THATCHER ISLAND

CLARK POINT
JACK ISLAND
INDIAN VILLAGE
GUEMES ISLAND
SHORE DR
GUEMES ISLAND
BOAT HARBOR
EDENS RD
S SHORE DR
HOLIDAY
HUCKLEBERRY
CHANNEL VIEW BLVD
GUEMES
GUEMES CHANNEL
KELLYS POINT
DEADMAN BAY
COOKS COVE
SOUTHEAST POINT

WILLIAM POINT
SAMISH ISLAND
HALLORAN RD
FISH POINT
SCOTTS POINT
SAMISH ISLAND

PADILLA
SADDLEBAG ISLAND
SADDLEBAG ISLAND STATE PARK
DOT ISLAND
HAT ISLAND
MARCH POINT LIGHT

PADILLA BAY

VIEW EDISON RD

FROST ISLAND
LOPEZ ISLAND
THATCHER PASS
THATCHER PASS RD
FAULTLEROY POINT
SYLVAN COVE
SAN ELMO
DAVIS BAY
DECATUR ISLAND
DECATUR
BOWERS BLVD
DECATUR HEAD
JAMES ISLAND STATE PARK
BELLE ROCK LIGHT
CENTER ISLAND
WHITE CLIFF
BIRD ROCKS
READS BAY
TRUMP ISLAND
BRIGANTINE BAY

STATE TOLL
FERRY
259
SHANNON POINT
SHIP HARBOR
SUNSET BEACH
GREEN POINT
WASHINGTON PARK
20
OAKES AV
FIDALGO HEAD
SHORT BAY
FLOUNDER BAY
BURROWS ISLAND LIGHTHOUSE
BURROWS ISLAND
ALICE BIGHT
YOUNG ISLAND
BURROWS BAY
ALLEN ISLAND
PEARTREE BAY
WILLIAMSON ROCKS
GUEMES
CRANBERRY LAKE
ANACORTES
COMMERCIAL AV
41ST
HAVEMOST
FIDALGO
A AV
R AV
MARINE DR
CAP SANTE
MARCH POINT
N TEXAS RD
MARCH POINT RD
PERSONS RD
JOSH WILSON RD
BAY VIEW
FIDALGO BAY

LOPEZ PASS
SPERRY POINT
JASPER BAY
HUNTER BAY
SHOAL BIGHT
SPERRY RD
ELIZA DR
CAPE SAINT MARY
MUD BAY
MUD BAY RD
COLE RD
ALECK BAY RD
CHADWICK HILL
LOPEZ ISLAND
TELEGRAPH BAY
CAPE SAINT MARY RD
ALECK ROCKS
POINT COLVILLE
COLVILLE ISLAND
DAVIDSON ROCK LIGHT

ROSARIO
WASHINGTON

ANACORTES
FIDALGO ISLAND
MOUNT ERIE PARK
WHISTLE LAKE
HEART LAKE
LAKE ERIE
MOUNT ERIE
ALEXANDER BEACH
MARINE DR
ROSARIO RD
SHARPE RD
BIZ POINT
BIZ POINT RD
SARES HEAD
ROSARIO BEACH
DECEPTION PASS STATE PARK
GINNETT
GINNETT HILL
CAMPBELL LAKE
CAMPBELL LAKE RD
SIMILK BEACH
DEWEY
4TH ST
NORTHWEST ISLAND
DECEPTION ISLAND
PASS ISLAND
MACS COVE
GOOSE ROCK
BEN URE ISLAND
BOWMAN BAY
YOKEKO
YOKEKO POINT
DECEPTION
HOYPUS POINT
HOYPUS HILL
DECEPTION PASS STATE PARK
LANG BAY
SKAGIT BAY

CHRISTIANSON RD
STEVENSON RD
SATTERLEE RD
GIBRALTAR RD
SIMILK BAY
TURNERS BAY
MEMORIAL HWY
20
WHITMARSH
WHITNEY
SWINOMISH
RESERVATION
SWINOMISH CHANNEL
SNEE-OOSH RD
FLAGSTAFF LN
SNEE OOSH
SWINOMISH INDIAN RESERVATION
SWINOMISH VILLAGE
KIKET ISLAND
KIKET BAY
SKAGIT ISLAND
INDIAN RD
LA CONNER RD
DOWNEY RD
VIEW EDISON BAY RD

SKAGIT CO
ISLAND CO

0 1 2 3 4 miles   1 in. = 2.5 mi.

BELLINGHAM

SEDRO-WOOLLEY

BURLINGTON

MOUNT VERNON

WHATCOM COUNTY

SKAGIT COUNTY

WASHINGTON

WHATCOM CO / SKAGIT CO

METRO

SEE 160 MAP

SEE 102 MAP

SEE 168 MAP

SEE 258 MAP

Stewart Mountain
Hard Scrabble Falls
Strand Rd
Homesteader Rd
Blue Mountain
Mosquito Lake
Acme
Blue Mountain
Lookout Mountain
South Bay
Park
Wickersham
Eddys Mountain
Nooksack River
Chuckanut Mountain
Larrabee State Park
Cain Lake
Anderson Mountain
Dogfish Point
Pigeon Point
Windy Point
Alger
Prairie
Thornwood
Lyman Hill
Lyman Pass
Blanchard
Samish Bay
Bay View
Edison
Edison Station
Bow
Skagit Valley Casino
Double Creek Ln
Park Ridge Ln
Hoogdal
Avalon Golf Club
Butler Hill
Bridgewater
Bacus Rd
Bacus Hill
Cookedale
Lyman Hamilton
Skagit River
KOA Burlington
Sterling
Clear Lake
Barney Lake
Beaver Lake
Haystack Mountain
Cultus Mountain
Big Rock
Fredonia
Avon
Skagit Regional Bay View Airport
Happy Valley
Geneva
Sudden Valley
Reveille Island
Lake Louise
Lake Whatcom
Lake Padden

MOUNT VERNON-BIG LAKE RD

miles 1 in. = 2.5 mi.
0 1 2 3 4

METRO

SEE 100 MAP

| A | B | C | D |

1

WAATCH POINT

HOBUCK BEACH

MAKAH

BAHOBOHOSH POINT

MAKAH BAY

WAATCH PEAK

INDIAN

SOOES BEACH

SHIPWRECK POINT

112

CHITO BEACH

CHEEKA PEAK

ANDERSON POINT

MAKAH PEAKS

RESERVATION

PORTAGE HEAD

MAKAH NATIONAL SALMON HATCHERY

SOOES

SOOES PEAK

2

MAIN LINE

RD

CLALLAM

COUNTY

FLATTERY

WASHBURN HILL

RIVER

7000

3

ROCKS

SEKIU MOUNTAIN

NATIONAL

SNAG PEAK

RD

RIVER

HOKO FALLS

4

BODELTEH ISLANDS

FLATTERY ROCKS

WASHINGTON

FR.D

RD

TSKAWAHYAH ISLAND

OZETTE INDIAN RESERVATION

1400

STOLZENBERG MOUNTAIN

OZETTE

HOKO

OZETTE ISLAND

OLYMPIC

WEDDING ROCKS

OZETTE CAMPGROUND

HOKO

SEE 100 MAP

SEE 163 MAP

BLOOMS BAY

WHITE ROCK

NORTH END

WILDLIFE

SAND POINT

DEER BAY

DEER POINT

ERICKSONS BAY CAMPGROUND

OZETTE

5

NATIONAL

UMBRELLA BAY

JERSTED POINT

DICKEY LAKE

REFUGE

ERICKSONS BAY

SHAFERS POINT

ROCKY POINT

SWAN BAY

OZETTE

GARDEN ISLAND

YELLOW BANKS

BOOT BAY

PREACHERS POINT

LAKE

MAINLINE

6

PARK

CEMETERY POINT

ALLENS BAY

TIVOLI ISLAND

RD

WEST

FORK

BABY ISLAND

KAYOSTIA BEACH

SOUTH END

FORK

7

QUILLAYUTE

NEEDLES

NATIONAL

RIVER

WILDLIFE

CARROLL ISLAND

REFUGE

EAST

JAGGED ISLAND

DICKEY

DICKEY

RIVER

GUNDERSON MOUNTAIN

SEA LION ROCK

| A | B | C | D |

0 1 2 3 4 miles 1 in. = 2.5 mi.

SEE 169 MAP

SEE 100 MAP

A · B · C · D

1

BRITISH COLUMBIA

CLALLAM CO

BRITISH COLUMBIA

WASHINGTON

CANADA

USA

2

STRAIT OF JUAN DE FUCA

EAGLE POINT

Hoko

112

SEKIU AIRPORT

Sekiu

CLALLAM BAY

MIDDLE POINT

SLIP POINT

SLIP POINT LIGHTHOUSE

Clallam Bay

RIVER

RD

3

HOKO

HOKO OZETTE

CLALLAM COUNTY

BLUE CANYON

CLALLAM RIVER CAMPGROUND

PILLAR POINT

WASHINGTON

112

4

SEE 164 MAP

BUTLER COVE

112

HERMAN FALLS

ELLIS MOUNTAIN

RD

GIBSON FARM

RIVER

BURNT MOUNTAIN

113

NFD RD 3117

NFD RD 3116

NFD RD 3031

NFD RD 3029

5

BEAR CREEK FALLS

NELSON HILL

HOKO

MOUNTAIN

OLYMPIC

NFD RD 3016

NFD RD 3031

NFD RD 3028

DICKEY HOKO SUMMIT

DEADMANS HILL

BEAVER FALLS

NFD RD 30

NFD RD 3067

3040

TYEE HILL

BURNT

NATIONAL

NFD

RD

DICKEY EAST RIVER FORK

NFD RD 3007

NFD RD 3040

NFD RD 3069

6

BOAT LAUNCH

LAKE PLEASANT RD

BEAVER HILL

Sappho

BEAR CREEK CAMPGROUND

NFD RD 3041

KLAHOWA CAMPGROUND

Beaver

LAKE PLEASANT RD

LAKE PLEASANT

E

CLARK

RD

RIVER

101

SOL

DUC

RIVER

PAYEL

RD

SOL DUC SALMON HATCHERY

SUL

DUC

EAGLE CREEK RANCH

RD

NFD RD 2929

101

WHEELER RD

EAGLE POINT

2902

NFD RD 2930

VALLEY

RD

FOREST

NFD RD 29

NFD RD 2929

NFD RD 2933

2903

BIGLER MOUNTAIN

NFD RD 2922

NFD RD

7

NFD

RD

SCHUTZ PASS

NFD RD 2923

29

NFD RD 2978

CALAWAH RIDGE

NFD RD 2937

SOL DUC VALLEY

SEE 108 MAP

A · B · C · D

0 1 2 3 4 miles 1 in. = 2.5 mi.

METRO

SEE 101 MAP
SEE 163 MAP
SEE 165 MAP
SEE 109 MAP

A   B   C   D

1   2   3   4   5   6   7

14

COAST

KEMP LAKE RD

WEST

SOOKE INDIAN RESERVE 2

SOOKE BAY

GRANT RD

WIFFIN SPIT RD

SOOKE HARBOR

East Sooke

EAST SOOKE RD

SOOKE BASIN

BRITISH COLUMBIA

EAST SOOKE REGIONAL PARK

STRAIT OF

CLALLAM CO

BRITISH COLUMBIA

WASHINGTON

CANADA

USA

JUAN DE FUCA

TREE BLUFF

LOW POINT

AGATE BAY

TONGUE POINT

SALT CREEK CAMPGROUND

SALT CREEK RECREATION AREA

STRIPED PEAK

LYRE RIVER RD

LYRE RIVER CAMPGROUND

REYNOLD RD

FARRINGTON RD

SCHMITT RD

CRESCENT BEACH RD

CAMP

HAYDEN

SEAGULL DR

FRESHWATER BAY BOAT LAUNCH RAMP

FRESHWATER BAY RD

112

CLALLAM COUNTY

WASHINGTON

GOSSETT RD

Disque

RD

Joyce

PIEDMONT RD

MILLER RD

BISHOP RD

DREPSEN RD

Ramapo

GRAUL RD

DURRWACHTER RD

WASANKARI RD

RD

PIEDMONT RD

SPRUCE TRAIL RD

Piedmont

SARATOGA POINT

HARRIGAN POINT

DEVIL POINT

PYRAMID MOUNTAIN

EAST BEACH

EAST BEACH RD

OLYMPIC

Maple Grove

LAKE SUTHERLAND

EDEN VALLEY

RD

NFD RD 30

NFD RD 3040

OLYMPIC

NFD RD 3068

Fairholm

CAMP

DAVID

JR RD

OLYMPIC

Fairholm Campground

EAGLE POINT

LAKE CRESCENT

BARNES POINT

LAPOEL POINT

MAPLE POINT

HWY

SLEDGE HAMMER POINT

101

MARYMERE FALLS

BARNES

CREEK

Snug Harbor

SOUTH SHORE RD

OLYMPIC NATIONAL FOREST

BALDY RIDGE

NATIONAL PARK

NFD RD 2946

SOL DUC RIVER

SOURDOUGH MOUNTAIN

AURORA PEAK

HWY

0 1 2 3 4 miles 1 in. = 2.5 mi.

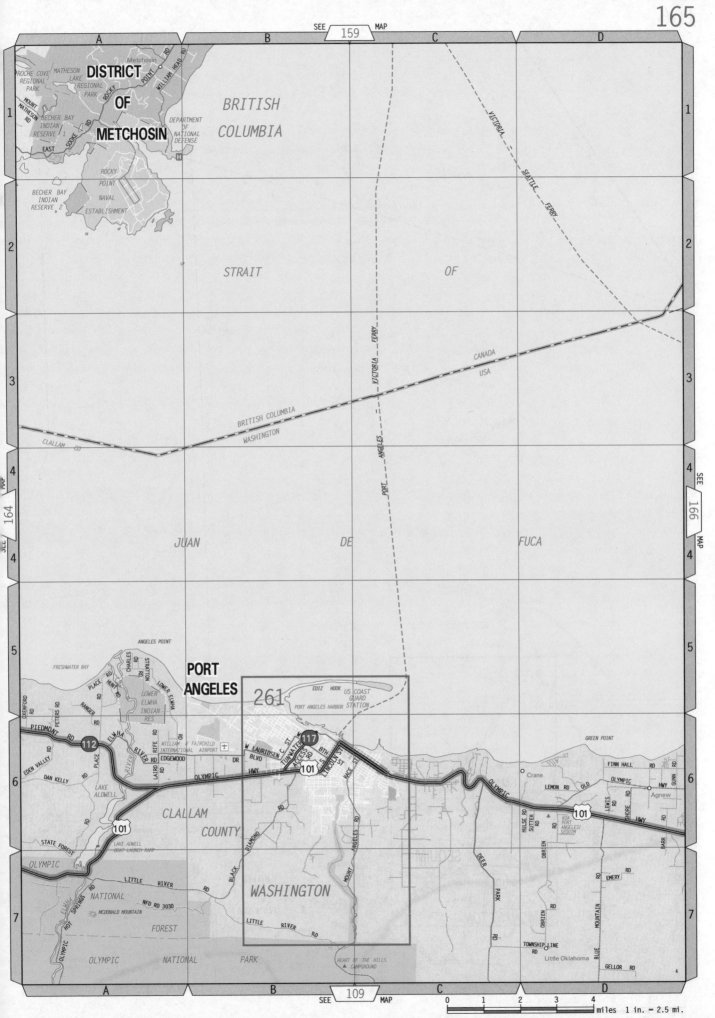

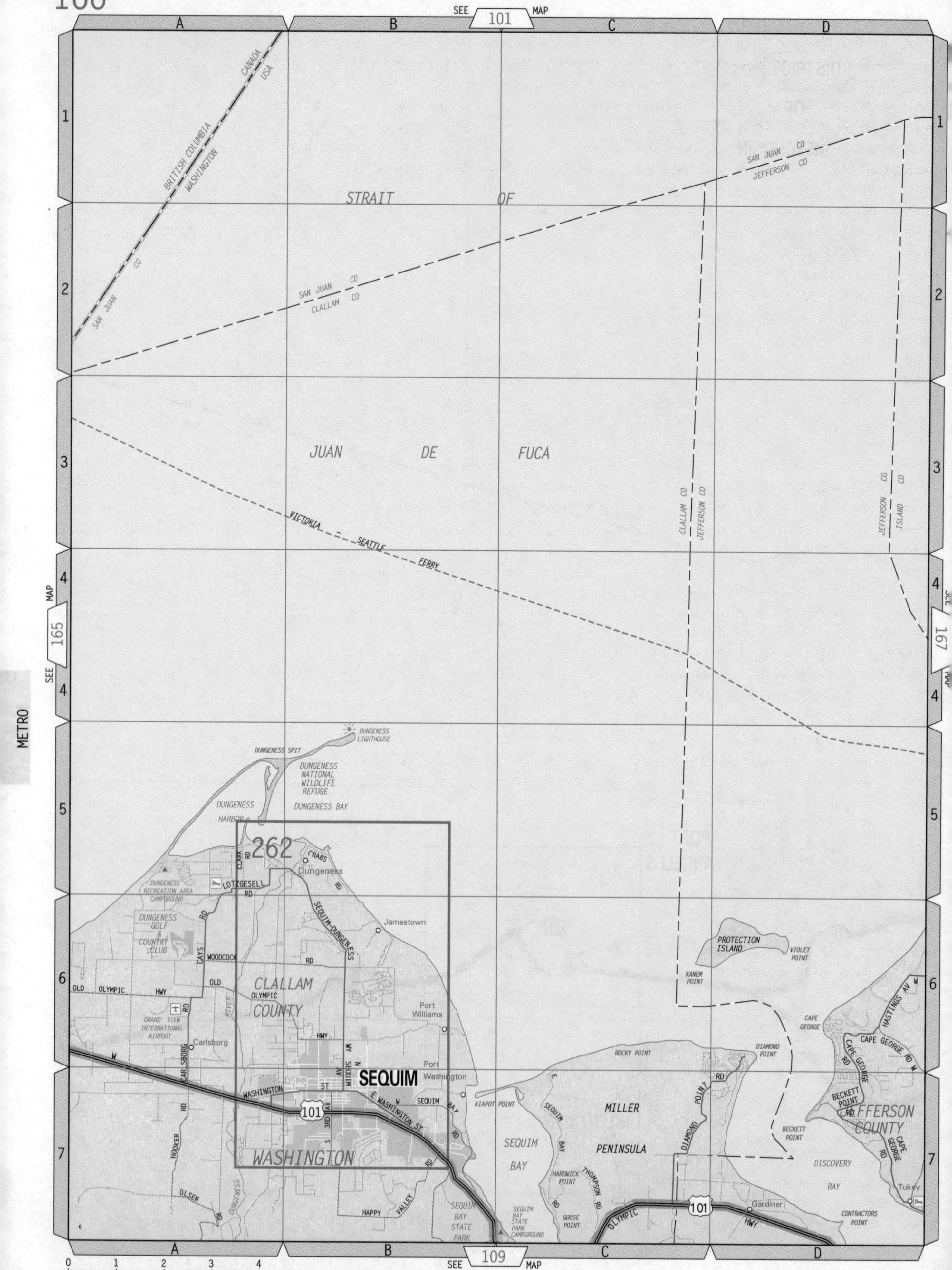

SEE 101 MAP

A | B | C | D

BRITISH COLUMBIA
CANADA
USA
WASHINGTON

SAN JUAN CO

STRAIT OF

SAN JUAN CO
JEFFERSON CO

1

SAN JUAN CO
CLALLAM CO

2

JUAN DE FUCA

CLALLAM CO
JEFFERSON CO

JEFFERSON CO
ISLAND CO

3

VICTORIA — SEATTLE FERRY

SEE 165 MAP

METRO

4

SLC 167 HWY

DUNGENESS LIGHTHOUSE
DUNGENESS SPIT
DUNGENESS NATIONAL WILDLIFE REFUGE
DUNGENESS BAY
DUNGENESS HARBOR

5

262
CLARK RD
CRABS
Dungeness
SEQUIM-DUNGENESS RD
LOTZGESELL RD
DUNGENESS RECREATION AREA CAMPGROUND
DUNGENESS GOLF & COUNTRY CLUB
CAYS
WOODCOCK
RD
Jamestown

PROTECTION ISLAND
VIOLET POINT

6

OLD OLYMPIC HWY
CLALLAM COUNTY
OLD OLYMPIC HWY
RIVER
CARLSBORG RD
GRAND VIEW INTERNATIONAL AIRPORT
Carlsborg
Port Williams
KANEM POINT

CAPE GEORGE
DIAMOND POINT
HASTINGS AV W
CAPE GEORGE RD

SEQUIM
S 3RD AV
Port Washington
E WASHINGTON ST
W SEQUIM BAY
KIAPOT POINT
ROCKY POINT
DIAMOND POINT RD
CAPE GEORGE RD
BECKETT POINT RD
JEFFERSON COUNTY

WASHINGTON
HOOKER RD
DUNGENESS RD
SEQUIM BAY
SEQUIM BAY
MILLER PENINSULA
DIAMOND POINT RD
BECKETT POINT
CAPE GEORGE RD
DISCOVERY BAY
Tukey

7

OLSEN
HAPPY VALLEY
SEQUIM BAY STATE PARK
SEQUIM BAY STATE PARK CAMPGROUND
HARDWICK POINT
THOMPSON RD
GOOSE POINT
OLYMPIC HWY
101
Gardiner
CONTRACTORS POINT

SEE 109 MAP

0 1 2 3 4 miles   1 in. = 2.5 mi.

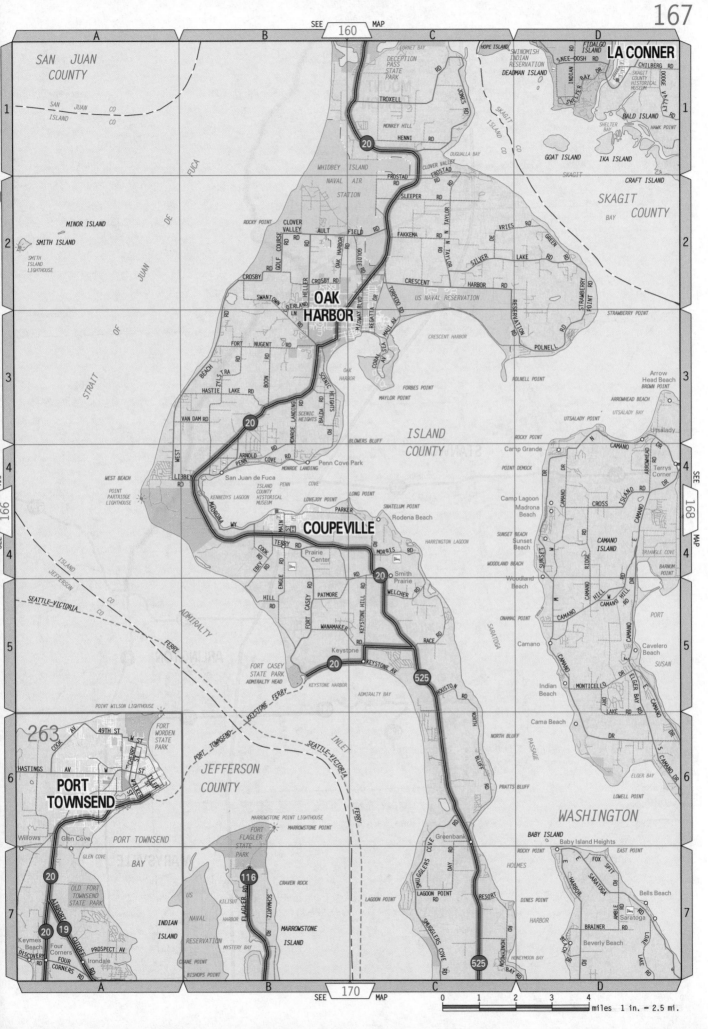

METRO

SEE 161 MAP

MOUNT VERNON

STANWOOD

ARLINGTON

MARYSVILLE

SKAGIT COUNTY

ISLAND COUNTY

SNOHOMISH COUNTY

WASHINGTON

TULALIP INDIAN RESERVATION

SEE 167 MAP

SEE 102 MAP

SEE 171 MAP

Split Rock
Table Mountain
Big Lake
Montborne
Little Mountain
Mountain View Rd
Scott Mountain
Devils Mountain
Cedardale
Skagit City
Conway
Milltown
Monson Corner
Cedarhome
Corner
Brandstrom
Pilchuck
Bryant
McMurray
Lake McMurray
Pilchuck Bridge Campground
Stimson Hill
Cavanaugh Creek
Peter Burns Rd
Walker Valley Rd
Finn Settlement Rd
Grandstrom Rd
Udell
Cedarvale Loop Rd
Heiner Rd
Grandview
Stillaguamish River
Armstrong Lake
Stanwood-Bryant Rd
Florence
Silvana
Norman
Prestliens Bluff
Happy Hollow
Lake Martha
Warm Beach
Lakewood
Island School Crossing
Smokey Point
Arlington Airport
Edgecomb
Sisco
Sisco Heights
Crossing
Kruse
Getchell Hill
Getchell
Camano Island
Livingston Bay
Utsalady
Lona Beach
Mountain View Beach
Cornell
Sunny Shore Acres
Sunny Shores
Tulare Beach
Kayak Point County Park
Kayak Point
Wenberg Campground
Lake Goodwin
Warm Beach
Mabana
Dallman
Tyee Beach
Spee-bi-dah
Pebble Beach
Tulalip Shores
Tulalip
Tulalip Marina
Skiou Point
Camano Head
Hermosa Point
Possession Sound
Saratoga Passage
Port Susan
Skagit Bay
Fir Island
Mann Island
Skagit River
Stillaguamish River

Highways: 5, 9, 161, 171, 167, 102, 224, 221, 218, 215, 212, 210, 208, 206, 202, 200, 530, 531, 532, 534

miles 1 in. = 2.5 mi.
0 1 2 3 4

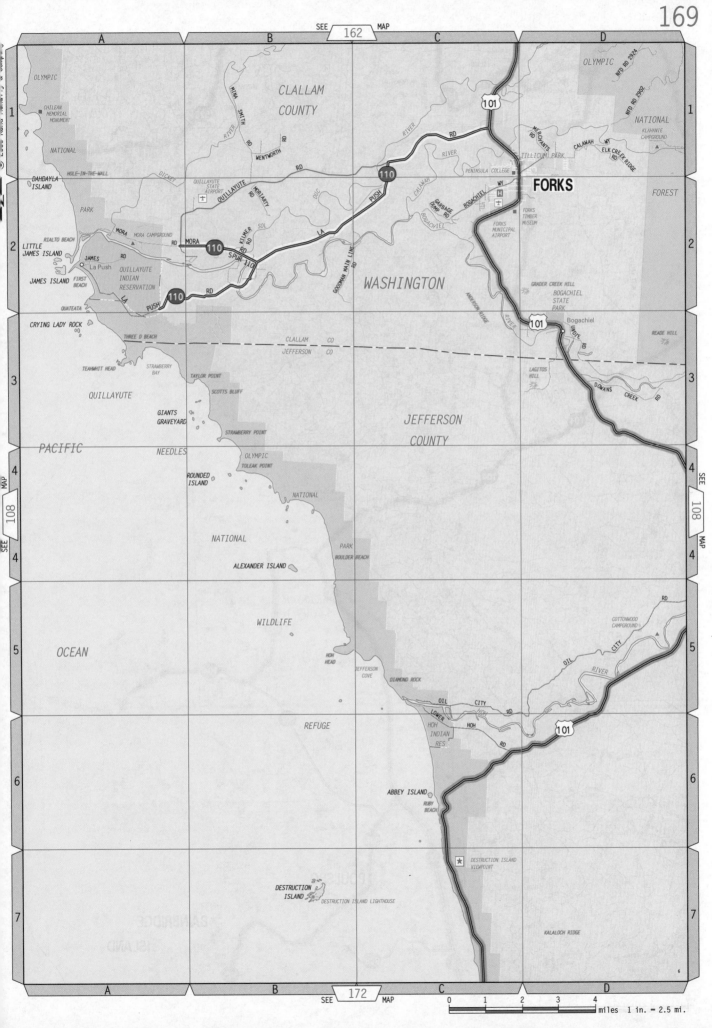

METRO

SEE MAP 162

A   B   C   D

OLYMPIC

CLALLAM
COUNTY

NATIONAL

NFD. RD 2924

NFD. RD 2902

KLAHANIE
CAMPGROUND

FOREST

CHILEAN
MEMORIAL
MONUMENT

101

MIMA

SMITH

RD

RD

WENTWORTH

RD

RIVER

RD

RIVER

RD

MERCANTS
RD

CALAWAH

ELK CREEK RIDGE

CALAWAH

WY

DAHDAYLA
ISLAND

HOLE-IN-THE-WALL

DICKEY

QUILLAYUTE
STATE AIRPORT

QUILLAYUTE

MORIARTY RD

RD

DIC

RD

110

PUSH

CALAWAH

PENINSULA COLLEGE

TILLICUM PARK

BOGACHIEL

GARBAGE
DUMP

DUMP RD

FORKS

FORKS
TIMBER
MUSEUM

PARK

RIALTO BEACH

MORA

MORA CAMPGROUND

RD

MORA

110

SOL

KLIMER RD

LA

RD

BOGACHIEL

FORKS
MUNICIPAL
AIRPORT

LITTLE
JAMES ISLAND

JAMES

RD

SPUR 110

JAMES ISLAND

FIRST
BEACH

La Push

QUILLAYUTE
INDIAN
RESERVATION

GOODMAN MAIN LINE

RD

WASHINGTON

GRADER CREEK HILL

BOGACHIEL
STATE
PARK

QUATEATA

LA

PUSH

110

RD

ANDERSON RIDGE

101

Bogachiel

READE HILL

CRYING LADY ROCK

THREE D BEACH

CLALLAM   CO

JEFFERSON   CO

UNOTE RD

LAGITOS
HILL

RIVER

PACIFIC

TEAHWHIT HEAD

STRAWBERRY
BAY

TAYLOR POINT

SCOTTS BLUFF

QUILLAYUTE

DOWANS   CREEK   RD

GIANTS
GRAVEYARD

STRAWBERRY POINT

JEFFERSON
COUNTY

NEEDLES

OLYMPIC
TOLEAK POINT

ROUNDED
ISLAND

NATIONAL

SEE MAP 108

SEE MAP 108

NATIONAL

PARK
BOULDER BEACH

ALEXANDER ISLAND

RD

COTTONWOOD
CAMPGROUND

WILDLIFE

OCEAN

HOH
HEAD

JEFFERSON
COVE

DIAMOND ROCK

CITY

OIL

RIVER

101

REFUGE

OIL   CITY

HOH

RD

LOWER

HOH
INDIAN
RES

HOH

RD

101

ABBEY ISLAND

RUBY
BEACH

DESTRUCTION ISLAND
VIEWPOINT

DESTRUCTION
ISLAND

DESTRUCTION ISLAND LIGHTHOUSE

KALALOCH RIDGE

A   B   C   D

0 1 2 3 4

miles 1 in. = 2.5 mi.

METRO

SEE 167 MAP

A B C D

19
20

ANDERSON
LAKE
STATE
PARK

QUIMPER
PENINSULA

IRONDALE
Irondale
NESS CORNER
JORGENSON HILL
CHIMACUM RD
Hadlock

INDIAN
ISLAND
US NAVAL
RESERVATION

FLAGLER

SCOW BAY RESERVATION
NODULE POINT
MARROWSTONE
ISLAND
E MARROWSTONE RD

116

Woodmans
ANDERSON LAKE

1

Chimacum

LIPLIP POINT

KINNEY POINT

PUGET

ADMIRALTY

INLET

BUSH
POINT
LIGHT
BUSH POINT

WHIDBEY
SMUGGLERS COVE

HONEYMOON BAY

HOLMES
HARBOR

GOSS
LAKE
LONE
LAKE

ISLAND
COUNTY

GOSS
LAKE RD

BEAVER VALLEY RD

VAN TROJAN RD

GIBBS
LAKE
RD

GIBBS
LAKE

WEST VALLEY
WEST VALLEY RD

CENTER RD

EGG AND I RD

OAK BAY RD

SWANSONVILLE RD

OLYMPUS BLVD

19

OLELE POINT

MATS MATS BAY
BASALT POINT
BURNER POINT

COLVOS ROCKS LIGHT

BUSH
ISLAND

POINT

SEATTLE-VICTORIA

KITSAP CO
JEFFERSON CO

MUTINY BAY
Austin
LANCASTER RD

DOUBLE BLUFF

DEER
LAGOON

Sunlight
Beach

USELESS BAY

WAHL RD

DOUBLE BLUFF

DOUBLE BLUFF LIGHT

FERRY

525

Freeland
NEWMAN RD
WOODARD
MAIN ST
SCENIC DR

Bayview

MILLMAN RD

BAYVIEW RD

EWING RD

STILLS RD

2

EAGLEMOUNT RD

CENTER RD

Center

SANDY SHORE LAKE RD

LARSON LAKE RD
LARSON LAKE

BEAVER VALLEY RD

PARADISE BAY RD

Swansonville

Port Ludlow

BULLS HEAD

OAK BAY RD

TALA POINT

E LUDLOW RD
E LUDLOW RIDGE RD
WATSON RD
LUDLOW BAY RD
TALA SHORE DR

FOULWEATHER BLUFF

Foulweather
Bluff

SKUNK BAY LIGHT

NE TWIN
SPITS RD
Hansville
NORWEGIAN POINT

POINT NO POINT LIGHT

3

JEFFERSON
COUNTY

104

104

THORNDIKE RD

TEAL LAKE RD

S POINT RD

PARADISE RD

PARADISE RD

WHITE ROCK

Shine

POINT HANNON LIGHT

HOOD HEAD

TERMINATION POINT
BYWATER BAY

SQUAMISH HARBOR

HOOD CANAL DR NE

NE 360TH ST

PILOT POINT

NE EGLON RD

HOFFMAN RD NE

Eglon

POINT LIGHT

4

SEE 109 MAP

DABOB RD

COYLE RD

DABOB POST OFFICE

Dabob

COYLE RD

RIVER

CREEK

HOOD CANAL

JEFFERSON CO
KITSAP CO

PORT GAMBLE HISTORIC MUSEUM

Port Gamble
NE BABCOCK ST

PORT
GAMBLE

OF SEA AND SHORE MUSEUM

LITTLE BOSTON

NE 288TH ST

PORT GAMBLE
RD

PORT GAMBLE RD NE

GAMBLE PL NE

Hansville
PARCELL RD NE

SANDY BEACH LN NE

APPLE COVE
POINT LIGHT
APPLE COVE POINT

SEE 171 MAP

4

3

104

KITSAP
COUNTY

WASHINGTON

Four
Corners

BEACH DR NE

PORT GAMBLE

GAMBLE BAY RD NE

NE SHORTY CAMPBELL RD

104

KINGSTON
Kingston

EDMONDS-KINGSTON FERRY

KITSAP CO
SNOHOMISH CO

5

TARBOO BAY

Camp
Discovery

CAMP DISCOVERY RD

THORNDYKE RD

THORNDYKE BAY

TOANDOS RD

Lofall
Breidablick

WAGHORN RD

NW PIONEER HILL RD

BIG VALLEY RD

PIONEER RD

307

STRIEBELS CORNER
CRAWFORD DR

W KINGSTON RD NE

HIGHLAND RD NE

HANSVILLE RD NE

APPLETREE COVE

KINGSTON RD NE

PRESIDENT POINT

6

LINDSAYS BEACH

LEMONDS RD

TOANDOS
PENINSULA

HOOD CANAL LIGHT

BROWN POINT

THORNDYKE RD

Vinland
AMBERJACK AV

RHODODENDRON RON LN NW

NW DARTER RD

EASTERN BOUNDARY RD

NW FINN HILL RD

NW RUDE RD

NE SAWDUST HILL RD

NE ROVA RD

KEMPER BREWERY

NE IVERSON RD

NE GUNDERSON RD

MILLER BAY RD NE

INDIANOLA RD NE

Indianola

PORT
MADISON
INDIAN
RESERVATION

TULIN RD NE

7

TABOOK POINT

CAMP HARMONY RD

COYLE RD

ZELATCHED POINT RD

HAZEL POINT

HAZEL POINT RD

FISHERMAN HARBOR

Olympic
View

OLYMPIC VIEW LOOP RD

Bangor

US NAVAL RESERVATION

STURGEON ST

BULLHEAD RD

SEALION ST

ARCHERFISH RD

SCANDIA RD

FLIER AV

NW PARAULT RD

NW PUGH RD

LINCOLN RD NE

BOND RD NE

NE STOTTLEMEYER RD

BIG VALLEY RD

3

305

FRONT ST

3RD AV NE

VIKING WY NE

NE MESFORD RD
NE HOSTMARK ST

MARINE SCIENCE CENTER

POULSBO

LIBERTY INLET

Lemolo

SHORE DR NE

LEMOLO

Virginia
Keyport

NAVAL UNDERSEA MUSEUM

TOTTEN RD NE

WIDME RD

COLUMBIA ST NE

AUGUSTA AV NE

SUQUAMISH WY NE

Suquamish

SUQUAMISH CASINO

DIVISION AV NE

GATE POINT

MILLER BAY

MILLER BAY RD NE

BLOEDEL RESERVE

Port Madison

Seabold

SUNRISE DR NE

BAINBRIDGE

ISLAND

POINT MONROE LIGHT

PUGET

SOUND

KITSAP CO
KING CO

POINT BOLIN

305

7

CLEAR CREEK RD

THRESHER AV NW

SILVERDALE WY NW

LUOTO RD

308

SCAT

3

ANDERSON LAKE

0 1 2 3 4 miles 1 in. = 2.5 mi.

SEE 174 MAP

A B C D

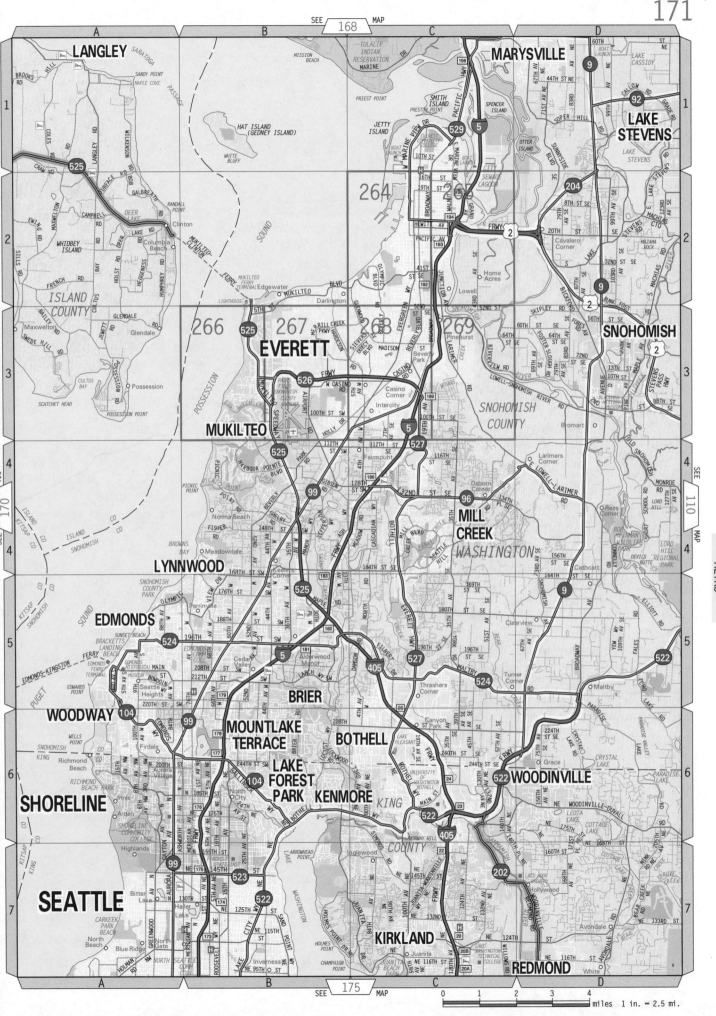

LANGLEY

MARYSVILLE

LAKE STEVENS

TULALIP INDIAN RESERVATION MARINE

MISSION BEACH

SMITH ISLAND

SPENCER ISLAND

264

WHIDBEY ISLAND

ISLAND COUNTY

SNOHOMISH

266 267 268 269

EVERETT

MUKILTEO

SNOHOMISH COUNTY

MILL CREEK

WASHINGTON

LYNNWOOD

EDMONDS

BRIER

WOODWAY

MOUNTLAKE TERRACE

LAKE FOREST PARK

BOTHELL

WOODINVILLE

SHORELINE

KENMORE

KING COUNTY

SEATTLE

KIRKLAND

REDMOND

METRO

0 1 2 3 4 miles   1 in. = 2.5 mi.

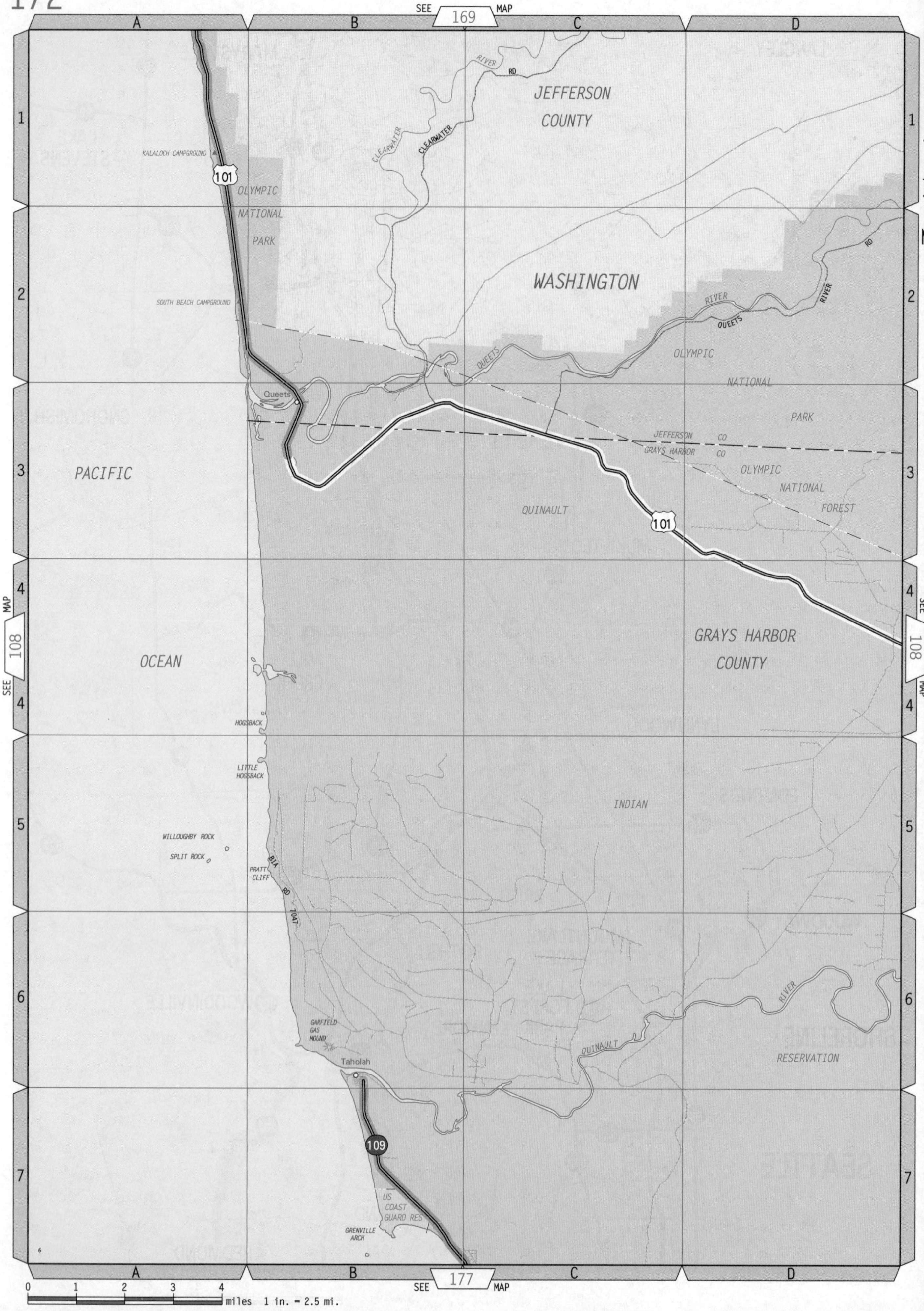

SEE 169 MAP

A   B   C   D

1

JEFFERSON
COUNTY

KALALOCH CAMPGROUND

101

OLYMPIC

NATIONAL

PARK

WASHINGTON

RIVER RD

CLEARWATER

CLEARWATER

RIVER

RD

2

SOUTH BEACH CAMPGROUND

RIVER

QUEETS

RIVER

OLYMPIC

NATIONAL

PARK

QUEETS

3

PACIFIC

Queets

QUINAULT

JEFFERSON   CO
GRAYS HARBOR   CO

OLYMPIC

NATIONAL

FOREST

101

SEE 108 MAP
SEE 108 MAP

4

OCEAN

GRAYS HARBOR
COUNTY

HOGSBACK

LITTLE
HOGSBACK

5

WILLOUGHBY ROCK

SPLIT ROCK

PRATT
CLIFF

BIA
RD
7047

INDIAN

6

GARFIELD
GAS
MOUND

Taholah

RIVER

QUINAULT

RESERVATION

7

109

US
COAST
GUARD RES

GRENVILLE
ARCH

SEE 177 MAP

A   B   C   D

METRO

0   1   2   3   4   miles   1 in. = 2.5 mi.

SEE MAP 109

A · B · C · D

METRO

OLYMPIC NATIONAL PARK

OLYMPIC NATIONAL FOREST

JEFFERSON COUNTY

SAINT PETERS DOME

TRAP PASS

NORTH ROCK

NFD RD 2530
NFD RD 2540
NFD RD 2546
NFD RD 2510

WEST ROCK
EAST ROCK
NFD RD 24 03
NFD RD 25 24
WEBB MOUNTAIN

JEFFERSON CO
MASON CO

LENA LAKE CAMPGROUND

DUCKABUSH RIVER
NFD RD 2515
NFD RD 2510

MOUNT JUPITER

DUCKABUSH RD
BLACK POINT
Duckabush

PLEASANT HARBOR

JEFFERSON CO
KITSAP CO

MISERY POINT
MIAMI BEACH
MAPLE BEACH
MISERY POINT LOOP
Seabeck

QUATSAP POINT

HOOD POINT

KITSAP COUNTY

STAVIS NW
LARSON LN NW
SEABECK-HOLLY RD NW

OLYMPIC NATIONAL FOREST

NFD RD
HAMMA
LENA CREEK CAMPGROUND
25
HAMMA HAMMA CAMPGROUND
NFD RD 2421

JEFFERSON RIDGE

HAMMA
HAMMA RD
NFD RD 2472
NFD RD 2510

SEAMOUNT DR

McDONALD COVE

TRITON COVE
TRITON HEAD

TEKIU POINT

Nellita
NELLITA RD NW

Hite Center
HITE CENTER RD NW
NW HOLLY
Camp Union
NW FOUR WHEEL DR
TAHUYA LAKE RD NW

OLYMPIC NATIONAL FOREST

NFD RD 2401
NFD RD 2420
NFD RD 2470
NFD 2469

WASHINGTON PASS

NFD RD 2480

RIVER

CUMMINGS POINT

Eldon

Holly

SEABECK HWY
HOLLY RD

PETER HAGEN RD NW
Crosby

HINTZVILLE RD NW

WASHINGTON

W WINTERGREEN LN

LEWIS RD NW

GOLD CREEK RD

NFD RD 2464
24

LILLIWAUP CREEK CAMPGROUND

SADDLE MOUNTAIN

AYOCK POINT

CAPSTAN ROCK

CHINOM POINT
KITSAP CO
MASON CO

DEWATTO RD

BEAR CREEK
BEAR CREEK
BEAR CREEK DR
DEWATTO RD

LOST RIVER

Morgan Marsh

McCaslin Marsh
NORTH MISSION RD NW
PANTHER LAKE
PANTHER RD

DEWATTO RD

SEE MAP 109

HOOD CANAL

LILLIWAUP FALLS
Lilliwaup
LILLIWAUP BAY
101

DOW MOUNTAIN

Dewatto
DEWATTO BAY
LONG POINT

HOLLY RD

DEWATTO RD

DEWATTO

TAHUYA BLACKSMITH
BELFAIR-TAHUYA

TOONERVILLE RD

ELFENDAHL PASS
SCARIFICATION RD
SAND HILL
PLANTATION RD

OLD BELFAIR HWY

3
Belfair
NORTH SHORE RD
300
LYNCH COVE
PLUM POINT

SEE MAP 174

HOODSPORT TRAIL STATE PARK

LAKE CUSHMAN RD
119
Hoodsport
101

NORTH SHORE RD

MUSQUETI POINT

MASON COUNTY

RED BLUFF

BELFAIR-TAHUYA
TAHUYA RIVER

TAHUYA RIVER RD

NORTH SHORE RD

HOOD CANAL

Sunset Beach
106
Forest Beach

3

OLD RD 302
302
Allyn

POTLATCH STATE PARK CAMPGROUND
ANNAS BAY

AYRES POINT
NORTH SHORE RD

101
Potlatch

Tahuya

SISTERS POINTS

TWANOH STATE PARK

TRAILS RD

NORTH BAY

SKOKOMISH INDIAN RES
SKOKOMISH VALLEY RD
101 106

Union
McREAVY RD
DALBY RD
Grahamsville
Fernwood
McREAVY RD

MASON LAKE DR W
MASON LAKE
MASON LAKE RD
MASON BENSON RD

3

Allyn-Grapeview
GRAPEVIEW LOOP RD
ROCKY POINT
REACH ISLAND

SEE MAP 180

0 1 2 3 4 miles   1 in. = 2.5 mi.

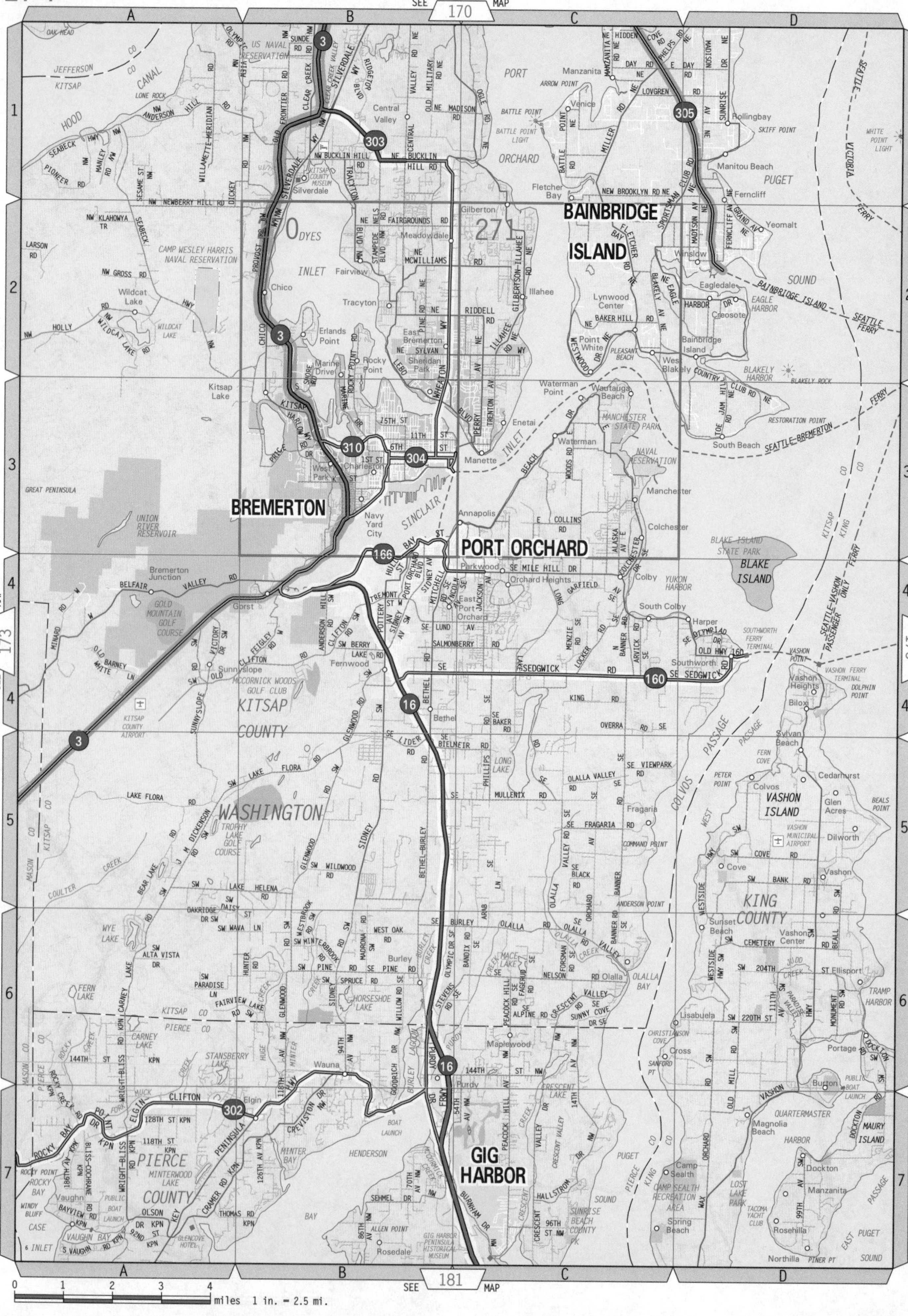

SEE MAP 170

BAINBRIDGE ISLAND

BREMERTON

PORT ORCHARD

GIG HARBOR

METRO

SEE MAP 173

SEE MAP 175

SEE MAP 181

KITSAP COUNTY
PIERCE COUNTY
KING COUNTY
MASON COUNTY
WASHINGTON

HOOD CANAL
JEFFERSON CO / KITSAP CO
DYES INLET
PORT ORCHARD
SINCLAIR INLET
PUGET SOUND
COLVOS PASSAGE
VASHON ISLAND
MAURY ISLAND
BLAKE ISLAND STATE PARK
BLAKELY HARBOR
EAGLE HARBOR
MANCHESTER STATE PARK
UNION RIVER RESERVOIR
GREAT PENINSULA

0   1   2   3   4
miles   1 in. = 2.5 mi.

© 1996 Rand McNally & Company

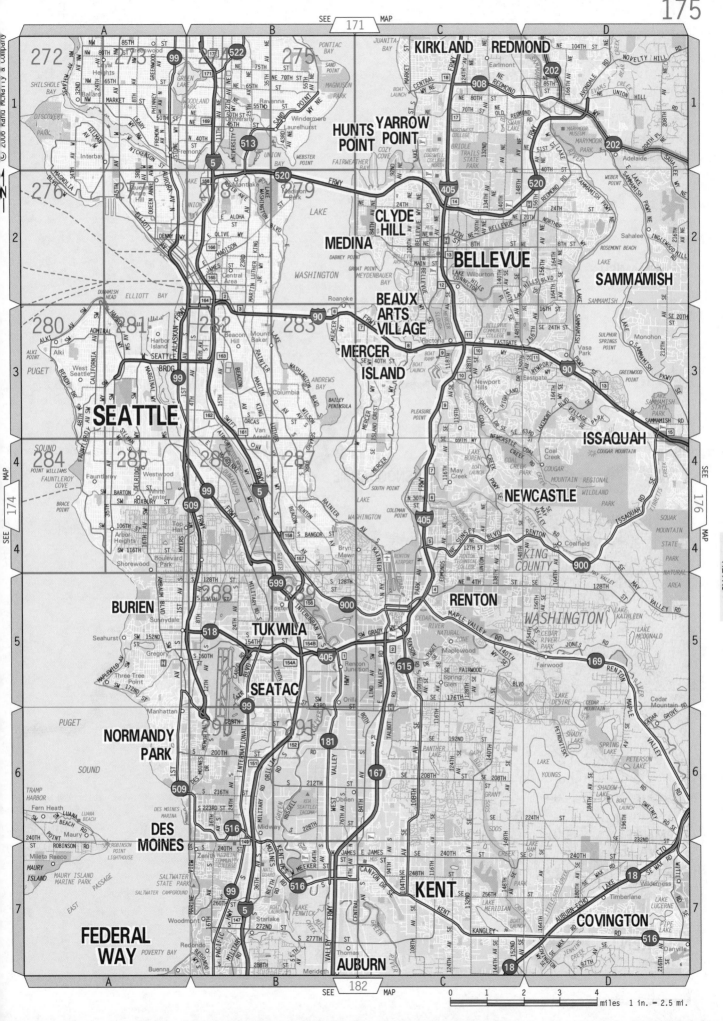

A   B   C   D

CARNATION

SAMMAMISH

KING COUNTY

WASHINGTON

1

2

3

4

5

6

7

TOLT RIVER HIGHLANDS AREA

TOLT RIVER RESERVOIR

BLACK LAKE

CALLIGAN LAKE

LAKE HANCOCK

METCALF MARSH

BRIDGES LAKE

KLAUS LAKE

FULLER MOUNTAIN

HANS LAKE

PLATT POND

LANGLOIS LAKE

LAKE JOY

LAKE MARCEL

Stillwater

CARNATION-DUVALL

Elwater Lake

SIKES LAKE

PETERSON POND

UNION HILL

NOVELTY HILL RD

UNION HILL RD

Carnation Farm

Carnation

HORSESHOE LAKE

TOLT HILL

MACDONALD MEMORIAL PARK

AMES LAKE

BEAVER LAKE

ISSAQUAH

PINE LAKE

DUTHIE HILL

REDMOND FALL CITY RD

TRINITY LUTHERAN COLLEGE

GRAND RIDGE

Mitchell Hill

Fall City

CARNATION RD NE

GRIFFIN CREEK

RUTHERFORD SLOUGH

TEN CREEK

PRESTON

Preston

TRADITION LAKE

High Point

ISSAQUAH STATE SALMON HATCHERY

TIGER MOUNTAIN

SQUAK TIGER MOUNTAIN CORRIDOR

SQUAK MOUNTAIN STATE PARK NATURAL AREA

WEST TIGER MOUNTAIN

STATE FOREST

SOUTH TIGER MOUNTAIN

TIGER MOUNTAIN

Mirrormont

Four Lakes

Hobart

SNOQUALMIE

SNOQUALMIE FALLS

LAKE ALICE

NORTHWEST RAILWAY MUSEUM

Tokul

BORST LAKE

THREE FORKS PARK

REINIG

Ernies Grove

MOON VALLEY

GREEN MOUNTAIN

NORTH BEND

Upper Preston

ECHO LAKE

Lake Creek

RATTLESNAKE MOUNTAIN SCENIC AREA

RATTLESNAKE MOUNTAIN

RAGING RIVER

TAYLOR MOUNTAIN

Taylor Mountain

CANYON CREEK

BREW HILL

Tanner

Edgewick

LITTLE SI

MUSEUM

BORLEY CREEK

GROUSE RIDGE

RATTLESNAKE LAKE

RATTLESNAKE LEDGE

CEDAR BUTTE

Cedar Falls

LOOKOUT MOUNTAIN

CEDAR LAKE

CHESTER MORSE LAKE

CHANGE CREEK

HALL CREEK

Bagley Jct

Barneston

MOUNT BAKER-SNOQUALMIE

NATIONAL FOREST

WEBSTER LAKE

FRANCIS LAKE

FRANCIS LAKE

WALSH LAKE

MAPLE VALLEY

KENT

Atkinson

Hobart

Trude

Selleck

Landsburg

Georgetown

Kangley

Ravensdale

RAVENSDALE LAKE

LAKE RETREAT

SUGARLOAF MOUNTAIN

Wilderness

Summit

DIVERSION DITCH

CEDAR RIVER

SNOQUALMIE RIVER

MIDDLE FORK

SOUTH FORK

NORTH FORK

TOLT RIVER

SOUTH FORK TOLT RIVER

PATTERSON CREEK

SEE 175 MAP

SEE 111 MAP

METRO

© 2006 Rand McNally & Company

0 1 2 3 4 miles   1 in. = 2.5 mi.

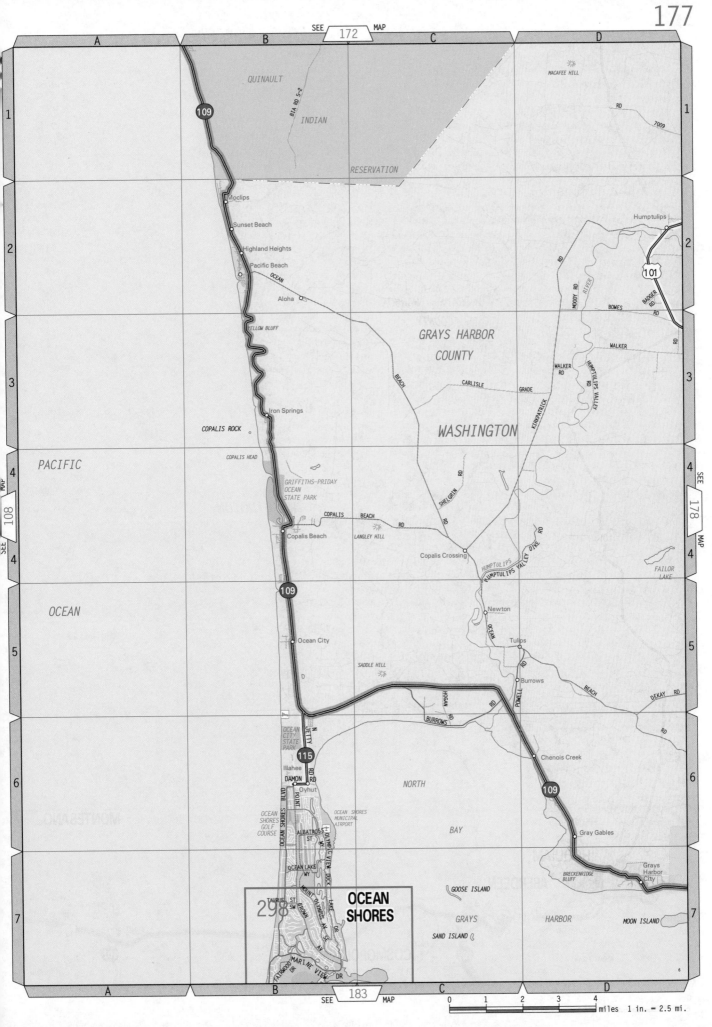

METRO

QUINAULT

B1A RD S-2

INDIAN

RESERVATION

MACAFEE HILL

RD

7009

109

Moclips

Sunset Beach

Humptulips

Highland Heights

Pacific Beach

101

OCEAN

MOODY RD

RIVER

BOWES

BADGER RD

Aloha

GRAYS HARBOR

COUNTY

WALKER

YELLOW BLUFF

BEACH

CARLISLE

GRADE

WALKER RD

HUMPTULIPS VALLEY RD

KIRPATRICK

WASHINGTON

Iron Springs

COPALIS ROCK

SHELGRIN RD

COPALIS HEAD

PACIFIC

GRIFFITHS-PRIDAY
OCEAN
STATE PARK

COPALIS   BEACH   RD

Copalis Beach

LANGLEY HILL

Copalis Crossing

HUMPTULIPS VALLEY DIKE RD

HUMPTULIPS

FAILOR
LAKE

109

Newton

OCEAN

OCEAN

Ocean City

Tulips

SADDLE HILL

RD

Burrows

POWELL RD

BEACH

DEKAY RD

HOGAN RD

BURROWS

RD

OCEAN
CITY
STATE PARK

N
JETTY
RD

Chenois Creek

115

Illahee

DAMON   RD

Oyhut

POINT

NORTH

109

OCEAN SHORES BLVD

OCEAN SHORES
GOLF
COURSE

Ocean Shores
Municipal
Airport

Gray Gables

ALBATROSS
ST

OLYMPIC VIEW DUCK

BAY

OCEAN LAKE
WY

LAKE
DR

BRECKENRIDGE
BLUFF

Grays
Harbor
City

298

TAURUS   ST
SW

MOUNT OLYMPUS AV SW

BRONN
AV

OCEAN
SHORES

GOOSE ISLAND

FAIRWOOD DR   MARINE VIEW   DR

GRAYS

HARBOR

MOON ISLAND

SAND ISLAND

0   1   2   3   4
miles   1 in. = 2.5 mi.

SEE 108 MAP

SEE 178 MAP

METRO

SEE 109 MAP

SEE 177 MAP

SEE 179 MAP

A | B | C | D

1

RD 8.02
DONKEY CREEK
REED HILL
COUGAR MOUNTAIN
OLYMPIC NATIONAL FOREST
ABERDEEN WATERSHED
RIVER

US 101

2

MCNUTT RD
TUFFRE RD
NEWBURY RD
HUMPTULIPS RIVER
E
HUMPTULIPS
WEST FORK HUMPTULIPS RIVER
EAST FORK
RD
WYNOOCHEE

GRAYS HARBOR COUNTY

3

HENSEL RD
YOUMANS RD
RIVER
WISHKAH RIVER
COUGAR SMITH RD
RD
VALLEY RD
A7200
RIVER

4

US 101
E HOQUIAM RD
GREENWOOD RD
W WISHKAH RD
RD
WISHKAH RD
WASHINGTON
Nisson
HOQUIAM WISHKAH RD
Greenwood
HAMILTON CANYON
WYNOOCHEE
A6000 RD
ROAD A-LINE
A7000
SAT SOP
WEST FORK
A5000 RD
ROAD D-LINE
A3000
CANYON RD

5

HOQUIAM RIVER
E FORK
New London
LYTLE LANDING
WISHKAH
EAST WYNOOCHEE WISHKAH
RD
OLD WYNOOCHEE
WYNOOCHEE
PRICES PEAK
Aberdeen Gardens
Wishkah
ABERDEEN GARDENS RD

6

OCEAN BEACH RD
WEST FORK
E FORK HOQUIAM
HOQUIAM RD
WISHKAH RD
GEISSLER VALLEY RD
WYNOOCHEE VALLEY
BLACK CREEK RD
MONTESANO

7

HOQUIAM
109
ABERDEEN
109
PERRY AV
BROADWAY
EMERSON AV
LINCOLN ST
SIMPSON AV
HOQUIAM CASTLE
OLYMPIC STADIUM
East Hoquiam
SUMNER AV
US 101
ADAMS ST
5TH ST
AIRPORT WY
PAULSON RD
ARNOLD POLSON PARK & MUSEUM
COW POINT
BAY AV
INDUSTRIAL
East Aberdeen
K ST
B ST
WISHKAH RIVER
Lake Aberdeen Hatchery
W GEISSLER RD
W GEISSLER RD
MONTESANO ABERDEEN RD
KATON RD
LAKE SYLVIA
LAKE SYLVIA STATE PARK
MCBRYDE AV E
SYLVIA LAKE RD
3RD ST N
1ST ST N
BEACON AV
CAMP CREEK RD
OLD 410 HWY
PIONEER AV W
107
12

GRAYS HARBOR
RENNIE ISLAND
105
HARDING RD
BOONE ST
South Aberdeen
GRAYS HARBOR COLLEGE
W HUNTLEY ST
US 101
W CURTIS ST
WEST ST BLVD
Junction City
GRAYS HARBOR HISTORICAL SEAPORT
COSMOPOLIS
CHEHALIS RIVER
SOLLI RD
12
Central Park
HIGGINS ISLAND
CHEHALIS RIVER
SOUTH BANK
CHEHALIS RIVER
SOUTH BANK RD

SEE 109 MAP
SEE 117 MAP

0 1 2 3 4 miles 1 in. = 2.5 mi.

SEE 109 MAP

A   B   C   D

METRO

NFD RD 2153

NFD RD 2199
NFD RD 239.9
NFD RD 2255
NFD RD 2341
SOUTH MOUNTAIN

SKOKOMISH RIVER
SKOKOMISH VALLEY
Mohrweis
SHELTON TROUT HATCHERY

WEST FORK SATSOP RIVER
KELLY RD
KELLY HALL RD
NFD RD
DRY CREEK
BEEVILLE LOOP RD
ANDERSON RD

WASHINGTON

CANYON
FORK
SATSOP
RIVER

FORD RD

NFD RD 1700
Matlock
NFD RD 2199
NFD RD

Frisken Wye
DECKERVILLE
Deckerville

NAHWATZEL LAKE
SHELTON-MATLOCK

DAYTON-AIRPORT RD
102
WASHINGTON CORRECTIONS CENTER
Dayton
RD

MIDDLE SATSOP RD
SATSOP FORK

CREEK
MARDEN RD
BINGHAM
FIRE

MASON COUNTY

MARY M KNIGHT RD

DELL RD
ADAMS RD

LITTLE EGYPT VALLEY
LITTLE EGYPT RD

COUGAR SMITH RD
MIDDLE SATSOP RD

FISH HATCHERY RD
DRY CREEK

HIGHLAND RD

DAYTON PEAK
GALLAGHER RD

RD B-LINE
RD A-LINE
MIDDLE FORK

FORD LOOP RD
FORD RD

RIVER
SA-760 P

STAR LAKE
SNAG HILL

LOST LAKE
WHITE STAR
LOST LAKE RD
CLOQUALLUM RD

SEE 180 MAP
I-8/T-8

A2000 RD

DECKER CREEK
RD C530
CLOQUALLUM RD

Cloquallum

A2000 RD
G-LINE RD
A-LINE RD
A1000 RD

BEERBOWER
PLUG MILL RD

SATSOP

CLOQUALLUM CREEK

SATSOP
G-LINE RD
G1100 RD

SCHAFER STATE PARK
MASON CO
GRAYS HARBOR CO

CLOQUALLUM
CLOQUALLUM CREEK

MASON CO
THURSTON CO
TORNQUIST RD
108

SATSOP
G100 RD

EAST FORK SATSOP RIVER
MIDDLE

GRAYS HARBOR COUNTY

A900 RD

FALLS CREEK RD

POWER CREEK RD
LOST LAKE RD
BUSH CREEK RD

Garden City
HICKLIN RD

Hillgrove
SUMMIT RD
ELMA-MCCLEARY RD
MCCLEARY

HICKLIN HILL
8

MONTESANO

STEPHEN RD

Whites
OLD 410 HWY
ELMA HWY
MCKNIGHT RD
FOREMAN RD
SINE RD

BOZY CREEK RD
GRAYS HARBOR CO
THURSTON CO

8
R
SOUTH UNION RD
OLD SAND CREEK RD

A4000 RD

CAPITOL STATE FOREST

MOORE RD
ONEILL RD
HURD RD
STANLEY RD
NEWMAN CREEK RD
STAMPER RD

W MARTIN ST
W MAIN ST
BUSHWELL

MOX-CHEHALIS RD

BUCK RIDGE

Satsop
OLD HWY 410
Brady Rd
KEYES RD
BRADY LOOP
HENRY FOSTER RD
BRADY LOOP RD

12
ELMA
WAKEFIELD RD

ELMA MUNICIPAL AIRPORT

RD A-LINE

RD B-1000

SATSOP RIVER
WENZEL SLOUGH RD
CHEHALIS RIVER
WORKMAN CREEK RD
SOUTH BANK RD

Damon
South Elma

12

Malone

PORTER CREEK RD
RD C-LINE

CHEHALIS RIVER

SEE 117 MAP

0 1 2 3 4 miles   1 in. = 2.5 mi.

METRO

A B C D

SKOKOMISH INDIAN RES
WEBB HILL
GEORGE ADAMS SALMON HATCHERY
PURDY CUTOFF
MEHB HILL
MCREAVY
BROCKDALE RD

MASON COUNTY

LAKE DR W
MASON LAKE
Little Hoquiam
MASON BENSON RD
GRAPEVIEW LOOP RD

STRETCH ISLAND

MCLANE COVE
DOUGALL POINT
INDIAN COVE

PIERCE COUNTY

CRANBERRY LAKE
LAKE LIMERICK
MASON LAKE RD W
MASON LAKE RD

MCEWAN
PRAIRIE RD
MASON LAKE RD W
JOHNS PRAIRIE RD
Bayshore

3
SPENCER LAKE
PICKERING
SPENCER LAKE RD
PHILLIPS LAKE
Graham Point

SUN POINT
JARRELL COVE
NORTH RD
Hartstene
YATES RD

HARTSTENE ISLAND
MCMICKEN ISLAND

HERRON BAY
HERRON ISLAND
Herron
205TH AV

101
DAYTON AIRPORT RD
102
SANDERSON FIELD AIRPORT

BROCKDALE HILL
SHELTON
CAPITOL HILL
N NORTHCLIFF PINE
W RAILROAD ST
MASON COUNTY MUSEUM
Oakland
OAKLAND BAY

CHAPMANS COVE
DANIELS RD
AGATE
CRESTVIEW DR
AGATE RD
CHURCH POINT
HAMMERSLEY INLET
ARCADIA
Arcadia

HUNGERFORD POINT
CAPE COD
ARCADIA POINT
HOPE ISLAND
POTLATCH POINT

HARTSTENE
LANSKY DR
ISLAND SHORE
WILSON POINT
JARED RD
SLIVA LN

JOEMMA BEACH CAMPGROUND
WHITMAN COVE
CASE INLET

SHELTON-MATLOCK RD
SHELTON VALLEY RD
DEEGAN
LOST LAKE
ISABELLA LAKE
OLD OLYMPIC HWY
3

WASHINGTON

SQUAXIN ISLAND INDIAN RES
BELSPECH POINT
BURGUNDY RD
HUIOS RD
THURSTON CO
PIERCE CO
JOHNSON POINT

CLOQUALLUM RD
MAINLINE
ISABELLA VALLEY
2900 RD
COLE RD
101

LYNCH
WINDY POINT
DEER HARBOR
MUD CAT POINT

TOTTEN INLET
HUNTER POINT
90TH AV NW
SALTY DR NW

TUCKSEL POINT
BRISCO POINT
DANA PASSAGE
FT STRAP
BAIRD COVE
PONCIN RD

HENDERSON INLET
BAIRD RD NE
78TH AV NE

181

LYNCH
LITTLE SKOOKUM INLET
KAMILCHE POINT
QUARTERS POINT
SLOCUM RIDGE
BLOOMFIELD
DEEPWATER POINT

85TH AV NW
78TH AV NW
79TH AV NW
COUGAR POINT
BALLAGHER COVE
HUDSON COVE
69TH AV NW

81ST
SANDERSON HARBOR
JEAL POINT
DOVER POINT
LIGHTHOUSE
Boston Harbor
73RD

81ST AV NE
77TH AV NE
CHAPMAN BAY
WOODARD BAY
POINT

BIG FISHTRAP
CLIFF POINT

Kamilche
LITTLE CREEK CASINO

NEW Kamilche
OLD OLYMPIC HWY

BURNS POINT
BURNS COVE
54TH AV NW
STIMPSON RD NW
HOFFMAN RD NW
FRYE COVE
61ST AV NW
YOUNG RD NW

66TH AV NW
64TH AV NW
57TH WY NW
BIG TYKLE COVE
LITTLE TYKLE COVE
46TH AV NE
43RD
GULL HARBOR
North Olympia

WOODARD BAY RD NE
BOSTON HARBOR RD NE
LIBBY RD NE
HEIGHTS RD
SHINCKE RD NE

63RD AV NE
61ST AV NE
46TH AV NE
SHINCKE
KINNEY RD
JOHNSON PUGET

108
KAMILCHE VALLEY
LITTLE SKOOKUM VALLEY
HURLEY-WALDRIP RD

OYSTER BAY
SHELLRIDGE RD NW
HOLIDAY VALLEY DR NW
SCOTT RD NW
42ND AV NW

STEAMBOAT ISLAND
GRAVELLY BEACH
KEATING RD NW
SUNRISE BEACH RD NW

YOUNG COVE
GREEN COVE
SNYDER COVE
BISCAY ST NW
COOPER POINT

BUDD INLET
GULL HARBOR

46TH AV NE
LIBBY
LEMMON
41ST AV NE

HAWKS PRAIRIE RD NE

MASON CO
THURSTON CO

Schneiders Prairie
WHITTAKER

THURSTON COUNTY

ROCKY POINT
BREMER RD NW
SIMMONS RD NW
STEDMAN

THE EVERGREEN STATE COLLEGE
DRIFTWOOD RD NW
36TH AV NW
28TH AV NW

BUTLER COVE
36TH AV
South Bay

ELLIS COVE
26TH AV NE
26TH AV NE
SLEATER

15TH AV NE

96

297

SUMMIT LAKE SHORE RD NW
SUMMIT LAKE
WILSON RD NW
SUMMIT LAKE RD NW

8
OLD OLYMPIC HWY
RANDALL RD SW
MCKENZIE

EVERGREEN PKWY
KAISER RD
MUD BAY
11TH AV NW
14TH AV NW
MUD BAY HWY SW
HARRISON AV

DIVISION ST
BAY DR
N BETHEL
PINE
STATE AV
4TH AV E
UNION AV
12TH AV NE
MARTIN WY

5
109
108
107
PACIFIC AV

FIVE FORKS RD SW
PORTER PASS
POWERLINE RD SW
ROCK CANDY MOUNTAIN RD SW

CEDAR FLATS
BAKER RD SW
MAPLE VALLEY RD SW
MUNSON DR SW

COOPER POINT
BLACK LAKE BLVD
PERCIVAL CREEK
SAPP RD SW

105
104
103
102
5

CAPITOL WY
22ND AV
FONES RD SW
37TH AV SE

OLYMPIA
LACEY

TUMWATER

CAPITOL STATE FOREST
LARCH MOUNTAIN
ROCK CANDY MOUNTAIN

DELPHI RD SW
62ND AV SW
49TH AV SW
54TH AV SW

LINWOOD AV
RURAL
NORTH ST SE
CLEVELAND
DESCHUTES

BOULEVARD RD SE
HOFFMAN RD SE
YELM
WIGGINS RD SE
COLLEGE ST SE
RICH RD SE
RAINIER

GRAYS HARBOR CO
THURSTON CO
BORDEAUX CAMPGROUND
CAPITOL PEAK

BLACK LAKE
66TH AV SW
70TH AV SW
ISRAEL RD
LITTLEROCK RD
101
YELM HWY
HENDERSON BLVD

0 1 2 3 4 miles 1 in. = 2.5 mi.

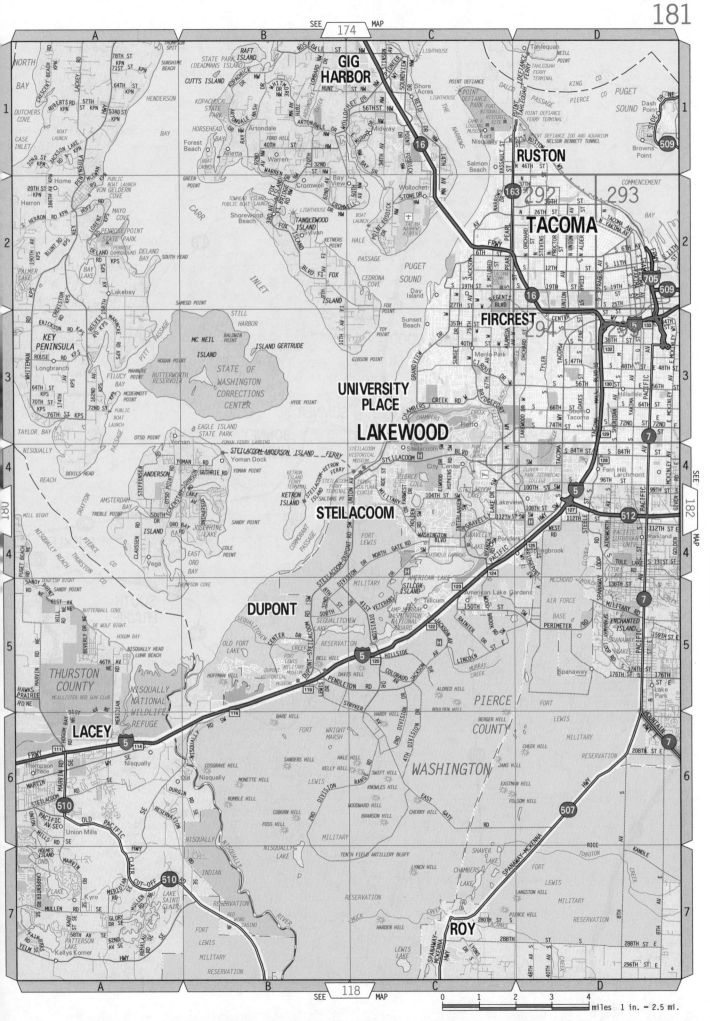

METRO

miles 1 in. = 2.5 mi.

182

SEE 175 MAP

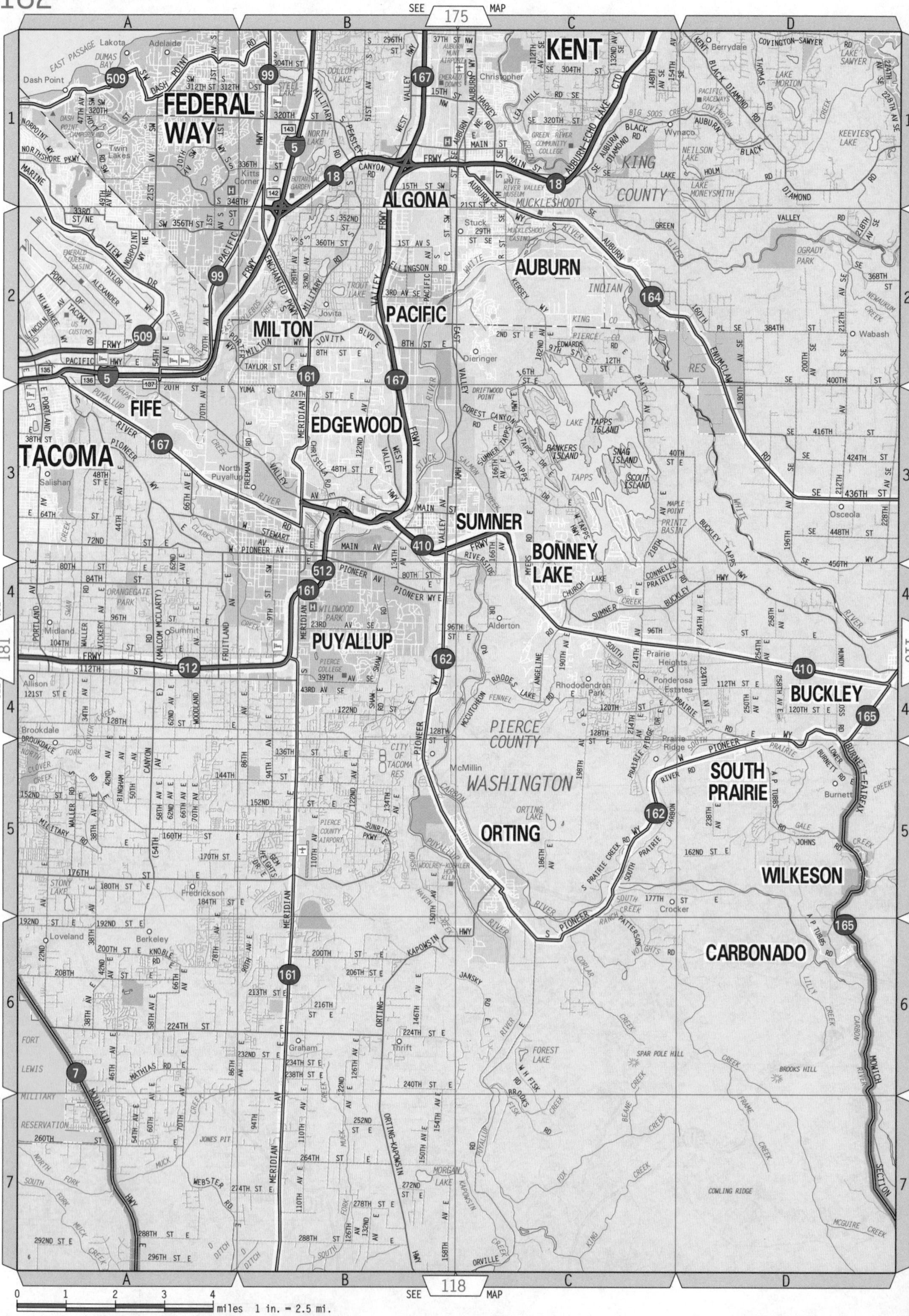

KENT

FEDERAL WAY

ALGONA

AUBURN

PACIFIC

MILTON

EDGEWOOD

FIFE

TACOMA

SUMNER

BONNEY LAKE

PUYALLUP

BUCKLEY

SOUTH PRAIRIE

WILKESON

ORTING

CARBONADO

KING COUNTY

MUCKLESHOOT

PIERCE COUNTY

WASHINGTON

METRO

SEE 181 MAP

SEE 118 MAP

0 1 2 3 4 miles   1 in. = 2.5 mi.

A   B   C   D

OCEAN SHORES

WASHINGTON STATE OYHUT GAME RANGE

298

OCEAN SHORES BLVD SW
OCEAN SHORES BLVD SW

GRAYS   HARBOR

STEARNS BLUFF

105

NEWSKAH RD

WESTHAVEN ST
ANEIS ST
MONTESANO

Westhaven

WESTPORT

WESTHAVEN
FOREST AV
OCEAN AV
VETERAN AV
FARRAGUT AV
CHEHALIS AV
NEEL ST
BOURNE ST
ROBERTS RD

Ophassett

WESTPORT LIGHT STATE PARK

TRAITORS INLET

WUSTENECKER RD

GEORGE CLARK RD

105

JOHNS   RIVER

Ocosta

SOUTH BAY
GRASS ISLAND

GRAYS HARBOR COUNTY

105

Bay City

HUNT CLUB RD

SOPUN INLET

RD

NORTH RIVER DIVIDE

ROBERTS FARM

CHESTER AV

105

WASHINGTON

PACIFIC

CRANBERRY RD
BLAKE RD

Grayland

AMERICAN MILL RD
BISHOP RD

EVERGREEN PARK RD

GRAYS HARBOR CO
PACIFIC CO

OCEAN

SEAHURST ACCESS RD
MIDWAY BEACH RD

Heather
LINDGREN RD
UDELL RD
HANSEN RD
JACOBSON RD
GOULD RD
LARKIN RD
SMITH RD
ANDERSON RD

SEASTRAND RIDGE

PACIFIC COUNTY

NORTH   RIVER

METRO

WILLAPA NATIONAL WILDLIFE REFUGE

SHOALWATER INDIAN RESERVATION

HAWKS POINT

105

Dexter By The Sea

NORTH COVE

TOKELAND RD

TOKE POINT

Tokeland

RANGE POINT

BRUCEPORT PARK

101

BUSH DR
ROBERT DR

WILLAPA   BAY

STONY POINT

SOUTH BEND

SNAG ISLANDS

PALIX RD

LEADBETTER POINT

WILSON POINT

KINGSLEY RD

WILLAPA

NATIONAL

GRASSY ISLAND

BUSH PIONEER COUNTY PARK
GOOSE POINT

Bay Center

BAY CENTER RD
BAY CENTER DIKE RD

HAROLD YOUNG RD

WILDLIFE

KOA BAY CENTER/ WILLAPA BAY

Rhodesia Beach

SOUTH BEND

RIXON

REFUGE

LEADBETTER POINT STATE PARK

103

STACKPOLE HARBOR

SANDY POINT

RHODESIA BEACH RD

PALIX RIVER

0 1 2 3 4 miles   1 in. = 2.5 mi.

SEE 180 MAP

A B C D

METRO

1

CAPITOL
STATE
FOREST

LITTLE LARCH MOUNTAIN
Fall Creek Campground
Mount Molly Campground
Fuzzy Top
Yew Tree Campground
Middle Waddel Campground
Margaret McKenny Campground
Mina Falls Trailhead Campground
Sherman Valley Campground
Lost Valley
Sherman Valley

GRAYS HARBOR CO
THURSTON CO

Delphi

101ST AV
103RD AV SW
110TH AV
113TH

WADDELL CREEK RD SW
FAIRVIEW
88TH AV
81ST AV SW
93RD AV SW
99
101ST AV SW
104TH AV SW
107TH AV SW

121

OLYMPIA AIRPORT
83RD AV SW
88TH

East Olympia
FIR TREE DR SE
89TH AV SE
RAINIER RD SE
RICH RD

FORT LEWIS MILITARY RESERVATION

103RD AV SE

2

Bordeaux
BORDEAUX
Bordeaux
MARKSHAM RD SW
Littlerock
MAYTOWN
133RD AV SW
140TH AV SW
143RD AV SW
Mumby

MILLER-SYLVANIA STATE PARK

MAYTOWN
95
GUN STONE ST
REEDER RD
140TH
143RD AV
MAYTOWN RD SW
131ST SE

121

South Union
100TH AV SE
BROOKS LN SE
SHELDON RD SE
McCORKLE RD SE
PATSY RD SE

OFFUTT LAKE
OFFUTT LAKE RD SE
WALDRICK RD SE
STEDMAN RD SE

ANGUS DR SE
Chain Hill
HYATT SE
VANTINE SE

3

Mima
152ND AV SW
MIMA RD
POLEHN RD SW
163RD AV SW
169TH AV SW
180TH
183RD

R
R

Sunnydale
TILLEY RD
PACIFIC HWY
171ST AV SE
MELVILLE RD SE

Tenino Junction

OREGON TRAIL MONUMENT
LEMON HILL
OLD MILITARY RD SE

TENINO
TENINO DEPOT MUSEUM
BLUMAUER RD SE
NORTHCRAFT RD SE
BLUMER HILL
NORTHCRAFT MOUNTAIN
CHURCHILL RD SE
STRAWN LN SE

507
KINMILES SE
McDUFF RD SE
MIMA ACRES SE
SUMNER ST SE

4

ANDERSON RD
175TH AV SW
176TH AV SW
173RD ST SW
JORDAN ST SW
ALBANY ST SW
183RD AV SW
Rochester
LUCKY EAGLE CASINO
188TH AV SW
CHEHALIS INDIAN RESERVATION
188TH AV SW
191ST AV
195TH AV SW
196TH AV SW
12
JOSELYN SW
SQUARE ST
NUTMEG ST
LEITNER
DANBY DR
MAKLY LN
WAKLY

THURSTON COUNTY

BUCODA

SKOOKUMCHUCK RD
507
TONO RD
TYRELL RD SE
Tono

SKOOKUMCHUCK RIVER

PENDLETON
SCHOOL LAND RD
LITTLEROCK
GATE
HUNTER RD SW
Gate
HOLM RD SW
MOON RD
BLACK LAND RD
SARGENT
ROSEBERG ST SW
DENMARK ST SW
CARPER ST SW
GRAND MOUND
88
Grand Mound
210TH AV SW
213TH
216TH AV SW
219TH AV SW
Meadows

HELSING JUNCTION
MANNERS RD
Helsing Junction
VAN DYKE RD SW
MICHIGAN HILL
LUNDEEN RD SW
Michigan Hill
LANGWORTHY RD
MICHIGAN HILL
PRATHER
JAMES
JORDAN ST SW

CHEHALIS RIVER

PACIFIC HWY
OLD HWY 99

DUNLAP RD SE
ZENKER
ZENNER VALLEY
OCONNER
GRADE ST SE
CONNER RD

LEWIS COUNTY
THURSTON CO
LEWIS CO

5

LINCOLN CREEK RD
TEAGUE RD
MATTSON RD
COOKS RD
Galvin
GALVIN
LINCOLN CREEK RD

PRAIRIE AV
HARRISON
DOWNING RD
Wabash
BIG HANAFORD RD
HANAFORD RD

CENTRALIA
299
PEARL ST
W REYNOLDS AV
82
W SIXTH ST
SIXTH ST
W FIRST ST
TOWER AV
MAIN ST
MELLEN ST
81
12
HILL RD
GOLD ST
KRESKY AV
HAM HILL
LITTLE HANAFORD RD
N SEMINARY HILL RD
SALZER VALLEY RD
GRIMES RD
TEITTEL RD
CENTRALIA ALPHA RD

Nulls Crossing
ANDERSON RD
JONES RD
LITTLE HANAFORD RD
Kopiah
Mendota

WASHINGTON

6

BUNKER CREEK RD
DEEP CREEK RD
CHILVERS RD
JEFFRIES RD
Claquato
BEACH AV
OCEAN BEACH HWY
CHEHALIS RIVER
Littell
Milburn
CERES HILL
MESKILL RD
SPOONER RD
CLINTON RD
CURTIS HILL RD
6
Adna
Chehalis Junction

CHEHALIS
5
79
AIRPORT RD
STATE AV
NATIONAL AV
MAIN ST
MARKET ST
77
76
ADAMS RD
JACKSON HWY
COAL CREEK RD
PROFFITT RD
ALPHA
Logan Hill
ROGERSON RD
POLLMAN RD
YATES RD
PATTEE RD
HEWITT RD
LOGAN HILL RD
NORTH FORK NEWAUKUM RIVER

STAN HEDWALL PARK
NEWAUKUM RIVER
Newaukum

7

SEE 117 MAP
SEE 118 MAP
SEE 187 MAP

0 1 2 3 4 miles   1 in. = 2.5 mi.

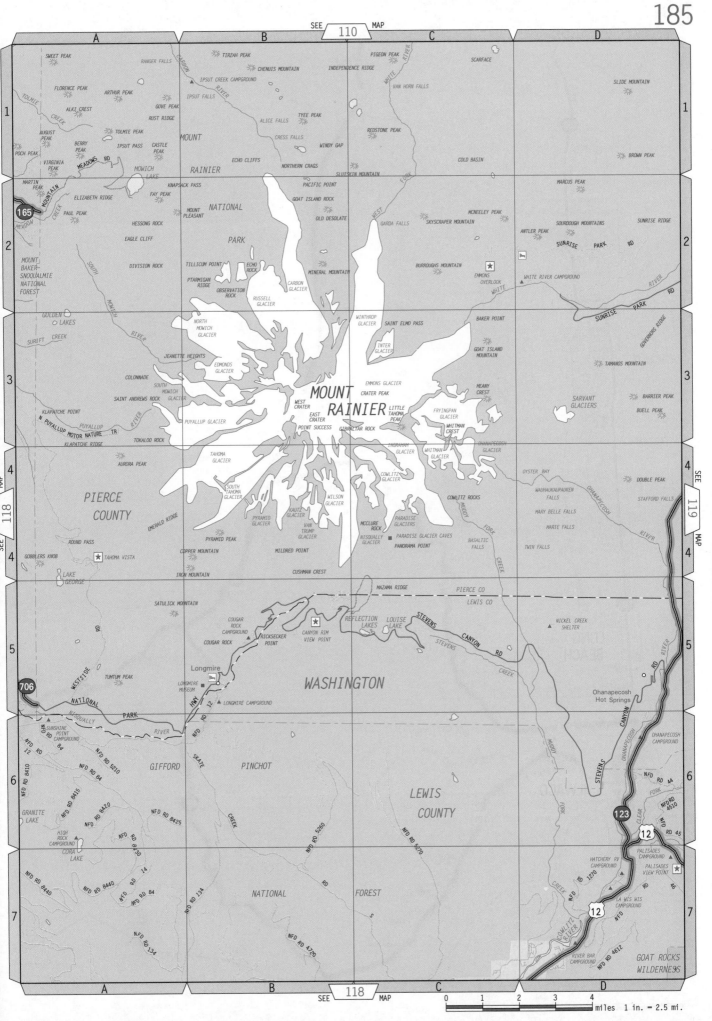

METRO

SEE 183 MAP

A B C D

1 1

WILLAPA

NORTH
STACKPOLE RD

101

RAMSEY POINT

103
BEACH
Oysterville
OYSTERVILLE RD
ESPY DR
PL
DOUGLAS DR

BAY

2 2

PENINSULA

JOE JOHNS RD

LYNN POINT

NEEDLE POINT

Nahcotta

BAY AV

Ocean Park

DIAMOND POINT

PACIFIC

245 ST

Klipsan Beach
227

ST
PL
PL
RD

3 3

SUNSHINE POINT

JENSEN POINT

WILLAPA

PARADISE POINT

CHETLO

LONG ISLAND

208 PL

198 PL

BIRCH ST

NATIONAL

STANLEY PENINSULA

STANLEY PENINSULA HARBOR

101

OCEAN

WILDLIFE

177TH ST

REFUGE

SMOKY HOLLOW

SEE 116 MAP

4 4

Oceanside

BIRCH

Pacific Beach
CRANBERRY RD

HIGH POINT

SHOALWATER BAY

PAR PALA

4

SEE 117 MAP

PL

SANDRIDGE

OMEARA POINT

ROUND ISLAND

NASELLE STATE SALMON HATCHERY

LONGFELLOW HILL

113 ST

101

101 PL

SPRUCE ST

Breakers

103

PIONEER RD

PACIFIC

PORTER POINT

RD

5 5

LONG BEACH

WASHINGTON AV S

WILLAPA

COUNTY

Naselle

4

WORLD KITE MUSEUM AND HALL OF FAME

WOODGATE RD

67TH

NATIONAL

VELDNESS RD

BEAR RIVER RIDGE

TARLATT RD

Moores Corner
55

WILDLIFE

JIM ST

BALD RIDGE

Seaview

REFUGE

FERRY RD

41 PL

101

WASHINGTON

6

PACIFIC CO

WAHKIAKUM CO

SALMON CREEK RD

ALT 101

101

NORTH HEAD RD

Holman

CHINOOK

BEAR RIVER RD

SHOALWATER BAY

6 6

NORTH HEAD LIGHT-HOUSE

100

KOA ILWACO

STRINGTOWN RD

BEAR RIVER

NASELLE RIDGE

401

BRIX BAY

BEARDS HOLLOW

NORTH HEAD LIGHTHOUSE RD

ROBERT GRAY DR

ILWACO

ILWACO HERITAGE MUSEUM

VALLEY RD

ROCKY POINT LIGHT

MCKENZIE HEAD

US NAVAL RESER- VATION

BAKER BAY

101

KNAPPTON

GRAYS POINT

GRAYS BAY LIGHT

GRAYS BAY

FORT CANBY STATE PARK

LINGENFELTER RD

BEAR MOUNTAIN

CAPE DISAPPOINTMENT LIGHTHOUSE

SAND ISLAND

PACIFIC CO
CLATSOP CO

Chinook

HOUTCHEN ST

FORT COLUMBIA STATE PARK

CLIFF POINT

GRAYS POINT LIGHT

7 7

WASHINGTON
OREGON

REAR ENTRANCE RANGE LIGHTHOUSE

COLUMBIA

RIVER

SCARBORO HILL

HUNGRY HARBOR

RIVER

SAND ISLAND DIKE MIDDLE LIGHT

SAND ISLAND DIKE LIGHT

CHINOOK POINT

COLUMBIA

PACIFIC CO
CLATSOP CO

CLATSOP COUNTY

CHINOOK DIKE LIGHT

FORT STEVENS STATE PARK

A B C D

SEE 188 MAP

0 1 2 3 4 miles 1 in. = 2.5 mi.

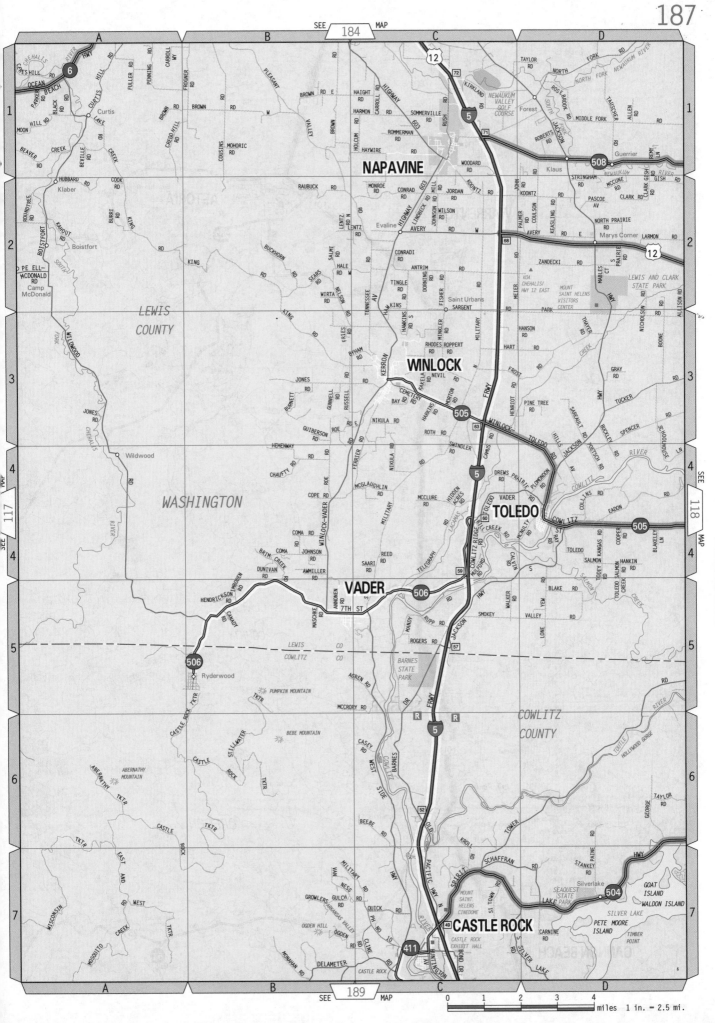

METRO

NAPAVINE

WINLOCK

TOLEDO

VADER

CASTLE ROCK

LEWIS COUNTY

WASHINGTON

COWLITZ COUNTY

miles 1 in. = 2.5 mi.

SEE MAP 186

A   B   C   D

1

COLUMBIA

RIVER

CLATSOP SPIT

JETTY

REAR RANGE LIGHT

FRONT RANGE LIGHT

GENERAL ANCHORAGE

TONGUE POINT LIGHTHOUSE

POINT ADAMS
Fort Stevens
Hammond
POINT ADAMS
COAST GUARD STATION
LOWER SANDS LIGHTHOUSE

TONGUE POINT
NAVAL BASE
(HISTORICAL)
Tongue Point Village

MOTT ISLAND

WEST LIGHT

LOIS ISLAND

FORT
STEVENS
STATE
PARK

300

KOA ASTORIA/SEASIDE

SKIPANON WATERWAY LIGHTHOUSE

YOUNGS BAY ENTRANCE LIGHT

Lexington
Irving
30 AV
COLUMBIA RIVER

NIAGARA AV
ALAMEDA AV
7TH ST

ASTORIA

Emerald Heights

Fern Hill

CLATSOP
STATE
FOREST

WARRENTON

2

COLUMBIA BEACH

E HARBOR ST

WARRENTON DUMP

SCHOOL RD

MAIN AV

7TH ST

OCEANVIEW CEMETERY

FORT STEVENS RD

CAMP RILEA

101

BUS 101

PORT OF ASTORIA AIRPORT

WARRENTON

YOUNGS BAY

Jeffers Garden

Miles Crossing

202

YOUNGS

NEHALEM HWY

WALLUSKI LOOP RD

LABISKE

3

PACIFIC

Clatsop Station
PERKINS RD

Glenwood

CAMP CLATSOP MILITARY RESERVATION

SOUTH POST RD

Carnahan

CULLABY LAKE RD

LEWIS AND CLARK NATIONAL HISTORICAL PARK

CLATSOP

FORT
CLATSOP RD

YOUNGS RIVER

FRY ISLAND

GRANT ISLAND

HAVEN ISLAND

TUCKER CREEK

LEWIS AND
CLARK RD

LOGAN RD

PETER JOHNSON LOOP

Olney

PALMER RD

LILLENAS RD

Sunset Beach

SUNSET BEACH RD

LEWIS AV

OCEAN

CULLABY LAKE COUNTY PARK

West Lake

CULLABY LAKE

DELLMOOR LP

SURF PINES RD

CLATSOP RIDGE

MAUGSWORTH RD

LEWIS AND CLARK HWY

LONE RIDGE

Melville

KLASKANINE FISH HATCHERY

GREEN MOUNTAIN

SADDLE MOUNTAIN RD

4

SEE MAP 116

METRO

OCEAN

301

GEARHART LOOP RD

Butterfield

MARION AV

PACIFIC WY

G ST

GEARHART

YOUNGS RIVER FALLS

YOUNGS RIVER

CLATSOP STATE FOREST

5

COTTAGE AV

Neawanna Station

BEACH DR

HOLLADAY DR

N WAHANNA RD

BROADWAY

AVE G

AVE S

SEASIDE

LEWIS AND CLARK HWY

**CLATSOP
COUNTY**

SISTER GREEN MOUNTAIN

GREEN MOUNTAIN

CLATSOP STATE FOREST

EELS RIDGE

CLARK

SADDLE
MOUNTAIN
STATE
PARK

6

ECOLA
STATE
PARK

TILLAMOOK HEAD DR

SUNSET BEACH

WEST POINT

RIPPET RD

Rippet Mountain

101

TWIN PEAKS

DAVIS POINT

OREGON

SADDLE MOUNTAIN

SADDLE MOUNTAIN RD

HUMBUG MOUNTAIN

TILLAMOOK HEAD

TILLAMOOK ROCK

BALD MOUNTAIN

BIRD POINT

Cannon Beach Junction

COAST HWY

7

INDIAN BEACH

SUBMARINE ROCK

SEA LION ROCK ARCH

CRESCENT BEACH

BIRD ROCKS

CHAPMAN BEACH

26

KLOOTCHIE CREEK CAMPGROUND

N HEMLOCK ST

OREGON COAST HWY

SUNSET HWY

NECANICUM

NECANICUM RIVER

Necanicum Junction

26

SUNSET HWY

CANNON BEACH

HAYSTACK ROCK

SUNSET BLVD

CLATSOP STATE FOREST

BAILEY POINT

53

Hamlet

SEE MAP 191

A   B   C   D

0 1 2 3 4 miles 1 in. = 2.5 mi.

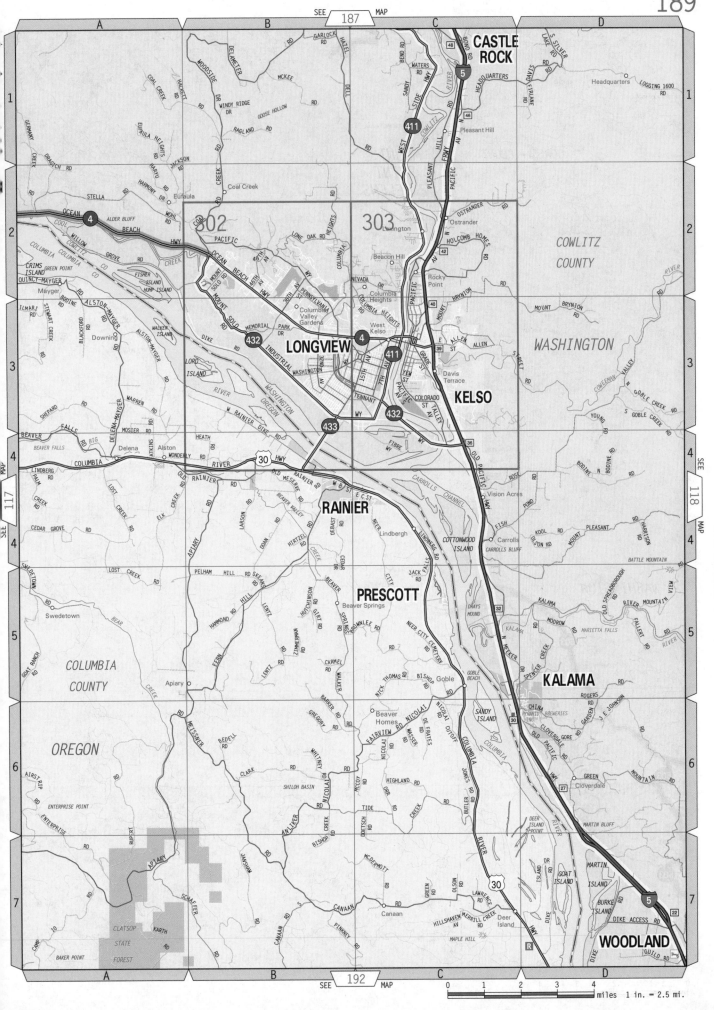

METRO

miles 1 in. = 2.5 mi.

A | B | C | D

SEE 118 MAP

METRO

MOUNT SAINT HELENS

SPOTTED BUCK MOUNTAIN

SPUD MOUNTAIN

CASTLE PEAK

CASTLE CREEK MARSH

JOHNSTON RIDGE

504

HARRYS RIDGE

SPIRIT LAKE

DUCK BAY

HARMONY VIEW POINT

CEDAR CREEK VIEW POINT

NFD RD 2560

NFD RD 2560

DENNY BROOK VIEW POINT

NFD RD 94

NFD RD 9403

WINDY RIDGE VIEW POINT

SMITH CREEK VIEW POINT

NORTH FORK TOUTLE RIVER

MOUNT SAINT HELENS

NATIONAL VOLCANIC MONUMENT

STUDEBAKER RIDGE

NFD RD 99

COWLITZ COUNTY

MOUNT SAINT

SOUTH FORK TOUTLE

TIMBERLINE CAMPGROUND

WISHBONE GLACIER

ALPINE BUTTE

NFD RD 270

RIVER

HELENS

SHEEP CANYON VIEW POINT

SHEEP CANYON

RIVER

NATIONAL

TALUS GLACIER

TOUTLE GLACIER

CRESCENT RIDGE

NELSON GLACIER

APE GLACIER

PUMICE BUTTE

APE CANYON

NFD RD 380

1980 CRATER

SHOESTRING GLACIER

NFD RD 83

MUDDY RIVER GORGE

NFD RD 700

CLEARWATER

GIFFORD

PINCHOT

NATIONAL

VOLCANIC

DRYER GLACIER

BUTTE CAMP DOME

MONITOR RIDGE

SWIFT GLACIER

WORM FLOWS

PINE

LAVA CANYON

NFD RD 810

RIVER RD

FOREST

GOAT MOUNTAIN

RD 81

NFD RD B123

MONUMENT

SWIFT CREEK FLOW

JACKPINE SHELTER

LAHAR VIEW POINT

NFD RD 8320

NFD RD 2588

NFD RD 2586

NFD RD 30

NFD RD 81

RIVER

BEDROCK PASS

NFD RD 81

NFD RD 83

GIFFORD

KALAMA

PINCHOT

MUDDY RIVER VIEW POINT

NFD RD 81

KALAMA FALLS

CINNAMON PEAK

NFD RD 8303

APE CAVE MUSEUM

MARBLE MOUNTAIN

NATIONAL

LEWIS

MERRILL LAKE CAMPGROUND

9015

FOREST

SEE 118 MAP

MERRILL LAKE

GREEN MOUNTAIN

LEWIS

NFD RD

SWIFT DAM OVERLOOK

RIVER

SWIFT FOREST CAMPGROUND

NFD RD 90

WASHINGTON

BEAVER BAY CAMPGROUND

CHRISTMAS CANYON

SWIFT CREEK RESERVOIR

Cougar

503

RD

LEWIS

RIVER

SKAMANIA COUNTY

COONEY POINT

RIVER

McCLELLAN MOUNTAIN

SPEELYAI STATE HATCHERY

CLARK CO

SKAMANIA CO

GIFFORD

NFD RD 3105

PARADISE VALLEY

503

SPEELYAI HILL VIEW POINT

WILLIAMS RD

YALE LAKE

CLARK COUNTY

NFD RD 6403

NFD RD 207

NFD RD 64

HAM RD

PRIVATE

SADDLE DAM CAMPGROUND

PINCHOT

NFD RD 64

NFD RD 6401

FRAZIER RD

COWLITZ CO

CLARK CO

TIMBERED PEAK

503

NFD RD 64

NATIONAL

NFD RD 203

RD

TUMTUM MOUNTAIN

FOREST

HEALY

NFD RD 5701

NFD RD 320

HORSESHOE RIDGE

NFD RD 6406

SISTER ROCKS

NFD RD 317

NFD RD 54

CALAMITY PEAK

RD

OBSERVATION BERRYFIELD CAMPGROUND

0 1 2 3 4 miles   1 in. = 2.5 mi.

A | B | C | D

SEE 188 MAP

A   B   C   D

© 2006 Rand McNally & Company

CANNON BEACH

CANNON BEACH
Tolovana Park
CLATSOP STATE FOREST

SILVER POINT
JOCKEY CAP
DOUBLE PEAK
SUGARLOAF MOUNTAIN

HUMBUG POINT
CLATSOP COUNTY

HAMLET

ARCADIA BEACH
CLATSOP STATE FOREST
SOUTH SUGARLOAF
CLATSOP
COLE MOUNTAIN

HUG POINT
HUG POINT STATE PARK
ADAIR POINT

AUSTIN POINT
COLE MOUNTAIN

CLATSOP STATE FOREST
ONION PEAK
CLATSOP STATE FOREST
STATE

ARCH CAPE
CASTLE ROCK
OREGON
BLACK BUTTE
NORTH FORK FALLS

OCEAN
ARCH CAPE
GULL ROCK

COVE BEACH
ANGORA PEAK
NORTH HWY
COUNTY LINE
FORK RD
FOREST

SHORT SAND CROSS OVER
CLATSOP CO.
TILLAMOOK CO.
GODS VALLEY RD

TIDE AV
OSWALD WEST STATE PARK
TILLAMOOK STATE FOREST
ALDERVALE
VALLEY

ARMSTEAD MEMORIAL
RD
GODS
RECTOR RIDGE

FALCON ROCK
TILLAMOOK STATE FOREST
ROCK MOUNTAIN

SMUGGLER COVE
OREGON COAST HWY
NEHALEM QUARRY RD
WILSON ANDERSON RD
NECANICUM

DEVILS CAULDRON
NEAHKAHNIE MOUNTAIN
CLASSIC RIDGE
RIVER
RD

NORTH FORK RD
MCDONALD RD
NEHALEM RIVER

Neahkahnie Beach
RD
MCKIMMENS RD
NEHALEM FALLS
FOSS RD

MANZANITA
NEHALEM RD
OCEAN RD
3RD ST
OCEAN AV
SPOOLINGTER
GRANGE GATEWAY RD
B ST
TIDELAND
NEHALEM

LANEDA
CAREY
Bayside Gardens
NEHALEM
53
Mohler
SHIFFMAN RD
FOSS
FOSS RD

VENNE BEACH
NEHALEM BAY STATE AIRPORT
DEAN POINT
3RD ST
Batterson
COOK RD

SUNSET BEACH
NEHALEM BAY
Foss

FISHERY POINT
WHEELER
HWY
Wheeler Heights
RIVER
CREEK RD

NEHALEM BAY STATE PARK
NEHALEM BEACH
Brighton
MIAMI
SHIFFMAN RD

PACIFIC
CRAB ROCK
NEHALEM FISH HATCHERY
TILLAMOOK

OREGON COAST HWY
Nedonna Beach
Barnesdale
CRAIG MOUNTAIN
STATE

101
Manhattan Beach
FRANK RD
CRANE RD

ROCKAWAY BEACH
RIVER

N 3RD AV
TILLAMOOK COUNTY
RIVER

S 2ND ST
S QUADRANT AV
S EASY ST
FOREST

TWIN ROCKS
CAPTAIN GRAY MOUNTAIN
MIAMI

PAINTED ROCK
Twin Rocks
GRAYS MOUNTAIN

Watseco
FOREST

Barview
GREEN HILL
TILLAMOOK
MOSS CREEK RD

GARIBALDI
AV
GARIBALDI
EKROTH RD
STATE

CRAB ROCK
MIAMI COVE
FOREST

BAYOCEAN DIKE RD
Tillamook Bay Coast Guard Station
Crab Harbor
HOBSONVILLE POINT
Hobsonville
KILCHIS RIVER RD

BAYOCEAN PENINSULA
TILLAMOOK BAY
HOBSONVILLE POINT DR HIGH ST
BAY CITY

Bayocean
LARSON COVE
SANDSTONE POINT

SEE 124 MAP
SEE 125 MAP

METRO

SEE 197 MAP

0 1 2 3 4 miles   1 in. = 2.5 mi.

SEE 189 MAP

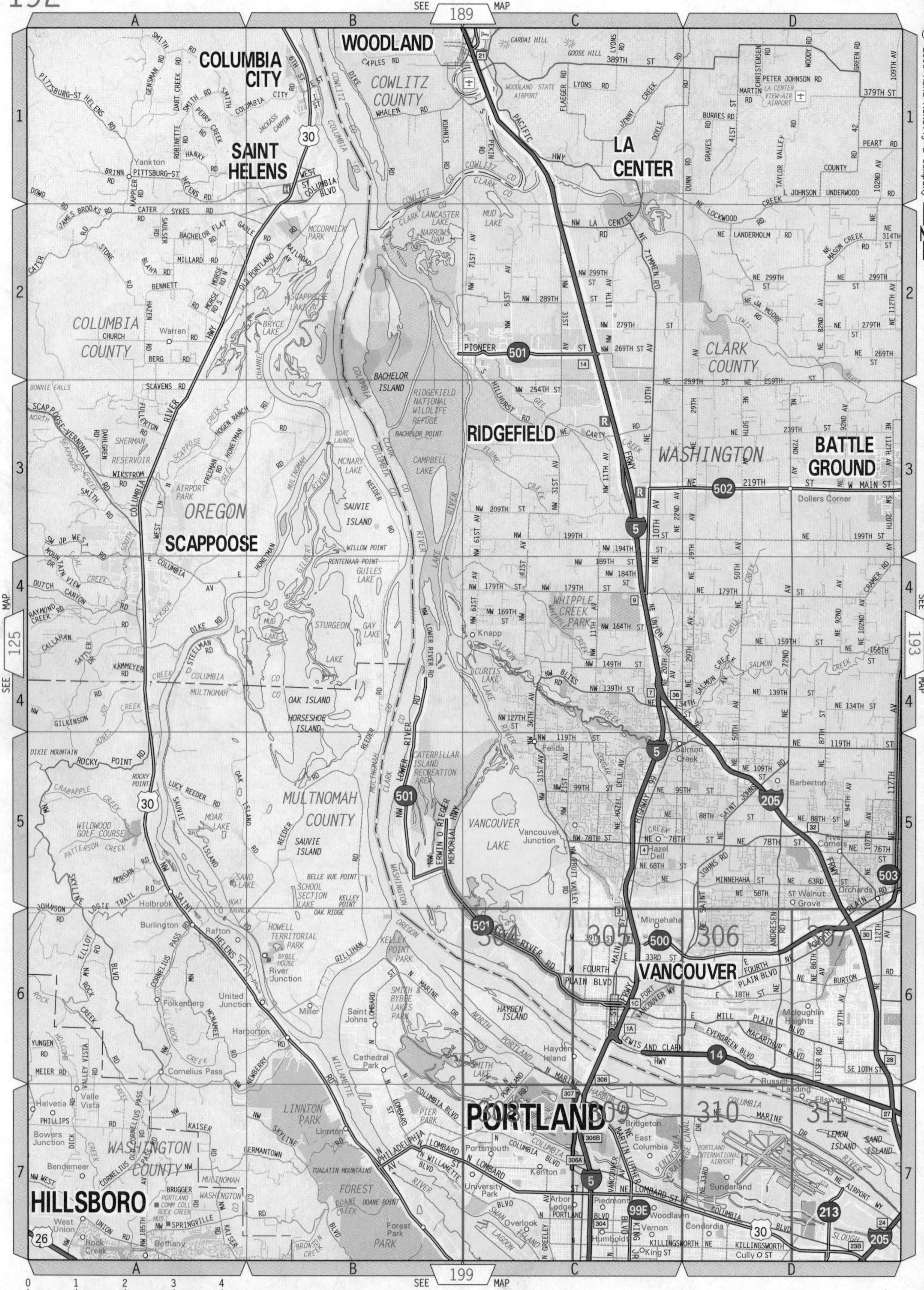

WOODLAND

COLUMBIA CITY

SAINT HELENS

COWLITZ COUNTY

LA CENTER

CLARK COUNTY

WASHINGTON

RIDGEFIELD

BATTLE GROUND

COLUMBIA COUNTY

CHURCH

SCAPPOOSE

OREGON

Ridgefield National Wildlife Refuge

Bachelor Island

Sauvie Island

MULTNOMAH COUNTY

Vancouver Lake

Vancouver Junction

VANCOUVER

PORTLAND

HILLSBORO

WASHINGTON COUNTY

FOREST PARK

Portland International Airport

METRO

SEE 125 MAP

SEE 193 MAP

SEE 199 MAP

0 1 2 3 4 miles 1 in. = 2.5 mi.

© 2008 Rand McNally & Company

501 502 503 500 304 305 306 307 308 310 311 213 205 99E 30 26 14 5

Map Labels

Cities/Places: YACOLT, BATTLE GROUND, VANCOUVER, CAMAS, WASHOUGAL, PORTLAND

Counties: CLARK COUNTY, SKAMANIA COUNTY, WASHINGTON

Parks/Forests: GIFFORD PINCHOT NATIONAL FOREST, WORMALD STATE PARK, MOULTON FALLS PARK, BATTLE GROUND STATE PARK, LEWISVILLE PARK, LACAMAS PARK

Features: Fargher Lake, Heisson, Venersborg, Dole, Hockinson, Brush Prairie, Proebstel, Creswell Heights, Round Lake, Lacamas Lake, Mill Plain, Oak Park

Mountains: Yacolt Mountain, Gumboot Mountain, Tatoosh Hills, Jack Mountain, Bells Mountain, Tukes Mountain, Spotted Deer Mountain, Rock Creek, Squaw Butte, Elkhorn Mountain, Larch Mountain, Camp Hill, Munsell Hill, Little Baldy, Livingston Mountain, Spud Mountain, Green Mountain, Brunner Hill, Pohls Hill, Bobs Mountain, Bluff Mountain, Hemlock, Nichols Hill, Mount Pleasant, Cape Horn

Campgrounds: Sunset Campground, Tarbell Campground, Cold Creek Campground, Rock Creek Campground, Jones Creek Campground

Highways: 503, 500, 14, 205, 190, 192, 194, 200

Rivers: Lewis River, Yacolt Creek, Cedar Creek, Columbia River, Washougal River, Lacamas Creek, Salmon Creek, Camas Creek, Burnt Bridge Creek, Campen Creek, Gibbons Creek, Washougal Falls

SEE 190 MAP / SEE 200 MAP / SEE 192 MAP / SEE 194 MAP

METRO

0 1 2 3 4 miles 1 in. = 2.5 mi.

LEWIS AND CLARK HWY, EVERGREEN HWY, WASHINGTON ST

SEE 190 MAP

METRO

A B C D

1

CALAMITY
CALAMITY PEAK
PEAK
NFD RD 58
NFD RD 58
NFD RD 54
CANYON
CREEK
NFD RD 527

BARE MOUNTAIN
RIDGE
TR
OBSERVATION PEAK
GIFFORD
HOWE RIDGE
MIDDLE BUTTE
NFD RD 64
RD
CREEK
NFD RD 6053
NFD RD 65

PINCHOT
MEADOW RD
SOUTH BUTTE
NFD RD
GULER
NFD RD 6052

SODA PEAKS
SODA PEAK
MINERAL SPRINGS RD
NFD RD
NATIONAL
CARSON
RD

2

SATURDAY ROCK
GREEN LOOKOUT MOUNTAIN
NFD RD 42
RIDGE
WEST CRATER
SODA
NFD RD 42
SODA PEAK
CARSON NATIONAL FISH HATCHERY
LITTLE SODA SPRINGS CAMPGROUND
NFD RD
BEAVER CAMPGROUND
LITTLE SODA SPRINGS
FOREST
GULER
PANTHER CREEK

FORK
GREEN
NFD RD 4306
TROUT CREEK HILL
CARSON
GOBBLERS KNOB
PANTHER
EXPERIMENTAL
FOREST

3

LITTLE LOOKOUT MOUNTAIN
HEMLOCK
NFD RD 413
WIND RIVER
NFD RD 43
NFD RD 417
TR
WARREN GAP
NFD RD 6517
PANTHER CREEK CAMPGROUND
WEIGLE HILL

SUNSET
RD
NFD RD 43
EXPERIMENTAL
CREST
RD Stabler
PILOT KNOB
RD

MCKINLEY RIDGE
SKAMANIA
COUNTY
SNAG
SUNSET
FOREST
HEMLOCK
GREEN KNOB
HEMLOCK RD
FOSTER RD
BLACKLEDGE RD
WIND
WIND RIVER
BATTLE GROUND

4

CREEK
PACIFIC
TR
WASHINGTON
STEVENSON RIDGE
SNAG
RD
TR
BEAR CREEK RD

SEE 193 MAP

RIVER
CREEK
ROCK CREEK BUTTE
SKAAR RD
CARSON
CARSON RIVER VALLEY

SEE 195 MAP

WASHOUGAL RIVER
HOT SPRINGS
GREENLEAF PEAK
AALVIK RD
KANAKA CREEK RD
STEVENSON RIDGE TR
HOT SPRINGS AV

5

RD
GREENLEAF BASIN
RYAN-ALLEN RD
LOOP RD
14
COLUMBIA RIVER
GOVERNMENT COVE
ANDERSON POINT
HERMAN CREEK RD

DOUGAN CREEK CAMPGROUND
TABLE MOUNTAIN
STEVENSON
ROCK COVE
HWY
SKAMANIA CO
HOOD RIVER CO
HWY 47
HWY

WASHOUGAL STATE SALMON HATCHERY
MINES
MCCLOSKEY
BEACON ROCK STATE PARK
ASH LAKE
CASCADE LOCKS HWY
CASCADE FOREST RD
ASH LAKE RD
BOW FISH HATCHERY
CASCADE LOCKS

6

MABEE CREEK RD
CEDAR CREEK RD
SWAMP RD
SCOTT RD
COUNTRY QUARRY
KUEFFLER RD
HAMILTON MOUNTAIN
HARDY FALLS
NORTH BONNEVILLE
EAGLE CREEK CAMPGROUND
EVERGREEN
Fort Rains
COLUMBIA
14
MARINE PARK AND CAMPGROUND
CASCADE LOCKS-STEVENSON STATE AIRPORT
HOOD RIVER COUNTY

MCCLOSKEY
DIMRILL RD
DALE RD
DUNCAN RD
MCDONALD CREEK
BEACON ROCK
Skamania
PIERCE ISLAND
30
84
40
Bonneville
TOOTH ROCK TUNNEL
WAUNA POINT
CASCADE SALMON HATCHERY
RD
CABLE
CASCADE FALLS
METLAKO FALLS
BENSON PLATEAU
PACIFIC
PUNCH BOWL FALLS

7

RYAN-TAVELLI RD
SNEIDER-BARKS
ARCHER MOUNTAIN
FRANZ RD
DEVILLE RD
WASHINGTON
OREGON
TOMMIT RD
COLUMBIA RIVER
HWY 37
Dodson
WAUNEKA POINT
ELOWAH FALLS
MUNRA POINT
MOFFETT FALLS
TANNER CREEK RD
HOOD RIVER CO
MULTNOMAH CO
LOOWIT FALLS
COLUMBIA
WILDERNESS
LOOWIT FALLS

14
EVERGREEN HWY
SKAMANIA ISLAND
36
HWY
Cruzatt
Pringle
SKAMANIA CO
MULTNOMAH CO
31
CROWN POINT MIST FALLS
DALTON POINT WAHKEENA FALLS
ONEONTA FALLS
HORSETAIL FALLS
YEON MOUNTAIN
WAESPE POINT
NESMITH POINT
NE SMITH POINT RD
MOUNT HOOD
NATIONAL FOREST
PALMER PEAK
MULTNOMAH COUNTY
OREGON
TALAPUS RIDGE
WY'EAST CAMPSITE
BLUE GROUSE CAMPSITE
TUNNEL FALLS
SEVEN-AND-A-HALF MILE CAMPSITE
TR

0 1 2 3 4 miles   1 in. = 2.5 mi.

SEE 118 MAP

A B C D

1

CARSON GULER RD
FORLORN LAKES RD
CAVE CREEK RD
COUGAR WY
TRAIL PEAK
GULER MOUNTAIN
DRY CREEK RIDGE
BEAR VALLEY
CASCADE CREST TR
LUSK CREEK
MONTE CRISTO
CAMP FIVE HILL
NFD RD 6610
WHITE
141
ETON RIDGE

GIFFORD PINCHOT
BIG LAVA BED
S PRAIRIE
OKLAHOMA CAMPGROUND
LITTLE WHITE SALMON RIVER
MONTE CARLO
SALMON RIVER
CORNER
GLENWOOD RD
Gilmer
B Z

2
BIG HUCKLEBERRY MOUNTAIN
NATIONAL FOREST
BIG
OKLAHOMA RD
PENNY RIDGE
TIMBERHEAD MOUNTAIN
B Z Corner
MCILROY CANYON
OAK RIDGE RD
POSTGREN RD
PANTHER CREEK EXPERIMENTAL FOREST
S PRAIRIE
MCILROY SADDLE
BALDY PEAK
NFD RD 68
PACIFIC CREST
HUCKLEBERRY
KLICKITAT
COUNTY
NESTOR PEAK
RATTLESNAKE

3
GRASSY KNOLL
SHINGLE MOUNTAIN
LITTLE WHITE SALMON RD
MOSS CREEK CAMPGROUND RD
WHISTLING RIDGE
NORTHWESTERN LAKE
Husum
SANBORN
LOST RD
GOAT POINT
CREEK
BLUE
OX LOGGING RD
SALMON RIVER
WHITE SALMON RIVER
WASHINGTON

4
BUSH CREEK
TRIANGLE PASS
HAUK BUTTE
Willard
SKAMANIA COUNTY
WILLARD NATIONAL FISH HATCHERY
WILLARD RIVER
KLICKITAT CO
SKAMANIA CO
GREEN MOUNTAIN
POWERHOUSE RD
BALD MOUNTAIN
WHITE SALMON RD
WNUK RD
SNOWDEN
BATES RD
BERGE RD
Mill A
COOK-UNDERWOOD RD
UNDERWOOD MOUNTAIN
141
GRANGEVIEW RD
BURDOIN MOUNTAIN
TUNNEL
SHIPHERD FALLS
AUGSPURGER MOUNTAIN
BUNKER KEYS
CHEMAWA HILL
SPUR 141
HOT SPRINGS AV
BERGE RD
CARSON
Saint Martins Hot Springs
COOK HILL
KOLLOCK-KNAPP
COOK-UNDERWOOD HWY
Underwood
Underwood Heights
141
MAIN AV
PINE ESTES AV
SPRING ST
WHITE SALMON
RAMSEY LN

5
Home Valley
WIND MOUNTAIN
GIRL SCOUT
Collins
LITTLE WHITE SALMON NATIONAL FISH HATCHERY
Cook
EVERGREEN HWY
LEWIS & CLARK
14
WASHINGTON
OREGON
RUTHTON POINT
WELLS ISLAND
HOOD RIVER CO
BAUCOMA BASIN
KLICKITAT CO
H
BINGEN
CEDAR ST
SKAMANIA CO
HOOD RIVER CO
COLUMBIA RIVER
HOOD RIVER
RUTHTON COVE
62
RAND RD
30
84
WASCO LIGHT
84 30
HERMAN CREEK RD
Wyeth 51
WYETH CAMPGROUND
COLUMBIA RIVER
56
WYGANT STATE PARK
SENECA FOUTS MEMORIAL STATE PARK
POST CANYON
Clifton
MAY ST
BELMONT DR
FAIRVIEW DR
BELMONT DR
12TH ST
HOOD RIVER
84
30
SHELLROCK MOUNTAIN
LINDSEY CREEK STATE PARK
STARVATION CREEK STATE PARK
WARREN CREEK FALLS
VIENTO STATE PARK
POST CANYON
METHODIST DR
MULTNOMAH DR
INDIAN CREEK RD
PANORAMA POINT
COLUMBIA RIVER GORGE

6
NICK EATON RIDGE
COLUMBIA WILDERNESS
VIENTO RIDGE
COLUMBIA RIVER GORGE NATIONAL SCENIC AREA
RUCKMAN HILL DR
YORK HILL
HOOD RIVER GOLF COURSE
DR
COUNTRY CLUB
Rockford
BARRETT DR
TUCKER RD
Windmaster
HOOD RIVER COUNTY AIRPORT
NATIONAL SCENIC AREA
OLD DALLES DR
HOOD RIVER COUNTY
WOOLLY HORN RIDGE
MOUNT HOOD
LARCH MOUNTAIN RD
BINNS HILL RD
PORTLAND DR
Oak Grove
REED RD
TUCKER RD
ODELL HWY
35
Van Horn
VAN HORN BUTTE
RIDGE DR
Pine Grove
WHISKEY CREEK
EASTSIDE RD
VAN HORN RD
HOOD RIVER MOUNTAIN
OLD DALLES RD
HOOD RIVER CO
WASCO CO
CEDAR SWAMP CAMPSITE
KINGSLEY CAMPGROUND
KINGSLEY
HOOD RIVER
SUMMIT DR
Summit
Lenz
FIR RD
NEAL CREEK RD
THOMSEN RD

7
SEVEN-AND-A-HALF MILE CAMPSITE
TOMLIKE MOUNTAIN
WAHTUM LAKE
NFD RD 2810
OREGON NATIONAL FOREST
DEAD POINT
HOOD RIVER HATCHERY
PUNCHBOWL FALLS
PUNCH
DEAD POINT
Odell
DAVIS DR
Dukes Valley
WYEAST RD
CENTRAL VALE
MOUNT HOOD HWY
BOOTH HILL
MOUNT HOOD NATIONAL FOREST
HUSKEY MOUNTAIN
WAHTUM LAKE CAMPGROUND
BLOWDOWN RIDGE
COOK RD
WEST
GREEN RD
LOST LAKE
BONE RD
HOOD RIVER HWY
HILLCREST RD
NEAL CREEK RD
GILMOUR RD
PINE MOUNT DR

0 1 2 3 4 miles   1 in. = 2.5 mi.

SEE 194 MAP

SEE 196 MAP

METRO

METRO

SEE MAP 119

A B C D

SEE MAP 195

SEE MAP 127

1

2

3

4

5

6

7

CORNER–GLENWOOD RD

YAKAMA INDIAN RESERVATION

Panakanic

PANAKANIC

GLENWOOD–GOLDENDALE HWY

SODA SPRINGS RD

SODA SPRINGS CAMPGROUND

BATTLESNAKE RD

WILLIS CANYON

MAHKIACUS HEIGHTS

WILLIS CANYON

BEEKS CANYON RD

BEEKS CANYON

LOG

DUNKARD RD

FISHER

CORRAL FENCE RD

DIVISION RD

RATHERT RD

SKOOKUM CANYON RD

SPRING

WAHKIACUS

LEGALL

KLICKITAT RIVER

BILL MOORE RD

STAUCH RD

LAYALL RD

ONEAL RD

TITH HILL RD

BREWER

PARADISE RD

HOME ACRES RANCH RD

BREWER

MILL HEIGHTS DR

Woodruff Mill

LONG RD

SNYDER SWALE

KLICKITAT COUNTY

SKOOKUM CANYON

LONG BUTTE

WAHKIACUS CANYON

SNOWDEN RD

Snowden

SALMON

WHITE

SLEEPY HOLLOW

SNOWDEN RD

LYLE

SLEEPY HOLLOW RD

PYLE RD

Appleton

OLD APPLETON GRADE RD

SNYDER CANYON

Klickitat Springs

Klickitat

WAHKIACUS

Horseshoe Bend RD

142

ACME RD

DORSEY RD

BAKER RD

APPLETON CANYON RD

FISHER HILL RD

KLICKITAT APPLETON RD

KLICKITAT RIVER

PRAIRIE SWALE

PEARCE RD

CYMIOTTI RD

CANYON RD

SHADY LN

Pitt

LOGGING CAMP CANYON

WASHINGTON

WAHKIACUS HIGH RD

PLATT RD

COLUMBIA RIVER GORGE NATIONAL SCENIC AREA

JOHNSON RD

MCKINNEN RD

LYLE SNOWDEN RD

FISHER HILL RD

WHEELER CANYON RD

PAT MARX RD

JOHNSON CANYON RD

MORRIS RD

SCHILLING RD

Laws Corner

JOHNSON RD

TRACY HILL

LAZY B RD

ALLEN OAKS RD

HIGH

PRAIRIE RD

CLARK RD

Hartland

CREEK

127

Bristol

Bristol

ATWOOD RD

MAJOR CREEK RD

MCCLAIN TUTHILL RD

KNIGHT RD

GREEN CANYON RD

CENTERVILLE HWY

MANSFIELD BARKER RD

RIM VIEW RD

ROWLAND LAKE OLD

BALCH RD

HWY

CHAMBERLAIN LAKE

142

STR UCK HWY

MUD SPRING CANYON

DILLACORT CANYON

STACKER BUTTE

BINGEN GAP

14

R

R

Lyle

INDIAN POINT

KNIGHT CANYON RD

WIDE SKY CANYON

84

30

84

30

MOSIER-THE DALLES

MEMALOOSE STATE PARK

CANYON WY

DOUGS BEACH

CENTERVILLE

COLUMBIA RIVER GORGE NATIONAL

3RD AV

69

Hood River

MOSIER

STATE

MARSH CTO

DELL

MAYER STATE PARK

HWY

76

Rowena

RONDA DELL

COLUMBIA RIVER

MAYER STATE PARK

COLD SPRING FLAT

LEWIS RD

WINDY POINT

SCENIC AREA

STANLEY CANYON

TWIN OAK RD

DALLES MOUNTAIN RD

MOSIER RD

DRY CREEK RD

BEHRN RD

MORGANSON RD

CATLON RD

CAROL RD

MCCALL POINT

30

WASCO AND KLICKITAT CO.

Murdock

Smithville

CLARK

14

HORSETHIEF BUTTE HWY

HORSETHIEF LAKE STATE PARK

HUSKEY RD

WILSON RD

DIGGER RD

CREEK

SEVENMILE HILL

SEVENMILE HILL RD

CRATES POINT

DALLESPORT

WASHINGTON OREGON

COLUMBIA RIVER HWY

WASCO COUNTY

SNYDER CANYON

BAKER RD

WOODS BACKBONE

OSBURN CUTOFF RD

HIDDEN VALLEY

82

Crates Point

RIVER RD

HILL ST

TYADMAN

THE DALLES MUNICIPAL AIRPORT

DALLESPORT

PARALLEL AV

DOCK

CUSHING FALLS

Petersburg

SIGNAL HILL

88

WYSE RD

WASCO BUTTE

CHENOWETH CREEK RD

CHENOWETH RD

Chenoweth

83

2ND ST

LOWER EIGHTMILE RD

GOODERTSON RD

SUGARLOAF

LUCKY CANYON RD

KETCHUM RD

BROWNS CREEK RD

MARTONKA RD

SANDLIN RD

CHERRY HEIGHTS RD

LUTZ LN

Cherry Heights

CHERRY ST

KNOB HILL

10TH ST

13TH ST

84

85

86

87

84

197

THE DALLES DAM

COLUMBIA VIEW DR

LOWER EIGHTMILE

FIFTEENMILE RD

FIVEMILE CREEK

EIGHTMILE CREEK

OREGON

MILL CREEK

HILL CREEK RD

SKYLINE

SCENIC DR

E 10TH

E 13TH ST

E 19TH ST

H ST

OLD DUFUR RD

197

THE DALLES

SEE MAP 127

0 1 2 3 4 miles 1 in. = 2.5 mi.

SEE MAP 191

| A | B | C | D |

BAY CITY

TILLAMOOK

TILLAMOOK STATE FOREST

TILLAMOOK BAY

TILLAMOOK STATE FOREST

STANLEY PEAK

TILLAMOOK STATE FOREST

RANDALL HILL

BASELINE RD
DOUGHTY RD
VAUGHN RD
daville
OREGON COAST HWY
ALDERBROOK
101

PYRAMID ROCK

CAPE MEARES STATE PARK
PILLAR ROCK
CAPE MEARES LIGHTHOUSE
Cape Meares

PITCHER POINT
FLOWER POT (HISTORICAL)
GOOSE POINT
BOULDER POINT
ROCK POINT
Juno
SQUEEDUNK RIVER
MAKINSTER
MING POINT
HWY RIVER

KILCHIS FOREST
KILCHIS RIVER
KILCHIS POINT
MCCOYS COVE
BAYOCEAN RD
GOODSPEED
WILSON

AGATE BEACH
LATIMER RD
WILSON RIVER LP
LATIMIER RD
LATIMIER OUTLET AND TEXTILE CENTER
RIVER WILSON HWY
BLUE RIDGE
6

THREE ARCH ROCKS
LOST BOY CAVE
SEAL ROCK
Oceanside

TILLAMOOK
TILLAMOOK COUNTY PIONEER MUSEUM
NETARTS HWY
3RD ST
12TH ST
Hathaway Mead
WILSON
FAIRVIEW RD
HUGHEY LN
Fairview
BALMER HILL
GINGER PEAK
TILLAMOOK STATE FOREST
RIVER

CAPE MEARES LOOP
NETARTS HWY
Netarts
TOMLINSON RD
FENK RD
IONE RD
ELM AV
MAIN AV
RIVER RD
MATEJECK RD
W NELSON RD
GIENGER RD
TILLAMOOK COUNTY FAIRGROUNDS
MCCORMICK LP
TRASK
TRASK
TRASK RIVER STATE FISH HATCHERY

NETARTS
NETARTS RD
BURTON-FRASER RD
LONG PRAIRIE
CHANCE RD
NORTH FORK RD
GOLD CREEK RD

OCEAN
WILSON BEACH
CAPE LOOKOUT
NETARTS BAY
NETARTS BAY DR
WHISKEY CREEK
ELKOFF RD
SUTTON CREEK RD
BEWLEY CREEK RD
STEINER RD
TILLAMOOK HWY
BLIMP BLVD
TILLAMOOK AIRPORT
BRICKYARD
TILLAMOOK NAVAL AIR STATION MUSEUM
SOUTH PRAIRIE RD
EDWARDS BUTTE RD
EDWARDS BUTTE
STONE RD

TILLAMOOK COUNTY

STATE
PARK
NETARTS BAY CAMPGROUND
101
COAST
FANCETT CREEK RD
SIMMONS CREEK RD
TILLAMOOK STATE FOREST

SEE 124 MAP

OREGON
YELLOW FIR RD
Pleasant Valley
MUNSON CREEK RD
MUNSON CREEK FALLS
BEAVER POINT
GRINDSTONE MOUNTAIN

SEE 125 MAP

METRO

CAPE LOOKOUT STATE
SIUSLAW NATIONAL FOREST
CAPE LOOKOUT RD
SAND LAKE SUMMIT RD
SAND LAKE RD
NEWBERG RD
SAND LAKE
GREEN TIMBER RD
OREGON COAST HWY
BLANCHARD RD
NFD RD 8170
NFD 9171
BEAVER CREEK
HIGH PEAK
HARDSCRABBLE MOUNTAIN

PACIFIC
NFD RD 8008
Sandlake
GALLOWAY RD
Hemlock
SIUSLAW
EAST BEAVER RD
NFD RD 8112
CAMELBACK BLUFF
MOON CREEK
CARSON RD
NFD 8377

SAND BEACH CAMPGROUND
SAND LAKE
BUZZARD BUTTE
BIXBY
Beaver
BLAINE
NESTUCCA RD
BOULDER CREEK RD
Blaine
EAST CREEK RD
NFD RD 8376

Tierra Del Mar
FOREST
FARMER CREEK RD
MILES MOUNTAIN
OLD CONDOR RD
EVERGREEN RD
SIUSLAW
UPPER NESTUCCA RIVER RD
POWDER CREEK RD
NFD RD 8594

CAPE KIWANDA STATE PARK
MCPHILLIPS RD
FERRY RD
Hebo
THREE RIVERS
NATIONAL
NFD RD 14
HEBO LAKE CAMPGROUND
NFD RD 1492
MOUNT HEBO CAMPGROUND
MOUNT HEBO
NFD RD 14
FOREST
TILLAMOOK CO
YAMHILL CO
BURNT RIDGE

HAYSTACK ROCK
Pacific City
Woods
ROUND TOP
101
COAST HWY
CEDAR CREEK RD
1491
CASTLE ROCK
YAMHILL COUNTY
SOUTH LAKE CAMPGROUND
NFD RD 14
NFD RD 2283

BOB STRAUB STATE PARK
NESTUCCA BAY
BOOTEN RD
RESORT DR
OREGON RD
JENCK
WOODS RD
NESTUCCA RIVER
ALDERMAN BUTTE
Cloverdale
22
CASTLE ROCK CAMPGROUND
NFD RD 1590
CASTLE ROCK CAMPGROUND
HWY
SOUTH POINT

PACIFIC CITY STATE AIRPORT

SEE MAP 203

| A | B | C | D |

0 1 2 3 4 miles   1 in. = 2.5 mi.

SEE 125 MAP

A | B | C | D

FOREST GROVE

HILLSBORO

CORNELIUS

TILLAMOOK STATE FOREST

Pacific University Old College Hall Museum

PACIFIC AV

Portland-Hillsboro Airport

National Guard Armory

OREGON

WASHINGTON COUNTY

GASTON

Scoggins Valley Park

Stimson Mill

Cherry Grove

Dellwood

Laurelwood

Burkhalter Reservoir

Farmington

Jacktown

North Scholls

Midway

Laurel

Scholls

YAMHILL COUNTY

Dewey

Bald Peak

Cove Orchard

Keona

Lunnville

YAMHILL

CARLTON

Carlton Lake State Game Refuge

Alecs Butte

Mountain Home

NEWBERG

Springbrook

Sunnycrest

Rex

DUNDEE

Ash Island

Skookum Lake

Champoeg

MARION COUNTY

LAFAYETTE

Saint Joseph

Warmington

Evers Lake

DAYTON

SAINT PAUL

Horseshoe Lake

MCMINNVILLE

Linfield College

McMinnville Municipal Airport

Yamhill County Fairgrounds

Booth Bend

SEE 125 MAP

SEE 204 MAP

METRO

199

0 1 2 3 4 miles   1 in. = 2.5 mi.

Highways: 8, 47, 10, 219, 210, 240, 99W, 18, 233, 221

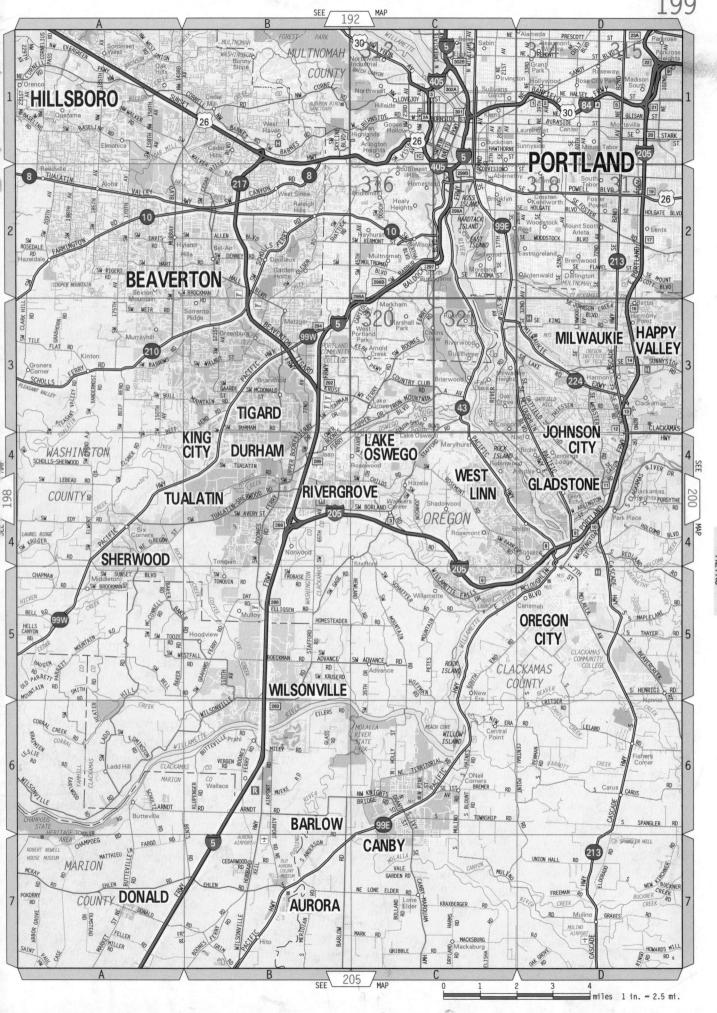

METRO

SEE 193 MAP

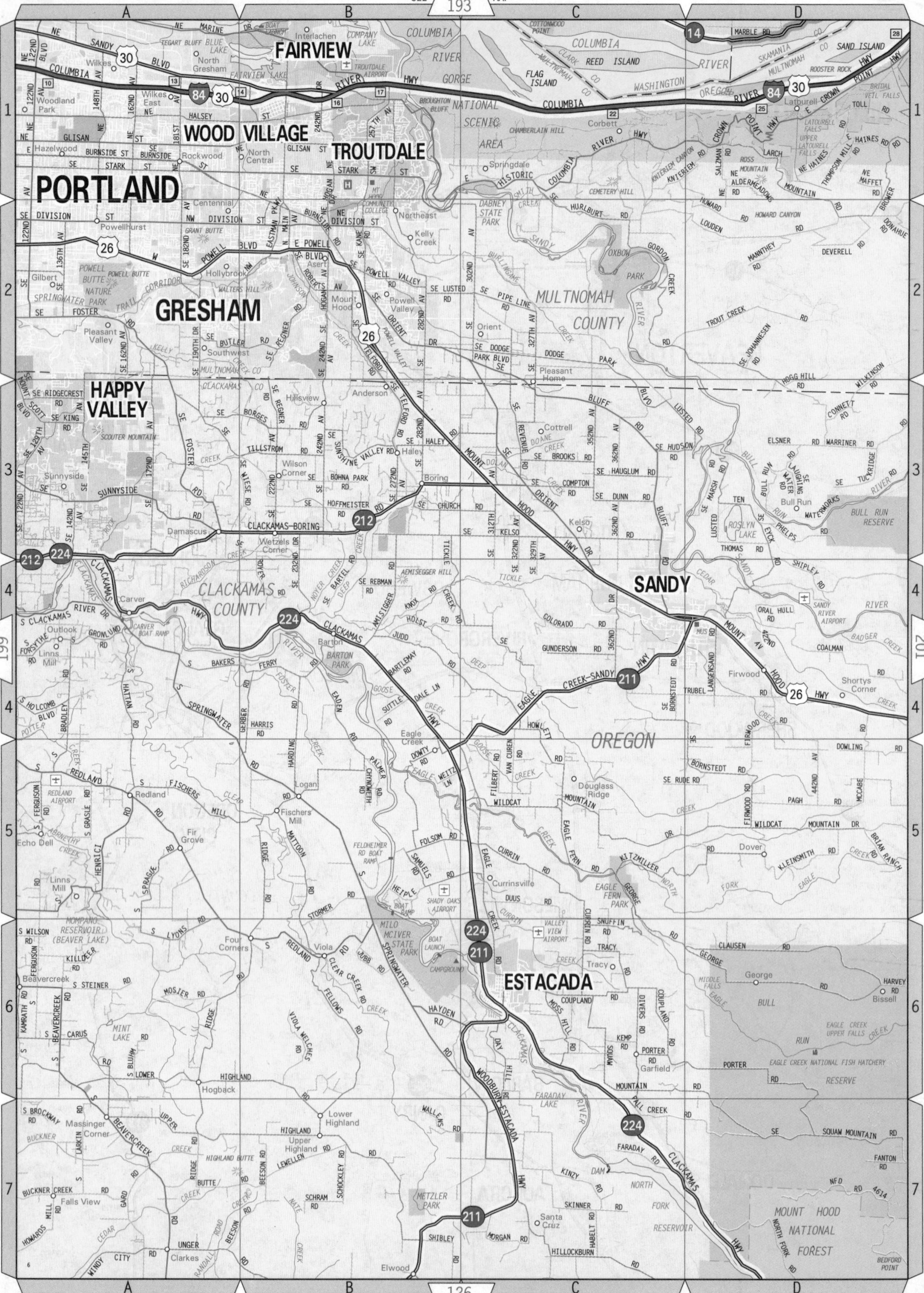

FAIRVIEW

WOOD VILLAGE

TROUTDALE

PORTLAND

GRESHAM

HAPPY VALLEY

CLACKAMAS COUNTY

MULTNOMAH COUNTY

SANDY

OREGON

ESTACADA

COLUMBIA RIVER GORGE NATIONAL SCENIC AREA

COLUMBIA RIVER

WASHINGTON

BULL RUN RESERVE

MOUNT HOOD NATIONAL FOREST

EAGLE CREEK NATIONAL FISH HATCHERY

SEE 199 MAP

SEE 201 MAP

SEE 126 MAP

0 1 2 3 4 miles   1 in. = 2.5 mi.

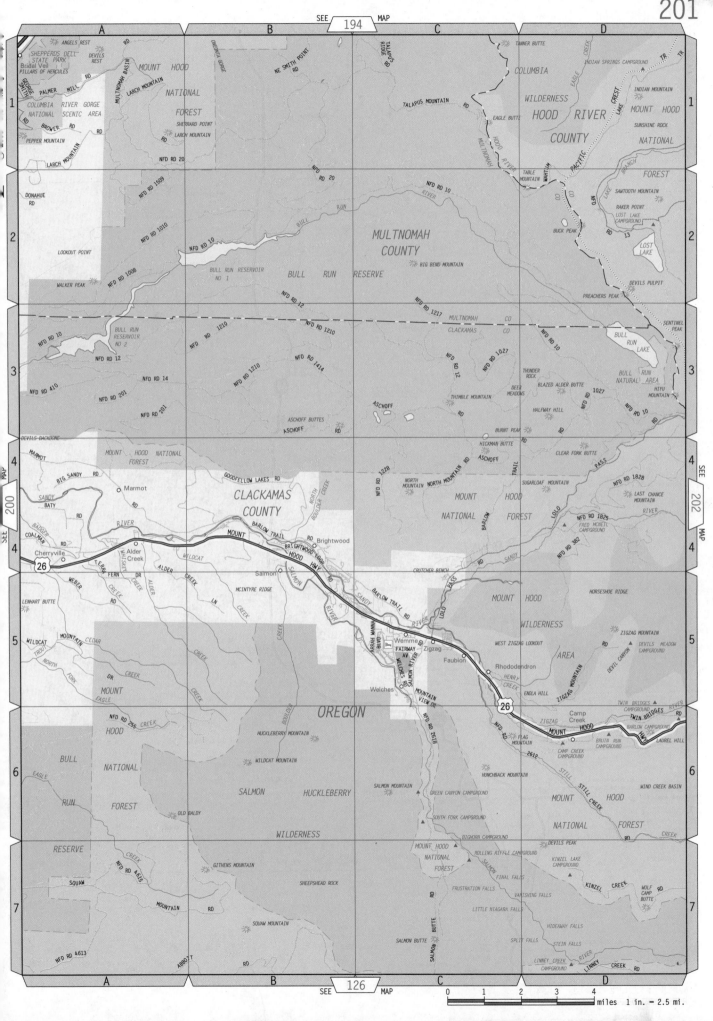

METRO

SEE 200 MAP

SEE 202 MAP

0 1 2 3 4 miles   1 in. = 2.5 mi.

METRO

SEE 195 MAP

SEE MAP 201

SEE 127 MAP

A B C D

1

NFD RD 1310
INDIANHEAD ROCK
NFD RD 13
LOST LAKE BRANCH 13
WEST LAKE FORK RD
TROUT CREEK RD
TONY CREEK RD
HOOD RIVER RD
WOODWORTH
HWY
Mount Hood
PINE MOUNT DR
BOOTH HILL
NFD RD 1710
FIR MOUNTAIN
FIR MOUNTAIN
BALD BUTTE
NFD RD 1711

2

NFD RD
NFD RD 16
BLUE RIDGE
MOUNT
NFD RD 16
RED
NFD RD 16
1610
Parkdale
BASE LINE
DR
CULBERTSON
CREEK DR
COOPER SPUR
HUTSON DR
MCINTOSH RD
LONDON DR
CLEAR
SURVEYORS RIDGE
RIM ROCK
12
JOHNS MILL
MILL RIDGE
MILL CREEK LOOKOUT RD
NORTH
HILLARY GRADE
HILLARY GRADE
NFD RD 1340
WEST PASS
LOLO
NFD RD 1670
NFD RD 1640
RED
NFD RD
1611
NFD RD 1610
BUTCHER PEAK
LADD CREEK CAMPGROUND
NFD RD 1810
NFD RD 1660
RED HILL
NFD RD 1650
NFD RD 1611
RESERVOIR CAMPGROUND
LAURANCE LAKE DR
KINNIKINNICK CAMPGROUND
NFD RD 2840
OREGON

3

LOLO PASS
NFD RD 1810
VISTA RIDGE
INSPIRATION POINT
NFD RD 3512
COOPER SPUR
MOUNT HOOD
MCGIBBOT
CANYON
ROUTSON COUNTY PARK CAMPGROUND
35
HWY
HOOD RIVER COUNTY
SHELLROCK MOUNTAIN
SOUTH FORK
WASCO
HOOD RIVER
MILL CREEK BUTTES
1720
NFD RD
KNEBAL SPRING CAMPGROUND
NFD RD 4440
FIVEMILE
FIVEMILE RD
BROOKS MEADOW
CREEK
LOWER EIGHTMILE CAMPGROUND

4

BALD MOUNTAIN SHELTER
CATHEDRAL RIDGE
CAIRN BASIN
ELK COVE
STRANAHAN RIDGE
BALD MOUNTAIN
COOPER SPUR SKI AREA
SAND CANYON
TAMANAWAS FALLS
CLINGER CAMPGROUND
POLALLIE CAMPGROUND
44
NFD RD
NFD RD 4410
PERRY POINT
44
RAIL HOLLOW RD
EIGHTMILE
FIVEMILE BUTTE
PEBBLE FORD CAMPGROUND
MOUNT HOOD
MCNEIL POINT
LADD GLACIER
BARRETT SPUR
CLOUD CAP SADDLE CAMPGROUND
LANGILLE CRAGS
SHERWOOD CAMPGROUND
NFD RD 4450

WILDERNESS
SLISAN GLACIER
YOCUM RIDGE
LANGILLE GLACIER
MOUNT
HOOD
RAMONA FALLS
SANDY RIVER
SANDY GLACIER
REID GLACIER
ELIOT GLACIER
MOUNT HOOD
BULO POINT
COLD SPRINGS
MARION POINT
NATIONAL

5

AREA
SLIDE MOUNTAIN
LEUTHOLD COULOIR
MISSISSIPPI HEAD
PALMER GLACIER
ZIGZAG GLACIER
MOUNT HOOD
STEEL CLIFF
NEWTON CLARK GLACIER
LAMBERSON BUTTE
GNARL RIDGE
BLUEGRASS RIDGE
NOTTINGHAM CAMPGROUND
NATIONAL
FOREST
NFD RD
FIFTEENMILE
4420
FIFTEEN MILE CAMPGROUND
COLD SPRINGS
COLD POINT
JORDAN CREEK
NFD RD 2720

PACIFIC
CREST
TRIANGLE MORAINE
SILCOX WARMING HUT
WHITE RIVER GLACIER
STEEL CLIFF GLACIER
WHITE RIVER
ELK MOUNTAIN
ROBINHOOD CAMPGROUND
3550
LOOKOUT MOUNTAIN
GUMJUWAC SADDLE
JORDAN
FLAG POINT
BADGER

CLACKAMAS
COUNTY
ZIGZAG RIVER
LITTLE ZIGZAG CANYON
SAND CANYON
PHLOX POINT CAMPGROUND
TR
LEG
MOUNT HOOD MEADOW SKI AREA
UMBRELLA FALLS
MOUNT HOOD
GUNSIGHT BUTTE
RD 3540
BADGER
TIGH BURN RD
FLAG POINT

6

YOCUM FALLS
ALPINE CAMPGROUND
SWITCHBACK FALLS
SAHALE FALLS
35
BENNETT PASS
NFD RD 3540
BADGER LAKE CAMPGROUND
BADGER BUTTE
CREEK
WILDERNESS
GORDON BUTTE
26
MOUNT
Government Camp
MANITCH CAMPGROUND
TIMBERLINE
TIMBERLINE HWY
HOOD
SUMMIT MEADOW
CLACKAMAS CO
HOOD RIVER CO
BENNETT PASS
WHITE RIVER PARK CAMPGROUND
NFD
RD 3540
NFD
NFD RD 4860
AREA
SKI BOWL AND MULTORPOR WINTER SPORTS AREA
MULTORPOR MOUNTAIN
STILL CREEK CAMPGROUND
TIMBERLINE EASTLEG
HWY
RD 48

TOM DICK AND HARRY MOUNTAIN
STILL
EUREKA PEAK
CREEK
BARLOW BUTTE
BUZZARD POINT
NFD RD 4811

7

VEDA BUTTE
KINZEL CREEK
TRILLIUM LAKE
WARM SPRINGS RIVER
TRILLIUM LAKE CAMPGROUND
DEVILS HALF ACRE MEADOW CAMPGROUND
BARLOW
BARLOW RIDGE
BONNEY BUTTE
BONNEY MEADOWS CAMPGROUND
ECHO POINT
BUCK DRAW
GRASSHOPPER POINT
THREEMILE
CREEK
NFD RD 4811
ROCKY BUTTE
NAMIC MILL RD

SALMON HUCKLEBERRY WILDERNESS
MUD CREEK RIDGE
SALMON RIVER
SALMON RIVER MEADOWS
26
FROG LAKE CAMPGROUND
CLACKAMAS CO
WASCO CO
WAPINITIA PASS
BIRD BUTTE
FROG LAKE BUTTE
FROG LAKE BUTTES
WASCO COUNTY
LOWER TWIN CAMPGROUND
NFD RD 48
BONNEY MEADOWS
NFD RD 4880
NFD RD 4970
BOULDER RIDGE RD
NAMIC
GRASSHOPPER RD
NFD RD 4820
GATE CREEK

SEE 126 MAP

A B C D

0 1 2 3 4 miles 1 in. = 2.5 mi.

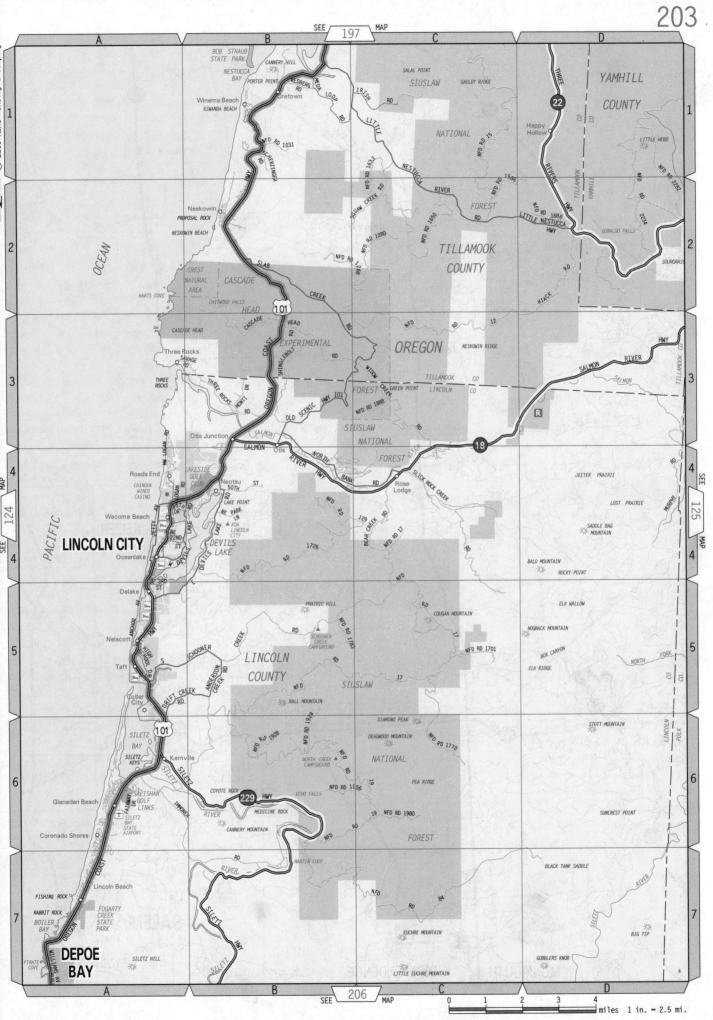

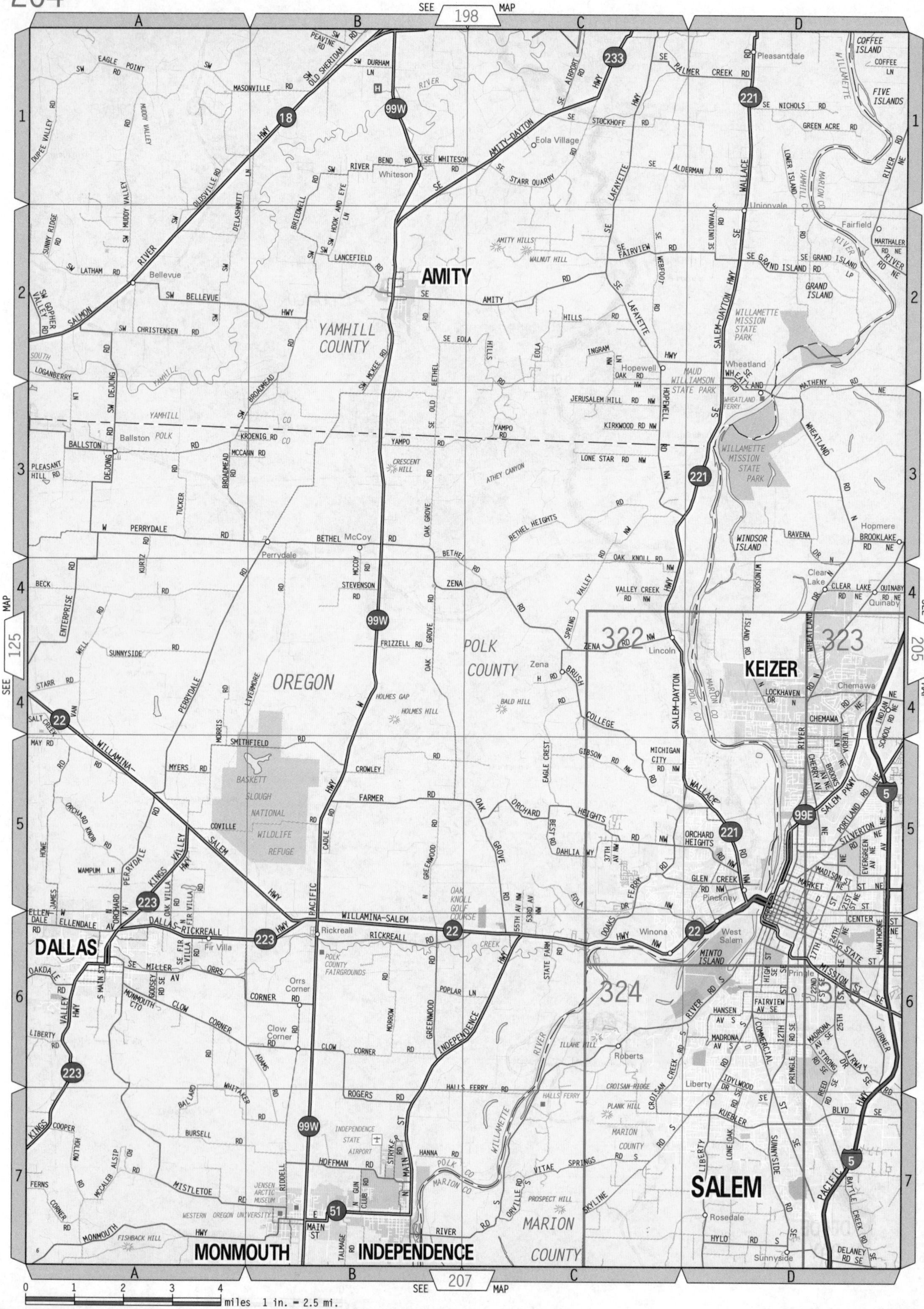

SEE 198 MAP

A   B   C   D

METRO

SEE 125 MAP

SEE 205 MAP

AMITY

YAMHILL COUNTY

OREGON

POLK COUNTY

KEIZER

DALLAS

SALEM

233

221

18

99W

322

323

324

223

22

99E

5

51

99W

WILLAMETTE MISSION STATE PARK

MAUD WILLIAMSON STATE PARK

BASKETT SLOUGH NATIONAL WILDLIFE REFUGE

OAK KNOLL GOLF COURSE

POLK COUNTY FAIRGROUNDS

INDEPENDENCE STATE AIRPORT

JENSEN ARCTIC MUSEUM

WESTERN OREGON UNIVERSITY

MARION COUNTY

MONMOUTH   INDEPENDENCE

SEE 207 MAP

0 1 2 3 4 miles   1 in. = 2.5 mi.

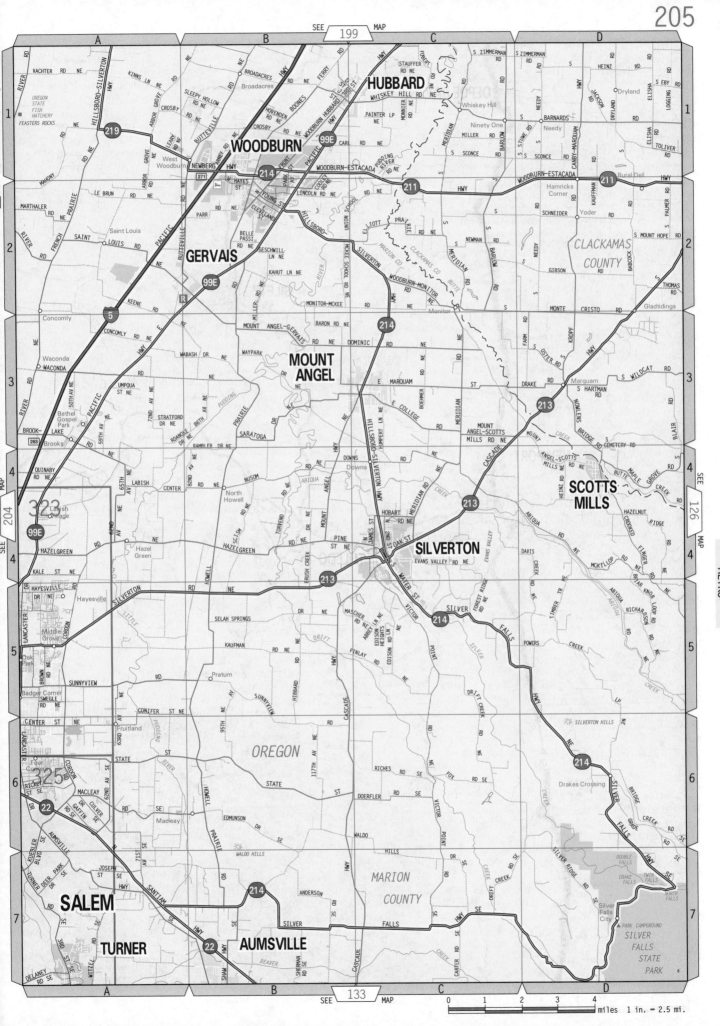

METRO

SEE 204 MAP

SEE 126 MAP

HUBBARD

WOODBURN

GERVAIS

MOUNT ANGEL

SCOTTS MILLS

SILVERTON

SALEM

TURNER

AUMSVILLE

OREGON

MARION COUNTY

CLACKAMAS COUNTY

SILVER FALLS STATE PARK

miles 1 in. = 2.5 mi.
0 1 2 3 4

METRO

SEE 203 MAP

A   B   C   D

DEPOE BAY AQUARIUM
DEPOE BAY
WINCHELL ST
AINSLEE AV
DEPOE BAY
WHALE COVE

BUTTERFIELD RIFFLE
LAMBERT POINT

SILETZ HWY
229

LOWER GORGE
MOONSHINE PARK RD

THE MAPLES
KOSYDAR RD

101
OTTER CREST

MILLER RD
SILETZ

UPPER FARM

GULL ROCK
FINGER ROCK
DEVILS PUNCH BOWL STATE PARK
Otter Rock

OREGON

OJALLA RD
HUHTALA RD
RIVER
RD

OTTER ROCK
BEVERLY BEACH STATE PARK
Beverly Beach

DEWEY CREEK

SILETZ AIRPORT
OLD SILETZ INDIAN RESERVATION
Government Hill
SWAN AV

RIVER
HAMER
RD

100TH
WY

NEWTON HILL

SILETZ
Camp Twelve
Camp Twelve LP

RD
CREEK
RD
RIVER

PACIFIC

MOOLACK BEACH
SCHOONER POINT
IRON MOUNTAIN

LINCOLN COUNTY

LOGSDEN

STARFISH COVE
LIGHTHOUSE
YAQUINA HEAD
MARTIN FALLS
Agate Beach

PIONEER SUMMIT
COOKS RD
SAMS
THORNTON CREEK
HIGHWAY 20

20
PIONEER MOUNTAIN

NEWPORT
HARNEY NE
NE BIG CREEK RD
OCEAN VIEW DR

BIG CREEK RESERVOIR

JACOBSON RD
ELK CITY RD
VINGEN
TRAP CREEK RD

JUMPOFF JOE
NW 12TH ST
12TH ST
BEACH NYE
W OLIVE ST
Newport Heights
LINCOLN COUNTY FAIRGROUNDS
YAQUINA HEIGHTS DR
BUFORD HILL
FRUITVALE

CHRISTIANSEN RD
HIGHWAY 20
BUS 20

HIGHWAY 20

ELK CITY
DEVILS WELL

SW ELIZABETH ST
OREGON COAST HISTORY CENTER
UNDERSEA GARDENS
HATFIELD MARINE BLVD SCIENCE CENTER
BENTON
YAQUINA BAY
OREGON STATE UNIVERSITY MARINE SCIENCE CENTER
OREGON COAST AQUARIUM

20
SKYLINE DR
ARCADIA RD
STURDAVENT RD

TOLEDO
SLOTE RD
Elk City

YAQUINA RIVER

SOUTH BEACH STATE PARK
South Beach

COQUILLE POINT
VALLEY RD

TOLEDO STATE AIRPORT
ELK CITY
SUNNYRIDGE
MILL CREEK

HARLAN RD

OCEAN

YAQUINA BAY LIGHTHOUSE

HIDDEN
Yaquina
WEISER POINT
ONEATTA POINT
Winant
BOONE ISLAND
BOONE SLOUGH

YAQUINA
CRAIGIE POINT
STRAWBERRY MOUNTAIN

UPDIKE RD

NEWPORT MUNICIPAL AIRPORT

MCCAFFREY ISLAND
Oysterville
YAQUINA BAY
SOUTH
GRASSY POINT

SUNNYRIDGE RD
TOLEDO RESERVOIR

HARLAN

Holiday Beach

WRIGHT CREEK RD
PETERSON RIDGE
PALMER MOUNTAIN
ERROL RIDGE RD
CREEK

LOST CREEK STATE RECREATION SITE
Fortar

WOLKAV CREEK RD
BEAVER RD
MILL CREEK DIVIDE
BEAVER RD

CAPE HORN RIDGE

101

ONA BEACH
SIUSLAW

NFD RD 3120
GOPHER RIDGE

N BEAVER CREEK RD
S
BEAVER CREEK RD
ELKHORN CREEK RD

NATIONAL
NFD RD 50
NFD RD 5087
FIVEMILE SHELTER
NFD RD 1030
NFD RD 1014 RD

ELEPHANT ROCK
Seal Rock
Ona
N BEAVER VALLEY DR

NFD RD S2
FOREST
TABLE MOUNTAIN
NFD RD 1000

OREGON
HOLLY BEACH
BEAVER CREEK
HOME CANYON RD

DRIFT CREEK WILDERNESS
DRIFT CREEK
PEAVINE RIDGE

SEE 132 MAP
SEE 133 MAP
SEE 209 MAP

0 1 2 3 4 miles   1 in. = 2.5 mi.

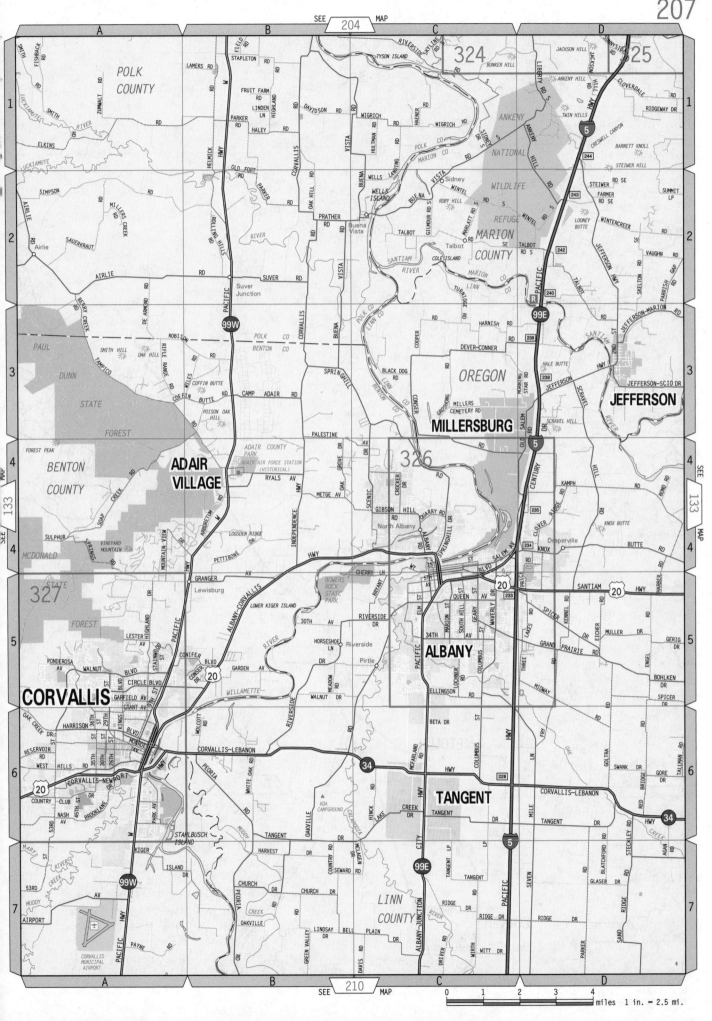

METRO

POLK COUNTY

324

25

244

243

242

240

99E

239

238

OREGON COUNTY

MARION COUNTY

MILLERSBURG

JEFFERSON

99W

Polk Co
Benton Co

Marion Co
Linn Co

BENTON COUNTY

ADAIR VILLAGE

326

133 SEE MAP

PAUL DUNN STATE FOREST

MCDONALD

327 STATE FOREST

North Albany

ALBANY

235

234

CORVALLIS

20

99W

20

34

228

TANGENT

5

LINN COUNTY

99E

34

0 1 2 3 4 miles 1 in. = 2.5 mi.

CORVALLIS MUNICIPAL AIRPORT

SEE 127 MAP

A B C D

METRO

SEE 135 MAP

SEE 135 MAP

1

2

3

4

5

6

7

WASCO COUNTY

KLAWHOP BUTTE

WARM SPRINGS RIVER

Kahneeta Hot Springs

HELLGATE

WARM SPRING

SIMNASHO HOT SPRINGS RD

EAGLE BUTTE

South Junction

SOUTH JUNCTION

RD

WARM SPRINGS

INDIAN RESERVATION

WEBSTER FLAT RD

WASCO CO

JEFFERSON CO

GATE SPRING CANYON

DRY CREEK TRAIL

UPPER DRY CREEK RD

TEE WEES BUTTE

DRY CREEK RD

DESCHUTES

COLEMAN POINT

NE COLEMAN

COLEMAN RD

NE COOK LN

BAKER CANYON

TROUT

OREGON

WARM SPRINGS HWY 26

WOLFORD CANYON RD

THE MUSEUM AT WARM SPRINGS

MILLER HEIGHTS

AGENCY-HOT SPRINGS

DRY CREEK CAMPGROUND

MECCA GRADE

FROG SPRINGS CANYON

NE GATEWAY GRADE

NE MARKET ST

CLEMENS DR NE

NE MCFARLAND

Gateway

NE NEFF

EAGLE LN

CREEK

97

WEST HILLS

Warm Springs

ELLIOT HEIGHTS

NW TENINO RD

NW JUNIPER LN

NE JUNIPER LN

BUCKLEY LN

NE EMERSON DR

QUAALE

IVY LN

HWY 97

OLD HWY

DESCHUTES DR

COLUMBIA DR

NW IVY LN

NW HICKORY DR

NW ADAMS DR

CLARK DR

NE FERN LN

DALLES-CALIFORNIA

NE IVY

JEFFERSON

TRAIL

RD

NW RIMROCK RD WARM 26

NW BOISE DR

NW GUMWOOD LN

NE BARNES DR

NE EMERSON DR

OLD MAUDS CANYON

HAY

JEFFERSON COUNTY

DRY HOLLOW RD

RD P-110 JACKSON

DRY HOLLOW RD

SEEKSEEQUA

LUNA BUTTE

NEGRO BROWN CANYON

DESCHUTES DR

ELBE DR

NW FIR LN

NW ELM LN

NE ADAMS

THE OLD SPRINGS VALLEY RD

NE FERN LN

NE ELM LN

NE EMERSON

HEREFORD LN

NT

CROOKED

HAY CREEK

SEEKSEEQUA CREEK OLD

Seekseequa Junction

JACKSON BUTTES

WILLOW CREEK RD

DOGWOOD LN

NW DOGWOOD

NE DOGWOOD

LN

METOLIUS BENCH RD

BOX CANYON TRAIL

JACKSON

HUBERS CANYON

CLACKAMAS

MADRAS CITY-COUNTY AIRPORT

NE CHERRY LN

RIVER

LOUCKS

RED SHED CANYON

COLEMAN CANYON

ELK DR NW

ELK DR

WILLOW CREEK CANYON

Madras Station

BIRCH LN

NE LOUCKS RD

LOUCKS

HENDERSON DR

SW ALMA LN

ALMA LN

DESCHUTES DR

SW ASHWOOD LN

NE B ST ASHWOOD

ASHWOOD RD

DENTES CANYON

CORVALLIS

MADRAS

SW BELMONT LN

ELBE DR

JEFFERSON COUNTY FAIRGROUNDS

SE BUFF ST

SE J ST

GRIZZLY RD

BUCK BUTTE

NFD RD 1176

NATIONAL

MOUNTAIN VIEW DR

DRY CANYON

ROUND BUTTE

CROOKED RIVER NATIONAL GRASSLAND

METOLIUS

CULVER

BEAR

MADRAS-PRINEVILLE DR

SE ADAMS DR

SE BALDWIN DR

DOVER LN

SE DIXON DR

BALDWIN HILLS

WAGONBLAST CANYON

RD M-110

RIVERVIEW OBSERVATORY

THE COVE PALISADES STATE PARK

CANADIAN BENCH

ROUND BUTTE DR

SW DOVER LN

SW JEFFERSON AV

9TH ST

BUTTE AV

SW COLUMBIA

DR

SE

GRIZZLY

GLOVER RD

CROOKED RIVER

JUNIPER BENCH

SW GALLOWAY LN

SW EUREKA AV

SW EUREKA LN

CROOKED RIVER GORGE

97

26 FRANKLIN LN

FOSTER LN

MADRAS-PRINEVILLE HWY

MUD SPRINGS CREEK

GRASSLAND

NATIONAL GRASSLAND

FRANKLIN DR

FEATHER DR

SW GEM LN

CULVER HWY

FALCON LN

361

97

BEAR DR

FORD LN

SE ADAMS DR

SE HOLLY LN

SE JASPER LN

FRANK FOREST RD

SW PECK RD

SW FRAZIER

HIGHLAND

DALLES-CALIFORNIA

SE GRIZZLY LN

LAKE BILLY CHINOOK STATE AIRPORT

JORDAN

CULVER

SW GREEN DR

SW IRIS LN

1ST AV

6TH AV

D ST

C ST

VIEWPOINT DR

SW IRIS LN

SW COLUMBIA DR

THE

SW IRVING LN

SW IMBLER LN

RIVER

0 1 2 3 4 miles 1 in. = 2.5 mi.

SEE 212 MAP

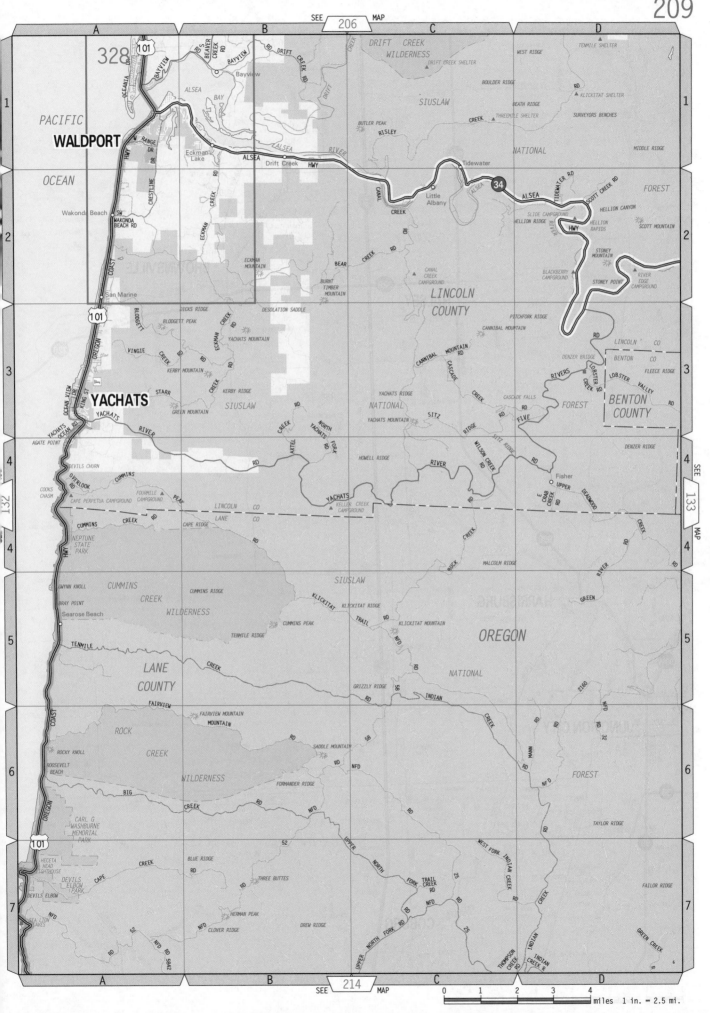

METRO

SEE 207 MAP

SEE 133 MAP

SEE 133 MAP

SEE 215 MAP

A B C D

BRATTAIN DR
GREEN VALLEY RD
GREENBACK RD
FAYETTEVILLE DR
Shedd
BOSTON
Fayetteville
PECKENPAUGH RD
Peoria
HOACUM ISLAND
ABRAHAM
MUDDY DR
SHEDD CEMETERY RD
BOSTON MILL DR
ROBERTS RD
99E
PLAINVIEW
Plainview DR
MORGAN DR
WARD BUTTE
ROCK HILL RD
ROCK HILL
TY VALLEY RD
SAND RIDGE RD
BROWNSVILLE
MIDDLE RD
OAK CREEK

PEORIA RD
POTTER RD
OAK
PLAIN DR
LINN WEST
DANNEN DR
BEND RD
HARMONY CREEK RD
CREEK DR
LINN COUNTY
MANNING RD
HARRISON DR
POWELL HILLS
SEVEN MILE LN
LONE PINE BUTTE
WASHBURN BUTTE
COCHRAN CREEK DR
CEDAR BUTTE
ROBE HILL
SNAKE HILL
KIRK DR
HOME DR

AMERICAN DR
NICEWOOD DR
IRISH BEND LP
NICEWOOD LN
CROOK DR
American
CREEK DR
CROOK DR
HALSEY-SWEET
228
216
HALSEY
HOME
SEEFELD DR
FALK DR
LAKE CREEK DR
SEEFELD DR
WEBER CREEK DR
OAKVIEW
KIRK AV
BROWNSVILLE
NORTHERN DR
228
HWY
RIVER

IRISH BEND LP
LAKE CREEK DR
POWERLINE RD
ALBANY-JUNCTION CITY
BRANDON RD
TWIN BUTTES W DR
OREGON
NIXON DR
SCHOOL RD
DINWIDDIE VALLEY
COURTNEY CREEK RD
TIMBER RD
COURTNEY CREEK DR
CARTNEY DR

MALPASS RD
CARTNEY RD
ISOM DR
SUBSTATION
BOND BUTTE DR
WAGGENER RD
CENTER RD
TWIN BUTTES
INDIAN HEAD
GAP RD
NORTHERNWOOD DR
HORSE ROCK
LITTLE VALLEY RD

WILLAMETTE
RICKARD DR
BENTON CO
LANE CO
TALBOTT LN
TANDY LN
POWERLINE RD
HARRIS DR
ROWLAND RD
BELTS RD
99E HWY
DIAMOND DR
DIAMOND HILL RD
209
HILL DR
DIAMOND HILL
COUGAR RIDGE

JAGER LN
MCMULLEN RD
HOWARD LN
MORATEN RD
9TH ST
TERRITORIAL ST
HARRISBURG
WEATHERFORD DR
PRICEBORO DR
GAP RD
BALD MOUNTAIN
CROOKED CREEK RD
15-2-26-1
RD 15-2-25
15-1-31
15-2-25-1

LINGO
LANCASTER
99W
OAKLEA
PACIFIC
LINK LN
TOFTDAHL RD N
ALBANY-JUNCTION CITY
WILLAMETTE RIVER
COBURG RD
STRODA DR
CURTIS RD
PRICEBORO DR
5
CREEK RD
ROUND MOUNTAIN
15-2-31
RD 15-2-10-2

W 18TH AV
W 6TH AV
JUNCTION CITY
DANE RD
DALE DR
BOWERS RD
WYATT DR
COBURG RD
BUSH GARDEN DR
MOUNT TOM DR
WEST POINT HILL
TOM MOUNT
15-2-10

PITNEY LN
PRAIRIE RD
36
EL RIO DR
CURTIS RD
LINN CO
LANE CO
HERMAN LN
POWERLINE RD
Wilkins
PACIFIC
LANE COUNTY
ROCK HILL DR
BUCK MOUNTAIN
16-2-7-1
RD 16-2-16-1
16-2-17-1
MOUNT TOM RD
PARSONS CREEK RD
ROSE RD
PLOCH CREEK RD

CULVER RD
HAYES LN
HARPER LN
MORGAN RD
MARSHALL ISLAND
E CROSSROAD
LANES TURN RD
COMPTON DR
SOVERN LN
99 HWY
MILLIRON RD
MEADOWVIEW RD
HEATHER OAK DR
MONTMORENCE DR
BISHOP LN
LONE PINE DR
MAPLE DR
COUNTRY LN
CENTENNIAL BUTTE
WILKINS RD
LENON HILL
COBURG
PEARL ST
VAN DUYN
HERFORD RD
TRIPLE OAK DR
OAK CREST RD
16-2-27
RD 16-3-32
16-3-13
Marcola
MOHAWK RIVER
16-2-18
16-2-29

GREEN HILL RD
VICTORY RD
LASSEN LN
GREEN ISLAND RD
GREEN ISLAND RD
COBURG RD
COBURG BOTTOM LOOP RD
FUNKE RD
W BEACON DR E
199
MCGOWAN CREEK
16-2-28
MOHAWK HILL
SUNDERMAN RD
CALOINE RD
MOHAWK VALLEY RD

0 1 2 3 4 miles   1 in. = 2.5 mi.

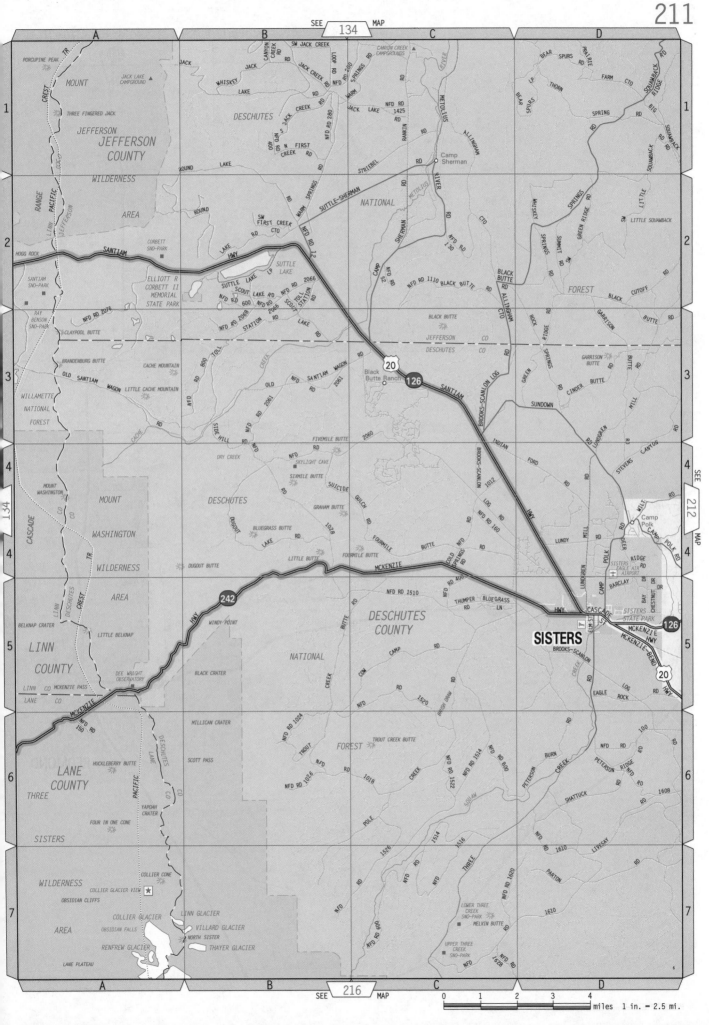

METRO

SEE 212 MAP

0 1 2 3 4 miles   1 in. = 2.5 mi.

SEE 208 MAP

METRO

DESCHUTES

NATIONAL

FOREST

SQUAWBACK RIDGE

SW SQUAW FLAT RD

CROOKED

GREEN MOUNTAIN

NFD RD 1399

GENEVA OVERLOOK

POTTER CANYON

RIVER

TRAHAN CANYON

JEFFERSON COUNTY

SQUAW FLAT CANYON

SQUAW CREEK CANYON

SW SQUAW CREEK RD

NATIONAL

GRASSLAND

NFD RD 1393

PENINSULA DR

CRATER LP

CHIPMUNK

GOLDEN MANTEL

HORNY HOLLOW

SW KEENEY

SHAD RD

SWALLOW DR

RIM RD

CHICKADEE DR

ROBIN DR

STEELHEAD RD

PERCH RD

MEADOWLARK DR

SPARROW DR

RAINBOW DR

STEELHEAD FALLS

ERMINE DR

DINGO

COUGAR RD

BLACKTAIL DR

JEFFERSON CO

DESCHUTES CO

PARKEY DR

GALENA

BIG FALLS

DESCHUTES COUNTY

TERREBONNE - LOWER BRIDGE

W LAMBERT

LAFOLLETTE BUTTE

BESSIE BUTTE

NW TEATER AV

SMITH ROCK STATE PARK

NE WILCOX AV

SMITH ROCK

Terrebonne

NW SEDGEWICK

NW ODEM AV

NW KNICKERBOCKER AV

NW COYNER AV

PERSHALL

NE YUCCA AV

Prineville Junction

UPAS AV

SPRUCE ST

HAYSTACK RESERVOIR

JERICHO

KOA MADRAS/CULVER

KING LN

SW KING LN

JUNIPER BUTTE

HAYSTACK BUTTE

MONROE LN

Opal City

OPAL LN

PARK LN

NORRIS LN

SHERWOOD DR

THE DALLES - CALIFORNIA

DONEY

COYOTE BUTTE

NE EBY

10TH ST

NW FLUME

WIMP

NW 43RD ST

NW 27TH ST

13TH ST

NW 9TH ST

NW 31ST ST

NW 19TH ST

NW 11TH ST

NE 1ST AV

NE 5TH ST

NE ICH RD

ONEIL

NE 17TH ST

NW 10TH ST

NW 5TH ST

KING ST

REDMOND - POWELL BUTTE RD

JUNIPER GOLF CLUB

REDMOND

DESCHUTES REDMOND CAVE CO. FAIR-GROUNDS

REDMOND MUNICIPAL AIRPORT

SE AIRPORT

SW SALMON AV

SW 27TH ST

SW 35TH

SW WICKIUP AV

SW YEW AV

SW ZENITH

SW COYOTE

SW HARVEST LN

MCVEY

QUARRY AV

NEWCOMB RD

HARPER

77TH

YOUNG AV

6TST

GIFT AV

GIFT RD

LIMESTONE AV

MORRILL

HORNER RD

OREGON

McKENZIE HWY

126

Cloverdale

ASPENS LAKES GOLF CLUB

CAMP POLK RD

HURTLEY RANCH RD

GOODRICH

HOLMES

EDMUNDSON RD

FADJUR

BUTTE DR

NASHUA LN

GREEN RIDGE DR

HENKLE

SQUAW CREEK

GEO CYRUS

A J WARRIN RD

FRYREAR BUTTE

FORKED HORN

KENT RD

CLOVERDALE

IVY LN

JORDAN

KOA SISTERS/BEND

HARRINGTON LP

TROUT

VARCO RD

CASCADE ESTATES DR

Plainview

THIRD ST

2ND AV

1ST ST

WEST ST

CENTRAL ST

20

SIEMORE

BRANDYWINE

McKENZIE - BEND HWY

DELICIOUS ST

BARBARA WY

BROOKS SCALON LN

KOHFELD

SNOW CREEK RD

DUSTY LP

OLSIN

INNES

SW BROWN RD

WHITE ROCK LOOP RD

MARSH RD

WHITE ROCK LOOP

SWALLEY

REDMOND - BEND HWY

93RD

ARID

CONNARN RD

DAYTON RD

RUDI RD

SMOKEY BUTTE RD

GEKLING MARKET RD

COLLINS RD

ALLEN RD

TWEED

COUCH

MARKET RD

CLINE

FALLS

STURGEON RD

84TH

85TH

TUMALO - DESCHUTES HWY

DESCHUTES - PLEASANT RIDGE MARKET RD

361

97

97

HWY

CULVER HWY

126 HWY

McKENZIE HWY

SISTERS

ORCHARD HWY

BLVD

CANAL

97

DALLES - CALIFORNIA

EAGLE CREST GOLF COURSES

CLINE FALLS STATE PARK

EAGLE DR

CLINE BUTTES

CLINE FALLS

FRANK

DEEP CANYON

BUCKHORN

HOLMES

BARR

STEVENS CANYON

FREMONT CANYON RD

WILT VIEW

SQUAW MOUNTAIN RD

BUFFALO DR

HENKLE BUTTE

CANYON CREST DR

McKENZIE CANYON

BUCKHORN CANYON

HUNT RD

JAEGER RD

NW 91ST ST

NW 74TH ST

HOMESTEAD ST

ATKINSON AV

8380 ST

ODIN FALLS

NW COYER AV

NW ATKINSON AV

YUCCA AV

NW KACHINA

NW SPRUCE AV

QUINCE AV

CASHMUR CT

REASON

OAK RD

POPLAR DR

TULLAR DR

LARCH DR

TETHEROW RD

RIVER

HELMHOLTZ

NW MAPLE

NE MAPLE

NW HEMLOCK AV

ANTLER AV

OBSIDIAN

58TH

51ST

SW 23RD ST

SW 35TH ST

DESCHUTES

SEE 211 MAP / 213

0 1 2 3 4 miles   1 in. = 2.5 mi.

A   B   C   D

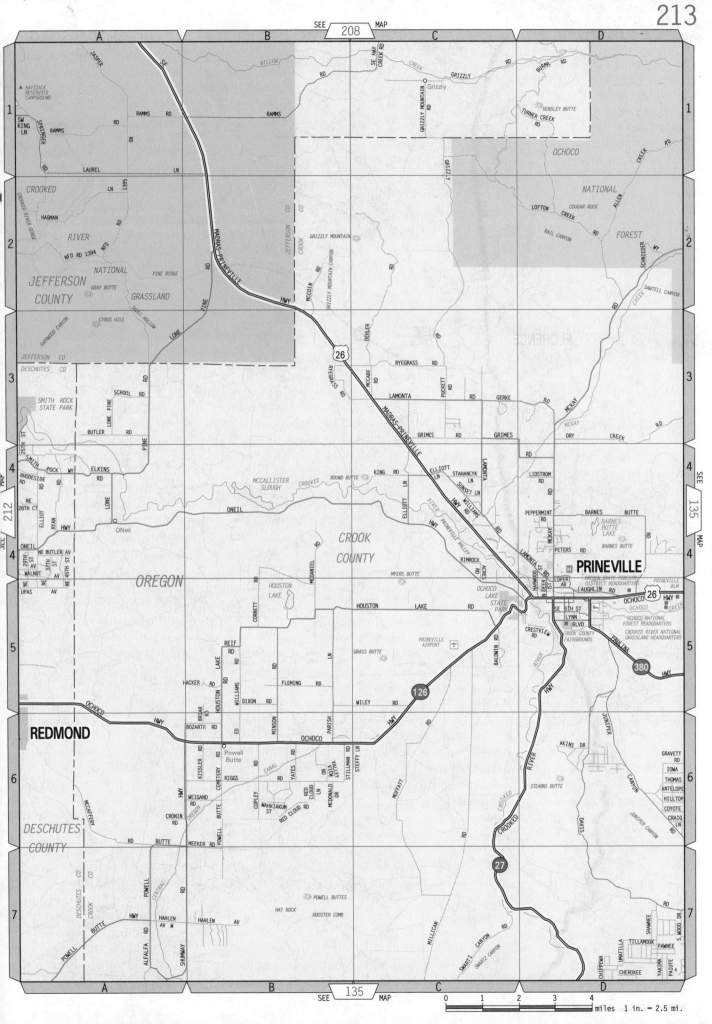

METRO

SEE 209 MAP

A B C D

SEE 132 MAP

METRO

SIUSLAW NATIONAL FOREST

CAPE MOUNTAIN

NORTH FORK SIUSLAW CAMPGROUND

UPPER NORTH FORK RD

THOMPSON CREEK RD

5842

SUTTON LAKE
BEN BUNCH LN
RUSTIC RD
MERCER LAKE RD
ENCHANTED VALLEY

Minerva
FORK SIUSLAW
STOUT CANYON
DAVIS RAPIDS
Rainrock
36
ROCK CANYON
Brickerville

SUTTON BEACH
SUTTON LAKE CAMPGROUND
SUTTON LAKE
SUTTON CREEK CAMPGROUND
SUTTON RD
COAST HWY

Heceta Beach
HECETA BEACH RD
RHODODENDRON DR
MERCER LAKE
CLEAR LAKE
COLLARD LAKE
THE PORTAGE

NORTH
DAVID RIDGE
719
NFD
NFD RD
BALD MOUNTAIN
NEELY MOUNTAIN
2610 NFD RD 719
BELLSTROM CANYON
HANSON RIDGE
MISERY RIDGE
MAPLETON JUNCTION CITY HWY
E MAPLETON RD
Mapleton
2610

Heceta Junction
101
MUNSEL LAKE RD
SIUSLAW
35TH ST
MUNSEL LAKE
BENDER LANDING
FLORENCE-EUGENE
Tiernan
CREEK
Point Terrace
RD
NFD RD

LANE COMMUNITY COLLEGE
DOLLY WARES DOLL MUS
NORTH FORK
BULL ISLAND
Wendson
126
BERNHARDT
KANOWSKY CREEK
HENDERSON CANYON

FLORENCE
FLORENCE MUNICIPAL AIRPORT
9TH ST
Cushman
SKUNK HOLLOW
COX ISLAND
NATIONAL
LANE COUNTY
831

OREGON
SIUSLAW VISTA
SIUSLAW RIVER
SOUTH INLET
CREEK
HENDERSON CREEK
HENDERSON
FOREST
MOUNT PETER
SWEET CREEK FALLS
SWEET CREEK FALLS
831

Glenada
SIUSLAW PIONEER MUSEUM
DUNES
JESSIE M HONEYMAN MEMORIAL STATE PARK
SOUTH SLOUGH
953 RD
NFD RD
MAPLE CREEK RD
SUNSET MOUNTAIN
2480
BEAVER CREEK FALLS
SWEET CREEK RD
ROCKY POINT
GOODWIN PEAK
NFD RD 48

NATIONAL
CANARY RD
RECREATION
WOAHINK LAKE
DUNES CITY
Canary
UPPER CANARY RD
4830
4811
908 RD
FIDDLE CREEK RIDGE
MOUNT GRAYBACK

AREA
CLEAR LAKE
NorthBeach
NORTH BEACH BAY
Siltcoos
Siltcoos STATION
Ada
FIDDLE CREEK
NFD RD
OREGON
4820
RIVER

DRIFTWOOD CAMPGROUND
DRIFTWOOD II CAMPGROUND
LAGOON CAMPGROUND
Westlake
TYEE CAMPGROUND
WAXMYRTLE CAMPGROUND
LODGEPOLE CAMPGROUND
SILTCOOS LAKE
BOOTH ISLAND
SILTCOOS
CANARY RD S
MILES CANYON
HENDERSON CANYON
NFD
FORK
ROBINSON RIDGE

CARTER LAKE CAMPGROUND
EAST CARTER CAMPGROUND
EAST CARTER BOAT RAMP
COUNTY LINE RD
HWY
REED ISLAND
ADA
HARMONY BAY
CREEK
59
LANE CO
DOUGLAS CO
BOOTH RIDGE
4811
SULPHUR RIDGE
NORTH

CROWN ZELLERBACK CAMPGROUND
OREGON DUNES OVERLOOK
LOST LAKE CAMPGROUND
101
COAST
BOOTH RD
CATFISH HOLE
NFD RD
RD
NFD RD
RD 23
BLM RD 2-3
BLM RD 33-0
LITTLE BURMA
SPENCER CREEK
BLM

CLAY POINT
HALFWAY POINT
HENDERSON PEAK
4811
NORTH FORK SMITH RIVER
BLM RD 2-

TAHKENITCH LANDING
TAHKENITCH LAKE
SNARE POINT
BUZZARDS BUTTE
North Fork
SMITH
RD
BLM RD 36-0
Sulphur Springs

ELBOW LAKE CAMPGROUND
OREGON DUNES NATIONAL RECREATION AREA
MIDDLE POINT
FIVEMILE
DOUGLAS COUNTY
SMITH RIVER
SMITH RIVER
WASSON RIDGE

HOME POINT
GARDINER LANDING
FOURMILE PARK RD
FOURMILE LIGHT
SPARROW LIGHT
THREEMILE LIGHT
CLEAR LAKE
OREGON
UMPQUA RIVER
LOWER SMITH RIVER

SEE 218 MAP

0 1 2 3 4 miles 1 in. = 2.5 mi.

SEE 210 MAP

A B C D

MAHLON SWEET MUNICIPAL AIRPORT

GREEN HILL   E ENID RD   FIR GROVE
IRVINGTON   WILKES DR
AIRPORT RD   IRVING   NORTHWEST   CROCKER   RD
CLEAR LAKE RD   SANTA CLARA   RD   SCENIC DR

MCKENZIE   RIVER

RIVERIDGE GOLF COURSE   SPORES POINT   COBURG RIDGE

BLACK CANYON RD   HILL   SUNDERMAN RD   TREE FARM RD

CAMP CREEK RIDGE

1

99   MAXWELL RD   RIVER AV   CRESCENT   AV   COBURG   N GAME FARM RD   MCKENZIE   VIEW DR

HILL   BARGER   PARK   AV   HOWARD   AV   LAKE DR   HORN LN
BELTLINE   DELTA HWY   CAL YOUNG RD   GAME FARM RD   OLD MOHAWK RD   MOHAWK   MARCOLA RD
ROYAL   AV   BETHEL   COBURG RD   OAKWAY   HARLOW RD   PIONEER PKWY   HAYDEN BRIDGE   MOHAWK VALLEY

329   330   331

GREEN   N DANEBO AV   S DANEBO AV   BERTELSEN RD   EUGENE   NORTH SPRINGFIELD   YOLANDA   VITUS BUTTE   CAMP CREEK RD
BETHEL   105   SPRINGFIELD   31ST ST   UPPER CAMP CREEK RD

2

126   W 5TH AV   W 6TH AV   W 11TH AV   CENTENNIAL   194B   WALNUT   CENTENNIAL BLVD   OLYMPIC   32ND ST   THURSTON RD   MCKENZIE   HWY
CROW RD   W 11TH   POLK ST   13TH   JASPER ST   MAIN ST   COMMERCIAL ST   N 28TH ST   THURSTON
BAILEY HILL RD   W 18TH   FRANKLIN BLVD   192   GLENWOOD   191   SPRINGFIELD JUNCTION   BOOTH KELLY RD   126   SPRINGFIELD
W 24TH AV   HILYARD ST   AGATE ST   189   JASPER   WEYERHAEUSER RD

EUGENE   CHAMBERS   FRIENDLY   CREST DR   28TH   HENDRICKS PARK   30TH AV   188A   188B   SEAVEY LOOP   WILLAMETTE   MIDDLE   WEYERHAEUSER RD   WALLACE CREEK   PANORAMA RD

3

GIMPL HILL RD   BAILEY HILL RD   LORANE RD   MCBETH RD   WILLAMETTE   RIDGELINE TR   FOX HOLLOW RD   HULT PARK   GOSHEN   WILLAMETTE   RIVER   JASPER   FORD RD   JASPER LOWELL RD

SPENCER CREEK RD   SPENCER BUTTE PARK   99   EDENVALE   VALLEY RD   Hills

4

LORANE HWY   DILLARD RD   SHORT MOUNTAIN   186   58   HWY   PLEASANT HILL   PHEASANT LN   HILLTOP DR   WHEELER RD   IMMIGRANT RD   TRENT   WILLAMETTE RIVER

133   LOWER FOX HOLLOW RD   PERRY RD   ROUND MOUNTAIN   ROCK HILL DR   CAMAS SWALE   KOA CAMPGROUND   SELLERS BUTTE   BUENA VISTA   N MORNING STAR RD   RATTLESNAKE BUTTE   SUMMER CREEK   SHOSHONI LN

4   HAMM RD   WEISS RD   CLAYTON RD   SHER KHAN RD   CAMAS SWALE RD   HARVEY RD   EMERALD VALLEY RESORT GOLF COURSE   ENTERPRISE RD   RODGERS RD   BEAR CREEK RD   BEAR MOUNTAIN RD   WILLS RD   KIMBALL RD
CRESWELL   182   CLOVERDALE

LANE COUNTY

5   MUNGRY HILL RD   DE BERRY RD   NONE RD   LN   5   GOSHEN-DIVIDE HWY   PACIFIC HWY   HILLVIEW RD   RIVER RD   99   SEARS RD   BEAR MOUNTAIN RD   ROUND MOUNTAIN

MELODY LN   LYNX HOLLOW RD   BEACH RD   LYNX HOLLOW RD   TURKEY RUN RD   WALKER   RIVER RD   DAVISSON RD   SEARS RD   COUGAR MOUNTAIN   OREGON   PRUNE HILL   BEAR MOUNTAIN

6   HAWLEY CREEK   HAWLEY RIDGE   BENNETT CREEK RD   SAGINAW   WEST RD   176   WITCHER RD   GATEWAY RD   GOSHEN-DIVIDE HWY   WILLAMETTE RIVER   PACIFIC HWY   SEARS RD

BALD BUTTE   LORANE MOUNTAIN   ROUND MOUNTAIN   COTTAGE   LONG RIDGE   MOLITOR HILL RD   BALD MOUNTAIN   CREEK   HARMS CREEK

7   KELLY CREEK   GREEN RIDGE   GROVE-LORANE RD   MCFARLAND BUTTE   COTTAGE GROVE MUSEUM   COTTAGE GROVE STATE PARK AIRPORT   MOSBY CREEK RD   CEDAR PARK   BRYSON SEARS RD   ROSS RD   OLD SLOW AND EASY LANDING   RIVER

COTTAGE GROVE   174   99   S R ST   MAIN ST   S 6TH ST   S 10TH ST   RIVER RD   CEDAR PARK   ROW RIVER RD   DORENA LAKE

GOWDYVILLE   STIUSLAW   LANE CO   DOUGLAS   RIVER   5   LATHAM   LAYING RD   DORENA

SEE 219 MAP

0 1 2 3 4 miles   1 in. = 2.5 mi.

METRO

SEE 133 MAP

SEE 211 MAP

METRO

A   B   C   D

1

MIDDLE SISTER
HAYDEN GLACIER
DILLER GLACIER
SQUAW CREEK FALLS
IRVING GLACIER
SQUAW CREEK
THREE CREEK BUTTE
CARVER GLACIER
SNOW CREEK RD
NFD RD 1628
LANE COUNTY
SKINNER GLACIER
THREE CREEK
THREE CREEK MEADOW CAMPGROUND
NFD RD 370
EUGENE GLACIER
PROUTY GLACIER
DRIFTWOOD CAMPGROUND
BEAR
LOST CREEK GLACIER
SOUTH SISTER
JAMES CREEK SHELTER
HODGE CREST
LEWIS GLACIER
TAM MCARTHUR RIM
WALLOW
TRIANGLE HILL
CLARK GLACIER
THREE CREEK LAKE CAMPGROUND
BUTTE

2

THREE
SISTERS
BEND GLACIER
BROKEN TOP
BROKEN HAND
BEARWALLOW BUTTE
ROCK MESA
CROOK GLACIER
WILDERNESS
BALL BUTTE
BEARWALLOWS
LE CONTE CRATER
CAYUSE CRATER
AREA
HAPPY VALLEY
370
TUMALO
LOOP
NFD RD 4601

3

KALEETAN BUTTE
DEVILS HILL
CASCADE
RD
TUMALO FALLS
TUMALO FALLS
KOKOSTICK BUTTE
LAKES
TODD LAKE CAMPGROUND
TUMALO FALLS SHELTER
RED HILL
KOOSAH MOUNTAIN
TALAPUS BUTTE
NFD
CREEK
KATSUK BUTTE
HWY
TUMALO
SWEDE RIDGE SHELTER
SWEDE RIDGE
PACIFIC
CREST
SPARKS LAKE
TUMALO MOUNTAIN
SWAMPY LAKES SHELTER
RD
NFD RD 4615
NFD RD 4612
BIG SPRING BURN

4

SEE 134 MAP
NFD RD 450
MOOLACK BUTTE
MOUNT BACHELOR SKI LIFT
CENTURY
SWAMPY LAKES SNOWPARK
DRIVE
372
WANOGA SNOWMOBILE SNOWPARK
VIRGINIA MEISSNER SNOWPARK
HWY
SEE 217 MAP
Elk Lake
ELK LAKE CAMPGROUND
ELK LAKE
HOSMER LAKE
DESCHUTES
KAPKA BUTTE
ELK MOUNTAIN
LITTLE FAWN CAMPGROUND
TOT MOUNTAIN
OREGON
BIG
SPRING
POINT CAMPGROUND
SOUTH CAMPGROUND
MALLARD MARSH CAMPGROUND
NATIONAL
BEACH CAMPGROUND
MUD LAKE RD
RED CRATER
KATALO BUTTE
NFD RD 4613
KIWA BUTTE
CASCADE
KWOLH BUTTE

5

FOREST
DESCHUTES COUNTY
EDISON BUTTE
KAPKA BUTTE
WILLIAMSON MOUNTAIN
LAVA LAKE
EDISON SNO-PARK
ICE
WANOGA LOOKOUT
PITSUA BUTTE
LAVA LAKE CAMPGROUND
EDISON ICE CAVE
RD
NFD RD 4180
LITTLE LAVA LAKE
KUAMAKSI BUTTE
LAKES
LAVA LAKE RD
LITTLE LAVA LAKE CAMPGROUND
SHERIDAN MOUNTAIN
EDISON
TELEPHONE

6

WILLIAMSON MOUNTAIN
UPPER CAMPGROUND
MILE CAMPGROUND
BUTTE
RD
EDISON ICE CAVE
PITSUA BUTTE
HWY
SIAH
LOLO BUTTE
KLAK BUTTE
NFD RD 160
RD
KLAK BUTTE RD
BUTTE
PRATER RD
MARK
SIAH BUTTE
LOLO BUTTE
DESCHUTES
ANNS BUTTE
BENCH MARK BUTTE
NFD RD 4220

7

CULTUS LAKE
LOLAH BUTTE
LUMRUM BUTTE
WAKE BUTTE
UPPER
CULTUS LAKE CAMPGROUND
CENTURY
LOLAH BUTTE RD
THREE
TRAPPER
SITKUM BUTTE
BENCH
LOOKOUT
MOUNTAIN
RD
LOOKOUT
LLOYD
NFD RD 4630
LOOKOUT RD
DRY BUTTE
PISTOL BUTTE
NFD RD 4635
COW CAMP CAMPGROUND
DR
UPPER DESCHUTES
PISTOL BUTTE RD
CENTURY DR
BIG RIVER CAMPGROUND
NFD
CRANE PRAIRIE RESERVOIR
CRANE PRAIRIE CAMPGROUND
PRINGLE FALLS EXPERIMENTAL
LOOKOUT MOUNTAIN
FOREST ADDITION
INDIAN CREEK RD
MOUNTAIN R
BATES BUTTE
LAVA

A   B   C   D

SEE 142 MAP

0 1 2 3 4 miles   1 in. = 2.5 mi.

METRO

A B C D

SEE MAP 212

1

SNOW CREEK RD
BULL FLAT RD
BROOKS-SCANLON
SOUTHERN RD
SPRING RD
BULL
WALTON RD PINEHURST RD
COLLINS PINEHURST RD
HORSESHOE LN
MOCK RD
TUMALO RESERVOIR RD
LAIDLAW BUTTE
TYLER RD
MCKNIGHT RD
COOK
LOB
REDMOND-BEND HWY
Tumalo
THE DALLES-CALIFORNIA HWY
HWY
BLACK ROCK
HUNNELL RD
SUNDANCE
BEND-DESCHUTES
MARKET RD
MCGRATH RD
POWELL BUTTE HWY

2

TRIANGLE HILL RD
HIGHLINE RD
CONCH RD
COLUMBIA RD
DESCHUTES
COLUMBIA RD
NATIONAL RD
JOHNSON RD
NW SHEVLIN MARKET
SHEVLIN PARK
MOUNT PARK
NW COLLEGE WAY
WASHINGTON
DESCHUTES
332
BEND
NW PORTLAND AV
RIVER DR
STUDIO
NE BOYD ACRES
NE NEFF RD
BUTLER
NEFF
27TH ST
MARKET ST
PIONEER
STILVIS
CARWELL RD
DICKEY RD
ERICKSON RD
BUTLER MARKET RD
BARLOW CAVE
WILSON CAVE
NELSON
BEND MUNICIPAL AIRPORT
STENKAMP RD
MAUGH
STENKAMP
DIXON LP
MARKET RD
ALFALFA
WALKER RD
HORSE CAVE

3

TUMALO LOOP RD
SKYLINERS RD
TUMALO CREEK
SKYLINERS RD
TUMALO RD
FOREST
NFD RD 300
NFD RD 4610
SWEDE RIDGE RD
CENTURY DRIVE
372
DESCHUTES HWY
BROKEN TOP GOLF COURSE
NW NEWPORT AV
GALVESTON AV
14TH ST
SE WILSON AV
SE REED
MURPHY
SE 15TH
KNOTT
97
20
E BEAR CREEK RD
CENTRAL
OREGON HWY
20
BEAR CREEK RD
PETTIGREW
ORION DR
FERGUSON RD
MARKET RD
OREGON ST
21ST ST
STEVENS RD
WARD
CANAL
WARD RD
MCARDLE RD
GOSNEY RD
TEAL RD
BENNETT RD
TEN BAR
GRIBBLING
SAINT CLAIR
RICKARD
HAMBY
BYRAM

4

SEE 216 MAP
NFD RD 4130
DILLON FALLS
SPRING RD
KIWA RD
LAVA ISLAND SHELTER
LAVA ISLAND SHELTER (PREHISTORIC)
LAVA ISLAND CAMPGROUND
UPPER FALLS DESCHUTES RIVER
ASPEN CAMPGROUND
DILLON FALLS CAMPGROUND
DESCHUTES RIVER
THE HIGH DESERT MUSEUM
Deschutes River Woods
KNOTT RD
CHINA
NFD RD 600
NFD RD 9701
HORSE BUTTE
COYOTE BUTTE
NFD RD 230
CABIN BUTTE
SKELETON CAVE
BOYD CAVE
NFD RD 1815
NFD RD 1818
ARNOLD MARKET RD
ARNOLD MARKET
BILLADEAU
STIRLING DR
HORSE BUTTE
FORD RD
DARK HOLE WIND CAVE
ARNOLD ICE CAVE
SEE 135 MAP

5

NEWBERRY
SLOUGH CAMPGROUND
BENHAM FALLS
BENHAM FALLS CAMPGROUND
NATIONAL
NFD RD 200
NFD RD 200
BENHAM FALLS RD
LAVA LANDS VISITOR CENTER
BENHAM FALLS
HWY
SWAMP
WELLS
DESCHUTES CO
DESCHUTES
NFD RD 30
LOCKITT BUTTE
NFD RD 1814
NFD RD 1814
KELSEY BUTTE
HAT
CHARCOAL CAVE
NFD RD 1820
NATIONAL

6

CONKLIN SPRING RD
RIVER RD
FIRE RD
Sunriver
BESSON CAMPGROUND
HARPER BRIDGE RD
97
S CENTURY DR
CRAWFORD
LAVA RIVER CAVES
VOLCANIC
LAVA
CAST
FOREST
SWAMP
WELLS
OREGON
NATIONAL
LAVA TOP BUTTE
FUZZTAIL BUTTE
SWAMP WELLS
FOREST
NFD RD 1825

7

LLOYD WY
Three Rivers
DESCHUTES
S CENTURY DR
VANDEVERT
LAMBERTIANA
CENTURY DR
PENGR A-HUNTINGTON RD
THE DALLES-CALIFORNIA
NFD RD 4000
NFD RD 9720
NFD RD 9720
NFD RD 9724
NFD RD 9724
SUGARPINE BUTTE
LAVA CAST FOREST
NFD RD 9723
IKT BUTTE
NFD RD 9720
MOKST BUTTE
LAVA CAST FOREST
LAVA CAST FOREST CAMPGROUND
KLONE BUTTE
KWINNUM BUTTE
LAVA CAST FOREST
MONUMENT
NFD RD 1810
LOCKITT BUTTE
1818
NFD RD 250
SWAMP WELLS BUTTE
HUNTER BUTTE
NFD RD 1825

0 1 2 3 4 miles   1 in. = 2.5 mi.

METRO

SEE 214 MAP

A | B | C | D

REEDSPORT

LAKESIDE

NORTH BEND

COOS BAY

333

Gardiner
East Gardiner
STEAMBOAT ISLAND
LEEDS ISLAND
BOLON ISLAND STATE PARK

BARRETTS LANDING
BRUSHY HILL
OREGON DUNES NATIONAL RECREATION AREA
HENDERSON COVE
DOUBLE COVE POINT
HUNT COVE
MACEY COVE
ARMY HILL

SIUSLAW NATIONAL FOREST

SMITH RIVER
SOUTH SIDE RD
OTTER SLOUGH
BUTLER CREEK RD
LOWER SMITH
SMITH RIVER LIGHT
DISCOVER CENTER
UMPQUA RIVER

JERDEN COVE
RIDGEWAY DR
H
CORNWALL POINT
Winchester Bay
LONGWOOD
BOWMAN RD
COAST HWY

38 HWY

DOUGLAS COUNTY

UMPQUA LIGHTHOUSE
UMPQUA LIGHTHOUSE STATE PARK

HARBOR DR
SALMON
OREGON DUNES NATIONAL RECREATION AREA

LAKE MARIE CAMPGROUND

CLEAR LAKE
LAKE EDNA
WILLIAM M TUGMAN STATE PARK
EEL LAKE

SCHOLFIELD RIDGE RD
DEAN MOUNTAIN RD

ELLIOTT

TWIN SISTERS

OCEAN

DOUGLAS CO
COOS CO
BLACKS ARM
CARSON ARM

NORTH TENMILE LAKE

BIG CREEK RD
NOBLE CREEK RD

NORTH EEL CAMPGROUND

BIG CREEK ARM
LINDROS ARM
BIG CREEK ARM

STATE

MIDDLE EEL CAMPGROUND
EEL CREEK CAMPGROUND
SOUTH EEL CREEK CAMPGROUND
SPINREEL CAMPGROUND
Tenmile

NORTH LAKE RD

SCHOOL LAND BAY
DEVORE ARM
WILLOW POINT
COLEMAN ARM

BENSON CREEK RD

SHUTTER ARM
TENMILE LAKE
TEMPLETON ARM
TEMPLETON RD
Templeton
ROBERT CREEK RD

FOREST

OREGON DUNES NATIONAL RECREATION AREA

SHUTTERS LANDING

COAST RD
STAGE RD

COOS COUNTY

OREGON

TENMILE BUTTE

Saunders Lake

WILLWOOD DR
OREGON
NORTH ZARA DR
HAYNES

HWY

TRAIL BUTTE
BUTTE RD
FORK-MILLICOMA RIVER
HENRYS FALLS
ESTELL FALLS
PIDGEON FALLS

Hauser
KOA OREGON DUNES

RIDGE DR
MEADOW LN
LARSON
BAY
LARSON
KETTMAN CREEK RD
BALDY BUTTE
DEAN MOUNTAIN

MILLICOMA TRAIL
WEST FORK
WEST FORK MILLICOMA RIVER

HORSEFALL BEACH
BLUEBILL LAKE CAMPGROUND

Shorewood
HAYNES INLET

DEVILS ELBOW

ELK MOUNTAIN HWY

TRANS PACIFIC PKWY

Glasgow
KENTUCK GOLF COURSE
KENTUCK INLET

JORDAN COVE
COOS BAY
EAST BAY DR

KENTUCK WY

COOS MILLICOMA RIVER

NORTH BAY
Cooston
NOAH BUTTE

Allegany

Empire
ARAGO
COLORADO AV
VIRGINIA AV
FENWICK ST
EMPIRE COOS BAY HWY
NEWMARK ST
SHERMAN ST
TREMONT ST

WILLANCH WY

MCKEEVER MOUNTAIN

PACIFIC

0 1 2 3 4 miles 1 in. = 2.5 mi.

SEE 220 MAP

SEE 140 MAP

1 | 2 | 3 | 4 | 5 | 6 | 7

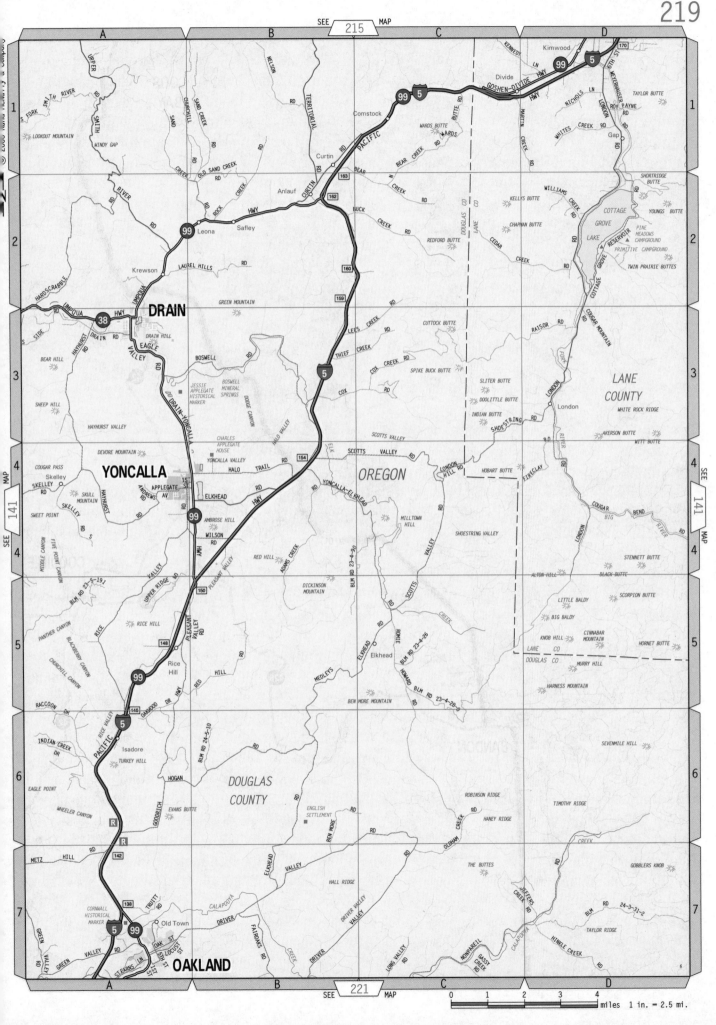

METRO

METRO

SEE MAP 140

SEE MAP 140

A | B | C | D

1
2
3
4
5
6
7

© 2000 Rand McNally & Company

N

COOS BAY

333

UPPER PONY CREEK RES

Empire-Coos Bay Hwy

EMPIRE

Eastside

101

ELROD ST
5TH ST
ELROD AV
SOUTHWEST BLVD
LOCKART AV
Englewood
Bay Park
McCormac
Bunker Hill
COOS RIVER HWY

Millington
Cleo
OLIVE BARBER RD
ROSS INLET RD
EASTSIDE-SUMNER RD
CITY-SUMNER RD

COOS COUNTY
OREGON

BOONE CREEK RD

42
DELMAR RD
UPPER LOOP RD
TIMBER WY
GREEN ACRES RD
Green Acres

OVERLAND RD
Overland

BEAVER CREEK RD
Coaledo

OLD BEAVER HILL RD
BANK RD
Leneve
Chrome
COOS GARDEN VALLEY RD

COOS BAY-ROSEBURG HWY

BUDD MOUNTAIN
COQUILLE-FAIRVIEW RD

COQUILLE
W CENTRAL BLVD
Cedar Point
E 2ND ST
E 1ST ST
H
SHELLEY RD
FISHTRAP RD
DUTCH JOHN RAVINE
RINK CREEK RD

42S
COQUILLE RIVER
HWY
GATEWAY RD

Riverton
42S
BAKER RD
COQUILLE-FAT ELK RD
COQUILLE-FAT ELK RD
GLEN AIKEN CREEK RD
Johnson

COQUILLE VALLEY RD
LANDING RD
42
BAY-ROSEBURG HWY

HATCHET SLOUGH RD
BANK RD

COQUILLE-BANDON HWY

MYRTLE RD
LAMPA MOUNTAIN
POINT-LAMPA RD
MYRTLE RD
Norway
Arago
ARAGO LN
LOWER NORWAY RD

LAMPA VALLEY RD
POINT-LAMPA RD

PLEASANT VALLEY RD
HALL CREEK RD
PLEASANT VALLEY RD
WEST SIDE RD
MATHENY CREEK RD

OCEAN

COOS HEAD US NAVAL FACILITY
OREGON INST OF MARINE BIOLOGY
Barview
CAPE ARAGO HWY
Charleston
MCLAIN-

BASTENDORFF BEACH
YOAKAM POINT COUNTY PARK

SQUAW ISLAND
ARAGO LIGHT
SUNSET BAY
SUNSET BAY STATE PARK

SHELL ISLAND
NORTH COVE
CAPE ARGO STATE PARK
CAPE ARAGO
SHORE ACRES STATE PARK
SEA LION VIEW POINT
DRAKE POINT
SOUTH COVE

COLLVER POINT
YOUNKER POINT
CROWN POINT
Crown Point
JOE NEY-DAVIS SL RD

SALAL LN
SOUTH SLOUGH NATIONAL ESTUARY
LONG ISLAND POINT
YOAKAM HILL
THE BUTTES

SEVEN DEVILS RD
FINCH RD
COX CANYON RD

BEAVER HILL RD
COOS COUNTY FOREST

AGATE BEACH

FIVEMILE POINT
WHISKEY RUN RD
SEVEN DEVILS RD
E HUMPHREYS RD

COAST RD

BRANDON DUNES GOLF COURSE

W HUMPHREYS RD

BEAVER HILL RD
101
BEAVER HILL RD

COQUILLE RIVER

PACIFIC

BULLARDS BEACH STATE PARK

SEVEN MILE RD
Rocky Point
BANK RD

PARKERSBURG-PROSPER JUNCTION RD
Prosper
Parkersburg

PARK RD
N BANK RD
RIVERSIDE DR
SPRUCE HOLLOW RD
TOM SMITH RD

FIVE FOOT ROCK
COQUILLE POINT
BANDON BEACH
CAT AND KITTENS ROCK

8TH ST SW
BANDON LOOP
BEACH LOOP DR SW
1ST ST
2ND ST SE
BATES RD
BANDLL RD
Winterville
BEAR CREEK RD

BANDON
SEA BIRD DR

HAYSTACK ROCK

BANDON STATE AIRPORT
WINDHURST RD
MORRISON RD

BEACH LOOP RD
ROSA RD
BOAT RD
BARNEKOFF RD

TWOMILE
DEW VALLEY RD
TWOMILE RD

BANDON STATE PARK
DEW VALLEY RD
101
Laurel Grove

0 1 2 3 4 miles 1 in. = 2.5 mi.

GRIGSBY ROCK
WAPLO CREEK RD
HORSE HOLLOW RD
CATCHING CREEK RD

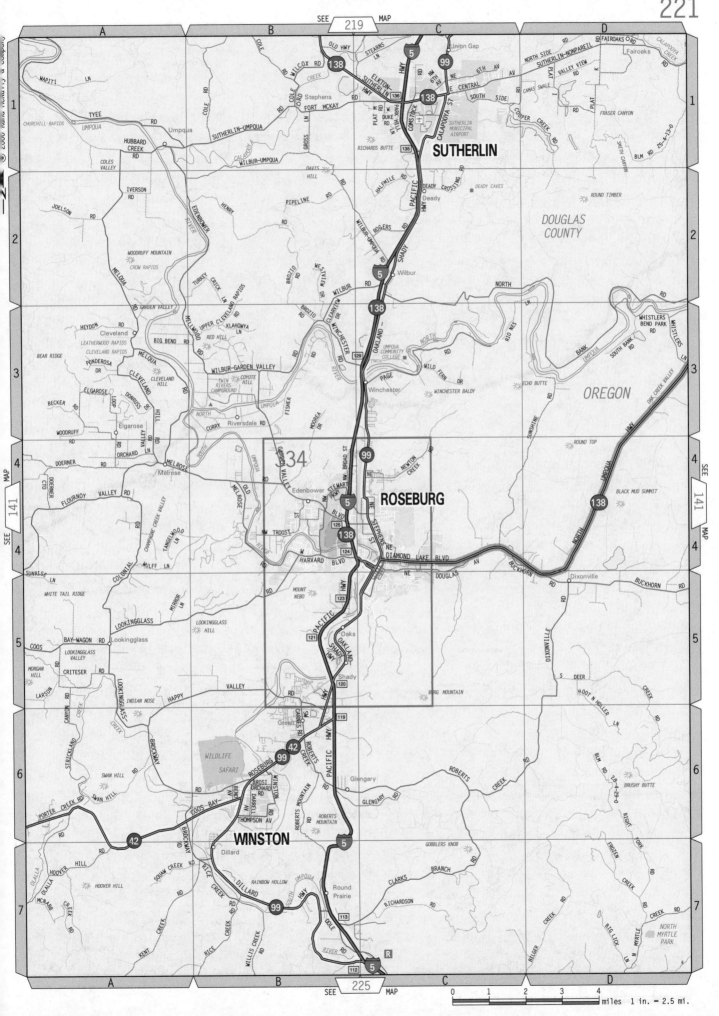

SEE 219 MAP

SUTHERLIN

DOUGLAS
COUNTY

OREGON

ROSEBURG

METRO

SEE 141 MAP

SEE 141 MAP

WINSTON

SEE 225 MAP

0 1 2 3 4 miles   1 in. = 2.5 mi.

A B C D

1 2 3 4 5 6 7

N

METRO

NFD RD 3817
NFD RD 100
GRANDDAD BUTTE
REYNOLDS CREEK RD
BULLDOG RD
REYNOLDS RIDGE
REYNOLDS BUTTE
BULLDOG ROCK
LOST PRAIRIE ROCK
STALEY RIDGE
COAL CREEK
WILLAMETTE
NATIONAL
FOREST
WABASH RD
REYNOLDS CREEK
CREEK
REYNOLDS SHELTER
STEAMBOAT
STEAMBOAT FALLS CAMPGROUND
SILVER ROCK
BALM MOUNTAIN
NFD RD 34
UMPQUA
STEAMBOAT
LITTLE FALLS
SINGLE CREEK RD
QUARTZ POINT
WILD ROSE POINT
HARDING BUTTE
DEVILS STAIRWAY
BEAR POINT
SPRING MOUNTAIN
BOULDER CREEK WILDERNESS
NORTH UMPQUA RIVER
NFD RD 500
NFD RD 200
ILLAHEE ROCK
DOUGLAS COUNTY
NATIONAL
DOG MOUNTAIN
RAGGED RIDGE
RAGGED BUTTE
BARTRUMS ROCK
BOULDER CREEK
PERRY BUTTE
THORN MOUNTAIN
JACK FALLS
JACK POINT
LIMPY ROCK
INDIAN CAVE
BRADLEY RIDGE
REYNOLDS RIDGE
EAGLE RIDGE
PINE POINT
RATTLESNAKE RIDGE
PINE BENCH
BOULDER FLAT CAMPGROUND
CAMEL HUMP
OREGON
FOREST
138
NORTH UMPQUA RIVER
PANTHER LEAP
NORTH
WEEPING ROCK CAMPGROUND
EAGLE ROCK CAMPGROUND
RATTLESNAKE ROCK
EAGLE ROCK
OLD MAN ROCK
NORTH UMPQUA RD
LEMOLO TWO FOREBAY CAMPGROUND
UMPQUA RD
HORSESHOE BEND CAMPGROUND
CHARCOAL POINT
BIG
FLATIRON POINT
LINCOLN HWY
TOKETEE FALLS
TOKETEE LAKE CAMPGROUND
CALF RIDGE
CAMAS CREEK RD
SNUFF SHELTER
FISH CREEK
RIVER
TOKETEE RESERVOIR
NFD RD 75
138
CLEARWATER
WATSON FALLS
FAIRY SHELTER
BACHELOR BUTTE
COPELAND CREEK
BRINK RD
CLEARWATER RD
LIMPY MOUNTAIN
BIG
NFD RD 35
CODWATER CAMPGROUND
OK BUTTE
BIG TWIN LAKES CAMPGROUND
UMPQUA
CAMAS
FISH CREEK CAMPGROUND
YAKSO FALLS
TWIN LAKES
CAMAS CREEK CAMPGROUND
FISH CREEK DESERT
LITTLE RIVER RD
CALF CREEK
TWIN LAKES MOUNTAIN
FISH CREEK
HEMLOCK FALLS
QUARTZ MOUNTAIN
SNOWBIRD SHELTER
DOEHEAD MOUNTAIN
COPELAND CREEK
NATIONAL
RHODODENDRON RIDGE
ROUGH CREEK
HEMLOCK LAKE CAMPGROUND
LITTLE RIVER RD
SNOWBIRD MOUNTAIN
RAVEN ROCK
MUD LAKE MOUNTAIN
HEMLOCK MEADOW CAMPGROUND
BUCKHEAD MOUNTAIN
BEAR WALLOW
SNOWBIRD RD
NFD RD
BUCKHEAD MOUNTAIN CAMPGROUND
FOREST
BLACK ROCK
ROLLING GROUNDS CAMP
BEAVER SHELTER
QUARTZ MOUNTAIN
BLACK ROCK FORK
NFD RD 950
MOUNTAIN RD
FLAGSTONE PEAK
QUARTZ CREEK RD
ROCK RD
BOZE SHELTER
DEER LICK FALLS
BLACK FORK
CASTLE CREEK
ROGUE-UMPQUA
QUARTZ CANYON
HAPPY VALLEY
FISH CREEK VALLEY
FISH CREEK SHELTER
RATTLESNAKE MOUNTAIN
DIVIDE
BUCKNECK MOUNTAIN
QUARTZ
BLACK FISH RIVER LAKE
BEAVER SWAMP CAMPGROUND
WINDY GAP
TILLER-SOUTH UMPQUA CAMP RD
SOUTH UMPQUA RD
EMERSON RD
ROCKY RIDGE
CASTLE ROCK
DEVILS SLIDE
WILEY CAMP
WILDERNESS
SKIMMERHORN CAMPGROUND
FISH LAKE CAMPGROUND
FISH LAKE
ROGUE RIVER NATIONAL FOREST
BUCK CANYON

0 1 2 3 4 miles 1 in. = 2.5 mi.

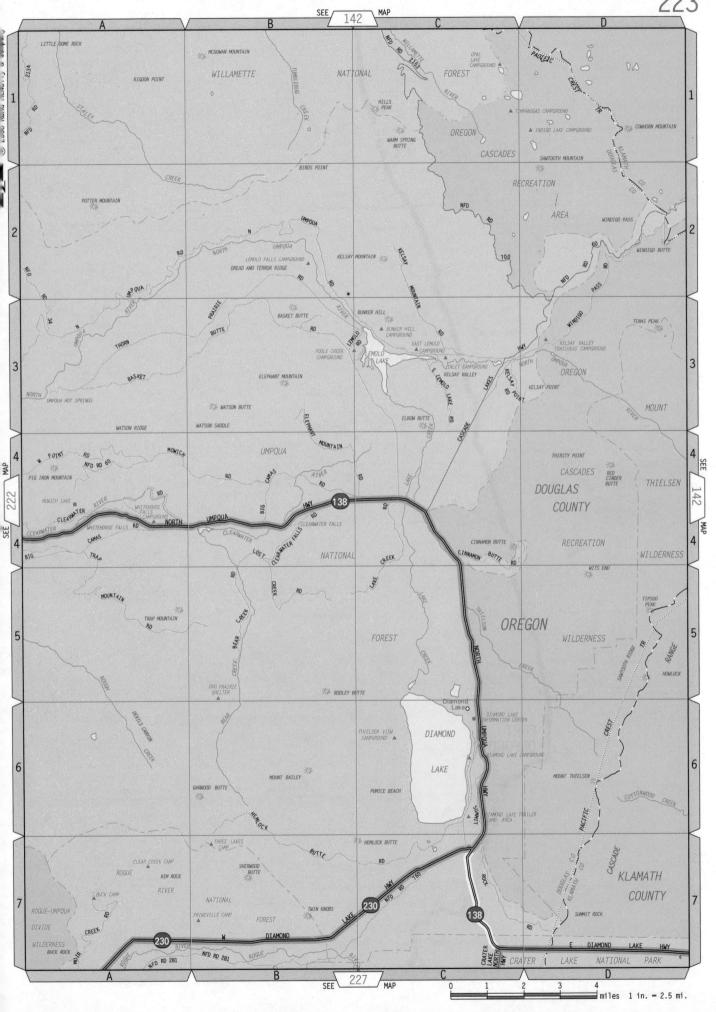

METRO

miles 1 in. = 2.5 mi.

A   B   C   D

© 2008 Rand McNally & Company

METRO

SEE 140 MAP

SEE 140 MAP

COOS COUNTY

NEW RIVER PARK

STEWART RD

LOWER FOURMILE RD

Fourmile

NORTH FOURMILE RD

CROFT LAKE RD

101

SYDNAW RD

BUZZARD BUTTE

NEW LAKE RD

COOS CO

CURRY CO

COTTON BUTTE

BENNETT BUTTE

MORTON BUTTE

RD

WATCHES BUTTE

HWY

LANGLOIS

ROUND TOP MOUNTAIN

Langlois

FLORAS CREEK

LOOP RD

FLORAS

GROUSE LN

CREEK

RD

CALF RANCH MOUNTAIN

FLORAS LAKE RD

FLORAS LAKE

PACIFIC HWY

FERN RIDGE RD

PACIFIC OCEAN

KOA BANDON-PORT ORFORD

Denmark

WHITE MOUNTAIN

TOWER ROCK

FLORAS LAKE

COAST

STONE BUTTE

SUMMIT MOUNTAIN

BLACKLOCK POINT

CASTLE ROCK

CAPE BLANCO STATE AIRPORT

OREGON

EIGHTMILE PRAIRIE MOUNTAIN

CURRY COUNTY

GULL ROCK

SIXES BEACH

AIRPORT RD

OREGON

CAPE BLANCO

MADDEN BUTTE

RD

CAPE BLANCO LIGHTHOUSE

CAPE BLANCO STATE PARK

CAPE BLANCO

CRYSTAL CREEK

SQUAW BLUFF

HEREFORD RD

SUGARLOAF MOUNTAIN

RIVER

SIXES

BLANCO HWY

Sixes

SADDLE ROCK

SIXES

RD

SIXES RIVER

RIVER

McKENZIE RD

GRASSY KNOB

RIVER

POVERTY RIDGE

SISKIYOU

MOON MOUNTAIN

CHINA PEAK

RUSTY BUTTE

SILVER BUTTE

ELK

GRASSY

NATIONAL

FOREST

RIVER

ELK

KNOB

AGATE BEACH

PORT ORFORD

SISKIYOU

WILDERNESS

KLOOQUEH ROCK

PORT ORFORD HWY

OREGON ST

RIVER

NATIONAL

ANVIL MOUNTAIN

FORT POINT

NELLIES COVE

OREGON

FOREST

NELLIES POINT

CHINA MOUNTAIN

ELK RIVER STATE FISH HATCHERY

BUTLER BAR CAMPGROUND

TICHENOR ROCK

101

COAST

ROCKY POINT

RD

CHINA MOUNTAIN

NFD RD 20

McGRIBBLE CAMPGROUND

PANTHER CREEK CAMPGROUND

MILBURY MOUNTAIN

COAL POINT

HUMBUG MOUNTAIN STATE PARK

NFD RD 5400

RD

FATHER MOUNTAIN

HWY

HUMBUG MOUNTAIN CAMPGROUND

HUMBUG MOUNTAIN

0 1 2 3 4 miles   1 in. = 2.5 mi.

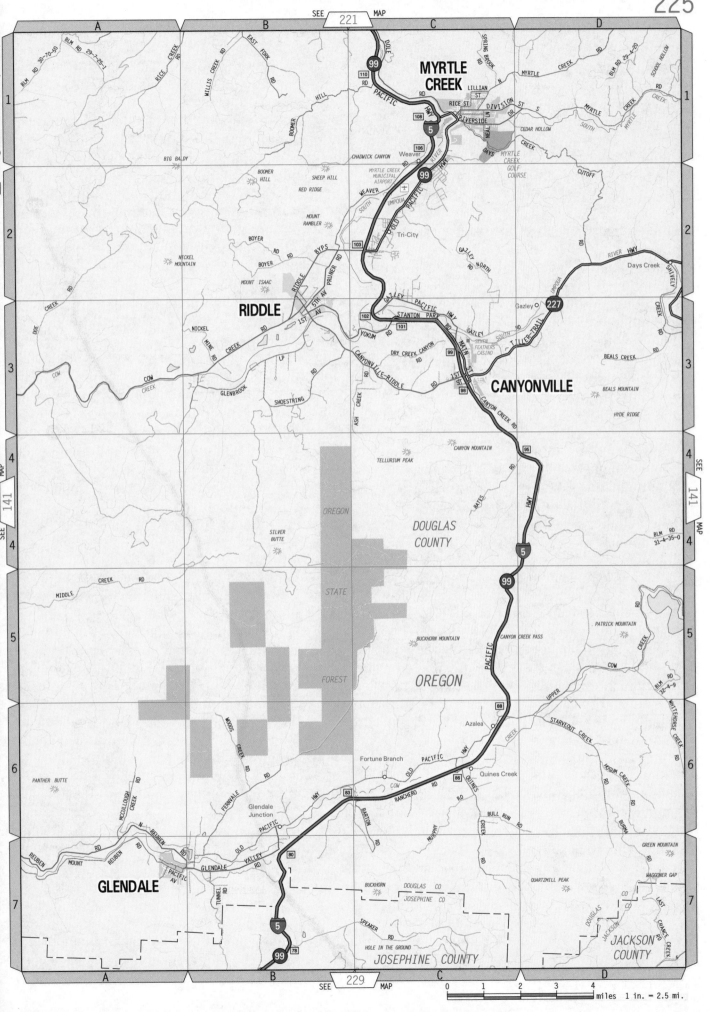

METRO

A B C D

1

TILLER–SOUTH
SOUTH UMPQUA FALLS
UMPQUA CAMP RD
RIVER
SOUTH
BUCKEYE CREEK RD
BUCKEYE CREEK
ACKER ROCK
TWINBUCK SHELTER
DOUGLAS COUNTY
UMPQUA
ROGUE–UMPQUA
BUCKEYE LAKE CAMPGROUND
GRASSHOPPER MOUNTAIN
HIGHROCK MOUNTAIN
JACKASS MOUNTAIN
DIVIDE
WEAVER MOUNTAIN
FISH MOUNTAIN
HOLE IN THE GROUND
ALKALI CAMP
LEWIS CAMP
ROGUE
FOSTER CREEK
RIVER
HERSHBERGER MOUNTAIN
HERSHBERGER RD
HWY

2

TALLOW BUTTE
CLIFF LAKE CAMPGROUND
FIVESTICKS RD
JACKSON
JACKSON
NATIONAL
WILDERNESS
CREEK
ANDERSON MOUNTAIN
RABBIT EARS
PRAIRIE CREEK RD
RD
230
LAKE
NATIONAL
DIAMOND
COPELAND CREEK
N

3

COW HORN ARCH
COUGAR BUTTE
CREEK
RD
SQUAW CREEK
FALCON BUTTE
ELEPHANT HEAD
ABBOTT BUTTE
ABBOTT
CREEK
OREGON
WOLF PEAK
MOUNT STELLA RD
MOUNT STELLA
DOUGLAS CO
JACKSON CO
FOREST
DIAMOND
OLD BYBEE CREEK
BYBEE CREEK RD
CREEK
DEER CREEK RD
CASTLE
WHISKEY CASTLE CREEK RD
CREEK
CRATER LAKE
62
HWY

4

WINDY GAP
NFD RD 950
HUCKLEBERRY GAP
NEAL SPRINGS CAMPGROUND
QUARTZ MOUNTAIN
HUCKLEBERRY LAKE CAMPGROUND
WHALEBACK
FOREST
ROGUE
CREEK
NATURAL
RESEARCH AREA
RIVER
ABBOTT CREEK RD
SUNSHINE CREEK RD
ABBOTT CREEK CAMPGROUND
KNOB HILL
WOODRUFF
NATURAL BRIDGE
UNION CREEK CAMPGROUND
ROGUE GORGE VIEW POINT
UNION CREEK
NATURAL BRIDGE VIEW POINT
62
ROGUE
UNION CREEK
HUCKLEBERRY RD
CREEK RD

4
BUTLER BUTTE
SUGARPINE SHELTER
TUCKER GAP
GREY ROCK
COLD SPRING
TRIPOD
CAMP RD
OLD
WEST SPUR
HWY
NATIONAL
JACKSON COUNTY

5

GOODVIEW POINT
GREY
GRUB BOX GAP
BUCK BASIN
JIM CREEK SPUR
HOP CREEK
BUZZARD MINE RD
ROUND TOP
NEEDLE ROCKS RD
BUZZARD MINE RD
NEEDLE
ROCK RD
NEEDLE RIDGE
GRAVEL BUTTE
LICK ROCK
NEEDLE CREEK RD
BUZZARD MINE RD
ABBOTT
TAKELMA GORGE
CREEK RD
LAKE
LOOP RD
MILL
CREEK RD
ELK
MILL CREEK
RIDGE
ELK RD
GINKGO
RIVER BRIDGE CAMPGROUND
UPPER INJUN CREEK RD
GINKGO

6

ELKHORN RIDGE RD
TIMBER CREEK RD
MILLER MOUNTAIN
SUGAR PINE RD
MULE HILL
ELK CREEK RD
GREY RD
HIBBARD POINT
BALD MOUNTAIN
SANDOZ GAP
HALLS POINT
KITER CREEK
KITER CREEK SPUR
LARSON CREEK RD
GRAHAM CREEK RD
ROGUE RIVER
WHETSTONE POINT
MILL CREEK
MILL CREEK CAMPGROUND
RED BLANKET MOUNTAIN
RED BLANKET CREEK
RED BLANKET RD
FOREST

7

ELK CREEK
ELK CREEK
BAILEY BUTTE
DORES CREEK RD
BURNT PEAK
WILLITS RIDGE
ULRICH RD
CASCADE GORGE
FLOUNCE ROCK
TATOUCHE PEAK
WHITE POINT
SCHOOLMARM SPUR
CRATER LAKE
MILL CREEK DR
RED BLANKET
PROSPECT
MILL CREEK FALLS
BESSIE RD
BESSIE CREEK
RED CREEK
S RED BLANKET RD
MIDDLE FORK
BUTTE FALLS–PROSPECT RD
ROGUE RIVER
PARKER MEADOWS RD
62

0 1 2 3 4 miles   1 in. = 2.5 mi.

SEE 223 MAP

DOUGLAS COUNTY

A B C D

CRATER

CRATER LAKE

CRATER LAKE NATIONAL PARK

KLAMATH COUNTY

OREGON

NATIONAL PARK

WINEMA NATIONAL FOREST

CASCADE RANGE

SKY LAKES WILDERNESS

Muir Creek Falls
Hamaker Campground
Hamaker Butte
Hamaker Bluff
Hurryon Camp
Muir Creek Rd
Rogue River
Diamond Lake
Old National
Douglas Co / Klamath Co
Crescent Ridge
Bald Crater
Oasis Butte
Stream
Douglas Co / Jackson Co
Crater Creek Rd
Crater Creek Mtwy
Bybee Creek
Bybee Creek Rd
Deer Branch Rd
Copeland
Rock Creek
Castle Creek
Whiskey Creek
Castle Creek Rd
Huckleberry Rd
Union Creek
Thousand Springs Rd
National Park
Elephants Back
Llaos Hallway
Whitehorse Bluff
Castle Point
Castle Creek
North Ginko Spur
Union
Alder Spring Rd
Huckleberry Mountain
Rocktop Butte
Dead Soldier Creek
Ginko Rd
Red Blanket Mountain
Blanket Rd
Red Mountain
Red Blanket Creek
Red Blanket Falls
Stuart Falls
Bald Top
Bessie Rock
Jerry Mountain
Tom Mountain
Cinnamon Peak
Bessie Creek
Bessie Shelter
Mudjekeewis Mountain
Kerby Creek
Kerby Hill
Middle Fork Rogue River
Jackson Co / Klamath Co

Gaywas Peak
Desert Ridge
Klamath Ridge
Desert Cone
Pumice Desert
Timber Crater
Rogue River
North Hwy
Pacific Crest Tr
Red Cone
Grouse Hill
Williams Crater
The Watchman
Hillman Peak
Llao Rock
Steel Bay
Pumice Point
Rim of the Crater
Lido Bay
Merriam Point
Devils Backbone
Wizard Island
Fumarole Bay
Governors Bay
Discovery Point
Eagle Cove
Rim Dr
Sinnott Memorial Overlook
Castle Crest
Crater Lake National Park Headquarters
Garfield Peak
Eagle Crags
Applegate Peak
Munson Ridge
Munson Point
Cascade Divide
Mazama Campground
Duwee Falls
Godfrey Glen
Arant Point
Cold Springs Campground
Union Peak
Red Blanket
Crest Tr
Goose Nest
Rogue Watershed
Goose Egg
Oregon Desert
Lone Wolf
Ruth Mountain

Cleetwood Cove
Palisade Point
Palisades Dr
Roundtop
Wineglass
Grotto Cove
Skell Head
Scott Bluffs
Redcloud Cliff
Cloudcap
Cloudcap Bay
Pumice Castle
Castle Rock
Victor View
Mount Scott
Phantom Ship
Chaski Bay
Dutton Cliff
Phantom Ship Overlook
Dutton Ridge
Danger Bay
Rim Dr
Sand Creek
Pinnacle Valley
Vidae Ridge
Tututni Pass
Munson Valley
Grayback Ridge
Maklaks Pass
Crater Peak
Sun Creek
Annie Creek
Maklaks Crater
Annie Falls
Scoria Cone
Crater Lake Hwy
62

230
62
77
142 SEE MAP
METRO

miles 1 in. = 2.5 mi.
0 1 2 3 4

SEE 231 MAP

A | B | C | D

METRO

SEE 148 MAP

SEE 148 MAP

OREGON COAST HWY

ELK RIVER

NFD RD 150

ROCKY PEAK

SUNSHINE CREEK CAMPGROUND

RD

ELK RIVER RD

PANTHER MOUNTAIN

CHISMORE BUTTE

SISKIYOU

MCCURDY CAMPGROUND

OPHIR MOUNTAIN

NFD RD 110

RD 3310

3402

NFD RD

NATIONAL

FOREST

LOOKOUT ROCK

FRANKPORT

COLEBROOK BUTTE

COFFEE BUTTE

FALL MOUNTAIN

NFD RD

LAKE OF THE WOODS MOUNTAIN

SISTERS ROCKS

PREHISTORIC GARDENS

CREEK RD

3340

DEVILS BACKBONE

PACIFIC

Ophir EUCHRE

CURRY COUNTY

CREEK

SOLDIER CAMP MOUNTAIN

OCEAN

RD

R

OPHIR RD

SQUAW

ULMER MOUNTAIN

BRUSHY BALD MOUNTAIN

FIRST PRAIRIE MOUNTAIN

SECOND PRAIRIE MOUNTAIN

POTATO ILLAHE MOUNTAIN

RD

LOBSTER

LOBSTER HILL

RIVER

AGNESS RD

VALLEY

NORTH ROCK

Nesika Beach

VONDERGREEN HILL

NFD RD

3533

QUOSATANA CAMPGROUND

ROGUE RIVER

AGNESS

NESIKA RD

RD

CANFIELD HILL

LOBSTER CREEK CAMPGROUND

WAKEMAN BEACH

EDSON

RIVER

RD

RD

AGATE BEACH

CREEK

RUMLEY HILL

NORTH BANK RD

ROGUE

FLAT

KIMBALL HILL

SISKIYOU

3313

SKOOKUMHOUSE BUTTE

OTTER POINT

RD

JERRYS

BARLEY BEACH

RACETRACK HILL

NORTH BANK ROGUE RIVER

SAUNDERS CREEK

RD

NFD RD

NATIONAL

150

WILDHORSE CAMPGROUND

101

Wedderburn

ROGUE RIVER

JERRYS FLAT RD

OREGON

DOYLE POINT

GOLD BEACH

INDIAN CREEK CAMPGROUND

TOMCAT HILL

H

SIGNAL BUTTES

NFD RD

QUOSATANA BUTTE

FOREST

GOLD BEACH MUNICIPAL AIRPORT

CURRY COUNTY FAIRGROUNDS

SADDLE MOUNTAIN

GRIZZLY MOUNTAIN

RD

SUGARLOAF MOUNTAIN

Hunter Creek

BUENA VISTA OCEAN WAYSIDE STATE PARK

OREGON HUNTER

3680

RIVER

KALMIOPSIS WILDERNESS

FAIRVIEW MOUNTAIN

COLLIER BUTTE

RD

CREEK

CREEK

NFD RD

PISTOL

FAIRVIEW CAMPGROUND

JACOBY BUTTE

COAST

CAPE SEBASTIAN FRONTAGE RD HWY

SNOW CAMP MOUNTAIN

CAPE SEBASTIAN STATE PARK

6

A | B | C | D

0 1 2 3 4 miles 1 in. = 2.5 mi.

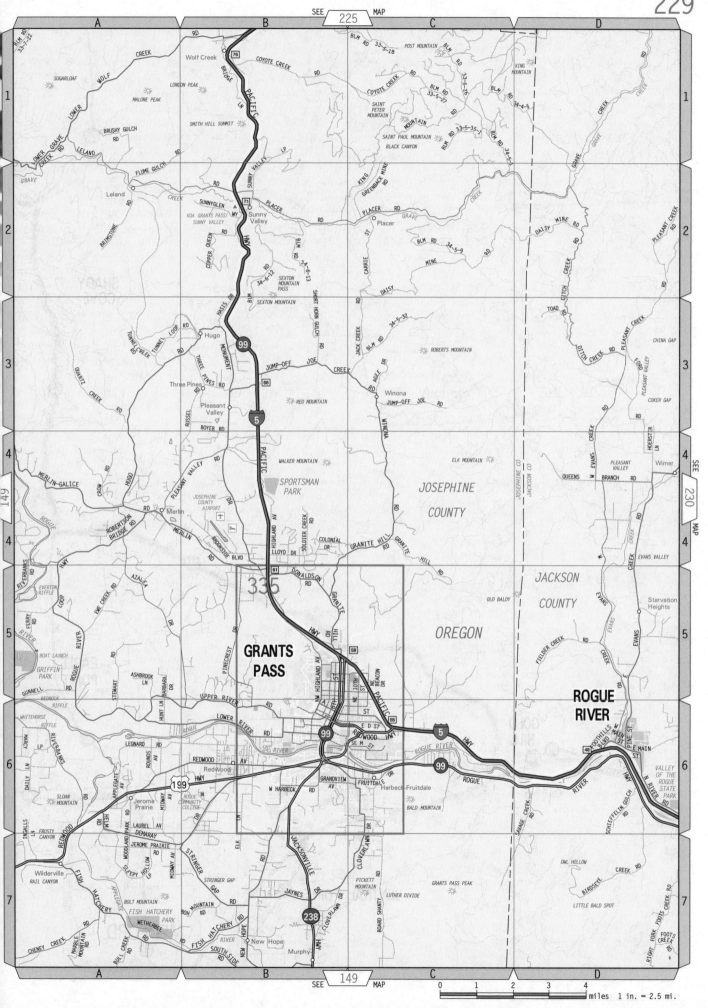

METRO

SEE MAP 141

A B C D

SEE MAP 229

SEE MAP 149

JACKSON COUNTY

OREGON

SHADY COVE

GOLD HILL

EAGLE POINT

CENTRAL POINT

MEDFORD

336

White Rock Mountain
West Fork
Evans
Cold Spring Rd
Rock Creek
Salt Creek
Round Top Rd
Round Top
Peavine Ridge
Horse Mountain
Misty
Cleveland Ridge
East Fork Evans Creek
Romine Creek Rd
Tiller-Trail Hwy
Willy Rock
Willy Mountain
227
Board Mountain
Rogue National Forest
Old Trail Creek Rd
River
Trail
Battle Mountain
Little Battle Mountain
Battle Creek
Bear Wallow
Spignet Butte
Mill Hollow
Boswell Mountain
Evans Creek
Pomeroy
Sawyer Rd
Fry Peak
Black Butte
Mays
Lucky Hollow Creek
Snake Creek
Fawn Creek Rd
False Face Mountain
Neathammer Gulch
Bald Mountain
Maple Gulch Rd
Ramsey Canyon
Hull Mountain
Evans Rd
Cinnabar Mountain
Antioch
Meadows
62
Rogue River
Lake
Shady Cove Dr
Lover Peak
Evans Creek
Braton Hollow
Elkhorn Butte
Ramsey Canyon Rd
Chimney Rock Butte
Jones Rd
Debenger Gap
Ironwood Dr
Leafwood Dr
Hammell Rd
Butte Falls Rd
Evans
Murphy Gulch Rd
McConville Peak
Sardine Mountain
Right Fork Sardine Creek
Turtle Rock
Neil Rock
Eagle Dr
Beagle
New Jones Rd
Shiloh Rd
Mosser Mountain
Ball Rd
Crater Lake Hwy
Hillis Peak
Sardine
Wilcox Peak
Dodge Rd
234
Glass Ln
Perry Rd
Antioch Rd
Rattlesnake Rapids
Long Mountain
Reese Creek
The Oregon Vortex & House of Mystery
Sardine Creek Rd
Fork
Left Creek
Boyd Rd
Lyman Mountain
Sams Valley
Old Sams Valley Rd
Ramsey Rd
Tresham Ln
Wheeler Rd
Table Rock Trail Rd
Upper Table Rock
Modoc Rd
River
W Linn Rd
Young Rd
Nick Rd
Agate Rd
Lake
S Shasta Ave
Royal Ave
Alta Vista
Wards
River Rd
Sardine Creek
Galls Creek
Dillon Falls
Sams Valley
John Day
Hardy Riffle
Valley
Upper River Rd
Gold Hill
Table Rock Rd
Lower Table Rock
Table Rock
Tou Velle State Park
62
Big Ham Brown Rd
99
234
4th Ave
Old Stage Rd
40
Blackwell
Gold Ray Rd
Blackwell Hill
Kirtland
Bear Creek
Agate Desert
Antelope Rd
White City
Kershaw Rd
140
45
43
5
Pacific Hwy
35
Newland Rd
Antelope
Lake of the Woods Hwy
Corey Rd
Foots Creek Rd
Rough & Rugged
Kane Creek
Stage Rd
Scenic
Tolo Rd
Crater Rock Museum
Seven Oaks
Gibbon Rd
Midway
Ham Black Rd
Vilas Rd
Four Corners
Coker Butte
Foothill Rd
Left Fork Foots Creek
Middle Fork Foots Creek Rd
Millpond Campground
Old Stage
Taylor
99
3rd St
Rogue Valley Hwy
Upton Rd
33
Biddle Rd
McLaughlin
Lake
Crater Lake Hwy
Beall Ln
K Pine
Freeman Rd
Beall Ln
Table Rock Rd
62
Delta Waters Rd

SEE MAP 234

0 1 2 3 4 miles 1 in. = 2.5 mi.

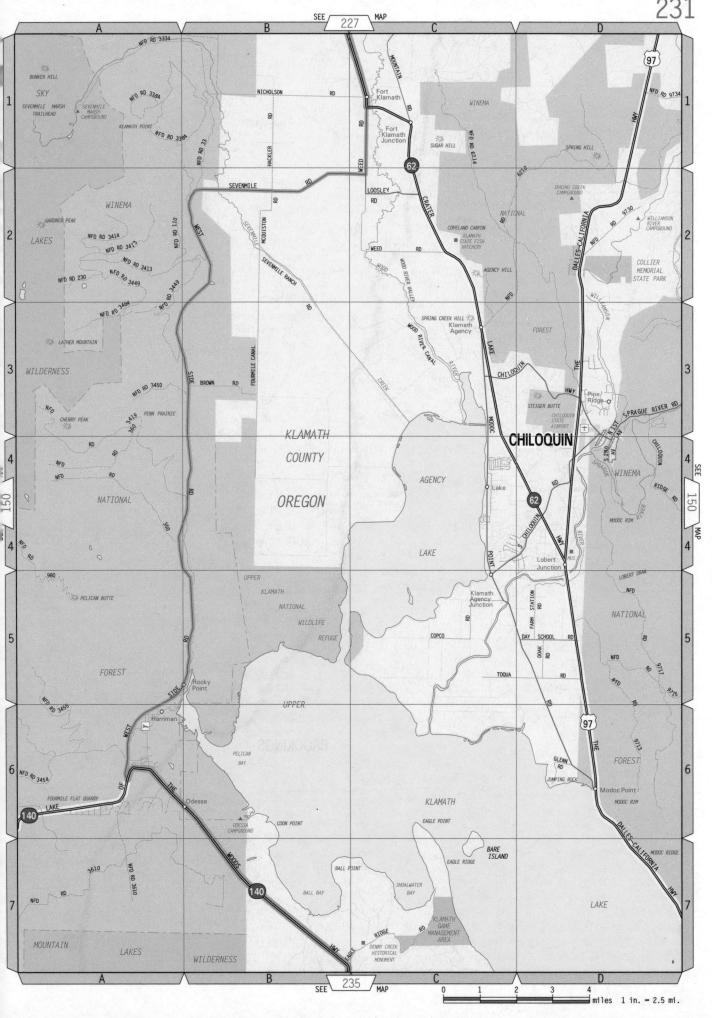

METRO

METRO

SEE 228 MAP

A

CAVE ROCK

MYERS

B

HENRY ROCK

CREEK RD

SUNDOWN
MOUNTAIN

SISKIYOU

C

RIVER

PINE POINT

NFD RD 230

STACK YARDS

D

1

PISTOL
RIVER
STATE

PARK

Pistol
River

NORTH BANK

PISTOL RIVER

PISTOL

RIVER

RD

NATIONAL

NFD RD

70

THREE TREES

THREE TREES CAMP
(HISTORICAL)

1

SADDLE ROCK

MACK POINT

RED ROCK

FOREST

HOG
MOUNTAIN

NFD RD 130

NFD RD
1846

BUZZARD ROOST

2

MACK ARCH
COVE

101

OREGON

RIDGE KNOB

S FORK
RIVER

PISTOL
RD

Carpenterville

BURNT HILL SUMMIT

BOSLEY
BUTTE

HAZEL CAMP

2

YELLOW ROCK

ARCH ROCK
WINDY POINT

BLACK ROCK

LEANING ROCK

CARPENTERVILLE

FITZPATRICK RIDGE

COLEGROVE BUTTE

INDIAN ROCK

CASSIDAY BUTTE

CASHNER BUTTE

RD

3

SEE 148 MAP

SEAL
COVE

COAST

NATURAL BRIDGES

THOMAS
HILL

FRONTAGE

RD

3

PACIFIC

THOMAS POINT

SAMUEL H
BOARDMAN
STATE

PARK

HWY

R

SMITH HILL

WHALEHEAD

GREENHILL

BUSH MOUND

CURRY
COUNTY

RIDGE

4

JCT 148

4

WHALEHEAD
ISLAND

SHORE PINE
RD

MARTIN RANCH
RD

SUNDOWN RD

SUN RAY

CAPE
FERRELO

SAND HILL

RD

MORTON BUTTE

RED MOUND

PALMER BUTTE

OREGON

GARDNER

ALFRED A LOEB
STATE PARK

4

OCEAN

BARNACLE ROCK

HOUSE ROCK

OREGON

101

COAST

OULEY CREEK
RD

RAINBOW ROCK

RD

BLACK MOUND

GARDNER RIDGE

CHETCO RIVER

RIVER

5

LONE RANCH BEACH

BLACK POINT

TWIN
ROCKS

RD

5

WHITE ROCK

GOAT
ISLAND

HWY

HARRIS
BUTTE

HARRIS BEACH
STATE PARK
CAMPGROUND

BROOKINGS STATE
AIRPORT

HARRIS BEACH

TIDE ROCK

NORTH

BANK

SOUTH

BANK

CHETCO

CHETCO RIVER

SALMON
RUN
GOLF
COURSE

ARCH ROCK

HARRIS BEACH
STATE PARK

FOUNTAIN ROCK

BROOKINGS

EASY ST

CHETCO

AZALEA
PK

AV

Harbor

6

DIVER ROCK

CHETCO POINT

CHETCO COVE

RED POINT

TWIN COUSINS

OREGON

COAST

HWY

OCEAN
VIEW
DR

WINCHUCK

RIVER

RD

6

CAMEL ROCK

OCEAN
VIEW

CURRY CO

NFD RD

1101

7

DEL
NORTE
CO

REDWOOD

HWY

CALIFORNIA

GILBERT CREEK

DR

D5

7

A

B

SEE 148 MAP

C

D

miles   1 in. = 2.5 mi.

0   1   2   3   4

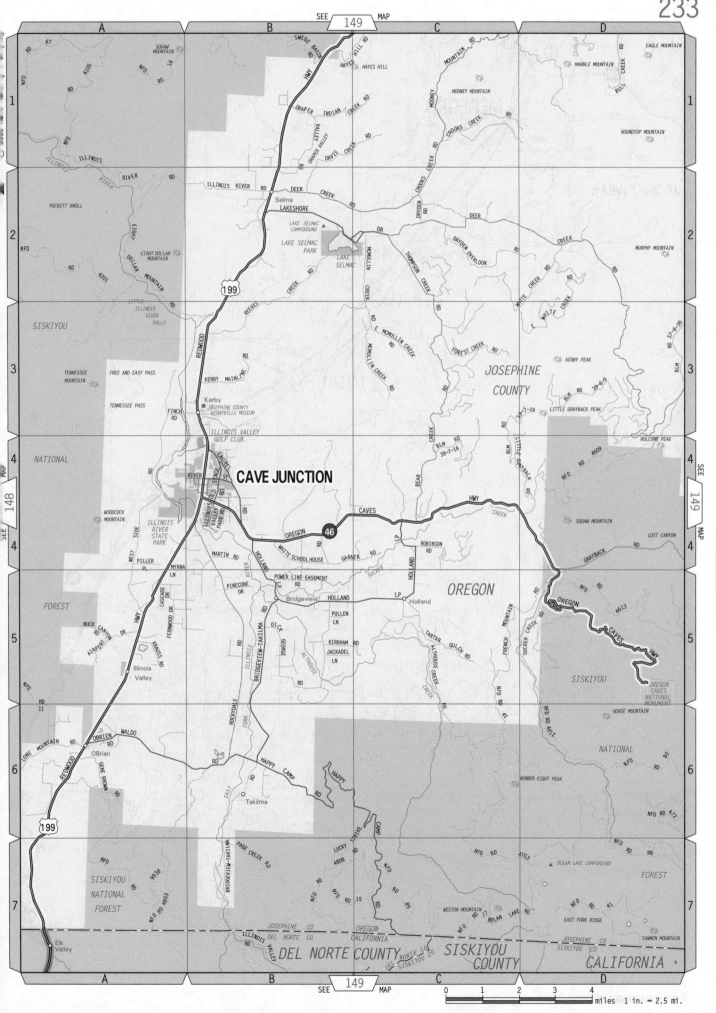

SEE 149 MAP

METRO

CAVE JUNCTION

JOSEPHINE
COUNTY

OREGON

SISKIYOU
NATIONAL
FOREST

NATIONAL
FOREST

SISKIYOU

DEL NORTE COUNTY • SISKIYOU COUNTY
CALIFORNIA

SEE 149 MAP

SEE 148 MAP

SEE 149 MAP

0 1 2 3 4 miles 1 in. = 2.5 mi.

METRO

A | B | C | D

1

OLD STAGE RD
HANLEY RD
238 ROSSANLEY DR
62
30
19
56
CEDAR LINKS RD
CRATER LAKE AV
SPRINGBROOK
LONE PINE RD
SPRING ST
HILLCREST
HILLCREST
ROXY ANN
RD CANYON
VALLEY VIEW
E. ANTELOPE RD
ANTELOPE RD
LAKE CREEK RD
E. ANTELOPE CREEK RD

JACKSONVILLE HWY
ARNOLD LN
BELLINGER LN
BEELMAN HOUSE
HULL RD
STEWART
DOZIER LN
McANDREWS RD
CENTRAL AV
DAKOTA AV
BARNETT
SISKIYOU BLVD
BLACK OAK DR
PHOENIX RD
LARSON CREEK
CHERRY LN

MEDFORD

2

JACKSONVILLE

W GRIFFIN CREEK RD
KNOWLES RD
GRIFFIN CREEK RD
DARK HOLLOW RD
NEVILLE LN
ANDREWS LN
GRIFFIN LN
CARPENTER
DARK HOLLOW
HILL
PIONEER
CREEK
STAGE RD
BRAGG RD
VOORHIES RD
VOORHIES
Voorhies
Gas Works
ROSE RD
BAKER RD
HOUSTON RD
4TH ST
COLVER RD
COAL MINE RD
CAMPBELL RD
FERN VALLEY
FERN VALLEY RD
PHOENIX
N PHOENIX RD
PAYNE RD
TERRI DR
PAYNE
TOMBSTONE
PAYNE CLIFFS
BALDY
GRIZZLY PEAK

PHOENIX

ROGUE VALLEY
BEAR CREEK
PACIFIC HWY
5
24
21

3

NELSON MOUNTAIN LN
GRIFFIN CREEK RD
GRIFFIN CREEK
COLEMAN CREEK RD
DEER TRAIL LN
ADAMS RD
ZEMKE RD
FOSS RD
COLEMAN CREEK
WAGNER CREEK RD
ANDERSON CREEK
HOLTON RD
WAGNER CREEK
337
W VALLEY VIEW RD
19
EAGLE MILL RD
MULTNOMAH AV
MOUNTAIN AV
WALKER AV
INDIAN CREEK RD
BLACK ROCK
DEAD WALKER
99

TALENT

4

STERLING CREEK RD
GRIFFIN CREEK RD
ANDERSON CREEK RD
YANK GULCH
WAGNER CREEK RD
WIMER ST
OREGON SHAKESPEARE THEATRES
N MAIN ST
OAK ST
IOWA
MAIN ST
WALKER AV
CLAY ST
SISKIYOU BLVD
66
14
GREEN SPRINGS HWY
KUB ASHLAND
DUNN BUTTE
EMIGRANT CREEK
WALKER
EMIGRANT LAKE
EMIGRANT LAKE REC AREA
66
11

JACKSON COUNTY

ASHLAND

TUNNEL RIDGE
APPLEGATE
BALD MOUNTAIN

OREGON

5

LITTLE
YALE CREEK RD
BRICK RD
PILE RD
WAGNER BUTTE
WAGNER
ASHLAND
WINBURN MOUNTAIN
2060 RD
ASHLAND CREEK
COGGINS SADDLE
SISKIYOU LOOP
SUMMIT
Klamath Junction
2059 RD
ROGUE RIVER
99
5

ROGUE RIVER NATIONAL FOREST
WATERSHED
NATIONAL FOREST

6

SUMMIT RD
SQUAW CREEK GAP
DEADMANS POINT
LITTLE RED MOUNTAIN
CREEK
ASHLAND MOUNTAIN
WAGNER GAP
2040 RD
NFD RD
NATIONAL
McDONALD PEAK
ASHLAND LOOP RD
TRAIL RD
GROUSE GAP SHELTER
MOUNT ASHLAND SKI AREA
GROUSE CREEK GAP
BULL GAP CAMPGROUND
BULL GAP
MOUNT ASHLAND RD
4050 RD
COLESTIN RD
SKI RD
Siskiyou
OLD SISKIYOU HWY
PACIFIC HWY

FOREST
SISKIYOU PEAK

7

MAPLE DELL GAP
DONOMORE PEAK
MAPLE DELL
ASHLAND LOOP RD
2025 RD
ASHLAND LOOP
DUTCHMAN PEAK
SILVER FORK GAP
SILVER FORK BASIN
JACKSON GAP
SISKIYOU RD
OBSERVATION GAP
WRANGLE GAP
SUMMIT
SISKIYOU GAP
BIG RED MOUNTAIN
NFD RD
DOE PEAK
KLAMATH NATIONAL FOREST
4050 RD
FOUR CORNERS RD
Four Corners
MILL CREEK
4050 RD
NFD RD
COLESTIN RD
Colestin
COLESTIN RD
99
5

0 1 2 3 4 miles 1 in. = 2.5 mi.

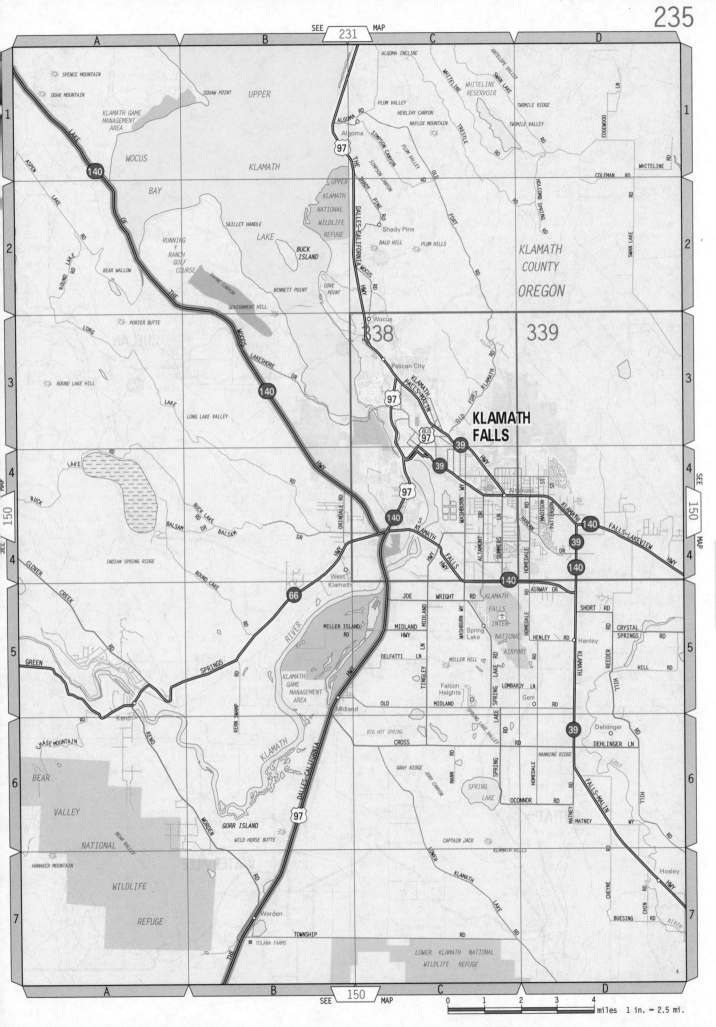

235

METRO

SEE 231 MAP

KLAMATH FALLS

KLAMATH COUNTY OREGON

338

339

SEE 150 MAP

miles 1 in. = 2.5 mi.

236

SEE 112 MAP

A   B   C   D

1

RAMONA PARK CAMPGROUND

8410

WENATCHEE

Hollywood Beach
SLIDE RIDGE
Shrine Beach
SLIDE PEAK

NATIONAL

FIRST CREEK

FOREST

FOREST MOUNTAIN

WASHINGTON

NFD RD

8410

5300

GOMAN PEAK

OKLAHOMA GULCH

PALMICH CANYON

SMITHERS CANYON

BYERS CANYON

McKINSTRY CANYON

BYRD CANYON

RIBBON MESA

EARTHQUAKE POINT

CRUM CANYON

DICK MESA

HANAH CANYON

SAUNDERS CANYON

ENTIAT RIVER

ENTIAT

McLEISH CANYON

MOODY CANYON

MILLS CANYON

KEYSTONE POINT

PETERS POINT

WENATCHEE NATIONAL FOREST

SPENCER CANYON

SPENCER LAKE

Orondo

ALT 97   97

LAKESHORE

LOWER JOE CREEK   GRADE CREEK   UPPER JOE CREEK
WAPATO LAKE
DRY LAKE
WASHINGTON ST
GREEN AV
MANSON BLVD
WILLOW POINT
ROSES LAKE
WAPATO LAKE RD
IVAN MORSE RD

COOLEY

WINESAP AV

NORTHSHORE RD

BOYD RD

WAPATO
Manson
150
WAPATO POINT

CHELAN-STEHEKIN FERRY

LAKE   CHELAN

S LAKESHORE RD

MINNEAPOLIS BEACH

971

BEAR MOUNTAIN

NFD RD

BEAR MOUNTAIN

NAVARRE RD

NAVARRE COULEE

FISHER CANYON

COULEE RD

971

MOWREY RD

KNAPP COULEE

DOWNEY GULCH RD

8550

STAYMAN RD

ALT 97

SPADERS BAY

150

Lakeside

WOODIN AV

GIBSON

CHELAN

ALT 97

WILLMORTH RD

GORGE RIVER RD

PUB

150

CHELAN STATE FISH HATCHERY

Beebe

McNEIL CANYON RD

CHELAN BUTTE

CHELAN RD

DOWNEY GULCH

DAYBREAK CANYON

CHELAN BUTTE

Chelan Falls

HOMESTEAD CANYON

CHELAN BUTTE

WASHINGTON AV

COLUMBIA   RIVER

97

BIG BENCH

JACKSON CANYON

HIGH RIM RD

ROCKY

CHELAN HILL

FARNHAM CANYON

OLMSTEAD RD NW

10   RD NW

DOUGLAS COUNTY

BRAYS CANYON

BROWNS CANYON

HIGGINS LOOP RD NW

BARBER RD NW

8 RD NW

7 3/4 RD NW

7 1/2 RD NW

BRAYS

BROWNS

RD NW

97

GREENS CANYON

9   RD   NW

8 1/2   RD   NW

LAMOINE

RD   NW

7 1/2 RD NW

7   RD   NW

JOHN LONG   RD

LUDEMAN

GIBSON

PIERCE

7   RD NW

PORTER   RD

NELS NELSON RD NW

HARDIN

PINE CANYON

CLOSE

JONES   RD

ROCK

5   RD   NW

NORTH

SLUSSER   RD   NW

CARLOCK   RD

BARNES   RD

GOLL

BALLARD

TOLER

WATERVILLE

2

DOUGLAS COUNTY HISTORICAL MUSEUM

STANDPIPE HILL

2

Douglas

CORBALEY CANYON

McGINNIS CANYON

PLANETE CANYON

BASELINE

239

SEE   MAP

112

150

97

WENATCHEE NATIONAL FOREST

CHELAN COUNTY

ANTOINE CREEK

HIGHLAND BENCH

BRONNFIELD CANYON

BURGELON CANYON

APPLE ACRES

HOWARD

FLAT

CHELAN MUNICIPAL AIRPORT

DEER MOUNTAIN

97

NFD RD 8020

ECHO VALLEY SKI AREA

SWANSON GULCH

COOPER MOUNTAIN

PURTEMAN GULCH

UNION VALLEY LOOP

ROGERS AND HOBSON RD

UNION VALLEY LOOP RD

CHELAN COUNTY

DOUGLAS CO

0 1 2 3 4 miles 1 in. = 2.5 mi.

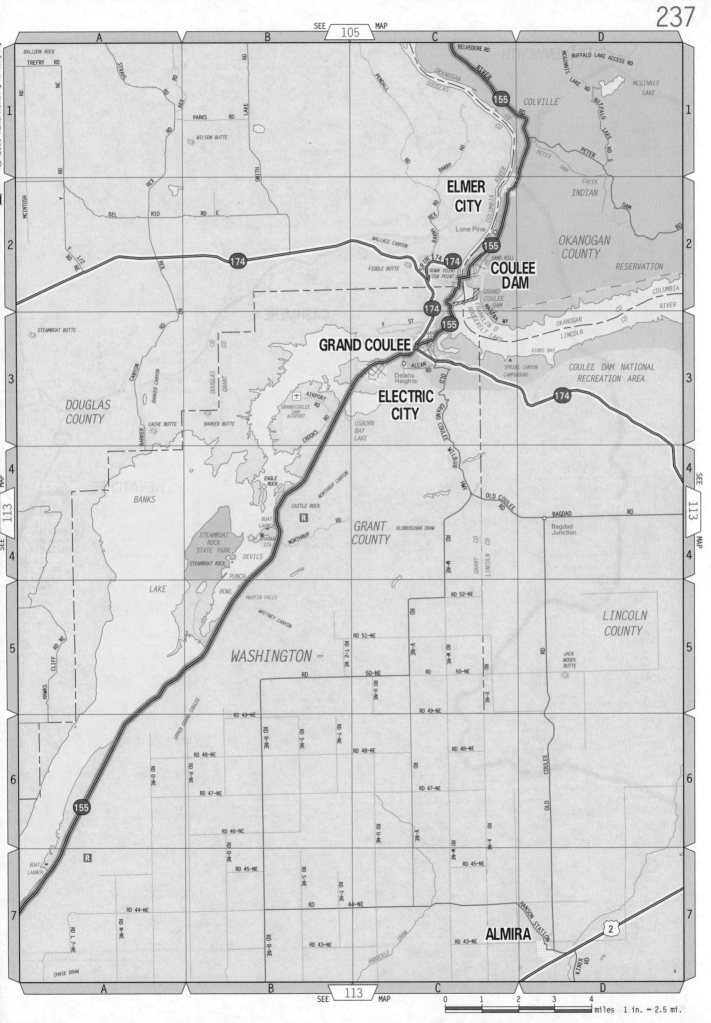

SEE 105 MAP

A B C D

BALLOON ROCK
TREFRY RD
NE
RD
STRAHL RD
RD
PENDALL
LAKE RD
SMITH RD E
BELVEDERE RD
OKANOGAN
DOUGLAS
COLUMBIA RIVER
155
COLVILLE
McGINNIS LAKE ACCESS RD
BUFFALO LAKE ACCESS RD
McGINNIS LAKE
MCINTOSH
PARKS RD
WILSON BUTTE
BARRY
RD
RD
PETER
PETER DAM
DAM CREEK
RD S

1

DEL RIO RD E
REX
Y RD
Y 1/2 RD NE
REX
WALLACE CANYON
FIDDLE BUTTE
174
REX
BARKER
SPUR 174
174
CROWN POINT VIEW POINT
Lone Pine
ELMER CITY
SAND HILL
155
COULEE DAM
155
GRAND COULEE DAM
FRANKLIN D ROOSEVELT LAKE
MIANA WY
INDIAN
OKANOGAN COUNTY
RESERVATION
COLUMBIA CO
CO RIVER

2

STEAMBOAT BUTTE
CANYON
BARKER CANYON
DOUGLAS CO
GRANT CO
174
155
F ST
GRAND COULEE
OLD GRAND COULEE RD
ALCAN RD
Delano Heights
SPRING CANYON CAMPGROUND
GIBBS BAY
OKANOGAN CO
LINCOLN CO
COLUMBIA RIVER
COULEE DAM NATIONAL RECREATION AREA
174

3

DOUGLAS COUNTY
CACHE BUTTE
BARKER
BARKER BUTTE
AIRPORT RD
GRAND COULEE DAM AIRPORT
CROOKS RD
ELECTRIC CITY
OSBORN BAY LAKE
WILBUR
OLD COULEE RD
HWY

4

SEE 113 MAP

BANKS
EAGLE ROCK
CASTLE ROCK
R
BOAT LAUNCH
RANGER STA
STEAMBOAT ROCK STATE PARK
DEVILS
STEAMBOAT ROCK
NORTHRUP CANYON
NORTHRUP
KLOBUSCHAR DRAW
GRANT COUNTY
RD N-NE
OLD COULEE RD
BAGDAD RD
BAGDAD Junction
LINCOLN CO
GRANT CO

4

PUNCH
BOWL
LAKE
MARTIN FALLS
WHITNEY CANYON
WASHINGTON
HAWKS CLIFF RD NE
RD
50-NE
RD 51-NE
RD T-2 NE
RD
V-NE
RD
RD
RD U-NE
RD
RD 52-NE
RD W-NE
RD
50-NE
RD
X-NE
RD
LINCOLN COUNTY
JACK WOODS BUTTE

5

UPPER GRAND COULEE
RD 49-NE
RD R-NE
RD S-NE
RD T-NE
RD 49-NE
RD 48-NE
RD
RD 47-NE
RD 48-NE
OLD COULEE RD

6

155
R
BOAT LAUNCH
RD O-NE
RD P-NE
RD 48-NE
RD 47-NE
RD 46-NE
RD Q-NE
RD 45-NE
RD S-NE
RD U-NE
RD V-NE
RD 45-NE
RD W-NE
RD X-NE
RD 45-NE

6

RD 44-NE
RD L-7-NE
RD N-NE
RD R-NE
RD 43-NE
RD
44-NE
RD T-NE
ARBUCKLE DRAW
RD 43-NE
HANSON STATION RD
ALMIRA
2
KINER RD

7

CHASE DRAW

SEE 113 MAP

A B C D

0 1 2 3 4 miles   1 in. = 2.5 mi.

METRO

238

SEE 111 MAP

LEAVENWORTH

CASHMERE

WENATCHEE

West Wenatchee

KOA LEAVENWORTH/WENATCHEE

PINE ST

WENATCHEE RIVER

ICICLE RD
WILSON ST
SHORE ST
PROWELL ST
PETERS AV
E LEAVENWORTH RD
MOUNTAIN HOME RD

Peshastin

LEAVENWORTH NATIONAL FISH HATCHERY

ICICLE CREEK

BEACHER HILL RD
SAUNDERS RD

ANDERSON CANYON RD

WILLIAMS CANYON RD
JUDGE CANYON

BLAG MOUNTAIN

OLALLA CANYON RD

TIBBETS MOUNTAIN RD

WENATCHEE

NAHAHUM CANYON RD

NFD RD 7412
NFD RD 7413

SWAKANE

BURCH MOUNTAIN

CANYON

NFD RD 5215

NATIONAL

FOREST

CHELAN COUNTY

EAGLE ROCK

WARNER CANYON

MUNDUN CANYON RD

DEAD MAN RD

NORTH RD
N DRYDEN RD

Dryden

OLLALA RD

STINEHILL RD

SUNSET HWY

PIONEER DR
TIGNER RD

SHY MEADOW

BRENDER CANYON

CAMAS CREEK

TRIPP CANYON

POISON CANYON

MISSION CREEK

SHERMAN CANYON

YAKSUM CANYON RD

YAKSUM CANYON

WILLIS CAREY HISTORICAL MUSEUM

EELS RD
HUGHES RD
SUNSET LV
KELLY RD
ZAGER RD

Monitor

E MAIN ST

SLEEPY HOLLOW

SUNSET HWY

AMERICAN FRUIT RD
CRESTVIEW RD
SCHOOL ST
Sunnyslope

EASY ST
PETERS ST
LOWER SUNNYSLOPE RD

COLUMBIA AV
EUCLID AV

MAPLE ST
SPRINGWATER AV
NINTH ST
FIFTH ST
ORCHARD AV
WASHINGTON ST
CASTLEROCK AV
CHERRY ST
WESTERN AV
SKYLINE DR
RED APPLE RD

WENATCHEE VALLEY JUNIOR COLLEGE

NUMBER TWO CANYON

OLD BUTTE
CRAWFORD ST
OKANOGAN AV

HORSE LAKE MOUNTAIN

ROOSTER COMB

PITCHER CANYON RD
SQUILCHUCK RD
WENATCHEE HEIGHTS RD

WASHINGTON

WENATCHEE

NATIONAL

CEDAR GROVE CAMPGROUND

WINDMILL POINT
TIPTOP

SHEEP MOUNTAIN

Blewett

FOREST

RED HILL

BONANZA CAMPGROUND

TRONSEN RIDGE

STUMP CAMPGROUND

PINE CAMPGROUND

MISSION RIDGE

SHEEP ROCK

PENDLETON CANYON

PEAVINE CANYON

WHEELER HILL

STEMILT LOOP

SCOTTY CREEK CAMPGROUND

NFD RD 7320

NFD RD 7324

NFD 200

SWAUK PASS SNO-PARK

TRONSEN CAMPGROUND

ALPINE CAMPGROUND

BEEHIVE MOUNTAIN

PARK CAMPGROUND

SWAUK CAMPGROUND

BLEWETT PASS

Mountain Home

NFD RD 9715
NFD RD 9714

NFD RD 9711

NFD RD 116

NFD RD 9116

NFD RD 9712

HANEY MEADOW CAMPGROUND

MEADOW CAMPGROUND

SPRING CAMPGROUND

BEEHIVE SPRING CAMPGROUND

CHELAN CO
KITTITAS CO

NFD RD 9705
NFD RD 9718
NFD RD 9712
NFD RD 118
NFD RD 115

SWAUK RIDGE

KITTITAS

NANEUM RD
NFD RD 3530
NFD RD 35

MISSION PEAK

MISSION RIDGE WINTER SPORTS AREA

NFD RD 125

SNOWSHOE RIDGE

COUNTY

WENATCHEE MOUNTAIN

NANEUM POINT

Meaghersville

0 1 2 3 4 miles 1 in. = 2.5 mi.

SEE 241 MAP

SEE 239 MAP

SEE 111 MAP

METRO

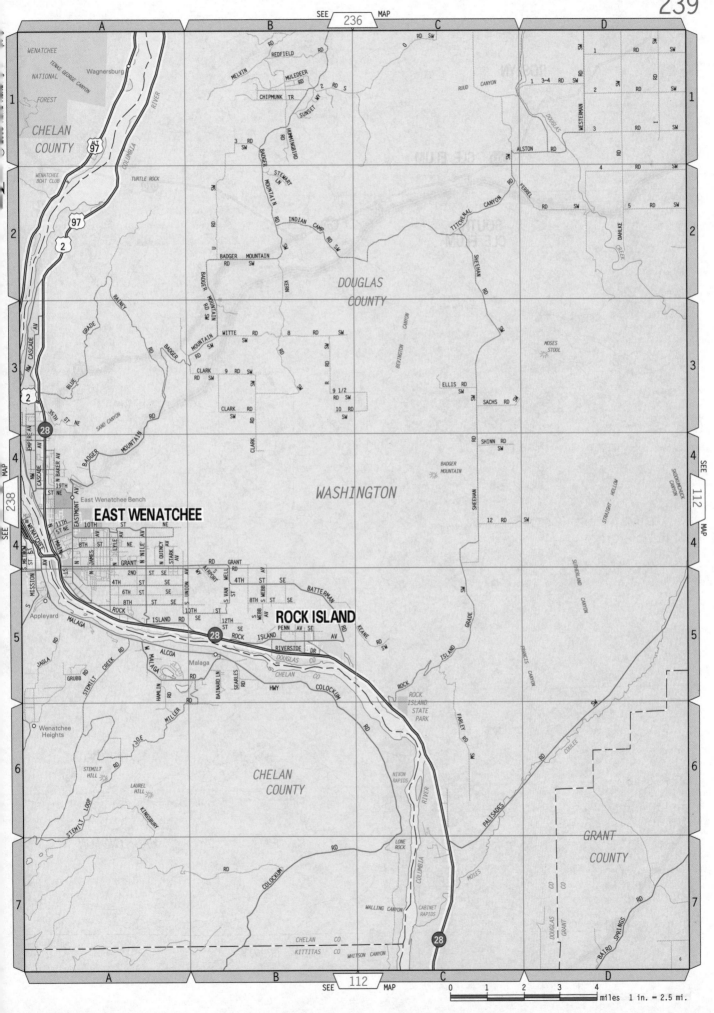

METRO

A B C D

CHELAN COUNTY

WENATCHEE

TENAS GEORGE CANYON

NATIONAL

FOREST

Wagnersburg

COLUMBIA RIVER

ALT 97

97

2

WENATCHEE BOAT CLUB

TURTLE ROCK

REDFIELD RD

MELVIN

MULEDEER RD

CHIPMUNK TR

SUNSET WY

HUMMINGBIRD

BADGER MOUNTAIN RD

STEWART LN

MOUNTAIN N RD

INDIAN CAMP RD SW

KERN

RD SW

RD SW

RUUD CANYON

1 3-4 RD SW

ALSTON RD

DOUGLAS

WESTERMAN RD

TITCHENAL CANYON

FERREL RD SW

DAHLKE CREEK

1

2

DOUGLAS COUNTY

BADGER MOUNTAIN RD SW

BADGER MOUNTAIN RD SW

WITTE RD

8 RD SW

U RD SW

R RD SW

CLARK 9 RD SW

9 1/2 RD SW

10 RD SW

CLARK RD SW

CLARK SW

BEVINGTON CANYON

SHEEHAN RD

ELLIS RD SW

SACHS RD SW

MOSES STOOL

3

WASHINGTON

SHINN RD SW

BADGER MOUNTAIN

12 RD SW

SHEEHAN RD

STRAIGHT HOLLOW

SADDOW CHECK CANYON

SEE [112] MAP

SEE [238] MAP

BLUE GRADE

NW CASCADE AV

RAINEY GRADE

BADGER

MOUNTAIN RD SW

SAND CANYON

BADGER MOUNTAIN

35TH ST NE

2

28

EMPIRE AV

NW CASCADE

N BAKER AV

19TH ST NE

East Wenatchee Bench

EAST WENATCHEE

EASTMONT AV

10TH ST NE

11TH ST NE

8TH ST NE

JAMES N LYLE

N NILE AV

N QUINCY AV

STARK AV

GRANT AV

2ND ST SE

4TH ST SE

6TH ST SE

8TH ST SE

ROCK ISLAND RD

10TH ST SE

RD

AIRPORT

GRANT RD

S VAN WELL

S UNION AV

4TH ST SE

WEBB AV

8TH ST SE

S WEBB ST

12TH ST SE

ROCK ISLAND

PENN AV SE

BATTERMAN

KEANE RD SW

RIVERSIDE DR

ROCK ISLAND RD

GRADE SW

FRANCIS CANYON

SUTHERLAND CANYON

4

S METHOW ST

S MISSION ST

WENATCHEE

Appleyard

MALAGA

W MALAGA

ALCOA

Malaga

STEMILT CREEK RD

HAMLIN RD

BATNARD LN

SEARLES RD

CHELAN HWY

COLOCKUM RD

DOUGLAS CO

CHELAN CO

ROCK ISLAND STATE PARK

FARLEY RD

PALLISADES RD

COULEE SW

ROCK ISLAND

GRANT COUNTY

5

JAGLA RD

GRUBB RD

MILLER

30 E

Wenatchee Heights

STEMILT LOOP

STEMILT HILL

LAUREL HILL

KINGSBURY

COLOCKUM RD

CHELAN COUNTY

NIXON RAPIDS

LONE ROCK

COLUMBIA RIVER

MOSES

DOUGLAS CO

GRANT CO

6

COLOCKUM RD

WALLING CANYON

CABINET RAPIDS

28

BAIRD SPRINGS RD

7

CHELAN CO

KITTITAS CO

WHITSON CANYON

A B C D

miles 1 in. = 2.5 mi.

0 1 2 3 4

METRO

SEE 111 MAP

	A	B	C	D

ROSLYN

Ronald

ROSLYN MUSEUM

CLE ELUM RIDGE

TEANAWAY

MASON CREEK RD

WENATCHEE NATIONAL FOREST

Liberty

903

CLE ELUM

CLE ELUM TELEPHONE MUSEUM

97

LEY RD

HARTMAN RD

SWAUK PRAIRIE RD

Virden

W BALLARD DR

970

97

Nelson

80

90

SOUTH CLE ELUM

85

AIRPORT RD

MASTERSON RD

Teanaway

RED BRIDGE RD

970

HIDDEN VALLEY

HIDDEN VALLEY RD

HORSE CANYON RD

BETTAS RD

AIRPORT RD

LAMBERT RD

R

HART RD

LOOKOUT MOUNTAIN

YAKIMA

LOWER PEOH POINT RD

INDIAN JOHN HILL

THORP PRAIRIE

R

Bristol

UPPER PEOH POINT

CLE ELUM POINT

SOUTH CLE ELUM RIDGE

TANEUM POINT

MOONLIGHT CANYON

MORRISON CANYON

RD

93

Horlick

RIVER

Kountze

SHAUK

HAYWARD RD

10

NORTH FORK TANEUM

CREEK

TANEUM CAMPGROUND

TANEUM CANYON

HORLICK RD

BRUKETTA RD

Dudley

DUDLEY RD

WENATCHEE

TANEUM RIDGE

CREEK

QUARTZ MOUNTAIN RD

LEWIS AND CLARK TRAIL STATE PARK

TANEUM

TANEUM CANYON

RD

SOUTH FORK

MOLE MOUNTAIN

TANEUM

SEE 111 MAP

NATIONAL

FROST MOUNTAIN

YAHNE CANYON

TANEUM RD

SEE 241 MAP

90

TAMARACK SPRING CAMPGROUND

RATTLESNAKE CANYON

WATT CANYON

WATT CANYON RD

ERNY

MINEGAR CANYON

WASHER CANYON

KITTITAS

COUNTY

PAGE CANYON

FOREST

SHELL

ROCK

WHISKY CANYON

ROBINSON CANYON

AINSLEY CANYON

KLOSS RD

COLEMAN CANYON

NFD RD 1708

MANASTASH

MANASTASH RD

NORTH RIGGS CANYON

BALD MOUNTAIN

CREEK

NFD RD

1703

Cliffdell

HOG

NENAS

WASHINGTON

SOUTH RIGGS CANYON

NFD RD

1720

RD

1701

RANCH

CREEK

KITTITAS CO

YAKIMA CO

NFD RD

410

1721

NFD RD

COTTONWOOD CAMPGROUND

NACHES RIVER

MOUNT BAKER-SNOQUALMIE NATIONAL FOREST

YAKIMA COUNTY

WENAS

WENAS RD

	A	B	C	D

SEE 119 MAP

0 1 2 3 4 miles 1 in. = 2.5 mi.

METRO

SEE 238 MAP

SEE 112 MAP

SEE 240 MAP

A B C D

1 2 3 4 5 6 7

LIBERTY RD

LION ROCK
LION ROCK
SPRING CAMPGROUND
TABLE MOUNTAIN
NFD RD 35-07

NFD RD 9726
NFD RD 9726
NFD RD 213

WENATCHEE

113

NFD RD 3521

NATIONAL

TEANAWAY WILSON STOCK TR.

WENATCHEE NATIONAL FOREST

NANEUM RIDGE RD

JUMPOFF RIDGE RD

KITTITAS
COUNTY

NANEUM BASIN

NFD RD 3506

RD 114

NFD RD 111

NFD RD 3517

NFD RD 112
NFD RD 113

NFD RD 114
NFD RD 115
NFD RD 116

HABBERMAN RD

GREEN CANYON

UPPER GREEN CANYON RD

REECER CREEK RD

RD

FOREST

CURRIER CANYON

WILSON CREEK

NATURAL

SWAG CANYON RD

CAVE CANYON

CREEK

WASHINGTON

LILLARD HILL

NANEUM

CAVE CANYON

SCHNEBLY CANYON

COLEMAN CANYON

DINING CANYON

COLOCKUM CANYON

SMITHSON RD

PUMP RD

SMITHSON

HOWARD RD

DRY

ROBBINS RD

97

REECER CREEK RD

RD

LOWER GREEN CANYON RD

CANAL

CASCADE

YAKIMA

THORP

Thorp

GOODWIN RD

PASSMORE RD

MCHANNY

10

101

HUNTER RD

RD

COVE RD

THORP HWY

90

CEM

RIVER

FAUST

FAUST RD

DRY CREEK RD

KILLMORE RD

ROBINSON CANYON

97

WEAVER RD

106
ELLENSBURG

CLARKE RD

KERR RD

HUNGRY JUNCTION RD
Waldale

BENDER RD

AIRPORT RD

UNIVERSITY WY

ELLENSBURG

W 15TH AV
14TH AV
E

DOLARWAY RD

97

HANSON RD

COVE

HANSON RD

BARNES RD

BROWN

STRANDE

SUSAN RD

BRONDT

DAMMAN RD

90

MANASTASH

MANASTASH

SOUTH FORK

CREEK

RD

MAIN ST

MOUNTAIN VIEW AV

CLYMER MUSEUM
CENTRAL WASHINGTON UNIVERSITY
NICHOLSON PAVILION
FAIRGROUNDS
KITTITAS COUNTY HISTORICAL MUSEUM

KITTITAS HWY

110

Regal

WILSON CREEK RD

FIELDS RD

NANEUM

GAME FARM RD

WILLOWDALE RD

LYONS RD

BRICK RD

MILL RD

ALFORD RD

TIPTON RD

RADER RD

BRICK MILL RD

CHARLTON RD

THOMAS RD

LEWIS LN

BAR 14 RD

THOMAS RD

COLEMAN

FAIRVIEW

LYONS RD

WATSON RD

VANTAGE RD

PUMP RD

SCHNEBLY RD

SCHNEBLY DITCH

LESTER RD

COOKE RD

COLOCKUM RD

BRICK RD

MILL RD

81

GILBERT RD

GRINROD RD

VENTURE RD

CARIBOU CREEK

SNODGRASS RD

NUMBER RD

81 RD

COOKE RD

GAGE RD

CANYON RD

CREEK RD

CHRISTENSEN RD

PARK RD

CARIBOU RD

VANPRY
FOX
MT HWY LN

ELLENSBURG

MOUNTAIN VIEW AV

KITTITAS HWY

OLMSTEAD PLACE STATE PARK

KITTITAS

HWY

4TH AV

MAIN ST

FRWY

HANSON RD

HOLMES

STONE QUARRY CANYON RD

LONG TOM CANYON

UMPTANUM

BENNY CANYON

DURR RD

THRALL
Thrall

SKOOKUMCHUCK CANYON

STRANDE RD

YAKIMA RIVER

CANYON RD

BOTTOM RD

NANEUM CREEK

COLEMAN CREEK

RD

CLEMAN RD

THRALL RD

CASCADE

East Kittitas

90

BADGER POCKET

PUMP DITCH

CANAL

821

82

97

KITTITAS CO
YAKIMA CO

WENAS

RD

0 1 2 3 4
miles 1 in. = 2.5 mi.

242

A · B · C · D

MOSES LAKE

GRANT COUNTY

WASHINGTON

THE POTHOLES RESERVOIR

Grant County International Airport

Moses Lake Municipal Airport

Grant County Fairgrounds

Moses Lake Community Park

Cascade Valley

Crest Island
Marsh Island
Goat Island
Gaileys Island
Sand Dunes

Potholes State Park

Corral Lake
Soda Lake
Columbia National Wildlife Refuge
Big Goose Lake

Frenchman Hills

Columbia National Wildlife Refuge

GRANT CO
ADAMS CO
ADAMS COUNTY

Lind Coulee
Rocky Coulee
Crab Creek
Winchester Wasteway
Drumheller
O'Sullivan Dam Rd

Roads: CANAL W-20, RD 9-NW, RD 8-NW, RD 7-NW, RD 10-NE, Neppel Rd, Stonecrest Rd, Lake Vista Dr, Westshore Dr, McConihe, Hansen Dr, Randolph, Chanute St, 2nd St, Patton Blvd, Stratford, Tyndall, Parkway Dr, Dick Rd, Maple, Park Orchard Dr, Kinder, Ottmar, Airway Dr, Valley Rd, Central Dr, Pioneer Wy, Division St, Broadway, Marina Dr, Peninsula Dr, Potato Hill, Baseline Rd, Nelson Rd, Hill Av, Hiawatha, Mae, Valley, Sage Rd

Highways: 17, 171, 90, 112, 113, 120, 169, 175, 179, 182, 262

N FRONTAGE RD / FRONTAGE RD

METRO
SEE 112 MAP

SEE 120 MAP

0 1 2 3 4 miles 1 in. = 2.5 mi.

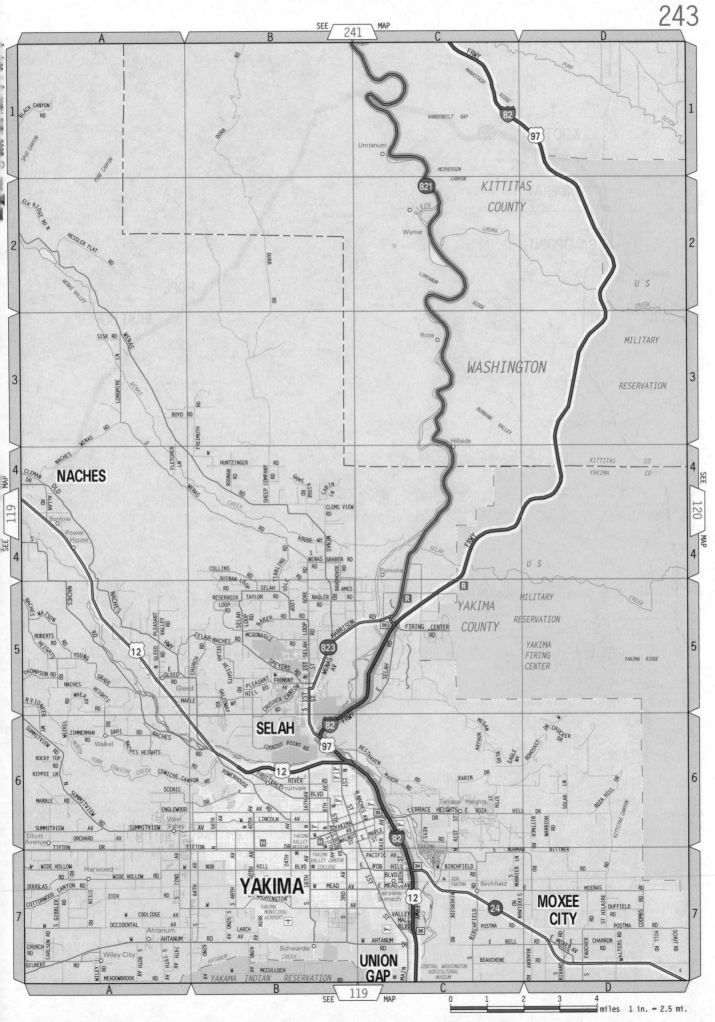

METRO

A | B | C | D

NACHES

SELAH

YAKIMA

UNION GAP

MOXEE CITY

KITTITAS COUNTY

WASHINGTON

YAKIMA COUNTY

MILITARY RESERVATION

YAKIMA FIRING CENTER

US MILITARY RESERVATION

YAKAMA INDIAN RESERVATION

SEE 119 MAP

SEE 120 MAP

0 1 2 3 4 miles   1 in. = 2.5 mi.

METRO

SEE MAP 107

SEE 107 MAP

SEE 107 MAP

SEE 245 MAP

A B C D

KOOTENAI

PONDERAY

SANDPOINT

DOVER

HOPE

EAST HOPE

95
2
200

HIDDEN VALLEY RD
SCHWEITZER BASIN RD
E BRONX RD
E SHINGLE MILL RD
W SHINGLE MILL RD
N KOOTENAI RD
N KOOTENAI RD
HICKEY RD
COLBURN CULVER RD
LOWER PACK RIVER RD
PACK RIVER
TROUT CREEK

KANIKSU

TROUT PEAK
TRESTLE PEAK

SANDPOINT AIRPORT
MOUNTAIN VIEW DR
MOUNTAIN VIEW DR
BALDY MOUNTAIN RD
KOOTENAI CTO
1ST AV
WHISKEY JACK RD
PONDER POINT
KOOTENAI BAY
KOOTENAI POINT
ODEN BAY
SUNNYSIDE
SUNNYSIDE
SUNNYSIDE MOUNTAIN
GRIEF MOUNTAIN

NATIONAL

TRESTLE CREEK
COCHRAN DRAW
ROUND TOP MOUNTAIN
NFD 489
AUXOR BASIN

LARCH ST
PINE ST
ONTARIO ST
N DIVISION ST
S DIVISION ST
BOYER AV
N BOYER AV

FISHERMAN ISLAND
HAWKINS POINT
PACK RIVER BOAT RAMP
TRESTLE CREEK
TRESTLE CREEK BOAT RAMP

FOREST

PEND OREILLE RIVER
ROCKY POINT
LAKESHORE DR
SPADES
SPRING POINT CAMPGROUND
MURPHY BAY
OSPREY NESTS VIEWPOINT
SANDPOINT FISH HATCHERY
GUN CLUB RD
LIGNITE
SAGLE
CONTEST POINT
SOURDOUGH POINT
GOLD HILL RD
GOLD HILL
GOLD HILL CTR
BOTTLE BAY RD
BOTTLE BAY
BOTTLE BAY
YUANCY LAKE
BOTTLE BAY POINT
ANDERSON POINT
RD
SUNRISE BAY
GLENGARY BAY RD
MARTIN BAY
PRINGLE BOAT LAUNCH
DAVID THOMPSON HISTORICAL MONUMENT
COUGAR PEAK

WARREN ISLAND
COTTAGE ISLAND
PEARL ISLAND
OWENS BAY
ELLISPORT BAY
RED FIR
HOPE PENINSULA
SPRING CREEK RD

GOLD MOUNTAIN
GOLD MOUNTAIN RD
GLENGARY BAY RD
GLENGARY BAY RD
CAMP BAY RD
PICARD POINT
ELLIOT BAY
MEMALOOSE ISLAND
SHEEPHERDER POINT
HOWE MOUNTAIN

95
BONNER COUNTY
ALGOMA SPUR
REED HILL
S SAGLE
TALACHE
SHEPHERD LAKE ACCESS AREA
GARFIELD BAY
GARFIELD BAY ACCESS AREA
GARFIELD BAY CTO
GARFIELD BAY
GREEN BAY RD
GREEN BAY
MINERAL POINT
LONG POINT
CAMP BAY
LAKE PEND OREILLE
PETROGLYPHS
200
DERR ISLAND

HEATH LAKE RD
E DUFORT RD
MIRROR LAKE ACCESS
GROUSE MOUNTAIN
GROUSE MOUNTAIN POINT
PONDEROSA RD
NFD RD 2233

BEEKS RD
COCOLALLA LAKE ACCESS AREA
WESTMOND
WESTMOND
TALACHE
BIMETALLIC RIDGE

KANIKSU
BUTLER CREEK RD
BUTLER MOUNTAIN
BLACKTAIL MOUNTAIN
UPPER COCOLALLA CREEK
MAIDEN ROCK

KILROY BAY
PINE COVE
ECHO ROCK
GRANITE POINT
WINDY POINT
INDIAN POINT
DEADMAN POINT
GREEN MONARCH MOUNTAIN
GREEN MONARCH RIDGE
SHAFER PEAK
SHERMAN RIDGE
WHITE QUARTZ RIDGE

IDAHO

JAKES MOUNTAIN
JOHNSON POINT VISTA
NFD RD 278
JOHNSON PEAK

COCOLALLA CREEK RD
LITTLE BLACKTAIL MOUNTAIN
NATIONAL
LITTLE BLACKTAIL MOUNTAIN
NFD RD
278
RD
FLEMING POINT
KANIKSU
MINERVA PEAK
MINERVA RIDGE
NFD RD 1088
TOMS RIDGE
PEEP A DAY RIDGE
1066 RD
JOHNSON SADDLE
RD 332

WHISKEY ROCK BAY
WHISKEY ROCK
NFD RD 1050
BARTON HUMP
PACKSADDLE MOUNTAIN
NATIONAL
FOREST
COEUR D'ALENE
BONNER CO
SHOSHONE CO
COEUR D'ALENE RIVER
NFD RD 306

THREE SISTERS PEAKS
SUNSET RD
FOREST
NFD RD 22
LARCH MOUNTAIN
NATIONAL FOREST
SHOSHONE COUNTY
POWER MOUNTAIN

0 1 2 3 4 miles   1 in. = 2.5 mi.

SEE 244 MAP

KANISKU NATIONAL FOREST
CAPE HORN PEAK
LAKE PEND OREILLE

KANISKU NATIONAL FOREST

BONNER COUNTY

95

PERIMETER RD
CAPE HORN RD
Bayview
SCENIC BAY
BLACKWELL POINT
GRAHAM POINT
Lakeview
NFD RD 278

FARRAGUT STATE PARK
HILL CAMPGROUND
BENNION CAMPGROUND
WILLOW DAY USE AREA
SUNRISE DAY USE AREA
PETERSON CAMPGROUND
WARD CAMPGROUND
SNOWBERRY CAMPGROUND
ECHO BAY
BERNARD OVERLOOK
SCOTT CAMPGROUND
BRIDGE CAMPGROUND
WHITETAIL CAMPGROUND
NIGHTHAWK CAMPGROUND
WALDRON CAMPGROUND
KESTREL CAMPGROUND
BEAVER BAY SWIM AREA

ATHOL
54

HOWARD RD
E SAINT JOE DR

KANISKU NATIONAL FOREST

BERNARD PEAK
NFD RD 278
NATIONAL FOREST
NFD RD 1017
KOOTENAI CO / BONNER CO

REMINGTON RD
CLAGSTONE
LINDSEY RD
CARAVELLE RD
LEWELLEN CREEK
GOOD HOPE RD
PARKS RD
BUNCO RD
NFD RD 209
NFD RD 1080
PROSPECT PEAK
NFD RD 332

RAMSEY RD
RANCH RD
SEASONS RD
BRUNNER RD
BUNCO RD
NUNN RD
HONEY MOUNTAIN

CHILCO MOUNTAIN

D MOUNTAIN
TRENT RD
BENCH RD
PURCELL TRENCH
KOOTENAI COUNTY
CEDAR SADDLE
GREEN MOUNTAIN
SOUTH CHILCO MOUNTAIN
SOLITARE SADDLE
NFD RD 6728
JACKKNIFE PEAK
NFD RD 258
NFD RD 209

Ramsey
Chilco
E CHILCO AV
FIRST ST
95
RIMROCK
HOLLISTER MOUNTAIN TR
NFD RD 406
SAGE CREEK SADDLE
NFD RD 794

OHIO MATCH RD
RAMSEY RD
GARWOOD RD
HUDLOW RD
RIMROCK RD
PINEWOOD WY
NFD RD 2302
NFD RD 625
BUCKLES MOUNTAIN
NFD RD 437
HUDLOW SADDLE
NFD RD 1594

247
53
KNUDSEN
DODD RD
BOOTHILL RD
KOA COEUR D'ALENE NORTH HAYDEN LAKE
TRIANGLE RD
HUDLOW MOUNTAIN
BURNT CABIN RD
STUMP RD
IDAHO
HELLS CANYON
BADGER MOUNTAIN
COLT MOUNTAIN
NFD RD 392
NFD RD 437
NFD RD 406
NFD RD 209

HAYDEN LAKE RD
MCLEAN RD
HAYDEN LAKE
MOKINS BAY CAMPGROUND
E NEILSON RD
DEERFOOT RIDGE
TENDERFOOT RIDGE
SPADES MOUNTAIN
NFD RD 206
NFD RD 1587

LANCASTER RD
COEUR D'ALENE AIR TERMINAL
GOVERNMENT
95
HAYDEN LAKE
HAYDEN
STRAHORN
LAKEVIEW
ENGLISH PT
CRAMPS BAY
BERVEN BAY
MOKINS BAY
YELLOWSTONE POINT
COEUR D'ALENE
HUCKLEBERRY MOUNTAIN
NFD RD 612
ECHO PEAK
FLORA MILLER HILL
NFD RD 209
NFD RD 411
NFD RD 616
NFD RD 206
NFD RD 209
NFD RD 610
NFD RD 3027

MILES AV
E MILES AV
HAYDEN AV
REED RD
HAYDEN WY
HONEYSUCKLE BAY
Clarkesville
WINDY BAY
O-ROURKE BAY
HAYDEN LAKE

HONEYSUCKLE
35
PRAIRIE AV
DALTON GARDENS
WEST CANFIELD BUTTE
CANFIELD LOOP
CANFIELD BUTTE VISTA
NFD RD 268
FERNAN SADDLE
TREASURE MOUNTAIN
NATIONAL
WINDY RIDGE
HONEYSUCKLE CAMPGROUND
SHADY DRAW
NFD RD 434

HANLEY AV
DALTON AV
RAMSEY RD
REED RD
GOVERNMENT
MARGARET AV
ATLAS RD
W KATHLEEN AV
COEUR D'ALENE
STACKEL DRAW
TREASURE SADDLE
WOLF LODGE MOUNTAIN
NFD RD 2320
SKITWISH PEAK

BEST AV
11
12
13
15TH ST
14TH ST
FRENCH GULCH RD
FERNAN
FERNAN HILL RD
BLUE CREEK
KELLY MOUNTAIN
FOREST

SPOKANE RIVER
EMMA
HARRISON AV
ST FOSTER AV
15
FERNAN LAKE SADDLE DR
MARIE CREEK RD
MEYERS SADDLE
SKITWISH RIDGE
NFD RD 413

E SHERMAN AV
FERNAN LAKE VILLAGE
90
KERN BUTTE
BLUE CREEK RD
FOLSOM RIDGE
COPPER MOUNTAIN
MARIE SADDLE

COEUR D'ALENE LAKE

SEE 248 MAP

miles 1 in. = 2.5 mi.
0 1 2 3 4

METRO
SEE 115 MAP

SEE 114 MAP

346

347

STEVENS COUNTY

RIVERSIDE

CORKSCREW CANYON RD
SWENSON RD
STEVENS CO
SPOKANE CO

W PINE BLUFF RD
W CARLSON RD
CHARLES RD

291

NINE MILE FALLS
Nine Mile Falls

W FOUR MOUND RD
W SEVEN MILE RD
Seven Mile
CAMP SEVEN MILE MILITARY RESERVATION

RUTTER PKWY
INDIAN TRAIL RD

FIVE MILE RD
FIVE MILE RD
Town & Country

Dartford

LITTLE SPOKANE DR
SHADY SLOPE RD
NEWPORT HWY

395

2

W WAIKIKI
Fairwood

HAWTHORNE RD

Country Homes
Morgan Acres

COUNTRY HOMES BLVD
MILL RD

2
395

LINCOLN RD

FRANCIS AV
FRANCIS AV

348

349

SPOKANE

350

MILLWOOD

SPOKANE COUNTY

RIVERSIDE STATE PARK

GARFIELD RD
OLD TRAILS RD

RIVERSIDE PARK DR
AUBREY L WHITE PKWY

DRISCOLL BLVD
WELLESLEY AV

ASH ST
GARLAND AV
MAPLE ST
EUCLID AV

WALL ST
DIVISION ST
RUBY ST

WELLESLEY
Hillyard

CRESTLINE ST
NEVADA ST
PERRY ST
EUCLID

MARKET ST
HAVANA ST

UPRIVER DR
Pasadena Park
ARGONNE RD
EMPIRE WY
PINES RD

287
289

MAXWELL AV
West Spokane
MISSION
SPOKANE
Orchard Avenue
Parkwater
Orchard Park

27

DENO RD

CRAIG RD
FLINT RD
GROVE RD

GREENWOOD RD
GOVERNMENT WY
GREENWOOD RD
BASALT RD

TRENT AV
290
FRWY
FREYA ST
SPRAGUE
BROADWAY AV
MISSION
BROADWAY
286
90
University
4TH

Dishman
DISHMAN HILLS NATURAL AREA

8TH
16TH
32ND AV

McDONALD RD
BLAKE RD
PINES RD

AIRWAY HEIGHTS

Northern Quest Casino

W 12TH AV
W 14TH AV
SUNSET HWY
2

AIRPORT DR
FRWY
GEIGER BLVD
277
90
279

281
395

2

Opportunity

SPOKANE VALLEY
Chester

SPOKANE INTERNATIONAL AIRPORT

276

INLAND EMPIRE WY
14TH AV
29TH
SOUTHEAST BLVD
37TH

GRAND BLVD
PERRY ST
RAY ST
FREYA ST
HAVANA ST
CARNAHAN RD

HARTSON AV
8TH
East Spokane

GLENROSE RD

W McFARLANE
LYONS RD
HAYFORD RD

Hayford
ELECTRIC RD
GEIGER BLVD
90
395

53RD AV
ABBOTT RD
DORSET RD
THORPE RD

BERNARD ST
195

E 44TH AV
E 57TH
E 63RD AV
HIGH DR
HATCH RD

BROWNE MOUNTAIN

902
272
HALLETT

Geiger Heights

REGAL RD
PALOUSE HWY

E JANIESON RD

KRELL HILL
BIG ROCK

DISHMAN-MICA RD

W THORPE RD
SPOTTED RD

THOMAS-MALLEN RD
MELVILLE

GRIFFIN RD

CHENEY-SPOKANE RD
SPOKANE RD
CEDAR RD
WHITE RD

INLAND RD
HANGMAN
REGAL RD

E WILLOW SPRINGS RD
WILLOW SPRINGS
SILVER HILL
BIG ROCK RD
KIESLING RD
STEVENS CREEK

SANDS RD
GIBBS RD

270

Four Lakes
WASHINGTON
Needham Hill
WRIGHTS HILL

ANDRUS

Marshall

E TAYLOR RD
GIBBS RD

SHERMAN RD
AUSTIN RD

VALLEY RD
HANGMAN
EMPIRE HWY
HANGMAN VALLEY GOLF CLUB

S BALTIMORE RD
E GIBBS RD
E VALLEY RD

PALOUSE RD
S BRUNA RD
NOSION RD

WEGER RD
E WASHINGTON RD

Valleyford
CONNOR
STOUGHTON

904
JENSEN
PROSSER HILL

Scribner
GARDNER RD
SCRIBNER RD

ROSA BUTTE

CHAPEL RD
STOUGHTON RD

E PARADISE RD
DUNN RD
SANDS RD
ELDER RD

CHENEY
EASTERN WASHINGTON UNIVERSITY
ELM ST
WASHINGTON ST
BETZ RD
Cheney Flour Mill

ANDRIS RD
ANDERSON RD
ANDERSON RD

LOIS DR
Dynamite

SMYTHE RD

195

SPANGLE CREEK
STENTZ RD
Duncan

YALE RD
SMYTHE RD

E VALLEY RD
CHAPEL
BAKER RD

COLUMBIA BASIN HWY

0 1 2 3 4 miles   1 in. = 2.5 mi.

SEE 114 MAP

SEE 114 MAP

SEE 247 MAP

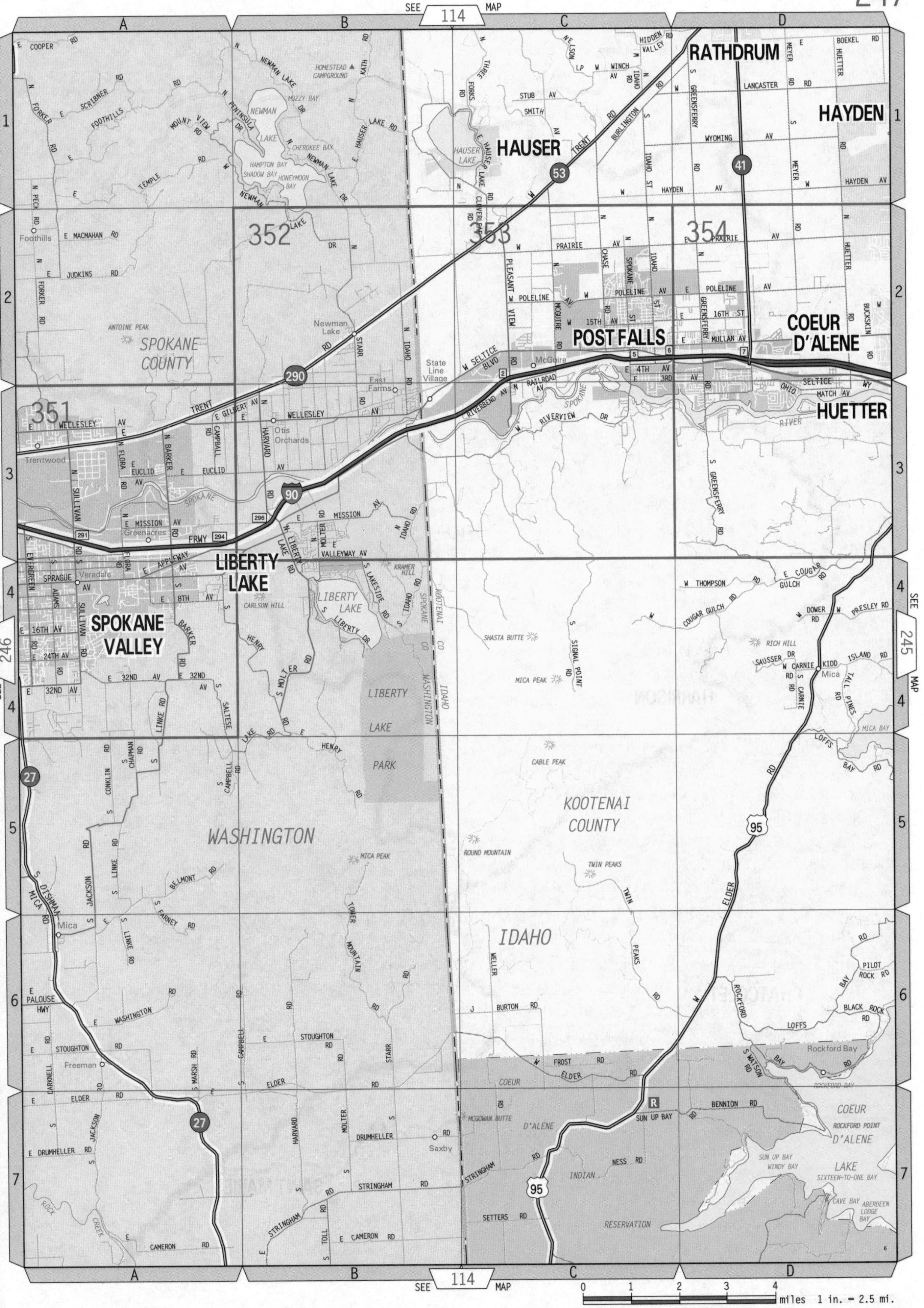

SEE 114 MAP

A	B	C	D

RATHDRUM

HAYDEN

HAUSER

POST FALLS

COEUR D'ALENE

HUETTER

352

353

354

351

LIBERTY LAKE

SPOKANE VALLEY

SPOKANE COUNTY

WASHINGTON

IDAHO

KOOTENAI COUNTY

LIBERTY LAKE PARK

LIBERTY LAKE

COEUR D'ALENE LAKE

COEUR D'ALENE INDIAN RESERVATION

SEE 114 MAP

SEE 246 MAP

SEE 245 MAP

METRO

miles 1 in. = 2.5 mi.

0 1 2 3 4

SEE 245 MAP

A   B   C   D

METRO

SEE 247 MAP

SEE 115 MAP

KID ISLAND BAY
KID ISLAND
W PRESLEY RD
WENIGER HILL RD
ARROW POINT
Twin Beaches
KIDD ISLAND
W VALHALLA RD
ECHO BAY
EVERWELL BAY
SQUAW BAY
EDDYVILLE
Eddyville
GOZZIER RD
BENNETT BAY
90
E YELLOWSTONE TR
BLUE CREEK BAY
BLUE POINT PUBLIC BOAT RAMP
MOSCOW BAY
22
KOA COEUR D'ALENE
MINERAL RIDGE BOAT RAMP
BEAUTY CREEK
BEAUTY CREEK CAMPGROUND
Wolf Lodge
ALDER CREEK
RD
FOURTH OF JULY SUMMIT
BOGIE DRAW
AUBREY DRAW
28
90

COEUR
LOFFS BAY
DELCARDO BAY
HAPPY COVE
TURNER BAY
97
D'ALENE
GAND BAY
LOFFS BAY
GOTHAM BAY
GOTHAM BAY RD
BURMA RD
CARLIN BAY
TURNER PEAK
GOTHAM BAY RD
COEUR D'ALENE
KOOTENAI COUNTY
NATIONAL FOREST
BEAUTY SADDLE
NFD RD 438
RED HORSE MOUNTAIN
NFD RD 810
ELK MOUNTAIN
HAGGMAN DRAW
LAKES DIVIDE RD
WARD RIDGE
WARD RIDGE
KILLARNEY MOUNTAIN
ROSE LAKE ACCESS AREA
DOYLE RD
OLD ROSE CREEK
ROSE LAKE
Rose Lake

PILOT ROCK RD
CRESCENT BAY
LAKE
CARLIN BAY
MARTIN BAY
BLACK BAY
BLACK ROCK BAY
ROUND BAY RD
HALF ROUND BAY
HALF
DEER DR
CARLIN CREEK
ASBURY RD
NFD
CARILL PEAK
RD
RD 810
COTTONWOOD PEAK
POPCORN ISLAND
SWAN SADDLE
CHATFIELD SADDLE
KILLARNEY LAKE
HOGBACK RIDGE
SWAN PEAK
IDAHO
COEUR
D'ALENE RIVER
Lane Cemetery
CANARY CREEK
BLACK ROCK RD
INITIAL PEAK
CANARY CREEK

POWDERHORN BAY
EAST POINT
BELL BAY CAMPGROUND
BELL BAY
HARLOW POINT
COEUR
HARLOW POINT
LITTLE COTTONWOOD BAY
THOMPSON LAKE RD
THOMPSON LAKE
SPRINGSTON RD
ANDERSON LAKE
HART AV
D'ALENE
HARRISON
HARRISON BOAT LANDING
BLUE LAKE
COEUR D'ALENE RIVER
Springston
LAMB RD
LAMB CANYON
LAMB PEAK
VAN DUSEN RD
MEDICINE MOUNTAIN
Medimont
SIRAN LAKE
CAVE LAKE
RAINY HILL CAMPGROUND
MEDIMONT RD
EVANS CREEK
3
EAGLE PEAK
PETIT PEAK
EAGLE PEAK
RD
SMITH RIDGE
BUTLER CREEK
RD

COTTONWOOD BAY
D'ALENE
COTTONWOOD
ATOR HILL
CLELAN BAY
LOWHEISTER BAY
FULLERS BAY
BLOOMSBURG BAY
ZEHM HILL
BROWNS BAY
LAKE
SHINGLE BAY
CAREY BAY
TALBOT HILL CEMETERY
INDIAN
HARRISON RD
SUNRISE DR
SUNSET DR
COEUR
D'ALENE
SOLOA PEAK
GRASSY MOUNTAIN
KOOTENAI CO
BENEWAH CO
BENEWAH COUNTY
ROUND TOP

CONKLING PARK
KYRUS BAY RD
SHOEFFLER BUTTE
SUNNY SLOPE
CHATCOLET
LITTLE
PARK RD
O-GARA BAY
O-GARA
BEEDLE POINT
INDIAN MOUNTAIN RD
INDIAN MOUNTAIN
3
HELLS GULCH RD
INDIAN RESERVATION
HOLLY GULCH RD
SHARP TOP
CEDAR DRAW

CHATCOLET LAKE
PLUMMER PENINSULA
Rocky Point
HEYBURN RD
ROUND LAKE
BENEWAH LAKE
HELLS GULCH
HELLS GULCH RD
CEDAR ST
5
BENEWAH ST
SAINT MARIES MUNICIPAL AIRPORT
SAINT JOE RIVER
SAINT JOE RIVER

ELLIS LN
CEDAR ST
MINALOOSA
HEYBURN STATE PARK
NEGRO BROWN HILL
SHAY HILL
SHAY HILL RD
5
SAINT MARIES RIVER ACCESS AREA
JACOT

MINALOOSA VALLEY
MINALOOSA RD
COON CREEK RD
BENEWAH RD
CHERRY CREEK
KINGS PEAK
SAINT MARIES
SAINT MARIES RIVER
3

0 1 2 3 4 miles   1 in. = 2.5 mi.

SEE 115 MAP

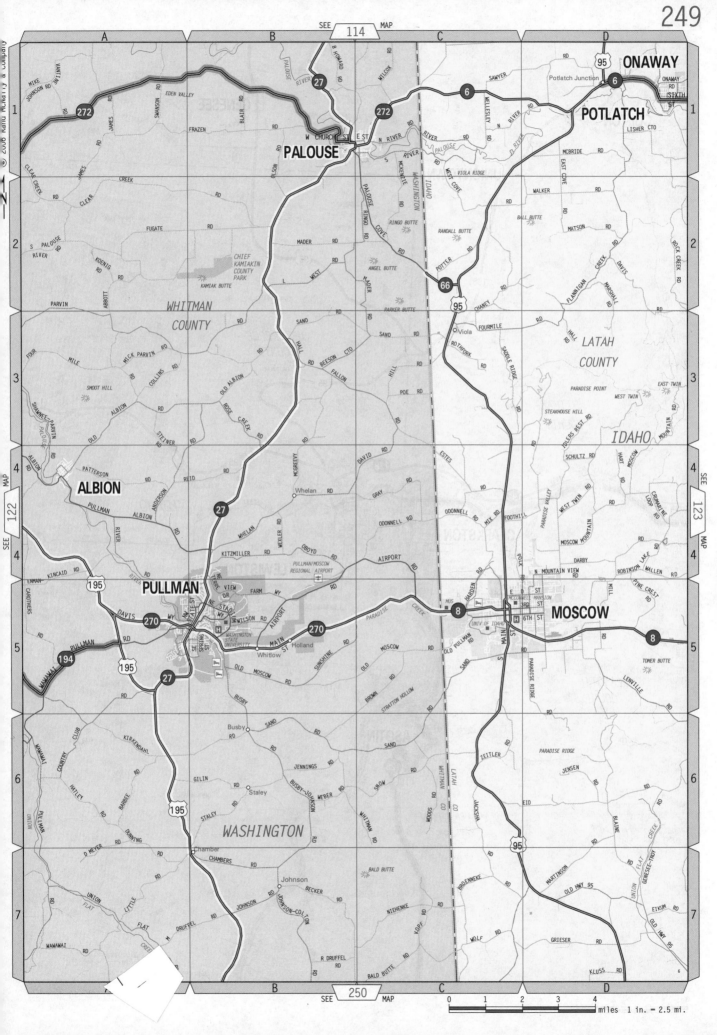

COLTON

UNIONTOWN

GENESEE

LATAH COUNTY

LEWISTON

CLARKSTON

ASOTIN

NEZ PERCE COUNTY

WHITMAN COUNTY

ASOTIN COUNTY

WASHINGTON

IDAHO

NEZ PERCE

INDIAN RESERVATION

Lewiston Hill

North Lewiston

Hatwai

Silcott

Clarkston Heights

Vineland

Lewis-Clark State College

Walla Walla Com. College

Lewiston Orchards

Lewiston Airport

Hells Gate State Park

Asotin Museum

Mann Lake

Mann Lake Public Fishing Area

Beaver Rd

Waha Prairie

Tenmile Rapids

Tenmile Canyon

Ayers Ridge

Short Canyon

Locust Grove Rd

Weissenfels Ridge

George Creek

Meyers

Cloverland Rd

Parson Rd

Bowman Rd

Hostetler Rd

SEE 249 MAP

SEE 123 MAP

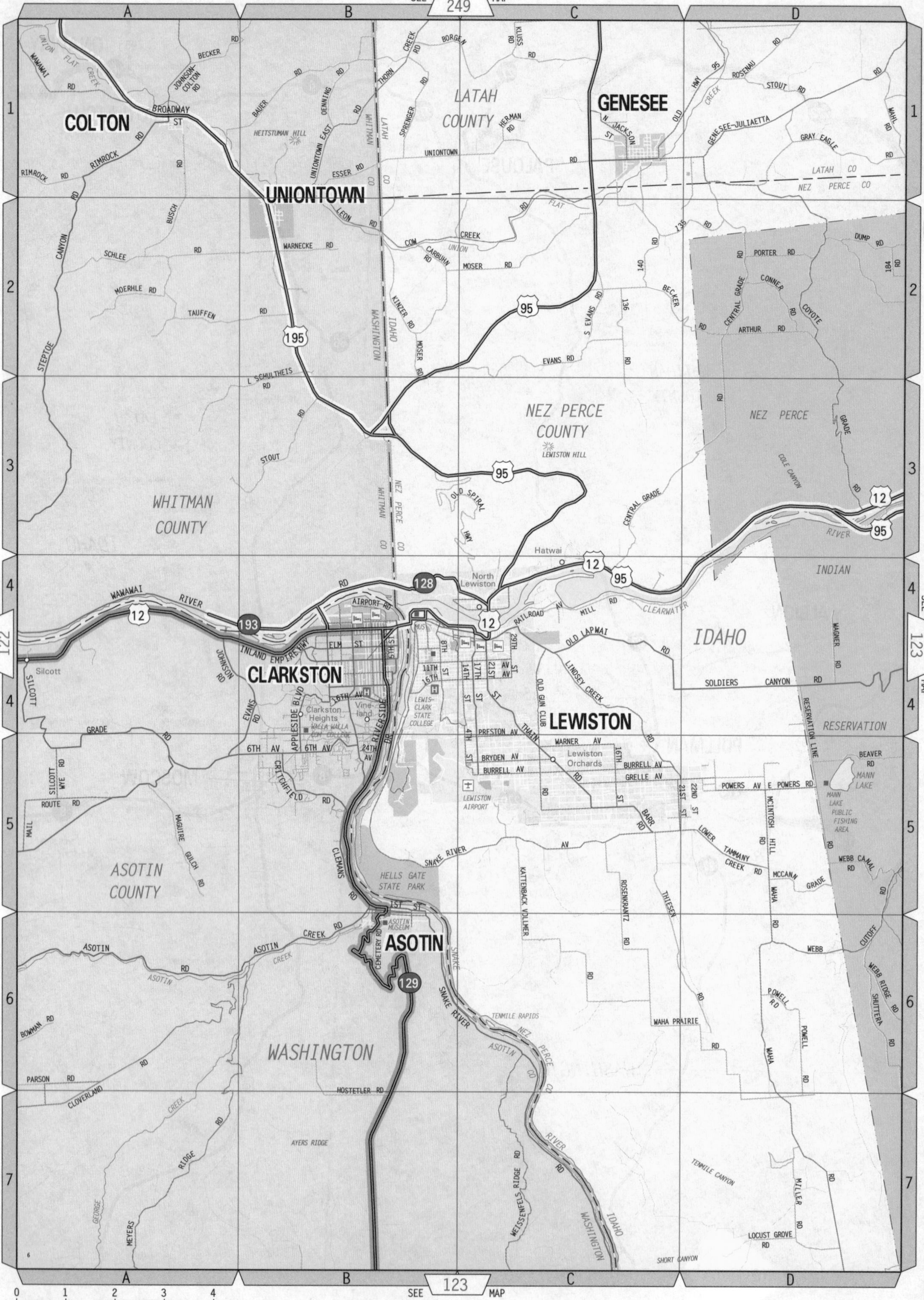

SEE 122 MAP

SEE 123 MAP

Roads and labels: BROADWAY ST, RIMROCK RD, MAMMAI RD, JOHNSON-COLTON RD, BECKER RD, BAUER RD, DENNING RD, THORN RD, SPRENGER, BORGEN, KLUSS RD, HERMAN RD, N JACKSON ST, OLD HWY 95, ROSENAU, STOUT, WAHL RD, GRAY EAGLE, GENESEE-JULIAETTA, LATAH CO, NEZ PERCE CO, UNIONTOWN EAST, ESSER RD, LEON RD, UNIONTOWN, HEITSTUMAN HILL, WARNECKE RD, COM, CARBUHN RD, UNION CREEK, MOSER RD, SCHLEE RD, MOERHLE RD, TAUFFEN, STEPTOE, CANYON, BUSCH RD, L SCHULTHEIS RD, STOUT, S EVANS RD, EVANS RD, FLAT, BECKER, PORTER RD, CONNER, DUMP RD, COYOTE, CENTRAL GRADE, ARTHUR, COLE CANYON, GRADE, WHITMAN, IDAHO, WASHINGTON, KINER RD, MOSER RD, OLD SPIRAL HWY, RAILROAD AV, MILL, CLEARWATER, OLD LAPWAI, LINDSEY CREEK, SOLDIERS CANYON RD, WAGNER RD, WAWAWAI, RIVER, INLAND EMPIRE HWY, JOHNSON RD, SILCOTT, GRADE, EVANS RD, CRITCHFIELD RD, APPLESIDE BLVD, ELM ST, 6TH AV, 24TH AV, 11TH ST, 16TH ST, 8TH ST, 14TH ST, 17TH ST, 21ST AV, 29TH ST, THAIN, PRESTON AV, WARNER AV, BRYDEN AV, BURRELL AV, GRELLE AV, 16TH ST, 22ND ST, 21ST ST, POWERS AV, E POWERS RD, MCINTOSH HILL RD, WEBB CANAL, WEBB RD, SILCOTT, WYE RD, MAGUIRE GULCH RD, MAIL ROUTE RD, CLEMANS RD, RIVERSIDE, CEMETERY RD, 1ST ST, SNAKE RIVER, KATTENBACK VOLLMER RD, ROSENKRANTZ RD, THIESEN, LOWER, TAMMANY CREEK RD, MCCANN GRADE, WAHA GRADE, POWELL RD, WEBB, CUTOFF, WEBB RIDGE, SMITTERA, MILLER, NEZ PERCE CO, ASOTIN CO, WASHINGTON, IDAHO

Route markers: 249, 195, 95, 12, 128, 193, 129, 136, 139, 140

Scale: 0 1 2 3 4 miles 1 in. = 2.5 mi.

Grid: A B C D / 1 2 3 4 5 6 7

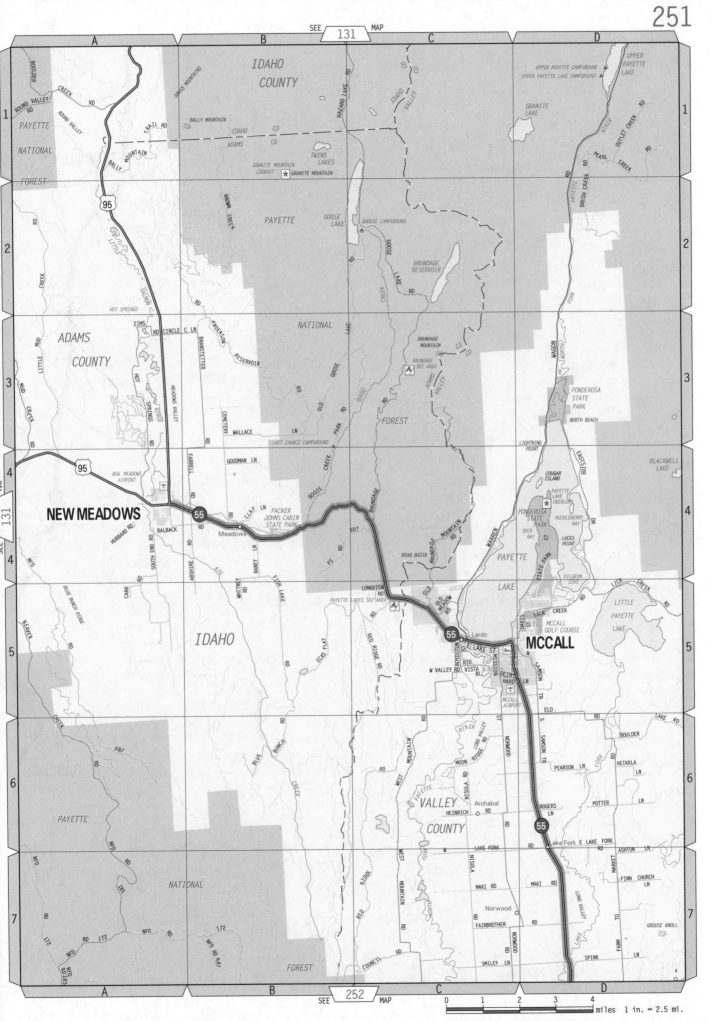

METRO

SEE 251 MAP

A   B   C   D

METRO

SEE 139 MAP

1

NFD RD 183

NFD RD 151

COLD SPRING SUMMIT

NFD RD 481

NFD RD 165

NO BUSINESS MOUNTAIN

NFD RD

WEST MOUNTAIN

PAYETTE RIVER

NISULA RD

NORWOOD

SCHELINE LN

PADDY FLAT RD

PADDY FLAT RD

NASI LN

MARKET LN

TITUS LN

55

WALLACE LN

DONNELLY

2

PAYETTE

NFD RD 199

NFD RD 200

NFD RD

COUNCIL MOUNTAIN

NATIONAL

ADAMS COUNTY

218

NFD RIVER RD

186

ADAMS CO

VALLEY CO

RAINBOW POINT CAMPGROUND

WEST MOUNTAIN

AMANITA CAMPGROUND

TAMARACK FALLS

FALLS RD

W ROSEBERRY RD

E ROSEBERRY RD

To Roseberry

DONNELLY AIRPORT

LOOMIS

OLD STATE LN

BARKER LN

FARM RD

GOLD FORK RD

GOLD FORK RIVER

DAVIS CREEK LN

KOSKELLA RD

3

NFD RD

ARBUCKLE BASIN

HOT SPRINGS

WHITE LICKS

FOREST

CABIN CREEK CAMPGROUND

WEISER

MICA HILL

MIDDLE FORK

NFD RD 186

E MIDDLE FORK RD

FALL CREEK RD

SUGARLOAF

206

LONE TREE

WEISER RIVER

POISON CREEK CAMPGROUND

VALLEY COUNTY

W 4TH LN

KANTOLA RD

OLD STATE

ARLING HOT SPRING

4

GRAYS CREEK RD

NFD RD

NFD RD 214

217

WEISER RIVER

NFD RD 243

INDIAN MOUNTAIN

COUGAR BASIN

LITTLE

BURNT WAGON BASIN

POISON TIMBER POINT

IDAHO

NFD RD 116

SUGARLOAF

SUGARLOAF ISLAND

STONE BREAKER LN

CASCADE

55

5

TELEPHONE DRAW

NFD RD

NFD RD 214

RD

POTATO KNOB

NFD RD 835

NFD RD

WEST RD

BOISE

RESERVOIR

CROWN POINT

55

6

RIDGE

TIFF LINDSAY DRAW

KING HILL

WEISER RIVER

RD

TWIN SISTERS

LITTLE WEISER RIVER

LITTLE WEISER RD

LOOKOUT PEAK

ADAMS CO

GEM CO

CREEK

VALLEY CO

GEM CO

NATIONAL

MOUNTAIN

COLLIER PEAK

CASCADE

MAIN ST

OLD STATE HWY

IDAHO 55

LAKESHORE DR

RD 422

7

LITTLE

SQUAW CREEK RD

MILL CREEK SUMMIT

FOUR BIT SUMMIT

BUCK MOUNTAIN

NFD RD 625

GEM COUNTY

WILSON PEAK

SNOWBANK MOUNTAIN

CABARTON RD

RD

NFD RD 618

SQUAW RD

NFD RD 625

GABES PEAK

FOREST

ADAMS CO

WASHINGTON CO

WASHINGTON CO

0 1 2 3 4 miles   1 in. = 2.5 mi.

SEE 139 MAP

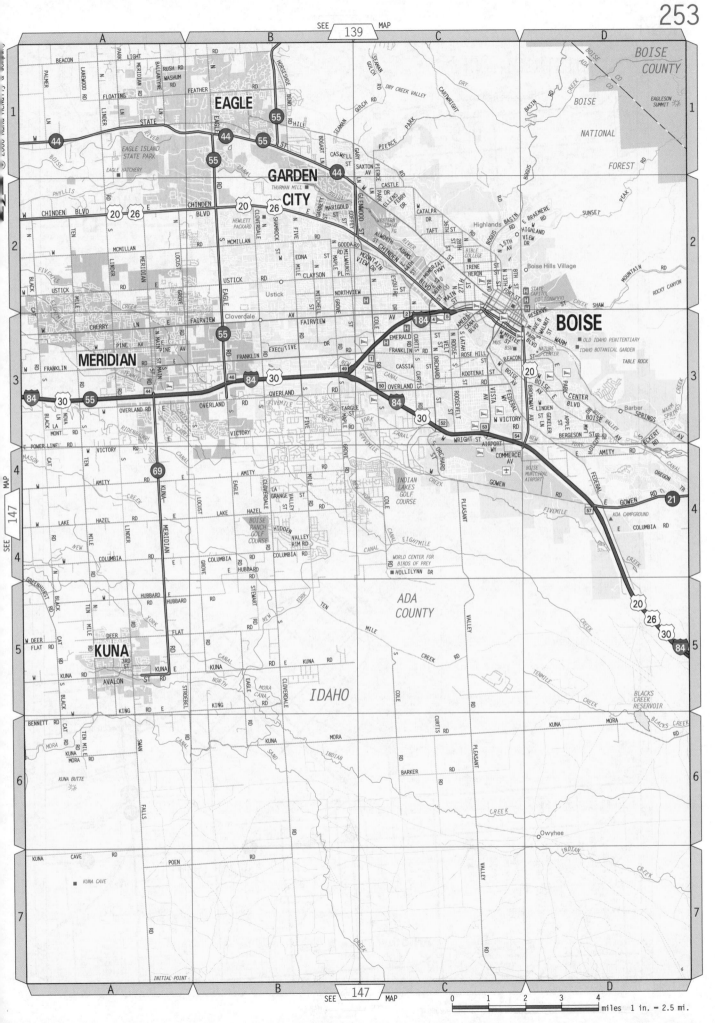

METRO

0 1 2 3 4 miles 1 in. = 2.5 mi.

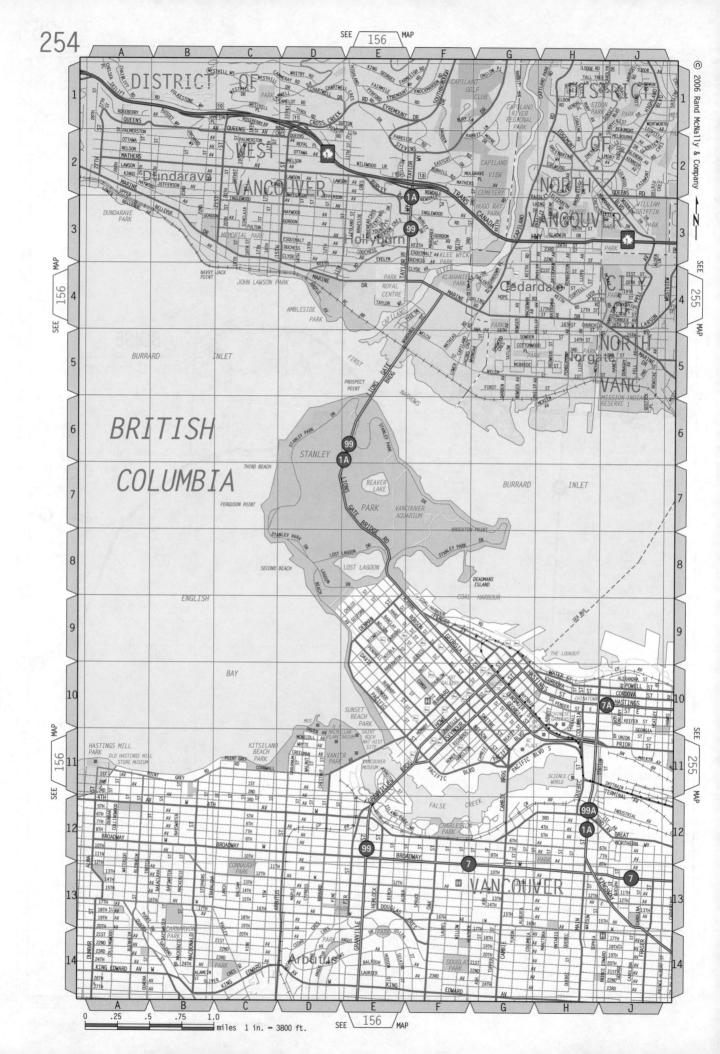

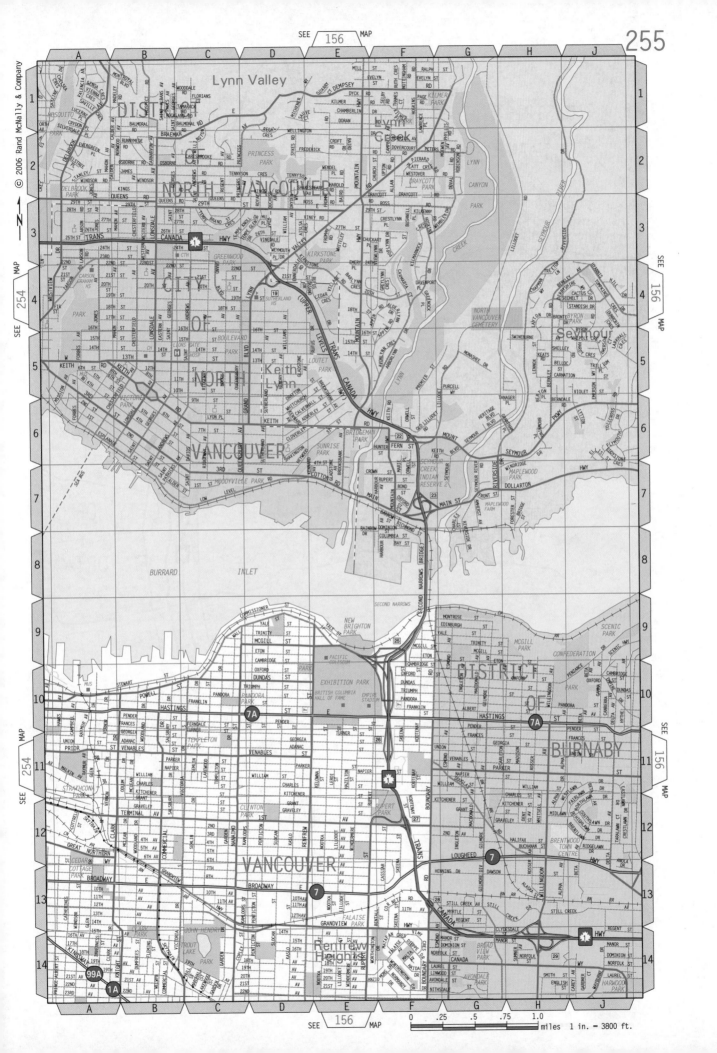

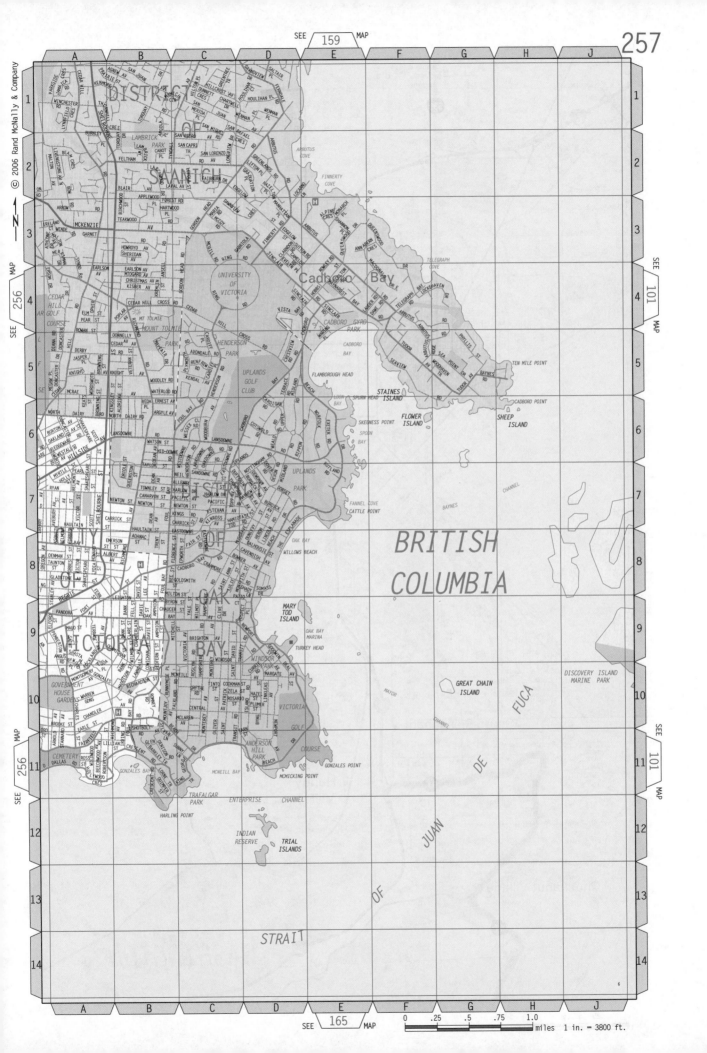

N

SEE 256 MAP

SEE 101 MAP

DETAIL

BRITISH

COLUMBIA

SEE 256 MAP

SEE 101 MAP

0   .25   .5   .75   1.0
miles 1 in. = 3800 ft.

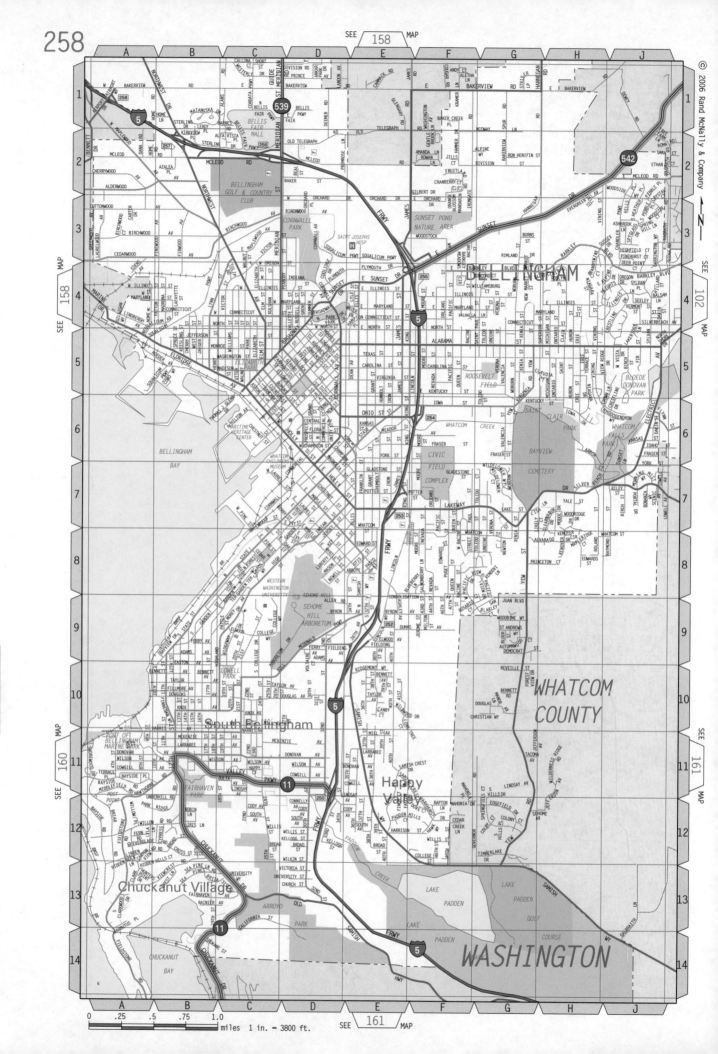

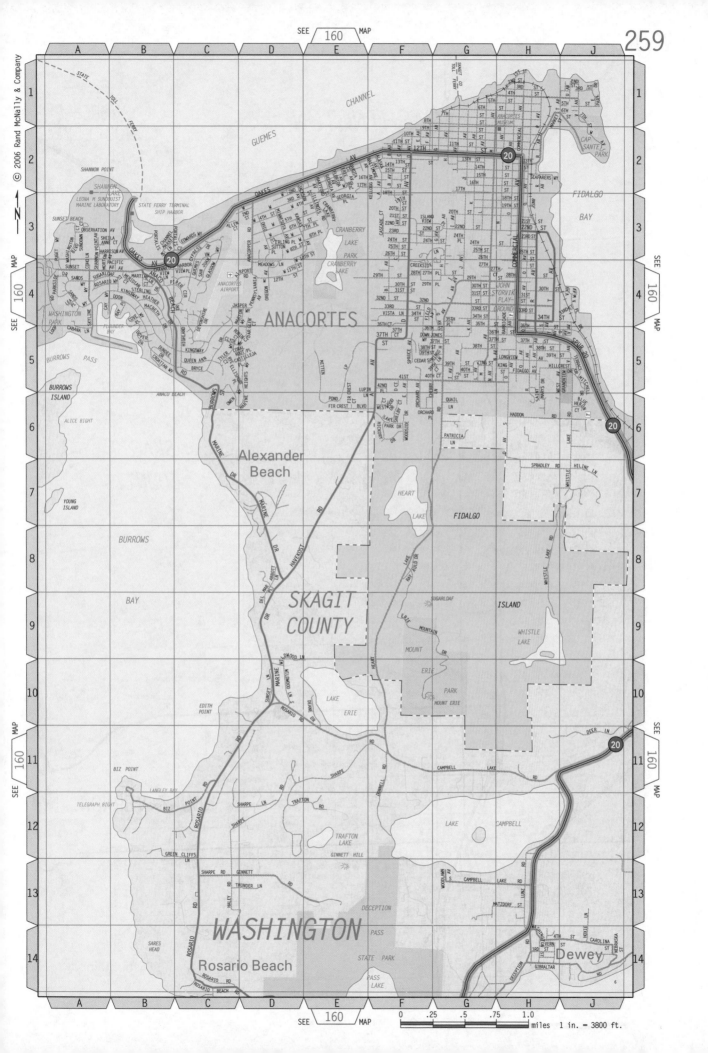

DETAIL

SEE 160 MAP

SEE 160 MAP

SEE 160 MAP

SEE 160 MAP

SEE 160 MAP

CHANNEL

GUEMES

FIDALGO
BAY

ANACORTES

BURROWS
PASS

BURROWS
ISLAND

ALICE BIGHT

YOUNG
ISLAND

BURROWS
BAY

Alexander
Beach

SKAGIT
COUNTY

HEART
LAKE

FIDALGO

ISLAND

WHISTLE
LAKE

MOUNT
ERIE
PARK

MOUNT ERIE

LAKE
ERIE

EDITH
POINT

BIZ POINT

LANGLEY BAY

TELEGRAPH BIGHT

GREEN CLIFFS

CAMPBELL LAKE

LAKE
CAMPBELL

TRAFTON
LAKE

GINNETT HILL

WASHINGTON

SARES
HEAD

DECEPTION
PASS

STATE PARK

PASS
LAKE

Rosario Beach

Dewey

0   .25   .5   .75   1.0
miles   1 in. = 3800 ft.

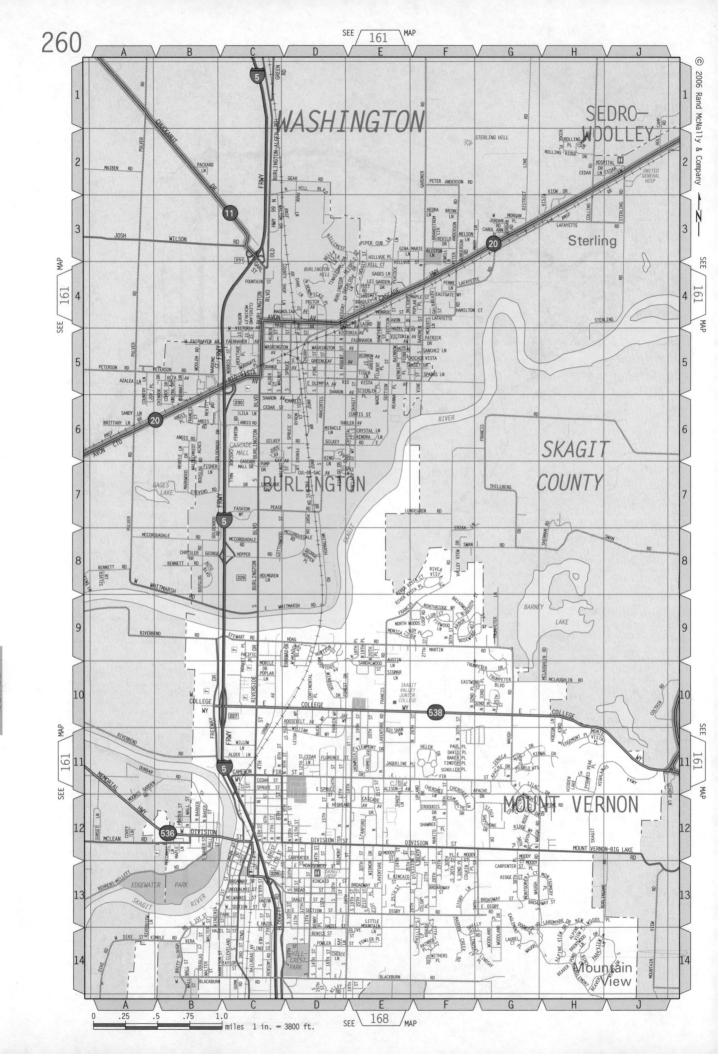

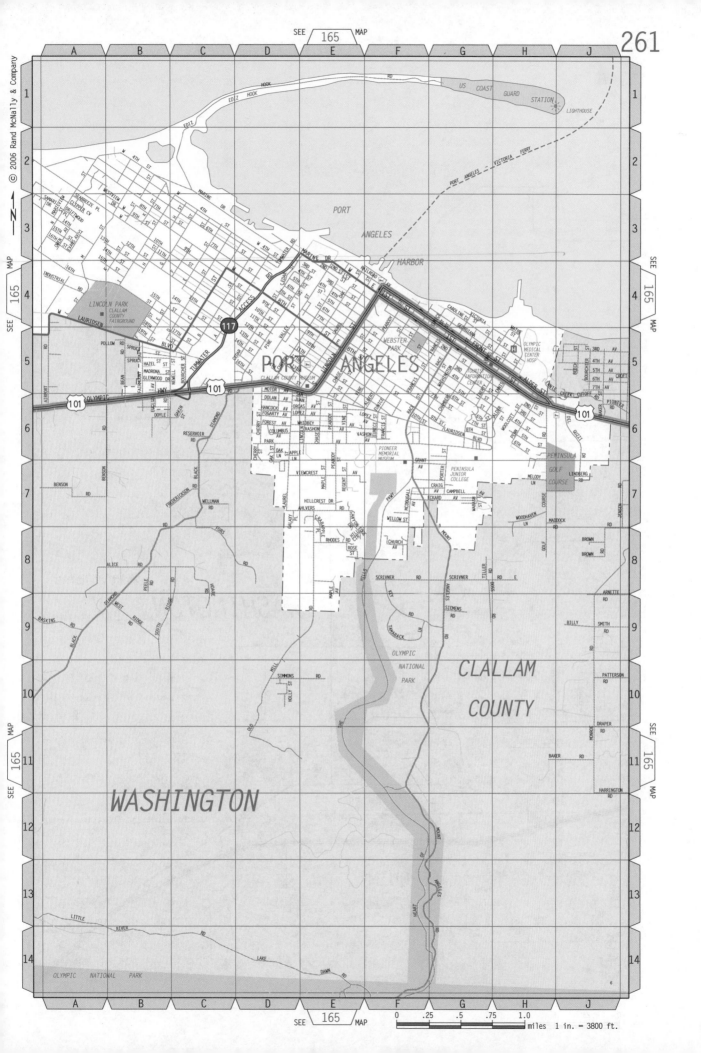

© 2006 Rand McNally & Company

N

DETAIL

SEE 165 MAP

SEE 165 MAP

SEE 165 MAP

SEE 165 MAP

A B C D E F G H J

PORT ANGELES HARBOR

US COAST GUARD STATION

LIGHTHOUSE

PORT ANGELES — VICTORIA FERRY

EDIZ HOOK

LINCOLN PARK
CLALLAM COUNTY FAIRGROUND

PORT ANGELES

WEBSTER PARK

OLYMPIC MEDICAL CENTER HOSP

TOURIST INFORMATION CENTER

CLALLAM COUNTY MUSEUM

PIONEER MEMORIAL MUSEUM

PENINSULA JUNIOR COLLEGE

PENINSULA GOLF COURSE

OLYMPIC NATIONAL PARK

CLALLAM COUNTY

WASHINGTON

OLYMPIC NATIONAL PARK

0 .25 .5 .75 1.0
miles   1 in. = 3800 ft.

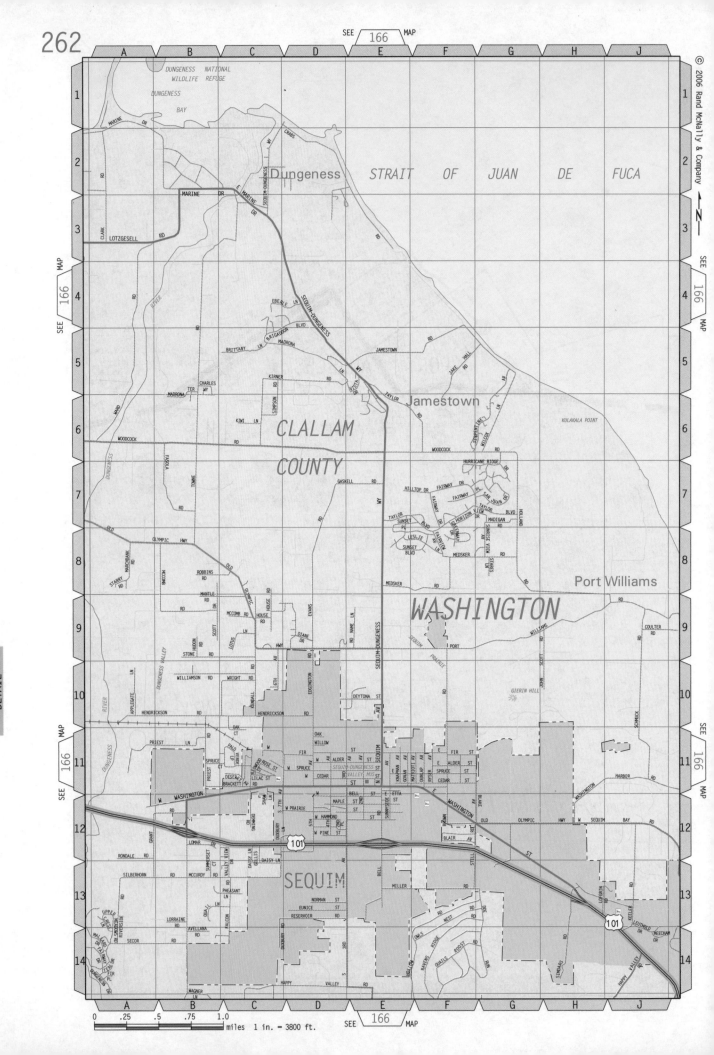

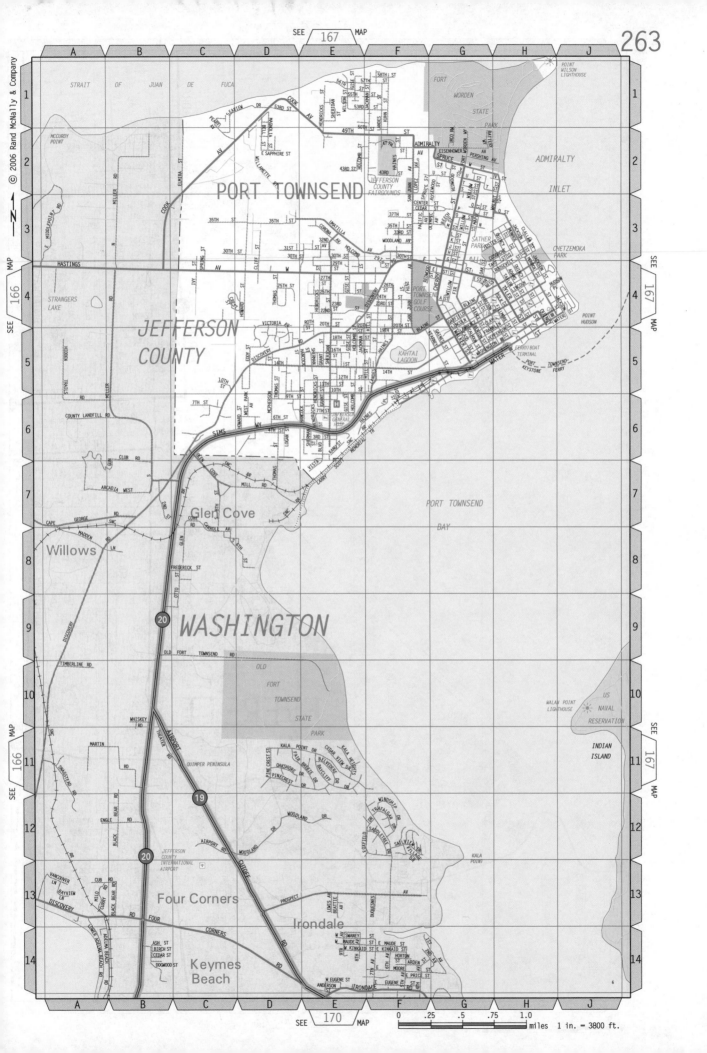

DETAIL

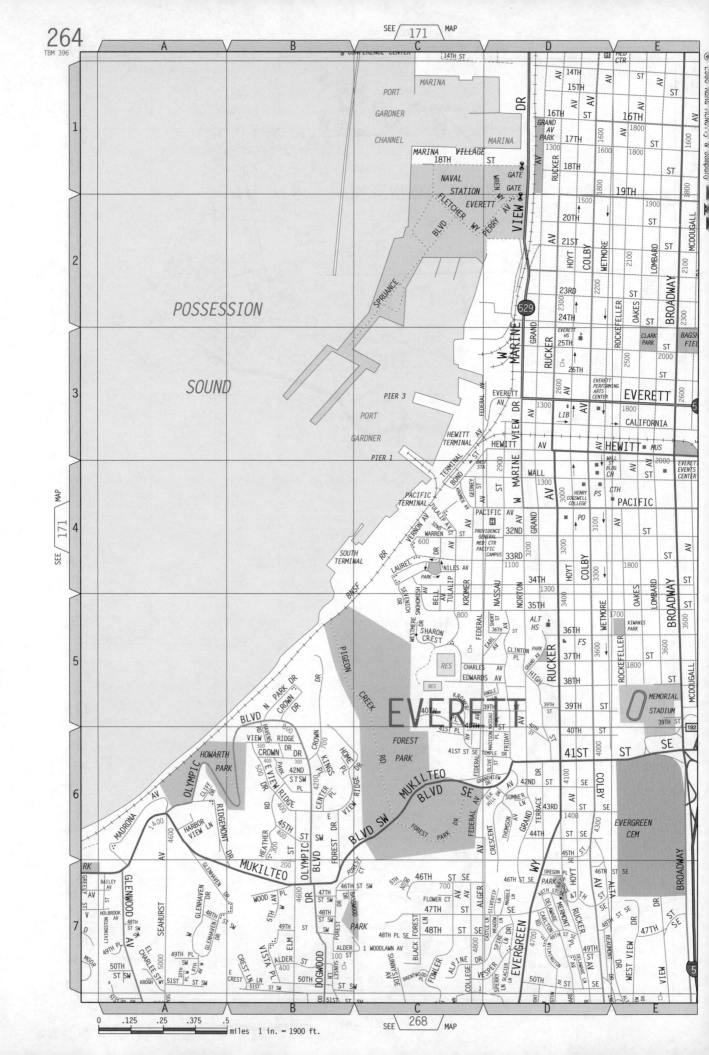

SEE 171 MAP

A   B   C   D   E

& CONFERENCE CENTER
14TH ST

MARINA

PORT
GARDNER
CHANNEL

MARINA

MARINA VILLAGE

18TH   ST

NAVAL
STATION
EVERETT

GATE
GATE

FLETCHER WY

PERRY AV

WREN AV

MARINE VIEW DR

14TH AV
15TH AV
16TH
17TH
18TH
19TH
20TH
21ST
23RD
24TH

GRAND AV PARK
1300
1600

1500

1600
1800
1800

1800

1900

RUCKER

HOYT
COLBY
WETMORE
ROCKEFELLER
OAKES
LOMBARD
BROADWAY
MCDOUGALL

MED CTR

ST AV ST AV

16TH

2100

2100

SPRUANCE

POSSESSION

SOUND

PIER 3

PORT

GARDNER

PIER 1

HEWITT
TERMINAL

W MARINE DR

GRAND AV

529

RUCKER

25TH
26TH

EVERETT HS

2200
2300

2300

2500

ROCKEFELLER

OAKES ST

BROADWAY

CLARK PARK

BAGSHE FIELD

EVERETT
PERFORMING
ARTS
CENTER

EVERETT

2600

5

EVERETT AV

1300
LIB

1800

CALIFORNIA

2600

HEWITT

TERMINAL ST

BOND

HEWITT AV

WALL ST

W MARINE AV

HEWITT AV

WALL AV

MUS

2900

1300

3000

PS

HENRY COGSWELL
COLLEGE

CTH

WALL
BLDG CH

2000

PACIFIC

EVERETT
EVENTS
CENTER

PACIFIC
TERMINAL

SOUTH
TERMINAL

TULALIP AV

VERNON AV

GEDNEY ST

KROMER AV

32ND

WARREN   600

PACIFIC AV

PROVIDENCE
GENERAL
MED CTR
PACIFIC CAMPUS

GRAND AV

3200

PO

3100

PACIFIC

RR

LAUREL

NILES AV

BELL
TULALIP
PARK

DR

33RD

3200

1100

3300

COLBY

HOYT

1800

BNSF

SEVENTH DR

SNOHOMISH DR

WESTMORE DR

KROMER

NASSAU

NORTON

34TH
35TH

800

1300

3400

1800

SHARON
CREST

RES

RES

CHARLES
EDWARDS AV

FEDERAL AV

EARL SHORT ST

CLINTON PL

ANGLE AV

ALT HS

CLINTON PARK

GRAND AV

HIGH ST

RUCKER

36TH

FS

37TH

38TH

39TH

3600

1700

3600

WETMORE

OAKES

ROCKEFELLER

LOMBARD

BROADWAY

1800

KIWANIS PARK

3500

MCDOUGALL

EVERETT

PIGEON CREEK

BLVD N PARK DR

CROWN DR

CROWN DR

FOREST PARK

40TH PL

39TH ST

NASSAU ST

40TH

39TH

MEMORIAL
STADIUM
39TH ST

192

MADRONA AV

OLYMPIC

HOWARTH
PARK

CLIFF DR

RIDGEMONT DR

HARBOR VIEW LN

HAVENS RD

VIEW RIDGE DR

CROWN DR

E VIEW RIDGE DR

KINGS PL

500
400

800

700

300

42ND
ST SW

CENTER PL

HOME PL

VIEW RIDGE DR

FOREST

ROD DR

MUKILTEO BLVD SW

FOREST PARK DR

TIMOTHY TEMPLE OLIVE

GRANDVIEW PL

ELK HILL DR

FRIDAY PL

FEDERAL AV

SUMNER LN

GRAND AV

CRESCENT

THOMSON

TERRACE

41ST PL SE

41ST ST SE

42ND

43RD

44TH

4000

4100

SE

SE

SE

4200

1400

41ST

ST

COLBY SE

EVERGREEN
CEM

1400

4300

MUKILTEO

BLVD SE

4600

14 00

MUKILTEO

FOREST DR

OLYMPIC BLVD

HEATHER ST

45TH ST

400
200

45TH
ST SE

BROADWAY

GREELY AV

BAILEY AV

HOLBROOK AV

LIVINGSTON

GLENWOOD AV

SEAHURST AV

GLENHAVEN DR

GLENHAVEN DR

WOOD PL

5TH AV W

VISTA PL

ALDER ST

ELM

DOGWOOD

SUNSET

FOREST CT

BASSWOOD DR

46TH ST SW

47TH ST SW

48TH ST SW

FOREST PARK

46TH ST SE

5TH DR SE

700

FLOWER CT

ALGER

SILVERTIP LN

MARBLE LN

MEADOW LN

CASTLE LN

SPIRE LN

BLACK FOREST LN

46TH ST SE

46TH ST SE

OREGON PL

PARK PL

HOYT

DELAMARE

CARLTON

MERMONT

46TH AV SE

ALTA

4700

BEAUMONT

WEST VIEW DR

RUCKER

VIEW DR

BROADWAY

RK

5000
1400

4600

100 ST

EL CHARLEE ST

KROGH WY

10TH

GLENHAVEN DR

E CREST LN

SUNSET LN

47TH
ST SW

ALDER ST

1 WOODLAWN AV

47TH

48TH

SUNNYSIDE AV

COLLEGE

FOWLER

ALPINE DR

VESPER

SPERRY LN

GLACIER DR

WILMINGTON DR

EVERGREEN WY

BEAUMONT

DELAMARE

WEST VIEW DR

47TH

49TH

49TH

50TH

5

MOOR

HOLBROOK AV

48TH ST SW

49TH PL

49TH ST SW

50TH ST SW

51ST ST SW

51ST ST SW

51ST

50TH

DETAIL

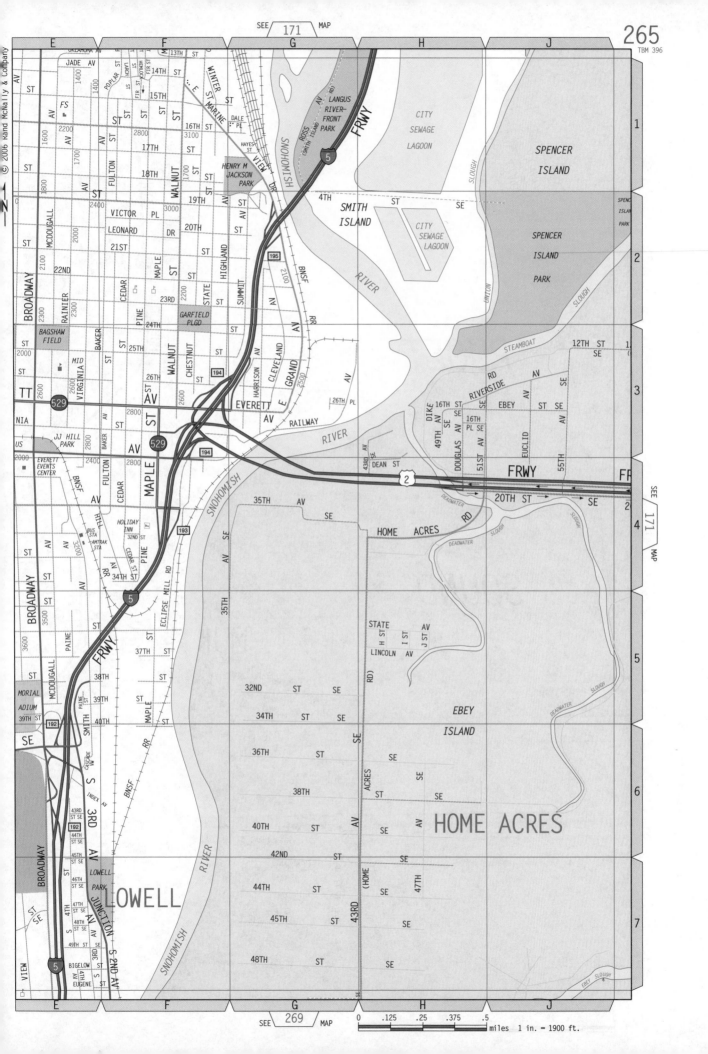

DETAIL

© 2006 Rand McNally & Company

SPENCER
ISLAND

CITY
SEWAGE
LAGOON

LANGUS
RIVER-
FRONT
PARK

HENRY M
JACKSON
PARK

SMITH
ISLAND

CITY
SEWAGE
LAGOON

SPENCER
ISLAND
PARK

SPENC
ISLAN
PARK

4TH   ST   SE

STEAMBOAT   12TH ST

RIVERSIDE RD

16TH ST SE

DIKE
16TH
PL SE

EBEY   ST SE

RR   RIVER

DEAN ST

FRWY   FR

20TH ST   SE

HOME ACRES   RD

DEADWATER   SLOUGH

DEADWATER RD

SLOUGH

HOME ACRES

STATE
LINCOLN AV

EBEY
ISLAND

SLOUGH

DEADWATER   SLOUGH

HOME ACRES

LOWELL

MORIAL
ADIUM

BROADWAY

BAGSHAW
FIELD

JJ HILL
PARK

EVERETT
EVENTS
CENTER

GARFIELD
PLGD

HOLIDAY
INN

LOWELL
PARK

JUNCTION

EBEY SLOUGH

SNOHOMISH RIVER

SNOHOMISH RIVER

0   .125   .25   .375   .5
miles   1 in. = 1900 ft.

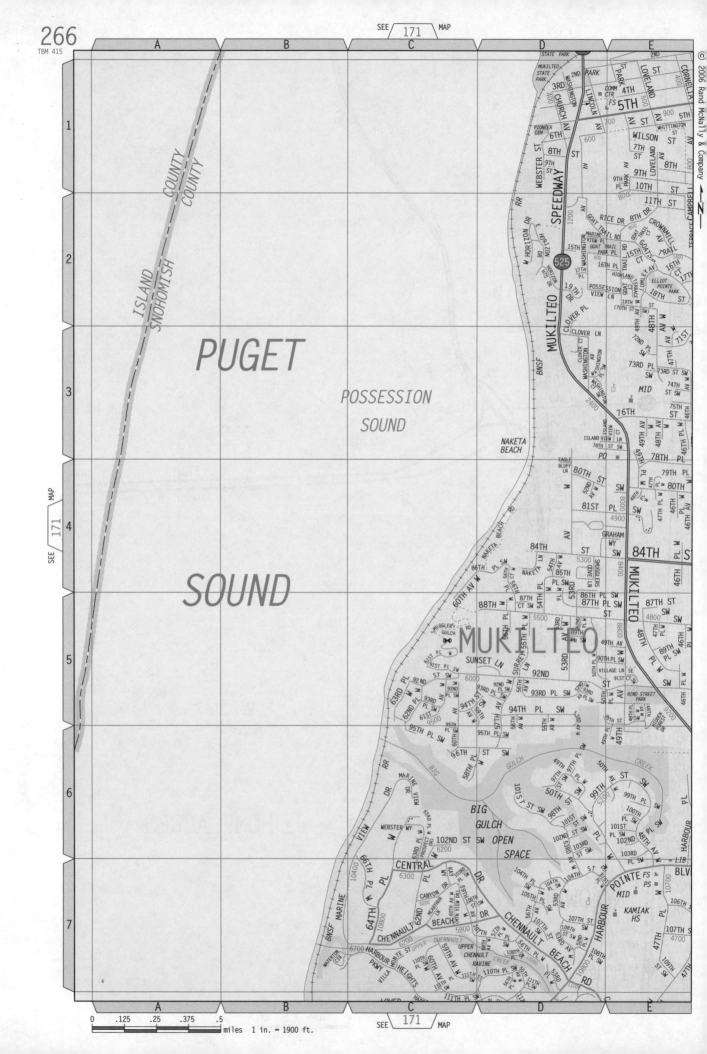

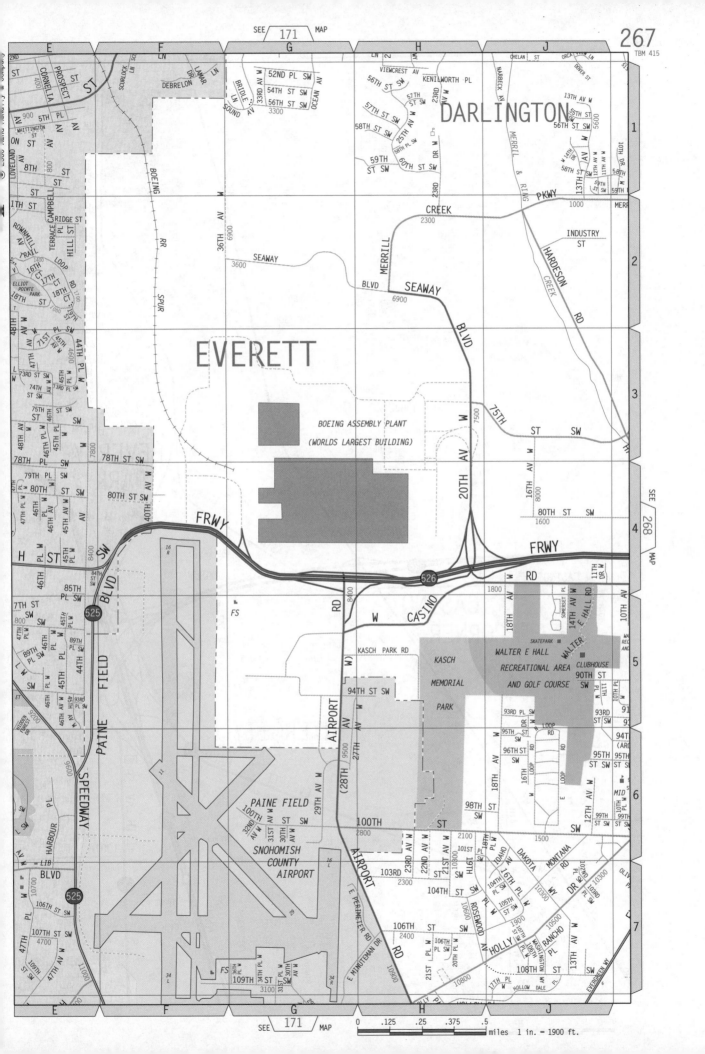

SEE 171 MAP

DARLINGTON

EVERETT

BOEING ASSEMBLY PLANT
(WORLDS LARGEST BUILDING)

CREEK

SEAWAY BLVD

FRWY

526

FRWY

W CASINO RD

PAINE FIELD

SPEEDWAY

KASCH PARK RD

KASCH
MEMORIAL
PARK

WALTER E HALL
RECREATIONAL AREA
AND GOLF COURSE

SKATEPARK

CLUBHOUSE

PAINE FIELD

SNOHOMISH
COUNTY
AIRPORT

AIRPORT RD

SEE 268 MAP

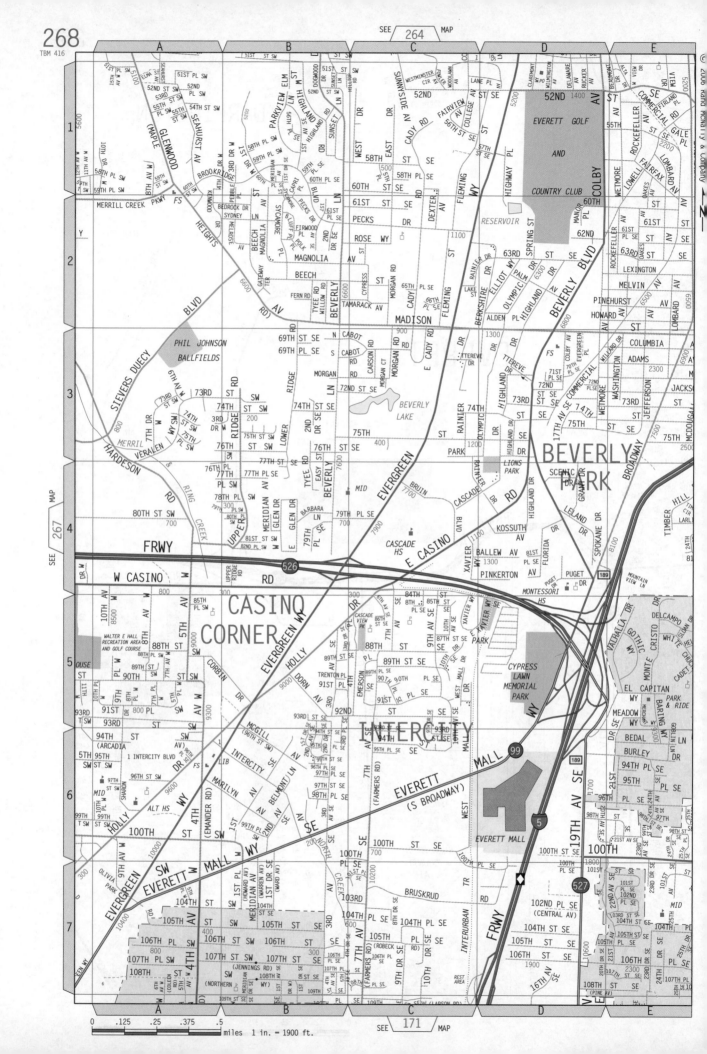

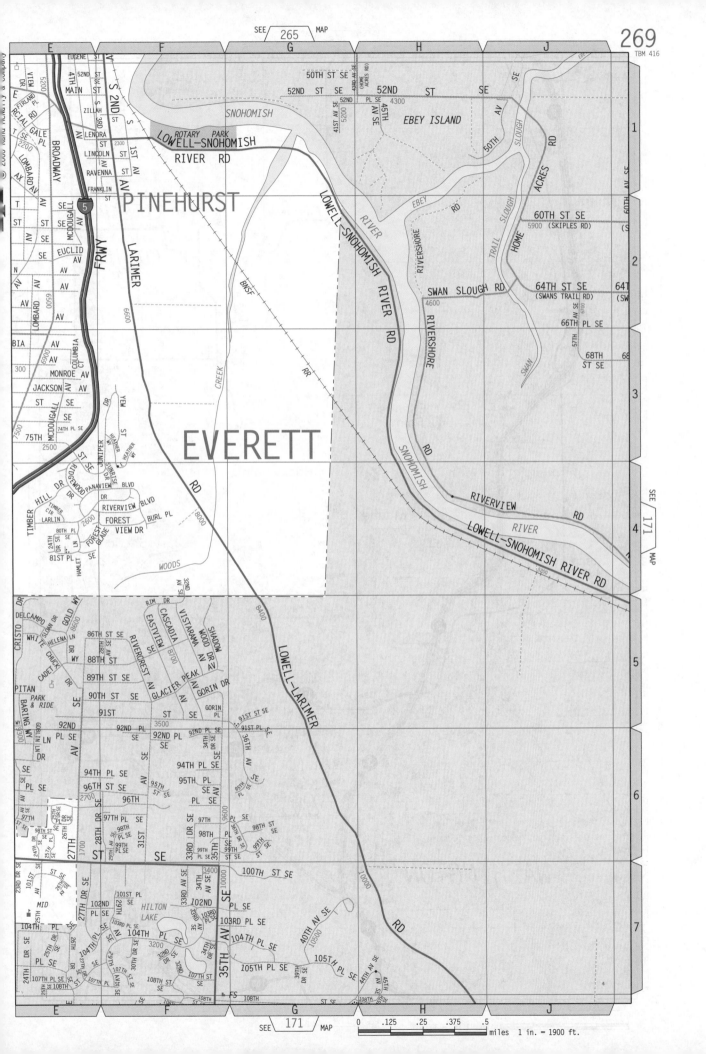

E   F   G   H   J

EUGENE

50TH ST SE

52ND ST SE   52ND   ST   SE

VIEW DR

52ND ST

4TH ST

MAIN ST

S 2ND AV

ZILLAH

5200

FTIRLAND RD SE

5200

41ST AV SE

52ND PL SE

45TH AV SE

4300

EBEY ISLAND

50TH AV

SE

60TH AV

1

GALE PL

2200

LOMBARD AV

3RD ST

LENORA ST

LINCOLN AV

1ST AV

2300

ROTARY PARK

LOWELL–SNOHOMISH

RIVER RD

SNOHOMISH

RIVER

60TH ST SE

5900 (SKIPLES RD)

(S

2

BROADWAY

RAVENNA

FRANKLIN

5

PINEHURST

LARIMER

BNSF

LOWELL–SNOHOMISH RIVER RD

EBEY RD

RIVERSHORE

SWAN SLOUGH RD

4600

RIVERSHORE

HOME ACRES RD

TRAIL

SWAN SLOUGH

RIVERSHORE RD

64TH ST SE

(SWANS TRAIL RD)

64T

(SW

66TH PL SE

68TH

ST SE

68

T

ST

AV

AV SE

SE

AV

N

AV

AV

AV

6000

LOMBARD

AV

BIA

AV

6900

AV

300

MONROE AV

JACKSON AV

MCDOUGALL SE

EUCLID AV

COLUMBIA CT

6600

FRWY

CREEK

RR

SNOHOMISH

RD

SWAN

SE

57TH AV

3

7500

75TH

2500

MCDOUGALL SE

74TH PL SE

YEM ST

JUNIPER DR

HEATHER ST

SUNRISE

EVERETT

RIVERVIEW

RD

RIVERVIEW

RD

LOWELL–SNOHOMISH RIVER RD

RIVER

SEE 171 MAP

4

TIMBER HILL DR

TIMBER CIR

LARLIN

DR

2600

REDWOOD RD SE

ST SE

PANAVIEW DR

RIVERVIEW BLVD

FOREST GLADE

BLVD

BURL PL

FOREST VIEW DR

8000

WOODS

8200

80TH PL SE

24TH DR SE

LN SE

HAMLET

81ST PL SE

32ND AV SE

8400

DELCAMPO DR

GOLD WY

8600

RIM DR

CASCADIA

VISTARAMA AV

SHADOW WOOD DR

5

CRISTO DR

WHITE DR

HELENA DR

SUNNY DR

86TH ST SE

88TH ST

EASTVIEW WY

8700

 GLACIER PEAK AV

GORIN DR

LOWELL–LARIMER

CHUCK DR

CADET DR

RIVERCREST AV

89TH ST SE

90TH ST SE

ST

GORIN PL

PITAN

PARK & RIDE

BARING WY

9300

91ST

91ST ST SE

91ST PL SE

92ND

92ND PL SE

92ND PL SE

34TH DR SE

36TH AV SE

6

92ND PL SE

LN SE

LN DR

3500

92ND PL SE

SE

94TH PL SE

95TH PL SE

AV SE

PL SE

94TH PL SE

95TH PL

SE

96TH ST SE

2700

96TH

95TH ST SE

PL SE

9600

AV

SE

PL SE

AV

97TH

97TH PL SE

98TH PL SE

28TH DR SE

31ST DR SE

33RD DR SE

97TH

98TH

99TH PL SE

35TH

99TH

98TH ST SE

99TH ST SE

36TH PL SE

7

1700

27TH ST SE

98TH PL SE

99TH PL SE

100TH ST SE

10000

RD

10000

23RD DR SE

101ST

24TH AV SE

MID

101ST PL

102ND

29TH

102ND

HILTON LAKE

33RD AV SE

34TH AV SE

103RD PL SE

103RD PL SE

PL SE

40TH AV SE

10500

104TH PL

25TH AV SE

102ND PL SE

103RD DR SE

104TH

PL SE

34TH DR SE

35TH AV SE

104TH PL SE

39TH DR SE

45TH AV SE

44TH AV SE

107TH PL SE

24TH DR SE

25TH

104TH PL SE

30TH DR SE

107TH ST SE

108TH

105TH PL SE

105TH PL SE

108TH

108TH ST SE

FS

E   F   G   H   J

0   .125   .25   .375   .5   miles   1 in. = 1900 ft.

DETAIL

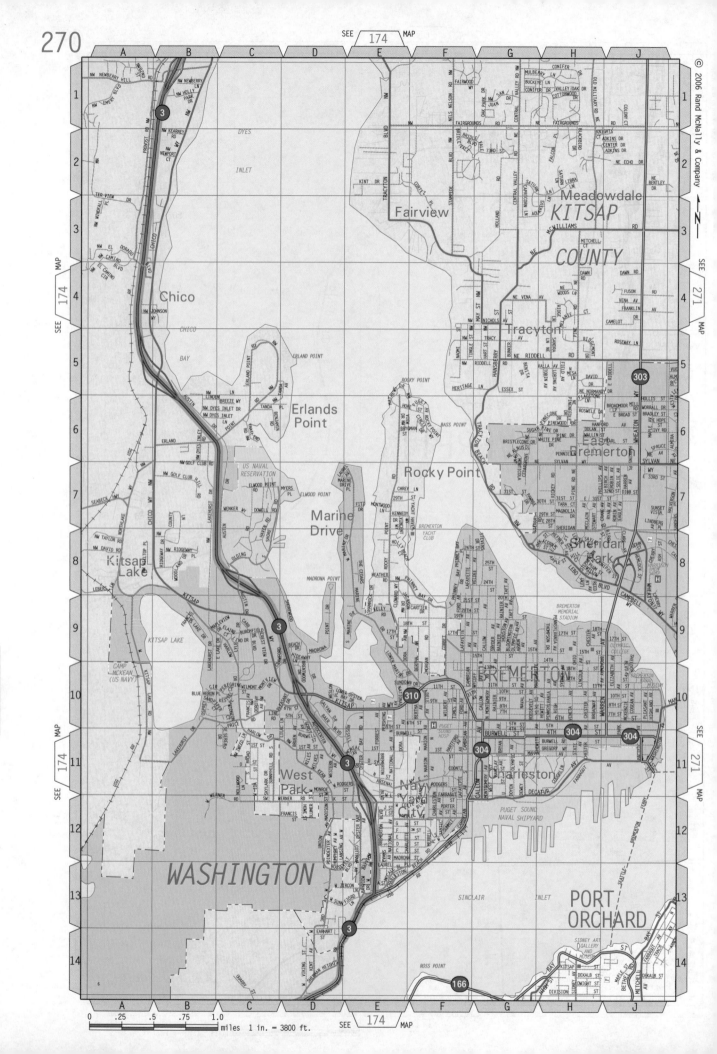

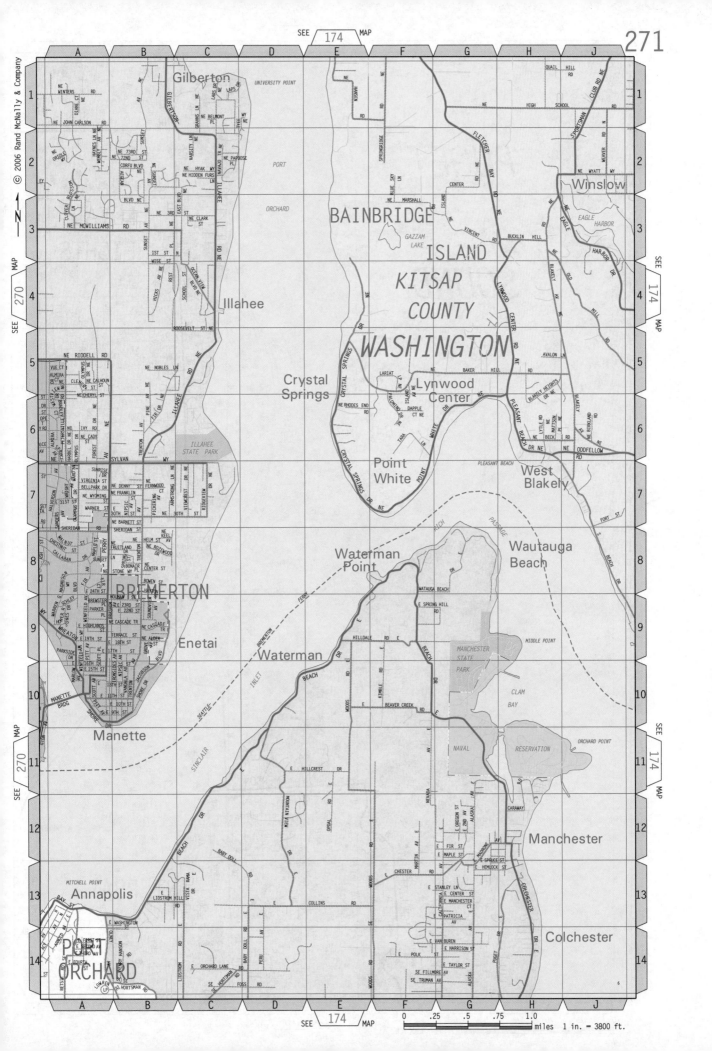

DETAIL

SEE 174 MAP

SEE 270 MAP

SEE 174 MAP

SEE 270 MAP

SEE 174 MAP

SEE 174 MAP

© 2006 Rand McNally & Company

N

Gilberton

UNIVERSITY POINT

PORT

ORCHARD

BAINBRIDGE

ISLAND

KITSAP

COUNTY

WASHINGTON

Winslow

EAGLE HARBOR

Illahee

ILLAHEE STATE PARK

Crystal
Springs

Lynwood
Center

Point
White

West
Blakely

BREMERTON

Waterman
Point

Wautauga
Beach

Enetai

Waterman

MANCHESTER STATE PARK

MIDDLE POINT

Manette

CLAM BAY

NAVAL   RESERVATION

ORCHARD POINT

Manchester

Annapolis

MITCHELL POINT

PORT
ORCHARD

Colchester

0   .25   .5   .75   1.0
miles   1 in. = 3800 ft.

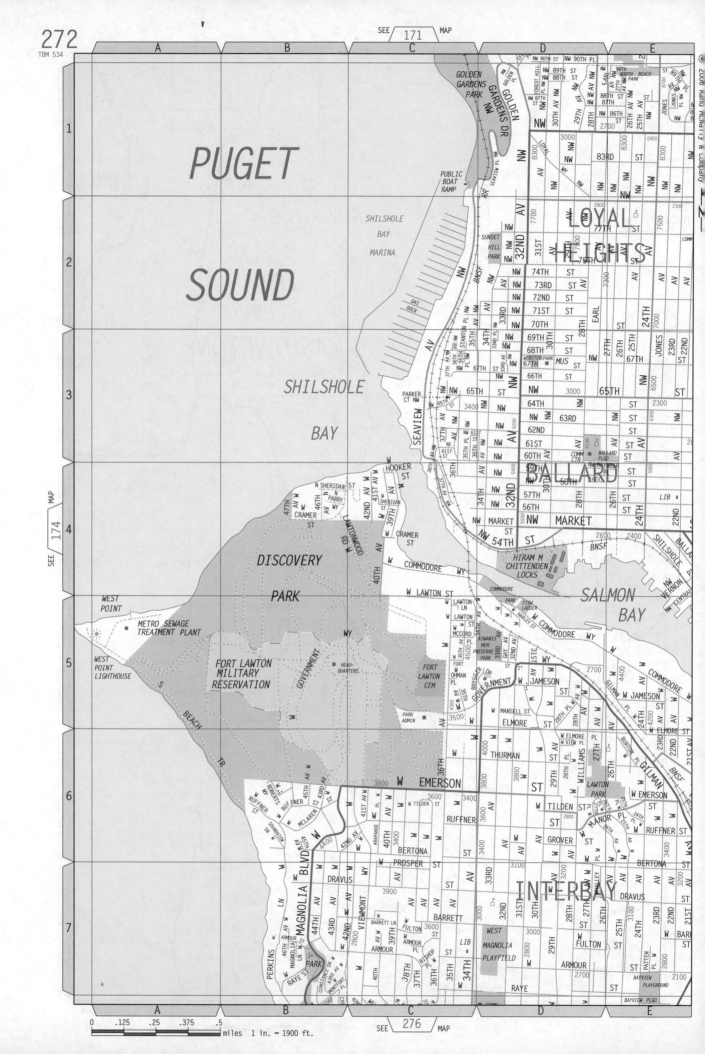

SEE 171 MAP

A   B   C   D   E

PUGET

SOUND

GOLDEN GARDENS PARK

GOLDEN GARDENS DR NW

PUBLIC BOAT RAMP

SHILSHOLE BAY MARINA

SHILSHOLE

BAY

GAS DOCK

LOYAL HEIGHTS

BALLARD

SUNSET HILL PARK

HIRAM M CHITTENDEN LOCKS

SALMON BAY

DISCOVERY

PARK

WEST POINT

METRO SEWAGE TREATMENT PLANT

WEST POINT LIGHTHOUSE

FORT LAWTON MILITARY RESERVATION

HEAD-QUARTERS

FORT LAWTON CEM

KIWANIS MEM PRESERVE PARK

LAWTON PARK

BEACH TR

PARK ADMIN

W EMERSON

INTERBAY

MAGNOLIA BLVD

WEST MAGNOLIA PLAYFIELD

BAYVIEW PLAYGROUND

0   .125   .25   .375   .5

miles   1 in. = 1900 ft.

DETAIL

SEE 174 MAP

E F G H J

GREENWOOD

CROWN HILL

SEATTLE

GREEN LAKE

GREEN LAKE PARK

GREEN LAKE GOLF COURSE

WOODLAND PARK

WOODLAND PARK ZOO

ROSE GARDEN

BALLARD HS PLGD

GILMAN PLGD

COMM CTR LOYAL HEIGHTS PLAYFIELD

SALMON BAY PARK

SWEDISH HEALTH SERVICES BALLARD

ROSS PLGD

BRIGHT ST

B F DAY PLGD

MENFORD WALLINGFORD PLGD

MARKET ST

LEARY WY NW

BALLARD WY

BOAT LAUNCH

OMMODORE WY

FISHERMAN'S TERMINAL

EMERSON ST

INTERBAY ATHLETIC FIELD

SEATTLE PACIFIC UNIV

ROYAL BROUGHAM PAVILION

FREMONT CANAL PARK

LAKE WASHINGTON SHIP CANAL

NICKERSON ST

N CANAL ST

FREMONT

LAKE UNION

MT PLEASANT CEM

HILLS OF ETERNITY CEM

DAVID RODGERS PARK

QUEEN ANNE BOWL PLFD

CROWN HILL CEMETERY NW

BAKER PARK ON CROWN HILL

SANDEL PLGD

GREENWOOD PARK

AMERICAN INDIAN HERITAGE HS

AURORA 99

WINONA AV N

GREEN LAKE DR

NORTHLAKE WY

BRIDGE WY

DETAIL

1 2 3 4 5 6 7

SEE 274 MAP

SEE 277 MAP

0 .125 .25 .375 .5 miles   1 in. = 1900 ft.

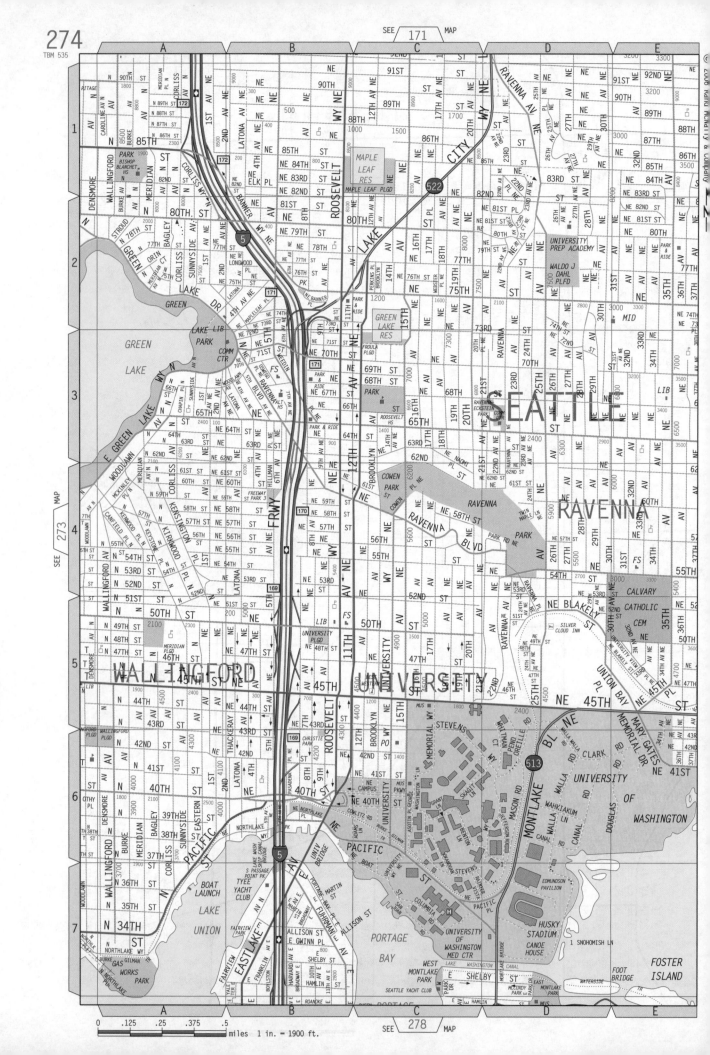

DETAIL

© 2006 Rand McNally & Company

0 .125 .25 .375 .5
miles 1 in. = 1900 ft.

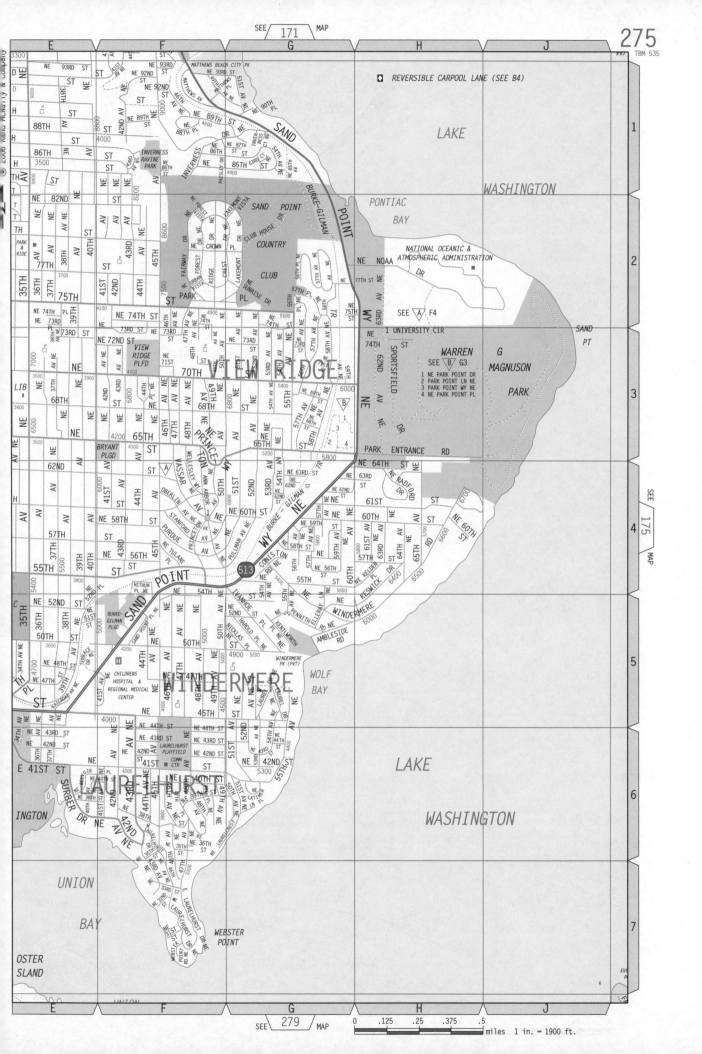

REVERSIBLE CARPOOL LANE (SEE B4)

LAKE

WASHINGTON

PONTIAC
BAY

NATIONAL OCEANIC &
ATMOSPHERIC ADMINISTRATION

SEE F4

1 UNIVERSITY CIR

WARREN
SEE B G3

1 NE PARK POINT DR
2 PARK POINT LN NE
3 PARK POINT WY NE
4 NE PARK POINT PL

G MAGNUSON PARK

SAND PT

MATTHEWS BEACH CITY PK

SAND POINT

BURKE-GILMAN

SAND POINT COUNTRY CLUB

INVERNESS RAVINE PARK

VIEW RIDGE

VIEW RIDGE PLFD

BRYANT PLGD

PRINCETON WY

PARK ENTRANCE RD

513

WINDERMERE

BURKE-GILMAN PLGD

CHILDRENS HOSPITAL & REGIONAL MEDICAL CENTER

WINDERMERE PK (PVT)

WOLF BAY

WINDERMERE

LAURELHURST PLAYFIELD
COMM CTR

LAURELHURST

LAKE

WASHINGTON

UNION BAY

SURBER DR NE

WEBSTER POINT

OSTER SLAND

0 .125 .25 .375 .5
miles 1 in. = 1900 ft.

SEE 175 MAP

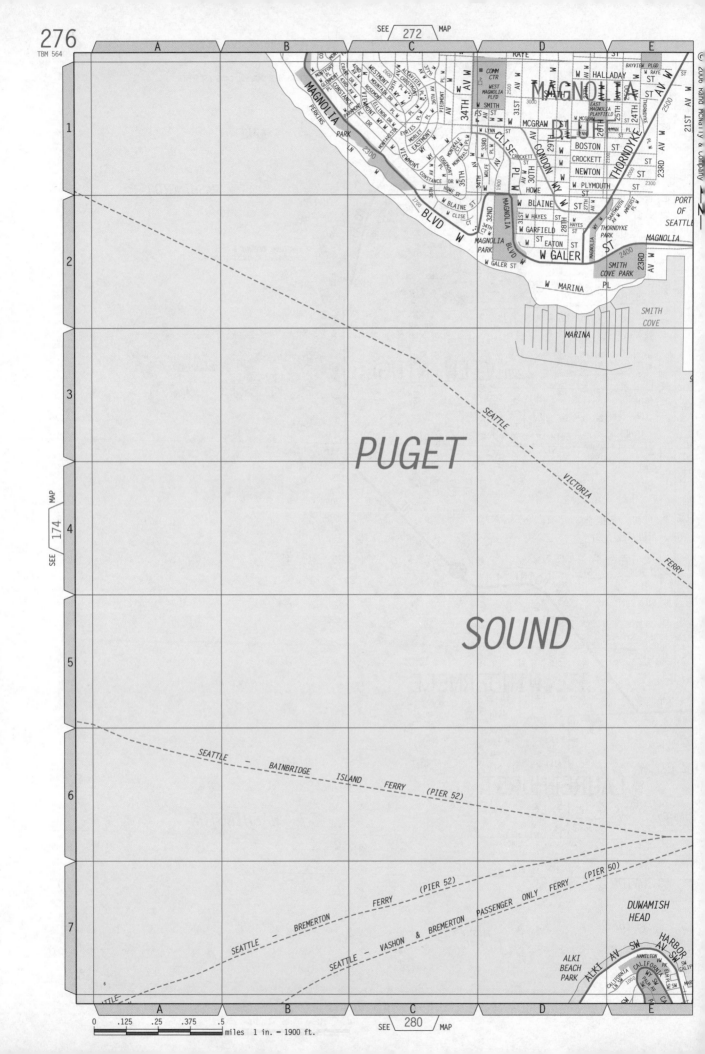

SEE 272 MAP

© 2006 Rand McNally & Company

A   B   C   D   E

MAGNOLIA

MAGNOLIA BLUFF

COMM CTR

WEST MAGNOLIA PLFD

EAST MAGNOLIA PLAYFIELD

RAYE ST

W HALLADAY ST

BAYVIEW PLGD

SMITH

McGRAW

BOSTON

CROCKETT

NEWTON

PLYMOUTH ST

PORT OF SEATTLE

34TH AV W

CLISE

CONDON WY

THORNDYKE AV W

W BLAINE ST

W HAYES

W GARFIELD

EATON

W GALER

MAGNOLIA BLVD

MAGNOLIA PARK

W GALER ST

THORNDYKE PARK

SMITH COVE PARK

MAGNOLIA

23RD AV

2400

W MARINA PL

MAGNOLIA PARK

PERKINS LN

MAGNOLIA BLVD W

SMITH COVE

MARINA

1

2

3

4

5

6

7

PUGET

SOUND

SEATTLE — VICTORIA FERRY

SEATTLE — BAINBRIDGE ISLAND FERRY (PIER 52)

FERRY (PIER 52)

SEATTLE — BREMERTON FERRY (PIER 52)

SEATTLE — VASHON & BREMERTON PASSENGER ONLY FERRY (PIER 50)

DUWAMISH HEAD

ALKI BEACH PARK

ALKI AV SW

HARBOR AV SW

CALIFORNIA AV SW

SEE 174 MAP

DETAIL

0   .125   .25   .375   .5   miles   1 in. = 1900 ft.

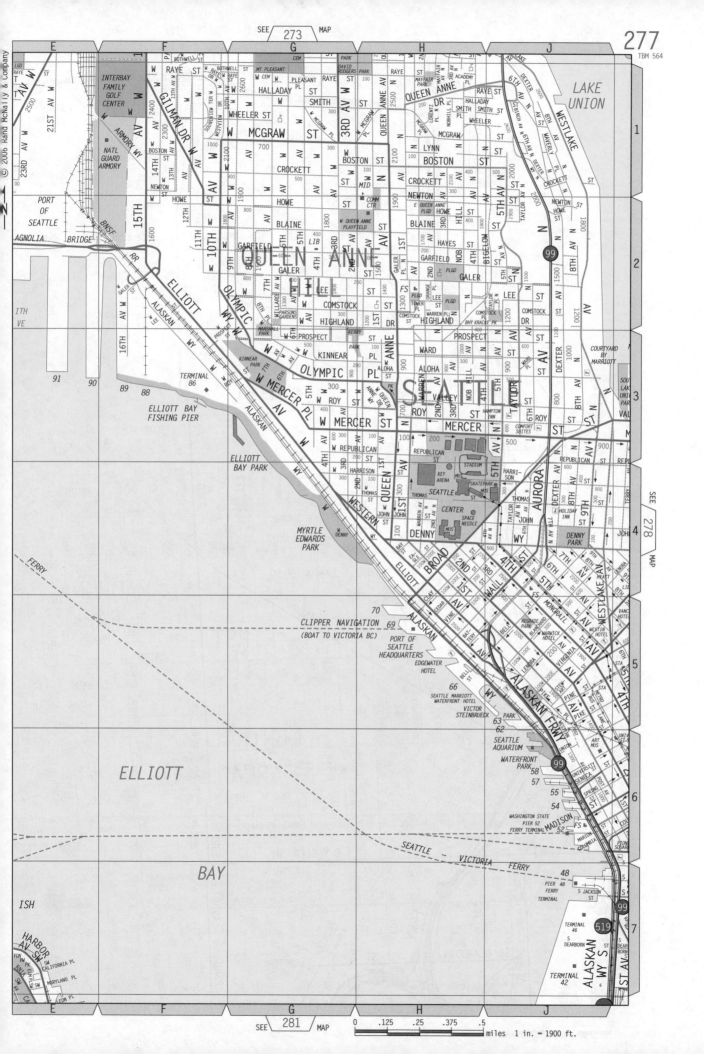

© 2006 Rand McNally & Company

LAKE
UNION

PORT OF
SEATTLE

AGNOLIA
BRIDGE

ITH
VE

PORT OF
SEATTLE

INTERBAY
FAMILY GOLF
CENTER

NATL
GUARD
ARMORY

QUEEN ANNE
HILL

SEATTLE

ELLIOTT BAY
FISHING PIER

TERMINAL
86

ELLIOTT
BAY PARK

MYRTLE
EDWARDS
PARK

SEATTLE
CENTER

KEY
ARENA

STADIUM

SPACE
NEEDLE

DENNY
PARK

ELLIOTT

BAY

FERRY

70
CLIPPER NAVIGATION   69
(BOAT TO VICTORIA BC)

PORT OF
SEATTLE
HEADQUARTERS

EDGEWATER
HOTEL

66
SEATTLE MARRIOTT
WATERFRONT HOTEL
VICTOR
STEINBRUECK
63
62

SEATTLE
AQUARIUM

WATERFRONT
PARK
58
57
55
54

WASHINGTON STATE
PIER 52
FERRY TERMINAL
52

SEATTLE   VICTORIA   FERRY

48
PIER 4B
FERRY
TERMINAL

99

COURTYARD
BY
MARRIOTT

SOU
LAK
UNI
PAR

HAMPTON
INN

COMFORT
SUITES

HOLIDAY
INN

REGRADE
PARK

WARWICK
HOTEL

WESTIN
HOTEL

VANC
HOTEL

MONORAIL

ART
MUS

UNIV
ST ST

PIONE
SQUARE

ISH

HARBOR
AV SW
CALIFORNIA PL

MARYLAND PL

LEON PL

TERMINAL
46

S DEARBORN
ST

TERMINAL
42

99

519

ALASKAN WY S

ST AV S

0   .125   .25   .375   .5
miles 1 in. = 1900 ft.

DETAIL

SEE 278 MAP

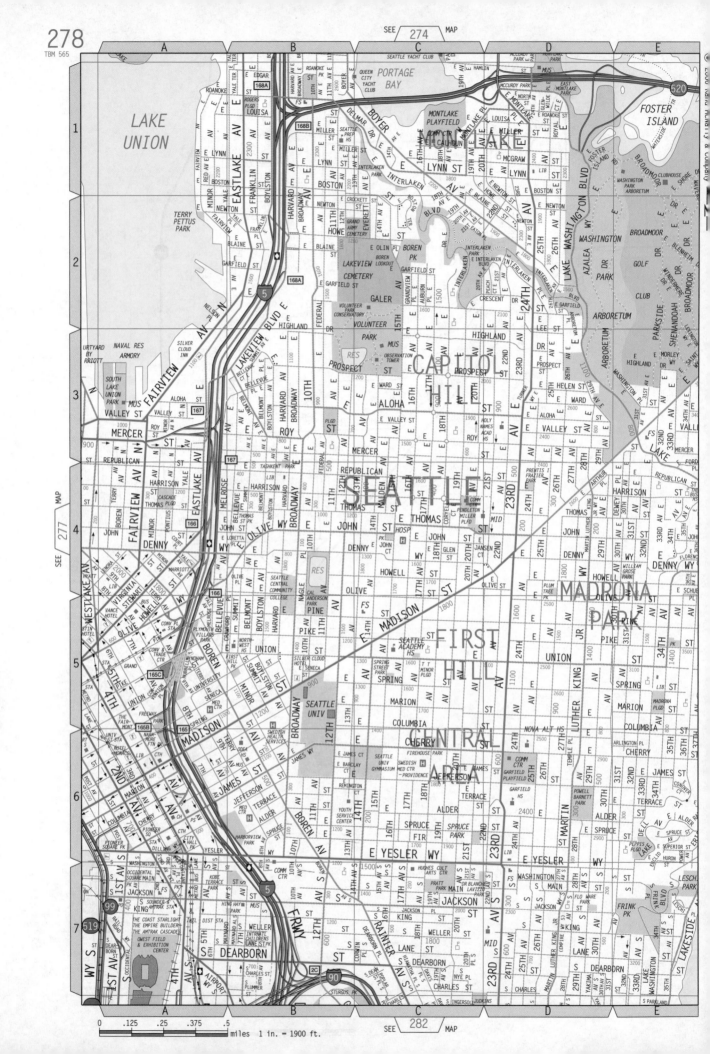

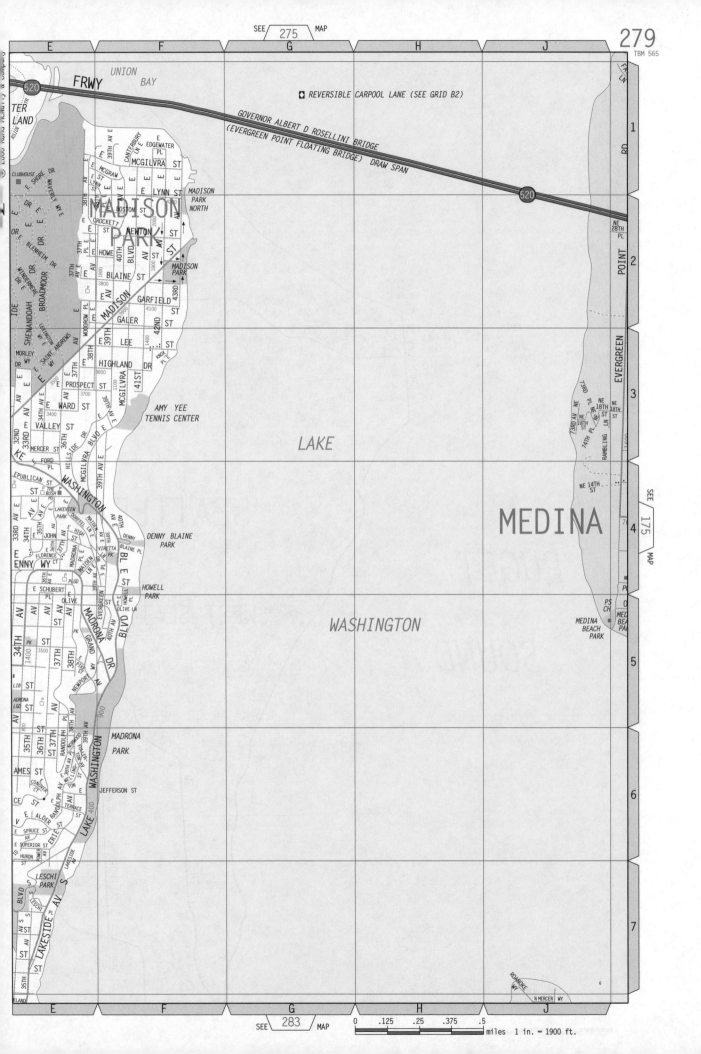

E   F   G   H   J

⬡ REVERSIBLE CARPOOL LANE (SEE GRID B2)

520 FRWY   UNION BAY

GOVERNOR ALBERT D ROSELLINI BRIDGE
(EVERGREEN POINT FLOATING BRIDGE) DRAW SPAN

520

1

TER LAND
CLUBHOUSE

E SHORE DR
WAVERLY WY E

39TH AV E
CANTERBURY LN E
E EDGEWATER PL

MCGILVRA ST

E MCGRAW

E LYNN ST
MADISON PARK NORTH

MADISON PARK

E BOSTON ST

NEWTON ST
E CROCKETT ST

HOWE ST
40TH AV E
MADISON BLVD

E BLAINE ST
MADISON PARK

GARFIELD ST
43RD ST

MADISON ST

GALER ST

LEE ST
39TH

HIGHLAND DR
41ST
KNOX

E PROSPECT ST
MCGILVRA
37TH

E WARD ST
34TH AV E

VALLEY ST
33RD
32ND

MERCER ST
FORD PL
HILLSIDE DR
36TH
39TH AV

MCGILVRA BLVD E

AMY YEE TENNIS CENTER

LAKE

NE 28TH PL

POINT

EVERGREEN

73RD AV NE
NE 18TH ST
NE 18TH PL NE
74TH AV NE
RAMBLING LN

NE 14TH ST

MEDINA

2

3

4

SEE 175 MAP

REPUBLICAN ST
THE BUSH
LAKEVIEW PARK
DORFFEL DR E

33RD AV
34TH
E 35TH
37TH
HIGH
JOHN
MADRONA
FLORENCE CT
VIRETTA PK
DENNY BLAINE PL
DENNY BLAINE PARK

WASHINGTON

36TH
MALDEN
37TH
38TH
40TH AV
EVERGREEN
HOWELL PL
OLIVE LN

HOWELL PARK

E SCHUBERT PL
OLIVE ST
MADRONA
BLVD

34TH AV
ST

37TH
38TH
GRAND WY
NEWPORT

LIB ST
ADRONA LGD ST

AV
35TH
36TH
37TH
RANDOLPH
38TH AV
39TH AV

MADRONA DR

MADRONA PARK

AMES ST

CE ST

E ALDER
E SPRUCE ST
E SUPERIOR ST
HURON

LESCHI PARK
BLVD

LAKESIDE AV S

35TH

MEDINA BEACH PARK

PS CH

5

6

7

E   F   G   H   J

0   .125   .25   .375   .5
miles   1 in. = 1900 ft.

DETAIL

SEE 276 MAP

© 2006 Rand McNally & Company

DETAIL

SEE 174 MAP

PUGET

SOUND

SEATTLE

WEST SEATTLE

ALKI
POINT

ALKI
POINT
LIGHTHOUSE

ALKI
BEACH PARK

SEATTLE
BIRTHPLACE
MONUMENT

SCHMITZ
PRESERVE
PARK

EMMA
SCHMITZ
MEMORIAL
OVERLOOK
PARK

FAIRM
PLGD

0 .125 .25 .375 .5
miles 1 in. = 1900 ft.

SEE 284 MAP

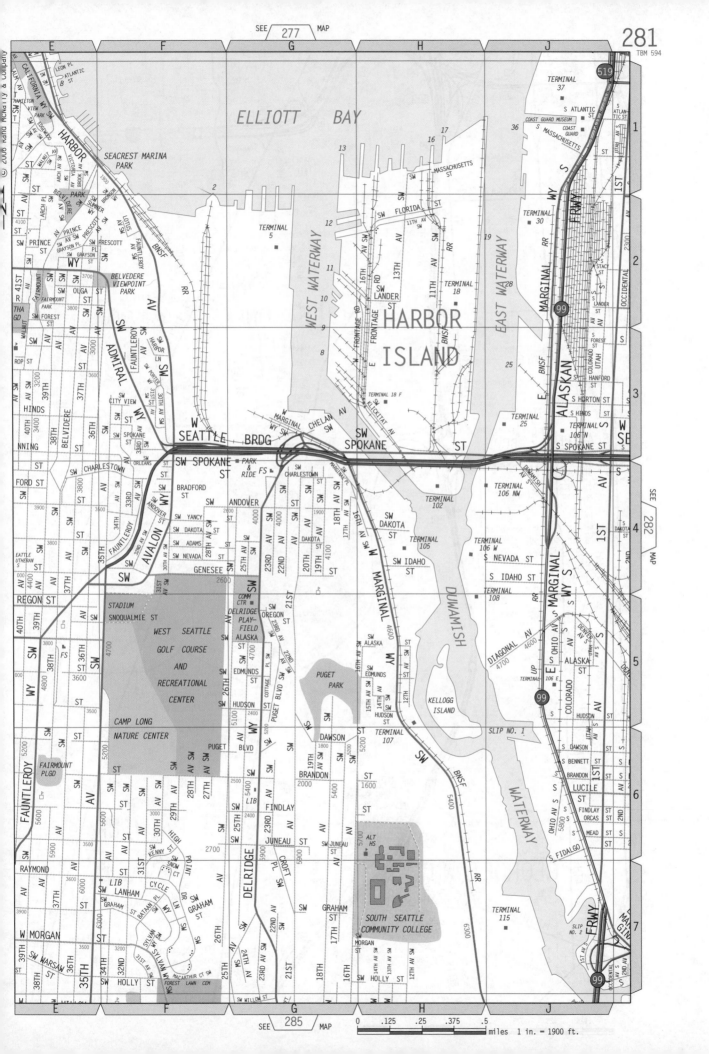

ELLIOTT BAY

HARBOR ISLAND

WEST SEATTLE BRDG

SW SPOKANE ST

DUWAMISH

WEST SEATTLE GOLF COURSE AND RECREATIONAL CENTER

CAMP LONG NATURE CENTER

SOUTH SEATTLE COMMUNITY COLLEGE

WATERWAY

KELLOGG ISLAND

SEACREST MARINA PARK

BELVEDERE VIEWPOINT PARK

PUGET PARK

DETAIL

0 .125 .25 .375 .5

miles   1 in. = 1900 ft.

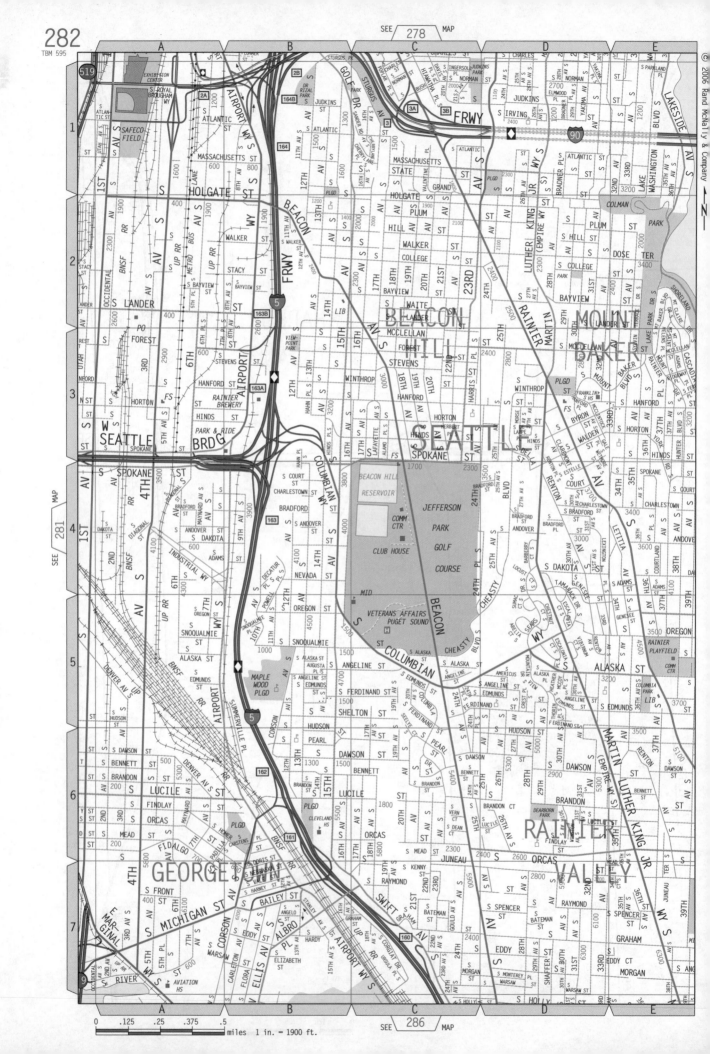

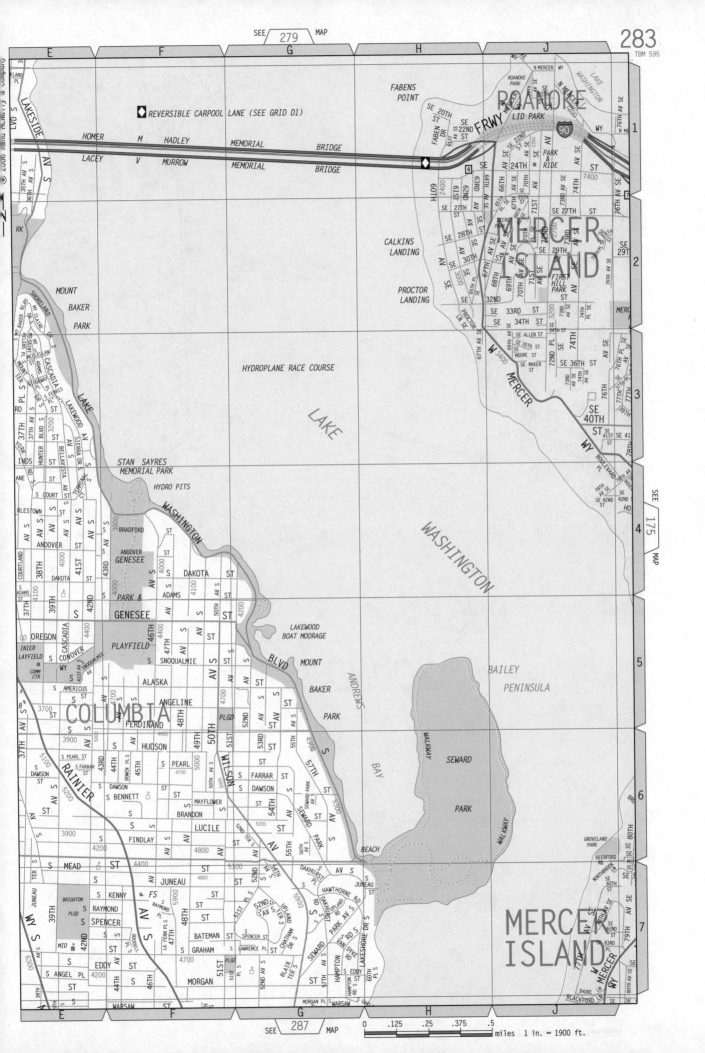

◆ REVERSIBLE CARPOOL LANE (SEE GRID D1)

ROANOKE

FABENS
POINT

ROANOKE
PARK

LID PARK

PARK & RIDE

HOMER M HADLEY MEMORIAL BRIDGE

LACEY V MURROW MEMORIAL BRIDGE

MERCER
ISLAND

CALKINS
LANDING

PROCTOR
LANDING

FIRST
HILL
PARK

MOUNT
BAKER
PARK

LAKESIDE AV S

MOUNT
BAKER
PARK

LAKE

HYDROPLANE RACE COURSE

WASHINGTON

MERCER

SE
40TH
ST

STAN SAYRES
MEMORIAL PARK

HYDRO PITS

BRADFORD

ANDOVER
GENESEE

DAKOTA ST

BAILEY
PENINSULA

GENESEE

PARK &

LAKEWOOD
BOAT MOORAGE

MOUNT
BAKER
PARK

ANDREWS

WALKWAY

SEWARD
PARK

COLUMBIA

ALASKA

FERDINAND

HUDSON

BAY

WALKWAY

RAINIER

PEARL

FARRAR

DAWSON

BENNETT

MAYFLOWER

BRANDON

SEWARD PARK

BEACH

GROVELAND
PARK

LUCILE

FINDLAY

DEERFORD
RD

NORTHBROOK

MEAD ST

JUNEAU ST

OAKHURST

HAWTHORNE RD

JUNEAU
ST

BRIGHTON
PLGD

KENNY

RAYMOND

SPENCER

BATEMAN

GRAHAM

UPLAND

PARK AV S

MERCER
ISLAND

MID

EDDY ST

S ANGEL PL

MORGAN

WARSAW ST

LAKESHORE DR S

BLACKFORD

0 .125 .25 .375 .5
miles 1 in. = 1900 ft.

DETAIL

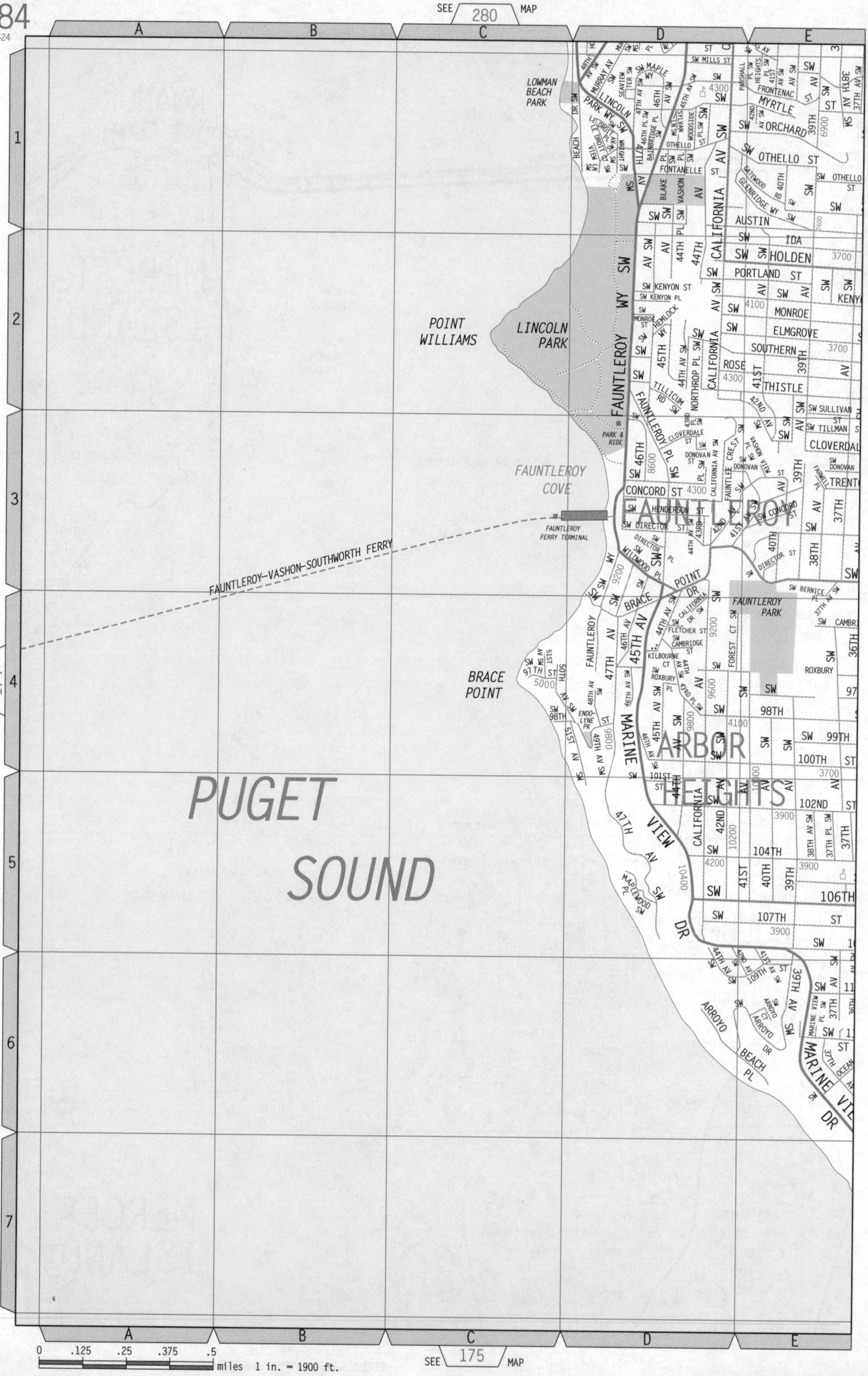

SEE 280 MAP

DETAIL

© 2006 Rand McNally & Company

PUGET

SOUND

POINT
WILLIAMS

LINCOLN
PARK

LOWMAN
BEACH
PARK

FAUNTLEROY
COVE

FAUNTLEROY
FERRY TERMINAL

FAUNTLEROY–VASHON–SOUTHWORTH FERRY

BRACE
POINT

FAUNTLEROY

FAUNTLEROY
PARK

ARBOR
HEIGHTS

PARK & RIDE

CALIFORNIA AV SW

MARINE VIEW DR

MARINE VIEW DR

ARROYO
BEACH
PL

MYRTLE

ORCHARD

OTHELLO ST

AUSTIN

IDA

HOLDEN

PORTLAND ST

MONROE

ELMGROVE

SOUTHERN

THISTLE

ROSE

CLOVERDALE

TRENT

CONCORD ST

HENDERSON ST

DIRECTOR ST

ROXBURY

98TH

99TH

100TH

102ND

104TH

106TH

107TH
ST

SEE 174 MAP

0   .125   .25   .375   .5
miles   1 in. = 1900 ft.

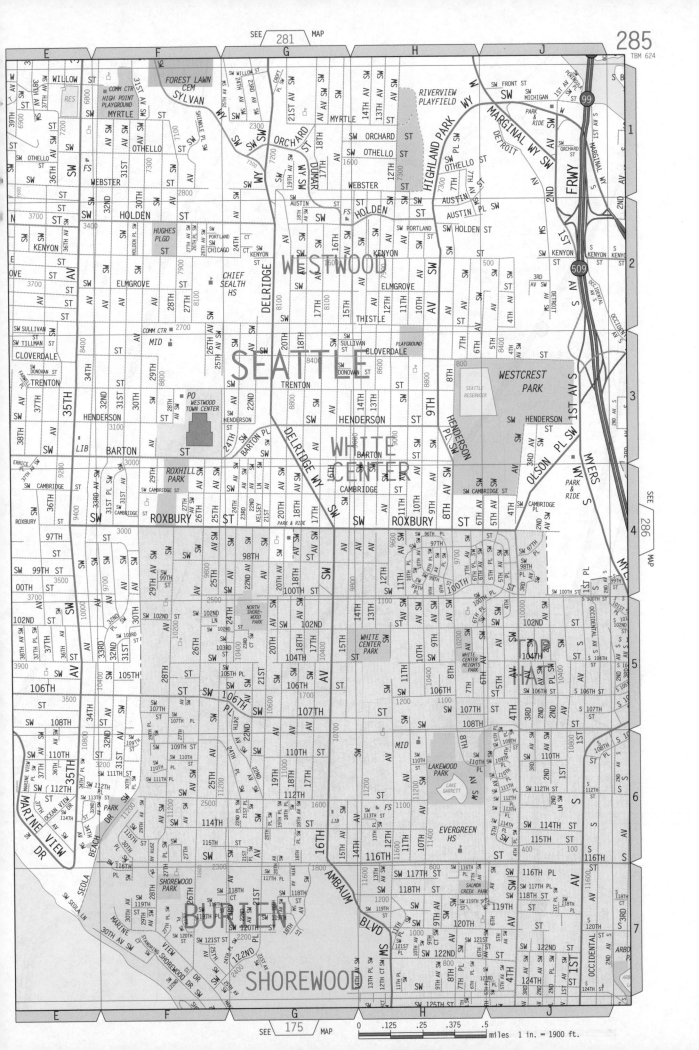

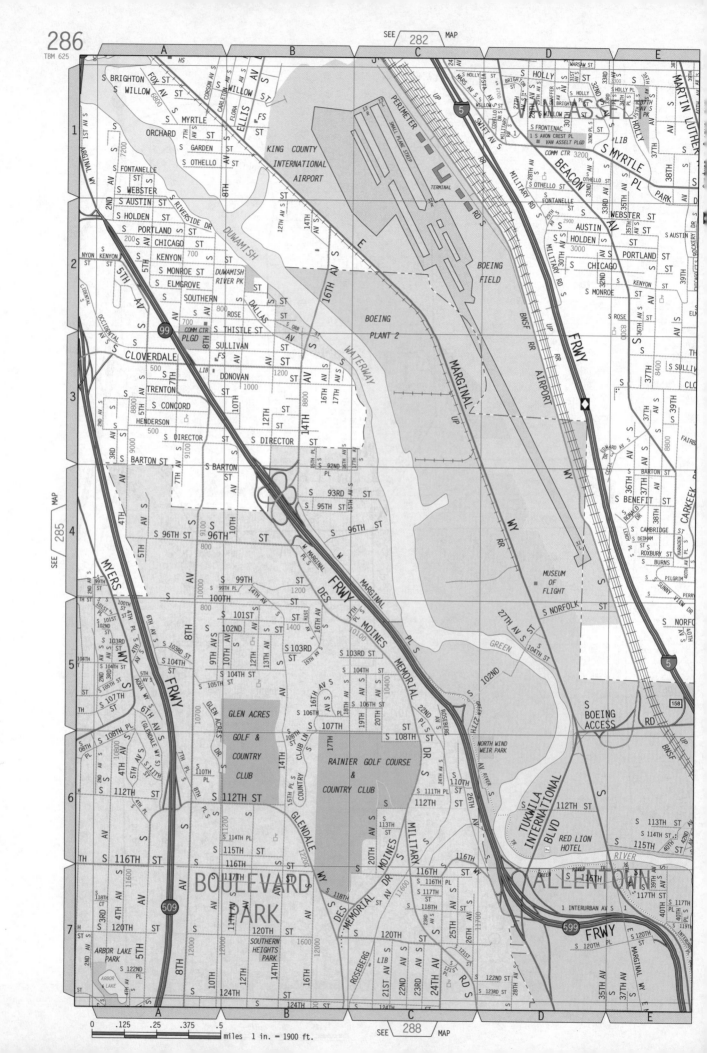

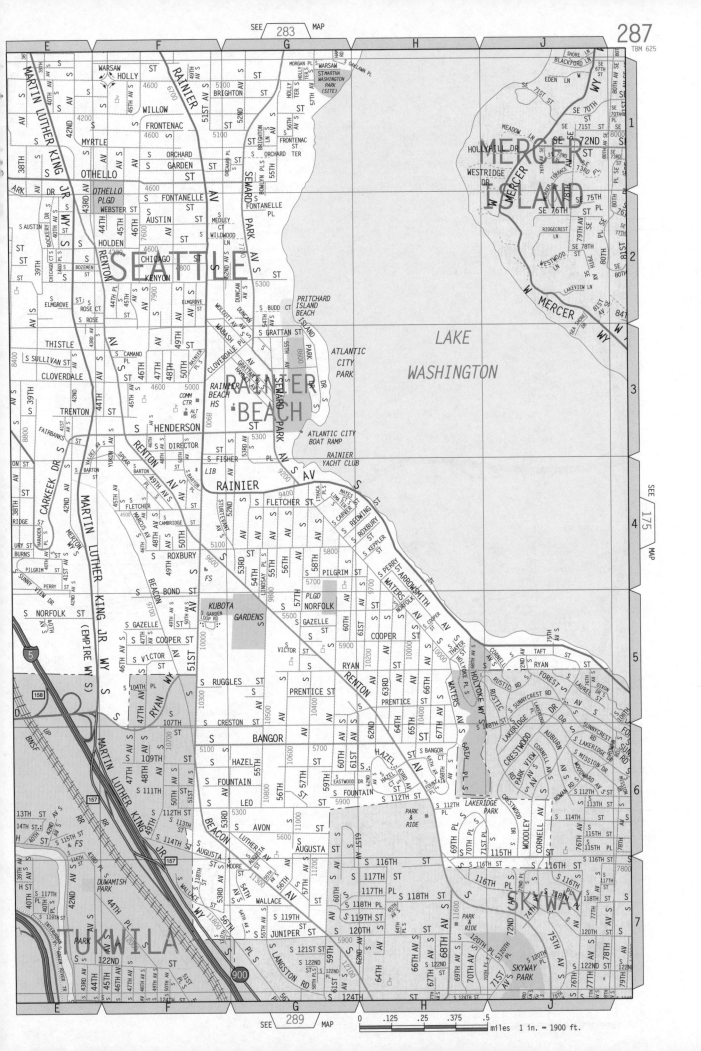

DETAIL

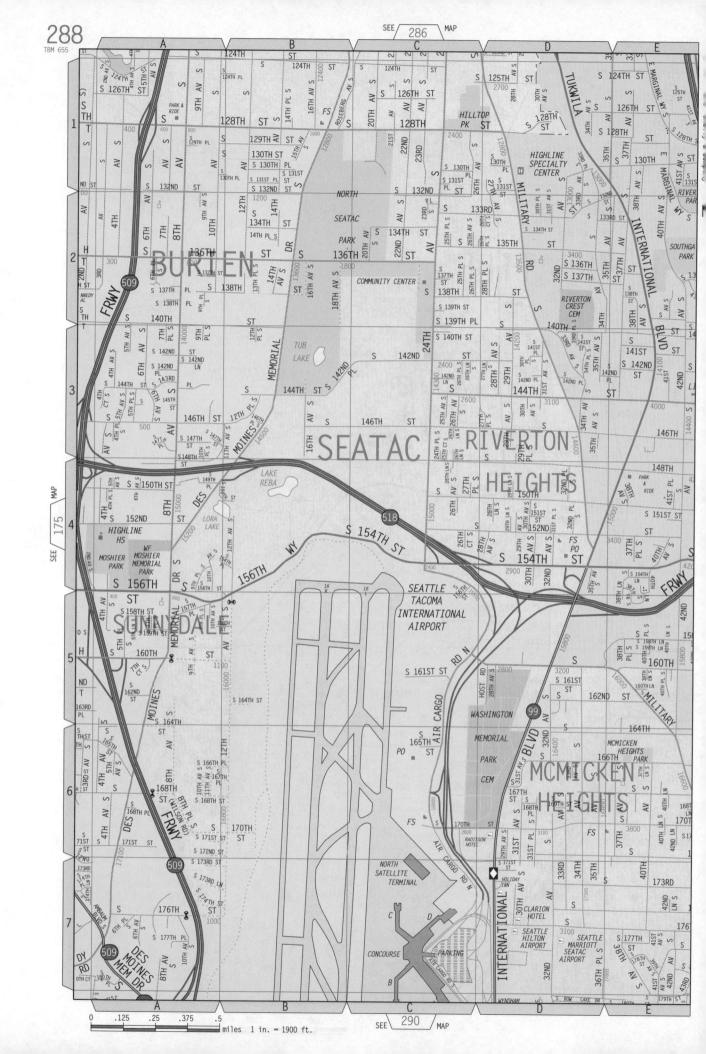

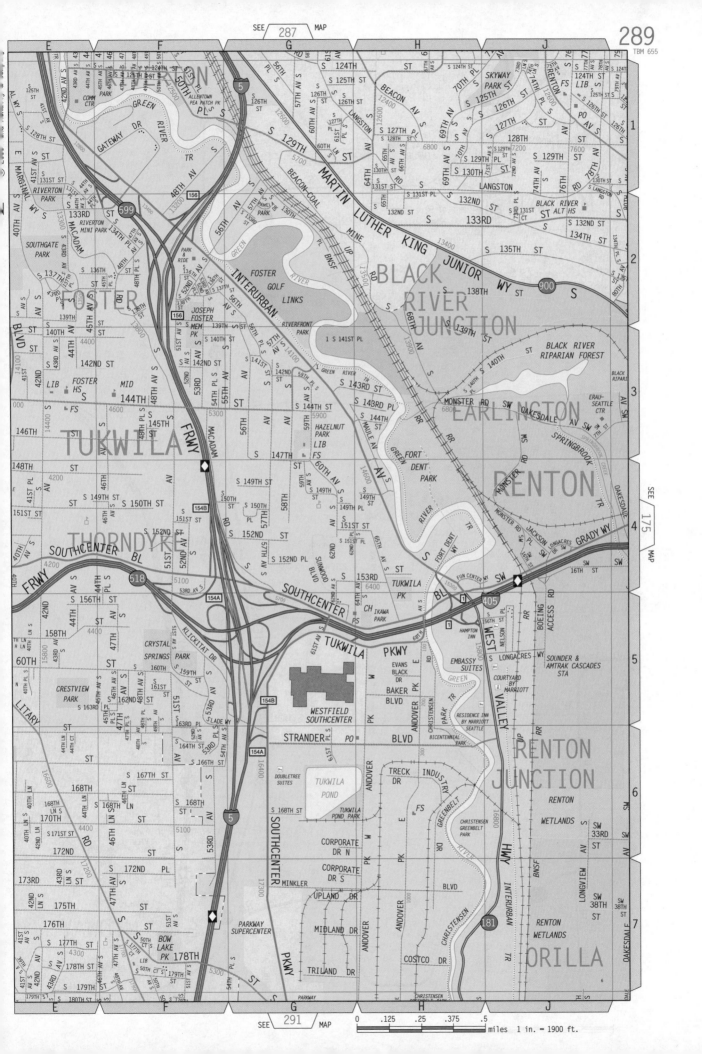

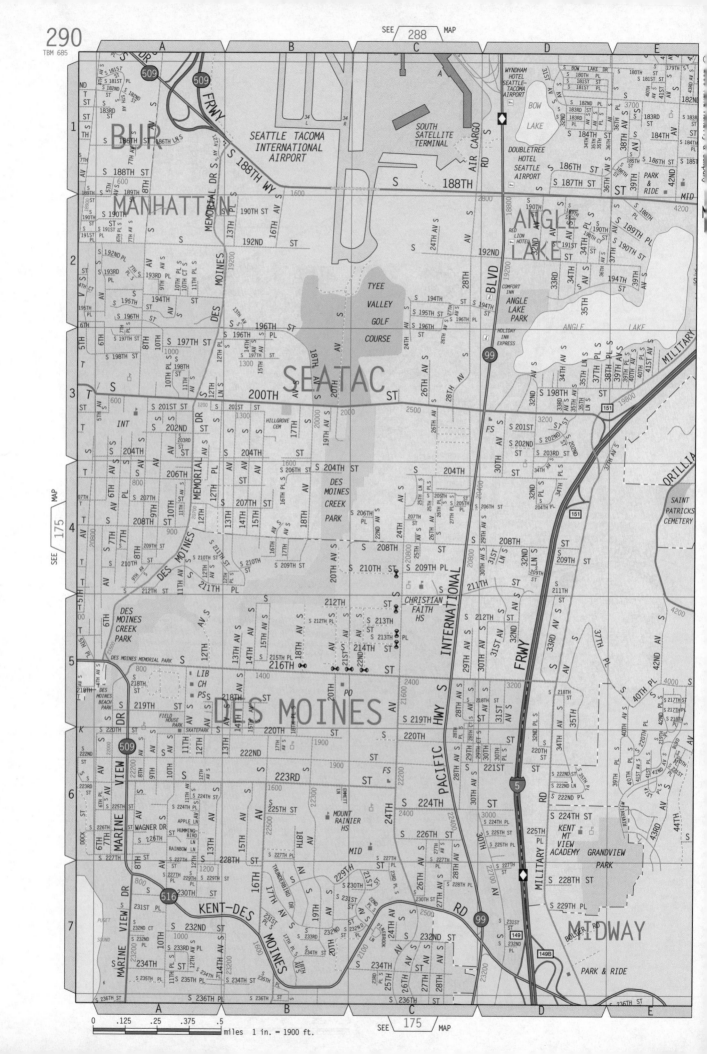

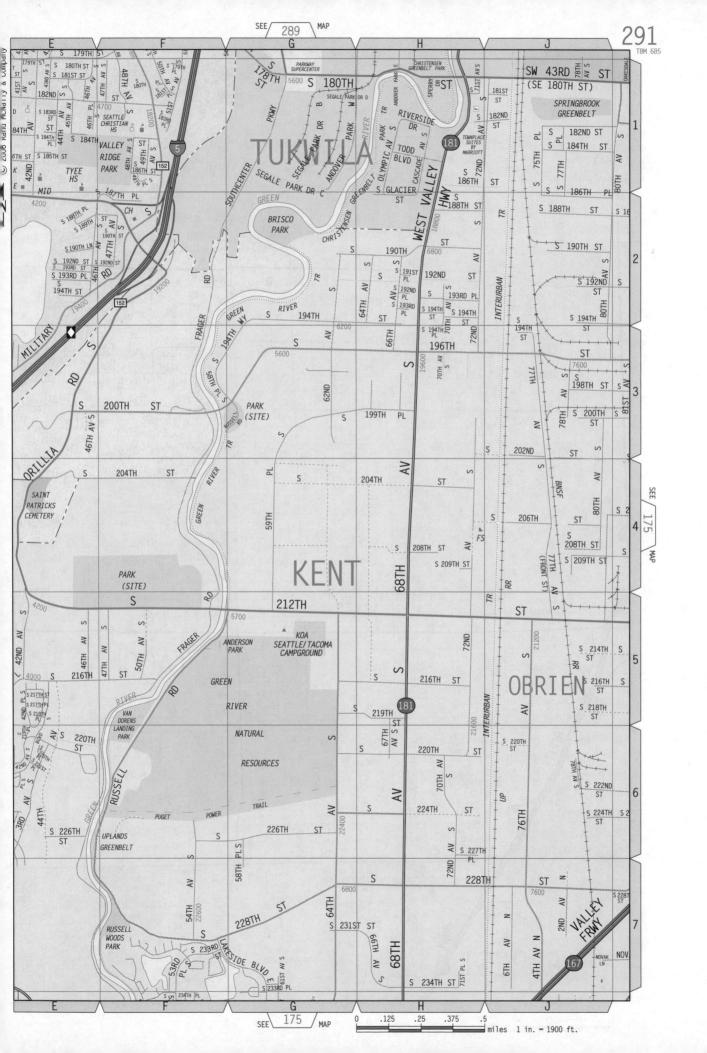

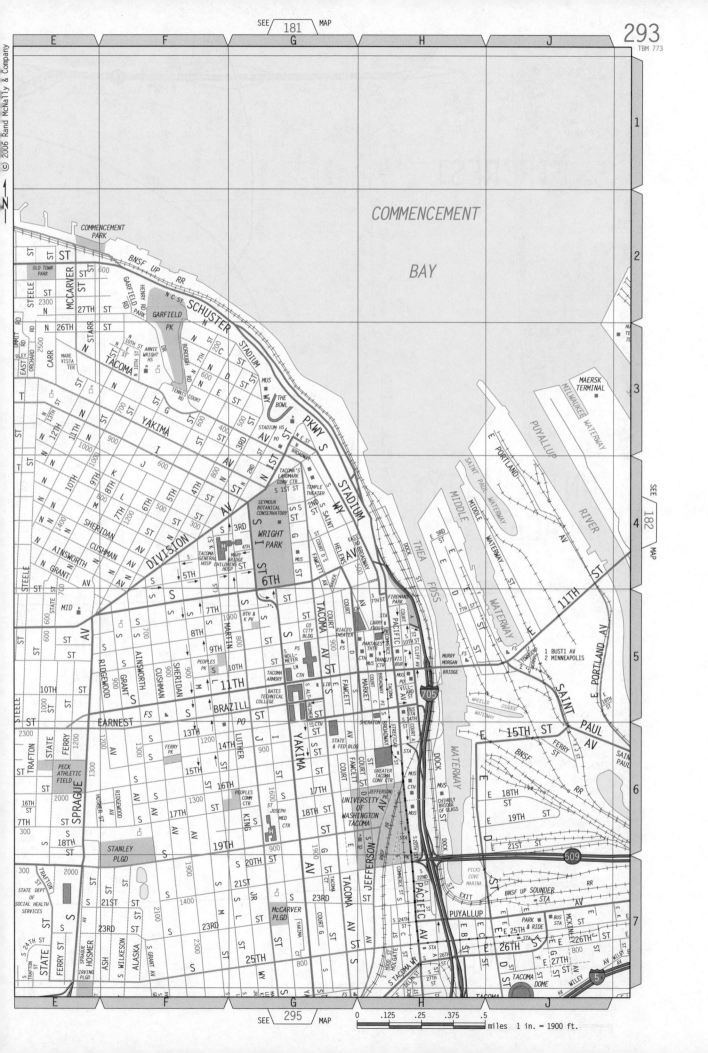

© 2006 Rand McNally & Company

E   F   G   H   J

COMMENCEMENT

BAY

1

2

3

4

5

6

7

SEE 182 MAP

DETAIL

COMMENCEMENT PARK

OLD TOWN PARK

GARFIELD PARK

SCHUSTER PKWY S

STADIUM

THE BOWL

WRIGHT PARK

MAERSK TERMINAL

MILWAUKEE WATERWAY

PUYALLUP RIVER

SAINT PAUL WATERWAY

PORTLAND AV

MIDDLE WATERWAY

THEA FOSS WATERWAY

SEYMOUR BOTANICAL CONSERVATORY

TACOMA'S LANDMARK CONV CTR

TEMPLE THEATER

TACOMA GENERAL HOSP

MARY BRIDGE CHILDRENS HOSP

FIREMANS PARK

RIALTO THEATER

PANTAGES THTR

CO CITY BLDG

8TH & K PK

PEOPLES PK

TACOMA ARMORY

BATES TECHNICAL COLLEGE

LARRY FROST

11TH ST

E PORTLAND AV

1 BUSTI AV
2 MINNEAPOLIS

MURRY MORGAN BRIDGE

WHEELER OSGOOD WATERWAY

705

SAINT PAUL AV

SHERATON

STATE & FED BLDG

GREATER TACOMA CONV CTR

UNIVERSITY OF WASHINGTON TACOMA

JEFFERSON PK

CHIHULY BRIDGE OF GLASS

JOSEPH MED CTR

PEOPLES COMM CTR

STANLEY PLGD

STATE DEPT OF SOCIAL HEALTH SERVICES

PECK ATHLETIC FIELD

SPRAGUE HOSMER

IRVING PLGD

McCARVER PLGD

PICKS COVE MARINA

BNSF UP SOUNDER STA

PARK & RIDE

TACOMA DOME

609

5

PUYALLUP

0   .125   .25   .375   .5
miles   1 in. = 1900 ft.

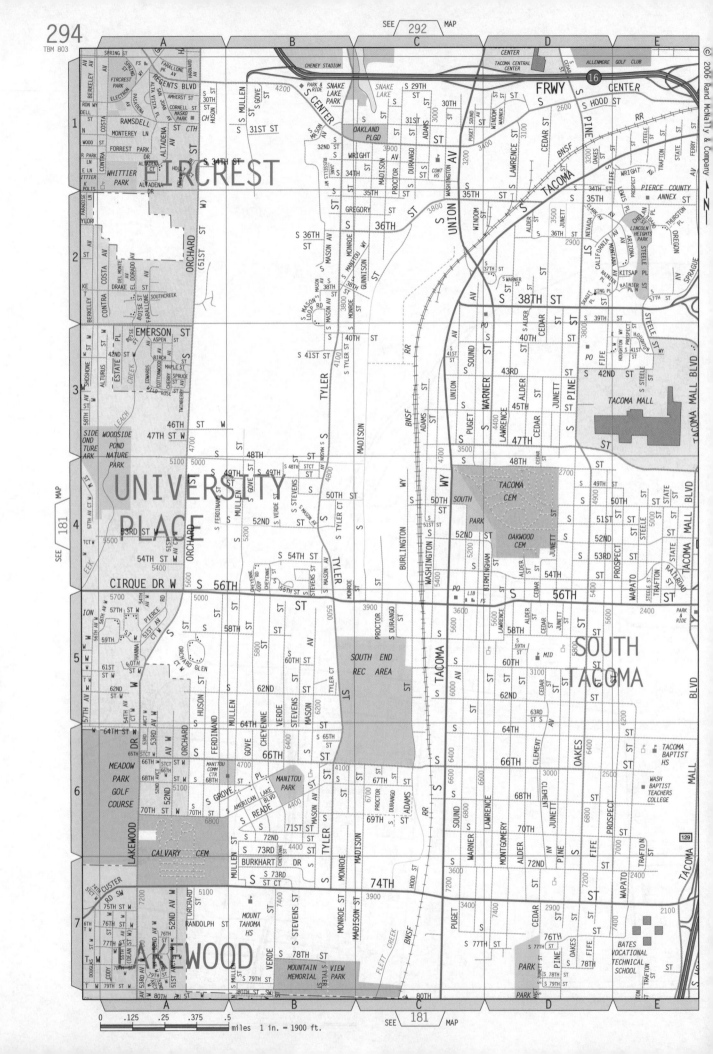

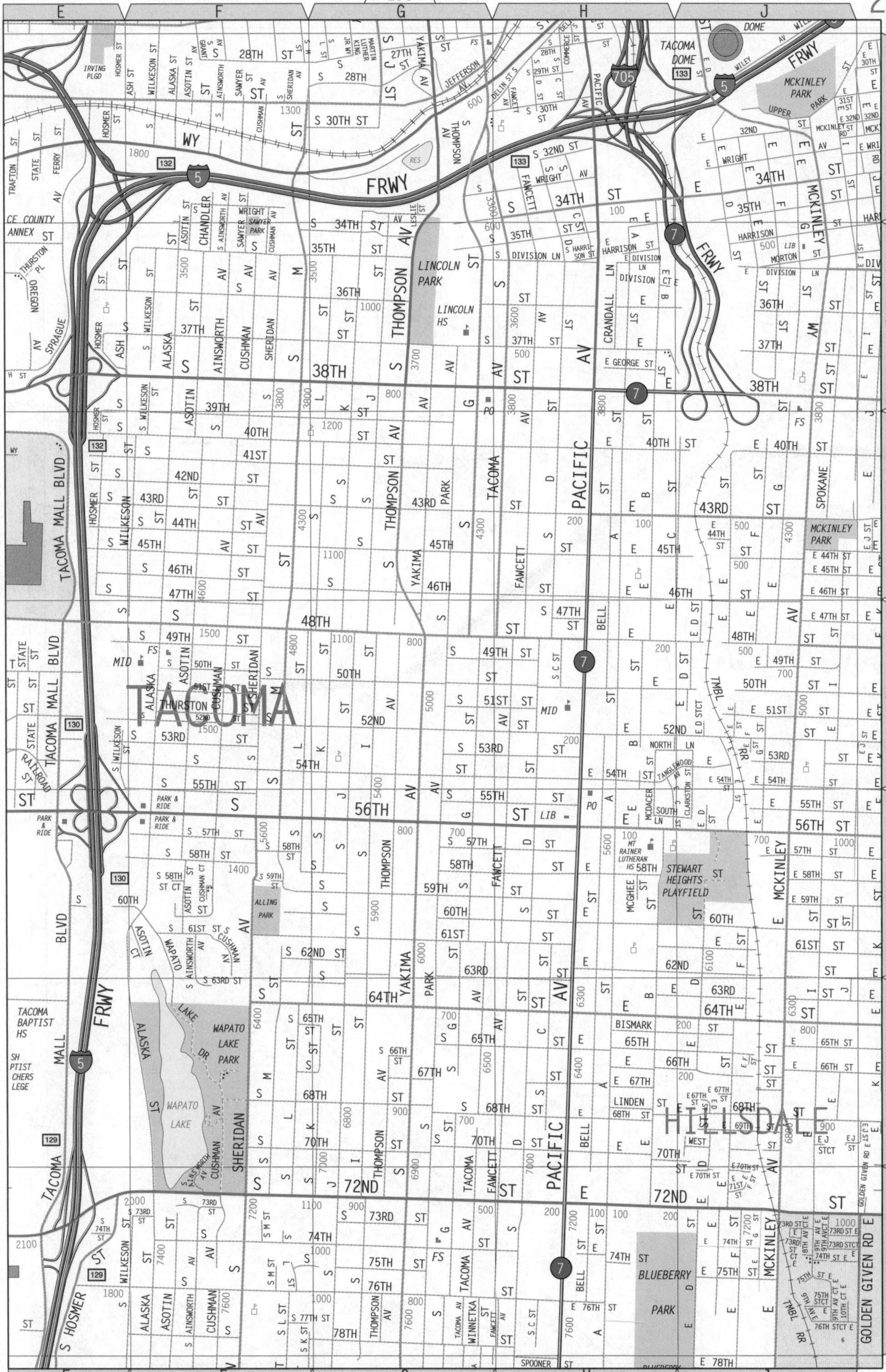

© 2006 Rand McNally & Company

E F G H J

TACOMA

TACOMA DOME

MCKINLEY PARK

LINCOLN PARK

LINCOLN HS

TACOMA MALL BLVD

MID

PARK & RIDE

ALLING PARK

WAPATO LAKE PARK

WAPATO LAKE

TACOMA BAPTIST HS

SH PTIST CHERS LEGE

MT RAINER LUTHERAN HS

STEWART HEIGHTS PLAYFIELD

HILLSDALE

BISMARK

LINDEN

MCKINLEY PARK

BLUEBERRY PARK

DETAIL

FRWY

TACOMA MALL BLVD

GOLDEN GIVEN RD

0 .125 .25 .375 .5 miles 1 in. = 1900 ft.

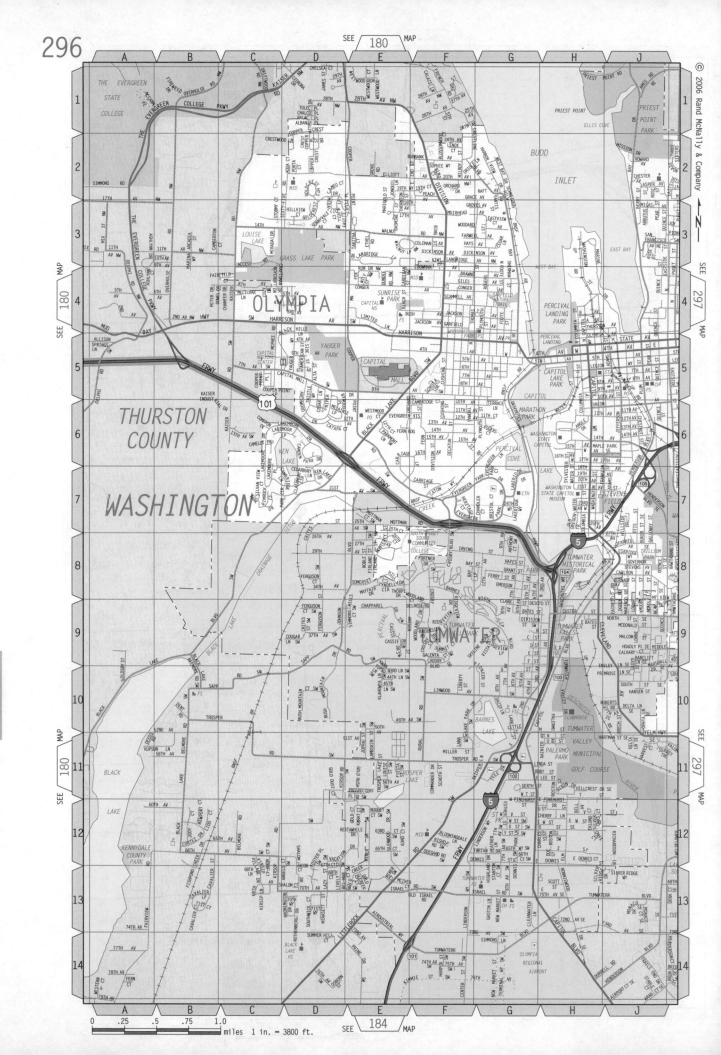

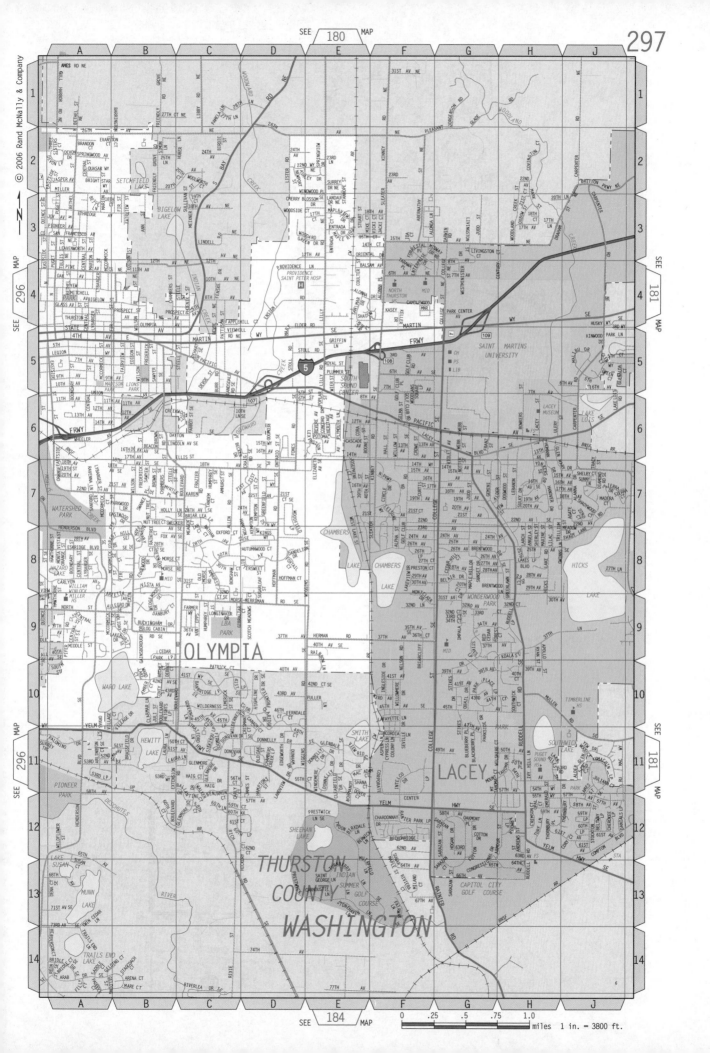

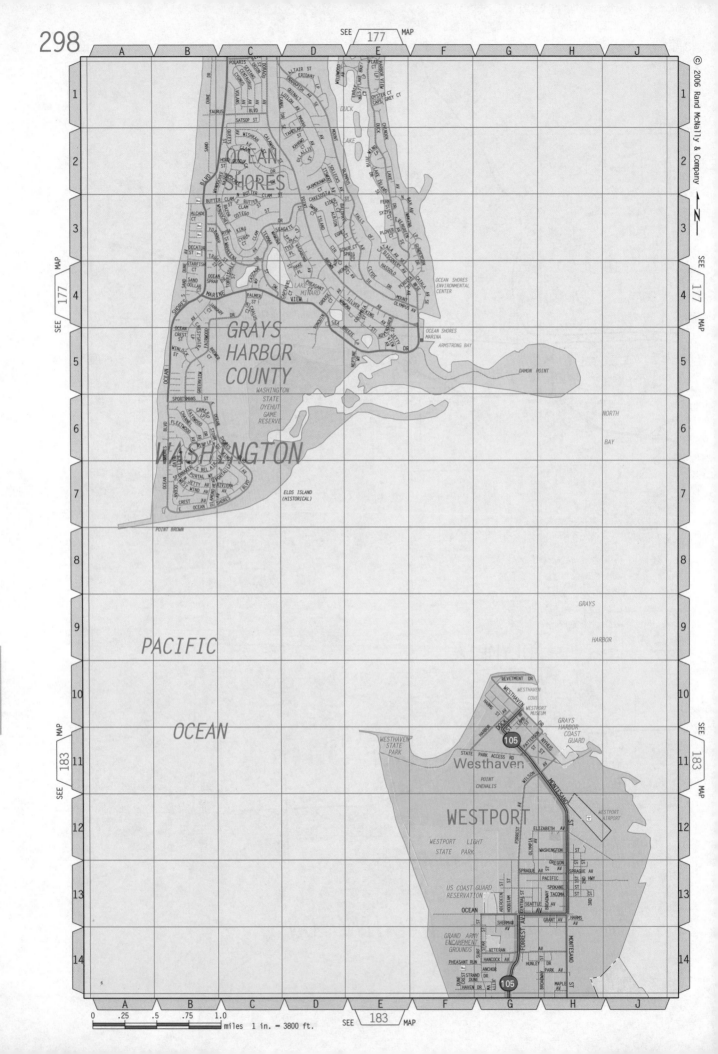

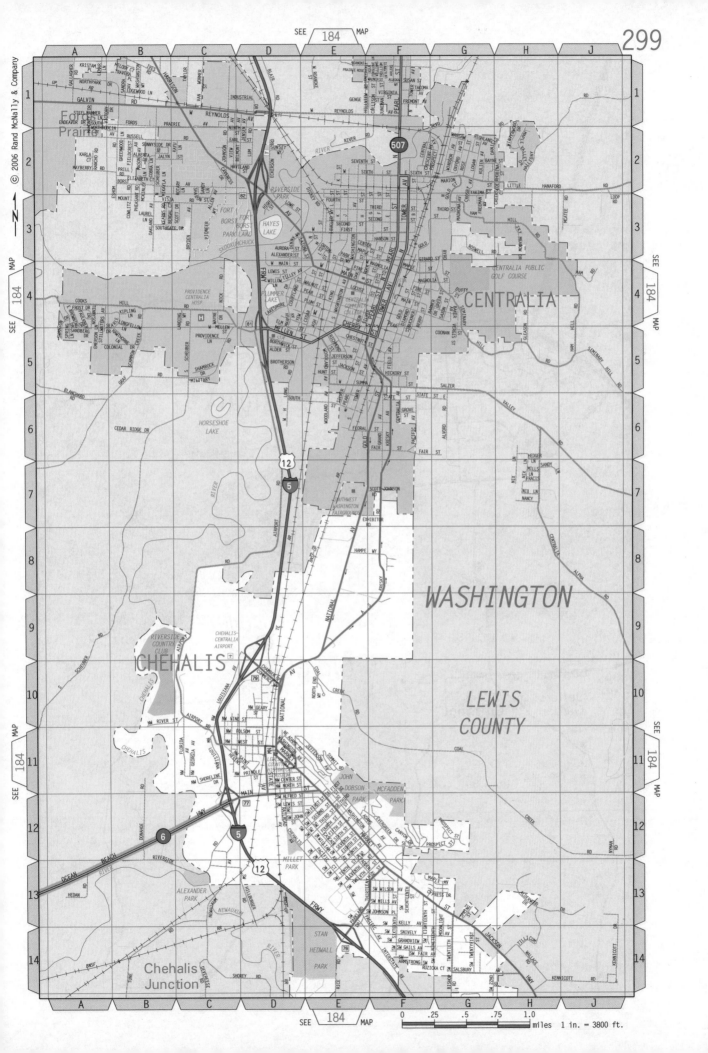

CENTRALIA

CHEHALIS

WASHINGTON

LEWIS
COUNTY

Fort Borst
Prairie

Chehalis
Junction

DETAIL

0   .25   .5   .75   1.0
miles 1 in. = 3800 ft.

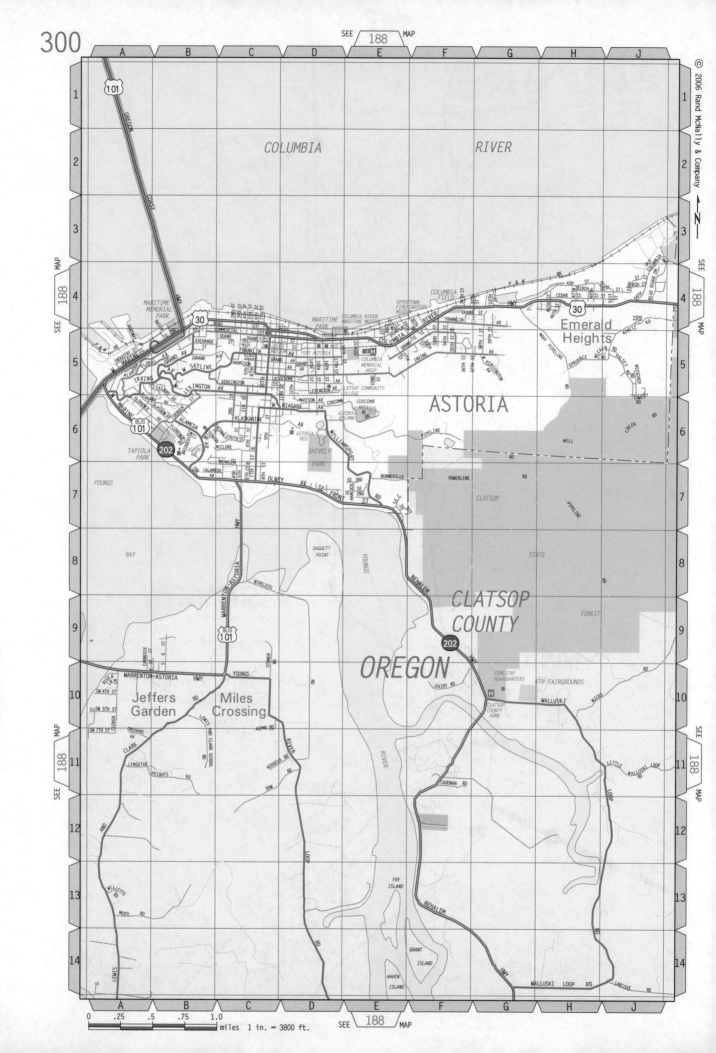

COLUMBIA   RIVER

ASTORIA

Emerald
Heights

CLATSOP
COUNTY

OREGON

Jeffers
Garden

Miles
Crossing

YOUNGS

BAY

DETAIL

SEE 188 MAP

SEE 188 MAP

SEE 188 MAP

SEE 188 MAP

0   .25   .5   .75   1.0
miles 1 in. = 3800 ft.

SEE 188 MAP

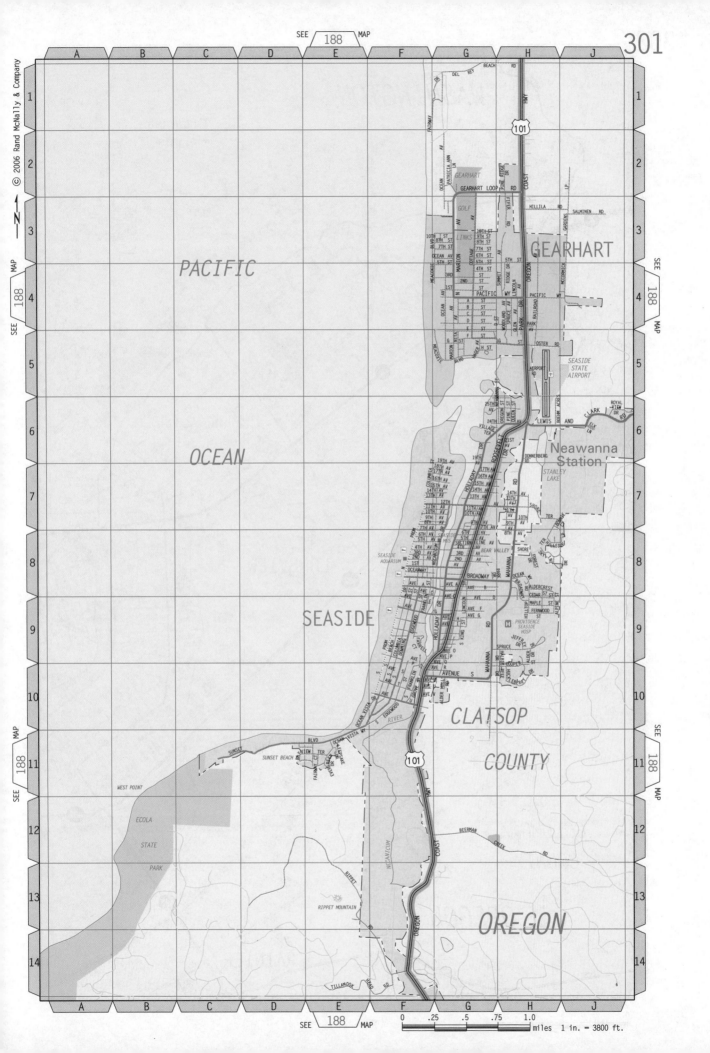

SEE 188 MAP

N

PACIFIC

OCEAN

SEASIDE

GEARHART

Neawanna Station

CLATSOP

COUNTY

OREGON

WEST POINT

ECOLA

STATE

PARK

RIPPET MOUNTAIN

SEE 188 MAP

0 .25 .5 .75 1.0

miles   1 in. = 3800 ft.

DETAIL

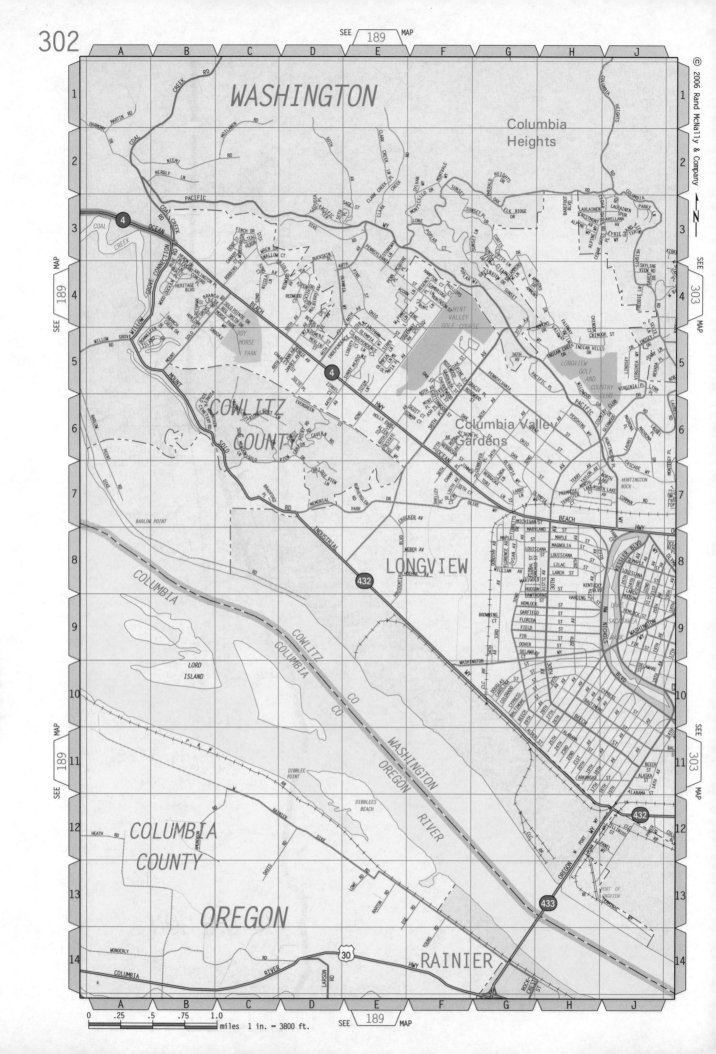

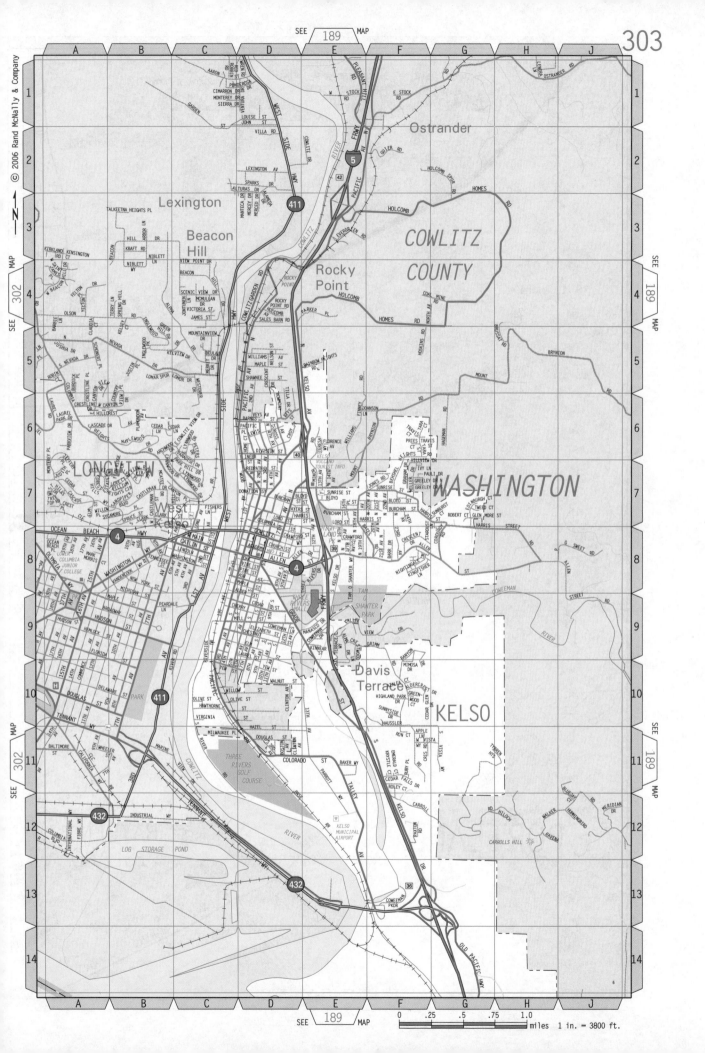

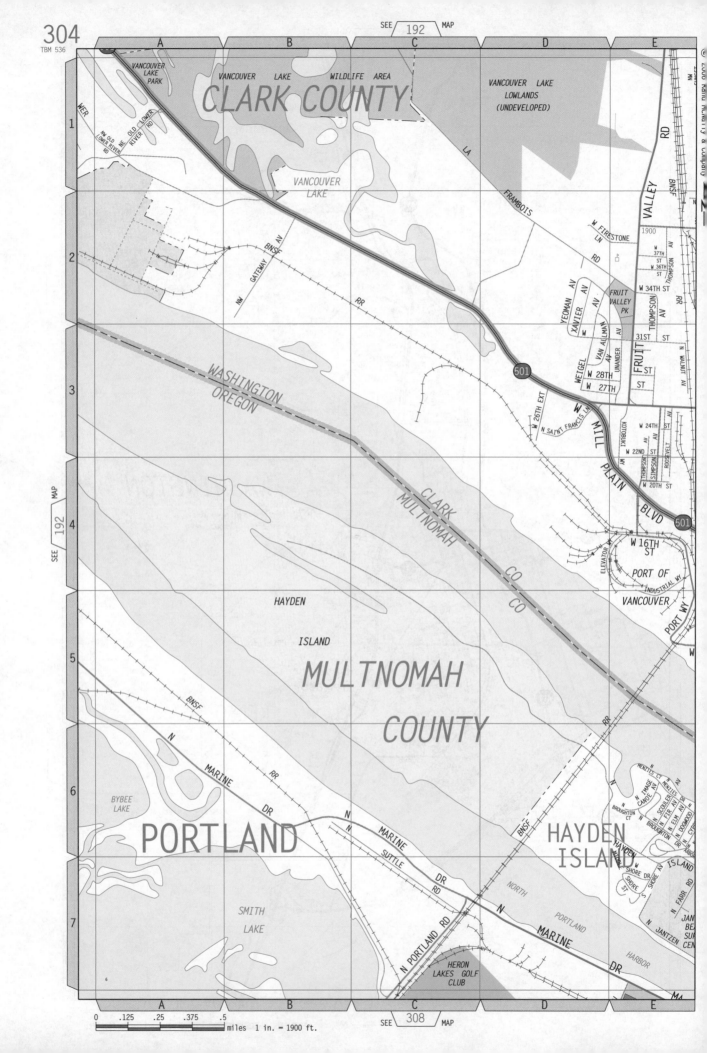

SEE 192 MAP

A   B   C   D   E

VANCOUVER
LAKE
PARK

VANCOUVER   LAKE   WILDLIFE   AREA

CLARK COUNTY

VANCOUVER LAKE
LOWLANDS
(UNDEVELOPED)

VANCOUVER
LAKE

1900

W FIRESTONE LN

W 37TH ST
W 36TH ST
W 34TH ST

FRUIT
VALLEY
PK

NW GATEWAY AV
BNSF AV

NW RR

W 31ST ST

W 28TH ST
W 27TH ST

WASHINGTON
OREGON

501

W 26TH EXT

N SAINT FRANCIS LN

W 24TH AV
W 22ND AV
W 20TH

SEE 192 MAP

CLARK
MULTNOMAH
CO
CO

HAYDEN

ISLAND

ELEVATOR W
W 16TH ST

PORT OF
VANCOUVER

INDUSTRIAL WY

PORT WY

MULTNOMAH

COUNTY

BYBEE
LAKE

N MARINE DR
BNSF RR

N
MARINE
DR

PORTLAND

N SUTTLE RD

N MARINE DR

BNSF

RR

HAYDEN

HAYDEN
ISLAND

N MENZIES CT
N MENZIES DR
N SCOULER
N IMAGE AV
N CANOE AV
N BROUGHTON CT
N FIR AV
N BROUGHTON DR
N ELM AV
N DOGWOOD
N CYPRESS

SHORE DR
SHORE ST
SHORE DR

ISLAND

N FARR RD

SMITH
LAKE

NORTH

N PORTLAND RD

N
MARINE
DR

PORTLAND

JAN
BEA
SUN
CEN

N JANTZEN AV

HARBOR

HERON
LAKES GOLF
CLUB

A   B   C   D   E

SEE 308 MAP

0 .125 .25 .375 .5
miles 1 in. = 1900 ft.

DETAIL

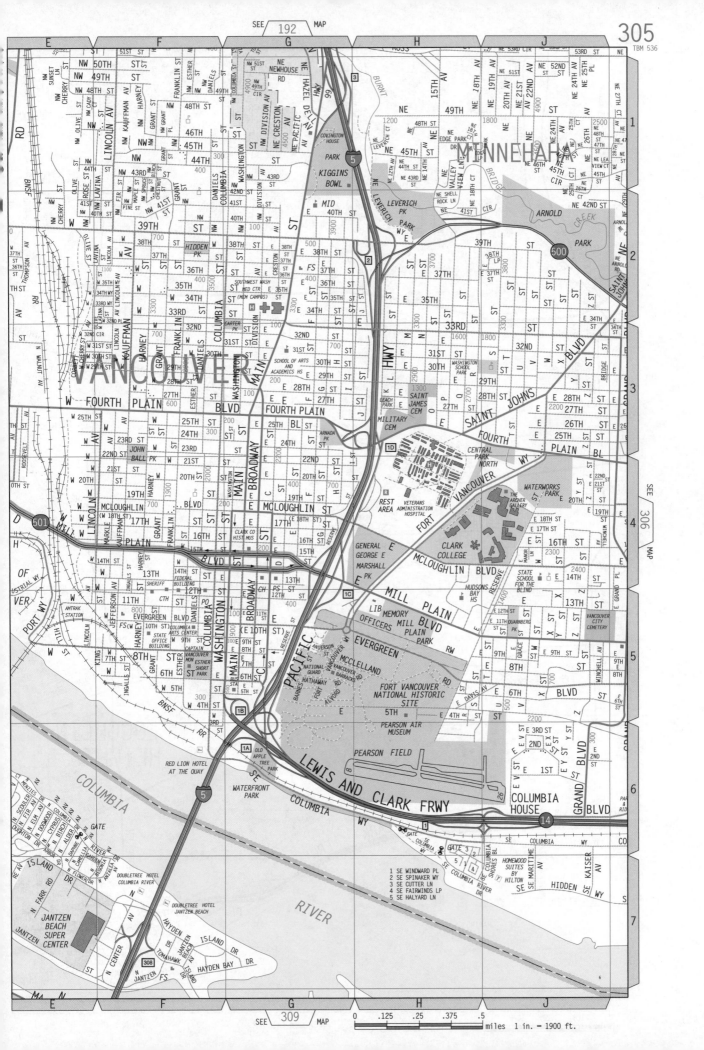

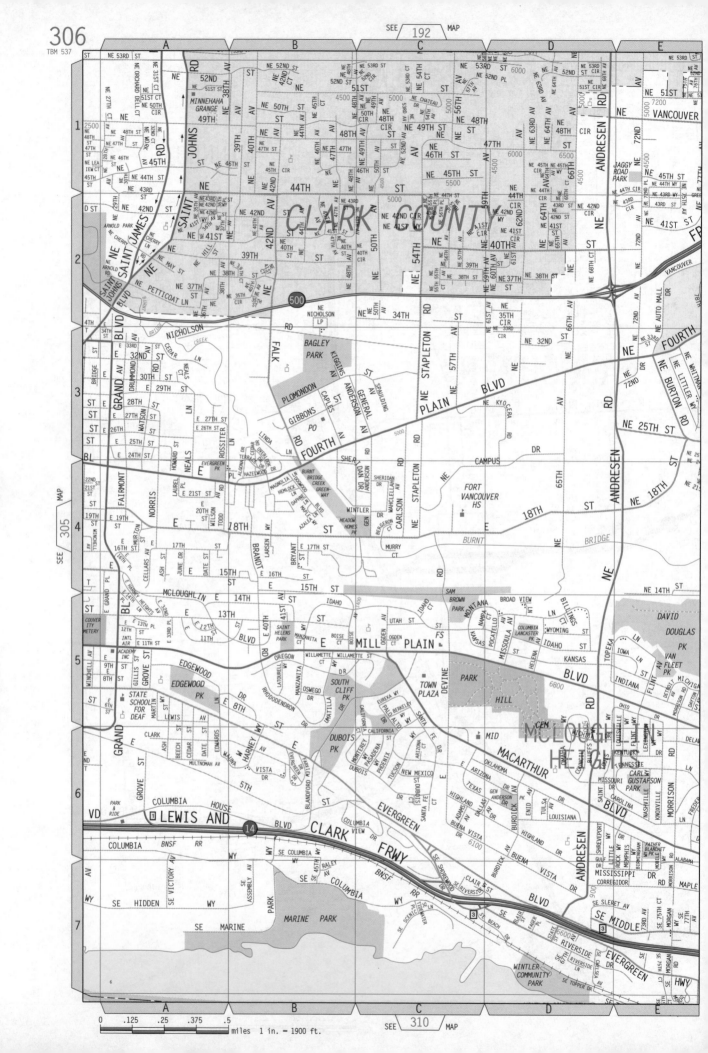

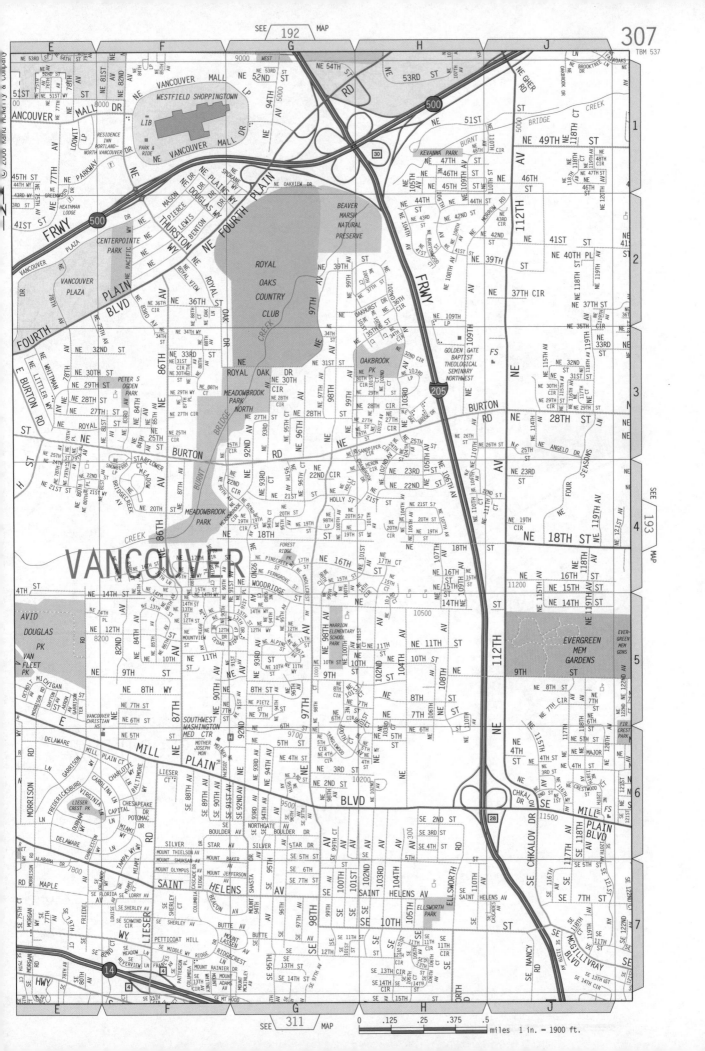

VANCOUVER

0   .125   .25   .375   .5
miles   1 in. = 1900 ft.

DETAIL

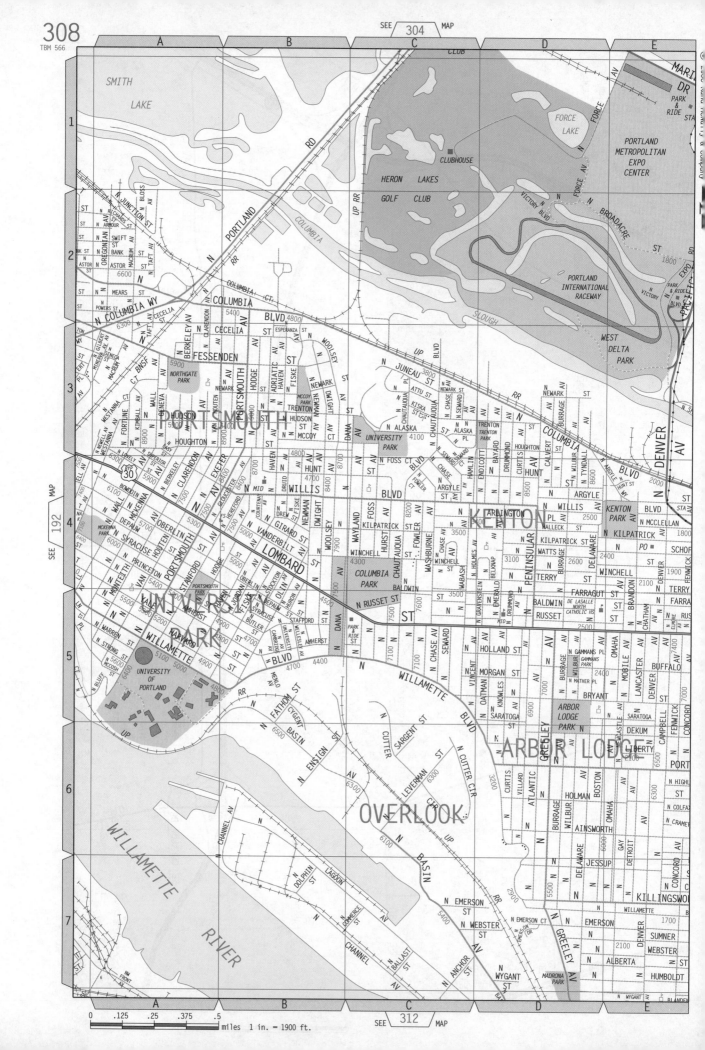

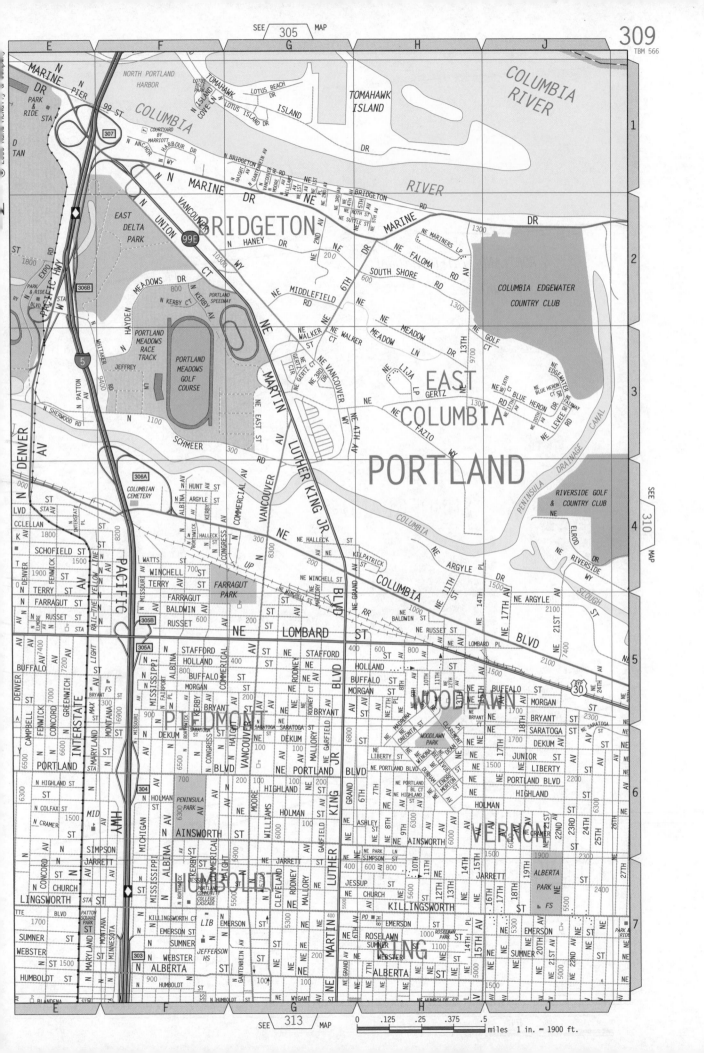

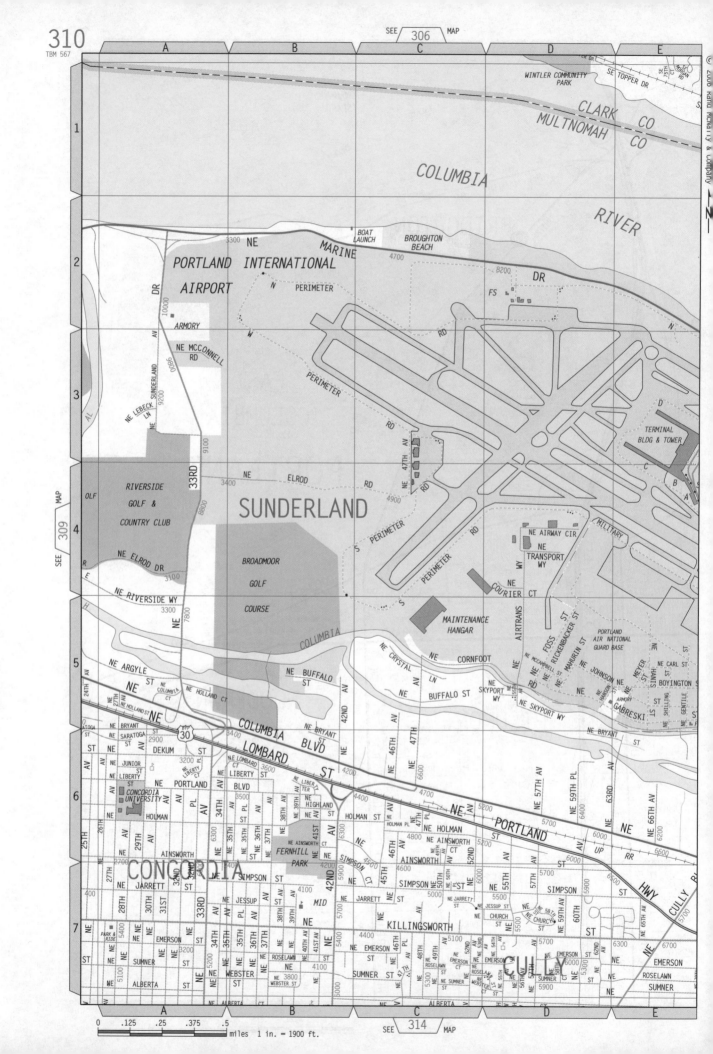

310
TBM 567

SEE 306 MAP
SEE 309 MAP
SEE 314 MAP

0 .125 .25 .375 .5
miles 1 in. = 1900 ft.

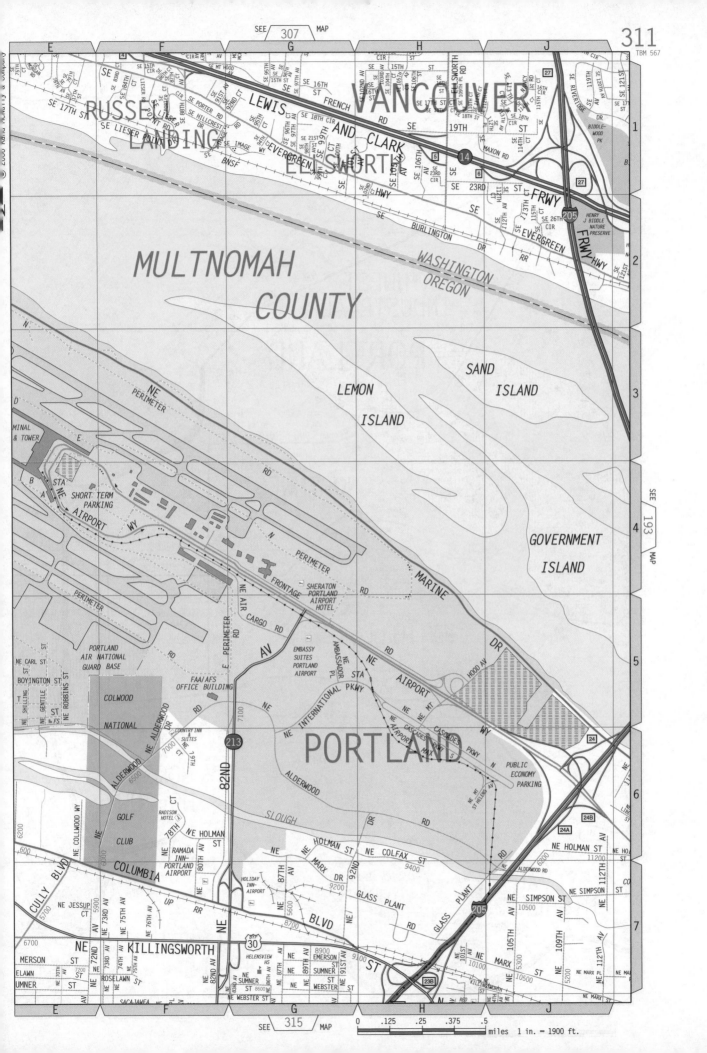

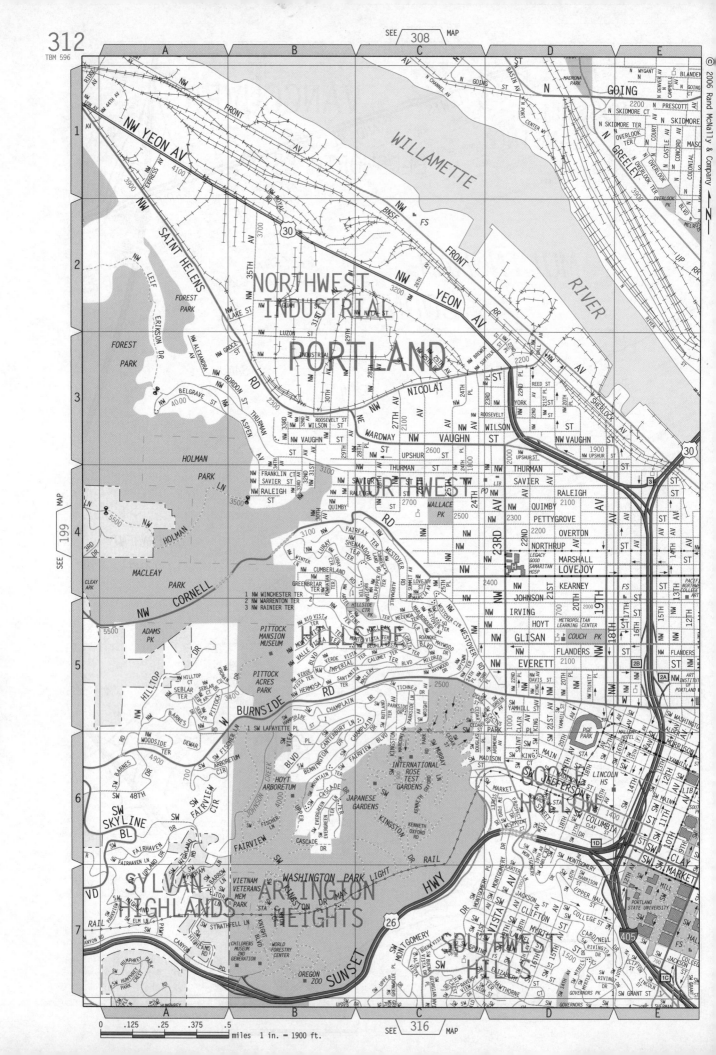

© 2006 Rand McNally & Company

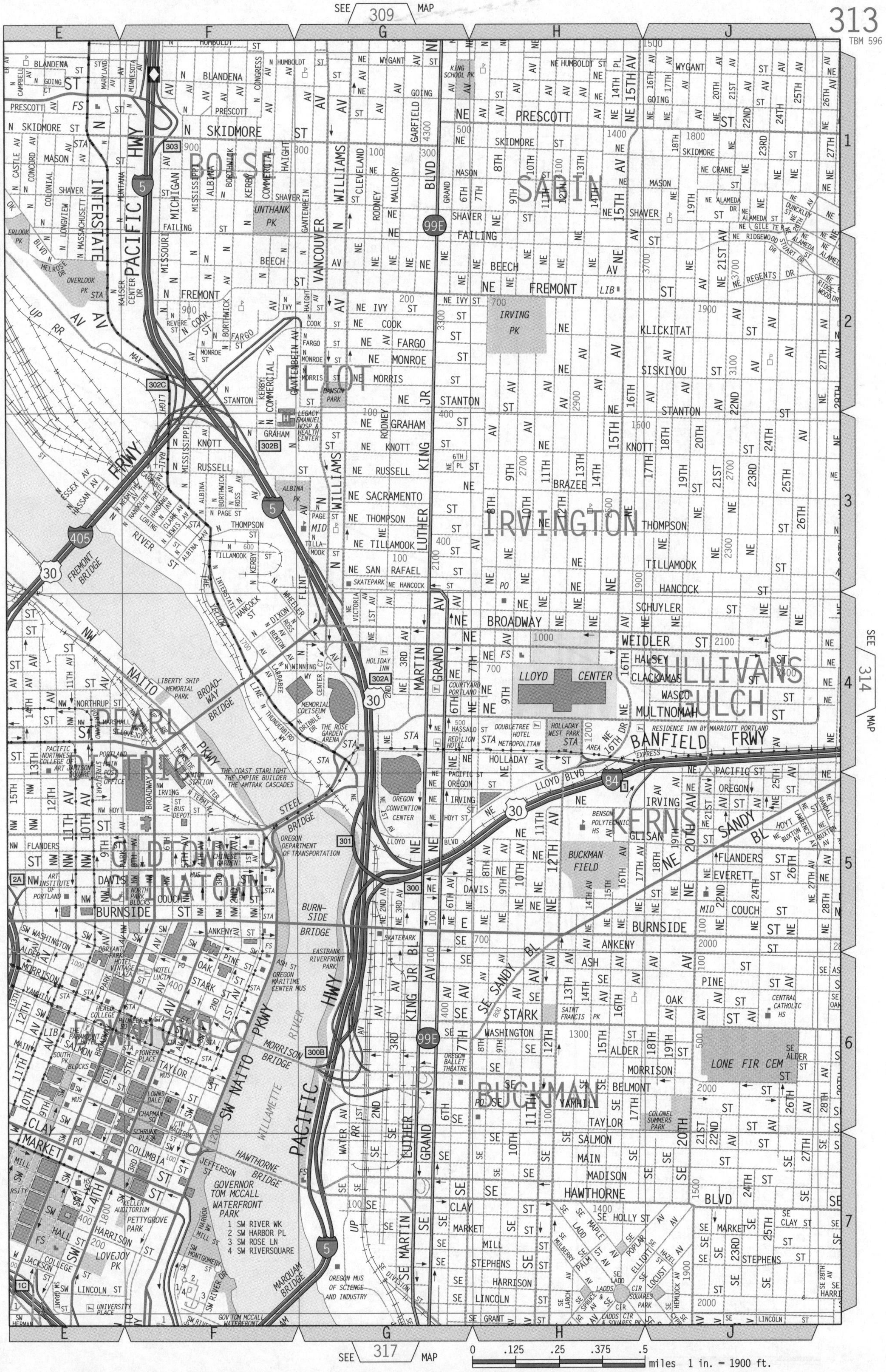

E F G H J

BOISE

ELIOT

SABIN

IRVINGTON

KERNS

BUCKMAN

SULLIVANS GULCH

DOWNTOWN

OLD TOWN / CHINATOWN

PEARL DISTRICT

INTERSTATE

PACIFIC HWY

FREMONT BRIDGE

BROADWAY BRIDGE

STEEL BRIDGE

BURNSIDE BRIDGE

MORRISON BRIDGE

HAWTHORNE BRIDGE

MARQUAM BRIDGE

BANFIELD FRWY

LLOYD CENTER

MEMORIAL COLISEUM

THE ROSE GARDEN ARENA

OREGON CONVENTION CENTER

LONE FIR CEM

IRVING PK

UNTHANK PK

KING SCHOOL PK

LEGACY EMANUEL HOSP & HEALTH CENTER

OREGON MUSEUM OF SCIENCE AND INDUSTRY

GOVERNOR TOM McCALL WATERFRONT PARK

WILLAMETTE RIVER

1 2 3 4 5 6 7

SEE 314 MAP

0 .125 .25 .375 .5 miles   1 in. = 1900 ft.

DETAIL

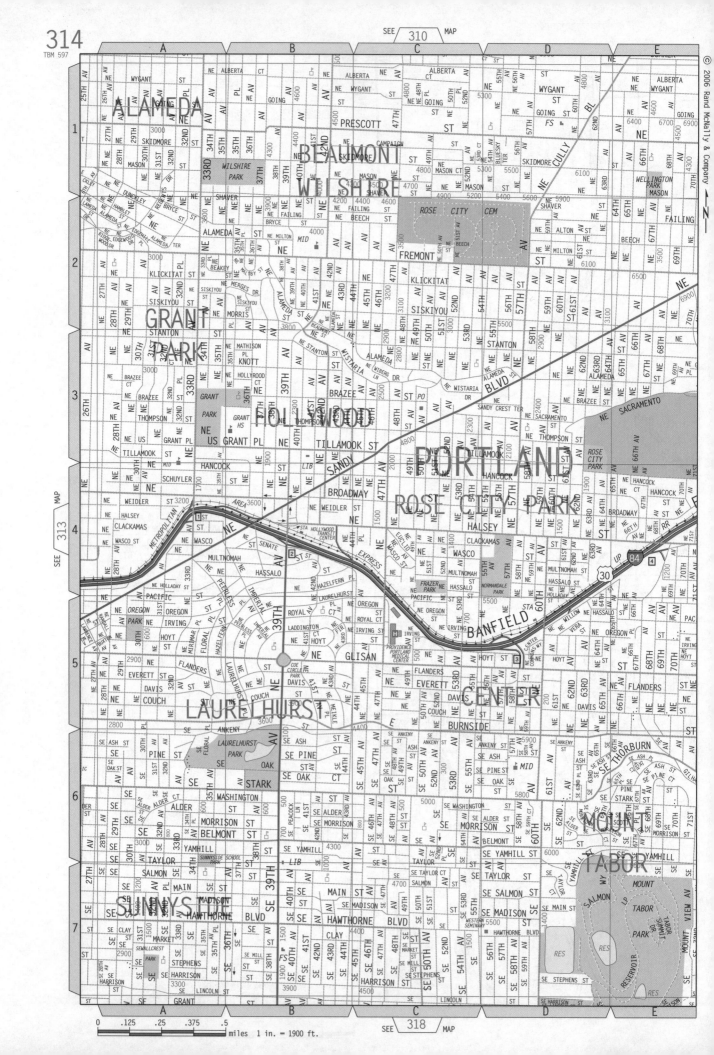

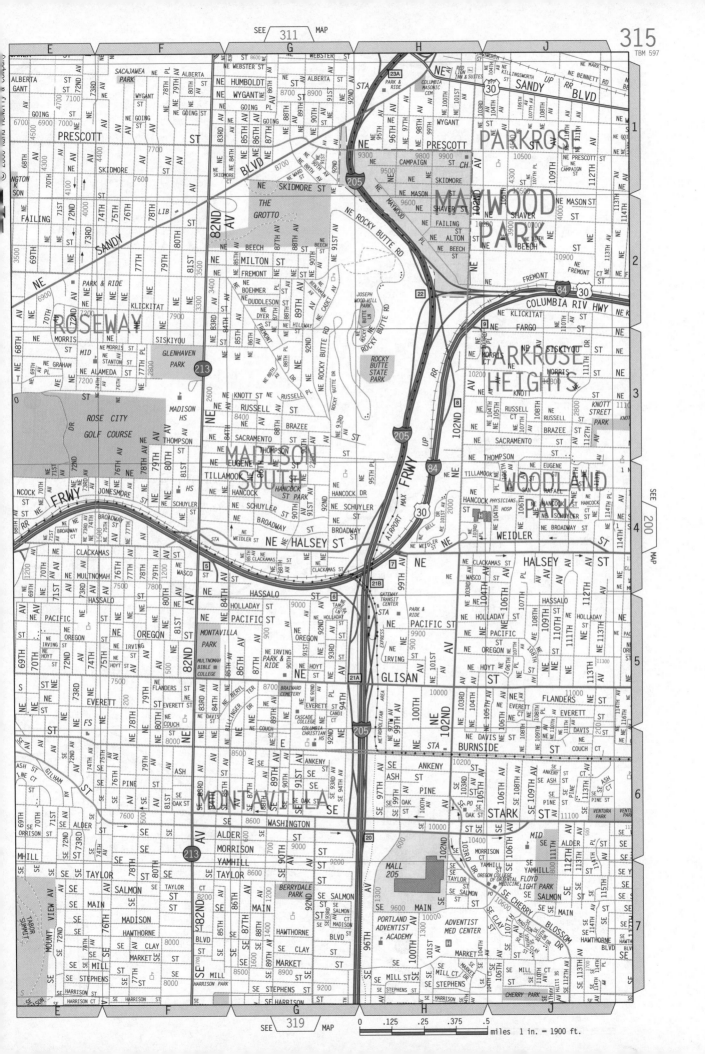

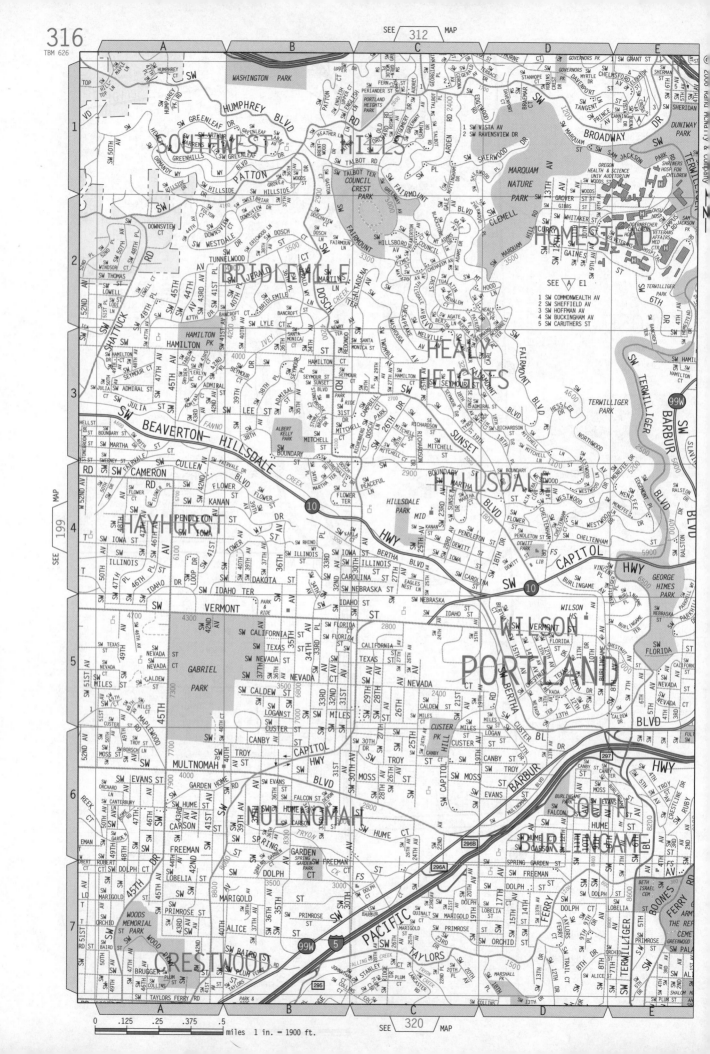

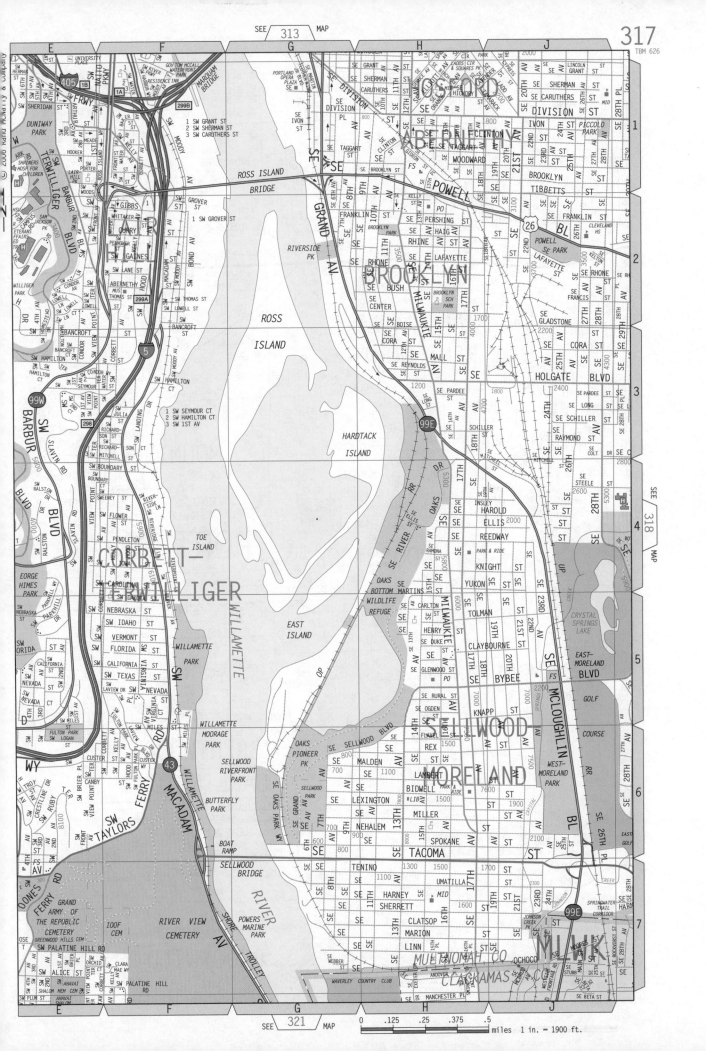

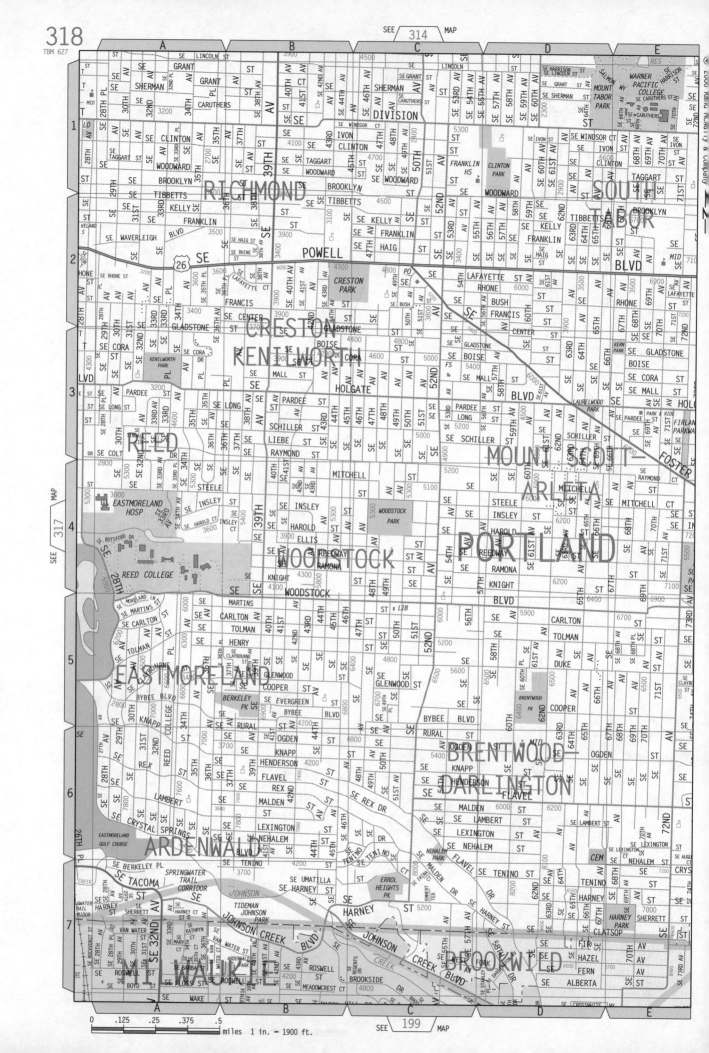

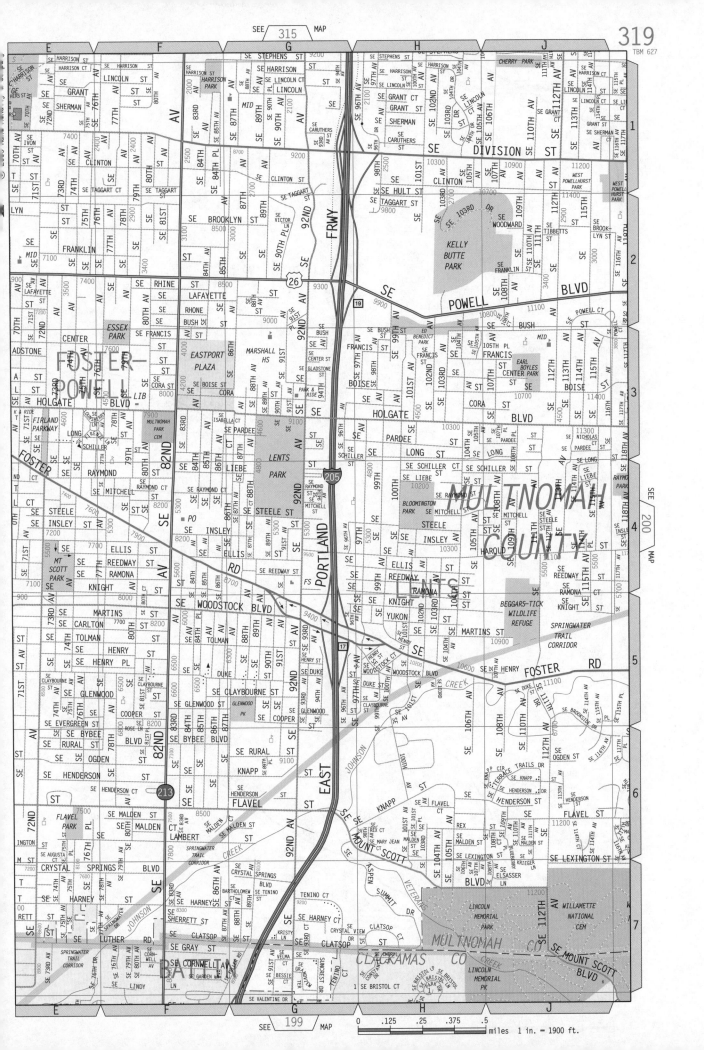

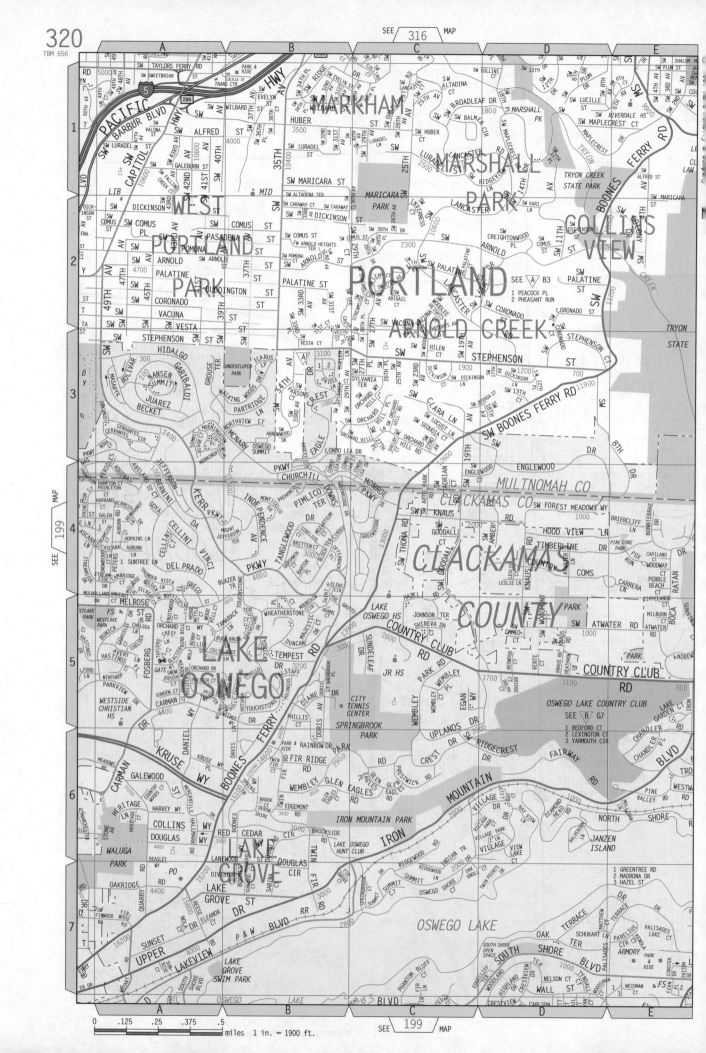

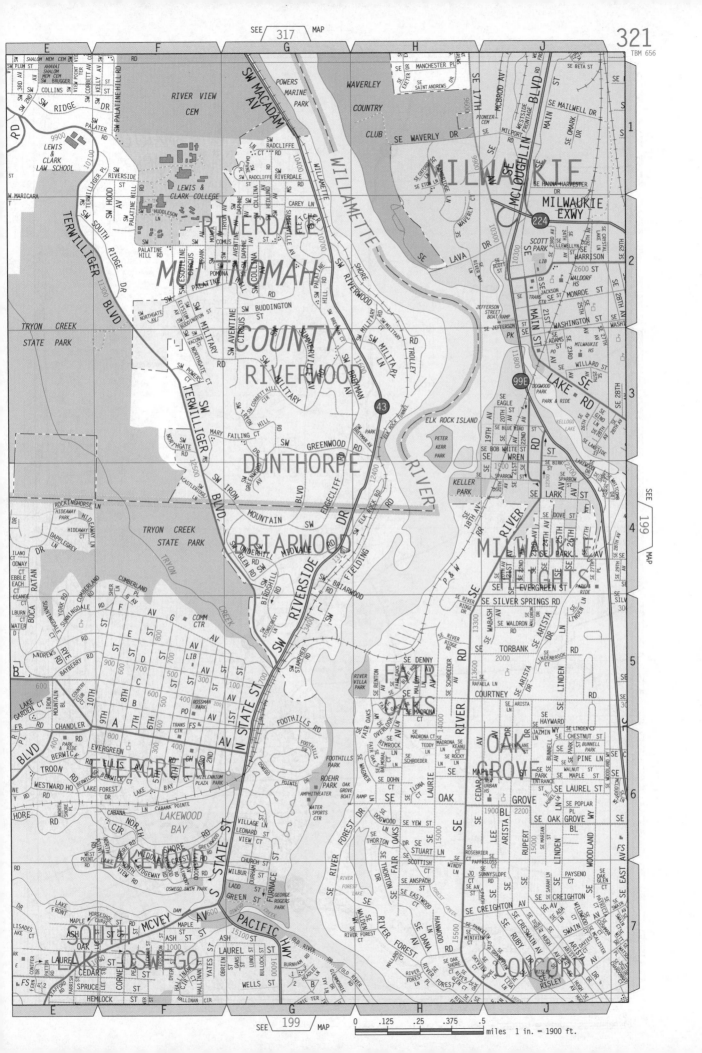

SEE 317 MAP

SEE 199 MAP

DETAIL

SEE 199 MAP

0   .125   .25   .375   .5
miles   1 in. = 1900 ft.

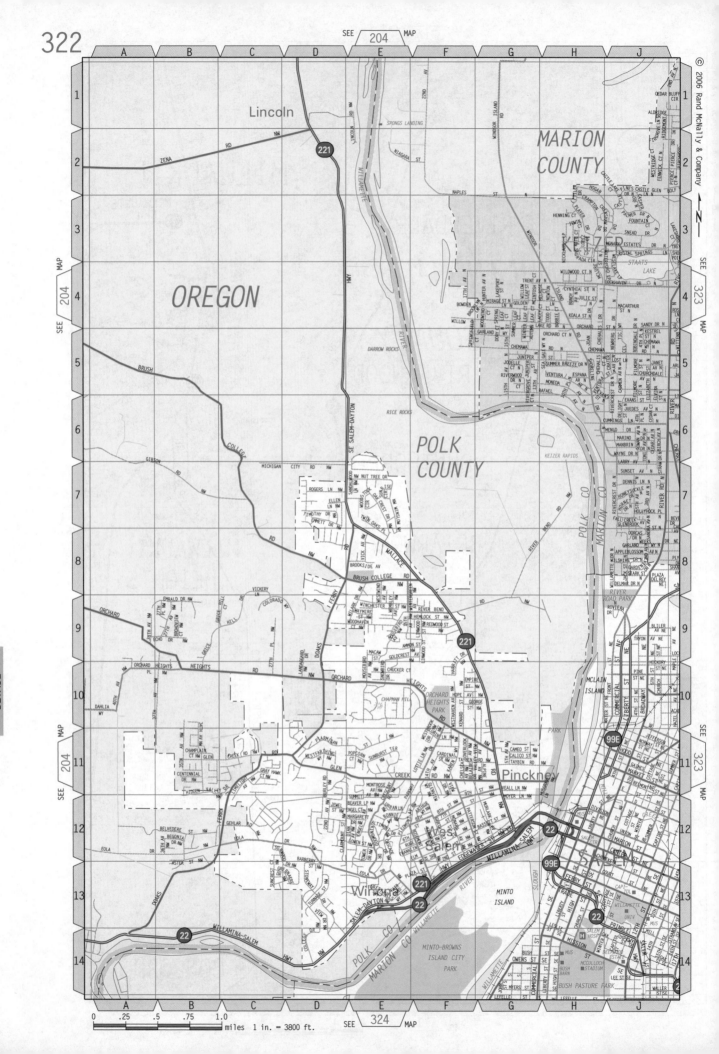

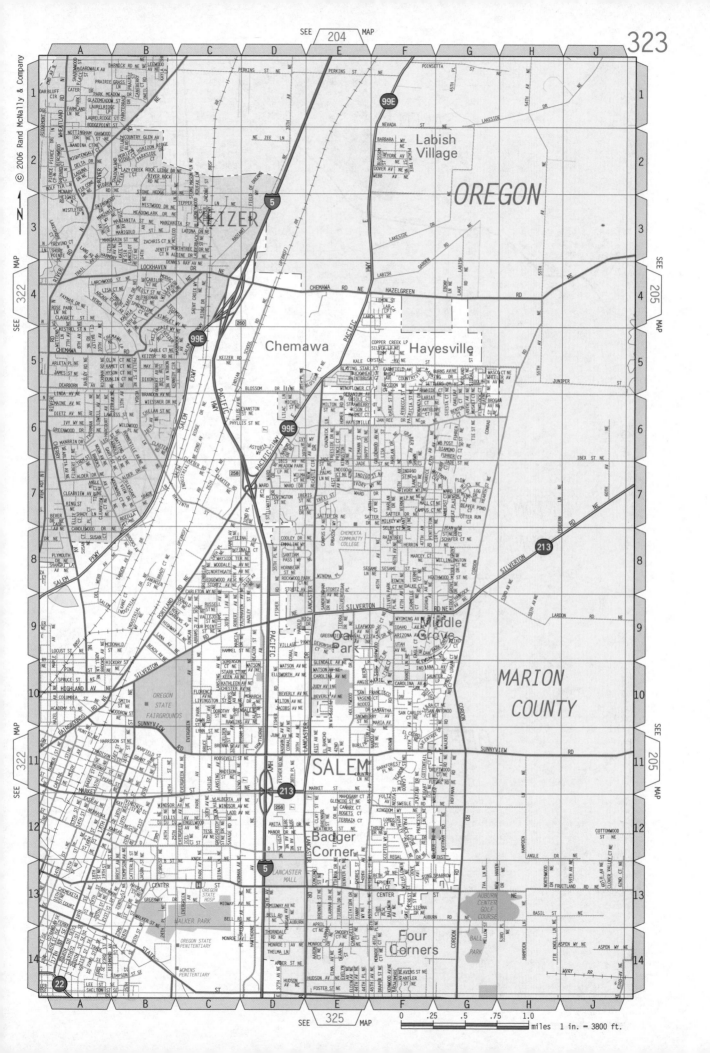

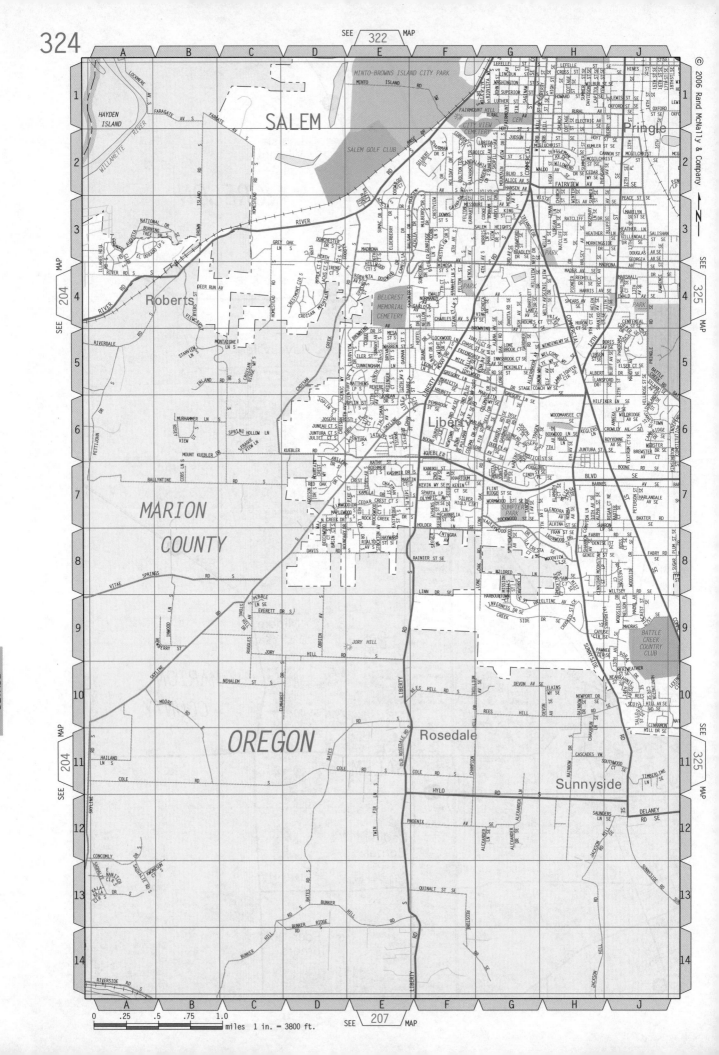

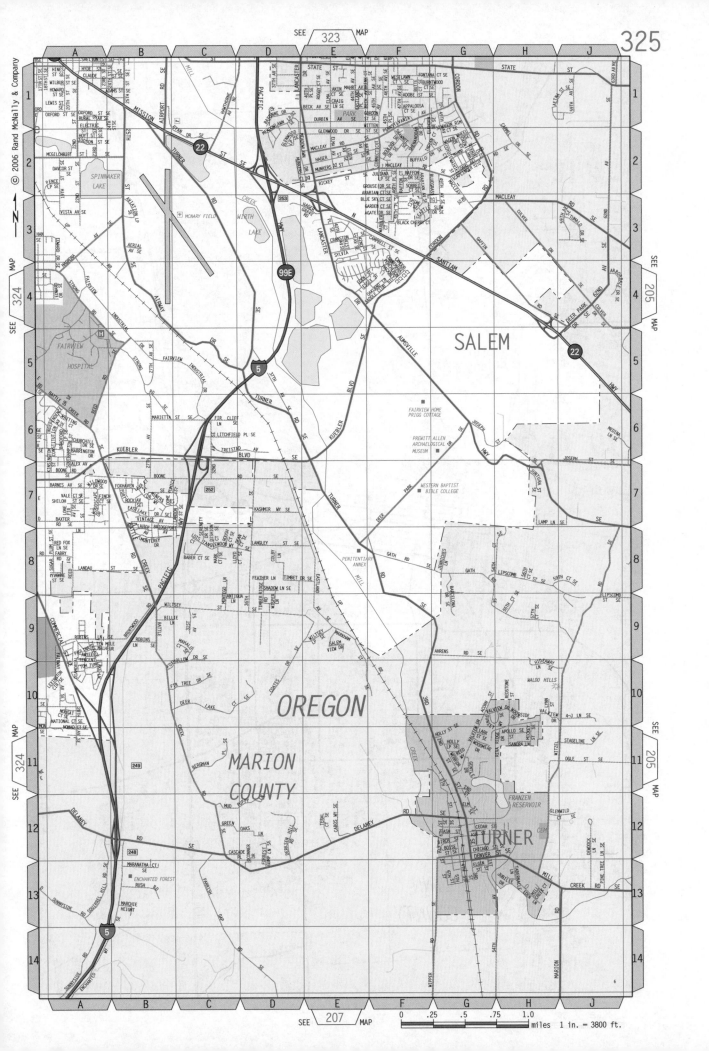

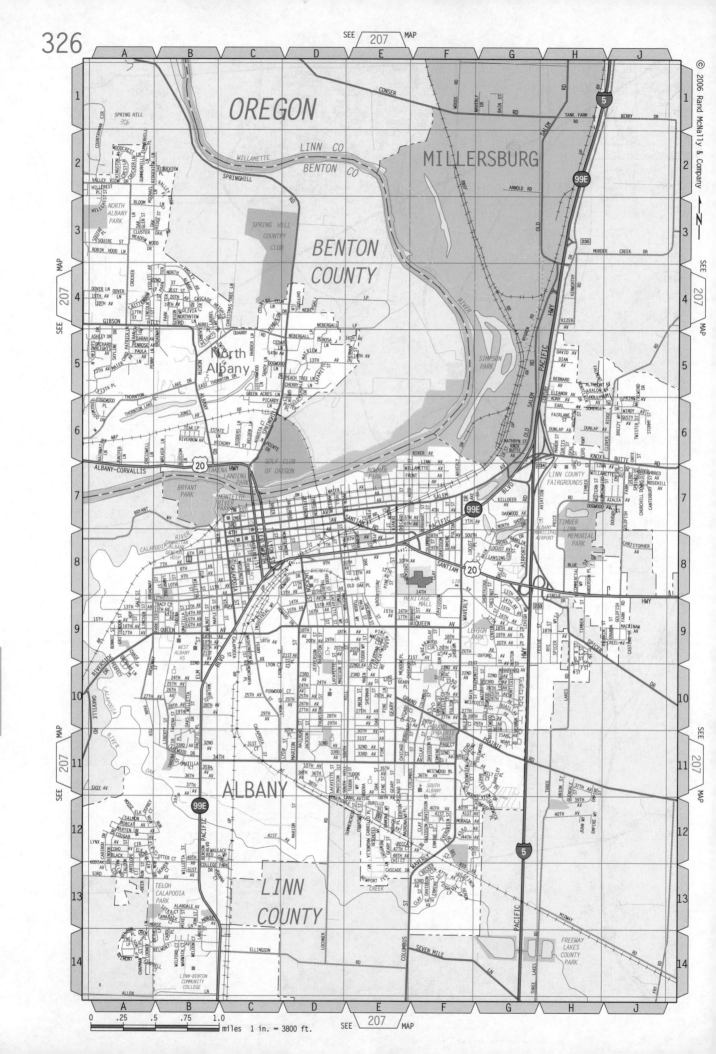

OREGON

MILLERSBURG

BENTON COUNTY

North Albany

ALBANY

LINN COUNTY

DETAIL

0   .25   .5   .75   1.0
miles 1 in. = 3800 ft.

SEE 207 MAP

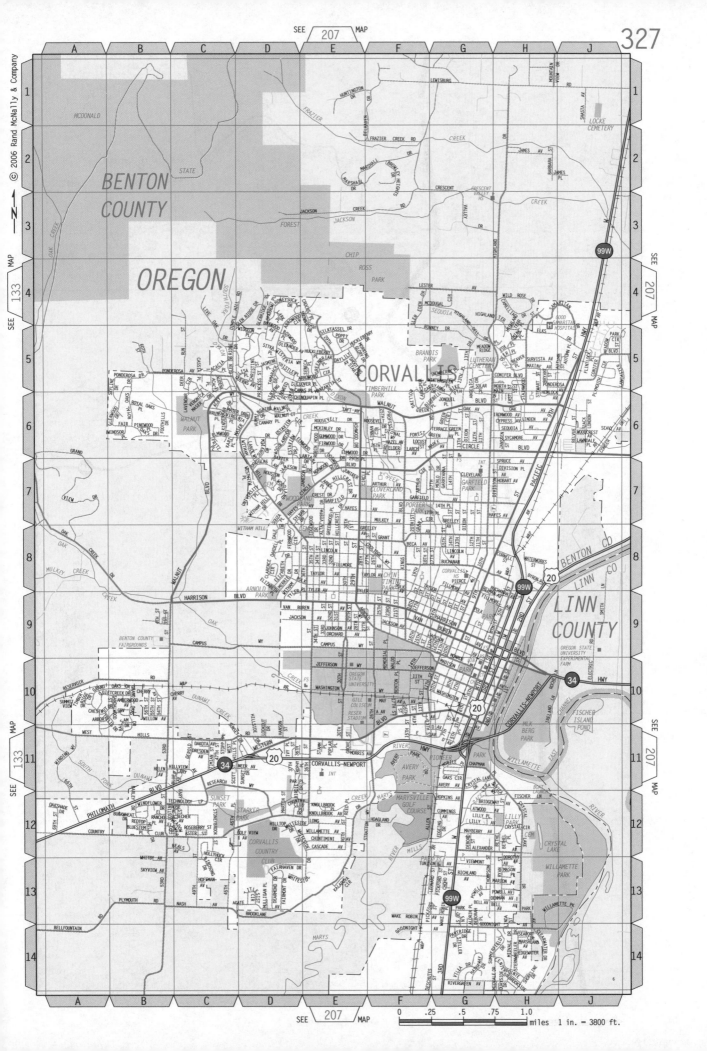

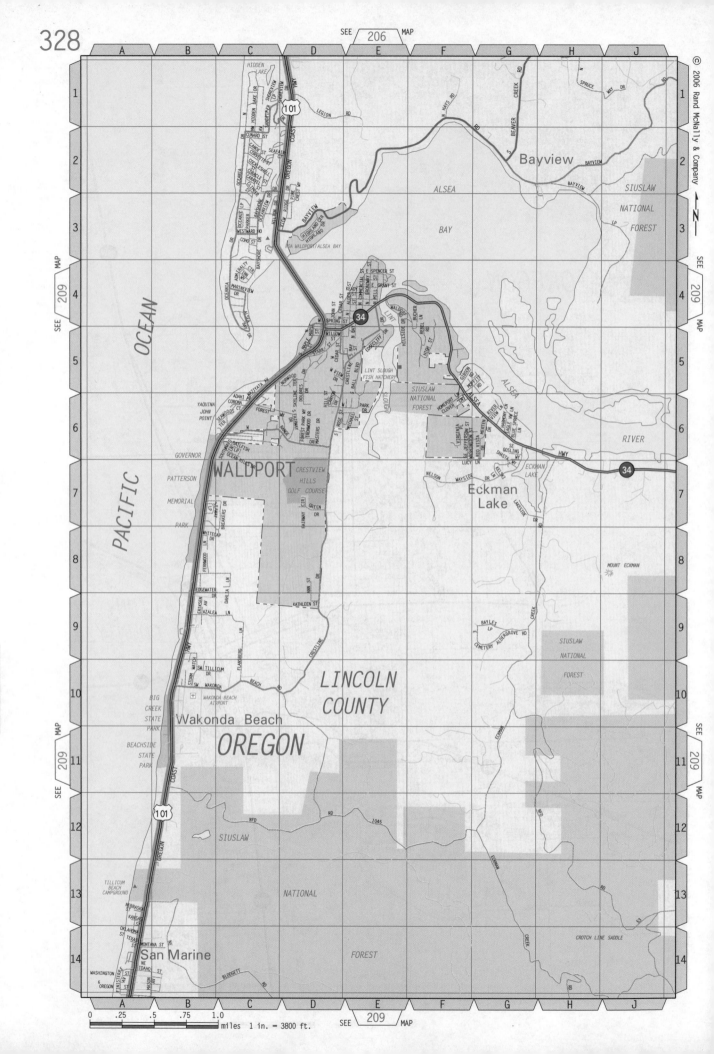

SEE 206 MAP

© 2006 Rand McNally & Company

DETAIL

PACIFIC OCEAN

Bayview

ALSEA BAY

SIUSLAW NATIONAL FOREST

WALDPORT

CRESTVIEW HILLS GOLF COURSE

LINT SLOUGH FISH HATCHERY

SIUSLAW NATIONAL FOREST

ALSEA RIVER

Eckman Lake

MOUNT ECKMAN

GOVERNOR PATTERSON MEMORIAL PARK

YAQUINA JOHN POINT

SIUSLAW NATIONAL FOREST

LINCOLN COUNTY

OREGON

BIG CREEK STATE PARK

Wakonda Beach

WAKONDA BEACH AIRPORT

BEACHSIDE STATE PARK

SIUSLAW

NATIONAL

FOREST

TILLICUM BEACH CAMPGROUND

CROTCH LINE SADDLE

San Marine

SEE 209 MAP

SEE 209 MAP

SEE 209 MAP

0   .25   .5   .75   1.0
miles 1 in. = 3800 ft.

SEE 209 MAP

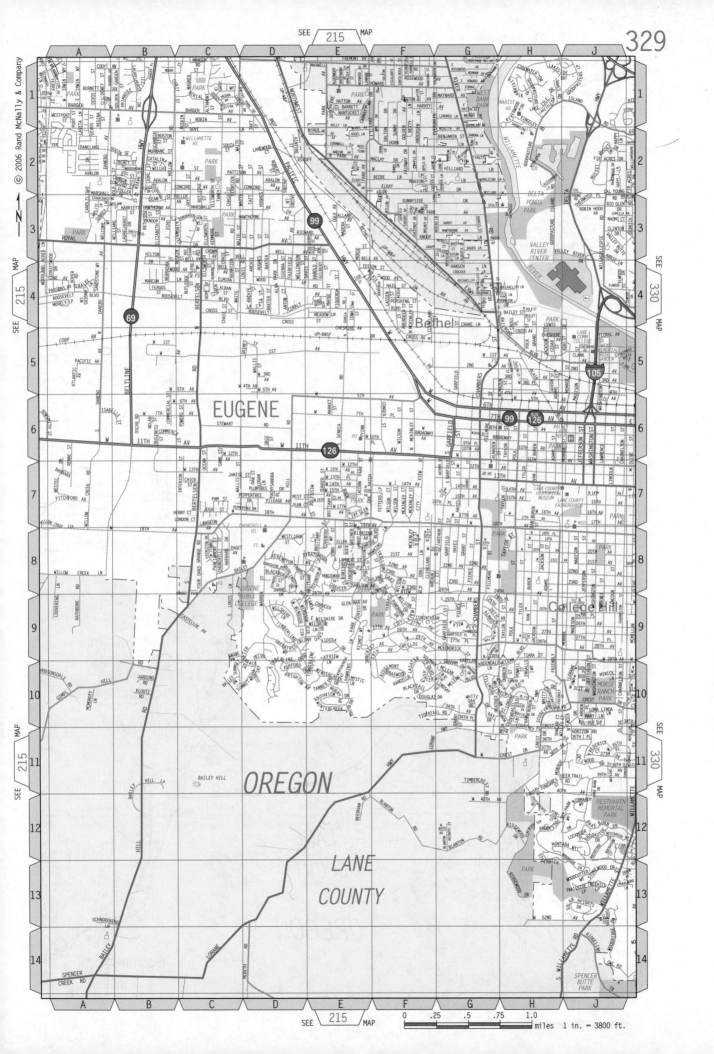

DETAIL

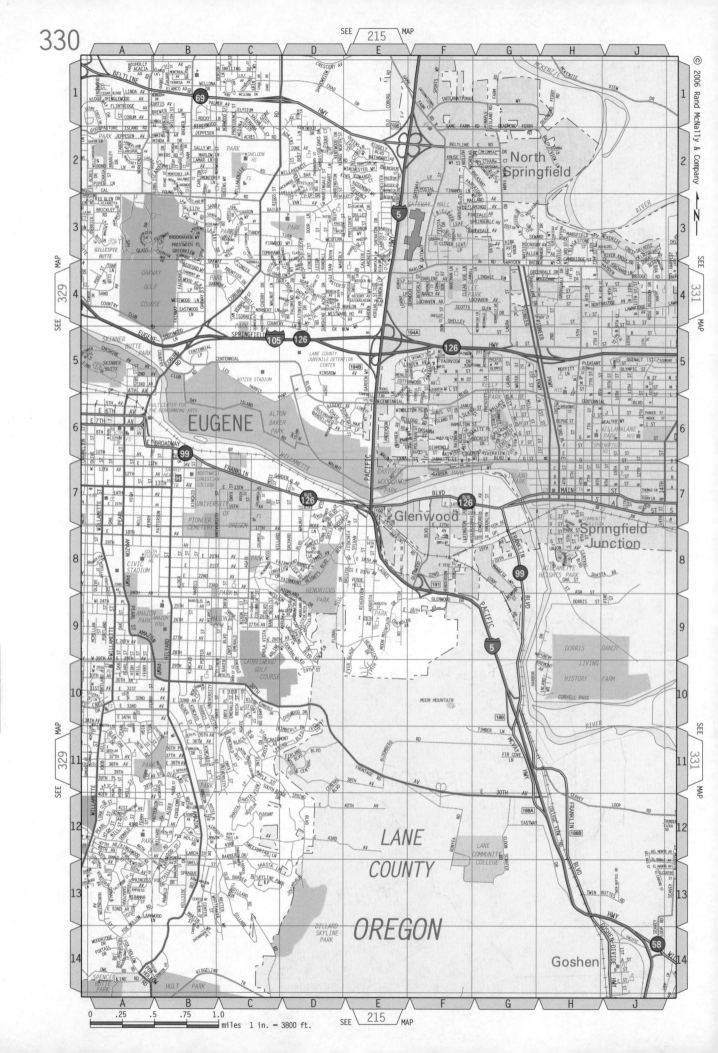

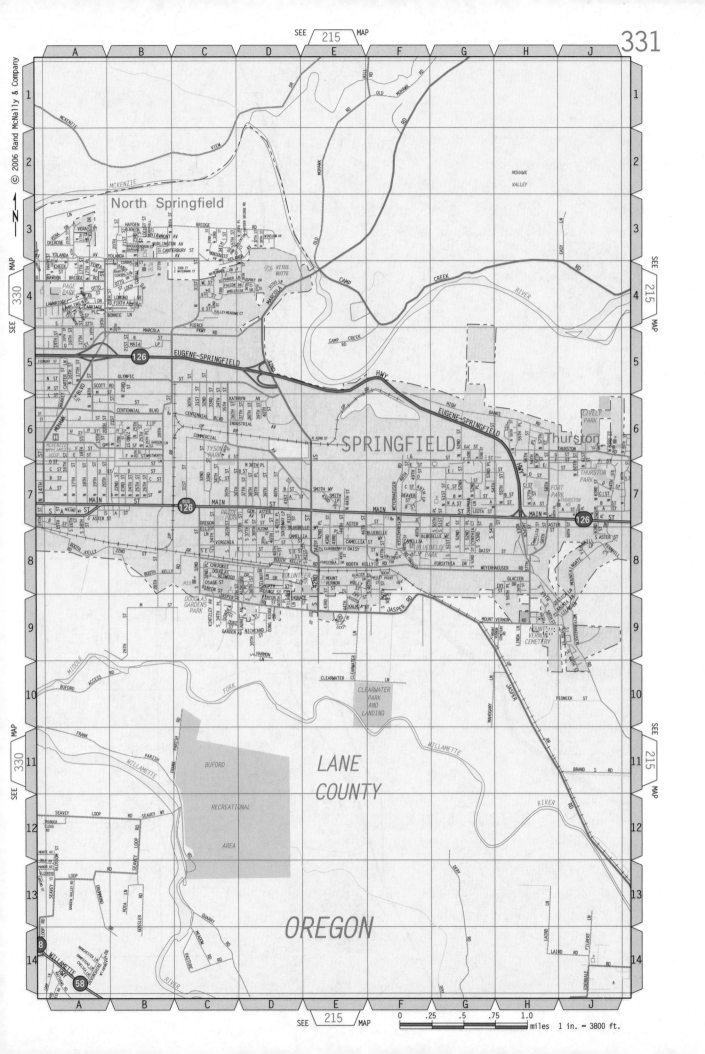

DETAIL

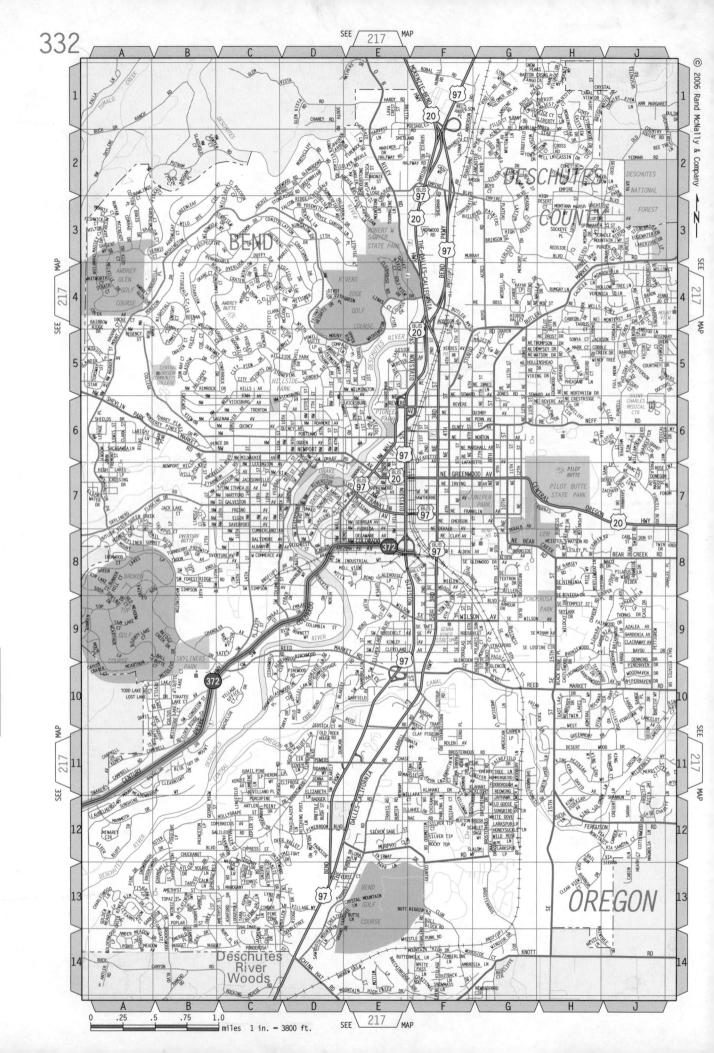

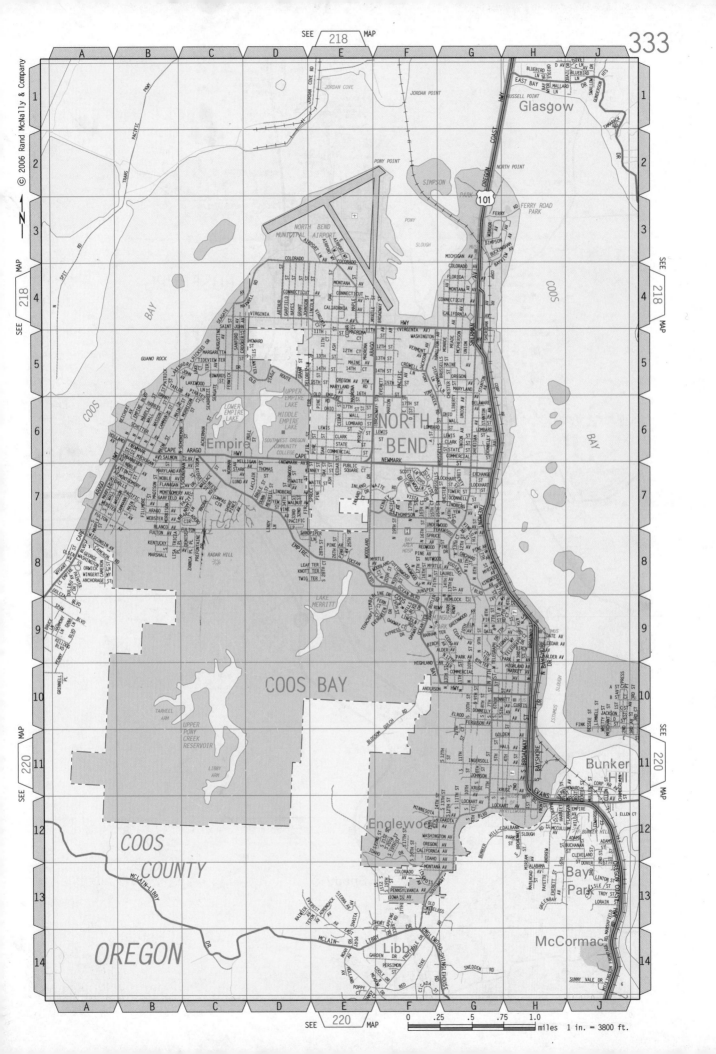

DETAIL

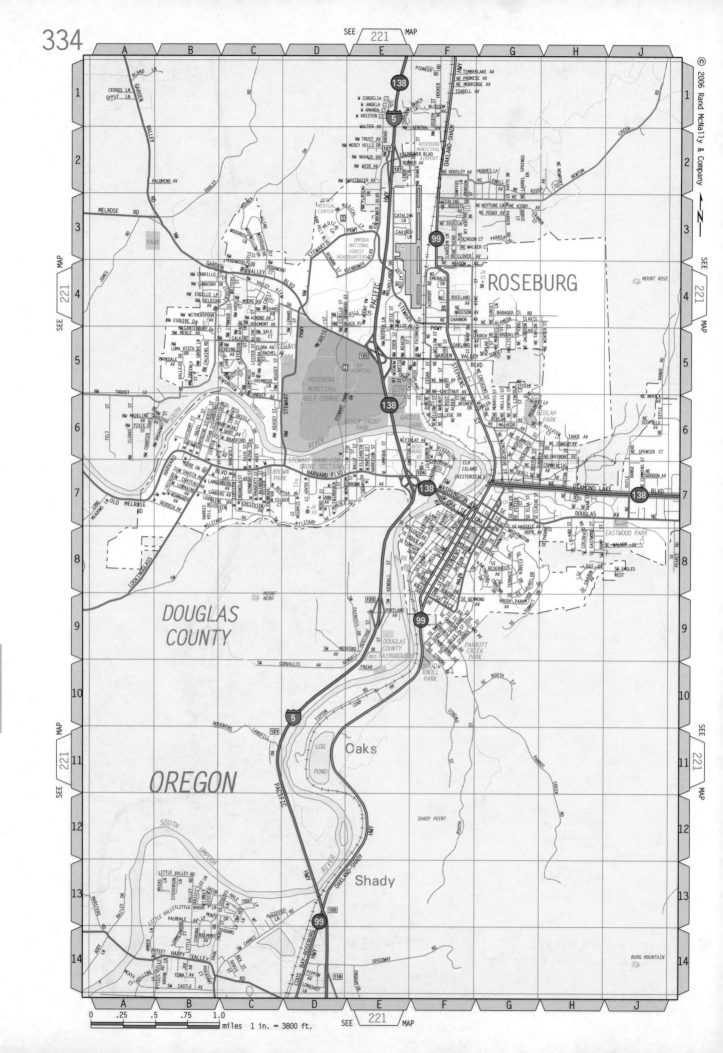

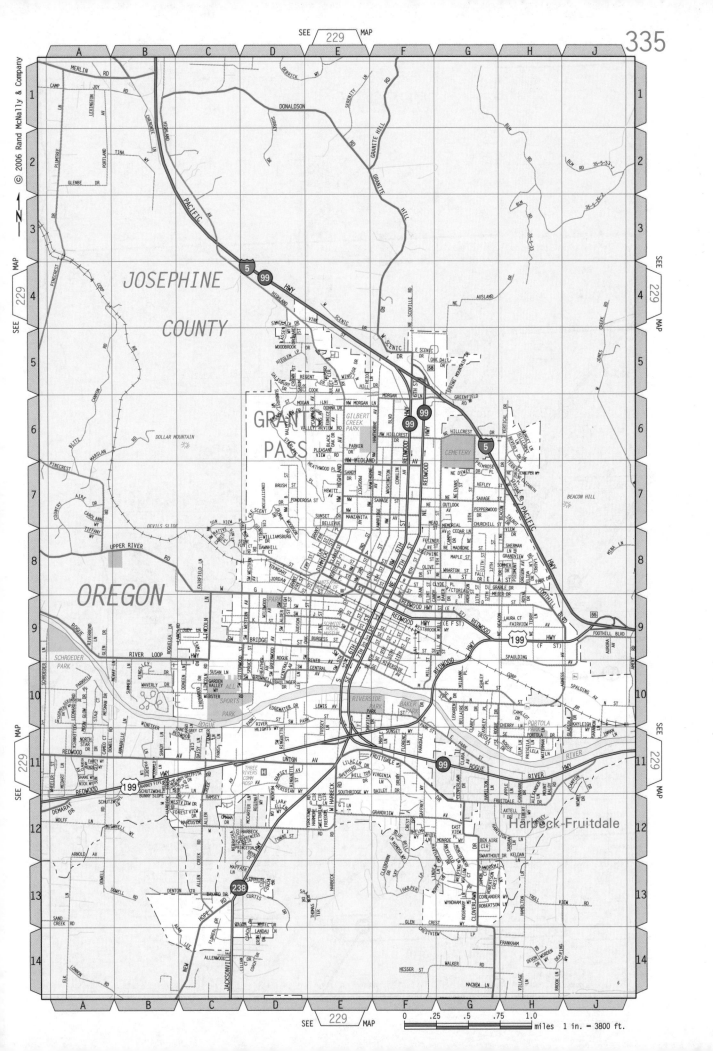

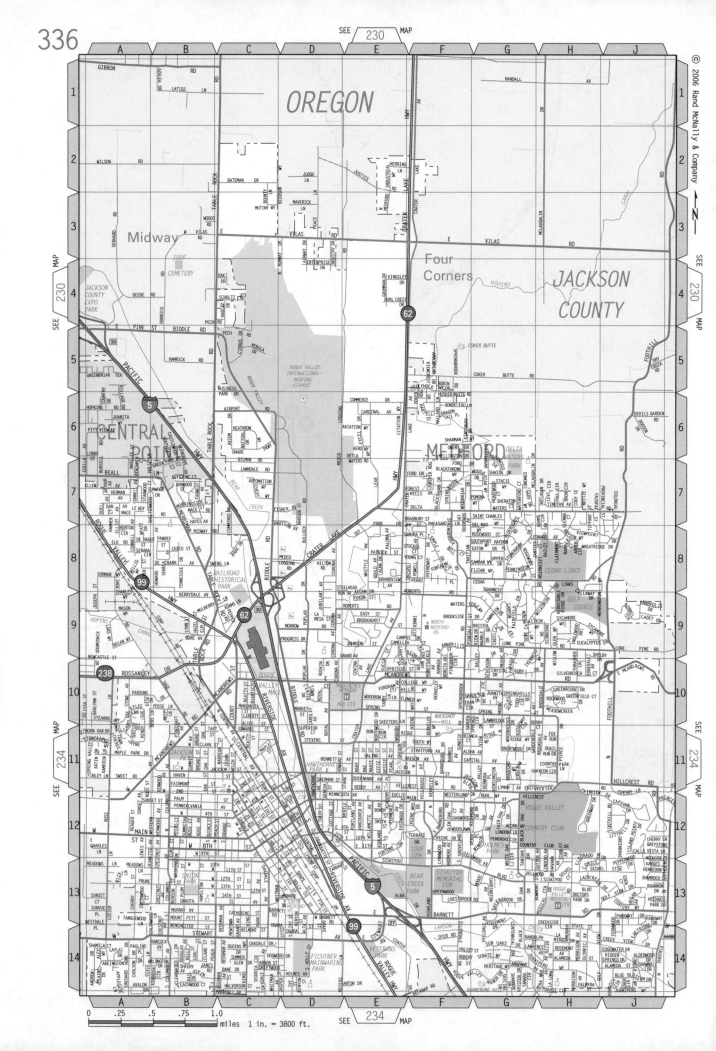

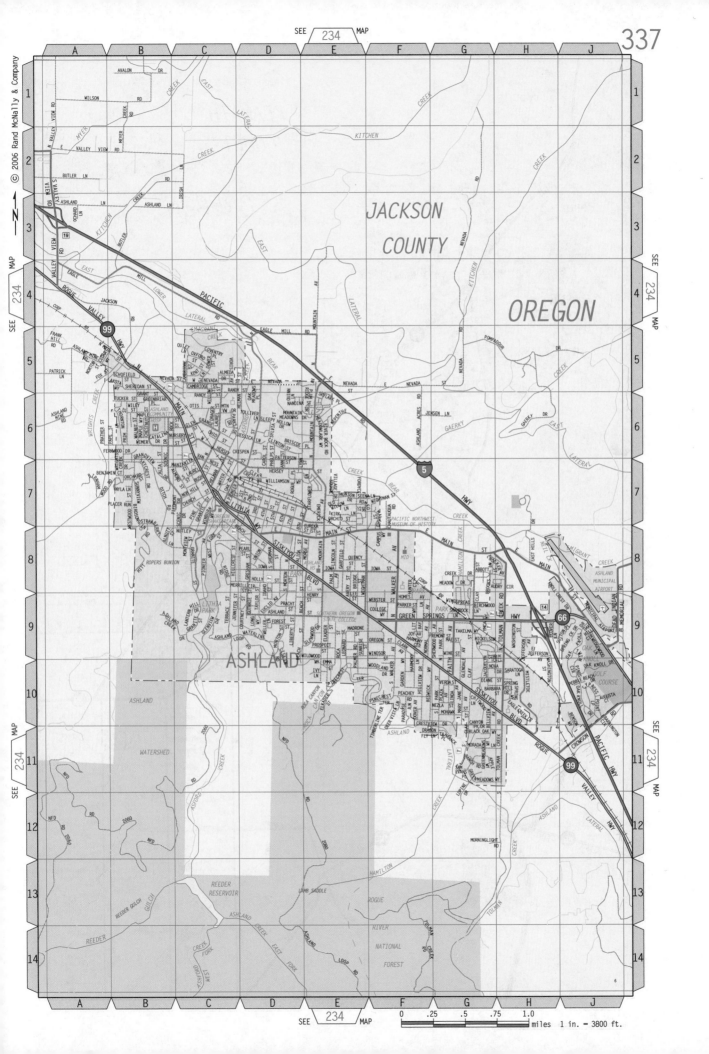

© 2006 Rand McNally & Company

SEE 234 MAP

A   B   C   D   E   F   G   H   J

JACKSON

COUNTY

OREGON

ASHLAND

DETAIL

SEE 234 MAP

SEE 234 MAP

SEE 234 MAP

SEE 234 MAP

0   .25   .5   .75   1.0
miles 1 in. = 3800 ft.

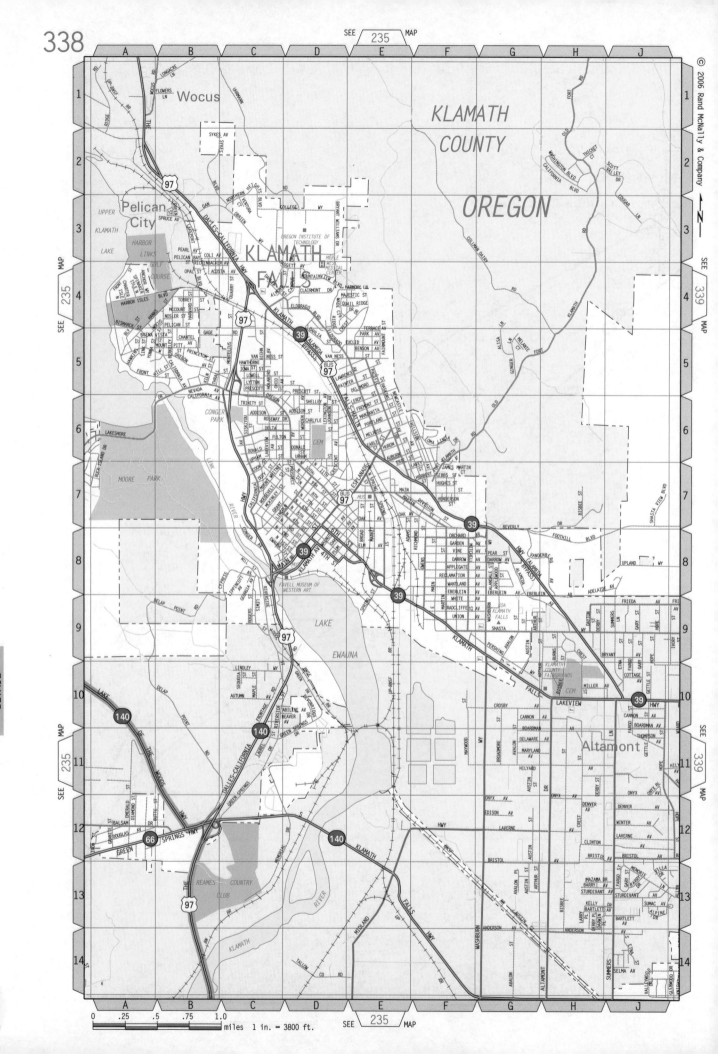

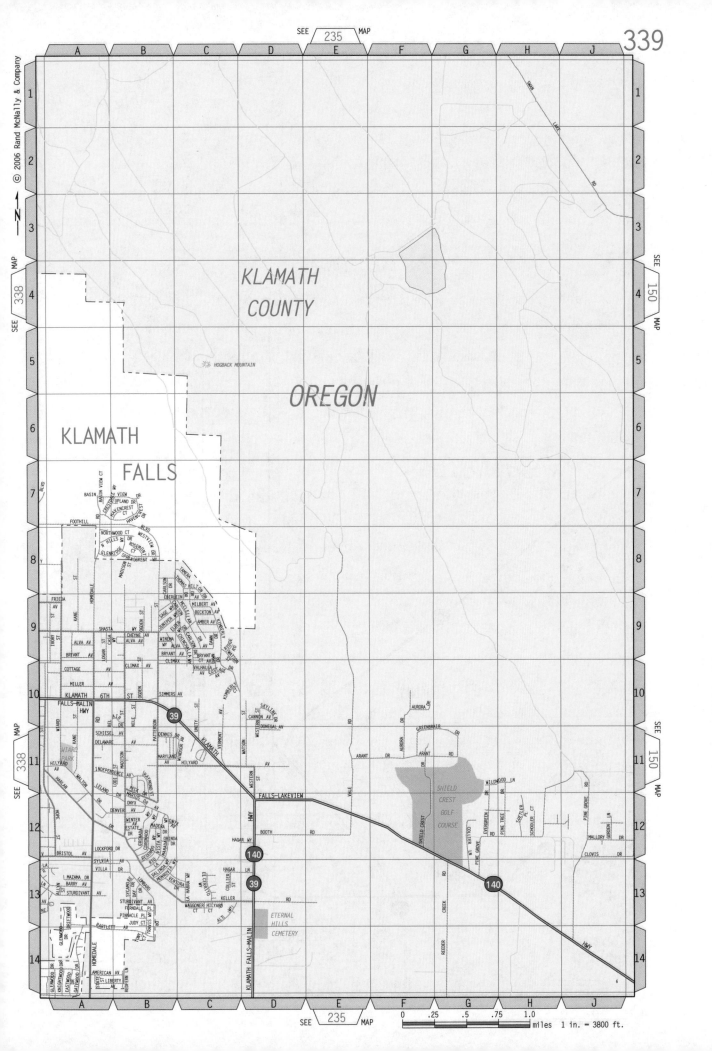

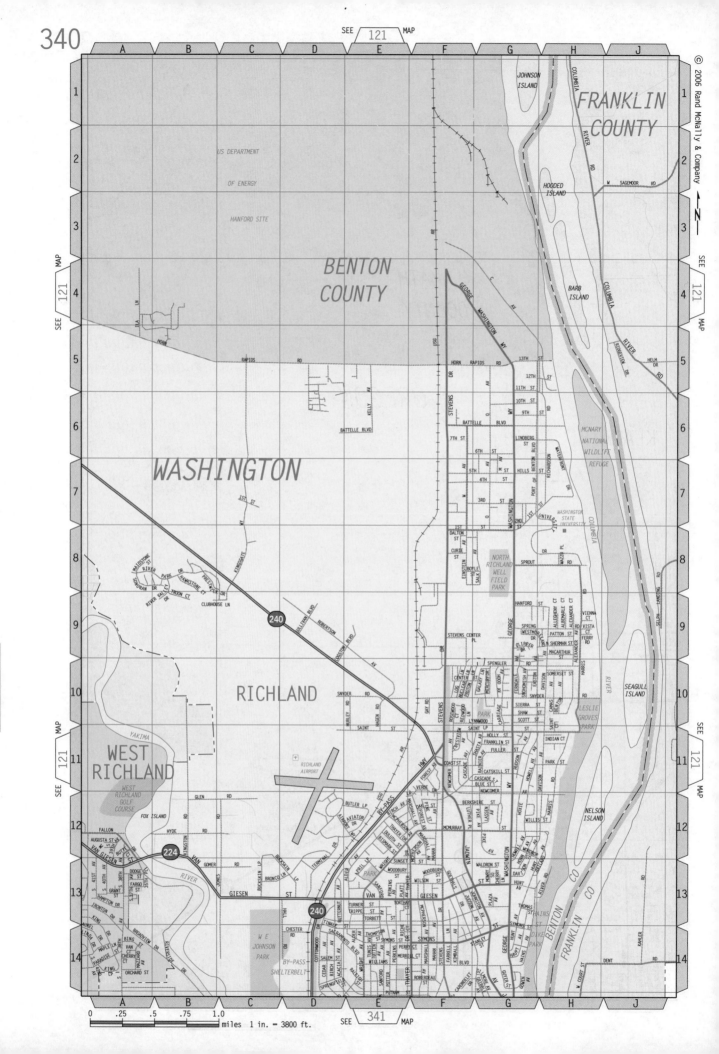

SEE 121 MAP

SEE 121 MAP

SEE 121 MAP

SEE 121 MAP

SEE 121 MAP

SEE 341 MAP

DETAIL

FRANKLIN COUNTY

BENTON COUNTY

US DEPARTMENT OF ENERGY

HANFORD SITE

WASHINGTON

RICHLAND

WEST RICHLAND

WEST RICHLAND GOLF COURSE

YAKIMA

JOHNSON ISLAND

HOODED ISLAND

BARB ISLAND

MCNARY NATIONAL WILDLIFE REFUGE

SEAGULL ISLAND

LESLIE GROVES PARK

NELSON ISLAND

WASHINGTON STATE UNIVERSITY

NORTH RICHLAND WELL FIELD PARK

RICHLAND AIRPORT

W E JOHNSON PARK

0   .25   .5   .75   1.0
miles   1 in. = 3800 ft.

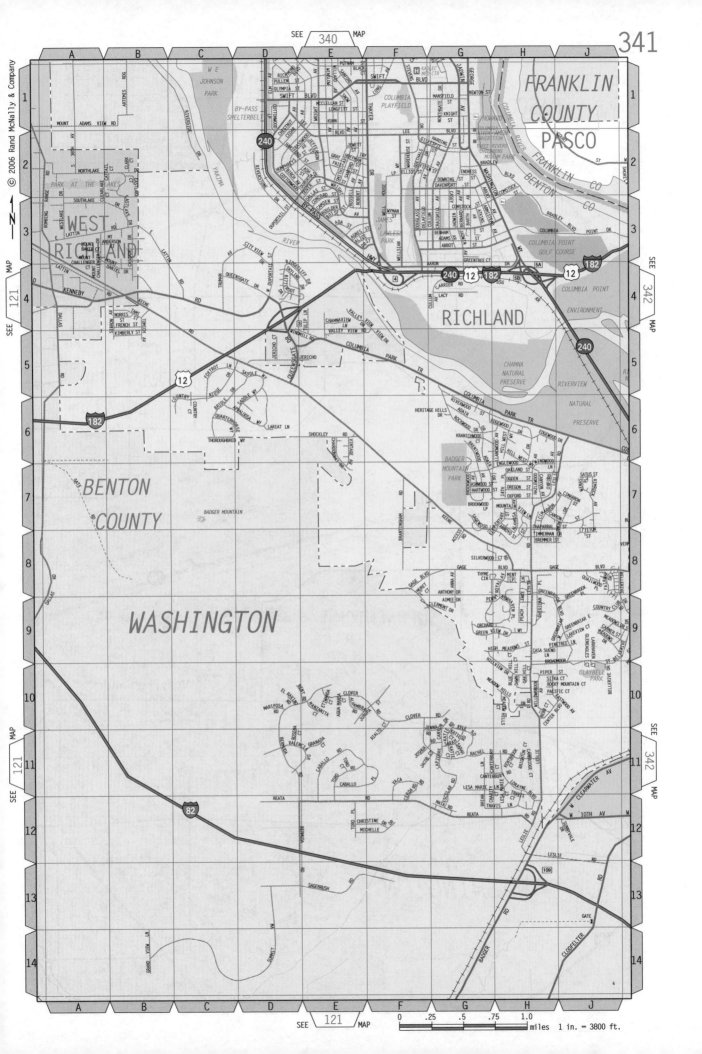

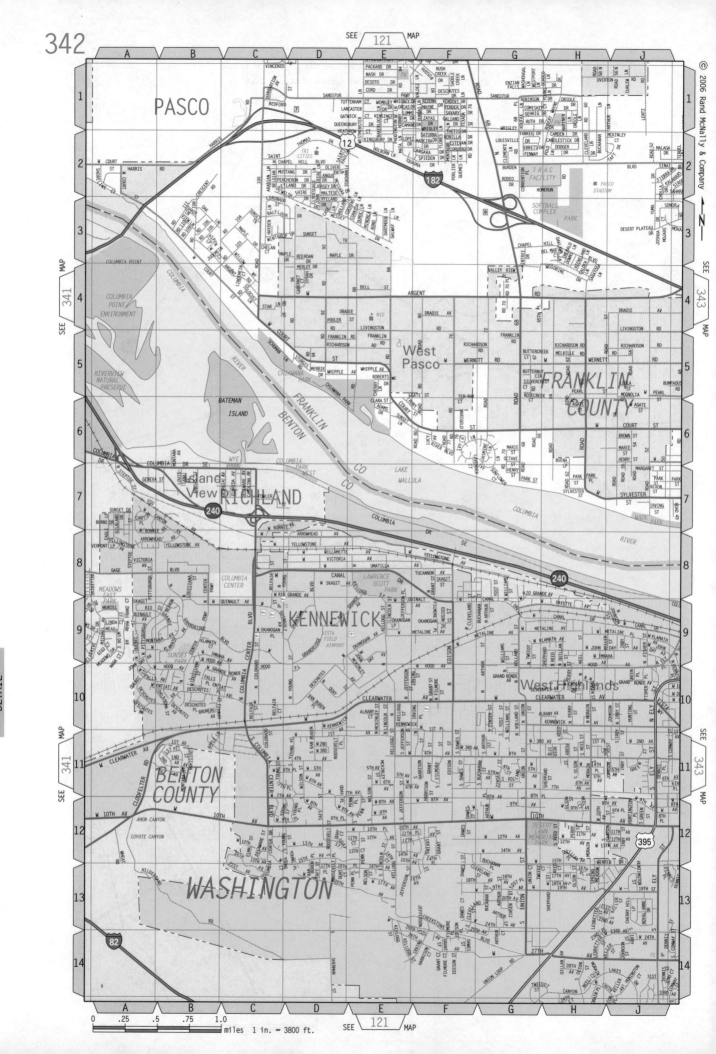

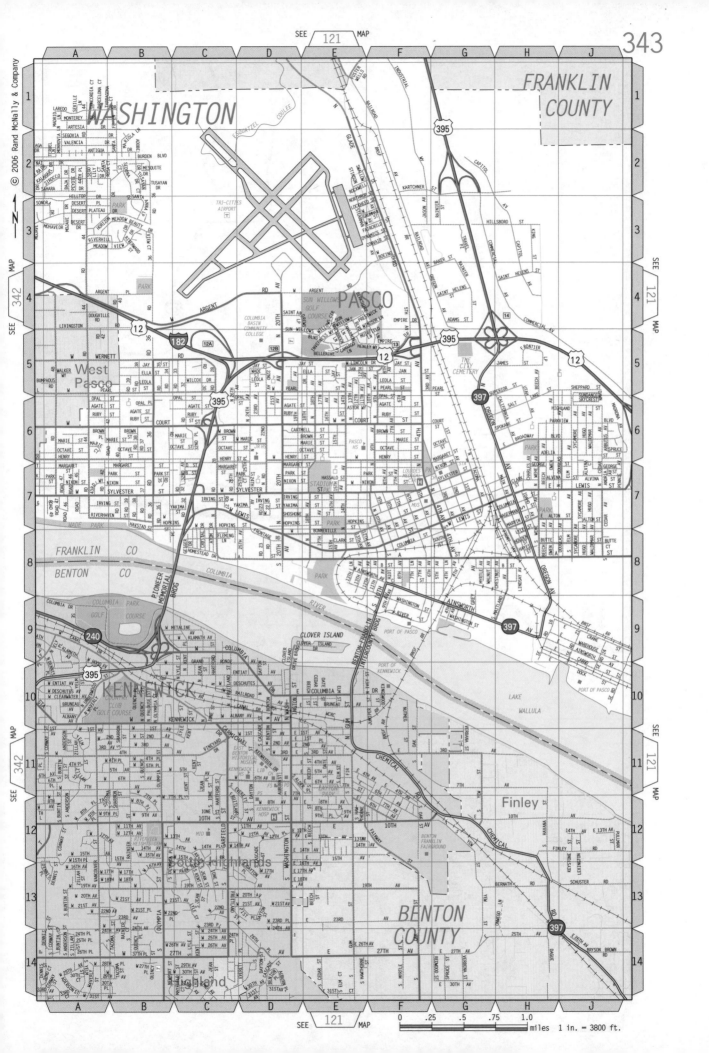

FRANKLIN COUNTY

WASHINGTON

TRI-CITIES AIRPORT

PASCO

SUN WILLOWS GOLF COURSE

COLUMBIA BASIN COMMUNITY COLLEGE

West Pasco

THE CITY CEMETERY

FRANKLIN CO
BENTON CO

COLUMBIA PARK GOLF COURSE

PIONEER MEMORIAL BRDG

COLUMBIA RIVER

CLOVER ISLAND

PORT OF PASCO

PORT OF KENNEWICK

BENTON-FRANKLIN INTERCOUNTY BRDG

LAKE WALLULA

PORT OF PASCO

KENNEWICK

COUNTRY CLUB GOLF COURSE

EAST BENTON HISTORICAL MUSEUM

Finley

BENTON FRANKLIN FAIRGROUND

South Highlands

BENTON COUNTY

© 2006 Rand McNally & Company

N

SEE 121 MAP

SEE 342 MAP

SEE 121 MAP

DETAIL

0 .25 .5 .75 1.0
miles   1 in. = 3800 ft.

SEE 121 MAP

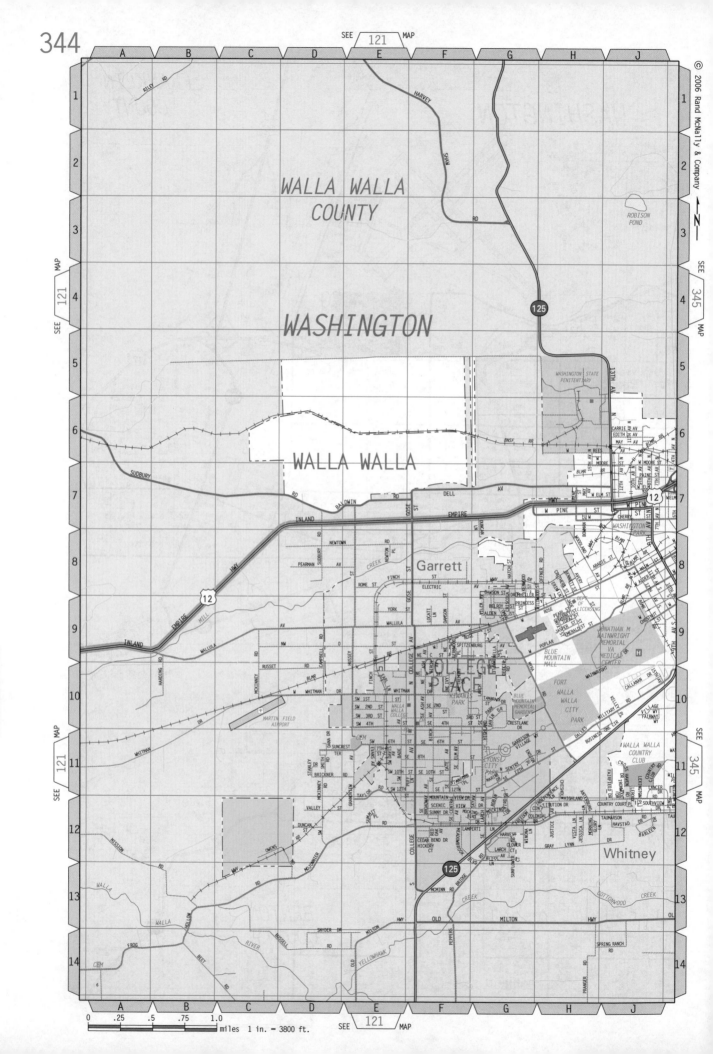

344

SEE 121 MAP

SEE 121 MAP

SEE 345 MAP

SEE 345 MAP

SEE 121 MAP

DETAIL

WALLA WALLA
COUNTY

WASHINGTON

WALLA WALLA

Garrett

COLLEGE PLACE

Whitney

ROBISON POND

WASHINGTON STATE PENITENTIARY

JONATHAN M WAINWRIGHT MEMORIAL VA MEDICAL CENTER

BLUE MOUNTAIN MALL

FORT WALLA WALLA CITY PARK

WALLA WALLA COUNTRY CLUB

MARTIN FIELD AIRPORT

0 .25 .5 .75 1.0
miles 1 in. = 3800 ft.

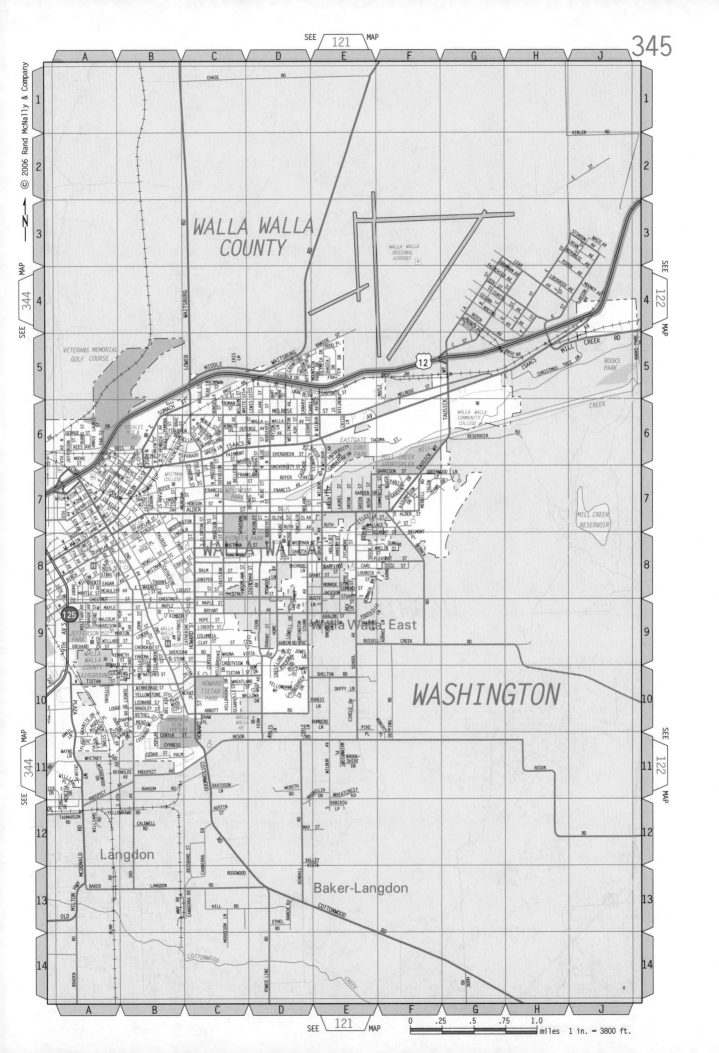

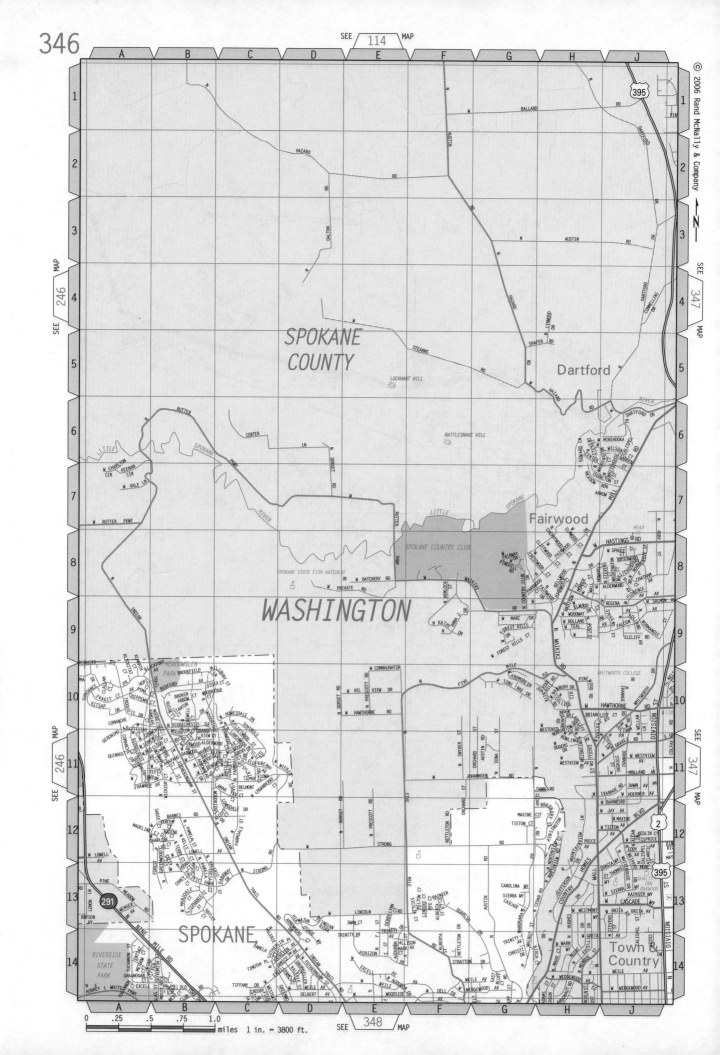

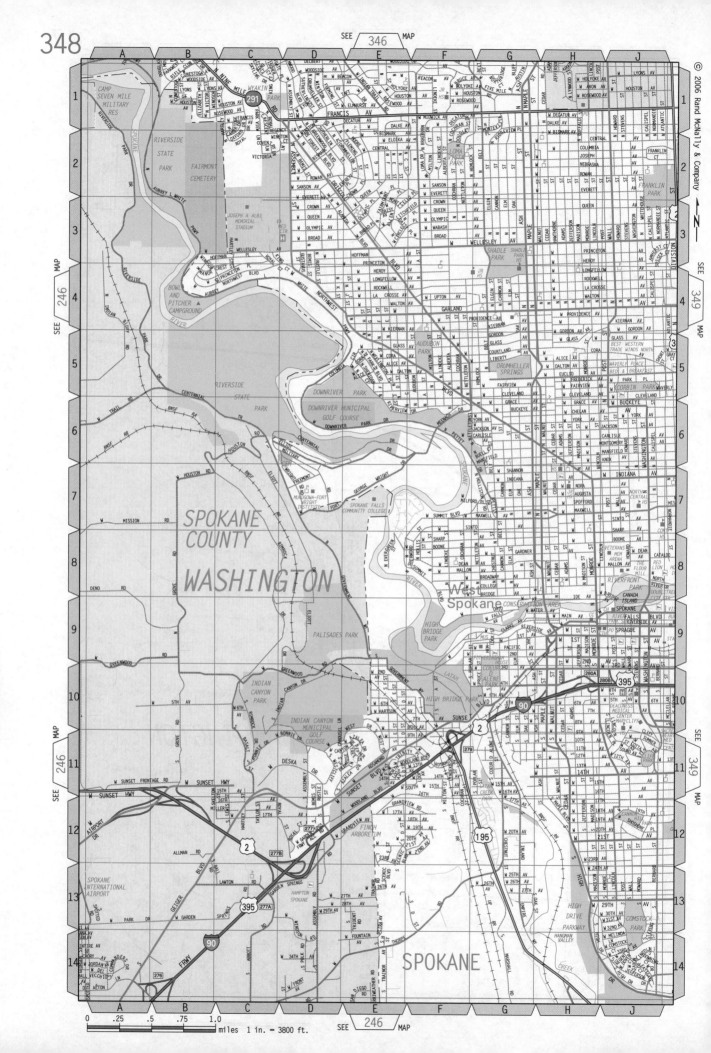

SPOKANE COUNTY

WASHINGTON

SPOKANE

West Spokane

DETAIL

0   .25   .5   .75   1.0
miles 1 in. = 3800 ft.

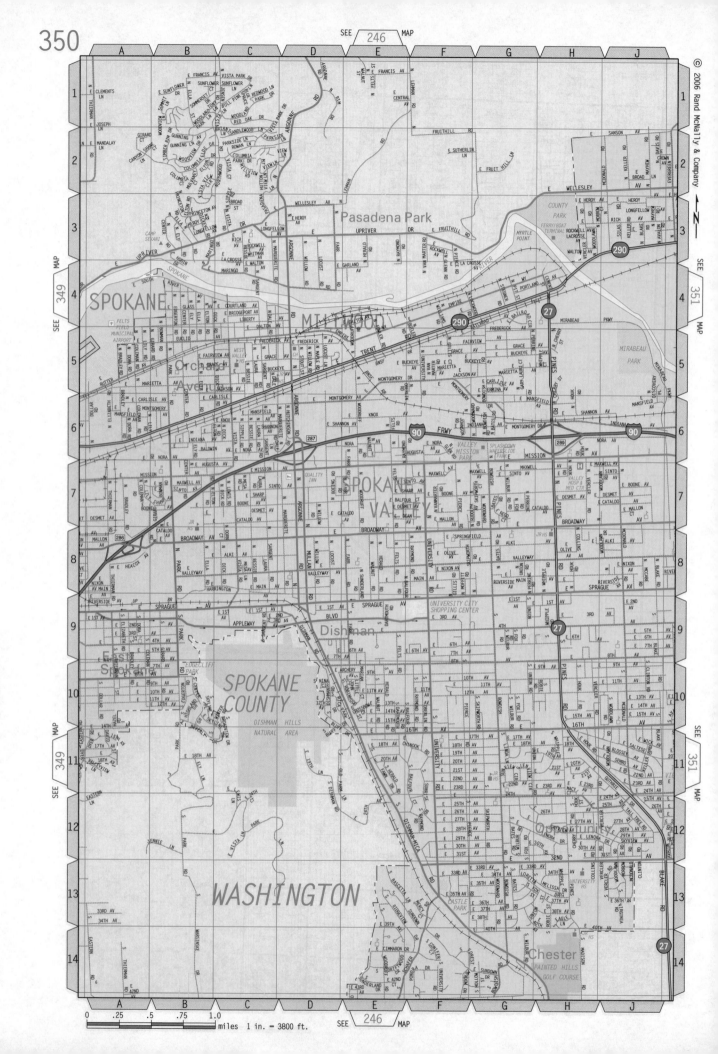

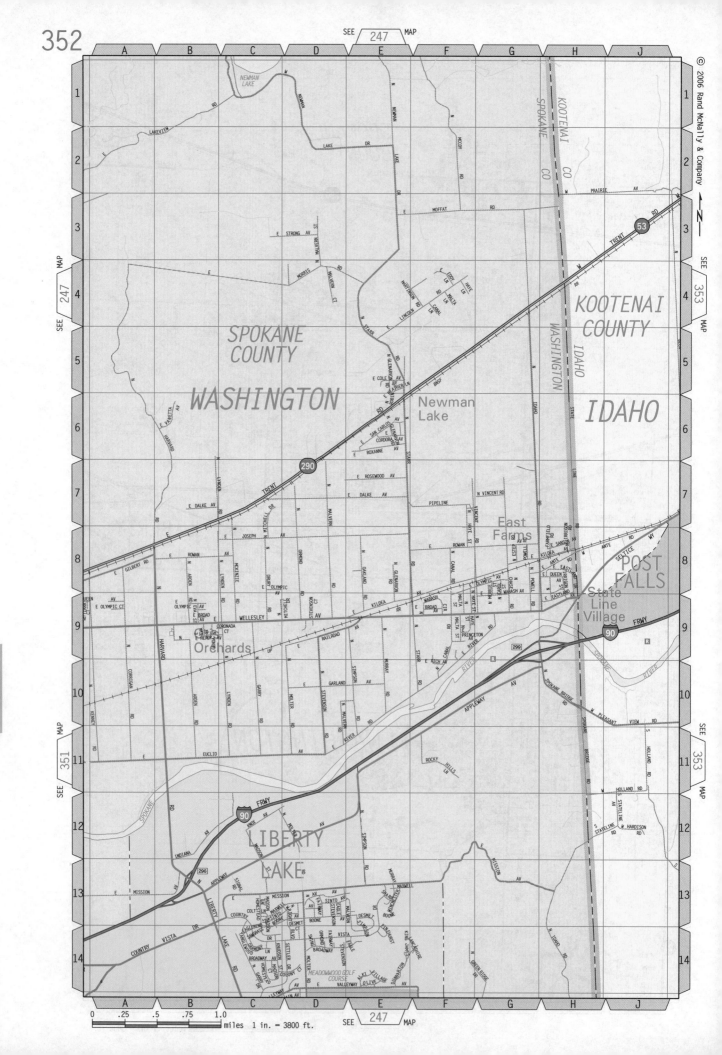

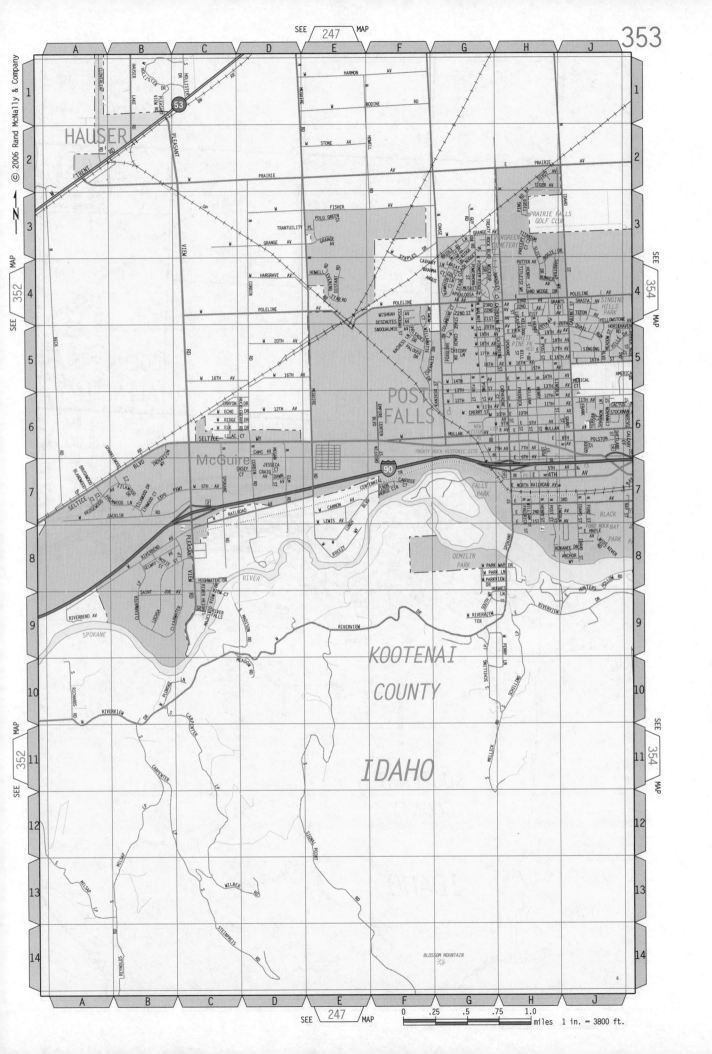

DETAIL

HAUSER

POST FALLS

McGuire

KOOTENAI

COUNTY

IDAHO

SPOKANE

© 2006 Rand McNally & Company

SEE 247 MAP

SEE 352 MAP

SEE 354 MAP

SEE 247 MAP

0   .25   .5   .75   1.0
miles   1 in. = 3800 ft.

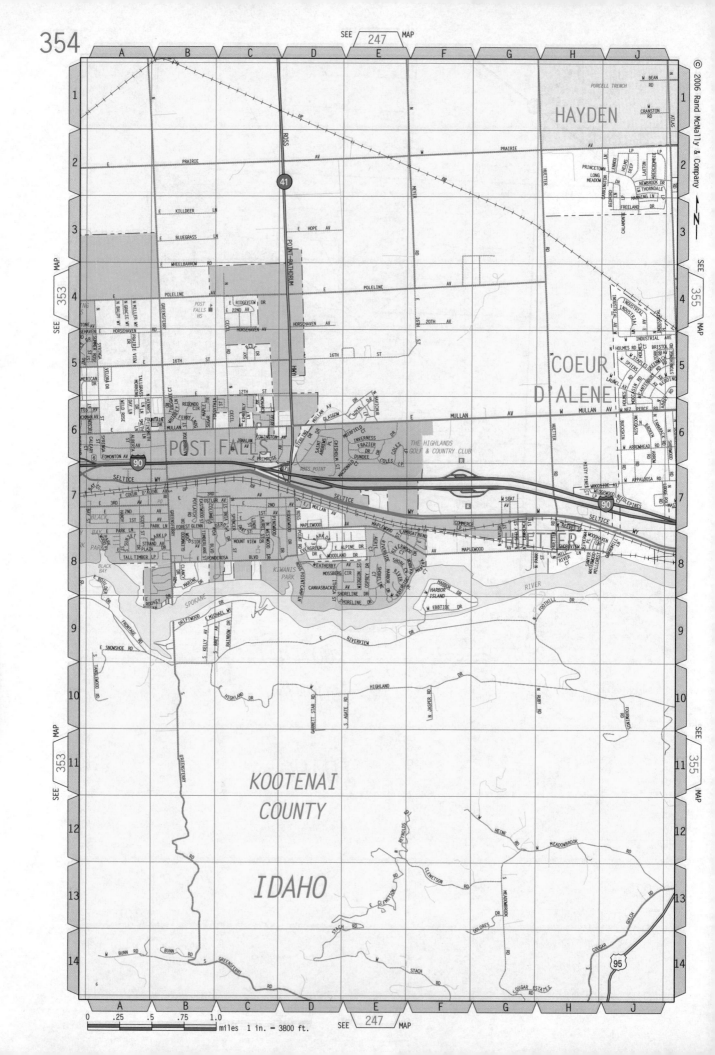

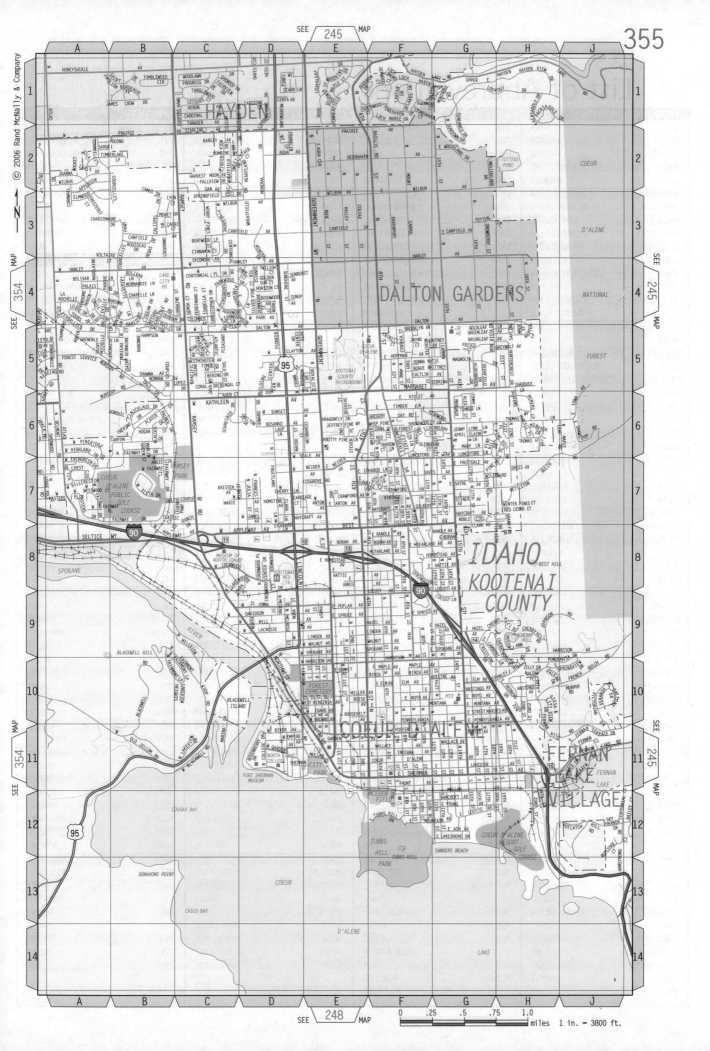

HAYDEN

DALTON GARDENS

IDAHO

KOOTENAI
COUNTY

COEUR D'ALENE

FERNAN
LAKE
VILLAGE

DETAIL

miles 1 in. = 3800 ft.
0 .25 .5 .75 1.0

List of Abbreviations

PREFIXES AND SUFFIXES

Abbreviation	Full	Abbreviation	Full	Abbreviation	Full
AL	ALLEY	CTST	COURT STREET	PZ D LA	PLAZA DE LA
ARC	ARCADE	CUR	CURVE	PZ D LAS	PLAZA DE LAS
AV, AVE	AVENUE	CV	COVE	PZWY	PLAZA WAY
AVCT	AVENUE COURT	DE	DE	RAMP	RAMP
AVD	AVENIDA	DIAG	DIAGONAL	RD	ROAD
AVD D LA	AVENIDA DE LA	DR	DRIVE	RDAV	ROAD AVENUE
AVD D LOS	AVENIDA DE LOS	DRAV	DRIVE AVENUE	RDBP	ROAD BYPASS
AVD DE	AVENIDA DE	DRCT	DRIVE COURT	RDCT	ROAD COURT
AVD DE LAS	AVENIDA DE LAS	DRLP	DRIVE LOOP	RDEX	ROAD EXTENSION
AVD DEL	AVENIDA DEL	DVDR	DIVISION DR	RDG	RIDGE
AVDR	AVENUE DRIVE	EXAV	EXTENSION AVENUE	RDSP	ROAD SPUR
AVEX	AVENUE EXTENSION	EXBL	EXTENSION BOULEVARD	RDWY	ROAD WAY
AV OF	AVENUE OF	EXRD	EXTENSION ROAD	RR	RAILROAD
AV OF THE	AVENUE OF THE	EXST	EXTENSION STREET	RUE	RUE
AVPL	AVENUE PLACE	EXT	EXTENSION	RUE D	RUE D
BAY	BAY	EXWY	EXPRESSWAY	RW	ROW
BEND	BEND	FOREST RT	FOREST ROUTE	RY	RAILWAY
BL, BLVD	BOULEVARD	FRWY, PZ	FREEWAY	SKWY	SKYWAY
BLCT	BOULEVARD COURT	FRY	FERRY	SQ	SQUARE
BLEX	BOULEVARD EXTENSION	GDNS	GARDENS	ST	STREET
BRCH	BRANCH	GN, GLN	GLEN	STAV	STREET AVENUE
BRDG	BRIDGE	GRN	GREEN	STCT	STREET COURT
BYPS	BYPASS	GRV	GROVE	STDR	STREET DRIVE
BYWY	BYWAY	HTS	HEIGHTS	STEX	STREET EXTENSION
CIDR	CIRCLE DRIVE	HWY	HIGHWAY	STLN	STREET LANE
CIR	CIRCLE	ISL	ISLE	STLP	STREET LOOP
CL	CALLE	JCT	JUNCTION	ST OF	STREET OF
CL DE	CALLE DE	LN	LANE	ST OF THE	STREET OF THE
CL DL	CALLE DEL	LNCR	LANE CIRCLE	STOV	STREET OVERPASS
CL D LA	CALLE DE LA	LNDG	LANDING	STPL	STREET PLACE
CL D LAS	CALLE DE LAS	LNDR	LAND DRIVE	STPM	STREET PROMENADE
CL D LOS	CALLE DE LOS	LNLP	LANE LOOP	STWY	STREET WAY
CL EL	CALLE EL	LP	LOOP	STXP	STREET EXPRESSWAY
CLJ	CALLEJON	MNR	MANOR	TER	TERRACE
CL LA	CALLE LA	MT	MOUNT	TFWY	TRAFFICWAY
CL LAS	CALLE LAS	MTWY	MOTORWAY	THWY	THROUGHWAY
CL LOS	CALLE LOS	MWCR	MEWS COURT	TKTR	TRUCK TRAIL
CLTR	CLUSTER	MWLN	MEWS LANE	TPKE	TURNPIKE
CM	CAMINO	NFD	NAT'L FOREST DEV	TRC	TRACE
CM DE	CAMINO DE	NK	NOOK	TRCT	TERRACE COURT
CM DL	CAMINO DEL	OH	OUTER HIGHWAY	TR, TRL	TRAIL
CM D LA	CAMINO DE LA	OVL	OVAL	TRWY	TRAIL WAY
CM D LAS	CAMINO DE LAS	OVLK	OVERLOOK	TTSP	TRUCK TRAIL SPUR
CM D LOS	CAMINO DE LOS	OVPS	OVERPASS	TUN	TUNNEL
CMTO	CAMINITO	PAS	PASEO	UNPS	UNDERPASS
CMTO DEL	CAMINITO DEL	PAS DE	PASEO DE	VIA D	VIA DE
CMTO D LA	CAMINITO DE LA	PAS DE LA	PASEO DE LA	VIA DL	VIA DEL
CMTO D LAS	CAMINITO DE LAS	PAS DE LAS	PASEO DE LAS	VIA D LA	VIA DE LA
CMTO D LOS	CAMINITO DE LOS	PAS DE LOS	PASEO DE LOS	VIA D LAS	VIA DE LAS
CNDR	CENTER DRIVE	PAS DL	PASEO DEL	VIA D LOS	VIA DE LOS
COM	COMMON	PASG	PASSAGE	VIA LA	VIA LA
COMS	COMMONS	PAS LA	PASEO LA	VW	VIEW
CORR	CORRIDOR	PAS LOS	PASEO LOS	VWY	VIEW WAY
CRES	CRESCENT	PASS	PASS	VIS	VISTA
CRLO	CIRCULO	PIKE	PIKE	VIS D	VISTA DE
CRSG	CROSSING	PK	PARK	VIS D L	VISTA DE LA
CST	CIRCLE STREET	PKDR	PARK DRIVE	VIS D LAS	VISTA DE LAS
CSWY	CAUSEWAY	PKWY, PKY	PARKWAY	VIS DEL	VISTA DEL
CT	COURT	PL	PLACE	WK	WALK
CTAV	COURT AVENUE	PLWY	PLACE WAY	WY	WAY
CTE	CORTE	PLZ, PZ	PLAZA	WYCR	WAY CIRCLE
CTE D	CORTE DE	PT	POINT	WYDR	WAY DRIVE
CTE DEL	CORTE DEL	PTAV	POINT AVENUE	WYLN	WAY LANE
CTE D LAS	CORTE DE LAS	PTH	PATH	WYPL	WAY PLACE
CTO	CUT OFF	PZ DE	PLAZA DE		
CTR	CENTER	PZ DEL	PLAZA DEL		

DIRECTIONS

E	EAST
KPN	KEY PENINSULA NORTH
KPS	KEY PENINSULA SOUTH
N	NORTH
NE	NORTHEAST
NW	NORTHWEST
S	SOUTH
SE	SOUTHEAST
SW	SOUTHWEST
W	WEST

BUILDINGS

CH	CITY HALL
CHP	CALIFORNIA HIGHWAY PATROL
COMM CTR	COMMUNITY CENTER
CON CTR	CONVENTION CENTER
CONT HS	CONTINUATION HIGH SCHOOL
CTH	COURTHOUSE
FAA	FEDERAL AVIATION ADMIN
FS	FIRE STATION
HOSP	HOSPITAL
HS	HIGH SCHOOL
INT	INTERMEDIATE SCHOOL
JR HS	JUNIOR HIGH SCHOOL
LIB	LIBRARY
MID	MIDDLE SCHOOL
MUS	MUSEUM
PO	POST OFFICE
PS	POLICE STATION
SR CIT CTR	SENIOR CITIZENS CENTER
STA	STATION
THTR	THEATER
VIS BUR	VISITORS BUREAU

OTHER ABBREVIATIONS

BCH	BEACH
BLDG	BUILDING
CEM	CEMETERY
CK	CREEK
CO	COUNTY
COMM	COMMUNITY
CTR	CENTER
EST	ESTATE
HIST	HISTORIC
HTS	HEIGHTS
LK	LAKE
MDW	MEADOW
MED	MEDICAL
MEM	MEMORIAL
MHP	MOBILE HOME PARK
MT	MOUNT
MTN	MOUNTAIN
NATL	NATIONAL
PKG	PARKING
PLGD	PLAYGROUND
RCH	RANCH
RCHO	RANCHO
REC	RECREATION
RES	RESERVOIR
RIV	RIVER
RR	RAILROAD
SPG	SPRING
STA	SANTA
VLG	VILLAGE
VLY	VALLEY
VW	VIEW

A U.S.-95 STREET INDEX ANTIOCH RD 357

STREET City State Page-Grid

A

A U.S.-95
COTTONWOOD ID 123-C3
GRANGEVILLE ID 123-C3
IDAHO CO ID 123-B3
A AV
ANACORTES WA 259-F6
LAKE OSWEGO OR 321-F5
A RD SW
DOUGLAS CO WA 112-B2
A ST
ASHLAND OR 337-D7
GRANTS PASS OR 335-E8
PIERCE CO WA 181-D5
TACOMA WA 293-H5
WALLA WALLA CO WA 345-G4
A ST Rt#-38
DOUGLAS CO OR 141-A1
ELKTON OR 141-A1
A ST Rt#-411
CASTLE ROCK WA 187-C7
E A ST
GRANTS PASS OR 335-G8
PASCO WA 121-A3
PASCO WA 343-H8
N A ST
ELLENSBURG WA 241-B5
SPOKANE WA 348-F2
S A ST
SPOKANE WA 348-F10
S A ST Rt#-126 Bus
LANE CO OR 330-J7
SPRINGFIELD OR 330-J7
SPRINGFIELD OR 331-A7
W A ST
PASCO WA 343-D8
A ST E U.S.-20
VALE OR 139-A3
A ST SE
AUBURN WA 182-B1
EPHRATA WA 112-C3
GRANT CO WA 112-C3
A ST W
MALHEUR CO OR 138-C3
VALE OR 138-C3
A ST W U.S.-20
VALE OR 139-A3
A900 RD
GRAYS HARBOR CO WA 179-B6
A1000 RD
GRAYS HARBOR CO WA 179-A5
A2000 RD
GRAYS HARBOR CO WA 179-A5
A3030 RD
GRAYS HARBOR CO WA 178-D4
A4000 RD
GRAYS HARBOR CO WA 179-D7
A5000 RD
GRAYS HARBOR CO WA 178-D4
A6000 RD
GRAYS HARBOR CO WA 178-D4
A7200 RD
GRAYS HARBOR CO WA 178-D3
AALVIK RD
SKAMANIA CO WA 194-C5
AARON DR
RICHLAND WA 341-F4
ABBEY RD
YAMHILL CO OR 198-B6
ABBOT ST
RICHLAND WA 341-G3
ABBOTSFORD-MISSION HWY Rt#-11
DISTRICT OF ABBOTSFORD BC 102-B1
DISTRICT OF MATSQUI BC 94-B3
DISTRICT OF MATSQUI BC 102-B1
ABBOTT RD
CLACKAMAS CO OR 126-C3
CLACKAMAS CO OR 201-A7
WALLA WALLA WA 345-C10
WALLA WALLA CO WA 122-A3
Walla Walla East WA 345-D10
WHITMAN CO WA 249-A2
S ABBOTT RD
SPOKANE CO WA 246-B5
SPOKANE CO WA 348-C13
ABBOTT CREEK RD
JACKSON CO OR 226-C4
ABERDEEN GARDENS RD
GRAYS HARBOR CO WA 178-B6
ABERNATHY ST NE
LACEY WA 297-F3
THURSTON CO WA 297-F3
ABERNATHY TKTR
COWLITZ CO WA 187-A6
ABIQUA RD NE
MARION CO OR 205-D4
ABRAHAM DR
LINN CO OR 210-A1
ABSHIRE RD
ADAMS CO ID 251-B4
ACADEMY ST
KELSO WA 303-D8
LEBANON OR 133-C1
ACADIA RD
UNIVERSITY ENDOWMENT LAND BC 156-A4
ACCESS RD
SISKIYOU CO CA 149-C3
ACKLEY CAMP RD
HARNEY CO OR 153-A2
ACME RD
KLICKITAT CO WA 196-A3
ADA RD
DOUGLAS CO OR 214-B5
N ADAIR ST Rt#-8
CORNELIUS OR 198-C1
FOREST GROVE OR 198-C1
ADAMS AV U.S.-30
LA GRANDE OR 130-A2
ADAMS DR
MADRAS OR 208-C5
N ADAMS DR
JEFFERSON CO OR 208-C3
S ADAMS DR
JEFFERSON CO OR 208-C6
MADRAS OR 208-C6
ADAMS RD
JACKSON CO OR 234-B3
POLK CO OR 204-B6
N ADAMS RD
SPOKANE VALLEY WA 351-B8
S ADAMS RD
SPOKANE CO WA 351-B11
SPOKANE VALLEY WA 351-B11
ADAMS ST
HOQUIAM WA 178-A7
ADAMS ST
OLYMPIA WA 296-J5
E ADAMS ST
GARDEN CITY ID 253-C2
N ADAMS ST
SPOKANE WA 348-H9
N ADAMS ST Rt#-42
COQUILLE OR 220-D5
NE ADAMS ST Rt#-14B
CAMAS WA 193-B7
NW ADAMS ST Rt#-99W
MCMINNVILLE OR 198-A7
SW ADAMS ST Rt#-99W
MCMINNVILLE OR 198-A7
W ADAMS ST
GARDEN CITY ID 253-C2
ADAMS CREEK RD
DOUGLAS CO OR 219-B4
ADCOCK RD
YAMHILL CO OR 198-B4
E ADDISON DR
SPOKANE WA 349-A1
N ADDISON ST
SPOKANE WA 349-A1
ADDY-GIFFORD RD
STEVENS CO WA 106-A3
ADELE AV
BREMERTON WA 270-F10
ADKISSON MARKET RD
WASCO CO OR 127-B2
SW ADMIRAL WY
SEATTLE WA 280-D2
SEATTLE WA 281-F3
ADMIRALS RD
BRITISH COLUMBIA BC 256-B6
DISTRICT OF SAANICH BC 256-C5
TOWN OF ESQUIMALT BC 256-B6
TOWN OF VIEW ROYAL BC 256-C5
ADMIRALTY AV
PORT TOWNSEND WA 263-F2
ADOBE WY
YAKIMA CO WA 243-B4
ADRIAN BLVD Rt#-201
NYSSA OR 139-A3
SW ADVANCE RD
CLACKAMAS CO OR 199-B5
WILSONVILLE OR 199-B5
ADVENT RD
PITT MEADOWS BC 157-B5
AENEAS VALLEY RD
OKANOGAN CO WA 105-A2
AGAN RD
LINN CO OR 207-D7
AGATE RD
JACKSON CO OR 230-D6
MASON CO WA 180-B3
AGATE ST
ASTORIA OR 300-A5
EUGENE OR 330-C8
AGATE POINT RD NE
BAINBRIDGE ISLAND WA 170-C7
AGEE DR
JOSEPHINE CO OR 229-C3
AGENCY-HOT SPRINGS RD
JEFFERSON CO OR 208-A2
Warm Springs OR 208-A2
AGER RD
MONTAGUE CA 150-A3
SISKIYOU CO CA 150-A3
AGER BESWICK RD
SISKIYOU CO CA 150-A3
NE AGNESS AV
GRANTS PASS OR 335-J9
AGNESS RD
CURRY CO OR 148-B1
CURRY CO OR 228-C4
AGNESS-ILLAHE RD
CURRY CO OR 148-B1
AGREN RD
COWLITZ CO WA 187-B5
AHSAHKA RD Rt#-7
OROFINO ID 123-C2
AHTANUM RD
UNION GAP WA 243-A7
YAKIMA CO WA 119-C2
YAKIMA CO WA 243-A7
W AHTANUM RD
UNION GAP WA 243-C7
AINSLEE AV
DEPOE BAY OR 206-B1
E AINSWORTH AV Rt#-397
PASCO WA 343-G9
W AINSWORTH AV Rt#-397
PASCO WA 343-F8
AINSWORTH AV S
PIERCE CO WA 181-D4
N AINSWORTH ST
PORTLAND OR 309-G6
NE AINSWORTH ST
PORTLAND OR 309-G6
AIR CARGO RD N
SEATAC WA 288-C4
AIRDUSTRIAL WY
TUMWATER WA 296-E13
AIRLIE RD
POLK CO OR 133-B1
POLK CO OR 207-A2
AIRPLANE RESERVOIR RD
MALHEUR CO OR 154-C2
MALHEUR CO OR 155-A2
AIRPORT AV
BENTON CO OR 133-B1
BENTON CO OR 207-A7
AIRPORT DR
BELLINGHAM WA 258-A1
JOSEPHINE CO OR 233-A5
LEBANON OR 133-C1
LINN CO OR 133-C1
WHATCOM CO WA 158-D7
WHATCOM CO WA 258-A1
W AIRPORT DR
SPOKANE CO WA 246-A4
SPOKANE CO WA 348-B11
AIRPORT RD
ALBANY OR 326-G8
BENTON CO OR 133-B1
CANYON CO ID 147-C1
CENTRALIA WA 299-D8
CHEHALIS WA 299-C9
CLALLAM CO WA 261-A4
CLARKSTON WA 250-B4
CURRY CO OR 224-A4
EUGENE OR 215-A1
EVERETT WA 171-B4
EVERETT WA 267-G6
GRANT CO WA 237-B3
HARNEY CO OR 145-B1
KITTITAS CO WA 240-C2
AIRPORT RD
KITTITAS CO WA 241-B5
LEWIS CO WA 299-D8
MALHEUR CO OR 138-C3
MEDFORD OR 336-C6
OKANOGAN WA 104-C3
OKANOGAN CO WA 104-C3
PORT ANGELES WA 261-A4
PULLMAN WA 249-C4
SNOHOMISH CO WA 171-B4
SNOHOMISH CO WA 267-G6
WHITMAN CO WA 249-C4
NE AIRPORT RD
CLACKAMAS CO OR 199-B6
ROSEBURG OR 334-F4
SE AIRPORT RD
YAMHILL CO OR 204-C1
W AIRPORT RD
BAKER CO OR 130-B3
BAKER CO OR 138-B1
AIRPORT RD NE
MARION CO OR 199-B6
AIRPORT RD SE
SALEM OR 323-B14
SALEM OR 325-B1
AIRPORT WY
BELLINGHAM WA 258-A1
HOQUIAM WA 178-A7
LAKESIDE OR 218-B4
SNOHOMISH CO WA 171-D3
TILLAMOOK CO OR 197-A7
NE AIRPORT WY
PORTLAND OR 311-E4
S AIRPORT WY
DOUGLAS CO WA 239-B5
SE AIRPORT WY
REDMOND OR 212-D6
W AIRPORT WY
BOISE ID 253-C4
AIRPORT WY S
SEATTLE WA 278-A7
SEATTLE WA 282-B1
SEATTLE WA 286-D3
TUKWILA WA 286-D3
AIRPORT CUTOFF RD Rt#-19
Irondale WA 263-B11
JEFFERSON CO WA 263-B11
AIRSTRIP RD
COLUMBIA CO OR 189-A6
MALHEUR CO OR 146-B3
AIRWAY DR
GRANT CO WA 242-C2
KLAMATH CO OR 235-D5
MOSES LAKE WA 242-C2
AIRWAY DR SE
SALEM OR 325-B4
A J WARRIN RD
DESCHUTES CO OR 212-A5
AKINS DR
CROOK CO OR 213-D6
ALABAMA ST
BELLINGHAM WA 258-F5
LONGVIEW WA 302-G10
ALAMEDA AV
ASTORIA OR 300-A5
FIRCREST WA 181-C3
NE ALAMEDA AV
ROSEBURG OR 334-F4
ALAMO LN
CANYON CO ID 147-B1
ALASKA AV E
Colby WA 271-G14
S ALASKA ST
SEATTLE WA 282-D5
SW ALASKA ST
SEATTLE WA 280-D5
SEATTLE WA 281-E5
ALASKA ST SE
Colby WA 271-G14
ALASKAN FRWY Rt#-99
SEATTLE WA 277-J5
SEATTLE WA 278-A6
SEATTLE WA 281-J3
SEATTLE WA 282-A1
ALASKAN WY
SEATTLE WA 277-H5
ALASKAN WY S Rt#-519
SEATTLE WA 277-J7
SEATTLE WA 278-A7
SEATTLE WA 281-J1
ALASKAN WY W
SEATTLE WA 277-H5
ALBANY RD U.S.-2
BONNER CO ID 107-A3
PRIEST RIVER ID 107-A3
ALBANY ST Rt#-82
ELGIN OR 130-A1
ALBANY ST SW
Rochester WA 184-A3
THURSTON CO WA 184-A3
ALBANY-CORVALLIS HWY U.S.-20
ALBANY OR 207-B5
ALBANY OR 326-A7
BENTON CO OR 207-B5
BENTON CO OR 326-A7
BENTON CO OR 327-J8
CORVALLIS OR 207-B5
CORVALLIS OR 327-J8
ALBANY-JCT CITY HWY Rt#-9E
ALBANY OR 207-C7
ALBANY OR 326-C14
HALSEY OR 210-B3
HARRISBURG OR 210-A5
JUNCTION CITY OR 210-A5
LANE CO OR 210-A5
LINN CO OR 207-C7
LINN CO OR 210-B3
TANGENT OR 207-C7
ALBANY-LYONS HWY Rt#-226
LINN CO OR 133-C1
LINN CO OR 134-A1
SCIO OR 133-C1
ALBATROSS ST
OCEAN SHORES WA 177-B6
ALBERT ST
NANAIMO BC 93-A3
N ALBERTA ST
PORTLAND OR 309-F7
NE ALBERTA ST
PORTLAND OR 309-H7
SE ALBERTA ST
CLACKAMAS CO OR 318-E7
ALBERTSON RD
YAMHILL CO OR 198-C4
N ALBINA AV
PORTLAND OR 309-F7
ALBION RD
ALBION WA 249-A4
WHITMAN CO WA 122-C1
WHITMAN CO WA 249-A4
S ALBRO PL
SEATTLE WA 282-B7
ALCAN RD
GRAND COULEE WA 237-C3
ALCORT RD
MALHEUR CO OR 154-B2
ALDER
PIERCE CO WA 182-A4
ALDER AV
SUMNER WA 182-B3
N ALDER AV
GRANITE FALLS WA 102-C3
S ALDER AV
GRANITE FALLS WA 102-C3
ALDER DR NE
KEIZER OR 323-A7
ALDER RD
FRANKLIN CO WA 121-A2
ALDER ST
CATHLAMET WA 117-B3
LA GRANDE OR 130-A2
MOSES LAKE WA 242-C3
ALDER ST Rt#-507
CENTRALIA WA 299-E4
E ALDER ST
WALLA WALLA WA 345-C7
Walla Walla East WA 345-F7
N ALDER ST
TACOMA WA 292-D4
N ALDER ST U.S.-101
ABERDEEN WA 178-B7
S ALDER ST Rt#-21
ODESSA WA 113-B3
S ALDER ST U.S.-101
ABERDEEN WA 178-B7
SW ALDER ST
GRANTS PASS OR 335-D9
PORTLAND OR 313-F6
ALDER BRANCH RD
LANE CO OR 215-D1
ALDERBRIDGE WY
CITY OF RICHMOND BC 156-B6
ALDERBROOK RD
BAY CITY OR 197-B1
TILLAMOOK CO OR 197-B1
ALDER CREEK LN
CLACKAMAS CO OR 201-A4
ALDER CREEK RD
BAKER CO OR 138-B1
KOOTENAI CO ID 248-C1
WHEELER CO OR 128-B3
WHEELER CO OR 136-B1
ALDER CUTOFF RD
EATONVILLE WA 118-B1
PIERCE CO WA 118-B1
ALDERDALE RD
KLICKITAT CO WA 120-B3
KLICKITAT CO WA 128-B1
YAKIMA CO WA 120-B3
ALDERDALE WYE
YAKIMA CO WA 120-B3
ALDERGROVE RD
Birch Bay WA 158-B5
WHATCOM CO WA 158-C5
SE ALDERMAN RD
YAMHILL CO OR 204-C1
NE ALDERMEADOWS RD
MULTNOMAH CO OR 200-D1
ALDER SPRING RD
JACKSON CO OR 226-D5
JACKSON CO OR 227-A5
ALDERWOOD AV
BELLINGHAM WA 258-A2
WHATCOM CO WA 158-D7
WHATCOM CO WA 258-A2
ALDERWOOD MALL PKWY
LYNNWOOD WA 171-B5
SNOHOMISH CO WA 171-B4
ALDRICH RD
WHATCOM CO WA 158-D5
ALECK BAY RD
SAN JUAN CO WA 160-A7
ALEXANDER AV
BENTON CO OR 327-G12
CORVALLIS OR 327-G12
TACOMA WA 182-A2
ALEXANDER RD
SUNNYSIDE WA 120-B2
YAKIMA CO WA 120-B2
ALEXANDER RD Rt#-241
SUNNYSIDE WA 120-B2
YAKIMA CO WA 120-B2
ALFALFA RD
CROOK CO OR 135-B3
CROOK CO OR 213-A7
ALFALFA-GRANGER RD Rt#-223
YAKIMA CO WA 120-A2
ALFALFA MARKET RD
DESCHUTES CO OR 135-B3
DESCHUTES CO OR 217-D2
ALFORD RD
KITTITAS CO WA 241-B4
ALFRED JOHNSON RD
MOUNT VERNON WA 168-B1
MOUNT VERNON WA 260-C14
ALGER HILL LOGGING TR
SKAGIT CO WA 161-B3
ALGOMA RD
KLAMATH CO OR 235-B1
ALGOMA SPUR RD
BONNER CO ID 244-A4
ALICE AV S
SALEM OR 324-G2
ALKALI GULCH RD
MALHEUR CO OR 139-A2
ALKI AV SW
SEATTLE WA 276-D7
SEATTLE WA 280-D1
ALLAN RD
YAKIMA CO WA 243-A4
ALLARD CRES
TOWNSHIP OF LANGLEY BC 157-C6
SW ALLEN BLVD
BEAVERTON OR 199-B2
ALLEN RD
DESCHUTES CO OR 212-B7
LEWIS CO WA 187-D1
SUNNYSIDE WA 120-B2
YAKIMA CO WA 120-B2
ALLEN ST
KELSO WA 303-C8
ALLEN ST Rt#-4
KELSO WA 303-D8
E ALLEN ST
COWLITZ CO WA 303-F8
KELSO WA 303-F8
ALLEN CREEK RD
CROOK CO OR 213-D2
GRANTS PASS OR 335-C12
JOSEPHINE CO OR 335-C12
ALLEN WEST RD
SKAGIT CO WA 161-A5
ALLINGHAM CTO
JEFFERSON CO OR 211-C1
ALLISON RD
LEWIS CO WA 187-D3
NE ALLWORTH RD
CLARK CO WA 193-A3
ALMA LN
JEFFERSON CO OR 208-B5
SW ALMA LN
JEFFERSON CO OR 208-A5
ALMA ST
UNIVERSITY ENDOWMENT LAND BC 254-A13
VANCOUVER BC 254-A13
NW ALMETER WY
DESCHUTES CO OR 212-D4
ALMIRA RD S
LINCOLN CO WA 113-B2
ALM LANE RD
STEVENS CO WA 106-B3
ALMOTA RD
WHITMAN CO WA 122-C1
ALMOTA RD Rt#-194
WHITMAN CO WA 122-B1
ALMOTA ST Rt#-27
PALOUSE WA 249-B1
ALMOTA FERRY RD
GARFIELD CO WA 122-B1
E ALOHA ST
SEATTLE WA 278-C3
ALPINE DR SW
THURSTON CO WA 180-B7
ALPINE RD
BENTON CO OR 133-B2
SE ALPINE RD
KITSAP CO WA 174-C6
ALSEA HWY Rt#-34
BENTON CO OR 133-A1
LINCOLN CO OR 133-A2
LINCOLN CO OR 209-D2
LINCOLN CO OR 328-F6
WALDPORT OR 328-F6
ALSEA BAY DR
LINCOLN CO OR 328-C4
ALSEA-DEADWOOD HWY
BENTON CO OR 133-A2
ALSIP RD
POLK CO OR 204-A7
ALSTON RD W
DOUGLAS CO WA 239-D1
ALSTON-MAYGER RD
COLUMBIA CO OR 189-A3
ALTA LAKE RD
BRITISH COLUMBIA BC 93-C1
WHISTLER BC 93-C1
ALTAMONT DR
Altamont OR 235-C5
Altamont OR 338-H14
KLAMATH FALLS OR 338-H14
SW ALTA VISTA DR
KITSAP CO WA 174-A6
ALTA VISTA RD
EAGLE POINT OR 230-D6
JACKSON CO OR 230-D6
S ALTHEIMER ST
TACOMA WA 293-G6
ALTHOUSE CREEK RD
JOSEPHINE CO OR 233-C5
SE ALTMAN RD
CLACKAMAS CO OR 200-C3
MULTNOMAH CO OR 200-C2
ALTNOW-BEULAH RD
HARNEY CO OR 138-A3
ALTO RD
COLUMBIA CO WA 122-A2
E ALTON ST
PASCO WA 343-H7
ALTOONA PILLAR ROCK RD
WAHKIAKUM CO WA 117-A2
ALVADORE RD
LANE CO OR 133-B2
ALVADORE RD S
LANE CO OR 133-B3
NE ALVAS RD
CLARK CO WA 193-B3
ALVILLE LN
GILLIAM CO OR 128-A2
ALWARD COUNTY RD
PIERCE CO WA 182-C5
W ALWORTH ST
GARDEN CITY ID 253-C2
W AMAZON DR
EUGENE OR 330-B12
AMAZON PKWY
EUGENE OR 330-A8
AMBAUM BLVD S Rt#-509
BURIEN WA 175-A5
BURIEN WA 288-A7
AMBAUM BLVD SW
BURIEN WA 175-A5
BURIEN WA 285-G7
KING CO WA 175-A5
KING CO WA 285-G7
AMBERJACK AV
KITSAP CO WA 170-B6
AMBLE RD
ISLAND CO WA 167-D7
AMBOY Rt#-503
CLARK CO WA 193-B1
AMBOY RD
CLARK CO WA 193-B1
AMERICAN DR
HALSEY OR 210-A2
LINN CO OR 210-A2
N AMERICANA BLVD
BOISE ID 253-C3
AMERICAN FRUIT RD
Sunnyslope WA 238-D3
AMERICAN LAKE AV
PIERCE CO WA 181-C5
AMERICAN MILL RD
GRAYS HARBOR CO WA 183-D3
AMES RD
YAKIMA CO WA 243-B5
AMES RD NE
OLYMPIA WA 296-J1
THURSTON CO WA 296-J1
THURSTON CO WA 297-A1
NE AMES LAKE RD
KING CO WA 176-A2
AMES LAKE CARNATION RD NE
KING CO WA 176-A1
AMICK RD
SKAGIT CO WA 168-C1
AMISIGGER RD
CLACKAMAS CO OR 200-B4
E AMITY RD
ADA CO ID 253-B4
BOISE ID 253-D4
SE AMITY RD
AMITY OR 204-C2
YAMHILL CO OR 204-C2
W AMITY RD
ADA CO ID 253-A4
AMITY DAYTON HWY
DAYTON OR 198-C7
YAMHILL CO OR 198-B7
AMITY DAYTON HWY Rt#-233
YAMHILL CO OR 198-B7
YAMHILL CO OR 204-C1
SE AMITY-DAYTON HWY Rt#-233
YAMHILL CO OR 204-C1
NE AMMETER RD
CLARK CO WA 193-C6
ANACO BEACH RD
ANACORTES WA 259-B4
ANACOPPER RD
ANACORTES WA 259-D3
N ANACORTES AV
BURLINGTON WA 260-D4
S ANACORTES ST
BURLINGTON WA 260-D6
SW ANCHOR AV
LINCOLN CITY OR 203-A5
ANDERSON AV
Altamont OR 338-H14
COOS BAY OR 333-G10
ANDERSON RD
GRAYS HARBOR CO WA 184-A3
LEWIS CO WA 184-D6
MASON CO WA 179-B2
THURSTON CO WA 184-A3
WHITMAN CO WA 249-A4
S ANDERSON RD
CLACKAMAS CO OR 199-B7
W ANDERSON RD
SPOKANE CO WA 246-B7
ANDERSON RD SE
MARION CO OR 205-B7
ANDERSON RD SE Rt#-214
MARION CO OR 205-B7
ANDERSON CANYON RD
CHELAN CO WA 238-A1
ANDERSON CREEK RD
JACKSON CO OR 234-B3
LINCOLN CO OR 203-B5
NW ANDERSON HILL RD
KITSAP CO WA 174-A1
ANDERSON HILL RD SW
KITSAP CO WA 174-B4
ANDERSON LAKE RD
JEFFERSON CO WA 170-A1
ANDERSON RESERVOIR RD
ADAMS CO ID 251-B3
ANDERSON VALLEY RD
HARNEY CO OR 145-C2
ANDRAIN
PIERCE CO WA 182-A6
ANDRESEN RD
VANCOUVER WA 306-D7
NE ANDRESEN RD
CLARK CO WA 192-D5
CLARK CO WA 306-D1
VANCOUVER WA 306-D1
ANDREWS RD
DOUGLAS CO OR 219-A4
JACKSON CO OR 234-A2
S ANDRUS RD
SPOKANE CO WA 246-A6
ANGELINE RD
BONNEY LAKE WA 182-C4
ANGUS DR
THURSTON CO WA 184-D2
ANKENY HILL RD
MARION CO OR 207-D1
ANKENY HILL RD SE
MARION CO OR 207-D2
ANKERTON RD
SHERMAN CO OR 127-C2
ANLIKER RD
COLUMBIA CO OR 189-B6
ANNACIS HWY Rt#-91
CITY OF RICHMOND BC 156-D6
DISTRICT OF DELTA BC 101-C1
DISTRICT OF DELTA BC 156-D6
NEW WESTMINSTER BC 156-D6
ANNACIS HWY Rt#-91A
CITY OF RICHMOND BC 156-D6
ANNASIS HWY
DISTRICT OF DELTA BC 101-C1
ANNAWALT RD
MALHEUR CO OR 146-C3
ANNEX RD
MALHEUR CO OR 139-A2
ANNONEN RD
LEWIS CO WA 187-B5
ANSELL ST
MAPLE RIDGE BC 157-D5
ANTELOPE
CROOK CO OR 213-D6
ANTELOPE HWY Rt#-293
JEFFERSON CO OR 135-C1
WASCO CO OR 127-C3
WASCO CO OR 135-C1
ANTELOPE RD
JACKSON CO OR 230-C6
White City OR 230-D6
E ANTELOPE RD
JACKSON CO OR 149-C1
JACKSON CO OR 234-D1
ANTELOPE CANAL RD
MALHEUR CO OR 147-A3
ANTELOPE FLAT RD
MALHEUR CO OR 146-B2
ANTELOPE SPRINGS RD
OWYHEE CO ID 147-C3
ANT FLAT RD
ENTERPRISE OR 130-C2
WALLOWA CO OR 130-C2
ANTHONY LAKES HWY
BAKER CO OR 130-A3
HAINES OR 130-A3
ANTHONY LAKES RD
BAKER CO OR 130-A3
ANTIOCH RD
JACKSON CO OR 230-C5

INDEX

358 W ANTLER AV STREET INDEX SE BARTEL RD

STREET City State Page-Grid

W ANTLER AV
DESCHUTES CO OR 212-D5
REDMOND OR 212-D5
ANTLES RD
UNION CO OR 130-B2
ANTOINE CREEK RD
CHELAN CO WA 236-D1
ANTRIM RD
LEWIS CO WA 187-C2
A-P-A RD
WHATCOM CO WA 101-C1
APEL DR
PORT COQUITLAM BC 157-B4
APIARY RD
COLUMBIA CO OR 117-B3
COLUMBIA CO OR 189-B4
S APPLE ST
BOISE ID 253-D3
APPLE ACRES RD
CHELAN CO WA 112-B1
CHELAN CO WA 236-D2
APPLEFORD RD
ASOTIN CO WA 123-A3
APPLEGATE AV
DOUGLAS CO OR 219-A4
JOSEPHINE CO OR 229-A6
APPLEGATE RD
JACKSON CO OR 149-B2
N APPLEGATE RD
JACKSON CO OR 149-B2
JOSEPHINE CO OR 149-B2
APPLEGATE ST
JACKSON CO OR 149-B2
JACKSONVILLE OR 149-B2
APPLESIDE BLVD
ASOTIN CO WA 250-B5
Vineland WA 250-B5
APPLETON RD
KLICKITAT CO WA 196-B3
APPLE VALLEY RD
CANYON CO ID 139-A3
APPLEWAY AV
LIBERTY LAKE WA 352-B13
SPOKANE CO WA 352-F10
E APPLEWAY AV
SPOKANE CO WA 351-G8
SPOKANE VALLEY WA 351-G8
W APPLEWAY AV
COEUR D'ALENE ID 355-C8
APPLEWAY BLVD
SPOKANE VALLEY WA 350-C9
A P TUBBS RD
PIERCE CO WA 182-D5
ARAGO LN
COOS CO OR 220-D6
ARAGO-ARAGO JCT
COOS CO OR 220-D6
ARAGO CROSS RD
COOS CO OR 220-D6
ARBORETUM RD
BENTON CO OR 207-B4
ARBOR GROVE RD
MARION CO OR 199-A7
MARION CO OR 205-B1
ARBOR GROVE RD NE
MARION CO OR 205-A1
ARBORLYNN DR
DISTRICT OF NORTH VANCOUV BC 255-F5
ARBUTUS RD
DISTRICT OF SAANICH BC 257-D2
ARBUTUS ST
VANCOUVER BC 156-B5
VANCOUVER BC 254-D13
E ARCADIA AV
MASON CO WA 180-A3
SHELTON WA 180-A3
ARCADIA DR NE
LINCOLN CO OR 206-C4
ARCADIA RD
MASON CO WA 180-B3
ARCHERFISH RD
KITSAP CO WA 170-B7
ARCHER MOUNTAIN RD
SKAMANIA CO WA 194-B6
ARCHIE MYERS RANCH RD
MALHEUR CO OR 154-B2
ARDENA RD
FIFE WA 182-A2
ARDMORE DR
LAKEWOOD WA 181-C4
W ARGENT RD
FRANKLIN CO WA 342-E4
FRANKLIN CO WA 343-C4
PASCO WA 342-E4
PASCO WA 343-C4
N ARGONNE RD
MILLWOOD WA 350-D3
SPOKANE CO WA 246-D2
SPOKANE CO WA 350-D2
SPOKANE VALLEY WA 350-D6
ARGYLE DR
VANCOUVER BC 156-C5
ARGYLE DR S
SALEM OR 324-G3
ARGYLE ST
VANCOUVER BC 156-C5
ARID AV
DESCHUTES CO OR 212-C7
W ARLINGTON ST
GLADSTONE OR 199-D4
ARLINGTON HEIGHTS RD
SNOHOMISH CO WA 168-D4
ARMAR RD
ARLINGTON WA 168-C7
MARYSVILLE WA 168-C7
SNOHOMISH CO WA 168-C7
ARMITAGE RD
SAN JUAN CO WA 160-A5
ARMSTRONG RD
TOWNSHIP OF LANGLEY BC 157-D7
ARMSTRONG ST
PACIFIC CO WA 117-A1
ARMSWORTHY ST
WASCO OR 127-C1
ARMSWORTHY ST Rt#-206
WASCO OR 127-C1
ARNDT RD
CLACKAMAS CO OR 199-B6
MARION CO OR 199-A6
ARNEY RD NE
MARION CO OR 205-B1
ARNIE RD
WHATCOM CO WA 158-B4
ARNOLD LN
JACKSON CO OR 234-A1
ARNOLD RD
ISLAND CO WA 167-B4
ARNOLD WY
CORVALLIS OR 327-E9
ARNOLD MARKET RD
DESCHUTES CO OR 217-C4
ARNOT RD
SNOHOMISH CO WA 168-D4
AROCK RD
MALHEUR CO OR 146-C3
ARRAH WANNA BLVD
CLACKAMAS CO OR 201-C5
ARRITOLA PLACE RD
MALHEUR CO OR 146-C3
MALHEUR CO OR 147-A3
ARROW AV U.S.-12
NEZ PERCE CO ID 123-A2
W ARROWHEAD AV
BENTON CO WA 342-D8
KENNEWICK WA 342-D8
ARROWHEAD RD
ISLAND CO WA 167-D4
ARSENAL WY E
BREMERTON WA 270-E11
Navy Yard City WA 270-E11
ART DALZELL RD
MORROW CO OR 128-B2
ARTHUR BLVD
YAKIMA CO WA 243-C6
ARTHUR DR
DISTRICT OF DELTA BC 101-C1
ARTHUR RD
NEZ PERCE CO ID 250-D2
ARTHUR ST
NORTH BEND OR 333-D4
S ARTHUR ST
SPOKANE WA 349-B10
SW ARTHUR ST
PORTLAND OR 317-E1
ARTHUR LAING BRDG
CITY OF RICHMOND BC 156-B5
ARTHUR V GOLTZ
PIERCE CO WA 182-B5
ARTONDALE DR NW
PIERCE CO WA 181-B1
ARVICK RD SE
KITSAP CO WA 174-C4
ARVID NELSON RD
CROOK CO OR 136-A2
ASBURY RD
KOOTENAI CO ID 248-A3
ASCHOFF RD
CLACKAMAS CO OR 201-B3
N ASH AV
WARDEN WA 121-A1
S ASH AV
WARDEN WA 121-A1
ASH RD
DISTRICT OF SAANICH BC 159-D5
ASH ST
BROWNSVILLE OR 210-C2
KELSO WA 303-D8
SODAVILLE OR 133-C2
N ASH ST
SPOKANE WA 346-G14
SPOKANE WA 348-G1
NE ASH ST
PULLMAN WA 249-B5
ASH ST N
OMAK WA 104-C2
ASH ST S
OMAK WA 104-C3
ASH WY
SNOHOMISH CO WA 171-B4
ASHBROOK LN
JOSEPHINE CO OR 229-A5
ASH CREEK RD
DOUGLAS CO OR 225-C3
ASH LAKE RD
SKAMANIA CO WA 194-C5
ASHLAND ST
ASHLAND OR 337-D9
ASHLAND LOOP RD
JACKSON CO OR 234-C6
ASHTON LN
VALLEY CO ID 251-D7
SW ASHWOOD LN
JEFFERSON CO OR 208-B5
ASHWOOD RD
JEFFERSON CO OR 208-C5
ASHWORTH AV N
SHORELINE WA 171-A7
A S KRESKY RD
CHEHALIS WA 299-E9
LEWIS CO WA 299-E9
ASOTIN RD
ASOTIN CO WA 122-C2
ASOTIN CO WA 250-A6
ASOTIN CREEK RD
ASOTIN WA 250-B6
ASOTIN CO WA 250-B6
ASPEN ST
LANE CO OR 330-F7
SPRINGFIELD OR 330-F7
N ASPEN ST Rt#-231
LINCOLN CO WA 114-A2
REARDAN WA 114-A2
ASPEN WY
NEWBERG OR 198-D5
YAMHILL CO OR 198-D5
ASPEN LAKE RD
KLAMATH CO OR 235-A1
ASPENWALL RD
THURSTON CO WA 180-B6
S ASSEMBLY RD
SPOKANE CO WA 246-B5
SPOKANE CO WA 348-D13
N ASSEMBLY ST
SPOKANE WA 348-D2
ATHENA-HOLDMAN HWY
ATHENA OR 129-C1
UMATILLA CO OR 129-B1
E ATHENA-HOLDMAN HWY
ATHENA OR 129-C1
ATKINS AV
DISTRICT OF LANGFORD BC 159-B6
TOWN OF VIEW ROYAL BC 159-B6
ATKINS RD
COLUMBIA CO OR 189-A4
ATKINSON AV
DESCHUTES CO OR 212-C4
NW ATKINSON AV
DESCHUTES CO OR 212-C4
N ATLAS RD
COEUR D'ALENE ID 355-A4
HAYDEN ID 355-A1
KOOTENAI CO ID 355-A6
ATOR HILL RD
KOOTENAI CO ID 248-A5
ATWOOD RD
KLICKITAT CO WA 196-A5
AUBREY L WHITE PKWY
SPOKANE WA 348-B4
SPOKANE CO WA 348-B4
N AUBREY L WHITE PKWY
SPOKANE WA 346-A14
SPOKANE WA 348-B2
SPOKANE CO WA 348-B2
AUBURN AV
BAKER CITY OR 138-B1
AUBURN AV U.S.-30
BAKER CITY OR 138-B1
AUBURN AV NE
AUBURN WA 182-C1
AUBURN ST
KLAMATH FALLS OR 338-E6
AUBURN WY N
AUBURN WA 175-C7
AUBURN WA 182-C1
AUBURN WY S
AUBURN WA 182-C1
AUBURN WY S Rt#-164
AUBURN WA 182-C1
AUBURN BLACK DIAMOND RD
AUBURN WA 182-D1
BLACK DIAMOND WA 110-C3
KING CO WA 110-C3
KING CO WA 182-D1
SE AUBURN BLACK DIAMOND RD
KING CO WA 182-C1
AUBURN-ECHO LAKE CTO Rt#-18
AUBURN WA 182-C1
COVINGTON WA 175-D7
KENT WA 175-D7
KING CO WA 175-D7
KING CO WA 176-A6
KING CO WA 182-C1
MAPLE VALLEY WA 175-D7
AUBURN-ECHO LAKE CTO SE Rt#-18
KING CO WA 176-A6
AUBURN ENUMCLAW RD Rt#-164
AUBURN WA 182-C2
KING CO WA 182-C2
S AUDUBON ST
SPOKANE WA 348-F10
AUFDERHEIDE SCENIC BYWY
LANE CO OR 134-A3
LANE CO OR 142-A1
WESTFIR OR 142-A1
W AUGUSTA AV
SPOKANE WA 348-J7
AUGUSTA AV NE
Suquamish WA 170-C7
AULT FIELD RD
Ault Field WA 167-B2
ISLAND CO WA 167-B2
AUMSVILLE HWY SE
AUMSVILLE OR 133-C1
AUMSVILLE OR 205-B7
MARION CO OR 205-A7
MARION CO OR 325-F5
SALEM OR 325-F5
AUNE HALL RD
WHITMAN CO WA 122-A1
AURORA AV N Rt#-99
SEATTLE WA 171-A7
SEATTLE WA 273-J2
SEATTLE WA 277-J4
SHORELINE WA 171-A7
AUSTIN AV
COQUITLAM BC 157-A5
DISTRICT OF COQUITLAM BC 156-D5
AUSTIN DR
BREMERTON WA 270-C8
AUSTIN RD
DISTRICT OF BURNABY BC 156-D5
DISTRICT OF COQUITLAM BC 156-D5
SKAGIT CO WA 161-C7
N AUSTIN RD
SPOKANE WA 346-F2
S AUSTIN RD
SPOKANE CO WA 246-B6
AUTOCENTER WY
BREMERTON WA 270-D10
AVALON ST Rt#-69
ADA CO ID 253-A5
KUNA ID 253-A5
W AVALON ST
KUNA ID 253-A5
SW AVALON WY
SEATTLE WA 281-F4
AVENUE A
SEASIDE OR 301-F8
AVENUE B
GRANDVIEW WA 120-B3
SEASIDE OR 301-G8
N AVENUE B
BOISE ID 253-D3
GRANDVIEW WA 120-B3
AVENUE D
SNOHOMISH WA 171-D3
SNOHOMISH CO WA 171-D3
AVENUE G
SEASIDE OR 301-G9
AVENUE S
SEASIDE OR 301-G10
CLATSOP CO OR 301-F10
AVENUE U
CLATSOP CO OR 301-F10
SEASIDE OR 301-F10
AVERY RD E
LEWIS CO WA 187-D2
AVERY RD W
LEWIS CO WA 187-C2
SW AVERY ST
TUALATIN OR 199-B4
AVON AV Rt#-20
BURLINGTON WA 260-C4
AVON CTO Rt#-20
SKAGIT CO WA 161-A6
SKAGIT CO WA 260-A6
AVON-ALLEN RD
SKAGIT CO WA 161-A6
AVON CUT-OFF Rt#-20
SKAGIT CO WA 161-A7
AVONDALE PL NE
KING CO WA 171-D7
AVONDALE RD NE
KING CO WA 171-D7
KING CO WA 175-D1
REDMOND WA 171-D7
REDMOND WA 175-D1
AVONDALE WY NE
REDMOND WA 175-D1
AWMILLER RD
YAKIMA CO WA 187-B4
AXFORD RD
BATTLE GROUND WA 193-A3
CLARK CO WA 193-A3
AXLING RD
WHATCOM CO WA 158-D3
AXTEL CREEK RD
LINCOLN CO OR 209-B4
E AXTON RD
WHATCOM CO WA 102-B1
WHATCOM CO WA 158-D6
W AXTON RD
FERNDALE WA 158-D6
WHATCOM CO WA 158-D6
AYER RD
WALLA WALLA CO WA 121-C2
AZALEA DR
JOSEPHINE CO OR 229-A5

B

B AV
DESCHUTES CO OR 212-D4
Terrebonne OR 212-D4
W B AV Rt#-99
DRAIN OR 219-A3
B ST
ABERDEEN WA 178-B7
ASHLAND OR 337-D7
FOREST GROVE OR 198-B1
TILLAMOOK CO OR 191-B4
WASHINGTON CO OR 198-B1
B ST Rt#-82
ISLAND CITY OR 130-A2
E B ST U.S.-30
RAINIER OR 189-C4
NE B ST
MADRAS OR 208-C5
S B ST
ISLAND CITY OR 130-A2
W B ST
RAINIER OR 189-B4
W B ST U.S.-30
RAINIER OR 189-C4
B ST E
PIERCE CO WA 181-D5
B 1/2-NE RD
GRANT CO WA 112-C3
B 5-NE
GRANT CO WA 112-C2
E BABB RD
SPOKANE CO WA 114-C3
BABCOCK RD
WALLA WALLA CO WA 121-C2
S BABCOCK RD
CLACKAMAS CO OR 205-D2
NE BABCOCK ST
KITSAP CO WA 170-C4
B A BENSON RD
SKAGIT CO WA 161-A5
BABY DOLL RD E
KITSAP CO WA 271-D14
BABY DOLL RD SE
KITSAP CO WA 271-D14
BACHELOR DR
LINCOLN CO WA 113-C1
BACHELOR FLAT RD
COLUMBIA CO OR 192-A2
SAINT HELENS OR 192-A2
BACONA RD
WASHINGTON CO OR 125-C1
BACON CAMP RD
HARNEY CO OR 144-B3
BACUS RD
SKAGIT CO WA 161-D5
BADGER RD
BENTON CO WA 120-C3
BENTON CO WA 121-A3
BENTON CO WA 341-G14
GRAYS HARBOR CO WA 177-D2
KENNEWICK WA 341-G14
E BADGER RD Rt#-546
WHATCOM CO WA 102-B1
WHATCOM CO WA 158-D3
E BADGER RD Rt#-547
WHATCOM CO WA 102-B1
W BADGER RD
WHATCOM CO WA 158-D3
BADGER CANYON RD
BENTON CO WA 120-C3
BADGER CREEK RD
CROOK CO OR 136-A2
WASCO CO OR 127-A3
WHEELER CO OR 136-B2
BADGER MOUNTAIN RD
DOUGLAS CO WA 239-A4
BADGER MOUNTAIN RD SW
DOUGLAS CO WA 239-B2
BADGER POCKET RD
KITTITAS WA 241-C6
KITTITAS CO WA 241-C6
BAGBY RD
CLACKAMAS CO OR 126-B3
BAGDAD RD
LINCOLN CO WA 113-B1
LINCOLN CO WA 237-D4
BAILER HILL RD
SAN JUAN CO WA 101-C2
BAILEY RD
CITY OF CHILLIWACK BC 94-C3
ISLAND CO WA 171-A3
S BAILEY ST
SEATTLE WA 282-B7
BAILEY HILL RD
EUGENE OR 329-C8
LANE CO OR 329-A14
BAINARD LN
CHELAN CO WA 239-B5
BAINBRIDGE IS-SEATTLE FERRY
KING CO WA 174-D2
BAIRD RD NE
THURSTON CO WA 180-D4
BAIRD SPRINGS RD
GRANT CO WA 112-C3
GRANT CO WA 239-D7
BAKEOVEN RD
MAUPIN OR 127-B3
WASCO CO OR 127-B3
N BAKER AV
East Wenatchee Bench WA 239-A4
BAKER RD
CLACKAMAS CO OR 199-A5
COOS CO OR 220-C5
JACKSON CO OR 234-B2
KLICKITAT CO WA 196-B3
MORROW CO OR 128-B1
YAKIMA CO WA 243-B5
E BAKER RD
SPOKANE CO WA 246-D7
SE BAKER RD
KITSAP CO WA 174-C4
SW BAKER RD
CLACKAMAS CO OR 199-A5
BAKER RD SW
THURSTON CO WA 180-B6
NE BAKER ST
MCMINNVILLE OR 198-A7
NE BAKER ST Rt#-99W
MCMINNVILLE OR 198-A7
SE BAKER ST Rt#-99W
MCMINNVILLE OR 198-A7
BAKER-COPPERFIELD HWY Rt#-86
BAKER CO OR 130-B3
BAKER CO OR 131-A3
BAKER CO OR 138-C1
BAKER CO OR 139-A1
RICHLAND OR 139-A1
NW BAKER CREEK RD
MCMINNVILLE OR 198-A7
YAMHILL CO OR 198-A7
BAKER HEIGHTS RD
SKAGIT CO WA 161-C7
NE BAKER HILL RD
BAINBRIDGE ISLAND WA 271-G5
BAKER LAKE HWY
WHATCOM CO WA 102-C2
BAKER LAKE RD
SKAGIT CO WA 102-C2
BAKER LANGDON RD
WALLA WALLA CO WA 345-A13
S BAKERS FERRY RD
CLACKAMAS CO OR 200-A4
E BAKERVIEW RD
BELLINGHAM WA 258-F1
WHATCOM CO WA 258-F1
BALBACK RD
ADAMS CO ID 251-A4
BALCH RD
KLICKITAT CO WA 196-B5
BALDA RD
ISLAND CO WA 167-B3
BALD BUTTE RD
WHITMAN CO WA 249-C7
BALD HILLS RD SE
THURSTON CO WA 118-A1
BALD PEAK RD
WASHINGTON CO OR 198-C3
YAMHILL CO OR 198-C4
BALD RIDGE RD N
LINCOLN CO WA 114-A1
S BALDWIN DR
JEFFERSON CO OR 208-C6
BALDWIN RD
CROOK CO OR 213-C5
Garrett WA 344-D7
WALLA WALLA WA 344-D7
BALDY MOUNTAIN RD
BONNER CO ID 107-A3
BONNER CO ID 244-A2
BALL RD
JACKSON CO OR 230-D4
BALL ST
MOUNT VERNON WA 260-B12
N BALLANTYNE LN
ADA CO ID 253-A1
EAGLE ID 253-A1
W BALLARD DR
KITTITAS CO WA 240-D2
BALLARD RD
POLK CO OR 204-A7
BALLARD RD NW
DOUGLAS CO WA 236-D7
BALLINGER DR
GRANTS PASS OR 335-D10
BALLINGER WY NE Rt#-104
LAKE FOREST PARK WA 171-B6
SHORELINE WA 171-B6
BALL MTN LTLE SHASTA RD Rt#-3
MONTAGUE CA 150-A3
SISKIYOU CO CA 150-A3
SISKIYOU CO CA 150-A3
BALLOW RD
MASON CO WA 180-D2
BALLSTON RD
POLK CO OR 204-A3
YAMHILL CO OR 204-A3
SW BALLSTON RD
YAMHILL CO OR 125-B3
YAMHILL CO OR 204-A3
BALLY MOUNTAIN TRAIL RD
ADAMS CO ID 251-A1
BALM FORK RD
MORROW CO OR 128-C2
BALSAM DR
KLAMATH CO OR 235-A4
KLAMATH CO OR 338-A12
KLAMATH FALLS OR 338-A12
BALSAM DR S
SALEM OR 324-F3
S BALTIMORE RD
SPOKANE CO WA 246-C6
BALTIMORE ST
LONGVIEW WA 302-H10
LONGVIEW WA 303-A11
BANDIX RD SE
KITSAP CO WA 174-C6
BANDY RD
BONNER CO ID 107-A3
BANFIELD FRWY I-84
PORTLAND OR 313-H4
PORTLAND OR 314-C5
PORTLAND OR 315-J2
S BANGOR ST
SEATTLE WA 287-G6
N BANK RD
COOS CO OR 220-C4
S BANK RD
GRAYS HARBOR CO WA 117-B1
S BANK RD Rt#-107
GRAYS HARBOR CO WA 117-A1
SW BANK RD
KING CO WA 174-D5
NE BANNER PL
SEATTLE WA 274-B2
N BANNER RD
KITSAP CO WA 174-C4
BANNER RD SE
KITSAP CO WA 174-C5
BANNER WY NE
SEATTLE WA 274-B2
BANNISTER RD
UMATILLA CO OR 129-C1
WESTON OR 129-C1
BANTA RD
BAKER CO OR 130-B3
BAPTIST CHURCH DR
LINN CO OR 133-C1
BAR 14 RD
KITTITAS CO WA 241-C4
BARBARA DR
JOSEPHINE CO OR 229-A5
BARBARA WY
DESCHUTES CO OR 212-A7
BARBEE RD
WHITMAN CO WA 249-A6
BARBER RD NW
DOUGLAS CO WA 236-B5
SW BARBUR BLVD
PORTLAND OR 317-E1
SW BARBUR BLVD Rt#-99W
PORTLAND OR 199-B3
PORTLAND OR 316-E3
PORTLAND OR 317-E2
PORTLAND OR 320-A1
TIGARD OR 199-B3
BARCLAY DR
DESCHUTES CO OR 211-D5
BARGER AV
EUGENE OR 329-A1
BARKER LN
VALLEY CO ID 252-D2
BARKER RD
COLUMBIA CO OR 189-B5
LANE CO OR 133-B3
N BARKER RD
SPOKANE VALLEY WA 351-G3
S BARKER RD
SPOKANE CO WA 351-G10
SPOKANE VALLEY WA 351-G8
W BARKER RD
ADA CO ID 253-C6
BARKER CANYON RD
DOUGLAS CO WA 237-A3
BARKES RD
HARRAH WA 119-C2
BARKLEY BLVD
BELLINGHAM WA 258-J4
E BARKLEY BLVD
BELLINGHAM WA 258-H3
BARLOW RD
BARLOW OR 199-B7
CLACKAMAS CO OR 199-B7
CLACKAMAS CO OR 205-C1
HOOD RIVER CO OR 202-B7
S BARLOW RD
CLACKAMAS CO OR 205-C1
S BARLOW MONTE CRISTO RD
CLACKAMAS CO OR 205-C2
MARION CO OR 205-C2
BARLOW TRAIL RD
CLACKAMAS CO OR 201-B4
BARNARDS RD
CLACKAMAS CO OR 126-A3
CLACKAMAS CO OR 205-D1
S BARNARDS RD
CLACKAMAS CO OR 205-D1
S BARNEBURG RD
MEDFORD OR 336-F12
BARNEKOFF RD
COOS CO OR 220-B7
BARNES AV U.S.-395
SENECA OR 137-B3
BARNES DR
COWLITZ CO WA 187-C6
LEWIS CO WA 187-C6
NE BARNES DR
JEFFERSON CO OR 208-C3
BARNES RD
KITTITAS CO WA 241-B6
NW BARNES RD
BEAVERTON OR 199-B1
WASHINGTON CO OR 199-B1
SW BARNES RD
BEAVERTON OR 199-B1
WASHINGTON CO OR 199-B1
BARNES RD NW
DOUGLAS CO WA 236-D7
BARNES ST
KELSO WA 303-D6
BARNES BUTTE RD
CROOK CO OR 213-D4
BARNET HWY Rt#-7A
COQUITLAM BC 157-A4
PORT MOODY BC 157-A4
BARNET RD Rt#-7A
DISTRICT OF BURNABY BC 156-D4
BARNETT RD
GILLIAM CO OR 128-A2
E BARNETT RD
MEDFORD OR 234-B1
MEDFORD OR 336-F13
W BARNETT RD
MEDFORD OR 336-D13
BARNHART RD
WHATCOM CO WA 158-D3
YAKIMA CO WA 120-A2
BARNSTON DR E
CITY OF SURREY BC 157-B6
BARNSTON DR W
CITY OF SURREY BC 157-B6
BARON RD NE
MARION CO OR 205-B3
BARR RD
CLALLAM CO WA 165-D6
DESCHUTES CO OR 212-B5
LEWISTON ID 250-C5
NEZ PERCE CO ID 250-C5
WHATCOM CO WA 158-C6
BARR-ALEX RD Rt#-219
WASHINGTON CO OR 198-D3
BARRELL SPRINGS RD
SKAGIT CO WA 161-B3
BARRETT RD
HOOD RIVER CO OR 195-C5
SW BARROWS RD
BEAVERTON OR 199-A3
WASHINGTON CO OR 199-A3
BARRY RD
DOUGLAS CO WA 237-C1
BARRY REX RD
DOUGLAS CO WA 237-C2
BARSTOW-PIERRE LAKE RD
STEVENS CO WA 105-C1
SE BARTEL RD
CLACKAMAS CO OR 200-B4

INDEX

BARTLEMAY RD STREET INDEX BIGHAM BROWN RD 359

STREET City State Page-Grid

BARTLEMAY RD
CLACKAMAS CO OR 200-B4
BARTLETTE RD
PEND OREILLE CO WA 106-B3
SW BARTON PL
SEATTLE WA 285-G3
BARTON RD
DOUGLAS CO OR 225-C6
SW BARTON ST
SEATTLE WA 284-D3
SEATTLE WA 285-F3
S BASALT ST
SPOKANE CO WA 348-C11
BASE LINE DR
HOOD RIVER CO OR 202-C2
BASE LINE RD
GILLIAM CO OR 128-A2
BASELINE RD
BAY CITY OR 197-B1
DOUGLAS CO WA 236-C7
GRANT CO WA 112-B3
W BASELINE RD
HILLSBORO OR 198-D1
HILLSBORO OR 199-A1
WASHINGTON CO OR 198-D1
WASHINGTON CO OR 199-A1
BASELINE RD E
GRANT CO WA 242-C4
BASELINE ST Rt#-8
CORNELIUS OR 198-C1
SE BASELINE ST Rt#-8
HILLSBORO OR 198-D1
SW BASELINE ST Rt#-8
HILLSBORO OR 198-D1
BASELINE .5 RD SE
GRANT CO WA 242-D4
BASELINE RIDGE RD
WASHINGTON CO OR 198-A1
BASEY CANYON RD
MORROW CO OR 128-C2
N BASIN AV
PORTLAND OR 308-C7
PORTLAND OR 312-D1
W BASIN RD
DESCHUTES CO OR 135-B3
BASIN ST N Rt#-28
EPHRATA WA 112-C3
GRANT CO WA 112-C3
BASIN ST NW Rt#-28
EPHRATA WA 112-C3
GRANT CO WA 112-C3
BASIN ST S Rt#-28
EPHRATA WA 112-C3
GRANT CO WA 112-C3
BASKET BUTTE RD
DOUGLAS CO OR 223-A3
NE BASKET FLAT RD
CLARK CO WA 193-B2
BASL HILL RD
MARION CO OR 134-A1
BASSET RD
SKAGIT CO WA 161-C5
BATES RD
COOS CO OR 220-B6
DOUGLAS CO OR 225-C4
KELSO WA 303-E8
KLICKITAT CO WA 195-D4
BATES RD E
LINCOLN CO WA 113-B3
BATH
PIERCE CO WA 182-B6
BATTELLE BLVD
RICHLAND WA 340-F6
BATTERMAN RD
DOUGLAS CO WA 239-B5
BATTERY ST
SEATTLE WA 277-J4
BATTLE CREEK RD
JACKSON CO OR 230-A2
OWYHEE CO ID 155-C1
BATTLE CREEK RD SE
MARION CO OR 325-B9
SALEM OR 324-J5
SALEM OR 325-A5
BATTLE CREEK RANCH RD
MALHEUR CO OR 154-B2
BATTLE POINT RD NE
BAINBRIDGE ISLAND WA 174-C1
BATUM RD
ADAMS CO WA 113-B3
LINCOLN CO WA 113-B3
BATY RD
CLACKAMAS CO OR 201-A4
BAUER RD
WHITMAN CO WA 250-B1
BAUMAN RD
ADAMS CO WA 113-C3
ADAMS CO WA 121-C1
RITZVILLE WA 113-C3
BAUMEISTER DR
ASOTIN WA 250-B5
BAY AV
HOQUIAM WA 178-A7
BAY AV Rt#-103
Ocean Park WA 186-A2
SE BAY BLVD
NEWPORT OR 206-B4
SW BAY BLVD
NEWPORT OR 206-B4
E BAY DR
OLYMPIA WA 296-J2
W BAY DR
OLYMPIA WA 296-G3
E BAY DR NW
PIERCE CO WA 181-C1
S BAY LP NE
THURSTON CO WA 180-D5
BAY PL
DESCHUTES CO OR 211-D5
BAY RD
Birch Bay WA 158-B4
LEWIS CO WA 187-C3
S BAY RD NE
OLYMPIA WA 297-C2
THURSTON CO WA 180-D5
THURSTON CO WA 297-C2
BAY ST
CITY OF VICTORIA BC 256-H7
CITY OF VICTORIA BC 257-A8
PORT ORCHARD WA 270-J14
PORT ORCHARD WA 271-A13
BAY ST Rt#-166
PORT ORCHARD WA 174-B4
PORT ORCHARD WA 270-H14
BAY ST Rt#-167
TACOMA WA 182-A2
S BAY ST
WALDPORT OR 328-E5

SW BAY ST
NEWPORT OR 206-B4
BAYARD ST Rt#-206
CONDON OR 128-A2
E BAYARD ST Rt#-206
CONDON OR 128-A2
BAY CENTER RD
PACIFIC CO WA 183-C7
BAY CENTER DIKE RD
PACIFIC CO WA 183-C7
BAYLEY RD
YAMHILL CO OR 198-C5
BAYLISS RD
YAMHILL CO OR 198-B6
BAYNES RD
DISTRICT OF SAANICH BC 257-G5
BAYOCEAN RD NW
TILLAMOOK CO OR 197-B1
BAYOCEAN DIKE RD
TILLAMOOK CO OR 191-A7
TILLAMOOK CO OR 197-A1
BAYSHORE DR
LINCOLN CO OR 328-C3
N BAYSHORE DR
COOS BAY OR 333-H9
S BAYSHORE DR
COOS BAY OR 333-H11
BAYVIEW DR
WHATCOM CO WA 101-C1
BAYVIEW DR W
BREMERTON WA 270-E13
Navy Yard City WA 270-E13
BAYVIEW RD
ISLAND CO WA 170-D2
LINCOLN CO OR 328-H2
SKAGIT CO WA 161-A6
WALDPORT OR 328-D3
BAYVIEW RD KPN
PIERCE CO WA 174-A7
BAY VIEW EDISON RD
SKAGIT CO WA 160-D5
SKAGIT CO WA 161-A5
B D MINKLER RD
SKAGIT CO WA 161-C5
BEACH DR
DISTRICT OF OAK BAY BC 257-E5
ISLAND CO WA 167-D7
S BEACH DR
BAINBRIDGE ISLAND WA 271-J8
SEASIDE OR 301-F10
BEACH DR E
Colby WA 271-F9
KITSAP CO WA 271-F9
PORT ORCHARD WA 271-C12
BEACH DR NE
KITSAP CO WA 170-B5
BEACH DR SW
SEATTLE WA 280-C5
SEATTLE WA 284-D1
BEACH RD
LANE CO OR 215-B6
BEACH ST
ASHLAND OR 337-E9
BEACHER HILL RD
CHELAN CO WA 238-A1
BEACH LOOP DR SW
BANDON OR 220-A6
BEACH LOOP RD
BANDON OR 220-A7
COOS CO OR 220-A7
BEACON AV S
KING CO WA 287-F6
KING CO WA 289-H1
SEATTLE WA 282-B2
SEATTLE WA 286-D1
SEATTLE WA 287-F6
E BEACON DR
LANE CO OR 210-A7
Santa Clara OR 210-A7
NE BEACON DR
GRANTS PASS OR 335-H7
W BEACON DR
LANE CO OR 210-A7
BEACON LN
DISTRICT OF WEST VANCOUVE BC 156-A3
BEACON RD
GRAYS HARBOR CO WA 178-D7
WHITMAN CO WA 122-A1
W BEACON ST
BOISE ID 253-C3
E BEACON LIGHT RD
ADA CO ID 253-B1
EAGLE ID 253-B1
W BEACON LIGHT RD
ADA CO ID 253-A1
BEAGLE RD
JACKSON CO OR 230-C4
E BEAKMAN ST Rt#-203
UNION OR 130-B2
BEALL LN
CENTRAL POINT OR 230-C7
CENTRAL POINT OR 336-A7
JACKSON CO OR 230-C7
MEDFORD OR 230-C7
MEDFORD OR 336-A7
BEALL RD SW
KING CO WA 174-D6
BEALS CREEK RD
DOUGLAS CO OR 225-D3
BEAM RD
YAKIMA CO WA 120-A2
BEAR AV
CITY OF HARRISON HOT SPRI BC 94-C3
BEAR DR
JEFFERSON CO OR 208-B7
SW BEAR DR
JEFFERSON CO OR 208-B6
BEAR CREEK RD
COOS CO OR 220-B6
CROOK CO OR 136-A1
DESCHUTES CO OR 217-D3
DOUGLAS CO OR 219-C1
DOUGLAS CO OR 223-B5
GRANT CO OR 137-B2
JOSEPHINE CO OR 233-C4
LANE CO OR 215-C5
LINCOLN CO OR 203-C4
LINCOLN CO OR 209-B2
SKAMANIA CO WA 194-D4
WALLOWA CO OR 130-B2
E BEAR CREEK RD
BEND OR 217-C3
BEND OR 332-J8
DESCHUTES CO OR 217-C3
N BEAR CREEK RD
DOUGLAS CO OR 219-C1
NE BEAR CREEK RD
BEND OR 332-G8

W BEAR CREEK RD
KITSAP CO WA 173-C4
MASON CO WA 173-C4
BEAR CREEK RD NE
KING CO WA 171-D7
BEAR CREEK DEWATTO RD
KITSAP CO WA 173-C4
MASON CO WA 173-C4
BEAR CREEK-FIFE RD
CROOK CO OR 135-C3
CROOK CO OR 136-A3
CROOK CO OR 144-B1
BEAR CREST DR Rt#-99
JACKSON CO OR 234-B2
PHOENIX OR 234-B2
BEAR FLAT RD
KLAMATH CO OR 143-A2
LAKE CO OR 143-A2
BEAR LAKE RD
KITSAP CO WA 174-A5
BEAR MOUNTAIN RD
CHELAN CO WA 236-B3
LANE CO OR 215-C5
BEAR RIVER RD
PACIFIC CO WA 186-B6
BEAR SPURS LP
JEFFERSON CO OR 211-D1
BEAR SPURS RD
JEFFERSON CO OR 211-D1
BEAR WALLOW BUTTE RD
DESCHUTES CO OR 216-D1
BEATYS BUTTE RD
LAKE CO OR 152-C2
E BEAUCHENE RD
YAKIMA CO WA 243-C7
S BEAUDRY RD
YAKIMA CO WA 243-D7
BEAUTY CREEK RD
KOOTENAI CO ID 248-B1
BEAVER RD
DISTRICT OF NORTH VANCOUV BC 255-B1
NEZ PERCE CO ID 250-D5
BEAVERBROOK DR
CITY OF BURNABY BC 156-D4
NE BEAVER BROOK RD
CLARK CO WA 193-A1
BEAVER BUTTE RD
WASCO CO OR 127-A3
BEAVER CREEK RD
ADAMS CO ID 131-C3
ADAMS CO ID 251-A5
COOS CO OR 220-D3
CROOK CO OR 136-B3
LEWIS CO WA 187-A1
LINCOLN CO OR 206-B6
WAHKIAKUM CO WA 117-B3
E BEAVER CREEK RD
Colby WA 271-F10
KITSAP CO WA 271-F10
N BEAVER CREEK RD
LINCOLN CO OR 206-B6
S BEAVER CREEK RD
LINCOLN CO OR 206-B7
LINCOLN CO OR 328-G2
S BEAVERCREEK RD
CLACKAMAS CO OR 126-A3
CLACKAMAS CO OR 199-D5
CLACKAMAS CO OR 200-A6
OREGON CITY OR 199-D5
BEAVER FALLS RD
CLATSKANIE OR 117-B3
COLUMBIA CO OR 117-B3
COLUMBIA CO OR 189-A4
E BEAVER HILL RD
COOS CO OR 220-C4
W BEAVER HILL RD
COOS CO OR 220-B3
BEAVER LAKE RD
SKAGIT CO WA 161-C7
BEAVER MARSH RD
SKAGIT CO WA 168-A1
BEAVER SPRINGS RD
COLUMBIA CO OR 189-B5
SW BEAVRTN-HLLSDLE HWY Rt#-10
BEAVERTON OR 199-B2
PORTLAND OR 199-B2
PORTLAND OR 316-A3
WASHINGTON CO OR 199-B2
BEAVERTON-TGRD FRWY Rt#-217
BEAVERTON OR 199-B3
LAKE OSWEGO OR 199-B3
TIGARD OR 199-B3
WASHINGTON CO OR 199-B3
BEAVERTON VALLEY RD
SAN JUAN CO WA 101-C2
N BEAVER VALLEY DR
LINCOLN CO OR 206-B7
BEAVER VALLEY RD Rt#-19
JEFFERSON CO WA 170-A1
BEBER RANCH RD
MALHEUR CO OR 154-B1
BECK RD
BENTON CO WA 121-A3
POLK CO OR 204-A4
STEVENS CO WA 106-A3
NE BECK RD
BAINBRIDGE ISLAND WA 271-H6
BECKER RD
DOUGLAS CO OR 221-A3
NEZ PERCE CO ID 250-C2
WHITMAN CO WA 249-B7
WHITMAN CO WA 250-A1
BECKETT POINT RD
JEFFERSON CO WA 166-D7
BECKLEY RD
ADAMS CO WA 122-A1
BEDELL RD
COLUMBIA CO OR 189-B6
BED ROCK FLAT RD
WASHINGTON CO ID 139-B1
BEDWELL BAY RD
ANMORE BC 157-A3
BELCARRA BC 157-A3
CITY OF PORT MOODY BC 156-D3
MAPLE RIDGE BC 157-A3
PORT MOODY BC 157-A3
VILLAGE OF BELCARRA BC 156-D3
BEEBE RD
COWLITZ CO WA 187-C6
BEECH AV
WALLA WALLA CO WA 345-G4
BEECH ST
ARLINGTON OR 128-A1
LONGVIEW WA 302-H10
E BEECH CREEK RD
GRANT CO OR 137-B1

SW BEEF BEND RD
KING CITY OR 199-A4
WASHINGTON CO OR 199-A4
BEEKS RD
BONNER CO ID 244-A5
BEEKS CANYON RD
KLICKITAT CO WA 196-C1
BEE MILL RD
JEFFERSON CO WA 109-C1
BEERBOWER RD
MASON CO WA 179-A5
BEESON CTO
WHITMAN CO WA 249-B3
BEESON RD
CLACKAMAS CO OR 200-A7
BEET RD
CANYON CO ID 147-B1
BEEVILLE LOOP RD
MASON CO WA 179-B2
BEGBIE ST
CITY OF VICTORIA BC 256-J9
CITY OF VICTORIA BC 257-A9
BEHME RD
WHATCOM CO WA 158-C3
BEHRENS LN
UNION CO OR 130-A2
BEHRENS-MILLETT RD
MOUNT VERNON WA 260-A13
SKAGIT CO WA 260-A13
BEHRN RD
WASCO CO OR 196-A6
BEIRMAN RD
ADAMS CO WA 113-C3
BEITEY RD
STEVENS CO WA 106-B3
BELFAIR-TAHUYA RD
MASON CO WA 173-C5
W BELFAIR VALLEY RD
BREMERTON WA 174-A4
KITSAP CO WA 174-A4
BELKNAP SPRINGS HWY Rt#-126
LANE CO OR 134-B2
LINN CO OR 134-B2
SE BELL AV
CLACKAMAS CO OR 318-E7
BELL RD
WASHINGTON CO OR 199-A5
YAMHILL CO OR 198-D5
E BELL RD
YAKIMA CO WA 243-C7
SW BELL RD
CLACKAMAS CO OR 199-A5
BELL ST
DISTRICT OF MISSION BC 94-B3
BELLE CENTER RD
SKAMANIA CO WA 193-D7
BELLE PASSI RD NE
MARION CO OR 205-B2
BELLEVILLE ST
CITY OF VICTORIA BC 256-G9
BELLEVUE HWY
AMITY OR 204-B2
YAMHILL CO OR 204-B2
SW BELLEVUE HWY
YAMHILL CO OR 204-A2
BELLEVUE WY NE
BELLEVUE WA 175-C2
BELLEVUE WY SE
BELLEVUE WA 175-C2
NE BELLEVUE REDMOND RD
BELLEVUE WA 175-C2
REDMOND WA 175-C2
BELLFOUNTAIN RD
BENTON CO OR 133-B2
BENTON CO OR 327-A14
BELLINGER LN
JACKSON CO OR 234-A1
BELLINGER SCALE RD
LINN CO OR 133-C1
BELL PLAIN DR
LINN CO OR 207-B7
BELL PLAIN RD
GARFIELD CO WA 122-B2
N BELLWOOD ST
UNION OR 130-B2
S BELLWOOD ST
UNION OR 130-B2
BELMONT AV E
SEATTLE WA 278-B3
BELMONT DR
HOOD RIVER CO OR 195-C5
SW BELMONT LN
JEFFERSON CO OR 208-B5
MADRAS OR 208-B5
BELMONT RD
HOOD RIVER OR 195-C5
HOOD RIVER CO OR 195-C5
E BELMONT RD
SPOKANE CO WA 247-A5
SE BELMONT ST
PORTLAND OR 313-G6
PORTLAND OR 314-A6
BELMONT-FARMINGTON RD
FARMINGTON WA 115-A3
NW BELT RD
YAMHILL CO OR 198-A4
N BELT ST
SPOKANE WA 348-G2
BELTLINE HWY
EUGENE OR 329-B2
BELTLINE HWY Rt#-69
EUGENE OR 215-B1
EUGENE OR 329-B5
EUGENE OR 330-A1
LANE CO OR 215-B1
Santa Clara OR 215-B1
SPRINGFIELD OR 330-A1
BELTLINE E RD
SPRINGFIELD OR 330-F2
BELTS DR
LINN CO OR 210-B4
BELVEDERE RD
OKANOGAN CO WA 237-C1
BEN BUNCH RD
LANE CO OR 214-B1
S BEN BURR BLVD
SPOKANE WA 349-F11
N BENCH RD
KOOTENAI CO ID 245-A3
W BENCH RD
ADAMS CO WA 121-A1
BENCH MARK BUTTE RD
DESCHUTES CO OR 216-A7
BEND AV
WINSTON OR 221-B6
BEND PKWY U.S.-97
BEND OR 332-F3

BEND PKWY U.S.-97
DESCHUTES CO OR 332-F3
BEN DAY GULCH RD
GARFIELD CO WA 122-B2
BEND-DESCHUTES MARKET RD
BEND OR 217-C1
DESCHUTES CO OR 212-C7
DESCHUTES CO OR 217-C1
BENDER RD
KITTITAS CO WA 241-B5
LYNDEN WA 102-B1
WHATCOM CO WA 102-B1
BENDIGO BLVD N Rt#-202
NORTH BEND WA 176-C4
SNOQUALMIE WA 176-C4
BENDIGO BLVD S Rt#-202
NORTH BEND WA 176-C5
BENDIRE RD
MALHEUR CO OR 138-A3
BEND ON RD N
OKANOGAN CO WA 104-C3
BENEKE RD
CLATSOP CO OR 117-B3
BENEWAH RD
BENEWAH CO ID 115-A3
BENEWAH CO ID 248-B7
S BEN GARNETT WY
SPOKANE WA 348-J10
BENGE WASHTUCNA RD
ADAMS CO WA 122-A1
BENGE-WASHTUCNA RD
ADAMS CO WA 121-C1
BENGE WINONA RD
ADAMS CO WA 122-A1
BENGOA RD
HUMBOLDT CO NV 154-A3
BENHAM ST
RICHLAND WA 341-G3
BENHAM FALLS RD
DESCHUTES CO OR 217-A5
BEN HOWARD RD
SNOHOMISH CO WA 110-C1
BENJAMIN RD
YAMHILL CO OR 198-D5
BEN MORE RD
DOUGLAS CO OR 219-B6
BENNETT DR
WHATCOM CO WA 158-D7
WHATCOM CO WA 258-A1
BENNETT RD
CANYON CO ID 147-C1
COLUMBIA CO OR 192-A2
DESCHUTES CO OR 217-D3
PEND OREILLE CO WA 106-C3
WASCO CO OR 127-C3
BENNETT CREEK RD
LANE CO OR 215-B6
BENNION RD
KOOTENAI CO ID 247-D7
BENSON DR S Rt#-515
KING CO WA 175-C5
RENTON WA 175-C5
BENSON RD Rt#-515
KENT WA 175-C6
KING CO WA 175-C6
SE BENSON RD
LINCOLN CO OR 206-B4
NEWPORT OR 206-B4
BENSON RD S
KING CO WA 175-C5
RENTON WA 175-C5
BENSON RD SE Rt#-515
KING CO WA 175-C6
BENSON CREEK RD
COOS CO OR 218-D4
OKANOGAN CO WA 104-B3
BENSTON CORNER CLEAR LAKE
PIERCE CO WA 118-B1
BENSTON-KAPOWSIN
PIERCE CO WA 182-A7
BENTON ST
PORT TOWNSEND WA 263-G5
N BENTON ST
KENNEWICK WA 343-D10
S BENTON ST
KENNEWICK WA 343-D11
BENTON-FRANKLIN INTERCNTY BRDG
KENNEWICK WA 343-E10
PASCO WA 343-F9
BENTS RD
MARION CO OR 199-B6
BENVENUTO AV
DISTRICT OF CENTRAL SAANI BC 159-B4
BERCOT RD
Freeland WA 170-D1
BERG RD
COLUMBIA CO OR 192-A2
DOUGLAS CO WA 112-C2
BERGE RD
SKAMANIA CO WA 195-A4
BERGER-FEELEY RD
HARNEY CO OR 136-C3
E BERGESON ST
BOISE ID 253-D3
BERKELEY AV SW
LAKEWOOD WA 181-C5
PIERCE CO WA 181-C5
BERKLEY AV
DISTRICT OF NORTH VANCOUV BC 255-H4
BERKLEY RD
DISTRICT OF NORTH VANCOUV BC 255-H5
BERLIN RD
CRESWELL OR 133-C1
LEBANON OR 133-C1
LINN CO OR 133-C1
LOWELL OR 133-C1
BERMUDA RD
BENTON CO WA 341-D12
S BERNARD ST
SPOKANE WA 348-J13
BERNARDS LN
MARION CO OR 198-D7
S BERNEY DR
WALLA WALLA WA 345-F8
WALLA WALLA CO WA 345-F8
Walla Walla East WA 345-F8
BERNHARDT CREEK RD
LANE CO OR 214-C3
BERRY DR
LINN CO OR 326-J1
NE BERRY RD
CLARK CO WA 193-B3
BERRY CREEK RD
POLK CO OR 207-A2
NW BERRY CREEK RD
YAMHILL CO OR 198-A6

SW BERRY LAKE RD
KITSAP CO WA 174-B4
N BERTELSEN RD
EUGENE OR 329-C4
S BERTELSEN RD
EUGENE OR 329-C7
LANE CO OR 329-C7
SW BERTHA BLVD
PORTLAND OR 316-D5
BERTHUSEN RD
WHATCOM CO WA 158-D4
BERT JAMES RD
BENTON CO WA 120-C3
BESSEN RD
DESCHUTES CO OR 217-A6
BESSIE CREEK RD
JACKSON CO OR 226-C7
JACKSON CO OR 227-A7
E BEST AV
COEUR D'ALENE ID 355-E8
BEST RD
POLK CO OR 204-C5
SKAGIT CO WA 161-A7
SKAGIT CO WA 168-A1
BETA DR
ALBANY OR 207-C6
BETHANY RD
YAKIMA CO WA 120-B2
BETHANY-ALEXANDER WYE
YAKIMA CO WA 120-B2
BETHEL RD
East Port Orchard WA 174-B4
KITSAP CO WA 174-B4
POLK CO OR 204-B3
BETHEL RD Rt#-166
PORT ORCHARD WA 174-B4
PORT ORCHARD WA 270-J14
N BETHEL ST
OLYMPIA WA 297-A3
BETHEL BURLEY RD SE
KITSAP CO WA 174-B5
BETHEL-BURLEY RD SE
KITSAP CO WA 174-B5
BETHEL HEIGHTS RD
POLK CO OR 204-C3
BETTAS RD
KITTITAS CO WA 240-D2
S BETTMAN RD
SPOKANE VALLEY WA 349-J11
W BETZ RD
CHENEY WA 246-A7
SPOKANE CO WA 246-A6
BEULAH RD
MALHEUR CO OR 138-A3
MALHEUR CO OR 146-A1
BEVERLY BLVD
EVERETT WA 268-D2
BEVERLY DR NE
THURSTON CO WA 181-A5
BEVERLY LN
EVERETT WA 268-B2
BEVERLY BURKE RD
GRANT CO WA 120-B1
BEVERLY PARK RD
EVERETT WA 171-B4
MUKILTEO WA 171-B4
SNOHOMISH CO WA 171-B4
BEVILLE RD
LEWIS CO WA 187-A1
BEWLEY CREEK RD
TILLAMOOK CO OR 197-C3
BEWLEYS ST
BAY CITY OR 197-B1
B HOWARD RD
WHITMAN CO WA 249-B1
BIA RD 33
JEFFERSON CO OR 134-C1
JEFFERSON CO OR 135-A1
BIA RD 108
YAKIMA CO WA 119-A2
BIA RD 140
YAKIMA CO WA 119-B3
BIA RD 255
YAKIMA CO WA 119-A3
BIA RD 7047
GRAYS HARBOR CO WA 172-B5
BIA RD S-2
GRAYS HARBOR CO WA 177-B1
BIBLE CREEK RD
TILLAMOOK CO OR 125-A2
SW BIBLE CREEK RD
TILLAMOOK CO OR 125-A2
YAMHILL CO OR 125-A2
BICKFORD AV
SNOHOMISH WA 171-D2
SNOHOMISH CO WA 171-D2
BIDDLE RD
JACKSON CO OR 336-B5
MEDFORD OR 336-C8
BIEHN ST
KLAMATH FALLS OR 338-C5
SE BIELMEIR RD
KITSAP CO WA 174-B5
BIG ALKALI RD
WHITMAN CO WA 122-A1
BIG BENCH RD
DOUGLAS CO WA 236-D4
BIG BEND RD
DOUGLAS CO OR 221-A3
BIG BUTTER CREEK RD
MORROW CO OR 128-C1
MORROW CO OR 129-A2
BIG CAMAS RD
DOUGLAS CO OR 222-C3
DOUGLAS CO OR 223-B4
BIG CREEK RD
BONNER CO ID 107-A3
COOS CO OR 218-D3
LANE CO OR 209-A6
SHOSHONE CO ID 115-C2
NE BIG CREEK RD
LINCOLN CO OR 206-B3
BIG ELK RD
JACKSON CO OR 150-A2
BIGELOW ST NE
OLYMPIA WA 297-B4
E BIGELOW GULCH RD
SPOKANE CO WA 246-D2
SPOKANE CO WA 347-H14
SPOKANE CO WA 349-G1
BIG FALL CREEK RD
LANE CO OR 133-C3
LANE CO OR 134-A3
BIG FLAT RD
BAKER CO OR 138-A1
WASHINGTON CO OR 139-C2
BIGHAM BROWN RD
JACKSON CO OR 230-D6

INDEX

360 BIG HANAFORD RD — STREET INDEX — BRICK PILE RD

STREET — City State Page-Grid

BIG HANAFORD RD
LEWIS CO WA 184-C5
BIG HUCKLEBERRY RD
SKAMANIA CO WA 195-A2
W BIG LAKE BLVD
SKAGIT CO WA 168-C1
BIG LICK LN
DOUGLAS CO OR 221-D7
E BIG MEADOWS RD
SPOKANE CO WA 114-C1
E BIG ROCK RD
SPOKANE CO WA 246-D5
BIG SANDY RD
CLACKAMAS CO OR 201-A4
BIG SPRING RD
DESCHUTES CO OR 216-D4
BIG SPRING BURN RD
DESCHUTES CO OR 216-D3
E BIG SPRINGS RD
SPOKANE CO WA 349-G11
BIG SQUAWBACK RD
JEFFERSON CO OR 211-D1
BIG STICK RD
HARNEY CO OR 144-C2
HARNEY CO OR 145-A2
BIG VALLEY RD NE
KITSAP CO WA 170-B6
BIG WILLOW RD
PAYETTE CO ID 139-B3
BILGER CREEK RD
DOUGLAS CO OR 221-D7
BILLADEAU RD
DESCHUTES CO OR 217-D4
BILL CREEK RD
LEWIS CO WA 187-C4
BILL MCDONALD PKWY
BELLINGHAM WA 258-C10
BILL MOORE RD
KLICKITAT CO WA 196-B2
BILYEU CREEK RD
LINN CO OR 134-A1
BINGHAM AV E
PIERCE CO WA 182-A5
BINGHAM RD
UMATILLA CO OR 129-C1
BINGHAMPTON ST Rt#-507
RAINIER WA 118-A1
THURSTON CO WA 118-A1
BINNS HILL DR
HOOD RIVER CO OR 195-B6
BIRCH AV
HARRAH WA 119-C2
LAPWAI ID 123-A2
NW BIRCH LN
JEFFERSON CO OR 208-B5
BIRCH PL
PACIFIC CO WA 186-A3
BIRCH RD
DISTRICT OF NORTH SAANICH BC 159-B2
FRANKLIN CO WA 121-A2
BIRCH ST
BAKER CITY OR 138-B1
JUNCTION CITY OR 210-A6
PACIFIC CO WA 186-A4
N BIRCH ST Rt#-42S
COQUILLE OR 220-D5
BIRCH BAY DR
Birch Bay WA 158-B5
BIRCH BAY-LYNDEN RD
Birch Bay WA 158-B4
LYNDEN WA 158-D4
WHATCOM CO WA 158-C4
BIRCH CREEK RD
MALHEUR CO OR 146-C2
UMATILLA CO OR 121-C3
E BIRCH CREEK RD
PILOT ROCK OR 129-B2
UMATILLA CO OR 129-B2
S BIRCHFIELD RD
YAKIMA CO WA 243-C7
W BIRCHFIELD RD
YAKIMA WA 243-C7
YAKIMA CO WA 243-C7
BIRCH POINT RD
Birch Bay WA 158-A4
BIRCHWOOD AV
BELLINGHAM WA 258-C3
S BIRD RD
CLACKAMAS CO OR 126-A3
BIRDSEYE CREEK RD
JACKSON CO OR 229-D7
BISCAY ST NW
THURSTON CO WA 180-C5
BISCUIT BUTTE RD
MALHEUR CO OR 146-C2
BISHOP LN
LANE CO OR 210-A7
BISHOP RD
CLALLAM CO WA 164-D6
COLUMBIA CO OR 189-C5
GRAYS HARBOR CO WA 183-D3
BISHOP CREEK RD
COLUMBIA CO OR 189-B7
NW BISHOP-SCOTT RD
YAMHILL CO OR 198-A4
BISSELL RD
STEVENS CO WA 105-C3
BISSINGER RD
UMATILLA CO OR 129-B1
BITTERS RD
KOOTENAI CO ID 115-A2
BITTNER RD
YAKIMA CO WA 243-D6
E BITTNER RD
YAKIMA CO WA 243-D7
BIXBY RD
TILLAMOOK CO OR 197-C6
BIZ POINT RD
SKAGIT CO WA 259-B12
BJORN RD
SNOHOMISH CO WA 168-C5
BJORNDAHL RD
SNOHOMISH CO WA 168-C3
BLACK RD
LEWIS CO WA 187-A1
N BLACK RD
SPOKANE CO WA 347-F4
SE BLACK RD
KITSAP CO WA 174-C5
W BLACK RD
COUPEVILLE WA 167-B4
ISLAND CO WA 167-B4
BLACK BRIDGE RD
PAYETTE CO ID 139-B3
BLACKBURN RD
CITY OF CHILLIWACK BC 102-C1
YAMHILL CO OR 198-B5
E BLACKBURN RD
MOUNT VERNON WA 260-E14
SKAGIT CO WA 260-E14
W BLACKBURN RD
MOUNT VERNON WA 260-B14
SKAGIT CO WA 260-B14
BLACK BUTTE LN
WHEELER CO OR 128-A3
BLACK BUTTE RD
JEFFERSON CO OR 211-C2
JEFFERSON CO OR 212-A2
E BLACK CANYON HWY Rt#-52
GEM CO ID 139-C3
W BLACK CANYON HWY
GEM CO ID 139-B3
BLACK CANYON RD
LANE CO OR 215-C1
YAKIMA CO WA 243-A1
N BLACK CAT RD
ADA CO ID 253-A2
MERIDIAN ID 253-A2
S BLACK CAT RD
ADA CO ID 253-A3
BLACK CREEK RD
GRAYS HARBOR CO WA 178-D6
BLACK DIAMOND RD
CLALLAM CO WA 261-C7
BLACK DOG RD
LINN CO OR 207-C3
BLACKFORD RD
COLUMBIA CO OR 189-A3
BLACK LAKE BLVD SW
OLYMPIA WA 296-E6
THURSTON CO WA 296-A10
TUMWATER WA 296-E6
BLACK LAKE BELMORE RD SW
THURSTON CO WA 296-B9
BLACKLEDGE RD
SKAMANIA CO WA 194-C3
BLACK MOUNTAIN RD
BAKER CO OR 138-A1
BLACK OAK DR
MEDFORD OR 336-G12
BLACK ROCK LN
DESCHUTES CO OR 217-C1
BLACK ROCK RD
DOUGLAS CO OR 222-B7
KOOTENAI CO ID 247-D6
KOOTENAI CO ID 248-D3
BLACKTAIL DR
JEFFERSON CO OR 212-C3
BLACKWELL RD
JACKSON CO OR 230-B6
BLAHA RDEX
COLUMBIA CO OR 192-A2
BLAINE RD
LATAH CO ID 249-D6
PAYETTE CO ID 139-B3
TILLAMOOK CO OR 197-C6
WHATCOM CO WA 158-B3
BLAINE RD Rt#-548
Birch Bay WA 158-B4
BLAINE WA 158-B3
WHATCOM CO WA 158-B3
BLAINE ST
PORT TOWNSEND WA 263-G4
BLAINE ST U.S.-30
CALDWELL ID 147-B1
W BLAINE ST
SEATTLE WA 276-D2
BLAIR RD
WHITMAN CO WA 249-B1
NE BLAIR RD
CLARK CO WA 193-B6
S BLAIR RD
CLACKAMAS CO OR 205-D3
SE BLAIR RD
CLARK CO WA 193-B6
BLAKE RD
GRAYS HARBOR CO WA 183-B3
LEWIS CO WA 187-D5
BLAKE RD Rt#-27
SPOKANE CO WA 351-A12
SPOKANE VALLEY WA 350-H10
SPOKANE VALLEY WA 351-A12
BLAKELEY LN
LEWIS CO WA 187-D4
BLAKELY AV NE
BAINBRIDGE ISLAND WA 174-D2
BAINBRIDGE ISLAND WA 271-H4
W BLAKELY AV NE
BAINBRIDGE ISLAND WA 271-J6
NE BLAKELY ST
SEATTLE WA 274-D5
BLALOCK CANYON RD
GILLIAM CO OR 128-A1
BLANCA ST
UNIVERSITY ENDOWMENT LAND BC 156-A4
BLANCHARD RD
TILLAMOOK CO OR 197-C5
E BLANCHARD RD
SPOKANE CO WA 114-C1
BLANK RD
WHITMAN CO WA 114-C3
BLANSHARD ST
CITY OF VICTORIA BC 256-H9
DISTRICT OF SAANICH BC 256-F4
BLANSHARD ST Rt#-17
CITY OF VICTORIA BC 256-G6
DISTRICT OF SAANICH BC 256-G5
BLANTON RD
FRANKLIN CO WA 121-B2
BLANTON RD Rt#-260
FRANKLIN CO WA 121-B1
BLATCHFORD RD
LINN CO OR 207-D7
BLENHEIM ST
VANCOUVER BC 156-B5
VANCOUVER BC 254-A13
BLENKINSOP RD
DISTRICT OF SAANICH BC 159-C5
DISTRICT OF SAANICH BC 256-J1
BLIMP BLVD
TILLAMOOK CO OR 197-C3
NW BLISS RD
CLARK CO WA 192-C4
N BLISS ST
PORTLAND OR 192-B7
BLISS-COCHRANE RD KPN
PIERCE CO WA 174-A7
BLIZZARD RD
WHATCOM CO WA 160-B1
BLM ACCESS RD
MAUPIN OR 127-B3
BLM RD 2-3
DOUGLAS CO OR 214-D6
BLM RD 23-4-26
DOUGLAS CO OR 219-C5
BLM RD 23-4-28-0
DOUGLAS CO OR 219-C5
BLM RD 23-4-90
DOUGLAS CO OR 219-B5
BLM RD 23-5-191
DOUGLAS CO OR 219-A5
BLM RD 24-1
DOUGLAS CO OR 214-D6
BLM RD 24-3-31-2
DOUGLAS CO OR 219-D7
BLM RD 24-5-10
DOUGLAS CO OR 219-B6
BLM RD 25-4-13-0
DOUGLAS CO OR 221-D1
BLM RD 25-7-5-1
DOUGLAS CO OR 141-A1
BLM RD 28-4-29-0
DOUGLAS CO OR 221-D6
BLM RD 29-4-20
DOUGLAS CO OR 225-D1
BLM RD 29-7-25-1
DOUGLAS CO OR 225-A1
BLM RD 30-70-50
DOUGLAS CO OR 225-A1
BLM RD 31-4-35-0
DOUGLAS CO OR 225-D4
BLM RD 32-4-9
DOUGLAS CO OR 225-D5
BLM RD 32-9-3
COOS CO OR 140-C3
BLM RD 33-0
DOUGLAS CO OR 214-D6
BLM RD 33-5-18
JOSEPHINE CO OR 229-C1
BLM RD 33-5-26
JOSEPHINE CO OR 229-C1
BLM RD 33-5-27
JOSEPHINE CO OR 229-C1
BLM RD 33-5-35-1
JOSEPHINE CO OR 229-C1
BLM RD 33-7-22
JOSEPHINE CO OR 229-A1
BLM RD 34-4-5
JOSEPHINE CO OR 229-C1
BLM RD 34-5-1
JOSEPHINE CO OR 229-C1
BLM RD 34-5-32
JOSEPHINE CO OR 229-C3
BLM RD 34-5-9
JOSEPHINE CO OR 229-C2
BLM RD 34-6-12
JOSEPHINE CO OR 229-B3
BLM RD 34-6-13
JOSEPHINE CO OR 229-B2
BLM RD 34-8-1
JOSEPHINE CO OR 141-A3
BLM RD 36-0
DOUGLAS CO OR 214-C7
BLM RD 37-6-36
JOSEPHINE CO OR 233-D3
BLM RD 39-6-9
JOSEPHINE CO OR 233-D3
BLM RD 39-7-16
JOSEPHINE CO OR 233-C4
BLM RD 61064
LAKE CO OR 152-C2
BLODGETT RD
LINCOLN CO OR 209-A3
MOUNT VERNON WA 260-C13
SKAGIT CO WA 168-B1
BLOMBERG RD SW
THURSTON CO WA 184-C1
BLOODGOOD RD
KLICKITAT CO WA 127-C1
BLOOMFIELD RD
MASON CO WA 180-B5
BLOOMING-FERN HILL RD
WASHINGTON CO OR 198-C2
BLOSSOM DR NE
Hayesville OR 323-D5
SALEM OR 323-D5
S BLOUNT RD
CLACKAMAS CO OR 199-C6
BLOWOUT RESERVOIR RD
MALHEUR CO OR 146-C2
MALHEUR CO OR 147-A2
BLUE BUNCH RD
ADAMS CO ID 251-B6
BLUE CREEK RD
KOOTENAI CO ID 245-C6
KOOTENAI CO ID 248-B1
BLUE CREEK RD W
STEVENS CO WA 106-A3
BLUE CREEK WEST RD
STEVENS CO WA 106-A3
BLUE GRADE
DOUGLAS CO WA 239-A3
BLUEGRASS LN
DESCHUTES CO OR 211-C5
BLUE LAKE RD
OKANOGAN CO WA 104-C1
BLUE MOUNTAIN RD
CLALLAM CO WA 165-D7
WHATCOM CO WA 161-D1
BLUE MOUNTAIN ST
COQUITLAM BC 157-A5
BLUE MOUNTAIN LOGGING RD
WHATCOM CO WA 161-C1
BLUE OX LOGGING RD
SKAMANIA CO WA 195-B3
BLUESTEM RD
LINCOLN CO WA 114-A2
BLUFF RD
CLACKAMAS CO OR 200-C3
PAYETTE CO ID 139-B3
SANDY OR 200-C3
N BLUFF RD
CITY OF SURREY BC 158-A2
CITY OF WHITE ROCK BC 158-A2
SE BLUFF RD
CLACKAMAS CO OR 200-C3
MULTNOMAH CO OR 200-C3
BLUFF ST
WINTHROP WA 104-A2
S BLUHM RD
CLACKAMAS CO OR 200-A6
BLUMAUER RD SE
THURSTON CO WA 184-D3
BLUNDELL RD
CITY OF RICHMOND BC 156-B6
BLUNT RD KPS
PIERCE CO WA 181-A2
BLY MOUNTAIN CTO
KLAMATH CO OR 151-A2
BOARDMAN IRRIGON RD
MORROW CO OR 128-C1
BOARDMAN-IRRIGON RD
MORROW CO OR 128-C1
BOARD SHANTY RD
JOSEPHINE CO OR 229-C7
BOAT RD
COOS CO OR 220-A7
BOB GALBREATH RD
Clinton WA 171-A2
BOB HALL RD
WHATCOM CO WA 158-D4
BODINE RD
COLUMBIA CO OR 189-A3
COWLITZ CO WA 189-D4
N BODINE RD
COWLITZ CO WA 189-D4
BOE RD
SNOHOMISH CO WA 168-A4
SW BOECKMAN RD
WILSONVILLE OR 199-B5
BOEHMER RD NE
MARION CO OR 205-C3
S BOEING ACCESS RD
TUKWILA WA 286-D5
TUKWILA WA 287-E5
E BOEKEL RD
KOOTENAI CO ID 247-D1
BOGACHIEL WY
CLALLAM CO WA 169-C2
N BOGART LN
ADA CO ID 253-B1
BOG CREEK RD
BOUNDARY CO ID 106-C1
BOUNDARY CO ID 107-A1
N BOGUS BASIN RD
ADA CO ID 253-D2
BOISE ID 253-C2
BOGUS RANCH RD
MALHEUR CO OR 146-C3
BOHLKEN DR
LINN CO OR 133-C1
LINN CO OR 207-D5
BOH MOUNTAIN RD
JOSEPHINE CO OR 229-B7
SE BOHNA PARK RD
DAMASCUS OR 200-B3
BOHOSKEY DR W
YAKIMA CO WA 243-D6
BOISE AV
BENTON CO OR 133-B2
E BOISE AV
ADA CO ID 253-D3
BOISE ID 253-D3
W BOISE AV
BOISE ID 253-C3
NW BOISE DR
JEFFERSON CO OR 208-B3
BOISE ST
KOOTENAI ID 244-A1
BOISTFORT RD
LEWIS CO WA 187-A2
BOLAN LAKE RD
JOSEPHINE CO OR 233-C7
BOLEN RD
CLARK CO WA 192-C1
LA CENTER WA 192-C1
BOLESKINE RD
DISTRICT OF SAANICH BC 256-F5
BOLLAND RD
CLACKAMAS CO OR 199-C7
N BOLLENBAUGH HILL RD
SNOHOMISH CO WA 110-C1
BOLTON HILL RD
LANE CO OR 133-B3
VENETA OR 133-B3
BOMBING RANGE RD
MORROW CO OR 128-C2
WEST RICHLAND WA 341-A3
BONAPARTE RD
OKANOGAN CO WA 105-A1
BONAPARTE LAKE RD
OKANOGAN CO WA 105-A2
BOND DR
COWLITZ CO WA 187-C7
COWLITZ CO WA 189-C1
BOND RD
COWLITZ CO WA 189-C1
LINN CO OR 207-D4
BOND RD NE
POULSBO WA 170-B6
BOND RD NE Rt#-307
KITSAP CO WA 170-C6
POULSBO WA 170-C6
BOND ST
ASTORIA OR 300-C4
COWLITZ CO WA 187-C7
DISTRICT OF BURNABY BC 156-C5
NW BOND ST
BEND OR 332-E6
W BOND ST
ASTORIA OR 300-B4
BOND BUTTE DR
LINN CO OR 210-B4
BOND CREEK RD
SHOSHONE CO ID 115-B2
BOND MILL RD
SAN JUAN CO WA 160-A3
BONITA RD
MALHEUR CO OR 138-B3
W BONNEVILLE ST
PASCO WA 343-E8
BONNEY MEADOWS TR
WASCO CO OR 202-C7
BONNIEWOOD DR SE
TUMWATER WA 296-H13
BONSON RD
BRITISH COLUMBIA BC 157-C6
PITT MEADOWS BC 157-C5
BONY RD
YAMHILL CO OR 198-B4
BOOKER RD
ADAMS CO WA 121-A1
BOOMER HILL RD
DOUGLAS CO OR 225-B1
BOON RD
ISLAND CO WA 167-B3
BOONE RD
LEWIS CO WA 187-D3
N BOONE ST Rt#-105
ABERDEEN WA 178-B7
S BOONE ST Rt#-105
ABERDEEN WA 117-A1
ABERDEEN WA 178-B7
GRAYS HARBOR CO WA 117-A1
BOONE CREEK RD
COOS CO OR 220-D3
BOONES FERRY RD
CLACKAMAS CO OR 199-B6
CLACKAMAS CO OR 320-B6
LAKE OSWEGO OR 199-B6
LAKE OSWEGO OR 320-B6
BOONES FERRY RD
LAKE OSWEGO OR 320-B6
MARION CO OR 205-B1
MULTNOMAH CO OR 320-B6
PORTLAND OR 320-B6
SW BOONES FERRY RD
DURHAM OR 199-B4
PORTLAND OR 316-E7
PORTLAND OR 317-E7
PORTLAND OR 320-D2
TUALATIN OR 199-B4
TUALATIN OR 199-B4
WASHINGTON CO OR 199-B4
WILSONVILLE OR 199-B4
BOONES FERRY RD NE
MARION CO OR 199-B7
MARION CO OR 205-B1
WOODBURN OR 205-B1
BOOTH LN
UNION CO OR 130-A2
BOOTH RD
DOUGLAS CO OR 214-A6
SW BOOTH BEND RD
MCMINNVILLE OR 198-A7
BOOTH HILL RD
HOOD RIVER CO OR 202-D1
N BOOTHILL RD
KOOTENAI CO ID 245-B4
BOOTH KELLY RD
SPRINGFIELD OR 331-D8
W BORAH ST
BOISE ID 253-C2
BORBA RD
TILLAMOOK CO OR 197-C5
BORDEAUX RD SW
THURSTON CO WA 184-A2
BOREN AV
SEATTLE WA 278-A5
BOREN AV S
SEATTLE WA 278-B6
BORGEN RD
LATAH CO ID 250-B1
WALLA WALLA CO WA 121-C3
SE BORGES RD
DAMASCUS OR 200-B3
NE BORIN RD
CLARK CO WA 193-D6
SE BORING RD
GRESHAM OR 200-B2
SW BORLAND RD
CLACKAMAS CO OR 199-C4
TUALATIN OR 199-C4
WEST LINN OR 199-C4
SE BORNSTEDT RD
CLACKAMAS CO OR 200-C4
N BORSETH ST Rt#-9
SEDRO-WOOLLEY WA 161-C5
BOSK RD
SNOHOMISH CO WA 168-B3
BOSSBURG RD
STEVENS CO WA 106-A1
BOSTIAN RD
SNOHOMISH CO WA 171-D6
BOSTON ST
SEATTLE WA 277-H1
BOSTON HARBOR RD NE
THURSTON CO WA 180-C5
BOSTON MILL DR
LINN CO OR 210-B1
BOSWELL RD
DOUGLAS CO OR 219-B3
NE BOTHELL WY Rt#-522
BOTHELL WA 171-B6
KENMORE WA 171-B6
KING CO WA 171-B6
LAKE FOREST PARK WA 171-B6
BOTHELL WY NE Rt#-522
BOTHELL WA 171-C6
LAKE FOREST PARK WA 171-B6
SHORELINE WA 171-B7
BOTHELL WY NE Rt#-527
BOTHELL WA 171-C6
BOTHELL WA 171-C6
BOTHELL EVERETT HWY Rt#-527
BOTHELL WA 171-C4
EVERETT WA 171-C4
MILL CREEK WA 171-C4
SNOHOMISH CO WA 171-C4
BOTTLE BAY RD
BONNER CO ID 244-A3
BOULDER CREEK RD
ADAMS CO ID 131-C3
ADAMS CO ID 251-A1
TILLAMOOK CO OR 197-C6
BOULDER LAKE RD
VALLEY CO ID 251-D6
BOULDER RIDGE RD
WASCO CO OR 202-C7
BOULEVARD PL
MERCER ISLAND WA 283-J3
BOULEVARD RD SE
OLYMPIA WA 297-C7
THURSTON CO WA 297-C7
BOUNDARY HWY Rt#-22A
NORTHPORT WA 106-B1
STEVENS CO WA 106-B1
BOUNDARY RD
CITY OF CHILLIWACK BC 102-C1
DISTRICT OF BURNABY BC 156-C5
DISTRICT OF BURNABY BC 255-F12
JACKSON CO OR 150-A1
PEND OREILLE CO WA 106-B1
VANCOUVER BC 156-C5
VANCOUVER BC 255-F12
W BOUNDARY RD
KLAMATH CO OR 142-C3
LANE CO OR 134-A3
BOUNDARY RD S
DISTRICT OF BURNABY BC 156-C5
VANCOUVER BC 156-C5
BOUNDARY BAY RD
DISTRICT OF DELTA BC 101-C1
WHATCOM CO WA 101-C1
BOUNDARY CREEK RD
BOUNDARY CO ID 107-A1
BOURBON RD
SHERMAN CO OR 127-C2
BOW RD
SKAGIT CO WA 161-A5
BOWDEN RANCH RD
MALHEUR CO OR 154-B1
N BOWDISH RD
SPOKANE VALLEY WA 350-G7
S BOWDISH RD
SPOKANE VALLEY WA 350-G10
BOWDOIN WY
EDMONDS WA 171-A5
BOWE LN SE
KITSAP CO WA 174-C5
BOWEN RD
NANAIMO BC 93-A3
BOWERS BLVD
SAN JUAN CO WA 160-A5
BOWERS DR
LINN CO OR 210-B5
BOWES RD
GRAYS HARBOR CO WA 177-D2
BOW HILL RD
SKAGIT CO WA 161-A4
BOWLES RD
Finley WA 121-A3
BOWMAN RD
ASOTIN CO WA 250-A6
REEDSPORT OR 218-C2
WHATCOM CO WA 161-C2
BOWMAN HILL RD
COLUMBIA CO WA 122-A2
BOWMONT AV
KELSO WA 303-D6
BOWMONT RD
CANYON CO ID 147-B1
BOX CANYON RD
PEND OREILLE CO WA 106-B1
BOYD RD
CHELAN WA 236-C2
CHELAN CO WA 236-C2
JACKSON CO OR 230-A5
YAKIMA CO WA 243-A3
BOYD ST
NEW WESTMINSTER BC 156-D6
BOYD ACRES RD
BEND OR 332-G4
BOYD LOOP RD
DUFUR OR 127-B2
WASCO CO OR 127-B2
BOYDSTUN ST
VALLEY CO ID 251-C5
N BOYER AV
SANDPOINT ID 244-A2
BOYER AV E
SEATTLE WA 274-B7
SEATTLE WA 278-B1
BOYER RD
DOUGLAS CO OR 225-B2
JOSEPHINE CO OR 229-B3
BOYLSTON AV E
SEATTLE WA 278-B2
BOZARTH RD
CROOK CO OR 213-B6
BOZY CREEK RD
GRAYS HARBOR CO WA 179-D6
SW BRACE POINT DR
SEATTLE WA 284-D3
BRADEN RD
WALLA WALLA CO WA 345-A14
BRADLEY RD
SKAGIT CO WA 161-A5
S BRADLEY RD
CLACKAMAS CO OR 200-A4
BRADNER RD
DISTRICT OF MATSQUI BC 102-B1
BRADSHAW RD
SKAGIT CO WA 161-A7
SKAGIT CO WA 168-A1
E BRADSHAW RD
SPOKANE CO WA 114-C2
BRADY LOOP RD
GRAYS HARBOR CO WA 179-A7
BRAEMAR RD E
DISTRICT OF NORTH VANCOUV BC 255-B2
E BRAEMERE RD
BOISE ID 253-D2
BRAGG RD
JACKSON CO OR 234-B2
BRAID ST
NEW WESTMINSTER BC 156-D5
NEW WESTMINSTER BC 157-A5
BRAINER RD
ISLAND CO WA 167-D7
BRAMHALL RD
COLUMBIA CO WA 122-A2
BRANCH RD
HARRAH WA 119-C2
YAKIMA CO WA 119-C2
YAKIMA CO WA 120-A2
BRANDON RD
LINN CO OR 210-B3
BRANDSTROM RD
SNOHOMISH CO WA 168-B3
BRANDYWINE RD
DESCHUTES CO OR 212-A7
BRANSTETTER RD
ADAMS CO ID 251-B3
BRATHOVDE RD
YAKIMA CO WA 243-B5
BRATTAIN DR
LINN CO OR 210-A1
BRAYS RD NW
DOUGLAS CO WA 236-B5
BRECHIN RD
NANAIMO BC 93-A3
BREITENBUSH RD
DETROIT OR 134-B1
MARION CO OR 134-B1
S BREMER RD
CLACKAMAS CO OR 199-C6
BRENNER RD NW
THURSTON CO WA 180-B6
BRENNER CANYON RD
MORROW CO OR 128-B2
BRETZ MINE RD
MALHEUR CO OR 154-B2
BREWER RD
KLICKITAT CO WA 196-C2
BREWERY GRADE ST
THE DALLES OR 196-C7
BREWSTER RD
LEBANON OR 133-C1
LINN CO OR 133-C1
BREYMAN ORCHARDS RD
YAMHILL CO OR 198-C6
BRIAN RANCH RD
CLACKAMAS CO OR 200-D5
BRIAR RD
CROOK CO OR 213-B6
BRIAR KNOB LOOP RD
MARION CO OR 205-D4
BRICE CREEK RD
LANE CO OR 141-C1
BRICKEL CREEK RD
KOOTENAI CO ID 115-A1
BRICK MILL RD
KITTITAS CO WA 241-B5
BRICK PILE RD
JACKSON CO OR 234-B5

INDEX

INDEX

CEMETERY RD U.S.-95 STREET INDEX CLODFELTER RD 363

STREET City State Page-Grid

CEMETERY RD U.S.-95
OWYHEE CO ID 147-B1
S CEMETERY RD
CLACKAMAS CO OR 205-D4
SW CEMETERY RD
KING CO WA 174-D6
CEMETERY HILL RD
COLUMBIA CO WA 122-A2
CENTENNIAL BLVD
EUGENE OR 330-C5
SPRINGFIELD OR 330-H6
SPRINGFIELD OR 331-B6
W CENTENNIAL BLVD
LANE CO OR 330-E6
SPRINGFIELD OR 330-E6
E CENTENNIAL ST
CALDWELL ID 147-B1
CENTENNIAL TR
SPOKANE CO WA 348-B5
CENTENNIAL WY U.S.-30
CALDWELL ID 147-B1
CENTER AV Rt#-25
NORTHPORT WA 106-A1
STEVENS CO WA 106-A1
E CENTER AV
PAYETTE ID 139-A3
CENTER DR
DUPONT WA 181-B5
N CENTER PKWY
KENNEWICK WA 342-B8
CENTER RD
JEFFERSON CO WA 109-C1
JEFFERSON CO WA 170-A2
CENTER ST
SUBLIMITY OR 133-C1
N CENTER ST
SPOKANE WA 349-C6
S CENTER ST
TACOMA WA 294-B1
TACOMA WA 295-E1
CENTER ST E
EATONVILLE WA 118-B1
CENTER ST NE
Four Corners OR 204-D6
Four Corners OR 323-F13
MARION CO OR 323-F13
SALEM OR 322-J12
SALEM OR 323-B13
CENTER ST NE Rt#-22
SALEM OR 322-H12
CENTER ST W
EATONVILLE WA 118-B1
CENTER RIDGE RD
WASCO CO OR 127-B2
CENTER SCHOOL RD
LINN CO OR 210-C3
CENTER ST BRDG Rt#-22
SALEM OR 322-H12
CENTER ST BRDG NE Rt#-22
SALEM OR 322-H12
CENTERVILLE HWY
KLICKITAT CO WA 196-D5
CENTRAL
DESCHUTES CO OR 212-A6
CENTRAL AV
COOS BAY OR 333-G10
GRANTS PASS OR 335-D10
E CENTRAL AV
DOUGLAS CO OR 221-C1
SUTHERLIN OR 221-C1
N CENTRAL AV
JACKSON CO OR 336-B10
MEDFORD OR 336-C10
S CENTRAL AV
MEDFORD OR 336-D12
S CENTRAL AV U.S.-2
WATERVILLE WA 236-C7
SW CENTRAL AV
GRANTS PASS OR 335-E10
CENTRAL AV N
KENT WA 175-C6
CENTRAL AV N Rt#-516
KENT WA 175-C7
CENTRAL AV S
AUBURN WA 175-B7
GRANT CO WA 112-B3
KENT WA 175-B7
KING CO WA 175-B7
QUINCY WA 112-B3
CENTRAL AV S Rt#-281
GRANT CO WA 112-B3
QUINCY WA 112-B3
CENTRAL AV S Rt#-516
KENT WA 175-C7
CENTRAL AV W
OROVILLE WA 104-C1
CENTRAL BLVD U.S.-95
CAMBRIDGE ID 139-B1
WASHINGTON CO ID 139-B1
N CENTRAL BLVD Rt#-42
COQUILLE OR 220-D4
W CENTRAL BLVD Rt#-42
COQUILLE OR 220-D4
CENTRAL DR
MOSES LAKE WA 242-C3
MUKILTEO WA 266-C7
CENTRAL RD
LANE CO OR 133-B3
CENTRAL WY
KIRKLAND WA 175-C1
CENTRAL FERRY CANYON RD
DOUGLAS CO WA 112-B1
CENTRAL GRADE RD
NEZ PERCE CO ID 250-C3
CENTRALIA ALPHA RD
LEWIS CO WA 118-A1
LEWIS CO WA 184-C6
LEWIS CO WA 299-H8
CENTRAL OREGON HWY U.S.-20
BEND OR 217-C2
BEND OR 332-G7
BURNS OR 145-A1
DESCHUTES CO OR 135-B3
DESCHUTES CO OR 143-C1
DESCHUTES CO OR 144-A1
DESCHUTES CO OR 217-C2
HARNEY CO OR 138-A3
HARNEY CO OR 144-B1
HARNEY CO OR 145-A1
HARNEY CO OR 146-A1
HINES OR 145-A1
LAKE CO OR 144-A1
MALHEUR CO OR 138-C3
MALHEUR CO OR 139-A3
MALHEUR CO OR 146-A1
NYSSA OR 139-A3
VALE OR 138-C3

CENTRAL OREGON HWY U.S.-20
VALE OR 139-A3
S CENTRAL POINT RD
CLACKAMAS CO OR 199-C6
CENTRAL RIDGE RD
LEWIS CO ID 123-C2
NEZ PERCE CO ID 123-C2
PECK ID 123-C2
CENTRAL SAANICH RD
DISTRICT OF CENTRAL SAANI BC 159-C4
CENTRAL VALE DR
HOOD RIVER CO OR 195-C7
CENTRAL VALLEY RD NE
KITSAP CO WA 174-B1
KITSAP CO WA 270-G3
Tracyton WA 270-G3
CENTRAL VALLEY RD NW
KITSAP CO WA 270-G1
CENTURY DR
ALBANY OR 326-H6
LINN CO OR 326-H6
S CENTURY DR
DESCHUTES CO OR 143-A1
DESCHUTES CO OR 216-D7
DESCHUTES CO OR 217-A6
Three Rivers OR 216-D7
Three Rivers OR 217-A7
CENTURY LN
WALLOWA CO OR 130-C2
CENTURY DRIVE HWY Rt#-372
BEND OR 217-B3
BEND OR 332-A11
DESCHUTES CO OR 216-C4
DESCHUTES CO OR 217-B3
DESCHUTES CO OR 332-A11
CERES HILL RD
LEWIS CO WA 184-A7
LEWIS CO WA 187-A1
SE CHADWICK ST
ROSEBURG OR 334-G8
CHAIN LAKE RD
SNOHOMISH CO WA 110-C1
CHALET RD
DISTRICT OF NORTH SAANICH BC 159-B1
CHALK BUTTE RD
MALHEUR CO OR 139-A3
CHALK HILLS RD NE
DOUGLAS CO WA 112-C1
CHAMBER OF COMMERCE WY
CHEHALIS WA 299-D10
CHAMBERS LN W
UNIVERSITY PLACE WA 181-C3
CHAMBERS RD
WHITMAN CO WA 249-B7
CHAMBERS ST
EUGENE OR 329-G6
LANE CO OR 329-G9
CHAMBERS CREEK RD
PIERCE CO WA 181-C3
STEILACOOM WA 181-C3
UNIVERSITY PLACE WA 181-C3
CHAMBERS CREEK RD W
UNIVERSITY PLACE WA 181-C3
CHAMPOEG RD
MARION CO OR 198-D6
MARION CO OR 199-A7
CHANCE RD
TILLAMOOK CO OR 197-C3
CHANCELLOR BLVD
UNIVERSITY ENDOWMENT LAND BC 156-A4
CHANDLER LN
BAKER CO OR 130-B3
CHANDLER RD
LAKE OSWEGO OR 321-E5
CHANEY RD
LATAH CO ID 249-C2
CHANNEL DR
SKAGIT CO WA 160-D7
CHANNEL VIEW DR
SKAGIT CO WA 160-C5
CHANUTE ST
GRANT CO WA 242-C2
CHAPEL DR
BENTON CO OR 133-B1
PHILOMATH OR 133-B1
W CHAPIN AV
ADA CO ID 253-B4
CHAPMAN PL
CORVALLIS OR 327-G11
CHAPMAN RD
WASHINGTON CO OR 199-A5
S CHAPMAN RD
LATAH WA 114-C3
SPOKANE CO WA 114-C3
SPOKANE CO WA 247-A5
CHARLES RD
CLALLAM CO WA 165-A5
W CHARLES RD
SPOKANE CO WA 114-B1
SPOKANE CO WA 246-A1
CHARLES ST
PORT MOODY BC 157-A4
CHARLESTON BEACH RD W
Navy Yard City WA 270-E13
CHARLOTTE AV W
Navy Yard City WA 270-F12
CHARLTON RD
KITTITAS CO WA 241-C3
CHAROLAIS RD
WALLOWA CO OR 130-C1
E CHARRON RD
YAKIMA CO WA 243-D7
CHARTWELL DR
DISTRICT OF WEST VANCOUVE BC 254-D1
N CHASE RD
KOOTENAI CO ID 353-G3
POST FALLS ID 353-G3
CHASE MOUNTAIN RD
KLAMATH CO OR 235-A6
CHATCOLET RD
KOOTENAI CO ID 115-A2
CHATHAM HILL DR
Sunnyslope WA 238-D3
CHAUFTY RD
LEWIS CO WA 187-B4
CHEAM AV Rt#-9
DISTRICT OF KENT BC 94-C3
CHEESE FACTORY RD
KLAMATH CO OR 151-A2
CHEHALEM DR
NEWBERG OR 198-D5
YAMHILL CO OR 198-D5
CHEHALIS AV
GRAYS HARBOR CO WA 183-A2
N CHELAN AV
DOUGLAS CO WA 236-C7
WATERVILLE WA 236-C7

N CHELAN AV Rt#-285
WENATCHEE WA 238-D4
N CHELAN AV U.S.-2
WATERVILLE WA 236-C7
S CHELAN AV
WATERVILLE WA 236-C7
S CHELAN AV Rt#-285
WENATCHEE WA 238-D4
WENATCHEE WA 239-A4
S CHELAN ST
RITZVILLE WA 113-C3
CHELAN BUTTE RD
CHELAN CO WA 236-C3
CHELAN FALLS RD
CHELAN CO WA 236-D3
CHELAN FALLS RD Rt#-150
CHELAN CO WA 236-D3
CHELAN FALLS RD U.S.-97
CHELAN CO WA 236-D3
CHELAN-OKANOGAN HWY U.S.-97
Sunnyslope WA 238-D3
CHELAN-STEHEKIN FERRY
CHELAN WA 236-B2
CHELAN CO WA 236-B2
CHEMAWA RD N
KEIZER OR 322-H5
KEIZER OR 323-A5
CHEMAWA RD NE
KEIZER OR 323-A5
MARION CO OR 204-D4
MARION CO OR 323-E4
SALEM OR 204-D4
SALEM OR 323-E4
CHEMEKETA ST NE
SALEM OR 322-H12
CHEMICAL RD Rt#-397
Finley WA 121-A3
Finley WA 343-G12
KENNEWICK WA 343-F11
CHENEY CREEK RD
JOSEPHINE CO OR 229-A7
CHENEY-PLAZA RD
SPOKANE CO WA 114-B2
S CHENEY-PLAZA RD
CHENEY WA 246-A7
SPOKANE CO WA 114-B3
SPOKANE CO WA 246-A7
W CHENEY-SPANGLE RD
CHENEY WA 246-A7
SPOKANE CO WA 114-B2
SPOKANE CO WA 246-A7
S CHENEY-SPOKANE RD
SPOKANE WA 246-A7
SPOKANE WA 348-H14
SPOKANE CO WA 246-A7
W CHENEY-SPOKANE RD
SPOKANE WA 246-B5
SPOKANE CO WA 246-B5
CHENNAULT BEACH DR
MUKILTEO WA 266-C7
CHENNAULT BEACH RD
MUKILTEO WA 266-D7
MUKILTEO WA 267-E7
CHENOWETH RD
WASCO CO OR 196-B7
CHENOWETH CREEK RD
THE DALLES OR 196-B7
WASCO CO OR 196-B7
CHEROKEE
CROOK CO OR 213-D7
CHEROKEE RD
GRANT CO WA 242-D2
CHEROKEE CREEK RD
MALHEUR CO OR 154-B2
CHERRY AV NE
KEIZER OR 322-J6
KEIZER OR 323-A6
SALEM OR 323-A6
CHERRY LN
CANYON CO ID 147-B1
LINN CO OR 207-C5
MEDFORD OR 234-B1
E CHERRY LN
CANYON CO ID 147-C1
NE CHERRY LN
JEFFERSON CO OR 208-C4
W CHERRY LN
ADA CO ID 253-A3
MERIDIAN ID 253-A3
CHERRY ST
PORT TOWNSEND WA 263-G4
WENATCHEE WA 238-D4
E CHERRY ST
SEATTLE WA 278-C6
WALLA WALLA WA 345-A7
W CHERRY ST
WALLA WALLA WA 344-J7
WALLA WALLA WA 345-A7
W CHERRY ST Rt#-507
CENTRALIA WA 299-E4
SE CHERRY BLOSSOM DR
PORTLAND OR 315-J7
CHERRY CREEK RD
BENEWAH CO ID 248-C7
WHITMAN CO WA 114-B3
CHERRY HEIGHTS RD
THE DALLES OR 196-C7
WASCO CO OR 196-B7
CHERRY HILL RD
GRANGER WA 120-A2
CHERRY LANE RD
NEZ PERCE CO ID 123-B2
CHESAW RD
OKANOGAN CO WA 104-C1
OKANOGAN CO WA 105-A1
OROVILLE WA 104-C1
CHESNIMNUS LN
WALLOWA CO OR 131-A1
CHESTER AV
GRAYS HARBOR CO WA 183-B3
E CHESTER RD
Colby WA 271-F13
KITSAP CO WA 271-F13
CHESTERFIELD AV
CITY OF NORTH VANCOUVER BC 255-B5
E CHESTNUT AV
GENESEE ID 250-C1
NE CHESTNUT AV
ROSEBURG OR 334-F5
W CHESTNUT AV
GENESEE ID 250-C1
LATAH CO ID 250-C1
CHESTNUT DR
DESCHUTES CO OR 211-D5
WALLA WALLA WA 345-D9
Walla Walla East WA 345-D9

CHESTNUT ST
ASHLAND OR 337-B6
ASOTIN CO WA 250-B4
CLARKSTON WA 250-B4
KELSO WA 303-C9
E CHESTNUT ST
WALLA WALLA WA 345-C8
Walla Walla East WA 345-C8
S CHESTNUT ST
SPOKANE WA 348-G12
W CHESTNUT ST
WALLA WALLA WA 344-J9
WALLA WALLA WA 345-A9
CHETCO AV U.S.-101
BROOKINGS OR 232-C6
W CHEWACK RD
OKANOGAN CO WA 104-A2
CHEWILIKEN RD
OKANOGAN CO WA 105-A2
CHEWILIKEN VALLEY RD
OKANOGAN CO WA 104-C2
E CHEWUCH RD
OKANOGAN CO WA 104-A2
CHEYNE RD
KLAMATH CO OR 235-D7
CHICAGO ST SE
TURNER OR 325-G12
CHICKADEE DR
JEFFERSON CO OR 212-C2
CHICKAHOMINY RD
LANE CO OR 133-A3
CHICKEN DINNER RD
CANYON CO ID 147-B1
CHICO WY NW
BREMERTON WA 270-A7
KITSAP CO WA 270-B3
Silverdale WA 270-B3
Tracyton WA 270-A7
CHIEF MARTIN RD
WHATCOM CO WA 158-C7
CHILBERG RD
LA CONNER WA 167-D1
SKAGIT CO WA 167-D1
E CHILCO AV
KOOTENAI CO ID 245-A3
SW CHILDS RD
CLACKAMAS CO OR 199-C4
CHILKO DR
COQUITLAM BC 157-A5
CHILLIWACK LAKE RD
BRITISH COLUMBIA BC 102-C1
BRITISH COLUMBIA BC 103-A1
CITY OF CHILLIWACK BC 102-C1
CHILOQUIN HWY
CHILOQUIN OR 231-C3
KLAMATH CO OR 231-C3
S CHILOQUIN RD
CHILOQUIN OR 231-D4
KLAMATH CO OR 231-D4
CHILOQUIN CAMP RD
KLAMATH CO OR 142-C3
CHILOQUIN RIDGE RD
KLAMATH CO OR 231-D4
CHILVERS RD
LEWIS CO WA 184-A7
CHIMACUM RD
Hadlock-Irondale WA 170-A1
JEFFERSON CO WA 170-A1
CHIMNEY CREEK RD
MALHEUR CO OR 138-A3
MALHEUR CO OR 146-A1
CHIN RD
KLAMATH CO OR 235-D7
CHINA CREEK RD
DOUGLAS CO WA 105-A3
CHINA GARDEN RD
KALAMA WA 189-D6
CHINA GRADE RD
SISKIYOU CO CA 149-A3
CHINA HAT RD
BEND OR 217-C4
BEND OR 332-D14
DESCHUTES CO OR 135-B3
DESCHUTES CO OR 143-B1
DESCHUTES CO OR 217-C4
DESCHUTES CO OR 332-D14
CHINA MOUNTAIN RD
CURRY CO OR 224-B6
CHINA PEAK LOOKOUT RD
SISKIYOU CO CA 149-B3
CHINDEN BLVD U.S.-20
CANYON CO ID 147-C1
E CHINDEN BLVD U.S.-20
ADA CO ID 253-B2
BOISE ID 253-B2
EAGLE ID 253-B2
W CHINDEN BLVD U.S.-20
ADA CO ID 147-C1
ADA CO ID 253-A2
BOISE ID 253-B2
CANYON CO ID 147-C1
EAGLE ID 253-B2
GARDEN CITY ID 253-C2
CHINOOK PASS HWY Rt#-410
PIERCE CO WA 111-A3
CHINOOK VALLEY RD
PACIFIC CO WA 186-B6
CHIPMUNK
JEFFERSON CO OR 212-C2
CHIPMUNK TR
DOUGLAS CO WA 239-B1
CHIPPEWA
CROOK CO OR 213-D7
CHIWAWA LP
CHELAN CO WA 111-C1
CHIWAWA RIVER RD
CHELAN CO WA 103-C3
CHELAN CO WA 111-C1
NE CHKALOV DR
VANCOUVER WA 307-J6
SE CHKALOV DR
VANCOUVER WA 307-J7
E CHOCKTOOT ST
CHILOQUIN OR 231-D4
N CHOCKTOOT ST
CHILOQUIN OR 231-D4
W CHOCKTOOT ST
CHILOQUIN OR 231-D3
E CHRIS CT
SPOKANE CO WA 347-F5
CHRISELLA RD E
EDGEWOOD WA 182-B3
CHRISTENSEN RD
CLARK CO WA 192-D1
KITTITAS CO WA 241-D5
SW CHRISTENSEN RD
YAMHILL CO OR 204-A2

CHRISTIANSEN RD
LINCOLN CO OR 206-C4
CHRISTIANSON RD
SKAGIT CO WA 160-C7
CHRISTIE RD
BENTON CO WA 120-C3
BENTON CO WA 121-A3
BENTON CO WA 128-C1
CHRISTMAS VALLEY-WAGONTIRE RD
LAKE CO OR 143-B2
LAKE CO OR 144-A2
CHROME RIDGE RD
JOSEPHINE CO OR 148-C1
CHUCKANUT DR Rt#-11
BELLINGHAM WA 258-B12
SKAGIT CO WA 160-D2
SKAGIT CO WA 161-A3
SKAGIT CO WA 260-B1
WHATCOM CO WA 160-D2
WHATCOM CO WA 258-B14
CHUCKER DR
YAKIMA CO WA 243-D6
CHURCH AV Rt#-219
MARION CO OR 198-D7
SAINT PAUL OR 198-D7
CHURCH DR
LINN CO OR 207-B7
CHURCH RD
COLUMBIA CO OR 192-A2
WHATCOM CO WA 158-C5
YAKIMA CO WA 243-B5
SE CHURCH RD
CLACKAMAS CO OR 200-B3
W CHURCH RD
MARION CO OR 205-B3
MOUNT ANGEL OR 205-B3
YAKIMA CO WA 243-A7
CHURCH ST Rt#-165
WILKESON WA 182-D5
CHURCH ST Rt#-216
GRASS VALLEY OR 127-C2
W CHURCH ST
MONMOUTH OR 204-B7
W CHURCH ST Rt#-272
PALOUSE WA 249-B1
WHITMAN CO WA 249-B1
CHURCH ST NE
SALEM OR 322-J12
CHURCH ST SE
SALEM OR 322-H13
CHURCH HILL RD
WHITMAN CO WA 122-B1
CHURCHILL RD
DOUGLAS CO OR 219-A1
CHURCHILL RD SE
THURSTON CO WA 184-D3
CHURCH LAKE RD E
BONNEY LAKE WA 182-C4
PIERCE CO WA 182-C4
CHYNOWETH RD
CLACKAMAS CO OR 200-B5
CINDER BUTTE RD
DESCHUTES CO OR 211-D3
CINDER HILL RD
DESCHUTES CO OR 135-B3
DESCHUTES CO OR 143-B1
CINEBAR RD
LEWIS CO WA 118-A2
CINNAMON BUTTE RD
DOUGLAS CO OR 223-C4
CIRCLE BLVD
BENTON CO OR 207-B5
BENTON CO OR 327-G6
CORVALLIS OR 207-B5
CORVALLIS OR 327-G6
CIRCLE C LN
ADAMS CO ID 251-A3
CIRQUE DR W
TACOMA WA 294-A4
UNIVERSITY PLACE WA 181-C3
UNIVERSITY PLACE WA 294-A4
CISPUS RD Rt#-131
LEWIS CO WA 118-C2
CITADEL DR
PORT COQUITLAM BC 157-A5
NW CLACKAMAS DR
JEFFERSON CO OR 208-B4
CLACKAMAS HWY Rt#-211
CLACKAMAS CO OR 200-B4
ESTACADA OR 200-C5
CLACKAMAS HWY Rt#-212
CLACKAMAS CO OR 199-D3
CLACKAMAS CO OR 200-A4
DAMASCUS OR 200-A4
HAPPY VALLEY OR 200-A4
CLACKAMAS HWY Rt#-224
CLACKAMAS CO OR 126-B3
CLACKAMAS CO OR 200-B4
DAMASCUS OR 200-B4
ESTACADA OR 200-C7
CLACKAMAS-BORING RD Rt#-212
CLACKAMAS CO OR 200-B3
DAMASCUS OR 200-B3
HAPPY VALLEY OR 200-B3
S CLACKAMAS RIVER DR
CLACKAMAS CO OR 199-D4
CLACKAMAS CO OR 200-A4
OREGON CITY OR 199-D4
CLACKAMAS RIVER RD
CLACKAMAS CO OR 126-B3
MARION CO OR 126-C3
CLAGSTONE RD
KOOTENAI CO ID 245-A2
CLAIR CUT-OFF RD Rt#-510
THURSTON CO WA 181-A7
CLAREMONT DR
JEFFERSON CO OR 208-C5
MADRAS OR 208-C5
S CLARK AV Rt#-20
REPUBLIC WA 105-B2
CLARK BLVD
MALHEUR CO OR 139-A3
CLARK DR
VANCOUVER BC 255-A12
NE CLARK DR
JEFFERSON CO OR 208-C3
CLARK LN
HARNEY CO OR 137-C3
CLARK RD
CLALLAM CO WA 163-B6
COLUMBIA CO OR 189-B6
FRANKLIN CO WA 121-A2
KLICKITAT CO WA 196-D4
LEWIS CO WA 187-D2
CLARK RD SW
DOUGLAS CO WA 239-B3

CLARK ST
BAKER CITY OR 138-B1
SHERMAN CO OR 127-C1
WASCO OR 127-C1
CLARK ST U.S.-95
LEWIS CO ID 123-B2
WINCHESTER ID 123-B2
E CLARK ST
CONNELL WA 121-B1
W CLARK ST
CONNELL WA 121-B1
FRANKLIN CO WA 121-B1
CLARK CREEK RD
PIERCE CO WA 182-A3
UNION CO OR 130-B1
CLARKE RD
COQUITLAM BC 157-A4
DISTRICT OF COQUITLAM BC 156-D4
KITTITAS CO WA 241-A4
PORT MOODY BC 157-A4
SW CLARK HILL RD
WASHINGTON CO OR 199-A3
CLARKS BRANCH RD
DOUGLAS CO OR 221-C7
CLARKS CANYON RD
MORROW CO OR 128-C2
CLARKS CREEK RD
BAKER CO OR 138-B1
CLAUSSEN RD
PIERCE CO WA 181-A4
CLAY LN
ADAMS CO ID 251-B4
CLAY ST
ASHLAND OR 337-G9
DISTRICT OF MISSION BC 94-B3
JACKSON CO OR 337-G9
SW CLAY ST
PORTLAND OR 312-E6
PORTLAND OR 313-E7
CLAYBURN RD
DISTRICT OF MATSQUI BC 102-B1
NW CLAY PIT RD
YAMHILL CO OR 198-A5
CLAYTON RD
LANE CO OR 215-B5
CLEARBROOK RD
DISTRICT OF MATSQUI BC 102-B1
CLEAR CREEK RD
CLACKAMAS CO OR 200-B6
HOOD RIVER CO OR 202-C2
WHITMAN CO WA 249-A1
CLEAR CREEK RD NW
KITSAP CO WA 170-B7
KITSAP CO WA 174-B1
Olympic View WA 170-B7
Silverdale WA 174-B1
CLEAR LAKE RD
DOUGLAS CO OR 214-A7
DUNES CITY OR 214-B4
LANE CO OR 133-B3
LANE CO OR 215-A1
MODOC CO CA 151-A3
CLEAR LAKE RD NE
KEIZER OR 204-D4
CLEARVIEW DR
DOUGLAS CO OR 221-B3
W CLEARWATER AV
BENTON CO WA 341-J12
KENNEWICK WA 341-J12
KENNEWICK WA 342-E10
NE CLEARWATER DR
CLARK CO WA 193-C3
CLEARWATER RD
DOUGLAS CO OR 222-D4
DOUGLAS CO OR 223-A4
JEFFERSON CO WA 108-C1
JEFFERSON CO WA 172-B1
CLEARWATER FALLS RD
DOUGLAS CO OR 223-B4
CLEMAN RD
KITTITAS CO WA 241-C7
CLEMANS RD
ASOTIN WA 250-B5
ASOTIN CO WA 250-B5
NE CLEMENS DR
JEFFERSON CO OR 208-C2
CLEMENTS RD
TILLAMOOK CO OR 197-C3
CLEMS VIEW RD
YAKIMA CO WA 243-B4
CLETO RD
MALHEUR CO OR 154-B2
CLEVELAND AV
TUMWATER WA 296-H9
CLEVELAND BLVD U.S.-30
CALDWELL ID 147-B1
CANYON CO ID 147-B1
NAMPA ID 147-B1
CLEVELAND ST Rt#-202
REDMOND WA 175-D1
E CLEVELAND ST
WOODBURN OR 205-B2
CLEVELAND HILL RD
DOUGLAS CO OR 221-A3
CLEVELAND RIDGE RD
JACKSON CO OR 230-C1
CLIFFRIDGE AV
DISTRICT OF NORTH VANCOUV BC 156-B2
CLIFTON RD
CLATSOP CO OR 117-B3
CLIFTON RD SW
KITSAP CO WA 174-B4
PORT ORCHARD WA 174-B4
CLINE RD
COWLITZ CO WA 187-C7
CLINE FALLS HWY
DESCHUTES CO OR 212-B7
DESCHUTES CO OR 217-B1
CLINTON RD
LEWIS CO WA 184-A7
N CLINTON ST
WALLA WALLA WA 345-C6
S CLINTON ST
WALLA WALLA WA 345-C8
CLINTON FERRY
MUKILTEO WA 171-B2
SNOHOMISH CO WA 171-B2
CLISE PL W
SEATTLE WA 276-D1
CLIVEDEN AV
DISTRICT OF DELTA BC 156-D6
CLODFELTER RD
BENTON CO WA 121-A3
BENTON CO WA 341-J14
BENTON CO WA 342-A12
KENNEWICK WA 341-J14
KENNEWICK WA 342-A12

INDEX

364 CLOQUALLUM RD — STREET INDEX — COUGAR RD

STREET / City State / Page-Grid

CLOQUALLUM RD
MASON CO WA 179-D4
MASON CO WA 180-A4
CLOQUALLUM LOST LAKE RD
GRAYS HARBOR CO WA 179-B5
CLOSE RD NW
DOUGLAS CO WA 236-C7
WATERVILLE WA 236-C7
CLOVER BLOSSOM LN NE
KITSAP CO WA 271-A3
CLOVER CREEK RD
KLAMATH CO OR 150-B2
KLAMATH CO OR 235-A4
CLOVERDALE AV
DISTRICT OF SAANICH BC 256-G5
CLOVERDALE BYPS Rt#-15
CITY OF SURREY BC 157-B7
CLOVERDALE RD
COWLITZ CO WA 189-D6
CRESWELL OR 215-C5
DESCHUTES CO OR 212-A5
LANE CO OR 215-C5
LINCOLN CO WA 114-A2
MARION CO OR 207-D1
N CLOVERDALE RD
BOISE ID 253-B2
S CLOVERDALE RD
ADA CO ID 253-B4
BOISE ID 253-B4
COWLITZ CO WA 189-D6
S CLOVERDALE ST
SEATTLE WA 285-J3
SEATTLE WA 286-A3
CLOVER ISLAND DR
KENNEWICK WA 343-D9
CLOVER ISLAND DRIVE BRDG
KENNEWICK WA 343-D9
CLOVERLAND RD
ASOTIN CO WA 122-C2
ASOTIN CO WA 250-A7
CLOVERLAWN DR
GRANTS PASS OR 335-G13
JOSEPHINE CO OR 229-B7
JOSEPHINE CO OR 335-G13
N CLOVERLEAF RD
HAUSER ID 247-C1
KOOTENAI CO ID 247-C1
CLOVER RIDGE RD
ALBANY OR 326-J6
LINN CO OR 326-J6
CLOVER VALLEY RD
Ault Field WA 167-B2
ISLAND CO WA 167-B2
CLOW CORNER RD
POLK CO OR 204-A6
E CLUB CT
SPOKANE WA 246-C5
CLUGSTON CREEK-ONION CREEK RD
STEVENS CO WA 106-A2
COAL CREEK PKWY SE
BELLEVUE WA 175-C3
NEWCASTLE WA 175-C3
RENTON WA 175-C3
COAL CREEK RD
COWLITZ CO WA 189-A1
COWLITZ CO WA 302-B3
LONGVIEW WA 302-B3
COALMAN RD
CLACKAMAS CO OR 200-D4
CLACKAMAS CO OR 201-A4
COAL MINE RD
JACKSON CO OR 234-B2
COAL MINE HILL RD
MORROW CO OR 129-A3
COAST DR
DEPOE BAY OR 206-B1
SW COAST CREEK RD
YAMHILL CO OR 125-A3
COAST MERIDIAN RD
COQUITLAM BC 157-B4
PORT COQUITLAM BC 157-B4
COBBLE HILL RD
BRITISH COLUMBIA BC 159-A2
COBURG RD
COBURG OR 210-B7
EUGENE OR 215-B1
EUGENE OR 330-C4
LANE CO OR 210-B6
LANE CO OR 215-B1
LINN CO OR 210-A5
COBURG RD Rt#-99
EUGENE OR 330-A6
N COBURG RD
COBURG OR 210-B7
LANE CO OR 210-B7
LINN CO OR 210-B5
COBURG BOTTOM LOOP RD
LANE CO OR 210-B7
N COCHRAN ST
SPOKANE WA 348-F5
COCHRAN CREEK DR
LINN CO OR 210-C2
COCOLALLA CREEK RD
BONNER CO ID 244-A6
W COE AV
STANFIELD OR 129-A1
E COEUR D'ALENE AV Rt#-97
HARRISON ID 248-A4
KOOTENAI CO ID 248-A4
E COEUR D'ALENE AV U.S.-95
BENEWAH CO ID 115-A3
TENSED ID 115-A3
COFFEE LN NE
MARION CO OR 204-D1
COFFEEPOT RD
LINCOLN CO WA 113-B2
COFFEY RD
BAKER CO OR 130-B3
N COFFEY ST
ADA CO ID 253-B2
GARDEN CITY ID 253-B2
COFFIN RD
BENTON CO WA 121-A3
COFFIN BUTTE RD
BENTON CO OR 207-A3
COGLAN BUTTE RD
LAKE CO OR 144-A3
LAKE CO OR 151-C1
LAKE CO OR 152-A1
COLBURN CULVER RD
BONNER CO ID 107-B2
BONNER CO ID 244-B1
COLBURN-MCCUTCHEON RD
PIERCE CO WA 182-B4
COLBY AV
EVERETT WA 264-D2
COLBY AV
EVERETT WA 268-D1
COLCHESTER DR E
Colby WA 271-H13
COLCHESTER DR SE
Colby WA 174-C4
Colby WA 271-H13
COLD CAMP RD
WASCO CO OR 135-C1
COLD SPRING RD
JACKSON CO OR 226-B4
JACKSON CO OR 230-B1
COLD SPRINGS RD
DESCHUTES CO OR 211-C4
LANE CO OR 214-B1
LEWIS CO ID 123-B2
WASCO CO OR 202-D4
S COLD SPRINGS RD
UMATILLA CO OR 129-B1
COLE RD
DOUGLAS CO OR 221-B1
MASON CO WA 180-B3
SAN JUAN CO WA 160-A7
N COLE RD
BOISE ID 253-C3
S COLE RD
ADA CO ID 253-C4
BOISE ID 253-C4
COLE ST
ENUMCLAW WA 110-C3
HAINES OR 130-A3
COLEMAN RD
KLAMATH CO OR 235-D1
MALHEUR CO OR 138-C3
NE COLEMAN RD
JEFFERSON CO OR 208-C1
COLEMAN CREEK RD
JACKSON CO OR 234-B3
KITTITAS CO WA 241-D4
COLEMAN VALLEY RD
LAKE CO OR 152-B2
COLE MOUNTAIN RD
CLATSOP CO OR 191-D2
COLES RD
ISLAND CO WA 171-A1
COLESTIN RD
JACKSON CO OR 234-D6
COLINWOOD RD
TOWN OF SIDNEY BC 159-C2
COLLAWASH RIVER RD
CLACKAMAS CO OR 126-B3
COLLEGE AV Rt#-5
SAINT MARIES ID 248-D7
N COLLEGE AV
COLLEGE PLACE WA 344-F10
Garrett WA 344-F9
S COLLEGE AV
COLLEGE PLACE WA 344-F12
WALLA WALLA CO WA 344-F12
E COLLEGE RD
MARION CO OR 205-C3
MOUNT ANGEL OR 205-C3
COLLEGE ST Rt#-219
NEWBERG OR 198-D5
YAMHILL CO OR 198-D5
N COLLEGE ST Rt#-219
NEWBERG OR 198-D5
S COLLEGE ST
NEWBERG OR 198-D5
SW COLLEGE ST
MILTON-FREEWATER OR 121-C3
COLLEGE ST NE
LACEY WA 297-G4
COLLEGE ST SE
LACEY WA 297-G7
THURSTON CO WA 297-F11
COLLEGE WY
FOREST GROVE OR 198-B1
COLLEGE WY Rt#-538
MOUNT VERNON WA 260-J11
SKAGIT CO WA 161-C7
SKAGIT CO WA 260-J11
E COLLEGE WY Rt#-538
MOUNT VERNON WA 260-D10
SKAGIT CO WA 260-H10
NW COLLEGE WY
BEND OR 332-A5
W COLLEGE WY Rt#-538
MOUNT VERNON WA 260-B10
E COLLINS DR
KLICKITAT CO WA 127-C1
COLLINS RD
DESCHUTES CO OR 212-B7
DESCHUTES CO OR 217-B1
LEWIS CO WA 187-D4
SEDRO-WOOLLEY WA 260-H3
SKAGIT CO WA 161-B5
SKAGIT CO WA 260-H3
UNION CO OR 130-B3
WHITMAN CO WA 249-A3
YAKIMA CO WA 243-B4
E COLLINS RD
KITSAP CO WA 271-E13
COLOCKUM RD
CHELAN CO WA 239-B5
KITTITAS CO WA 112-A3
KITTITAS CO WA 239-B7
KITTITAS CO WA 241-D3
COLONIAL DR
JOSEPHINE CO OR 229-B4
COLONIAL RD
DOUGLAS CO OR 221-A5
COLONY RD
SKAGIT CO WA 161-B4
COLONY MOUNTAIN RD
SKAGIT CO WA 161-A4
COLORADO AV
NORTH BEND OR 333-D3
PIERCE CO WA 181-C5
NW COLORADO AV Rt#-372
BEND OR 332-E8
SW COLORADO AV Rt#-372
BEND OR 332-D9
COLORADO RD
CLACKAMAS CO OR 200-C4
COLORADO ST
KELSO WA 303-D11
NE COLORADO ST
PULLMAN WA 249-B5
COLTON RD
BAKER CO OR 130-B3
N COLTON ST
SPOKANE WA 347-A13
COLUMBIA AV
BRIDGEPORT WA 112-C1
DOUGLAS CO WA 112-C1
COLUMBIA AV Rt#-155
COULEE DAM WA 237-C2
COLUMBIA AV Rt#-173
BRIDGEPORT WA 112-C1
E COLUMBIA AV
COLUMBIA CO OR 192-A4
COLUMBIA BLVD
SAINT HELENS OR 192-B1
N COLUMBIA BLVD
PORTLAND OR 192-B7
PORTLAND OR 308-D3
PORTLAND OR 309-E4
NE COLUMBIA BLVD
PORTLAND OR 309-H4
PORTLAND OR 310-B5
PORTLAND OR 311-F7
COLUMBIA DR
JEFFERSON CO OR 208-B7
E COLUMBIA DR
KENNEWICK WA 343-E10
NW COLUMBIA DR
JEFFERSON CO OR 208-B3
SW COLUMBIA DR
JEFFERSON CO OR 208-B6
W COLUMBIA DR
KENNEWICK WA 343-C9
COLUMBIA DR SE
RICHLAND WA 341-H6
RICHLAND WA 342-A6
COLUMBIA RD
DESCHUTES CO OR 217-A2
E COLUMBIA RD
ADA CO ID 253-D4
BOISE ID 253-D4
W COLUMBIA RD
ADA CO ID 253-A4
COLUMBIA ST
CATHLAMET WA 117-B3
DOUGLAS CO WA 112-B2
MESA WA 121-A2
NEW WESTMINSTER BC 156-D6
POMEROY WA 122-B2
VANCOUVER BC 254-H11
VANCOUVER WA 305-F3
COLUMBIA ST Rt#-150
CHELAN WA 236-D3
COLUMBIA ST Rt#-544
NOOKSACK WA 102-B1
NE COLUMBIA ST
KITSAP CO WA 170-C6
Suquamish WA 170-C6
NW COLUMBIA ST
BEND OR 332-D7
SW COLUMBIA ST
BEND OR 332-C9
PORTLAND OR 312-D6
COLUMBIA WY
WALLA WALLA CO WA 121-B3
N COLUMBIA WY
PORTLAND OR 308-A3
SE COLUMBIA WY
VANCOUVER WA 305-G6
COLUMBIA BASIN HWY I-90
ADAMS CO WA 113-C3
COLUMBIA BASIN HWY Rt#-904
CHENEY WA 246-A7
SPOKANE CO WA 246-A7
N COLUMBIA CENTER BLVD
KENNEWICK WA 342-C10
RICHLAND WA 342-C7
S COLUMBIA CENTER BLVD
KENNEWICK WA 342-C11
COLUMBIA HEIGHTS RD
COWLITZ CO WA 189-B2
COWLITZ CO WA 302-H1
COWLITZ CO WA 303-A5
KELSO WA 303-A5
LONGVIEW WA 303-A5
COLUMBIA HOUSE BLVD
VANCOUVER WA 305-J6
VANCOUVER WA 306-A6
S COLUMBIAN WY
SEATTLE WA 282-B4
COLUMBIA PARK TR
BENTON CO WA 341-E5
RICHLAND WA 341-G5
COLUMBIA RIVER HWY I-84
ARLINGTON OR 128-A1
BOARDMAN OR 128-B1
CASCADE LOCKS OR 194-C6
FAIRVIEW OR 200-A1
GILLIAM CO OR 127-C1
GILLIAM CO OR 128-A1
GRESHAM OR 200-A1
HOOD RIVER OR 195-A5
HOOD RIVER CO OR 194-D6
HOOD RIVER CO OR 195-A5
MORROW CO OR 128-B1
MOSIER OR 196-D7
MULTNOMAH CO OR 194-B7
MULTNOMAH CO OR 200-C1
MULTNOMAH CO OR 201-A1
PORTLAND OR 200-A1
PORTLAND OR 315-J2
RUFUS OR 127-C1
SHERMAN CO OR 127-C1
THE DALLES OR 196-D7
TROUTDALE OR 200-A1
WASCO CO OR 127-B1
WASCO CO OR 195-A5
WASCO CO OR 196-D7
WOOD VILLAGE OR 200-A1
COLUMBIA RIVER HWY Rt#-730
UMATILLA CO OR 121-A3
WALLA WALLA CO WA 121-A3
COLUMBIA RIVER HWY U.S.-30
ASTORIA OR 188-D1
ASTORIA OR 300-E5
CLATSKANIE OR 117-B3
CLATSOP CO OR 117-A3
CLATSOP CO OR 188-D1
COLUMBIA CITY OR 192-A3
COLUMBIA CO OR 117-B3
COLUMBIA CO OR 189-A4
COLUMBIA CO OR 192-A3
COLUMBIA CO OR 302-A14
RAINIER OR 189-A4
SAINT HELENS OR 192-A3
SCAPPOOSE OR 192-A3
COLUMBIA RIVER HWY U.S.-730
IRRIGON OR 128-C1
MORROW CO OR 128-C1
UMATILLA OR 129-A1
UMATILLA CO OR 128-C1
UMATILLA CO OR 129-A1
COLUMBIA RIVER RD
FRANKLIN CO WA 121-A2
FRANKLIN CO WA 340-H1
OKANOGAN CO WA 104-C3
OKANOGAN CO WA 105-A3
COLUMBIA SCHOOL RD
Burbank WA 121-A3
COLUMBIA TIE RD
CLARK CO WA 118-A3
COLUMBIA VIEW DR
THE DALLES OR 196-D7
N COLUMBUS AV
GOLDENDALE WA 127-C1
MEDFORD OR 336-B12
S COLUMBUS AV
GOLDENDALE WA 127-C1
JACKSON CO OR 234-A2
KLICKITAT CO WA 127-C1
MEDFORD OR 234-A2
MEDFORD OR 336-B13
S COLUMBUS AV Rt#-238
MEDFORD OR 336-B12
COLUMBUS ST
ALBANY OR 326-F11
LINN CO OR 207-C6
LINN CO OR 326-E14
COLVER RD
JACKSON CO OR 234-B2
PHOENIX OR 234-B2
TALENT OR 234-B2
COLVILLE RD
TOWN OF ESQUIMALT BC 256-C7
COLVILLE-ALADDIN-NORTHPORT RD
NORTHPORT WA 106-B1
STEVENS CO WA 106-B1
COLVILLE-TIGER RD Rt#-20
STEVENS CO WA 106-A2
COLWOOD DR
DISTRICT OF NORTH VANCOUV BC 254-H2
COMA RD
LEWIS CO WA 187-B4
COMMERCE AV
LONGVIEW WA 303-A8
W COMMERCE AV
BOISE ID 253-C4
S COMMERCE ST
TACOMA WA 293-H4
COMMERCIAL AV
ANACORTES WA 259-H2
COOS BAY OR 333-G10
SPRINGFIELD OR 331-C6
COMMERCIAL AV Rt#-20
ANACORTES WA 259-H2
COMMERCIAL DR
VANCOUVER BC 156-C5
VANCOUVER BC 255-B12
COMMERCIAL ST
ASTORIA OR 300-C5
HARNEY CO OR 137-C3
SPOKANE CO WA 114-C2
WAVERLY WA 114-C2
COMMERCIAL ST U.S.-30
ASTORIA OR 300-C5
E COMMERCIAL ST
WEISER ID 139-A2
W COMMERCIAL ST
ASTORIA OR 300-B5
WEISER ID 139-A2
COMMERCIAL ST NE
SALEM OR 322-J9
COMMERCIAL ST NE Rt#-99E
SALEM OR 322-J10
COMMERCIAL ST SE
SALEM OR 322-H13
SALEM OR 324-G2
SALEM OR 325-A9
COMMERICAL AV Rt#-20
ANACORTES WA 160-C6
ANACORTES WA 259-H3
SKAGIT CO WA 259-J6
COMO LAKE AV
COQUITLAM BC 157-A4
DISTRICT OF COQUITLAM BC 156-D4
COMOX RD
NANAIMO BC 93-A3
COMPTON LN
LANE CO OR 210-A6
COMPTON RD
BRITISH COLUMBIA BC 159-B5
SE COMPTON RD
CLACKAMAS CO OR 200-C3
COMSTOCK RD
SUTHERLIN OR 221-C1
CONCOMLY RD NE
MARION CO OR 205-A3
CONCONULLY RD
CONCONULLY WA 104-B2
OKANOGAN CO WA 104-B2
CONCRETE SAUK VALLEY RD
CONCRETE WA 102-C2
SKAGIT CO WA 102-C2
SKAGIT CO WA 103-A2
CONDON RD
CLARK CO WA 193-A1
CONDON WY W
SEATTLE WA 276-D1
CONGER CREEK RD
OKANOGAN CO WA 104-B2
CONIFER BLVD
CORVALLIS OR 207-B5
CORVALLIS OR 327-J5
CONIFER ST NE
MARION CO OR 205-A5
CONKLIN RD
DESCHUTES CO OR 217-A5
S CONKLIN RD
SPOKANE CO WA 247-A5
CONKLING PARK RD
KOOTENAI CO ID 115-A2
KOOTENAI CO ID 248-A6
CONNARN RD
DESCHUTES CO OR 212-B7
CONNECTICUT AV
NORTH BEND OR 333-G4
CONNECTICUT AV SE
Four Corners OR 325-F2
SALEM OR 325-F2
W CONNECTICUT ST
BELLINGHAM WA 258-C4
CONNECTING RD
MAPLE RIDGE BC 157-C5
PITT MEADOWS BC 157-C5
CONNELL HILL RD
GARFIELD CO WA 122-C2
CONNELLS PRAIRIE RD
PIERCE CO WA 182-C4
CONNELLY RD
SNOHOMISH CO WA 171-D4
CONNER RD
NEZ PERCE CO ID 250-D2
CONNER RD SE
THURSTON CO WA 184-C4
CONNETT RD
CLACKAMAS CO OR 200-D3
E CONNOR RD
SPOKANE CO WA 246-D6
CONRAD RD
LEWIS CO WA 187-C2
CONRADI RD
LEWIS CO WA 187-C2
CONSER DR
CORVALLIS OR 207-B5
CONSER RD
LINN CO OR 207-C3
LINN CO OR 326-E1
MILLERSBURG OR 326-E1
CONWAY RD
SKAGIT CO WA 168-B2
COOK AV
DESCHUTES CO OR 217-B1
JEFFERSON CO WA 263-B3
PORT TOWNSEND WA 263-B3
NE COOK LN
JEFFERSON CO OR 208-C2
COOK RD
BAKER CO OR 130-C3
ISLAND CO WA 167-B4
LEWIS CO WA 187-A2
SEDRO-WOOLLEY WA 161-B5
SKAGIT CO WA 161-B5
YAKIMA CO WA 120-A2
SW COOK RD
WASHINGTON CO OR 198-C1
COOK ST
CITY OF VICTORIA BC 256-J6
DISTRICT OF SAANICH BC 256-H5
COOK CREEK RD
TILLAMOOK CO OR 191-D4
COOKE RD
KLICKITAT CO WA 196-A4
COOKE CANYON RD
KITTITAS CO WA 241-D4
COOKS RD
LINCOLN CO OR 206-D3
COOKS HILL RD
CENTRALIA WA 299-A4
LEWIS CO WA 299-A4
COOK-UNDERWOOD RD
SKAMANIA CO WA 195-B4
COOLEY RD
BEND OR 217-C1
DESCHUTES CO OR 217-C1
COOLEY RD NE
MARION CO OR 205-B2
WOODBURN OR 205-B2
W COOLIDGE AV
YAKIMA CO WA 243-A7
COOMBS RD
YAKIMA CO WA 243-D7
COOMBS CANYON RD
UMATILLA CO OR 129-B1
COOPER RD
LEWIS CO WA 187-D4
LINN CO OR 207-C3
COOPER CREEK RD
DOUGLAS CO OR 221-C1
COOPER HOLLOW RD
POLK CO OR 204-A7
COOPER MOUNTAIN RD
CHELAN CO WA 236-C2
COOPER POINT RD NW
OLYMPIA WA 296-E2
THURSTON CO WA 180-C5
THURSTON CO WA 296-E2
COOPER POINT RD SW
OLYMPIA WA 296-E5
COOPER SPUR RD
HOOD RIVER CO OR 202-C2
COOS BAY-ROSEBURG HWY Rt#-42
COOS CO OR 140-C2
COOS CO OR 220-D4
COQUILLE OR 220-D4
DOUGLAS CO OR 140-C3
DOUGLAS CO OR 141-A2
DOUGLAS CO OR 221-A6
MYRTLE POINT OR 140-C2
WINSTON OR 221-B6
COOS BAY-ROSEBURG HWY Rt#-99
DOUGLAS CO OR 221-B6
DOUGLAS CO OR 334-D14
WINSTON OR 221-B6
COOS BAY-WAGON RD
DOUGLAS CO OR 141-A2
DOUGLAS CO OR 221-A5
COOS CITY-SUMNER RD
COOS CO OR 140-B2
COOS CO OR 220-D2
COOS RIVER HWY
COOS BAY OR 220-D1
COOS CO OR 140-B2
COOS CO OR 218-D7
COOS CO OR 220-D1
COOS RIVER RD
COOS CO OR 140-B2
S COOS RIVER RD
COOS CO OR 140-C2
COPALIS BEACH RD
GRAYS HARBOR CO WA 177-B4
COPCO RD
KLAMATH CO OR 231-C5
SISKIYOU CO CA 150-A3
COPE RD
LEWIS CO WA 187-B4
COPELAND CREEK RD
DOUGLAS CO OR 222-C4
COPLEY RD
CROOK CO OR 213-B6
COPPEI AV U.S.-12
WAITSBURG WA 122-A2
COPPER QUEEN RD
JOSEPHINE CO OR 229-B2
COQUILLE-BANDON HWY Rt#-42S
BANDON OR 220-C6
COOS CO OR 220-C6
COQUILLE OR 220-C6
COQUILLE-FAIRVIEW RD
COOS CO OR 140-C2
COOS CO OR 220-D4
COQUILLE OR 220-D4
COQUILLE-FAT ELK RD
COOS CO OR 220-D5
CORAL SEA AV
OAK HARBOR WA 167-C3
CORBET DR
BREMERTON WA 270-F9
KITSAP CO WA 270-F9
SW CORBETT AV
PORTLAND OR 317-F1
CORDATA PKWY
BELLINGHAM WA 158-D7
CORDON RD
Four Corners OR 323-G14
Four Corners OR 325-G1
Hayesville OR 323-G8
MARION CO OR 323-G10
MARION CO OR 325-G1
SALEM OR 323-G10
SALEM OR 325-G3
CORDOVA ST
VANCOUVER BC 254-H10
VANCOUVER BC 255-A10
CORDOVA BAY RD
DISTRICT OF SAANICH BC 159-C5
CORDUROY RD
KELSO WA 303-G8
COREY RD
JACKSON CO OR 230-D6
CORKSCREW CANYON RD
STEVENS CO WA 114-A1
CORKSCREW CANYON RD Rt#-291
STEVENS CO WA 114-B1
STEVENS CO WA 246-A1
CORLISS WY N
SEATTLE WA 274-A1
NW CORNELIUS PASS RD
HILLSBORO OR 199-A1
MULTNOMAH CO OR 192-A6
WASHINGTON CO OR 192-A7
WASHINGTON CO OR 199-A1
NW CORNELIUS-SCHEFFLIN RD
WASHINGTON CO OR 198-C1
NE CORNELL RD
HILLSBORO OR 198-D1
HILLSBORO OR 199-A1
NW CORNELL RD
BEAVERTON OR 199-B1
HILLSBORO OR 199-B1
MULTNOMAH CO OR 199-B1
PORTLAND OR 199-B1
PORTLAND OR 199-B1
PORTLAND OR 312-A5
WASHINGTON CO OR 199-B1
CORNETT RD
CROOK CO OR 213-B5
CORNWALL AV
BELLINGHAM WA 258-D5
VANCOUVER BC 254-C11
W CORNWALL RD
SPOKANE CO WA 114-B2
CORONA AV
MEDFORD OR 336-D9
CORRAL CREEK RD
MALHEUR CO OR 154-C2
YAMHILL CO OR 198-D5
YAMHILL CO OR 199-A6
CORSON AV S
SEATTLE WA 282-B7
CORVALLIS RD
INDEPENDENCE OR 204-B7
POLK CO OR 204-B7
POLK CO OR 207-B2
CORVALLIS-LEBANON HWY Rt#-34
LEBANON OR 133-C1
LINN CO OR 133-C1
LINN CO OR 207-B6
TANGENT OR 207-B6
CORVALLIS-NEWPORT HWY Rt#-34
CORVALLIS OR 327-H11
LINN CO OR 207-B6
LINN CO OR 327-H11
CORVALLIS-NEWPORT HWY U.S.-20
BENTON CO OR 133-A1
CORVALLIS OR 133-A1
CORVALLIS OR 327-E11
PHILOMATH OR 133-A1
COTTAGE AV
CASHMERE WA 238-C2
CLATSOP CO OR 301-G3
GEARHART OR 301-G3
COTTAGE ST
MEDFORD OR 336-D12
E COTTAGE GROVE CONN
COTTAGE GROVE OR 215-B7
COTTAGE GROVE-LORANE RD
COTTAGE GROVE OR 215-A6
LANE CO OR 133-B3
LANE CO OR 215-A6
COTTAGE GROVE RESERVOIR RD
LANE CO OR 219-D2
COTTON RD
CITY OF NORTH VANCOUVER BC 255-E7
DISTRICT OF NORTH VANCOUV BC 255-E7
COTTONWOOD BAY
KOOTENAI CO ID 115-A2
KOOTENAI CO ID 248-A5
COTTONWOOD DR
Birch Bay WA 158-B4
MAPLE RIDGE BC 157-D6
RICHLAND WA 341-D2
COTTONWOOD RD
ADAMS CO ID 139-C1
STEVENS CO WA 114-A1
WALLA WALLA CO WA 121-C3
WALLA WALLA CO WA 122-A3
WALLA WALLA CO WA 345-C11
COTTONWOOD ST Rt#-19
ARLINGTON OR 128-A1
SW COTTONWOOD ST
GRANTS PASS OR 335-C10
COTTONWOOD BUTTE RD
IDAHO CO ID 123-B3
COTTONWOOD CANYON RD
YAKIMA CO WA 119-C2
YAKIMA CO WA 243-A7
COTTONWOOD CREEK RD
NEZ PERCE CO ID 123-B2
STEVENS CO WA 106-B3
COUCH RD
DESCHUTES CO OR 217-A2
COUCH MARKET RD
DESCHUTES CO OR 212-B7
COUGAR RD
CROOK CO OR 135-C1
JEFFERSON CO OR 212-C3

INDEX

OUGAR WY STREET INDEX NW DAVID HILL RD 365

STREET
City State Page-Grid

COUGAR WY
SKAMANIA CO WA 195-B1
COUGAR BEND RD
LANE CO OR 219-D4
COUGAR CREEK RD
ASOTIN CO WA 122-C3
E COUGAR GULCH RD
KOOTENAI CO ID 247-D4
KOOTENAI CO ID 354-J13
KOOTENAI CO ID 355-A13
W COUGAR GULCH RD
KOOTENAI CO ID 247-D4
COUGAR MOUNTAIN RD
LANE CO OR 219-D3
COUGAR SMITH RD
GRAYS HARBOR CO WA 178-D3
GRAYS HARBOR CO WA 179-A3
COUGHANOUR LN
UNION CO OR 130-A3
COULEE BLVD Rt#-155
ELECTRIC CITY WA 237-C3
GRANT CO WA 237-C3
COULSON RD
LEWIS CO WA 187-D2
COUNCIL RD
ADAMS CO ID 139-C1
VALLEY CO ID 251-C7
COUNCIL ST
FOREST GROVE OR 198-B1
COUNTRY LN
LANE CO OR 210-B7
COUNTRY RD
LINN CO OR 207-B7
COUNTRY CLUB DR
BENTON CO OR 327-A12
CORVALLIS OR 327-A12
COUNTRY CLUB RD
EUGENE OR 329-J4
EUGENE OR 330-A4
HOOD RIVER CO OR 195-C6
LAKE OSWEGO OR 320-C5
LAKE OSWEGO OR 321-E5
WHITMAN CO WA 249-A6
COUNTRY CLUB RD NE
BAINBRIDGE ISLAND WA 174-D2
N COUNTRY HOMES BLVD
Country Homes WA 346-H13
SPOKANE WA 346-H13
SPOKANE WA 347-A12
Town and Country WA 346-H13
COUNTRY QUARRY RD
SKAMANIA CO WA 194-B6
COUNTRYSIDE RD
CLACKAMAS CO OR 199-B6
COUNTRY VISTA DR
LIBERTY LAKE WA 351-J7
LIBERTY LAKE WA 352-A14
SPOKANE CO WA 351-J7
COUNTY RD Rt#-27
WHITMAN CO WA 114-C3
COUNTY 1 RD
LA CENTER WA 192-C1
COUNTY LINE RD
BENTON CO WA 120-B3
CLATSOP CO OR 191-D2
DOUGLAS CO OR 214-A5
GEM CO ID 139-B3
SKAGIT CO WA 168-B3
WASCO CO OR 135-A1
COUNTY RD 5
CLARK CO WA 193-A1
COUNTY RD 12
CLARK CO WA 193-C2
COUNTY RD 722
UMATILLA CO OR 129-C1
COUNTY RD 725
UMATILLA CO OR 129-C1
COUNTY RD 802
UMATILLA CO OR 129-B1
COUNTY RD 821
UMATILLA CO OR 129-B1
COUNTY RD 900
Mission OR 129-B1
UMATILLA CO OR 129-B1
COUNTY RD 900 U.S.-30
PENDLETON OR 129-B1
UMATILLA CO OR 129-B1
COUNTY RD 1046
UMATILLA CO OR 129-C2
COUNTY WELL RD
BENTON CO WA 120-C3
COUPLAND RD
CLACKAMAS CO OR 200-C6
ESTACADA OR 200-C6
N COURT AV U.S.-20
BURNS OR 145-B1
NW COURT AV
PENDLETON OR 129-B1
NW COURT AV U.S.-30
PENDLETON OR 129-B1
SE COURT AV U.S.-30
PENDLETON OR 129-B1
SW COURT AV U.S.-30
PENDLETON OR 129-B1
SE COURT PL
PENDLETON OR 129-B1
SW COURT PL
PENDLETON OR 129-B1
SW COURT PL Rt#-37
PENDLETON OR 129-B1
COURT ST
DUFUR OR 127-B2
MEDFORD OR 336-C10
COURT ST Rt#-74
HEPPNER OR 128-C2
E COURT ST
GOLDENDALE WA 127-C1
NE COURT ST
DUFUR OR 127-B2
W COURT ST
FRANKLIN CO WA 340-H14
FRANKLIN CO WA 341-J2
FRANKLIN CO WA 342-A2
FRANKLIN CO WA 343-B6
GOLDENDALE WA 127-C1
PASCO WA 341-J2
PASCO WA 342-A2
PASCO WA 343-B6
COURT ST NE
SALEM OR 322-H13
COURTNEY RD
WASHINGTON CO OR 198-D5
YAMHILL CO OR 198-D5
COURTNEY CREEK DR
LINN CO OR 210-D3
COURTNEY CREEK RD
LINN CO OR 210-D3

COUSE CREEK RD
ASOTIN CO WA 123-A3
COUSINS RD
LEWIS CO WA 187-B1
COVE HWY Rt#-237
COVE OR 130-A2
UNION OR 130-A2
UNION CO OR 130-A2
E COVE HWY Rt#-237
UNION OR 130-B2
COVE RD
KITTITAS CO WA 241-A5
WASHINGTON CO ID 139-B2
SW COVE RD
KING CO WA 174-D5
COVE ORCHARD RD
YAMHILL CO OR 198-B4
COVERED BRIDGE RD
WAHKIAKUM CO WA 117-A2
COVILLE RD
POLK CO OR 204-A5
NE COVINGTON RD
CLARK CO WA 192-D5
COVINGTON WY SE
COVINGTON WA 175-D7
COVINGTON-SAWYER RD
KING CO WA 182-D1
COW CAMP RD
DESCHUTES CO OR 211-C5
WASHINGTON CO ID 139-A1
COW CREEK RD
DOUGLAS CO OR 141-A3
DOUGLAS CO OR 225-A3
NEZ PERCE CO ID 250-B2
RIDDLE OR 225-A3
WASHINGTON CO ID 139-B1
W COW CREEK RD
MALHEUR CO OR 146-C3
COWEN PL NE
SEATTLE WA 274-C4
COW HOLLOW RD
MALHEUR CO OR 139-A3
N COWICHE RD
YAKIMA CO WA 119-C1
W COWICHE CANYON RD
YAKIMA CO WA 243-A6
COWICHE MILL RD
YAKIMA CO WA 119-C1
COWICHE-TIETON RD
TIETON WA 119-C1
YAKIMA CO WA 119-C1
COWLITZ AV
CASTLE ROCK WA 187-C7
COWLITZ CO WA 187-C7
E COWLITZ AV
CASTLE ROCK WA 187-C7
COWLITZ ST Rt#-505
LEWIS CO WA 187-D4
TOLEDO WA 187-D4
COWLITZ WY
KELSO WA 303-D8
COWLITZ WY Rt#-4
KELSO WA 303-D8
COWLITZ GARDEN RD
COWLITZ CO WA 303-D4
COWLITZ LOOP RD
LEWIS CO WA 187-C4
COWLITZ RIDGE RD
LEWIS CO WA 187-C4
COX RD
DOUGLAS CO OR 219-B3
COX CREEK RD
DOUGLAS CO OR 219-C3
NW COYER AV
DESCHUTES CO OR 212-C4
COYLE RD
JEFFERSON CO WA 170-A4
NW COYNER AV
DESCHUTES CO OR 212-D4
Terrebonne OR 212-D4
COYOTE
CROOK CO OR 213-D6
SW COYOTE
DESCHUTES CO OR 212-C6
COYOTE CREEK RD
JOSEPHINE CO OR 229-B1
COYOTE GRADE RD
NEZ PERCE CO ID 250-D2
COYOTE POINT RD
HUMBOLDT CO NV 154-A3
E COZZA DR U.S.-2
SPOKANE WA 347-A14
CRAB CREEK RD
GRANT CO WA 120-C1
E CRAB CREEK RD
LINCOLN CO WA 209-D4
CRACKER CREEK RD
BAKER CO OR 138-A1
CRAIG LN
CROOK CO OR 213-D6
N CRAIG RD
SPOKANE CO WA 246-A4
S CRAIG RD
SPOKANE CO WA 246-A4
CRAIGFLOWER RD
BRITISH COLUMBIA BC 256-D6
CITY OF VICTORIA BC 256-E7
TOWN OF ESQUIMALT BC 256-D6
TOWN OF VIEW ROYAL BC 256-D6
CRAIG JUNCTION RD
LEWIS CO ID 123-B2
CRAMER RD
CLARK CO WA 192-D4
CRAMER RD KPN
PIERCE CO WA 174-A7
CRANBERRY RD
GRAYS HARBOR CO WA 183-B3
PACIFIC CO WA 186-A4
N CRANE RD
WASHINGTON CO ID 139-C2
CRANE-BUCHANAN RD
HARNEY CO OR 145-C1
CRANE CREEK RD
WASHINGTON CO ID 139-B2
CRANE CREEK RESERVOIR RD
WASHINGTON CO ID 139-B2
CRANE ORCHARD
DOUGLAS CO WA 112-B1
CRANE ORCHARD RD
DOUGLAS CO WA 104-B3
CRANES RD NW
DOUGLAS CO WA 104-B3
CRANE-VENATOR RD
HARNEY CO OR 145-C2
HARNEY CO OR 146-A2
MALHEUR CO OR 146-A2
CRANLEY DR
CITY OF SURREY BC 158-A2

CRATER LP
JEFFERSON CO OR 212-C2
CRATER CREEK MTWY
JACKSON CO OR 226-D2
JACKSON CO OR 227-A2
CRATER CREEK RD
JACKSON CO OR 226-D2
KLAMATH CO OR 227-C5
CRATER LAKE AV
JACKSON CO OR 336-F3
MEDFORD OR 336-E11
CRATER LAKE HWY Rt#-62
EAGLE POINT OR 230-D4
JACKSON CO OR 149-C1
JACKSON CO OR 150-A1
JACKSON CO OR 226-C7
JACKSON CO OR 227-D7
JACKSON CO OR 230-D4
JACKSON CO OR 336-F3
KLAMATH CO OR 227-D7
KLAMATH CO OR 231-C2
MEDFORD OR 336-F3
SHADY COVE OR 230-D4
White City OR 230-D6
CRATER LAKE RD
MALHEUR CO OR 146-C2
CRATER LAKE NORTH HWY
DOUGLAS CO OR 223-C7
DOUGLAS CO OR 227-C2
KLAMATH CO OR 227-C2
CRAW RD
ISLAND CO WA 171-A1
NE CRAWFORD DR
KITSAP CO WA 170-C5
CRAWFORD LN
YAMHILL CO OR 198-C6
CRAWFORD RD
DESCHUTES CO OR 217-A6
CRAWFORD ST
WENATCHEE WA 238-D5
WENATCHEE WA 239-A5
E CRAWFORD ST
DEER PARK WA 114-B1
W CRAWFORD ST
DEER PARK WA 114-B1
CREASY RD
WHATCOM CO WA 158-C4
CREEK DR
LINN CO OR 210-A2
CREEK RD
HARNEY CO OR 137-B3
E CREEK RD
TILLAMOOK CO OR 197-D5
CREEK BEND RD
LINN CO OR 210-A2
CREGO HILL RD
LEWIS CO WA 187-A1
CRESCENT AV
EUGENE OR 215-B1
CRESCENT RD
CITY OF SURREY BC 158-A1
CITY OF VICTORIA BC 257-B11
DISTRICT OF OAK BAY BC 257-B11
LINCOLN CO WA 114-A1
CRESCENT RD NW
SALEM OR 322-E12
CRESCENT BEACH RD
CLALLAM CO WA 164-C5
CRESCENT BEACH RD KPN
PIERCE CO WA 181-A1
CRESCENT CUT-OFF RD
KLAMATH CO OR 142-C1
CRESCENT HARBOR RD
ISLAND CO WA 167-C2
OAK HARBOR WA 167-C2
CRESCENT LAKE HWY
KLAMATH CO OR 142-B1
CRESCENT VALLEY DR NW
PIERCE CO WA 174-C7
CRESCENT VALLEY RD SE
KITSAP CO WA 174-C6
CREST DR
EUGENE OR 329-J10
EUGENE OR 330-A10
LANE CO OR 329-H11
W CREST DR
EUGENE OR 329-H11
LANE CO OR 329-H11
CRESTLINE BLVD NW
OLYMPIA WA 296-G2
CRESTLINE DR
LINCOLN CO OR 328-D9
WALDPORT OR 328-E5
S CRESTLINE DR
WALDPORT OR 328-E5
N CRESTLINE ST
SPOKANE WA 347-D13
SPOKANE WA 349-D2
SPOKANE CO WA 347-D13
CRESTLOCH RD
FRANKLIN CO WA 121-A2
CRESTVIEW DR
MASON CO WA 180-B3
CRESTVIEW LN
SKAGIT CO WA 161-A6
CRESTVIEW RD
CROOK CO OR 213-D5
Sunnyslope WA 238-D3
CRESWELL RD
SNOHOMISH CO WA 110-C1
CREVISTON DR NW
PIERCE CO WA 174-B7
CREVISTON RD KPS
PIERCE CO WA 181-A3
CRISP LN
LANE CO OR 215-B5
CRITCHFIELD RD
ASOTIN CO WA 250-B5
Vineland WA 250-B5
CRITES RD
SHERMAN CO OR 127-C2
CRITESER RD
DOUGLAS CO OR 221-A5
S CRITSER RD
CLACKAMAS CO OR 199-D6
CROCKER LN
ALBANY OR 326-A4
CROCKER RD
Santa Clara OR 215-A1
CROFT AV U.S.-2
GOLD BAR WA 110-C1
SNOHOMISH CO WA 110-C1
CROFT LAKE RD
COOS CO OR 224-B1
CROISAN CREEK RD S
MARION CO OR 324-D5
SALEM OR 324-D5

CROMWELL DR NW
PIERCE CO WA 181-B2
CRONIN RD
CROOK CO OR 213-A6
CROOK DR
LINN CO OR 210-A3
CROOKED CREEK RD
LANE CO OR 210-D5
MALHEUR CO OR 146-B3
MALHEUR CO OR 154-B1
CROOKED CREEK RANGE RD
MALHEUR CO OR 154-A1
CROOKED FINGER RD
MARION CO OR 205-D4
CROOKED FINGER RD NE
MARION CO OR 126-A3
CROOKED RIVER HWY Rt#-27
CROOK CO OR 135-C3
CROOK CO OR 213-C6
DESCHUTES CO OR 135-C3
PRINEVILLE OR 213-C6
CROOKS RD
GRANT CO WA 237-B3
CROOKS CREEK RD
JOSEPHINE CO OR 233-C1
CROSBY RD
Ault Field WA 167-B2
BENTON CO WA 120-C2
ISLAND CO WA 167-B2
CROSBY RD NE
MARION CO OR 205-A1
CROSBY ST Rt#-27
TEKOA WA 114-C3
CROSS RD
KLAMATH CO OR 235-C6
CROSS CREEK RD
DISTRICT OF WEST VANCOUVE BC 254-D1
CROSS ISLAND RD
ISLAND CO WA 167-D4
E CROSSROAD LN
LANE CO OR 210-A6
N CROSS STATE HWY Rt#-20
SEDRO-WOOLLEY WA 161-C5
SKAGIT CO WA 161-C5
CROSSWINDS
DESCHUTES CO OR 217-C1
CROW RD
JOSEPHINE CO OR 229-A4
LANE CO OR 133-B3
LANE CO OR 215-A2
CROW CREEK RD
WALLOWA CO OR 130-C2
WALLOWA CO OR 131-A1
CROWELL LN
NORTH BEND OR 333-F5
CROWFOOT RD
JACKSON CO OR 149-C1
CROWLEY RD
MALHEUR CO OR 138-B3
MALHEUR CO OR 146-B1
POLK CO OR 204-B5
CROWLEY-RIVERSIDE RD
MALHEUR CO OR 146-A1
SE CROWN RD
CAMAS WA 193-B7
CLARK CO WA 193-B7
CROWN ST
VANCOUVER BC 156-A5
CROWN POINT HWY
MULTNOMAH CO OR 194-A7
MULTNOMAH CO OR 200-D1
MULTNOMAH CO OR 201-A1
E CROWN POINT HWY
MULTNOMAH CO OR 200-D1
MULTNOMAH CO OR 201-A1
CROWN POINT RD Rt#-174
DOUGLAS CO WA 237-C2
CROWN PT RD
COOS CO OR 220-C2
CROWSNEST HWY Rt#-3
BRITISH COLUMBIA BC 103-C1
CROWSON RD
JACKSON CO OR 234-D4
JACKSON CO OR 337-J11
W CROW VALLEY RD
SAN JUAN CO WA 101-C2
CROW-VAUGHN RD
LANE CO OR 133-A3
CRUMARINE LOOP RD
LATAH CO ID 249-D4
CRUM CANYON RD
CHELAN CO WA 236-A6
CRUSH CRES
TOWNSHIP OF LANGLEY BC 157-C7
CRUSHER CANYON RD
YAKIMA CO WA 243-B5
CRYSTAL CREEK RD
CROOK CO OR 136-A2
CURRY CO OR 224-B4
CRYSTAL LAKE DR
BENTON CO OR 327-H12
CORVALLIS OR 327-H12
CRYSTAL LAKE RD
SNOHOMISH CO WA 171-D6
CRYSTAL MOUNTAIN BLVD
PIERCE CO WA 119-A1
CRYSTAL SPRINGS DR NE
BAINBRIDGE ISLAND WA 271-E6
CRYSTAL SPRINGS RD
KLAMATH CO OR 150-C2
KLAMATH CO OR 235-D5
CRYSTAL SPRINGS RD NE
BAINBRIDGE ISLAND WA 271-G6
CSP RR
WHITMAN CO WA 250-A4
C-SW DODSON RD
GRANT CO WA 120-C1
ROYAL CITY WA 120-C1
CUB CREEK RD
OKANOGAN CO WA 104-A2
CULBERTSON DR
HOOD RIVER CO OR 202-C2
CULDESAC CUTOFF RD
CULDESAC ID 123-B2
CULLABY LAKE RD
CLATSOP CO OR 188-B3
CULLEN RD
YAMHILL CO OR 198-D5
CULLUM AV
RICHLAND WA 341-G3
NE CULLY BLVD
PORTLAND OR 310-E7
PORTLAND OR 311-E7
PORTLAND OR 314-D1
CULTUS BAY RD
ISLAND CO WA 171-A3
CULTUS LAKE RD
BRITISH COLUMBIA BC 102-C1

CULTUS LAKE RD
CITY OF CHILLIWACK BC 102-C1
CULVER DR SE
MARION CO OR 325-H3
CULVER HWY Rt#-361
CULVER OR 208-B7
JEFFERSON CO OR 208-B6
JEFFERSON CO OR 212-D1
MADRAS OR 208-B6
METOLIUS OR 208-B6
SW CULVER HWY
JEFFERSON CO OR 212-D2
CULVER RD
LANE CO OR 210-A6
CUMBERLAND ST
NEW WESTMINSTER BC 156-D5
CUMBERLAND-KANASKAT RD
KING CO WA 110-C3
CUMMINGS LN N
KEIZER OR 322-H6
CUMMINS CREEK RD
LANE CO OR 209-A4
CUMMINS PEAK RD
LINCOLN CO OR 209-A4
CUNNINGHAM LN
YAMHILL CO OR 198-C4
CUNNINGHAM RD
ADAMS CO WA 121-C1
W CUNNINGHAM RD
ADAMS CO WA 121-B1
W CURLEW LAKE RD
FERRY CO WA 105-B2
CURLY CREEK RD
SKAMANIA CO WA 118-C3
CURRIN RD
CLACKAMAS CO OR 200-C5
CURRY RD
DOUGLAS CO OR 221-B3
CURTIN RD
DOUGLAS CO OR 219-B2
CURTIS RD
HARRAH WA 119-C2
LINN CO OR 210-A6
WHATCOM CO WA 158-D7
N CURTIS RD
BOISE ID 253-C3
S CURTIS RD
ADA CO ID 253-C3
BOISE ID 253-C3
W CURTIS RD
SPOKANE CO WA 246-B7
CURTIS ST
DISTRICT OF BURNABY BC 156-D4
W CURTIS ST U.S.-101
ABERDEEN WA 178-B7
CURTIS HILL RD
LEWIS CO WA 184-A7
LEWIS CO WA 187-A1
W CUSTER DR
SPOKANE WA 348-F6
CUSTER RD SW
LAKEWOOD WA 181-C3
LAKEWOOD WA 294-A7
CUSTER RD W
LAKEWOOD WA 181-C3
CUSTER ST
TUMWATER WA 296-H9
CUSTER SCHOOL RD
WHATCOM CO WA 158-C4
CUTHBERTSON RD
LAKE STEVENS WA 110-C1
LAKE STEVENS WA 171-D1
CUTOFF RD
JEFFERSON CO OR 211-D2
JEFFERSON CO OR 212-A2
C W HUGHES RD
WHITMAN CO WA 114-C3
C WILLIAMS RD
BENTON CO WA 121-A3
CY BINGHAM RD
HARNEY CO OR 137-C3
CYMIOTTI RD
KLICKITAT CO WA 196-B3
CYPRESS WY
SNOHOMISH CO WA 171-B5
W CYPRESS WY
SNOHOMISH CO WA 171-B5
CYPRESS BOWL RD
DISTRICT OF WEST VANCOUVE BC 156-A2

D

D AV
ANACORTES WA 259-F4
D ST
BAKER CITY OR 138-B1
CULVER OR 208-B7
GRANTS PASS OR 335-E8
HUBBARD OR 205-B1
SALEM OR 322-J12
SALEM OR 323-B12
SPRINGFIELD OR 330-H7
D ST Rt#-14
WASHOUGAL WA 193-C7
D ST Rt#-14B
WASHOUGAL WA 193-C7
D ST Rt#-218
SHANIKO OR 127-C3
D ST Rt#-507
TENINO WA 184-D3
D ST Rt#-548
BLAINE WA 158-B3
D ST U.S.-12
LEWISTON ID 250-B4
E D ST
GRANTS PASS OR 335-G9
MOSCOW ID 249-D5
TACOMA WA 293-H6
TACOMA WA 295-J1
SW D ST Rt#-361
MADRAS OR 208-C5
W D ST
LANE CO OR 330-F7
SPRINGFIELD OR 330-G7
DABOB RD
JEFFERSON CO WA 170-A3
DABOB POST OFFICE RD
JEFFERSON CO WA 170-A4
DAHL RD
YAKIMA CO WA 243-A6
DAHLGREN RD
COLUMBIA CO OR 192-A3
DAHLIA WY
POLK CO OR 204-C5
POLK CO OR 322-A10
DAHLKE RD SW
DOUGLAS CO WA 239-D2

DAILY LN
JOSEPHINE CO OR 229-A6
DAIRY-BONANZA HWY Rt#-70
BONANZA OR 151-A2
KLAMATH CO OR 151-A2
SW DAISY ST
KITSAP CO WA 174-A6
DAISY ST N Rt#-17
GRANT CO WA 112-C2
SOAP LAKE WA 112-C2
DAISY ST S Rt#-17
SOAP LAKE WA 112-C2
DAISY MINE RD
JACKSON CO OR 229-D2
JOSEPHINE CO OR 229-C2
STEVENS CO WA 105-C3
STEVENS CO WA 106-A3
DAKIN ST
BELLINGHAM WA 258-J4
DAKOTA AV
MEDFORD OR 336-B13
DALBY RD
MASON CO WA 173-B7
DALE DR
LINN CO OR 210-B5
DALE LN
CLACKAMAS CO OR 200-B4
DALE RD
BRITISH COLUMBIA BC 94-B3
DALLAS RD
BENTON CO WA 341-A4
CITY OF VICTORIA BC 256-F10
CITY OF VICTORIA BC 257-A11
RICHLAND WA 341-A4
WEST RICHLAND WA 341-A4
NE DALLAS ST Rt#-500
CAMAS WA 193-B7
DALLAS-RICKREALL HWY Rt#-223
DALLAS OR 204-A6
POLK CO OR 204-A6
DALLES MOUNTAIN RD
KLICKITAT CO WA 127-B1
KLICKITAT CO WA 196-D6
DALLESPORT RD
KLICKITAT CO WA 196-C6
DALLMAN RD
ISLAND CO WA 168-A7
E DALTON AV
COEUR D'ALENE ID 355-F4
DALTON GARDENS ID 355-F4
KOOTENAI CO ID 355-F4
W DALTON AV
COEUR D'ALENE ID 355-D5
DALY CREEK RD
BAKER CO OR 139-A1
DAMMAN RD
KITTITAS CO WA 241-B6
DAMON RD
ADAMS CO WA 113-B3
ADAMS CO WA 121-B1
DAMON RD Rt#-115
GRAYS HARBOR CO WA 177-B6
OCEAN SHORES WA 177-B6
DAMSON RD
SNOHOMISH CO WA 171-C5
DANBY DR SW
THURSTON CO WA 184-C3
DANE LN
LANE CO OR 210-A6
N DANEBO AV
EUGENE OR 329-A4
S DANEBO AV
EUGENE OR 329-A6
DANEKAS RD
ADAMS CO WA 113-C3
ADAMS CO WA 114-A3
RITZVILLE WA 113-C3
DANIELS RD
MASON CO WA 180-B2
DAN KELLY RD
CLALLAM CO WA 165-A6
DANNEN RD
LINN CO OR 210-B2
DANNER LP
MALHEUR CO OR 147-A3
DANNER RD
MALHEUR CO OR 146-C3
MALHEUR CO OR 147-A3
SNOHOMISH CO WA 168-C5
DARBY RD
LATAH CO ID 249-D4
DARK HOLLOW RD
JACKSON CO OR 234-A2
S DARKNELL RD
SPOKANE CO WA 247-A6
E DARLAND ST
GOLDENDALE WA 127-C1
DARLEY RD
MARION CO OR 133-C1
DARRELL AV
WINSTON OR 221-B6
DARRNGTN BENTTS STR RD Rt#-530
DARRINGTON WA 103-A3
SKAGIT CO WA 103-A3
SNOHOMISH CO WA 103-A3
DARRINGTON CLEAR CREEK RD
DARRINGTON WA 103-A3
SNOHOMISH CO WA 103-A3
DART CREEK RD
COLUMBIA CO OR 192-A1
DARTER RD
KITSAP CO WA 170-B6
W DARTFORD DR
Fairwood WA 346-J6
Fairwood WA 347-A6
SPOKANE CO WA 346-J6
DARTMOUTH ST U.S.-95
ADAMS CO ID 139-C1
COUNCIL ID 139-C1
S DASH POINT RD Rt#-509
FEDERAL WAY WA 182-B1
SW DASH POINT RD Rt#-509
FEDERAL WAY WA 182-A1
SE DATE AV
COLLEGE PLACE WA 344-F11
DAVENPORT ST
RICHLAND WA 341-G2
DAVID AV
COQUITLAM BC 157-B4
PORT MOODY BC 157-A4
DAVID RD
WHITMAN CO WA 249-C4
NW DAVID HILL RD
FOREST GROVE OR 198-B1
WASHINGTON CO OR 198-B1

INDEX

366 DAVIDSON AV
STREET INDEX
DOUBLE O RD

STREET
City State Page-Grid

DAVIDSON AV
COWLITZ CO WA 192-B1
WOODLAND WA 192-B1
DAVIDSON RD
POLK CO OR 207-B1
DAVIE ST
VANCOUVER BC 254-E9
DAVIES
PIERCE CO WA 182-B7
DAVIES RD
BRITISH COLUMBIA BC 159-B5
N DAVIES RD
SNOHOMISH CO WA 171-D1
S DAVIES RD
SNOHOMISH CO WA 171-D2
DAVIS DR
HOOD RIVER CO OR 195-C6
DAVIS RD
ADAMS CO WA 113-B3
ASOTIN CO WA 123-A3
COWLITZ CO WA 189-D1
CROOK CO OR 213-D6
LATAH CO ID 249-D2
LINCOLN CO WA 113-B3
LINN CO OR 207-C7
SISKIYOU CO CA 150-C3
SW DAVIS RD
BEAVERTON OR 199-A2
DAVIS ST
MCCALL ID 251-D5
DAVIS WY Rt#-270
PULLMAN WA 249-A5
WHITMAN CO WA 249-A5
DAVIS CREEK LN
VALLEY CO ID 252-D2
DAVIS CREEK RD
JOSEPHINE CO OR 233-B1
DAVIS CREEK RD NE
MARION CO OR 205-D4
DAVIS PEAK RD
COWLITZ CO WA 118-A3
DAVISSON RD
LANE CO OR 215-C6
S DAVIS SPUR RD
COWLITZ CO WA 189-D1
DAWES HILL RD
COQUITLAM BC 157-A5
DAWSON RD
BENTON CO OR 133-B2
DAY RD
IDAHO CO ID 123-C3
ISLAND CO WA 167-C7
WASHINGTON CO OR 199-B5
WILSONVILLE OR 199-B5
E DAY RD
SPOKANE CO WA 246-D1
NE DAY RD E
BAINBRIDGE ISLAND WA 174-D1
NE DAY RD W
BAINBRIDGE ISLAND WA 174-C1
DAY HILL RD
CLACKAMAS CO OR 200-C6
DAY ISLAND RD
EUGENE OR 330-B6
DAY-MT SPOKANE RD
SPOKANE CO WA 246-D1
SPOKANE CO WA 347-J3
DAY SCHOOL RD
KLAMATH CO OR 231-D5
DAYS CREEK RD
DOUGLAS CO OR 141-B3
DAYS CREEK CUTOFF RD
DOUGLAS CO OR 225-C1
E DAYTON AV
DAYTON WA 122-A2
W DAYTON AV
DAYTON WA 122-A2
DAYTON AV N
SHORELINE WA 171-A7
DAYTON RD
DESCHUTES CO OR 212-B7
DAYTON ST
Altamont OR 338-H9
S DAYTON ST
KENNEWICK WA 343-D14
DAYTON-AIRPORT RD
MASON CO WA 179-D2
DAYTON-AIRPORT RD Rt#-102
MASON CO WA 179-D2
MASON CO WA 180-A2
SE DAYTON BYPASS RD Rt#-18
DAYTON OR 198-B7
YAMHILL CO OR 198-B7
DEAD INDIAN RD
JACKSON CO OR 150-A2
JACKSON CO OR 234-D4
KLAMATH CO OR 150-B2
DEAD INDIAN MEMORIAL RD
ASHLAND OR 337-J9
JACKSON CO OR 234-D4
JACKSON CO OR 337-J9
DEAD MAN RD
CHELAN CO WA 238-B2
N DEADMAN RD
GARFIELD CO WA 122-B2
DEADMAN CREEK RD
DOUGLAS CO OR 141-C3
DEADMAN GULCH RD
MALHEUR CO OR 146-C1
DEADMOND FERRY RD
SPRINGFIELD OR 330-G2
DEAD POINT RD
HOOD RIVER CO OR 195-B7
DEADY CROSSING RD
DOUGLAS CO OR 221-C2
DEAL RD
ADAMS CO WA 113-B3
ADAMS CO WA 121-B1
DEAN MOUNTAIN RD
COOS CO OR 218-C6
DOUGLAS CO OR 218-D2
DEAN PARK RD
DISTRICT OF NORTH SAANICH BC 159-C3
DEARBORN AV NE
KEIZER OR 322-J5
KEIZER OR 323-A5
S DEARBORN ST
SEATTLE WA 278-A7
DE ARMOND RD
POLK CO OR 207-A3
DEBAST RD
COLUMBIA CO OR 189-B4
DE BERRY RD
LANE CO OR 215-B5
DECATUR AV
BREMERTON WA 270-G11
DECEPTION RD
SKAGIT CO WA 160-C7
SKAGIT CO WA 259-H14
DECKER RD
BENTON CO OR 133-B2
DECKERVILLE RD
MASON CO WA 179-B2
DEEGAN RD W
MASON CO WA 180-A3
DEEP CREEK RD
CLACKAMAS CO OR 200-B3
DAMASCUS OR 200-B3
LEWIS CO WA 184-A7
DEEP LAKE BOUNDARY RD
STEVENS CO WA 106-B1
DEEP RIVER VALLEY RD
WAHKIAKUM CO WA 117-A2
DEER DR
KOOTENAI CO ID 248-A3
DEER RD
WHEELER CO OR 136-B2
N DEER ST
PRINEVILLE OR 213-D5
DEER CREEK RD
JACKSON CO OR 226-D3
JACKSON CO OR 227-A3
JOSEPHINE CO OR 233-B2
KLAMATH CO OR 227-A3
STEVENS CO WA 106-A3
S DEER CREEK RD
DOUGLAS CO OR 221-D5
DEER CREEK-BOULDER CREEK RD
FERRY CO WA 105-B1
DEER FLAT RD
CANYON CO ID 147-B1
E DEER FLAT RD
ADA CO ID 253-A5
KUNA ID 253-A5
W DEER FLAT RD
ADA CO ID 253-A5
DEERHORN RD
LANE CO OR 133-C3
DEER LAKE AV
DISTRICT OF BURNABY BC 156-D5
DEER LAKE PL
DISTRICT OF BURNABY BC 156-D5
DEER LAKE RD
Clinton WA 171-A2
DEER LAKE LOOP RD
STEVENS CO WA 106-B3
DEER PARK DR SE
MARION CO OR 325-J5
SALEM OR 325-J5
DEER PARK RD
CLALLAM CO WA 165-C7
DEER PARK-MILAN RD
DEER PARK WA 114-B1
SPOKANE CO WA 114-B1
E DEER PARK-MILAN RD
SPOKANE CO WA 114-B1
W DEER PARK-MILAN RD
SPOKANE CO WA 114-B1
DEER RIDGE RD
DESCHUTES CO OR 211-D4
DEER TRAIL LN
JACKSON CO OR 234-B3
DEER VALLEY RD
NEWPORT WA 106-C3
PEND OREILLE CO WA 106-C3
DE FRATES RD
COLUMBIA CO OR 189-C6
DEGGLER RD
LEWIS CO WA 118-A2
SW DEHAVEN ST
MILTON-FREEWATER OR 121-C3
DEHLER RD
CROOK CO OR 213-C3
DEHLINGER LN
KLAMATH CO OR 235-D6
DEINHARD LN
MCCALL ID 251-C5
DEJEE RD N
LINCOLN CO WA 113-B2
DEJONG RD
POLK CO OR 204-A3
YAMHILL CO OR 204-A3
SW DEJONG RD
YAMHILL CO OR 204-A2
DEKAY RD
GRAYS HARBOR CO WA 177-D5
DEKKER RD
YAKIMA CO WA 120-A2
DELAMETER RD
COWLITZ CO WA 187-B7
COWLITZ CO WA 189-B1
DELANEY RD
FRANKLIN CO WA 121-B2
DELANEY RD SE
MARION CO OR 207-D1
MARION CO OR 324-J12
MARION CO OR 325-A12
TURNER OR 325-E12
DELANO RD KPS
PIERCE CO WA 181-A2
SW DELASHMUTT LN
YAMHILL CO OR 204-A2
DELBROOK AV
DISTRICT OF NORTH VANCOUV BC 255-A2
DELENA-MAYGER RD
COLUMBIA CO OR 189-A4
DELEZENNE RD
GRAYS HARBOR CO WA 117-B1
DELFATTI LN
KLAMATH CO OR 235-C5
DELICIOUS ST
DESCHUTES CO OR 212-A7
DELINTMENT LAKE RD
HARNEY CO OR 136-C3
DELL AV
Garrett WA 344-F7
WALLA WALLA WA 344-F7
DELL RD W
WASCO CO OR 196-B6
DELL ADAMS RD
MASON CO WA 179-C3
DELLMOOR LP
CLATSOP CO OR 188-B4
DELMAR DR E
SEATTLE WA 278-B1
DELMAR RD
COOS CO OR 220-D3
DELPHI RD NW
THURSTON CO WA 296-A3
DELPHI RD SW
THURSTON CO WA 180-B7
THURSTON CO WA 184-B1
THURSTON CO WA 296-A6
DELRIDGE WY SW
KING CO WA 285-G3
SEATTLE WA 281-G7
SEATTLE WA 285-G2
DEL RIO RD
DOUGLAS CO WA 113-A1
DEL RIO RD E
DOUGLAS CO WA 237-A2
DEL RIO COULEE CITY RD
DOUGLAS CO WA 113-A1
DELTA AV
DISTRICT OF BURNABY BC 255-J13
DELTA HWY
EUGENE OR 329-J3
DELTA ST
KLAMATH FALLS OR 338-C6
DELTA LINE RD
WHATCOM CO WA 158-C4
DELTAPORT WY
DISTRICT OF DELTA BC 101-C1
DELTA WATERS RD
JACKSON CO OR 336-F7
MEDFORD OR 336-F7
DEMARAY DR
JOSEPHINE CO OR 229-A7
JOSEPHINE CO OR 335-A12
DEMPSEY RD
CLALLAM CO WA 164-D6
DISTRICT OF NORTH VANCOUV BC 255-E1
DENBROOK RD
CLACKAMAS CO OR 199-B6
E DENISON-CHATTAROY RD
SPOKANE CO WA 114-C1
W DENISON-CHATTAROY RD
SPOKANE CO WA 114-B1
DENMAN ST
VANCOUVER BC 254-E9
DENMARK ST SW
THURSTON CO WA 184-B4
SW DENNEY RD
BEAVERTON OR 199-B2
DENNIS RD
BENTON CO WA 120-C3
DENNY WY
SEATTLE WA 277-H4
SEATTLE WA 278-A4
E DENNY WY
SEATTLE WA 278-A4
SEATTLE WA 279-E4
W DENNY WY
SEATTLE WA 277-H4
DENNY SCHOOL RD
LINN CO OR 133-C1
W DENO RD
SPOKANE CO WA 246-A4
DENT RD
FRANKLIN CO WA 340-J14
N DENVER AV
PORTLAND OR 308-E4
DENVER RD
IDAHO CO ID 123-C3
S DENVER ST
ASTORIA OR 300-B6
DENVER ST SE
TURNER OR 325-G12
DEPARTURE BAY RD
NANAIMO BC 93-A3
DERRICK CAVES RD
LAKE CO OR 143-B2
DESCHUTES AV U.S.-197
MAUPIN OR 127-B3
DESCHUTES DR
JEFFERSON CO OR 208-B5
NW DESCHUTES DR
JEFFERSON CO OR 208-B3
DESCHUTES PKWY
OLYMPIA WA 296-G6
TUMWATER WA 296-G6
E DESCHUTES RD
DESCHUTES CO OR 142-C1
DESCHUTES ST
WASCO CO OR 127-C1
DESCHUTES WY
TUMWATER WA 296-H9
DESCHUTES RIVER RD
MAUPIN OR 127-B3
WASCO CO OR 127-B3
DESERT RD
GEM CO ID 139-B3
W DESKA DR
SPOKANE CO WA 348-C11
DES MOINES MEMORIAL DR S
BURIEN WA 288-A4
DES MOINES WA 290-A2
KING CO WA 286-B4
KING CO WA 288-A4
SEATAC WA 288-A4
SEATAC WA 290-A2
DES MOINES MEM DR S Rt#-509
BURIEN WA 288-A7
BURIEN WA 290-A1
SEATAC WA 290-A1
NW DESPAIN AV
PENDLETON OR 129-B1
DESPAIN GULCH RD
UMATILLA CO OR 129-A1
DETHMAN RIDGE DR
HOOD RIVER CO OR 195-C6
DETROIT BLVD S
PACIFIC WA 182-B2
DEVER-CONNER RD
LINN CO OR 207-C3
DEVERELL RD
MULTNOMAH CO OR 200-D2
DEVILLE RD
SKAMANIA CO WA 194-A6
DEVILS CANYON RD Rt#-263
FRANKLIN CO WA 121-C2
KAHLOTUS WA 121-C2
DEVILS GAP RD
LINCOLN CO WA 114-A1
E DEVILS LAKE RD
LINCOLN CITY OR 203-B4
LINCOLN CO OR 203-B4
W DEVILS LAKE RD
LINCOLN CITY OR 203-A4
LINCOLN CO OR 203-A4
DEVILS MTN RD
SKAGIT CO WA 168-B1
DEVILS WELL RD
LINCOLN CO OR 206-D4
DEVINE RIDGE RD
HARNEY CO OR 137-B3
DE VRIES RD
ISLAND CO WA 167-C2
DEWATO RD W
KITSAP CO WA 173-C3
DEWATTO RD
KITSAP CO WA 173-D4
MASON CO WA 173-D4
MASON CO WA 174-A4
DEWATTO-HOLLY RD
MASON CO WA 173-B5
DEWDNEY TRUNK RD
DISTRICT OF MISSION BC 94-B3
MAPLE RIDGE BC 94-B3
MAPLE RIDGE BC 157-C5
PITT MEADOWS BC 157-B5
DEWEY AV Rt#-7
BAKER CITY OR 138-B1
DEWEY ST
BREMERTON WA 270-G11
DEWEY CREEK LP
LINCOLN CO OR 206-C2
DEW VALLEY RD
COOS CO OR 220-A7
S DHOOGHE RD
CLACKAMAS CO OR 126-A3
DIAGONAL ST Rt#-129
CLARKSTON WA 250-B4
DIAL LN
UNION CO OR 130-A2
DIAMOND LN
HARNEY CO OR 145-B3
DIAMOND HILL DR
LINN CO OR 210-A4
DIAMOND HILL RD
HARRISBURG OR 210-A5
LINN CO OR 210-A5
NE DIAMOND LAKE BLVD Rt#-138
ROSEBURG OR 221-C4
ROSEBURG OR 334-H7
E DIAMOND LAKE HWY Rt#-138
DOUGLAS CO OR 223-D7
KLAMATH CO OR 142-B2
KLAMATH CO OR 223-D7
W DIAMOND LAKE HWY Rt#-230
DOUGLAS CO OR 223-B7
DOUGLAS CO OR 226-D3
DOUGLAS CO OR 227-A1
JACKSON CO OR 226-D3
KLAMATH CO OR 142-C3
DIAMOND MATCH CAMP RD
CLEARWATER CO ID 123-C1
DIAMOND POINT RD
CLALLAM CO WA 166-C7
JEFFERSON CO WA 166-C7
DICK RD
GRANT CO WA 242-C2
NW DICK RD
WASHINGTON CO OR 192-A7
DICKENSHEET RD
BONNER CO ID 107-A2
DICKENSON RD
BRITISH COLUMBIA BC 93-A3
NANAIMO BC 93-A3
DICKEY RD
DESCHUTES CO OR 217-D2
S DICKEY RD
SPOKANE VALLEY WA 349-J10
DICKEY RD NW
KITSAP CO WA 174-A1
DICKEY PRAIRIE RD
CLACKAMAS CO OR 126-A3
DICK GEORGE RD
JOSEPHINE CO OR 233-B5
DIETZ AV NE
KEIZER OR 322-J6
KEIZER OR 323-A6
E DIGBY RD
MOUNT VERNON WA 260-E13
DIGGER RD
WASCO CO OR 196-A6
DIKE BYPS U.S.-12
LEWISTON ID 250-B4
DIKE RD
COLUMBIA CO OR 189-D7
COLUMBIA CO OR 192-A4
COWLITZ CO WA 189-D7
COWLITZ CO WA 192-B1
SKAGIT CO WA 168-B1
SKAGIT CO WA 260-A14
SNOHOMISH CO WA 168-D5
WHATCOM CO WA 161-D1
W DIKE ST
MOUNT VERNON WA 260-A14
SKAGIT CO WA 260-A14
DIKE ACCESS RD
COWLITZ CO WA 189-D7
WOODLAND WA 189-D7
DILLARD HWY Rt#-99
DOUGLAS CO OR 221-B7
WINSTON OR 221-B7
DILLARD RD
LANE CO OR 215-B4
SW DILLEY RD
WASHINGTON CO OR 198-B1
DILLON FALLS RD
DESCHUTES CO OR 217-A4
NW DIMMICK ST
GRANTS PASS OR 335-E8
SW DIMMICK ST
GRANTS PASS OR 335-E8
DIMRILL DALE RD
SKAMANIA CO WA 194-A6
DINGO
JEFFERSON CO OR 212-C3
DINSMORE BRDG
CITY OF RICHMOND BC 156-B6
DINWITTY LN
MALHEUR CO OR 147-A3
DISASTER PEAK RD
MALHEUR CO OR 154-B2
DISCOVERY AV SE
OCEAN SHORES WA 298-F4
DISCOVERY RD
JEFFERSON CO WA 166-D7
JEFFERSON CO WA 263-A9
PORT TOWNSEND WA 263-F4
S DISHMAN RD
SPOKANE VALLEY WA 350-D9
E DISHMAN-MICA RD
SPOKANE CO WA 246-D5
SPOKANE CO WA 247-A5
S DISHMAN-MICA RD
SPOKANE CO WA 246-D5
SPOKANE VALLEY WA 246-D5
SPOKANE VALLEY WA 350-E12
S DISHMAN-MICA RD Rt#-27
SPOKANE CO WA 247-A5
DISTRICT LINE RD
BENTON CO WA 120-C3
DITCH RD
DESCHUTES CO OR 212-D4
DITCH CREEK RD
JACKSON CO OR 229-D3
DIVERS RD
CLACKAMAS CO OR 200-C6
NE DIVIDE RD
JEFFERSON CO OR 135-C1
DIVISION AV
EPHRATA WA 112-C3
TACOMA WA 293-F4
S DIVISION AV Rt#-225
BENTON CITY WA 120-C3
DIVISION AV E
EPHRATA WA 112-C3
DIVISION AV NE
Suquamish WA 170-C7
DIVISION AV W
EPHRATA WA 112-C3
E DIVISION LN
TACOMA WA 295-J2
N DIVISION RD
DOUGLAS CO WA 112-B2
GRANT CO WA 242-A3
S DIVISION RD
DOUGLAS CO WA 112-B2
GRANT CO WA 242-A4
DIVISION ST
BEND OR 332-F9
CASHMERE WA 238-C2
DOUGLAS CO OR 225-C1
GRANT CO WA 242-C3
KELSO WA 303-D6
MOSES LAKE WA 242-C3
MYRTLE CREEK OR 225-C1
OLYMPIA WA 296-F2
PORT ORCHARD WA 270-H14
THURSTON CO WA 296-F2
DIVISION ST Rt#-20
TWISP WA 104-A3
DIVISION ST Rt#-204
ELGIN OR 130-A1
UNION CO OR 130-A1
DIVISION ST U.S.-20
BEND OR 332-F5
DIVISION ST U.S.-97
BEND OR 332-F9
DESCHUTES CO OR 332-D12
E DIVISION ST
MOUNT VERNON WA 260-D12
N DIVISION ST
CASHMERE WA 238-C2
CHELAN CO WA 238-C2
RITZVILLE WA 113-C3
SANDPOINT ID 244-A2
WALLA WALLA WA 345-C7
N DIVISION ST Rt#-21
ODESSA WA 113-B3
N DIVISION ST Rt#-27
PALOUSE WA 249-B1
N DIVISION ST U.S.-2
SPOKANE WA 346-J12
SPOKANE WA 347-A14
SPOKANE WA 349-A3
Town and Country WA 346-J12
Town and Country WA 347-A14
Town and Country WA 349-A3
N DIVISION ST U.S.-395
Country Homes WA 346-J11
Country Homes WA 347-A8
Fairwood WA 347-A8
SPOKANE WA 346-J11
Town and Country WA 346-J11
NE DIVISION ST
BEND OR 332-F4
CHEHALIS WA 299-D11
GRESHAM OR 200-B2
NW DIVISION ST
GRESHAM OR 200-A2
MYRTLE CREEK OR 225-C1
S DIVISION ST
ADAMS CO WA 113-C3
CASHMERE WA 238-C2
MOSES LAKE WA 242-C3
RITZVILLE WA 113-C3
SANDPOINT ID 244-A2
WALLA WALLA WA 345-C8
Walla Walla East WA 345-C8
S DIVISION ST Rt#-225
BENTON CITY WA 120-C3
S DIVISION ST U.S.-2
SPOKANE WA 349-A9
SE DIVISION ST
GRESHAM OR 200-A2
PORTLAND OR 200-A2
PORTLAND OR 313-G7
PORTLAND OR 317-G1
PORTLAND OR 318-C1
PORTLAND OR 319-H1
W DIVISION ST Rt#-536
MOUNT VERNON WA 260-B12
DIVISION ST E
QUINCY WA 112-B3
DIVISION ST N
SOAP LAKE WA 112-C2
DIVISION ST NE
SALEM OR 322-H12
DIVISION ST S
GRANT CO WA 112-C2
KELLOGG ID 115-C2
SOAP LAKE WA 112-C2
DIVISION FENCE RD
KLICKITAT CO WA 196-C1
DIXIE CREEK RD
BAKER CO OR 138-C2
GRANT CO OR 137-B2
WASHINGTON CO ID 139-B1
DIXIE MOUNTAIN RD
WASHINGTON CO OR 125-C1
SE DIXON DR
JEFFERSON CO OR 208-C6
DIXON LP
DESCHUTES CO OR 217-D2
DIXON RD
CROOK CO OR 213-B5
DIXON MILL RD
WASHINGTON CO OR 198-C3
DIXONVILLE RD
DOUGLAS CO OR 221-D5
D MEYER RD
WHITMAN CO WA 249-A7
DOAK RD
KLAMATH CO OR 231-D5
DOAKS FERRY RD
POLK CO OR 322-D9
SALEM OR 322-D9
DOAN RD
COLUMBIA CO OR 189-B4
E DOBBIE POINT LN
SHERMAN CO OR 127-C3
DOBBIN RD
WALLOWA CO OR 130-C2
DOBER RD
WASHINGTON CO OR 198-C2
DOCK RD
KLICKITAT CO WA 196-D7
DOCK ST Rt#-105
WESTPORT WA 298-G11
DOCKTON RD SW
KING CO WA 174-D6
E DODD RD
KOOTENAI CO ID 245-A4
DODDS RD
DESCHUTES CO OR 135-B3
DODES CREEK RD
JACKSON CO OR 226-A7
DODGE RD
JACKSON CO OR 230-C4
SE DODGE PARK BLVD
MULTNOMAH CO OR 200-C2
DODGE VALLEY RD
SKAGIT CO WA 167-D1
DODSON RD
EPHRATA WA 112-C3
GRANT CO WA 112-C3
DOE CREEK RD
DOUGLAS CO OR 225-A3
DOERFLER RD SE
MARION CO OR 205-C6
DOERNER CTO
DOUGLAS CO OR 221-A4
DOERNER RD
DOUGLAS CO OR 221-A4
DOERSCHLAG RD
LINCOLN CO WA 114-A2
DOETSCH RD
COLUMBIA CO OR 189-C6
DOG RD
GRANT CO OR 137-B2
DOG LAKE RD
LAKE CO OR 151-C2
LAKE CO OR 152-A2
DOG RIDGE RD
NEWBERG OR 198-D6
YAMHILL CO OR 198-D6
DOGWOOD AV
ALBANY OR 326-H7
DOGWOOD DR
EVERETT WA 264-B7
EVERETT WA 268-B1
DOGWOOD LN
JEFFERSON CO OR 208-B4
NE DOGWOOD LN
JEFFERSON CO OR 208-C4
E DOGWOOD RD
FRANKLIN CO WA 121-A2
W DOLARWAY RD
ELLENSBURG WA 241-B5
DOLE RD
DOUGLAS CO OR 221-B7
DOUGLAS CO OR 225-C1
MYRTLE CREEK OR 225-C1
NE DOLE VALLEY RD
CLARK CO WA 193-C3
DOLLARHIDE RD
WHEELER CO OR 136-B1
DOLLARTON HWY
DISTRICT OF NORTH VANCOUV BC 156-D3
DISTRICT OF NORTH VANCOUV BC 255-H7
DOMINIC RD
MARION CO OR 205-C3
DONAHUE RD
MULTNOMAH CO OR 200-D2
MULTNOMAH CO OR 201-A2
DONALD RD
MARION CO OR 199-A7
WAPATO WA 120-A2
YAKIMA CO WA 120-A2
DONALDSON RD
JOSEPHINE CO OR 335-D1
DONALD-WAPATO RD
YAKIMA CO WA 120-A2
DONELLY RD
HARNEY CO OR 136-C3
HARNEY CO OR 144-C1
HARNEY CO OR 145-A1
DONEY RD
DESCHUTES CO OR 212-D3
JEFFERSON CO OR 212-D3
DONKEY CREEK RD
GRAYS HARBOR CO WA 109-A2
GRAYS HARBOR CO WA 178-A1
DONNELLY RD
SKAGIT CO WA 161-A7
DONOVAN AV
BELLINGHAM WA 258-D11
DONRUSS DR
DOUGLAS CO OR 221-A3
DOOLEY MOUNTAIN HWY Rt#-245
BAKER CO OR 138-A1
DOPP RD
YAMHILL CO OR 198-C4
DORAN RD
WHATCOM CO WA 161-C2
SE DORION AV U.S.-30
PENDLETON OR 129-B1
SW DORION AV U.S.-30
PENDLETON OR 129-B1
DORMAIER RD
SHERMAN CO OR 127-C1
DORNING RD
LEWIS CO WA 187-C2
DORRANCE MEADOW RD
DESCHUTES CO OR 143-A1
DORRIS BROWNELL RD
SISKIYOU CO CA 150-C3
S DORSET RD
SPOKANE CO WA 246-B5
DORSEY RD
KLICKITAT CO WA 196-A3
SW DOSCH RD
PORTLAND OR 316-B2
DOSEWALLIPS RD
JEFFERSON CO WA 109-C1
DOT RD
KLICKITAT CO WA 120-A3
KLICKITAT CO WA 128-A1
DOUBLE BLUFF RD
ISLAND CO WA 170-D2
DOUBLE CREEK LN
SKAGIT CO WA 161-B4
DOUBLEDAY RD
JACKSON CO OR 150-A1
DOUBLE O RD
HARNEY CO OR 145-A2

INDEX

DOUGHERTY DR STREET INDEX ELKTON-SUTHERLIN HWY 367

STREET City State Page-Grid

DOUGHERTY DR
CASTLE ROCK WA 187-C7
COWLITZ CO WA 187-C7
DOUGHTY RD
BAY CITY OR 197-B1
TILLAMOOK CO OR 197-B1
DOUGLAS AV
GERVAIS OR 205-A2
MARION CO OR 205-A2
SNOHOMISH CO WA 265-H4
N DOUGLAS AV
PASCO WA 343-J7
NE DOUGLAS AV
DOUGLAS CO OR 221-C5
ROSEBURG OR 221-C5
ROSEBURG OR 334-J7
SE DOUGLAS AV
ROSEBURG OR 334-H7
N DOUGLAS BLVD Rt#-99
WINSTON OR 221-B6
W DOUGLAS BLVD Rt#-42
WINSTON OR 221-B6
DOUGLAS CRES
LANGLEY BC 158-C1
VANCOUVER BC 254-E13
DOUGLAS DR
PACIFIC CO WA 186-A2
DOUGLAS RD
DISTRICT OF BURNABY BC 156-D4
DISTRICT OF BURNABY BC 255-G11
FERNDALE WA 158-C6
WHATCOM CO WA 158-B6
YAKIMA CO WA 243-A7
DOUGLAS ST
LONGVIEW WA 302-J10
LONGVIEW WA 303-A10
DOUGLAS ST Rt#-1
CITY OF VICTORIA BC 256-G6
DISTRICT OF SAANICH BC 256-G6
DOUGLAS FALLS RD
STEVENS CO WA 106-A2
SE DOVER LN
JEFFERSON CO OR 208-C6
SW DOVER LN
JEFFERSON CO OR 208-B6
S DOVER RD
SPOKANE CO WA 114-B2
DOVER ST
DISTRICT OF BURNABY BC 156-C5
DOW RD
KLICKITAT CO WA 196-D6
DOWANS CREEK RD
JEFFERSON CO WA 169-D3
DOWD RD
COLUMBIA CO OR 192-A1
W DOWER RD
KOOTENAI CO ID 247-D4
SE DOWLING RD
CLACKAMAS CO OR 200-D5
DOWNES RD
DISTRICT OF MATSQUI BC 102-B1
DOWNEY RD
DISTRICT OF NORTH SAANICH BC 159-B2
SKAGIT CO WA 160-D7
DOWNEY GULCH RD
CHELAN CO WA 236-C3
S DOWNING DR
SEASIDE OR 301-F10
E DOWNING RD Rt#-507
CENTRALIA WA 184-C5
LEWIS CO WA 184-C5
S DOWNING ST
SEASIDE OR 301-F9
DOWN RIVER RD Rt#-128
LEWISTON ID 250-B4
W DOWNRIVER PARK DR
SPOKANE WA 348-D6
DOWNS RD NE
MARION CO OR 205-B4
SE DOWTY RD
CLACKAMAS CO OR 200-B5
DOYLE RD
CLARK CO WA 192-C1
N DOYLE RD
KOOTENAI CO ID 248-D2
DRAGICH RD
COWLITZ CO WA 189-A1
DRAHAM ST NE
THURSTON CO WA 297-H3
DRAIN RD
DOUGLAS CO OR 219-A3
DRAIN 10 RD
MODOC CO CA 151-A3
DRAIN-YONCALLA HWY Rt#-99
DOUGLAS CO OR 219-A3
DRAIN OR 219-A3
YONCALLA OR 219-A3
DRAKE RD
CLACKAMAS CO OR 205-D3
NW DRAKE RD
BEND OR 332-D6
DRAKE RD NE
CLACKAMAS CO OR 205-C3
MARION CO OR 205-C3
DRAPER SPRINGS RD
KLICKITAT CO WA 119-A3
DRAPER VALLEY RD
JOSEPHINE CO OR 233-B1
W DRAVUS ST
SEATTLE WA 273-E7
DRAYTON ST
LYNDEN WA 102-B1
DRAYTON HARBOR RD
Birch Bay WA 158-A3
BLAINE WA 158-A3
WHATCOM CO WA 158-A3
DRAZIL RD
KLAMATH CO OR 151-A2
DREGER RD E
LINCOLN CO WA 113-B1
DRESSER RD Rt#-500
CLARK CO WA 193-B6
DREWS RD
KLAMATH CO OR 151-A1
DREWSEY RD
HARNEY CO OR 137-C3
HARNEY CO OR 145-C1
DREWSEY MARKET RD
HARNEY CO OR 137-C3
DREWS PRAIRIE RD
LEWIS CO WA 187-C4
D REX RD
DOUGLAS CO WA 105-A3
DRIFT CREEK RD
LINCOLN CO OR 203-A5
LINCOLN CO OR 209-B1
DRIFT CREEK RD NE
MARION CO OR 205-C5

DRIFT CREEK RD SE
MARION CO OR 205-C7
DRIFTWOOD RD NW
THURSTON CO WA 180-C5
THURSTON CO WA 296-C1
N DRISCOLL BLVD
SPOKANE WA 348-D2
DRIVER RD
LINN CO OR 207-C7
DRIVER VALLEY RD
DOUGLAS CO OR 219-B7
DRUMHELLAR RD
GRANT CO WA 242-A1
DRUMHELLER RD
SPOKANE CO WA 247-B7
E DRUMHELLER RD
SPOKANE CO WA 247-A7
DRY COULEE RD
GRANT CO WA 112-C2
DRY CREEK CTO
MALHEUR CO OR 146-B1
DRY CREEK LN
UNION CO OR 130-A2
DRY CREEK RD
CROOK CO OR 213-D3
IDAHO CO ID 131-B1
JEFFERSON CO OR 208-B2
KITTITAS CO WA 241-B5
MALHEUR CO OR 146-C1
PAYETTE CO ID 139-B2
Warm Springs OR 208-B2
WASCO CO OR 196-A6
WHITMAN CO WA 114-C3
DRY CREEK RD U.S.-97
KITTITAS CO WA 241-A4
DRY CREEK CANYON RD
DOUGLAS CO OR 225-C3
DRY CREEK TRAIL RD
Warm Springs OR 208-A2
DRYDEN RD
JOSEPHINE CO OR 233-C2
N DRYDEN RD
CHELAN CO WA 238-B2
DRYDEN OVERLOOK RD
JOSEPHINE CO OR 233-C2
DRY HOLLOW RD
JEFFERSON CO OR 208-A4
THE DALLES OR 196-C7
WASCO CO OR 196-C7
WHEELER CO OR 136-A1
DRY LAKE RD
CHELAN CO WA 236-B1
ISLAND CO WA 167-D5
MALHEUR CO OR 146-B2
DRYLAND RD
CLACKAMAS CO OR 199-C7
S DRYLAND RD
CLACKAMAS CO OR 205-D1
DRY SLOUGH RD
SKAGIT CO WA 168-A2
DRY VALLEY HWY
HARNEY CO OR 144-B2
DRY VALLEY RD
HARNEY CO OR 144-C2
N DUBOIS RD
COWLITZ CO WA 118-A3
DUBUQUE RD
SNOHOMISH CO WA 110-C1
SNOHOMISH CO WA 171-D2
DUCKABUSH RD
JEFFERSON CO WA 173-C1
DUCK CREEK RD
BAKER CO OR 131-A3
DUCK LAKE DR
OCEAN SHORES WA 177-B7
DUCK LAKE DR SE
OCEAN SHORES WA 298-E1
DUCK LAKE RD
LINCOLN CO WA 113-B2
ODESSA WA 113-B2
DUDLEY RD
KITTITAS CO WA 240-D3
KOOTENAI CO ID 115-B2
YAMHILL CO OR 198-C5
E DUFFIELD RD
YAKIMA CO WA 243-D7
DUFORT RD
BONNER CO ID 107-A3
E DUFORT RD
BONNER CO ID 244-A4
DUFUR BYPASS RD
WASCO CO OR 127-B2
DUFUR GAP RD
WASCO CO OR 127-B2
DUFUR VALLEY RD
WASCO CO OR 127-A2
WASCO CO OR 202-D4
DUGOUT LAKE RD
DESCHUTES CO OR 211-B4
DUKE LN
MARION CO OR 198-D7
W DUKE RD
DOUGLAS CO OR 221-C1
DUKE POINT HWY Rt#-19
BRITISH COLUMBIA BC 93-A3
NANAIMO BC 93-A3
DULEY CREEK RD
CURRY CO OR 232-C5
DUMAR WY SW
SEATTLE WA 285-G1
DUMP RD
NEZ PERCE CO ID 250-D2
DUNBAR RD
SKAGIT CO WA 161-A7
DUNBAR ST
UNIVERSITY ENDOWMENT LAND BC 156-A5
VANCOUVER BC 156-A5
VANCOUVER BC 254-A14
DUNBAR DIV
VANCOUVER BC 254-A13
DUNCAN CREEK RD
SKAMANIA CO WA 194-B6
DUNDAS ST
VANCOUVER BC 255-D10
SW DUNDEE RD
WASHINGTON CO OR 198-A2
DUNIVAN RD
LEWIS CO WA 187-B4
DUNIWAY RD
YAMHILL CO OR 198-B6
DUNKARD RD
KLICKITAT CO WA 196-B1
DUNLAP RD SW
THURSTON CO WA 184-C4
DUNN RD
CLARK CO WA 192-D1
S DUNN RD
SPOKANE CO WA 246-D6

SE DUNN RD
CLACKAMAS CO OR 200-C3
DUNNING RD
WHITMAN CO WA 249-A6
DUNSMUIR ST
VANCOUVER BC 254-G10
DUPONT ST
BELLINGHAM WA 258-C5
DUPONT-STEILACOOM RD SW
DUPONT WA 181-B5
PIERCE CO WA 181-B5
DUPORTAIL ST
RICHLAND WA 341-E2
DURBIN CREEK RD
BAKER CO OR 138-C2
SW DURHAM LN
YAMHILL CO OR 204-B1
SW DURHAM RD
TIGARD OR 199-B3
DURR RD
KITTITAS CO WA 241-B7
KITTITAS CO WA 243-B1
YAKIMA CO WA 243-B2
DURRWACHTER RD
CLALLAM CO WA 164-D5
DURY RD
ADAMS CO WA 113-C3
DUSTY LP
DESCHUTES CO OR 212-B6
DUTCH CANYON RD
COLUMBIA CO OR 125-C1
COLUMBIA CO OR 192-A4
DUTCH HENRY RD
DOUGLAS CO OR 141-A3
DUTCHY CREEK RD
JOSEPHINE CO OR 148-C1
DUTHIE AV
DISTRICT OF BURNABY BC 156-D4
SE DUTHIE HILL RD
KING CO WA 176-A3
SAMMAMISH WA 176-A3
DUTTON RD
UNION CO OR 130-B2
DUUS RD
CLACKAMAS CO OR 200-C5
DUVAL RD
DISTRICT OF NORTH VANCOUV BC 255-G2
DUVALL AV NE
RENTON WA 175-C4
DUVALL-MONROE RD Rt#-203
KING CO WA 110-C1
SNOHOMISH CO WA 110-C1
DUVALL-MONROE RD NE Rt#-203
DUVALL WA 110-C1
KING CO WA 110-C1
DWIGHT HALSEY RD
ASOTIN CO WA 123-A3
DYKE RD
CITY OF RICHMOND BC 156-B7
PITT MEADOWS BC 157-B5

E

E RD
COTTONWOOD ID 123-C3
IDAHO CO ID 123-C3
E RD SE
DOUGLAS CO WA 112-C2
E ST
COLUMBIA CITY OR 192-B1
CULVER OR 208-B7
ENDICOTT WA 122-B1
GRANTS PASS OR 335-E8
NESPELEM WA 105-A3
NORTH POWDER OR 130-B3
SISKIYOU CO CA 151-A3
TULELAKE CA 151-A3
WALLA WALLA CO WA 345-H4
WHITMAN CO WA 122-B1
E ST Rt#-8
FOREST GROVE OR 198-B1
E ST Rt#-14B
WASHOUGAL WA 193-C7
E ST Rt#-207
LEXINGTON OR 128-C2
E ST Rt#-272
PALOUSE WA 249-C1
E ST U.S.-97
SHANIKO OR 127-C3
E E ST
GRANTS PASS OR 335-G9
N E ST
TACOMA WA 293-G3
N E ST Rt#-272
PALOUSE WA 249-C1
S E ST
ABERDEEN WA 178-B7
E ST NE
GRANT CO WA 112-C2
EADEN RD
CLACKAMAS CO OR 200-B4
EADON RD
LEWIS CO WA 187-D4
NE EADS ST
NEWPORT OR 206-B4
EAGAR RD
COLUMBIA CO WA 122-A2
EAGLE DR
DESCHUTES CO OR 212-C5
JACKSON CO OR 230-C4
EAGLE LN
COLUMBIA CO OR 208-C2
E EAGLE RD
BAKER CO OR 130-C3
N EAGLE RD
EAGLE ID 253-B1
S EAGLE RD
ADA CO ID 253-B4
MERIDIAN ID 253-B4
S EAGLE RD Rt#-55
ADA CO ID 253-B2
BOISE ID 253-B2
EAGLE ID 253-B2
MERIDIAN ID 253-B2
EAGLE WY
YAKIMA CO WA 243-C6
EAGLE CREEK DR
BAKER CO OR 130-C3
EAGLE CREEK LN
UNION CO OR 130-B3
EAGLE CREEK RD
CHELAN CO WA 111-C2
CLACKAMAS CO OR 200-C5
EAGLE CREEK RANCH RD
CLALLAM CO WA 163-C7

EAGLE CREEK-SANDY HWY Rt#-211
CLACKAMAS CO OR 200-C4
SANDY OR 200-C4
EAGLE CREST RD
POLK CO OR 204-C5
EAGLE FERN RD
CLACKAMAS CO OR 200-C5
NE EAGLE HARBOR DR
BAINBRIDGE ISLAND WA 174-D2
BAINBRIDGE ISLAND WA 271-J3
EAGLE MILL RD
JACKSON CO OR 337-A4
N EAGLE MILL RD
JACKSON CO OR 337-D5
EAGLEMOUNT RD
JEFFERSON CO WA 170-A2
EAGLE PEAK RD
KOOTENAI CO ID 248-D4
SW EAGLE POINT RD
YAMHILL CO OR 204-A1
EAGLE RIDGE RD
KLAMATH CO OR 231-B7
EAGLE ROCK RD
DESCHUTES CO OR 211-D5
EAGLE SPRINGS RD E
LINCOLN CO WA 113-B2
EAGLE VALLEY RD Rt#-99
DOUGLAS CO OR 219-A3
EARLES ST
VANCOUVER BC 156-C5
EARLWOOD RD
CLACKAMAS CO OR 199-A6
YAMHILL CO OR 199-A6
EARNEST S BRAZILL ST
TACOMA WA 293-F6
EAST BLVD NE
KITSAP CO WA 271-C3
EAST MALL
UNIVERSITY ENDOWMENT LAND BC 156-A4
EAST RD
ANMORE BC 157-A3
KLICKITAT CO WA 120-A3
KLICKITAT CO WA 128-A1
EAST AND WEST TKTR
COWLITZ CO WA 187-A7
EAST BAY DR
COOS BAY OR 220-D1
COOS CO OR 140-B2
COOS CO OR 218-B7
COOS CO OR 220-D1
COOS CO OR 333-H1
EAST BEACH RD
CLALLAM CO WA 164-C6
EAST BEAVER CREEK RD
TILLAMOOK CO OR 197-C5
EAST COVE RD
LATAH CO ID 249-D1
EASTERDAY RD
WASHINGTON CO OR 198-B1
EASTERN BOUNDARY RD
KITSAP CO WA 170-B6
EAST FORK RD
DOUGLAS CO OR 225-B1
JOSEPHINE CO OR 149-B2
EAST FORK EVANS CREEK RD
JACKSON CO OR 230-C1
EAST FORK GLENN CREEK RD
COOS CO OR 140-C1
EAST FORK PINE CREEK RD
SHOSHONE CO ID 115-C2
EAST GATE RD
PIERCE CO WA 181-C6
WASCO CO OR 126-C3
WASCO CO OR 127-A3
SE EASTGATE WY
BELLEVUE WA 175-C3
EASTLAKE AV E
SEATTLE WA 274-B7
SEATTLE WA 278-B1
EASTLAKE DR
DISTRICT OF BURNABY BC 156-D4
NW EASTMAN PKWY
GRESHAM OR 200-B2
N EASTMONT AV
DOUGLAS CO WA 239-A4
EAST WENATCHEE WA 239-A4
East Wenatchee Bench WA 239-A4
EASTON CANYON RD
WASCO CO OR 127-B2
EAST POINT RD
KOOTENAI CO ID 248-A4
EAST PORTLAND FRWY I-205
CLACKAMAS CO OR 199-D4
CLACKAMAS CO OR 319-G6
GLADSTONE OR 199-D4
OREGON CITY OR 199-D4
PORTLAND OR 319-G6
TUALATIN OR 199-D4
WASHINGTON CO OR 199-D4
WEST LINN OR 199-D4
EAST SAANICH RD
DISTRICT OF NORTH SAANICH BC 159-C3
EAST SHORE RD
BONNER CO ID 107-A1
EASTSIDE DR
VALLEY CO ID 251-D4
EASTSIDE DR NE Rt#-509
PIERCE CO WA 181-D1
PIERCE CO WA 182-A1
EAST SIDE RD
UMATILLA CO OR 121-C3
EASTSIDE RD
BONNER CO ID 107-A2
HOOD RIVER CO OR 195-D6
OKANOGAN CO WA 104-C1
EASTSIDE ST
OLYMPIA WA 297-A5
N EASTSIDE ST
OLYMPIA WA 296-J5
OLYMPIA WA 297-A5
EASTSIDE ACCESS RD
OKANOGAN CO WA 104-C3
EASTSIDE CHEWACK RD
OKANOGAN CO WA 104-A2
WINTHROP WA 104-A2
EASTSIDE OROVILLE RD
OKANOGAN CO WA 104-C1
EASTSIDE-SUMNER RD
COOS CO OR 140-B2
COOS CO OR 220-D2
EAST SOOKE RD
BRITISH COLUMBIA BC 164-D1
BRITISH COLUMBIA BC 165-A1
DISTRICT OF METCHOSIN BC 165-A1
EAST TWISP-WINTHROP RD
OKANOGAN CO WA 104-A2
TWISP WA 104-A2

EAST VALLEY HWY
AUBURN WA 182-B2
AUBURN WA 182-B2
PACIFIC WA 182-B2
SUMNER WA 182-B2
EAST WEST RD
SISKIYOU CO CA 150-C3
SISKIYOU CO CA 151-A3
EASY ST
BROOKINGS OR 232-C6
SISKIYOU CO CA 149-C3
Sunnyslope WA 238-D3
S EASY ST
ROCKAWAY BEACH OR 191-B6
EATON RD
CLARK CO WA 118-A3
CLARK CO WA 193-B1
EATONVILLE HWY
EATONVILLE WA 118-B1
PIERCE CO WA 118-B1
EATONVILLE CUT-OFF RD
PIERCE CO WA 118-B1
EBELL CREEK RD
BAKER CO OR 138-B1
EBEY RD
ISLAND CO WA 167-B4
NE EBY AV
DESCHUTES CO OR 212-D3
Terrebonne OR 212-D3
S EBY RD
CLACKAMAS CO OR 205-D1
ECHAVE RANCH RD
MALHEUR CO OR 154-B2
ECHO LAKE CTO SE Rt#-18
KING CO WA 176-B5
ECHO LAKE RD
SNOHOMISH CO WA 171-D5
ECHO LAKE-SNOQUALMIE CTO SE
KING CO WA 176-B4
SNOQUALMIE WA 176-B4
ECKENSTAM-JOHNSON RD
PIERCE CO WA 181-A4
S ECKERT RD
ADA CO ID 253-D3
BOISE ID 253-D3
ECKLER MOUNTAIN RD
COLUMBIA CO WA 122-B2
ECKMAN CREEK RD
LINCOLN CO OR 209-B3
ECKS FLAT RD
ADAMS CO ID 251-B5
EDDYVILLE RD
KOOTENAI CO ID 248-B1
EDDYVILLE BLODGETT HWY
BENTON CO OR 133-A1
LINCOLN CO OR 133-A1
EDENBOWER MILLWOOD RD
DOUGLAS CO OR 221-B2
EDENS RD
SKAGIT CO WA 160-C5
EDENVALE RD
LANE CO OR 215-D3
LANE CO OR 331-J14
EDEN VALLEY RD
CLALLAM CO WA 164-D6
CLALLAM CO WA 165-A6
WAHKIAKUM CO WA 117-A2
EDER RD
OKANOGAN CO WA 104-C1
EDGEMONT BLVD
DISTRICT OF NORTH VANCOUV BC 254-H2
EDGEWATER ST NW Rt#-221
SALEM OR 322-F12
EDGEWOOD DR
CLALLAM CO WA 165-A6
CLALLAM CO WA 261-A5
PORT ANGELES WA 165-A6
PORT ANGELES WA 261-A5
EDGEWOOD LN
KLAMATH CO OR 235-D1
EDINBOWER BLVD
DOUGLAS CO OR 334-E2
ROSEBURG OR 334-E3
EDISON AV SW
BANDON OR 220-B6
N EDISON ST
BENTON CO WA 342-F9
KENNEWICK WA 342-F9
S EDISON ST
KENNEWICK WA 342-F11
EDISON HEIGHTS LN
MARION CO OR 205-C5
EDISON ICE CAVE RD
DESCHUTES CO OR 216-C5
EDLER RD
KLAMATH CO OR 151-B1
SW EDMINSTON RD
CLACKAMAS CO OR 199-A6
EDMONDS AV NE
RENTON WA 175-C5
EDMONDS ST
DISTRICT OF BURNABY BC 156-D5
EDMONDS WY Rt#-104
EDMONDS WA 171-A6
SNOHOMISH CO WA 171-A6
WOODWAY WA 171-A6
EDMONDS-KINGSTON FERRY
EDMONDS WA 171-A5
Kingston WA 170-D5
KITSAP CO WA 170-D5
SNOHOMISH CO WA 171-A5
EDMUNDSON RD
DESCHUTES CO OR 212-A4
EDMUNSON DR SE
MARION CO OR 205-B6
W EDNA ST
BOISE ID 253-B2
EDSON CREEK RD
CURRY CO OR 228-A4
EDWARDS DR
WHATCOM CO WA 101-C1
EDWARDS RD E
PIERCE CO WA 182-C2
EDWARDS BUTTE RD
TILLAMOOK CO OR 197-D3
SW EDY RD
WASHINGTON CO OR 199-A4
EELLS ST
TACOMA WA 182-A2
EELS RD
CHELAN CO WA 238-C2
S EGAN AV
BURNS OR 145-B1
HARNEY CO OR 145-B1
EGAN SPRINGS RD
KLAMATH CO OR 142-C3

EGBERS KALSO RD
SKAGIT CO WA 161-A6
EGG AND I RD
JEFFERSON CO WA 170-A2
NE EGLON RD
KITSAP CO WA 170-D4
EGYPT CANYON RD
HARNEY CO OR 144-C1
EHLEN RD
AURORA OR 199-B7
MARION CO OR 199-A7
N EHORN LN
CHEWELAH WA 106-B3
EICHER RD
LINN CO OR 207-D5
EID RD
LATAH CO ID 249-D6
EIGHT DOLLAR MOUNTAIN RD
JOSEPHINE CO OR 233-A2
EILERS RD
CLACKAMAS CO OR 199-B6
SW EISCHEN DR
WASHINGTON CO OR 198-C2
S EKELMAN RD
YAKIMA CO WA 243-C7
EKROTH RD
TILLAMOOK CO OR 191-B7
ELBE DR
JEFFERSON CO OR 212-D2
NW ELBE DR
JEFFERSON CO OR 208-B4
SW ELBE DR
JEFFERSON CO OR 208-B7
ELDER RD
WHATCOM CO WA 158-C6
E ELDER RD
SPOKANE CO WA 246-D7
SPOKANE CO WA 247-A7
W ELDER RD
KOOTENAI CO ID 247-C6
W ELDER RD U.S.-95
KOOTENAI CO ID 247-D5
ELDORADO AV
KLAMATH FALLS OR 338-D5
ELDORADO BLVD
KLAMATH FALLS OR 338-D4
NW EL DORADO BLVD
KITSAP CO WA 270-A3
ELDORADO RD
CLACKAMAS CO OR 199-D7
ELDRIDGE AV
BELLINGHAM WA 258-B5
ELDRIDGE-FRAZIER RD
PIERCE CO WA 182-C4
ELECTRIC AV
BELLINGHAM WA 258-J6
W ELECTRIC AV
SPOKANE CO WA 246-A5
ELEPHANT MOUNTAIN RD
DOUGLAS CO OR 223-B3
ELFENDAHL PASS RD
MASON CO WA 173-C5
ELGAROSE LOOP RD
DOUGLAS CO OR 221-A3
ELGER BAY RD
ISLAND CO WA 167-D5
ELGIN AV U.S.-20
CANYON CO ID 147-B1
NOTUS ID 147-B1
ELGIN RD
CITY OF SURREY BC 158-A1
PAYETTE CO ID 139-B3
ELGIN-CLIFTON Rt#-302
PIERCE CO WA 174-A7
ELIJAH RD
STEVENS CO WA 114-A1
ELISHA RD
CLACKAMAS CO OR 199-C7
CLACKAMAS CO OR 205-D1
ELIZA DR
SAN JUAN CO WA 160-A6
ELIZABETH ST Rt#-27
TEKOA WA 114-C3
NE ELIZABETH ST
MILTON-FREEWATER OR 121-C3
SW ELIZABETH ST
NEWPORT OR 206-A4
NW ELK DR
JEFFERSON CO OR 208-B5
SW ELK DR
JEFFERSON CO OR 208-B5
ELK RD
JACKSON CO OR 226-C5
ELK BUTTE RD
CLEARWATER CO ID 123-C1
N ELK- CHATTAROY RD
SPOKANE CO WA 114-C1
ELK CITY RD
LINCOLN CO OR 206-D4
ELK CREEK RD
COLUMBIA CO OR 189-A4
JACKSON CO OR 226-B6
ELK CREEK RIDGE RD
CLALLAM CO WA 169-D1
ELKHEAD RD
DOUGLAS CO OR 219-B4
ELKHORN CREEK RD
LINCOLN CO OR 206-B6
ELKHORN RIDGE RD
JACKSON CO OR 226-A5
ELKINS RD
CROOK CO OR 213-A4
POLK CO OR 207-A1
N ELKINS RD
SPOKANE CO WA 114-B1
ELK LAKE RD
IDAHO CO ID 131-C2
ELK MOUNTAIN RD
COOS CO OR 218-D7
ELKOFF RD
TILLAMOOK CO OR 197-B3
ELK PRAIRIE RD
PACIFIC CO WA 117-A2
ELK RIDGE RD N
YAKIMA CO WA 243-A2
ELK RIVER RD
CLEARWATER CO ID 123-C1
CURRY CO OR 140-B3
CURRY CO OR 224-B6
CURRY CO OR 228-C1
ELK RIVER RD Rt#-3
LATAH CO ID 123-B1
ELKTON-SUTHERLIN HWY Rt#-138
DOUGLAS CO OR 141-A1
DOUGLAS CO OR 221-C1
ELKTON OR 141-A1
SUTHERLIN OR 221-C1

INDEX

368 E ELKTON-SUTHERLIN HWY
STREET INDEX
S FEDERAL WY

STREET
City State Page-Grid

E ELKTON-SUTHERLIN HWY Rt#-99
SUTHERLIN OR 221-C1
W ELKTON-SUTHERLIN HWY Rt#-138
DOUGLAS CO OR 221-C1
SUTHERLIN OR 221-C1
ELK VALLEY RD Rt#-D2
CRESCENT CITY CA 148-B3
DEL NORTE CO CA 148-B3
ELK VALLEY CROSS RD Rt#-D2
DEL NORTE CO CA 148-B3
ELK VIEW RD
CITY OF CHILLIWACK BC 102-C1
ELLA RD
MORROW CO OR 128-B2
E ELLENDALE AV Rt#-223
DALLAS OR 204-A6
W ELLENDALE AV
DALLAS OR 204-A6
ELLENDALE RD
DALLAS OR 204-A6
POLK CO OR 125-B3
POLK CO OR 204-A6
W ELLENDALE RD
POLK CO OR 125-B3
W ELLENS FERRY DR
BOISE ID 253-C2
ELLIGSEN RD
WASHINGTON CO OR 199-B5
WILSONVILLE OR 199-B5
ELLINGSON RD
ALBANY OR 326-C14
ALGONA WA 182-B2
AUBURN WA 182-B2
KING CO WA 182-B2
LINN CO OR 326-C14
PACIFIC WA 182-B2
ELLIOT DR
SPOKANE WA 348-D6
ELLIOT RD
CLARK CO WA 193-B1
DESCHUTES CO OR 213-A4
MULTNOMAH CO OR 192-A6
ELLIOT ST
DISTRICT OF DELTA BC 101-C1
ELLIOTT AV
SEATTLE WA 277-H4
ELLIOTT AV W
SEATTLE WA 277-F2
ELLIOTT LN
CROOK CO OR 213-C4
ELLIOTT RD
SNOHOMISH CO WA 171-D5
ELLIOTT PRAIRIE RD NE
MARION CO OR 205-C2
ELLIS AV S
SEATTLE WA 282-B7
SEATTLE WA 286-B1
ELLIS LN
BENEWAH CO ID 248-A7
ELLIS RD
BAKER CO OR 130-A3
UNION CO OR 130-A3
ELLIS RD SW
DOUGLAS CO WA 239-C3
ELLIS ST
BELLINGHAM WA 258-E4
SE ELLSWORTH RD
VANCOUVER WA 307-H7
VANCOUVER WA 311-H1
ELLSWORTH ST U.S.-20
ALBANY OR 326-C8
ELM AV
TILLAMOOK OR 197-B2
E ELM AV
COEUR D'ALENE ID 355-G10
HERMISTON OR 129-A1
UMATILLA CO OR 129-A1
S ELM AV
PASCO WA 343-J8
W ELM AV
HERMISTON OR 129-A1
ELM LN
CANYON CO ID 147-C1
NE ELM LN
JEFFERSON CO OR 208-C4
NW ELM LN
JEFFERSON CO OR 208-B4
ELM ST
ALBANY OR 326-B8
ASOTIN CO WA 250-B4
BELLINGHAM WA 258-C5
CANNON BEACH OR 188-B7
CHENEY WA 246-A7
CLARKSTON WA 250-B4
SISTERS OR 211-D5
SUMNER WA 182-B3
WHATCOM CO WA 101-C1
ELM ST U.S.-30
BAKER CITY OR 138-B1
E ELM ST
DOUGLAS CO WA 236-C7
WATERVILLE WA 236-C7
S ELM ST Rt#-22
TOPPENISH WA 120-A2
ELMA-GATE RD
GRAYS HARBOR CO WA 117-B1
ELMA-HICKLIN RD
GRAYS HARBOR CO WA 179-C6
ELMA-MCCLEARY RD
GRAYS HARBOR CO WA 179-C6
ELMA-MCCLEARY RD Rt#-108
GRAYS HARBOR CO WA 179-C6
MCCLEARY WA 179-C6
ELMORE RD
PAYETTE CO ID 139-A3
ELMWAY Rt#-20
OKANOGAN WA 104-C3
OKANOGAN CO WA 104-C3
OMAK WA 104-C3
ELO RD
VALLEY CO ID 251-D5
EL RIO LN
LANE CO OR 210-A6
ELROD AV
COOS BAY OR 333-G10
ELSNER RD
CLACKAMAS CO OR 200-D3
SW ELSNER RD
WASHINGTON CO OR 199-A4
ELTOPIA WEST RD
FRANKLIN CO WA 121-A2
ELTOPIA WEST RD W
FRANKLIN CO WA 121-A2
SW ELWERT RD
WASHINGTON CO OR 199-A4
ELWHA RIVER RD
CLALLAM CO WA 165-A6
ELWOOD DR SW
LAKEWOOD WA 181-C4
N ELY PL
KENNEWICK WA 342-J9
KENNEWICK WA 343-A9
N ELY ST U.S.-395
KENNEWICK WA 342-J10
S ELY ST
KENNEWICK WA 342-J13
KENNEWICK WA 343-A12
S ELY ST U.S.-395
KENNEWICK WA 342-J11
EMANDER RD
EVERETT WA 268-A6
SNOHOMISH CO WA 268-A6
EMENS AV
DARRINGTON WA 103-A3
EMENS AV Rt#-530
DARRINGTON WA 103-A3
EMERALD RD
GRANGER WA 120-B2
YAKIMA CO WA 120-B2
W EMERALD ST
BOISE ID 253-C3
EMERSON AV Rt#-109
HOQUIAM WA 178-A7
NE EMERSON DR
JEFFERSON CO OR 208-D3
EMERSON LN
JEFFERSON CO OR 208-D4
W EMERSON PL
SEATTLE WA 272-E6
SEATTLE WA 273-E6
EMERSON RD
DOUGLAS CO OR 222-B7
EMERSON ST
FIRCREST WA 294-A3
UNIVERSITY PLACE WA 294-A3
W EMERSON ST
SEATTLE WA 272-C6
SEATTLE WA 273-E6
EMERSON LOOP RD
WASCO CO OR 127-B2
WASCO CO OR 196-D7
EMERY RD
CLALLAM CO WA 165-D7
SE EMIGRANT AV Rt#-37
PENDLETON OR 129-B1
SW EMIGRANT AV Rt#-37
PENDLETON OR 129-B1
EMIGRANT CREEK RD
HARNEY CO OR 136-C3
HARNEY CO OR 137-A3
EMIGRANTS RD
UMATILLA CO OR 129-B1
EMIGRANT SPRINGS RD
SHERMAN CO OR 127-C1
W EMMA AV
COEUR D'ALENE ID 355-D9
EMMA ST Rt#-278
ROCKFORD WA 114-C2
EMMETT HWY Rt#-16
ADA CO ID 139-C3
GEM CO ID 139-C3
N EMMETT HWY Rt#-16
ADA CO ID 139-C3
ADA CO ID 147-C1
EMMETT RD
ADAMS CO ID 139-C1
CANYON CO ID 147-B1
NW EMPIRE AV
East Wenatchee Bench WA 239-A4
EMPIRE BLVD
BEND OR 332-F2
S EMPIRE BLVD
COOS BAY OR 333-A8
COOS CO OR 220-C1
COOS CO OR 333-A8
E EMPIRE WY
MILLWOOD WA 350-D5
SPOKANE VALLEY WA 350-F4
EMPIRE WY S
SEATTLE WA 278-D7
SEATTLE WA 282-D2
SEATTLE WA 283-E7
SEATTLE WA 287-E5
TUKWILA WA 287-E5
EMPIRE CENTER BLVD
POST FALLS ID 353-F6
EMPIRE-COOS BAY HWY
COOS BAY OR 333-D8
ENCHANTED PKWY Rt#-161
FEDERAL WAY WA 182-B1
ENCHANTED PKWY S Rt#-161
EDGEWOOD WA 182-B2
FEDERAL WAY WA 182-B2
KING CO WA 182-B2
MILTON WA 182-B2
S ENDICOTT RD
ENDICOTT WA 122-B1
WHITMAN CO WA 122-B1
ENDICOTT RD E
WHITMAN CO WA 122-B1
ENDICOTT RD SW
THURSTON CO WA 184-B2
ENDICOTT RD W
ENDICOTT WA 122-A1
WHITMAN CO WA 122-A1
ENDICOTT-SAINT JOHN RD
ENDICOTT WA 122-B1
WHITMAN CO WA 114-B3
WHITMAN CO WA 122-B1
ENDICOTT-ST JOHN RD
WHITMAN CO WA 114-B3
ENDICOTT-ST JOHN RD Rt#-23
SAINT JOHN WA 114-B3
WHITMAN CO WA 114-B3
ENDRESEN RD
HOQUIAM WA 178-A7
ENGEL RD
LINN CO OR 207-D5
ENGLE RD
ISLAND CO WA 167-B5
ENGLEWOOD AV
YAKIMA WA 243-A6
YAKIMA CO WA 243-A6
ENGLEWOOD-SHINGLEHOUSE RD
COOS CO OR 220-D2
COOS CO OR 333-F14
ENGLISH RD
SKAGIT CO WA 168-B2
ENGLISH BLUFF RD
DISTRICT OF DELTA BC 101-C1
ENGLISH GRADE RD
SNOHOMISH CO WA 168-B3
ENGLISH PT RD
KOOTENAI CO ID 245-A5
E ENID RD
LANE CO OR 215-A1
ENMAN-KINCAID RD
WHITMAN CO WA 249-A5
ENNIS CREEK RD
WHATCOM CO WA 161-C3
W ENOCH RD
SPOKANE CO WA 114-B1
ENTERPRISE AV
MALHEUR CO OR 139-A3
ENTERPRISE RD
COLUMBIA CO OR 189-A6
FERNDALE WA 158-C5
POLK CO OR 125-B3
POLK CO OR 204-A4
WHATCOM CO WA 158-C5
E ENTERPRISE RD
LANE CO OR 215-C5
N ENTERPRISE RD
WHATCOM CO WA 158-D4
ENTERPRISE-LEWISTON HWY Rt#-3
WALLOWA CO OR 122-C3
WALLOWA CO OR 130-C1
ENTIAT RIVER RD
CHELAN CO WA 112-A1
CHELAN CO WA 236-A6
ENTRANCE MOUNTAIN RD
SAN JUAN CO WA 160-A3
ENUMCLAW BLK DMD RD SE Rt#-169
BLACK DIAMOND WA 110-C3
KING CO WA 110-C3
ENUMCLAW CHNOOK PSS RD Rt#-410
KING CO WA 110-C3
SE ENMCLAW CHNK PSS RD Rt#-410
KING CO WA 110-C3
PIERCE CO WA 110-C3
PIERCE CO WA 111-A3
EOLA DR NW
POLK CO OR 322-C12
SALEM OR 322-E13
SE EOLA HILLS RD
YAMHILL CO OR 204-B2
ERICKSON RD
DESCHUTES CO OR 217-D2
ERICKSON RD KPS
PIERCE CO WA 181-A3
ERIE ST
CITY OF VICTORIA BC 256-F9
ERLAND POINT RD NW
Tracyton WA 270-C5
ERMINE DR
JEFFERSON CO OR 212-C3
ERSHING RD
SKAGIT CO WA 161-A5
ERSKINE RD SW
THURSTON CO WA 184-B2
ERSKINE WY SW
SEATTLE WA 280-D6
NW E O RIEGER MEM HWY Rt#-501
VANCOUVER WA 192-B5
ESCOLAR RD
KITSAP CO WA 170-A7
ESPANOLA RD
MEDICAL LAKE WA 114-B2
SPOKANE CO WA 114-B2
S ESPANOLA RD
SPOKANE CO WA 114-B2
ESPLANADE AV
CITY OF HARRISON HOT SPRI BC 94-C3
ESPLANADE ST
CITY OF NORTH VANCOUVER BC 255-A6
KLAMATH FALLS OR 338-E6
ESPLANADE ST U.S.-97 Bus
KLAMATH FALLS OR 338-E7
ESPY DR
PACIFIC CO WA 186-A1
ESQUIMALT RD
CITY OF VICTORIA BC 256-E8
TOWN OF ESQUIMALT BC 256-C8
N ESQUIRE DR
BOISE ID 253-C2
ESSER RD
WHITMAN CO WA 250-B1
NE ESTES AV
WHITE SALMON WA 195-D4
ESTES RD
LATAH CO ID 249-C4
EUCHRE CREEK RD
CURRY CO OR 228-B3
EUCLID AV
GRANDVIEW WA 120-B3
Sunnyslope WA 238-D3
YAKIMA CO WA 120-B3
E EUCLID AV
Otis Orchards WA 352-B11
SPOKANE WA 349-A5
SPOKANE CO WA 351-F4
SPOKANE CO WA 352-A11
SPOKANE VALLEY WA 350-B5
SPOKANE VALLEY WA 351-C4
W EUCLID AV
SPOKANE WA 348-H5
SPOKANE WA 349-A5
EUCLID RD
GRANDVIEW WA 120-B3
MABTON WA 120-B3
YAKIMA CO WA 120-B3
E EUCLID RD
YAKIMA CO WA 120-B3
N EUCLID RD
GRANDVIEW WA 120-B3
S EUCLID RD
YAKIMA CO WA 120-B3
EUFAULA HEIGHTS RD
COWLITZ CO WA 189-A1
EUGENE ST
HOOD RIVER OR 195-D5
EUGENE-SPRINGFIELD HWY I-105
EUGENE OR 329-J4
EUGENE OR 330-A5
SPRINGFIELD OR 330-A5
EUGENE-SPRINGFIELD HWY Rt#-126
EUGENE OR 330-E5
LANE CO OR 331-G6
SPRINGFIELD OR 330-E5
SPRINGFIELD OR 331-C5
SW EUREKA LN
JEFFERSON CO OR 208-B6
EUREKA RD N
WALLA WALLA CO WA 121-C2
EVANS BLVD U.S.-101
COOS BAY OR 333-H11
EVANS RD
ASOTIN CO WA 250-B4
HARRAH WA 119-C2
KLAMATH CO OR 151-A3
YAKIMA CO WA 119-C2
S EVANS RD
NEZ PERCE CO ID 250-C2
EVANS CREEK RD
JACKSON CO OR 229-D4
JACKSON CO OR 230-C1
KOOTENAI CO ID 248-C4
E EVANS CREEK RD
JACKSON CO OR 229-D5
JACKSON CO OR 230-C3
ROGUE RIVER OR 229-D5
W EVANS CREEK RD
JACKSON CO OR 229-D4
EVANS HILL CUTOFF RD
STEVENS CO WA 106-A2
EVANS-LEAP RD
WALLOWA CO OR 130-C2
EVANS VALLEY LP
MARION CO OR 205-C4
EVANS VALLEY RD NE
MARION CO OR 205-C4
EVERETT AV
EVERETT WA 265-G3
EVERETT AV Rt#-529
EVERETT WA 264-E3
EVERETT WA 265-E3
SE EVERETT RD Rt#-500
CAMAS WA 193-B6
CLARK CO WA 193-B6
NE EVERETT ST
PORTLAND OR 313-F5
NE EVERETT ST Rt#-500
CAMAS WA 193-B7
NW EVERETT ST
PORTLAND OR 312-D5
PORTLAND OR 313-F5
EVERETT MALL WY Rt#-99
EVERETT WA 268-D5
SE EVERETT MALL WY Rt#-99
EVERETT WA 268-C6
SW EVERETT MALL WY Rt#-99
EVERETT WA 268-A7
SE EVERGREEN AV Rt#-126
REDMOND OR 212-D5
EVERGREEN AV NE
SALEM OR 323-C11
E EVERGREEN BLVD
VANCOUVER WA 305-G5
VANCOUVER WA 306-B6
SE EVERGREEN BLVD Rt#-14B
CLARK CO WA 193-C7
WASHOUGAL WA 193-C7
W EVERGREEN BLVD
VANCOUVER WA 305-G5
EVERGREEN DR Rt#-9
DISTRICT OF KENT BC 94-C3
EVERGREEN HWY
VANCOUVER WA 306-D7
EVERGREEN HWY Rt#-14
CARSON WA 194-C6
CARSON WA 195-B5
CLARK CO WA 193-D7
CLARK CO WA 200-C1
NORTH BONNEVILLE WA 194-C6
SKAMANIA CO WA 193-D7
SKAMANIA CO WA 194-A7
SKAMANIA CO WA 195-B5
SKAMANIA CO WA 200-D1
STEVENSON WA 194-C6
EVERGREEN HWY Rt#-22
TOPPENISH WA 120-A2
YAKIMA CO WA 120-A2
EVERGREEN HWY U.S.-97
TOPPENISH WA 120-A2
YAKIMA CO WA 120-A2
SE EVERGREEN HWY
VANCOUVER WA 193-A7
VANCOUVER WA 306-E7
VANCOUVER WA 307-E7
VANCOUVER WA 311-G1
EVERGREEN LN
SKAGIT CO WA 160-C5
NW EVERGREEN PKWY
HILLSBORO OR 199-A1
EVERGREEN RD
TILLAMOOK CO OR 197-B6
N EVERGREEN RD
SPOKANE VALLEY WA 351-A2
NW EVERGREEN RD
HILLSBORO OR 198-D1
WASHINGTON CO OR 198-D1
S EVERGREEN RD
SPOKANE CO WA 351-A12
SPOKANE VALLEY WA 351-A10
EVERGREEN WY
EVERETT WA 264-D7
EVERETT WA 268-C4
EVERGREEN WY Rt#-14B
WASHOUGAL WA 193-C7
EVERGREEN WY Rt#-99
EVERETT WA 171-B4
EVERETT WA 267-J7
EVERETT WA 268-A7
SNOHOMISH CO WA 171-B4
EVERGREEN PARK DR
OLYMPIA WA 296-F7
S EVERGREEN PARK DR
OLYMPIA WA 296-F7
EVERGREEN PARK RD
PACIFIC CO WA 183-B4
EVERSON AV Rt#-544
EVERSON WA 102-B1
NOOKSACK WA 102-B1
EVERSON GOSHEN RD
WHATCOM CO WA 102-B1
EVERSON GOSHEN RD Rt#-544
EVERSON WA 102-B1
WHATCOM CO WA 102-B1
EWARTSVILLE RD
WHITMAN CO WA 122-C1
WHITMAN CO WA 249-A6
EWE CREEK RD
JOSEPHINE CO OR 229-A5
EWING RD
ISLAND CO WA 170-D2
ISLAND CO WA 171-A2
NE EXCHANGE DR
ROSEBURG OR 334-F4
W EXECUTIVE DR
BOISE ID 253-B3
EXTENSION RD
BRITISH COLUMBIA BC 93-A3
NANAIMO BC 93-A3
EXTROM RD
CITY OF CHILLIWACK BC 102-C1
EYREMOUNT DR
DISTRICT OF WEST VANCOUVE BC 254-E1
EYREMOUNT RD
DISTRICT OF WEST VANCOUVE BC 156-B2
DISTRICT OF WEST VANCOUVE BC 254-E1

F

F ST
BELLINGHAM WA 258-D5
CHENEY WA 246-A7
GEARHART OR 301-G5
GRANT CO WA 237-C3
GRANTS PASS OR 335-D8
PORT TOWNSEND WA 263-F4
WALLA WALLA CO WA 345-H5
F ST U.S.-95
WORLEY ID 115-A2
F ST U.S.-199
GRANTS PASS OR 335-H9
JOSEPHINE CO OR 335-H9
E F ST
TACOMA WA 293-J5
E F ST U.S.-199
GRANTS PASS OR 335-G9
N F ST
ELMA WA 179-B7
F ST N U.S.-395
LAKEVIEW OR 152-A2
F ST S U.S.-395
LAKE CO OR 152-A2
LAKEVIEW OR 152-A2
F ST SE Rt#-28
GRANT CO WA 112-B3
QUINCY WA 112-B3
F ST SW Rt#-28
GRANT CO WA 112-B3
QUINCY WA 112-B3
FACTORIA BLVD SE
BELLEVUE WA 175-C3
FACTORY RD
YAKIMA CO WA 120-B2
FADJUR LN
DESCHUTES CO OR 212-A4
FAGAN RD
SKAGIT CO WA 168-B3
FAGERUD RD SE
KITSAP CO WA 174-C6
FAIL RD
SNOHOMISH CO WA 171-D3
FAIR AV
YAKIMA WA 243-C6
YAKIMA CO WA 243-C6
FAIRBANKS RD
WHITMAN CO WA 114-C3
FAIRBANKS-SEABURY RD
WHITMAN CO WA 114-C3
FAIRBROTHER RD
VALLEY CO ID 251-C7
FAIRFIELD RD
CITY OF VICTORIA BC 256-J10
CITY OF VICTORIA BC 257-A11
DISTRICT OF OAK BAY BC 257-A11
NE FAIRGROUNDS RD
KITSAP CO WA 270-H1
NW FAIRGROUNDS RD
KITSAP CO WA 270-F1
FAIRGROUNDS RD NE
SALEM OR 322-J11
SALEM OR 323-A11
E FAIRHAVEN AV
BURLINGTON WA 260-E5
SKAGIT CO WA 260-E5
FAIROAKS RD
DOUGLAS CO OR 219-B7
DOUGLAS CO OR 221-D1
FAIROAKS RD SE
THURSTON CO WA 181-A7
FAIRVIEW AV
PAYETTE CO ID 139-A3
E FAIRVIEW AV
ADA CO ID 253-B3
BOISE ID 253-B3
MERIDIAN ID 253-B3
N FAIRVIEW AV
BOISE ID 253-B3
SW FAIRVIEW AV Rt#-223
DALLAS OR 204-A6
W FAIRVIEW AV
ADA CO ID 253-B3
BOISE ID 253-B3
GARDEN CITY ID 253-B3
FAIRVIEW AV N
SEATTLE WA 278-A3
FAIRVIEW AV SE
SALEM OR 324-H2
FAIRVIEW DR
HOOD RIVER CO OR 195-C5
SNOHOMISH CO WA 171-D2
YAMHILL CO OR 198-C6
FAIRVIEW LN
GILLIAM CO OR 128-B1
FAIRVIEW RD
COLUMBIA CO OR 189-C6
KITTITAS CO WA 241-C5
LINN CO OR 133-C2
TILLAMOOK CO OR 197-C2
SE FAIRVIEW RD
YAMHILL CO OR 204-C2
FAIRVIEW RD SW
THURSTON CO WA 184-B1
N FAIRVIEW ST
PRINEVILLE OR 213-D5
S FAIRVIEW ST
CROOK CO OR 213-D5
PRINEVILLE OR 213-D5
FAIRVIEW CANYON RD
CHELAN CO WA 238-C3
FAIRVIEW LAKE RD SW
KITSAP CO WA 174-A6
FAIRVIEW-MCKINLEY RD
COOS CO OR 140-C2
FAIRVIEW MOUNTAIN RD
LANE CO OR 209-A5
E FAIRWAY AV
CLACKAMAS CO OR 201-C5
FAIRWAY DR
LINCOLN CO OR 203-A6
FAIRWAY ST
Finley WA 343-F12
KENNEWICK WA 343-F12
SE FAIRWOOD BLVD
KING CO WA 175-C5
FAIRWOOD DR
OCEAN SHORES WA 298-B5
FAITH AV
ASHLAND OR 337-G10
FAKKEMA RD
ISLAND CO WA 167-C2
FALCON LN
JEFFERSON CO OR 208-B7
FALES RD
SNOHOMISH CO WA 171-D5
FALK RD
CLARK CO WA 306-B3
LINN CO OR 210-B3
VANCOUVER WA 306-B3
FALL CITY-CRNTN RD NE Rt#-203
CARNATION WA 176-B2
KING CO WA 176-B2
FALL CITY-CRNTN RD SE Rt#-203
KING CO WA 176-B3
FALL CITY-SNOQUALM RD Rt#-203
KING CO WA 176-B3
SNOQUALMIE WA 176-B3
FALL CREEK RD
ADAMS CO ID 252-A3
CLACKAMAS CO OR 200-C7
LINCOLN CO OR 133-A2
FALLERT RD
COWLITZ CO WA 189-D5
FALLON DR
WEST RICHLAND WA 340-A12
FALLON RD
WHITMAN CO WA 249-B3
FALLS CITY HWY
MONMOUTH OR 204-B7
POLK CO OR 204-B7
FALLS CITY RD
FALLS CITY OR 125-B3
POLK CO OR 125-B3
FALLS CREEK RD
GRAYS HARBOR CO WA 179-B6
N FANCHER RD
SPOKANE WA 349-J8
SPOKANE VALLEY WA 349-J8
S FANCHER RD
SPOKANE VALLEY WA 349-J9
FANDANGO PASS RD
MODOC CO CA 152-A3
F AND S GRADE RD
SEDRO-WOOLLEY WA 161-B5
SKAGIT CO WA 161-B5
FANTON RD
CLACKAMAS CO OR 200-D7
FARADAY RD
CLACKAMAS CO OR 200-C7
FARGO RD
MARION CO OR 199-A7
FARLEY RD SW
DOUGLAS CO WA 239-C6
FARM RD
CLACKAMAS CO OR 205-D3
FARM WY
WHITMAN CO WA 249-B5
FARMER RD
POLK CO OR 204-B5
FARMER RD SE
MARION CO OR 207-D2
FARMER CREEK RD
TILLAMOOK CO OR 197-B6
FARMERS RD
EVERETT WA 268-C6
SW FARMINGTON RD Rt#-10
BEAVERTON OR 199-A2
WASHINGTON CO OR 198-D3
WASHINGTON CO OR 199-A2
FARMS RD
BRITISH COLUMBIA BC 94-B3
FARM STATION RD
KLAMATH CO OR 231-D5
FARM TO MARKET RD
VALLEY CO ID 251-D7
VALLEY CO ID 252-D2
WASHINGTON CO ID 139-B2
FARM TO MARKET LOOP RD
STEVENS CO WA 106-A3
FARMWAY RD
CANYON CO ID 147-B1
S FARNEY RD
SPOKANE CO WA 247-A6
FARR RD
CLARK CO WA 193-A1
N FARR RD
SPOKANE CO WA 350-D3
SPOKANE VALLEY WA 350-E8
S FARR RD
SPOKANE VALLEY WA 350-E9
FARRAGUT AV
BREMERTON WA 270-H11
WESTPORT WA 298-G14
FARRAGUT ST
BREMERTON WA 270-F12
FARRELL RD
ADAMS CO ID 251-B4
FARRINGTON RD
CLALLAM CO WA 164-C5
FARWELL RD
LINCOLN CO WA 114-A1
E FARWELL RD
Fairwood WA 347-C7
SPOKANE CO WA 246-D1
SPOKANE CO WA 347-C7
W FARWELL RD
SPOKANE CO WA 114-B1
FARWEST DR SW
LAKEWOOD WA 181-C4
S FAUCHER RD
YAKIMA CO WA 243-D7
FAUNTLEROY WY SW
SEATTLE WA 280-E6
SEATTLE WA 281-F4
SEATTLE WA 284-D2
FAUST RD
KITTITAS CO WA 241-B5
FAUST RD U.S.-97
KITTITAS CO WA 241-B5
FAWCETT CREEK RD
TILLAMOOK CO OR 197-C3
FAWN CREEK RD
JACKSON CO OR 230-A3
FAYETTEVILLE DR
LINN CO OR 210-A1
SW FEATHER DR
JEFFERSON CO OR 208-B7
JEFFERSON CO OR 212-D1
S FEDERAL WY
ADA CO ID 253-D4

INDEX

STREET INDEX

S GARFIELD ST Rt#-126 STREET INDEX GRANT AV 371

STREET
City State Page-Grid

S GARFIELD ST Rt#-126
EUGENE OR 329-G6
GARFIELD BAY CTO
BONNER CO ID 244-B4
GARFIELD BAY RD
BONNER CO ID 244-B4
GARFIELD-FARMINGTON RD
FARMINGTON WA 115-A3
GARFIELD WA 114-C3
WHITMAN CO WA 114-C3
WHITMAN CO WA 115-A3
GARIBALDI AV U.S.-101
GARIBALDI OR 191-B7
TILLAMOOK CO OR 191-B7
N GARL ST
BURLINGTON WA 260-C4
W GARLAND AV
SPOKANE WA 348-F4
SPOKANE WA 349-A4
GARLOCK RD
COWLITZ CO WA 189-B1
GARNER RD
CLARK CO WA 193-B2
JOSEPHINE CO OR 233-B4
KLICKITAT CO WA 127-B1
YACOLT WA 193-B2
NE GARNER RD
CLARK CO WA 193-B1
GARRARD CREEK RD
GRAYS HARBOR CO WA 117-B1
OAKVILLE WA 117-B1
N GARRETT ST
GARDEN CITY ID 253-B2
GARRISON RD Rt#-547
WHATCOM CO WA 102-B1
GARRISON ST
WALLA WALLA WA 345-F7
Walla Walla East WA 345-F7
GARRISON BUTTE RD
JEFFERSON CO OR 211-D3
GARRITY BLVD U.S.-30
CANYON CO ID 147-C1
NAMPA ID 147-C1
S GARRY RD
SPOKANE CO WA 247-B4
E GARWOOD RD
KOOTENAI CO ID 245-A4
N GARY LN
ADA CO ID 253-C1
BOISE ID 253-C1
GASSY CREEK RD
DOUGLAS CO OR 219-C7
SW GASTON RD
GASTON OR 198-B3
WASHINGTON CO OR 198-B3
GATE CREEK RD
WASCO CO OR 202-D7
GATE MIMA RD
THURSTON CO WA 184-A3
GATENSBURY RD
COQUITLAM BC 157-A5
PORT MOODY BC 157-A5
GATENSBURY ST
COQUITLAM BC 157-A4
GATEWAY DR
COOS CO OR 220-C4
GATEWAY RD
COOS CO OR 220-C5
GATEWAY ST
SPRINGFIELD OR 330-F4
NE GATEWAY GRADE
JEFFERSON CO OR 208-C2
GATFIELD
GEM CO ID 139-C3
GAZLEY RD
DOUGLAS CO OR 225-C3
GAZLEY BRIDGE RD
DOUGLAS CO OR 225-C3
GAZLEY NORTH RD
DOUGLAS CO OR 225-C2
GAZLEY PACIFIC HWY
DOUGLAS CO OR 225-C3
GEARHART LOOP RD
CLATSOP CO OR 301-G2
GEARHART OR 301-G2
GEARY ST
ALBANY OR 326-E10
GEHRING RD
PIERCE CO WA 182-A3
S GEIGER BLVD
SPOKANE CO WA 246-B5
SPOKANE CO WA 348-B13
W GEIGER BLVD
SPOKANE CO WA 246-A5
SPOKANE CO WA 348-C11
SW GEIGER RD
FOREST GROVE OR 198-C1
WASHINGTON CO OR 198-C1
GEISSLER RD
GRAYS HARBOR CO WA 178-C6
W GEISSLER RD
GRAYS HARBOR CO WA 178-C7
GEKELER LN
LA GRANDE OR 130-B2
UNION CO OR 130-B2
S GEKELER LN
BOISE ID 253-D3
GELLOR RD
CLALLAM CO WA 165-D7
GEM AV
MALHEUR CO OR 139-A3
SW GEM LN
JEFFERSON CO OR 208-B7
GEM HEIGHTS DR E
PIERCE CO WA 182-B5
GENE BROWN RD
JOSEPHINE CO OR 233-A6
S GENESEE ST
SEATTLE WA 282-E5
SEATTLE WA 283-F5
SW GENESEE ST
SEATTLE WA 281-F4
S GENESEE WY
SEATTLE WA 283-G5
GENESEE-JULIAETTA RD
LATAH CO ID 250-D1
GENESEE-TROY RD
LATAH CO ID 249-D7
GENSMAN RD
COLUMBIA CO OR 192-A1
GENZER RD
WASHINGTON CO OR 125-B1
GEO CYRUS RD
DESCHUTES CO OR 212-A5
GEORGE RD
CLACKAMAS CO OR 200-C5
GEORGE CLARK RD
GRAYS HARBOR CO WA 183-C2

GEORGE KNOTT RD
WHITMAN CO WA 114-A3
GEORGE MASSEY TUN Rt#-99
CITY OF RICHMOND BC 156-B7
DISTRICT OF DELTA BC 156-C7
GEORGE SMITH RD
MULTNOMAH CO OR 200-D1
GEORGE TAYLOR RD
COWLITZ CO WA 187-D6
GEORGE WASHINGTON WY
BENTON CO WA 340-F4
RICHLAND WA 340-G9
RICHLAND WA 341-G1
GEORGIA ST
VANCOUVER BC 254-G10
GEORGIA ST Rt#-99
VANCOUVER BC 254-F9
GERBER RD
CLACKAMAS CO OR 200-B4
KLAMATH CO OR 151-A2
NE GERBER RD
CLARK CO WA 193-B1
GERBER-MCKEE RD
CLARK CO WA 193-B1
GERBER RANCH RD
KLAMATH CO OR 151-B2
GERIG DR
LINN CO OR 207-D5
GERKE RD
CROOK CO OR 213-C3
GERKING MARKET RD
DESCHUTES CO OR 212-B7
NW GERMANTOWN RD
MULTNOMAH CO OR 192-B7
WASHINGTON CO OR 192-B7
GERMANY CREEK RD
COWLITZ CO WA 117-B3
COWLITZ CO WA 189-A1
NW GERRISH VALLEY RD
YAMHILL CO OR 198-A3
GERTH ST NW
SALEM OR 322-F12
GERTLER RD
FRANKLIN CO WA 121-B2
GESCHWILL LN NE
MARION CO OR 205-B2
GETCHELL RD
MARYSVILLE WA 168-D7
SNOHOMISH CO WA 102-C3
SNOHOMISH CO WA 168-D7
NE GHER RD
CLARK CO WA 192-D5
CLARK CO WA 307-J1
VANCOUVER WA 307-J1
S GIBBLER RD
YAKIMA CO WA 243-A7
GIBBON RD
JACKSON CO OR 230-C7
JACKSON CO OR 336-A1
E GIBBS RD
SPOKANE CO WA 246-C6
W GIBBS RD
SPOKANE CO WA 246-B6
GIBBS LAKE RD
JEFFERSON CO WA 170-A2
GIBRALTAR RD
SKAGIT CO WA 259-H14
GIBSON RD
COWLITZ CO WA 187-D7
SNOHOMISH CO WA 171-B4
WASHINGTON CO OR 198-C3
S GIBSON RD
CLACKAMAS CO OR 205-D2
SE GIBSON RD
CLARK CO WA 193-C7
GIBSON RD NW
DOUGLAS CO WA 236-D5
POLK CO OR 204-C5
GIBSON RD SW
THURSTON CO WA 184-C3
GIBSON ST
CHELAN WA 236-C3
GIBSON CREEK RD
CROOK CO OR 135-C3
GIBSON HILL RD
ALBANY OR 207-C4
ALBANY OR 326-A4
GIBSON PASS RD
BRITISH COLUMBIA BC 103-B1
GIENGER RD
TILLAMOOK CO OR 197-C2
GIFFORD RD SW
THURSTON CO WA 184-B2
GIFFORD LENORE GRADE
NEZ PERCE CO ID 123-B2
GIFFORD REUBENS RD
NEZ PERCE CO ID 123-B2
GIFT AV
DESCHUTES CO OR 212-C7
GIFT RD
DESCHUTES CO OR 212-C7
KLAMATH CO OR 151-A2
GILBERT AV
GLENDALE OR 225-A7
GILBERT RD
CITY OF RICHMOND BC 156-B7
KITTITAS CO WA 241-D5
SNOHOMISH CO WA 168-C4
YAKIMA CO WA 243-A7
E GILBERT RD
Otis Orchards WA 351-J2
Otis Orchards WA 352-A8
GILBERT CREEK RD
YAMHILL CO OR 125-A2
SW GILBERT CREEK RD
YAMHILL CO OR 125-A2
GILBERT GRADE Rt#-7
CLEARWATER CO ID 123-C2
GILBERTSON-ILLAHEE RD NE
KITSAP CO WA 174-C1
KITSAP CO WA 271-B1
NW GILCHRIST ST
BEND OR 332-D8
GILES RD
WHATCOM CO WA 158-C4
GILHAM RD
EUGENE OR 330-B2
GILHOULEY RD
HOOD RIVER CO OR 195-C7
GILIN RD
WHITMAN CO WA 249-B6
GILKEY RD
LINN CO OR 133-C1
GILKEY RD E
BURLINGTON WA 260-D6
NW GILKISON RD
MULTNOMAH CO OR 192-A4

GILLESPIE RD
BRITISH COLUMBIA BC 159-A7
BRITISH COLUMBIA BC 164-D1
BRITISH COLUMBIA BC 165-A1
DISTRICT OF METCHOSIN BC 159-A7
GILLESPIE ST
RICHLAND WA 341-F2
GILLEY AV
DISTRICT OF BURNABY BC 156-D5
GILLIHAN RD
MULTNOMAH CO OR 192-B6
W GILLIS RD
ADAMS CO WA 120-C1
ADAMS CO WA 121-A1
GILMAN AV W
SEATTLE WA 272-E6
SEATTLE WA 273-E6
NW GILMAN BLVD
ISSAQUAH WA 175-D4
ISSAQUAH WA 176-A4
GILMAN DR W
SEATTLE WA 277-F1
GILMORE AV
DISTRICT OF BURNABY BC 255-G12
GILMORE WY
DISTRICT OF BURNABY BC 255-G14
GILMORE DIV
DISTRICT OF BURNABY BC 255-G13
GILMOUR RD S
MARION CO OR 207-C2
GIMPL HILL RD
EUGENE OR 329-B10
LANE CO OR 215-A3
LANE CO OR 329-A10
GINKGO RD
JACKSON CO OR 226-D6
JACKSON CO OR 227-A5
GINKGO ELK RD
JACKSON CO OR 226-C5
GINNETT RD
SKAGIT CO WA 259-C13
GIRL SCOUT RD
SKAMANIA CO WA 195-A5
GIRT RD
COLUMBIA CO OR 189-B5
GISH RD
LEWIS CO WA 187-D2
N GLADE RD
FRANKLIN CO WA 121-A2
FRANKLIN CO WA 343-D1
PASCO WA 343-E1
GLADE CREEK RD
JACKSON CO OR 234-B7
GLADIOLA DR
GRANTS PASS OR 335-J11
JOSEPHINE CO OR 335-J11
GLADWIN RD
DISTRICT OF MATSQUI BC 102-B1
GLANFORD AV
DISTRICT OF SAANICH BC 159-C5
DISTRICT OF SAANICH BC 256-E2
GLASER DR
LINN CO OR 207-D7
GLASS LN
JACKSON CO OR 230-C5
GLASS RD
CLACKAMAS CO OR 199-B6
GLASSER HILL RD
STEVENS CO WA 106-B3
E GLEED RD
YAKIMA CO WA 243-A5
N GLEED RD
YAKIMA CO WA 243-A5
GLEN DR
COQUITLAM BC 157-A4
GLEN ST
ASHLAND OR 337-C6
GLEN AIKEN CREEK RD
COOS CO OR 220-D5
GLENAYRE DR
PORT MOODY BC 157-A4
GLENBROOK LP
DOUGLAS CO OR 225-B3
GLENBROOK RD
BENTON CO OR 133-A2
NW GLENCOE RD
HILLSBORO OR 198-D1
GLEN COVE MILL RD
JEFFERSON CO WA 263-C6
PORT TOWNSEND WA 263-C6
GLEN CREEK RD NW
SALEM OR 322-D11
GLENDALE RD
ISLAND CO WA 171-A3
WHATCOM CO WA 158-D4
GLENDALE WY S
KING CO WA 286-B6
GLENDALE VALLEY RD
DOUGLAS CO OR 225-B7
GLENGARY BAY
BONNER CO ID 244-B3
GLENGARY RD
DOUGLAS CO OR 221-C6
GLENGARY BAY RD
BONNER CO ID 244-C3
GLENN ST S
VALE OR 139-A3
GLEN RIDGE DR
CORVALLIS OR 327-C5
E GLENROSE RD
SPOKANE WA 349-G11
SPOKANE CO WA 349-G11
S GLENROSE RD
SPOKANE CO WA 246-C5
SPOKANE CO WA 349-J13
GLENWAY AV
PAYETTE CO ID 139-A3
GLENWOOD AV
EVERETT WA 264-A7
EVERETT WA 268-A1
GLENWOOD BLVD
EUGENE OR 330-F8
SPRINGFIELD OR 330-F8
GLENWOOD DR
LONGVIEW WA 302-J6
GLENWOOD RD SW
KITSAP CO WA 174-B5
N GLENWOOD ST
BOISE ID 253-C2
GARDEN CITY ID 253-C2
N GLENWOOD ST Rt#-44
ADA CO ID 253-C2
GARDEN CITY ID 253-C2
GLENWOOD-GOLDENDALE HWY
KLICKITAT CO WA 127-B1
KLICKITAT CO WA 196-D1
GLENWOOD-GOLDENDALE RD
KLICKITAT CO WA 119-A3

G-LINE RD
GRAYS HARBOR CO WA 179-A5
NE GLISAN ST
FAIRVIEW OR 200-B1
GRESHAM OR 200-B1
MULTNOMAH CO OR 200-A1
PORTLAND OR 200-A1
PORTLAND OR 313-J5
PORTLAND OR 314-B5
PORTLAND OR 315-H5
NW GLISAN ST
PORTLAND OR 312-D5
PORTLAND OR 313-E5
GLORY DR SE
THURSTON CO WA 181-A7
GLOVER RD
TOWNSHIP OF LANGLEY BC 157-C7
GLOVER RD Rt#-10
LANGLEY BC 157-C7
TOWNSHIP OF LANGLEY BC 157-C7
SW GLOVER RD
JEFFERSON CO OR 208-A7
G L WILLIAMS RD
CLARK CO WA 118-A3
GNAT CREEK RD
CLATSOP CO OR 117-A3
GNOS RD
WASHINGTON CO OR 198-C2
GOAT RANCH RD
COLUMBIA CO OR 189-A5
N GOBLE CREEK RD
COWLITZ CO WA 189-D3
S GOBLE CREEK RD
COWLITZ CO WA 189-D3
GODBERTSON RD
WASCO CO OR 196-A7
SW GODDARD RD
WASHINGTON CO OR 198-C2
W GODDARD RD
BOISE ID 253-B2
GODOWA SPRINGS RD
KLAMATH CO OR 151-A1
SE GODSEY RD
DALLAS OR 204-A6
GODS VALLEY RD
TILLAMOOK CO OR 191-C3
GOERIG ST
WOODLAND WA 118-A3
WOODLAND WA 192-C1
GOERIG ST Rt#-503
WOODLAND WA 118-A3
WOODLAND WA 192-C1
GOETHALS DR
RICHLAND WA 341-F2
N GOING ST
PORTLAND OR 312-D1
PORTLAND OR 313-E1
GOLD ST
CENTRALIA WA 299-E6
LEWIS CO WA 299-E6
N GOLD ST
CENTRALIA WA 299-G3
GOLD CREEK RD
TILLAMOOK CO OR 197-D3
GOLD CREEK RD W
KITSAP CO WA 173-D3
GOLDENDALE BICKLETON RD
KLICKITAT CO WA 120-A3
KLICKITAT CO WA 127-C1
KLICKITAT CO WA 128-A1
YAKIMA CO WA 120-A3
GOLDENDALE-CENTERVILLE RD
KLICKITAT CO WA 127-C1
GOLDENDALE-GLENWOOD HWY
KLICKITAT CO WA 119-A3
GOLDENDALE GOODNOE HILLS RD
KLICKITAT CO WA 127-C1
KLICKITAT CO WA 128-A1
GOLDEN GARDENS DR NW
SEATTLE WA 272-D1
GOLDEN GIVEN RD E
PIERCE CO WA 181-D4
PIERCE CO WA 295-J7
GOLDEN MANTEL
JEFFERSON CO OR 212-C2
GOLDFISH FARM RD
ALBANY OR 326-J7
LINN CO OR 326-J7
GOLD FORK RD
VALLEY CO ID 252-D2
GOLD HILL CIR
BONNER CO ID 244-B3
GOLD HILL SPUR Rt#-99
GOLD HILL OR 230-B6
JACKSON CO OR 230-B6
GOLDIE RD
ISLAND CO WA 167-C2
GOLD LAKE RD
OKANOGAN CO WA 105-A3
GOLD MOUNTAIN RD
BONNER CO ID 244-B3
GOLD RAY RD
JACKSON CO OR 230-B6
GOLDSTREAM AV Rt#-1A
CITY OF COLWOOD BC 159-B6
DISTRICT OF LANGFORD BC 159-B6
GOLF DR
SEATTLE WA 278-B7
SEATTLE WA 282-B1
GOLF CLUB RD
MARION CO OR 133-C1
STAYTON OR 133-C1
GOLF CLUB RD SE
LACEY WA 297-F6
MARION CO OR 133-C1
STAYTON OR 133-C1
GOLF COURSE RD
Ault Field WA 167-B2
ISLAND CO WA 167-B2
PACIFIC CO WA 117-A1
WALLOWA CO OR 130-C2
N GOLF COURSE RD U.S.-101
PORT ANGELES WA 261-H6
SW GOLF COURSE RD
WASHINGTON CO OR 198-C2
GOLL RD NW
DOUGLAS CO WA 236-D7
GOLTRA RD
LINN CO OR 207-D6
GOOD RD
BENTON CO WA 120-C3
ISLAND CO WA 168-A3
GOODACRE-BENSTON
PIERCE CO WA 182-A7
GOODFELLOW LAKES RD
CLACKAMAS CO OR 201-B4

N GOOD HOPE RD
KOOTENAI CO ID 245-C2
S GOOD HOPE RD
KOOTENAI CO ID 245-C2
GOODMAN LN
ADAMS CO ID 251-B4
GOODMAN MAIN LINE RD
CLALLAM CO WA 169-B2
GOODNIGHT AV
BENTON CO OR 327-G14
CORVALLIS OR 327-G14
GOODNOE STATION RD
KLICKITAT CO WA 127-C1
KLICKITAT CO WA 128-A1
GOODPASTURE ISLAND RD
EUGENE OR 329-H2
EUGENE OR 330-A2
GOODRICH DR NW
PIERCE CO WA 174-B7
GOODRICH HWY
DOUGLAS CO OR 219-A6
GOODRICH RD
DESCHUTES CO OR 212-A5
WASHINGTON CO ID 139-B1
GOODRICH CREEK RD
ADAMS CO ID 139-B1
GOODSPEED RD
TILLAMOOK CO OR 197-B1
SE GOODWIN AV
PENDLETON OR 129-B1
SW GOODWIN AV
PENDLETON OR 129-B1
SW GOODWIN LN
PENDLETON OR 129-B1
GOODWIN RD
KITTITAS CO WA 241-A4
NE GOODWIN RD
CAMAS WA 193-A6
CLARK CO WA 193-A6
GOOSEBERRY RD
IONE OR 128-B2
MORROW CO OR 128-B2
GOOSE CREEK RD Rt#-194
WHITMAN CO WA 122-C1
GOOSE CREEK PARK RD
ADAMS CO ID 251-B4
GOOSE LAKE RD
ADAMS CO ID 251-C2
GOPHER VALLEY RD
YAMHILL CO OR 125-B3
SW GOPHER VALLEY RD
YAMHILL CO OR 125-B3
YAMHILL CO OR 204-A2
GORDON CREEK RD
MULTNOMAH CO OR 200-C2
GORDON HEAD RD
DISTRICT OF SAANICH BC 257-C3
GORDON RIDGE RD
SHERMAN CO OR 127-C1
GORE DR
LINN CO OR 207-D6
GORE RD
COWLITZ CO WA 189-D6
YAKIMA CO WA 243-B5
GORGE RD
CHELAN CO WA 236-D3
GORGE RD E Rt#-1A
CITY OF VICTORIA BC 256-F6
GORGE RD W Rt#-1A
CITY OF VICTORIA BC 256-C5
DISTRICT OF SAANICH BC 256-C5
GOSE ST
Garrett WA 344-F7
GOSHEN-DIVIDE HWY Rt#-99
COTTAGE GROVE OR 215-B6
CRESWELL OR 215-C4
LANE CO OR 215-C4
LANE CO OR 219-C1
LANE CO OR 330-J14
N GOSHEN-DIVIDE HWY Rt#-99
COTTAGE GROVE OR 215-B7
N GOSHEN-DIVIDE ST Rt#-99
COTTAGE GROVE OR 215-B7
S GOSHEN-DIVIDE ST Rt#-99
CRESWELL OR 215-C5
GOSNER RD
JEFFERSON CO OR 136-A1
NE GOSNER RD
JEFFERSON CO OR 135-C1
GOSNEY RD
DESCHUTES CO OR 217-D3
GOSSETT RD
CLALLAM CO WA 164-C5
GOSS LAKE RD
ISLAND CO WA 170-D1
GOTHAM BAY RD
KOOTENAI CO ID 248-A2
GOULD
PIERCE CO WA 182-A6
GOULD RD
PACIFIC CO WA 183-B4
GOULD CITY-MAYVIEW RD
GARFIELD CO WA 122-B2
GOVERNMENT RD
GRANT CO WA 120-B1
LANE CO OR 141-C1
LANE CO OR 215-C7
MATTAWA WA 120-B1
GOVERNMENT ST
BRITISH COLUMBIA BC 101-A1
CITY OF VICTORIA BC 256-G8
DISTRICT OF BURNABY BC 156-D5
DUNCAN BC 101-A1
N GOVERNMENT WY
COEUR D'ALENE ID 355-E5
DALTON GARDENS ID 355-E5
HAYDEN ID 245-A5
HAYDEN ID 355-E5
KOOTENAI CO ID 245-A5
KOOTENAI CO ID 355-E5
SPOKANE WA 348-E8
SPOKANE CO WA 348-E8
S GOVERNMENT WY
SPOKANE WA 348-E10
SPOKANE CO WA 348-E9
W GOVERNMENT WY
SEATTLE WA 272-D5
GOWDYVILLE RD
LANE CO OR 215-A7
E GOWEN RD Rt#-21
ADA CO ID 253-D4
BOISE ID 253-D4
W GOWEN RD
ADA CO ID 253-C4
BOISE ID 253-C4
GOZZER RD
KOOTENAI CO ID 248-A1

GRABER RD
YAKIMA CO WA 243-B4
GRABHORN RD
WASHINGTON CO OR 199-A3
GRADE CRES
LANGLEY BC 158-C1
GRADE RD
LAKE STEVENS WA 171-D1
GRADE RD SE
MARION CO OR 205-D6
GRADE ST
COWLITZ CO WA 303-D9
KELSO WA 303-D9
GRADE ST SE
THURSTON CO WA 184-C4
GRADE CREEK RD
CHELAN CO WA 236-B1
S GRADY WY
RENTON WA 175-C5
S GRADY WY Rt#-515
RENTON WA 175-C5
SW GRADY WY
RENTON WA 175-C5
RENTON WA 289-J4
TUKWILA WA 289-J4
GRAHAM BLVD
MALHEUR CO OR 138-C3
SW GRAHAM RD
JEFFERSON CO OR 135-A1
GRAHAM CREEK RD
JACKSON CO OR 226-C6
SW GRAHAMS FERRY RD
CLACKAMAS CO OR 199-B5
GRAN RD
SNOHOMISH CO WA 168-B3
GRAND AV
ASTORIA OR 300-E5
E GRAND AV
EVERETT WA 265-G3
N GRAND AV Rt#-27
PULLMAN WA 249-B5
NE GRAND AV Rt#-99E
PORTLAND OR 313-G4
S GRAND AV Rt#-27
PULLMAN WA 249-B5
SE GRAND AV Rt#-99E
PORTLAND OR 313-G7
PORTLAND OR 317-G2
W GRAND AV
ASTORIA OR 300-B5
GRAND AV NE
BAINBRIDGE ISLAND WA 174-D2
GRAND BLVD
CITY OF NORTH VANCOUVER BC 255-C4
VANCOUVER WA 305-J6
VANCOUVER WA 306-A3
S GRAND BLVD
SPOKANE WA 246-C5
SPOKANE WA 349-B13
GRAND COULEE AV Rt#-155
ELECTRIC CITY WA 237-C3
GRAND COULEE WA 237-C3
GRANT CO WA 237-C3
GRAND COULEE AV E Rt#-174
GRAND COULEE WA 237-C3
GRANT CO WA 237-C3
GRAND COULEE AV W Rt#-174
GRAND COULEE WA 237-C3
GRAND COULEE HWY Rt#-155
GRAND COULEE WA 237-C3
GRANDE RONDE RD
ASOTIN CO WA 122-C3
WALLOWA CO OR 122-C3
GRANDE RONDE RIVER RD
UNION CO OR 129-C2
SE GRAND ISLAND LP
YAMHILL CO OR 204-D2
SE GRAND ISLAND RD
YAMHILL CO OR 204-D2
GRAND PRAIRIE RD
ALBANY OR 326-E10
LINN CO OR 207-D5
LINN CO OR 326-G11
GRAND RONDE RD
POLK CO OR 125-A3
YAMHILL CO OR 125-A3
SW GRAND RONDE RD
YAMHILL CO OR 125-A3
GRANDSTROM RD
SKAGIT CO WA 168-C3
GRANDVIEW AV
GRANTS PASS OR 335-F12
JOSEPHINE CO OR 335-F12
GRANDVIEW DR
DISTRICT OF SAANICH BC 257-D1
GRANDVIEW DR W
UNIVERSITY PLACE WA 181-C3
GRANDVIEW HWY
VANCOUVER BC 255-B13
GRANDVIEW RD
Birch Bay WA 158-B5
SNOHOMISH CO WA 168-D4
WHATCOM CO WA 158-C5
GRANDVIEW RD Rt#-548
Birch Bay WA 158-B5
WHATCOM CO WA 158-B5
SW GRANDVIEW LOOP RD
JEFFERSON CO OR 212-A2
GRANDVIEW PAVEMENT RD
GRANDVIEW WA 120-B3
YAKIMA CO WA 120-B3
GRANGE RD NE
DOUGLAS CO WA 104-C3
GRANGE ST
DISTRICT OF BURNABY BC 156-C5
GRANGEMONT RD
CLEARWATER CO ID 123-C2
OROFINO ID 123-C2
GRANGER AV
BENTON CO OR 207-B5
GRANGEVIEW RD
KLICKITAT CO WA 195-D4
GRANITE RD
GRANITE OR 137-C1
GRANT CO OR 137-C1
GRANITE CREEK RD
MALHEUR CO OR 146-A1
GRANITE FALLS HWY Rt#-92
GRANITE FALLS WA 102-C3
SNOHOMISH CO WA 102-C3
SNOHOMISH CO WA 110-C1
GRANITE HILL RD
BAKER CO OR 138-A1
JOSEPHINE CO OR 229-C4
JOSEPHINE CO OR 335-F2
SUMPTER OR 138-A1
GRANT AV
CORVALLIS OR 327-F8

INDEX

HARRISON AV — STREET INDEX — HIGHWAY Rt#-8 373

STREET
City State Page-Grid

HARRISON AV
LEWIS CO WA 299-B1
OLYMPIA WA 296-E5
E HARRISON AV
COEUR D'ALENE ID 355-F10
W HARRISON AV
COEUR D'ALENE ID 355-E10
HARRISON AV SW
OLYMPIA WA 296-C4
HARRISON BLVD
BENTON CO OR 327-C9
CORVALLIS OR 327-C9
HARRISON BLVD Rt#-34
CORVALLIS OR 327-G9
LINN CO OR 327-G9
N HARRISON BLVD
BOISE ID 253-C2
HARRISON RD
COWLITZ CO WA 189-D4
LINN CO OR 210-C1
HARRISON RD Rt#-97
KOOTENAI CO ID 248-B5
HARRISON RD Rt#-823
YAKIMA CO WA 243-B5
HARRISON ST
SEATTLE WA 277-J4
SE HARRISON ST
MILWAUKIE OR 199-D3
MILWAUKIE OR 321-J2
HARRIS STREET RD
COWLITZ CO WA 303-G8
KELSO WA 303-G8
HARSTINE ISLAND RD N
MASON CO WA 180-D2
HARSTINE ISLAND RD S
MASON CO WA 180-D3
HART RD
KITTITAS CO WA 240-C2
LATAH CO ID 249-D4
LEWIS CO WA 187-C3
WALLA WALLA CO WA 121-C3
SW HART RD
BEAVERTON OR 199-A2
HART RD SE
THURSTON CO WA 184-C1
HARTEL RD
UMATILLA CO OR 121-B3
UMATILLA CO OR 129-B1
HARTFORD DR
LAKE STEVENS WA 110-C1
LAKE STEVENS WA 171-D1
HARTFORD ST
ELGIN OR 130-A1
HARTLEY RD
BRITISH COLUMBIA BC 94-B3
HARTMAN RD
KITTITAS CO WA 240-D1
S HARTMAN RD
CLACKAMAS CO OR 205-D3
HART MOUNTAIN RD
LAKE CO OR 152-B1
HARTS LAKE RD S
PIERCE CO WA 118-A1
HARTS LAKE LOOP RD
PIERCE CO WA 118-A1
PIERCE CO WA 181-D7
E HARTSON AV
SPOKANE WA 349-C10
W HARTSON AV
SPOKANE WA 348-F10
HARVARD AV E
SEATTLE WA 274-B7
SEATTLE WA 278-B1
SW HARVARD BLVD Rt#-138
ROSEBURG OR 334-F7
W HARVARD BLVD
ROSEBURG OR 334-B7
W HARVARD BLVD Rt#-138
ROSEBURG OR 334-E7
N HARVARD RD
LIBERTY LAKE WA 352-B9
Otis Orchards WA 352-B9
SPOKANE CO WA 352-B9
S HARVARD RD
SPOKANE CO WA 247-B7
HARVEST DR
LINN CO OR 207-B7
SW HARVEST LN
DESCHUTES CO OR 212-C6
HARVEY AV
ROSEBURG OR 334-C6
HARVEY RD
AUBURN WA 182-C1
CLACKAMAS CO OR 200-D6
LANE CO OR 215-C4
WHATCOM CO WA 158-B3
HARVEY SHAW RD
WALLA WALLA CO WA 121-C3
WALLA WALLA CO WA 344-F1
HARVIE RD
CITY OF SURREY BC 157-B7
HARWOOD ST
PRINEVILLE OR 213-D5
HARYU RD
COWLITZ CO WA 189-A2
HASIS DR
JOSEPHINE CO OR 229-B3
HASKINS RD
KLAMATH CO OR 151-A2
HASTIE LAKE RD
ISLAND CO WA 167-B3
HASTINGS AV W
JEFFERSON CO WA 166-D6
JEFFERSON CO WA 263-A4
PORT TOWNSEND WA 263-A4
E HASTINGS RD
Fairwood WA 346-J8
Fairwood WA 347-A8
SPOKANE CO WA 347-A8
W HASTINGS RD
Fairwood WA 346-J8
HASTINGS ST
DISTRICT OF BURNABY BC 156-D4
VANCOUVER BC 254-G10
HASTINGS ST Rt#-7A
DISTRICT OF BURNABY BC 156-D4
DISTRICT OF BURNABY BC 255-G10
VANCOUVER BC 255-F10
HASTINGS ST E Rt#-1
VANCOUVER BC 255-F10
HASTINGS ST E Rt#-7A
VANCOUVER BC 254-J10
VANCOUVER BC 255-B10
HASTINGS HILL RD
GARFIELD CO WA 122-B1
S HATCH RD
SPOKANE WA 246-C5
SPOKANE CO WA 246-C5
HATCHET SLOUGH RD
COOS CO OR 220-C5
HATFIELD HWY Rt#-39
KLAMATH CO OR 151-A2
SISKIYOU CO CA 151-A3
NW HATHAWAY RD
CLARK CO WA 192-C4
HATLEY RD
WHITMAN CO WA 249-A6
S HATTAN RD
CLACKAMAS CO OR 200-A4
W HATTON RD
ADAMS CO WA 121-A1
HAUGEN RD
SKAGIT CO WA 168-B3
WASHINGTON CO OR 199-A5
YAMHILL CO OR 199-A5
SE HAUGLUM RD
CLACKAMAS CO OR 200-C3
HAUSER LAKE RD
HAUSER ID 353-B1
KOOTENAI CO ID 353-B1
E HAUSER LAKE RD
HAUSER ID 247-C1
SPOKANE CO WA 247-B1
N HAVANA ST
SPOKANE WA 349-G2
SPOKANE CO WA 349-G2
SPOKANE VALLEY WA 349-G8
S HAVANA ST
SPOKANE WA 246-C5
SPOKANE WA 349-G12
SPOKANE CO WA 246-C5
SPOKANE CO WA 349-G12
SPOKANE VALLEY WA 349-G12
HAVANA-HELIX HWY
HELIX OR 129-B1
UMATILLA CO OR 129-B1
HAVEKOST RD
ANACORTES WA 259-D8
SKAGIT CO WA 259-D8
HAVERLAND KOONTZ RD
FRANKLIN CO WA 121-B2
HAVILLAH RD
OKANOGAN CO WA 104-C2
OKANOGAN CO WA 105-A1
TONASKET WA 104-C2
HAVLINA RD Rt#-260
FRANKLIN CO WA 121-B1
HAWKINS RD
LEWIS CO WA 187-C3
HAWKINS RD S
LEWIS CO WA 187-C3
HAWKS CLIFF RD NE
DOUGLAS CO WA 113-A1
DOUGLAS CO WA 237-A5
HAWKS PRAIRIE RD NE
LACEY WA 181-A5
THURSTON CO WA 180-D5
THURSTON CO WA 181-A5
HAWLEY CREEK RD
LANE CO OR 215-A6
HAWN CREEK RD
YAMHILL CO OR 198-B6
HAWORTH AV
NEWBERG OR 198-D5
HAWTHORNE AV
MEDFORD OR 336-D12
NW HAWTHORNE AV
GRANTS PASS OR 335-F6
HAWTHORNE AV NE
SALEM OR 323-D11
SALEM OR 325-C1
SE HAWTHORNE BLVD
PORTLAND OR 313-H7
PORTLAND OR 314-A7
HAWTHORNE RD
BELLINGHAM WA 258-A12
E HAWTHORNE RD
Country Homes WA 346-J10
Country Homes WA 347-A10
SPOKANE WA 347-B10
SPOKANE CO WA 347-C10
W HAWTHORNE RD
Country Homes WA 346-J10
S HAWTHORNE ST
Finley WA 343-E12
KENNEWICK WA 343-E12
HAXTON WY
WHATCOM CO WA 158-C7
WHATCOM CO WA 160-C1
NE HAY CREEK RD
JEFFERSON CO OR 135-B1
JEFFERSON CO OR 208-D4
SE HAY CREEK RD
JEFFERSON CO OR 135-B1
JEFFERSON CO OR 213-C1
E HAYDEN AV
HAYDEN ID 245-A5
W HAYDEN AV
HAYDEN ID 245-A5
HAYDEN ID 247-D1
KOOTENAI CO ID 247-C1
HAYDEN RD
CLACKAMAS CO OR 200-B6
LINCOLN CO WA 113-B1
LINN CO OR 133-C1
HAYDEN BRIDGE RD
LANE CO OR 330-J4
LANE CO OR 331-A4
SPRINGFIELD OR 330-J4
SPRINGFIELD OR 331-A4
HAYDEN BRIDGE WY
LANE CO OR 330-G4
SPRINGFIELD OR 330-G4
E HAYDEN LAKE RD
KOOTENAI CO ID 245-B6
N HAYDEN LAKE RD
KOOTENAI CO ID 245-B4
S HAYDEN LAKE RD
HAYDEN ID 355-F1
KOOTENAI CO ID 355-F1
HAYES LN
LANE CO OR 210-A6
HAYES RD
CLARK CO WA 118-A3
CLARK CO WA 192-C1
S HAYES ST
MOSCOW ID 249-D5
W HAYES ST
WOODBURN OR 205-B2
HAYES HILL RD
JOSEPHINE CO OR 233-B1
HAYESVILLE DR NE
Hayesville OR 323-E6
MARION CO OR 323-E6
SALEM OR 323-E6
S HAYFORD RD
AIRWAY HEIGHTS WA 246-A4
SPOKANE CO WA 246-A5
HAYHURST RD
DOUGLAS CO OR 219-A3
HAY-LA CROSSE RD
WHITMAN CO WA 122-A1
HAYNES WY
COOS CO OR 218-C6
HAYNIE RD
WHATCOM CO WA 158-C3
HAYSTACK DR
JEFFERSON CO OR 212-D1
HAYSTACK ROCK RD
MALHEUR CO OR 146-C1
HAYWARD RD
KITTITAS CO WA 240-D3
HAYWIRE RD
LEWIS CO WA 187-C1
N HAZARD RD
SPOKANE CO WA 346-G4
W HAZARD RD
SPOKANE CO WA 346-H5
HAZARD LAKE RD
IDAHO CO ID 251-B1
HAZEL AV
BENTON CITY WA 120-C3
W HAZEL ST
MOUNT VERNON WA 260-B14
HAZEL CAMP RD
CURRY CO OR 232-D3
NE HAZEL DELL AV
CLARK CO WA 192-C5
CLARK CO WA 305-G1
VANCOUVER WA 305-G1
HAZEL DELL RD
COWLITZ CO WA 187-B7
COWLITZ CO WA 189-B1
HAZELGREEN RD NE
Hayesville OR 323-F4
MARION CO OR 205-B4
MARION CO OR 323-F4
SALEM OR 323-F4
HAZELNUT RIDGE RD NE
MARION CO OR 205-D4
HAZEL POINT RD
JEFFERSON CO WA 170-A7
HAZEN RD
CLARK CO WA 193-A1
COLUMBIA CO OR 192-A2
HEADQUARTERS RD
COWLITZ CO WA 189-C1
HEADQUATERS RD
COWLITZ CO WA 189-C1
HEALY RD
CLARK CO WA 190-A7
HEART LAKE RD
ANACORTES WA 259-F10
SKAGIT CO WA 259-F10
HEART OF THE HILLS
CLALLAM CO WA 109-B1
HEART OF THE HILLS PKWY
CLALLAM CO WA 261-G14
HEATER RD
CLACKAMAS CO OR 199-A6
WASHINGTON CO OR 199-A6
HEATHER OAK DR
LANE CO OR 210-A7
HEATH LAKE RD
BONNER CO ID 244-A4
HEBER RD
UNION CO OR 130-A3
HECETA BEACH RD
LANE CO OR 214-A2
HECKARD RD
PACIFIC CO WA 117-A1
E HEDGER AV Rt#-225
BENTON CITY WA 120-C3
E HEGLAR RD
SPOKANE CO WA 246-D1
HEIGHTS LN NE
THURSTON CO WA 180-D5
HEIKKLA LN
VALLEY CO ID 251-D6
HEIMER RD
SNOHOMISH CO WA 168-D3
HEIMRICH ST
DUFUR OR 127-B2
WASCO CO OR 127-B2
HEINE RD
STEVENS CO WA 106-A3
HEINEMAN RD
ADAMS CO WA 113-C3
HEINRICH RD
VALLEY CO ID 251-C6
HEINZ BLVD
MALHEUR CO OR 139-A3
S HEINZ RD
CLACKAMAS CO OR 205-D1
HEINZ RD NE
MARION CO OR 205-D4
HEIPLE RD
CLACKAMAS CO OR 200-B5
HEISSON RD
BATTLE GROUND WA 193-A3
CLARK CO WA 193-A3
HELIX-VANCYCLE RD
HELIX OR 129-B1
UMATILLA CO OR 121-B3
UMATILLA CO OR 129-B1
HELLER RD
Ault Field WA 167-B2
ISLAND CO WA 167-B2
OAK HARBOR WA 167-B2
HELLS CANYON RD
WASHINGTON CO OR 198-D5
WASHINGTON CO OR 199-A5
HELLS GULCH RD
BENEWAH CO ID 248-C6
KOOTENAI CO ID 248-C6
HELM RD
JOSEPHINE CO OR 229-A6
HELMAN ST
ASHLAND OR 337-C7
HELMCKEN RD
DISTRICT OF SAANICH BC 256-C2
TOWN OF VIEW ROYAL BC 256-A4
NW HELMHOLTZ WY
DESCHUTES CO OR 212-D5
SW HELMHOLTZ WY
DESCHUTES CO OR 212-D5
HELMICK RD
POLK CO OR 207-B1
SKAGIT CO WA 161-C5
NW HELVETIA RD
WASHINGTON CO OR 125-C1
HEMENWAY RD
LEWIS CO WA 187-B4
NE HEMLOCK AV
REDMOND OR 212-D5
NW HEMLOCK AV
DESCHUTES CO OR 212-D5
HEMLOCK RD
SKAMANIA CO WA 194-C3
HEMLOCK ST
LONGVIEW WA 302-G9
VANCOUVER BC 254-E13
N HEMLOCK ST
CANNON BEACH OR 188-A7
S HEMLOCK ST
CANNON BEACH OR 188-A7
CANNON BEACH OR 191-A1
W HEMLOCK ST Rt#-34
WALDPORT OR 328-E4
HEMLOCK BUTTE RD
DOUGLAS CO OR 223-B6
HEMLOCK VALLEY RD
BRITISH COLUMBIA BC 94-C3
HEMMERING RD
LINCOLN CO WA 113-B2
W HEMMI RD
WHATCOM CO WA 158-D5
HENDERER RD
DOUGLAS CO OR 141-A1
HENDERSON BLVD
OLYMPIA WA 296-J7
HENDERSON BLVD SE
OLYMPIA WA 296-J7
OLYMPIA WA 297-A8
THURSTON CO WA 296-J7
THURSTON CO WA 297-A8
TUMWATER WA 297-A8
NE HENDERSON DR
JEFFERSON CO OR 208-C5
HENDERSON LN
OWYHEE CO ID 147-C2
HENDERSON PL SW
SEATTLE WA 285-H3
HENDERSON RD
DISTRICT OF OAK BAY BC 257-C5
S HENDERSON ST
SEATTLE WA 287-F3
SW HENDERSON ST
SEATTLE WA 285-G3
HENDERSON CREEK RD
LANE CO OR 214-C3
HENDRICKS RD
FRANKLIN CO WA 121-A1
YAMHILL CO OR 198-B5
HENDRICKSON RD
LEWIS CO WA 187-B5
HENKLE ST Rt#-6
PACIFIC CO WA 117-A1
RAYMOND WA 117-A1
HENKLE BUTTE DR
DESCHUTES CO OR 212-A4
HENLEY RD
KLAMATH CO OR 235-D5
HENLEY HORNBROOK RD
SISKIYOU CO CA 150-A3
HENNI RD
ISLAND CO WA 167-C1
HENRICHS RD
SHERMAN CO OR 127-C2
S HENRICI RD
CLACKAMAS CO OR 199-D5
CLACKAMAS CO OR 200-A5
HENRIOT RD
LEWIS CO WA 187-C3
HENRY RD
DOUGLAS CO OR 221-B2
LINCOLN CO OR 133-A1
WHATCOM CO WA 158-B5
E HENRY RD
SPOKANE CO WA 247-B5
N HENRY RD
LIBERTY LAKE WA 247-B4
LIBERTY LAKE WA 351-J8
LIBERTY LAKE WA 352-A14
SPOKANE CO WA 351-J8
S HENRY RD
SPOKANE CO WA 247-B4
SPOKANE CO WA 351-J9
W HENRY ST
FRANKLIN CO WA 342-J6
PASCO WA 342-J6
PASCO WA 343-D6
HENRY CREEK RD
WHEELER CO OR 128-B3
HENRY FOSTER RD
GRAYS HARBOR CO WA 179-A7
HENSEL RD
GRAYS HARBOR CO WA 178-A3
HENSON RD
BENTON CO OR 120-C3
HEPPNER HWY Rt#-74
GILLIAM CO OR 128-B1
HEPPNER OR 128-C2
IONE OR 128-B1
LEXINGTON OR 128-C2
MORROW CO OR 128-B1
MORROW CO OR 129-A2
UMATILLA CO OR 129-A2
HEPPNER-SPRAY HWY Rt#-207
MORROW CO OR 128-C3
WHEELER CO OR 128-C3
WHEELER CO OR 136-C1
HERBERT HOOVER HWY Rt#-99W
NEWBERG OR 198-D5
YAMHILL CO OR 198-D5
HERD RD
YAMHILL CO OR 198-D5
NE HEREFORD LN
JEFFERSON CO OR 208-D4
HEREFORD RD
CURRY CO OR 224-B4
HERFERD RD
LANE CO OR 210-C7
SW HERGERT RD
WASHINGTON CO OR 198-C2
HERITAGE MOUNTAIN BLVD
PORT MOODY BC 157-A4
HERMAN RD
ADAMS CO WA 121-C1
LANE CO OR 210-B6
LATAH CO ID 250-C1
OLYMPIA WA 297-E9
HERMAN CREEK RD
HOOD RIVER CO OR 194-D5
HOOD RIVER CO OR 195-A5
W HERMISTON AV Rt#-207
HERMISTON OR 129-A1
HERMISTON HWY Rt#-207
HERMISTON OR 129-A1
UMATILLA CO OR 129-A1
HERMISTON-HINKLE RD
HERMISTON OR 129-A1
UMATILLA CO OR 129-A1
HERMISTON LOOP RD
HERMISTON OR 129-A1
UMATILLA CO OR 129-A1
E HERON ST U.S.-101
ABERDEEN WA 178-B7
W HERON ST U.S.-101
ABERDEEN WA 178-B7
HERRIN RD
SHERMAN CO OR 127-C1
HERRING LN
YAMHILL CO OR 198-C5
HERRING RD
WASHINGTON CO OR 198-A2
S HERRON RD KPN
PIERCE CO WA 181-A2
E HERSEY ST
ASHLAND OR 337-D7
W HERSEY ST
ASHLAND OR 337-C6
HERSHBERGER RD
DOUGLAS CO OR 226-C1
HESS RD
BENTON CO WA 120-C3
HESSELTINE RD
STEVENS CO WA 106-A3
HESSLER FLAT RD
YAKIMA CO WA 243-A2
HEWITT AV
EVERETT WA 264-D3
EVERETT WA 265-F3
E HEWITT AV
SNOHOMISH CO WA 171-D2
HEWITT PARK HWY
BAKER CO OR 139-A1
HEYBURN RD
CHATCOLET ID 248-A6
KOOTENAI CO ID 248-A6
HEYDON RD
DOUGLAS CO OR 221-A3
HIACK RD
TILLAMOOK CO OR 203-D2
HIAWATHA RD NE
GRANT CO WA 242-B3
HIBBARD RD NE
MARION CO OR 205-B5
HICKEY RD
BONNER CO ID 244-B1
NW HICKORY LN
JEFFERSON CO OR 208-B3
HICKOX RD
SKAGIT CO WA 168-B1
HIDDEN ACRES RD
LEWIS CO WA 187-C4
NE HIDDEN COVE LN
BAINBRIDGE ISLAND WA 174-C1
NE HIDDEN COVE RD
BAINBRIDGE ISLAND WA 174-C1
HIDDEN FALLS RD
CLARK CO WA 193-C7
HIDDEN SPRINGS RD
YAMHILL CO OR 198-C5
HIDDEN VALLEY RD
BONNER CO ID 244-A1
KITTITAS CO WA 240-D2
LINCOLN CO OR 206-B5
W HIDDEN VALLEY RD
KOOTENAI CO ID 247-C1
HIGGINS AIRPORT WY
SKAGIT CO WA 161-A7
HIGGINS LOOP RD NW
DOUGLAS CO WA 236-B5
E HIGH DR
SPOKANE WA 246-C5
S HIGH DR
SPOKANE WA 246-C5
SPOKANE WA 348-H13
SPOKANE CO WA 246-C5
W HIGH DR
SPOKANE WA 246-C5
SPOKANE WA 348-J14
SPOKANE WA 349-A14
HIGH ST
BAY CITY OR 191-B7
BELLINGHAM WA 258-C8
PORT ORCHARD WA 270-H14
PRIEST RIVER ID 107-A3
SW HIGH ST
GRANTS PASS OR 335-D9
HIGH ST NE
SALEM OR 322-H13
HIGH ST SE
SALEM OR 322-H14
SALEM OR 324-H1
HIGH BRIDGE RD
SNOHOMISH CO WA 110-C1
HIGHGRADE RD
MODOC CO CA 152-A3
HIGHLAND AV
ASOTIN CO WA 250-B4
CLARKSTON WA 250-B4
GRANTS PASS OR 335-D4
JOSEPHINE CO OR 335-B1
E HIGHLAND AV
HERMISTON OR 129-A1
NW HIGHLAND AV
GRANTS PASS OR 335-E7
SW HIGHLAND AV Rt#-126
REDMOND OR 212-D5
W HIGHLAND AV
HERMISTON OR 129-A1
UMATILLA CO OR 129-A1
HIGHLAND AV NE
SALEM OR 322-J10
SALEM OR 323-A10
HIGHLAND BLVD
DISTRICT OF NORTH VANCOUV BC 156-B2
DISTRICT OF NORTH VANCOUV BC 254-J1
E HIGHLAND BLVD
SPOKANE WA 349-B12
HIGHLAND DR
BELLEVUE WA 175-C3
BELLINGHAM WA 258-C10
BENTON CO OR 327-H3
CORVALLIS OR 327-H3
ISLAND CO WA 168-A6
MEDFORD OR 336-F13
YAKIMA CO WA 120-A2
E HIGHLAND DR
ARLINGTON WA 168-D5
SW HIGHLAND LN
JEFFERSON CO OR 208-B7
HIGHLAND RD
BRITISH COLUMBIA BC 159-B6
COLUMBIA CO OR 189-C6
COLUMBIA CO WA 122-B2
HIGHLAND RD
MASON CO WA 179-D4
POLK CO OR 207-B1
TOWN OF VIEW ROYAL BC 159-B6
HIGHLAND RD NE
KITSAP CO WA 170-C5
HIGHLAND FLATS RD
BOUNDARY CO ID 107-B2
HIGHLAND PARK WY SW
SEATTLE WA 285-H1
HIGHLANDS DR NE
ISSAQUAH WA 176-A4
HIGHLAND SCHOOL RD SE
DOUGLAS CO WA 112-C2
E HIGHLAND VIEW DR
BOISE ID 253-D2
N HIGHLAND VIEW DR
BOISE ID 253-C2
S HIGHLINE DR
EAST WENATCHEE WA 239-A4
East Wenatchee Bench WA 239-A4
HIGHLINE RD
DESCHUTES CO OR 217-A2
HIGH PASS RD
JUNCTION CITY OR 210-A6
LANE CO OR 133-A2
LANE CO OR 210-A6
SE HIGH POINT WY
KING CO WA 176-A4
HIGH PRAIRIE RD
KLICKITAT CO WA 196-C4
LANE CO OR 134-A3
HIGH RIM RD
DOUGLAS CO WA 236-D4
HIGH SCHOOL DR
LINCOLN CITY OR 203-A5
NE HIGH SCHOOL RD
BAINBRIDGE ISLAND WA 271-H1
HIGH VALLEY RD
UNION CO OR 130-B2
HIGHWAY
BEND OR 332-D13
HIGHWAY 7
OKANOGAN CO WA 104-C1
OROVILLE WA 104-C1
HIGHWAY I-18
BRITISH COLUMBIA BC 101-A1
HIGHWAY I-82
YAKIMA CO WA 120-A2
HIGHWAY Rt#-1
BOUNDARY CO ID 107-B1
HIGHWAY Rt#-1A
CITY OF VICTORIA BC 256-F6
DISTRICT OF SAANICH BC 256-B5
LANGLEY BC 158-C1
HIGHWAY Rt#-3
BENEWAH CO ID 115-B3
BENEWAH CO ID 248-B6
BREMERTON WA 174-B4
BRITISH COLUMBIA BC 95-C3
BRITISH COLUMBIA BC 104-B1
BRITISH COLUMBIA BC 105-C1
BRITISH COLUMBIA BC 106-C1
GRAND FORKS BC 105-C1
GREENWOOD BC 105-B1
HOPE BC 95-A3
JULIAETTA ID 123-B2
KENDRICK ID 123-B1
KITSAP CO WA 170-C4
KITSAP CO WA 174-B4
KITSAP CO WA 270-D14
KOOTENAI CO ID 115-B2
KOOTENAI CO ID 248-D2
LATAH CO ID 115-B3
LATAH CO ID 123-B1
MASON CO WA 173-D5
MASON CO WA 174-A5
MASON CO WA 180-D1
MONTAGUE CA 150-A3
Navy Yard City WA 270-E14
NEZ PERCE CO ID 123-A2
PRINCETON BC 95-C3
SAINT MARIES ID 248-D7
SHOSHONE CO ID 115-B3
SISKIYOU CO CA 149-C3
SISKIYOU CO CA 150-A3
YREKA CA 149-C3
HIGHWAY Rt#-3B
BRITISH COLUMBIA BC 106-A1
MONTROSE BC 106-B1
ROSSLAND BC 106-A1
HIGHWAY Rt#-4
BRITISH COLUMBIA BC 92-A3
CATHLAMET WA 117-B3
PACIFIC CO WA 186-C4
PORT ALBERNI BC 92-B3
SHOSHONE CO ID 115-C2
WAHKIAKUM CO WA 117-A2
WAHKIAKUM CO WA 186-D5
WALLACE ID 115-C2
HIGHWAY Rt#-5
BENEWAH CO ID 248-A7
BRITISH COLUMBIA BC 95-C1
CHATCOLET ID 248-B6
HOPE BC 95-A3
SAINT MARIES ID 248-C7
HIGHWAY Rt#-5A
BRITISH COLUMBIA BC 95-C1
PRINCETON BC 95-C3
HIGHWAY Rt#-6
BRITISH COLUMBIA BC 106-C1
LATAH CO ID 123-B1
LATAH CO ID 249-D1
LEWIS CO WA 117-B2
PACIFIC CO WA 117-A1
PE ELL WA 117-B2
POTLATCH ID 249-D1
HIGHWAY Rt#-7
BRITISH COLUMBIA BC 95-A3
CLEARWATER CO ID 123-C2
LEWIS CO WA 118-B1
OROFINO ID 123-C2
PIERCE CO WA 118-B1
HIGHWAY Rt#-7A
DISTRICT OF BURNABY BC 156-D4
HIGHWAY Rt#-8
BEAVERTON OR 199-B1
BOVILL ID 123-B1
BRITISH COLUMBIA BC 95-C1
CLEARWATER CO ID 123-B1
ELK RIVER ID 123-C1
ELMA WA 179-B7
GRAYS HARBOR CO WA 179-C6
LATAH CO ID 123-B1
LATAH CO ID 249-D5
MCCLEARY WA 179-C6
MOSCOW ID 249-C5
THURSTON CO WA 179-D6

INDEX

INDEX

HIGHWAY U.S.-95 STREET INDEX HUNTER RD SW 375

STREET City State Page-Grid

HIGHWAY U.S.-95
HAYDEN ID 355-D1
HOMEDALE ID 147-A1
IDAHO CO ID 123-B3
IDAHO CO ID 131-C1
IDAHO CO ID 251-A1
KOOTENAI CO ID 115-A2
KOOTENAI CO ID 245-B1
KOOTENAI CO ID 247-D4
KOOTENAI CO ID 354-J13
KOOTENAI CO ID 355-D2
LAPWAI ID 123-A2
LATAH CO ID 115-A3
LATAH CO ID 249-D1
LATAH CO ID 250-C1
LEWIS CO ID 123-B2
LEWISTON ID 250-C4
MALHEUR CO OR 139-A2
MIDVALE ID 139-B1
MOSCOW ID 249-C5
NEZ PERCE CO ID 123-A2
NEZ PERCE CO ID 250-C1
OWYHEE CO ID 147-A1
PAYETTE ID 139-A3
PAYETTE CO ID 139-A2
PLUMMER ID 115-A2
PONDERAY ID 244-A1
RIGGINS ID 131-C2
SANDPOINT ID 244-A2
WASHINGTON CO ID 139-B1
WEISER ID 139-A2
WILDER ID 147-A1
WINCHESTER ID 123-B2
WORLEY ID 115-A2
HIGHWAY U.S.-97
BREWSTER WA 104-B3
CHELAN WA 236-C3
CHELAN CO WA 112-B1
CHELAN CO WA 236-D2
CHELAN CO WA 238-B1
CHELAN CO WA 239-A1
DORRIS CA 150-B3
DOUGLAS CO WA 236-D3
ELLENSBURG WA 241-B5
ENTIAT WA 236-B6
GOLDENDALE WA 127-C1
KITTITAS CO WA 111-C3
KITTITAS CO WA 238-B6
KITTITAS CO WA 240-D1
KITTITAS CO WA 241-A1
KLAMATH CO OR 150-C3
KLAMATH FALLS OR 338-C4
KLICKITAT CO WA 119-C3
KLICKITAT CO WA 127-C1
OKANOGAN WA 104-C3
OKANOGAN CO WA 104-C1
OKANOGAN CO WA 112-B1
OMAK WA 104-C2
OROVILLE WA 104-C1
PATEROS WA 104-B3
PATEROS WA 112-B1
RIVERSIDE WA 104-C2
SHERMAN CO OR 127-C1
SISKIYOU CO CA 150-C3
Sunnyslope WA 238-D3
TONASKET WA 104-C2
TOPPENISH WA 120-A2
WAPATO WA 120-A2
YAKIMA CO WA 119-C3
YAKIMA CO WA 120-A2
HIGHWAY U.S.-101
CLALLAM CO WA 109-C1
CLALLAM CO WA 162-D7
CLALLAM CO WA 163-B6
CLALLAM CO WA 164-A6
CLALLAM CO WA 165-A6
CLALLAM CO WA 166-A7
CLALLAM CO WA 169-C1
CLALLAM CO WA 262-A12
COSMOPOLIS WA 117-A1
FORKS WA 169-C1
GRAYS HARBOR CO WA 108-C2
GRAYS HARBOR CO WA 109-A2
GRAYS HARBOR CO WA 117-A1
GRAYS HARBOR CO WA 172-B3
GRAYS HARBOR CO WA 177-D2
GRAYS HARBOR CO WA 178-A1
HOQUIAM WA 178-A6
ILWACO WA 186-A6
JEFFERSON CO WA 108-C1
JEFFERSON CO WA 109-C1
JEFFERSON CO WA 169-D3
JEFFERSON CO WA 172-A1
JEFFERSON CO WA 173-D1
MASON CO WA 173-C2
MASON CO WA 180-A1
PACIFIC CO WA 117-A1
PACIFIC CO WA 183-C6
PACIFIC CO WA 186-B1
PACIFIC CO WA 188-C1
RAYMOND WA 117-A1
SEQUIM WA 166-B7
SEQUIM WA 262-E12
SHELTON WA 180-A2
SOUTH BEND WA 117-A1
THURSTON CO WA 180-B5
HIGHWAY U.S.-195
COLFAX WA 122-C1
COLTON WA 250-A1
NEZ PERCE CO ID 250-B3
SPOKANE WA 348-F11
SPOKANE CO WA 114-C2
SPOKANE CO WA 246-C6
UNIONTOWN WA 250-B1
WHITMAN CO WA 114-C3
WHITMAN CO WA 122-C1
WHITMAN CO WA 249-A4
WHITMAN CO WA 250-A1
HIGHWAY U.S.-197
KLICKITAT CO WA 196-C6
HIGHWAY U.S.-395
ADAMS CO WA 121-B1
BENTON CO WA 121-A3
COLVILLE WA 106-A2
CONNELL WA 121-B1
DEER PARK WA 114-B1
Fairwood WA 347-A6
FERRY CO WA 105-C1
FERRY CO WA 106-A1
Finley WA 121-A3
FRANKLIN CO WA 121-B1
KENNEWICK WA 121-A3
KENNEWICK WA 342-J10
KENNEWICK WA 343-B10
KETTLE FALLS WA 106-A2
MODOC CO CA 152-A3
PASCO WA 121-A2
SPOKANE CO WA 114-B1

HIGHWAY U.S.-395
SPOKANE CO WA 346-J1
SPOKANE CO WA 347-A2
STEVENS CO WA 106-A2
STEVENS CO WA 114-B1
HIGHWAY ADRIAN RD
CANYON CO ID 139-A3
HILDERBRAND LN
SHERMAN CO OR 127-C1
HILL AV
MOSES LAKE WA 242-C3
E HILL AV
MOSES LAKE WA 242-C3
HILL RD
ISLAND CO WA 167-B5
KLAMATH CO OR 235-D5
LANE CO OR 215-C1
LANE CO OR 331-F1
MODOC CO CA 151-A3
OWYHEE CO ID 147-A1
SISKIYOU CO CA 150-C3
SISKIYOU CO CA 151-A3
WASHINGTON CO ID 139-A2
WHITMAN CO WA 249-C3
YAKIMA CO WA 243-D7
N HILL RD
YAMHILL CO OR 198-A6
NW HILL RD
YAMHILL CO OR 198-A6
SW HILL RD
YAMHILL CO OR 198-A7
W HILL RD
ADA CO ID 253-B1
BOISE ID 253-B1
HILL RD NE
THURSTON CO WA 181-A5
HILL ST
ALBANY OR 326-D7
KLICKITAT CO WA 196-C7
HILL ST Rt#-162
KAMIAH ID 123-C2
HILLAIRE RD
WHATCOM CO WA 158-C7
HILLARY GRADE
WASCO CO OR 202-D2
E HILLCREST DR
KITSAP CO WA 271-D11
NE HILLCREST DR
GRANTS PASS OR 335-G6
JOSEPHINE CO OR 335-G6
NW HILLCREST DR
GRANTS PASS OR 335-F6
HILLCREST RD
HOOD RIVER CO OR 195-C7
JACKSON CO OR 234-C1
JACKSON CO OR 336-J11
MEDFORD OR 234-C1
MEDFORD OR 336-G12
HILLCREST LOOP RD
CLATSOP CO OR 117-A3
HILLDALE RD E
KITSAP CO WA 271-E9
S HILLHURST RD
RIDGEFIELD WA 192-C3
HILL LOOP RD
STEVENS CO WA 106-A1
HILLOCKBURN RD
CLACKAMAS CO OR 200-C7
HILL PASSAGE
PIERCE CO WA 181-B1
HILLS AV
LEWIS CO WA 187-D3
S HILLS DR
WENATCHEE WA 238-D4
West Wenatchee WA 238-D4
HILLS RD
ADAMS CO WA 113-C3
HILLSBORO HWY Rt#-219
NEWBERG OR 198-D5
WASHINGTON CO OR 198-D5
YAMHILL CO OR 198-D5
SW HILLSBORO HWY Rt#-219
HILLSBORO OR 198-D2
WASHINGTON CO OR 198-D2
HILLSBORO-SLVERTON HWY Rt#-214
MARION CO OR 205-B1
MARION CO OR 205-B2
MOUNT ANGEL OR 205-C3
SILVERTON OR 205-C3
WOODBURN OR 205-B2
HLLSBORO-SLVRTN HWY NE Rt#-219
MARION CO OR 205-A1
HILLSHAVEN AV
COLUMBIA CO OR 189-C7
HILLSIDE AV
CITY OF VICTORIA BC 256-H7
CITY OF VICTORIA BC 257-A6
HILLSIDE DR
PIERCE CO WA 181-C5
YAMHILL CO OR 198-C5
NW HILLSIDE RD
WASHINGTON CO OR 125-B1
HILLTOP
CROOK CO OR 213-D6
HILLTOP DR
LANE CO OR 215-D4
HILLVIEW RD
GEM CO ID 139-B3
LANE CO OR 215-C5
HILYARD AV
Altamont OR 339-C11
HILYARD ST
EUGENE OR 330-B9
HINCH RD
COOS CO OR 220-C3
HINCK RD
LINN CO OR 207-C6
HINES ST SE
SALEM OR 324-J1
SALEM OR 325-A1
HINES LOGGING RD
HARNEY CO OR 137-A3
HARNEY CO OR 145-A1
HINKLE CREEK RD
DOUGLAS CO OR 219-D7
NE HINNESS RD
CLARK CO WA 193-B4
HINTON RD
WASCO CO OR 127-C3
HINTZVILLE RD NW
KITSAP CO WA 173-D3
HIPKINS RD SW
LAKEWOOD WA 181-C4
HIRTZEL RD
COLUMBIA CO OR 189-B4

E HISTORIC COLUMBIA RIVER HWY
MULTNOMAH CO OR 200-C1
TROUTDALE OR 200-C1
NW HITE CENTER RD
KITSAP CO WA 173-D2
H LAWRENCE RD
CLARK CO WA 193-A1
HOAG RD
MOUNT VERNON WA 260-D9
HOBART RD NE
MARION CO OR 205-C4
SILVERTON OR 205-C4
NW HOBBS RD
CORNELIUS OR 198-C1
WASHINGTON CO OR 198-C1
HOBO PASS RD
SHOSHONE CO ID 115-C3
HOBSON RD
SKAGIT CO WA 161-B5
HOBSON RD SW
THURSTON CO WA 184-B4
HOBSONVILLE POINT DR
BAY CITY OR 191-B7
TILLAMOOK CO OR 191-B7
HODGEN RD
UMATILLA CO OR 121-C3
NW HODGEN RD
MILTON-FREEWATER OR 121-C3
HOEHN RD
SKAGIT CO WA 161-D6
HOERSTER LN
JACKSON CO OR 229-D4
HOFF RD
PIERCE CO WA 181-A2
HOFFMAN RD
CLACKAMAS CO OR 199-C5
INDEPENDENCE OR 204-B7
POLK CO OR 204-B7
WASHINGTON CO OR 125-B1
HOFFMAN RD NE
KITSAP CO WA 170-D4
HOFFMAN RD NW
THURSTON CO WA 180-C5
HOFFMAN RD SE
OLYMPIA WA 297-D8
SE HOFFMEISTER RD
DAMASCUS OR 200-B3
NE HOGAN DR
GRESHAM OR 200-B1
HOGAN RD
DAMASCUS OR 200-B3
DOUGLAS CO OR 219-A6
GRAYS HARBOR CO WA 177-C5
SE HOGAN RD
GRESHAM OR 200-B2
HOGAN RANCH RD
COLUMBIA CO OR 192-B3
HOGBACK RD
LAKE CO OR 144-B3
LAKE CO OR 152-B1
HOG CREEK RD
WASHINGTON CO ID 139-B1
HOGG HILL RD
MULTNOMAH CO OR 200-D3
HOG RANCH RD
KITTITAS CO WA 240-B6
HOGUM BAY RD NE
LACEY WA 181-A6
HOGUM CREEK RD
DOUGLAS CO OR 225-D6
HOIER RD
WHATCOM CO WA 158-B3
HOKO OZETTE RD
CLALLAM CO WA 162-C4
CLALLAM CO WA 163-A3
HOLBROOK RD
COLUMBIA CO OR 189-C6
S HOLCOMB BLVD
CLACKAMAS CO OR 199-D4
CLACKAMAS CO OR 200-A4
S HOLCOMB RD
ADA CO ID 253-D3
BOISE ID 253-D3
HOLCOMB HOMES RD
COWLITZ CO WA 303-F3
HOLCOMB SPRING RD
KLAMATH CO OR 235-D2
HOLCUM RD
LEWIS CO WA 187-C1
HOLDEN RD SW
LAKEWOOD WA 181-C4
SW HOLDEN ST
SEATTLE WA 284-E2
SEATTLE WA 285-F2
HOLDER LN SE
MARION CO OR 324-F7
SALEM OR 324-F7
HOLDMAN RD
HELIX OR 129-B1
UMATILLA CO OR 129-B1
HOLDOM AV
DISTRICT OF BURNABY BC 156-D4
SE HOLGATE BLVD
PORTLAND OR 317-J3
PORTLAND OR 318-B3
PORTLAND OR 319-E3
S HOLGATE ST
SEATTLE WA 282-A2
HOLIDAY BLVD
SKAGIT CO WA 160-C5
HOLIDAY VALLEY DR NW
THURSTON CO WA 180-B5
N HOLLADAY DR
SEASIDE OR 301-G7
S HOLLADAY DR
SEASIDE OR 301-G9
E HOLLAND AV
SPOKANE WA 346-J11
SPOKANE WA 347-A11
W HOLLAND AV
Country Homes WA 346-J11
HOLLAND LP
JOSEPHINE CO OR 233-B4
W HOLLILYNN DR
ADA CO ID 253-C4
HOLLINGSWORTH RD
FRANKLIN CO WA 121-A2
HOLLY DR
EVERETT WA 267-J7
EVERETT WA 268-B5
SE HOLLY LN
JEFFERSON CO OR 208-C7
HOLLY RD
MALHEUR CO OR 139-A2
NW HOLLY RD
KITSAP CO WA 173-D2
KITSAP CO WA 174-A2

HOLLY ST
MAPLE RIDGE BC 157-C5
E HOLLY ST
BELLINGHAM WA 258-D7
N HOLLY ST
CLACKAMAS CO OR 199-C6
MEDFORD OR 336-C12
S HOLLY ST
MEDFORD OR 336-C12
W HOLLY ST
BELLINGHAM WA 258-D6
HOLLY GULCH RD
BENEWAH CO ID 248-C6
HOLLY HILL RD
WASHINGTON CO OR 198-C3
HOLLYWOOD CRES
CITY OF VICTORIA BC 257-A11
HOLLYWOOD DR NE
Hayesville OR 323-E9
SALEM OR 323-E10
HOLM RD SW
THURSTON CO WA 184-A3
HOLMAN RD NW
SEATTLE WA 171-A7
SEATTLE WA 273-F1
HOLMES RD
DESCHUTES CO OR 212-B4
HOLMES POINT DR NE
KING CO WA 171-B7
HOLST RD
CLACKAMAS CO OR 200-B4
ISLAND CO WA 171-A2
HOLTON RD
JACKSON CO OR 234-B3
HOME AV
WALLA WALLA WA 345-D9
Walla Walla East WA 345-D9
HOME ACRES RD
SNOHOMISH CO WA 265-H4
SNOHOMISH CO WA 269-H1
HOME ACRES RANCH RD
KLICKITAT CO WA 196-D2
HOMEDALE RD
Altamont OR 235-D5
Altamont OR 339-A14
CANYON CO ID 147-B1
KLAMATH CO OR 235-D6
KLAMATH CO OR 339-A14
KLAMATH FALLS OR 339-A14
W HOMER LN
ADA CO ID 139-C3
HOMESTEAD RD
MORROW CO OR 128-C1
SAN JUAN CO WA 160-A3
HOMESTEAD WY
DESCHUTES CO OR 212-C4
HOMESTEADER RD
CLACKAMAS CO OR 199-B5
WASHINGTON CO OR 199-B5
WHATCOM CO WA 161-C1
E HONEYMAN RD
COLUMBIA CO OR 192-B4
N HONEYMAN RD
COLUMBIA CO OR 192-A3
SCAPPOOSE OR 192-A3
HONEYMOON BAY RD
Freeland WA 170-C1
ISLAND CO WA 167-C7
HONEYSUCKLE AV
HAYDEN ID 355-A1
KOOTENAI CO ID 355-A1
N HONEYSUCKLE DR
COEUR D'ALENE ID 355-F6
W HOOD AV
KENNEWICK WA 342-H10
HOOD ST NE
SALEM OR 322-J11
HOOD CANAL DR NE
KITSAP CO WA 170-C3
HOOD RIVER HWY
HOOD RIVER CO OR 195-B7
HOOD RIVER CO OR 202-C1
HOOD RIVER RD
MOSIER OR 196-A5
WASCO CO OR 196-A5
HOOGDAL RD
SKAGIT CO WA 161-C5
SW HOOK AND EYE LN
YAMHILL CO OR 204-B2
HOOKER RD
CLALLAM CO WA 166-A7
HOOPER WOOLAM RD
CLARK CO WA 193-A1
HOOT N HOLLER LN
DOUGLAS CO OR 221-D5
HOOVER RD
FRANKLIN CO WA 121-B1
HOOVER CREEK LN
WHEELER CO OR 128-A3
HOOVER HILL RD
DOUGLAS CO OR 221-A7
HOP CREEK RD
JACKSON CO OR 226-B5
HOPE ST
Altamont OR 338-J11
Altamont OR 339-A12
HOPE PENINSULA RD
BONNER CO ID 244-D3
HOPEWELL RD Rt#-9
WHATCOM CO WA 102-B1
HOPEWELL RD NW
POLK CO OR 204-C3
YAMHILL CO OR 204-C3
W HOPKINS ST
PASCO WA 343-B7
HOPP RD N
LINCOLN CO WA 113-B3
HOPPER AV Rt#-71
CAMBRIDGE ID 139-B1
WASHINGTON CO ID 139-B1
E HOQUIAM RD
GRAYS HARBOR CO WA 178-A6
HOQUIAM WA 178-A6
HOQUIAM WISHKAH RD
GRAYS HARBOR CO WA 178-B4
HORLICK RD
KITTITAS CO WA 240-D3
HORN LN
EUGENE OR 329-F2
LANE CO OR 329-F2
HORN RD Rt#-225
BENTON CITY WA 120-C2
BENTON CO WA 120-C2
HORNBROOK RD
SISKIYOU CO CA 150-A3
NW HORNECKER RD
WASHINGTON CO OR 198-C1

HORNER RD
DESCHUTES CO OR 212-D7
N HORNET CREEK RD
ADAMS CO ID 131-B3
ADAMS CO ID 139-B1
WASHINGTON CO ID 131-B3
HORNY HOLLOW TR
JEFFERSON CO OR 212-C2
HORRIGAN RD
BENTON CO WA 120-B3
HORSE BUTTE RD
DESCHUTES CO OR 217-D4
HORSE CREEK RD
HUMBOLDT CO NV 154-A3
WALLOWA CO OR 123-A3
HORSEFALL BEACH RD
COOS CO OR 218-A6
HORSEHEAD BAY DR
PIERCE CO WA 181-B1
HORSEMAN LN
DESCHUTES CO OR 217-B1
HORSESHOE LN
LINN CO OR 207-B5
HORSESHOE BEND RD
KLICKITAT CO WA 196-D3
SHERMAN CO OR 127-C3
HORSESHOE BEND RD Rt#-55
BOISE CO ID 139-C3
HORSESHOE BEND ID 139-C3
N HORSESHOE BEND RD
ADA CO ID 139-C3
ADA CO ID 253-B1
EAGLE ID 253-B1
N HORSESHOE BEND RD Rt#-55
ADA CO ID 139-C3
ADA CO ID 253-B1
BOISE CO ID 139-C3
EAGLE ID 253-B1
HORSESHOE LAKE RD
MARION CO OR 198-C7
HORTON RD
LANE CO OR 133-A2
HORTON GRADE RD
WHITMAN CO WA 122-B1
SE HORTSMAN RD
KITSAP CO WA 271-C14
PORT ORCHARD WA 271-B14
HOSKINS RD
DISTRICT OF NORTH VANCOUV BC 255-F1
HOSKINS-SUMMIT RD
BENTON CO OR 133-A1
S HOSMER ST
PIERCE CO WA 181-D4
TACOMA WA 181-D4
TACOMA WA 295-E7
HOSPITAL WY
BREWSTER WA 104-B3
HOSTETLER RD
ASOTIN CO WA 250-B7
HOSTETLER ST W
THE DALLES OR 196-C7
WASCO CO OR 196-C7
NE HOSTMARK ST
POULSBO WA 170-B7
HOTCHKISS LN
HARNEY CO OR 145-A1
HOT SPRINGS AV
CARSON WA 194-D4
CARSON WA 195-A4
HOT SPRINGS RD
ADAMS CO ID 251-A3
MALHEUR CO OR 154-B2
HOT SPRINGS RD Rt#-9
CITY OF HARRISON HOT SPRI BC 94-C3
DISTRICT OF KENT BC 94-C3
HOUSER WY S Rt#-900
RENTON WA 175-C5
NE HOUSLEY AV
DOUGLAS CO OR 334-F2
ROSEBURG OR 334-F2
HOUSTON RD
ISLAND CO WA 167-C5
JACKSON CO OR 234-B2
LEWIS CO ID 123-B3
SPOKANE CO WA 348-C6
N HOUSTON RD
SPOKANE CO WA 348-B6
W HOUSTON RD
SPOKANE CO WA 348-B7
HOUSTON LAKE RD
CROOK CO OR 213-C5
HOUTCHEN ST
PACIFIC CO WA 186-B7
HOVANDER RD
FERNDALE WA 158-C6
HOVENDEN RD NE
MARION CO OR 205-B1
HOWARD AV
EUGENE OR 329-F1
LANE CO OR 329-F1
HOWARD LN
LANE CO OR 210-A5
HOWARD RD
KITTITAS CO WA 241-A4
E HOWARD RD
KOOTENAI CO ID 245-B1
SE HOWARD RD
MULTNOMAH CO OR 200-D2
HOWARD ST
WALLA WALLA WA 345-C9
Walla Walla East WA 345-C9
S HOWARD ST
WALLA WALLA WA 345-C11
HOWARD CREEK RD
CROOK CO OR 136-A2
HOWARD FLAT RD
CHELAN CO WA 236-D2
HOWARDS MILL RD
CLACKAMAS CO OR 199-D7
CLACKAMAS CO OR 200-A7
HOWE
PIERCE CO WA 182-B6
HOWE LN
LANE CO OR 215-B5
HOWE ST
VANCOUVER BC 254-G9
HOWE ST Rt#-99
VANCOUVER BC 254-F10
W HOWE ST
SEATTLE WA 276-D1
SEATTLE WA 277-F2
HOWELL ST
SEATTLE WA 278-A5
HOWELL GRADE RD
GARFIELD CO WA 122-C2
HOWELL PRAIRIE RD
MARION CO OR 205-B4

HOWLETT RD
CLACKAMAS CO OR 200-C4
E HOXIE RD
SPOKANE CO WA 115-A2
E HOXIE RD Rt#-278
ROCKFORD WA 114-C2
SPOKANE CO WA 114-C2
HOYT RD SW
FEDERAL WAY WA 182-A1
NW HOYT ST
PORTLAND OR 313-E5
HOYT ST S
SALEM OR 324-G2
HOYT ST SE
SALEM OR 324-H2
H STREET RD
BLAINE WA 158-C3
WHATCOM CO WA 158-D3
HUBBARD RD
ADAMS CO ID 251-A4
LEWIS CO WA 187-A2
E HUBBARD RD
ADA CO ID 253-B4
N HUBBARD ST
COEUR D'ALENE ID 355-D11
HUBBARD CREEK RD
DOUGLAS CO OR 221-A1
HUBBARD GULCH RD
NEZ PERCE CO ID 123-B2
HUBER LN
JEFFERSON CO OR 208-B7
HUBER RD
PACIFIC CO WA 117-B2
HUCKELBERRY LN
COOS CO OR 220-B4
HUCKLEBERRY RD
JACKSON CO OR 226-D5
JACKSON CO OR 227-A4
HUDDLESTON RD
WHEELER CO OR 128-B3
E HUDLOW RD
KOOTENAI CO ID 245-A4
HUDSON RD
SKAMANIA CO WA 193-D7
SE HUDSON RD
CLACKAMAS CO OR 200-C3
HUDSON ST
CITY OF RICHMOND BC 156-B5
LONGVIEW WA 303-A9
VANCOUVER BC 156-B5
SW HUDSON ST
SEATTLE WA 280-C5
HUETTER RD
HAYDEN ID 354-H2
KOOTENAI CO ID 354-H2
N HUETTER RD
COEUR D'ALENE ID 354-H8
KOOTENAI CO ID 354-H6
NE HUFF RD
CLARK CO WA 193-A1
HUGHES AV
BLAINE WA 158-B3
WHATCOM CO WA 158-B3
HUGHES RD
CHELAN CO WA 238-C2
NE HUGHES RD
CLARK CO WA 193-C6
HUGHEY LN
TILLAMOOK CO OR 197-C2
HUGO RD
JOSEPHINE CO OR 229-A4
HUHTALA RD
LINCOLN CO OR 206-C2
HULL RD
JACKSON CO OR 234-A2
HULL ST
PORT ORCHARD WA 174-B4
PORT ORCHARD WA 270-G14
HULSE RD
CLALLAM CO WA 165-D6
HULTMAN RD
POLK CO OR 207-C1
HUMBOLDT ST
CITY OF VICTORIA BC 256-H9
HUME RD
WHITMAN CO WA 114-C3
HUMMINGBIRD RD
DOUGLAS CO OR 239-B1
HUMORIST RD
Burbank WA 121-B3
WALLA WALLA CO WA 121-B3
HUMPBACK RD
BRITISH COLUMBIA BC 159-A6
DISTRICT OF LANGFORD BC 159-A6
HUMPERT LN NE
MARION CO OR 205-C3
SW HUMPHREY BLVD
MULTNOMAH CO OR 316-B1
PORTLAND OR 316-B1
HUMPHREY RD
ISLAND CO WA 171-A2
HUMPHREY HILL RD
SKAGIT CO WA 161-B4
E HUMPHREYS RD
COOS CO OR 220-B4
W HUMPHREYS RD
COOS CO OR 220-B4
E HUMPTULIPS RD
GRAYS HARBOR CO WA 178-B2
HUMPTULIPS VALLEY RD
GRAYS HARBOR CO WA 177-D3
HUNGRY HILL RD
LANE CO OR 215-B5
HUNGRY HOLLOW RD
OKANOGAN CO WA 105-A1
HUNGRY JUNCTION RD
KITTITAS CO WA 241-B5
HUNNELL RD
DESCHUTES CO OR 217-C1
HUNT LN
JOSEPHINE CO OR 229-A6
HUNT RD
CLALLAM CO WA 165-A5
DESCHUTES CO OR 212-B4
HUNT ST NW
GIG HARBOR WA 181-B1
PIERCE CO WA 181-B1
HUNT CLUB RD
GRAYS HARBOR CO WA 183-B2
HUNTER RD
ISLAND CITY OR 130-A2
KITTITAS CO WA 241-A5
UNION CO OR 130-A2
SW HUNTER RD
KITSAP CO WA 174-B6
HUNTER RD SW
THURSTON CO WA 184-A3

INDEX

376 HUNTER CREEK LP — STREET INDEX — SE JOHANNESEN RD

STREET / City State / Page-Grid

HUNTER CREEK LP
CURRY CO OR 228-A6
HUNTER CREEK RD
CURRY CO OR 228-A6
HUNTER POINT RD NW
THURSTON CO WA 180-C4
HUNTINGDON RD
DISTRICT OF ABBOTSFORD BC 102-B1
DISTRICT OF MATSQUI BC 102-B1
HUNTINGTON AV
CASTLE ROCK WA 187-C7
CASTLE ROCK WA 189-C1
COWLITZ CO WA 189-C1
HUNTINGTON AV Rt#-411
CASTLE ROCK WA 187-C7
COWLITZ CO WA 187-C7
HUNTINGTON HWY U.S.-30
BAKER CO OR 138-C2
BAKER CO OR 139-A2
HUNTINGTON OR 138-C2
MALHEUR CO OR 139-A2
HUNTINGTON PL
LONGVIEW WA 302-J6
HUNTINGTON RD
MALHEUR CO OR 138-C2
W HUNTLEY ST
ABERDEEN WA 178-B7
COSMOPOLIS WA 178-B7
W HUNTZINGER RD
YAKIMA CO WA 243-B4
HURD RD
GRAYS HARBOR CO WA 179-B7
SE HURLBURT RD
MULTNOMAH CO OR 200-C2
HURLEY-WALDRIP RD
MASON CO WA 180-A5
HURRICANE CREEK RD
ENTERPRISE OR 130-C2
JOSEPH OR 130-C2
WALLOWA CO OR 130-C2
HURTLEY RANCH RD
DESCHUTES CO OR 212-A5
HUSKEY RD
HOOD RIVER CO OR 195-D7
WASCO CO OR 196-A6
HUSSEY ST
COLLEGE PLACE WA 344-E9
Garrett WA 344-E9
WALLA WALLA CO WA 344-E9
HUTCHENS HILL RD
GARFIELD CO WA 122-B2
HUTCHINSON RD
BRITISH COLUMBIA BC 159-A1
COLUMBIA CO OR 189-B5
HUTSON DR
HOOD RIVER CO OR 202-C2
HYACINTH ST NE
SALEM OR 323-B7
HYANNIS DR
DISTRICT OF NORTH VANCOUV BC 255-J4
HYATT RD SE
THURSTON CO WA 184-D2
HYATT PRAIRIE RD
JACKSON CO OR 150-A2
HYLINE RD
MALHEUR CO OR 139-A2
HYLO RD S
MARION CO OR 324-F11

I

I AV
ANACORTES WA 259-G4
I RD SW
DOUGLAS CO WA 239-D1
I ST
COLUMBIA CITY OR 192-B1
NEHALEM OR 191-B4
N I ST
LIND WA 121-B1
TACOMA WA 293-F3
S I ST
TACOMA WA 293-G4
SW I ST
GRANTS PASS OR 335-D9
ICE HARBOR DR
WALLA WALLA CO WA 121-B3
ICE HARBOR DR Rt#-124
WALLA WALLA CO WA 121-B3
ICICLE RD
CHELAN CO WA 238-A1
IDAHO AV U.S.-30
ONTARIO OR 139-A3
E IDAHO AV U.S.-95
HOMEDALE ID 147-A1
W IDAHO AV
ONTARIO OR 139-A3
W IDAHO AV Rt#-19
HOMEDALE ID 147-A1
W IDAHO BLVD
GEM CO ID 139-B3
N IDAHO RD
KOOTENAI CO ID 247-C1
Otis Orchards WA 352-G6
SPOKANE CO WA 352-G6
S IDAHO RD
SPOKANE CO WA 247-B4
IDAHO ST
CASCADE ID 252-D6
E IDAHO ST
BOISE ID 253-C3
N IDAHO ST
KOOTENAI CO ID 353-J3
POST FALLS ID 353-J3
S IDAHO ST
KOOTENAI CO ID 247-C1
W IDAHO ST
BOISE ID 253-C2
W IDAHO ST U.S.-95
WEISER ID 139-A2
IDAHO-OREGON-NEVADA HWY U.S.-9
HUMBOLDT CO NV 154-B3
JORDAN VALLEY OR 147-A3
MALHEUR CO OR 146-B3
MALHEUR CO OR 147-A2
MALHEUR CO OR 154-B1
OWYHEE CO ID 147-A2
IDAHO POWER RD
BAKER CO OR 131-A3
IDLERS REST RD
LATAH CO ID 249-D4
IDYLWOOD DR SE
SALEM OR 324-F5
IGO RD
GILLIAM CO OR 128-A2
IHRIG RD
WASHINGTON CO OR 198-B1

S ILER ST
MOXEE WA 243-D7
ILLAHEE RD NE
KITSAP CO WA 174-C1
KITSAP CO WA 271-C6
ILLINOIS AV U.S.-95
COUNCIL ID 139-C1
S ILLINOIS AV
PASCO WA 343-E8
ILLINOIS RIVER RD
JOSEPHINE CO OR 233-A1
ILLINOIS VALLEY RD
DEL NORTE CO CA 233-B7
ILLINOIS VALLEY PARK RD
CAVE JUNCTION OR 233-B4
JOSEPHINE CO OR 233-B4
ILMARI RD
COLUMBIA CO OR 189-A3
IMBLER LN
JEFFERSON CO OR 208-C7
IMBODEN RD
LEWIS CO WA 187-B5
IMHOFF RD
WHATCOM CO WA 158-C6
IMMIGRANT RD
LANE CO OR 215-D4
S IMMONEN RD
LINCOLN CO OR 203-A6
IMPERIAL ST
DISTRICT OF BURNABY BC 156-C5
INCHELIUM-KETTLE FALLS RD
FERRY CO WA 105-C2
Inchelium WA 105-C2
INDEPENDENCE HWY
BENTON CO OR 207-B4
INDEPENDENCE HWY Rt#-51
POLK CO OR 204-B6
INDEPENDENCE RD
YAKIMA CO WA 120-B2
INDEPENDENCE RD SW
LEWIS CO WA 117-B1
INDEX-GALENA RD
SNOHOMISH CO WA 111-A1
INDIAN RD
Shelter Bay WA 167-D1
SKAGIT CO WA 160-D7
SKAGIT CO WA 167-D1
INDIAN ST
BELLINGHAM WA 258-D8
E INDIANA AV
SPOKANE WA 349-A7
SPOKANE VALLEY WA 350-J6
SPOKANE VALLEY WA 351-A6
S INDIANA AV
CALDWELL ID 147-B1
CANYON CO ID 147-B1
W INDIANA AV
SPOKANE WA 348-J7
SPOKANE WA 349-A7
INDIAN CAMP RD SW
DOUGLAS CO WA 239-B2
INDIAN CEMETERY RD
KOOTENAI CO ID 248-A5
INDIAN CHURCH RD
GRANGER WA 120-A2
YAKIMA CO WA 120-A2
INDIAN CREEK DR
DOUGLAS CO OR 219-A6
INDIAN CREEK RD
DESCHUTES CO OR 216-C7
GRANT CO OR 137-B2
HOOD RIVER CO OR 195-C5
JOSEPHINE CO OR 233-B1
LANE CO OR 209-D7
SISKIYOU CO CA 149-A3
INDIAN FORD RD
DESCHUTES CO OR 211-C4
INDIAN FORT CREEK RD
MALHEUR CO OR 146-C3
INDIAN GULCH RD
MALHEUR CO OR 138-B2
INDIAN HEAD RD
WASHINGTON CO ID 139-A2
INDIAN MOUNTAIN RD
KOOTENAI CO ID 248-B6
INDIANOLA RD NE
Indianola WA 170-C6
INDIAN RIVER DR
DISTRICT OF NORTH VANCOUV BC 156-D3
INDIAN SCHOOL RD NE
SALEM OR 323-C5
N INDIAN TRAIL RD
SPOKANE WA 346-C12
SPOKANE CO WA 346-A9
W INDIAN TRAIL RD
SPOKANE WA 346-D14
SPOKANE WA 348-E1
INDIAN VALLEY RD
ADAMS CO ID 139-C1
INDUSTRIAL RD
ABERDEEN WA 178-A7
CITY OF SURREY BC 157-A5
HOQUIAM WA 178-A7
INDUSTRIAL WY Rt#-432
COWLITZ CO WA 302-D8
LONGVIEW WA 302-D8
LONGVIEW WA 303-A12
INGALLS LN
JOSEPHINE CO OR 229-A7
INGALLS RD
LEWIS CO WA 117-B1
WAHKIAKUM CO WA 117-B2
INGLE CREEK RD
GRANT CO OR 137-A2
INGLEWOOD AV
DISTRICT OF WEST VANCOUVE BC 254-C3
INGLEWOOD HILL RD
SAMMAMISH WA 175-D2
INGRAM LN NW
YAMHILL CO OR 204-C2
INGRAM ISLAND RD
BENTON CO OR 133-B2
INITIAL PEAK RD
KOOTENAI CO ID 248-D3
INLAND ST U.S.-195
WHITMAN CO WA 114-C3
N INLAND ST
SPOKANE CO WA 246-A2
INLAND EMPIRE HWY
GRANDVIEW WA 120-B3
SUNNYSIDE WA 120-B2
YAKIMA CO WA 120-A2
INLAND EMPIRE HWY U.S.-12
ASOTIN CO WA 250-B4
Garrett WA 344-D7
WALLA WALLA CO WA 344-D7

S INLAND EMPIRE HWY U.S.-195
SPOKANE WA 246-C5
SPOKANE CO WA 246-C5
N INLAND EMPIRE RD
GRANDVIEW WA 120-B3
S INLAND EMPIRE WY
SPOKANE WA 348-G12
INLAND ISLAND HWY Rt#-19
BRITISH COLUMBIA BC 92-A1
NW INLET AV
LINCOLN CITY OR 203-A4
INLET DR Rt#-7A
DISTRICT OF BURNABY BC 156-D4
INNES RD
DESCHUTES CO OR 212-B7
INTERLAAKEN DR SW
LAKEWOOD WA 181-C4
INTERNATIONAL BLVD Rt#-99
DES MOINES WA 290-C5
SEATAC WA 288-D7
SEATAC WA 290-C5
TUKWILA WA 288-D7
INTERNATIONAL WY
LANE CO OR 330-F1
SPRINGFIELD OR 330-F1
INTER-PROVINCIAL HWY
DISTRICT OF ABBOTSFORD BC 94-B3
DISTRICT OF ABBOTSFORD BC 102-B1
DISTRICT OF MATSQUI BC 102-B1
N INTERSTATE AV
PORTLAND OR 308-E4
PORTLAND OR 309-E6
PORTLAND OR 313-E1
INTERURBAN AV S
TUKWILA WA 286-D7
TUKWILA WA 287-E7
TUKWILA WA 289-G2
INTERURBAN RD
DISTRICT OF SAANICH BC 256-D1
INTERVALE RD
YAMHILL CO OR 198-B6
IOCO RD
PORT MOODY BC 157-A4
IOLANDA PL
WHATCOM CO WA 101-C1
IONE RD
FRANKLIN CO WA 121-A2
N IONE ST
KENNEWICK WA 343-C10
IONE-BOARDMAN RD
MORROW CO OR 128-B2
IONE-GOOSEBERRY RD
MORROW CO OR 128-B2
IOWA
CROOK CO OR 213-D6
S IOWA AV
East Wenatchee Bench WA 239-A5
PAYETTE ID 139-A3
PAYETTE CO ID 139-A3
IOWA AV N
PAYETTE ID 139-A3
PAYETTE CO ID 139-A3
IOWA ST
ASHLAND OR 337-D8
BELLINGHAM WA 258-F6
IOWA HEIGHTS RD
WHATCOM CO WA 161-B2
IOWA HILL RD
WASHINGTON CO OR 198-C2
IRBY RD
LINCOLN CO WA 113-B2
IRBY RD N
LINCOLN CO WA 113-B2
IRELAND RD
WALLA WALLA CO WA 121-C3
NE IRELAND RD
CLARK CO WA 193-C6
IRENE ST
WALLA WALLA WA 344-H7
W IRENE ST
BOISE ID 253-C2
SW IRIS LN
CULVER OR 208-B7
JEFFERSON CO OR 208-A7
IRISH RD
TILLAMOOK CO OR 203-C1
IRISH BEND LP
LINN CO OR 210-A3
IRONDALE RD
Hadlock-Irondale WA 170-A1
Irondale WA 263-E14
IRON MOUNTAIN BLVD
LAKE OSWEGO OR 320-E6
LAKE OSWEGO OR 321-E6
IRON MOUNTAIN RD
MALHEUR CO OR 146-A3
IRONWOOD DR
JACKSON CO OR 230-D4
W IRONWOOD DR
COEUR D'ALENE ID 355-C8
IRVING AV
ASTORIA OR 300-F5
W IRVING AV
ASTORIA OR 300-B5
SW IRVING LN
JEFFERSON CO OR 208-B7
IRVING RD
EUGENE OR 215-A1
LANE CO OR 215-A1
Santa Clara OR 215-A1
IRVINGTON DR
Santa Clara OR 215-A1
SE ISAAC AV
PENDLETON OR 129-B1
SW ISAAC AV
PENDLETON OR 129-B1
E ISAACS AV
WALLA WALLA WA 345-C6
WALLA WALLA WA 345-H5
ISLAND DR
COLUMBIA CO OR 189-D7
N ISLAND DR
MASON CO WA 180-C2
S ISLAND DR
MASON CO WA 180-C2
ISLAND HWY Rt#-1
BRITISH COLUMBIA BC 101-A1
BRITISH COLUMBIA BC 159-B6
DISTRICT OF LANGFORD BC 159-B6
DISTRICT OF SAANICH BC 256-D4
DUNCAN BC 101-A1
TOWN OF VIEW ROYAL BC 159-B6
TOWN OF VIEW ROYAL BC 256-D4
ISLAND HWY Rt#-1A
TOWN OF VIEW ROYAL BC 256-A5
ISLAND HWY N Rt#-19
BRITISH COLUMBIA BC 93-A3

ISLAND HWY N Rt#-19
NANAIMO BC 93-A3
ISLAND HWY N Rt#-19A
BRITISH COLUMBIA BC 93-A3
NANAIMO BC 93-A3
SE ISLAND CREST WY
MERCER ISLAND WA 175-C3
ISLAND SHORE RD
MASON CO WA 180-D3
ISOM RD
LINN CO OR 210-A4
ISRAEL RD SW
TUMWATER WA 296-E13
SE ISSAQUAH FALL CITY RD
KING CO WA 176-A3
ISSAQUAH HOBART RD
ISSAQUAH WA 176-A5
KING CO WA 176-A5
ISSAQUAH PINE LAKE RD SE
KING CO WA 176-A3
SAMMAMISH WA 176-A3
IVANHOE AV
MALHEUR CO OR 139-A3
N IVANHOE ST U.S.-30
PORTLAND OR 192-B7
IVAN MORSE RD
CHELAN CO WA 236-B1
IVERSON RD
DOUGLAS CO OR 221-A2
ISLAND CO WA 168-A4
SNOHOMISH CO WA 110-C1
YAKIMA CO WA 120-A2
NE IVERSON RD
KITSAP CO WA 170-C6
IVORY PINE RD
KLAMATH CO OR 151-B1
IVY AV
GERVAIS OR 205-B2
IVY LN
DESCHUTES CO OR 212-A6
JEFFERSON CO OR 208-D3
NW IVY LN
JEFFERSON CO OR 208-B3
IVY ST Rt#-99
JUNCTION CITY OR 210-A5
N IVY ST
CANBY OR 199-C6
S IVY ST
CANBY OR 199-C6
IZEE-OFFICER RANCH RD
GRANT CO OR 137-A3
IZEE RD TO BUSH RANCH RD
GRANT CO OR 137-A3

J

J ST
COSMOPOLIS WA 178-B7
HUBBARD OR 205-B1
MARION CO OR 205-B1
E J ST
HUBBARD OR 205-C1
S J ST
TACOMA WA 293-G6
TACOMA WA 295-G1
SE J ST
GRANTS PASS OR 335-F9
MADRAS OR 208-C5
SW J ST
GRANTS PASS OR 335-E9
MADRAS OR 208-C5
J ST SE
QUINCY WA 112-B3
J ST SW
QUINCY WA 112-B3
JACKADEL LN
JOSEPHINE CO OR 233-B5
JACK CREEK RD
JEFFERSON CO OR 211-B1
JOSEPHINE CO OR 229-C3
S JACK CREEK RD
JEFFERSON CO OR 211-B1
SW JACK CREEK LOOP RD
JEFFERSON CO OR 211-B1
JACK FALLS RD
COLUMBIA CO OR 189-C5
JACK LAKE RD
JEFFERSON CO OR 211-B1
JACKLIN RD
DISTRICT OF LANGFORD BC 159-B6
JACKMAN RD
WHATCOM CO WA 158-D3
JACK MOUNTAIN RD
HARNEY CO OR 145-B3
JACK MOUNTAIN SPUR
HARNEY CO OR 145-B2
JACKSHA RD
LATAH CO ID 249-C6
JACKSON AV
KITSAP CO WA 174-C4
PIERCE CO WA 181-C5
TACOMA WA 181-C5
S JACKSON AV
TACOMA WA 181-C2
E JACKSON BLVD
MEDFORD OR 336-F11
JACKSON HWY
CHEHALIS WA 299-G14
LEWIS CO WA 184-C7
LEWIS CO WA 187-D1
LEWIS CO WA 299-G14
JACKSON HWY S
LEWIS CO WA 187-C5
JACKSON RD
Birch Bay WA 158-B5
COWLITZ CO WA 189-A2
WASHINGTON CO ID 139-A2
E JACKSON RD
SPOKANE CO WA 247-A5
S JACKSON RD
CLACKAMAS CO OR 205-D1
SPOKANE CO WA 114-C2
SPOKANE CO WA 247-A5
JACKSON ST
ALBANY OR 326-D8
PORT TOWNSEND WA 263-H3
E JACKSON ST
MEDFORD OR 336-E11
N JACKSON ST
GENESEE ID 250-C1
N JACKSON ST U.S.-95
MOSCOW ID 249-C5
NE JACKSON ST
ROSEBURG OR 334-G7
S JACKSON ST
SEATTLE WA 277-J7
SEATTLE WA 278-A7

S JACKSON ST U.S.-95
MOSCOW ID 249-C5
SE JACKSON ST
ROSEBURG OR 334-F8
W JACKSON ST
MEDFORD OR 336-B11
JACKSON CANYON RD
DOUGLAS CO WA 236-D4
JACKSON CREEK RD
DOUGLAS CO OR 141-C3
DOUGLAS CO OR 226-A2
MALHEUR CO OR 154-B2
JACKSON HILL RD
MARION CO OR 207-D1
JACKSON LAKE RD KPN
PIERCE CO WA 181-A1
NE JACKSON SCHOOL RD
HILLSBORO OR 198-D1
NW JACKSON SCHOOL RD
WASHINGTON CO OR 125-C1
JACKSON TRAIL RD
JEFFERSON CO OR 208-A5
JACKSONVILLE HWY
JACKSON CO OR 234-A1
JACKSONVILLE HWY Rt#-238
GRANTS PASS OR 229-B7
GRANTS PASS OR 335-C14
JACKSON CO OR 149-B2
JACKSON CO OR 234-A1
JACKSONVILLE OR 149-B2
JACKSONVILLE OR 234-A1
JOSEPHINE CO OR 149-B2
JOSEPHINE CO OR 229-B7
JOSEPHINE CO OR 335-C14
JACK VAUGHN RD
GRANT CO OR 137-A1
SW JACOBSEN RD
SEATTLE WA 280-C5
JACOBSON BLVD
BREMERTON WA 271-B10
KITSAP CO WA 271-B9
JACOBSON RD
PACIFIC CO WA 183-B4
JACOMBS RD
CITY OF RICHMOND BC 156-C6
JACOT RD
BENEWAH CO ID 248-D7
JADWIN AV
RICHLAND WA 340-F12
RICHLAND WA 341-G1
JAEGER RD
DESCHUTES CO OR 212-B4
JAGER LN
LANE CO OR 210-A5
JAGLA RD
CHELAN CO WA 239-A5
N JAMES AV
East Wenatchee Bench WA 239-A4
JAMES RD
BELLINGHAM WA 258-E3
CLALLAM CO WA 169-A2
WHATCOM CO WA 258-E3
WHITMAN CO WA 249-A1
JAMES RD SW
THURSTON CO WA 184-A4
JAMES ST
BELLINGHAM WA 258-E5
SEATTLE WA 278-A6
E JAMES ST
KENT WA 175-C7
E JAMES ST U.S.-195
COLFAX WA 122-C1
N JAMES ST
MARION CO OR 205-C4
SILVERTON OR 205-C4
S JAMES ST
SILVERTON OR 205-C4
W JAMES ST
KENT WA 175-B7
E JAMES WY
SEATTLE WA 278-B6
JAMES BROOKS RD
COLUMBIA CO OR 192-A2
JAMES HOWE RD
POLK CO OR 204-A5
JAMESON ST
SEDRO-WOOLLEY WA 161-C6
JAMESON LAKE RD
DOUGLAS CO WA 112-C2
JAMESON LAKE EAST ACCESS RD NE
DOUGLAS CO WA 112-C2
JAMES SCHOOLHOUSE LN
BAKER CO OR 138-B1
JAMESTOWN AV
BENTON CO OR 133-B2
E JAMIESON RD
SPOKANE CO WA 246-C5
NE JA MOORE RD
CLARK CO WA 192-D2
JANETA AV
MALHEUR CO OR 139-A3
JANICE AV NE
Hayesville OR 323-F7
JANICKI RD
SKAGIT CO WA 161-C7
JANSHAW RD
COLUMBIA CO OR 189-B7
JANSKY RD E
PIERCE CO WA 182-C6
JANTZ RD
ADAMS CO WA 121-B1
JAPANESE HOLLOW RD
WASCO CO OR 127-B2
JAQUITH RD
WASHINGTON CO OR 198-D4
YAMHILL CO OR 198-D4
JARE ST SW
Grand Mound WA 184-B4
THURSTON CO WA 184-B4
JARED RD
MASON CO WA 180-D3
JASPER RD
JEFFERSON CO OR 208-C7
JEFFERSON CO OR 213-A1
LANE CO OR 215-D3
LANE CO OR 331-F9
SPRINGFIELD OR 331-C9
JASPER RDEX
SPRINGFIELD OR 331-H7
JASPER-LOWELL RD
LANE CO OR 133-C3
LANE CO OR 215-D3
LOWELL OR 133-C3
JAYNES DR
JOSEPHINE CO OR 229-B7
J BURTON RD
KOOTENAI CO ID 247-C6

JEFFERS CREEK RD
DOUGLAS CO OR 219-C7
JEFFERSON AV
CORVALLIS OR 327-G10
JEFFERSON AV Rt#-361
JEFFERSON CO OR 208-B6
METOLIUS OR 208-B6
S JEFFERSON AV
TACOMA WA 293-H7
TACOMA WA 295-G1
JEFFERSON DR
MALHEUR CO OR 139-A3
JEFFERSON HWY
JEFFERSON OR 207-D3
LINN CO OR 207-D3
MARION CO OR 207-D2
JEFFERSON ST
EUGENE OR 329-J7
OLYMPIA WA 296-J6
PORT TOWNSEND WA 263-G5
E JEFFERSON ST
STAYTON OR 133-C1
N JEFFERSON ST
BENTON CO WA 342-E8
NW JEFFERSON ST
ROSEBURG OR 334-C5
SE JEFFERSON ST Rt#-223
DALLAS OR 204-A6
SW JEFFERSON ST
PORTLAND OR 312-D6
JEFFERSON WY
CORVALLIS OR 327-E10
SNOHOMISH CO WA 171-B4
JEFFERSON-MARION RD
JEFFERSON OR 207-D3
MARION CO OR 133-C1
MARION CO OR 207-D3
JEFFERSON-SCIO DR
JEFFERSON OR 207-D3
LINN CO OR 133-C1
MARION CO OR 133-C1
MARION CO OR 207-D3
SCIO OR 133-C1
JEFFRIES RD
LEWIS CO WA 184-A7
J E JOHNSON RD
COWLITZ CO WA 189-D6
JELDNESS RD
PACIFIC CO WA 186-B5
JEMTEGAARD RD
SKAMANIA CO WA 193-D7
JENCK RD
TILLAMOOK CO OR 197-B7
JENKINS CREEK RD
WASHINGTON CO ID 139-A2
JENNINGS RD
WHITMAN CO WA 249-B6
JENNY CREEK RD
CLARK CO WA 192-C1
JENSEN RD
LATAH CO ID 249-D6
SNOHOMISH CO WA 168-B4
W JENSEN RD
SPOKANE CO WA 246-A6
JENTGES RD
IDAHO CO ID 123-C3
JEPPESEN ACRES RD
EUGENE OR 330-B2
JERICHO LN
JEFFERSON CO OR 212-D1
JERNSTEDT RD
YAMHILL CO OR 198-B6
JEROME PRAIRIE RD
JOSEPHINE CO OR 229-A7
JERRYS FLAT RD
CURRY CO OR 228-A5
GOLD BEACH OR 228-A5
JERUSALEM HILL RD NW
YAMHILL CO OR 204-C3
JERVIS ST
VANCOUVER BC 254-F9
JESS RD
WHATCOM CO WA 158-C4
JESSUP RD
IDAHO CO ID 123-C3
NE JESSUP ST
PORTLAND OR 309-G7
JETTY AV
LINCOLN CITY OR 203-A4
JETTY RD
CLATSOP CO OR 188-A1
N JETTY RD Rt#-115
GRAYS HARBOR CO WA 177-B6
JEWELL RD
SNOHOMISH CO WA 171-C5
E JEWETT BLVD Rt#-141
WHITE SALMON WA 195-D4
W JEWETT BLVD Rt#-141
KLICKITAT CO WA 195-D4
WHITE SALMON WA 195-D4
JEWETT RD
ISLAND CO WA 171-A3
JIM ST
PACIFIC CO WA 186-A5
JIM CREEK RD
SNOHOMISH CO WA 102-C3
JIM CREEK SPUR
JACKSON CO OR 226-B5
JIM DAVIS RD
WHITMAN CO WA 114-B3
JIM TOWN LN
LOSTINE OR 130-C1
WALLOWA CO OR 130-C1
JINGLE POT RD
BRITISH COLUMBIA BC 93-A3
NANAIMO BC 93-A3
J LINE RD
GRAYS HARBOR CO WA 117-B1
J M DICKENSON RD SW
KITSAP CO WA 174-A5
JOE JOHNS RD
Ocean Park WA 186-A2
PACIFIC CO WA 186-A2
JOELSON RD
DOUGLAS CO OR 221-A2
JOE MILLER RD
CHELAN CO WA 239-A6
JOE MOSES RD
OKANOGAN CO WA 105-B3
JOE NEY-DAVIS SL RD
COOS CO OR 220-C2
JOE SHERWOOD RD
STEVENS CO WA 114-A1
JOE WRIGHT RD
KLAMATH CO OR 235-C5
SE JOHANNESEN RD
MULTNOMAH CO OR 200-D2

INDEX

INDEX

INDEX

E MAIN ST U.S.-12 STREET INDEX MAUPIN RD 381

STREET
City State Page-Grid

E MAIN ST U.S.-12
LEWISTON ID 250-C4
E MAIN ST U.S.-26
GRANT CO OR 137-B2
JOHN DAY OR 137-B2
E MAIN ST U.S.-95
WEISER ID 139-A2
E MAIN ST U.S.-395
MOUNT VERNON OR 137-A2
N MAIN ST
BOARDMAN OR 128-C1
EAST WENATCHEE WA 239-A4
East Wenatchee Bench WA 239-A4
FALLS CITY OR 125-B3
MABTON WA 120-B3
MERIDIAN ID 253-A3
MILTON-FREEWATER OR 121-C3
MOSCOW ID 249-C5
PENDLETON OR 129-B1
PRINEVILLE OR 213-D4
SPANGLE WA 114-C2
TOLEDO OR 206-C4
N MAIN ST Rt#-47
BANKS OR 125-B1
N MAIN ST Rt#-51
INDEPENDENCE OR 204-B7
POLK CO OR 204-B7
N MAIN ST Rt#-82
JOSEPH OR 130-C2
WALLOWA CO OR 130-C2
N MAIN ST Rt#-99
ASHLAND OR 337-C6
CANYONVILLE OR 225-C3
JACKSON CO OR 337-C6
PHOENIX OR 234-B2
N MAIN ST Rt#-203
UNION OR 130-B2
N MAIN ST Rt#-214
MOUNT ANGEL OR 205-C3
N MAIN ST Rt#-231
SPRINGDALE WA 106-B3
N MAIN ST Rt#-240
NEWBERG OR 198-D5
N MAIN ST U.S.-95
LATAH CO ID 249-C4
MOSCOW ID 249-C5
N MAIN ST U.S.-195
COLFAX WA 122-C1
N MAIN ST U.S.-395
COLVILLE WA 106-A2
S MAIN ST
BOARDMAN OR 128-C1
DALLAS OR 204-A6
FALLS CITY OR 125-B3
INDEPENDENCE OR 204-A6
JEFFERSON OR 207-D3
KLAMATH CO OR 150-C3
MARION CO OR 205-C3
MARION CO OR 207-D3
MERIDIAN ID 253-A3
MERRILL OR 150-C2
MILTON-FREEWATER OR 121-C3
MOUNT ANGEL OR 205-C3
PENDLETON OR 129-B1
SPANGLE WA 114-C2
SPOKANE CO WA 114-C2
TOLEDO OR 206-C4
S MAIN ST Rt#-11
MILTON-FREEWATER OR 121-C3
S MAIN ST Rt#-18
WILLAMINA OR 125-A3
S MAIN ST Rt#-19
CONDON OR 128-A2
S MAIN ST Rt#-47
BANKS OR 125-B1
WASHINGTON CO OR 125-B1
S MAIN ST Rt#-51
INDEPENDENCE OR 204-B7
S MAIN ST Rt#-82
JOSEPH OR 130-C2
S MAIN ST Rt#-99
CANYONVILLE OR 225-C3
S MAIN ST Rt#-223
DALLAS OR 204-A6
S MAIN ST Rt#-237
UNION OR 130-B2
S MAIN ST U.S.-95
BONNERS FERRY ID 107-B2
MOSCOW ID 249-C5
S MAIN ST U.S.-195
COLFAX WA 122-C1
S MAIN ST U.S.-395
COLVILLE WA 106-A2
SE MAIN ST
MILWAUKIE OR 321-J2
ROSEBURG OR 334-F8
SW MAIN ST
PORTLAND OR 313-E6
SHERWOOD OR 199-A4
W MAIN ST
ALMIRA WA 237-D7
AUBURN WA 182-B1
BATTLE GROUND WA 193-A3
BOISE ID 253-C2
CENTRALIA WA 299-E4
COTTAGE GROVE OR 215-B7
ELMA WA 179-B7
GRANDVIEW WA 120-B3
JACKSON CO OR 234-A1
JACKSON CO OR 336-A12
KELSO WA 303-C8
LANE CO OR 215-B7
LONG CREEK OR 137-A1
LYNDEN WA 158-D4
MARION CO OR 205-C4
MEDFORD OR 234-A1
MEDFORD OR 336-C12
MONMOUTH OR 204-B7
MONROE WA 110-C1
PULLMAN WA 249-A5
ROGUE RIVER OR 229-D6
SANDPOINT ID 244-A2
SILVERTON OR 205-C4
SNOHOMISH CO WA 110-C1
WALLA WALLA WA 344-J8
WALLA WALLA WA 345-A8
WHATCOM CO WA 158-D4
WHITMAN CO WA 249-A5
WILLAMINA OR 125-A3
W MAIN ST Rt#-13
GRANGEVILLE ID 123-C3
IDAHO CO ID 123-C3
W MAIN ST Rt#-18
SHERIDAN OR 125-B3
W MAIN ST Rt#-27
GARFIELD WA 114-C3
W MAIN ST Rt#-44
CANYON CO ID 147-B1

W MAIN ST Rt#-44
MIDDLETON ID 147-B1
W MAIN ST Rt#-47
CARLTON OR 198-B6
W MAIN ST Rt#-99
CANYONVILLE OR 225-C3
W MAIN ST Rt#-211
CLACKAMAS CO OR 126-A3
MOLALLA OR 126-A3
W MAIN ST Rt#-213
SILVERTON OR 205-C4
W MAIN ST Rt#-502
BATTLE GROUND WA 192-D3
BATTLE GROUND WA 193-A3
W MAIN ST U.S.-12
DAYTON WA 122-B2
W MAIN ST U.S.-26
MOUNT VERNON OR 137-A2
W MAIN ST U.S.-95
WEISER ID 139-A2
W MAIN ST U.S.-395
GRANT CO OR 137-B2
JOHN DAY OR 137-B2
MAIN ST E
SUMNER WA 182-B3
MAIN ST N
COUPEVILLE WA 167-B4
MAIN ST S
MONTESANO WA 178-D7
MAIN ST S Rt#-20
OMAK WA 104-C3
MAIN EAST WEST RD
MODOC CO CA 151-A3
MAIN LINE RD
CLALLAM CO WA 162-C2
MAINLINE RD
MASON CO WA 180-A4
S MAITLAND AV
PASCO WA 343-H9
MAJOR CREEK RD
KLICKITAT CO WA 196-A4
MAKI RD
VALLEY CO ID 251-C7
MAKINSTER RD
TILLAMOOK CO OR 197-B1
W MALAGA RD
CHELAN CO WA 239-A5
MALAGA ALCOA HWY
Appleyard WA 239-A5
CHELAN CO WA 239-A5
MALAVIEW ST
TOWN OF SIDNEY BC 159-C2
MALCOM MCCLARTY
PIERCE CO WA 182-A4
MALDEN RD
MALDEN WA 114-C3
WHITMAN CO WA 114-C3
NE MALHEUR AV
ROSEBURG OR 334-G6
MALHEUR CAVE RD
HARNEY CO OR 146-A2
MALHEUR LINE RD
BAKER CO OR 138-C2
MALHEUR RESERVOIR RD
BAKER CO OR 138-B2
MALHEUR CO OR 138-B2
MALIN LP
KLAMATH CO OR 151-A2
N MALIN RD
KLAMATH CO OR 151-A2
MALLIS LANDING RD
PACIFIC CO WA 117-A1
MALONEY MOUNTAIN RD
COLUMBIA CO WA 122-B2
MALPASS RD
LINN CO OR 210-A4
MALTBY RD Rt#-524
BOTHELL WA 171-C5
SNOHOMISH CO WA 171-C5
MANASTASH RD
KITTITAS CO WA 240-C6
KITTITAS CO WA 241-A6
MANDY RD
LEWIS CO WA 187-C5
MANETTE BRDG
BREMERTON WA 270-J10
BREMERTON WA 271-A10
MANILA CREEK RD
FERRY CO WA 113-B1
MANION RD
CLATSOP CO OR 188-B4
NE MANITOU BEACH DR
BAINBRIDGE ISLAND WA 174-D1
MANLEY RD
WHATCOM CO WA 161-B2
MANLEY RD NW
KITSAP CO WA 174-A1
MANN RD
KLAMATH CO OR 235-C6
LANE CO OR 209-D6
LINCOLN CO WA 114-A2
SKAGIT CO WA 168-A2
SNOHOMISH CO WA 110-C1
UMATILLA CO OR 129-C1
MANN CREEK RD
WASHINGTON CO ID 139-B2
MANNERS RD
LEWIS CO WA 117-B1
LEWIS CO WA 184-A4
THURSTON CO WA 184-A4
MANNERS RD SW
LEWIS CO WA 117-B1
MANNING DR
LINN CO OR 210-C1
MANNING BASIN RD
BAKER CO OR 138-C1
MANNTHEY RD
MULTNOMAH CO OR 200-D2
W MANOR PL
SEATTLE WA 272-D6
MANOR WY
SNOHOMISH CO WA 171-B4
MANSFIELD RD NE
DOUGLAS CO WA 112-C1
MANSFIELD BARKER RD
KLICKITAT CO WA 196-A5
MANSON BLVD
CHELAN CO WA 236-B2
MANSON RD
DISTRICT OF MISSION BC 94-B3
NW MANZANITA AV
GRANTS PASS OR 335-E7
MANZANITA RD NE
BAINBRIDGE ISLAND WA 174-C1
MANZER ST
DISTRICT OF MISSION BC 94-B3
MAPLE AV
LA CONNER WA 167-D1

MAPLE AV
SNOHOMISH WA 171-D3
NE MAPLE AV
DESCHUTES CO OR 212-D5
REDMOND OR 212-D5
NW MAPLE AV
DESCHUTES CO OR 212-D5
REDMOND OR 212-D5
MAPLE AV E
PORT ORCHARD WA 271-A14
MAPLE CRES
MAPLE RIDGE BC 157-C5
MAPLE CT
BOTHELL WA 171-C6
MAPLE DR
GRANT CO WA 242-C2
LANE CO OR 210-A7
MAPLE RD
SNOHOMISH CO WA 171-B5
MAPLE ST
ASHLAND OR 337-B6
LONGVIEW WA 302-J8
LONGVIEW WA 303-B9
NORTH BEND OR 333-E4
SODAVILLE OR 133-C2
WENATCHEE WA 238-D4
West Wenatchee WA 238-D4
MAPLE ST Rt#-173
BRIDGEPORT WA 112-C1
DOUGLAS CO WA 112-C1
MAPLE ST Rt#-529
EVERETT WA 265-F4
E MAPLE ST
BELLINGHAM WA 258-D7
CENTRALIA WA 299-F4
YAKIMA WA 243-C6
N MAPLE ST
SPOKANE WA 348-G1
WALDPORT OR 328-D5
N MAPLE ST Rt#-47
YAMHILL OR 198-B4
NE MAPLE ST
PULLMAN WA 249-B5
S MAPLE ST
SPOKANE WA 348-H10
WALDPORT OR 328-D5
S MAPLE ST Rt#-47
YAMHILL OR 198-B5
MAPLE WY
YAKIMA CO WA 243-A5
MAPLE DELL RD
JACKSON CO OR 234-A7
MAPLE GROVE RD
CLACKAMAS CO OR 205-D4
POLK CO OR 133-B1
N MAPLE GROVE RD
BOISE ID 253-B2
S MAPLE GROVE RD
ADA CO ID 253-B3
BOISE ID 253-B3
CLACKAMAS CO OR 126-A3
MAPLE GULCH RD
JACKSON CO OR 230-B3
MAPLE HEIGHTS RD
EVERETT WA 268-A1
S MAPLELANE RD
CLACKAMAS CO OR 199-D5
OREGON CITY OR 199-D5
MAPLE PARK AV SE
OLYMPIA WA 296-H6
E MAPLETON RD
LANE CO OR 214-D2
MAPLETON-JCT CITY HWY
Rt#-36
LANE CO OR 132-C3
LANE CO OR 133-B2
LANE CO OR 210-A6
LANE CO OR 214-D2
MAPLE VALLEY HWY Rt#-169
KING CO WA 175-C5
RENTON WA 175-C5
MAPLE VALLEY RD SW
THURSTON CO WA 180-B6
MAPLE VLY BLCK DIAMND RD
BLACK DIAMOND WA 110-C3
KING CO WA 110-C3
MAPLE VLY BLCK DMND RD
Rt#-169
MAPLE VALLEY WA 110-C3
MAPLE VALLEY WA 175-D7
MAPLE VALLEY WA 176-A7
MAPLEWILD AV SW
BURIEN WA 175-A5
MAPLEWOOD AV
COEUR D'ALENE ID 354-F8
KOOTENAI CO ID 354-D7
POST FALLS ID 354-E7
W MAPLEWOOD AV
BELLINGHAM WA 258-A2
WHATCOM CO WA 158-D7
WHATCOM CO WA 258-A2
MAPLEWOOD RD
DISTRICT OF SAANICH BC 256-J4
MAP ROCK RD
CANYON CO ID 147-B1
MARBLE RD
SKAMANIA CO WA 200-D1
W MARBLE RD
YAKIMA CO WA 243-A6
MARBLE CREEK RD
SHOSHONE CO ID 115-C3
MARBLE FRONT RD
CALDWELL ID 147-B1
MARBLE MOUNTAIN RD
JOSEPHINE CO OR 229-A7
MARBLE VALLEY SOUTH
BASIN RD
STEVENS CO WA 106-A2
MARCELLUS RD
ADAMS CO WA 113-C3
ADAMS CO WA 121-C1
RITZVILLE WA 113-C3
MARCH POINT RD
SKAGIT CO WA 160-C6
E MARCH POINT RD
SKAGIT CO WA 160-D6
S MARCH POINT RD
ANACORTES WA 160-D6
SKAGIT CO WA 160-D6
W MARCH POINT RD
ANACORTES WA 160-C6
MARCOLA RD
LANE CO OR 133-C2
LANE CO OR 210-D7
LANE CO OR 215-D1
LANE CO OR 331-D4
SPRINGFIELD OR 331-D4

MARCY LP
JOSEPHINE CO OR 229-A6
MARGARET AV
COEUR D'ALENE ID 355-F5
KOOTENAI CO ID 355-F5
MARGIN ST
ENDICOTT WA 122-B1
E MARGINAL WY S
SEATTLE WA 281-J2
SEATTLE WA 282-A7
SEATTLE WA 286-C3
TUKWILA WA 286-C3
E MARGINAL WY S Rt#-99
SEATTLE WA 281-J5
W MARGINAL WY S
SEATTLE WA 285-J1
W MARGINAL WY SW
SEATTLE WA 281-H4
SEATTLE WA 285-J1
S MARGUERITE RD
SPOKANE VALLEY WA 350-D9
W MARIE ST
PASCO WA 343-D6
MARIE CREEK RD
KOOTENAI CO ID 245-C7
W MARIGOLD ST
GARDEN CITY ID 253-B2
MARIHUGH RD
SKAGIT CO WA 161-A6
MARINA DR
WHATCOM CO WA 101-C1
W MARINA DR
MOSES LAKE WA 242-C3
MARINE DR
ANACORTES WA 259-C6
BELLINGHAM WA 258-A4
BREMERTON WA 270-E8
CITY OF NORTH VANCOUVER BC 254-J5
CITY OF SURREY BC 158-A2
CITY OF WHITE ROCK BC 158-A2
CLALLAM CO WA 262-B3
DISTRICT OF BURNABY BC 156-C5
DISTRICT OF NORTH VANCOUV BC 254-F4
DISTRICT OF WEST VANCOUVE BC 156-A2
DISTRICT OF WEST VANCOUVE BC 254-A2
NEW WESTMINSTER BC 156-C5
PORT ANGELES WA 261-E3
SKAGIT CO WA 259-C6
SNOHOMISH CO WA 168-B4
SNOHOMISH CO WA 171-C1
WHATCOM CO WA 101-C1
WHATCOM CO WA 158-C7
WHATCOM CO WA 258-A4
MARINE DR Rt#-99
DISTRICT OF WEST VANCOUVE BC 254-E4
MARINE DR U.S.-30
ASTORIA OR 300-C5
E MARINE DR
CLALLAM CO WA 262-C3
N MARINE DR
PORTLAND OR 192-B6
PORTLAND OR 304-A6
PORTLAND OR 308-E1
PORTLAND OR 309-F1
N MARINE DR Rt#-99E
PORTLAND OR 309-E1
NE MARINE DR
FAIRVIEW OR 200-A1
GRESHAM OR 200-A1
PORTLAND OR 193-A7
PORTLAND OR 200-A1
PORTLAND OR 309-H2
PORTLAND OR 310-B2
PORTLAND OR 311-H4
NW MARINE DR
TROUTDALE OR 200-B1
UNIVERSITY ENDOWMENT LAND BC 156-A4
SE MARINE DR
VANCOUVER BC 156-C5
SW MARINE DR
UNIVERSITY ENDOWMENT LAND BC 156-A5
VANCOUVER BC 156-B5
W MARINE DR Rt#-202
ASTORIA OR 300-A6
W MARINE DR U.S.-30
ASTORIA OR 300-B4
W MARINE DR U.S.-101
ASTORIA OR 300-A5
MARINE DR NE
SNOHOMISH CO WA 168-C7
SNOHOMISH CO WA 171-C1
MARINE WY
DISTRICT OF BURNABY BC 156-C5
NEW WESTMINSTER BC 156-C5
VANCOUVER BC 156-C5
MARINER WY
COQUITLAM BC 157-A5
MARINE VIEW DR
DES MOINES WA 290-A7
OCEAN SHORES WA 298-B4
SEATTLE WA 284-D4
SEATTLE WA 285-E6
MARINEVIEW DR
LINCOLN CO OR 328-C4
MARINE VIEW DR Rt#-509
DES MOINES WA 290-A6
TACOMA WA 181-D1
TACOMA WA 182-A1
E MARINE VIEW DR
EVERETT WA 171-C1
EVERETT WA 265-F1
E MARINE VIEW DR Rt#-529
EVERETT WA 171-C1
W MARINE VIEW DR
EVERETT WA 264-D4
W MARINE VIEW DR Rt#-529
EVERETT WA 171-C1
EVERETT WA 264-D3
MARINE VIEW DR S
DES MOINES WA 175-B7
DES MOINES WA 290-A7
N MARINGO DR
SPOKANE CO WA 350-B3
E MARINGO RD
SPOKANE CO WA 350-C4
N MARION AV
CLATSOP CO OR 301-G4
GEARHART OR 301-G4
S MARION AV
BREMERTON WA 270-F11
MARION AV N
BREMERTON WA 270-F10
MARION RD
DISTRICT OF ABBOTSFORD BC 102-B1
MARION CO OR 133-C1
MARION CO OR 325-H14
MARION ST
ALBANY OR 326-D11

MARION ST
CENTRALIA WA 299-G2
SALEM OR 322-J12
SALEM OR 323-A13
SEATTLE WA 277-J6
SEATTLE WA 278-A6
MARION ST Rt#-22
SALEM OR 322-H12
MARION DRAIN RD
YAKIMA CO WA 120-A2
MARION ST BRDG Rt#-22
SALEM OR 322-H12
MARK RD
CLACKAMAS CO OR 199-C7
N MARKET EXT
SPOKANE WA 349-E5
MARKET LN
UNION CO OR 130-A2
MARKET RD
SHERMAN CO OR 127-C3
E MARKET RD
OWYHEE CO ID 147-B1
MARKET ST
ANACORTES WA 259-H1
BONANZA OR 151-A2
CHEHALIS WA 299-D11
KIRKLAND WA 175-C1
KLAMATH CO OR 151-A2
KLICKITAT CO WA 120-A3
MALIN OR 151-A3
MARKET ST Rt#-27
LATAH WA 114-C3
E MARKET ST
ABERDEEN WA 178-B7
N MARKET ST
SEATTLE WA 273-H5
SPOKANE WA 349-E2
SPOKANE CO WA 347-F6
SPOKANE CO WA 349-E2
NE MARKET ST
JEFFERSON CO OR 208-C2
NW MARKET ST
SEATTLE WA 272-D4
SEATTLE WA 273-G4
S MARKET ST
TACOMA WA 293-H5
SW MARKET ST
PORTLAND OR 312-E7
PORTLAND OR 313-E7
MARKET ST NE
DONALD OR 199-A7
SALEM OR 322-J11
SALEM OR 323-A11
MARKET ST NE Rt#-213
SALEM OR 323-D11
MARKSMAN ST SW
THURSTON CO WA 184-B2
MARKWORTH RD
WHATCOM CO WA 158-D3
MARLATT RD S
MARION CO OR 207-C2
MARMONT ST
COQUITLAM BC 157-A5
MARMOT RD
CLACKAMAS CO OR 201-A4
E MARQUAM ST
MARION CO OR 205-C3
MOUNT ANGEL OR 205-C3
W MARQUAM ST
MARION CO OR 205-B3
MOUNT ANGEL OR 205-B3
E MARROWSTONE RD
JEFFERSON CO WA 170-B1
MARSH CTO
WASCO CO OR 196-B5
MARSH RD
DESCHUTES CO OR 212-B7
YAKIMA CO WA 243-C6
S MARSH RD
SPOKANE CO WA 114-C2
SPOKANE CO WA 247-A6
SE MARSH RD
CLACKAMAS CO OR 200-D3
MARSHALL AV
MAPLE RIDGE BC 157-D5
SW MARSHALL AV
PENDLETON OR 129-B1
MARSHALL RD
CHENEY WA 246-A7
DISTRICT OF ABBOTSFORD BC 102-B1
DISTRICT OF MATSQUI BC 102-B1
LATAH CO ID 249-D2
SPOKANE CO WA 246-A7
NW MARSHALL ST
PORTLAND OR 312-D4
MARSING RD
CANYON CO ID 147-B1
MARSING-MURPHY RD Rt#-78
MARSING ID 147-B1
OWYHEE CO ID 147-B1
MARTHA BOARDMAN RD
STEVENS CO WA 114-A1
MARTHALER RD NE
MARION CO OR 204-D2
MARION CO OR 205-A2
MARTIN RD
CLARK CO WA 192-D1
JOSEPHINE CO OR 233-B4
MOUNT VERNON WA 260-F9
SHERMAN CO OR 127-C2
SKAGIT CO WA 260-F9
NW MARTIN RD
WASHINGTON CO OR 198-C1
W MARTIN RD
SPOKANE CO WA 114-B3
MARTIN ST
KLAMATH FALLS OR 338-E7
W MARTIN ST
ELMA WA 179-B7
MARTIN WY SE
LACEY WA 181-A6
LACEY WA 297-F5
OLYMPIA WA 297-C5
THURSTON CO WA 181-A6
THURSTON CO WA 297-F5
MARTIN CREEK RD
LANE CO OR 219-D1
NE M L KING JR BLVD
Rt#-99E
PORTLAND OR 309-G3
PORTLAND OR 313-G4
SE M L KING JR BLVD
Rt#-99E
PORTLAND OR 313-G7
PORTLAND OR 317-G1
MARTIN LUTHER KING JR WY
SEATTLE WA 278-D6

MARTIN LUTHER KING JR WY
E
SEATTLE WA 278-D4
MARTIN LUTHER KING JR WY
S
SEATTLE WA 278-D7
SEATTLE WA 282-D3
SEATTLE WA 283-E7
SEATTLE WA 287-E4
TUKWILA WA 287-E4
MARTIN L KING JR WY S
Rt#-900
KING CO WA 175-C5
KING CO WA 287-E6
KING CO WA 289-G1
RENTON WA 175-C5
RENTON WA 289-G1
SEATTLE WA 287-E6
TUKWILA WA 287-E6
TUKWILA WA 289-G1
MARTIN RANCH RD
CURRY CO OR 232-C4
MARTINSON RD
LATAH CO ID 249-D7
MARTLETT DR
BRITISH COLUMBIA BC 159-B5
MARVIN RD NE
LACEY WA 181-A5
THURSTON CO WA 181-A5
MARVIN RD NE Rt#-510
LACEY WA 181-A6
MARVIN RD SE
THURSTON CO WA 181-A7
MARVIN RD SE Rt#-510
LACEY WA 181-A6
THURSTON CO WA 181-A6
E MARVIN ST
PASCO WA 343-H7
MARX ST U.S.-95
IDAHO CO ID 131-C2
RIGGINS ID 131-C2
MARY GATES MEMORIAL DR
SEATTLE WA 274-E5
MARY HILL BYPS
PORT COQUITLAM BC 157-B5
MARYHILL DR
EVERETT WA 171-B4
SNOHOMISH CO WA 171-B4
MARY HILL RD
PORT COQUITLAM BC 157-A5
MARYLAND AV Rt#-42
MYRTLE POINT OR 140-B2
MARY M KNIGHT RD
MASON CO WA 179-B3
MARYS PEAK RD
BENTON CO OR 133-A1
MARYS RIVER RD
BENTON CO OR 133-A1
MASCHER RD NE
MARION CO OR 205-B5
MASCHKE RD
LEWIS CO WA 187-B5
MASHELL AV S Rt#-161
EATONVILLE WA 118-B1
E MASON AV
BUCKLEY WA 110-C3
BUCKLEY WA 182-D4
W MASON AV
BUCKLEY WA 182-D4
MASON DR
CROOK CO OR 213-D5
PRINEVILLE OR 213-D5
MASON RD
WASCO CO OR 127-B2
MASON ANDERSON RD
TILLAMOOK CO OR 191-B3
MASON BENSON RD
MASON CO WA 173-C7
MASON CO WA 180-C1
MASON CREEK RD
KITTITAS CO WA 240-C1
NE MASON CREEK RD
CLARK CO WA 192-D2
MASON LAKE DR W
MASON CO WA 173-C7
MASON CO WA 180-C1
MASON LAKE RD
MASON CO WA 173-C7
MASON CO WA 180-C1
MASON LAKE RD W
MASON CO WA 180-B1
SW MASONVILLE RD
YAMHILL CO OR 204-A1
S MASSACHUSETTS ST
SEATTLE WA 282-C1
MASTERSON RD
KITTITAS CO WA 240-C2
MATEJECK RD
TILLAMOOK CO OR 197-B2
MATHENY RD N
MARION CO OR 204-D3
YAMHILL CO OR 204-D3
MATHENY RD NE
MARION CO OR 204-D3
MARION CO OR 205-A3
MATHENY CREEK RD
COOS CO OR 220-D7
MATHER MEMORIAL PKWY
Rt#-410
PIERCE CO WA 119-A1
MATHERS AV
DISTRICT OF WEST VANCOUVE BC 254-A2
MATHIAS RD E
PIERCE CO WA 182-A6
MATLOCK-BRADY RD
MASON CO WA 179-A4
MATNEY RD
KLAMATH CO OR 235-D6
MATNEY WY
KLAMATH CO OR 235-D6
MATSEN RD
KLICKITAT CO WA 120-A3
MATSON RD
LATAH CO ID 249-D2
MATTESON RD
YAMHILL CO OR 198-B3
MATTHIEU LN
MARION CO OR 199-A7
MATTOON RD
CLACKAMAS CO OR 200-B5
MATTSON RD
LEWIS CO WA 184-B5
MAUI AV
OAK HARBOR WA 167-C3
MAUPIN RD
DOUGLAS CO OR 141-A1
SKAGIT CO WA 168-A2

INDEX

E MILE HILL DR Rt#-166 STREET INDEX MOUNT OLYMPUS AV 383

STREET
City State Page-Grid

SE MILE HILL DR Rt#-166
East Port Orchard WA 174-C4
KITSAP CO WA 174-C4
PORT ORCHARD WA 174-B4
E MILES AV
HAYDEN ID 245-A5
W MILES AV
HAYDEN ID 245-A5
MILES RD
STEVENS CO WA 106-A3
MILES BRIDGE RD
BAKER CO OR 130-B3
MILES CRESTON RD
LINCOLN CO WA 113-C1
MILEY RD
WILSONVILLE OR 199-B6
MILITARY RD
COWLITZ CO WA 187-B7
FEDERAL WAY WA 175-B7
FEDERAL WAY WA 182-B1
KING CO WA 182-B1
LAKEWOOD WA 181-C4
N MILITARY RD
LEWIS CO WA 187-C3
S MILITARY RD
LEWIS CO WA 187-C4
MILITARY RD E
PIERCE CO WA 181-D5
PIERCE CO WA 182-A5
MILITARY RD S
FEDERAL WAY WA 175-B7
FEDERAL WAY WA 182-B1
KENT WA 175-B7
KENT WA 290-D7
KING CO WA 175-B7
KING CO WA 182-B1
KING CO WA 286-C6
KING CO WA 288-D1
MILTON WA 182-B2
PIERCE CO WA 181-D5
SEATAC WA 288-E5
SEATAC WA 289-E6
SEATAC WA 290-E3
SEATAC WA 291-F1
TUKWILA WA 288-D1
MILITARY CROSSING RD
KLAMATH CO OR 142-C3
MILL AV S Rt#-900
RENTON WA 175-C5
MILL DR
KLICKITAT CO WA 196-D2
MILL RD
ASOTIN CO WA 122-C3
LATAH CO ID 249-D5
LEWIS CO WA 187-C2
NEZ PERCE CO ID 250-C4
WASHINGTON CO ID 139-B1
N MILL RD
Fairwood WA 346-J7
Fairwood WA 347-A6
SPOKANE CO WA 347-A6
MILL ST
CHENEY WA 246-A7
CLEARWATER CO ID 123-C1
ELK RIVER ID 123-C1
GRANTS PASS OR 335-F10
KELSO WA 303-C9
MAPLE RIDGE BC 157-D5
SPOKANE CO WA 246-A7
NE MILL ST
GRANTS PASS OR 335-G9
SE MILL ST
DALLAS OR 204-A6
GRANTS PASS OR 335-G9
SW MILL ST
SHERIDAN OR 125-B3
YAMHILL CO OR 125-B3
MILLARD RD
COLUMBIA CO OR 192-A2
MILL BAY RD
BRITISH COLUMBIA BC 159-B2
MILL CREEK BLVD
MILL CREEK WA 171-C4
MILL CREEK DR
JACKSON CO OR 226-C7
MILL CREEK RD
ADAMS CO ID 139-C1
AUMSVILLE OR 133-C1
COWLITZ CO WA 117-B3
CROOK CO OR 135-C2
JACKSON CO OR 234-C7
LINCOLN CO OR 206-C5
MARION CO OR 133-C1
MARION CO OR 325-H13
PACIFIC CO WA 117-A1
POLK CO OR 125-B3
THE DALLES OR 196-C7
TURNER OR 325-H13
UNION CO OR 130-B2
WALLA WALLA WA 122-A3
WALLA WALLA WA 345-H5
WALLA WALLA CO WA 122-A3
WALLA WALLA CO WA 345-H5
WASCO CO OR 127-A2
WASCO CO OR 196-C7
MILL CREEK RD SE
TURNER OR 325-H12
MILL CREEK LOOKOUT RD
WASCO CO OR 202-D2
MILL CREEK RIDGE RD
JACKSON CO OR 226-C5
SE MILLER AV
DALLAS OR 204-A6
POLK CO OR 204-A6
MILLER RD
CITY OF RICHMOND BC 156-B6
CLACKAMAS CO OR 205-C1
CLALLAM CO WA 164-C6
JEFFERSON CO WA 263-B7
LINCOLN CO OR 206-C1
MARION CO OR 199-A7
NEZ PERCE CO ID 250-D7
SNOHOMISH CO WA 168-B4
S MILLER RD
JEFFERSON CO WA 263-B6
MILLER RD NE
BAINBRIDGE ISLAND WA 174-C1
MARION CO OR 205-B3
MILLER RD NW
BAINBRIDGE ISLAND WA 174-C1
N MILLER ST
WENATCHEE WA 238-D4
N MILLER ST Rt#-285
WENATCHEE WA 238-D4
S MILLER ST
WENATCHEE WA 238-D4
MILLER BAY RD NE
KITSAP CO WA 170-C6

STREET
City State Page-Grid

MILLER BAY RD NE
Suquamish WA 170-C6
MILLER CANYON RD
HARNEY CO OR 144-C1
MILLER CEMETERY RD
LINN CO OR 133-C1
MILLER ISLAND RD
KLAMATH CO OR 235-B5
MILLERS CEMETERY RD
LINN CO OR 207-C3
MILLERS CREEK RD
POLK CO OR 207-A2
MILLICAN RD
CROOK CO OR 135-B3
CROOK CO OR 213-C7
LAKE CO OR 143-C1
W MILLIRON RD
LANE CO OR 210-A7
MILLMAN RD
ISLAND CO WA 170-D1
MILL PLAIN BLVD Rt#-501
VANCOUVER WA 305-G4
E MILL PLAIN BLVD
VANCOUVER WA 305-H5
VANCOUVER WA 306-C5
VANCOUVER WA 307-F6
E MILL PLAIN BLVD Rt#-501
VANCOUVER WA 305-G4
SE MILL PLAIN BLVD
CLARK CO WA 193-A6
VANCOUVER WA 193-A6
VANCOUVER WA 307-J6
W MILL PLAIN BLVD Rt#-501
VANCOUVER WA 304-D3
VANCOUVER WA 305-E4
SE MILL PLAIN RD
VANCOUVER WA 307-J6
MILL RIDGE RD
WASCO CO OR 202-D2
MILLS RD
DISTRICT OF NORTH SAANICH BC 159-C2
TOWN OF SIDNEY BC 159-C2
MILLS CANYON RD
CHELAN CO WA 236-A7
MILLSTREAM RD
DISTRICT OF LANGFORD BC 159-B5
MILLSTREAM LAKE RD
BRITISH COLUMBIA BC 159-B5
MILLTOWN RD
SKAGIT CO WA 168-B2
MILTON WY
MILTON WA 182-B2
MILTON CEMETERY RD
MILTON-FREEWATER OR 121-C3
UMATILLA CO OR 121-C3
MILWAUKEE DR
COEUR D'ALENE ID 355-E10
N MILWAUKEE ST
BOISE ID 253-B2
MILWAUKEE WY
TACOMA WA 182-A2
SE MILWAUKIE AV
PORTLAND OR 317-H2
MILWAUKIE EXWY Rt#-224
CLACKAMAS CO OR 199-D3
MILWAUKIE OR 199-D3
MILWAUKIE OR 321-J2
MILWAUKIE-FOSTER RD
CLACKAMAS CO OR 199-D3
MIMA ACRES RD SE
THURSTON CO WA 184-D3
MINALOOSA RD
BENEWAH CO ID 248-A7
MINARD RD W
KITSAP CO WA 174-A4
MINA SMITH RD
CLALLAM CO WA 169-B1
MINERAL RD
WASHINGTON CO ID 139-A1
MINERAL SPRINGS RD
SKAMANIA CO WA 194-C1
YAMHILL CO OR 198-B6
MINK RD
CANYON CO ID 147-B1
MINK RD NE
KING CO WA 171-D7
MINKLER RD
LEWIS CO WA 187-C3
NE MINNEHAHA ST
CLARK CO WA 192-D5
MINNESOTA AV
RAINIER WA 118-A1
MINOR RD
KELSO WA 303-E7
MINSON RD
CROOK CO OR 213-B6
SW MINTERBROOK RD
KITSAP CO WA 174-B6
MIRROR LN
DOUGLAS CO OR 221-A5
MISERY POINT LOOP RD NW
KITSAP CO WA 173-D1
MISSIMER RD
BENTON CO OR 120-B2
E MISSION AV
LIBERTY LAKE WA 352-C13
SPOKANE WA 349-D7
SPOKANE CO WA 352-G13
SPOKANE VALLEY WA 349-J7
SPOKANE VALLEY WA 350-G6
SPOKANE VALLEY WA 351-A7
W MISSION AV
SPOKANE WA 348-J7
SPOKANE WA 349-A7
MISSION RD
MARION CO OR 198-D7
SAINT PAUL OR 198-D7
MISSION ST
MCCALL ID 251-C5
N MISSION ST Rt#-285
WENATCHEE WA 238-D4
S MISSION ST
Appleyard WA 239-A5
WENATCHEE WA 239-A5
S MISSION ST Rt#-285
WENATCHEE WA 238-D4
WENATCHEE WA 239-A4
MISSION ST SE
SALEM OR 322-H14
MISSION ST SE Rt#-22
SALEM OR 322-J14
SALEM OR 323-A14
SALEM OR 325-B1
MISSION CREEK RD
CHELAN CO WA 238-C3
MISSOULA AV U.S.-2
LINCOLN CO MT 107-C2
TROY MT 107-C2

STREET
City State Page-Grid

E MISSOULA AV U.S.-2
TROY MT 107-C2
MISSOURI AV
CANYON CO ID 147-B1
MIST DR Rt#-47
COLUMBIA CO OR 125-B1
VERNONIA OR 125-B1
MIST-CLATSKANIE HWY Rt#-47
CLATSKANIE OR 117-B3
COLUMBIA CO OR 117-B3
MISTLETOE RD
ASHLAND OR 337-H10
DALLAS OR 204-A7
MONMOUTH OR 204-A7
POLK CO OR 204-A7
MISTY CREEK RD
JACKSON CO OR 230-B1
MITCHELL AV
PORT ORCHARD WA 174-B4
PORT ORCHARD WA 270-J14
MITCHELL RD
PIERCE CO WA 181-D6
MITCHELL RD SE
East Port Orchard WA 174-B4
PORT ORCHARD WA 174-B4
MITCHELL ST
KLAMATH FALLS OR 338-F8
N MITCHELL ST
BOISE ID 253-B2
MITCHELL BUTTE RD
MALHEUR CO OR 139-A3
MALHEUR CO OR 146-C1
MIX RD
LATAH CO ID 249-C4
MIX ST NW
THURSTON CO WA 296-A3
MOCK RD
DESCHUTES CO OR 217-B1
MOCLIPS HWY
GRAYS HARBOR CO WA 108-C2
GRAYS HARBOR CO WA 109-A2
MOCTILEME RD Rt#-60
BENEWAH CO ID 115-A3
MODOC RD
JACKSON CO OR 230-C6
MODOC POINT RD
KLAMATH CO OR 231-C3
MODROW RD
COWLITZ CO WA 189-D5
MOE RD NE
DOUGLAS CO WA 104-C3
MOELLERING RD
LINCOLN CO WA 113-C2
MOERHLE RD
WHITMAN CO WA 250-A2
E MOFFAT RD
SPOKANE CO WA 246-D2
MOFFATT RD
CROOK CO OR 213-C6
SE MOFFET RD
CLARK CO WA 193-D7
MOHAWK BLVD
SPRINGFIELD OR 330-J6
SPRINGFIELD OR 331-A6
MOHAWK HILL RD
LANE CO OR 210-D7
MOHLER RD
LINCOLN CO WA 113-C2
LINCOLN CO WA 114-A2
MOHLER CHEESE FACTORY RD
TILLAMOOK CO OR 191-B7
MOHORIC RD
LEWIS CO WA 187-B1
MOJONNIER RD
COLLEGE PLACE WA 344-D13
WALLA WALLA CO WA 344-D13
MOLALLA AV
CLACKAMAS CO OR 126-A3
OREGON CITY OR 199-D5
N MOLALLA AV
MOLALLA OR 126-A3
S MOLALLA AV
CLACKAMAS CO OR 126-A3
MOLALLA OR 126-A3
MOLALLA FOREST RD
CANBY OR 199-C6
CLACKAMAS CO OR 199-C6
MOLITOR HILL RD
LANE CO OR 215-C7
MOLSON RD
OKANOGAN CO WA 105-A1
N MOLTER RD
LIBERTY LAKE WA 352-D14
S MOLTER RD
SPOKANE CO WA 247-B4
MONAHAN RD
COWLITZ CO WA 187-B7
MONCTON ST
CITY OF RICHMOND BC 156-B7
MONDOVI RD
LINCOLN CO WA 114-A1
NE MONEY CREEK RD
KING CO WA 111-A2
MONITOR-MCKEE RD NE
MARION CO OR 205-B2
MONKLAND RD
SHERMAN CO OR 127-C2
N MONMOUTH AV
MONMOUTH OR 204-B7
MONMOUTH CTO
DALLAS OR 204-A6
POLK CO OR 204-A6
MONMOUTH HWY
POLK CO OR 125-B3
POLK CO OR 133-B1
POLK CO OR 204-A7
POLK CO OR 207-A1
MONMOUTH ST Rt#-51
INDEPENDENCE OR 204-B7
MONMOUTH-INDPNDNCE HWY Rt#-51
INDEPENDENCE OR 204-B7
MONMOUTH OR 204-B7
POLK CO OR 204-B7
MONNIER RD NE
MARION CO OR 205-C1
MONROE AV
CORVALLIS OR 327-G10
LA GRANDE OR 130-A2
NORTH BEND OR 333-G4
SW MONROE LN
JEFFERSON CO OR 212-C1
MONROE RD
LEWIS CO WA 187-C2
N MONROE RD
SPOKANE CO WA 114-B1

STREET
City State Page-Grid

W MONROE RD
DEER PARK WA 114-B1
SPOKANE CO WA 114-B1
MONROE ST
PORT TOWNSEND WA 263-H4
E MONROE ST Rt#-78
BURNS OR 145-B1
HARNEY CO OR 145-B1
N MONROE ST
SPOKANE WA 348-H8
Town and Country WA 346-H14
Town and Country WA 348-H8
S MONROE ST
SPOKANE WA 348-H9
W MONROE ST U.S.-20
BURNS OR 145-B1
MONROE CREEK RD
WASHINGTON CO ID 139-A2
MONROE LANDING RD
ISLAND CO WA 167-B3
MONSE SOUTH RD
OKANOGAN CO WA 104-C3
MONSON RD
LINCOLN CO WA 113-B2
MONSOR RD Rt#-21
LINCOLN CO WA 113-B2
MONTAGUE GRENADA RD
MONTAGUE CA 150-A3
SISKIYOU CO CA 150-A3
MONTE CRISTO RD
SNOHOMISH CO WA 111-A1
S MONTE CRISTO RD
CLACKAMAS CO OR 205-D2
SW MONTEE DR
PENDLETON OR 129-B1
UMATILLA CO OR 129-B1
MONTERAY AV
DISTRICT OF NORTH VANCOUV BC 255-B1
MONTEREY DR NE
RENTON WA 175-C5
MONTESANO ST
GRAYS HARBOR CO WA 183-B2
WESTPORT WA 183-B2
WESTPORT WA 298-H14
MONTESANO ST Rt#-105
WESTPORT WA 298-H11
MONTESANO-ABERDEEN RD
GRAYS HARBOR CO WA 178-D7
E MONTGOMERY AV
SPOKANE VALLEY WA 350-D6
SPOKANE VALLEY WA 351-F5
E MONTGOMERY DR
SPOKANE VALLEY WA 350-E5
MONTGOMERY RD
DESCHUTES CO OR 136-A3
DESCHUTES CO OR 144-A1
JEFFERSON CO OR 135-A1
MONTGOMERY RIDGE RD
ASOTIN CO WA 123-A3
MONTI DR
LINCOLN CO OR 203-B3
MONTICELLO DR
ISLAND CO WA 167-D5
MONTLAKE BLVD NE Rt#-513
SEATTLE WA 274-D6
SEATTLE WA 278-D1
E MONTLAKE PL E
SEATTLE WA 278-D1
W MONTLAKE PL E
SEATTLE WA 278-C1
MONTMORENCE DR
LANE CO OR 210-A7
MONTOUR RD
GEM CO ID 139-C3
MONTREAL ST
CITY OF VICTORIA BC 256-F9
MONTROYAL BLVD
DISTRICT OF NORTH VANCOUV BC 156-B2
DISTRICT OF NORTH VANCOUV BC 255-A1
MONUMENT DR
JOSEPHINE CO OR 229-B3
JOSEPHINE CO OR 335-B1
MONUMENT RD
GRANT CO OR 136-C1
GRANT CO WA 112-B3
MONUMENT RD SW
KING CO WA 174-D6
MONUMENT TO COUNTY LINE
GRANT CO OR 128-C3
GRANT CO OR 136-C1
MONUMENT TO COURTROCK RD
GRANT CO OR 136-C1
GRANT CO OR 137-A1
MOODY RD
GRAYS HARBOR CO WA 177-D2
MOODY ST
PORT MOODY BC 157-A4
MOON RD
FRANKLIN CO WA 121-B1
MOON RD SW
THURSTON CO WA 184-A3
MOON CREEK RD
TILLAMOOK CO OR 197-D5
MOONEY MOUNTAIN RD
JOSEPHINE CO OR 233-C1
MOON HILL RD
LEWIS CO WA 187-A1
MOON RIDGE RD
VALLEY CO ID 251-C6
MOONSHINE PARK RD
LINCOLN CO OR 206-D1
MOON VALLEY RD
KING CO WA 176-D4
MOORE LN
SHERMAN CO OR 127-C2
MOORE RD
GRAYS HARBOR CO WA 179-A7
SKAGIT CO WA 168-A1
MOORE ST Rt#-9
SEDRO-WOOLLEY WA 161-C5
MOOREA DR
DOUGLAS CO OR 221-B3
MOOREHOUSE RD
UMATILLA CO OR 129-A1
MOORES HOLLOW RD
MALHEUR CO OR 139-A2
NW MOORES VALLEY RD
YAMHILL CO OR 198-A5
MORA RD
CLALLAM CO WA 169-A2
MORA RD Rt#-110
CLALLAM CO WA 169-B2
N MORAIN ST
KENNEWICK WA 342-H10
S MORAIN ST
BENTON CO WA 342-H11
KENNEWICK WA 342-H11

STREET
City State Page-Grid

MORAY BRDG
CITY OF RICHMOND BC 156-B6
MORCOM RD
MALHEUR CO OR 146-C2
MORELAND AV
MALDEN WA 114-B3
MORFORD RD
SKAGIT CO WA 161-C6
MORGAN AV
MALHEUR CO OR 139-A3
MORGAN DR
Birch Bay WA 158-B4
LINN CO OR 210-C1
MORGAN LN
LANE CO OR 210-A6
NE MORGAN LN
GRANTS PASS OR 335-F6
NW MORGAN LN
GRANTS PASS OR 335-E6
MORGAN RD
CLACKAMAS CO OR 200-C7
MORROW CO OR 128-B2
MULTNOMAH CO OR 192-A5
E MORGAN RD
SPOKANE CO WA 246-D2
MORGAN ST U.S.-2
DAVENPORT WA 114-A2
LINCOLN CO WA 114-A2
SW MORGAN ST
SEATTLE WA 280-E7
SEATTLE WA 281-F7
MORGAN LAKE RD
ADAMS CO WA 242-D7
MORGANSON RD
WASCO CO OR 196-A6
MORIARTY RD
CLALLAM CO WA 169-B2
MORMON BASIN RD
MALHEUR CO OR 138-B2
MORMON BASIN CUTOFF RD
MALHEUR CO OR 138-B2
MORNING STAR RD
LINN CO OR 207-D3
N MORNING-STAR RD
LANE CO OR 215-D4
MORRELLI DR
YAMHILL CO OR 198-B5
MORRILL RD
DESCHUTES CO OR 212-D7
MORRIS RD
ISLAND CO WA 167-C4
KLICKITAT CO WA 196-D4
POLK CO OR 204-A5
MORRIS ST
LA CONNER WA 167-D1
MORRISON RD
COOS CO OR 220-B6
SE MORRISON ST
PORTLAND OR 313-G6
MORRIS VALLEY RD
BRITISH COLUMBIA BC 94-C3
MORROW RD
MEDFORD OR 336-D9
POLK CO OR 204-B6
MORSE RD N
COLUMBIA CO OR 192-A2
MORSE RD S
COLUMBIA CO OR 192-A2
MORSE ST
COWLITZ CO WA 187-B5
MORSE-MERRIMAN RD SE
OLYMPIA WA 297-C9
MORTON RD
LEWIS CO WA 187-C3
MORTON RD Rt#-7
LEWIS CO WA 118-B2
MORTON WA 118-B2
MORTON ST Rt#-34
LEBANON OR 133-C1
N MORTON ST
COLFAX WA 122-C1
MORTON-BEAR CANYON RD Rt#-508
LEWIS CO WA 118-B2
MORTON WA 118-B2
MOSBY CREEK RD
COTTAGE GROVE OR 215-B7
LANE CO OR 141-C1
LANE CO OR 215-B7
MOSCOW RD Rt#-27
PALOUSE WA 249-B1
MOSCOW MOUNTAIN RD
LATAH CO ID 249-D4
MOSCROP ST
DISTRICT OF BURNABY BC 156-C5
MOSER RD
NEZ PERCE CO ID 250-B2
MOSES RD
SNOHOMISH CO WA 168-D4
MOSES COULEE RD SE
DOUGLAS CO WA 112-C2
MOSES CREEK LN
UNION CO OR 130-A1
SE MOSHER AV
ROSEBURG OR 334-F8
MOSIER RD
CLACKAMAS CO OR 200-A6
COLUMBIA CO OR 189-A3
SKAGIT CO WA 161-C5
MOSIER CREEK RD
WASCO CO OR 196-A6
MOSIER-THE DALLES HWY U.S.-30
MOSIER OR 196-A5
THE DALLES OR 196-A5
WASCO CO OR 196-A5
MOSQUITO CREEK RD
COWLITZ CO WA 187-A7
MOSQUITO LAKE RD
WHATCOM CO WA 102-B1
WHATCOM CO WA 161-D1
MOSS ST
CITY OF VICTORIA BC 256-J11
MOSS CREEK RD
TILLAMOOK CO OR 191-B7
MOSS HILL RD
CLACKAMAS CO OR 200-C6
MOULTON RD
FRANKLIN CO WA 121-B2
MOUNT ADAMS RD
KLICKITAT CO WA 119-A3
MOUNT ADAMS ST
HARRAH WA 119-C2
YAKIMA CO WA 119-C2
MOUNT ADAMS RECREATION AREA RD
KLICKITAT CO WA 119-A3
YAKIMA CO WA 119-A3

STREET
City State Page-Grid

N MOUNTAIN AV
ASHLAND OR 337-E6
JACKSON CO OR 337-E6
S MOUNTAIN AV
ASHLAND OR 337-E8
MOUNTAIN BLVD U.S.-395
MOUNT VERNON OR 137-A2
MOUNTAIN HWY
DISTRICT OF NORTH VANCOUV BC 255-E2
MOUNTAIN HWY E Rt#-7
PIERCE CO WA 118-B1
PIERCE CO WA 181-D6
PIERCE CO WA 182-A7
MOUNTAIN HWY E Rt#-706
PIERCE CO WA 118-B1
PIERCE CO WA 185-A5
MOUNTAIN RD
ASOTIN CO WA 122-C3
GARFIELD CO WA 122-B2
KLAMATH CO OR 231-C1
SW MOUNTAIN RD
CLACKAMAS CO OR 199-C5
MOUNTAIN HOME DR
LINN CO OR 210-D2
MOUNTAIN HOME RD
CHELAN CO WA 238-A1
WASHINGTON CO OR 198-D4
NE MOUNTAIN HOME RD
YAMHILL CO OR 198-D5
MOUNTAIN LOOP HWY
DARRINGTON WA 103-A3
GRANITE FALLS WA 102-C3
SNOHOMISH CO WA 102-C3
SNOHOMISH CO WA 103-A3
SNOHOMISH CO WA 111-A1
MOUNTAIN MEADOWS RD
PIERCE CO WA 185-A2
MOUNTAIN MEADOWS RD Rt#-165
PIERCE CO WA 118-C1
PIERCE CO WA 185-A2
MOUNTAIN TOP RD
YAMHILL CO OR 198-D4
E MOUNTAIN VIEW AV
ELLENSBURG WA 241-B6
KITTITAS CO WA 241-B6
W MOUNTAIN VIEW AV
ELLENSBURG WA 241-B6
MOUNTAIN VIEW DR
BENTON CO OR 207-A4
BENTON CO OR 327-H1
BONNER CO ID 244-A2
CLACKAMAS CO OR 201-C5
MOUNTAINVIEW DR
NEWBERG OR 198-D5
YAMHILL CO OR 198-D5
N MOUNTAIN VIEW DR
BOISE ID 253-C2
SW MOUNTAIN VIEW DR
JEFFERSON CO OR 208-A6
W MOUNTAIN VIEW DR
BOISE ID 253-C2
MOUNTAIN VIEW DR E
KITSAP CO WA 271-D12
MOUNTAIN VIEW DR S
SALEM OR 324-G2
MOUNTAIN VIEW RD
COLUMBIA CO OR 192-A3
COWLITZ CO WA 189-D5
DESCHUTES CO OR 212-A4
FERNDALE WA 158-B6
SKAGIT CO WA 260-J14
WHATCOM CO WA 158-B6
N MOUNTAIN VIEW RD
LATAH CO ID 249-D4
MOUNTAIN VISTA RD
FRANKLIN CO WA 121-A2
MOUNT ANGEL HWY NE
MARION CO OR 205-B4
MOUNT ANGELES RD
CLALLAM CO WA 261-G8
PORT ANGELES WA 261-G8
MOUNT ANGEL-GERVAIS RD NE
MARION CO OR 205-B3
MOUNT ANGEL-SCOTTS MILLS RD NE
MARION CO OR 205-C3
MOUNT ASHLAND SKI RD
JACKSON CO OR 234-D6
MOUNT BAKER HWY Rt#-542
WHATCOM CO WA 102-B1
WHATCOM CO WA 103-A1
MOUNT BALDY LOOKOUT RD
SISKIYOU CO CA 149-A3
MOUNT BRYNION RD
COWLITZ CO WA 189-D3
COWLITZ CO WA 303-H5
KELSO WA 303-F6
N MOUNT CARROL ST
DALTON GARDENS ID 355-F2
MOUNT GLEN RD
UNION CO OR 130-A2
MOUNT HOOD AV Rt#-214
MARION CO OR 205-B1
WOODBURN OR 205-B1
MOUNT HOOD HWY Rt#-35
CLACKAMAS CO OR 202-C5
HOOD RIVER CO OR 195-C7
HOOD RIVER CO OR 202-C1
MOUNT HOOD HWY U.S.-26
CLACKAMAS CO OR 200-C3
CLACKAMAS CO OR 201-B4
CLACKAMAS CO OR 202-A6
DAMASCUS OR 200-C3
GRESHAM OR 200-C3
MULTNOMAH CO OR 200-C3
SANDY OR 200-C3
SE MOUNT HOOD HWY U.S.-26
MULTNOMAH CO OR 200-A2
PORTLAND OR 200-A2
MOUNT HOOD ST
THE DALLES OR 196-C7
S MOUNT HOPE RD
CLACKAMAS CO OR 205-D2
MOUNT HOREB RD SE
MARION CO OR 134-A1
MOUNT JUPITER RD
JEFFERSON CO WA 173-C1
MOUNT LEHMAN RD
DISTRICT OF MATSQUI BC 102-B1
MOUNT MATHESON RD
BRITISH COLUMBIA BC 165-A1
DISTRICT OF METCHOSIN BC 165-A1
MOUNT NEWTON CROSS RD
DISTRICT OF CENTRAL SAANI BC 159-B3
MOUNT OLYMPUS AV
OCEAN SHORES WA 298-E4

INDEX

384 MOUNT OLYMPUS AV SE STREET INDEX NFD RD 5

STREET City State Page-Grid

MOUNT OLYMPUS AV SE
OCEAN SHORES WA 298-D2
MOUNT PLEASANT RD
COWLITZ CO WA 189-D4
SKAMANIA CO WA 193-D7
MOUNT REUBEN RD
DOUGLAS CO OR 225-A7
NW MOUNT RICHMOND RD
YAMHILL CO OR 198-A4
SE MOUNT SCOTT BLVD
CLACKAMAS CO OR 200-A3
CLACKAMAS CO OR 319-J7
HAPPY VALLEY OR 200-A3
MULTNOMAH CO OR 319-H6
PORTLAND OR 200-A3
PORTLAND OR 319-H6
PORTLAND OR 319-J7
MOUNT SEYMOUR PKWY
DISTRICT OF NORTH VANCOUV BC 156-D3
DISTRICT OF NORTH VANCOUV BC 255-H6
MOUNT SEYMOUR RD
DISTRICT OF NORTH VANCOUV BC 156-D3
MOUNT SHASTA DR
VANCOUVER WA 307-G7
MOUNT SOLO RD
COWLITZ CO WA 302-B5
LONGVIEW WA 302-B5
MOUNT SOLO RD Rt#-432
COWLITZ CO WA 302-C6
LONGVIEW WA 302-C6
E MOUNT SPOKANE PARK DR Rt#-20
SPOKANE CO WA 114-C1
SPOKANE CO WA 246-D1
SPOKANE CO WA 247-A1
SPOKANE CO WA 347-H5
N MOUNT SPOKANE PARK DR Rt#-20
SPOKANE CO WA 114-C1
MOUNT STELLA RD
JACKSON CO OR 226-D3
MOUNT TOM DR
LINN CO OR 210-B6
MOUNT TOM RD
LANE CO OR 210-C7
MOUNT VERNON RD
LANE CO OR 331-H9
SPRINGFIELD OR 331-H9
MOUNT VERNON RD S
MOUNT VERNON WA 168-B1
SKAGIT CO WA 168-B1
MOUNT VERNON-BIG LAKE RD
MOUNT VERNON WA 260-H12
SKAGIT CO WA 161-C7
SKAGIT CO WA 260-H12
MOUNT VIEW RD
SPOKANE CO WA 247-A1
NW MOUNT WASHINGTON DR
BEND OR 332-B3
E MOUTAIN RD
BENTON CO WA 341-A4
MOWICH RD
DOUGLAS CO OR 223-A4
MOWICH SECTION Rt#-165
CARBONADO WA 182-D6
PIERCE CO WA 110-C3
PIERCE CO WA 118-C1
PIERCE CO WA 182-D6
MOWREY RD
CHELAN CO WA 236-B3
MOX-CHEHALIS RD
GRAYS HARBOR CO WA 117-B1
GRAYS HARBOR CO WA 179-C7
E MOXEE AV
MOXEE WA 243-D7
YAKIMA CO WA 243-D7
MOYIE RIVER RD
BOUNDARY CO ID 107-B1
MUCK-KAPOWSIN
PIERCE CO WA 182-A6
MUD BAY HWY SW
OLYMPIA WA 296-A4
THURSTON CO WA 180-B6
THURSTON CO WA 296-A4
MUD BAY RD
SAN JUAN CO WA 160-A7
MUD CREEK RD
ADAMS CO ID 251-A3
MUDDY RD
WASCO CO OR 135-C1
MUDDY CREEK RD
BAKER CO OR 130-A3
SW MUDDY VALLEY RD
YAMHILL CO OR 204-A2
MUD FLAT RD
MALHEUR CO OR 146-C2
OWYHEE CO ID 147-C3
OWYHEE CO ID 155-B1
WHITMAN CO WA 122-B1
MUD LAKE RD
DESCHUTES CO OR 216-A4
SKAGIT CO WA 161-C6
MUD SPRING RD
MALHEUR CO OR 154-A2
MUD SPRINGS RD NE
DOUGLAS CO WA 112-C1
MUD SPRINGS RD NW
DOUGLAS CO WA 112-B1
MUEKE RD
CLACKAMAS CO OR 199-B6
MUELLER RD
UMATILLA CO OR 121-C3
MUFFORD AV
LANGLEY BC 157-C7
TOWNSHIP OF LANGLEY BC 157-C7
MUIR CREEK RD
DOUGLAS CO OR 223-A7
DOUGLAS CO OR 227-A1
MUKILTEO BLVD
EVERETT WA 171-B2
EVERETT WA 264-A7
MUKILTEO WA 171-B2
MUKILTEO BLVD SE
EVERETT WA 264-C6
MUKILTEO BLVD SW
EVERETT WA 264-B7
MUKILTEO SPEEDWAY Rt#-525
MUKILTEO WA 171-B2
MUKILTEO WA 266-D3
MUKILTEO WA 267-E5
SNOHOMISH CO WA 171-B4
SNOHOMISH CO WA 267-E6
MULEDEER RD
DOUGLAS CO WA 239-B1
MULE SPRING RD
HARNEY CO OR 144-C3
MULFORD RD
LEWIS CO WA 187-C4

NW MULHOLLAND DR
ROSEBURG OR 334-E4
MULINO RD
CLACKAMAS CO OR 199-C7
S MULINO RD
CANBY OR 199-C6
CLACKAMAS CO OR 199-C6
MULKEY RD
WHITMAN CO WA 114-B3
E MULLAN AV
KOOTENAI CO ID 353-H6
KOOTENAI CO ID 354-F6
OSBURN ID 115-C2
POST FALLS ID 353-H6
POST FALLS ID 354-B6
W MULLAN AV
KOOTENAI CO ID 354-H6
POST FALLS ID 353-G6
MULLAN RD
ADAMS CO WA 122-A1
N MULLAN RD
SPOKANE VALLEY WA 350-D8
MULLEN RD SE
LACEY WA 297-H10
THURSTON CO WA 181-A7
THURSTON CO WA 297-J11
SE MULLENIX RD
KITSAP CO WA 174-C5
MULLER DR
LINN CO OR 207-D5
S MULLINIX RD
SPOKANE CO WA 114-B2
SW MULTNOMAH BLVD
PORTLAND OR 199-B2
PORTLAND OR 316-A6
MULTNOMAH DR
HOOD RIVER CO OR 195-C5
NE MULTNOMAH ST
PORTLAND OR 313-H4
PORTLAND OR 314-A4
MULTNOMAH BASIN RD
MULTNOMAH CO OR 201-A1
MUNCH RD
CLARK CO WA 193-A1
MUNDUN CANYON RD
CHELAN CO WA 238-A2
MUNDY ST
COQUITLAM BC 157-A5
MUNDY LOSS RD
PIERCE CO WA 182-D4
MUNN RD
BRITISH COLUMBIA BC 159-B5
DISTRICT OF SAANICH BC 256-A1
MUNSEL LAKE RD
FLORENCE OR 214-B2
LANE CO OR 214-B2
MUNSON DR SW
THURSTON CO WA 180-B6
MUNSON CREEK RD
TILLAMOOK CO OR 197-C4
MURCHIE RD
TOWNSHIP OF LANGLEY BC 158-C2
MURDER CREEK DR
LINN CO OR 326-H3
MURPHY DR NW
PIERCE CO WA 181-C1
MURPHY RD
BEND OR 332-E12
DOUGLAS CO OR 225-C7
FRANKLIN CO WA 121-B2
LINCOLN CO OR 203-D4
S MURPHY RD
SPOKANE CO WA 246-A6
MURPHY CREEK RD
JOSEPHINE CO OR 149-A2
MURPHY-GRANDVIEW RD Rt#-78
OWYHEE CO ID 147-C2
MURPHY GULCH RD
JACKSON CO OR 230-A4
NW MURRAY BLVD
BEAVERTON OR 199-B1
WASHINGTON CO OR 199-B1
SW MURRAY BLVD
BEAVERTON OR 199-A2
WASHINGTON CO OR 199-A2
MURRAY RD SW
LAKEWOOD WA 181-C5
PIERCE CO WA 181-C5
MURRAY ST
PORT MOODY BC 157-A4
MUSTANG RESERVOIR RD
MALHEUR CO OR 154-C1
MUTINY BAY RD
Clinton WA 171-A2
Freeland WA 170-C1
MYERS RD
POLK CO OR 204-A5
TOPPENISH WA 120-A2
YAKIMA CO WA 120-A2
MYERS RD E
BONNEY LAKE WA 182-C4
MYERS WY S
KING CO WA 285-J3
KING CO WA 286-A4
SEATTLE WA 285-J3
SEATTLE WA 286-A4
MYERS CREEK RD
CURRY CO OR 232-B1
MYRA RD
COLLEGE PLACE WA 344-G9
WALLA WALLA WA 344-G9
WALLA WALLA CO WA 344-G9
MYRNA LN
JOSEPHINE CO OR 233-A4
S MYRTLE PL
SEATTLE WA 286-D1
E MYRTLE ST
BOISE ID 253-C3
S MYRTLE ST
SEATTLE WA 286-D1
W MYRTLE ST
BOISE ID 253-C3
MYRTLE CREEK RD
COOS CO OR 140-C3
N MYRTLE CREEK RD
DOUGLAS CO OR 141-B2
DOUGLAS CO OR 221-D7
DOUGLAS CO OR 225-D1
S MYRTLE CREEK RD
DOUGLAS CO OR 225-D1
MYRTLE PARK RD
HARNEY CO OR 137-A3
MYRTLE POINT-COOPER BRIDGE RD
COOS CO OR 140-B2
MYRTLE POINT OR 140-B2

MYRTLE POINT-LAMPA RD
COOS CO OR 140-B2
COOS CO OR 220-C6
MYRTLE POINT OR 140-B2
MYRTLE POINT-SITKUM RD
COOS CO OR 140-C2

N

N ST
GRANTS PASS OR 335-G10
JOSEPHINE CO OR 335-H10
SE N ST
GRANTS PASS OR 335-G10
NACHES AV
TIETON WA 119-C1
E NACHES AV Rt#-823
SELAH WA 243-B5
S NACHES AV
YAKIMA WA 243-C6
S NACHES RD
NACHES WA 119-C1
YAKIMA CO WA 119-C1
YAKIMA CO WA 243-A5
S NACHES WY
YAKIMA CO WA 119-C1
W NACHES WY
YAKIMA CO WA 119-C1
NACHES HEIGHTS RD
YAKIMA CO WA 243-A5
NACHES-TIETON RD
TIETON WA 119-C1
YAKIMA CO WA 119-C1
NACHES WENAS RD
YAKIMA CO WA 243-A4
NAGLER RD
YAKIMA CO WA 243-B5
NAHAHUM CANYON RD
CHELAN CO WA 238-C2
NW NAITO PKWY
PORTLAND OR 312-E3
PORTLAND OR 313-F4
SW NAITO PKWY
PORTLAND OR 313-F6
PORTLAND OR 317-F1
SW NAITO PKWY Rt#-99W
PORTLAND OR 317-F1
NAMPA BLVD Rt#-55
NAMPA ID 147-B1
NANAIMO PKWY Rt#-19
NANAIMO BC 93-A3
NANAIMO ST
VANCOUVER BC 156-C5
VANCOUVER BC 255-C12
NANAIMO-HORSESHOE FERRY
BRITISH COLUMBIA BC 93-A3
NANAIMO LAKES RD
NANAIMO BC 93-A3
NANAIMO-TSAWWASSEN FERRY
BRITISH COLUMBIA BC 93-A3
BRITISH COLUMBIA BC 101-B1
NANAIMO BC 93-A3
NANCY GREENE WY
DISTRICT OF NORTH VANCOUV BC 156-B2
NANEUM RD
KITTITAS CO WA 241-C4
NANEUM RIDGE RD
KITTITAS CO WA 241-D1
NAPOLEON-BARSTOW RD
STEVENS CO WA 106-A1
NARROWS DR
TACOMA WA 181-C2
NARROWS-PRINCETON RD
HARNEY CO OR 145-B2
NASH AV
BENTON CO OR 327-C13
NASH LN
CANYON CO ID 147-B1
NASHUA LN
DESCHUTES CO OR 212-A4
NW NASHVILLE AV
BEND OR 332-D6
NASI LN
VALLEY CO ID 252-D1
NASTY FLAT RD
HARNEY CO OR 144-B3
SW NATERLIN DR
NEWPORT OR 206-B4
NATIONAL AV
CHEHALIS WA 299-E9
LEWIS CO WA 299-E9
S NATIONAL AV
Navy Yard City WA 270-E12
NATIONAL AV N
BREMERTON WA 270-E11
Navy Yard City WA 270-E11
NATIONAL PARK HWY
LEWIS CO WA 185-A5
PIERCE CO WA 185-A5
NATIONAL PARK HWY Rt#-62
KLAMATH CO OR 227-B4
NATIONAL PARK HWY U.S.-12
LEWIS CO WA 118-B2
MORTON WA 118-B2
NAVAL AV
BREMERTON WA 270-G10
NAVARRE ST
CHELAN WA 236-D3
NAVARRE COULEE RD Rt#-971
CHELAN CO WA 236-B3
NEACOXIE DR
GEARHART OR 301-G5
NEAH BAY RD
CLALLAM CO WA 100-B2
Neah Bay WA 100-B2
NEAH BAY RD Rt#-112
CLALLAM CO WA 100-B2
Neah Bay WA 100-B2
NEAL LN
DOUGLAS CO OR 225-C1
NEAL CREEK RD
HOOD RIVER CO OR 195-C7
NEALEY RD
OKANOGAN CO WA 105-A1
NEATHAMMER GULCH RD
JACKSON CO OR 230-A3
NEAVES RD
PITT MEADOWS BC 157-C5
NEBRASKA ST
SKAGIT CO WA 259-J14
NECANICUM DR
SEASIDE OR 301-G8
NECANICUM HWY Rt#-53
CLATSOP CO OR 188-D7
CLATSOP CO OR 191-C3
TILLAMOOK CO OR 191-C3
NECK RD
YAMHILL CO OR 198-C7

NEEDLE CREEK RD
JACKSON CO OR 226-C5
NEEDLE RIDGE RD
JACKSON CO OR 226-C5
NEEDLE ROCK RD
JACKSON CO OR 226-B5
S NEEDY RD
CLACKAMAS CO OR 205-D1
NEER CITY RD
COLUMBIA CO OR 189-C4
NEER CITY CEMETERY RD
COLUMBIA CO OR 189-C5
NEERGAARD RD
ADAMS CO WA 113-B3
NEFF RD
BEND OR 217-C2
DESCHUTES CO OR 217-C2
JEFFERSON CO OR 208-C3
NE NEFF RD
BEND OR 217-C2
BEND OR 332-H6
NEGUS WY
DESCHUTES CO OR 212-D5
NEHALEM DR
CLATSOP CO OR 191-D1
NEHALEM HWY Rt#-47
COLUMBIA CO OR 117-B3
COLUMBIA CO OR 125-B1
WASHINGTON CO OR 125-B1
NEHALEM HWY Rt#-202
CLATSOP CO OR 117-B3
CLATSOP CO OR 188-D3
CLATSOP CO OR 300-F8
COLUMBIA CO OR 117-B3
NEHALEM RD
TILLAMOOK CO OR 191-A4
NEHALEM ST
CLATSKANIE OR 117-B3
NEHALEM QUARRY RD
TILLAMOOK CO OR 191-B3
E NEIDER AV
COEUR D'ALENE ID 355-E7
NEILL RD
WASHINGTON CO OR 198-D5
NEILSEN RD
WHATCOM CO WA 158-C6
E NEILSON RD
KOOTENAI CO ID 245-B5
NELLITA RD NW
KITSAP CO WA 173-C2
NELS NELSON RD NW
DOUGLAS CO WA 236-B6
KITSAP CO WA 174-B1
KITSAP CO WA 270-F1
Silverdale WA 174-B1
NELSON AV
DISTRICT OF BURNABY BC 156-C5
NELSON LP
KOOTENAI CO ID 247-C1
NELSON RD
DESCHUTES CO OR 217-D2
DOUGLAS CO OR 219-B1
LEWIS CO WA 187-B2
WALLA WALLA CO WA 121-B3
WASHINGTON CO OR 198-A1
E NELSON RD
GRANT CO WA 242-D3
SE NELSON RD
KITSAP CO WA 174-C6
NELSON ST
VANCOUVER BC 254-E9
NELSON SIDING RD
KITTITAS CO WA 111-B3
NEPPEL RD
GRANT CO WA 242-B1
NESIKA RD
CURRY CO OR 228-A4
NESS RD
KOOTENAI CO ID 247-C7
NESS RD Rt#-116
Hadlock-Irondale WA 170-A1
JEFFERSON CO WA 170-A1
NESS CORNER RD Rt#-116
Hadlock-Irondale WA 170-A1
NESTUCCA RIVER RD
TILLAMOOK CO OR 125-B2
YAMHILL CO OR 125-B2
NW NESTUCCA RIVER RD
YAMHILL CO OR 125-B2
NETARTS HWY
TILLAMOOK OR 197-B2
TILLAMOOK CO OR 197-A2
NETARTS BAY DR
TILLAMOOK CO OR 197-A2
N NETTLETON ST
SPOKANE WA 348-F5
SW NEUGEBAUER RD
WASHINGTON CO OR 198-D4
NEVADA AV
KLAMATH FALLS OR 338-B5
W NEVADA AV Rt#-903
ROSLYN WA 240-A1
N NEVADA DR
COWLITZ CO WA 302-J5
COWLITZ CO WA 303-A5
E NEVADA ST
ASHLAND OR 337-D5
N NEVADA ST
SPOKANE WA 347-B11
SPOKANE WA 349-B4
SPOKANE CO WA 347-B12
W NEVADA ST
ASHLAND OR 337-C5
NEVADA STATE ROUTE Rt#-140
HARNEY CO OR 153-A3
HUMBOLDT CO NV 153-C3
NEVADA STATE ROUTE Rt#-292
HUMBOLDT CO NV 153-C3
NEVIL RD
LEWIS CO WA 187-C3
NEVILLE LN
JACKSON CO OR 234-A2
NEVIN RD
CITY OF CHILLIWACK BC 94-C3
E NEWARK AV
SPOKANE WA 349-C10
NEWBERG HWY Rt#-214
WOODBURN OR 205-B1
NEWBERG HWY Rt#-219
MARION CO OR 205-B1
WASHINGTON CO OR 198-D2
WOODBURN OR 205-B1
NEWBERG RD
TILLAMOOK CO OR 197-B5
NW NEWBERRY RD
MULTNOMAH CO OR 192-B6

NW NEWBERRY RD
PORTLAND OR 192-B6
NEWBERRY CRATER RD
DESCHUTES CO OR 143-A1
NW NEWBERRY HILL RD
KITSAP CO WA 174-A2
Silverdale WA 270-A1
NEW BRIDGE RD
BAKER CO OR 139-A1
NE NEW BROOKLYN RD
BAINBRIDGE ISLAND WA 174-C1
NEWBURY RD
GRAYS HARBOR CO WA 178-A2
NEWCASTLE WY
BELLEVUE WA 175-C4
NEWCASTLE WA 175-C4
NEWCASTLE GOLF CLUB RD
NEWCASTLE WA 175-C3
NEWCOMB RD
DESCHUTES CO OR 212-C6
NEW CREEK RD
MALHEUR CO OR 146-B1
S NEW ERA RD
CLACKAMAS CO OR 199-C6
NEW HOPE RD
GRANTS PASS OR 335-C14
JOSEPHINE CO OR 149-A2
JOSEPHINE CO OR 229-B7
JOSEPHINE CO OR 335-C14
NEW JONES RD
JACKSON CO OR 230-C4
S NEW KIRCHNER RD
CLACKAMAS CO OR 199-D7
NEW LAKE RD
COOS CO OR 224-B2
NEWLAND RD
CLACKAMAS CO OR 199-C5
JACKSON CO OR 230-C6
NEWMAN RD
ISLAND CO WA 170-D1
S NEWMAN RD
CLACKAMAS CO OR 205-C2
NEWMAN CREEK RD
GRAYS HARBOR CO WA 179-B7
N NEWMAN LAKE DR
SPOKANE CO WA 247-B1
SPOKANE CO WA 352-E1
W NEWMAN LAKE DR
SPOKANE CO WA 247-B1
SPOKANE CO WA 352-D1
NEWMARK AV
COOS BAY OR 333-B6
NORTH BEND OR 333-D7
NEWMARK ST
NORTH BEND OR 333-F6
NEWPORT AV
COOS CO OR 220-D1
COOS CO OR 333-J12
DISTRICT OF OAK BAY BC 257-D9
NEWPORT AV U.S.-101
COOS BAY OR 333-H12
COOS CO OR 333-H12
NW NEWPORT AV
BEND OR 332-D6
N NEWPORT HWY U.S.-2
Country Homes WA 347-B9
Fairwood WA 347-B9
SPOKANE CO WA 347-E5
NW NEWPORT WY
ISSAQUAH WA 175-D4
SE NEWPORT WY
BELLEVUE WA 175-D3
NEWPORT WY NW
ISSAQUAH WA 175-D4
ISSAQUAH WA 176-A4
NEWSKAH RD
GRAYS HARBOR CO WA 183-D1
NEWSOME CREEK RD
CROOK CO OR 136-A3
NEWTON RD
STEVENS CO WA 106-B3
NEWTON ST
CITY OF VICTORIA BC 257-B7
DISTRICT OF SAANICH BC 257-B7
E NEWTON ST
SEATTLE WA 278-B2
NE NEWTON CREEK RD
DOUGLAS CO OR 334-H2
ROSEBURG OR 334-G3
NEWTON HILL RD
LINCOLN CO OR 206-B3
NEZ PERCE AV
WINCHESTER ID 123-B2
W NEZ PERCE RD
COEUR D'ALENE ID 354-J6
COEUR D'ALENE ID 355-A6
NEZPERCE-CRAIGMONT RD
LEWIS CO ID 123-B2
NFD DUFUR VALLEY RD
WASCO CO OR 202-D4
NFD RD 2
ADAMS CO ID 131-B3
NFD RD 9
SHOSHONE CO ID 115-C1
WASHINGTON CO ID 139-A1
NFD RD 10
CLACKAMAS CO OR 201-A3
GRANT CO OR 129-B3
GRANT CO OR 137-B1
MULTNOMAH CO OR 201-B2
NFD RD 11
JOSEPHINE CO OR 233-A5
NFD RD 12
CLACKAMAS CO OR 201-A3
JEFFERSON CO OR 134-C1
JEFFERSON CO OR 211-B2
LEWIS CO WA 185-A6
MULTNOMAH CO OR 201-B2
TILLAMOOK CO OR 203-C3
NFD RD 13
BAKER CO OR 137-C2
GRANT CO OR 137-C2
HOOD RIVER CO OR 201-D2
HOOD RIVER CO OR 202-A1
NFD RD 14
CLACKAMAS CO OR 201-A3
GRANT CO OR 137-C3
LEWIS CO WA 185-A7
TILLAMOOK CO OR 197-C6
YAMHILL CO OR 197-D7
NFD RD 15
GRANT CO OR 137-B3
JOSEPHINE CO OR 233-B7
TILLAMOOK CO OR 203-C2
NFD RD 16
BAKER CO OR 138-A2
GRANT CO OR 137-C2
HOOD RIVER CO OR 202-A2

NFD RD 16
JOSEPHINE CO OR 233-A1
NFD RD 17
HOOD RIVER CO OR 202-C3
JOSEPHINE CO OR 233-C7
LINCOLN CO OR 203-C4
NFD RD 18
LAKE CO OR 143-B1
NFD RD 19
LINCOLN CO OR 203-B6
NFD RD 20
CURRY CO OR 224-B7
MULTNOMAH CO OR 201-A1
NFD RD 21
GRANT CO OR 137-A2
LANE CO OR 142-A1
MORROW CO OR 128-C3
UMATILLA CO OR 129-C3
UNION CO OR 129-C2
NFD RD 22
BONNER CO ID 244-A7
KLAMATH CO OR 143-A1
LAKE CO OR 143-A1
LANE CO OR 142-A1
NFD RD 23
CURRY CO OR 148-C1
DOUGLAS CO OR 214-C6
LANE CO OR 142-B1
LEWIS CO WA 118-C2
MASON CO WA 109-B2
SKAMANIA CO WA 119-A3
NFD RD 24
GRANT CO OR 136-C2
GRANT CO OR 137-A2
LAKE CO OR 143-A1
LANE CO OR 142-B1
MASON CO WA 109-B2
MASON CO WA 173-A4
NFD RD 25
LANE CO OR 209-C6
LEWIS CO WA 118-C2
MASON CO WA 173-A2
SKAMANIA CO WA 118-C2
WASHINGTON CO ID 139-A1
WHEELER CO OR 128-B3
NFD RD 28
GRANT CO OR 137-B3
NFD RD 29
CLALLAM CO WA 163-C7
NFD RD 30
CLALLAM CO WA 163-C6
CLALLAM CO WA 164-A5
COWLITZ CO WA 190-A3
DESCHUTES CO OR 217-C5
NFD RD 31
GRANT CO OR 137-A3
UMATILLA CO OR 130-A1
WASHINGTON CO ID 139-B1
NFD RD 32
LANE CO OR 209-D6
OKANOGAN CO WA 105-A1
UMATILLA CO OR 130-A1
NFD RD 33
CURRY CO OR 148-B1
KLAMATH CO OR 231-B1
NFD RD 34
DOUGLAS CO OR 222-D2
DOUGLAS CO OR 223-A2
NFD RD 35
DOUGLAS CO OR 222-D4
KITTITAS CO WA 238-B7
NFD RD 36
GRANT CO OR 137-B1
NFD RD 37
GRANT CO OR 137-A3
NFD RD 38
LANE CO OR 142-A1
OKANOGAN CO WA 104-B2
NFD RD 40
GARFIELD CO WA 122-B2
NFD RD 41
JOSEPHINE CO OR 233-D7
NFD RD 42
JOSEPHINE CO OR 233-C5
SKAMANIA CO WA 194-A2
NFD RD 43
KLAMATH CO OR 142-C3
SKAMANIA CO WA 194-B3
NFD RD 44
HOOD RIVER CO OR 202-C4
LEWIS CO WA 185-D6
OKANOGAN CO WA 104-A3
WASCO CO OR 202-D4
NFD RD 44 RD
HOOD RIVER CO OR 202-D4
WASCO CO OR 202-D4
NFD RD 46
KLAMATH CO OR 151-A1
LEWIS CO WA 185-D7
MARION CO OR 126-C3
MARION CO OR 134-C1
NFD RD 48
HOOD RIVER CO OR 202-B6
LANE CO OR 214-D4
WASCO CO OR 127-A3
WASCO CO OR 202-C7
NFD RD 48N
KLAMATH CO OR 151-B3
LAKE CO OR 151-B3
NFD RD 49
KLAMATH CO OR 143-A3
NFD RD 50
KING CO WA 176-D7
LINCOLN CO OR 206-C7
SHOSHONE CO ID 115-B2
NFD RD 51
GRANT CO OR 129-C3
UNION CO OR 129-C3
NFD RD 52
GRANT CO OR 129-C3
JEFFERSON CO OR 211-C2
LANE CO OR 209-A7
LINCOLN CO OR 206-D7
UMATILLA CO OR 129-B3
NFD RD 53
MORROW CO OR 129-A3
SKAMANIA CO WA 193-D2
UMATILLA CO OR 129-A3
NFD RD 54
LANE CO OR 209-C4
SKAMANIA CO WA 190-B7
SKAMANIA CO WA 193-D1
SKAMANIA CO WA 194-A1
NFD RD 55
WASHINGTON CO ID 131-B3
NFD RD 58
CROOK CO OR 136-C2
GRANT CO OR 136-C2

INDEX

NFD RD 58 STREET INDEX NFD RD 4601 385

STREET City State Page-Grid

NFD RD 58
LANE CO OR 209-C5
SKAMANIA CO WA 194-A1
NFD RD 59
DOUGLAS CO OR 214-B6
NFD RD 60
DOUGLAS CO OR 223-D2
KLAMATH CO OR 142-B1
NFD RD 62
UNION CO OR 130-B1
NFD RD 63
UNION CO OR 130-A1
NFD RD 64
SKAMANIA CO WA 190-D6
UNION CO OR 130-A1
NFD RD 65
CHELAN CO WA 111-B1
SKAMANIA CO WA 194-D1
NFD RD 67
JOSEPHINE CO OR 233-A1
NFD RD 68
SKAMANIA CO WA 195-A3
NFD RD 70
CURRY CO OR 232-C1
NFD RD 73
GRANITE OR 137-C1
GRANT CO OR 129-C3
GRANT CO OR 130-A3
GRANT CO OR 137-C1
UNION CO OR 130-A3
NFD RD 75
DOUGLAS CO OR 222-D4
NFD RD 77
BAKER CO OR 130-C3
NFD RD 80
GRAYS HARBOR CO WA 109-A2
JOSEPHINE CO OR 233-D6
NFD RD 81
COWLITZ CO WA 190-A3
SKAMANIA CO WA 190-B3
NFD RD 83
HUMBOLDT CO NV 154-C3
HUMBOLDT CO NV 155-A3
SKAMANIA CO WA 190-D2
NFD RD 84
HUMBOLDT CO NV 154-C3
LEWIS CO WA 185-A6
LINCOLN CO OR 203-C7
NFD RD 85
JOSEPHINE CO OR 233-C7
TILLAMOOK CO OR 125-A2
TILLAMOOK CO OR 197-D6
NFD RD 87
HUMBOLDT CO NV 154-C3
NFD RD 89
ADAMS CO ID 131-C3
NFD RD 90
SKAMANIA CO WA 118-C3
SKAMANIA CO WA 190-D5
NFD RD 92 Rt#-508
LINCOLN CO MT 107-C1
NFD RD 94
SKAMANIA CO WA 190-D1
NFD RD 96
HUMBOLDT CO NV 154-C3
HUMBOLDT CO NV 155-A3
NFD RD 98
JOSEPHINE CO OR 233-D7
NFD RD 99
SKAMANIA CO WA 190-C1
NFD RD 100
DESCHUTES CO OR 211-D6
DOUGLAS CO OR 222-B1
OKANOGAN CO WA 105-B2
NFD RD 105
ADAMS CO ID 131-B3
NFD RD 110
CURRY CO OR 228-D1
KLAMATH CO OR 231-A2
NFD RD 111
KITTITAS CO WA 241-B1
NFD RD 112
CHELAN CO WA 111-C2
KITTITAS CO WA 241-A2
TILLAMOOK CO OR 125-A2
NFD RD 113
KITTITAS CO WA 241-B1
NFD RD 114
KITTITAS CO WA 241-A1
NFD RD 115
KITTITAS CO WA 238-A7
KITTITAS CO WA 241-B2
NFD RD 116
KITTITAS CO WA 238-A6
KITTITAS CO WA 241-B2
VALLEY CO ID 252-C4
NFD RD 118
KITTITAS CO WA 238-A7
NFD RD 128
ADAMS CO ID 131-B3
NFD RD 129
LINCOLN CO OR 203-B4
NFD RD 130
CURRY CO OR 232-D2
JEFFERSON CO OR 211-C2
NFD RD 134
LEWIS CO WA 185-A7
NFD RD 150
CURRY CO OR 228-B1
GRANT CO OR 129-A3
LANE CO OR 211-A6
NFD RD 151
SHOSHONE CO ID 115-C1
NFD RD 160
DESCHUTES CO OR 211-C4
DESCHUTES CO OR 216-D6
NFD RD 165
ADAMS CO ID 139-C1
ADAMS CO ID 252-A1
NFD RD 172
ADAMS CO ID 251-A7
NFD RD 181
ADAMS CO ID 251-A7
NFD RD 183
ADAMS CO ID 251-A7
ADAMS CO ID 252-A1
NFD RD 186
ADAMS CO ID 252-B2
VALLEY CO ID 252-C1
NFD RD 199
ADAMS CO ID 252-A2
NFD RD 200
ADAMS CO ID 252-A2
CHELAN CO WA 238-B3
DESCHUTES CO OR 217-A5
DOUGLAS CO OR 222-B2
JEFFERSON CO OR 211-B1
OKANOGAN CO WA 105-B2
NFD RD 201
CLACKAMAS CO OR 201-A3
NFD RD 203
SKAMANIA CO WA 190-D7
NFD RD 206
ADAMS CO ID 252-B4
KOOTENAI CO ID 245-C4
NFD RD 207
SKAMANIA CO WA 190-D6
NFD RD 208
SHOSHONE CO ID 115-C1
NFD RD 209
KOOTENAI CO ID 245-C2
NFD RD 213
KITTITAS CO WA 241-A1
NFD RD 214
ADAMS CO ID 252-A4
NFD RD 217
ADAMS CO ID 252-A4
NFD RD 218
ADAMS CO ID 252-C2
NFD RD 230
CURRY CO OR 232-D1
DESCHUTES CO OR 217-D5
KLAMATH CO OR 231-A2
NFD RD 231
BOUNDARY CO ID 107-A2
NFD RD 243
ADAMS CO ID 252-B5
NFD RD 250
DESCHUTES CO OR 217-D7
NFD RD 255
CLACKAMAS CO OR 201-A6
NFD RD 258
KOOTENAI CO ID 245-D3
NFD RD 268
KOOTENAI CO ID 245-B6
NFD RD 270
SKAMANIA CO WA 190-D2
NFD RD 278
BONNER CO ID 244-D5
BONNER CO ID 245-D1
KOOTENAI CO ID 245-D2
NFD RD 280
JEFFERSON CO OR 211-B1
NFD RD 281
DOUGLAS CO OR 223-A7
DOUGLAS CO OR 227-A1
NFD RD 288
KLAMATH CO OR 143-B3
KLAMATH CO OR 151-B1
LAKE CO OR 143-B3
NFD RD 291
BOUNDARY CO ID 107-B2
NFD RD 294
BOUNDARY CO ID 107-B2
NFD RD 300
DESCHUTES CO OR 217-A3
NFD RD 301
SHOSHONE CO ID 115-C3
NFD RD 302
BONNER CO ID 106-C2
NFD RD 306
SHOSHONE CO ID 244-D7
NFD RD 317
SKAMANIA CO WA 190-D7
NFD RD 320
SKAMANIA CO WA 190-C7
NFD RD 331
KLAMATH CO OR 151-B1
NFD RD 332
BONNER CO ID 244-C7
BONNER CO ID 245-D2
SHOSHONE CO ID 244-D6
NFD RD 348
KLAMATH CO OR 151-B1
LAKE CO OR 151-C1
NFD RD 350
KLAMATH CO OR 231-A4
NFD RD 360
KLAMATH CO OR 231-A4
NFD RD 370
DESCHUTES CO OR 216-C1
NFD RD 375
KLAMATH CO OR 151-B2
NFD RD 380
SKAMANIA CO WA 190-D2
NFD RD 381
KLAMATH CO OR 151-B2
NFD RD 382
CLACKAMAS CO OR 201-D4
NFD RD 392
KOOTENAI CO ID 245-C4
NFD RD 400
CHELAN CO WA 238-A2
DESCHUTES CO OR 211-C5
DESCHUTES CO OR 216-D5
JEFFERSON CO OR 211-B1
SHOSHONE CO ID 115-C1
NFD RD 406
KOOTENAI CO ID 245-C3
NFD RD 410
CLACKAMAS CO OR 201-A3
NFD RD 411
KOOTENAI CO ID 245-D5
NFD RD 413
KOOTENAI CO ID 245-D7
SKAMANIA CO WA 194-B2
NFD RD 422
VALLEY CO ID 252-D7
NFD RD 434
KOOTENAI CO ID 245-D6
NFD RD 435
VALLEY CO ID 252-C5
NFD RD 437
KOOTENAI CO ID 245-C4
NFD RD 438
KOOTENAI CO ID 248-C2
NFD RD 450
DESCHUTES CO OR 216-A3
NFD RD 456
SHOSHONE CO ID 115-C2
NFD RD 471
HUMBOLDT CO NV 154-C3
NFD RD 472
JOSEPHINE CO OR 233-D6
NFD RD 480
LANE CO OR 142-A1
NFD RD 487
ADAMS CO ID 251-B7
ADAMS CO ID 252-B1
NFD RD 489
BONNER CO ID 244-D2
NFD RD 500
DOUGLAS CO OR 222-B2
NFD RD 503
SHOSHONE CO ID 115-C1
NFD RD 508 Rt#-508
LINCOLN CO MT 107-C2
NFD RD 510
CHELAN CO WA 238-A2
NFD RD 527
SKAMANIA CO WA 194-A1
NFD RD 529
HUMBOLDT CO NV 154-C3
NFD RD 531
HUMBOLDT CO NV 154-C3
NFD RD 587
ADAMS CO ID 251-A5
NFD RD 600
DESCHUTES CO OR 211-C7
DESCHUTES CO OR 217-C4
JEFFERSON CO OR 211-B2
NFD RD 610
KOOTENAI CO ID 245-D5
NFD RD 612
KOOTENAI CO ID 245-C5
NFD RD 616
KOOTENAI CO ID 245-D5
NFD RD 618
GEM CO ID 252-B7
NFD RD 625
GEM CO ID 252-B7
KOOTENAI CO ID 245-B4
NFD RD 700
DOUGLAS CO OR 223-C2
LINN CO OR 134-A2
SKAMANIA CO WA 190-D3
NFD RD 719
LANE CO OR 214-C2
NFD RD 760
DOUGLAS CO OR 223-C7
NFD RD 794
KOOTENAI CO ID 245-D3
NFD RD 800
DESCHUTES CO OR 211-B3
NFD RD 808
KOOTENAI CO ID 248-B3
NFD RD 810
KOOTENAI CO ID 248-C2
SKAMANIA CO WA 190-D3
NFD RD 831
LANE CO OR 214-D3
NFD RD 835
ADAMS CO ID 252-B5
NFD RD 855
KLAMATH CO OR 142-C1
NFD RD 950
DOUGLAS CO OR 222-C6
DOUGLAS CO OR 226-B3
NFD RD 953
LANE CO OR 214-B4
NFD RD 958
LANE CO OR 214-D4
NFD RD 980
KLAMATH CO OR 231-A4
NFD RD 1000
LINCOLN CO OR 206-D7
NFD RD 1008
MULTNOMAH CO OR 201-A2
NFD RD 1010
MULTNOMAH CO OR 201-A2
NFD RD 1012
DESCHUTES CO OR 211-C4
NFD RD 1013
BOUNDARY CO ID 106-C1
NFD RD 1014
LINCOLN CO OR 206-D7
NFD RD 1017
BONNER CO ID 245-D2
NFD RD 1018
DESCHUTES CO OR 211-B6
NFD RD 1024
DESCHUTES CO OR 211-B6
NFD RD 1026
DESCHUTES CO OR 211-B6
NFD RD 1027
CLACKAMAS CO OR 201-C3
NFD RD 1028
DESCHUTES CO OR 211-B4
NFD RD 1030
LINCOLN CO OR 206-D7
NFD RD 1031
TILLAMOOK CO OR 203-B1
NFD RD 1050
BONNER CO ID 244-B7
NFD RD 1066
BONNER CO ID 244-D6
NFD RD 1080
BONNER CO ID 245-D2
NFD RD 1088
BONNER CO ID 244-C6
NFD RD 1101
CURRY CO OR 232-D7
NFD RD 1110
JEFFERSON CO OR 211-C2
NFD RD 1176
JEFFERSON CO OR 208-C5
NFD RD 1179
JEFFERSON CO OR 212-A2
NFD RD 1207
YAKIMA CO WA 119-A2
NFD RD 1210
CLACKAMAS CO OR 201-B3
NFD RD 1217
MULTNOMAH CO OR 201-C2
NFD RD 1228
CLACKAMAS CO OR 201-C4
NFD RD 1268
TILLAMOOK CO OR 203-B2
NFD RD 1270
LEWIS CO WA 185-D7
NFD RD 1280
TILLAMOOK CO OR 203-C2
NFD RD 1310
HOOD RIVER CO OR 202-A1
NFD RD 1340
HOOD RIVER CO OR 202-A2
NFD RD 1341
BONNER CO ID 107-A1
NFD RD 1376
CURRY CO OR 148-B2
NFD RD 1393
JEFFERSON CO OR 212-B3
NFD RD 1394
JEFFERSON CO OR 213-A2
NFD RD 1395
JEFFERSON CO OR 213-A2
NFD RD 1399
JEFFERSON CO OR 212-B1
NFD RD 1414
CLACKAMAS CO OR 201-B3
NFD RD 1425
JEFFERSON CO OR 211-C1
NFD RD 1441
CHELAN CO WA 103-C3
NFD RD 1491
TILLAMOOK CO OR 197-C7
NFD RD 1509
MULTNOMAH CO OR 201-A2
NFD RD 1510
DESCHUTES CO OR 211-C5
NFD RD 1514
DESCHUTES CO OR 211-C6
NFD RD 1516
DESCHUTES CO OR 211-C7
NFD RD 1520
DESCHUTES CO OR 211-C5
NFD RD 1522
DESCHUTES CO OR 211-C6
NFD RD 1526
DESCHUTES CO OR 211-C7
NFD RD 1587
KOOTENAI CO ID 245-C4
NFD RD 1590
TILLAMOOK CO OR 197-B7
NFD RD 1594
KOOTENAI CO ID 245-D4
NFD RD 1608
DESCHUTES CO OR 211-D6
NFD RD 1610
DESCHUTES CO OR 211-D7
HOOD RIVER CO OR 202-B2
NFD RD 1611
HOOD RIVER CO OR 202-B2
NFD RD 1614
IDAHO CO ID 131-C2
NFD RD 1620
DESCHUTES CO OR 211-C7
NFD RD 1628
DESCHUTES CO OR 211-C7
DESCHUTES CO OR 216-C1
NFD RD 1631
HOOD RIVER CO OR 202-B3
NFD RD 1633
TILLAMOOK CO OR 203-C2
NFD RD 1640
HOOD RIVER CO OR 202-A2
NFD RD 1650
HOOD RIVER CO OR 202-A3
TILLAMOOK CO OR 203-C2
NFD RD 1660
HOOD RIVER CO OR 202-A3
NFD RD 1670
HOOD RIVER CO OR 202-A3
NFD RD 1686
TILLAMOOK CO OR 203-D2
NFD RD 1700
MASON CO WA 179-B2
NFD RD 1701
LINCOLN CO OR 203-C5
YAKIMA CO WA 240-B7
NFD RD 1703
KITTITAS CO WA 240-A7
NFD RD 1708
KITTITAS CO WA 240-A6
NFD RD 1710
HOOD RIVER CO OR 202-D1
NFD RD 1711
HOOD RIVER CO OR 202-D1
NFD RD 1720
HOOD RIVER CO OR 202-D3
KITTITAS CO WA 240-B7
NFD RD 1721
KITTITAS CO WA 240-A7
NFD RD 1726
LINCOLN CO OR 203-B4
NFD RD 1770
LINCOLN CO OR 203-C6
NFD RD 1783
LINCOLN CO OR 203-B5
NFD RD 1800
YAKIMA CO WA 119-B1
NFD RD 1810
DESCHUTES CO OR 217-C7
HOOD RIVER CO OR 202-A3
NFD RD 1814
DESCHUTES CO OR 217-C5
NFD RD 1815
DESCHUTES CO OR 217-C4
NFD RD 1818
DESCHUTES CO OR 217-D7
NFD RD 1819
DESCHUTES CO OR 217-D5
NFD RD 1820
DESCHUTES CO OR 217-D6
NFD RD 1825
CLACKAMAS CO OR 201-D4
DESCHUTES CO OR 217-D6
NFD RD 1828
CLACKAMAS CO OR 201-D4
NFD RD 1846
CURRY CO OR 232-D2
NFD RD 1888
LINCOLN CO OR 203-C3
Rose Lodge OR 203-C3
NFD RD 1928
LINCOLN CO OR 203-B6
NFD RD 1929
LINCOLN CO OR 203-B6
NFD RD 1956
LINCOLN CO OR 203-B6
NFD RD 1980
LINCOLN CO OR 203-C6
NFD RD 2022
LINN CO OR 134-A2
NFD RD 2025
JACKSON CO OR 234-A7
NFD RD 2026
LINN CO OR 134-A2
NFD RD 2040
JACKSON CO OR 234-B5
NFD RD 2050
JEFFERSON CO OR 212-A3
NFD RD 2060
DESCHUTES CO OR 211-B4
JACKSON CO OR 234-C5
NFD RD 2061
DESCHUTES CO OR 211-B3
NFD RD 2066
JEFFERSON CO OR 211-B2
NFD RD 2068
JEFFERSON CO OR 211-B3
NFD RD 2076
JEFFERSON CO OR 211-A3
NFD RD 2134
DOUGLAS CO OR 223-A1
LANE CO OR 142-A1
NFD RD 2153
DOUGLAS CO OR 223-C1
GRAYS HARBOR CO WA 179-A1
NFD RD 2160
LANE CO OR 209-D6
NFD RD 2199
MASON CO WA 179-C1
NFD RD 2207
MARION CO OR 134-A1
NFD RD 2210
YAMHILL CO OR 197-D7
NFD RD 2233
BONNER CO ID 244-B4
NFD RD 2234
YAMHILL CO OR 203-D2
NFD RD 2255
MASON CO WA 179-B1
NFD RD 2260
GRAYS HARBOR CO WA 109-B2
NFD RD 2282
YAMHILL CO OR 203-D1
NFD RD 2283
YAMHILL CO OR 197-D7
NFD RD 2302
GRAYS HARBOR CO WA 109-A2
KOOTENAI CO ID 245-C3
NFD RD 2308
CURRY CO OR 148-C1
NFD RD 2312
GRAYS HARBOR CO WA 109-B2
NFD RD 2320
KOOTENAI CO ID 245-D6
NFD RD 2341
MASON CO WA 179-B1
NFD RD 2399
MASON CO WA 179-B1
NFD RD 2401
MASON CO WA 173-A3
NFD RD 2403
JEFFERSON CO WA 173-B2
NFD RD 2420
MASON CO WA 173-A3
NFD RD 2421
MASON CO WA 173-A2
NFD RD 2464
MASON CO WA 173-A4
NFD RD 2469
MASON CO WA 173-A3
NFD RD 2470
MASON CO WA 173-A3
NFD RD 2472
MASON CO WA 173-B2
NFD RD 2480
LANE CO OR 214-D4
MASON CO WA 173-B3
NFD RD 2510
JEFFERSON CO WA 109-C1
JEFFERSON CO WA 173-B1
NFD RD 2512
BONNER CO ID 107-A2
NFD RD 2515
JEFFERSON CO WA 173-C1
NFD RD 2516
KLAMATH CO OR 143-A2
LAKE CO OR 143-A2
NFD RD 2524
JEFFERSON CO WA 173-B2
NFD RD 2530
JEFFERSON CO WA 173-B1
NFD RD 2540
JEFFERSON CO WA 173-B1
NFD RD 2546
JEFFERSON CO WA 173-B1
NFD RD 2550
BONNER CO ID 107-A3
NFD RD 2560
SKAMANIA CO WA 190-D1
NFD RD 2586
SKAMANIA CO WA 190-D3
NFD RD 2588
SKAMANIA CO WA 190-D3
NFD RD 2605
BOUNDARY CO ID 107-A2
NFD RD 2610
LANE CO OR 214-C2
NFD RD 2612
CLACKAMAS CO OR 201-C6
NFD RD 2618
CLACKAMAS CO OR 201-C6
NFD RD 2652
BONNER CO ID 245-A1
NFD RD 2654
LINN CO OR 134-B2
NFD RD 2720
WASCO CO OR 202-D5
NFD RD 2820
HOOD RIVER CO OR 195-A6
NFD RD 2823
LAKE CO OR 143-B3
LAKE CO OR 151-C1
NFD RD 2840
HOOD RIVER CO OR 202-B3
NFD RD 2902
CLALLAM CO WA 163-B7
CLALLAM CO WA 169-D1
NFD RD 2903
CLALLAM CO WA 163-B7
NFD RD 2918
CLALLAM CO WA 109-A1
NFD RD 2922
CLALLAM CO WA 163-C7
NFD RD 2923
CLALLAM CO WA 163-C7
NFD RD 2924
CLALLAM CO WA 169-D1
NFD RD 2929
CLALLAM CO WA 163-D7
NFD RD 2933
CLALLAM CO WA 163-A7
NFD RD 2937
CLALLAM CO WA 163-B7
NFD RD 2938
CLALLAM CO WA 163-B7
NFD RD 2946
CLALLAM CO WA 164-A7
NFD RD 2978
CLALLAM CO WA 163-D7
NFD RD 3006
CLALLAM CO WA 163-B5
NFD RD 3007
CLALLAM CO WA 163-B6
NFD RD 3010
OKANOGAN CO WA 105-A2
NFD RD 3027
KOOTENAI CO ID 245-D5
NFD RD 3028
CLALLAM CO WA 163-D5
NFD RD 3029
CLALLAM CO WA 163-D5
NFD RD 3030
CLALLAM CO WA 165-A7
NFD RD 3031
CLALLAM CO WA 163-C5
NFD RD 3040
CLALLAM CO WA 163-C6
CLALLAM CO WA 164-A6
NFD RD 3041
CLALLAM CO WA 163-C6
NFD RD 3062
SKAMANIA CO WA 194-C1
NFD RD 3067
CLALLAM CO WA 163-D6
NFD RD 3068
CLALLAM CO WA 164-A6
NFD RD 3069
CLALLAM CO WA 163-D6
NFD RD 3080
SKAMANIA CO WA 194-C2
NFD RD 3105
SKAMANIA CO WA 190-D6
NFD RD 3116
CLALLAM CO WA 163-B5
NFD RD 3117
CLALLAM CO WA 163-B5
NFD RD 3120
LINCOLN CO OR 206-D6
NFD RD 3142
LAKE CO OR 143-B3
NFD RD 3230
DOUGLAS CO OR 141-C3
NFD RD 3310
CURRY CO OR 228-D1
NFD RD 3312
KLAMATH CO OR 151-B1
NFD RD 3313
CURRY CO OR 228-C5
NFD RD 3334
KLAMATH CO OR 231-A1
NFD RD 3340
CURRY CO OR 228-D3
NFD RD 3348
COOS CO OR 140-C3
NFD RD 3384
KLAMATH CO OR 231-A1
NFD RD 3402
CURRY CO OR 228-B1
NFD RD 3413
KLAMATH CO OR 231-A2
NFD RD 3414
KLAMATH CO OR 231-A2
NFD RD 3419
KLAMATH CO OR 231-A4
NFD RD 3449
KLAMATH CO OR 231-A2
NFD RD 3450
KLAMATH CO OR 231-A3
NFD RD 3454
KLAMATH CO OR 231-A6
NFD RD 3455
KLAMATH CO OR 231-A5
NFD RD 3484
KLAMATH CO OR 231-A3
NFD RD 3506
KITTITAS CO WA 241-A2
NFD RD 3507
KITTITAS CO WA 241-A1
NFD RD 3512
HOOD RIVER CO OR 202-B3
NFD RD 3517
KITTITAS CO WA 241-B2
NFD RD 3521
KITTITAS CO WA 241-B1
NFD RD 3530
KITTITAS CO WA 238-B7
NFD RD 3533
CURRY CO OR 228-C4
NFD RD 3540
HOOD RIVER CO OR 202-C6
NFD RD 3550
HOOD RIVER CO OR 202-C6
NFD RD 3610
KLAMATH CO OR 231-A7
NFD RD 3640
GRANT CO OR 137-B1
NFD RD 3660
GRANT CO OR 137-B1
NFD RD 3670
GRANT CO OR 137-B1
NFD RD 3680
CURRY CO OR 228-B6
NFD RD 3817
DOUGLAS CO OR 222-B1
NFD RD 4000
DESCHUTES CO OR 217-A6
NFD RD 4017
LAKE CO OR 151-C3
NFD RD 4050
JACKSON CO OR 234-C7
NFD RD 4104
SKAMANIA CO WA 193-D3
NFD RD 4105
JOSEPHINE CO OR 233-A1
NFD RD 4109
CLARK CO WA 193-D3
SKAMANIA CO WA 193-D3
NFD RD 4130
DESCHUTES CO OR 217-A4
NFD RD 4180
DESCHUTES CO OR 216-D5
NFD RD 4201
JOSEPHINE CO OR 233-A2
NFD RD 4211
SKAMANIA CO WA 193-D2
NFD RD 4220
DESCHUTES CO OR 216-D6
NFD RD 4235
CROOK CO OR 136-A2
NFD RD 4240
WALLOWA CO OR 131-B2
NFD RD 4260
WALLOWA CO OR 131-B1
NFD RD 4273
DESCHUTES CO OR 142-C1
NFD RD 4305
UNION CO OR 129-C3
NFD RD 4306
SKAMANIA CO WA 194-B2
NFD RD 4410
HOOD RIVER CO OR 202-C4
NFD RD 4420
HOOD RIVER CO OR 202-D5
NFD RD 4430
WASCO CO OR 202-D3
NFD RD 4450
WASCO CO OR 202-D4
NFD RD 4510
LEWIS CO WA 185-D6
NFD RD 4601
DESCHUTES CO OR 216-D3

INDEX

INDEX

OCEAN SHORES BLVD — STREET INDEX — OREGON COAST HWY U.S.-101 387

STREET
City State Page-Grid

OCEAN SHORES BLVD
OCEAN SHORES WA 298-B5
E OCEAN SHORES BLVD
OCEAN SHORES WA 298-B6
OCEAN SHORES BLVD SW
OCEAN SHORES WA 177-B7
OCEAN VIEW BLVD NE
KITSAP CO WA 271-C4
OCEAN VIEW DR
CURRY CO OR 232-D6
Harbor OR 232-D6
NEWPORT OR 206-B4
YACHATS OR 209-A3
OCEAN VIEW DR Rt#-D5
DEL NORTE CO CA 148-B3
DEL NORTE CO CA 232-D7
OCEANVIEW CEMETERY RD
CLATSOP CO OR 188-B2
WARRENTON OR 188-B2
OCEAN VISTA WY
SEASIDE OR 301-E11
OCHOCO HWY Rt#-126
CROOK CO OR 213-A5
DESCHUTES CO OR 213-A5
PRINEVILLE OR 213-B6
REDMOND OR 212-D5
REDMOND OR 213-A5
OCHOCO HWY U.S.-26
CROOK CO OR 135-C2
CROOK CO OR 136-A2
CROOK CO OR 213-D5
GRANT CO OR 136-B1
MITCHELL OR 136-B1
PRINEVILLE OR 213-D5
WHEELER CO OR 136-B1
OCHOCO CREEK RD
CROOK CO OR 135-C2
CROOK CO OR 136-A2
OCONNER RD SE
THURSTON CO WA 184-C4
OCONNOR RD
KLAMATH CO OR 235-C6
NE ODDFELLOW RD
BAINBRIDGE ISLAND WA 271-J6
ODELL HWY
HOOD RIVER CO OR 195-C6
ODELL RD
DESCHUTES CO OR 142-C1
ODELL ST
BLAINE WA 158-B3
WHATCOM CO WA 158-B3
NW ODEM AV
DESCHUTES CO OR 212-D4
Terrebonne OR 212-D4
ODENS
PIERCE CO WA 182-B4
ODEY
PIERCE CO WA 182-B6
ODONNELL RD
LATAH CO ID 249-C4
WHITMAN CO WA 249-C4
OENNING RD
WHITMAN CO WA 250-B1
OFFUTT LAKE RD SE
THURSTON CO WA 184-D2
O-GARA RD
KOOTENAI CO ID 248-B5
OGDEN RD
COWLITZ CO WA 187-B7
OGLE RD NE
KITSAP CO WA 174-C1
OHARA RD
UMATILLA CO OR 129-C1
WESTON OR 129-C1
OHIO ST
BELLINGHAM WA 258-E6
E OHIO MATCH RD
KOOTENAI CO ID 245-A4
OHOP VALLEY RD E
PIERCE CO WA 118-B1
OIL CITY RD
JEFFERSON CO WA 169-C5
OJALLA RD
LINCOLN CO OR 206-C2
S OKANOGAN AV
WENATCHEE WA 238-D4
OKLAHOMA RD
SKAMANIA CO WA 195-B2
OKLAHOMA GULCH RD
CHELAN CO WA 236-A4
OK MILL RD
SNOHOMISH CO WA 110-C1
OKOMA DR Rt#-20
OKANOGAN CO WA 104-C3
OMAK WA 104-C3
OLA HWY
GEM CO ID 139-C3
OLALLA RD
DOUGLAS CO OR 141-A2
DOUGLAS CO OR 221-A7
LINCOLN CO OR 206-C4
SE OLALLA VALLEY RD
KITSAP CO WA 174-C6
OLALLA VALLEY RD SE
KITSAP CO WA 174-C5
OLANDER RD
LEWIS CO ID 123-B3
OLD HWY
DOUGLAS CO OR 221-B1
KLICKITAT CO WA 196-A5
OLD 26 RD
ADAMS CO WA 122-A1
OLD 302 Rt#-302
MASON CO WA 173-D6
OLD 410 HWY
ELMA WA 179-A7
GRAYS HARBOR CO WA 178-D7
GRAYS HARBOR CO WA 179-C6
OLD 99 HWY
SISKIYOU CO CA 149-C3
SISKIYOU CO CA 150-A3
OLD ALBION RD
WHITMAN CO WA 249-A3
OLD ALTURAS HWY
KLAMATH CO OR 151-A3
MODOC CO CA 151-A3
OLD APPLETON GRADE RD
KLICKITAT CO WA 196-C3
SW OLD BARNEY WHITE LN
KITSAP CO WA 174-A4
OLD BEAVER HILL RD
COOS CO OR 220-C4
OLD BELFAIR HWY
MASON CO WA 173-D5
MASON CO WA 174-A4
OLD BELFAIR HWY Rt#-300
MASON CO WA 173-D5
NE OLD BELFAIR HWY
MASON CO WA 174-A4
SE OLD BETHEL RD
YAMHILL CO OR 204-B3
OLD BRIDGE DR
LINN CO OR 133-C1
OLD BRUNDAGE MOUNTAIN RD
MCCALL ID 251-C5
OLD BUZZARD MINE RD
JACKSON CO OR 226-B4
SW OLD CLIFTON RD
KITSAP CO WA 174-A4
OLD CONDOR RD N
TILLAMOOK CO OR 197-B6
NW OLD CORNELIUS PASS RD
WASHINGTON CO OR 192-A7
OLD COULEE RD
ALMIRA WA 237-D6
GRANT CO WA 237-C4
LINCOLN CO WA 237-C4
OLD CRATER LAKE HWY
EAGLE POINT OR 230-D5
JACKSON CO OR 230-D5
OLD DALLES DR
HOOD RIVER CO OR 195-D5
OLD DALLES RD
HOOD RIVER CO OR 195-D6
OLD DAY CREEK RD
SKAGIT CO WA 161-C6
OLD DIAMOND LAKE RD
DOUGLAS CO OR 227-A2
JACKSON CO OR 226-D3
OLD DUFUR RD
THE DALLES OR 196-D7
WASCO CO OR 196-D7
OLD EASTSIDE RD
BONNER CO ID 107-A3
OLD EMIGRANT HILL SCENIC FRNTG
UNION CO OR 129-C2
OLD EMPIRE RD
NORTH BEND OR 333-E6
OLD EXPERIMENT RD
HARNEY CO OR 145-B1
OLD FAIRHAVEN PKWY Rt#-11
BELLINGHAM WA 258-B11
OLDFIELD RD
DISTRICT OF CENTRAL SAANI BC 159-C5
DISTRICT OF SAANICH BC 159-C5
OLD FORT RD
KLAMATH CO OR 235-C1
KLAMATH CO OR 338-H2
POLK CO OR 207-B1
OLD FORT HARNEY RD
HARNEY CO OR 145-B1
OLD FORT KLAMATH RD
KLAMATH CO OR 338-G6
OLD FRONTIER RD NW
KITSAP CO WA 174-B1
OLD GED BROWN
PIERCE CO WA 182-A6
OLD GOOSE LAKE RD
ADAMS CO ID 251-B3
OLD GRAND COULEE WILBUR HWY
GRANT CO WA 237-C3
OLD GUN CLUB RD
LEWISTON ID 250-C4
NEZ PERCE CO ID 250-C4
OLDHAM CREEK RD
DOUGLAS CO OR 219-C7
OLD HIGHWAY RD
WASHINGTON CO ID 139-B1
OLD HWY RD
MIDVALE ID 139-B1
WASHINGTON CO ID 139-B1
OLD HIGHWAY 22 CUTOFF RD
STEVENS CO WA 113-C1
OLD HWY 30 E
BAKER CITY OR 138-B1
BAKER CO OR 138-B1
OLD HIGHWAY 47
WASHINGTON CO OR 198-B2
SW OLD HIGHWAY 47 Rt#-8
FOREST GROVE OR 198-B1
OLD HWY 95
LATAH CO ID 249-D7
OLD HWY 97
BREWSTER WA 104-C3
JEFFERSON CO OR 208-D3
OKANOGAN CO WA 104-C3
OLD HWY 99
SKAGIT CO WA 168-B3
SNOHOMISH CO WA 168-B3
THURSTON CO WA 184-D1
OLD HWY 99 N
BURLINGTON WA 260-C3
SKAGIT CO WA 161-B3
SKAGIT CO WA 168-B2
WHATCOM CO WA 161-B3
OLD HWY 99 SE
THURSTON CO WA 296-H14
OLD HWY 99 SW
Grand Mound WA 184-B4
THURSTON CO WA 184-B4
OLD HWY 101
CANNON BEACH OR 188-B7
CLATSOP CO OR 188-B7
OLD HWY 160
KITSAP CO WA 174-D4
OLD HWY 195
WHITMAN CO WA 114-C3
OLD HWY EAST SPRINGDALE RD
STEVENS CO WA 106-B3
OLD HWY NORTHPORT RD
STEVENS CO WA 106-A1
OLD HWY-NW CHEWELAH RD
CHEWELAH WA 106-B3
OLD IDAHO-OREGON-NEVADA HWY
MALHEUR CO OR 146-B3
MALHEUR CO OR 154-B1
OLD IMNAHA RD
WALLOWA CO OR 131-A2
OLDING RD
BREMERTON WA 270-C8
OLD INLAND EMPIRE HWY
BENTON CITY WA 120-C3
BENTON CO WA 120-C3
OLD ISLAND HWY
CITY OF COLWOOD BC 159-B6
OLD ISLAND HWY Rt#-1A
CITY OF COLWOOD BC 159-B6
DISTRICT OF SAANICH BC 256-B5
TOWN OF ESQUIMALT BC 256-B5
TOWN OF VIEW ROYAL BC 159-B6
TOWN OF VIEW ROYAL BC 256-A4
OLD KETTLE RD
STEVENS CO WA 106-A2
W OLD KETTLE RD
KETTLE FALLS WA 106-A2
STEVENS CO WA 106-A2
OLD LAKE RD
LAKE CO OR 143-C2
OLD LAPWAI RD
LEWISTON ID 250-C4
NEZ PERCE CO ID 250-C4
OLD LORANE RD
LANE CO OR 133-B3
OLD MARINE DR
WHATCOM CO WA 158-D7
OLD MCMINNVILLE HWY
YAMHILL CO OR 198-B6
OLD MEADOW RD
MCCALL ID 251-C5
OLD MEHAMA RD SE
MARION CO OR 133-C1
STAYTON OR 133-C1
OLD MELROSE RD
DOUGLAS CO OR 221-B4
DOUGLAS CO OR 334-A7
ROSEBURG OR 334-A7
OLD MIDLAND RD
KLAMATH CO OR 235-C5
OLD MILITARY RD
FEDERAL WAY WA 175-B7
OLD MILITARY RD NE
KITSAP CO WA 174-B1
KITSAP CO WA 270-H1
OLD MILITARY RD SE
THURSTON CO WA 184-D3
NE OLD MILL RD
BAINBRIDGE ISLAND WA 271-J4
OLD MILL RD SW
KING CO WA 174-D7
OLD MILL SCHOOLIE RD
WASCO CO OR 127-A3
OLD MILTON HWY
WALLA WALLA WA 344-F13
WALLA WALLA CO WA 345-A13
OLD MOHAWK RD
LANE CO OR 215-D1
LANE CO OR 331-E3
OLD MONITOR RD
CASHMERE WA 238-C2
CHELAN CO WA 238-C2
OLD MOSCOW RD
WHITMAN CO WA 249-B5
OLD NACHES HWY
NACHES WA 119-C1
YAKIMA CO WA 119-C1
YAKIMA CO WA 243-A4
OLD NORTHERN STATE HOSPITAL RD
SKAGIT CO WA 161-C4
OLD NORTHPORT HWY
STEVENS CO WA 106-A1
OLD OCHOCO HWY
CROOK CO OR 136-A2
OLD OLYMPIC HWY
CLALLAM CO WA 165-D6
CLALLAM CO WA 166-A6
CLALLAM CO WA 262-A8
MASON CO WA 180-A4
OLD OLYMPIC HWY Rt#-3
MASON CO WA 180-A3
SHELTON WA 180-A3
OLD OLYMPIC HWY SW
THURSTON CO WA 180-B6
OLD OREGON TRAIL HWY I-84
BAKER CITY OR 138-B1
BAKER CO OR 130-A3
BAKER CO OR 138-B1
LA GRANDE OR 130-A2
MALHEUR CO OR 138-B1
MALHEUR CO OR 139-A2
MORROW CO OR 128-C1
NORTH POWDER OR 130-A3
ONTARIO OR 139-A2
PAYETTE CO ID 139-A2
PENDLETON OR 129-A1
UMATILLA CO OR 128-C1
UMATILLA CO OR 129-A1
UNION CO OR 129-C2
UNION CO OR 130-A2
OLD OWEN RD
MONROE WA 110-C1
SNOHOMISH CO WA 110-C1
OLD PACIFIC HWY
COWLITZ CO WA 118-A3
COWLITZ CO WA 187-C6
COWLITZ CO WA 189-C4
DOUGLAS CO OR 225-C6
KELSO WA 189-C4
KELSO WA 303-G14
SNOHOMISH CO WA 168-A4
WOODLAND WA 118-A3
WOODLAND WA 189-D7
OLD PACIFIC HWY Rt#-99
DOUGLAS CO OR 225-C2
MYRTLE CREEK OR 225-C2
Tri-City OR 225-C2
OLD PACIFIC HWY Rt#-432
KELSO WA 303-F13
OLD PACIFIC HWY N
CASTLE ROCK WA 187-C7
COWLITZ CO WA 187-C6
OLD PACIFIC HWY S
COWLITZ CO WA 189-D6
OLD PACIFIC HWY SE
THURSTON CO WA 181-A6
OLD PARRETT MOUNTAIN RD
YAMHILL CO OR 199-A5
OLD PENDLETON RIVER RD
ECHO OR 129-A1
UMATILLA CO OR 129-A1
OLD PENGRA RD
LANE CO OR 133-C3
LOWELL OR 133-C3
OLD PORTLAND RD
COLUMBIA CO OR 192-A2
SAINT HELENS OR 192-A2
OLD PULLMAN RD
MOSCOW ID 249-C5
OLD RAINIER RD
COLUMBIA CO OR 189-A4
NE OLD REDMOND RD
KING CO WA 175-C1
REDMOND WA 175-C1
OLD REDWOOD HWY
JOSEPHINE CO OR 229-A7
OLD RIVER RD
BENTON CO OR 133-B2
BENTON CO OR 210-A4
LINCOLN CO OR 206-C2
OLD ROSE CREEK RD
KOOTENAI CO ID 248-D2
OLD RR GRADE
YAMHILL CO OR 198-A4
NW OLD RR GRADE
YAMHILL CO OR 198-A5
OLD SALEM RD
MILLERSBURG OR 207-D3
MILLERSBURG OR 326-H3
OLD SAMISH HWY
BELLINGHAM WA 258-D13
WHATCOM CO WA 161-A2
WHATCOM CO WA 258-D13
OLD SAMS VALLEY RD
JACKSON CO OR 230-B5
OLD SAND CREEK RD
DOUGLAS CO OR 219-B2
GRAYS HARBOR CO WA 179-C6
OLD SANDERS RD
BENEWAH CO ID 115-A3
OLD SANTIAM WAGON RD
DESCHUTES CO OR 211-A3
OLD SCENIC HWY 101
LINCOLN CO OR 203-B3
Rose Lodge OR 203-B3
OLD SEEKSEEQUA RD
JEFFERSON CO OR 208-A4
OLDS FERRY RD
WASHINGTON CO ID 139-A2
OLDS FERRY-ONTARIO HWY Rt#-201
MALHEUR CO OR 139-A2
ONTARIO OR 139-A2
OLDS FERRY-ONTARIO HWY U.S.-30
MALHEUR CO OR 139-A3
ONTARIO OR 139-A3
SW OLD SHERIDAN RD
MCMINNVILLE OR 204-B1
YAMHILL CO OR 204-B1
OLD SHERMAN HWY
SHERMAN CO OR 127-C1
OLD SISKIYOU HWY
JACKSON CO OR 234-D5
OLD SNOHOMISH MONROE RD
SNOHOMISH CO WA 110-C1
SNOHOMISH CO WA 171-D4
NW OLD SOLDIERS RD
YAMHILL CO OR 198-A5
OLD SOLDIERS GRADE
LAPWAI ID 123-A2
NEZ PERCE CO ID 123-A2
NEZ PERCE CO ID 250-D4
OLD SOUTH RD
CLEARWATER CO ID 123-B2
OLD SPIRAL HWY
NEZ PERCE CO ID 250-B3
OLD SPIRAL HWY Rt#-128
LEWISTON ID 250-B4
OLD SPREADBOROUGH RD
COWLITZ CO WA 189-D5
OLD SR 195
SPOKANE CO WA 114-C2
OLD STAGE RD
CAVE JUNCTION OR 233-B4
JACKSON CO OR 149-B2
JACKSON CO OR 230-B6
JACKSON CO OR 234-A1
JOSEPHINE CO OR 233-B4
OLD STAGE RD Rt#-99
JACKSON CO OR 230-B6
OLD STAGE ROUTE
COOS BAY OR 333-D5
COOS CO OR 333-D5
NORTH BEND OR 333-D5
OLD STATE HWY
CASCADE ID 252-D6
LINCOLN CO WA 114-C3
SISKIYOU CO CA 150-B3
SPRAGUE WA 114-C3
WHITMAN CO WA 114-C3
OLD STATE RD
VALLEY CO ID 252-D2
OLD STITES STAGE RD
IDAHO CO ID 123-C3
SW OLDSVILLE RD
YAMHILL CO OR 204-A1
OLD THORNTON HWY
WHITMAN CO WA 114-C3
N OLD TRAIL RD
SPOKANE CO WA 246-A3
OLD TRAIL CREEK RD
JACKSON CO OR 230-D2
OLD TYGH MARKET RD
WASCO CO OR 127-B2
OLD US HWY 2
BOUNDARY CO ID 107-B1
MOYIE SPRINGS ID 107-B1
OLD US HWY 30
CLATSOP CO OR 117-A3
OLD WAPINITIA RD
WASCO CO OR 127-A3
OLD WILLAMETTE HWY
LANE CO OR 142-A1
OLD WILLAPA
PACIFIC CO WA 117-A1
OLD WOODS RD
TILLAMOOK CO OR 197-A7
OLD WYNOOCHEE RD
GRAYS HARBOR CO WA 178-C5
OLD YALE RD
CITY OF SURREY BC 157-A6
DISTRICT OF ABBOTSFORD BC 102-B1
DISTRICT OF MATSQUI BC 102-B1
TOWNSHIP OF LANGLEY BC 158-C1
SW OLESON RD
BEAVERTON OR 199-B2
PORTLAND OR 199-B2
WASHINGTON CO OR 199-B2
OLEX-MCNAB RD
MORROW CO OR 128-B2
OLGA TO PT LAWRENCE RD
SAN JUAN CO WA 160-A3
E OLIPHANT RD
COLUMBIA CO WA 122-B2
GARFIELD CO WA 122-B2
OLIVE ST
LINCOLN CO OR 206-B4
NEWPORT OR 206-B4
OLIVE ST U.S.-20
NEWPORT OR 206-B4
E OLIVE ST U.S.-20
NEWPORT OR 206-B4
W OLIVE ST
NEWPORT OR 206-A4
OLIVE WY
LONGVIEW WA 302-F7
SEATTLE WA 277-J5
OLIVE WY
SEATTLE WA 278-A5
E OLIVE WY
SEATTLE WA 278-B4
OLIVE BARBER RD
COOS CO OR 220-D2
OLIVER RD
COQUITLAM BC 157-B4
OLLALA CANYON RD
CHELAN CO WA 238-B2
OLMSTEAD RD
MARION CO OR 199-A7
OLMSTEAD RD NW
DOUGLAS CO WA 236-D4
OLNEY AV Rt#-202
ASTORIA OR 300-C7
NE OLNEY AV
BEND OR 332-F6
OLNEY AV SE
KITSAP CO WA 271-A14
PORT ORCHARD WA 271-A14
OLNEY CUTOFF RD
CLATSOP CO OR 188-D3
OLSEN RD
CLALLAM CO WA 166-A7
SNOHOMISH CO WA 168-B4
TILLAMOOK CO OR 197-C2
SE OLSEN ST Rt#-270
PULLMAN WA 249-B5
OLSON DR KPN
PIERCE CO WA 174-A7
OLSON PL SW
SEATTLE WA 285-J4
OLSON RD
COLUMBIA CO OR 189-C7
COWLITZ CO WA 189-D4
DESCHUTES CO OR 212-B7
WHATCOM CO WA 158-C6
WHITMAN CO WA 249-B1
NW OLSON RD
YAMHILL CO OR 198-B3
S OLYMPIA ST
KENNEWICK WA 121-A3
KENNEWICK WA 343-B11
OLYMPIA WY
COWLITZ CO WA 302-D4
LONGVIEW WA 302-J8
LONGVIEW WA 303-A8
SE OLYMPIAD DR
KITSAP CO WA 174-D4
OLYMPIA TENINO HWY N
TENINO WA 184-D3
OLYMPIA-YELM HWY Rt#-510
THURSTON CO WA 118-A1
THURSTON CO WA 181-B7
YELM WA 118-A1
N OLYMPIC AV
ARLINGTON WA 168-D5
S OLYMPIC AV
ARLINGTON WA 168-D5
OLYMPIC BLVD
EVERETT WA 264-A6
OLYMPIC DR NW
GIG HARBOR WA 181-C1
OLYMPIC DR SE
KITSAP CO WA 174-B6
OLYMPIC HWY U.S.-101
CLALLAM CO WA 164-C6
CLALLAM CO WA 165-B6
CLALLAM CO WA 166-C7
CLALLAM CO WA 261-A6
JEFFERSON CO WA 109-C1
JEFFERSON CO WA 166-C7
PORT ANGELES WA 261-A6
OLYMPIC PL
ARLINGTON WA 168-D5
W OLYMPIC PL
SEATTLE WA 277-G3
OLYMPIC ST
SPRINGFIELD OR 331-B5
OLYMPIC WK NE
SHORELINE WA 171-B6
OLYMPIC WY SE Rt#-305
BAINBRIDGE ISLAND WA 174-D2
OLYMPIC WY W
SEATTLE WA 277-F2
OLYMPIC HOT SPRINGS RD
CLALLAM CO WA 109-A1
CLALLAM CO WA 165-A7
OLYMPIC VIEW DR
EDMONDS WA 171-A5
LYNNWOOD WA 171-A5
SNOHOMISH CO WA 171-A5
OLYMPIC VIEW RD NW
KITSAP CO WA 174-A1
OLYMPIC VIEW WY
OCEAN SHORES WA 177-B6
OLYMPIC VIEW LOOP RD NW
KITSAP CO WA 170-A7
OLYMPUS BLVD
JEFFERSON CO WA 170-B2
OLYMPUS DR
BREMERTON WA 271-A7
KITSAP CO WA 271-A7
OMAK AV E Rt#-155
OKANOGAN CO WA 104-C3
OMAK WA 104-C3
OMAK LAKE RD
OKANOGAN CO WA 104-C3
OMAK RIVERSIDE EASTSIDE RD
OKANOGAN CO WA 104-C2
ONAWAY RD
LATAH CO ID 249-D1
ONEAL RD
KLICKITAT CO WA 196-B2
ONEIL HWY
CROOK CO OR 213-B4
DESCHUTES CO OR 212-D4
DESCHUTES CO OR 213-A4
ONEILL RD
GRAYS HARBOR CO WA 179-A7
ONION MOUNTAIN RD
JOSEPHINE CO OR 148-C1
ONTARIO ST
SANDPOINT ID 244-A2
VANCOUVER BC 156-B5
OPAL LN
JEFFERSON CO OR 212-D2
OPHIR RD
CURRY CO OR 228-A3
NW OPPENLANDER LN
WASHINGTON CO OR 198-B1
ORAL HULL RD
CLACKAMAS CO OR 200-D4
ORANGE ST
ASHLAND OR 337-C6
S ORCAS ST
SEATTLE WA 282-D6
SEATTLE WA 283-E6
ORCAS TO OLGA RD
SAN JUAN CO WA 101-C2
SAN JUAN CO WA 160-A2
ORCHARD AV
CANYON CO ID 147-B1
KLAMATH CO OR 338-F8
KLAMATH FALLS OR 338-F8
WENATCHEE WA 238-D4
YAKIMA CO WA 243-A6
N ORCHARD AV
DALLAS OR 204-A6
POLK CO OR 204-A6
ORCHARD AV SE
KITSAP CO WA 174-C6
ORCHARD LN
DOUGLAS CO OR 221-A4
N ORCHARD ST
BOISE ID 253-C2
GARDEN CITY ID 253-C2
TACOMA WA 292-A4
S ORCHARD ST
BOISE ID 253-C3
FIRCREST WA 292-A7
FIRCREST WA 294-A2
TACOMA WA 292-A6
TACOMA WA 294-A4
UNIVERSITY PLACE WA 294-A2
SW ORCHARD ST
SEATTLE WA 285-G1
ORCHARD GRADE
OKANOGAN CO WA 104-C3
ORCHARD HEIGHTS PL NW
POLK CO OR 322-A10
ORCHARD HEIGHTS RD NW
POLK CO OR 204-C5
POLK CO OR 322-A9
SALEM OR 322-D10
ORCHARD KNOB RD
POLK CO OR 204-A5
ORCUTT RD
SNOHOMISH CO WA 168-B5
OREANA RD
OWYHEE CO ID 147-C2
OREGON AV
FRANKLIN CO WA 343-E1
KLAMATH FALLS OR 338-C6
PASCO WA 343-E1
E OREGON AV
CRESWELL OR 215-C5
N OREGON AV Rt#-397
PASCO WA 343-G6
S OREGON AV Rt#-397
PASCO WA 343-H8
W OREGON AV
CRESWELL OR 215-C5
OREGON RD
SISKIYOU CO CA 150-A3
OREGON ST
ASTORIA OR 300-A5
BENTON CO WA 120-C2
OREGON ST Rt#-231
LINCOLN CO WA 114-A2
OREGON ST U.S.-30
MALHEUR CO OR 139-A3
ONTARIO OR 139-A3
OREGON ST U.S.-101
PORT ORFORD OR 224-A6
N OREGON ST
JACKSON CO OR 149-B2
JACKSONVILLE OR 149-B2
N OREGON ST U.S.-30
ONTARIO OR 139-A3
NE OREGON ST
PORTLAND OR 313-G5
S OREGON ST
ONTARIO OR 139-A3
SW OREGON ST
SEATTLE WA 280-E5
SEATTLE WA 281-E5
SHERWOOD OR 199-A4
OREGON WY
LONGVIEW WA 302-H13
LONGVIEW WA 303-A10
OREGON WY Rt#-433
COLUMBIA CO OR 189-B4
COWLITZ CO WA 302-H13
LONGVIEW WA 302-J12
RAINIER OR 189-B4
RAINIER OR 302-H13
OREGON CANYON RD
MALHEUR CO OR 154-B2
OREGON CAVES HWY Rt#-46
CAVE JUNCTION OR 233-B4
JOSEPHINE CO OR 233-B4
OREGON CENTRAL HWY U.S.-20
CANYON CO ID 139-A3
OREGON COAST HWY
CLATSOP CO OR 188-B6
OREGON COAST HWY U.S.-101
ASTORIA OR 188-C1
ASTORIA OR 300-A1
BANDON OR 220-C4
BAY CITY OR 191-B5
BAY CITY OR 197-B1
BROOKINGS OR 232-C5
CANNON BEACH OR 188-B7
CANNON BEACH OR 191-A2
CLATSOP CO OR 188-C1
CLATSOP CO OR 191-A2
CLATSOP CO OR 300-A1
CLATSOP CO OR 301-F14
COOS CO OR 218-B5
COOS CO OR 220-C4
COOS CO OR 224-B4
COOS CO OR 333-J13
CURRY CO OR 224-B4
CURRY CO OR 228-A1
CURRY CO OR 232-B2
DEPOE BAY OR 203-A7
DEPOE BAY OR 206-B3
DOUGLAS CO OR 214-A7
DOUGLAS CO OR 218-B2
DUNES CITY OR 214-B4
FLORENCE OR 214-B4
GARIBALDI OR 191-B5
GEARHART OR 301-H4
GOLD BEACH OR 228-A6
Harbor OR 232-D6
LAKESIDE OR 218-B2
LANE CO OR 132-B2
LANE CO OR 209-A6
LANE CO OR 214-B4
Lincoln Beach OR 203-A7
LINCOLN CITY OR 203-B3

INDEX

INDEX

390 POPLAR LN **STREET INDEX** REDMOND FALL CITY RD

STREET City State Page-Grid

POPLAR LN
POLK CO OR 204-B6
POPLAR ST
POWERS OR 140-B3
E POPLAR ST U.S.-2
DOUGLAS CO WA 236-C7
WATERVILLE WA 236-C7
NW POPLAR ST
MILTON-FREEWATER OR 121-C3
W POPLAR ST
WALLA WALLA WA 344-H9
WALLA WALLA WA 345-A8
POPULAR ST Rt#-27
TEKOA WA 114-C3
POPULAR ST Rt#-274
TEKOA WA 114-C3
PORCUPINE BAY RD
LINCOLN CO WA 114-A1
PORCUPINE RIDGE RD
MORROW CO OR 129-A3
PORT WY
VANCOUVER WA 304-E5
VANCOUVER WA 305-E4
PORTAL WY
FERNDALE WA 158-C5
WHATCOM CO WA 158-C4
PORT ANGELES-VICTORIA FERRY
BRITISH COLUMBIA BC 165-C3
PORTER RD
CLACKAMAS CO OR 200-C6
NEZ PERCE CO ID 250-D2
NW PORTER RD
WASHINGTON CO OR 198-C1
PORTER RD NW
DOUGLAS CO WA 236-B6
PORTER ST
ENUMCLAW WA 110-C3
PORTER ST Rt#-169
ENUMCLAW WA 110-C3
KING CO WA 110-C3
PORTER WY
MILTON WA 182-A2
PORTER CREEK RD
DOUGLAS CO OR 221-A6
GRAYS HARBOR CO WA 117-B1
GRAYS HARBOR CO WA 179-C7
PORT GAMBLE RD NE
KITSAP CO WA 170-C5
PORT INDUSTRIAL RD
ABERDEEN WA 178-B7
PORTLAND AV
FAIRFIELD WA 114-C2
SPOKANE CO WA 114-C2
E PORTLAND AV
TACOMA WA 182-A3
TACOMA WA 293-J5
NW PORTLAND AV
BEND OR 332-D6
PORTLAND AV E
PIERCE CO WA 182-A4
TACOMA WA 182-A4
N PORTLAND BLVD
PORTLAND OR 308-D6
PORTLAND OR 309-G6
NE PORTLAND BLVD
PORTLAND OR 309-G6
PORTLAND DR
HOOD RIVER CO OR 195-C6
E PORTLAND FRWY I-205
CLACKAMAS CO OR 319-G7
NE PORTLAND HWY U.S.-30
PORTLAND OR 310-D6
PORTLAND OR 311-E7
PORTLAND RD Rt#-99W
NEWBERG OR 198-D5
WASHINGTON CO OR 199-A5
YAMHILL CO OR 198-D5
YAMHILL CO OR 199-A5
N PORTLAND RD
PORTLAND OR 304-C7
PORTLAND OR 308-B2
PORTLAND RD NE
SALEM OR 323-B9
N PORTLAND ST
WILBUR WA 113-B1
PORTLAND HUBBARD HWY
CLACKAMAS CO OR 199-B6
W PORT MADISON RD
BAINBRIDGE ISLAND WA 170-C7
PORT OF TACOMA RD
FIFE WA 182-A2
TACOMA WA 182-A2
SE PORTOLA DR
GRANTS PASS OR 335-H11
JOSEPHINE CO OR 335-H11
PORT ORCHARD BLVD
PORT ORCHARD WA 174-B4
PORT ORCHARD WA 270-H14
PORT ORFORD HWY
CURRY CO OR 224-A6
PORT ORFORD OR 224-A6
N PORTSMOUTH AV
PORTLAND OR 308-B3
PORT TOWNSEND-KEYSTONE FRY
ISLAND CO WA 167-B5
POSSESSION RD
ISLAND CO WA 171-A3
N POST ST
SPOKANE WA 348-J5
POST CANYON DR
HOOD RIVER CO OR 195-C5
POSTGREN RD
KLICKITAT CO WA 195-D2
POSTMA RD
YAKIMA CO WA 243-D7
E POSTMA RD
YAKIMA CO WA 243-C7
POTATO HILL RD
GRANT CO WA 242-C4
POTOMAC RANCH RD
MALHEUR CO OR 154-C1
POTTER LN
VALLEY CO ID 251-D6
POTTER RD
LATAH CO ID 249-C2
LINN CO OR 210-A2
POTTERY AV
PORT ORCHARD WA 174-B4
POTTS RD
WHITMAN CO WA 114-A3
POVERTY BEND RD
YAMHILL CO OR 198-A6
POWDER CREEK RD
TILLAMOOK CO OR 197-D6
E POWELL BLVD U.S.-26
GRESHAM OR 200-B2

SE POWELL BLVD U.S.-26
GRESHAM OR 200-A2
PORTLAND OR 200-A2
PORTLAND OR 317-H1
PORTLAND OR 318-B2
PORTLAND OR 319-H2
W POWELL BLVD U.S.-26
GRESHAM OR 200-A2
POWELL RD
COWLITZ CO WA 187-C7
GRAYS HARBOR CO WA 177-C5
NEZ PERCE CO ID 250-D6
NE POWELL RD
CLARK CO WA 193-B4
POWELL ST
VANCOUVER BC 254-J10
VANCOUVER BC 255-B10
POWELL BUTTE HWY
CROOK CO OR 213-A7
DESCHUTES CO OR 135-B3
DESCHUTES CO OR 213-A7
DESCHUTES CO OR 217-D1
POWELL BUTTE CEMETERY RD
CROOK CO OR 213-B6
SE POWELL VALLEY RD
GRESHAM OR 200-B2
POWER RD
MALHEUR CO OR 139-A2
POWER CREEK RD
GRAYS HARBOR CO WA 179-C6
POWERHOUSE RD
KLICKITAT CO WA 195-C4
YAKIMA WA 243-B6
YAKIMA CO WA 243-B6
POWER LINE RD
UMATILLA CO OR 121-C3
WALLA WALLA CO WA 345-D14
POWERLINE RD
IDAHO CO ID 123-C3
LANE CO OR 210-B6
LEWIS CO ID 123-C2
LINN CO OR 210-B3
POWERLINE RD SW
THURSTON CO WA 180-A7
POWER LINE EASEMENT RD
JOSEPHINE CO OR 233-B5
POWERS AV
NEZ PERCE CO ID 250-D5
POWERS HWY
COOS CO OR 140-B3
POWERS RD
BEND OR 332-D11
COLUMBIA CO WA 122-A2
E POWERS RD
NEZ PERCE CO ID 250-D5
POWERS CREEK LP NE
MARION CO OR 205-D5
POWERS SOUTH RD
COOS CO OR 140-B3
CURRY CO OR 140-B3
POWERS OR 140-B3
POW WAH KEE RD
GARFIELD CO WA 122-C2
PRAIRIE AV
LEWIS CO WA 184-B5
PORT COQUITLAM BC 157-B4
PRAIRIE AV U.S.-95
CRAIGMONT ID 123-B2
E PRAIRIE AV
DALTON GARDENS ID 355-E2
KOOTENAI CO ID 353-H2
KOOTENAI CO ID 354-B2
KOOTENAI CO ID 355-E2
W PRAIRIE AV
COEUR D'ALENE ID 354-G2
COEUR D'ALENE ID 355-B2
DALTON GARDENS ID 355-B2
HAYDEN ID 354-G2
HAYDEN ID 355-B2
KOOTENAI CO ID 353-D2
KOOTENAI CO ID 355-B2
PRAIRIE RD
JUNCTION CITY OR 210-A6
LANE CO OR 210-A7
LANE CO OR 215-A1
SKAGIT CO WA 161-B4
S PRAIRIE RD
LEWIS CO WA 187-D2
SKAMANIA CO WA 195-A1
PRAIRIE CTY S SDE OF RIV RD
GRANT CO OR 137-C2
PRAIRIE CITY OR 137-C2
PRAIRIE CREEK RD
DOUGLAS CO OR 226-D2
S PRAIRIE CREEK RD
PIERCE CO WA 182-C5
PRAIRIE FARM CTO
JEFFERSON CO OR 211-D1
PRAIRIE FARM RD
JEFFERSON CO OR 135-A1
PRAIRIE PKWY LN SW
THURSTON CO WA 184-B2
PRAIRIE RIDGE DR E
PIERCE CO WA 182-C5
PRAIRIE ROAD CONN
LANE CO OR 210-A6
PRAIRIE ROAD CONN Rt#-36
LANE CO OR 210-A6
S PRAIRIE VIEW RD
SPOKANE CO WA 114-C2
PRATER RD
DESCHUTES CO OR 216-C6
PRATHER RD
POLK CO OR 207-B2
PRATHER RD SW
THURSTON CO WA 184-A4
PRATT RD
WALLOWA CO OR 130-C2
PREACHER CREEK RD
LANE CO OR 133-A2
PREBLE ST
BREMERTON WA 270-E12
Navy Yard City WA 270-E12
NE PRESCOTT ST
MAYWOOD PARK OR 315-H1
PORTLAND OR 313-H1
PORTLAND OR 314-B1
PORTLAND OR 315-E1
PRESLEY
PIERCE CO WA 182-B6
W PRESLEY RD
KOOTENAI CO ID 247-D4
KOOTENAI CO ID 248-A1
PRESTON AV
LEWISTON ID 250-C5
PRESTON AV U.S.-12
WAITSBURG WA 122-A2

PRESTON-FALL CITY RD SE
KING CO WA 176-B4
W PREWETT RD
SPOKANE CO WA 114-B1
W PRICE AV
Town and Country WA 346-J12
PRICE RD
ALBANY OR 326-H7
BREMERTON WA 270-C10
KITSAP CO WA 270-C10
LINN CO OR 326-H7
YAKIMA CO WA 120-B2
N PRICE RD
YAKIMA CO WA 120-B2
PRICEBORO DR
LINN CO OR 210-A5
PRICE-TWELVEMILE RD
CROOK CO OR 136-B3
PRIEST RAPIDS RD
BENTON CO WA 120-B2
YAKIMA CO WA 120-B2
PRINCESS AV
DISTRICT OF NORTH VANCOUV BC 255-C2
PRINCETON AV NE
SEATTLE WA 275-F4
NE PRINCETON WY
SEATTLE WA 275-F3
PRINGLE PKWY SE Rt#-22
SALEM OR 322-J13
PRINGLE RD
WASHINGTON CO ID 139-A2
PRINGLE RD SE
SALEM OR 324-J5
PRINGLE FALLS LP
DESCHUTES CO OR 142-C1
DESCHUTES CO OR 143-A1
PRINGLE FLAT RD
CROOK CO OR 136-A3
PRIOR ST
VANCOUVER BC 254-J11
VANCOUVER BC 255-A11
PRIVATE RD
CLARK CO WA 190-A7
PROCTOR BLVD U.S.-26
SANDY OR 200-C4
N PROCTOR ST
TACOMA WA 292-C4
S PROCTOR ST
TACOMA WA 292-C6
PROFFITT RD
LEWIS CO WA 184-D6
N PROGRESS RD
SPOKANE CO WA 351-B2
SPOKANE VALLEY WA 351-B2
W PROGRESS RD
UMATILLA CO OR 129-A1
PROGRESSIVE RD
HARRAH WA 119-C2
N PROM
SEASIDE OR 301-F7
PROMISE RD
WALLOWA CO OR 130-B1
PROMONTORY RD
CITY OF CHILLIWACK BC 102-C1
PROSPECT AV
Irondale WA 263-D13
WALLA WALLA WA 345-B11
WALLA WALLA CO WA 345-B11
PROSPECT DR
BENTON CITY WA 120-C3
PROSPECT RD
DISTRICT OF NORTH VANCOUV BC 255-B1
PROSPECT ST
BELLINGHAM WA 258-D6
PROSPECT LAKE RD
DISTRICT OF SAANICH BC 159-B5
DISTRICT OF SAANICH BC 256-A1
PROVIDENCE RD
ADAMS CO WA 121-C1
PROVIDENCE RD Rt#-261
ADAMS CO WA 121-C1
PROVOST RD NW
KITSAP CO WA 270-A2
Silverdale WA 270-A2
PROWELL ST
CHELAN CO WA 238-A1
PRUNEDALE RD
UMATILLA CO OR 121-C3
PRUNER RD
DOUGLAS CO OR 225-B2
RIDDLE OR 225-B2
P S OGDEN RD
DESCHUTES CO OR 212-D3
SW PUCKER HUDDLE RD Rt#-141
KLICKITAT CO WA 195-D4
PUCKETT RD
CROOK CO OR 213-C3
PUDDING RIVER RD NE
MARION CO OR 205-C1
NW PUDDY GULCH RD
YAMHILL CO OR 198-A5
PUGET DR
VANCOUVER BC 254-B14
PUGET DR Rt#-524
EDMONDS WA 171-A5
PUGET DR E
Colby WA 271-G14
PUGET DR SE
Colby WA 271-G14
RENTON WA 175-C5
PUGET RD NE
THURSTON CO WA 180-D5
N PUGET ST
OLYMPIA WA 297-A4
PUGET BEACH RD NE
THURSTON CO WA 181-A4
PUGH RD NE
KITSAP CO WA 170-C6
PUITT RD
CROOK CO OR 136-B2
PULLEN LN
JOSEPHINE CO OR 233-B5
PULLMAN ALBION RD
ALBION WA 249-A4
WHITMAN CO WA 249-A4
PULVER RD
BURLINGTON WA 260-A5
SKAGIT CO WA 260-A2
SW PUMA DR
WASHINGTON CO OR 198-B2
PUMP RD
CANYON CO ID 147-B1
NW PUMPKIN RIDGE RD
WASHINGTON CO OR 125-C1
PUNCH BOWL RD
HOOD RIVER CO OR 195-B7

PUNKIN CENTER RD
UMATILLA CO OR 129-A1
NW PURDIN RD
WASHINGTON CO OR 198-B1
PURDY DR Rt#-302
KITSAP CO WA 174-B6
PIERCE CO WA 174-B6
PURDY CRESCENT
PIERCE CO WA 174-C6
PURDY CUTOFF RD
MASON CO WA 180-A1
PURDY KITSAP RD
PIERCE CO WA 174-C6
PURTTEMAN GULCH RD
CHELAN CO WA 236-C2
PUYALLUP AV
TACOMA WA 182-A2
TACOMA WA 293-H7
PUYALLUP ST
STEILACOOM WA 181-C4
N PUYALLUP MOTOR NATURE TR
PIERCE CO WA 185-A3
PYLE RD
KLICKITAT CO WA 196-B3

Q

Q RD NW
DOUGLAS CO WA 236-C7
Q ST
PORT TOWNSEND WA 263-H3
SPRINGFIELD OR 330-G5
SPRINGFIELD OR 331-A5
NE QUAALE RD
JEFFERSON CO OR 208-D3
QUADRA ST
CITY OF VICTORIA BC 256-H6
DISTRICT OF SAANICH BC 159-C5
DISTRICT OF SAANICH BC 256-F1
VANCOUVER BC 254-A13
S QUADRANT ST
ROCKAWAY BEACH OR 191-B6
QUARRY AV
DESCHUTES CO OR 212-C6
QUARRY RD
ALBANY OR 326-C5
COQUITLAM BC 157-B3
YAMHILL CO OR 198-D5
QUARTZ CREEK RD
DOUGLAS CO OR 222-B7
JOSEPHINE CO OR 229-A3
QUARTZ MOUNTAIN RD
DOUGLAS CO OR 222-A5
KITTITAS CO WA 240-C4
QUARTZVILLE DR
LINN CO OR 134-A1
QUEBEC ST
CITY OF VICTORIA BC 256-F9
VANCOUVER BC 254-H11
QUEEN AV
ALBANY OR 326-B9
LINN CO OR 326-B9
S QUEEN ANN BLVD
YAKIMA WA 243-B7
QUEEN ANNE AV N
SEATTLE WA 277-H1
QUEEN ANNE DR
SEATTLE WA 277-H1
W QUEEN ANNE DR WY
SEATTLE WA 277-H3
QUEEN MARY BLVD
CITY OF SURREY BC 157-A6
QUEENS AV
DISTRICT OF WEST VANCOUVE BC 254-A1
QUEENS RD
DISTRICT OF NORTH VANCOUV BC 254-J2
DISTRICT OF NORTH VANCOUV BC 255-B3
QUEENSBOROUGH BRDG Rt#-91A
CITY OF RICHMOND BC 156-D6
NEW WESTMINSTER BC 156-D6
QUEENS BRANCH RD
JACKSON CO OR 229-D4
QUEENSBURY AV
CITY OF NORTH VANCOUVER BC 255-C7
QUEENSGATE DR
BENTON CO WA 341-D5
RICHLAND WA 341-D5
QUEETS RIVER RD
JEFFERSON CO WA 172-D2
QUESNEL DR
VANCOUVER BC 254-B14
QUICK RD
COWLITZ CO WA 187-C7
QUILCEDA RD
SNOHOMISH CO WA 168-C7
E QUILCENE RD
JEFFERSON CO WA 109-C1
QUILLAYUTE RD
CLALLAM CO WA 169-B2
QUINABY RD NE
MARION CO OR 204-D4
MARION CO OR 205-A4
W QUINAULT AV
KENNEWICK WA 342-C9
QUINCE AV
DESCHUTES CO OR 212-C5
QUINCE ST Rt#-47
FOREST GROVE OR 198-C1
WASHINGTON CO OR 198-C1
N QUINCY AV
DOUGLAS CO WA 239-A4
QUINCY ST
PORT TOWNSEND WA 263-H4
QUINCY-MAYGER RD
COLUMBIA CO OR 117-B3
COLUMBIA CO OR 189-A2
QUINES CREEK RD
DOUGLAS CO OR 225-C6
QUINN RD
GILLIAM CO OR 128-A3
QUIRK RD E
LINCOLN CO WA 113-B2

R

R AV
ANACORTES WA 259-H2
R RD NE Rt#-17
DOUGLAS CO WA 112-C1
R RD SW
DOUGLAS CO WA 239-B3
S R ST
COTTAGE GROVE OR 215-B7
R ST SE
AUBURN WA 182-C2

NW RABAUL DR
KITSAP CO WA 170-B7
RABBIT CAMP RD
LINN CO OR 134-B2
RABY LN
PAYETTE CO ID 139-A3
RACCOON DR
DOUGLAS CO OR 219-A5
RACE RD
EPHRATA WA 112-C3
GRANT CO WA 112-C3
ISLAND CO WA 167-C5
RACE ST
PORT ANGELES WA 261-G5
RADAR RD
HARNEY CO OR 145-A1
RADAR HILL RD
ADAMS CO WA 121-A1
FRANKLIN CO WA 121-A1
RADER RD
KITTITAS CO WA 241-C4
RAFT AV
OLYMPIA WA 296-G2
RAGER RD
CROOK CO OR 136-B2
RAGLAND RD
COWLITZ CO WA 189-B1
RAIL HOLLOW RD
WASCO CO OR 127-B2
WASCO CO OR 202-D4
RAILROAD AV
DEL NORTE CO CA 148-B3
JOSEPHINE CO OR 225-B7
JOSEPHINE CO OR 229-B1
KITTITAS WA 241-C6
LEWISTON ID 250-C4
MOUNT ANGEL OR 205-C3
POWERS OR 140-B3
RAILROAD AV Rt#-200
KOOTENAI ID 244-A1
E RAILROAD AV
Otis Orchards WA 352-D9
N RAILROAD AV
COOS CO OR 140-B3
KOOTENAI CO ID 353-C7
POST FALLS ID 353-C7
POWERS OR 140-B3
SAINT HELENS OR 192-B2
NE RAILROAD AV
CLARK CO WA 193-B2
W RAILROAD AV
MASON CO WA 180-A3
SHELTON WA 180-A3
RAILROAD AV SE Rt#-202
SNOQUALMIE WA 176-C4
RAILROAD BLVD
EUGENE OR 329-H4
RAILROAD ST Rt#-27
ROCKFORD WA 114-C2
SPOKANE CO WA 114-C2
RAILROAD ST U.S.-95
MIDVALE ID 139-B1
SW RAILROAD ST
SHERIDAN OR 125-B3
SHERWOOD OR 199-A4
RAILWAY AV
CITY OF RICHMOND BC 156-B7
RAINBOW DR
JEFFERSON CO OR 212-C2
NW RAINBOW DR
DESCHUTES CO OR 212-C3
RAINBOW RD
WHATCOM CO WA 158-B5
RAINBOW ROCK RD
CURRY CO OR 232-C5
RAINEY RD
DOUGLAS CO WA 239-A2
RAINIER AV N
KING CO WA 175-C5
RENTON WA 175-C5
RAINIER AV S
KING CO WA 175-C4
KING CO WA 287-F1
RENTON WA 175-C4
SEATTLE WA 278-C7
SEATTLE WA 282-D2
SEATTLE WA 283-E6
SEATTLE WA 287-F1
RAINIER AV S Rt#-167
RENTON WA 175-C5
RAINIER DR
PIERCE CO WA 181-C5
RAINIER RD
LACEY WA 297-G13
THURSTON CO WA 297-G13
RAINIER RD SE
RAINIER WA 118-A1
THURSTON CO WA 118-A1
THURSTON CO WA 184-D1
THURSTON CO WA 297-G14
RAINIER ST
STEILACOOM WA 181-C4
RAINIER DIKE RD
RAINIER OR 302-G14
W RAINIER DIKE RD
COLUMBIA CO OR 302-C12
RAINIER OR 302-C12
RAINIER-YELM HWY Rt#-507
THURSTON CO WA 118-A1
YELM WA 118-A1
RAISOR RD
LANE CO OR 219-D3
RALSTON-BENGE RD
ADAMS CO WA 121-C1
ADAMS CO WA 122-A1
RAMBLER DR NE
MARION CO OR 205-B4
N RAMBO RD
SPOKANE CO WA 114-B2
RAMMS RD
JEFFERSON CO OR 213-A1
S RAMSBY RD
CLACKAMAS CO OR 126-A3
RAMSEY LN
KLICKITAT CO WA 195-D5
RAMSEY RD
COEUR D'ALENE ID 355-C3
HAYDEN ID 245-A5
HAYDEN ID 355-C3
JACKSON CO OR 230-B4
KOOTENAI CO ID 245-A5
KOOTENAI CO ID 355-C3
N RAMSEY RD
COEUR D'ALENE ID 355-C6
KOOTENAI CO ID 245-A2
RAMSEY RD E
LINCOLN CO WA 113-B1

S RAMSEY ST Rt#-27
TEKOA WA 114-C3
RAMSEY-CANYON RD
JACKSON CO OR 230-B3
RANCH RD
DESCHUTES CO OR 144-B1
DOUGLAS CO OR 218-C1
KOOTENAI CO ID 245-A2
RANCHERIA CIRCLE RD
SISKIYOU CO CA 150-A3
RANCHERO RD
DOUGLAS CO OR 225-C6
RAND RD
HOOD RIVER OR 195-C5
RANDAL RD
COOS CO OR 220-B6
RANDALL RD SW
THURSTON CO WA 180-B6
RANDOLPH RD
GRANT CO WA 242-C2
RANEY LN
ADAMS CO ID 251-B4
W RANGE DR
LINCOLN CO OR 328-D6
WALDPORT OR 328-D6
RANGER RD
CLALLAM CO WA 165-A5
RANKIN RD
JEFFERSON CO OR 211-C1
RANKIN HILL RD
Vineland WA 250-B5
RAT CREEK RD
LANE CO OR 215-D7
RATHERT RD
KLICKITAT CO WA 196-C1
RATTLESNAKE RD
HARNEY CO OR 145-B1
KLICKITAT CO WA 195-D3
KLICKITAT CO WA 196-A2
RATTLESNAKE CREEK RD
MALHEUR CO OR 154-B1
RAUBUCK RD
LEWIS CO WA 187-B2
RAVENA DR N
MARION CO OR 204-D3
RAVENNA AV NE
SEATTLE WA 274-D1
NE RAVENNA BLVD
SEATTLE WA 274-B3
RAWLINS RD
SKAGIT CO WA 168-A1
RAWLISON CRES
TOWNSHIP OF LANGLEY BC 157-D7
RAWLISON CRES Rt#-10
TOWNSHIP OF LANGLEY BC 157-C7
NE RAWSON RD
CLARK CO WA 193-B4
RAY RD
LEWIS CO WA 187-D4
S RAY ST
SPOKANE WA 349-F12
RAY BELL RD
MARION CO OR 198-D6
RAYE ST
SEATTLE WA 277-H1
RAYMOND CREEK RD
COLUMBIA CO OR 192-A4
RAY NASH DR NW
PIERCE CO WA 181-B1
RAZOR CLAM DR
OCEAN SHORES WA 298-C3
R DRUFFEL RD
WHITMAN CO WA 249-B7
REASON CT
DESCHUTES CO OR 212-C5
REATA RD
BENTON CO WA 341-D12
REAVIS LN
WALLOWA CO OR 130-C2
SE REBMAN RD
CLACKAMAS CO OR 200-B4
RECORD ST
BAKER CO OR 131-A3
HALFWAY OR 131-A3
RECREATIONAL CORR
GRANT CO WA 121-A1
RED APPLE RD
WENATCHEE WA 238-D4
REDBERG RD
TILLAMOOK CO OR 203-B1
RED BLANKET RD
JACKSON CO OR 226-C7
S RED BLANKET RD
JACKSON CO OR 226-D7
JACKSON CO OR 227-A6
RED BLANKET MOUNTAIN RD
JACKSON CO OR 226-D6
JACKSON CO OR 227-A6
RED BRIDGE RD
KITTITAS CO WA 240-C2
LINN CO OR 207-D6
RED CLOUD LN
CROOK CO OR 213-B6
RED CLOUD RD
CROOK CO OR 213-B6
REDDING RD
MORROW CO OR 128-B2
REDFIELD RD
DOUGLAS CO WA 239-B1
RED FIR RD
BONNER CO ID 244-D3
KLAMATH CO OR 151-B1
RED HILL RD
DOUGLAS CO OR 219-B5
HOOD RIVER CO OR 202-B2
WALLOWA CO OR 131-A1
RED HILLS RD
YAMHILL CO OR 198-C6
RED HOUSE RD
LAKE CO OR 152-A1
S REDLAND RD
CLACKAMAS CO OR 199-D4
CLACKAMAS CO OR 200-A5
OREGON CITY OR 199-D4
RED MARBLE RD
STEVENS CO WA 106-A3
NE REDMOND WY Rt#-202
REDMOND WA 175-D1
NE REDMOND WY Rt#-908
REDMOND WA 175-C1
REDMOND-BEND HWY
DESCHUTES CO OR 212-C7
DESCHUTES CO OR 217-C1
REDMOND FALL CITY RD Rt#-202
KING CO WA 175-D1
KING CO WA 176-A1
REDMOND WA 175-D1

INDEX

REDMOND FALL CITY RD — STREET INDEX — ROAD 42-NE 391

STREET / City State / Page-Grid

REDMOND FALL CITY RD Rt#-202
- SAMMAMISH WA 175-D1

SE REDMND FALL CITY RD Rt#-202
- KING CO WA 176-B3

REDMND FALL CITY RD NE Rt#-202
- KING CO WA 176-A2

REDMND FALL CITY RD SE Rt#-202
- KING CO WA 176-A2

REDMOND GRADE RD
- WALLOWA CO OR 122-C3

SW REDMOND HILL RD
- MCMINNVILLE OR 198-A7
- YAMHILL CO OR 198-A7

REDMOND-POWELL BUTTE RD
- DESCHUTES CO OR 212-D5
- REDMOND OR 212-D5

REDONDO WY S
- DES MOINES WA 175-B7
- FEDERAL WAY WA 175-B7

RED RIDGE RD
- ADAMS CO ID 251-C5
- VALLEY CO ID 251-C7

N RED RIVER RD
- WHATCOM CO WA 158-C6

RED ROCK RD
- SISKIYOU CO CA 150-B3

REDWOOD AV
- GRANTS PASS OR 335-A11
- JOSEPHINE CO OR 229-B6
- JOSEPHINE CO OR 335-A11

REDWOOD HWY
- GRANTS PASS OR 335-F9

REDWOOD HWY Rt#-99
- GRANTS PASS OR 335-F6

REDWOOD HWY U.S.-101
- CRESCENT CITY CA 148-B3
- DEL NORTE CO CA 148-B3
- DEL NORTE CO CA 232-D7

REDWOOD HWY U.S.-199
- CAVE JUNCTION OR 233-B3
- DEL NORTE CO CA 148-C3
- DEL NORTE CO CA 233-A6
- GRANTS PASS OR 335-F9
- JOSEPHINE CO OR 149-A1
- JOSEPHINE CO OR 229-A7
- JOSEPHINE CO OR 233-B3
- JOSEPHINE CO OR 335-A12

NE REDWOOD HWY Rt#-99
- GRANTS PASS OR 335-F7

REECER CREEK RD
- KITTITAS CO WA 241-B2

REED RD
- BEND OR 332-E10
- HOOD RIVER CO OR 195-C6
- LEWIS CO WA 187-C4

N REED RD
- HAYDEN ID 245-A5
- HAYDEN ID 355-D1

REED RD SE
- SALEM OR 325-A6

REEDER RD
- COLUMBIA CO OR 192-B3
- KLAMATH CO OR 235-D5
- MULTNOMAH CO OR 192-B5

REEDER RD SW
- THURSTON CO WA 184-C2

SE REED MARKET RD
- BEND OR 217-C3
- BEND OR 332-G10

SW REED MARKET RD
- BEND OR 332-D9

REESE RD
- LAKE OSWEGO OR 320-A7

REESE CREEK RD
- JACKSON CO OR 230-D5

REESE HILL RD Rt#-547
- WHATCOM CO WA 102-B1

REEVES RD KPS
- PIERCE CO WA 181-A3

REEVES CREEK RD
- JOSEPHINE CO OR 233-B3

S REGAL RD
- SPOKANE CO WA 246-C5

S REGAL ST
- SPOKANE WA 349-E14

REGATTA DR
- OAK HARBOR WA 167-C3

REGENTS BLVD
- FIRCREST WA 181-C2
- FIRCREST WA 292-A7
- FIRCREST WA 294-A1

E REGINA AV
- Fairwood WA 346-J8
- Fairwood WA 347-A8

W REGINA AV
- Fairwood WA 346-J9

SE REGNER RD
- GRESHAM OR 200-B2
- MULTNOMAH CO OR 200-B2

REHKLAU RD SE
- THURSTON CO WA 181-A7

REHN RD
- ADAMS CO WA 113-C3

REICHENBACK RD
- PITT MEADOWS BC 157-B5

REID DR NW
- GIG HARBOR WA 181-C1
- PIERCE CO WA 181-C1

REID RD
- CLARK CO WA 193-A1
- WHITMAN CO WA 249-A4

REIF RD
- CROOK CO OR 213-B5

REIMANN ST NE
- Hayesville OR 323-E6

SE REINIG RD
- KING CO WA 176-C4

REITER RD
- SNOHOMISH CO WA 111-A1

REITH RD
- KENT WA 175-B7

REKDAL RD
- ISLAND CO WA 168-A4

W REMINGTON RD
- KOOTENAI CO ID 245-A2

REMY LN
- LEWIS CO WA 187-D1

RENANN ST
- ROSEBURG OR 334-D3

RENFREW ST
- VANCOUVER BC 255-D12

RENFRO CREEK RD
- BENEWAH CO ID 115-B3

RENNE RD
- YAMHILL CO OR 198-D6

RENTON AV S
- KING CO WA 287-G5
- KING CO WA 289-J1
- SEATTLE WA 287-F2

SE RENTON ISSAQUAH RD Rt#-900
- KING CO WA 175-D4
- RENTON WA 175-D4

RENTON ISSAQUAH RD SE
- ISSAQUAH WA 175-D4

RENTON ISSAQUAH RD SE Rt#-900
- ISSAQUAH WA 175-D4
- KING CO WA 175-D4

RENTON MAPLE VALLEY RD Rt#-169
- KING CO WA 175-D5
- KING CO WA 176-A6
- MAPLE VALLEY WA 175-D5

RESEARCH WY
- CORVALLIS OR 327-C11

RESERVATION RD
- ANACORTES WA 160-D7
- ISLAND CO WA 167-C2
- OAK HARBOR WA 167-C2
- SKAGIT CO WA 160-D7
- WASCO CO OR 127-A3

RESERVATION RD Rt#-241
- YAKIMA CO WA 120-B3

W RESERVATION RD Rt#-241
- YAKIMA CO WA 120-B3

RESERVATION RD SE
- THURSTON CO WA 181-A6

RESERVATION LINE RD
- IDAHO CO ID 123-C3
- NEZ PERCE CO ID 250-D4

E RESERVE ST
- BOISE ID 253-D3

RESERVOIR RD
- BENTON CO OR 327-A10
- CORVALLIS OR 327-A10
- CROOK CO OR 135-B3
- MALHEUR CO OR 138-C3
- MALHEUR CO OR 146-A1

RESERVOIR LOOP RD
- YAKIMA CO WA 243-B5

RESOR RD
- WALLA WALLA CO WA 345-H11
- Walla Walla East WA 345-C11

RESORT DR
- TILLAMOOK CO OR 197-A7

RESTHAVEN DR
- TOWN OF SIDNEY BC 159-C2

RESTON RD
- DOUGLAS CO OR 141-A2

RETREAT KANASKAT RD
- KING CO WA 110-C3

RETSIL RD SE
- PORT ORCHARD WA 271-A14

REUBEN RD
- DOUGLAS CO OR 225-A7

N REUBEN RD
- DOUGLAS CO OR 225-A6

REUBENS RD
- LEWIS CO ID 123-B2

REUBENS GRADE
- NEZ PERCE CO ID 123-B2

SE REVENUE RD
- CLACKAMAS CO OR 200-C3

NE REVERE AV
- BEND OR 332-F6

NE REVERE AV U.S.-20
- BEND OR 332-F6

NW REVERE AV
- BEND OR 332-E6

REVETMENT DR
- WESTPORT WA 298-G10

REX RD
- DOUGLAS CO WA 237-B1

REYNOLD RD
- CLALLAM CO WA 164-B5

W REYNOLDS AV
- CENTRALIA WA 299-C1
- LEWIS CO WA 299-E1

REYNOLDS RD
- FRANKLIN CO WA 121-B2

REYNOLDS CREEK RD
- DOUGLAS CO OR 222-B1

REYNOLDS CREEK STAGE RD
- OWYHEE CO ID 147-B2

REYNOLDS RIDGE RD
- DOUGLAS CO OR 222-B3

RHEA RD
- GILLIAM CO OR 128-A1

RHEA CREEK RD
- MORROW CO OR 128-B2

RHINEHART RD
- UNION CO OR 130-A2

RHODES RD
- LEWIS CO WA 187-C3

RHODESIA BEACH RD
- PACIFIC CO WA 183-C7

RHODESIDE RD
- DESCHUTES CO OR 213-A4

RHODODENDRON DR
- FLORENCE OR 214-A2
- LANE CO OR 214-A2

RHODODENDRON LN NW
- KITSAP CO WA 170-B6

RHODODENDRON RD
- DOUGLAS CO OR 222-C5

RHODY DR Rt#-19
- Hadlock-Irondale WA 170-A1
- Irondale WA 263-E14
- JEFFERSON CO WA 170-A1
- JEFFERSON CO WA 263-E14

RIBBON RIDGE RD
- YAMHILL CO OR 198-C4

SE RICE AV
- ROSEBURG OR 334-F9

RICE RD
- BAKER CO OR 138-A1

RICE ST
- MYRTLE CREEK OR 225-C1

RICE CREEK RD
- DOUGLAS CO OR 221-B7
- DOUGLAS CO OR 225-A1

RICE KANDLE
- PIERCE CO WA 181-D7

RICE-ORIN RD
- STEVENS CO WA 105-C2
- STEVENS CO WA 106-A2

RICE VALLEY RD
- DOUGLAS CO OR 219-A5

RICH RD SE
- THURSTON CO WA 184-D1
- THURSTON CO WA 297-C12

RICHARDS RD
- BELLEVUE WA 175-C2

RICHARDSON RD
- DOUGLAS CO OR 221-C7
- LINCOLN CO WA 113-C2
- PITT MEADOWS BC 157-C4
- SISKIYOU CO CA 150-B3

RICHARDSON RD NE
- MARION CO OR 205-D5

RICHARDSONS GAP RD
- LINN CO OR 133-C1

RICHES RD SE
- MARION CO OR 205-C6

RICHMOND AV
- CITY OF VICTORIA BC 257-B8
- DISTRICT OF SAANICH BC 257-B8

N RICHMOND AV U.S.-30
- PORTLAND OR 192-B7

RICHMOND FRWY Rt#-91
- CITY OF RICHMOND BC 156-C6

RICHMOND RD
- DISTRICT OF SAANICH BC 257-B4
- GILLIAM CO OR 128-A2

N RICHMOND BEACH RD
- SHORELINE WA 171-A6

NW RICHMOND BEACH RD
- SHORELINE WA 171-A6

RICHMOND SIXSHOOTER RD
- WHEELER CO OR 136-B1

RICKARD RD
- BENTON CO OR 210-A4
- DESCHUTES CO OR 217-C3

RICKEY ST SE
- SALEM OR 325-E2

RICKREALL RD
- POLK CO OR 204-B6

RIDDELL RD
- POLK CO OR 204-B7

NE RIDDELL RD
- BREMERTON WA 270-G5
- KITSAP CO WA 270-G5
- KITSAP CO WA 271-A5
- Tracyton WA 270-G5

NW RIDDELL RD
- KITSAP CO WA 270-G5

RIDDLE BYPS
- DOUGLAS CO OR 225-B2
- RIDDLE OR 225-B2
- Tri-City OR 225-B2

RIDGE DR
- ASTORIA OR 300-C6
- HOOD RIVER CO OR 195-C6
- LINN CO OR 207-C7
- OROVILLE WA 104-C1

RIDGE DR NE
- KEIZER OR 323-C4

RIDGE RD
- ADAMS CO ID 252-A6
- CLACKAMAS CO OR 200-B5
- COOS CO OR 218-B6
- GILLIAM CO OR 128-B2
- HARNEY CO OR 137-B3
- MORROW CO OR 128-B2
- WARRENTON OR 188-B2
- YAMHILL CO OR 198-B4

RIDGE TR
- SKAMANIA CO WA 194-B1

SE RIDGECREST RD
- CLACKAMAS CO OR 200-A3
- HAPPY VALLEY OR 200-A3

RIDGELINE TR
- EUGENE OR 329-J14
- EUGENE OR 330-B14
- LANE CO OR 215-B3
- LANE CO OR 329-J14

RIDGETOP BLVD
- Silverdale WA 174-B1

RIDGEVIEW DR NE
- KITSAP CO WA 271-C7

RIDGEWAY DR
- REEDSPORT OR 218-C1

RIDGEWAY DR SE
- MARION CO OR 207-D1

SW RIEDWEG RD
- WASHINGTON CO OR 198-C2

RIETH RD
- UMATILLA CO OR 129-A1

RIFE RD
- CLALLAM CO WA 165-A6

RIFLE RANGE RD
- BENTON CO OR 207-A3

NE RIFLE RANGE RD
- ROSEBURG OR 334-J7

RIGDON RD
- LANE CO OR 142-A1

SW RIGERT RD
- WASHINGTON CO OR 199-A2

RIGGS RD
- CROOK CO OR 213-B6
- WALLA WALLA CO WA 121-B3

RIGHT FORK RD
- DOUGLAS CO OR 221-D6

RIGHT FORK FOOTS CREEK RD
- JACKSON CO OR 229-D7

RIGHT FORK SARDINE CREEK RD
- JACKSON CO OR 230-B4

RIM DR
- KLAMATH CO OR 227-C2

RIM RD
- CANYON CO ID 147-B1
- JEFFERSON CO OR 212-C2
- MODOC CO CA 151-A3

RIMROCK RD
- COLTON WA 250-A1
- WHITMAN CO WA 250-A1

N RIMROCK RD
- KOOTENAI CO ID 245-A4

NW RIMROCK RD
- JEFFERSON CO OR 208-B3

RIMROCK RD E
- LINCOLN CO WA 113-B2

RIMROCK ACRES RD
- CROOK CO OR 213-C4

RIM VIEW RD
- KLICKITAT CO WA 196-A5

RINEHART RD
- MALHEUR CO OR 146-C2

RINEHART RANCH RD
- MALHEUR CO OR 146-B2

RINGO RD
- CLACKAMAS CO OR 199-D7
- WHITMAN CO WA 249-C2

RINGOLD RD
- FRANKLIN CO WA 121-A2

RINK CREEK RD
- COOS CO OR 220-D5

RIO NES LN
- DOUGLAS CO OR 221-C3

RIORDAN HILL DR
- HOOD RIVER CO OR 195-B6

RIO VISTA AV
- BURLINGTON WA 260-D5
- SKAGIT CO WA 260-D5

RIO VISTA AV Rt#-20
- BURLINGTON WA 260-C5

RIO VISTA BLVD
- VALLEY CO ID 251-C5

RIPON AV
- LEWISTON ID 250-C5

RIPPEE LN
- YAKIMA CO WA 243-A6

RIPPINGTON RD
- PITT MEADOWS BC 157-B5

RISLEY CREEK RD
- LINCOLN CO OR 209-C1

NE RISTO RD
- CLARK CO WA 193-A3

RITCHEY RD
- WASHINGTON CO OR 198-B1

RITTER RD
- WHATCOM CO WA 158-D5

RITTER SPRINGS RD
- GRANT CO OR 129-A3

S RIVARD RD
- YAKIMA CO WA 243-D7

RIVER AV
- EUGENE OR 215-B1
- TILLAMOOK CO OR 197-A7

RIVER DR
- LANE CO OR 215-C5

RIVER DR Rt#-155
- COULEE DAM WA 237-C2
- OKANOGAN CO WA 237-C2

N RIVER DR
- LINN CO OR 133-C2

RIVER RD
- CITY OF RICHMOND BC 156-B6
- CITY OF SURREY BC 156-D6
- CLALLAM CO WA 262-B12
- DISTRICT OF DELTA BC 156-C7
- EUGENE OR 215-A1
- EUGENE OR 329-G1
- JACKSON CO OR 150-A1
- JACKSON CO OR 226-C6
- JACKSON CO OR 230-B3
- JUNCTION CITY OR 210-A6
- KOOTENAI CO ID 115-B2
- LAKE CO OR 151-C1
- LANE CO OR 210-A6
- LANE CO OR 215-A1
- LANE CO OR 329-G1
- LINN CO OR 134-B2
- MARION CO OR 198-D7
- MARION CO OR 205-A1
- Santa Clara OR 210-A7
- Santa Clara OR 215-A1
- SEQUIM WA 262-B12
- SKAGIT CO WA 161-C6
- TOWNSHIP OF LANGLEY BC 157-D6
- UMATILLA OR 129-A1
- UMATILLA CO OR 129-A1
- WASCO CO OR 196-C6
- WHITMAN CO WA 249-A4
- YAKIMA WA 243-B6

RIVER RD Rt#-155
- ELMER CITY WA 237-C1
- OKANOGAN CO WA 237-C1

RIVER RD Rt#-167
- PIERCE CO WA 182-A3
- PUYALLUP WA 182-A3
- TACOMA WA 182-A3

E RIVER RD
- PUYALLUP WA 182-B3

N RIVER RD
- JACKSON CO OR 229-D6
- JACKSON CO OR 230-A6
- LATAH CO ID 249-C1
- ROGUE RIVER OR 229-D6
- WHITMAN CO WA 249-C1

S RIVER RD
- COTTAGE GROVE OR 215-B7
- WHITMAN CO WA 249-C1

SE RIVER RD
- CLACKAMAS CO OR 199-C4
- CLACKAMAS CO OR 321-J4
- GLADSTONE OR 199-D4
- HILLSBORO OR 198-D2
- MILWAUKIE OR 321-J4
- WASHINGTON CO OR 198-D2

SW RIVER RD
- HILLSBORO OR 198-D2
- WASHINGTON CO OR 198-D2

RIVER RD N
- KEIZER OR 322-J7
- KEIZER OR 323-A4
- SALEM OR 322-J7

RIVER RD NE
- KEIZER OR 323-A2
- MARION CO OR 204-D1
- MARION CO OR 205-A1
- MARION CO OR 323-A2

RIVER RD S
- MARION CO OR 204-B7
- MARION CO OR 324-D3
- SALEM OR 322-G14
- SALEM OR 324-D3

S RIVER RD S
- INDEPENDENCE OR 204-B7

RIVER RD W
- DISTRICT OF DELTA BC 101-C1

RIVER ST
- CAVE JUNCTION OR 233-B4
- JOSEPHINE CO OR 233-B4
- LEBANON OR 133-C1

N RIVER ST Rt#-82
- ENTERPRISE OR 130-C2

N RIVER ST Rt#-99W
- NEWBERG OR 198-D5

S RIVER ST Rt#-82
- ENTERPRISE OR 130-C2

W RIVER ST
- CAVE JUNCTION OR 233-A4

RIVERBANKS RD
- JOSEPHINE CO OR 149-A1
- JOSEPHINE CO OR 229-A5

RIVER BEND RD
- SALEM OR 322-F9

RIVERBEND RD
- MOUNT VERNON WA 260-A9
- SKAGIT CO WA 161-A7
- SKAGIT CO WA 260-A9

SW RIVER BEND RD
- YAMHILL CO OR 204-B1

RIVER BOTTOM RD
- KITTITAS CO WA 241-B6

RIVERCREST DR N
- KEIZER OR 322-J6

NW RIVERFRONT BLVD
- BEND OR 332-D7

RIVERFRONT RD
- COLUMBIA CO OR 117-B3

RIVERHAVEN ST
- PASCO WA 343-A7

RIVERIA RD
- COLUMBIA CO WA 122-A2

RIVERSHORE RD
- SNOHOMISH CO WA 269-H2

RIVERSIDE AV Rt#-7
- OROFINO ID 123-C2

RIVERSIDE AV Rt#-20
- OKANOGAN CO WA 104-A2
- WINTHROP WA 104-A2

RIVERSIDE AV U.S.-101
- HOQUIAM WA 178-A7

N RIVERSIDE AV Rt#-99
- MEDFORD OR 336-C10

S RIVERSIDE AV Rt#-99
- MEDFORD OR 336-D13

W RIVERSIDE AV
- SPOKANE WA 348-H9

NW RIVERSIDE BLVD
- BEND OR 332-D7

RIVERSIDE DR
- BANDON OR 220-B5
- BURLINGTON WA 260-C9
- COOS CO OR 220-B5
- DISTRICT OF NORTH VANCOUV BC 255-J3
- DOUGLAS CO OR 225-C1
- DOUGLAS CO WA 239-B5
- LINN CO OR 207-C5
- LINN CO OR 326-A10
- MARION CO OR 198-D6
- MOUNT VERNON WA 260-C10
- MYRTLE CREEK OR 225-C1
- PIERCE CO WA 182-C3

RIVERSIDE DR Rt#-20
- OKANOGAN CO WA 104-C2
- OMAK WA 104-C2

RIVERSIDE DR Rt#-129
- ASOTIN CO WA 250-B5
- Vineland WA 250-B5

RIVERSIDE DR U.S.-101
- NEHALEM OR 191-B4

NE RIVERSIDE DR
- MCMINNVILLE OR 198-B7

SE RIVERSIDE DR
- VANCOUVER WA 306-C7

SW RIVERSIDE DR Rt#-43
- CLACKAMAS CO OR 321-G5
- LAKE OSWEGO OR 321-G5
- MULTNOMAH CO OR 321-G5

RIVERSIDE DR NE
- BANDON OR 220-B6

S RIVERSIDE RD
- YAKIMA CO WA 243-C7

RIVERSIDE RD S
- MARION CO OR 207-C1
- MARION CO OR 324-A14

RIVERSIDE ST
- BONNERS FERRY ID 107-B2
- BOUNDARY CO ID 107-B2

RIVERSIDE CUTOFF RD
- OKANOGAN CO WA 104-C2
- RIVERSIDE WA 104-C2

RIVERSIDE PARK DR
- SPOKANE CO WA 348-A1

RIVERVIEW BLVD
- CLARKSTON WA 250-B4

RIVERVIEW DR
- DESCHUTES CO OR 143-A1
- LANE CO OR 210-A7
- ROSEBURG OR 334-C5

W RIVERVIEW DR
- KOOTENAI CO ID 353-E9

RIVERVIEW RD
- JEFFERSON CO OR 208-A6
- SNOHOMISH WA 171-D3
- SNOHOMISH CO WA 171-D3
- SNOHOMISH CO WA 269-H4

SE RIVERWOOD RD
- YAMHILL CO OR 198-C7

RIXIE DR SE
- THURSTON CO WA 184-D1

RIXON RD
- PACIFIC CO WA 183-D7

ROAD 1-NE
- GRANT CO WA 242-D3

ROAD 1-NW
- GRANT CO WA 112-B3

ROAD 1-SW
- GRANT CO WA 112-B3
- GRANT CO WA 242-A4

ROAD 2-NE
- GRANT CO WA 242-A3

ROAD 2-NW
- GRANT CO WA 112-B3
- GRANT CO WA 242-A3

ROAD 3-NE
- GRANT CO WA 113-A2
- GRANT CO WA 242-A3
- MOSES LAKE WA 242-D3

ROAD 3-NW
- GRANT CO WA 242-A3

ROAD 3-SE
- GRANT CO WA 113-A3
- GRANT CO WA 242-D4

ROAD 3-SW
- GRANT CO WA 112-B3

ROAD 4-NE
- GRANT CO WA 242-B2

ROAD 4-NW
- GRANT CO WA 112-C3
- GRANT CO WA 242-A2

ROAD 4-SE
- GRANT CO WA 242-D5

ROAD 4-SW
- GRANT CO WA 112-C3

ROAD 4-10-NE
- GRANT CO WA 113-A2

ROAD 5-NE
- GRANT CO WA 242-A2

ROAD 5-NW
- GRANT CO WA 112-C3
- GRANT CO WA 242-A2

ROAD 5-SE
- GRANT CO WA 242-C5

ROAD 5-SW
- GRANT CO WA 112-B3

ROAD 6-NE
- GRANT CO WA 242-D2

ROAD 6-NW
- GRANT CO WA 112-B3

ROAD 6-SE
- GRANT CO WA 242-D5

ROAD 6-SW
- GRANT CO WA 112-B3

ROAD 7-NE
- GRANT CO WA 113-A3
- GRANT CO WA 242-D2

ROAD 7-NW
- GRANT CO WA 112-C3
- GRANT CO WA 242-A2

ROAD 7-SW
- GRANT CO WA 120-B1
- GRANT CO WA 242-A6

W ROAD 7-10-NE
- GRANT CO WA 113-A2

ROAD 8-NE
- GRANT CO WA 242-D1

ROAD 8-NW
- GRANT CO WA 242-A1

ROAD 8-SE Rt#-170
- GRANT CO WA 121-A1
- WARDEN WA 121-A1

ROAD 9-NE
- GRANT CO WA 113-A3
- GRANT CO WA 242-D1

ROAD 9-NW
- GRANT CO WA 112-C3
- GRANT CO WA 242-A1

ROAD 10-NE
- GRANT CO WA 242-C1

ROAD 10-NW Rt#-28
- GRANT CO WA 112-B3

ROAD 10-NW Rt#-281
- GRANT CO WA 112-B3

ROAD 11-NW Rt#-28
- GRANT CO WA 112-C3

ROAD 11-SW
- GRANT CO WA 120-B1
- GRANT CO WA 242-A7

ROAD 12 SE
- ADAMS CO WA 242-C7
- GRANT CO WA 242-C7

ROAD 12-NE
- GRANT CO WA 113-A3

ROAD 12-NW
- GRANT CO WA 112-C3

ROAD 12-SE
- GRANT CO WA 242-B7

ROAD 13-SE
- GRANT CO WA 242-B7

ROAD 13-SW
- GRANT CO WA 242-A7

ROAD 13-SW Rt#-26
- GRANT CO WA 120-B1

ROAD 15-NE
- GRANT CO WA 113-A3

ROAD 15-1-31
- LANE CO OR 210-D5
- LINN CO OR 210-D5

ROAD 15-2-25
- LANE CO OR 210-D5

ROAD 15-2-25-1
- LANE CO OR 210-D6

ROAD 15-2-26-1
- LINN CO OR 210-D5

ROAD 16-NE
- GRANT CO WA 113-A3

ROAD 16-2-10
- LANE CO OR 210-D6

ROAD 16-2-10-2
- LANE CO OR 210-D6

ROAD 16-2-17-1
- LANE CO OR 210-C6

ROAD 16-2-18
- LANE CO OR 210-D7

ROAD 16-2-18-1
- LANE CO OR 210-C6

ROAD 16-2-27
- LANE CO OR 210-C7

ROAD 16-2-28
- LANE CO OR 210-D7
- LANE CO OR 215-D1

ROAD 16-2-29
- LANE CO OR 210-C7

ROAD 16-2-7-1
- LANE CO OR 210-C6

ROAD 16-3-13-2
- LANE CO OR 210-C7

ROAD 19-NE
- GRANT CO WA 112-C2

ROAD 19-NW
- GRANT CO WA 112-C2

ROAD 20-NE
- GRANT CO WA 112-C2
- GRANT CO WA 113-A2

ROAD 20-NW
- GRANT CO WA 112-C2

ROAD 21 1/2-NE
- GRANT CO WA 113-A2

ROAD 22-NE
- GRANT CO WA 113-A2

N ROAD 22ND
- PASCO WA 343-D6

ROAD 23 SW
- GRANT CO WA 120-B1

ROAD 23-NE
- GRANT CO WA 112-C2
- GRANT CO WA 113-A2

ROAD 24-NW
- GRANT CO WA 112-B2

ROAD 24-SW
- GRANT CO WA 120-B1
- MATTAWA WA 120-B1

ROAD 25-NE
- GRANT CO WA 112-C2

N ROAD 26TH
- PASCO WA 343-C6

ROAD 27-SW
- GRANT CO WA 120-B1

ROAD 28
- PASCO WA 343-C5

N ROAD 28
- PASCO WA 343-C7

ROAD 29-NE
- GRANT CO WA 112-C2

ROAD 31-NE
- GRANT CO WA 113-A2

ROAD 36
- PASCO WA 343-B6

ROAD 36-NE
- GRANT CO WA 113-A2

ROAD 42-NE
- GRANT CO WA 113-A2

INDEX

392 ROAD 43-NE — STREET INDEX — SAGE RD

STREET
City State Page-Grid

ROAD 43-NE
GRANT CO WA 237-B7
ROAD 44
FRANKLIN CO WA 343-A4
PASCO WA 343-A6
N ROAD 44
PASCO WA 343-A3
ROAD 44-NE
GRANT CO WA 237-A7
ROAD 46-NE
GRANT CO WA 237-B6
ROAD 45-NE
GRANT CO WA 237-B7
ROAD 47-NE
GRANT CO WA 237-B6
ROAD 48
FRANKLIN CO WA 343-A5
PASCO WA 343-A5
ROAD 48-NE
GRANT CO WA 237-B6
ROAD 49-NE
GRANT CO WA 237-C5
ROAD 50-NE
GRANT CO WA 237-C5
ROAD 51-NE
GRANT CO WA 237-C5
ROAD 52-NE
GRANT CO WA 237-C5
ROAD 60
FRANKLIN CO WA 342-H5
PASCO WA 342-H5
ROAD 68
FRANKLIN CO WA 342-G4
PASCO WA 342-G6
ROAD 68 N
FRANKLIN CO WA 121-A2
PASCO WA 121-A2
PASCO WA 342-G1
ROAD 76
FRANKLIN CO WA 342-F5
PASCO WA 342-F6
ROAD 84
FRANKLIN CO WA 342-E4
PASCO WA 342-E4
ROAD 92
FRANKLIN CO WA 342-D4
PASCO WA 342-D4
ROAD 100
PASCO WA 342-C2
ROAD 170
FRANKLIN CO WA 121-A2
ROAD 4370
LINCOLN CO WA 113-B1
WILBUR WA 113-B1
ROAD 7009
GRAYS HARBOR CO WA 177-D1
ROAD 8002
GRAYS HARBOR CO WA 178-A1
ROAD A-LINE
GRAYS HARBOR CO WA 117-B1
GRAYS HARBOR CO WA 178-D4
GRAYS HARBOR CO WA 179-A4
ROAD A-NE
GRANT CO WA 112-C2
GRANT CO WA 242-A2
ROAD A-NW
GRANT CO WA 242-A1
ROAD A-SE
GRANT CO WA 120-C1
GRANT CO WA 242-A4
ROAD A-SE Rt#-262
GRANT CO WA 120-C1
GRANT CO WA 242-A7
ROAD B-1000
GRAYS HARBOR CO WA 179-D7
ROAD B-210
WASCO CO OR 135-A1
ROAD B-LINE
GRAYS HARBOR CO WA 179-A4
ROAD B-NE
GRANT CO WA 112-C2
ROAD B-NW
GRANT CO WA 112-C2
GRANT CO WA 242-A2
ROAD B-SE
GRANT CO WA 120-C1
GRANT CO WA 242-B7
ROAD C-LINE RD
GRAYS HARBOR CO WA 179-D7
ROAD C-NW
EPHRATA WA 112-C3
GRANT CO WA 112-C3
ROAD CS30
MASON CO WA 179-B4
ROAD C-SE
GRANT CO WA 242-B4
ROAD D-LINE
GRAYS HARBOR CO WA 178-D4
ROAD D-NE
GRANT CO WA 112-C2
GRANT CO WA 242-B3
ROAD D-SE
GRANT CO WA 120-C1
ROAD E-NE
GRANT CO WA 242-B3
ROAD E-NW
GRANT CO WA 112-C3
ROAD E-SW
GRANT CO WA 120-C1
ROAD F-NE
GRANT CO WA 112-C2
GRANT CO WA 242-B2
ROAD H SE
GRANT CO WA 242-C7
ROAD I-NE
GRANT CO WA 242-C2
ROAD J-NE
GRANT CO WA 113-A2
ROAD K-NE
GRANT CO WA 113-A3
GRANT CO WA 242-D2
ROAD K-NW
GRANT CO WA 112-C3
ROAD K-SE
GRANT CO WA 242-D4
ROAD K-SW
GRANT CO WA 112-C3
ROAD L-5-SW
GRANT CO WA 112-B3
GRANT CO WA 120-B1
ROAD L-7-NE
GRANT CO WA 237-A7
ROAD L-NE
GRANT CO WA 113-A2
GRANT CO WA 242-D1
ROAD L-SE
GRANT CO WA 242-D5
ROAD L-SW
GRANT CO WA 120-B1
ROAD M-110
JEFFERSON CO OR 208-A6
ROAD M-NW
GRANT CO WA 112-B3
ROAD M-SE
GRANT CO WA 242-D5
ROAD M-SW
GRANT CO WA 112-B3
GRANT CO WA 120-B1
ROAD N-NE
GRANT CO WA 237-A7
GRANT CO WA 242-D1
ROAD N-SE
GRANT CO WA 242-D4
ROAD O-NE
GRANT CO WA 237-A6
GRANT CO WA 242-D1
ROAD O-SE
GRANT CO WA 242-D4
ROAD O-SW
GRANT CO WA 120-B1
ROAD P-110
JEFFERSON CO OR 208-A4
ROAD P-NE
GRANT CO WA 113-A3
GRANT CO WA 237-B6
ROAD P-NW
GRANT CO WA 112-B3
ROAD Q-NE
GRANT CO WA 113-A3
GRANT CO WA 237-B6
ROAD Q-SE
GRANT CO WA 113-A3
ROAD Q-SW
GEORGE WA 112-B3
GRANT CO WA 112-B3
GRANT CO WA 120-B1
ROAD R-NE
GRANT CO WA 113-A2
GRANT CO WA 237-B6
HARTLINE WA 113-A2
ROAD R-NW
GRANT CO WA 112-B3
ROAD R-SW
GRANT CO WA 112-B3
GRANT CO WA 120-B1
ROAD S-322
WASCO CO OR 127-B3
ROAD S-NE
GRANT CO WA 113-A3
GRANT CO WA 237-B6
ROAD S-NW
GRANT CO WA 112-B3
ROAD T-2 NE
GRANT CO WA 237-B5
ROAD T-NE
GRANT CO WA 237-B6
ROAD U-NE
GRANT CO WA 113-A3
GRANT CO WA 237-C5
ROAD U-NW
GRANT CO WA 112-B3
ROAD U-SE
GRANT CO WA 113-A3
GRANT CO WA 121-A1
WARDEN WA 121-A1
ROAD U-SW
GRANT CO WA 112-B3
GRANT CO WA 120-B1
ROAD V-NE
GRANT CO WA 237-C5
ROAD WA-NA-PA
CASCADE LOCKS OR 194-D6
ROAD W-NE
GRANT CO WA 113-A2
GRANT CO WA 237-C4
LINCOLN CO WA 113-A2
MARLIN WA 113-A2
ROAD W-SE
GRANT CO WA 121-A1
ROAD X-NE
GRANT CO WA 237-C5
LINCOLN CO WA 237-C5
ROANOKE DR NE
MARION CO OR 205-A3
E ROANOKE ST
SEATTLE WA 278-B1
ROARING CREEK RD
WASHINGTON CO OR 198-A3
ROBBINS RD
KITTITAS CO WA 241-B4
ROBERTA AV
LAKE CO OR 152-A2
ROBERT BUSH DR U.S.-101
PACIFIC CO WA 183-D6
SOUTH BEND WA 117-A1
SOUTH BEND WA 183-D6
ROBERT CREEK RD
COOS CO OR 218-D4
ROBERT GRAY DR Rt#-100
PACIFIC CO WA 186-A6
SE ROBERTS AV
GRESHAM OR 200-B2
ROBERTS DR
BLACK DIAMOND WA 110-C3
ROBERTS RD
CROOK CO OR 135-C3
CROOK CO OR 136-A3
GRAYS HARBOR CO WA 183-B2
LEWIS CO WA 187-D1
LINN CO OR 210-B1
MEDFORD OR 336-E9
YAKIMA CO WA 243-A5
ROBERTS RD KPN
PIERCE CO WA 181-A1
ROBERTS BANK SUPERPORT CSWY
DISTRICT OF DELTA BC 101-C1
ROBERTS BUTTE RD
WALLOWA CO OR 130-C1
ROBERTS CREEK RD
DOUGLAS CO OR 221-B6
ROBERTS MOUNTAIN RD
DOUGLAS CO OR 221-B6
ROBERTSON CRES
TOWNSHIP OF LANGLEY BC 158-D1
ROBERTSON ST
CITY OF VICTORIA BC 257-A11
ROBERTSON BRIDGE RD
JOSEPHINE CO OR 229-A4
ROBIN DR
JEFFERSON CO OR 212-C2
ROBINETTE RD
COLUMBIA CO OR 192-A1
ROBINSON RD
JOSEPHINE CO OR 233-C4
MARYSVILLE WA 168-C7
SNOHOMISH CO WA 168-C7
ROBINSON ST
COQUITLAM BC 157-A4
ROBINSON CANYON RD
KITTITAS CO WA 241-A5
ROBINSON LAKE RD
LATAH CO ID 249-D4
ROBINSON PARK RD
LATAH CO ID 249-D4
ROBISON RD
BENTON CO OR 207-A3
POLK CO OR 207-A3
ROBSON DR
COQUITLAM BC 157-B4
ROBSON ST
VANCOUVER BC 254-F9
ROCHAT RD
KOOTENAI CO ID 115-B2
ROCHAT DIVIDE RD
BENEWAH CO ID 115-B2
ROCHE HARBOR RD
FRIDAY HARBOR WA 101-C2
SAN JUAN CO WA 101-C2
ROCK RD Rt#-547
WHATCOM CO WA 102-B1
ROCK RD NW
DOUGLAS CO WA 236-C6
ROCKAWAY BEACH RD
BAINBRIDGE ISLAND WA 174-D2
ROCK CANDY MOUNTAIN RD SW
THURSTON CO WA 180-A7
ROCK CANYON RD
MALHEUR CO OR 146-C1
ROCK CREEK RD
COLUMBIA CO OR 125-B1
COOS CO OR 140-C3
DOUGLAS CO OR 141-C2
DOUGLAS CO OR 219-B2
HARNEY CO OR 145-A3
HARNEY CO OR 153-A1
JACKSON CO OR 227-A3
JACKSON CO OR 230-B1
KLICKITAT CO WA 128-A1
LINCOLN CO OR 133-A1
MALHEUR CO OR 146-C3
WASHINGTON CO ID 139-A2
NW ROCK CREEK RD
MULTNOMAH CO OR 192-A6
S ROCK CREEK RD
BAKER CO OR 130-A3
ROCK CREEK DAM RD
WASCO CO OR 127-A3
ROCKCREST ST
COLUMBIA CO OR 189-B4
RAINIER OR 189-B4
RAINIER OR 302-G14
ROCK CUT RD
STEVENS CO WA 105-C1
ROCKFORD BAY RD
KOOTENAI CO ID 247-D6
ROCK HILL DR
Crowfoot OR 133-C1
LANE CO OR 215-B4
LINN CO OR 133-C1
LINN CO OR 210-C1
ROCK ISLAND AV
DOUGLAS CO WA 239-B5
ROCK ISLAND WA 239-B5
ROCK ISLAND RD
DOUGLAS CO WA 239-A5
East Wenatchee Bench WA 239-A5
ROCK ISLAND GRADE SW
DOUGLAS CO WA 239-C5
ROCK LAKE RD
WHITMAN CO WA 114-B3
S ROCK LAKE RD
SPOKANE CO WA 114-B3
ROCKLAND AV
CITY OF VICTORIA BC 256-J10
CITY OF VICTORIA BC 257-A10
W ROCKLAND RD
DISTRICT OF NORTH VANCOUV BC 255-B1
ROCKLYN RD
LINCOLN CO WA 113-C2
ROCKPORT CASCADE RD
SKAGIT CO WA 103-A2
ROCK SPRINGS RD
JEFFERSON CO OR 211-D3
WHITMAN CO WA 122-A1
ROCKWELL DR
CITY OF HARRISON HOT SPRI BC 94-C3
DISTRICT OF KENT BC 94-C3
E ROCKWOOD BLVD
SPOKANE WA 349-A11
S ROCKWOOD BLVD
SPOKANE WA 349-B12
ROCKY RD
DOUGLAS CO WA 236-D4
ROCKY BAY PT Rt#-302
MASON CO WA 173-D7
ROCKY BAY POINT DR Rt#-302
MASON CO WA 174-A7
ROCKY BAY POINT DR KPN Rt#-302
MASON CO WA 174-A7
PIERCE CO WA 174-A7
ROCKY BUTTE RD
WASCO CO OR 202-D7
ROCKY CANYON RD
IDAHO CO ID 123-B3
IDAHO CO ID 131-C1
ROCKY CREEK RD KPN
PIERCE CO WA 174-A6
ROCKYDALE RD
JOSEPHINE CO OR 233-B6
ROCKY FORD RD
LINCOLN CO WA 113-C2
YAKIMA CO WA 120-A2
NW ROCKYFORD RD
YAMHILL CO OR 198-A4
ROCKY POINT RD
BREMERTON WA 270-E8
DISTRICT OF METCHOSIN BC 159-A7
DISTRICT OF METCHOSIN BC 165-A1
KITSAP CO WA 270-E8
MULTNOMAH CO OR 125-C1
MULTNOMAH CO OR 192-A5
ROCKY TOP RD
YAKIMA CO WA 243-A6
RODGERS RD
LANE CO OR 215-C5
RODMAN RD
YAKIMA CO WA 243-B4
ROE RD
LEWIS CO WA 187-B4
ROE RD E
LEWIS CO WA 187-B3
ROE ST
STEILACOOM WA 181-C4
ROGERS LN
VALLEY CO ID 251-D6
ROGERS RD
COWLITZ CO WA 189-D5
DOUGLAS CO OR 221-C2
LEWIS CO WA 187-C5
POLK CO OR 204-B7
ROGERS AND HOBSON RD
CHELAN CO WA 236-D2
ROGERSON RD
LEWIS CO WA 184-D7
SE ROGUE DR
GRANTS PASS OR 335-G11
ROGUE RIVER DR
JACKSON CO OR 230-D4
SHADY COVE OR 230-D4
ROGUE RIVER HWY Rt#-99
GRANTS PASS OR 335-J11
JACKSON CO OR 229-C6
JACKSON CO OR 230-A6
JOSEPHINE CO OR 229-C6
JOSEPHINE CO OR 335-J11
ROGUE RIVER OR 229-C6
ROGUE RIVER LOOP HWY
GRANTS PASS OR 335-A9
JOSEPHINE CO OR 149-A1
JOSEPHINE CO OR 229-A4
JOSEPHINE CO OR 335-A9
ROGUE VALLEY HWY
MEDFORD OR 336-C9
ROGUE VALLEY HWY Rt#-99
ASHLAND OR 337-A4
CENTRAL POINT OR 230-C7
JACKSON CO OR 230-C7
JACKSON CO OR 234-B2
JACKSON CO OR 337-A4
MEDFORD OR 230-C7
MEDFORD OR 234-B2
MEDFORD OR 336-A7
PHOENIX OR 234-B2
TALENT OR 234-B3
ROITZ RD
STEVENS CO WA 106-B3
ROLLING HILLS RD
POLK CO OR 207-B2
ROLOFF RD
ADAMS CO WA 113-C3
ROME RD
MALHEUR CO OR 146-C3
ROMIE HOWARD RD
DOUGLAS CO OR 219-C5
ROMINE CREEK RD
JACKSON CO OR 230-C1
ROMMERMAN RD
LEWIS CO WA 187-C1
RONDO RD
PIERCE CO WA 181-C7
SW ROOD BRIDGE RD
WASHINGTON CO OR 198-D2
W ROOSEVELT AV
CANYON CO ID 147-B1
ROOSEVELT DR U.S.-101
SEASIDE OR 301-G6
S ROOSEVELT DR U.S.-101
CLATSOP CO OR 301-F10
SEASIDE OR 301-G8
ROOSEVELT ST
ABERDEEN WA 178-B7
N ROOSEVELT ST
WALLA WALLA WA 345-D6
S ROOSEVELT ST
BOISE ID 253-C3
WALLA WALLA WA 345-D8
ROOSEVELT WY
WHATCOM CO WA 101-C1
ROOSEVELT WY NE
SEATTLE WA 171-B7
SEATTLE WA 274-B2
ROOSEVELT GRADE RD
KLICKITAT CO WA 128-A1
ROPPERT RD
LEWIS CO WA 187-C3
ROSA RD
COOS CO OR 220-B7
ROSALYNN SUMNERS BLVD
EDMONDS WA 171-A5
ROSARIO RD
SKAGIT CO WA 160-C7
SKAGIT CO WA 259-D10
ROSARIO BEACH RD
SKAGIT CO WA 259-C14
ROSE AV Rt#-47
COLUMBIA CO OR 125-B1
VERNONIA OR 125-B1
ROSE RD
LANE CO OR 210-D6
SNOHOMISH CO WA 168-C4
ROSE ST
PHOENIX OR 234-B2
N ROSE ST
WALLA WALLA WA 345-B6
W ROSE ST
COLLEGE PLACE WA 344-F9
WALLA WALLA WA 344-H9
ROSEBERG ST SW
THURSTON CO WA 184-A4
E ROSEBERRY RD
DONNELLY ID 252-D1
VALLEY CO ID 252-D1
W ROSEBERRY RD
VALLEY CO ID 252-D1
ROSEBROOK RD
LEWIS CO WA 187-D1
ROSE CREEK RD
MALHEUR CO OR 138-A2
WHITMAN CO WA 249-B3
ROSEDALE RD
CATHLAMET WA 117-B3
WAHKIAKUM CO WA 117-B3
SW ROSEDALE RD
WASHINGTON CO OR 198-D2
WASHINGTON CO OR 199-A2
ROSEDALE ST NW
GIG HARBOR WA 181-B1
PIERCE CO WA 181-B1
ROSEDALE BAY
PIERCE CO WA 181-B1
ROSEDALE PURDY
PIERCE CO WA 174-B7
W ROSE HILL ST
BOISE ID 253-C3
ROSEMONT AV NW
SALEM OR 322-F12
ROSEMONT RD
CLACKAMAS CO OR 199-C4
ROSENAU RD
LATAH CO ID 250-D1
ROSENKRANTZ RD
NEZ PERCE CO ID 250-C5
ROSENOFF RD
ADAMS CO WA 113-B3
RITZVILLE WA 113-B3
ROSENOFF RD Rt#-21
ADAMS CO WA 113-B3
ROSE VALLEY RD
COWLITZ CO WA 118-A3
COWLITZ CO WA 189-C4
ROSS LN
JACKSON CO OR 234-A1
JACKSON CO OR 336-A12
LANE CO OR 215-C7
MEDFORD OR 336-A12
ROSS LN Rt#-238
MEDFORD OR 336-A12
ROSS RD
DISTRICT OF MATSQUI BC 102-B1
DISTRICT OF NORTH VANCOUV BC 255-F3
ROSSANLEY DR Rt#-238
JACKSON CO OR 234-A1
JACKSON CO OR 336-B10
MEDFORD OR 336-A10
ROSS INLET RD
COOS CO OR 220-D2
S ROSS POINT RD
KOOTENAI CO ID 354-D7
POST FALLS ID 354-D7
ROSS POINT-RATHDRUM HWY Rt#-41
KOOTENAI CO ID 247-D1
KOOTENAI CO ID 354-D2
POST FALLS ID 354-D2
ROSWELL RD
MALHEUR CO OR 147-A1
ROTH RD
LEWIS CO WA 187-C3
ROTHFORK RD
LATAH CO ID 249-C3
ROTHROCK RD
BENTON CO WA 120-C2
NE ROTSCHY RD
CLARK CO WA 193-B1
ROUGH & RUGGED RD
JACKSON CO OR 230-B7
SW ROUND BUTTE DR
JEFFERSON CO OR 208-A6
ROUND BUTTE LOOP RD
KLAMATH CO OR 142-C3
ROUND LAKE RD
JEFFERSON CO OR 211-B1
KLAMATH CO OR 235-A2
ROUNDS AV
JOSEPHINE CO OR 229-A6
ROUND TOP RD
JACKSON CO OR 230-B1
ROUNDTREE RD
LEWIS CO WA 187-A2
ROUND VALLEY RD
ADAMS CO ID 131-C3
ADAMS CO ID 251-A1
ROUPE RD
ASOTIN CO WA 122-C2
ROUSE RD KPS
PIERCE CO WA 181-A3
NE ROVA RD
KITSAP CO WA 170-C6
ROWDY CREEK RD
DEL NORTE CO CA 148-B3
ROWE CREEK RD
WHEELER CO OR 128-A3
WHEELER CO OR 136-A1
ROWLAND RD
LINN CO OR 210-B4
YAMHILL CO OR 198-B5
ROW RIVER RD
COTTAGE GROVE OR 215-C7
LANE CO OR 141-C1
LANE CO OR 215-C7
ROW RIVER CUTOFF RD
COTTAGE GROVE OR 215-B7
SW ROXBURY ST
KING CO WA 285-F4
SEATTLE WA 285-F4
ROXY ANN RD
JACKSON CO OR 234-C1
ROY RD
WHATCOM CO WA 161-A2
NW ROY RD
WASHINGTON CO OR 125-C1
ROY ST
SEATTLE WA 277-H3
E ROY ST
SEATTLE WA 278-B3
W ROY ST
SEATTLE WA 277-G3
ROYAL AV
EUGENE OR 215-A2
EUGENE OR 329-A3
LANE CO OR 215-A2
MEDFORD OR 336-D11
NEW WESTMINSTER BC 156-D5
ROYAL AV N
EAGLE POINT OR 230-D5
JACKSON CO OR 230-D5
ROYAL AV S
EAGLE POINT OR 230-D5
S ROYAL BROUGHAM WY
SEATTLE WA 282-A1
S ROYAL BROUGHAM WY Rt#-519
SEATTLE WA 281-J1
SEATTLE WA 282-A1
ROYAL OAK AV
DISTRICT OF BURNABY BC 156-C5
ROYAL OAK DR
DISTRICT OF SAANICH BC 159-C5
ROY CHRISTIE
PIERCE CO WA 118-B1
SE ROYER RD
DAMASCUS OR 200-B4
ROY PAYNE RD
LANE CO OR 219-D1
ROY PETTIT
PIERCE CO WA 181-D7
SW ROY ROGERS RD
WASHINGTON CO OR 199-A3
ROZA HILL DR
YAKIMA CO WA 243-D6
E ROZA HILL DR
YAKIMA CO WA 243-C6
N RUBY ST U.S.-2
SPOKANE WA 349-A6
RUCKEL RD
UNION CO OR 130-A1
RUCKER AV
EVERETT WA 264-D3
RUCKMAN AV Rt#-82
IMBLER OR 130-A2
RUDDELL RD SE
LACEY WA 297-H11
THURSTON CO WA 297-H11
NW RUDE RD
KITSAP CO WA 170-B6
SE RUDE RD
CLACKAMAS CO OR 200-C5
RUDI RD
DESCHUTES CO OR 212-B7
RUE CREEK RD
PACIFIC CO WA 117-A1
RUEPPELL ST
TILLAMOOK CO OR 197-A7
RUMBLE ST
DISTRICT OF BURNABY BC 156-C5
SE RUPERT DR
CLACKAMAS CO OR 321-J6
RUPERT RD
COLUMBIA CO OR 189-A7
RUPERT ST
VANCOUVER BC 156-C5
VANCOUVER BC 255-E14
RUPP RD
LEWIS CO WA 187-C5
RUPPERT RD
BENTON CO WA 120-C2
RURAL AV
WHATCOM CO WA 158-C7
RURAL AV SE
SALEM OR 324-H1
RURAL RD SW
TUMWATER WA 296-F11
RURAL S ST
HARNEY CO OR 145-B2
RUSH AV
KLAMATH CO OR 151-A3
MALIN OR 151-A3
RUSH RD
NAPAVINE WA 187-C1
W RUSH RD
EAGLE ID 253-A1
RUSH CREEK RD
WASHINGTON CO ID 139-B1
RUSS BAKER WY
CITY OF RICHMOND BC 156-B6
RUSSEL RD
JOSEPHINE CO OR 229-B3
RUSSELL LN
JOSEPH OR 130-C2
WALLOWA CO OR 130-C2
RUSSELL RD
FRANKLIN CO WA 121-A2
KENT WA 291-F6
LEWIS CO WA 187-B3
MALHEUR CO OR 138-C3
RUSSELL ST
WENATCHEE WA 238-D4
RUSSELL CREEK RD
WALLA WALLA CO WA 345-E9
Walla Walla East WA 345-E9
RUSSELL RIDGE RD
LEWIS CO ID 123-C2
RUSSELL RIDGE RD Rt#-7
CLEARWATER CO ID 123-C2
RUSTEMEYER RD
GRAYS HARBOR CO WA 183-C1
RUSTIC LN
LANE CO OR 214-B1
S RUSTLE ST
SPOKANE WA 348-D12
RUSTON WY
TACOMA WA 181-D1
TACOMA WA 292-D1
TACOMA WA 293-E2
RUTLEDGE LN
SHERMAN CO OR 127-C2
RUTLEDGE RD
SHERMAN CO OR 127-C2
E RUTTER AV
SPOKANE WA 349-J6
SPOKANE WA 350-A5
SPOKANE VALLEY WA 349-J6
SPOKANE VALLEY WA 350-A5
N RUTTER PKWY
SPOKANE CO WA 346-B6
W RUTTER PKWY
Fairwood WA 346-E8
SPOKANE CO WA 246-A1
SPOKANE CO WA 346-B6
RUX RD E
LINCOLN CO WA 113-B1
RYALS AV
BENTON CO OR 207-B4
RYAN RD
DESCHUTES CO OR 213-A4
S RYAN WY
SEATTLE WA 287-F5
TUKWILA WA 287-F5
RYAN-ALLEN RD
SKAMANIA CO WA 194-C5
RYAN-TAVELLI RD
SKAMANIA CO WA 194-A7
RYE GRASS LN
HARNEY CO OR 145-B1
RYEGRASS RD
CROOK CO OR 213-B3
RYE VALLEY-MORMON BASIN RD
BAKER CO OR 138-C2

S

SAANICH RD
DISTRICT OF SAANICH BC 256-G5
SAARI RD
LEWIS CO WA 187-C4
SACHS RD SW
DOUGLAS CO WA 239-C3
SADDLE DR
KOOTENAI CO ID 245-B7
SADDLE BUTTE RD
HARNEY CO OR 145-C2
SADDLE MOUNTAIN RD
CLATSOP CO OR 188-D4
SADDLE RIDGE RD
LATAH CO ID 249-C3
SAGE RD
GRANT CO WA 242-C3
JACKSON CO OR 336-B10
MALHEUR CO OR 139-A3
OWYHEE CO ID 147-A1

INDEX

INDEX

394 W SEQUIM BAY RD
STREET INDEX
W SNOQUALMIE VALLEY RD NE

STREET City State Page-Grid

W SEQUIM BAY RD
CLALLAM CO WA 262-H12
SEQUIM WA 262-H12
SEQUIM-DUNGENESS WY
CLALLAM CO WA 262-D4
SERVICE CK-MITCHLL HWY Rt#-207
MITCHELL OR 136-A1
WHEELER CO OR 136-A1
NE SERWOLD RD
POULSBO WA 170-C7
SESAME ST NW
KITSAP CO WA 174-A1
SETHER AV
DOUGLAS CO OR 225-B7
GLENDALE OR 225-A7
SETTERS RD
KOOTENAI CO ID 247-C7
SETTLEMIER AV
MARION CO OR 205-B2
WOODBURN OR 205-B1
SEVEN DEVILS RD
COOS CO OR 220-B2
N SEVEN MILE EXT
SPOKANE CO WA 246-A2
SEVEN MILE LN
BROWNSVILLE OR 210-C2
LINN CO OR 207-D6
LINN CO OR 210-C1
LINN CO OR 326-F14
SEVEN MILE RD
COOS CO OR 220-B5
SEVENMILE RD
KLAMATH CO OR 231-B2
SEVEN MILE RD Rt#-162
IDAHO CO ID 123-C3
KAMIAH ID 123-C3
LEWIS CO ID 123-C3
W SEVEN MILE RD
SPOKANE CO WA 246-A2
SEVENMILE HILL RD
WASCO CO OR 196-B6
SEVENMILE RANCH RD
KLAMATH CO OR 231-B2
SEVEN SPRINGS DAIRY RD E
LINCOLN CO WA 113-C2
SEVENTH ST U.S.-101
HOQUIAM WA 178-A7
E SEVENTH ST
ROSALIA WA 114-C3
N SEVENTH ST Rt#-903
ROSLYN WA 240-A1
SEWARD DR
LINN CO OR 207-B7
NW SEWARD RD
CLARK CO WA 192-C4
SEWARD PARK AV S
SEATTLE WA 283-G7
SEATTLE WA 287-G1
SEYMOUR BLVD
DISTRICT OF NORTH VANCOUV BC 255-G6
SEYMOUR ST Rt#-99
VANCOUVER BC 254-F11
SHAD RD
JEFFERSON CO OR 212-C2
SHADY LN
KLICKITAT CO WA 196-B4
SHADY PINE RD
KLAMATH CO OR 235-C1
N SHADY SLOPE RD
SPOKANE CO WA 347-D5
SHAFF RD
MARION CO OR 133-C1
SHAFF RD SE
MARION CO OR 133-C1
STAYTON OR 133-C1
W SHAFFER AV Rt#-231
SPRINGDALE WA 106-B3
N SHAMROCK ST
BOISE ID 253-B2
SHANDROW
PIERCE CO WA 182-A7
SHANIKO-FOSSIL HWY Rt#-218
ANTELOPE OR 127-C3
FOSSIL OR 128-A3
SHANIKO OR 127-C3
WASCO CO OR 127-C3
WASCO CO OR 128-A3
WHEELER CO OR 128-A3
SHARON AV
BURLINGTON WA 260-C6
SHARON CREEK RESERVOIR RD
MALHEUR CO OR 155-A2
SHARPE RD
PITT MEADOWS BC 157-C5
SKAGIT CO WA 259-C13
SHARPS CREEK RD
LANE CO OR 141-C1
LANE CO OR 142-A1
S SHASTA AV
EAGLE POINT OR 230-D5
SHASTA WY
Altamont OR 338-G9
Altamont OR 339-A9
KLAMATH CO OR 338-G9
KLAMATH FALLS OR 338-G9
SHATTUCK RD
DESCHUTES CO OR 211-D6
SW SHATTUCK RD
MULTNOMAH CO OR 316-A3
PORTLAND OR 199-B2
PORTLAND OR 316-A3
SHAUGHNESSY ST
COQUITLAM BC 157-B4
PORT COQUITLAM BC 157-B4
SHAW HWY SE
AUMSVILLE OR 205-B7
MARION CO OR 205-B7
SHAW RD
PUYALLUP WA 182-B4
UMATILLA CO OR 129-B2
SHAW RD E
PIERCE CO WA 182-B4
SHAW-HOLMES RD
UMATILLA CO OR 129-B2
E SHAW MOUNTAIN RD
ADA CO ID 253-D2
SHAWNEE
CROOK CO OR 213-D7
SHAWNEE-PARVIN RD
WHITMAN CO WA 249-A3
SHAWNIGAN LAKE RD
BRITISH COLUMBIA BC 159-A3
SHAY LN
DESCHUTES CO OR 143-A1
SHAY HILL RD
BENEWAH CO ID 248-C7

SHEARERS BRIDGE HWY Rt#-216
WASCO CO OR 127-B2
SHEDD CEMETERY RD
LINN CO OR 210-B1
SHEEHAN RD SW
DOUGLAS CO WA 239-C2
NW SHEELAR LN
WASHINGTON CO OR 198-B1
SHEEP CANYON RD
GRANT CO WA 112-C2
SHEEP COMPANY RD
YAKIMA CO WA 243-B4
SHEEP CREEK RD
STEVENS CO WA 106-A1
WASHINGTON CO ID 139-C2
SHEFFIELD RD
FRANKLIN CO WA 121-A2
SHEFFLER RD
WALLA WALLA CO WA 121-B2
SHELBOURNE ST
CITY OF VICTORIA BC 257-A7
DISTRICT OF SAANICH BC 159-D5
DISTRICT OF SAANICH BC 257-A1
SHELBURN DR
LINN CO OR 133-C1
SHELBY RD
SNOHOMISH CO WA 171-B4
SHELDON RD SE
THURSTON CO WA 184-D1
SHELDON ST
FALLS CITY OR 125-B3
POLK CO OR 125-B3
SHELGRIN RD
GRAYS HARBOR CO WA 177-C4
SHELL RD
CITY OF RICHMOND BC 156-B6
SHELLER RD
YAKIMA CO WA 120-B2
SHELLEY RD
COOS CO OR 220-D5
SHELLRIDGE RD NW
THURSTON CO WA 180-B5
SHELL ROCK RD
CLACKAMAS CO OR 126-C3
KITTITAS CO WA 240-C6
SHELTER BAY DR
Shelter Bay WA 167-D1
SHELTON RD
Walla Walla East WA 345-E10
NW SHELTON RD
YAMHILL CO OR 198-A6
SHELTON-MATLOCK RD
MASON CO WA 179-C2
MASON CO WA 180-A3
SHELTON VALLEY RD
MASON CO WA 180-A3
SHEPARD RD
COLUMBIA CO OR 189-A3
SHERARS BRIDGE HWY Rt#-216
GRASS VALLEY OR 127-B2
SHERMAN CO OR 127-B2
SHERIDAN AV U.S.-101
NORTH BEND OR 333-G5
S SHERIDAN AV
TACOMA WA 295-F6
SHERIDAN RD
BREMERTON WA 270-H7
BREMERTON WA 271-A8
KITSAP CO WA 271-A8
SHERIDAN ST
PORT TOWNSEND WA 263-E5
SE SHERIDAN ST
POLK CO OR 125-B3
SW SHERIDAN ST
PORTLAND OR 317-E1
SHER KHAN RD
LANE CO OR 215-B4
NW SHERLOCK AV
PORTLAND OR 312-B1
E SHERLOCK ST Rt#-23
HARRINGTON WA 113-C2
SHERMAN AV
NORTH BEND OR 333-G5
SHERMAN AV U.S.-101
NORTH BEND OR 333-G5
E SHERMAN AV
COEUR D'ALENE ID 355-F11
KOOTENAI CO ID 355-F11
SHERMAN HWY U.S.-97
GRASS VALLEY OR 127-C2
MORO OR 127-C2
SHANIKO OR 127-C2
SHERMAN CO OR 127-C1
WASCO CO OR 127-B3
SHERMAN RD
ISLAND CO WA 167-B4
S SHERMAN RD
SPOKANE CO WA 246-B6
SHERMAN RD SE
MARION CO OR 205-B7
S SHERMAN ST
ASHLAND OR 337-D8
SPOKANE WA 349-B9
SHERMAN HEIGHTS RD
KITSAP CO WA 270-D14
Navy Yard City WA 270-D14
SHERWOOD DR
JEFFERSON CO OR 212-D2
SHERWOOD RD
CROOK CO OR 136-A3
NW SHEVLIN PARK MARKET RD
BEND OR 217-B2
BEND OR 332-A6
DESCHUTES CO OR 217-B2
SHIBLEY RD
CLACKAMAS CO OR 200-B7
SHIFFMAN RD
TILLAMOOK CO OR 191-C4
SHILOH RD
JACKSON CO OR 230-C4
SHINCKE RD NE
THURSTON CO WA 180-D5
SHINGLEBOLT RD
TILLAMOOK CO OR 203-B3
E SHINGLE MILL RD
BONNER CO ID 244-B1
W SHINGLE MILL RD
BONNER CO ID 244-B1
SHINN RD SW
DOUGLAS CO WA 239-C4
SHIPLEY RD
CLACKAMAS CO OR 200-D4
SHIRTTAIL CREEK RD
BAKER CO OR 138-C2
SHIVELY CREEK RD
DOUGLAS CO OR 225-D2

SHOALWATER BAY
PACIFIC CO WA 186-B6
SHOEPEG RD
WASHINGTON CO ID 139-B1
SHOESTRING RD
DOUGLAS CO OR 225-B3
LANE CO OR 219-C3
SHOLLMEYER RD
TILLAMOOK CO OR 191-B4
SHORE DR
BREMERTON WA 271-A10
S SHORE DR
SKAGIT CO WA 160-C5
W SHORE DR
SKAGIT CO WA 160-C4
WHATCOM CO WA 160-B1
SHORE RD
CLALLAM CO WA 165-D6
S SHORE RD
BREMERTON WA 270-C8
SKAGIT CO WA 160-C5
SHORE ST
CHELAN CO WA 238-A1
SHORELINE DR N
KEIZER OR 322-H5
SHORE PINE RD
CURRY CO OR 232-C4
SHOREVIEW DR
LINCOLN CO OR 328-C1
SHOREWOOD
SAN JUAN CO WA 160-A3
SE SHOREWOOD DR
VANCOUVER WA 306-C7
SHORT RD
KLAMATH CO OR 235-D5
N SHORT RD
SPOKANE CO WA 114-B1
SHORT ST
ASTORIA OR 300-B5
SHORT HORN GULCH RD
JOSEPHINE CO OR 229-B2
SHORT ROAD BEECH CREEK
GRANT CO OR 137-A1
SHORT ROAD IN FOX
GRANT CO OR 137-A1
SHORT SAND CROSS OVER RD
TILLAMOOK CO OR 191-B3
SHORT SCHOOL RD
SNOHOMISH CO WA 171-D4
NE SHORTY CAMPBELL RD
Kingston WA 170-D5
KITSAP CO WA 170-D5
SHOSHONI LN
LANE CO OR 215-D5
SHROPSHIRE RD
WHITMAN CO WA 122-A1
SHUFFIELD RD
LAKE CO OR 143-C3
SHUMAKER RD
ASOTIN CO WA 123-A3
SHUMWAY RD
CROOK CO OR 213-A7
MALHEUR CO OR 146-A1
SHUMWAY CUTOFF RD
MALHEUR CO OR 146-B1
SHUMWAY RANCH RD
MALHEUR CO OR 146-B1
NE SHUTE RD
HILLSBORO OR 198-D1
SHUTTERA RD
NEZ PERCE CO ID 250-D6
SHUTTERS LANDING RD
COOS CO OR 218-C4
SHY MEADOW
CHELAN CO WA 238-B2
SIAH BUTTE RD
DESCHUTES CO OR 216-C6
SIDAWAY RD
CITY OF RICHMOND BC 156-C7
S SIDE RD
DOUGLAS CO OR 219-A3
W SIDE RD
BOUNDARY CO ID 107-B1
SIDE HILL RD
DESCHUTES CO OR 211-B3
SIDNEY AV
PORT ORCHARD WA 174-B4
PORT ORCHARD WA 270-H14
SIDNEY AV SW
PORT ORCHARD WA 174-B4
SIDNEY RD S
MARION CO OR 207-C1
SIDNEY RD SW
KITSAP CO WA 174-B5
PIERCE CO WA 174-B6
PORT ORCHARD WA 174-B5
SIDNEY-ANACORTES FERRY
BRITISH COLUMBIA BC 101-C2
BRITISH COLUMBIA BC 159-C2
SAN JUAN CO WA 101-C2
TOWN OF SIDNEY BC 159-C2
SIEVERS DUECY BLVD
EVERETT WA 268-A3
SIGHTLY RD
COWLITZ CO WA 118-A2
SIGNAL PEAK RD
HARRAH WA 119-C2
SIGNAL PEAK RD Rt#-220
HARRAH WA 119-C2
S SIGNAL POINT RD
KOOTENAI CO ID 247-C4
SILCOTT GRADE RD
ASOTIN CO WA 250-A4
SILCOTT WYE RD
ASOTIN CO WA 250-A5
SILETZ HWY Rt#-229
LINCOLN CO OR 203-A6
LINCOLN CO OR 206-C1
SILETZ OR 206-C1
TOLEDO OR 206-C4
SILL RD
SNOHOMISH CO WA 168-C5
SILLS RD
ISLAND CO WA 170-D2
ISLAND CO WA 171-A2
SILTCOOS STATION RD
LANE CO OR 214-B5
SILVER ST
PORT TOWNSEND WA 263-E3
SILVER CITY RD
OWYHEE CO ID 147-B2
SILVER CREEK RD
FERRY CO WA 105-B3
HARNEY CO OR 144-C1
JOSEPHINE CO OR 148-C1
SILVERCREEK RD Rt#-122
LEWIS CO WA 118-A2

SILVER CROWN AV
NORTHPORT WA 106-A1
SILVERDALE WY NW
KITSAP CO WA 170-B7
KITSAP CO WA 174-B1
Silverdale WA 174-B1
Silverdale WA 170-B1
SILVER FALLS HWY Rt#-214
MARION CO OR 205-A7
SILVER FALLS HWY NE Rt#-214
MARION CO OR 205-C5
SILVERTON OR 205-C5
SILVER FALLS HWY NW Rt#-214
MARION CO OR 205-B7
SILVER FALLS HWY SE Rt#-214
MARION CO OR 205-D6
SILVER LAKE RD
ISLAND CO WA 167-C2
KLAMATH CO OR 142-C3
KLAMATH CO OR 143-A3
WHATCOM CO WA 102-C1
S SILVER LAKE RD
COWLITZ CO WA 187-C7
COWLITZ CO WA 189-D1
SILVERNAIL RD
SKAGIT CO WA 168-B3
SILVER RIDGE RD SE
MARION CO OR 205-D7
SILVERTON AV Rt#-214
MARION CO OR 205-B2
WOODBURN OR 205-B2
SILVERTON HWY Rt#-214
WOODBURN OR 205-B2
NE SILVERTON HWY Rt#-213
MARION CO OR 205-B4
SILVERTON RD NE
Hayesville OR 204-D5
Hayesville OR 323-H8
SALEM OR 323-B10
SILVERTON RD NE Rt#-213
Hayesville OR 323-E9
MARION CO OR 205-A5
MARION CO OR 323-E9
SILVER VALLEY RD
SHOSHONE CO ID 115-B2
SILVIES-HOPPER RANCH RD
GRANT CO OR 137-B3
SILVIS RD
DESCHUTES CO OR 217-D2
SIMCOE MOUNTAIN RD
KLICKITAT CO WA 127-B1
SIMILKAMEEN RD
OKANOGAN CO WA 104-C1
SIMMONS RD
KLICKITAT CO WA 195-D4
YAKIMA CO WA 119-C1
SIMMONS RD NW
THURSTON CO WA 180-B6
SIMMONS CREEK RD
TILLAMOOK CO OR 197-C3
SIMMONS RIDGE RD
TILLAMOOK CO OR 197-D3
SIMNASHO RD
WASCO CO OR 127-A3
SIMNASHO HOT SPRINGS RD
WASCO CO OR 127-B3
WASCO CO OR 208-B1
SIMONDS RD NE
KENMORE WA 171-C6
SIMPLOT BLVD Rt#-19
CALDWELL ID 147-B1
CANYON CO ID 147-B1
WILDER ID 147-B1
SIMPSON AV Rt#-108
MCCLEARY WA 179-D6
SIMPSON AV U.S.-101
ABERDEEN WA 178-B7
HOQUIAM WA 178-A7
SIMPSON RD
DISTRICT OF MATSQUI BC 102-B1
POLK CO OR 207-A2
UMATILLA CO OR 129-B1
SIMPSON RD NW
THURSTON CO WA 180-B5
SIMPSON CANYON RD
KLAMATH CO OR 235-C1
SIMS WY Rt#-20
PORT TOWNSEND WA 263-C6
SINCLAIR RD
BAKER CO OR 138-C1
CITY OF CHILLIWACK BC 102-C1
DISTRICT OF SAANICH BC 257-D3
SINE RD
GRAYS HARBOR CO WA 179-D6
MCCLEARY WA 179-D6
SINGLE CREEK RD
DOUGLAS CO OR 222-B2
SINGLE TREE TR
HUMBOLDT CO NV 154-C3
SINK RD
LAKE CO OR 143-C2
SINLAHEKIN RD
OKANOGAN CO WA 104-C2
SISCO HEIGHTS RD
SNOHOMISH CO WA 168-D7
SISCO HEIGHTS RD Rt#-531
ARLINGTON WA 168-D6
SNOHOMISH CO WA 168-D6
SISEMORE RD
DESCHUTES CO OR 212-A7
SISK RD
YAKIMA CO WA 243-A3
SISKIYOU BLVD
MEDFORD OR 336-E13
SISKIYOU BLVD Rt#-99
ASHLAND OR 337-D8
JACKSON CO OR 337-H10
SISKIYOU HWY
JACKSON CO OR 150-A2
SISKIYOU SUMMIT RD
JACKSON CO OR 234-D5
S SISTER RD
DOUGLAS CO OR 133-A3
LANE CO OR 133-A3
SISTERS AV
REDMOND OR 212-D5
SITKUM-COUNTY LINE RD
COOS CO OR 140-C2
COOS CO OR 141-A2
SI TOWN RD
COWLITZ CO WA 187-C7
SITZ RIDGE RD
LINCOLN CO OR 209-C3
SIUSLAW RIVER RD
LANE CO OR 133-A3

SIXES RIVER RD
CURRY CO OR 224-B5
SIX PRONG RD
KLICKITAT CO WA 128-A1
SIXTH ST Rt#-6
POTLATCH ID 249-D1
SIXTH ST Rt#-20
OKANOGAN CO WA 104-C2
TONASKET WA 104-C2
SIXTH ST Rt#-507
TENINO WA 184-D3
SIXTH ST U.S.-101
RAYMOND WA 117-A1
E SIXTH ST
CENTRALIA WA 299-F2
LANGLEY WA 171-A1
E SIXTH ST Rt#-507
CENTRALIA WA 299-F2
W SIXTH ST
CENTRALIA WA 299-F2
SKAAR RD
SKAMANIA CO WA 194-D4
S SKAGIT HWY
SKAGIT CO WA 102-C2
SKAGIT CO WA 161-C6
N SKAGIT ST
BURLINGTON WA 260-E4
S SKAGIT ST
BURLINGTON WA 260-E6
SKAGIT CITY RD
SKAGIT CO WA 168-A1
SKAMANIA MINES RD
SKAMANIA CO WA 193-D5
SKATE CREEK RD N
LEWIS CO WA 118-C1
SKATE CREEK RD S
LEWIS CO WA 185-B6
SKEANS RD
COLUMBIA CO OR 189-B5
SKELLEY RD
DOUGLAS CO OR 219-A4
SKELLEY RD S
DOUGLAS CO OR 219-A4
SKELTON RD SE
MARION CO OR 207-D2
N SKIDMORE ST
PORTLAND OR 313-F1
NE SKIDMORE ST
PORTLAND OR 313-G1
SKI HILL RD
CHELAN CO WA 238-A1
LEAVENWORTH WA 238-A1
SKINNER RD
CLACKAMAS CO OR 200-C7
SKINNER ST
CITY OF VICTORIA BC 256-E7
SKIPLES RD
SNOHOMISH CO WA 269-J2
SKIPLEY RD
SNOHOMISH CO WA 171-D3
SKI RUN RD
WALLOWA CO OR 130-C2
SKOKOMISH VALLEY RD
MASON CO WA 179-D1
SKOOKUM CANYON RD
KLICKITAT CO WA 196-C1
SKOOKUMCHUCK RD SE
THURSTON CO WA 184-D4
SKULL CREEK RD
MALHEUR CO OR 146-C3
MALHEUR CO OR 155-A1
SKYE RD
SKAMANIA CO WA 193-D6
W SKYLINE AV
ASTORIA OR 300-B5
NW SKYLINE BLVD
MULTNOMAH CO OR 192-A5
PORTLAND OR 192-B7
SW SKYLINE BLVD
MULTNOMAH CO OR 199-B1
MULTNOMAH CO OR 312-A6
PORTLAND OR 199-B1
PORTLAND OR 312-A6
SKYLINE DR
COLUMBIA CO WA 122-B3
WENATCHEE WA 238-D4
West Wenatchee WA 238-D4
NW SKYLINE DR
TOLEDO OR 206-C4
SKYLINE RD
BAKER CO OR 138-A1
CANYON CO ID 147-B1
WASCO CO OR 196-C7
SKYLINE RD S
MARION CO OR 207-C1
MARION CO OR 324-D8
SALEM OR 324-E6
SKYLINE WY
ANACORTES WA 259-A4
SKYLINERS RD
BEND OR 332-A7
DESCHUTES CO OR 217-A3
SLAB CREEK RD
TILLAMOOK CO OR 203-B2
SLACK CANYON RD SW
DOUGLAS CO WA 112-B2
SLATE CREEK RD
IDAHO CO ID 131-C1
SLATER RD
FERNDALE WA 158-C6
WHATCOM CO WA 158-B6
SLAVENS WY
COLUMBIA CO OR 192-A3
SLEATER KINNEY RD NE
LACEY WA 297-F3
OLYMPIA WA 297-F3
THURSTON CO WA 297-F3
SLEATER KINNEY RD SE
LACEY WA 297-F8
OLYMPIA WA 297-F8
SLEEPER RD
ISLAND CO WA 167-C2
SLEEPY HOLLOW LP
JOSEPHINE CO OR 229-A7
SLEEPY HOLLOW RD
CHELAN CO WA 238-C3
KLICKITAT CO WA 196-A3
SLEEPY HOLLOW RD NE
MARION CO OR 205-B1
N SLICK ROCK CREEK RD
LINCOLN CO OR 203-C4
SLIDE CREEK RD
COWLITZ CO WA 117-B3
SLIVA LN
MASON CO WA 180-D3
E SLOPE RD
LINCOLN CO OR 206-C4
TOLEDO OR 206-C4

E SLOPE RD SE
TOLEDO OR 206-C4
NE SLOPE ST
DOUGLAS CO OR 334-G2
SLUSSER RD NW
DOUGLAS CO WA 112-B2
DOUGLAS CO WA 236-C6
SMILEY LN
VALLEY CO ID 251-C7
SMITH AV
DISTRICT OF BURNABY BC 156-C5
DISTRICT OF BURNABY BC 255-G14
KOOTENAI CO ID 247-C1
SMITH LN
JEFFERSON CO OR 212-D1
SMITH RD
CLACKAMAS CO OR 199-A5
COLUMBIA CO OR 192-A1
HARRAH WA 119-C2
KLICKITAT CO WA 120-B3
POLK CO OR 207-A1
WALLA WALLA CO WA 121-C3
WALLA WALLA CO WA 122-A3
YAMHILL CO OR 199-A5
E SMITH RD
WHATCOM CO WA 102-B1
WHATCOM CO WA 158-D6
W SMITH RD
FERNDALE WA 158-D6
WHATCOM CO WA 158-D6
SMITH ST
HARRISBURG OR 210-A5
SEATTLE WA 277-H1
E SMITH ST Rt#-516
KENT WA 175-C7
W SMITH ST
KENT WA 175-B7
SMITH ANDERSON RD
PACIFIC CO WA 183-B5
SMITH CANYON RD
FRANKLIN CO WA 121-B2
SMITH COLUMBIA CITY RD
COLUMBIA CO OR 192-A1
SMITH CREEK RD
PACIFIC CO WA 117-A1
SMITHE ST
VANCOUVER BC 254-G10
SMITHFIELD RD
POLK CO OR 204-A5
SMITH HOLLOW RD
COLUMBIA CO WA 122-A2
SMITH LAKE RD
DOUGLAS CO WA 237-B2
NE SMITH POINT RD
MULTNOMAH CO OR 194-B7
MULTNOMAH CO OR 201-B1
SMITH RIVER RD
DOUGLAS CO OR 132-C3
DOUGLAS CO OR 133-A3
DOUGLAS CO OR 141-A1
DOUGLAS CO OR 214-D7
SMITH ROCK WY
DESCHUTES CO OR 212-D4
DESCHUTES CO OR 213-A4
SMITHSON RD
KITTITAS CO WA 241-A3
SMITH SPRINGS RD
PRESCOTT WA 121-C2
WALLA WALLA CO WA 121-C2
SMOCK RD
WASCO CO OR 127-A3
SMOKEHOUSE RD
WHATCOM CO WA 160-C1
SMOKEY BUTTE RD
DESCHUTES CO OR 212-B7
SMOKEY POINT BLVD
ARLINGTON WA 168-C5
MARYSVILLE WA 168-C5
SNOHOMISH CO WA 168-C5
SMOKEY VALLEY RD
LEWIS CO WA 187-C5
SMOOTHING IRON RD
ASOTIN CO WA 122-C3
SMUGGLERS COVE RD
ISLAND CO WA 167-C7
ISLAND CO WA 170-C1
S SMUGGLERS COVE RD
ISLAND CO WA 167-C7
S SMYTHE RD
SPOKANE CO WA 246-B7
SNAG CREEK TR
SKAMANIA CO WA 194-C4
SNAKE CREEK RD
JACKSON CO OR 230-A3
SNAKE RIVER AV
LEWISTON ID 250-B5
SNAKE RIVER RD
ASOTIN WA 250-B6
ASOTIN CO WA 123-A3
ASOTIN CO WA 250-B6
BAKER CO OR 138-C2
BAKER CO OR 139-A1
FRANKLIN CO WA 121-B2
HUNTINGTON OR 138-C2
N SNAKE RIVER RD
BAKER CO OR 139-A1
RICHLAND OR 139-A1
SNEE-OOSH RD
Shelter Bay WA 167-D1
SKAGIT CO WA 160-D7
SKAGIT CO WA 167-D1
Snee Oosh WA 167-D1
Swinomish Village WA 167-D1
SNEIDER-BARKS RD
SKAMANIA CO WA 194-A7
SNELLSTRON BUSH
PIERCE CO WA 182-A6
SNIPES RD
BENTON CO WA 120-B2
SNIVELY GULCH RD
MALHEUR CO OR 147-A1
SNODGRASS RD
KITTITAS CO WA 241-C5
SNOHOMISH AV
SNOHOMISH CO WA 171-D5
SNOHOMISH WOODINVILLE RD
SNOHOMISH CO WA 171-D6
SNOHOMISH WOODINVILLE RD Rt#-9
SNOHOMISH CO WA 171-D6
SNOQUALMIE PKWY
SNOQUALMIE WA 176-C4
W SNOQUALMIE VALLEY RD
KING CO WA 110-C1
W SNOQUALMIE VALLEY RD NE
KING CO WA 110-C1
KING CO WA 176-A1

INDEX

396 STEPTOE AV Rt#-27 — STREET INDEX — TAHUYA LAKE RD NW

STREET / City State Page-Grid

STEPTOE AV Rt#-27
- OAKESDALE WA 114-C3

STEPTOE ST
- COLTON WA 250-A1

STEPTOE CANYON RD
- WHITMAN CO WA 122-C2
- WHITMAN CO WA 250-A2

STERLING RD
- SEDRO-WOOLLEY WA 260-J3
- SKAGIT CO WA 260-J3

STERLING CREEK RD
- JACKSON CO OR 149-B2
- JACKSON CO OR 234-A4

STEUBEN ST Rt#-14
- BINGEN WA 195-D5

STEVENS DR
- BENTON CO WA 340-F5
- DISTRICT OF WEST VANCOUVE BC 156-B2
- DISTRICT OF WEST VANCOUVE BC 254-E2
- RICHLAND WA 340-F6
- RICHLAND WA 341-F1

STEVENS RD
- BEND OR 217-C3
- DESCHUTES CO OR 217-C3

STEVENS RD SE
- KITSAP CO WA 174-B6

STEVENS ST
- CHEWELAH WA 106-B3
- MEDFORD OR 336-D11
- STEVENS CO WA 106-B3

STEVENS ST Rt#-285
- WENATCHEE WA 239-A4

N STEVENS ST
- TACOMA WA 292-B1

S STEVENS ST
- SPOKANE WA 348-J9
- TACOMA WA 292-B5

STEVENS CANYON RD
- DESCHUTES CO OR 211-D4
- DESCHUTES CO OR 212-A3
- LEWIS CO WA 185-C5

S STEVENS CREEK RD
- SPOKANE CO WA 246-D6

STEVENSON AV
- ENUMCLAW WA 110-C3

STEVENSON RD
- ANACORTES WA 160-D6
- POLK CO OR 204-B4
- SKAGIT CO WA 160-D6

N STEVENSON RD
- Otis Orchards WA 352-D10

STEVENSON RIDGE TR
- CARSON WA 194-D4
- SKAMANIA CO WA 194-C3

STEVENS PASS HWY U.S.-2
- GOLD BAR WA 110-C1
- KING CO WA 111-B1
- MONROE WA 110-C1
- SNOHOMISH WA 171-D3
- SNOHOMISH CO WA 110-C1
- SNOHOMISH CO WA 111-A1
- SNOHOMISH CO WA 171-D3
- SULTAN WA 110-C1

NE STEVENS PASS HWY U.S.-2
- KING CO WA 111-A1
- SKYKOMISH WA 111-A1
- SNOHOMISH CO WA 111-A1

STEVENS PASS RD U.S.-2
- SNOHOMISH CO WA 171-D2

STEVESTON HWY
- CITY OF RICHMOND BC 156-B7

STEWARDSON WY
- NEW WESTMINSTER BC 156-D5

W STEWART
- PUYALLUP WA 182-B3

STEWART AV
- PIERCE CO WA 182-A3
- PUYALLUP WA 182-A3

E STEWART AV
- MEDFORD OR 336-E14

W STEWART AV
- JACKSON CO OR 234-A1
- JACKSON CO OR 336-B14
- MEDFORD OR 336-B14

STEWART LN
- DOUGLAS CO WA 239-B2

STEWART PKWY
- ROSEBURG OR 334-E4

NE STEWART PKWY
- ROSEBURG OR 334-F5

NW STEWART PKWY
- ROSEBURG OR 334-D3

STEWART RD
- COOS CO OR 224-B1
- JOSEPHINE CO OR 229-A5
- MOUNT VERNON WA 260-C9
- PIERCE CO WA 182-B2
- SUMNER WA 182-B2

S STEWART RD
- ADA CO ID 253-B5

STEWART RD SE
- PACIFIC WA 182-B2

STEWART RD SW
- PACIFIC WA 182-B2

STEWART ST
- SEATTLE WA 277-J5
- SEATTLE WA 278-A4

STEWART CREEK RD
- COLUMBIA CO OR 189-A3
- UMATILLA CO OR 129-B2

STIDMAN
- PIERCE CO WA 182-B7

S STILLAGUAMISH AV
- ARLINGTON WA 168-D5

STILL CREEK RD
- CLACKAMAS CO OR 201-D6
- CLACKAMAS CO OR 202-A6

STILLMAN RD
- CROOK CO OR 213-B6

STILLWATER TKTR
- COWLITZ CO WA 187-B6

STIMSON RD
- SNOHOMISH CO WA 168-C6

STINEHILL RD
- CHELAN CO WA 238-B2

STINSON AV
- GIG HARBOR WA 181-C1
- WALLA WALLA CO WA 345-J3

STIRLING DR
- DESCHUTES CO OR 217-D4

STITZEL RD
- MALHEUR CO OR 146-C3

STOCK DRIVE RD
- LAKE CO OR 152-A2

SE STOCKHOFF RD
- YAMHILL CO OR 204-C1

STOCKSHOW RD
- EVERETT WA 171-C4

STOCKYARD RD
- KLICKITAT CO WA 127-C1

STOLTE CANYON RD
- NEZ PERCE CO ID 123-B2

STOLTZ HILL RD
- Crowfoot OR 133-C1
- LEBANON OR 133-C1
- LINN CO OR 133-C1

STONE DR NW
- PIERCE CO WA 181-C2

STONE RD
- COLUMBIA CO OR 192-A2
- TILLAMOOK CO OR 197-D3
- YAMHILL CO OR 198-C5

STONE WY N
- SEATTLE WA 273-J7

STONE BREAKER LN
- VALLEY CO ID 252-D4

STONE CABIN RD
- WHEELER CO OR 128-A3

STONECIPHER RD
- WALLA WALLA CO WA 122-A3

STONECREST RD
- GRANT CO WA 242-B1

STONER
- PIERCE CO WA 182-B7

STOREY BLVD
- EUGENE OR 329-H10

N STORIE ST
- WALLOWA OR 130-C1

STORMER RD
- CLACKAMAS CO OR 200-B5

STOTTLEMEYER RD NE
- KITSAP CO WA 170-C6

STOTTS RD SW
- DOUGLAS CO WA 112-B2

E STOUGHTON RD
- SPOKANE CO WA 246-C6
- SPOKANE CO WA 247-B6

STOUT RD
- LATAH CO ID 250-D1
- WHITMAN CO WA 250-B3

E STOVER RD
- YAKIMA CO WA 120-B3

STRAHL RD
- DOUGLAS CO WA 105-A3
- DOUGLAS CO WA 237-A1

STRAHL CANYON RD
- DOUGLAS CO WA 105-A3

N STRAHORN RD
- HAYDEN ID 245-A5
- HAYDEN ID 355-F1
- HAYDEN LAKE ID 245-A5
- KOOTENAI CO ID 245-A5
- KOOTENAI CO ID 355-F1

STRAND RD
- WHATCOM CO WA 161-C1

STRANDE RD
- KITTITAS CO WA 241-A6

STRANDER BLVD
- TUKWILA WA 289-G6

STRATFORD DR NE
- MARION CO OR 205-A3

STRATFORD RD
- GRANT CO WA 113-A2
- GRANT CO WA 242-C1
- MOSES LAKE WA 242-C1

STRATTON RD
- CLALLAM CO WA 165-A5

STRAWBERRY RD
- GRANT CO WA 137-B2

STRAWBERRY POINT RD
- ISLAND CO WA 167-D2

STRAWN LN SE
- THURSTON CO WA 184-D3

STRICKLAND CANYON RD
- DOUGLAS CO OR 221-A6

STRIEBEL RD
- JEFFERSON CO OR 211-C1

STRIKER LN
- IMBLER OR 130-A2

STRINGER GAP RD
- JOSEPHINE CO OR 229-B7

STRINGHAM RD
- KOOTENAI CO ID 247-C7
- LEWIS CO WA 187-D2

E STRINGHAM RD
- ROCKFORD WA 114-C2
- SPOKANE CO WA 247-B7

STRINGTOWN RD
- PACIFIC CO WA 186-A6
- WASHINGTON CO OR 198-B1
- YAMHILL CO OR 198-C7

STRODA DR
- LINN CO OR 210-A5

S STROEBEL RD
- ADA CO ID 253-A5

STROME LN
- LANE CO OR 210-A6

STRONG RD SE
- SALEM OR 325-A4

STRUCK RD
- KLICKITAT CO WA 196-C5

STRYKER AV
- PIERCE CO WA 181-B5

STRYKER RD
- INDEPENDENCE OR 204-B7

STUB AV
- KOOTENAI CO ID 247-C1

STUBB RD
- SNOHOMISH CO WA 168-B4

NE STUDIO RD
- BEND OR 332-F5

N STUMP RD
- KOOTENAI CO ID 245-B4

STURDAVENT RD
- LINCOLN CO OR 206-C4
- TOLEDO OR 206-C4

STURGEON RD
- DESCHUTES CO OR 212-C7

STURGEON ST
- KITSAP CO WA 170-A7

STURM AV
- WALLA WALLA WA 345-D9
- Walla Walla East WA 345-D9

S STUWE RD
- CLACKAMAS CO OR 205-D1

SUBLIMITY RD
- MARION CO OR 133-C1
- SUBLIMITY OR 133-C1

SUBSTATION DR
- LINN CO OR 210-A4

SUCCOR CREEK HWY Rt#-201
- ADRIAN OR 147-A1
- MALHEUR CO OR 139-A3
- MALHEUR CO OR 147-A1
- NYSSA OR 139-A3

SUCCOR CREEK RD
- MALHEUR CO OR 147-A1

SUCIA DR
- WHATCOM CO WA 158-B6

SUCKER CREEK RD
- JOSEPHINE CO OR 233-D5

SUDBURY RD
- WALLA WALLA WA 344-A7
- WALLA WALLA CO WA 121-C3
- WALLA WALLA CO WA 344-A7

SUGAR PINE RD
- JACKSON CO OR 226-A6

SUGARPINE BUTTE RD
- DESCHUTES CO OR 217-B7

SUICIDE GULCH RD
- DESCHUTES CO OR 211-B4

SULLIVAN LN
- YAMHILL CO OR 198-C5

SULLIVAN RD
- SKAGIT CO WA 161-A5

N SULLIVAN RD
- SPOKANE VALLEY WA 351-C5

S SULLIVAN RD
- SPOKANE CO WA 351-C11
- SPOKANE VALLEY WA 351-C9

SULLIVAN CREEK RD
- PEND OREILLE CO WA 106-C1

SULLIVAN LAKE RD
- PEND OREILLE CO WA 106-B1

SULPHUR SPRINGS RD
- BENTON CO OR 207-A4

SULTAN BASIN RD
- SNOHOMISH CO WA 110-C1
- SULTAN WA 110-C1

E SUMACH ST
- WALLA WALLA WA 345-B6

SUMAS RD Rt#-547
- WHATCOM CO WA 102-B1

SUMAS WY
- DISTRICT OF ABBOTSFORD BC 102-B1
- DISTRICT OF MATSQUI BC 102-B1

E SUMMA ST
- CENTRALIA WA 299-F5
- LEWIS CO WA 299-F5

W SUMMA ST
- CENTRALIA WA 299-E5

SUMMER ST
- BELLINGHAM WA 258-D4

SUMMER ST NE
- SALEM OR 322-J12
- SALEM OR 323-A11

SUMMER CREEK RD
- LANE CO OR 215-D4

SUMMERHURST WK SW
- KING CO WA 174-D7

SUMMERLAND RD
- WHATCOM CO WA 161-A2

SUMMERS LN
- Altamont OR 235-C5
- Altamont OR 338-J14
- KLAMATH FALLS OR 235-C5
- KLAMATH FALLS OR 338-J14

SUMMERVILLE RD
- IMBLER OR 130-A2
- SUMMERVILLE OR 130-A2
- UNION CO OR 130-A2

SUMMIT AV
- WASHINGTON CO OR 198-A2

SUMMIT DR
- HOOD RIVER CO OR 195-C6

SUMMIT HWY
- BENTON CO OR 133-A1

SUMMIT LP
- MARION CO OR 207-D2

SUMMIT RD
- JACKSON CO OR 149-B2
- JACKSON CO OR 234-A6
- JEFFERSON CO OR 211-D2
- WHEELER CO OR 136-A2

SUMMIT RD Rt#-108
- GRAYS HARBOR CO WA 179-D6
- MCCLEARY WA 179-D6

SUMMIT LAKE RD NW
- THURSTON CO WA 180-A6

SUMMIT LAKE SHORE RD NW
- THURSTON CO WA 180-A6

SE SUMMIT LANDSBURG RD
- KING CO WA 176-A7

E SUMMIT MEADOW RD
- CLACKAMAS CO OR 202-A6

SUMMIT ROCK RD
- DOUGLAS CO OR 223-C6

SUMMIT VALLEY RD
- STEVENS CO WA 106-A3

SUMMITVIEW AV
- YAKIMA WA 243-A6
- YAKIMA CO WA 243-A6

W SUMMITVIEW AV
- YAKIMA CO WA 243-A6

SUMMITVIEW RD
- YAKIMA CO WA 119-C1
- YAKIMA CO WA 243-A6

N SUMMITVIEW RD
- YAKIMA CO WA 243-A6

SUMNER ST Rt#-507
- BUCODA WA 184-D4
- TENINO WA 184-D4
- THURSTON CO WA 184-D4

SUMNER ST U.S.-101
- ABERDEEN WA 178-A7
- HOQUIAM WA 178-A7

SUMNER-BUCKLEY HWY Rt#-410
- PIERCE CO WA 182-B3
- SUMNER WA 182-B3

SUMNER BUCKLEY HWY E
- BONNEY LAKE WA 182-C4
- BUCKLEY WA 182-C4
- PIERCE CO WA 182-C4

SUMNER-FAIRVIEW RD
- COOS CO OR 140-B2

SUMNER TAPPS HWY
- PIERCE CO WA 182-C3

SUMPTER HWY
- BAKER CO OR 138-A1
- SUMPTER OR 138-A1

SE SUN DR
- JEFFERSON CO OR 208-C5
- MADRAS OR 208-C5

SUNCREST TER
- WALLA WALLA CO WA 344-D11

NW SUNDE RD
- KITSAP CO WA 174-B1

SUNDERMAN RD
- LANE CO OR 210-D7

SUNDOWN RD
- CURRY CO OR 232-C4
- DESCHUTES CO OR 211-D3

SUNFLOWER RD
- MORROW CO OR 128-C3

SUNFLOWER FLAT RD
- MORROW CO OR 128-C3

SUN MOUNTAIN RD
- KLAMATH CO OR 142-B3

SUNNY COVE DR SE
- KITSAP CO WA 174-C6

SUNNYCREST RD
- NEWBERG OR 198-C5
- YAMHILL CO OR 198-C5

SUNNY DELL RD
- BAKER CO OR 131-A3

SUNNYGLEN WY
- JOSEPHINE CO OR 229-B2

SUNNYHILL RD S
- BREMERTON WA 270-C11
- KITSAP CO WA 270-C11

SUNNY RIDGE RD
- YAMHILL CO OR 204-A2

SUNNYRIDGE RD
- LINCOLN CO OR 206-C5

SUNNYSIDE AV
- GRANGER WA 120-A2

SUNNYSIDE BLVD
- MARYSVILLE WA 171-D1
- SNOHOMISH CO WA 171-D1

SUNNYSIDE BLVD NE
- MARYSVILLE WA 171-D1

SUNNYSIDE RD
- ANMORE BC 157-A3
- BONNER CO ID 244-B1
- LINN CO OR 134-A2
- POLK CO OR 204-A4

SE SUNNYSIDE RD
- CLACKAMAS CO OR 199-D3
- CLACKAMAS CO OR 200-A3
- DAMASCUS OR 200-A3
- HAPPY VALLEY OR 200-A3

SUNNYSIDE RD SE
- MARION CO OR 207-D1
- MARION CO OR 324-H9
- SALEM OR 324-H9

SUNNYSIDE-UMAPINE HWY
- UMATILLA CO OR 121-C3

SUNNY SLOPE LN
- BAKER CO OR 130-B3

SUNNYSLOPE LN
- BAKER CO OR 138-B1

SUNNY SLOPE RD Rt#-55
- CANYON CO ID 147-B1

SUNNYSLOPE RD SW
- KITSAP CO WA 174-A4

SUNNY VALLEY LP
- JOSEPHINE CO OR 229-B2

SUNNYVIEW RD
- MARION CO OR 205-B5
- MARION CO OR 323-G11
- SALEM OR 204-D5
- SALEM OR 323-B10

SUN RAY
- CURRY CO OR 232-C4

SUNRISE AV
- MEDFORD OR 336-F11

SUNRISE BLVD
- PIERCE CO WA 182-B5

N SUNRISE BLVD
- ISLAND CO WA 167-D4

SUNRISE BLVD E
- PIERCE CO WA 182-B5

SUNRISE DR
- KOOTENAI CO ID 248-B5

SUNRISE DR NE
- BAINBRIDGE ISLAND WA 170-D7
- BAINBRIDGE ISLAND WA 174-D1

SUNRISE LN
- DOUGLAS CO OR 221-A5

SUNRISE PKWY E
- PIERCE CO WA 182-B5

SUNRISE RD
- WALLOWA CO OR 130-C2
- WHATCOM CO WA 158-C3
- WHATCOM CO WA 160-B2

SUNRISE ST
- KELSO WA 303-F7

SUNRISE BEACH RD NW
- THURSTON CO WA 180-B5

SUNRISE PARK RD
- PIERCE CO WA 119-A1
- PIERCE CO WA 185-D2

SUNSET AV
- ANACORTES WA 259-A4

SUNSET AV N
- KEIZER OR 322-J7

SUNSET BLVD
- CANNON BEACH OR 188-B7
- CLATSOP CO OR 301-C11
- DISTRICT OF NORTH VANCOUV BC 254-J1
- SEASIDE OR 301-C11

E SUNSET BLVD
- CANNON BEACH OR 188-B7

NE SUNSET BLVD Rt#-900
- RENTON WA 175-C4

S SUNSET BLVD
- SPOKANE WA 348-G10

SW SUNSET BLVD
- PORTLAND OR 316-C3
- SHERWOOD OR 199-A5

SW SUNSET BLVD Rt#-900
- RENTON WA 175-C5

W SUNSET BLVD
- SPOKANE WA 348-F10
- SPOKANE CO WA 348-E11

SUNSET BLVD N Rt#-900
- RENTON WA 175-C5

SUNSET BLVD NE
- RENTON WA 175-C4

SUNSET DR
- BELLINGHAM WA 258-D4
- FOREST GROVE OR 198-B1
- ISLAND CO WA 167-D4
- KOOTENAI CO ID 248-B5
- LA GRANDE OR 130-A2
- WALLA WALLA CO OR 121-B3
- WASHINGTON CO OR 198-B1

E SUNSET DR
- BELLINGHAM WA 258-E4

E SUNSET DR Rt#-542
- BELLINGHAM WA 258-G3
- WHATCOM CO WA 102-B1
- WHATCOM CO WA 258-G3

SUNSET DR W
- UNIVERSITY PLACE WA 181-C3

SUNSET FRWY U.S.-2
- DOUGLAS CO WA 238-D3
- East Wenatchee Bench WA 238-D3
- Sunnyslope WA 238-D3

SUNSET HWY
- CHELAN CO WA 238-C2

SUNSET HWY Rt#-970
- KITTITAS CO WA 240-B2

SUNSET HWY U.S.-26
- BEAVERTON OR 199-A1
- CLATSOP CO OR 117-A3
- CLATSOP CO OR 125-A1
- CLATSOP CO OR 188-C7
- COLUMBIA CO OR 125-B1
- HILLSBORO OR 125-B1
- HILLSBORO OR 192-A7
- HILLSBORO OR 199-A1
- MULTNOMAH CO OR 312-B7
- NORTH PLAINS OR 125-B1
- PORTLAND OR 199-A1
- PORTLAND OR 312-B7
- PORTLAND OR 316-B1
- TILLAMOOK CO OR 125-B1
- WASHINGTON CO OR 125-B1
- WASHINGTON CO OR 199-A1

W SUNSET HWY
- SPOKANE WA 348-B11
- SPOKANE CO WA 348-B11

W SUNSET HWY U.S.-2
- AIRWAY HEIGHTS WA 246-A4
- SPOKANE CO WA 246-A4
- SPOKANE CO WA 348-A12

SUNSET LN
- CROOK CO OR 213-C4

SUNSET RD
- BONNER CO ID 244-A7
- SKAGIT CO WA 161-A5
- WHITMAN CO WA 114-B3

SUNSET WY
- CHELAN CO WA 238-C3
- DOUGLAS CO WA 239-B1

E SUNSET WY
- ISSAQUAH WA 176-A4

W SUNSET WY
- ISSAQUAH WA 176-A4

SUNSET BEACH RD
- CLATSOP CO OR 188-B3

SUNSET HEMLOCK RD
- SKAMANIA CO WA 193-D3
- SKAMANIA CO WA 194-A3

SUNSET HWY RD
- DAVENPORT WA 114-A2
- LINCOLN CO WA 114-A2

SUNSET HWY RD E
- LINCOLN CO WA 114-A2

SE SUNSET VIEW RD
- CLARK CO WA 193-C7
- WASHOUGAL WA 193-C7

SUNSHINE RD
- DOUGLAS CO OR 221-D3
- WHITMAN CO WA 249-B5

SUNSHINE CREEK RD
- JACKSON CO OR 226-C4

SE SUNSHINE VALLEY RD
- CLACKAMAS CO OR 200-B3

SUN UP BAY RD
- KOOTENAI CO ID 247-C7

SUPERIOR AV
- CONCRETE WA 102-C2

SUPERIOR ST
- CITY OF VICTORIA BC 256-F10

SUPERIOR ST U.S.-95
- CAMBRIDGE ID 139-B1
- SANDPOINT ID 244-A2

S SUPERIOR ST U.S.-95
- CAMBRIDGE ID 139-B1

SUQUAMISH WY NE
- Suquamish WA 170-C7

SURBER DR NE
- SEATTLE WA 275-E6

SURF ST
- WESTPORT WA 298-G14

SURFACE RD
- Clinton WA 171-A2
- ISLAND CO WA 171-A2

SURF PINES RD
- CLATSOP CO OR 188-B4

SURPRISE VALLEY RD
- LAKE CO OR 152-A3
- MODOC CO CA 152-A3

SUSAN RD
- KITTITAS CO WA 241-A6

NW SUSBAUER RD
- WASHINGTON CO OR 198-C1

SUSSEX ST Rt#-507
- TENINO WA 184-D3
- THURSTON CO WA 184-D3

SUTHERLIN-NONPAREIL RD
- DOUGLAS CO OR 141-B2
- DOUGLAS CO OR 221-D1

SUTHERLIN-UMPQUA RD
- DOUGLAS CO OR 221-B1

SUTTER RD
- CLALLAM CO WA 165-D6

SUTTLE RD
- CLACKAMAS CO OR 200-B4

SUTTLE LAKE LP
- JEFFERSON CO OR 211-B2

SUTTLE-SHERMAN RD
- JEFFERSON CO OR 211-B2

SUTTON RD
- ADAMS CO WA 121-C1

SUTTON BEACH RD
- LANE CO OR 214-B1

SUTTON CREEK RD
- TILLAMOOK CO OR 197-B3

SUTTON LAKE RD
- LANE CO OR 214-B1

SUVER RD
- POLK CO OR 207-B2

SWAKANE CANYON RD
- CHELAN CO WA 238-C1

SWALLEY RD
- DESCHUTES CO OR 212-C7

SWALLOW DR
- JEFFERSON CO OR 212-C2

SWALWELL RD
- SNOHOMISH CO WA 171-D2

SWAMP CREEK RD
- MALHEUR CO OR 146-A1

SWAMP CREEK TO COUNTY LINE RD
- GRANT CO OR 136-C3

SWAMP WELLS RD
- DESCHUTES CO OR 217-C6

E SWAN AV
- SILETZ OR 206-C2

SWAN RD
- SKAGIT CO WA 260-J8

S SWAN FALLS RD
- ADA CO ID 253-A6

SWAN HILL RD
- DOUGLAS CO OR 221-A6

SWANK DR
- LINN CO OR 207-D6

SWAN LAKE RD
- FERRY CO WA 105-B2
- KLAMATH CO OR 235-C1

SWAN SLOUGH RD
- SNOHOMISH CO WA 269-H2

SWANSON RD
- WHITMAN CO WA 249-A1

SWANSON GULCH RD
- CHELAN CO WA 236-C1

SWANSON LAKE RD N
- CRESTON WA 113-C1
- LINCOLN CO WA 113-C1

SWANSONVILLE RD
- JEFFERSON CO WA 170-B2

SWANS TRAIL RD
- SNOHOMISH CO WA 171-D3
- SNOHOMISH CO WA 269-J2

SWANTOWN RD
- ISLAND CO WA 167-B2
- OAK HARBOR WA 167-B2

SWARTZ BAY-TSAWWASSEN FERRY
- BRITISH COLUMBIA BC 101-B1
- BRITISH COLUMBIA BC 159-C1
- DISTRICT OF NORTH SAANICH BC 159-C1

SWARTZ CANYON RD
- CROOK CO OR 213-C7

SWAUK PRAIRIE RD
- KITTITAS CO WA 240-D1

SWAWILLA BASIN RD
- FERRY CO WA 113-B1

SWEDE BASIN RD
- JOSEPHINE CO OR 148-C1
- JOSEPHINE CO OR 233-B1

SWEDE HILL RD
- ISLAND CO WA 171-A3

SWEDE RIDGE RD
- DESCHUTES CO OR 216-D3
- DESCHUTES CO OR 217-A3

SWEDETOWN RD
- COLUMBIA CO OR 117-B3
- COLUMBIA CO OR 189-A5

SWEENEY RD SE
- KING CO WA 175-D6

SWEENEY GULCH RD
- GARFIELD CO WA 122-B2

SWEET RD
- WHATCOM CO WA 158-B3

SWEET CREEK RD
- LANE CO OR 214-D4

SWEGLE RD NE
- MARION CO OR 323-F12
- SALEM OR 323-F12

SWENSON RD
- STEVENS CO WA 114-B1
- STEVENS CO WA 246-A1

SWENSON-WILLIAMS VALLEY RD
- STEVENS CO WA 114-B1

SWIFT AV S
- SEATTLE WA 282-C7
- SEATTLE WA 286-C1

SWIFT BLVD
- RICHLAND WA 341-D1

SWINDLER RD
- LEWIS CO WA 187-C4

SYDNAM RD
- COOS CO OR 224-B1

SYKES RD
- SAINT HELENS OR 192-A2

NE SYLVAN WY
- BREMERTON WA 270-H7
- BREMERTON WA 271-B6
- KITSAP CO WA 271-B6

SYLVAN WY SW
- SEATTLE WA 281-F7
- SEATTLE WA 285-F1

SYLVESTER RD
- BRITISH COLUMBIA BC 94-B3

W SYLVESTER ST
- FRANKLIN CO WA 342-H7
- PASCO WA 342-H7
- PASCO WA 343-A7

SYLVIA LAKE RD
- MONTESANO WA 178-D7

SYMONS ST
- RICHLAND WA 340-F14

T

T AV
- ANACORTES WA 259-H4

T RD NW
- DOUGLAS CO WA 236-B5

T 1-2-SW ST
- GRANT CO WA 120-B1

TABLE ROCK RD
- JACKSON CO OR 230-C6
- JACKSON CO OR 336-C3
- MEDFORD OR 336-B8

TABLE ROCK TRAIL RD
- JACKSON CO OR 230-C5

N TACOMA AV
- PASCO WA 343-G7
- TACOMA WA 293-F3

S TACOMA AV
- TACOMA WA 293-G5

TACOMA AV S
- TACOMA WA 293-G7
- TACOMA WA 295-H3

SE TACOMA ST
- PORTLAND OR 317-H6
- PORTLAND OR 318-A7

S TACOMA WY
- LAKEWOOD WA 181-D4
- TACOMA WA 181-D4
- TACOMA WA 293-H7
- TACOMA WA 294-D2
- TACOMA WA 295-F1

TACOMA MALL BLVD
- TACOMA WA 294-E3
- TACOMA WA 295-E3

TACOMA-ORTING-PRAIRIE
- PIERCE CO WA 182-A6

TAFT ST Rt#-8
- ELK RIVER ID 123-C1

W TAFT ST
- BOISE ID 253-C2

TAHUYA BLACKSMITH RD
- MASON CO WA 173-B5

TAHUYA LAKE RD NW
- KITSAP CO WA 173-D2

INDEX

TAHUYA RIVER DR — STREET INDEX — TRANSFORMER RD 397

STREET
City State Page-Grid

TAHUYA RIVER DR
MASON CO WA 173-C6
TAHUYA RIVER RD
MASON CO WA 173-B6
TAKHOMA FARM LN
KITTITAS CO WA 241-D5
TALACHE RD
BONNER CO ID 244-A4
TALAPUS RIDGE RD
MULTNOMAH CO OR 194-C7
MULTNOMAH CO OR 201-C1
TALA SHORE DR
JEFFERSON CO WA 170-B3
TALBOT RD
MARION CO OR 207-D2
TALBOT RD S
KING CO WA 175-C6
MARION CO OR 207-D2
RENTON WA 175-C6
TALBOT RD S Rt#-515
RENTON WA 175-C5
TALBOT RD SE
MARION CO OR 207-C2
TALBOTT LN
LANE CO OR 210-A5
TALLEY AV
KELSO WA 303-E11
TALLEY WY
KELSO WA 303-F13
TALLMAN RD
LINN CO OR 207-D6
PIERCE CO WA 182-B7
TALL PINES RD
KOOTENAI CO ID 247-D4
TALMAGE RD
POLK CO OR 204-B7
TALMAKS RD
LEWIS CO ID 123-B3
TAMARACK LN
MAPLE RIDGE BC 157-D6
TAMARACK FALLS RD
VALLEY CO ID 252-C2
TAMPICO RD
BENTON CO OR 207-A3
TANDY LN
LINN CO OR 210-A4
TANEUM RD
KITTITAS CO WA 240-D4
TANGELWOOD LN
DOUGLAS CO OR 221-A4
TANGEN RD
YAMHILL CO OR 198-C5
TANGENT DR
LINN CO OR 207-B6
TANGENT OR 207-C6
TANGENT LP
LINN CO OR 207-C7
TANGENT ST Rt#-34
LEBANON OR 133-C1
TANKE RD
LINCOLN CO WA 113-C2
TANNER RD
DISTRICT OF CENTRAL SAANI BC 159-C4
TANNER CREEK RD
MULTNOMAH CO OR 194-C7
WASHINGTON CO OR 198-A1
S TAPPS DR E
PIERCE CO WA 182-C3
W TAPPS DR E
PIERCE CO WA 182-C3
W TAPPS HWY
BONNEY LAKE WA 182-C3
TARBOO LAKE RD
JEFFERSON CO WA 109-C1
W TARGEE ST
ADA CO ID 253-B3
TARLATT RD
PACIFIC CO WA 186-A5
TARTAR GULCH RD
JOSEPHINE CO OR 233-C5
TATLOW RD
DISTRICT OF NORTH SAANICH BC 159-C1
TATTERSALL DR
DISTRICT OF SAANICH BC 256-G4
TAUFFEN RD
WHITMAN CO WA 250-A2
TAUMARSON RD
COLLEGE PLACE WA 344-J12
WALLA WALLA WA 344-J12
WALLA WALLA CO WA 344-J12
WALLA WALLA CO WA 345-A12
TAURUS BLVD
OCEAN SHORES WA 298-B1
TAUSCHER RD
LEWIS CO WA 187-D1
TAUSICK WY
WALLA WALLA WA 345-G6
WALLA WALLA CO WA 345-G6
TAYLOR AV
ASTORIA OR 300-A5
BELLINGHAM WA 258-C10
TAYLOR AV N
SEATTLE WA 277-J2
TAYLOR RD
COLLEGE PLACE WA 344-E12
JACKSON CO OR 230-C7
LEWIS CO WA 187-D1
WALLA WALLA CO WA 344-E12
YAKIMA CO WA 243-B5
E TAYLOR RD
SPOKANE CO WA 246-B6
N TAYLOR RD
ISLAND CO WA 167-C2
TAYLOR ST E
MILTON WA 182-B2
TAYLOR WY
DISTRICT OF WEST VANCOUVE BC 254-F2
TACOMA WA 182-A2
TAYLOR WY Rt#-99
DISTRICT OF WEST VANCOUVE BC 254-E4
TAYLOR FLATS RD
FRANKLIN CO WA 121-A2
TAYLOR RICE
PIERCE CO WA 181-D7
SW TAYLORS FERRY RD
PORTLAND OR 316-B7
PORTLAND OR 317-F6
PORTLAND OR 320-A1
TAYLOR VALLEY RD
CLARK CO WA 192-D1
T CARRY RD
CLARK CO WA 193-A1
TEAGUE RD
LEWIS CO WA 184-A5
TEAL RD
DESCHUTES CO OR 217-D3
TEAL LAKE RD
JEFFERSON CO WA 170-B4
TEANAWAY RD
KITTITAS CO WA 240-C1
TEANAWAY WILSON STOCK TR
KITTITAS CO WA 241-B1
NW TEATER AV
DESCHUTES CO OR 212-C4
TEATERS RD
CROOK CO OR 136-A3
TECHNOLOGY LP
CORVALLIS OR 327-B12
TECHNOR ROBISON RD
SISKIYOU CO CA 150-C3
TEITZEL RD
LEWIS CO WA 184-C5
TEKOA-FARMINGTON RD
TEKOA WA 114-C3
WHITMAN CO WA 114-C3
WHITMAN CO WA 115-A3
TEKOA OAKSDALE RD Rt#-27
OAKESDALE WA 114-C3
WHITMAN CO WA 114-C3
TELEGRAPH RD
BRITISH COLUMBIA BC 159-A1
LEWIS CO WA 187-C4
TELEGRAPH TR
TOWNSHIP OF LANGLEY BC 157-C7
TELEPHONE RD
DESCHUTES CO OR 216-D5
TELEPHONE POLE RD
UMATILLA CO OR 121-C3
SE TELFORD RD
CLACKAMAS CO OR 200-B3
MULTNOMAH CO OR 200-B2
TELFORD RD N
LINCOLN CO WA 113-C2
TELOCASET LN
UNION CO OR 130-B3
E TEMPLE RD
SPOKANE CO WA 247-A1
TEMPLETON RD
COOS CO OR 218-C4
TEN BAR RD
DESCHUTES CO OR 217-D3
TEN EYCK RD
CLACKAMAS CO OR 200-D3
NW TENINO RD
JEFFERSON CO OR 135-A1
Warm Springs OR 208-A3
TENMILE RD
MALHEUR CO OR 154-B2
N TEN MILE RD
ADA CO ID 253-A2
MERIDIAN ID 253-A2
S TEN MILE RD
ADA CO ID 253-A4
TENMILE CREEK RD
LANE CO OR 209-A5
W TENMILE CREEK RD
ADA CO ID 253-B5
TENNANT WY
LONGVIEW WA 303-A10
TENNANT WY Rt#-432
COWLITZ CO WA 303-C12
LONGVIEW WA 303-C12
TENNESSEE RD
LEWIS CO WA 187-C3
LINN CO OR 133-C1
NE TENNY RD
CLARK CO WA 192-C4
TENT CREEK RD
MALHEUR CO OR 155-A2
TENTH ST
KETTLE FALLS WA 106-A2
NESPELEM WA 105-A3
TERMINAL AV
VANCOUVER BC 254-J11
VANCOUVER BC 255-B12
SW TERRA DR
JEFFERSON CO OR 212-C1
TERRACE HEIGHTS DR
YAKIMA WA 243-C6
YAKIMA CO WA 243-C6
TERRA FERN DR
CLACKAMAS CO OR 201-A4
TERREBONNE-LOWER BRIDGE WY
DESCHUTES CO OR 212-C3
Terrebonne OR 212-C3
NE TERRE VIEW DR
PULLMAN WA 249-B4
TERRI DR
JACKSON CO OR 234-C2
TERRITORIAL HWY
BENTON CO OR 133-B2
DOUGLAS CO OR 133-B3
LANE CO OR 133-B2
VENETA OR 133-B3
TERRITORIAL RD
COLUMBIA CO WA 122-A2
DOUGLAS CO OR 219-B1
NE TERRITORIAL RD
CANBY OR 199-C6
CLACKAMAS CO OR 199-C6
TERRITORIAL ST
HARRISBURG OR 210-A5
LINN CO OR 210-A5
TERRY RD
COUPEVILLE WA 167-B4
ISLAND CO WA 167-B4
SW TERWILLIGER BLVD
CLACKAMAS CO OR 321-F3
LAKE OSWEGO OR 321-F3
MULTNOMAH CO OR 321-F3
PORTLAND OR 316-E3
PORTLAND OR 317-E1
PORTLAND OR 320-E1
PORTLAND OR 321-E2
TETHEROW RD
DESCHUTES CO OR 212-C5
N TEXAS RD
SKAGIT CO WA 160-C6
TEXAS LAKE RD
WHITMAN CO WA 114-A3
TEXMAR ST SW
OCEAN SHORES WA 298-C3
THAIN RD
LEWISTON ID 250-C4
THATCHER RD
FOREST GROVE OR 198-B1
WASHINGTON CO OR 198-B1
NW THATCHER RD
WASHINGTON CO OR 125-B1
WASHINGTON CO OR 198-B1
THATCHER PASS RD
SAN JUAN CO WA 160-A5
THAYER DR
RICHLAND WA 340-F13
RICHLAND WA 341-F1
THAYER RD
LEWIS CO WA 187-D3
S THAYER RD
CLACKAMAS CO OR 199-D5
THE CRESCENT TR
INDEX WA 111-A1
THE DALLES-CALIF HWY U.S.-26
JEFFERSON CO OR 208-C6
MADRAS OR 208-C5
THE DALLES-CALIF HWY U.S.-97
BEND OR 217-C1
BEND OR 332-D13
BEND OR 332-F1
BEND OR 332-F3
CHILOQUIN OR 231-D3
DESCHUTES CO OR 143-A1
DESCHUTES CO OR 212-C7
DESCHUTES CO OR 217-C1
DESCHUTES CO OR 332-D14
DESCHUTES CO OR 332-F3
Deschutes River Woods OR 217-C1
Deschutes River Woods OR 332-D14
DUFUR OR 127-B2
JEFFERSON CO OR 135-B1
JEFFERSON CO OR 208-C4
JEFFERSON CO OR 212-D3
KLAMATH CO OR 142-C2
KLAMATH CO OR 143-A1
KLAMATH CO OR 150-C1
KLAMATH CO OR 231-D3
KLAMATH CO OR 235-C1
KLAMATH CO OR 338-A1
KLAMATH FALLS OR 338-A1
MADRAS OR 208-C4
MAUPIN OR 127-B3
REDMOND OR 212-D3
Terrebonne OR 212-D3
THE DALLES OR 196-D7
WASCO CO OR 127-B2
WASCO CO OR 127-B3
WASCO CO OR 135-B1
WASCO CO OR 196-D7
THE EVERGREEN COLLEGE PKWY
THURSTON CO WA 296-A2
THERMAL DR
COQUITLAM BC 157-A4
THIEF CREEK RD
DOUGLAS CO OR 219-B3
THIELSON ST
ECHO OR 129-A1
UMATILLA CO OR 129-A1
N THIERMAN RD
SPOKANE CO WA 350-A1
S THIERMAN ST
SPOKANE VALLEY WA 350-A10
THIESEN RD
NEZ PERCE CO ID 250-C5
SE THIESSEN RD
CLACKAMAS CO OR 199-D3
THILLBERG RD
SKAGIT CO WA 260-G7
THIRD
DESCHUTES CO OR 212-A6
THIRD AV
FERNDALE WA 158-C6
E THIRD AV
PORT ORCHARD WA 271-A14
THIRD AV NW
OKANOGAN WA 104-C3
THIRD AV SW
OKANOGAN WA 104-C3
THIRD ST
FARMINGTON WA 115-A3
LINCOLN CO WA 114-A2
WHITMAN CO WA 115-A3
THIRD ST Rt#-507
TENINO WA 184-D3
THIRD FORK RD
GEM CO ID 139-C2
SW THIRTEENTH ST
CHEHALIS WA 299-E13
THOMAS
CROOK CO OR 213-D6
THOMAS RD
CLACKAMAS CO OR 126-A3
CLACKAMAS CO OR 205-D2
KING CO WA 182-D1
KITTITAS CO WA 241-C4
SKAGIT CO WA 161-A5
STEVENS CO WA 105-C3
STEVENS CO WA 106-A3
SE THOMAS RD
CLACKAMAS CO OR 200-D3
THOMAS RD KPN
PIERCE CO WA 174-A7
E THOMAS ST
SEATTLE WA 278-C4
THOMAS CREEK DR
LINN CO OR 134-A1
THOMAS CREEK RD
LAKE CO OR 152-A2
S THOMAS-MALLEN RD
SPOKANE CO WA 246-A6
THOMLE RD
SNOHOMISH CO WA 168-A4
THOMPSON AV
DOUGLAS CO OR 221-B6
WINSTON OR 221-B6
S THOMPSON AV
TACOMA WA 295-G1
THOMPSON LN
YAMHILL CO OR 198-C7
THOMPSON RD
CLALLAM CO WA 166-C7
COOS BAY OR 333-F7
YAKIMA CO WA 243-A5
W THOMPSON RD
KOOTENAI CO ID 247-D4
THOMPSON ST
SUMNER WA 182-B3
THOMPSON CREEK RD
JACKSON CO OR 149-B2
JOSEPHINE CO OR 149-B2
JOSEPHINE CO OR 233-C2
LANE CO OR 209-C7
LANE CO OR 214-D1
THOMPSON LAKE RD
KOOTENAI CO ID 248-B4
THOMPSON MILL RD
MULTNOMAH CO OR 200-D1
THOMSEN RD
HOOD RIVER CO OR 195-D7
S THOR ST
SPOKANE WA 349-F10
SE THORBURN ST
PORTLAND OR 314-E6
PORTLAND OR 315-E6
THORMAN AV NE
KEIZER OR 323-A6
THORN CREEK RD
WHITMAN CO WA 114-B3
THORNDYKE AV W
SEATTLE WA 273-E7
SEATTLE WA 276-E1
SEATTLE WA 277-E1
THORNDYKE RD
JEFFERSON CO WA 170-B5
N THORNE LN SW
LAKEWOOD WA 181-C5
THORN HOLLOW RD
COLUMBIA CO WA 122-A2
THORN PRAIRIE RD
DOUGLAS CO OR 223-A3
THORN SPRING RD
JEFFERSON CO OR 211-D1
THORNTON RD
WHATCOM CO WA 158-C5
THORNTON CREEK RD
LINCOLN CO OR 206-D3
W THORNTON LAKE DR
ALBANY OR 326-A6
THORP HWY
KITTITAS CO WA 241-A4
S THORPE RD
SPOKANE WA 348-G12
W THORPE RD
SPOKANE WA 348-E14
SPOKANE CO WA 114-B2
SPOKANE CO WA 246-A5
SPOKANE CO WA 348-E14
THORP PRAIRIE RD
KITTITAS CO WA 240-C2
THOUSAND SPRINGS RD
JACKSON CO OR 227-A4
THRALL RD
KITTITAS CO WA 241-C7
THRALL RD Rt#-821
KITTITAS CO WA 241-B7
THREE CREEK RD
DESCHUTES CO OR 211-D5
DESCHUTES CO OR 216-C1
SISTERS OR 211-D5
THREE DEVILS GRADE RD SW
DOUGLAS CO WA 112-B2
THREE FORKS RD
MALHEUR CO OR 146-C3
MALHEUR CO OR 147-A3
MALHEUR CO OR 155-A1
N THREE FORKS RD
KOOTENAI CO ID 247-C1
THREE FORKS RESERVOIR RD
MALHEUR CO OR 146-A3
THREE LAKES RD
ALBANY OR 326-H11
LINN CO OR 326-H11
SNOHOMISH CO WA 110-C1
SNOHOMISH CO WA 171-D3
NE THREE MILE LN
MCMINNVILLE OR 198-A7
YAMHILL CO OR 198-A7
SE THREE MILE LN
MCMINNVILLE OR 198-A7
YAMHILL CO OR 198-A7
THREEMILE RD
WASCO CO OR 127-A2
WASCO CO OR 196-C7
THREE MILE LN HWY Rt#-18
MCMINNVILLE OR 198-B7
YAMHILL CO OR 198-B7
THREE PINES RD
JOSEPHINE CO OR 229-B3
THREE RIVERS HWY Rt#-22
POLK CO OR 125-A3
TILLAMOOK CO OR 197-B6
TILLAMOOK CO OR 203-D1
YAMHILL CO OR 125-A3
YAMHILL CO OR 203-D1
THREE ROCKS RD
LINCOLN CO OR 203-B3
THREE TRAPPER RD
DESCHUTES CO OR 216-C7
THRESHER AV
Olympic View WA 170-B7
THRIFT
PIERCE CO WA 182-B6
THUMPER RD
DESCHUTES CO OR 211-C5
NW THURMAN ST
PORTLAND OR 312-E4
THURSTON RD
LANE CO OR 215-D2
SPRINGFIELD OR 215-D2
SPRINGFIELD OR 331-J6
NE THURSTON WY
VANCOUVER WA 307-F2
TIBBETS MOUNTAIN RD
CHELAN CO WA 238-C1
TIBBLING RD
YAKIMA CO WA 243-B4
TICKLE CREEK RD
CLACKAMAS CO OR 200-B3
TICKNER RD
SISKIYOU CO CA 151-A3
TIDE AV
TILLAMOOK CO OR 191-A3
TIDE CREEK RD
COLUMBIA CO OR 189-C6
TIDELAND RD
TILLAMOOK CO OR 191-B4
TIDEWATER RD
LINCOLN CO OR 209-D2
TIEDMAN RD KPS
PIERCE CO WA 180-D2
E TIETAN ST
WALLA WALLA WA 345-C10
W TIETAN ST
WALLA WALLA WA 345-A10
WALLA WALLA CO WA 345-A10
W TIETON AV
Country Homes WA 346-J12
TIETON DR
YAKIMA WA 243-A6
YAKIMA CO WA 243-A7
TIETON RESERVOIR RD
YAKIMA CO WA 119-B2
SE TIGER MOUNTAIN RD
KING CO WA 176-A5
TIGNER RD
CHELAN CO WA 238-C2
W TILDEN ST
SEATTLE WA 272-D6
TILE FLAT RD
WASHINGTON CO OR 198-D3
WASHINGTON CO OR 199-A3
TILLAMOOK
CROOK CO OR 213-D7
TILLAMOOK AV
BAY CITY OR 197-B1
NE TILLAMOOK ST
PORTLAND OR 314-B3
TILLAMOOK RIVER RD
TILLAMOOK OR 197-B3
TILLAMOOK CO OR 197-B3
TILLER-SOUTH UMPQUA CAMP RD
DOUGLAS CO OR 141-C3
DOUGLAS CO OR 222-A7
DOUGLAS CO OR 226-A1
TILLER-TRAIL HWY Rt#-227
CANYONVILLE OR 225-D3
DOUGLAS CO OR 141-B3
DOUGLAS CO OR 225-D3
JACKSON CO OR 141-C3
JACKSON CO OR 230-D1
TILLEY RD SW
THURSTON CO WA 184-C3
TILLEY RD SW Rt#-121
THURSTON CO WA 184-C2
TILLICUM RD
DISTRICT OF SAANICH BC 256-D5
TOWN OF ESQUIMALT BC 256-D7
SE TILLSTROM RD
DAMASCUS OR 200-B3
TIMBER RD
COLUMBIA CO OR 125-B1
LINN CO OR 210-D3
WASHINGTON CO OR 125-B1
TIMBER ST
ALBANY OR 326-H7
TIMBER TR NE
MARION CO OR 205-D5
TIMBER WY
COOS CO OR 220-D3
TIMBER CREEK RD
JACKSON CO OR 226-A6
TIMBERLINE HWY
CLACKAMAS CO OR 202-A6
TIMBERLINE EAST LEG
CLACKAMAS CO OR 202-A6
TIMBERLINE WEST LEG
CLACKAMAS CO OR 202-A6
NE TIMMEN RD
CLARK CO WA 192-C2
NW TIMMEN RD
CLARK CO WA 192-C2
TIMOTHY LAKE RD
CLACKAMAS CO OR 126-C3
TINGLE RD
LEWIS CO WA 187-C2
TINGLEY LN
KLAMATH CO OR 235-C5
TIPTON RD
KITTITAS CO WA 241-B4
TISCH
PIERCE CO WA 118-A1
TITCHENAL CANYON RD SW
DOUGLAS CO WA 239-C2
TITUS LN
VALLEY CO ID 252-D1
TOAD RD
JACKSON CO OR 229-D3
TOANDOS RD
JEFFERSON CO WA 170-A5
TODEY RD
LEWIS CO WA 187-D5
TOE JAM HILL RD NE
BAINBRIDGE ISLAND WA 174-D3
TOFTDAHL RD N
LANE CO OR 210-A5
TOKELAND RD
PACIFIC CO WA 183-C5
TOKIO RD
ADAMS CO WA 113-B3
LINCOLN CO WA 113-C3
TOLEDO SALMON CREEK RD
LEWIS CO WA 187-D5
TOLEDO SALMON HANKIN RD
LEWIS CO WA 187-D4
TOLEDO VADER RD
LEWIS CO WA 187-C4
TOLEDO WA 187-C4
TOLER RD NW
DOUGLAS CO WA 236-D7
TOLIVER RD
CLACKAMAS CO OR 205-D1
TOLL RD
MULTNOMAH CO OR 200-D1
S TOLL RD
SPOKANE CO WA 247-B7
TOLL STATION RD
DESCHUTES CO OR 211-B3
JEFFERSON CO OR 211-B2
TOLMAN RD
LANE CO OR 215-A4
SE TOLMAN ST
PORTLAND OR 318-A5
TOLMAN CREEK RD
JACKSON CO OR 234-D5
N TOLMAN CREEK RD
ASHLAND OR 337-H9
JACKSON CO OR 337-H9
S TOLMAN CREEK RD
ASHLAND OR 337-H11
TOLMIE RD
DISTRICT OF ABBOTSFORD BC 102-B1
TOLO RD
JACKSON CO OR 230-B7
TOLONEN RD E
LINCOLN CO WA 113-B2
TOLT AV Rt#-203
CARNATION WA 176-B2
KING CO WA 176-B2
NE TOLT HILL RD
KING CO WA 176-A2
TOMLINSON RD
TILLAMOOK CO OR 197-B2
TOM SMITH RD
COOS CO OR 220-B5
TOM WRIGHT
PIERCE CO WA 182-A6
TONE RD
TILLAMOOK CO OR 197-B2
SW TONGUE LN
WASHINGTON CO OR 198-C2
TONO RD SE
THURSTON CO WA 184-D4
SW TONQUIN RD
WASHINGTON CO OR 199-B5
TONY CREEK RD
HOOD RIVER CO OR 202-B1
TOONERVILLE DR
MASON CO WA 173-D4
SW TOOZE RD
CLACKAMAS CO OR 199-A5
TOPE RD
WALLOWA CO OR 130-C1
E TOPPENISH AV
TOPPENISH WA 120-A2
S TOPPENISH AV
TOPPENISH WA 120-A2
TOPPENISH-ZILLAH RD
YAKIMA CO WA 120-A2
ZILLAH WA 120-A2
TOQUA RD
KLAMATH CO OR 231-C5
TORNQUIST RD
GRAYS HARBOR CO WA 179-D5
TORODA BRIDGE CUSTOMS RD
FERRY CO WA 105-B1
TORODA CREEK RD
FERRY CO WA 105-B1
OKANOGAN CO WA 105-A2
TORPEDO RD
ISLAND CO WA 167-C2
OAK HARBOR WA 167-C2
TORVEND RD NE
MARION CO OR 205-B4
TOTTEN RD NE
Suquamish WA 170-C7
TOUCHET RD
WALLA WALLA CO WA 121-B3
S TOUCHET RD
COLUMBIA CO WA 122-A3
TOUCHET-GARDENA RD
WALLA WALLA CO WA 121-B3
TOUVELLE RD
JACKSON CO OR 230-C5
N TOWER AV Rt#-507
CENTRALIA WA 299-F3
S TOWER AV Rt#-507
CENTRALIA WA 299-F4
TOWER RD
COWLITZ CO WA 118-A2
COWLITZ CO WA 187-C6
MORROW CO OR 128-B1
WHATCOM CO WA 161-A1
TOWER MOUNTAIN RD
SPOKANE CO WA 247-B5
TOWN RD
CITY OF CHILLIWACK BC 102-B1
DISTRICT OF ABBOTSFORD BC 102-B1
TOWNSEND-SACKMAN RD
STEVENS CO WA 106-A2
TOWNSHIP RD
KLAMATH CO OR 235-B7
TOWNSHIP RD Rt#-9
SEDRO-WOOLLEY WA 161-C5
SKAGIT CO WA 161-C5
S TOWNSHIP RD
CLACKAMAS CO OR 199-C6
TOWNSHIP LINE RD
CLALLAM CO WA 165-D7
N TRACK RD
WAPATO WA 120-A2
YAKIMA CO WA 120-A2
TRACY RD
CLACKAMAS CO OR 200-C6
TRACYTON BLVD NW
KITSAP CO WA 270-E3
Silverdale WA 174-B1
Silverdale WA 270-E3
Tracyton WA 270-E3
TRACYTON BEACH RD NW
BREMERTON WA 270-G6
KITSAP CO WA 270-G6
Tracyton WA 270-G6
TRADE ST SE Rt#-22
SALEM OR 322-H13
S TRAFTON ST
TACOMA WA 293-E7
W TRAIL RD
SPOKANE CO WA 246-A3
SPOKANE CO WA 348-A6
TRAIL BUTTE RD
COOS CO OR 218-D6
TRAIL CREEK RD
JACKSON CO OR 230-D1
LANE CO OR 209-C7
TRAIL FORK RD
GILLIAM CO OR 128-A3
TRAILS RD
MASON CO WA 173-C7
TRAM RD
IDAHO CO ID 123-C3
TRAM RD Rt#-162
IDAHO CO ID 123-C3
TRAMWAY RD
GARFIELD CO WA 122-C1
TRANS CANADA HWY Rt#-1
BRITISH COLUMBIA BC 93-C1
BRITISH COLUMBIA BC 94-C3
BRITISH COLUMBIA BC 95-A1
BRITISH COLUMBIA BC 101-A1
BRITISH COLUMBIA BC 102-B1
BRITISH COLUMBIA BC 156-A2
BRITISH COLUMBIA BC 159-A1
CITY OF CHILLIWACK BC 94-C3
CITY OF NORTH VANCOUVER BC 255-A3
CITY OF SURREY BC 157-B6
CITY OF VICTORIA BC 256-G11
COQUITLAM BC 157-B6
DISTRICT OF ABBOTSFORD BC 94-C3
DISTRICT OF ABBOTSFORD BC 102-B1
DISTRICT OF BURNABY BC 156-D4
DISTRICT OF BURNABY BC 255-F12
DISTRICT OF COQUITLAM BC 156-D4
DISTRICT OF LANGFORD BC 159-A6
DISTRICT OF MATSQUI BC 102-B1
DISTRICT OF NORTH VANCOUV BC 254-F2
DISTRICT OF NORTH VANCOUV BC 255-A3
DISTRICT OF SAANICH BC 256-G5
DISTRICT OF WEST VANCOUVE BC 156-A2
DISTRICT OF WEST VANCOUVE BC 254-F2
DUNCAN BC 101-A1
HOPE BC 95-A3
NANAIMO BC 93-A3
SQUAMISH BC 93-C1
TOWN OF VIEW ROYAL BC 159-A6
TOWN OF VIEW ROYAL BC 256-B3
TOWNSHIP OF LANGLEY BC 102-B1
TOWNSHIP OF LANGLEY BC 157-B6
TOWNSHIP OF LANGLEY BC 158-D1
VANCOUVER BC 255-F12
WHISTLER BC 93-C1
TRANSFORMER RD
KLAMATH CO OR 151-A2

INDEX

INDEX

400 E WAVERLY RD STREET INDEX WILLIS POINT RD

STREET City State Page-Grid

E WAVERLY RD
SPOKANE CO WA 114-C2
WAVERLY WA 114-C2
WAWAWAI RD
WHITMAN CO WA 249-A7
WHITMAN CO WA 250-A1
WAWAWAI GRADE RD
WHITMAN CO WA 122-C1
WAWAWAI-PULLMAN RD
PULLMAN WA 249-A6
WHITMAN CO WA 249-A6
WAWAWAI-PULLMAN RD Rt#-194
WHITMAN CO WA 249-A5
WAWAWAI RIVER RD
WHITMAN CO WA 122-C2
WHITMAN CO WA 250-A4
WAWAWAI RIVER RD Rt#-128
WHITMAN CO WA 250-B4
WAWAWAI RIVER RD Rt#-193
WHITMAN CO WA 250-B4
SE WAX RD
COVINGTON WA 175-D7
KING CO WA 175-D7
MAPLE VALLEY WA 175-D7
WAX ORCHARD RD SW
KING CO WA 174-D7
WAYBURNE DR
DISTRICT OF BURNABY BC 255-J14
WAYNE DR N
KEIZER OR 322-J6
WAYNITA WY NE
BOTHELL WA 171-C7
WAYPARK DR NE
MARION CO OR 205-B3
WEATHERFORD RD
LINN CO OR 210-B5
WEAVER RD
DOUGLAS CO OR 225-C2
KITTITAS CO WA 241-A5
WEAVER RD N
BAINBRIDGE ISLAND WA 271-J2
S WEBB AV
DOUGLAS CO WA 239-B5
WEBB ST Rt#-3
MONTAGUE CA 150-A3
WEBB CANAL RD
NEZ PERCE CO ID 250-D5
WEBB CUTOFF RD
NEZ PERCE CO ID 250-D6
WEBB DISTRICT RD
COLUMBIA CO OR 117-B3
WEBBER ST
THE DALLES OR 196-C7
WEBBER CANYON RD
BENTON CO WA 120-C3
WEBBER CANYON RD Rt#-224
BENTON CO WA 120-C3
WEBBER CANYON RD Rt#-225
BENTON CO WA 120-C3
WEBB HILL RD
MASON CO WA 180-A1
WEBB RIDGE RD
NEZ PERCE CO ID 250-D6
WEBER RD
ADAMS CO WA 113-C3
CLACKAMAS CO OR 201-A5
LINCOLN CO WA 113-C3
LINN CO OR 210-C3
WHITMAN CO WA 249-B6
S WEBER COULEE RD
ADAMS CO WA 113-B3
WEBERG RD
CROOK CO OR 136-C3
WEBFOOT RD
DAYTON OR 198-C7
YAMHILL CO OR 198-C7
SE WEBFOOT RD
YAMHILL CO OR 204-C2
WEBSTER AV
CHELAN WA 236-D3
WEBSTER AV U.S.-97
CHELAN WA 236-D3
W WEBSTER AV
CHEWELAH WA 106-B3
WEBSTER EXT
PIERCE CO WA 182-A6
WEBSTER RD
GLADSTONE OR 199-D4
PIERCE CO WA 118-B1
SE WEBSTER RD
CLACKAMAS CO OR 199-D3
GLADSTONE OR 199-D3
WEBSTER RD E
PIERCE CO WA 182-A7
WEBSTER FLAT RD
JEFFERSON CO OR 208-B1
W WEDGEWOOD AV
Town and Country WA 346-H14
Town and Country WA 347-A14
WEED RD
KLAMATH CO OR 231-C2
WEEDIN PL NE
SEATTLE WA 274-B3
S WEGER RD
SPOKANE CO WA 246-D6
N WEHE AV
PASCO WA 343-H7
S WEHE AV
PASCO WA 343-H8
WEHRLI CANYON RD
GILLIAM CO OR 128-A3
WEIDKAMP RD
WHATCOM CO WA 158-D3
NE WEIDLER ST
PORTLAND OR 313-H4
PORTLAND OR 315-J4
WEIGAND RD
CROOK CO OR 213-B6
WEIKEL RD
YAKIMA CO WA 243-A6
N WEIPERT DR
Country Homes WA 346-J12
Town and Country WA 346-J12
SW WEIR RD
BEAVERTON OR 199-A3
WEISER SPUR U.S.-95
MALHEUR CO OR 139-A2
WEISER RIVER RD
WASHINGTON CO ID 139-A2
WEISER ID 139-A2
WEISS RD
LANE CO OR 215-A5
WEISSENFELS RIDGE RD
ASOTIN CO WA 123-A3
ASOTIN CO WA 250-C7
WEITZ LN
CLACKAMAS CO OR 200-B5
WEITZ RD
CANYON CO ID 147-B1
WELCH ST
DISTRICT OF NORTH VANCOUV BC 254-G5
WELCH CREEK RD
LINCOLN CO WA 113-C1
WELCHER RD
ISLAND CO WA 167-C5
WELCHES RD
CLACKAMAS CO OR 201-C5
WELLER RD
KOOTENAI CO ID 247-C6
E WELLESLEY AV
Otis Orchards WA 351-H2
Otis Orchards WA 352-C9
SPOKANE WA 349-C3
SPOKANE CO WA 350-H2
SPOKANE CO WA 351-H2
SPOKANE VALLEY WA 350-H2
SPOKANE VALLEY WA 351-B2
W WELLESLEY AV
SPOKANE WA 348-F3
SPOKANE WA 349-A3
WELLESLEY RD
LATAH CO ID 249-C1
WELLINGTON AV
WALLA WALLA WA 345-D6
E WELLINGTON RD
NANAIMO BC 93-A3
WELLPINIT-LITTLE FALLS RD
STEVENS CO WA 114-A1
WELLPINIT-MCCOY LAKE RD
STEVENS CO WA 113-C1
STEVENS CO WA 114-A1
WELLS RD
DOUGLAS CO OR 141-A1
S WELLS RD
SPOKANE CO WA 114-B2
WELLSANDT RD
ADAMS CO WA 113-C3
ADAMS CO WA 114-A3
RITZVILLE WA 113-C3
WELLS BENCH RD
CLEARWATER CO ID 123-C2
WELLSIAN WY
RICHLAND WA 341-F3
WELLS LANDING RD
POLK CO OR 207-C2
WELLS LINE
DISTRICT OF ABBOTSFORD BC 102-B1
WELLS STATION RD
UMATILLA CO OR 129-A1
WEMBLEY DR
DISTRICT OF NORTH VANCOUV BC 255-G3
WENAS AV Rt#-823
SELAH WA 243-B5
YAKIMA CO WA 243-B5
WENAS RD
YAKIMA CO WA 119-C1
YAKIMA CO WA 240-D7
YAKIMA CO WA 241-A7
YAKIMA CO WA 243-A3
S WENAS RD
YAKIMA CO WA 243-B4
WENATCHEE AV
WENATCHEE WA 238-D4
WENATCHEE WA 239-A4
WENATCHEE AV Rt#-285
WENATCHEE WA 239-A4
N WENATCHEE AV Rt#-285
WENATCHEE WA 238-D4
West Wenatchee WA 238-D4
S WENATCHEE AV
Appleyard WA 239-A5
WENATCHEE WA 239-A4
S WENATCHEE AV Rt#-285
WENATCHEE WA 239-A4
WENATCHEE HEIGHTS RD
CHELAN CO WA 238-D6
WENIGER HILL RD
KOOTENAI CO ID 248-A1
WENTWORTH RD
CLALLAM CO WA 169-B1
WENTWORTH ST
NANAIMO BC 93-A3
WENZEL SLOUGH RD
GRAYS HARBOR CO WA 179-A7
SW WERNER RD
BREMERTON WA 270-D12
KITSAP CO WA 270-D12
W WERNETT RD
FRANKLIN CO WA 342-F5
FRANKLIN CO WA 343-A5
PASCO WA 342-F5
PASCO WA 343-A5
WERRON RD
PIERCE CO WA 182-D4
WESGATE PL
PENDLETON OR 129-B1
UMATILLA CO OR 129-B1
WESLEY RD
HARRAH WA 119-C2
WEST AV
ARLINGTON WA 168-D5
WEST BLVD
VANCOUVER BC 156-B5
N WEST BLVD U.S.-101
ABERDEEN WA 178-B7
COSMOPOLIS WA 178-B7
WEST LN
COLUMBIA CO OR 192-A3
WEST MALL
UNIVERSITY ENDOWMENT LAND BC 156-A4
WEST RD
PIERCE CO WA 181-D4
WEST SPUR
JACKSON CO OR 226-C4
WEST ST
DESCHUTES CO OR 212-A6
LINCOLN CO WA 114-A2
SAINT HELENS OR 192-B1
NW WEST ST
CHEHALIS WA 299-C11
S WEST ST Rt#-21
WILBUR WA 113-B1
WEST BEACH RD
Ault Field WA 167-A4
ISLAND CO WA 167-A4
WESTBROOK DR SW
KITSAP CO WA 174-B6
WESTBROOK MALL
UNIVERSITY ENDOWMENT LAND BC 156-A4
WEST COAST RD Rt#-14
BRITISH COLUMBIA BC 101-A2
BRITISH COLUMBIA BC 164-C1
WEST COVE RD
LATAH CO ID 249-C1
NE WESTERHOLM RD
CLARK CO WA 193-B4
WESTERMAN RD SW
DOUGLAS CO WA 239-D1
WESTERN AV
SEATTLE WA 277-G4
WENATCHEE WA 238-D4
West Wenatchee WA 238-D4
SW WESTERN AV
GRANTS PASS OR 335-D9
WESTERN BLVD
BENTON CO OR 327-D11
CORVALLIS OR 327-D11
WESTERN ST
Altamont OR 339-D11
WESTERN ROUTE RD
MORROW CO OR 128-C3
SW WESTFALL RD
CLACKAMAS CO OR 199-A5
WESTFIR RD
LANE CO OR 142-A1
WESTFIR OR 142-A1
WEST FORK RD
OKANOGAN CO WA 104-B2
WEST FORK EVANS CREEK RD
JACKSON CO OR 230-A1
WEST FORK INDIAN CREEK RD
LANE CO OR 209-C7
WEST FORK-MILLICOMA RD
COOS CO OR 218-D6
WESTGATE AV U.S.-30
PENDLETON OR 129-B1
WESTHAVEN DR
WESTPORT WA 298-G10
WEST HILLS RD
BENTON CO OR 133-B1
BENTON CO OR 327-A11
CORVALLIS OR 327-A11
WESTLAKE AV
SEATTLE WA 273-J7
SEATTLE WA 277-J1
WESTLAKE AV N
SEATTLE WA 277-J5
WESTLAKE RD
LEWIS CO ID 123-B2
WESTLAND RD
UMATILLA CO OR 129-A1
WESTMINSTER HWY
CITY OF RICHMOND BC 156-A6
WESTMINSTER HWY S
CITY OF RICHMOND BC 156-C6
WESTMINSTER WY N
SHORELINE WA 171-A7
WESTMOND RD
BONNER CO ID 244-A5
WEST MOUNTAIN RD
VALLEY CO ID 251-C5
VALLEY CO ID 252-C1
WESTON-ELGIN HWY Rt#-204
UMATILLA CO OR 129-C1
UMATILLA CO OR 130-A1
UNION CO OR 130-A1
WESTPORT RD Rt#-105
GRAYS HARBOR CO WA 117-A1
WESTPORT DOCK RD Rt#-409
CLATSOP CO OR 117-B3
WEST SAANICH RD
DISTRICT OF NORTH SAANICH BC 159-B2
WEST SAANICH RD Rt#-17A
DISTRICT OF CENTRAL SAANI BC 159-B3
DISTRICT OF NORTH SAANICH BC 159-B3
DISTRICT OF SAANICH BC 159-C5
WEST SHORE DR
WASHINGTON CO OR 198-A2
WESTSHORE DR
GRANT CO WA 242-C2
MOSES LAKE WA 242-C3
WEST SIDE HWY
COWLITZ CO WA 187-C6
LEWIS CO WA 187-C6
VADER WA 187-C6
WEST SIDE HWY Rt#-411
COWLITZ CO WA 187-C7
COWLITZ CO WA 189-C1
COWLITZ CO WA 303-C7
KELSO WA 303-C7
LONGVIEW WA 303-C7
WESTSIDE HWY SW
KING CO WA 174-D5
WEST SIDE RD
COOS CO OR 140-B3
COOS CO OR 220-D7
JOSEPHINE CO OR 233-A4
KLAMATH CO OR 231-B2
LAKE CO OR 151-C3
LAKE CO OR 152-A2
MODOC CO CA 151-C3
MODOC CO CA 152-A3
MYRTLE POINT OR 140-B3
WESTSIDE RD
PIERCE CO WA 185-A5
YAMHILL CO OR 198-A5
NE WESTSIDE RD
MCMINNVILLE OR 198-A7
YAMHILL CO OR 198-A6
WEST SIDE WOLLOCHET BAY
PIERCE CO WA 181-C2
WEST TWIN RD
LATAH CO ID 249-D4
NW WEST UNION RD
WASHINGTON CO OR 125-C1
WASHINGTON CO OR 192-A7
WASHINGTON CO OR 199-A1
WEST VALLEY HWY
AUBURN WA 175-B7
AUBURN WA 182-B1
EDGEWOOD WA 182-B1
KENT WA 175-B7
KING CO WA 175-B7
PACIFIC WA 182-B1
PACIFIC WA 182-B1
PIERCE CO WA 182-B1
SUMNER WA 182-B3
WEST VALLEY HWY Rt#-181
KENT WA 291-H2
TUKWILA WA 289-J5
TUKWILA WA 291-H2
WEST VALLEY HWY N
ALGONA WA 182-B1
WEST VALLEY HWY S
ALGONA WA 182-B2
KING CO WA 182-B2
PACIFIC WA 182-B2
WEST VALLEY RD
JEFFERSON CO WA 170-A2
WESTVIEW DR
CITY OF NORTH VANCOUVER BC 255-A4
DISTRICT OF DELTA BC 156-D7
WESTVIEW DR
DISTRICT OF NORTH VANCOUV BC 255-A4
DOUGLAS CO OR 221-B2
WESTWARD HO
LINCOLN CO OR 328-C3
WESTWICK RD
SNOHOMISH CO WA 110-C1
WESTWOOD ST
PORT COQUITLAM BC 157-A4
WETHERBEE RD
JOSEPHINE CO OR 229-A7
WEXLER RD
WHITMAN CO WA 249-B4
WEYERHAEUSER RD
SPRINGFIELD OR 331-G8
WEYERHAUSER RD
LANE CO OR 219-D1
WHALEN RD
COWLITZ CO WA 192-B1
WHARF ST
CITY OF VICTORIA BC 256-G9
WHATCOM RD
DISTRICT OF ABBOTSFORD BC 102-B1
SE WHEATLAND RD
YAMHILL CO OR 204-D2
WHEATLAND RD N
KEIZER OR 204-D3
KEIZER OR 323-A2
MARION CO OR 204-D3
WHEATON WY
BREMERTON WA 270-J8
BREMERTON WA 271-A9
WHEATON WY Rt#-303
BREMERTON WA 270-J6
KITSAP CO WA 270-J6
WHEELER RD
CLALLAM CO WA 163-A7
GRANT CO WA 242-D3
JACKSON CO OR 230-C5
LANE CO OR 215-D4
MOSES LAKE WA 242-D3
E WHEELER RD
MOSES LAKE WA 242-C3
S WHEELER RD
SPOKANE CO WA 114-C3
WHELAN RD
WHITMAN CO WA 249-B4
WHERRY RD
YAKIMA CO WA 243-A5
WHETSTONE RD
COLUMBIA CO WA 122-A2
WHIFFIN SPIT RD
BRITISH COLUMBIA BC 164-C1
WHISKEY CREEK DR
HOOD RIVER CO OR 195-D5
WHISKEY CREEK RD
COLUMBIA CO WA 122-A3
JACKSON CO OR 226-D3
MALHEUR CO OR 146-A1
TILLAMOOK CO OR 197-A3
WALLOWA CO OR 130-C1
WALLOWA CO OR 130-C1
E WHISKEY CREEK RD
WALLOWA CO OR 130-C1
S WHISKEY HILL RD
CLACKAMAS CO OR 205-C1
WHISKEY HILL RD NE
HUBBARD OR 205-C1
MARION CO OR 205-C1
WHISKEY JACK RD
BONNER CO ID 244-A1
JEFFERSON CO OR 211-B1
WHISKEY RUN RD
COOS CO OR 220-B4
WHISKEY SPRING CREEK RD
CROOK CO OR 135-C2
WHISKEY SPRINGS RD
JEFFERSON CO OR 211-D2
WHISTLE CREEK RD
HARNEY CO OR 136-C3
WHISTLERS LN
DOUGLAS CO OR 221-D3
WHISTLERS BEND PARK RD
DOUGLAS CO OR 221-D3
WHITAKER RD
POLK CO OR 204-A7
WHITCOMB AV U.S.-97
OKANOGAN CO WA 104-C2
TONASKET WA 104-C2
WHITE RD
WALLA WALLA CO WA 121-B3
W WHITE RD
SPOKANE CO WA 246-B5
E WHITEAKER AV
COTTAGE GROVE OR 215-B7
WHITE CREEK RD
JOSEPHINE CO OR 233-D3
E WHITE CREEK RD
JOSEPHINE CO OR 233-D3
WHITEHALL RD SE
DOUGLAS CO WA 112-C2
WHITEHORSE CTO
MALHEUR CO OR 154-B1
WHITEHORSE RD
MALHEUR CO OR 154-A1
WHITEHORSE CREEK RD
DOUGLAS CO OR 225-D6
WHITEHORSE RANCH RD
HARNEY CO OR 153-C2
HARNEY CO OR 154-A2
WHITELINE RD
KLAMATH CO OR 235-D1
WHITEMAN RD KPS
PIERCE CO WA 181-A3
WHITE OAK RD
LINN CO OR 207-B6
WHITE PINE DR Rt#-6
BENEWAH CO ID 115-B3
LATAH CO ID 115-B3
WHITE RIVER RD
CHELAN CO WA 111-C1
WASCO CO OR 127-A3
WHITE ROCK LOOP RD
DESCHUTES CO OR 212-B7
WHITE SCHOOL HOUSE RD
JOSEPHINE CO OR 233-B4
WHITES CREEK RD
LANE CO OR 219-D1
SE WHITESON RD
YAMHILL CO OR 204-B1
N WHITE SWAN RD
HARRAH WA 119-C2
W WHITE SWAN RD Rt#-220
HARRAH WA 119-C2
WHITHAM RD NE
THURSTON CO WA 180-D4
WHITING WY
DISTRICT OF COQUITLAM BC 156-D5
WHITLEY DR U.S.-95
FRUITLAND ID 139-A3
N WHITLEY DR U.S.-95
FRUITLAND ID 139-A3
PAYETTE CO ID 139-A3
E WHITMAN DR
COLLEGE PLACE WA 344-F10
W WHITMAN DR
COLLEGE PLACE WA 344-E10
WALLA WALLA CO WA 344-D10
WHITMAN RD
WHITMAN CO WA 249-C6
E WHITMAN RD
SPOKANE CO WA 114-C3
WHITMAN ST
WALLA WALLA WA 345-C8
S WHITMAN ST
MONMOUTH OR 204-B7
ROSALIA WA 114-C3
WHITMAN CO WA 114-C3
W WHITMAN ST
ROSALIA WA 114-C3
W WHITMARSH RD
BURLINGTON WA 260-A8
SKAGIT CO WA 260-A8
WHITMORE DR NW
PIERCE CO WA 181-B1
WHITMORE RD
WASHINGTON CO OR 198-C3
WHITNEY HWY Rt#-7
BAKER CITY OR 138-B1
BAKER CO OR 137-C1
BAKER CO OR 138-A1
GRANT CO OR 137-C1
WHITNEY RD
ADAMS CO ID 251-B5
COLUMBIA CO OR 189-B6
COOS CO OR 140-B3
E WHITNEY HILL RD
KING CO WA 110-C3
KING CO WA 182-D2
WHITNEY-LA CONNER RD
SKAGIT CO WA 160-D7
SKAGIT CO WA 167-D1
WHITTAKER RD NW
THURSTON CO WA 180-B5
N WHITWORTH DR
Country Homes WA 346-J10
Fairwood WA 346-J9
Fairwood WA 347-A9
WHOOPEMUP RD
COLUMBIA CO WA 122-A2
WIARD ST
Altamont OR 339-A9
WICKERSHAM TRUCK TR
WHATCOM CO WA 161-C2
WICKIEUP RD Rt#-1
BRITISH COLUMBIA BC 101-B1
BRITISH COLUMBIA BC 159-A1
DISTRICT OF LANGFORD BC 159-A5
SW WICKIUP AV
DESCHUTES CO OR 212-D6
WICKIUP RD
DESCHUTES CO OR 142-C1
W WIDE HOLLOW RD
YAKIMA CO WA 243-A7
WIDME RD NE
Suquamish WA 170-C7
WIDOW CREEK RD
LINCOLN CO OR 203-C3
Rose Lodge OR 203-C3
SE WIESE RD
DAMASCUS OR 200-B3
WIGGINS RD SE
OLYMPIA WA 297-D11
THURSTON CO WA 297-D11
WIGHTMAN ST
ASHLAND OR 337-E9
WIGRICH RD
POLK CO OR 207-C1
WIKSTROM RD
COLUMBIA CO OR 192-A3
N WILBUR AV
WALLA WALLA WA 345-E6
S WILBUR AV
WALLA WALLA WA 345-E7
Walla Walla East WA 345-E7
WILBUR RD
DOUGLAS CO OR 221-B2
WILBUR-GARDEN VALLEY RD
DOUGLAS CO OR 221-B3
WILBUR GULCH RD Rt#-194
WHITMAN CO WA 122-C1
WHITMAN CO WA 249-A5
WILBUR-UMPQUA RD
DOUGLAS CO OR 221-B1
WILCO RD
MARION CO OR 133-C1
STAYTON OR 133-C1
NE WILCOX AV
DESCHUTES CO OR 212-D4
WILCOX RD
DOUGLAS CO OR 221-B1
WHITMAN CO WA 122-B1
WHITMAN CO WA 249-C1
WILDCAT RD
MALHEUR CO OR 146-A3
S WILDCAT RD
CLACKAMAS CO OR 126-A3
CLACKAMAS CO OR 205-D3
NW WILDCAT LAKE RD
KITSAP CO WA 174-A2
WILDCAT MOUNTAIN DR
CLACKAMAS CO OR 200-C5
CLACKAMAS CO OR 201-A5
WILD FERN DR
DOUGLAS CO OR 221-C3
WILDHORSE RD
UMATILLA CO OR 129-C1
WILDWOOD DR
COOS CO OR 218-B5
SW WILDWOOD PL
SEATTLE WA 284-D3
WILDWOOD RD
LEWIS CO WA 187-A3
SW WILDWOOD RD
KITSAP CO WA 174-B5
WILES RD
BENTON CO OR 207-B3
WILEY RD
CROOK CO OR 213-C5
W WILEY RD
YAKIMA CO WA 243-A7
WILEY CREEK DR
LINN CO OR 134-A2
WILHOIT RD
CLACKAMAS CO OR 126-A3
WILKENSON RD
ISLAND CO WA 171-A1
WILKES DR
Santa Clara OR 215-A1
WILKINS RD
LANE CO OR 210-B7
WILKINSON RD
DISTRICT OF SAANICH BC 159-C5
DISTRICT OF SAANICH BC 256-D1
MALHEUR CO OR 154-C2
MULTNOMAH CO OR 200-D3
WILLAGILLESPIE RD
EUGENE OR 329-J4
WILLAMETTE AV
MEDFORD OR 336-E12
N WILLAMETTE BLVD
PORTLAND OR 192-B7
PORTLAND OR 308-A5
WILLAMETTE DR
LANE CO OR 210-A6
WILLAMETTE DR Rt#-43
LAKE OSWEGO OR 199-C4
WEST LINN OR 199-C4
WILLAMETTE HWY Rt#-58
KLAMATH CO OR 142-C2
LANE CO OR 133-C3
LANE CO OR 134-A3
LANE CO OR 142-B1
LANE CO OR 215-C3
LANE CO OR 330-J14
LANE CO OR 331-A14
OAKRIDGE OR 142-B1
S WILLAMETTE RD
LANE CO OR 215-B3
LANE CO OR 329-J14
WILLAMETTE ST
COBURG OR 210-B7
EUGENE OR 329-J13
EUGENE OR 330-A8
LANE CO OR 210-B7
LANE CO OR 329-H14
SAINT HELENS OR 192-B1
WILLAMETTE FALLS DR
WEST LINN OR 199-C5
WILLAMETTE FERRY ST
MARION CO OR 207-C2
POLK CO OR 207-C2
WILLAMETTE-MERIDIAN RD
KITSAP CO WA 174-A1
SW WILLAMINA CREEK RD
WILLAMINA OR 125-A3
YAMHILL CO OR 125-A3
WILLAMINA-SALEM HWY Rt#-22
POLK CO OR 125-B3
POLK CO OR 204-A5
POLK CO OR 322-G12
SALEM OR 322-G12
WILLAMINA-SALEM HWY NW Rt#-22
POLK CO OR 204-B6
POLK CO OR 322-B14
SALEM OR 322-B14
WILLAMINA-SHERIDAN HWY Rt#-18
POLK CO OR 125-A3
WILLAMINA OR 125-A3
WILLANCH WY
COOS CO OR 218-C7
WILLAPA RD
PACIFIC CO WA 117-A1
WILLAPA-MONOHAN LANDING RD
PACIFIC CO WA 117-A1
RAYMOND WA 117-A1
WILLARD RD
DESCHUTES CO OR 135-B3
SKAMANIA CO WA 195-B4
WILLEYS LAKE RD
WHATCOM CO WA 158-C4
WILLIAM H BUNDY BLVD U.S.-95
LAPWAI ID 123-A2
NEZ PERCE CO ID 123-A2
WILLIAM HEAD RD
DISTRICT OF METCHOSIN BC 165-A1
N WILLIAMS AV
PORTLAND OR 309-G7
PORTLAND OR 313-G1
WILLIAMS RD
ADAMS CO WA 121-B1
BENTON CO WA 120-B3
CITY OF RICHMOND BC 156-B7
COWLITZ CO WA 190-A6
CROOK CO OR 213-C4
LINCOLN CO WA 113-B1
WILLIAMS CANYON RD
CHELAN CO WA 238-B1
WILLIAMS CREEK RD
GRAYS HARBOR CO WA 117-B1
LANE CO OR 219-D2
WILLIAMS LAKE RD
STEVENS CO WA 106-A1
W WILLIAMS LAKE RD
SPOKANE CO WA 114-B2
WILLIAMSON RD
YAMHILL CO OR 198-C5
WILLIAMSON MOUNTAIN RD
DESCHUTES CO OR 216-A6
WILLIAMSON RIVER RD
KLAMATH CO OR 143-A3
KLAMATH CO OR 150-C1
KLAMATH CO OR 151-A1
WILLIAMSPORT RD
ASTORIA OR 300-D6
WILLIAMS VALLEY RD
STEVENS CO WA 114-B1
WILLIMINA CREEK RD
YAMHILL CO OR 125-A3
WILLINGDON AV
DISTRICT OF BURNABY BC 156-C5
DISTRICT OF BURNABY BC 255-H13
N WILLIS BLVD
PORTLAND OR 308-B4
E WILLIS RD
CANYON CO ID 147-B1
NW WILLIS RD
YAMHILL CO OR 198-A6
W WILLIS ST Rt#-516
KENT WA 175-C7
WILLIS CANYON RD
KLICKITAT CO WA 196-C1
WILLIS CREEK RD
DOUGLAS CO OR 221-B7
DOUGLAS CO OR 225-B1
WILLIS POINT RD
DISTRICT OF SAANICH BC 159-B4

INDEX

WILLOW AV Rt#-39 STREET INDEX 1ST AV S 401

STREET
City State Page-Grid

WILLOW AV Rt#-39
KLAMATH FALLS OR 338-D8
WILLOW RD SE
KITSAP CO WA 174-B6
PIERCE CO WA 174-B6
N WILLOW ST
LA GRANDE OR 130-A2
WILLOW CREEK RD
COLUMBIA CO WA 122-A2
JEFFERSON CO OR 208-B4
MALHEUR CO OR 138-B2
MORROW CO OR 128-C2
MORROW CO OR 129-A2
WILLOW CREEK RED ROCK RD
SISKIYOU CO CA 150-C3
WILLOWDALE RD
KITTITAS CO WA 241-B5
WILLOW GROVE RD
COWLITZ CO WA 189-A2
COWLITZ CO WA 302-A5
WILLOW GROVE RD Rt#-432
COWLITZ CO WA 302-A5
LONGVIEW WA 302-A5
WILLOW GROVE CONN RD Rt#-432
COWLITZ CO WA 302-A5
LONGVIEW WA 302-A5
WILLOWLAKE RD
GRANT CO WA 112-C2
WILLOWS RD
ILWACO WA 186-A6
PACIFIC CO WA 186-A6
REDMOND WA 171-C7
E WILLOW SPRINGS RD
SPOKANE CO WA 246-C5
WILLOW VALLEY RD
KLAMATH CO OR 151-B2
MODOC CO CA 151-B2
WILLS RD
LANE CO OR 215-D5
WILLWORTH RD Rt#-150
CHELAN CO WA 236-D3
WILSON AV
BEND OR 332-E9
WESTPORT WA 298-G11
SE WILSON AV
BEND OR 332-F9
WILSON AV S
SEATTLE WA 283-F6
WILSON HWY
YAKIMA CO WA 120-B2
WILSON LN
SKAGIT CO WA 161-A6
WILSON RD
BOARDMAN OR 128-C1
CLACKAMAS CO OR 126-C3
DOUGLAS CO OR 219-B4
GRANDVIEW WA 120-B3
LEWIS CO ID 123-C2
LEWIS CO WA 187-C2
MORROW CO OR 128-C1
WASCO CO OR 127-C3
WASCO CO OR 196-A6
WESTPORT WA 298-H11
WHITMAN CO WA 249-B5
YAKIMA CO WA 120-B3
YONCALLA OR 219-B4
S WILSON RD
CLACKAMAS CO OR 200-A6
WILSON RD NW
THURSTON CO WA 180-A6
WILSON ST
ASOTIN WA 250-B5
CHELAN CO WA 238-A1
DISTRICT OF MISSION BC 94-B3
MAPLE RIDGE BC 94-B3
THURSTON CO WA 297-B4
N WILSON ST
POST FALLS ID 353-F6
WILSON CREEK RD
KITTITAS CO WA 241-B2
LINCOLN CO OR 209-C4
WILSON RIVER HWY Rt#-6
BANKS OR 125-B1
TILLAMOOK OR 197-C2
TILLAMOOK CO OR 125-B1
TILLAMOOK CO OR 197-C2
WASHINGTON CO OR 125-B1
WILSON RIVER LP
TILLAMOOK CO OR 197-C2
WILSONVILLE RD
CLACKAMAS CO OR 199-B6
NEWBERG OR 198-D6
WILSONVILLE OR 199-B6
YAMHILL CO OR 198-D6
YAMHILL CO OR 199-A6
WILSONVILLE HUBBARD HWY
MARION CO OR 199-B7
MARION CO OR 205-C1
WILT RD
DESCHUTES CO OR 211-D4
DESCHUTES CO OR 212-A4
WIMER RD
JOSEPHINE CO OR 148-C2
WIMER ST
ASHLAND OR 337-B6
NW WIMP WY
DESCHUTES CO OR 212-D3
WINBURN WY
ASHLAND OR 337-C7
W WINCH AV
KOOTENAI CO ID 247-C1
WINCHELL ST
DEPOE BAY OR 206-B1
WINCHESTER AV
REEDSPORT OR 218-D1
WINCHESTER AV U.S.-101
REEDSPORT OR 218-C1
WINCHESTER RD
DOUGLAS CO OR 221-B3
LEWIS CO ID 123-B2
NE WINCHESTER ST
ROSEBURG OR 334-G6
WINCHUCK RIVER RD
CURRY CO OR 232-D7
WINDHURST RD
COOS CO OR 220-B6
WINDIGO PASS RD
DOUGLAS CO OR 223-D3
KLAMATH CO OR 142-B2
WIND MOUNTAIN RD
SKAMANIA CO WA 195-A5
WIND RIDGE RD
YAMHILL CO OR 198-C4
WIND RIVER RD
CARSON WA 194-D3
SKAMANIA CO WA 194-D3

WINDSOR RD
DISTRICT OF OAK BAY BC 257-D9
PITT MEADOWS BC 157-B5
WINDSOR ISLAND RD
KEIZER OR 322-G3
MARION CO OR 204-D4
MARION CO OR 322-G2
S WINDY CITY RD
CLACKAMAS CO OR 126-A3
CLACKAMAS CO OR 200-A7
WINDY RIDGE DR
COWLITZ CO WA 189-B1
WINESAP AV
CHELAN CO WA 236-C2
WINGVILLE RD
BAKER CO OR 130-A3
BAKER CO OR 138-A1
WINLOCK LN
WHEELER CO OR 128-B3
WINLOCK-TOLEDO RD Rt#-505
LEWIS CO WA 187-C3
WINLOCK-VADER RD
LEWIS CO WA 187-B4
WINLOCK WA 187-B4
WINONA AV N
SEATTLE WA 273-J2
WINONA RD
JOSEPHINE CO OR 229-C3
WINONA SOUTH RD
WHITMAN CO WA 122-A1
WINSLOW RD
WASCO CO OR 127-B2
WINSTON RD
DOUGLAS CO OR 221-B6
WINSTON OR 221-B6
WINSTON ST
DISTRICT OF BURNABY BC 156-D4
WINTEL RD S
MARION CO OR 207-C2
WINTER ST SE
SALEM OR 322-H14
WINTERCREEK RD
MARION CO OR 207-D2
WINTERGREEN AV NW
SALEM OR 322-F9
W WINTERGREEN LN
KITSAP CO WA 173-C3
WINTERS RD
WASHINGTON CO OR 198-C2
NE WINTERS RD
CLARK CO WA 193-C5
SW WINTERS RD
WASHINGTON CO OR 198-C2
WINTERS HILL RD
YAMHILL CO OR 198-C6
WIPPER RD SE
MARION CO OR 325-F14
TURNER OR 325-F14
WIRTA RD
LEWIS CO WA 187-B2
WIRTH RD
LINN CO OR 207-C7
WISCONSIN ST
PRIEST RIVER ID 107-A3
WISCONSIN TKTR
COWLITZ CO WA 117-B2
COWLITZ CO WA 187-A7
W WISER LAKE RD
WHATCOM CO WA 158-D5
WISHKAH RD
ABERDEEN WA 178-B6
GRAYS HARBOR CO WA 178-C3
W WISHKAH RD
GRAYS HARBOR CO WA 178-B4
WISHKAH ST
ABERDEEN WA 178-B7
WISHKAH ST U.S.-12
ABERDEEN WA 178-B7
GRAYS HARBOR CO WA 178-B7
WISHKAH ST U.S.-101
ABERDEEN WA 178-B7
E WISHKAH ST U.S.-101
ABERDEEN WA 178-B7
W WISHKAH ST U.S.-101
ABERDEEN WA 178-B7
NE WISTARIA DR
PORTLAND OR 314-B2
WITCHER GATEWAY RD
LANE CO OR 215-C6
WITHAM HILL DR
CORVALLIS OR 327-D6
WITHROW RD NW
DOUGLAS CO WA 112-B2
SW WITHYCOMBE RD
WASHINGTON CO OR 198-B2
WITT DR
LINN CO OR 207-C7
WITTE RD SE
KING CO WA 175-D7
MAPLE VALLEY WA 175-D7
WITTE RD SW
DOUGLAS CO WA 239-B3
WITTIG RD NE
DOUGLAS CO WA 112-C1
WITZEL RD SE
MARION CO OR 325-H11
TURNER OR 325-H11
NE W KINGSON RD
KITSAP CO WA 170-C5
WNUK RD
KLICKITAT CO WA 195-D4
WOCUS RD
KLAMATH CO OR 235-C2
KLAMATH CO OR 338-A1
WOHL RD
COWLITZ CO WA 189-A2
WOLCOTT AV S
SEATTLE WA 287-G3
WOLCOTT RD
LINN CO OR 207-B6
WOLF RD
LATAH CO ID 249-C7
WOLF CREEK LN
UNION CO OR 130-A3
WOLF CREEK RD
LANE CO OR 133-A3
WOLFE RD
CITY OF CHILLIWACK BC 94-C3
WOLF HOLLOW LN
GILLIAM CO OR 128-B2
WOLFORD CANYON RD
JEFFERSON CO OR 208-A2
N WOLKAV RD
LINCOLN CO OR 206-B6
WOLLOCHET DR NW
GIG HARBOR WA 181-B1
PIERCE CO WA 181-B1

WOLLOCHET-GIG HARBOR
GIG HARBOR WA 181-C1
PIERCE CO WA 181-C1
N WOLVERTON CT
SPOKANE WA 349-B5
WONDERLY RD
COLUMBIA CO OR 302-D14
S WOOD DR
CROOK CO OR 213-D7
WOOD RD
SKAGIT CO WA 161-A4
N WOOD RD
SPOKANE CO WA 114-B1
WOODARD RD
LEWIS CO WA 187-C1
WOODARD BAY RD NE
THURSTON CO WA 180-D5
WOODBROOK RD SW
LAKEWOOD WA 181-C5
WOODBROOK COUNTY PARK RD
COWLITZ CO WA 303-J1
WOODBURN-ESTACADA HWY Rt#-211
CLACKAMAS CO OR 126-A3
CLACKAMAS CO OR 200-C6
CLACKAMAS CO OR 205-D2
ESTACADA OR 200-C6
MARION CO OR 205-B1
MOLALLA OR 126-A3
WOODBURN OR 205-B1
WOODBURN HUBBARD HWY
HUBBARD OR 205-B1
MARION CO OR 205-B1
WOODBURN-MONITOR RD NE
MARION CO OR 205-C2
WOODCOCK RD
CLALLAM CO WA 262-A6
WOODELL LN
UNION CO OR 130-A2
WOODGATE RD
PACIFIC CO WA 186-A5
WOODIN AV
CHELAN WA 236-D3
CHELAN CO WA 236-C3
WOODIN AV Rt#-150
CHELAN WA 236-D3
WOODIN AV U.S.-97
CHELAN WA 236-C3
CHELAN CO WA 236-C3
SE WOODING RD
CLARK CO WA 193-C7
WOODINVILLE DR Rt#-522
BOTHELL WA 171-C6
NE WOODINVILLE-DUVALL RD
DUVALL WA 110-C1
KING CO WA 110-C1
KING CO WA 171-D6
WOODINVILLE WA 171-D6
WOODINVILLE REDMOND RD Rt#-202
KING CO WA 171-D7
REDMOND WA 171-D7
WOODINVILLE WA 171-D7
WOODINVILLE RDMND RD NE Rt#-20
REDMOND WA 171-D7
REDMOND WA 175-D1
WOODINVLLE SNOHOMISH RD Rt#-9
WOODINVILLE WA 171-C6
WOODINVLLE SNOHOMISH RD Rt#-20
WOODINVILLE WA 171-C6
WOODLAND AV
CENTRALIA WA 299-E5
WOODLAND AV E
PIERCE CO WA 182-A4
WOODLAND DR
COOS BAY OR 333-E8
NORTH BEND OR 333-E8
WOODLAND LP
YAMHILL CO OR 198-B4
WOODLAND RD
IDAHO CO ID 123-C2
SNOHOMISH CO WA 168-B4
WOODLAND GRADE RD
IDAHO CO ID 123-C2
WOODLAND PARK RD
JOSEPHINE CO OR 229-A7
WOODLAWN AV
SKAGIT CO WA 259-G13
WOODLAWN AV N
SEATTLE WA 274-A3
WOODLYN RD
WHATCOM CO WA 158-D5
WOODMONT DR S
DES MOINES WA 175-B7
WOODRIDGE PL
BRITISH COLUMBIA BC 159-B5
WOOD RIVER CANAL
KLAMATH CO OR 231-C3
WOODRUFF RD
DOUGLAS CO OR 221-A3
WOODRUFF CREEK RD
JACKSON CO OR 226-C4
WOODS RD
WHITMAN CO WA 249-C6
E WOODS RD
KITSAP CO WA 271-E9
WOODS RD E
KITSAP CO WA 271-E10
WOODS RD NE
DOUGLAS CO WA 112-C2
WOODS RD SE
KITSAP CO WA 271-F14
WOODS CREEK RD
DOUGLAS CO OR 225-B6
MONROE WA 110-C1
SNOHOMISH CO WA 110-C1
WOODS CREEK RD Rt#-131
LEWIS CO WA 118-C2
WOODSIDE DR
COWLITZ CO WA 189-B1
WOODS LAKE RD
SNOHOMISH CO WA 110-C1
SE WOODSTOCK BLVD
PORTLAND OR 318-B5
PORTLAND OR 319-F5
WOODWARD RD
Freeland WA 170-D1
SW WOODWARD RD
JEFFERSON CO OR 212-C1
WOODWARD CREEK RD
SKAMANIA CO WA 194-B6
WOODWORTH DR
HOOD RIVER CO OR 202-C1
WOODY RD
CLARK CO WA 192-D1

E WOOLARD RD
SPOKANE CO WA 114-C1
WOOLRIDGE RD
PITT MEADOWS BC 157-B5
NE WORDEN HILL RD
YAMHILL CO OR 198-C5
WORLINE RD
SKAGIT CO WA 161-A5
NE WORTHINGTON RD
CLARK CO WA 193-B1
WREN ST
DISTRICT OF MISSION BC 94-B3
WRENTHAM MARKET RD
WASCO CO OR 127-B2
WRIGHT AV
RICHLAND WA 340-E13
RICHLAND WA 341-E1
WRIGHT RD SE
THURSTON CO WA 184-C3
W WRIGHT ST
BOISE ID 253-C3
WRIGHT-BLISS RD KPN
PIERCE CO WA 174-A7
WRIGHT CREEK RD
LINCOLN CO OR 206-B6
WTC 8000 RD
DOUGLAS CO OR 140-C2
WULFF LN
DOUGLAS CO OR 221-A4
WYATT DR
LINN CO OR 210-A6
NE WYATT WY
BAINBRIDGE ISLAND WA 271-J2
WYATT WY NW
BAINBRIDGE ISLAND WA 271-J2
WYEAST RD
HOOD RIVER CO OR 195-C7
WYNOOCHEE VALLEY RD
GRAYS HARBOR CO WA 178-D4
WYNOOCHEE WISHKAH RD
GRAYS HARBOR CO WA 178-C5
S WYNOOSKI ST
NEWBERG OR 198-D6
YAMHILL CO OR 198-D6
WYOMING AV
HAYDEN ID 245-A5
KOOTENAI CO ID 245-A5
KOOTENAI CO ID 247-D1
WYOMING ST Rt#-3
DEARY ID 123-B1
LATAH CO ID 123-B1
WYSE RD
WASCO CO OR 196-A7

X

XL RANCH RD
LAKE CO OR 144-A3

Y

Y AV
LA GRANDE OR 130-A2
Y PL
PACIFIC CO WA 186-A4
Y RD
WHATCOM CO WA 102-B1
WHATCOM CO WA 161-B1
Y RD NE
DOUGLAS CO WA 237-A2
Y 1/2 RD NE
DOUGLAS CO WA 237-A2
YACHATS OCEAN RD
YACHATS OR 209-A3
YACHATS RIVER RD
LINCOLN CO OR 209-A3
YACHATS OR 209-A3
YAKIMA
CROOK CO OR 213-D7
E YAKIMA AV
YAKIMA WA 243-C6
N YAKIMA AV
TACOMA WA 292-E3
TACOMA WA 293-F3
S YAKIMA AV
TACOMA WA 293-G6
TACOMA WA 295-G1
W YAKIMA AV
YAKIMA WA 243-B6
YAKIMA VALLEY HWY
GRANGER WA 120-A2
SUNNYSIDE WA 120-A2
YAKIMA CO WA 120-A2
YAKSUM CANYON RD
CHELAN CO WA 238-C3
YALE RD E Rt#-1A
BRITISH COLUMBIA BC 94-C3
CITY OF CHILLIWACK BC 94-C3
YALE RD W Rt#-1A
CITY OF CHILLIWACK BC 94-C3
N YALE ST
SPOKANE CO WA 347-F5
YALE CREEK RD
JACKSON CO OR 234-A5
YAMHILL HWY Rt#-240
NEWBERG OR 198-B5
YAMHILL CO OR 198-B5
YAMHILL RD
YAMHILL CO OR 198-B5
N YAMHILL ST Rt#-47
CARLTON OR 198-B5
YAMPO RD
POLK CO OR 204-B3
YAMHILL CO OR 204-C3
YANK GULCH RD
JACKSON CO OR 234-B4
YAQUINA BAY RD
LINCOLN CO OR 206-B4
NEWPORT OR 206-B4
TOLEDO OR 206-B4
NE YAQUINA HEIGHTS DR
LINCOLN CO OR 206-B4
YARRINGTON RD
UNION CO OR 130-B1
YARROW CENTRAL RD
CITY OF CHILLIWACK BC 102-C1
YARROW POINT RD
YARROW POINT WA 175-C2
YATES RD
CROOK CO OR 213-B6
LEWIS CO WA 184-D7
MASON CO WA 180-D2
YATES ST
CITY OF VICTORIA BC 256-H9
YEAGENS LANDING RD NE
MARION CO OR 198-D6
YEAZELL RD KPS
PIERCE CO WA 181-A3

YELLOW FIR RD
TILLAMOOK CO OR 197-B4
YELLOW JACKET RD
UMATILLA CO OR 129-B2
YELLOWSTONE AV
OSBURN ID 115-C2
W YELLOWSTONE AV
BENTON CO WA 342-F8
E YELLOWSTONE TR
KOOTENAI CO ID 248-B1
YELM AV Rt#-507
YELM WA 118-A1
YELM AV Rt#-510
THURSTON CO WA 118-A1
YELM WA 118-A1
YELM HWY SE
LACEY WA 297-F12
OLYMPIA WA 296-J11
OLYMPIA WA 297-F12
THURSTON CO WA 181-A7
THURSTON CO WA 297-F12
TUMWATER WA 296-J11
NW YEON AV U.S.-30
PORTLAND OR 199-B1
PORTLAND OR 312-A1
YERGEN RD
MARION CO OR 199-A7
YESLER WY
SEATTLE WA 277-J6
SEATTLE WA 278-A6
E YESLER WY
SEATTLE WA 278-C6
YEW AV
OLYMPIA WA 297-B4
SW YEW AV
DESCHUTES CO OR 212-C6
YEW RD
WHATCOM CO WA 258-G12
YEW ST
BELLINGHAM WA 258-G5
KELSO WA 303-C10
WHATCOM CO WA 258-G8
S YEW ST
Finley WA 343-G12
YEW WY
SNOHOMISH CO WA 171-D5
YEW WY Rt#-524
SNOHOMISH CO WA 171-D5
YOAKUM GRADE RD
UMATILLA CO OR 129-B1
YOKEKO DR
SKAGIT CO WA 160-C7
YOKUM RD
DOUGLAS CO OR 225-C3
RIDDLE OR 225-C3
YOLANDA AV
LANE CO OR 331-B3
SPRINGFIELD OR 331-B3
YOMAN RD
PIERCE CO WA 181-A4
YONCALLA-ELKHEAD RD
DOUGLAS CO OR 219-B4
YORK RD
SISKIYOU CO CA 150-A3
SNOHOMISH CO WA 171-C5
UMATILLA CO OR 129-C1
WALLA WALLA CO WA 121-C3
YORK ST
BELLINGHAM WA 258-D6
YORK HILL DR
HOOD RIVER CO OR 195-C6
YOST RD
HARRAH WA 119-C2
YAKIMA CO WA 119-C2
YAKIMA CO WA 120-A2
YOUMANS RD
GRAYS HARBOR CO WA 178-A3
YOUNG AV
DESCHUTES CO OR 212-C7
YOUNG RD
CITY OF CHILLIWACK BC 94-C3
COWLITZ CO WA 189-D3
YOUNG RD NW
THURSTON CO WA 180-C5
YOUNG ST
ABERDEEN WA 178-B7
WOODBURN OR 205-B2
E YOUNG ST
ELMA WA 179-B7
YOUNG GRADE
YAKIMA CO WA 243-A5
YOUNGS RIVER LOOP RD
CLATSOP CO OR 188-C3
CLATSOP CO OR 300-C10
YTURRI BLVD
MALHEUR CO OR 147-A3
YUANCY LAKE RD
BONNER CO ID 244-B2
YUCCA AV
DESCHUTES CO OR 212-C4
NE YUCCA AV
DESCHUTES CO OR 212-D4
DESCHUTES CO OR 213-A4
YUMA ST
EDGEWOOD WA 182-B3
MILTON WA 182-B3
NW YUNGEN RD
WASHINGTON CO OR 192-A6

Z

ZAGER RD
CHELAN CO WA 238-C3
ZANDECKI RD
LEWIS CO WA 187-D2
ZANGLE RD NE
THURSTON CO WA 180-D4
ZARA DR
COOS CO OR 218-B5
ZAZA RD
NEZ PERCE CO ID 123-A3
ZEEK RD
CLARK CO WA 193-C6
ZEITLER RD
LATAH CO ID 249-C6
ZELATCHED POINT RD
JEFFERSON CO WA 170-A7
ZELL RD
WHATCOM CO WA 158-C4
ZEMKE RD
JACKSON CO OR 234-B3
ZENA RD
POLK CO OR 204-B4
ZENA RD NW
POLK CO OR 204-C4
POLK CO OR 322-B2
SW ZENITH
DESCHUTES CO OR 212-C6

ZENKER RD SW
THURSTON CO WA 184-C4
ZIAK-GNAT CREEK RD
CLATSOP CO OR 117-A3
W ZIER RD
YAKIMA CO WA 243-A7
ZIGZAG MOUNTAIN RD
CLACKAMAS CO OR 201-D5
E ZILLAH DR
YAKIMA CO WA 120-A2
ZILLIG RD
COWLITZ CO WA 118-A3
ZIMMER RD
STEVENS CO WA 106-A3
ZIMMERMAN RD
COLUMBIA CO OR 189-B5
YAKIMA CO WA 243-A6
S ZIMMERMAN RD
CLACKAMAS CO OR 205-C1
ZIMMERMAN RANCH RD
MALHEUR CO OR 154-A2
ZIMRI DR
NEWBERG OR 198-D5
YAMHILL CO OR 198-D5
ZIMS RD
ADAMS CO ID 251-A3
SE ZITZELSBERGER RD
CLARK CO WA 193-D7
SKAMANIA CO WA 193-D7
ZUMWALT RD
POLK CO OR 207-A1
WALLOWA CO OR 131-A2
ZYLSTRA RD
ISLAND CO WA 167-B3

#

1-2-SE RD
GRANT CO WA 121-A1
1/2-NE RD
GRANT CO WA 112-C2
SOAP LAKE WA 112-C2
1 AV
DISTRICT OF DELTA BC 101-C1
1ST AV
ALBANY OR 326-C7
1 RD NE
DOUGLAS CO WA 112-C2
1 RD SE U.S.-2
DOUGLAS CO WA 112-C2
1 RD SW
DOUGLAS CO WA 239-D1
1ST AV
ALGONA WA 182-B2
BONNER CO ID 244-A1
DISTRICT OF BURNABY BC 255-D12
KOOTENAI ID 244-A1
POWERS OR 140-B3
RIDDLE OR 225-B3
SEASIDE OR 301-F8
SEATTLE WA 277-H4
SEATTLE WA 278-A6
SHOSHONE CO ID 115-C2
SMELTERVILLE ID 115-C2
VANCOUVER BC 255-D12
1ST AV Rt#-3
BOVILL ID 123-B1
1ST AV Rt#-7
DISTRICT OF MISSION BC 94-B3
1ST AV Rt#-226
SCIO OR 133-C1
1ST AV Rt#-241
MABTON WA 120-B3
YAKIMA CO WA 120-B3
1ST AV Rt#-361
CULVER OR 208-B7
1ST AV Rt#-411
KELSO WA 303-C9
LONGVIEW WA 303-C9
E 1ST AV
JUNCTION CITY OR 210-A6
LANE CO OR 210-A6
RITZVILLE WA 113-C3
E 1ST AV Rt#-28
ODESSA WA 113-B3
N 1ST AV
CHILOQUIN OR 231-D3
KLAMATH CO OR 231-D3
STAYTON OR 133-C1
N 1ST AV Rt#-99
DRAIN OR 219-A3
N 1ST AV U.S.-95
SANDPOINT ID 244-A2
NW 1ST AV
CANBY OR 199-C6
MILTON-FREEWATER OR 121-C3
PAYETTE CO ID 139-B3
S 1ST AV
STAYTON OR 133-C1
S 1ST AV U.S.-95
SANDPOINT ID 244-A2
SE 1ST AV
CANBY OR 199-C6
CLACKAMAS CO OR 199-C6
SW 1ST AV
NEW PLYMOUTH ID 139-B3
PAYETTE CO ID 139-B3
PORTLAND OR 317-F1
W 1ST AV
ADAMS CO WA 113-C3
EUGENE OR 329-H5
JUNCTION CITY OR 210-A6
LANE CO OR 210-A6
RITZVILLE WA 113-C3
SPOKANE WA 348-H9
TOPPENISH WA 120-A2
YAKIMA CO WA 120-A2
W 1ST AV Rt#-21
ODESSA WA 113-B3
W 1ST AV Rt#-28
ODESSA WA 113-B3
1ST AV N
KELSO WA 303-D7
SEATTLE WA 277-H4
1ST AV N U.S.-101
ILWACO WA 186-A6
PACIFIC CO WA 186-A6
1ST AV NE
SEATTLE WA 171-B7
SHORELINE WA 171-B6
1ST AV NW
EPHRATA WA 112-C3
GRANT CO WA 112-C3
1ST AV NW Rt#-411
KELSO WA 303-C7
1ST AV S
BURIEN WA 175-A5
FEDERAL WAY WA 182-A1

INDEX

STREET INDEX

STREET — City State — Page-Grid

1ST AV S
KELSO WA 303-D8
KING CO WA 175-A5
KING CO WA 285-J6
NORMANDY PARK WA 175-A5
SEATTLE WA 278-A7
SEATTLE WA 281-J4
SEATTLE WA 282-A1
SEATTLE WA 285-J2
1ST AV S Rt#-509
BURIEN WA 175-A6
DES MOINES WA 175-A6
NORMANDY PARK WA 175-A6
1ST AV SW
QUINCY WA 112-B3
1ST PL
HERMISTON OR 129-A1
1ST PL W
EVERETT WA 268-B6
1ST RD
POWERS OR 140-B3
1ST ST
ASOTIN WA 250-B5
BANDON OR 220-B6
BREMERTON WA 270-D11
CANYONVILLE OR 225-C3
CITY OF NORTH VANCOUVER BC 254-H5
CLARKSTON WA 250-B5
DESCHUTES CO OR 212-A6
DISTRICT OF NORTH VANCOUV BC 254-H5
HERMISTON OR 129-A1
LINN CO OR 133-C1
LYNDEN WA 102-B1
MORO OR 127-C2
NEWPORT WA 106-C3
OAKLAND OR 219-A7
RICHLAND OR 139-A1
RICHLAND WA 340-F8
RUFUS OR 127-C1
WATERLOO OR 133-C1
WILSON CREEK WA 113-A2
YONCALLA OR 219-A4
1ST ST Rt#-4
SHOSHONE CO ID 115-C2
1ST ST Rt#-6
TILLAMOOK OR 197-B2
1ST ST Rt#-27
OAKESDALE WA 114-C3
1ST ST Rt#-82
ISLAND CITY OR 130-A2
1ST ST Rt#-129
ASOTIN WA 250-B5
1ST ST Rt#-214
SILVERTON OR 205-C4
1ST ST Rt#-237
ISLAND CITY OR 130-A2
UNION CO OR 130-A2
1ST ST Rt#-304
BREMERTON WA 270-J11
1ST ST U.S.-12
LEWISTON ID 250-B4
E 1ST ST
COLFAX WA 122-C1
COQUILLE OR 220-D5
PORT ANGELES WA 261-F4
WEISER ID 139-A2
E 1ST ST Rt#-82
WALLOWA OR 130-C1
E 1ST ST Rt#-99W
NEWBERG OR 198-D5
E 1ST ST Rt#-170
GRANT CO WA 121-A1
WARDEN WA 121-A1
E 1ST ST Rt#-219
NEWBERG OR 198-D5
YAMHILL CO OR 198-D5
E 1ST ST U.S.-101
PORT ANGELES WA 261-F4
N 1ST ST
AUMSVILLE OR 133-C1
AUMSVILLE OR 205-B7
MARION CO OR 205-B7
MOUNT VERNON WA 260-C12
SELAH WA 243-B5
TACOMA WA 293-G4
YAKIMA WA 243-B6
YAKIMA CO WA 243-B5
N 1ST ST Rt#-21
ODESSA WA 113-B3
N 1ST ST Rt#-99
OAKLAND OR 219-A7
N 1ST ST Rt#-214
SILVERTON OR 205-C4
N 1ST ST U.S.-395
HERMISTON OR 129-A1
NE 1ST ST
BELLEVUE WA 175-C2
DESCHUTES CO OR 212-D4
MEDINA WA 175-C2
NW 1ST ST Rt#-3
ENTERPRISE OR 130-C2
WALLOWA CO OR 130-C2
S 1ST ST
MOUNT VERNON WA 260-C13
SHELTON WA 180-A3
SUNNYSIDE WA 120-B2
UNION GAP WA 243-C7
YAKIMA WA 243-C7
S 1ST ST Rt#-823
SELAH WA 243-B5
YAKIMA CO WA 243-B5
SE 1ST ST
CLARK CO WA 193-A6
PENDLETON OR 129-B1
VANCOUVER WA 193-A6
SW 1ST ST
MADRAS OR 208-C5
ONTARIO OR 139-A3
PENDLETON OR 129-B1
W 1ST ST
MEDFORD OR 336-C11
NEWPORT WA 106-C3
PEND OREILLE CO WA 106-C3
PORT ANGELES WA 261-E4
WALLOWA OR 130-B1
WALLOWA CO OR 130-B1
W 1ST ST Rt#-82
WALLOWA OR 130-B1
W 1ST ST Rt#-170
WARDEN WA 121-A1
W 1ST ST Rt#-219
NEWBERG OR 198-D5
1ST ST N
MONTESANO WA 178-D7
1ST ST SW
BANDON OR 220-B6
1ST WY S
FEDERAL WAY WA 182-A1

1 1/2 RD NW
DOUGLAS CO WA 236-A7
1 3-4 RD SW
DOUGLAS CO WA 239-D1
2ND AV
ALBANY OR 326-C7
ASTORIA OR 300-C5
DESCHUTES CO OR 212-A6
SEATTLE WA 277-H4
SEATTLE WA 278-A6
TOWNSHIP OF LANGLEY BC 158-C3
VANCOUVER BC 254-J12
2ND AV Rt#-7
MORTON WA 118-B2
2ND AV Rt#-99
GOLD HILL OR 230-A6
2ND AV Rt#-903
KITTITAS CO WA 240-A1
E 2ND AV
SPOKANE WA 349-B9
NW 2ND AV
MYRTLE CREEK OR 225-C1
S 2ND AV
CHILOQUIN OR 231-D4
EVERETT WA 265-F7
EVERETT WA 269-F1
ROCKAWAY BEACH OR 191-B6
TUMWATER WA 296-G10
W 2ND AV
SPOKANE WA 348-H9
SPOKANE WA 349-A9
2ND AV N
WALLA WALLA WA 345-A7
2ND AV S
WALLA WALLA WA 345-B8
2ND AV S Rt#-52
PAYETTE ID 139-A3
2ND AV SE
SOAP LAKE WA 112-C2
2ND AV SW
SEATTLE WA 285-J2
SOAP LAKE WA 112-C2
2ND AV W
SEATTLE WA 277-H3
2ND AVEX S
SEATTLE WA 278-A6
NW 2ND DR
LINCOLN CITY OR 203-A4
2ND EXT
PIERCE CO WA 182-B6
2 RD NW
DOUGLAS CO WA 236-B7
WATERVILLE WA 236-B7
2 RD S
DOUGLAS CO WA 239-B1
2 RD SE
DOUGLAS CO WA 112-C2
2 RD SW
DOUGLAS CO WA 239-D1
2ND ST
ASOTIN WA 250-B5
CLARKSTON WA 250-B4
CORVALLIS OR 327-G10
HARRAH WA 119-C2
JEFFERSON OR 207-D3
LA GRANDE OR 130-A2
LEBANON OR 133-C1
MARION CO OR 207-D3
NACHES WA 119-C1
NEW WESTMINSTER BC 156-D5
SHERMAN CO OR 127-C3
SNOHOMISH WA 171-D3
YAKIMA CO WA 119-C1
2ND ST Rt#-30
NORTH POWDER OR 130-B3
2ND ST Rt#-34
LEBANON OR 133-C1
2ND ST Rt#-42S
COQUILLE OR 220-D5
2ND ST Rt#-99E
HALSEY OR 210-B2
2ND ST Rt#-100
ILWACO WA 186-A6
PACIFIC CO WA 186-A6
2ND ST Rt#-237
NORTH POWDER OR 130-B3
2ND ST U.S.-20
BENTON CO OR 327-H9
CORVALLIS OR 327-H9
E 2ND ST
COQUILLE OR 220-D5
WARDEN WA 121-A1
N 2ND ST
CENTRAL POINT OR 230-C7
LA GRANDE OR 130-A2
REEDSPORT OR 218-D1
SILVERTON OR 205-C4
NE 2ND ST
BEND OR 332-F6
NW 2ND ST
GRANTS PASS OR 335-E8
MCMINNVILLE OR 198-A7
S 2ND ST
MOUNT VERNON WA 260-C14
S 2ND ST Rt#-900
RENTON WA 175-C5
SE 2ND ST
BEND OR 332-F8
W 2ND ST
THE DALLES OR 196-C7
WARDEN WA 121-A1
WASCO CO OR 196-C7
W 2ND ST Rt#-124
WAITSBURG WA 122-A2
WALLA WALLA CO WA 122-A2
2ND ST E
PIERCE CO WA 182-C2
2ND ST NE
PUYALLUP WA 182-B3
2ND ST S
CANYON CO ID 147-B1
NAMPA ID 147-B1
2ND ST S U.S.-30
NAMPA ID 147-B1
2ND ST SE
DOUGLAS CO WA 239-A5
SNOHOMISH CO WA 110-C1
SNOHOMISH CO WA 171-D2
2ND ST SE U.S.-101
BANDON OR 220-B6
N 2ND ST W
CHEWELAH WA 106-B3
S 2ND ST W
CHEWELAH WA 106-B3
STEVENS CO WA 106-B3
2ND DIVISION DR
PIERCE CO WA 181-C6

2ND DIVISION RANGE RD
PIERCE CO WA 181-B6
2 1/2 RD NW U.S.-2
DOUGLAS CO WA 236-C7
WATERVILLE WA 236-C7
2 1/4 RD NW
DOUGLAS CO WA 236-B7
3 AV
DISTRICT OF DELTA BC 101-C1
3 RD NE
DOUGLAS CO WA 112-C2
3 RD NW
DOUGLAS CO WA 236-B7
3 RD SW
DOUGLAS CO WA 239-B1
3RD AV
ALBANY OR 326-C7
BREWSTER WA 104-B3
KELSO WA 303-C8
LONGVIEW WA 303-C8
MOSIER OR 196-A5
TOWNSHIP OF LANGLEY BC 158-C2
WASCO CO OR 196-A5
3RD AV Rt#-169
BLACK DIAMOND WA 110-C3
3RD AV Rt#-411
LONGVIEW WA 303-C9
3RD AV Rt#-432
LONGVIEW WA 303-B11
E 3RD AV
Finley WA 343-G11
KENNEWICK WA 343-E11
POST FALLS ID 353-J7
POST FALLS ID 354-A7
SPOKANE WA 349-B10
E 3RD AV Rt#-20
COLVILLE WA 106-A2
STEVENS CO WA 106-A2
N 3RD AV
ROCKAWAY BEACH OR 191-B6
STAYTON OR 133-C1
NE 3RD AV
GOLDENDALE WA 127-C1
KLICKITAT CO WA 127-C1
NE 3RD AV Rt#-14B
CAMAS WA 193-B7
CLARK CO WA 193-B7
WASHOUGAL WA 193-B7
NW 3RD AV
KELSO WA 303-C8
S 3RD AV
CLALLAM CO WA 262-D14
EVERETT WA 265-E6
SEQUIM WA 262-D14
UNION GAP WA 243-B7
YAKIMA WA 243-B7
YAKIMA CO WA 243-B7
SW 3RD AV
KELSO WA 303-C8
PAYETTE CO ID 139-A3
W 3RD AV
KENNEWICK WA 343-D11
SPOKANE WA 348-J10
SPOKANE WA 349-A10
3RD AV FI
PIERCE CO WA 181-B2
3RD AV N
KELSO WA 303-D7
PAYETTE ID 139-A3
3RD AV N Rt#-4
KELSO WA 303-D8
3RD AV N Rt#-524
EDMONDS WA 171-A5
3RD AV NE
SNOHOMISH CO WA 168-C5
S 3RD AV NE
POULSBO WA 170-B7
3RD AV NW
SHORELINE WA 171-A6
3RD AV S
KELSO WA 303-C9
WALLA WALLA WA 345-B9
WALLA WALLA CO WA 345-B13
3RD AV S Rt#-524
EDMONDS WA 171-A5
3RD AV SE
QUINCY WA 112-B3
3RD AV SW
EPHRATA WA 112-C3
PACIFIC WA 182-B2
3RD AV W
BREMERTON WA 270-D13
Navy Yard City WA 270-D13
SEATTLE WA 273-G7
SEATTLE WA 277-G1
SE 3RD DR
PENDLETON OR 129-B1
3RD PL
THE DALLES OR 196-C7
3RD ST
ASOTIN CO WA 250-B4
ASTORIA OR 300-C6
CANNON BEACH OR 188-B7
CITY OF NORTH VANCOUVER BC 254-J5
CITY OF NORTH VANCOUVER BC 255-A5
CLARKSTON WA 250-B4
HAINES OR 130-A3
HUBBARD OR 205-B1
LEAVENWORTH WA 238-A1
MANZANITA OR 191-B4
MARYSVILLE WA 171-C1
MCCLEARY WA 179-D6
NACHES WA 119-C1
NEWPORT WA 106-C3
OAKESDALE WA 114-C3
SEDRO-WOOLLEY WA 161-C6
THE DALLES OR 196-C7
TILLAMOOK OR 197-C2
TILLAMOOK CO OR 197-C2
WHEELER OR 191-B4
WHITMAN CO WA 114-C3
YAKIMA CO WA 119-C1
3RD ST Rt#-6
TILLAMOOK OR 197-C2
3RD ST Rt#-42
COQUILLE OR 220-D5
3RD ST Rt#-99E
HARRISBURG OR 210-A5
3RD ST Rt#-99W
LAFAYETTE OR 198-B6
3RD ST Rt#-112
Neah Bay WA 100-B2
3RD ST Rt#-221
DAYTON OR 198-C7
YAMHILL CO OR 198-C7
E 3RD ST
MOSCOW ID 249-D5

E 3RD ST Rt#-8
MOSCOW ID 249-C5
N 3RD ST
ALMIRA WA 237-D7
CENTRAL POINT OR 230-C7
DAYTON WA 122-A2
DUFUR OR 127-B2
JACKSON CO OR 230-C7
OSBURN ID 115-C2
WASCO CO OR 127-B2
NE 3RD ST
MALHEUR CO OR 139-A3
MCMINNVILLE OR 198-A7
ONTARIO OR 139-A3
RENTON WA 175-C5
NE 3RD ST Rt#-500
CLARK CO WA 193-B6
NE 3RD ST U.S.-20
BEND OR 332-F4
NE 3RD ST U.S.-97 Bus
BEND OR 332-F9
NW 3RD ST
GRANTS PASS OR 335-F8
S 3RD ST
ELMA WA 179-B7
S 3RD ST Rt#-23
HARRINGTON WA 113-C2
S 3RD ST Rt#-536
MOUNT VERNON WA 260-C12
S 3RD ST Rt#-900
RENTON WA 175-C5
S 3RD ST U.S.-95
FRUITLAND ID 139-A3
SE 3RD ST
LINCOLN CITY OR 203-A5
ONTARIO OR 139-A3
PENDLETON OR 129-B1
SE 3RD ST U.S.-97 Bus
BEND OR 332-F10
W 3RD ST
KUNA ID 253-A5
W 3RD ST Rt#-8
MOSCOW ID 249-C5
W 3RD ST Rt#-126
CROOK CO OR 213-D5
PRINEVILLE OR 213-D5
3RD ST N
MONTESANO WA 178-D7
3RD ST S
NAMPA ID 147-B1
3RD ST S U.S.-30
NAMPA ID 147-B1
3RD ST SE
MARION CO OR 325-F10
PUYALLUP WA 182-B3
TURNER OR 325-F10
3RD ST SW
AUBURN WA 182-B1
3RD ST W Rt#-99W
CORVALLIS OR 207-A7
CORVALLIS OR 327-G14
3RD ST W U.S.-20
CORVALLIS OR 327-G10
4TH AV
ALBANY OR 326-C8
GOLD HILL OR 230-A6
KITTITAS WA 241-C6
SCIO OR 133-C1
SEATTLE WA 277-J4
SEATTLE WA 278-A5
TOWNSHIP OF LANGLEY BC 158-C2
UNIVERSITY ENDOWMENT LAND BC 156-A4
4TH AV Rt#-234
GOLD HILL OR 230-B6
E 4TH AV
EUGENE OR 330-A5
POST FALLS ID 353-H7
POST FALLS ID 354-A7
SPOKANE WA 349-D10
SPOKANE VALLEY WA 349-J9
SPOKANE VALLEY WA 350-B9
SPOKANE VALLEY WA 351-B9
N 4TH AV
PASCO WA 343-F6
NW 4TH AV
ONTARIO OR 139-A3
S 4TH AV
PASCO WA 343-G7
YAKIMA WA 243-B7
SE 4TH AV
PAYETTE CO ID 139-B3
SW 4TH AV
PORTLAND OR 313-E7
PORTLAND OR 317-E1
SW 4TH AV Rt#-201
ONTARIO OR 139-A3
W 4TH AV
BENTON CO WA 342-G11
KENNEWICK WA 342-F11
KENNEWICK WA 343-B11
SPOKANE WA 348-H10
4TH AV E
OLYMPIA WA 296-J5
OLYMPIA WA 297-A5
4TH AV N
KELSO WA 303-D7
KENT WA 175-B7
KENT WA 291-J7
4TH AV NW
SNOHOMISH CO WA 168-C4
4TH AV S
SEATTLE WA 278-A7
SEATTLE WA 282-A4
4TH AV S Rt#-519
SEATTLE WA 278-A7
SEATTLE WA 282-A1
4TH AV SW
KING CO WA 285-J5
4TH AV W
BOTHELL WA 171-C6
EVERETT WA 268-A6
OLYMPIA WA 296-G5
SNOHOMISH CO WA 171-C4
SNOHOMISH CO WA 268-A6
UNIVERSITY ENDOWMENT LAND BC 156-A4
VANCOUVER BC 156-A4
VANCOUVER BC 254-A12
W 4TH LN
VALLEY CO ID 252-D3
4 RD SW
DOUGLAS CO WA 239-D2
4TH ST
ANACORTES WA 259-H1
GERVAIS OR 205-B2
GRANTS PASS OR 335-E8
HAINES OR 130-A3
LA GRANDE OR 130-A2
LEWISTON ID 250-C4

4TH ST
NANAIMO BC 93-A3
NORTHPORT WA 106-A1
PHOENIX OR 234-B2
SKAGIT CO WA 259-H14
SNOHOMISH CO WA 171-C1
SUMMERVILLE OR 130-A2
4TH ST Rt#-5
SAINT MARIES ID 248-D7
4TH ST Rt#-27
GARFIELD WA 114-C3
4TH ST Rt#-39
KLAMATH FALLS OR 338-D8
4TH ST Rt#-234
GOLD HILL OR 230-B6
4TH ST Rt#-304
BREMERTON WA 270-H11
4TH ST Rt#-528
MARYSVILLE WA 171-C1
SNOHOMISH CO WA 171-C1
4TH ST U.S.-97
GRASS VALLEY OR 127-C2
SHANIKO OR 127-C3
WASCO CO OR 127-C3
E 4TH ST
MEDFORD OR 336-C11
NEWBERG OR 198-D6
THE DALLES OR 196-C7
N 4TH ST
ALMIRA WA 237-D7
COEUR D'ALENE ID 355-E6
COULEE CITY WA 113-A2
DALTON GARDENS ID 355-F4
HAYDEN ID 355-E1
KLAMATH FALLS OR 338-D7
KOOTENAI CO ID 355-E1
MOUNT VERNON WA 260-C11
NE 4TH ST
BELLEVUE WA 175-C5
BEND OR 332-F6
ENTERPRISE OR 130-C2
RENTON WA 175-C5
NW 4TH ST U.S.-26
MADRAS OR 208-C5
S 4TH ST
COLUMBIA CO WA 122-A2
DAYTON WA 122-A2
SE 4TH ST
COLLEGE PLACE WA 344-F10
SW 4TH ST
COLLEGE PLACE WA 344-E10
MALHEUR CO OR 139-A3
ONTARIO OR 139-A3
PENDLETON OR 129-B1
SW 4TH ST U.S.-26
MADRAS OR 208-C5
W 4TH ST
MEDFORD OR 336-B12
THE DALLES OR 196-C7
4TH ST N Rt#-140
LAKE CO OR 152-A2
LAKEVIEW OR 152-A2
4TH ST NE
SNOHOMISH CO WA 171-D2
4TH ST NW
BREWSTER WA 104-B3
OKANOGAN CO WA 104-B3
4TH ST SE
DOUGLAS CO WA 239-B5
East Wenatchee Bench WA 239-A5
4TH ST SW
BANDON OR 220-A6
BREWSTER WA 104-B3
OKANOGAN CO WA 104-B3
4TH ST W Rt#-99W
CORVALLIS OR 327-H9
4TH ST W U.S.-20
CORVALLIS OR 327-H9
4TH DIVISION DR
PIERCE CO WA 181-C6
4TH ST GRADE
THE DALLES OR 196-C7
4 1/2 RD NW
DOUGLAS CO WA 112-B2
5TH AV
ALBANY OR 326-C8
BENTON CO OR 133-B2
MONROE OR 133-B2
OLYMPIA WA 296-G5
RIDDLE OR 225-B3
SEATTLE WA 277-J4
SEATTLE WA 278-A5
5TH AV Rt#-41
SPIRIT LAKE ID 115-A1
5TH AV Rt#-99W
MONROE OR 133-B2
5TH AV Rt#-109
Taholah WA 172-B6
5TH AV U.S.-95
SANDPOINT ID 244-A2
N 5TH AV
YAKIMA WA 243-B6
N 5TH AV U.S.-95
SANDPOINT ID 244-A2
S 5TH AV
YAKIMA WA 243-B6
SE 5TH AV
MALHEUR CO OR 139-A3
ONTARIO OR 139-A3
SW 5TH AV
ONTARIO OR 139-A3
PORTLAND OR 312-E7
PORTLAND OR 316-E1
PORTLAND OR 317-E1
W 5TH AV
EUGENE OR 329-E6
W 5TH AV U.S.-395
COLVILLE WA 106-A2
5TH AV N
KELSO WA 303-D7
SEATTLE WA 277-J2
5TH AV N Rt#-4
KELSO WA 303-D8
5TH AV NE
SEATTLE WA 171-B7
SEATTLE WA 274-B3
SHORELINE WA 171-B6
5TH AV NW
KELSO WA 303-C8
5TH AV S
EDMONDS WA 171-A5
KELSO WA 303-C10
KING CO WA 286-A1
SEATTLE WA 278-A7
SEATTLE WA 286-A2
5TH AV W
EVERETT WA 268-A5

5 RD NE
DOUGLAS CO WA 112-C2
5 RD NW
DOUGLAS CO WA 236-C6
5 RD SW
DOUGLAS CO WA 112-B2
DOUGLAS CO WA 239-D2
5TH ST
ASTORIA OR 300-C6
BAY CITY OR 197-B1
CLARKSTON WA 250-B4
CORVALLIS OR 327-H9
HOQUIAM WA 178-A7
LEWISTON ID 250-B4
MUKILTEO WA 171-B2
MUKILTEO WA 266-E1
MUKILTEO WA 267-E1
OAKLAND OR 219-A7
YAKIMA CO WA 120-B3
5TH ST Rt#-39
KLAMATH FALLS OR 338-E8
5TH ST Rt#-129
ASOTIN CO WA 250-B4
CLARKSTON WA 250-B4
5TH ST Rt#-162
KAMIAH ID 123-C2
5TH ST Rt#-226
LYONS OR 134-A1
MARION CO OR 134-A1
5TH ST U.S.-12
LEWISTON ID 250-B4
5TH ST U.S.-26
MADRAS OR 208-C5
5TH ST U.S.-95
CANYON CO ID 147-A1
WILDER ID 147-A1
N 5TH ST
DUFUR OR 127-B2
LANE CO OR 330-H5
SPRINGFIELD OR 330-H5
N 5TH ST Rt#-238
JACKSONVILLE OR 149-B2
N 5TH ST Rt#-505
LEWIS CO WA 187-D4
TOLEDO WA 187-D4
NE 5TH ST
CLATSKANIE OR 117-B3
DESCHUTES CO OR 212-D4
NW 5TH ST
CLATSKANIE OR 117-B3
COLUMBIA CO OR 117-B3
NW 5TH ST U.S.-97
REDMOND OR 212-D5
S 5TH ST
POMEROY WA 122-B2
SPRINGFIELD OR 330-H7
S 5TH ST Rt#-39
KLAMATH FALLS OR 338-D8
SE 5TH ST
PRINEVILLE OR 213-D5
SW 5TH ST
GRANTS PASS OR 335-E10
SW 5TH ST Rt#-99
CANYONVILLE OR 225-C3
SW 5TH ST U.S.-97
REDMOND OR 212-D5
W 5TH ST
GRANDVIEW WA 120-B3
WALLOWA OR 130-C1
YAKIMA CO WA 120-B3
5TH ST NE
East Wenatchee Bench WA 239-A4
SALEM OR 322-J11
6TH AV
ASOTIN CO WA 250-B5
NEW WESTMINSTER BC 156-D5
SEATTLE WA 278-A6
TACOMA WA 181-C2
TACOMA WA 292-B5
TACOMA WA 293-E5
TOWNSHIP OF LANGLEY BC 158-C2
VANCOUVER BC 254-G12
Vineland WA 250-B5
E 6TH AV
JUNCTION CITY OR 210-A6
E 6TH AV Rt#-21
ODESSA WA 113-B3
E 6TH AV Rt#-99
EUGENE OR 330-A6
N 6TH AV
RIDDLE OR 225-B3
YAKIMA WA 243-B6
NE 6TH AV
SUTHERLIN OR 221-C1
NW 6TH AV
SUTHERLIN OR 221-C1
NW 6TH AV Rt#-14B
CAMAS WA 193-B7
S 6TH AV
TACOMA WA 293-G4
SE 6TH AV Rt#-500
CAMAS WA 193-B7
SW 6TH AV
PORTLAND OR 312-E7
PORTLAND OR 316-E1
W 6TH AV
JUNCTION CITY OR 210-A6
KENNEWICK WA 343-D11
LANE CO OR 210-A6
W 6TH AV Rt#-99
EUGENE OR 329-G6
EUGENE OR 330-A6
6TH AV N
SEATTLE WA 277-J1
6TH AV NE
LACEY WA 297-F4
SEATTLE WA 274-B6
6TH AV NW
SHORELINE WA 171-A6
6TH AV S
SEATTLE WA 282-A3
6TH AV SE
GRANT CO WA 112-C2
LACEY WA 297-F5
SOAP LAKE WA 112-C2
6TH AV SW
GRANT CO WA 112-C2
SOAP LAKE WA 112-C2
NE 6TH DR
PORTLAND OR 309-G2
6 RD SE
DOUGLAS CO WA 112-C2
6TH ST
ANACORTES WA 259-J1
ASTORIA OR 300-C5
BREMERTON WA 270-D10
COLUMBIA CITY OR 192-B1
DESCHUTES CO OR 143-A1

6TH ST — STREET INDEX — 16TH ST 403

STREET / City State / Page-Grid

6TH ST
HARRISBURG OR 210-A5
HOOD RIVER OR 195-D5
LANE CO OR 219-D1
NEW WESTMINSTER BC 156-D5
THE DALLES OR 196-C7
WALLA WALLA CO WA 345-G4
6TH ST Rt#-39
KLAMATH FALLS OR 338-D8
6TH ST Rt#-129
CLARKSTON WA 250-B4
6TH ST Rt#-226
LINN CO OR 134-A1
LYONS OR 134-A1
6TH ST Rt#-310
BREMERTON WA 270-G10
6TH ST U.S.-2
NEWPORT WA 106-C3
6TH ST U.S.-730
UMATILLA OR 129-A1
UMATILLA CO OR 129-A1
E 6TH ST
COLFAX WA 122-C1
MOSCOW ID 249-D5
VANCOUVER WA 305-G5
N 6TH ST
GRANTS PASS OR 335-F6
KLAMATH FALLS OR 338-D7
SAINT HELENS OR 192-B1
N 6TH ST Rt#-52
PAYETTE ID 139-A3
NW 6TH ST U.S.-97
REDMOND OR 212-D5
S 6TH ST
COTTAGE GROVE OR 215-B7
LANE CO OR 215-B7
SUNNYSIDE WA 120-B2
S 6TH ST Rt#-39
KLAMATH FALLS OR 338-E8
SE 6TH ST
CLARK CO WA 193-C6
COLLEGE PLACE WA 344-F11
SW 6TH ST
COLLEGE PLACE WA 344-E11
WALLA WALLA CO WA 344-E11
SW 6TH ST U.S.-97
REDMOND OR 212-D5
W 6TH ST
MOSCOW ID 249-C5
VANCOUVER WA 305-G5
W 6TH ST Rt#-20
REPUBLIC WA 105-B2
6TH ST N
NAMPA ID 147-B1
6TH ST SE
DOUGLAS CO WA 239-A5
East Wenatchee Bench WA 239-A5
6TST ST
DESCHUTES CO OR 212-C7
7 RD NE
DOUGLAS CO WA 112-C1
7 RD NW
DOUGLAS CO WA 236-C5
7TH AV
ALBANY OR 326-B8
CITY OF RICHMOND BC 156-A7
DISTRICT OF MISSION BC 94-B3
KELSO WA 303-B9
LONGVIEW WA 303-B9
E 7TH AV
SPOKANE WA 349-C10
E 7TH AV Rt#-99
EUGENE OR 330-A6
N 7TH AV
YAKIMA WA 243-B6
S 7TH AV
YAKIMA WA 243-B6
SE 7TH AV
PORTLAND OR 313-G6
PORTLAND OR 317-G1
W 7TH AV
SPOKANE WA 348-F10
W 7TH AV Rt#-99
EUGENE OR 329-G6
EUGENE OR 330-A6
7TH AV N
KELSO WA 303-D8
PAYETTE ID 139-A3
PAYETTE CO ID 139-A3
SEATTLE WA 277-J4
7TH AV S
DES MOINES WA 290-A5
KELSO WA 303-D10
SEATTLE WA 278-B7
SEATTLE WA 282-B1
SEATTLE WA 286-A3
7TH AV SE
EVERETT WA 268-C7
7TH AV SW
KELSO WA 303-C8
OLYMPIA WA 296-C5
THURSTON CO WA 296-C5
7TH ST
GOLD HILL OR 230-B6
HARRISBURG OR 210-A5
NEHALEM OR 191-B4
OREGON CITY OR 199-D5
PROSSER WA 120-B3
7TH ST Rt#-43
OREGON CITY OR 199-D4
WEST LINN OR 199-D4
7TH ST Rt#-506
VADER WA 187-B5
7TH ST U.S.-101
NEHALEM OR 191-B4
7TH ST U.S.-95
WEISER ID 139-A2
E 7TH ST
PRINEVILLE OR 213-D5
E 7TH ST Rt#-19
FOSSIL OR 128-A3
E 7TH ST U.S.-95
WEISER ID 139-A2
N 7TH ST
BREWSTER WA 104-B3
COEUR D'ALENE ID 355-F8
COOS BAY OR 333-G10
SPRINGFIELD OR 330-H6
N 7TH ST Rt#-52
PAYETTE ID 139-A3
S 7TH ST
COOS BAY OR 333-G10
SPRINGFIELD OR 330-H7
TACOMA WA 293-H5
S 7TH ST Rt#-52
PAYETTE ID 139-A3
S 7TH ST U.S.-95
PAYETTE ID 139-A3

SE 7TH ST
WARRENTON OR 188-B2
7TH ST SW
BANDON OR 220-A6
7TH ST W
RAINIER OR 189-B4
7 1/2 RD NW
DOUGLAS CO WA 236-B5
7 3/4 RD NW
DOUGLAS CO WA 236-A5
8TH AV
CITY OF SURREY BC 158-B2
CITY OF WHITE ROCK BC 158-B2
LONGVIEW WA 303-B10
NEW WESTMINSTER BC 156-D5
TOWNSHIP OF LANGLEY BC 158-C2
8TH AV Rt#-162
NEZPERCE ID 123-C2
E 8TH AV
KENNEWICK WA 343-F12
SPOKANE WA 349-G10
SPOKANE CO WA 351-G9
SPOKANE VALLEY WA 349-H10
SPOKANE VALLEY WA 350-J9
SPOKANE VALLEY WA 351-B9
N 8TH AV Rt#-82
ELGIN OR 130-A1
NE 8TH AV
MILTON-FREEWATER OR 121-C3
NW 8TH AV
MILTON-FREEWATER OR 121-C3
ONTARIO OR 139-A3
S 8TH AV Rt#-82
ELGIN OR 130-A1
UNION CO OR 130-A1
SW 8TH AV
MILTON-FREEWATER OR 121-C3
W 8TH AV
SPOKANE WA 348-J10
SPOKANE WA 349-A10
8TH AV E
NEW WESTMINSTER BC 156-D5
PIERCE CO WA 118-A1
PIERCE CO WA 181-D7
8TH AV N Rt#-125
WALLA WALLA WA 344-J8
8TH AV NW
SEATTLE WA 273-G2
SHORELINE WA 171-A6
8TH AV S
BURIEN WA 288-A2
KING CO WA 286-A5
KING CO WA 288-A2
PIERCE CO WA 118-A1
PIERCE CO WA 181-D7
SEATAC WA 288-A4
SEATTLE WA 286-A5
8TH AV SW
SEATTLE WA 285-H4
8 RD NW
DOUGLAS CO WA 236-B5
8 RD SE
DOUGLAS CO WA 112-C2
8 RD SW
DOUGLAS CO WA 239-B3
8TH ST
ASHLAND OR 337-D8
ASTORIA OR 300-C5
LEWISTON ID 250-B4
NEW WESTMINSTER BC 156-D5
PIERCE CO WA 181-B5
8TH ST Rt#-42
MYRTLE POINT OR 140-B2
8TH ST U.S.-30
ASTORIA OR 300-C5
E 8TH ST
MEDFORD OR 336-D12
PORT ANGELES WA 261-E5
E 8TH ST Rt#-82
JOSEPH OR 130-C2
WALLOWA CO OR 130-C2
N 8TH ST
BOISE ID 253-C2
MOUNT VERNON WA 260-C12
PAYETTE ID 139-A3
NE 8TH ST
BELLEVUE WA 175-C2
BEND OR 332-G6
GRANTS PASS OR 335-F8
SAMMAMISH WA 176-A2
S 8TH ST
AUMSVILLE OR 133-C1
BOISE ID 253-C3
JEFFERSON CO WA 263-C7
PAYETTE ID 139-A3
SE 8TH ST
PENDLETON OR 129-B1
W 8TH ST
MEDFORD OR 336-B12
PORT ANGELES WA 261-D4
VANCOUVER WA 305-F5
8TH ST E
EDGEWOOD WA 182-B2
PACIFIC WA 182-B2
SUMNER WA 182-B2
8TH ST NE
East Wenatchee Bench WA 239-A4
8TH ST NW
SALEM OR 322-F12
8TH ST SE
DOUGLAS CO WA 239-B5
East Wenatchee Bench WA 239-A5
SNOHOMISH CO WA 171-D2
8TH ST SW
BANDON OR 220-A6
8 1/2 RD NW
DOUGLAS CO WA 236-C5
8-10-NE RD
GRANT CO WA 242-B1
9 RD NW
DOUGLAS CO WA 236-D5
9 RD SW
DOUGLAS CO WA 239-B3
9TH AV
ALBANY OR 326-D8
LONGVIEW WA 303-B8
SEATTLE WA 277-J4
N 9TH AV
PASCO WA 343-F6
SE 9TH AV
MILTON-FREEWATER OR 121-C3
W 9TH AV
SPOKANE WA 348-J10
SPOKANE WA 349-A10
9TH AV FI
PIERCE CO WA 181-B2
9TH AV N
SEATTLE WA 277-J4

9TH AV N Rt#-524
EDMONDS WA 171-A5
9TH AV S
EDMONDS WA 171-A5
9TH AV S Rt#-125
WALLA WALLA WA 344-J8
WALLA WALLA WA 345-A9
9TH AV SW
OLYMPIA WA 296-E5
SEATTLE WA 285-H3
9TH ST
CORVALLIS OR 327-H6
FLORENCE OR 214-B3
HARRISBURG OR 210-A5
HOOD RIVER OR 195-D5
JEFFERSON CO OR 208-B6
ONTARIO OR 139-A3
PORT ORFORD OR 224-A6
9TH ST Rt#-57
BONNER CO ID 107-A3
PRIEST RIVER ID 107-A3
9TH ST Rt#-225
BENTON CITY WA 120-C3
BENTON CO WA 120-C3
E 9TH ST
THE DALLES OR 196-C7
N 9TH ST
BOISE ID 253-C3
COEUR D'ALENE ID 355-F9
TACOMA WA 181-C2
NE 9TH ST
BEND OR 332-G8
CLARK CO WA 193-C6
DESCHUTES CO OR 212-D3
GRANTS PASS OR 335-G8
JOSEPHINE CO OR 335-G8
REDMOND OR 212-D5
Terrebonne OR 212-D3
S 9TH ST
BOISE ID 253-C3
SE 9TH ST
BEND OR 332-G8
9TH ST E
PIERCE CO WA 182-C2
9TH ST NE
East Wenatchee Bench WA 239-A4
9TH ST NW
SALEM OR 322-F12
9TH ST S
LAKE CO OR 152-A2
LAKEVIEW OR 152-A2
9TH ST SW
PUYALLUP WA 182-B4
9 1-2 RD SW
DOUGLAS CO WA 239-B3
10TH AV
DISTRICT OF BURNABY BC 156-A4
NEW WESTMINSTER BC 156-A4
TOWNSHIP OF LANGLEY BC 158-D2
VANCOUVER BC 156-A4
VANCOUVER BC 254-A12
10TH AV Rt#-99A
DISTRICT OF BURNABY BC 156-D5
NEW WESTMINSTER BC 156-D5
E 10TH AV
Finley WA 343-F12
KENNEWICK WA 343-F12
SPOKANE WA 349-B11
N 10TH AV
ELGIN OR 130-A1
PASCO WA 343-F7
STAYTON OR 133-C1
NE 10TH AV
CLARK CO WA 192-C3
PAYETTE ID 139-A3
PAYETTE CO ID 139-A3
RIDGEFIELD WA 192-C3
NE 10TH AV Rt#-502
CLARK CO WA 192-C3
NW 10TH AV
PORTLAND OR 313-E5
NW 10TH AV Rt#-503
BATTLE GROUND WA 193-A3
S 10TH AV
CALDWELL ID 147-B1
CANYON CO ID 147-B1
CORNELIUS OR 198-C1
PASCO WA 343-F8
S 10TH AV Rt#-397
PASCO WA 343-F9
SE 10TH AV
HILLSBORO OR 198-D1
SE 10TH AV Rt#-8
HILLSBORO OR 198-D1
SW 10TH AV
PORTLAND OR 312-E6
PORTLAND OR 313-E5
SW 10TH AV Rt#-503
BATTLE GROUND WA 193-A3
CLARK CO WA 193-A3
W 10TH AV
BENTON CO WA 341-J12
BENTON CO WA 342-B12
KENNEWICK WA 341-J12
KENNEWICK WA 342-A12
KENNEWICK WA 343-C12
10TH AV E
DISTRICT OF BURNABY BC 156-D5
NEW WESTMINSTER BC 156-D5
SEATTLE WA 278-B3
10TH AV NE
SHORELINE WA 171-B7
10TH AV SW
FEDERAL WAY WA 182-A1
QUINCY WA 112-B3
10TH AV W
SEATTLE WA 277-F2
10 RD NW
DOUGLAS CO WA 236-D5
10 RD SW
DOUGLAS CO WA 239-B3
10TH ST
CORVALLIS OR 327-G8
EVERETT WA 171-C1
NANAIMO BC 93-A3
SNOHOMISH WA 171-D3
10TH ST Rt#-173
BRIDGEPORT WA 112-C1
10TH ST U.S.-30
BAKER CITY OR 138-B1
E 10TH ST
MEDFORD OR 336-D12
THE DALLES OR 196-C7
N 10TH ST
CENTRAL POINT OR 230-C7
KLAMATH FALLS OR 338-D7
SPRINGFIELD OR 330-J6

NE 10TH ST
BEND OR 332-G7
GRANTS PASS OR 335-G7
JOSEPHINE CO OR 335-G7
NW 10TH ST
DESCHUTES CO OR 212-D3
PENDLETON OR 129-B1
Terrebonne OR 212-D4
NW 10TH ST U.S.-97
Terrebonne OR 212-D3
S 10TH ST
COTTAGE GROVE OR 215-B7
SPRINGFIELD OR 330-J7
SE 10TH ST
PENDLETON OR 129-B1
VANCOUVER WA 307-H7
SE 10TH ST Rt#-37
PENDLETON OR 129-B1
SW 10TH ST
PENDLETON OR 129-B1
W 10TH ST
MEDFORD OR 336-D12
PRINEVILLE OR 213-D5
THE DALLES OR 196-C7
WASCO CO OR 196-C7
10TH ST NE
DOUGLAS CO WA 239-A4
EAST WENATCHEE WA 239-A4
East Wenatchee Bench WA 239-A4
10TH ST SE
DOUGLAS CO WA 239-B5
10 5 SE RD
GRANT CO WA 242-C7
11TH AV
BREMERTON WA 270-F10
LEWISTON ID 250-B4
11TH AV Rt#-11
DISTRICT OF MISSION BC 94-B3
11TH AV U.S.-30
NAMPA ID 147-B1
E 11TH AV
EUGENE OR 330-A7
NE 11TH AV
PORTLAND OR 313-H4
NW 11TH AV
CLARK CO WA 192-C2
PORTLAND OR 313-E5
RIDGEFIELD WA 192-C2
SE 11TH AV
PORTLAND OR 313-H6
PORTLAND OR 317-H1
SW 11TH AV
PORTLAND OR 312-E6
PORTLAND OR 313-E6
W 11TH AV
EUGENE OR 329-H7
EUGENE OR 330-A7
W 11TH AV Rt#-126
EUGENE OR 215-A2
EUGENE OR 329-B6
LANE CO OR 215-A2
11TH AV FI
PIERCE CO WA 181-B3
11TH AV N U.S.-30
NAMPA ID 147-B1
11TH AV NE
SEATTLE WA 274-B5
SNOHOMISH CO WA 168-C6
THURSTON CO WA 297-B4
11TH AV NW
OLYMPIA WA 296-B3
THURSTON CO WA 296-A3
11TH ST
BELLINGHAM WA 258-B10
BREMERTON WA 270-G10
CORVALLIS OR 327-F10
DISTRICT OF WEST VANCOUVE BC 254-D4
MONTAGUE CA 150-A3
E 11TH ST
BREMERTON WA 271-A10
TACOMA WA 182-A2
TACOMA WA 293-J5
N 11TH ST
AUMSVILLE OR 133-C1
COEUR D'ALENE ID 355-G11
NE 11TH ST
DESCHUTES CO OR 212-D4
REDMOND OR 212-D5
NW 11TH ST Rt#-207
HERMISTON OR 129-A1
S 11TH ST
COEUR D'ALENE ID 355-G12
TACOMA WA 293-F5
SW 11TH ST Rt#-207
HERMISTON OR 129-A1
UMATILLA CO OR 129-A1
W 11TH ST
KETTLE FALLS WA 106-A2
STEVENS CO WA 106-A2
WARDEN WA 121-A1
11TH ST NE
EAST WENATCHEE WA 239-A4
12 AV
DISTRICT OF DELTA BC 101-C1
12TH AV
ALBANY OR 326-B9
CLATSOP CO OR 301-G7
SEASIDE OR 301-G7
SEATTLE WA 278-B6
TOWNSHIP OF LANGLEY BC 158-D2
VANCOUVER BC 254-J13
VANCOUVER BC 255-A13
E 12TH AV
SPOKANE WA 349-F11
NE 12TH AV
PORTLAND OR 313-H5
SE 12TH AV
PORTLAND OR 313-H6
PORTLAND OR 317-H1
SW 12TH AV
PORTLAND OR 312-E6
W 12TH AV
AIRWAY HEIGHTS WA 246-A4
12TH AV E
SEATTLE WA 278-B4
VANCOUVER BC 254-H13
12TH AV NE
SEATTLE WA 274-C4
THURSTON CO WA 297-B4
12TH AV S
SEATTLE WA 278-B7
WALLA WALLA WA 344-J8
12TH AV S Rt#-45
NAMPA ID 147-B1
12TH AV W
VANCOUVER BC 254-C13
12 RD NE
DOUGLAS CO WA 112-C2

12 RD NE U.S.-2
DOUGLAS CO WA 112-C2
12 RD SW
DOUGLAS CO WA 239-C4
12TH ST
BELLINGHAM WA 258-B10
HOOD RIVER OR 195-D5
LEBANON OR 133-C1
LINN CO OR 133-C1
NEW WESTMINSTER BC 156-D5
TILLAMOOK OR 197-C2
TILLAMOOK CO OR 197-C2
12TH ST Rt#-11
BELLINGHAM WA 258-B11
12TH ST Rt#-20
ANACORTES WA 259-F2
E 12TH ST
MEDFORD OR 336-D12
NE 12TH ST
BELLEVUE WA 175-C2
BEND OR 332-G6
CLYDE HILL WA 175-C2
MEDINA WA 175-C2
NEWPORT OR 206-B4
RENTON WA 175-C4
NW 12TH ST
LINCOLN CITY OR 203-A4
NEWPORT OR 206-A4
S 12TH ST
TACOMA WA 292-A6
TACOMA WA 293-E6
SE 12TH ST
COLLEGE PLACE WA 344-F11
PENDLETON OR 129-B1
WALLA WALLA CO WA 344-G11
SW 12TH ST
COLLEGE PLACE WA 344-E11
WALLA WALLA CO WA 344-E11
12TH ST E
PIERCE CO WA 182-C2
12TH ST N U.S.-26
MALHEUR CO OR 139-A3
VALE OR 139-A3
12TH ST NE
SALEM OR 322-J12
12TH ST SE
DOUGLAS CO WA 239-B5
SALEM OR 322-J14
SALEM OR 324-H5
12TH ST SE Rt#-22
SALEM OR 322-J14
12TH AVENUE RD Rt#-45
CANYON CO ID 147-B1
NAMPA ID 147-B1
OWYHEE CO ID 147-B1
13TH AV
TOWNSHIP OF LANGLEY BC 158-D2
E 13TH AV
EUGENE OR 330-A7
SPOKANE WA 349-F11
NE 13TH AV
PORTLAND OR 313-H4
SE 13TH AV
PORTLAND OR 317-H6
SW 13TH AV
PORTLAND OR 312-E6
W 13TH AV
EUGENE OR 329-G7
EUGENE OR 330-B7
13TH AV N Rt#-125
WALLA WALLA WA 344-J5
WALLA WALLA CO WA 344-J5
13TH AV S
SEATTLE WA 282-B7
13TH AV W
SNOHOMISH CO WA 171-B5
13 RD NE
DOUGLAS CO WA 113-A1
13TH ST
ANACORTES WA 259-H2
ASOTIN CO WA 250-B4
CITY OF NORTH VANCOUVER BC 255-B5
CLARKSTON WA 250-B4
DESCHUTES CO OR 212-D3
HOOD RIVER OR 195-D5
SNOHOMISH WA 171-D3
Vineland WA 250-B5
E 13TH ST
WASCO CO OR 196-D7
N 13TH ST
BOISE ID 253-C2
NE 13TH ST
DESCHUTES CO OR 212-D5
S 13TH ST
MOUNT VERNON WA 260-D13
TACOMA WA 293-G5
SW 13TH ST
PENDLETON OR 129-B1
W 13TH ST
THE DALLES OR 196-C7
WASCO CO OR 196-C7
13TH ST NE
SALEM OR 322-J13
SALEM OR 323-A13
14TH AV
OLYMPIA WA 296-H6
SEATTLE WA 278-C6
TOWNSHIP OF LANGLEY BC 158-D2
E 14TH AV
ELLENSBURG WA 241-B5
SPOKANE WA 349-D11
N 14TH AV
PASCO WA 343-E6
NE 14TH AV Rt#-500
CAMAS WA 193-B7
NW 14TH AV
PORTLAND OR 312-E4
W 14TH AV
SPOKANE WA 348-H11
SPOKANE WA 349-A11
W 14TH AV U.S.-2
AIRWAY HEIGHTS WA 246-A4
SPOKANE CO WA 246-A4
14TH AV NW
OLYMPIA WA 296-C3
PIERCE CO WA 174-C7
PIERCE CO WA 181-C1
THURSTON CO WA 296-C3
14TH AV S
KING CO WA 286-B3
SEATTLE WA 278-C7
SEATTLE WA 286-B3
14 RD NE
DOUGLAS CO WA 112-C1
14 RD NE Rt#-172
DOUGLAS CO WA 112-C1
14 RD NW Rt#-172
DOUGLAS CO WA 112-B1

14TH ST
LEWISTON ID 250-C4
PORT TOWNSEND WA 263-D5
REEDSPORT OR 218-C1
E 14TH ST
BREMERTON WA 271-A10
N 14TH ST
SPRINGFIELD OR 330-J7
NE 14TH ST
CLARK CO WA 193-B6
NW 14TH ST
BEND OR 332-C7
PENDLETON OR 129-B1
SE 14TH ST
VANCOUVER WA 193-C7
SW 14TH ST
BEND OR 332-C8
14TH ST NE
SALEM OR 322-J13
SALEM OR 323-A13
14TH ST SE
SALEM OR 322-J14
SALEM OR 324-J1
15 RD NE
DOUGLAS CO WA 112-C1
15TH AV
LONGVIEW WA 303-A8
E 15TH AV
POST FALLS ID 353-H5
NE 15TH AV
PORTLAND OR 309-H7
PORTLAND OR 313-H1
W 15TH AV
ELLENSBURG WA 241-B5
KITTITAS CO WA 241-B5
POST FALLS ID 353-H5
15TH AV E
SEATTLE WA 278-C4
15TH AV NE
LACEY WA 297-F3
LAKE FOREST PARK WA 171-B7
SEATTLE WA 171-B7
SEATTLE WA 274-C2
SHORELINE WA 171-B7
SNOHOMISH CO WA 168-C4
THURSTON CO WA 297-F3
15TH AV NW
SEATTLE WA 273-F2
SHORELINE WA 171-A6
15TH AV S
SEATTLE WA 282-B3
15TH AV SW
EPHRATA WA 112-C3
15TH AV W
SEATTLE WA 273-F7
SEATTLE WA 277-F2
15TH ST
ASOTIN CO WA 250-B4
BREMERTON WA 270-G9
CLARKSTON WA 250-B4
DISTRICT OF WEST VANCOUVE BC 254-D3
OROVILLE WA 104-C1
WASHOUGAL WA 193-C7
E 15TH ST
TACOMA WA 293-J6
N 15TH ST
BOISE ID 253-C2
COEUR D'ALENE ID 355-G8
DALTON GARDENS ID 355-G2
KOOTENAI CO ID 355-G2
S 15TH ST
BOISE ID 253-C2
POMEROY WA 122-B2
SE 15TH ST
BEND OR 332-H10
DESCHUTES CO OR 332-H12
SW 15TH ST
PENDLETON OR 129-B1
W 15TH ST Rt#-501
VANCOUVER WA 305-F4
15TH ST NE
AUBURN WA 182-C1
15TH ST NW
AUBURN WA 182-B1
East Wenatchee Bench WA 239-A4
15TH ST NW U.S.-2
East Wenatchee Bench WA 239-A4
15TH ST SW
AUBURN WA 182-B1
16TH AV
ASOTIN CO WA 250-B4
CITY OF SURREY BC 158-A2
CITY OF WHITE ROCK BC 158-A2
LEWISTON ID 250-B4
LONGVIEW WA 303-A9
TOWNSHIP OF LANGLEY BC 102-B1
TOWNSHIP OF LANGLEY BC 158-C2
E 16TH AV
SPOKANE VALLEY WA 349-H11
SPOKANE VALLEY WA 350-H10
SPOKANE VALLEY WA 351-A10
N 16TH AV
YAKIMA WA 243-B6
NE 16TH AV
PORTLAND OR 313-H4
S 16TH AV
YAKIMA WA 243-B7
YAKIMA CO WA 243-B7
W 16TH AV
SPOKANE VALLEY WA 349-J11
16TH AV NW
SNOHOMISH CO WA 168-C6
16TH AV S
DES MOINES WA 175-B7
DES MOINES WA 290-B7
FEDERAL WAY WA 175-B7
KING CO WA 286-B2
SEATTLE WA 286-B3
TUKWILA WA 286-B2
16TH AV S Rt#-99
FEDERAL WAY WA 182-B1
16TH AV S Rt#-161
FEDERAL WAY WA 182-B1
16TH AV SW
KING CO WA 285-G6
SEATTLE WA 285-G6
16TH AV W
UNIVERSITY ENDOWMENT LAND BC 156-A4
VANCOUVER BC 254-A13
NE 16TH DR
PORTLAND OR 313-H4
E 16TH PL
THE DALLES OR 196-C7
WASCO CO OR 196-C7
16 RD NE
DOUGLAS CO WA 112-C1
16TH ST
ASTORIA OR 300-D6

INDEX

404 16TH ST STREET INDEX 41ST DIVISION DR

STREET
City State Page-Grid

16TH ST
EVERETT WA 264-E1
EVERETT WA 265-F1
HOQUIAM WA 178-A7
LEWISTON ID 250-C5
NORTH BEND OR 333-E5
E 16TH ST
KOOTENAI CO ID 353-J5
KOOTENAI CO ID 354-B5
POST FALLS ID 353-J5
POST FALLS ID 354-B5
N 16TH ST
BOISE ID 253-C2
N 16TH ST U.S.-95
PAYETTE ID 139-A3
NE 16TH ST
FRUITLAND ID 139-A3
PAYETTE CO ID 139-A3
NE 16TH ST Rt#-30
FRUITLAND ID 139-A3
PAYETTE CO ID 139-A3
S 16TH ST
BOISE ID 253-C2
MOUNT VERNON WA 260-D13
SUNNYSIDE WA 120-B2
S 16TH ST U.S.-95
PAYETTE ID 139-A3
SE 16TH ST
BELLEVUE WA 175-D3
SW 16TH ST
RENTON WA 175-C5
W 16TH ST
VANCOUVER WA 304-E4
VANCOUVER WA 305-E4
16TH ST E
PIERCE CO WA 182-C2
16TH ST W
CITY OF NORTH VANCOUVER BC 254-J4
17TH AV
LONGVIEW WA 303-A9
SE 17TH AV
CLACKAMAS CO OR 321-H1
MILWAUKIE OR 317-H7
MILWAUKIE OR 321-H1
PORTLAND OR 317-H2
PORTLAND OR 317-H7
PORTLAND OR 321-H1
17TH AV NW
THURSTON CO WA 296-A3
17TH AV NW Rt#-900
ISSAQUAH WA 175-D3
17TH ST
ASOTIN CO WA 250-C4
BAKER CITY OR 138-B1
LEWISTON ID 250-C4
NORTH BEND OR 333-E6
WASHOUGAL WA 193-C7
17TH ST Rt#-173
BRIDGEPORT WA 112-C1
NE 17TH ST
DESCHUTES CO OR 212-D4
SE 17TH ST
PENDLETON OR 129-B1
SW 17TH ST Rt#-37
PENDLETON OR 129-B1
17TH ST NE
SALEM OR 323-A12
17TH ST SE
SALEM OR 323-A14
N 18 AV
PASCO WA 343-E6
18TH AV
LONGVIEW WA 302-J10
LONGVIEW WA 303-A9
TOWNSHIP OF LANGLEY BC 158-C2
E 18TH AV
EUGENE OR 330-B8
SPOKANE WA 349-B12
N 18TH AV
PASCO WA 343-E6
NW 18TH AV
PORTLAND OR 312-E5
SW 18TH AV
MALHEUR CO OR 139-A3
W 18TH AV
EUGENE OR 329-D7
EUGENE OR 330-A8
JUNCTION CITY OR 210-A5
LANE CO OR 210-A5
18TH AV N
KELSO WA 303-E7
18TH AV SE
OLYMPIA WA 297-C7
18TH ST
LEWISTON ID 250-C4
18TH ST U.S.-12
LEWISTON ID 250-C4
E 18TH ST
THE DALLES OR 196-C7
VANCOUVER WA 305-G4
VANCOUVER WA 306-B4
WASCO CO OR 196-C7
N 18TH ST
MOUNT VERNON WA 260-E11
SPRINGFIELD OR 331-A6
NE 18TH ST
VANCOUVER WA 193-A6
VANCOUVER WA 306-E4
VANCOUVER WA 307-J4
S 18TH ST
MOUNT VERNON WA 260-E13
POMEROY WA 122-B2
YAKIMA WA 243-C7
S 18TH ST Rt#-52
PAYETTE ID 139-A3
W 18TH ST
VANCOUVER WA 305-G4
19TH AV
TOWNSHIP OF LANGLEY BC 158-D2
19TH AV Rt#-8
FOREST GROVE OR 198-B1
E 19TH AV
Finley WA 343-E13
KENNEWICK WA 343-E13
NW 19TH AV
PORTLAND OR 312-D5
W 19TH AV
KENNEWICK WA 342-H13
KENNEWICK WA 343-C13
19TH AV E
SEATTLE WA 278-C1
19TH AV NE
SNOHOMISH CO WA 168-C4
19TH AV SE
BOTHELL WA 171-C6
19TH AV SE Rt#-527
EVERETT WA 171-C4
EVERETT WA 268-D6
19TH ST
BENTON CO OR 133-B1
CITY OF NORTH VANCOUVER BC 254-H4
CITY OF NORTH VANCOUVER BC 255-C4
DISTRICT OF BURNABY BC 156-D5
DISTRICT OF NORTH VANCOUV BC 254-H4
EVERETT WA 264-E2
EVERETT WA 265-E2
LANE CO OR 331-A5
PHILOMATH OR 133-B1
PORT TOWNSEND WA 263-F5
SPRINGFIELD OR 331-A5
E 19TH ST
THE DALLES OR 196-C7
NE 19TH ST
CLARK CO WA 193-B6
NW 19TH ST
DESCHUTES CO OR 212-D4
REDMOND OR 212-D5
Terrebonne OR 212-D4
S 19TH ST
FIRCREST WA 181-C2
FIRCREST WA 292-A6
TACOMA WA 181-C2
TACOMA WA 292-A6
TACOMA WA 293-F6
UNIVERSITY PLACE WA 181-C2
SW 19TH ST
REDMOND OR 212-D5
W 19TH ST
KENNEWICK WA 342-J13
19TH ST NE
East Wenatchee Bench WA 239-A4
19TH ST NW
East Wenatchee Bench WA 239-A4
19TH WY Rt#-8
FOREST GROVE OR 198-C1
20TH AV
CITY OF SURREY BC 158-A2
TOWNSHIP OF LANGLEY BC 158-D2
N 20TH AV
PASCO WA 343-D4
NE 20TH AV
CLARK CO WA 192-C4
PORTLAND OR 313-J5
NW 20TH AV
MALHEUR CO OR 139-A3
S 20TH AV
PASCO WA 343-D8
SE 20TH AV
PORTLAND OR 313-J7
PORTLAND OR 317-J1
SW 20TH AV
BATTLE GROUND WA 192-D3
CLARK CO WA 192-D3
20TH AV NE
SEATTLE WA 274-C1
20TH AV NW
OLYMPIA WA 296-F2
20TH AV W
EVERETT WA 267-H4
SEATTLE WA 273-E7
20 RD NE
DOUGLAS CO WA 112-C1
20TH ST
BELLINGHAM WA 258-C10
DISTRICT OF NORTH VANCOUV BC 255-E4
LA GRANDE OR 130-A2
NEW WESTMINSTER BC 156-D5
NE 20TH ST
BELLEVUE WA 175-D2
SE 20TH ST
CLARK CO WA 193-C7
SAMMAMISH WA 175-D3
SW 20TH ST
PENDLETON OR 129-B1
W 20TH ST
VANCOUVER WA 304-E4
20TH ST E
FIFE WA 182-A3
20TH ST KPN
PIERCE CO WA 181-A2
20TH ST NE
LAKE STEVENS WA 110-C1
LAKE STEVENS WA 171-D1
20TH ST SE
SNOHOMISH CO WA 171-D2
SNOHOMISH CO WA 265-J4
E 21 HWY
ADA CO ID 253-D3
BOISE ID 253-D3
21ST AV
LONGVIEW WA 302-J8
LONGVIEW WA 303-A8
TOWNSHIP OF LANGLEY BC 158-D2
E 21ST AV
SPOKANE WA 349-B12
NE 21ST AV
PORTLAND OR 313-J4
NW 21ST AV
CLARK CO WA 192-C5
SE 21ST AV
PORTLAND OR 317-J1
W 21ST AV
SPOKANE WA 348-J12
21ST AV SW
FEDERAL WAY WA 182-A1
OLYMPIA WA 296-E7
TUMWATER WA 296-E7
21ST ST
BELLINGHAM WA 258-C10
DISTRICT OF WEST VANCOUVE BC 254-C3
LEWISTON ID 250-C4
N 21ST ST
TACOMA WA 292-B3
TACOMA WA 293-E3
NW 21ST ST
LINCOLN CITY OR 203-A4
21ST ST NE
SALEM OR 323-B12
21ST ST SE
AUBURN WA 182-C2
22ND AV
GRANT CO WA 242-C2
OLYMPIA WA 297-A7
VANCOUVER BC 255-C14
N 22ND AV
PASCO WA 343-D5
NE 22ND AV
CLARK CO WA 192-C3
SE 22ND AV
MILWAUKIE OR 321-J3
22ND AV E
PIERCE CO WA 182-A6
SEATTLE WA 278-D1
22ND ST
ANACORTES WA 259-H3
DISTRICT OF NORTH VANCOUV BC 254-H3
EVERETT WA 264-D2
HOOD RIVER OR 195-C5
HOOD RIVER CO OR 195-C5
HOQUIAM WA 178-A7
LEWISTON ID 250-D5
NEZ PERCE CO ID 250-D5
NE 22ND ST
LINCOLN CITY OR 203-A4
S 22ND ST
REEDSPORT OR 218-C1
22ND ST SE
SALEM OR 325-A2
23RD AV
LONGVIEW WA 302-J8
SEATTLE WA 278-D6
NW 23RD AV
PORTLAND OR 312-D4
23RD AV E
SEATTLE WA 278-D4
23RD AV NE
SNOHOMISH CO WA 168-C5
23RD AV NW
SNOHOMISH CO WA 168-B4
23RD AV S
SEATTLE WA 278-D7
SEATTLE WA 282-C2
23RD AV SE
PUYALLUP WA 182-B4
23RD ST
CITY OF NORTH VANCOUVER BC 255-A3
S 23RD ST
COEUR D'ALENE ID 355-H12
SE 23RD ST
CLARK CO WA 193-B7
SW 23RD ST
REDMOND OR 212-D5
23RD ST NE
SALEM OR 323-B13
24TH AV
ALBANY OR 326-B10
ASOTIN CO WA 250-B5
CITY OF SURREY BC 158-A2
FOREST GROVE OR 198-C1
LONGVIEW WA 302-J8
SEASIDE OR 301-G6
TOWNSHIP OF LANGLEY BC 158-C2
WASHINGTON CO OR 198-C1
E 24TH AV
EUGENE OR 330-A9
SPOKANE CO WA 351-G11
SPOKANE VALLEY WA 350-J11
SPOKANE VALLEY WA 351-B11
N 24TH AV
PASCO WA 343-D6
NE 24TH AV
PORTLAND OR 313-J4
S 24TH AV
YAKIMA WA 243-B7
24TH AV E
SEATTLE WA 278-D2
24TH AV NE
SHORELINE WA 171-B6
24TH AV NW
SEATTLE WA 272-E2
24TH AV S
DES MOINES WA 290-C5
KING CO WA 286-C7
KING CO WA 288-C3
NAMPA ID 147-C1
SEATAC WA 288-C3
24TH PL S
DES MOINES WA 290-C6
24 RD NW
DOUGLAS CO WA 112-B2
GRANT CO WA 112-B2
N 24TH ST
TACOMA WA 292-D3
NE 24TH ST
CLYDE HILL WA 175-C2
REDMOND WA 175-D2
SE 24TH ST
BELLEVUE WA 175-D3
24TH ST E
EDGEWOOD WA 182-B3
24TH ST NE
SALEM OR 323-B14
E 25TH AV
SPOKANE VALLEY WA 350-J12
25TH AV NE
SEATTLE WA 274-D3
25TH AV S
SHORELINE WA 171-B7
25TH ST
DESCHUTES CO OR 213-A4
E 25TH ST
TACOMA WA 293-J7
NE 25TH ST
VANCOUVER WA 306-E3
VANCOUVER WA 307-E3
S 25TH ST
TACOMA WA 293-G7
25TH ST SE
SALEM OR 323-B14
SALEM OR 325-B1
26TH AV
LONGVIEW WA 302-H10
TOWNSHIP OF LANGLEY BC 158-D2
26TH AV NE
OLYMPIA WA 297-A2
THURSTON CO WA 297-D1
W 26TH PL
KENNEWICK WA 343-D14
26TH ST
CORVALLIS OR 327-F10
E 26TH ST
TACOMA WA 293-J7
N 26TH ST
TACOMA WA 181-C2
TACOMA WA 292-B3
S 26TH ST
TACOMA WA 293-H7
27B AV
DISTRICT OF DELTA BC 101-C1
27TH AV
ALBANY OR 326-A10
E 27TH AV
Finley WA 343-F14
KENNEWICK WA 343-F14
W 27TH AV
Finley WA 343-B14
KENNEWICK WA 342-G14
KENNEWICK WA 343-B14
27TH AV NE
SNOHOMISH CO WA 168-C4
27TH AV SE
SNOHOMISH CO WA 269-E6
27TH ST
DISTRICT OF WEST VANCOUVE BC 254-A2
N 27TH ST
BOISE ID 253-C2
NE 27TH ST
BEND OR 217-C2
DESCHUTES CO OR 217-C2
NW 27TH ST
DESCHUTES CO OR 212-D3
SE 27TH ST
BEND OR 217-C3
CLARK CO WA 193-C7
DESCHUTES CO OR 217-C3
SW 27TH ST
REDMOND OR 212-D6
27TH ST W
UNIVERSITY PLACE WA 181-C2
28 AV
DISTRICT OF DELTA BC 101-C1
28TH AV
TOWNSHIP OF LANGLEY BC 158-C2
SE 28TH AV
PORTLAND OR 317-J3
PORTLAND OR 318-A4
W 28TH AV
EUGENE OR 329-H9
28TH AV NW
SEATTLE WA 272-D1
SNOHOMISH CO WA 168-B4
THURSTON CO WA 296-E1
28TH AV S
KING CO WA 182-B2
28TH AV W
LYNNWOOD WA 171-B5
SEATTLE WA 272-D6
SNOHOMISH CO WA 171-B4
NE 28TH CT
DESCHUTES CO OR 213-A4
N 28TH ST
BOISE ID 253-C2
SPRINGFIELD OR 331-B6
NE 28TH ST
CLARK CO WA 193-B6
VANCOUVER WA 193-A6
VANCOUVER WA 307-J3
28TH ST NE
LAKE STEVENS WA 110-C1
SNOHOMISH CO WA 110-C1
29TH AV
VANCOUVER BC 156-B5
E 29TH AV
EUGENE OR 330-A10
SPOKANE WA 349-H13
SPOKANE CO WA 349-H13
NE 29TH AV
CLARK CO WA 192-D3
W 29TH AV
EUGENE OR 329-J10
EUGENE OR 330-A10
SPOKANE WA 348-J13
SPOKANE WA 349-C13
29TH AV W
SEATTLE WA 276-D2
29TH ST
ANACORTES WA 259-G4
CORVALLIS OR 327-E8
LEWISTON ID 250-C4
MANZANITA OR 191-B4
NE 29TH ST
DESCHUTES CO OR 213-A4
29TH ST E
DISTRICT OF NORTH VANCOUV BC 255-C3
29TH ST NE
FEDERAL WAY WA 182-A2
TACOMA WA 182-A2
29TH ST SE
AUBURN WA 182-C2
30TH AV
LINN CO OR 207-B5
LONGVIEW WA 302-H8
TOWNSHIP OF LANGLEY BC 158-D2
E 30TH AV
EUGENE OR 330-C10
LANE CO OR 330-G12
30TH AV NE
SEATTLE WA 274-D5
30TH AV W
SEATTLE WA 272-D6
30TH ST
BELLINGHAM WA 258-D12
CORVALLIS OR 327-E10
E 30TH ST
KITSAP CO WA 271-B7
N 30TH ST
RENTON WA 175-C4
TACOMA WA 181-C2
TACOMA WA 292-B2
TACOMA WA 293-E2
NE 30TH ST
KITSAP CO WA 271-C7
SE 30TH ST
CLARK CO WA 193-C7
SW 30TH ST
PENDLETON OR 129-B1
NW 31ST AV
CLARK CO WA 192-C2
RIDGEFIELD WA 192-C2
31ST AV NE
LACEY WA 181-A6
31ST AV SW Rt#-161
PUYALLUP WA 182-B4
N 31ST ST
LANE CO OR 331-C4
SPRINGFIELD OR 331-C4
NW 31ST ST
DESCHUTES CO OR 212-D4
31ST ST NE
TACOMA WA 182-A2
32ND AV
CITY OF SURREY BC 158-B1
LONGVIEW WA 302-G9
TOWNSHIP OF LANGLEY BC 158-C1
E 32ND AV
SPOKANE CO WA 350-H12
SPOKANE CO WA 351-B12
SPOKANE VALLEY WA 350-H12
NE 32ND AV
PORTLAND OR 314-A2
SE 32ND AV
HILLSBORO OR 198-D1
MILWAUKIE OR 199-D3
MILWAUKIE OR 318-A7
PORTLAND OR 318-A7
32ND AV NW
SEATTLE WA 272-D2
32ND AV S
FEDERAL WAY WA 175-B7
KENT WA 175-B7
KING CO WA 175-B7
KING CO WA 182-B2
32ND ST
ANACORTES WA 259-F4
BELLINGHAM WA 258-D11
WASHOUGAL WA 193-C7
E 32ND ST
VANCOUVER WA 305-J3
S 32ND ST
LANE CO OR 331-C8
SPRINGFIELD OR 331-C8
SE 32ND ST
KING CO WA 176-A3
SAMMAMISH WA 176-A3
32ND ST KPN
PIERCE CO WA 181-A1
32ND ST NW
PIERCE CO WA 181-B1
32ND ST SE
SNOHOMISH CO WA 171-D2
32ND DIVISION DR
PIERCE CO WA 181-B5
33RD AV
VANCOUVER BC 156-B5
E 33RD AV
EUGENE OR 330-A10
NE 33RD AV
PORTLAND OR 310-A7
PORTLAND OR 314-A1
NE 33RD DR
PORTLAND OR 310-A4
33RD ST
ASTORIA OR 300-F5
E 33RD ST
VANCOUVER WA 305-H3
VANCOUVER WA 306-A3
33RD ST NE
TACOMA WA 182-A2
33A AV
DISTRICT OF DELTA BC 101-C1
34TH AV
ALBANY OR 326-B11
SEATTLE WA 278-E5
SEATTLE WA 279-E4
TOWNSHIP OF LANGLEY BC 158-D1
34TH AV E
PIERCE CO WA 182-A4
34TH AV W
SEATTLE WA 272-C7
SEATTLE WA 276-C1
34TH ST
ANACORTES WA 259-H4
CLARK CO WA 193-C7
MOUNT VERNON WA 260-G13
WASHOUGAL WA 193-C7
E 34TH ST
TACOMA WA 295-J1
N 34TH ST
SEATTLE WA 273-H7
SEATTLE WA 274-A7
S 34TH ST
TACOMA WA 295-H1
SW 35TH AV
PORTLAND OR 316-B7
PORTLAND OR 320-B1
35TH AV NE
SEATTLE WA 274-E2
35TH AV S
SEATTLE WA 278-E7
SEATTLE WA 282-E1
35TH AV SE
BOTHELL WA 171-C6
MILL CREEK WA 171-C4
SNOHOMISH CO WA 171-C5
SNOHOMISH CO WA 269-F7
35TH AV SW
SEATTLE WA 281-E7
SEATTLE WA 285-E3
35TH AV W
SNOHOMISH CO WA 171-B4
SW 35TH DR
CLACKAMAS CO OR 199-C5
35TH ST
ASTORIA OR 300-F5
BENTON CO OR 327-E11
CORVALLIS OR 327-E11
FLORENCE OR 214-B2
SPRINGFIELD OR 331-C6
N 35TH ST
SEATTLE WA 273-H7
NW 35TH ST
DESCHUTES CO OR 212-D5
S 35TH ST
TACOMA WA 294-C2
SW 35TH ST
REDMOND OR 212-D5
35TH ST NE
DOUGLAS CO WA 239-A3
35TH ST W
UNIVERSITY PLACE WA 181-C3
36 AV
DISTRICT OF DELTA BC 101-C1
36TH AV
BELLINGHAM WA 258-E9
TOWNSHIP OF LANGLEY BC 158-C1
NW 36TH AV
CLARK CO WA 192-C4
S 36TH AV
YAKIMA WA 243-B7
YAKIMA CO WA 243-B7
36TH AV NE
THURSTON CO WA 180-D5
36TH AV NW
SNOHOMISH CO WA 168-B4
THURSTON CO WA 180-C5
36TH AV NW Rt#-531
SNOHOMISH CO WA 168-B6
36TH AV S
KENT WA 175-B7
KING CO WA 175-B7
36TH AV W
LYNNWOOD WA 171-B5
SNOHOMISH CO WA 171-B5
NE 36TH DR
LINCOLN CITY OR 203-A4
36TH ST
CORVALLIS OR 327-E8
E 36TH ST
GARDEN CITY ID 253-C2
N 36TH ST
BOISE ID 253-C2
SEATTLE WA 273-H6
NW 36TH ST
SEATTLE WA 273-H6
S 36TH ST
TACOMA WA 294-C2
W 36TH ST
GARDEN CITY ID 253-C2
37TH AV
LACEY WA 297-F9
TOWNSHIP OF LANGLEY BC 158-C1
E 37TH AV
SPOKANE WA 349-H14
SPOKANE CO WA 349-H14
W 37TH AV
SPOKANE WA 348-J14
SPOKANE WA 349-A14
37TH ST
ANACORTES WA 259-F5
N 37TH ST
TACOMA WA 292-A1
NE 37TH ST
DESCHUTES CO OR 213-A4
SW 37TH ST
PENDLETON OR 129-B1
UMATILLA CO OR 129-B1
37TH ST NE
AUBURN WA 182-C1
37TH ST NW
AUBURN WA 182-B1
38TH AV
COWLITZ CO WA 302-F6
LONGVIEW WA 302-F6
TOWNSHIP OF LANGLEY BC 158-C1
S 38TH AV
WEST RICHLAND WA 340-A13
38TH AV E
PIERCE CO WA 182-A5
38TH AV NW
GIG HARBOR WA 181-C1
PIERCE CO WA 181-C1
NE 38TH PL
KIRKLAND WA 175-C1
38TH ST
EVERETT WA 265-E5
E 38TH ST
TACOMA WA 182-A3
TACOMA WA 295-J2
E 38TH ST Rt#-7
TACOMA WA 295-H2
N 38TH ST
SEATTLE WA 273-H6
NE 38TH ST
CLARK CO WA 193-B6
S 38TH ST
TACOMA WA 294-D2
TACOMA WA 295-G2
39TH AV
SKAMANIA CO WA 193-D6
NE 39TH AV
PORTLAND OR 314-B5
SE 39TH AV
PORTLAND OR 314-B7
PORTLAND OR 318-B1
39TH AV S
SEATTLE WA 287-E4
39TH AV SE
PUYALLUP WA 182-B4
SNOHOMISH CO WA 171-C6
39TH AV SW
PIERCE CO WA 182-B4
PUYALLUP WA 182-B4
39TH ST
WASHOUGAL WA 193-C7
E 39TH ST
VANCOUVER WA 305-G2
N 39TH ST
SEATTLE WA 273-H6
NE 39TH ST
CLARK CO WA 193-D6
NW 39TH ST
SEATTLE WA 273-H6
W 39TH ST
VANCOUVER WA 304-E2
VANCOUVER WA 305-F2
40TH AV
CITY OF SURREY BC 158-B1
TOWNSHIP OF LANGLEY BC 158-C1
N 40TH AV
YAKIMA WA 243-B6
S 40TH AV
YAKIMA WA 243-B7
40TH AV NE
SEATTLE WA 274-B2
40TH AV NW
POLK CO OR 322-A10
SNOHOMISH CO WA 168-B3
40TH AV S
PIERCE CO WA 118-A1
PIERCE CO WA 181-D7
NE 40TH CIR
CLARK CO WA 193-C6
N 40TH ST
SEATTLE WA 273-J6
SEATTLE WA 274-A6
NE 40TH ST
CLARK CO WA 306-D2
REDMOND WA 175-D2
SEATTLE WA 274-B6
VANCOUVER WA 306-D2
NW 40TH ST
LINCOLN CITY OR 203-A4
SE 40TH ST
MERCER ISLAND WA 175-C3
MERCER ISLAND WA 283-J3
40TH ST E
PIERCE CO WA 182-C3
40TH ST NW
PIERCE CO WA 181-B1
40TH ST W
UNIVERSITY PLACE WA 181-C3
41ST AV
UNIVERSITY ENDOWMENT LAND BC 156-B5
VANCOUVER BC 156-B5
NE 41ST AV
PORTLAND OR 314-B2
NW 41ST AV
CLARK CO WA 192-C4
41ST AV NE
THURSTON CO WA 180-D5
41 PL
PACIFIC CO WA 186-A6
41ST ST
ANACORTES WA 259-F5
CLARK CO WA 192-D1
N 41ST ST
YAKIMA CO WA 243-C6
NE 41ST ST
SEATTLE WA 274-E6
SEATTLE WA 275-E6
41ST ST SE
AUBURN WA 182-B2
EVERETT WA 264-D6
EVERETT WA 265-E5
41ST DIVISION DR
PIERCE CO WA 181-C5

INDEX

406 87TH AV SE
STREET INDEX
163RD AV SW

STREET — City State Page-Grid

87TH AV SE
SNOHOMISH CO WA 171-D2
88TH AV
CITY OF SURREY BC 156-D6
CITY OF SURREY BC 157-A6
DISTRICT OF DELTA BC 156-D6
TOWNSHIP OF LANGLEY BC 157-C6
SE 88TH AV
VANCOUVER WA 311-F1
88TH AV NW
SNOHOMISH CO WA 168-B4
STANWOOD WA 168-B4
88TH AV SW
THURSTON CO WA 184-C1
TUMWATER WA 184-C1
88TH AV W
EDMONDS WA 171-A5
NE 88TH ST
CLARK CO WA 192-D5
SE 88TH ST
KING CO WA 176-D3
88TH ST NE
MARYSVILLE WA 168-C7
SNOHOMISH CO WA 168-C7
88TH ST SE
SNOHOMISH CO WA 171-D3
88TH ST SW
LAKEWOOD WA 181-C4
89TH AV SE
THURSTON CO WA 184-D1
89TH ST
BRITISH COLUMBIA BC 104-C1
89TH ST SW
LAKEWOOD WA 181-D4
90TH AV
DISTRICT OF DELTA BC 156-D6
S 90TH AV
YAKIMA CO WA 243-A7
90TH AV E
PIERCE CO WA 182-B6
90TH AV NE
KING CO WA 171-C7
90TH AV NW
THURSTON CO WA 180-C4
N 90TH ST
SEATTLE WA 273-J1
SEATTLE WA 274-A1
90TH ST SW
EVERETT WA 268-A5
91ST AV NE
SNOHOMISH CO WA 168-D6
NW 91ST ST
DESCHUTES CO OR 212-C4
91A AV
TOWNSHIP OF LANGLEY BC 157-C6
92A AV
TOWNSHIP OF LANGLEY BC 157-C6
92ND AV
CITY OF SURREY BC 157-A6
DISTRICT OF DELTA BC 156-D6
NE 92ND AV
CLARK CO WA 192-D3
SE 92ND AV
CLACKAMAS CO OR 319-G6
PORTLAND OR 315-G7
PORTLAND OR 319-G2
PORTLAND OR 319-G6
VANCOUVER WA 307-G6
92ND AV NE
SNOHOMISH CO WA 171-D1
YARROW POINT WA 175-C2
92ND AV NW
PIERCE CO WA 181-B1
SNOHOMISH CO WA 168-A5
92ND ST KPN
PIERCE CO WA 174-A7
92ND ST NW
SNOHOMISH CO WA 168-C7
92ND ST SE
SNOHOMISH WA 171-D3
SNOHOMISH CO WA 171-D3
93RD AV SE
THURSTON CO WA 184-C1
93RD AV SW
THURSTON CO WA 184-C1
93RD AV SW Rt#-121
THURSTON CO WA 184-C1
TUMWATER WA 184-C1
93RD ST
DESCHUTES CO OR 212-C7
93RD ST SW
LAKEWOOD WA 181-C4
94TH AV
CLARK CO WA 192-D1
NE 94TH AV
CLARK CO WA 192-D5
94TH AV E
PIERCE CO WA 182-B7
94TH AV S
KENT WA 175-C7
94TH ST
DESCHUTES CO OR 212-C7
95TH AV NE
MARION CO OR 205-B6
NE 95TH ST
SEATTLE WA 171-B7
96TH AV
CITY OF SURREY BC 156-D6
CITY OF SURREY BC 157-A6
DISTRICT OF DELTA BC 156-D6
MAPLE RIDGE BC 157-D6
TOWNSHIP OF LANGLEY BC 157-C6
96TH AV NE
BOTHELL WA 171-C6
96TH DR SE
SNOHOMISH WA 171-D3
SNOHOMISH CO WA 171-D3
S 96TH ST
KING CO WA 286-B4
PIERCE CO WA 181-D4
TACOMA WA 181-D4
96TH ST E
PIERCE CO WA 182-A4
96TH ST NW
GIG HARBOR WA 174-C7
NE 97TH AV
VANCOUVER WA 307-G5
98TH AV
MAPLE RIDGE BC 157-D6
TOWNSHIP OF LANGLEY BC 157-C6
NE 98TH AV
VANCOUVER WA 307-G3
SE 98TH AV
VANCOUVER WA 307-G7
98TH AV NE
KIRKLAND WA 171-C7
KIRKLAND WA 175-C1
99TH AV NE
SNOHOMISH CO WA 168-D4
SNOHOMISH CO WA 171-D1
99TH AV SE
SNOHOMISH CO WA 171-D2
99TH AV SW
KING CO WA 174-D7
LAKEWOOD WA 181-C4
NE 99TH ST
CLARK CO WA 192-C5
CLARK CO WA 193-A5
NW 99TH ST
CLARK CO WA 192-C5
99TH ST E
PIERCE CO WA 181-D4
100TH AV
CITY OF SURREY BC 157-A6
MAPLE RIDGE BC 157-D6
TOWNSHIP OF LANGLEY BC 157-C6
100TH AV NE
BELLEVUE WA 175-C2
BOTHELL WA 171-C7
KING CO WA 171-C7
KIRKLAND WA 171-C7
100TH AV SE
THURSTON CO WA 184-C1
100TH AV W
EDMONDS WA 171-A6
SW 100TH ST U.S.-101
NEWPORT OR 206-A5
100TH ST NE
GRANITE FALLS WA 102-C3
SNOHOMISH CO WA 102-C3
SNOHOMISH CO WA 168-C7
100TH ST SE
EVERETT WA 268-D6
EVERETT WA 269-G7
SNOHOMISH CO WA 268-D6
SNOHOMISH CO WA 269-G7
100TH ST SW
EVERETT WA 267-H6
EVERETT WA 268-A6
LAKEWOOD WA 181-D4
SNOHOMISH CO WA 267-H6
100TH WY
LINCOLN CO OR 206-B3
101ST AV
TOWNSHIP OF LANGLEY BC 157-C6
101ST AV SW
THURSTON CO WA 184-B1
NW 101 LN
DESCHUTES CO OR 212-C5
101 PL
PACIFIC CO WA 186-A5
102ND AV
CITY OF SURREY BC 157-B6
MAPLE RIDGE BC 157-D6
TOWNSHIP OF LANGLEY BC 157-C6
NE 102ND AV
CLARK CO WA 192-D1
MAYWOOD PARK OR 315-H2
PORTLAND OR 315-H2
SE 102ND AV
PORTLAND OR 315-H6
102ND AV NW
STANWOOD WA 168-A4
102B AV
TOWNSHIP OF LANGLEY BC 157-C6
103RD AV SE
SNOHOMISH CO WA 171-D2
THURSTON CO WA 184-D1
103RD AV SW
THURSTON CO WA 184-B1
SE 103RD DR
PORTLAND OR 315-H6
104 AV
CITY OF SURREY BC 156-D6
104TH AV
CITY OF SURREY BC 157-A6
104TH AV SE Rt#-515
KENT WA 175-C7
104TH AV SW
KING CO WA 174-D5
THURSTON CO WA 184-C1
104 ST
DISTRICT OF DELTA BC 156-D7
NE 104TH ST
REDMOND WA 175-D1
104TH ST E
PIERCE CO WA 182-A4
104TH ST NW
PIERCE CO WA 174-B7
104TH ST SW
LAKEWOOD WA 181-C4
N 105TH ST
SEATTLE WA 171-A7
NE 105TH ST
CLARK CO WA 193-B5
106TH AV SW
KING CO WA 174-D4
SW 106TH PL
KING CO WA 285-G5
SW 106TH ST
KING CO WA 285-E5
SEATTLE WA 284-D5
SEATTLE WA 285-E5
NE 107TH AV
CLARK CO WA 192-D5
107TH AV SW
THURSTON CO WA 184-C1
SW 107TH ST
KING CO WA 285-G5
108TH AV
CITY OF SURREY BC 157-A6
MAPLE RIDGE BC 157-D6
108TH AV SE
KENT WA 175-C7
108TH AV SE Rt#-515
KENT WA 175-C6
KING CO WA 175-C6
SW 108TH ST
SEATTLE WA 284-E5
108TH ST NE
SNOHOMISH CO WA 168-D7
108TH ST SW
LAKEWOOD WA 181-D4
109TH AV
CLARK CO WA 192-D1
NE 109TH AV
CLARK CO WA 192-D5
109TH AV SE
SNOHOMISH CO WA 171-D5
NE 109TH ST
CLARK CO WA 192-D5
CLARK CO WA 193-B5
110TH AV
CLACKAMAS CO OR 199-B5
MAPLE RIDGE BC 157-D6
110TH AV
WILSONVILLE OR 199-B5
110TH AV E
PIERCE CO WA 182-B5
110TH AV SW
THURSTON CO WA 184-B1
111TH AV SW
KING CO WA 174-D6
112TH AV
CITY OF SURREY BC 157-A5
MAPLE RIDGE BC 157-D6
NE 112TH AV
BATTLE GROUND WA 192-D3
CLARK CO WA 192-D2
VANCOUVER WA 307-J2
SE 112TH AV
MULTNOMAH CO OR 319-J7
PORTLAND OR 315-J7
PORTLAND OR 319-J1
112TH AV NE
BELLEVUE WA 175-C2
112TH AV SE
BELLEVUE WA 175-C2
KING CO WA 182-C1
112 ST
DISTRICT OF DELTA BC 156-D7
S 112TH ST
KING CO WA 286-A6
112TH ST E
PIERCE CO WA 181-D4
PIERCE CO WA 182-A4
112TH ST S
PIERCE CO WA 181-D4
112TH ST SE
EVERETT WA 171-C4
SNOHOMISH CO WA 171-C4
112TH ST SW
EVERETT WA 171-B4
LAKEWOOD WA 181-C4
SNOHOMISH CO WA 171-B4
113TH AV SW
THURSTON CO WA 184-B1
113 ST
PACIFIC CO WA 186-A5
114TH AV NE
MARION CO OR 205-B3
114TH ST NE
SNOHOMISH CO WA 168-C7
115TH AV NE
SNOHOMISH CO WA 168-D7
NE 115TH ST
SEATTLE WA 171-B7
116TH AV
CITY OF SURREY BC 157-A5
MAPLE RIDGE BC 157-D5
116TH AV NE
BELLEVUE WA 175-C2
116TH AV SE
BELLEVUE WA 175-C4
KENT WA 175-C7
KING CO WA 175-C6
NEWCASTLE WA 175-C4
116 ST
DISTRICT OF DELTA BC 156-D7
NE 116TH ST
KIRKLAND WA 171-C7
REDMOND WA 171-D7
S 116TH ST
KING CO WA 285-J6
KING CO WA 286-C7
SW 116TH ST
BURIEN WA 285-H6
KING CO WA 285-H6
116TH ST NE
MARYSVILLE WA 168-C7
SNOHOMISH CO WA 102-C3
SNOHOMISH CO WA 168-C7
116TH ST S
PIERCE CO WA 181-D4
116TH ST SE
SNOHOMISH CO WA 171-C4
S 116TH WY
KING CO WA 286-C6
TUKWILA WA 286-C6
117TH AV
MAPLE RIDGE BC 157-D5
NE 117TH AV Rt#-503
CLARK CO WA 192-D5
CLARK CO WA 193-A4
117TH AV NE
MARION CO OR 205-B6
NE 117TH ST
CLARK CO WA 192-D5
118TH AV
MAPLE RIDGE BC 157-D5
118TH AV NW
PIERCE CO WA 174-B7
118TH AV SE
BELLEVUE WA 175-C3
NE 118TH CIR
CLARK CO WA 193-B5
S 118TH ST
KING CO WA 286-B7
118TH ST KPN
PIERCE CO WA 174-A7
118TH ST NE
SNOHOMISH CO WA 168-C7
119TH AV
CLARK CO WA 193-A1
PITT MEADOWS BC 157-B5
119TH AV SE
BELLEVUE WA 175-C3
NE 119TH ST
CLARK CO WA 192-D5
CLARK CO WA 193-A5
NW 119TH ST
CLARK CO WA 192-C5
120TH AV NE
KIRKLAND WA 171-C7
NE 120TH PL
KIRKLAND WA 171-C7
120 ST
CITY OF SURREY BC 156-D7
DISTRICT OF DELTA BC 156-D7
S 120TH ST
KING CO WA 286-C7
120TH ST E
PIERCE CO WA 182-C4
SW 121ST AV
TIGARD OR 199-B3
121ST ST E
PIERCE CO WA 182-A4
122ND AV
MAPLE RIDGE BC 157-C5
NE 122ND AV
PORTLAND OR 200-A1
NE 122ND AV Rt#-503
BATTLE GROUND WA 193-A3
NE 122ND AV Rt#-503
CLARK CO WA 193-A3
SE 122ND AV
CLACKAMAS CO OR 200-A3
PORTLAND OR 200-A2
122ND AV E
EDGEWOOD WA 182-B3
PIERCE CO WA 182-B5
NE 122ND BLVD
PORTLAND OR 193-A7
PORTLAND OR 200-A1
NE 122ND ST
CLARK CO WA 193-B5
122ND ST E
PIERCE CO WA 182-B4
123RD AV
MAPLE RIDGE BC 157-C5
123RD AV NE
SNOHOMISH CO WA 168-D5
123RD AV SE
SNOHOMISH CO WA 171-D2
124TH AV
MAPLE RIDGE BC 157-C5
124TH AV NE
KING CO WA 171-C7
KIRKLAND WA 175-C1
WOODINVILLE WA 171-C7
124TH AV SE
KING CO WA 175-C6
NE 124TH ST
KING CO WA 171-C7
KIRKLAND WA 171-C7
REDMOND WA 171-C7
S 124TH ST
KING CO WA 289-H1
TUKWILA WA 289-H1
NE 124TH WY
KING CO WA 171-D7
REDMOND WA 171-D7
125TH AV
MAPLE RIDGE BC 157-D5
NE 125TH ST
SEATTLE WA 171-B7
126TH AV E
PIERCE CO WA 182-B6
126TH AV KPN
PIERCE CO WA 174-B7
126TH ST NW
SNOHOMISH CO WA 168-B6
127TH AV
MAPLE RIDGE BC 157-D5
127TH AV SE
SNOHOMISH CO WA 171-D4
127TH PL SE
BELLEVUE WA 175-C2
NW 127TH ST
CLARK CO WA 192-C4
128TH AV
MAPLE RIDGE BC 157-C5
128TH AV SE
BELLEVUE WA 175-C5
KING CO WA 175-C6
KING CO WA 175-C5
128TH ST
CITY OF SURREY BC 157-A7
CITY OF SURREY BC 158-A2
NE 128TH ST
KING CO WA 171-D7
S 128TH ST
BURIEN WA 288-B1
KING CO WA 288-B1
SEATAC WA 288-B1
SE 128TH ST
KING CO WA 175-D5
RENTON WA 175-D5
128TH ST E
PIERCE CO WA 182-A4
128TH ST KPN
PIERCE CO WA 174-A7
128TH ST NE
SNOHOMISH CO WA 168-C6
128TH ST SE Rt#-96
SNOHOMISH CO WA 171-C4
128TH ST SW
SNOHOMISH CO WA 171-C4
128TH ST SW Rt#-96
SNOHOMISH CO WA 171-C4
SE 128TH WY
KING CO WA 175-D5
129TH AV
MAPLE RIDGE BC 157-C5
PITT MEADOWS BC 157-B5
SE 129TH AV
CLACKAMAS CO OR 200-A3
HAPPY VALLEY OR 200-A3
129TH PL SE
BELLEVUE WA 175-C3
S 129TH ST
KING CO WA 289-G1
NE 130TH AV
CLARK CO WA 193-A5
130TH AV NE
BELLEVUE WA 175-C2
BOTHELL WA 171-C6
KING CO WA 171-C6
WOODINVILLE WA 171-C6
N 130TH ST
SEATTLE WA 171-A7
NE 130TH ST
KING CO WA 171-D7
SEATTLE WA 171-B7
NE 131ST AV
CLARK CO WA 193-A5
131ST AV NE
LAKE STEVENS WA 110-C1
SNOHOMISH CO WA 110-C1
131ST AV NE Rt#-92
SNOHOMISH CO WA 110-C1
131ST AV NE Rt#-202
BOTHELL WA 171-C6
WOODINVILLE WA 171-C6
131ST AV SE
THURSTON CO WA 184-C2
131ST ST E
PIERCE CO WA 181-D4
131ST ST NW
SNOHOMISH CO WA 168-C6
132ND AV
MAPLE RIDGE BC 157-C5
PITT MEADOWS BC 157-C5
NE 132ND AV
CLARK CO WA 193-A2
132ND AV E
PIERCE CO WA 182-B7
132ND AV NE
BOTHELL WA 171-C6
KING CO WA 171-C7
KIRKLAND WA 175-C1
REDMOND WA 175-C1
132ND AV NE
WOODINVILLE WA 171-C6
132ND AV SE
BELLEVUE WA 175-C7
KENT WA 175-C7
KING CO WA 175-C7
KING CO WA 182-C1
WOODINVILLE WA 171-C6
132ND ST
CITY OF SURREY BC 157-A7
NE 132ND ST
KING CO WA 171-C7
KIRKLAND WA 171-C7
S 132ND ST
KING CO WA 289-J2
132ND ST NE
SNOHOMISH CO WA 168-D6
132ND ST SE Rt#-96
EVERETT WA 171-C4
MILL CREEK WA 171-C4
SNOHOMISH CO WA 171-C4
133RD AV SE
NEWCASTLE WA 175-C4
133RD AV SW
THURSTON CO WA 184-B2
NE 133RD ST
KING CO WA 171-D7
S 133RD ST
KING CO WA 289-H2
TUKWILA WA 289-H2
134TH AV E
PIERCE CO WA 182-B5
134TH AV NE
BELLEVUE WA 175-C2
134TH PL SE
SNOHOMISH CO WA 171-C4
NE 134TH ST
CLARK CO WA 192-C4
135 RD
NEZ PERCE CO ID 250-C2
SE 136TH AV
PORTLAND OR 200-A2
136 RD
NEZ PERCE CO ID 250-C2
S 136TH ST
BURIEN WA 288-A2
SEATAC WA 288-B2
136TH ST E
PIERCE CO WA 182-B5
136TH ST NE
MARYSVILLE WA 168-C6
SNOHOMISH CO WA 168-C6
NE 137TH AV
CLARK CO WA 193-A5
138TH AV SE
RENTON WA 175-C4
138TH ST S
PIERCE CO WA 181-D5
NE 139TH ST
CLARK CO WA 192-D4
CLARK CO WA 193-A4
NW 139TH ST
CLARK CO WA 192-C4
140TH AV NE
BELLEVUE WA 175-C2
WOODINVILLE WA 171-C6
140TH AV SE
BELLEVUE WA 175-C2
KING CO WA 175-C6
140TH AV SW
THURSTON CO WA 184-B2
140TH PL NE
KING CO WA 171-C6
WOODINVILLE WA 171-C6
140 RD
NEZ PERCE CO ID 250-C2
140TH ST
CITY OF SURREY BC 157-A6
CITY OF SURREY BC 158-A2
CITY OF WHITE ROCK BC 158-A2
140TH ST NE
SNOHOMISH CO WA 168-C6
140TH ST NW
SNOHOMISH CO WA 168-B6
140TH WY SE
KING CO WA 175-C5
NE 142ND AV
CLARK CO WA 193-A4
SE 142ND AV
CLACKAMAS CO OR 200-A3
NW 143RD AV
WASHINGTON CO OR 199-A1
143RD AV SE
THURSTON CO WA 184-C2
143RD AV SW
THURSTON CO WA 184-C2
144TH AV SE
KENT WA 175-C7
144TH ST
CITY OF SURREY BC 158-A1
NE 144TH ST
CLARK CO WA 193-A4
S 144TH ST
SEATAC WA 288-D3
TUKWILA WA 288-D3
TUKWILA WA 289-F3
144TH ST E
PIERCE CO WA 182-A5
144TH ST KPN
PIERCE CO WA 174-A6
144TH ST NW
PIERCE CO WA 174-C6
145TH PL SE
BELLEVUE WA 175-C2
N 145TH ST
SEATTLE WA 171-A7
SHORELINE WA 171-A7
N 145TH ST Rt#-523
SEATTLE WA 171-A7
SHORELINE WA 171-A7
NE 145TH ST
KING CO WA 171-C7
NE 145TH ST Rt#-202
KING CO WA 171-D7
WOODINVILLE WA 171-C7
NE 145TH ST Rt#-523
SEATTLE WA 171-B7
SHORELINE WA 171-B7
146TH AV E
PIERCE CO WA 182-B6
NE 147TH AV
CLARK CO WA 193-A2
NE 148TH AV
PORTLAND OR 200-A1
148TH AV NE
BELLEVUE WA 175-C2
REDMOND WA 175-C2
148TH AV SE
BELLEVUE WA 175-C3
COVINGTON WA 175-C7
KENT WA 175-C7
KING CO WA 175-D4
KING CO WA 182-C1
RENTON WA 175-D4
148TH ST
CITY OF SURREY BC 157-A6
SW 148TH ST
BURIEN WA 175-A5
148TH ST SW
SNOHOMISH CO WA 171-B4
NW 149TH ST
CLARK CO WA 192-C4
150TH AV
PITT MEADOWS BC 157-C4
SW 150TH AV
WASHINGTON CO OR 199-A3
150TH AV E
PIERCE CO WA 182-B7
150TH AV SE
BELLEVUE WA 175-D3
KING CO WA 175-D3
150 NW ST
OAK HARBOR WA 167-B2
150TH ST SW
LAKEWOOD WA 181-C5
PIERCE CO WA 181-C5
NE 152ND AV
CLARK CO WA 193-A2
152ND AV SE
COVINGTON WA 175-C7
KENT WA 175-C7
KING CO WA 175-C7
152ND AV SW
THURSTON CO WA 184-B3
152ND ST
CITY OF SURREY BC 157-A6
CITY OF SURREY BC 158-A1
SW 152ND ST
BURIEN WA 175-A5
152ND ST E
PIERCE CO WA 182-A5
152ND ST NE
MARYSVILLE WA 168-C6
154TH AV E
PIERCE CO WA 182-B7
154TH AV SE
KING CO WA 182-C1
154TH PL SE
KING CO WA 175-D5
154TH ST
CITY OF SURREY BC 157-A6
S 154TH ST
SEATAC WA 288-C4
N 155TH ST
SHORELINE WA 171-B7
155TH ST SW
LAKEWOOD WA 181-C5
PIERCE CO WA 181-C5
156TH AV NE
BELLEVUE WA 175-D2
REDMOND WA 175-D2
WOODINVILLE WA 171-D6
156TH AV NE Rt#-202
KING CO WA 171-D7
REDMOND WA 171-D7
WOODINVILLE WA 171-D7
156TH AV SE
BELLEVUE WA 175-D3
KING CO WA 175-D5
156TH ST
CITY OF SURREY BC 157-A6
NE 156TH ST
CLARK CO WA 192-D4
S 156TH ST
BURIEN WA 175-A5
BURIEN WA 288-A4
SE 156TH ST
KING CO WA 176-A5
SW 156TH ST
BURIEN WA 175-A5
156TH ST NE
SNOHOMISH CO WA 168-C6
156TH ST SE
SNOHOMISH CO WA 171-D4
S 156TH WY
SEATAC WA 288-B4
157TH ST
CITY OF SURREY BC 158-A2
NW 158TH AV
BEAVERTON OR 199-A1
SW 158TH AV
BEAVERTON OR 199-A1
WASHINGTON CO OR 199-A1
158TH AV E
PIERCE CO WA 182-B7
158TH AV KPS
PIERCE CO WA 181-A3
159TH AV NE
SNOHOMISH CO WA 102-C3
NE 159TH ST
CLARK CO WA 192-D4
CLARK CO WA 193-A4
159TH ST E
PIERCE CO WA 181-D5
160TH AV E
SUMNER WA 182-C3
160TH PL SE
KING CO WA 182-D2
160TH ST
CITY OF SURREY BC 157-B6
NE 160TH ST
KING CO WA 171-D7
S 160TH ST
BURIEN WA 288-A5
SEATAC WA 288-D5
TUKWILA WA 288-D5
160TH ST E
PIERCE CO WA 182-A5
NE 162ND AV
CLARK CO WA 193-A5
GRESHAM OR 200-A1
PORTLAND OR 200-A1
VANCOUVER WA 193-A6
SE 162ND AV
MULTNOMAH CO OR 200-A2
PORTLAND OR 200-A2
162ND AV KPS
PIERCE CO WA 181-A3
162ND ST E
PIERCE CO WA 182-D5
163RD AV NE
SNOHOMISH CO WA 102-C3
163RD AV SW
THURSTON CO WA 184-C3

INDEX

408 296TH ST E STREET INDEX Rt#-7 E 38TH ST

STREET / City State Page-Grid

296TH ST E
PIERCE CO WA 182-A7
296TH ST S
PIERCE CO WA 181-D7
299TH AV SE
SNOHOMISH CO WA 110-C1
SULTAN WA 110-C1
NE 299TH ST
CLARK CO WA 192-D2
CLARK CO WA 193-A2
NW 299TH ST
CLARK CO WA 192-C2
300TH ST NE
SNOHOMISH CO WA 168-C3
300TH ST NW
SNOHOMISH CO WA 168-B3
SE 302ND AV
MULTNOMAH CO OR 200-C2
S 304TH ST
FEDERAL WAY WA 182-B1
SE 304TH ST
KING CO WA 182-C1
304TH ST E
PIERCE CO WA 118-A1
311TH AV SE
SNOHOMISH CO WA 110-C1
SULTAN WA 110-C1
NE 312TH AV
CLARK CO WA 193-C6
SE 312TH AV
CLACKAMAS CO OR 200-C3
S 312TH ST
FEDERAL WAY WA 182-A1
SE 312TH ST
KING CO WA 110-C3
SW 312TH ST
FEDERAL WAY WA 182-A1
NE 314TH ST
CLARK CO WA 192-D2
316TH ST NW
SNOHOMISH CO WA 168-C3
S 320TH ST
FEDERAL WAY WA 182-B1
KING CO WA 182-B1
SE 320TH ST
AUBURN WA 182-C1
SW 320TH ST
FEDERAL WAY WA 182-A1
320TH ST E
PIERCE CO WA 118-B1
SE 322ND AV
CLACKAMAS CO OR 200-C3
323RD AV SE
SNOHOMISH CO WA 110-C1
SULTAN WA 110-C1
324TH AV SE
KING CO WA 176-B3
324TH ST NW
SNOHOMISH CO WA 168-B3
SW 325TH AV
WASHINGTON CO OR 198-C1
SE 327TH AV
MULTNOMAH CO OR 200-C2
SE 329TH AV
CLACKAMAS CO OR 200-C4
SW 331ST AV
WASHINGTON CO OR 198-C1
332ND ST NW
SKAGIT CO WA 168-B3
NW 334TH AV
WASHINGTON CO OR 198-C1
S 336TH ST
FEDERAL WAY WA 182-B1
SW 336TH ST
FEDERAL WAY WA 182-A1
336TH ST S
PIERCE CO WA 118-A1
SW 345TH AV
WASHINGTON CO OR 198-C1
S 348TH ST
FEDERAL WAY WA 182-A1
349TH ST
CLARK CO WA 192-D1
352ND AV
CLACKAMAS CO OR 200-C3
S 352ND ST
KING CO WA 182-B2
352ND ST E
PIERCE CO WA 118-B1
S 356TH ST
FEDERAL WAY WA 182-A2
SW 356TH ST
FEDERAL WAY WA 182-A2
NE 360TH ST
KITSAP CO WA 170-D4
S 360TH ST
KING CO WA 182-B2
SE 362ND AV
CLACKAMAS CO OR 200-C3
SE 362ND DR
CLACKAMAS CO OR 200-C4
SE 368TH ST
KING CO WA 110-C3
KING CO WA 182-D2
379TH ST
CLARK CO WA 192-D1
CLARK CO WA 193-A1
SE 384TH ST
KING CO WA 182-D2
389TH ST
CLARK CO WA 192-C1
SE 400TH ST
KING CO WA 182-D2
412TH AV
CLARK CO WA 193-D6
SKAMANIA CO WA 193-D6
SE 416TH ST
KING CO WA 182-D3
422ND AV
CLACKAMAS CO OR 200-D4
SANDY OR 200-D4
SE 424TH ST
KING CO WA 110-C3
KING CO WA 182-D3
428TH AV SE
KING CO WA 176-C4
436TH AV SE
KING CO WA 176-C5
SE 436TH ST Rt#-164
KING CO WA 110-C3
KING CO WA 182-D3
SE 436TH WY Rt#-164
ENUMCLAW WA 110-C3
KING CO WA 110-C3
442ND AV
CLACKAMAS CO OR 200-D5
SE 448TH ST
KING CO WA 182-D3

SE 456TH WY
KING CO WA 182-D4
468TH AV SE
KING CO WA 176-D5
2900 RD
MASON CO WA 180-A4
7000 RD
CLALLAM CO WA 162-D3
I-5 FRWY
ARLINGTON WA 168-C5
BELLINGHAM WA 161-A2
BELLINGHAM WA 258-A1
BLAINE WA 158-B3
BURLINGTON WA 260-C3
CASTLE ROCK WA 187-C7
CENTRALIA WA 299-D1
CHEHALIS WA 299-D8
COWLITZ CO WA 187-C5
COWLITZ CO WA 189-C1
COWLITZ CO WA 303-F1
DES MOINES WA 290-D5
DUPONT WA 181-B5
EVERETT WA 171-C1
EVERETT WA 265-H1
EVERETT WA 268-E4
EVERETT WA 269-E1
FEDERAL WAY WA 175-B7
FEDERAL WAY WA 182-B1
FERNDALE WA 158-C5
FIFE WA 182-A2
Grand Mound WA 184-B3
KALAMA WA 189-C5
KELSO WA 189-C4
KELSO WA 303-D5
KENT WA 175-B7
KENT WA 290-D7
KING CO WA 289-G1
LACEY WA 181-A6
LACEY WA 297-J3
LAKEWOOD WA 181-D4
LEWIS CO WA 184-B5
LEWIS CO WA 187-C1
LEWIS CO WA 299-D1
LYNNWOOD WA 171-B5
MARYSVILLE WA 168-C6
MARYSVILLE WA 171-C1
MILTON WA 182-A2
MILTON WA 182-B2
MOUNT VERNON WA 168-B1
MOUNT VERNON WA 260-C9
MOUNTLAKE TERRACE WA 171-B5
NAPAVINE WA 187-C1
OLYMPIA WA 296-J6
OLYMPIA WA 297-G5
PIERCE CO WA 181-D4
PIERCE CO WA 182-A2
PORTLAND OR 313-G7
SEATAC WA 289-F7
SEATAC WA 290-E3
SEATAC WA 291-F1
SEATTLE WA 171-B7
SEATTLE WA 274-A1
SEATTLE WA 278-B1
SEATTLE WA 282-B1
SEATTLE WA 286-C1
SEATTLE WA 287-E5
SHORELINE WA 171-B6
SISKIYOU CO CA 149-C3
SISKIYOU CO CA 150-A3
SKAGIT CO WA 161-B3
SKAGIT CO WA 168-B1
SKAGIT CO WA 260-C1
SNOHOMISH CO WA 168-B3
SNOHOMISH CO WA 171-C1
TACOMA WA 181-D4
TACOMA WA 182-A2
TACOMA WA 293-J7
TACOMA WA 295-J1
THURSTON CO WA 181-A6
THURSTON CO WA 184-C1
THURSTON CO WA 296-E14
THURSTON CO WA 297-C6
TUKWILA WA 287-E5
TUKWILA WA 289-G1
TUKWILA WA 291-F1
TUMWATER WA 184-C1
TUMWATER WA 296-H8
WHATCOM CO WA 158-B3
WHATCOM CO WA 161-A2
WHATCOM CO WA 258-A1
WOODLAND WA 189-D7
YREKA CA 149-C3
I-5 PACIFIC HWY
ALBANY OR 326-H5
ASHLAND OR 337-C4
CANYONVILLE OR 225-C1
CENTRAL POINT OR 230-B6
CENTRAL POINT OR 336-A5
CLACKAMAS CO OR 199-B3
CLARK CO WA 192-C1
COBURG OR 210-B6
COBURG OR 215-C5
COTTAGE GROVE OR 215-B7
COWLITZ CO WA 192-C1
CRESWELL OR 215-C5
DOUGLAS CO OR 219-C1
DOUGLAS CO OR 221-C2
DOUGLAS CO OR 225-C1
DOUGLAS CO OR 334-C11
EUGENE OR 330-E7
Four Corners OR 323-D9
Four Corners OR 325-D1
GRANTS PASS OR 335-H7
Hayesville OR 323-D9
JACKSON CO OR 149-C3
JACKSON CO OR 150-A2
JACKSON CO OR 229-B4
JACKSON CO OR 230-B6
JACKSON CO OR 234-B2
JACKSON CO OR 336-A5
JACKSON CO OR 337-C4
JOSEPHINE CO OR 225-C5
JOSEPHINE CO OR 229-B1
JOSEPHINE CO OR 335-C3
KEIZER OR 323-C5
LAKE OSWEGO OR 199-B3
LANE CO OR 210-B6
LANE CO OR 215-C5
LANE CO OR 219-C1
LANE CO OR 330-G9
LINN CO OR 207-C7
LINN CO OR 210-B6
LINN CO OR 326-G14
MARION CO OR 199-B6
MARION CO OR 205-A2
MARION CO OR 207-D2
MARION CO OR 323-C5
MARION CO OR 325-B8

I-5 PACIFIC HWY
MARYSVILLE WA 168-C7
MARYSVILLE WA 171-C1
MEDFORD OR 234-B2
MEDFORD OR 336-E13
MILLERSBURG OR 326-H5
PHOENIX OR 234-B2
PORTLAND OR 199-B3
PORTLAND OR 305-G5
PORTLAND OR 309-F4
PORTLAND OR 313-F2
PORTLAND OR 316-C7
PORTLAND OR 317-F1
PORTLAND OR 320-A1
RIDGEFIELD WA 192-C2
ROGUE RIVER OR 229-B4
ROSEBURG OR 334-E4
SALEM OR 323-C5
SALEM OR 325-D1
SNOHOMISH CO WA 168-C7
SNOHOMISH CO WA 171-C1
SPRINGFIELD OR 330-E7
SUTHERLIN OR 221-C2
TIGARD OR 199-B3
Tri-City OR 225-C1
TUALATIN OR 199-B4
VANCOUVER WA 192-C5
VANCOUVER WA 305-G5
WASHINGTON CO OR 199-B4
WILSONVILLE OR 199-B5
WOODBURN OR 205-A2
WOODLAND WA 192-B1
I-18 HIGHWAY
BRITISH COLUMBIA BC 101-A1
I-82 FRWY
BENTON CO WA 120-C3
BENTON CO WA 121-A3
BENTON CO WA 341-A9
BENTON CO WA 342-A13
GRANDVIEW WA 120-B3
GRANGER WA 120-A2
KENNEWICK WA 341-H13
KITTITAS CO WA 241-B6
KITTITAS CO WA 243-C1
PROSSER WA 120-C3
SUNNYSIDE WA 120-B2
UNION GAP WA 120-A2
UNION GAP WA 243-C7
YAKIMA WA 243-B6
YAKIMA CO WA 120-A2
YAKIMA CO WA 243-D4
ZILLAH WA 120-A2
I-82 HIGHWAY
YAKIMA CO WA 120-A2
I-82 MCNARY HWY
UMATILLA OR 129-A1
UMATILLA CO OR 129-A1
I-84 E 184
BOISE ID 253-C2
I-84 W I84
BOISE ID 253-C2
I-84 BANFIELD FRWY
PORTLAND OR 313-H4
PORTLAND OR 314-C5
PORTLAND OR 315-J2
I-84 COLUMBIA RIVER HWY
ARLINGTON OR 128-A1
BOARDMAN OR 128-C1
CASCADE LOCKS OR 194-C6
FAIRVIEW OR 200-A1
GILLIAM CO OR 127-C1
GILLIAM CO OR 128-A1
GRESHAM OR 200-A1
HOOD RIVER OR 195-A5
HOOD RIVER CO OR 194-C6
HOOD RIVER CO OR 195-A5
MORROW CO OR 128-B1
MOSIER OR 196-D7
MULTNOMAH CO OR 194-B7
MULTNOMAH CO OR 200-C1
MULTNOMAH CO OR 201-A1
PORTLAND OR 200-A1
PORTLAND OR 315-J2
RUFUS OR 127-C1
SHERMAN CO OR 127-C1
THE DALLES OR 196-D7
TROUTDALE OR 200-A1
WASCO CO OR 127-B1
WASCO CO OR 195-A5
WASCO CO OR 196-D7
WOOD VILLAGE OR 200-A1
I-84 FRWY
ADA CO ID 147-C1
ADA CO ID 253-B3
BOISE ID 253-B3
CALDWELL ID 147-B1
CANYON CO ID 139-B3
CANYON CO ID 147-B1
MERIDIAN ID 253-B3
NAMPA ID 147-B1
PAYETTE CO ID 139-A3
I-84 OLD OREGON TRAIL HWY
BAKER CITY OR 138-B1
BAKER CO OR 130-A3
BAKER CO OR 138-B1
LA GRANDE OR 130-A2
MALHEUR CO OR 138-B1
MALHEUR CO OR 139-A2
MORROW CO OR 128-C1
NORTH POWDER OR 130-A3
ONTARIO OR 139-A2
PAYETTE CO ID 139-A2
PENDLETON OR 129-A1
UMATILLA CO OR 128-C1
UMATILLA CO OR 129-B1
UNION CO OR 129-C2
UNION CO OR 130-A2
I-90 COLUMBIA BASIN HWY
ADAMS CO WA 113-C3
I-90 FRWY
ADAMS CO WA 113-C3
ADAMS CO WA 114-A3
BELLEVUE WA 175-C3
CLE ELUM WA 240-B2
COEUR D'ALENE ID 245-B7
COEUR D'ALENE ID 354-J7
COEUR D'ALENE ID 355-A7
ELLENSBURG WA 241-B5
FERNAN LAKE VILLAGE ID 355-H11
GRANT CO WA 112-C3
GRANT CO WA 113-A3
GRANT CO WA 120-B1
GRANT CO WA 242-C3
ISSAQUAH WA 175-D3
ISSAQUAH WA 176-A4
KELLOGG ID 115-C2
KING CO WA 111-A2
KING CO WA 175-C3

I-90 FRWY
KING CO WA 176-A4
KITTITAS CO WA 111-A2
KITTITAS CO WA 120-A1
KITTITAS CO WA 240-A1
KITTITAS CO WA 241-A4
KOOTENAI CO ID 115-B2
KOOTENAI CO ID 245-B7
KOOTENAI CO ID 248-B1
KOOTENAI CO ID 352-J9
KOOTENAI CO ID 353-A8
KOOTENAI CO ID 354-C7
KOOTENAI CO ID 355-A7
LIBERTY LAKE WA 351-J7
LIBERTY LAKE WA 352-D11
LINCOLN CO WA 114-A2
MERCER ISLAND WA 175-C3
MERCER ISLAND WA 283-J1
MOSES LAKE WA 242-C3
NORTH BEND WA 176-C5
OSBURN ID 115-C2
PINEHURST ID 115-C2
POST FALLS ID 352-J9
POST FALLS ID 353-G6
POST FALLS ID 354-B7
SEATTLE WA 278-B7
SEATTLE WA 282-B1
SEATTLE WA 283-E1
SHOSHONE CO ID 115-C2
SNOQUALMIE WA 176-C4
SPOKANE WA 348-J10
SPOKANE WA 349-G9
SPOKANE CO WA 114-B2
SPOKANE CO WA 246-B5
SPOKANE CO WA 348-E12
SPOKANE CO WA 351-J7
SPOKANE CO WA 352-H9
SPOKANE VALLEY WA 349-J8
SPOKANE VALLEY WA 350-J6
SPOKANE VALLEY WA 351-A6
SPRAGUE WA 114-A3
WALLACE ID 115-C2
I-99 FRWY
CITY OF SURREY BC 101-C1
DISTRICT OF DELTA BC 101-C1
I-105 EUGENE-SPRINGFIELD HWY
EUGENE OR 329-J4
EUGENE OR 330-A5
SPRINGFIELD OR 330-A5
I-182 FRWY
BENTON CO WA 121-A3
BENTON CO WA 341-E4
FRANKLIN CO WA 342-B2
FRANKLIN CO WA 343-A4
PASCO WA 342-C1
PASCO WA 343-A4
RICHLAND WA 341-J3
RICHLAND WA 342-A3
I-184 184
BOISE ID 253-C3
I-205 E PORTLAND FRWY
CLACKAMAS CO OR 319-G7
I-205 EAST PORTLAND FRWY
CLACKAMAS CO OR 199-D4
CLACKAMAS CO OR 319-G6
GLADSTONE OR 199-D4
OREGON CITY OR 199-D4
PORTLAND OR 319-G6
TUALATIN OR 199-D4
WASHINGTON CO OR 199-D4
WEST LINN OR 199-D4
I-205 FRWY
CLARK CO WA 192-C4
CLARK CO WA 307-G1
MAYWOOD PARK OR 315-G1
PORTLAND OR 193-A7
PORTLAND OR 311-J2
PORTLAND OR 315-H1
PORTLAND OR 319-G1
VANCOUVER WA 192-D5
VANCOUVER WA 307-G1
VANCOUVER WA 311-J1
I-405 FRWY
BELLEVUE WA 175-C2
BOTHELL WA 171-C5
BOTHELL WA 171-C6
KING CO WA 171-C7
KING CO WA 175-C3
KIRKLAND WA 171-C7
KIRKLAND WA 175-C1
NEWCASTLE WA 175-C3
PORTLAND OR 312-E3
PORTLAND OR 313-F3
PORTLAND OR 317-E1
RENTON WA 175-C4
RENTON WA 289-J4
SNOHOMISH CO WA 171-B5
TUKWILA WA 289-J4
I-705 FRWY
TACOMA WA 293-H4
TACOMA WA 295-H1
Rt#-D1 WASHINGTON BLVD
CRESCENT CITY CA 148-B3
DEL NORTE CO CA 148-B3
Rt#-D1 E WASHINGTON BLVD
DEL NORTE CO CA 148-B3
Rt#-D2 ELK VALLEY CROSS RD
DEL NORTE CO CA 148-B3
Rt#-D2 ELK VALLEY RD
CRESCENT CITY CA 148-B3
DEL NORTE CO CA 148-B3
Rt#-D3 LAKE EARL DR
DEL NORTE CO CA 148-B3
Rt#-D3 NORTHCREST DR
CRESCENT CITY CA 148-B3
DEL NORTE CO CA 148-B3
Rt#-D4 FRED D HAIGHT DR
DEL NORTE CO CA 148-B3
Rt#-D5 OCEAN VIEW DR
DEL NORTE CO CA 148-B3
DEL NORTE CO CA 232-D7
Rt#-1 DOUGLAS ST
CITY OF VICTORIA BC 256-G6
DISTRICT OF SAANICH BC 256-G6
Rt#-1 HASTINGS ST E
VANCOUVER BC 255-F10
Rt#-1 HIGHWAY
BOUNDARY CO ID 107-B1
Rt#-1 ISLAND HWY
BRITISH COLUMBIA BC 101-A1
BRITISH COLUMBIA BC 159-B6
DISTRICT OF LANGFORD BC 159-B6
DISTRICT OF SAANICH BC 256-D4
DUNCAN BC 101-A1
TOWN OF VIEW ROYAL BC 159-B6
TOWN OF VIEW ROYAL BC 256-D4

Rt#-1 SECOND NARROWS BRDG
DISTRICT OF NORTH VANCOUV BC 255-F9
VANCOUVER BC 255-F9
Rt#-1 TRANS CANADA HWY
BRITISH COLUMBIA BC 93-C1
BRITISH COLUMBIA BC 94-C3
BRITISH COLUMBIA BC 95-A1
BRITISH COLUMBIA BC 101-A1
BRITISH COLUMBIA BC 102-B1
BRITISH COLUMBIA BC 156-A2
BRITISH COLUMBIA BC 159-A1
CITY OF CHILLIWACK BC 94-C3
CITY OF NORTH VANCOUVER BC 255-A3
CITY OF SURREY BC 157-B6
CITY OF VICTORIA BC 256-G11
COQUITLAM BC 157-B6
DISTRICT OF ABBOTSFORD BC 94-C3
DISTRICT OF ABBOTSFORD BC 102-B1
DISTRICT OF BURNABY BC 156-D4
DISTRICT OF BURNABY BC 255-F12
DISTRICT OF COQUITLAM BC 156-D4
DISTRICT OF LANGFORD BC 159-A6
DISTRICT OF MATSQUI BC 102-B1
DISTRICT OF NORTH VANCOUV BC 254-F2
DISTRICT OF NORTH VANCOUV BC 255-A3
DISTRICT OF SAANICH BC 256-G5
DISTRICT OF WEST VANCOUVE BC 156-A2
DISTRICT OF WEST VANCOUVE BC 254-F2
DUNCAN BC 101-A1
HOPE BC 95-A3
NANAIMO BC 93-A3
SQUAMISH BC 93-C1
TOWN OF VIEW ROYAL BC 159-A6
TOWN OF VIEW ROYAL BC 256-B3
TOWNSHIP OF LANGLEY BC 102-B1
TOWNSHIP OF LANGLEY BC 157-B6
TOWNSHIP OF LANGLEY BC 158-D1
VANCOUVER BC 255-F12
WHISTLER BC 93-C1
Rt#-1 UPPER LEVELS HWY
CITY OF NORTH VANCOUVER BC 255-D4
DISTRICT OF NORTH VANCOUV BC 254-H3
DISTRICT OF NORTH VANCOUV BC 255-D4
DISTRICT OF WEST VANCOUVE BC 156-A2
DISTRICT OF WEST VANCOUVE BC 254-A1
Rt#-1 WICKIEUP RD
BRITISH COLUMBIA BC 101-B1
BRITISH COLUMBIA BC 159-A1
DISTRICT OF LANGFORD BC 159-A5
Rt#-1A FRASER HWY
CITY OF SURREY BC 157-A6
DISTRICT OF MATSQUI BC 102-B1
LANGLEY BC 157-B7
LANGLEY BC 158-D1
TOWNSHIP OF LANGLEY BC 102-B1
TOWNSHIP OF LANGLEY BC 158-D1
Rt#-1A GOLDSTREAM AV
CITY OF COLWOOD BC 159-B6
DISTRICT OF LANGFORD BC 159-B6
Rt#-1A GORGE RD E
CITY OF VICTORIA BC 256-F6
Rt#-1A GORGE RD W
CITY OF VICTORIA BC 256-C5
DISTRICT OF SAANICH BC 256-C5
Rt#-1A HIGHWAY
CITY OF VICTORIA BC 256-F6
DISTRICT OF SAANICH BC 256-B5
LANGLEY BC 158-C1
Rt#-1A ISLAND HWY
TOWN OF VIEW ROYAL BC 256-A5
Rt#-1A KINGSWAY
VANCOUVER BC 156-C5
VANCOUVER BC 254-J13
VANCOUVER BC 255-A14
Rt#-1A OLD ISLAND HWY
CITY OF COLWOOD BC 159-B6
DISTRICT OF SAANICH BC 256-B5
TOWN OF ESQUIMALT BC 256-B5
TOWN OF VIEW ROYAL BC 159-B6
TOWN OF VIEW ROYAL BC 256-A4
Rt#-1A VEDDER RD
CITY OF CHILLIWACK BC 94-C3
Rt#-1A YALE RD E
BRITISH COLUMBIA BC 94-C3
CITY OF CHILLIWACK BC 94-C3
Rt#-1A YALE RD W
CITY OF CHILLIWACK BC 94-C3
Rt#-3 1ST AV
BOVILL ID 123-B1
Rt#-3 NW 1ST ST
ENTERPRISE OR 130-C2
WALLOWA CO OR 130-C2
Rt#-3 BALL MTN LTLE SHASTA RD
MONTAGUE CA 150-A3
SISKIYOU CO CA 150-A3
Rt#-3 CROWSNEST HWY
BRITISH COLUMBIA BC 103-C1
Rt#-3 ELK RIVER RD
LATAH CO ID 123-B1
Rt#-3 ENTERPRISE-LEWISTON HWY
WALLOWA CO OR 122-C3
WALLOWA CO OR 130-C1
Rt#-3 FRWY
BREMERTON WA 174-B4
BREMERTON WA 270-C6
KITSAP CO WA 170-B6
KITSAP CO WA 174-B1
KITSAP CO WA 270-B1
Navy Yard City WA 270-E11
PORT ORCHARD WA 174-B4
POULSBO WA 170-B6
Silverdale WA 174-B1
Silverdale WA 270-B1
Tracyton WA 270-A4
Rt#-3 HIGHWAY
BENEWAH CO ID 115-B3
BENEWAH CO ID 248-B6
BREMERTON WA 174-B4
BRITISH COLUMBIA BC 95-C3
BRITISH COLUMBIA BC 104-B1
BRITISH COLUMBIA BC 105-C1
BRITISH COLUMBIA BC 106-C1
GRAND FORKS BC 105-C1
GREENWOOD BC 105-B1
HOPE BC 95-A3
JULIAETTA ID 123-B2
KENDRICK ID 123-B1
KITSAP CO WA 170-C4
KITSAP CO WA 174-B4
KITSAP CO WA 270-D14
KOOTENAI CO ID 115-B2
KOOTENAI CO ID 248-D2
LATAH CO ID 115-B3
LATAH CO ID 123-B1
MASON CO WA 173-D5
MASON CO WA 174-A5

Rt#-3 HIGHWAY
MASON CO WA 180-D1
MONTAGUE CA 150-A3
Navy Yard City WA 270-E14
NEZ PERCE CO ID 123-A2
PRINCETON BC 95-C3
SAINT MARIES ID 248-D7
SHOSHONE CO ID 115-B3
SISKIYOU CO CA 149-C3
SISKIYOU CO CA 150-A3
YREKA CA 149-C3
Rt#-3 MAIN ST
BRITISH COLUMBIA BC 104-C1
JULIAETTA ID 123-B1
KENDRICK ID 123-B1
OSOYOOS BC 104-C1
Rt#-3 OLD OLYMPIC HWY
MASON CO WA 180-A3
SHELTON WA 180-A3
Rt#-3 PARK AV
BOVILL ID 123-B1
LATAH CO ID 123-B1
Rt#-3 E PINE ST
MASON CO WA 180-A3
SHELTON WA 180-A3
Rt#-3 SECOND AV
DEARY ID 123-B1
LATAH CO ID 123-B1
Rt#-3 WEBB ST
MONTAGUE CA 150-A3
Rt#-3 WYOMING ST
DEARY ID 123-B1
LATAH CO ID 123-B1
Rt#-3B HIGHWAY
BRITISH COLUMBIA BC 106-A1
MONTROSE BC 106-B1
ROSSLAND BC 106-A1
Rt#-4 1ST ST
SHOSHONE CO ID 115-C2
Rt#-4 3RD AV N
KELSO WA 303-D8
Rt#-4 5TH AV N
KELSO WA 303-D8
Rt#-4 ALLEN ST
KELSO WA 303-D8
Rt#-4 BURKE RD
SHOSHONE CO ID 115-C2
WALLACE ID 115-C2
Rt#-4 BURKE-CANYON CREEK RD
SHOSHONE CO ID 115-C2
Rt#-4 COWLITZ WY
KELSO WA 303-D8
Rt#-4 HIGHWAY
BRITISH COLUMBIA BC 92-A3
CATHLAMET WA 117-B3
PACIFIC CO WA 186-C4
PORT ALBERNI BC 92-B3
SHOSHONE CO ID 115-C2
WAHKIAKUM CO WA 117-A2
WAHKIAKUM CO WA 186-D5
WALLACE ID 115-C2
Rt#-4 OCEAN BEACH HWY
CATHLAMET WA 117-B3
COWLITZ CO WA 117-B3
COWLITZ CO WA 189-A2
COWLITZ CO WA 302-B3
LONGVIEW WA 302-F6
LONGVIEW WA 303-A8
WAHKIAKUM CO WA 117-B3
Rt#-5 4TH ST
SAINT MARIES ID 248-D7
Rt#-5 CEDAR ST
BENEWAH CO ID 115-A2
BENEWAH CO ID 248-A7
PLUMMER ID 115-A2
Rt#-5 COLLEGE AV
SAINT MARIES ID 248-D7
Rt#-5 HIGHWAY
BENEWAH CO ID 248-A7
BRITISH COLUMBIA BC 95-C1
CHATCOLET ID 248-B6
HOPE BC 95-A3
SAINT MARIES ID 248-C7
Rt#-5 MAIN AV
SAINT MARIES ID 248-C7
Rt#-5 MAIN ST
SAINT MARIES ID 248-D7
Rt#-5 NORTH FORK SIUSLAW RD
LANE CO OR 214-C1
Rt#-5A HIGHWAY
BRITISH COLUMBIA BC 95-C1
PRINCETON BC 95-C3
Rt#-6 1ST ST
TILLAMOOK OR 197-B2
Rt#-6 3RD ST
TILLAMOOK OR 197-C2
Rt#-6 W FOURTH AV
PE ELL WA 117-B2
Rt#-6 HENKLE ST
PACIFIC CO WA 117-A1
RAYMOND WA 117-A1
Rt#-6 HIGHWAY
BRITISH COLUMBIA BC 106-C1
LATAH CO ID 123-B1
LATAH CO ID 249-D1
LEWIS CO WA 117-B2
PACIFIC CO WA 117-A1
PE ELL WA 117-B2
POTLATCH ID 249-D1
Rt#-6 MAIN ST
PE ELL WA 117-B2
Rt#-6 OCEAN BEACH HWY
CHEHALIS WA 299-A13
LEWIS CO WA 117-B1
LEWIS CO WA 184-B7
LEWIS CO WA 187-A1
LEWIS CO WA 299-A13
PE ELL WA 117-B2
Rt#-6 SIXTH ST
POTLATCH ID 249-D1
Rt#-6 WHITE PINE DR
BENEWAH CO ID 115-B3
LATAH CO ID 115-B3
Rt#-6 WILSON RIVER HWY
BANKS OR 125-B1
TILLAMOOK OR 197-C2
TILLAMOOK CO OR 125-B1
TILLAMOOK CO OR 197-C2
WASHINGTON CO OR 125-B1
Rt#-7 1ST AV
DISTRICT OF MISSION BC 94-B3
Rt#-7 2ND AV
MORTON WA 118-B2
Rt#-7 E 38TH ST
TACOMA WA 295-H2

Rt#-7 AHSAHKA RD
STREET INDEX
Rt#-22A HIGHWAY 409

© 2006 Rand McNally & Company

STREET / City State Page-Grid

Rt#-7 AHSAHKA RD
OROFINO ID 123-C2
Rt#-7 BROADWAY E
VANCOUVER BC 254-H13
VANCOUVER BC 255-A13
Rt#-7 BROADWAY W
VANCOUVER BC 254-E12
Rt#-7 CAMPBELL ST
BAKER CITY OR 138-B1
Rt#-7 DEWEY AV
BAKER CITY OR 138-B1
Rt#-7 FRWY
TACOMA WA 295-H1
Rt#-7 GILBERT GRADE
CLEARWATER CO ID 123-C2
Rt#-7 HIGHWAY
BRITISH COLUMBIA BC 95-A3
CLEARWATER CO ID 123-C2
LEWIS CO WA 118-B1
OROFINO ID 123-C2
PIERCE CO WA 118-B1
Rt#-7 LOUGHEED HWY
BRITISH COLUMBIA BC 94-B3
COQUITLAM BC 157-A5
DISTRICT OF BURNABY BC 156-D4
DISTRICT OF BURNABY BC 255-G12
DISTRICT OF COQUITLAM BC 156-D4
DISTRICT OF KENT BC 94-B3
DISTRICT OF MISSION BC 94-B3
MAPLE RIDGE BC 94-B3
MAPLE RIDGE BC 157-D6
PITT MEADOWS BC 157-B4
PORT COQUITLAM BC 157-B4
Rt#-7 MAIN ST
BAKER CITY OR 138-B1
Rt#-7 MORTON RD
LEWIS CO WA 118-B2
MORTON WA 118-B2
Rt#-7 MOUNTAIN HWY E
PIERCE CO WA 118-B1
PIERCE CO WA 181-D6
PIERCE CO WA 182-A7
Rt#-7 NORTH RAILWAY AV
DISTRICT OF MISSION BC 94-B3
Rt#-7 PACIFIC AV
PIERCE CO WA 181-D4
TACOMA WA 181-D4
TACOMA WA 295-H3
Rt#-7 PACIFIC AV S
PIERCE CO WA 181-D5
Rt#-7 RIVERSIDE AV
OROFINO ID 123-C2
Rt#-7 RUSSELL RIDGE RD
CLEARWATER CO ID 123-C2
Rt#-7 WHITNEY HWY
BAKER CITY OR 138-B1
BAKER CO OR 137-C1
BAKER CO OR 138-A1
GRANT CO OR 137-C1
Rt#-7A BARNET HWY
COQUITLAM BC 157-A4
PORT MOODY BC 157-A4
Rt#-7A BARNET RD
DISTRICT OF BURNABY BC 156-D4
Rt#-7A HASTINGS ST
DISTRICT OF BURNABY BC 156-D4
DISTRICT OF BURNABY BC 255-G10
VANCOUVER BC 255-F10
Rt#-7A HASTINGS ST E
VANCOUVER BC 254-J10
VANCOUVER BC 255-B10
Rt#-7A HIGHWAY
DISTRICT OF BURNABY BC 156-D4
Rt#-7A INLET DR
DISTRICT OF BURNABY BC 156-D4
Rt#-7A SAINT JOHNS ST
DISTRICT OF BURNABY BC 156-D4
PORT MOODY BC 156-D4
PORT MOODY BC 157-A4
Rt#-8 E 3RD ST
MOSCOW ID 249-C5
Rt#-8 W 3RD ST
MOSCOW ID 249-C5
Rt#-8 SE 10TH AV
HILLSBORO OR 198-D1
Rt#-8 19TH AV
FOREST GROVE OR 198-B1
Rt#-8 19TH WY
FOREST GROVE OR 198-C1
Rt#-8 N ADAIR ST
CORNELIUS OR 198-C1
FOREST GROVE OR 198-C1
Rt#-8 BASELINE ST
CORNELIUS OR 198-C1
Rt#-8 SE BASELINE ST
HILLSBORO OR 198-D1
Rt#-8 SW BASELINE ST
HILLSBORO OR 198-D1
Rt#-8 SW BROADWAY
BEAVERTON OR 199-B2
Rt#-8 SW CANYON RD
BEAVERTON OR 199-B2
WASHINGTON CO OR 199-B2
Rt#-8 E ST
FOREST GROVE OR 198-B1
Rt#-8 FIRST ST
ELK RIVER ID 123-C1
Rt#-8 GALES CREEK RD
FOREST GROVE OR 198-B1
WASHINGTON CO OR 125-B1
WASHINGTON CO OR 198-B1
Rt#-8 NW GALES CREEK RD
WASHINGTON CO OR 125-B1
WASHINGTON CO OR 198-B1
Rt#-8 HIGHWAY
BEAVERTON OR 199-B1
BOVILL ID 123-B1
BRITISH COLUMBIA BC 95-C1
CLEARWATER CO ID 123-B1
ELK RIVER ID 123-C1
ELMA WA 179-B7
GRAYS HARBOR CO WA 179-C6
LATAH CO ID 123-B1
LATAH CO ID 249-D5
MCCLEARY WA 179-C6
MOSCOW ID 249-C5
THURSTON CO WA 179-D6
THURSTON CO WA 180-B6
TROY ID 123-A1
WASHINGTON CO OR 199-B1
Rt#-8 MAIN ST
TROY ID 123-A1
Rt#-8 SE OAK ST
HILLSBORO OR 198-D1
Rt#-8 SW OAK ST
HILLSBORO OR 198-D1
Rt#-8 SW OLD HIGHWAY 47
FOREST GROVE OR 198-B1
Rt#-8 PACIFIC AV
CORNELIUS OR 198-C1
FOREST GROVE OR 198-C1
Rt#-8 SECOND AV
DEARY ID 123-B1
LATAH CO ID 123-B1
Rt#-8 TAFT ST
ELK RIVER ID 123-C1
Rt#-8 TUALATIN VALLEY HWY
CORNELIUS OR 198-C1
HILLSBORO OR 198-D1
WASHINGTON CO OR 198-C1
Rt#-8 SE TUALATIN VALLEY HWY
HILLSBORO OR 198-D1
HILLSBORO OR 199-A2
WASHINGTON CO OR 199-A2
Rt#-8 SW TUALATIN VALLEY HWY
BEAVERTON OR 199-A2
HILLSBORO OR 199-A2
WASHINGTON CO OR 199-A2
Rt#-9 N BORSETH ST
SEDRO-WOOLLEY WA 161-C5
Rt#-9 CASCADE HWY
SEDRO-WOOLLEY WA 161-C6
Rt#-9 CHEAM AV
DISTRICT OF KENT BC 94-C3
Rt#-9 EVERGREEN DR
DISTRICT OF KENT BC 94-C3
Rt#-9 HAIG HWY
DISTRICT OF KENT BC 94-C3
Rt#-9 HIGHWAY
ARLINGTON WA 168-D5
BRITISH COLUMBIA BC 94-C3
DISTRICT OF KENT BC 94-C3
LATAH CO ID 123-A1
MARYSVILLE WA 168-D7
MARYSVILLE WA 171-D1
SEDRO-WOOLLEY WA 161-C6
SKAGIT CO WA 161-C3
SKAGIT CO WA 168-C1
SKAGIT CO WA 260-J11
SNOHOMISH WA 171-D3
SNOHOMISH CO WA 168-C3
SNOHOMISH CO WA 171-D1
Rt#-9 HOPEWELL RD
WHATCOM CO WA 102-B1
Rt#-9 HOT SPRINGS RD
CITY OF HARRISON HOT SPRI BC 94-C3
DISTRICT OF KENT BC 94-C3
Rt#-9 LAWRENCE RD
WHATCOM CO WA 102-B1
Rt#-9 MAIN ST
SKAGIT CO WA 168-C2
Rt#-9 MOORE ST
SEDRO-WOOLLEY WA 161-C5
Rt#-9 NOOKSACK AV
NOOKSACK WA 102-B1
Rt#-9 NOOKSACK RD
NOOKSACK WA 102-B1
WHATCOM CO WA 102-B1
Rt#-9 SNOHOMISH WOODINVLLE RD
SNOHOMISH CO WA 171-D6
Rt#-9 TOWNSHIP RD
SEDRO-WOOLLEY WA 161-C5
SKAGIT CO WA 161-C5
Rt#-9 VALLEY HWY
WHATCOM CO WA 102-B1
WHATCOM CO WA 161-C2
Rt#-10 56TH AV
CITY OF SURREY BC 157-A7
CITY OF SURREY BC 158-B1
Rt#-10 58TH AV
CITY OF SURREY BC 156-D7
CITY OF SURREY BC 157-A7
DISTRICT OF DELTA BC 156-D7
Rt#-10 232ND ST
TOWNSHIP OF LANGLEY BC 157-D7
Rt#-10 SW BEAVRTN-HLLSDLE
BEAVERTON OR 199-B2
PORTLAND OR 199-B2
PORTLAND OR 199-B2
PORTLAND OR 316-A3
WASHINGTON CO OR 199-B2
Rt#-10 SW CAPITOL HWY
PORTLAND OR 316-D4
PORTLAND OR 317-E4
Rt#-10 SW FARMINGTON RD
BEAVERTON OR 199-A2
WASHINGTON CO OR 198-D3
WASHINGTON CO OR 199-A2
Rt#-10 GLOVER RD
LANGLEY BC 157-C7
TOWNSHIP OF LANGLEY BC 157-C7
Rt#-10 HIGHWAY
KITTITAS CO WA 240-C2
KITTITAS CO WA 241-A3
TOWNSHIP OF LANGLEY BC 157-D7
Rt#-10 LADNER TRUNK RD
DISTRICT OF DELTA BC 101-C1
DISTRICT OF DELTA BC 156-D7
Rt#-10 LANGLEY BYPS
CITY OF SURREY BC 157-C7
CITY OF SURREY BC 158-B1
LANGLEY BC 157-C7
Rt#-10 RAWLISON CRES
TOWNSHIP OF LANGLEY BC 157-C7
Rt#-11 11TH AV
DISTRICT OF MISSION BC 94-B3
Rt#-11 12TH ST
BELLINGHAM WA 258-B11
Rt#-11 ABBOTSFORD-MISSION HWY
DISTRICT OF ABBOTSFORD BC 102-B1
DISTRICT OF MATSQUI BC 94-B3
DISTRICT OF MATSQUI BC 102-B1
Rt#-11 CHUCKANUT DR
BELLINGHAM WA 258-B12
SKAGIT CO WA 160-D2
SKAGIT CO WA 161-A3
SKAGIT CO WA 260-B1
WHATCOM CO WA 160-D2
WHATCOM CO WA 258-B14
Rt#-11 HIGHWAY
BURLINGTON WA 260-C3
CLEARWATER CO ID 123-B1
SKAGIT CO WA 161-A5
SKAGIT CO WA 260-A1
Rt#-11 S MAIN ST
MILTON-FREEWATER OR 121-C3
Rt#-11 OLD FAIRHAVEN PKWY
BELLINGHAM WA 258-B11
Rt#-11 OREGON-WASHINGTON HWY
ADAMS OR 129-B1
ATHENA OR 129-B1
Rt#-11 OREGON-WASHINGTON HWY
MILTON-FREEWATER OR 121-C3
PENDLETON OR 129-B1
UMATILLA CO OR 121-C3
UMATILLA CO OR 129-B1
WALLA WALLA CO WA 121-C3
Rt#-11 VALLEY PKWY
BELLINGHAM WA 258-C11
Rt#-12 HIGHWAY
CLEARWATER CO ID 123-C2
Rt#-13 264TH ST
TOWNSHIP OF LANGLEY BC 158-D2
Rt#-13 HARPSTER GRADE RD
IDAHO CO ID 123-C3
Rt#-13 HIGHWAY
TOWNSHIP OF LANGLEY BC 158-D2
Rt#-13 E MAIN ST
GRANGEVILLE ID 123-C3
IDAHO CO ID 123-C3
Rt#-13 W MAIN ST
GRANGEVILLE ID 123-C3
IDAHO CO ID 123-C3
Rt#-14 D ST
WASHOUGAL WA 193-C7
Rt#-14 EVERGREEN HWY
CARSON WA 194-C6
CARSON WA 195-B5
CLARK CO WA 193-D7
CLARK CO WA 200-C1
NORTH BONNEVILLE WA 194-C6
SKAMANIA CO WA 193-D7
SKAMANIA CO WA 194-A7
SKAMANIA CO WA 195-B5
SKAMANIA CO WA 200-D1
STEVENSON WA 194-C6
Rt#-14 HIGHWAY
BENTON CO WA 120-C3
BENTON CO WA 121-A3
BENTON CO WA 128-C1
BRITISH COLUMBIA BC 100-C2
IDAHO CO ID 123-C3
KLICKITAT CO WA 128-B1
Rt#-14 LEWIS AND CLARK FRWY
CAMAS WA 193-A7
CLARK CO WA 193-A7
VANCOUVER WA 193-A7
VANCOUVER WA 305-G6
VANCOUVER WA 306-A6
VANCOUVER WA 307-E7
VANCOUVER WA 311-G1
Rt#-14 LEWIS AND CLARK HWY
BINGEN WA 195-C5
CAMAS WA 193-C7
CLARK CO WA 193-C7
KLICKITAT CO WA 127-B1
KLICKITAT CO WA 195-C5
KLICKITAT CO WA 196-C6
SKAMANIA CO WA 195-C5
WASHOUGAL WA 193-C7
WHITE SALMON WA 195-C5
Rt#-14 SOOKE RD
BRITISH COLUMBIA BC 101-A2
BRITISH COLUMBIA BC 159-A7
DISTRICT OF LANGFORD BC 159-A7
DISTRICT OF METCHOSIN BC 159-A7
Rt#-14 STEUBEN ST
BINGEN WA 195-D5
Rt#-14 WEST COAST RD
BRITISH COLUMBIA BC 101-A2
BRITISH COLUMBIA BC 164-C1
Rt#-14B NE 3RD AV
CAMAS WA 193-B7
CLARK CO WA 193-B7
WASHOUGAL WA 193-B7
Rt#-14B NW 6TH AV
CAMAS WA 193-B7
Rt#-14B NE ADAMS ST
CAMAS WA 193-B7
Rt#-14B D ST
WASHOUGAL WA 193-C7
Rt#-14B E ST
WASHOUGAL WA 193-C7
Rt#-14B EVERGREEN WY
WASHOUGAL WA 193-C7
Rt#-14B SE EVERGREEN BLVD
CLARK CO WA 193-C7
WASHOUGAL WA 193-C7
Rt#-15 176TH ST
CITY OF SURREY BC 157-B7
CITY OF SURREY BC 158-B2
WHATCOM CO WA 158-B2
Rt#-15 CLOVERDALE BYPS
CITY OF SURREY BC 157-B7
Rt#-15 PACIFIC HWY
CITY OF SURREY BC 158-B1
Rt#-16 EMMETT HWY
ADA CO ID 139-C3
GEM CO ID 139-C3
Rt#-16 N EMMETT HWY
ADA CO ID 139-C3
ADA CO ID 147-C1
Rt#-16 FRWY
GIG HARBOR WA 174-B7
GIG HARBOR WA 181-C1
KITSAP CO WA 174-B4
PIERCE CO WA 174-B6
PIERCE CO WA 181-C1
PORT ORCHARD WA 174-B4
TACOMA WA 181-C2
TACOMA WA 292-A5
TACOMA WA 294-B1
TACOMA WA 295-E1
Rt#-16 HIGHWAY
BREMERTON WA 174-B4
GEM CO ID 139-C3
KITSAP CO WA 174-B4
Rt#-17 60 ST
DISTRICT OF DELTA BC 101-C1
Rt#-17 60TH ST
DISTRICT OF DELTA BC 156-C7
Rt#-17 BLANSHARD ST
CITY OF VICTORIA BC 256-G6
DISTRICT OF SAANICH BC 256-G5
Rt#-17 DAISY ST N
GRANT CO WA 112-C2
SOAP LAKE WA 112-C2
Rt#-17 DAISY ST S
SOAP LAKE WA 112-C2
Rt#-17 HIGHWAY
ADAMS CO WA 121-A1
BRIDGEPORT WA 112-C1
DOUGLAS CO WA 112-C1
DOUGLAS CO WA 113-A2
FRANKLIN CO WA 121-A1
GRANT CO WA 112-C2
Rt#-17 HIGHWAY
GRANT CO WA 113-A2
GRANT CO WA 121-A1
GRANT CO WA 242-B1
MESA WA 121-A2
MOSES LAKE WA 242-C2
OKANOGAN CO WA 104-C3
OKANOGAN CO WA 112-C1
SOAP LAKE WA 112-C2
Rt#-17 LEAHY RD S
DOUGLAS CO WA 112-C1
Rt#-17 PATRICIA BAY HWY
DISTRICT OF CENTRAL SAANI BC 159-C2
DISTRICT OF NORTH SAANICH BC 159-C2
DISTRICT OF SAANICH BC 159-C2
DISTRICT OF SAANICH BC 256-F2
TOWN OF SIDNEY BC 159-C2
Rt#-17 R RD NE
DOUGLAS CO WA 112-C1
Rt#-17 TSAWWASSEN FERRY CSWY
DISTRICT OF DELTA BC 101-C1
Rt#-17A HIGHWAY
DISTRICT OF SAANICH BC 159-C5
Rt#-17A MCTAVISH RD
DISTRICT OF NORTH SAANICH BC 159-C3
Rt#-17A WEST SAANICH RD
DISTRICT OF CENTRAL SAANI BC 159-B3
DISTRICT OF NORTH SAANICH BC 159-B3
DISTRICT OF SAANICH BC 159-C5
Rt#-18 AUBURN-ECHO LAKE CTO
AUBURN WA 182-C1
COVINGTON WA 175-D7
KENT WA 175-D7
KING CO WA 175-D7
KING CO WA 176-A6
KING CO WA 182-C1
MAPLE VALLEY WA 175-D7
Rt#-18 AUBURN-ECHO LAKE CTO S
KING CO WA 176-A6
Rt#-18 SE DAYTON BYPASS RD
DAYTON OR 198-B7
YAMHILL CO OR 198-B7
Rt#-18 ECHO LAKE CTO SE
KING CO WA 176-B5
Rt#-18 FRWY
AUBURN WA 182-B1
FEDERAL WAY WA 182-B1
KING CO WA 182-B1
Rt#-18 HIGHWAY
BRITISH COLUMBIA BC 100-C1
BRITISH COLUMBIA BC 101-A1
Lake Cowichan BC 100-C1
Rt#-18 HIGHWAY 99 S
YAMHILL CO OR 204-B1
Rt#-18 E MAIN ST
SHERIDAN OR 125-B3
WILLAMINA OR 125-A3
Rt#-18 S MAIN ST
WILLAMINA OR 125-A3
Rt#-18 W MAIN ST
SHERIDAN OR 125-B3
Rt#-18 SALMON RIVER HWY
LINCOLN CO OR 203-B4
MCMINNVILLE OR 198-A7
MCMINNVILLE OR 204-A2
POLK CO OR 125-A3
Rose Lodge OR 203-D3
SHERIDAN OR 125-B3
TILLAMOOK CO OR 125-A3
TILLAMOOK CO OR 203-D3
YAMHILL CO OR 125-B3
YAMHILL CO OR 198-A7
YAMHILL CO OR 204-A2
Rt#-18 NE SALMON RIVER HWY
YAMHILL CO OR 198-B7
Rt#-18 SE SALMON RIVER HWY
MCMINNVILLE OR 198-A7
YAMHILL CO OR 198-B7
Rt#-18 THREE MILE LN HWY
MCMINNVILLE OR 198-B7
YAMHILL CO OR 198-B7
Rt#-18 W VALLEY HWY
SHERIDAN OR 125-B3
WILLAMINA OR 125-B3
YAMHILL CO OR 125-B3
Rt#-18 WILLAMINA-SHERIDAN HWY
POLK CO OR 125-A3
WILLAMINA OR 125-A3
Rt#-19 E 7TH ST
FOSSIL OR 128-A3
Rt#-19 AIRPORT CUTOFF RD
Irondale WA 263-B11
JEFFERSON CO WA 263-B11
Rt#-19 BEAVER VALLEY RD
JEFFERSON CO WA 170-A1
Rt#-19 COTTONWOOD ST
ARLINGTON OR 128-A1
Rt#-19 DUKE POINT HWY
BRITISH COLUMBIA BC 93-A3
NANAIMO BC 93-A3
Rt#-19 E WALNUT ST
CONDON OR 128-A2
Rt#-19 HIGHWAY
BRITISH COLUMBIA BC 92-A1
CAMPBELL RIVER BC 92-A1
COURTENAY BC 92-A2
Rt#-19 W IDAHO AV
HOMEDALE ID 147-A1
Rt#-19 INLAND ISLAND HWY
BRITISH COLUMBIA BC 92-A1
Rt#-19 ISLAND HWY N
BRITISH COLUMBIA BC 93-A3
NANAIMO BC 93-A3
Rt#-19 JOHN DAY HWY
ARLINGTON OR 128-A2
CONDON OR 128-A2
FOSSIL OR 128-A3
GILLIAM CO OR 128-A2
GRANT CO OR 136-B1
SPRAY OR 136-B1
WHEELER CO OR 128-A3
WHEELER CO OR 136-B1
Rt#-19 LOCUST ST
ARLINGTON OR 128-A1
Rt#-19 N LOCUST ST
ARLINGTON OR 128-A1
GILLIAM CO OR 128-A1
Rt#-19 S LOCUST ST
ARLINGTON OR 128-A1
Rt#-19 MAIN ST
CANYON CO ID 147-B1
Rt#-19 MAIN ST
GREENLEAF ID 147-B1
Rt#-19 S MAIN ST
CONDON OR 128-A2
Rt#-19 NANAIMO PKWY
NANAIMO BC 93-A3
Rt#-19 OWYHEE BLVD
OWYHEE CO ID 147-A1
Rt#-19 RHODY DR
Hadlock-Irondale WA 170-A1
Irondale WA 263-E14
JEFFERSON CO WA 170-A1
JEFFERSON CO WA 263-E14
Rt#-19 SIMPLOT BLVD
CALDWELL ID 147-B1
CANYON CO ID 147-B1
WILDER ID 147-B1
Rt#-19 N WASHINGTON ST
CONDON OR 128-A2
Rt#-19 S WASHINGTON ST
CONDON OR 128-A2
Rt#-19A HIGHWAY
BRITISH COLUMBIA BC 92-A1
COURTENAY BC 92-A2
PARKSVILLE BC 92-C3
Rt#-19A ISLAND HWY N
BRITISH COLUMBIA BC 93-A3
NANAIMO BC 93-A3
Rt#-20 E 3RD AV
COLVILLE WA 106-A2
STEVENS CO WA 106-A2
Rt#-20 W 6TH ST
REPUBLIC WA 105-B2
Rt#-20 12TH ST
ANACORTES WA 259-F2
Rt#-20 AVON AV
BURLINGTON WA 260-C4
Rt#-20 AVON CTO
SKAGIT CO WA 161-A6
SKAGIT CO WA 260-A6
Rt#-20 AVON CUT-OFF
SKAGIT CO WA 161-A7
Rt#-20 BURLINGTON BLVD
BURLINGTON WA 260-C4
Rt#-20 S BURLINGTON BLVD
BURLINGTON WA 260-C6
Rt#-20 CASCADE HWY
SEDRO-WOOLLEY WA 161-C6
SEDRO-WOOLLEY WA 260-E4
SKAGIT CO WA 260-E4
Rt#-20 S CLARK AV
REPUBLIC WA 105-B2
Rt#-20 COLVILLE-TIGER RD
STEVENS CO WA 106-A2
Rt#-20 COMMERCIAL AV
ANACORTES WA 259-H2
Rt#-20 COMMERICAL AV
ANACORTES WA 160-C6
ANACORTES WA 259-H3
SKAGIT CO WA 259-J6
Rt#-20 N CROSS STATE HWY
SEDRO-WOOLLEY WA 161-C5
SKAGIT CO WA 161-C5
Rt#-20 DIVISION ST
TWISP WA 104-A3
Rt#-20 ELMWAY
OKANOGAN WA 104-C3
OKANOGAN CO WA 104-C3
OMAK WA 104-C3
Rt#-20 FOURTH AV W
OMAK WA 104-C3
Rt#-20 HIGHWAY
ANACORTES WA 160-C6
Ault Field WA 167-C2
BURLINGTON WA 260-C5
CONCRETE WA 102-C2
COUPEVILLE WA 167-B4
CUSICK WA 106-C3
FERRY CO WA 105-B2
FERRY CO WA 106-A2
HAMILTON WA 102-C2
ISLAND CO WA 160-C7
ISLAND CO WA 167-C1
JEFFERSON CO WA 109-C1
JEFFERSON CO WA 170-A1
JEFFERSON CO WA 263-C6
LYMAN WA 102-C2
NEWPORT WA 106-C3
OAK HARBOR WA 167-C2
OKANOGAN WA 104-C3
OKANOGAN CO WA 104-C2
OKANOGAN CO WA 105-A2
PEND OREILLE CO WA 106-B2
PORT TOWNSEND WA 263-C6
REPUBLIC WA 105-B2
SKAGIT CO WA 102-C2
SKAGIT CO WA 160-C6
SKAGIT CO WA 161-D5
SKAGIT CO WA 259-J11
SKAGIT CO WA 260-B6
WINTHROP WA 104-A2
Rt#-20 MAIN ST S
OMAK WA 104-C3
Rt#-20 MEMORIAL HWY
SKAGIT CO WA 160-D6
SKAGIT CO WA 161-A7
Rt#-20 E METHOW VALLEY HWY
OKANOGAN CO WA 104-B3
TWISP WA 104-A3
Rt#-20 NORTH CASCADES HWY
CHELAN CO WA 103-C2
OKANOGAN CO WA 103-C2
SKAGIT CO WA 103-A2
WHATCOM CO WA 103-A2
Rt#-20 OAKES AV
ANACORTES WA 259-B3
Rt#-20 OKOMA DR
OKANOGAN CO WA 104-C3
OMAK WA 104-C3
Rt#-20 PIONEER WY
OAK HARBOR WA 167-B3
Rt#-20 RIO VISTA AV
BURLINGTON WA 260-C5
Rt#-20 RIVERSIDE AV
OKANOGAN CO WA 104-A2
WINTHROP WA 104-A2
Rt#-20 RIVERSIDE DR
OKANOGAN CO WA 104-C2
OMAK WA 104-C2
Rt#-20 SECOND AV N
OKANOGAN WA 104-C3
Rt#-20 SECOND AV NW
OKANOGAN WA 104-C3
Rt#-20 SECOND AV SW
OKANOGAN WA 104-C3
Rt#-20 SIMS WY
PORT TOWNSEND WA 263-C6
Rt#-20 SIXTH ST
OKANOGAN CO WA 104-C2
TONASKET WA 104-C2
Rt#-20 SPUR 20
ANACORTES WA 160-C6
Rt#-20 WATER ST
PORT TOWNSEND WA 263-H5
Rt#-21 N 1ST ST
ODESSA WA 113-B3
Rt#-21 W 1ST AV
ODESSA WA 113-B3
Rt#-21 E 6TH AV
ODESSA WA 113-B3
Rt#-21 S ALDER ST
ODESSA WA 113-B3
Rt#-21 N DIVISION ST
ODESSA WA 113-B3
Rt#-21 W FIRST ST
LIND WA 121-B1
Rt#-21 W FRONT AV
LINCOLN CO WA 113-B1
WILBUR WA 113-B1
Rt#-21 E GOWEN RD
ADA CO ID 253-D4
BOISE ID 253-D4
Rt#-21 HIGHWAY
ADAMS CO WA 113-B3
ADAMS CO WA 121-B1
BOUNDARY CO ID 107-B1
BRITISH COLUMBIA BC 105-C1
BRITISH COLUMBIA BC 107-B1
FERRY CO WA 105-C1
FERRY CO WA 113-B1
GRAND FORKS BC 105-C1
LINCOLN CO WA 113-B1
LIND WA 121-B1
ODESSA WA 113-B3
REPUBLIC WA 105-B2
Rt#-21 LIND-KAHLOTUS RD
ADAMS CO WA 121-C1
FRANKLIN CO WA 121-C1
KAHLOTUS WA 121-C1
Rt#-21 W MAY AV
ODESSA WA 113-B3
Rt#-21 MONSOR RD
LINCOLN CO WA 113-B2
Rt#-21 ROSENOFF RD
ADAMS CO WA 113-B3
Rt#-21 E SECOND ST
LIND WA 121-B1
Rt#-21 VIOLET AV
KAHLOTUS WA 121-C1
Rt#-21 S WEST ST
WILBUR WA 113-B1
Rt#-22 12TH ST SE
SALEM OR 322-J14
Rt#-22 BUENA RD
YAKIMA CO WA 120-A2
Rt#-22 BUENA WY
TOPPENISH WA 120-A2
Rt#-22 CENTER ST BRDG
SALEM OR 322-H12
Rt#-22 CENTER ST BRDG NE
SALEM OR 322-H12
Rt#-22 CENTER ST NE
SALEM OR 322-H12
Rt#-22 S ELM ST
TOPPENISH WA 120-A2
Rt#-22 EVERGREEN HWY
TOPPENISH WA 120-A2
YAKIMA CO WA 120-A2
Rt#-22 FERRY ST SE
SALEM OR 322-H13
Rt#-22 FRONT ST NE
SALEM OR 322-H12
Rt#-22 FRONT ST SE
SALEM OR 322-H13
Rt#-22 HIGHWAY
BENTON CO WA 120-B3
BRITISH COLUMBIA BC 106-A1
MABTON WA 120-B3
PROSSER WA 120-C3
TOPPENISH WA 120-A2
YAKIMA CO WA 120-A2
Rt#-22 MARION ST
SALEM OR 322-H12
Rt#-22 MARION ST BRDG
SALEM OR 322-H12
Rt#-22 MISSION ST SE
SALEM OR 322-J14
SALEM OR 323-A14
SALEM OR 325-B1
Rt#-22 PRINGLE PKWY SE
SALEM OR 322-J13
Rt#-22 SALEM HWY
SALEM OR 322-J14
Rt#-22 N SANTIAM HWY
AUMSVILLE OR 205-A7
DETROIT OR 134-A1
GATES OR 134-A1
IDANHA OR 134-B1
LINN CO OR 134-C1
MARION CO OR 133-C1
MARION CO OR 134-A1
MARION CO OR 205-A7
MARION CO OR 325-G3
MILL CITY OR 134-A1
SALEM OR 204-D6
SALEM OR 325-G3
STAYTON OR 133-C1
SUBLIMITY OR 133-C1
Rt#-22 THREE RIVERS HWY
POLK CO OR 125-A3
TILLAMOOK CO OR 197-B6
TILLAMOOK CO OR 203-D1
YAMHILL CO OR 125-A3
YAMHILL CO OR 203-D1
Rt#-22 TRADE ST SE
SALEM OR 322-H13
Rt#-22 WAPENISH RD
YAKIMA CO WA 120-A2
Rt#-22 WILLAMINA-SALEM HWY
POLK CO OR 125-B3
POLK CO OR 204-A5
POLK CO OR 322-G12
SALEM OR 322-G12
Rt#-22 WILLAMINA-SALEM HWY NW
POLK CO OR 204-B6
POLK CO OR 322-B14
SALEM OR 322-B14
Rt#-22A BOUNDARY HWY
NORTHPORT WA 106-B1
STEVENS CO WA 106-B1
Rt#-22A HIGHWAY
BRITISH COLUMBIA BC 106-B1
STEVENS CO WA 106-A1

INDEX

INDEX

Rt#-97 HIGHWAY STREET INDEX Rt#-138 SW OAK AV 411

STREET INDEX

STREET
City State Page-Grid

Rt#-97 HIGHWAY
KOOTENAI CO ID 248-A1
OSOYOOS BC 104-C1
Rt#-97 LAKE AV
HARRISON ID 248-A4
Rt#-97C HIGHWAY
BRITISH COLUMBIA BC 95-C1
Rt#-99 N 1ST AV
DRAIN OR 219-A3
Rt#-99 N 1ST ST
OAKLAND OR 219-A7
Rt#-99 2ND AV
GOLD HILL OR 230-A6
Rt#-99 SW 5TH ST
CANYONVILLE OR 225-C3
Rt#-99 E 6TH AV
EUGENE OR 330-A6
Rt#-99 W 6TH AV
EUGENE OR 329-G6
EUGENE OR 330-A6
Rt#-99 E 7TH AV
EUGENE OR 330-A6
Rt#-99 W 7TH AV
EUGENE OR 329-G6
EUGENE OR 330-A6
Rt#-99 16TH AV S
FEDERAL WAY WA 182-B1
Rt#-99 54TH AV E
FIFE WA 182-A2
Rt#-99 70TH AV
VANCOUVER BC 156-B5
Rt#-99 ALASKAN FRWY
SEATTLE WA 277-J5
SEATTLE WA 278-A6
SEATTLE WA 281-J3
SEATTLE WA 282-A1
Rt#-99 AURORA AV N
SEATTLE WA 171-A7
SEATTLE WA 273-J2
SEATTLE WA 277-J4
SHORELINE WA 171-A7
Rt#-99 W B AV
DRAIN OR 219-A3
Rt#-99 BEAR CREST DR
JACKSON CO OR 234-B2
PHOENIX OR 234-B2
Rt#-99 BROADWAY
EVERETT WA 268-D5
Rt#-99 E BROADWAY
EUGENE OR 330-B6
Rt#-99 S BROADWAY
EVERETT WA 268-C6
Rt#-99 CALAPOOYA ST
DOUGLAS CO OR 221-C1
SUTHERLIN OR 221-C1
Rt#-99 N CEDAR ST
DRAIN OR 219-A3
Rt#-99 S CEDAR ST
DRAIN OR 219-A3
Rt#-99 COBURG RD
EUGENE OR 330-A6
Rt#-99 COOS BAY-ROSEBURG HWY
DOUGLAS CO OR 221-B6
DOUGLAS CO OR 334-D14
WINSTON OR 221-B6
Rt#-99 DILLARD HWY
DOUGLAS CO OR 221-B7
WINSTON OR 221-B7
Rt#-99 N DOUGLAS BLVD
WINSTON OR 221-B6
Rt#-99 DRAIN-YONCALLA HWY
DOUGLAS CO OR 219-A3
DRAIN OR 219-A3
YONCALLA OR 219-A3
Rt#-99 EAGLE VALLEY RD
DOUGLAS CO OR 219-A3
Rt#-99 E ELKTON-SUTHERLIN HWY
SUTHERLIN OR 221-C1
Rt#-99 EVERETT MALL WY
EVERETT WA 268-D5
Rt#-99 SE EVERETT MALL WY
EVERETT WA 268-C6
Rt#-99 SW EVERETT MALL WY
EVERETT WA 268-A7
Rt#-99 EVERGREEN WY
EVERETT WA 171-B4
EVERETT WA 267-J7
EVERETT WA 268-A7
SNOHOMISH CO WA 171-B4
Rt#-99 FRANKLIN BLVD
EUGENE OR 330-C7
LANE CO OR 330-H12
SPRINGFIELD OR 330-G8
Rt#-99 FRONT ST
YONCALLA OR 219-B4
Rt#-99 FRWY
CITY OF RICHMOND BC 156-B6
CITY OF SURREY BC 158-A1
DISTRICT OF DELTA BC 156-C7
KING CO WA 286-B4
SEATTLE WA 281-J7
SEATTLE WA 285-J1
SEATTLE WA 286-A2
TUKWILA WA 286-C5
WHATCOM CO WA 158-B3
Rt#-99 N FRONT ST
CENTRAL POINT OR 230-C7
Rt#-99 S FRONT ST
CENTRAL POINT OR 230-C7
OAKLAND OR 219-A7
Rt#-99 GEORGE MASSEY TUN
CITY OF RICHMOND BC 156-B7
DISTRICT OF DELTA BC 156-C7
Rt#-99 GEORGIA ST
VANCOUVER BC 254-F9
Rt#-99 GOLD HILL SPUR
GOLD HILL OR 230-B6
JACKSON CO OR 230-B6
Rt#-99 GOSHEN-DIVIDE HWY
COTTAGE GROVE OR 215-B6
CRESWELL OR 215-C4
LANE CO OR 215-C4
LANE CO OR 219-C1
LANE CO OR 330-J14
Rt#-99 N GOSHEN-DIVIDE HWY
COTTAGE GROVE OR 215-B7
Rt#-99 N GOSHEN-DIVIDE ST
COTTAGE GROVE OR 215-B7
Rt#-99 S GOSHEN-DIVIDE ST
CRESWELL OR 215-C5
Rt#-99 GRANVILLE BRDG
VANCOUVER BC 254-E12
Rt#-99 GRANVILLE ST
VANCOUVER BC 156-B5
VANCOUVER BC 254-E14
Rt#-99 GREEN LAKE DR N
SEATTLE WA 273-J2
Rt#-99 HIGHWAY
CITY OF RICHMOND BC 156-B5
EDMONDS WA 171-B5
KENDRICK ID 123-B1
LATAH CO ID 123-A1
LYNNWOOD WA 171-B4
MOUNTLAKE TERRACE WA 171-B5
SEATTLE WA 286-A2
SNOHOMISH CO WA 171-B4
TROY ID 123-A1
Rt#-99 HOWE ST
VANCOUVER BC 254-F10
Rt#-99 INTERNATIONAL BLVD
DES MOINES WA 290-C5
SEATAC WA 288-D7
SEATAC WA 290-C5
TUKWILA WA 288-D7
Rt#-99 IVY ST
JUNCTION CITY OR 210-A5
Rt#-99 LAKE OF THE WOODS HWY
CENTRAL POINT OR 230-C7
JACKSON CO OR 230-C7
MEDFORD OR 230-C7
Rt#-99 LIONS GATE BRDG
DISTRICT OF WEST VANCOUVE BC 254-E5
VANCOUVER BC 254-E5
Rt#-99 LIONS GATE BRIDGE RD
DISTRICT OF WEST VANCOUVE BC 254-E7
VANCOUVER BC 254-E7
Rt#-99 LITHIA WY
ASHLAND OR 337-C7
Rt#-99 MAIN ST
CANYONVILLE OR 225-C3
DOUGLAS CO OR 225-C3
PHOENIX OR 234-B2
Rt#-99 N MAIN ST
ASHLAND OR 337-C6
CANYONVILLE OR 225-C3
JACKSON CO OR 337-C6
PHOENIX OR 234-B2
Rt#-99 S MAIN ST
CANYONVILLE OR 225-C3
Rt#-99 W MAIN ST
CANYONVILLE OR 225-C3
Rt#-99 E MARGINAL WY S
SEATTLE WA 281-J5
Rt#-99 MARINE DR
DISTRICT OF WEST VANCOUVE BC 254-E4
Rt#-99 MCVAY HWY
LANE CO OR 330-G11
Rt#-99 OAK ST
CITY OF RICHMOND BC 156-B5
VANCOUVER BC 156-B5
Rt#-99 OAKLAND-SHADY HWY
DOUGLAS CO OR 219-A7
DOUGLAS CO OR 221-C3
DOUGLAS CO OR 334-F2
OAKLAND OR 219-A7
ROSEBURG OR 334-F2
SUTHERLIN OR 221-C3
Rt#-99 OLD PACIFIC HWY
DOUGLAS CO OR 225-C2
MYRTLE CREEK OR 225-C2
Tri-City OR 225-C2
Rt#-99 OLD STAGE RD
JACKSON CO OR 230-B6
Rt#-99 PACIFIC HWY
FEDERAL WAY WA 182-B1
Rt#-99 PACIFIC HWY E
FEDERAL WAY WA 182-A2
FIFE WA 182-A2
MILTON WA 182-A2
PIERCE CO WA 182-A2
Rt#-99 PACIFIC HWY S
DES MOINES WA 175-B7
DES MOINES WA 290-C6
FEDERAL WAY WA 175-B7
FEDERAL WAY WA 182-A2
KENT WA 175-B7
KENT WA 290-C6
Rt#-99 PACIFIC HWY W
EUGENE OR 215-A1
EUGENE OR 329-D2
JUNCTION CITY OR 210-A7
LANE CO OR 210-A7
LANE CO OR 215-A1
Rt#-99 SE PINE ST
ROSEBURG OR 334-F8
Rt#-99 REDWOOD HWY
GRANTS PASS OR 335-F6
Rt#-99 NE REDWOOD HWY
GRANTS PASS OR 335-F7
Rt#-99 N RIVERSIDE AV
MEDFORD OR 336-C10
Rt#-99 S RIVERSIDE AV
MEDFORD OR 336-D13
Rt#-99 ROGUE RIVER HWY
GRANTS PASS OR 335-J11
JACKSON CO OR 229-C6
JACKSON CO OR 230-A6
JOSEPHINE CO OR 229-C6
JOSEPHINE CO OR 335-J11
ROGUE RIVER OR 229-C6
Rt#-99 ROGUE VALLEY HWY
ASHLAND OR 337-A4
CENTRAL POINT OR 230-C7
JACKSON CO OR 230-C7
JACKSON CO OR 234-B2
JACKSON CO OR 337-A4
MEDFORD OR 230-C7
MEDFORD OR 234-B2
MEDFORD OR 336-A7
PHOENIX OR 234-B2
TALENT OR 234-B3
Rt#-99 SAMS VALLEY HWY
GOLD HILL OR 230-A6
JACKSON CO OR 230-A6
Rt#-99 NE STATE ST
DOUGLAS CO OR 221-C1
Rt#-99 SEYMOUR ST
VANCOUVER BC 254-F11
Rt#-99 SISKIYOU BLVD
ASHLAND OR 337-D8
JACKSON CO OR 337-H10
Rt#-99 STANTON PARK RD
DOUGLAS CO OR 225-C3
Rt#-99 NE STATE ST
SUTHERLIN OR 221-C1
Rt#-99 NE STEPHENS ST
ROSEBURG OR 334-F5
Rt#-99 SE STEPHENS ST
ROSEBURG OR 334-G7
Rt#-99 TAYLOR WY
DISTRICT OF WEST VANCOUVE BC 254-E4
Rt#-99 UMPQUA HWY
DOUGLAS CO OR 219-A2
DRAIN OR 219-A2
Rt#-99A 10TH AV
DISTRICT OF BURNABY BC 156-D5
NEW WESTMINSTER BC 156-D5
Rt#-99A HIGHWAY
CITY OF SURREY BC 156-D5
NEW WESTMINSTER BC 156-D5
Rt#-99A KING GEORGE HWY
CITY OF SURREY BC 156-D5
CITY OF SURREY BC 157-A7
CITY OF SURREY BC 158-A1
Rt#-99A KINGSWAY
DISTRICT OF BURNABY BC 156-C5
NEW WESTMINSTER BC 156-C5
Rt#-99A MCBRIDE BLVD
NEW WESTMINSTER BC 156-D5
Rt#-99A PATTULLO BRDG
CITY OF SURREY BC 156-D5
Rt#-99E 2ND ST
HALSEY OR 210-B2
Rt#-99E 3RD ST
HARRISBURG OR 210-A5
Rt#-99E ALBANY-JCT CITY HWY
ALBANY OR 207-C7
ALBANY OR 326-C14
HALSEY OR 210-B3
HARRISBURG OR 210-A5
JUNCTION CITY OR 210-A5
LANE CO OR 210-A5
LINN CO OR 207-C7
LINN CO OR 210-B3
TANGENT OR 207-C7
Rt#-99E COMMERCIAL ST NE
SALEM OR 322-J10
Rt#-99E FRONT ST NE
SALEM OR 322-H12
Rt#-99E NE GRAND AV
PORTLAND OR 313-G4
Rt#-99E SE GRAND AV
PORTLAND OR 313-G7
PORTLAND OR 317-G2
Rt#-99E HIGHWAY
MILWAUKIE OR 321-J2
SALEM OR 322-H12
Rt#-99E HIGHWAY 99
CLARK CO WA 192-C5
VANCOUVER WA 192-C5
VANCOUVER WA 305-G1
Rt#-99E LIBERTY ST NE
SALEM OR 322-J10
Rt#-99E N MARINE DR
PORTLAND OR 309-E1
Rt#-99E NE MLK JR BLVD
PORTLAND OR 309-G3
PORTLAND OR 313-G4
Rt#-99E SE MLK JR BLVD
PORTLAND OR 313-G7
PORTLAND OR 317-G1
Rt#-99E MCLOUGHLIN BLVD E
CLACKAMAS CO OR 199-D5
OREGON CITY OR 199-D5
Rt#-99E SE MCLOUGHLIN BLVD
CLACKAMAS CO OR 199-D3
CLACKAMAS CO OR 321-J2
GLADSTONE OR 199-D3
MILWAUKIE OR 317-J5
MILWAUKIE OR 321-J2
OREGON CITY OR 199-D3
PORTLAND OR 317-J5
Rt#-99E PACIFIC BLVD
ALBANY OR 326-F7
LINN CO OR 326-F7
MILLERSBURG OR 326-F7
Rt#-99E PACIFIC HWY
MARION CO OR 205-B2
WOODBURN OR 205-B1
Rt#-99E PACIFIC HWY E
AURORA OR 199-B7
BARLOW OR 199-C6
CANBY OR 199-C6
CLACKAMAS CO OR 199-D4
GERVAIS OR 205-B1
GLADSTONE OR 199-D4
Hayesville OR 204-D5
Hayesville OR 323-E5
HUBBARD OR 205-B1
MARION CO OR 199-B7
MARION CO OR 205-A3
MARION CO OR 323-E5
OREGON CITY OR 199-D4
SALEM OR 323-E5
WOODBURN OR 205-B1
Rt#-99E SALEM EXWY
KEIZER OR 323-C6
SALEM OR 323-C6
Rt#-99E SALEM PKWY
KEIZER OR 323-A8
MARION CO OR 323-A8
SALEM OR 322-J8
SALEM OR 323-A8
Rt#-99W E 1ST ST
NEWBERG OR 198-D5
Rt#-99W 3RD ST
LAFAYETTE OR 198-B6
Rt#-99W 3RD ST W
CORVALLIS OR 207-A7
CORVALLIS OR 327-G14
Rt#-99W 4TH ST W
CORVALLIS OR 327-H9
Rt#-99W 5TH AV
MONROE OR 133-B2
Rt#-99W NW ADAMS ST
MCMINNVILLE OR 198-A7
Rt#-99W SW ADAMS ST
MCMINNVILLE OR 198-A7
Rt#-99W NE BAKER ST
MCMINNVILLE OR 198-A7
Rt#-99W SE BAKER ST
MCMINNVILLE OR 198-A7
Rt#-99W SW BARBUR BLVD
PORTLAND OR 199-B3
PORTLAND OR 316-E3
PORTLAND OR 317-E2
PORTLAND OR 320-A1
TIGARD OR 199-B3
Rt#-99W E HANCOCK ST
NEWBERG OR 198-D5
Rt#-99W W HANCOCK ST
NEWBERG OR 198-D5
Rt#-99W HERBERT HOOVER HWY
NEWBERG OR 198-D5
YAMHILL CO OR 198-D5
Rt#-99W N HIGHWAY 99 W
DUNDEE OR 198-C6
YAMHILL CO OR 198-D6
Rt#-99W NE HIGHWAY 99 W
MCMINNVILLE OR 198-B7
YAMHILL CO OR 198-B7
Rt#-99W SW HIGHWAY 99 W
MCMINNVILLE OR 198-A7
MCMINNVILLE OR 204-B1
YAMHILL CO OR 198-A7
YAMHILL CO OR 204-B1
Rt#-99W SW NAITO PKWY
PORTLAND OR 317-F1
Rt#-99W N PACIFIC AV
MONMOUTH OR 204-B7
POLK CO OR 204-B7
Rt#-99W S PACIFIC AV
MONMOUTH OR 204-B7
Rt#-99W PACIFIC HWY W
ADAIR VILLAGE OR 207-B3
AMITY OR 204-B5
BENTON CO OR 133-B2
BENTON CO OR 207-B3
BENTON CO OR 327-H7
CORVALLIS OR 207-B3
CORVALLIS OR 327-H7
JUNCTION CITY OR 210-A5
KING CITY OR 199-B3
LANE CO OR 133-B2
LANE CO OR 210-A5
MONMOUTH OR 204-B5
MONROE OR 133-B2
NEWBERG OR 198-C6
POLK CO OR 204-B5
POLK CO OR 207-B3
TIGARD OR 199-B3
TUALATIN OR 199-B3
WASHINGTON CO OR 199-B3
YAMHILL CO OR 198-C6
YAMHILL CO OR 204-B5
Rt#-99W SW PACIFIC HWY W
SHERWOOD OR 199-A4
WASHINGTON CO OR 199-A4
Rt#-99W PORTLAND RD
NEWBERG OR 198-D5
WASHINGTON CO OR 199-A5
YAMHILL CO OR 198-D5
YAMHILL CO OR 199-A5
Rt#-99W N RIVER ST
NEWBERG OR 198-D5
Rt#-100 2ND ST
ILWACO WA 186-A6
PACIFIC CO WA 186-A6
Rt#-100 FORT CANBY RD
PACIFIC CO WA 186-A7
Rt#-100 HIGHWAY
ILWACO WA 186-A6
PACIFIC CO WA 186-A6
Rt#-100 NORTH HEAD RD
ILWACO WA 186-A6
PACIFIC CO WA 186-A6
Rt#-100 ROBERT GRAY DR
PACIFIC CO WA 186-A6
Rt#-100 SPRUCE ST E
ILWACO WA 186-A6
Rt#-100 SPRUCE ST W
ILWACO WA 186-A6
Rt#-101 HIGHWAY
BRITISH COLUMBIA BC 92-B1
BRITISH COLUMBIA BC 93-A1
Gibson BC 93-B3
PACIFIC CO WA 186-C4
POWELL RIVER BC 92-C1
Sechelt BC 93-A2
Rt#-102 DAYTON-AIRPORT RD
MASON CO WA 179-D2
MASON CO WA 180-A2
Rt#-103 BAY AV
Ocean Park WA 186-A2
Rt#-103 OCEAN BEACH HWY
LONG BEACH WA 186-A5
PACIFIC CO WA 186-A5
Rt#-103 PACIFIC HWY
Ocean Park WA 186-A2
PACIFIC CO WA 186-A3
Rt#-103 PACIFIC HWY S
LONG BEACH WA 186-A5
Rt#-103 PACIFIC HWY W
LONG BEACH WA 186-A5
Rt#-103 SANDRIDGE RD
Ocean Park WA 186-A2
PACIFIC CO WA 186-A1
Rt#-103 STACKPOLE RD
PACIFIC CO WA 183-B7
PACIFIC CO WA 186-A1
Rt#-104 244TH ST SW
MOUNTLAKE TERRACE WA 171-B6
SHORELINE WA 171-B6
Rt#-104 BALLINGER WY NE
LAKE FOREST PARK WA 171-B6
SHORELINE WA 171-B6
Rt#-104 EDMONDS WY
EDMONDS WA 171-A6
SNOHOMISH CO WA 171-A6
WOODWAY WA 171-A6
Rt#-104 HIGHWAY
JEFFERSON CO WA 109-C1
JEFFERSON CO WA 170-A3
Kingston WA 170-D5
KITSAP CO WA 170-C4
Rt#-104 LAKE BALLINGER WY
EDMONDS WA 171-B6
MOUNTLAKE TERRACE WA 171-B6
SHORELINE WA 171-B6
Rt#-104 NE 205TH ST
EDMONDS WA 171-B6
MOUNTLAKE TERRACE WA 171-B6
SHORELINE WA 171-B6
Rt#-105 N BOONE ST
ABERDEEN WA 178-B7
Rt#-105 S BOONE ST
ABERDEEN WA 117-A1
ABERDEEN WA 178-B7
GRAYS HARBOR CO WA 117-A1
Rt#-105 DOCK ST
WESTPORT WA 298-G11
Rt#-105 FORREST AV
WESTPORT WA 298-G14
Rt#-105 HIGHWAY
ABERDEEN WA 117-A1
GRAYS HARBOR CO WA 117-A1
GRAYS HARBOR CO WA 183-D1
PACIFIC CO WA 117-A1
PACIFIC CO WA 183-B3
RAYMOND WA 117-A1
WESTPORT WA 183-B2
WESTPORT WA 298-G11
Rt#-105 MONTESANO ST
WESTPORT WA 298-H11
Rt#-105 OCEAN AV
WESTPORT WA 298-F13
Rt#-105 PARK AV
RAYMOND WA 117-A1
Rt#-105 WESTPORT RD
GRAYS HARBOR CO WA 117-A1
Rt#-106 HIGHWAY
MASON CO WA 173-D5
MASON CO WA 180-A1
Rt#-107 HIGHWAY
GRAYS HARBOR CO WA 178-D7
MONTESANO WA 178-D7
Rt#-107 S BANK RD
GRAYS HARBOR CO WA 117-A1
Rt#-107 SOUTH BANK RD
GRAYS HARBOR CO WA 178-D7
Rt#-108 ELMA-MCCLEARY RD
GRAYS HARBOR CO WA 179-C6
MCCLEARY WA 179-C6
Rt#-108 HIGHWAY
GRAYS HARBOR CO WA 179-D5
MASON CO WA 179-D5
MASON CO WA 180-A4
Rt#-108 SIMPSON AV
MCCLEARY WA 179-D6
Rt#-108 SUMMIT RD
GRAYS HARBOR CO WA 179-D6
MCCLEARY WA 179-D6
Rt#-109 5TH AV
Taholah WA 172-B6
Rt#-109 EMERSON AV
HOQUIAM WA 178-A7
Rt#-109 FIR LP
Taholah WA 172-B6
Rt#-109 HIGHWAY
GRAYS HARBOR CO WA 172-B7
GRAYS HARBOR CO WA 177-B1
HOQUIAM WA 177-D7
HOQUIAM WA 178-A7
Taholah WA 172-B7
Rt#-109 NFD RD 7412
CHELAN CO WA 238-C1
Rt#-110 LA PUSH RD
CLALLAM CO WA 169-C1
FORKS WA 169-C1
Rt#-110 MORA RD
CLALLAM CO WA 169-B2
Rt#-112 3RD ST
Neah Bay WA 100-B2
Rt#-112 HIGHWAY
CLALLAM CO WA 100-B2
CLALLAM CO WA 162-C1
CLALLAM CO WA 163-A2
CLALLAM CO WA 164-A4
CLALLAM CO WA 165-A6
Neah Bay WA 100-B2
Rt#-112 NEAH BAY RD
CLALLAM CO WA 100-B2
Neah Bay WA 100-B2
Rt#-112 PIEDMONT RD
CLALLAM CO WA 164-C5
CLALLAM CO WA 165-A6
Rt#-113 BURNT MOUNTAIN RD
CLALLAM CO WA 163-B6
Rt#-115 DAMON RD
GRAYS HARBOR CO WA 177-B6
OCEAN SHORES WA 177-B6
Rt#-115 N JETTY RD
GRAYS HARBOR CO WA 177-B6
Rt#-116 FLAGLER RD
Hadlock-Irondale WA 170-B1
JEFFERSON CO WA 167-B7
JEFFERSON CO WA 170-B1
Rt#-116 NESS RD
Hadlock-Irondale WA 170-A1
JEFFERSON CO WA 170-A1
Rt#-116 NESS CORNER RD
Hadlock-Irondale WA 170-A1
Rt#-116 OAK BAY RD
Hadlock-Irondale WA 170-A1
JEFFERSON CO WA 170-A1
Rt#-117 TUMWATER ACCESS RD
CLALLAM CO WA 261-C5
PORT ANGELES WA 261-C5
Rt#-119 HIGHWAY
MASON CO WA 109-B2
MASON CO WA 173-A6
Rt#-119 LAKE CUSHMAN RD
MASON CO WA 109-B2
MASON CO WA 173-A6
Rt#-121 93RD AV SW
THURSTON CO WA 184-C1
TUMWATER WA 184-C1
Rt#-121 MAYTOWN RD SW
THURSTON CO WA 184-C2
Rt#-121 TILLEY RD SW
THURSTON CO WA 184-C2
Rt#-122 HARMONY RD
LEWIS CO WA 118-A2
MOSSYROCK WA 118-A2
Rt#-122 SILVERCREEK RD
LEWIS CO WA 118-A2
Rt#-123 HIGHWAY
LEWIS CO WA 185-D5
PIERCE CO WA 119-A1
PIERCE CO WA 185-D4
Rt#-124 W 2ND ST
WAITSBURG WA 122-A2
WALLA WALLA CO WA 122-A2
Rt#-124 HIGHWAY
PRESCOTT WA 121-C2
WALLA WALLA CO WA 121-C2
WALLA WALLA CO WA 122-A2
Rt#-124 ICE HARBOR DR
WALLA WALLA CO WA 121-B3
Rt#-124 LOWER WAITSBURG RD
WALLA WALLA CO WA 122-A2
Rt#-124 MAIN ST
WAITSBURG WA 122-A2
Rt#-124 SECOND ST
PRESCOTT WA 121-C2
WALLA WALLA CO WA 121-C2
Rt#-125 8TH AV N
WALLA WALLA WA 344-J8
Rt#-125 9TH AV S
WALLA WALLA WA 344-J8
WALLA WALLA WA 345-A9
Rt#-125 13TH AV N
WALLA WALLA WA 344-J5
WALLA WALLA CO WA 344-J5
Rt#-125 HIGHWAY
COLLEGE PLACE WA 344-H11
WALLA WALLA WA 344-H5
WALLA WALLA WA 345-A10
WALLA WALLA CO WA 121-C2
WALLA WALLA CO WA 344-G1
Rt#-125 W PINE ST
WALLA WALLA WA 344-J7
Rt#-126 W 3RD ST
CROOK CO OR 213-D5
PRINEVILLE OR 213-D5
Rt#-126 W 11TH AV
EUGENE OR 215-A2
EUGENE OR 329-B6
LANE CO OR 215-A2
Rt#-126 Bus S A ST
LANE CO OR 330-J7
SPRINGFIELD OR 330-J7
SPRINGFIELD OR 331-A7
Rt#-126 BELKNAP SPRINGS HWY
LANE CO OR 134-B2
LINN CO OR 134-B2
Rt#-126 EUGENE-SPRINGFLD HWY
EUGENE OR 330-E5
LANE CO OR 331-G6
SPRINGFIELD OR 330-E5
SPRINGFIELD OR 331-C5
Rt#-126 SE EVERGREEN AV
REDMOND OR 212-D5
Rt#-126 FLORENCE-EUGENE HWY
FLORENCE OR 214-C2
LANE CO OR 132-C3
LANE CO OR 133-A3
LANE CO OR 214-C2
LANE CO OR 215-A2
VENETA OR 133-A3
Rt#-126 Bus FRANKLIN BLVD
LANE CO OR 330-F7
Rt#-126 S GARFIELD ST
EUGENE OR 329-G6
Rt#-126 SW HIGHLAND AV
REDMOND OR 212-D5
Rt#-126 MAIN ST
LANE CO OR 330-H7
SPRINGFIELD OR 215-D2
SPRINGFIELD OR 330-H7
SPRINGFIELD OR 331-A7
Rt#-126 MCKENZIE HWY
DESCHUTES CO OR 211-D5
DESCHUTES CO OR 212-A5
LANE CO OR 133-C3
LANE CO OR 134-B2
LANE CO OR 215-D2
LINN CO OR 134-B2
REDMOND OR 212-D5
SISTERS OR 211-D5
SPRINGFIELD OR 215-D2
Rt#-126 OCHOCO HWY
CROOK CO OR 213-A5
DESCHUTES CO OR 213-A5
PRINEVILLE OR 213-B6
REDMOND OR 212-D5
REDMOND OR 213-A5
Rt#-126 OWSLEY GRADE RD
GARFIELD CO WA 122-B2
Rt#-127 HIGHWAY
GARFIELD CO WA 122-B1
WHITMAN CO WA 122-B1
Rt#-128 DOWN RIVER RD
LEWISTON ID 250-B4
Rt#-128 HIGHWAY
ASOTIN CO WA 250-B4
CLARKSTON WA 250-B4
LEWISTON ID 250-B4
WHITMAN CO WA 250-B4
Rt#-128 OLD SPIRAL HWY
LEWISTON ID 250-B4
Rt#-128 WAWAWAI RIVER RD
WHITMAN CO WA 250-B4
Rt#-129 1ST ST
ASOTIN WA 250-B5
Rt#-129 5TH ST
ASOTIN CO WA 250-B4
CLARKSTON WA 250-B4
Rt#-129 6TH ST
CLARKSTON WA 250-B4
Rt#-129 DIAGONAL ST
CLARKSTON WA 250-B4
Rt#-129 HIGHWAY
ASOTIN WA 250-B5
ASOTIN CO WA 122-C3
ASOTIN CO WA 123-A3
ASOTIN CO WA 250-B5
CLARKSTON WA 250-B4
Vineland WA 250-B5
Rt#-129 RIVERSIDE DR
ASOTIN CO WA 250-B5
Vineland WA 250-B5
Rt#-129 WASHINGTON ST
ASOTIN WA 250-B5
Rt#-131 CISPUS RD
LEWIS CO WA 118-C2
Rt#-131 WOODS CREEK RD
LEWIS CO WA 118-C2
Rt#-138 E DIAMOND LAKE HWY
DOUGLAS CO OR 223-D7
KLAMATH CO OR 142-B2
KLAMATH CO OR 223-D7
Rt#-138 NE DIAMOND LAKE BLVD
ROSEBURG OR 221-C4
ROSEBURG OR 334-H7
Rt#-138 ELKTON-SUTHERLIN HWY
DOUGLAS CO OR 141-A1
DOUGLAS CO OR 221-C1
ELKTON OR 141-A1
SUTHERLIN OR 221-C1
Rt#-138 W ELKTON-SUTHERLN HWY
DOUGLAS CO OR 221-C1
SUTHERLIN OR 221-C1
Rt#-138 SW HARVARD BLVD
ROSEBURG OR 334-F7
Rt#-138 W HARVARD BLVD
ROSEBURG OR 334-E7
Rt#-138 NORTH UMPQUA HWY
DOUGLAS CO OR 141-C2
DOUGLAS CO OR 221-D4
DOUGLAS CO OR 222-B3
DOUGLAS CO OR 223-A4
ROSEBURG OR 221-D4
Rt#-138 SE OAK AV
ROSEBURG OR 334-F7
Rt#-138 SW OAK AV
ROSEBURG OR 334-F7

INDEX

414 Rt#-503 NE LEWISVILLE HWY STREET INDEX U.S.-2 N WASHINGTON AV

STREET City State Page-Grid

Rt#-503 NE LEWISVILLE HWY
CLARK CO WA 193-A1
Rt#-504 HIGHWAY
COWLITZ CO WA 118-A2
SKAMANIA CO WA 118-B2
SKAMANIA CO WA 190-B1
Rt#-504 SPIRIT LAKE HWY
CASTLE ROCK WA 187-C7
COWLITZ CO WA 118-A2
COWLITZ CO WA 187-C7
Rt#-505 N 5TH ST
LEWIS CO WA 187-D4
TOLEDO WA 187-D4
Rt#-505 COWLITZ ST
LEWIS CO WA 187-D4
TOLEDO WA 187-D4
Rt#-505 HIGHWAY
COWLITZ CO WA 118-A2
LEWIS CO WA 118-A2
LEWIS CO WA 187-C3
TOLEDO WA 187-D4
WINLOCK WA 187-C3
Rt#-505 E WALNUT ST
WINLOCK WA 187-C3
Rt#-505 WINLOCK-TOLEDO RD
LEWIS CO WA 187-C3
Rt#-506 7TH ST
VADER WA 187-B5
Rt#-506 HIGHWAY
COWLITZ CO WA 187-B5
LEWIS CO WA 187-C4
VADER WA 187-C5
Rt#-507 ALDER ST
CENTRALIA WA 299-E4
Rt#-507 BINGHAMPTON ST
RAINIER WA 118-A1
THURSTON CO WA 118-A1
Rt#-507 BUCODA HWY
LEWIS CO WA 184-C5
Rt#-507 W CHERRY ST
CENTRALIA WA 299-E4
Rt#-507 D ST
TENINO WA 184-D3
Rt#-507 E DOWNING RD
CENTRALIA WA 184-C5
LEWIS CO WA 184-C5
Rt#-507 FRONT ST
BUCODA WA 184-D4
THURSTON CO WA 184-D4
Rt#-507 HIGHWAY
LEWIS CO WA 184-C5
THURSTON CO WA 118-A1
THURSTON CO WA 184-D3
Rt#-507 MCKENNA-YELM HWY
PIERCE CO WA 118-A1
THURSTON CO WA 118-A1
YELM WA 118-A1
Rt#-507 MCNAUGHT ST
ROY WA 181-C7
Rt#-507 MELLEN ST
CENTRALIA WA 299-D5
Rt#-507 N PEARL ST
CENTRALIA WA 184-C5
CENTRALIA WA 299-F1
LEWIS CO WA 184-C5
Rt#-507 S PEARL ST
CENTRALIA WA 299-F4
Rt#-507 RAINIER-YELM HWY
THURSTON CO WA 118-A1
YELM WA 118-A1
Rt#-507 SIXTH ST
TENINO WA 184-D3
Rt#-507 E SIXTH ST
CENTRALIA WA 299-F2
Rt#-507 SPANAWAY-MCKENNA HWY
PIERCE CO WA 118-A1
PIERCE CO WA 181-C7
ROY WA 181-C7
Rt#-507 SUMNER ST
BUCODA WA 184-D4
TENINO WA 184-D4
THURSTON CO WA 184-D4
Rt#-507 SUSSEX ST
TENINO WA 184-D3
THURSTON CO WA 184-D3
Rt#-507 THIRD ST
TENINO WA 184-D3
Rt#-507 N TOWER AV
CENTRALIA WA 299-F3
Rt#-507 S TOWER AV
CENTRALIA WA 299-F4
Rt#-507 YELM AV
YELM WA 118-A1
Rt#-508 HIGHWAY
LEWIS CO WA 118-A2
LEWIS CO WA 187-C1
MORTON WA 118-B2
Rt#-508 MAIN AV
MORTON WA 118-B2
Rt#-508 MORTON-BEAR CANYON RD
LEWIS CO WA 118-B2
MORTON WA 118-B2
Rt#-508 NFD RD 508
LINCOLN CO MT 107-C2
Rt#-508 NFD RD 92
LINCOLN CO MT 107-C1
Rt#-509 1ST AV S
BURIEN WA 175-A6
DES MOINES WA 175-A6
NORMANDY PARK WA 175-A6
Rt#-509 S 174TH ST
BURIEN WA 175-A5
Rt#-509 S 216TH ST
DES MOINES WA 175-A6
DES MOINES WA 290-A5
NORMANDY PARK WA 175-A6
NORMANDY PARK WA 290-A5
Rt#-509 AMBAUM BLVD S
BURIEN WA 175-A5
BURIEN WA 288-A7
Rt#-509 S DASH POINT RD
FEDERAL WAY WA 182-B1
Rt#-509 SW DASH POINT RD
FEDERAL WAY WA 182-A1
Rt#-509 DES MOINES MEM DR
BURIEN WA 288-A7
BURIEN WA 290-A1
SEATAC WA 290-A1
Rt#-509 EASTSIDE DR NE
PIERCE CO WA 181-D1
PIERCE CO WA 182-A1
Rt#-509 FRWY
BURIEN WA 175-A5
BURIEN WA 288-A1
BURIEN WA 290-A1
KING CO WA 286-A4
Rt#-509 FRWY
KING CO WA 288-A1
SEATAC WA 288-A6
SEATAC WA 290-A1
SEATTLE WA 285-J1
SEATTLE WA 286-A3
TACOMA WA 182-A2
TACOMA WA 293-J6
Rt#-509 N FRONTAGE RD
TACOMA WA 182-A2
Rt#-509 S FRONTAGE RD
TACOMA WA 182-A2
Rt#-509 MARINE VIEW DR
DES MOINES WA 290-A6
TACOMA WA 181-D1
TACOMA WA 182-A1
Rt#-510 CLAIR CUT-OFF RD
THURSTON CO WA 181-A7
Rt#-510 HIGHWAY
THURSTON CO WA 181-A6
Rt#-510 MARVIN RD NE
LACEY WA 181-A6
Rt#-510 MARVIN RD SE
LACEY WA 181-A6
THURSTON CO WA 181-A6
Rt#-510 OLYMPIA-YELM HWY
THURSTON CO WA 118-A1
THURSTON CO WA 181-B7
YELM WA 118-A1
Rt#-510 PACIFIC AV SE
THURSTON CO WA 181-A6
Rt#-510 PACIFIC HWY SE
THURSTON CO WA 181-A6
Rt#-510 YELM AV
THURSTON CO WA 118-A1
YELM WA 118-A1
Rt#-512 FRWY
LAKEWOOD WA 181-D4
PIERCE CO WA 181-D4
PIERCE CO WA 182-B3
PUYALLUP WA 182-B3
Rt#-513 NE 45TH ST
SEATTLE WA 274-D5
SEATTLE WA 275-E5
Rt#-513 MONTLAKE BLVD NE
SEATTLE WA 274-D6
SEATTLE WA 278-D1
Rt#-513 SAND POINT WY NE
SEATTLE WA 275-F5
Rt#-515 104TH AV SE
KENT WA 175-C7
Rt#-515 108TH AV SE
KENT WA 175-C6
KING CO WA 175-C6
Rt#-515 BENSON DR S
KING CO WA 175-C5
RENTON WA 175-C5
Rt#-515 BENSON RD
KENT WA 175-C6
KING CO WA 175-C6
Rt#-515 BENSON RD SE
KING CO WA 175-C6
Rt#-515 S GRADY WY
RENTON WA 175-C5
Rt#-515 HIGHWAY
RENTON WA 175-C5
Rt#-515 MAIN AV S
RENTON WA 175-C5
Rt#-515 TALBOT RD S
RENTON WA 175-C5
Rt#-516 SE 256TH ST
KENT WA 175-C7
Rt#-516 SE 272ND ST
COVINGTON WA 175-D7
KENT WA 175-C7
KING CO WA 175-D7
MAPLE VALLEY WA 175-D7
Rt#-516 CANYON DR SE
KENT WA 175-C7
Rt#-516 CENTRAL AV N
KENT WA 175-C7
Rt#-516 CENTRAL AV S
KENT WA 175-C7
Rt#-516 KENT KANGLEY RD
COVINGTON WA 175-C7
KENT WA 175-C7
KING CO WA 175-C7
KING CO WA 176-A7
MAPLE VALLEY WA 175-C7
MAPLE VALLEY WA 176-A7
Rt#-516 KENT-DES MOINES RD
DES MOINES WA 290-A7
KENT WA 175-B7
KENT WA 290-A7
Rt#-516 KENT-DES MOINES RD S
KENT WA 175-B7
KENT WA 290-E7
KING CO WA 175-B7
KING CO WA 290-E7
Rt#-516 E SMITH ST
KENT WA 175-C7
Rt#-516 W WILLIS ST
KENT WA 175-C7
Rt#-518 FRWY
BURIEN WA 175-A5
BURIEN WA 288-B4
SEATAC WA 288-B4
TUKWILA WA 288-D5
TUKWILA WA 289-F4
Rt#-519 4TH AV S
SEATTLE WA 278-A7
SEATTLE WA 282-A1
Rt#-519 ALASKAN WY S
SEATTLE WA 277-J7
SEATTLE WA 278-A7
SEATTLE WA 281-J1
Rt#-519 S ROYAL BROUGHAM WY
SEATTLE WA 281-J1
SEATTLE WA 282-A1
Rt#-520 FRWY
BELLEVUE WA 175-C2
CLYDE HILL WA 175-C2
HUNTS POINT WA 175-C2
KING CO WA 175-D1
MEDINA WA 175-C2
MEDINA WA 279-J2
REDMOND WA 175-D1
SEATTLE WA 278-D1
SEATTLE WA 279-E1
YARROW POINT WA 175-C2
Rt#-522 BOTHELL WY NE
BOTHELL WA 171-C6
LAKE FOREST PARK WA 171-B6
SHORELINE WA 171-B7
Rt#-522 NE BOTHELL WY
BOTHELL WA 171-B6
KENMORE WA 171-B6
KING CO WA 171-B6
LAKE FOREST PARK WA 171-B6
Rt#-522 FRWY
BOTHELL WA 171-C6
SNOHOMISH CO WA 171-D5
WOODINVILLE WA 171-C6
Rt#-522 HIGHWAY
MONROE WA 110-C1
SNOHOMISH CO WA 110-C1
SNOHOMISH CO WA 171-D5
Rt#-522 LAKE CITY WY NE
SEATTLE WA 171-B7
SEATTLE WA 274-C2
Rt#-522 WOODINVILLE DR
BOTHELL WA 171-C6
Rt#-523 N 145TH ST
SEATTLE WA 171-A7
SHORELINE WA 171-A7
Rt#-523 NE 145TH ST
SEATTLE WA 171-B7
SHORELINE WA 171-B7
Rt#-524 3RD AV N
EDMONDS WA 171-A5
Rt#-524 3RD AV S
EDMONDS WA 171-A5
Rt#-524 9TH AV N
EDMONDS WA 171-A5
Rt#-524 196TH ST SW
EDMONDS WA 171-B5
LYNNWOOD WA 171-B5
SNOHOMISH CO WA 171-B5
Rt#-524 208TH ST SE
BOTHELL WA 171-C5
SNOHOMISH CO WA 171-C5
Rt#-524 CASPERS ST
EDMONDS WA 171-A5
Rt#-524 FILBERT RD
BOTHELL WA 171-C5
LYNNWOOD WA 171-B5
SNOHOMISH CO WA 171-C5
Rt#-524 MAIN ST
EDMONDS WA 171-A5
Rt#-524 MALTBY RD
BOTHELL WA 171-C5
SNOHOMISH CO WA 171-C5
Rt#-524 PARADISE LAKE RD
SNOHOMISH CO WA 171-D5
Rt#-524 PINE ST
EDMONDS WA 171-A5
Rt#-524 PUGET DR
EDMONDS WA 171-A5
Rt#-524 YEW WY
SNOHOMISH CO WA 171-D5
Rt#-525 FRWY
SNOHOMISH CO WA 171-B4
Rt#-525 HIGHWAY
Clinton WA 171-A2
Freeland WA 170-C1
ISLAND CO WA 167-C5
ISLAND CO WA 170-C1
ISLAND CO WA 171-A1
SNOHOMISH CO WA 171-B4
Rt#-525 MUKILTEO SPEEDWAY
MUKILTEO WA 171-B2
MUKILTEO WA 266-D3
MUKILTEO WA 267-E5
SNOHOMISH CO WA 171-B4
SNOHOMISH CO WA 267-E6
Rt#-525 PAINE FIELD BLVD
MUKILTEO WA 267-F6
SNOHOMISH CO WA 267-F6
Rt#-526 84TH ST SW
MUKILTEO WA 266-E4
MUKILTEO WA 267-F4
Rt#-526 FRWY
EVERETT WA 267-F4
EVERETT WA 268-A4
MUKILTEO WA 267-F4
SNOHOMISH CO WA 267-F4
Rt#-527 19TH AV SE
EVERETT WA 171-C4
EVERETT WA 268-D6
Rt#-527 BOTHELL EVERETT HWY
BOTHELL WA 171-C4
EVERETT WA 171-C4
MILL CREEK WA 171-C4
SNOHOMISH CO WA 171-C4
Rt#-527 BOTHELL WY NE
BOTHELL WA 171-C6
BOTHELL WA 171-C6
Rt#-528 4TH ST
MARYSVILLE WA 171-C1
SNOHOMISH CO WA 171-C1
Rt#-528 64TH ST NE
MARYSVILLE WA 168-D7
MARYSVILLE WA 171-D1
SNOHOMISH CO WA 168-D7
SNOHOMISH CO WA 171-D1
Rt#-529 BROADWAY
EVERETT WA 171-C1
Rt#-529 EVERETT AV
EVERETT WA 264-E3
EVERETT WA 265-E3
Rt#-529 HIGHWAY
MARYSVILLE WA 171-C1
SNOHOMISH CO WA 171-C1
Rt#-529 MAPLE ST
EVERETT WA 265-F4
Rt#-529 E MARINE VIEW DR
EVERETT WA 171-C1
Rt#-529 W MARINE VIEW DR
EVERETT WA 171-C1
EVERETT WA 264-D3
Rt#-529 PACIFIC AV
EVERETT WA 265-F4
Rt#-529 PACIFIC HWY
EVERETT WA 171-C1
MARYSVILLE WA 171-C1
SNOHOMISH CO WA 171-C1
Rt#-529 STATE AV
MARYSVILLE WA 171-C1
Rt#-530 DARRNGTN BNTTS ST RD
DARRINGTON WA 103-A3
SKAGIT CO WA 103-A3
SNOHOMISH CO WA 103-A3
Rt#-530 EMENS AV
DARRINGTON WA 103-A3
Rt#-530 HIGHWAY
ARLINGTON WA 168-D5
DARRINGTON WA 103-A3
MARYSVILLE WA 168-D5
SNOHOMISH CO WA 102-C3
SNOHOMISH CO WA 103-A3
Rt#-530 HIGHWAY
SNOHOMISH CO WA 168-D4
Rt#-530 PIONEER HWY
SKAGIT CO WA 168-B2
Rt#-530 SAUK VALLEY RD
SKAGIT CO WA 103-A2
Rt#-530 SEEMANN ST
DARRINGTON WA 103-A3
Rt#-531 36TH AV NW
SNOHOMISH CO WA 168-B6
Rt#-531 172ND ST NE
ARLINGTON WA 168-C6
SNOHOMISH CO WA 168-C6
Rt#-531 E LAKE GOODWIN RD
SNOHOMISH CO WA 168-B5
Rt#-531 LAKEWOOD RD
ARLINGTON WA 168-B5
SNOHOMISH CO WA 168-B5
Rt#-531 SISCO HEIGHTS RD
ARLINGTON WA 168-D6
SNOHOMISH CO WA 168-D6
Rt#-532 268TH ST NW
ISLAND CO WA 167-D4
ISLAND CO WA 168-A4
SNOHOMISH CO WA 168-A4
STANWOOD WA 168-A4
Rt#-532 HIGHWAY
SNOHOMISH CO WA 168-A4
STANWOOD WA 168-A4
Rt#-534 HIGHWAY
SKAGIT CO WA 168-B2
Rt#-536 S 3RD ST
MOUNT VERNON WA 260-C12
Rt#-536 W DIVISION ST
MOUNT VERNON WA 260-B12
Rt#-536 KINCAID ST
MOUNT VERNON WA 260-C13
Rt#-536 MEMORIAL HWY
MOUNT VERNON WA 260-A11
SKAGIT CO WA 161-A7
SKAGIT CO WA 260-A11
Rt#-538 COLLEGE WY
MOUNT VERNON WA 260-J11
SKAGIT CO WA 161-C7
SKAGIT CO WA 260-J11
Rt#-538 E COLLEGE WY
MOUNT VERNON WA 260-D10
SKAGIT CO WA 260-H10
Rt#-538 W COLLEGE WY
MOUNT VERNON WA 260-B10
Rt#-539 GUIDE MERIDIAN RD
BELLINGHAM WA 158-D6
BELLINGHAM WA 258-C1
LYNDEN WA 158-D6
WHATCOM CO WA 158-D6
Rt#-539 MERIDIAN ST
BELLINGHAM WA 258-C2
Rt#-542 MOUNT BAKER HWY
WHATCOM CO WA 102-B1
WHATCOM CO WA 103-A1
Rt#-542 E SUNSET DR
BELLINGHAM WA 258-G3
WHATCOM CO WA 102-B1
WHATCOM CO WA 258-G3
Rt#-543 HIGHWAY
BLAINE WA 158-B3
WHATCOM CO WA 158-B3
Rt#-544 COLUMBIA ST
NOOKSACK WA 102-B1
Rt#-544 EVERSON AV
EVERSON WA 102-B1
NOOKSACK WA 102-B1
Rt#-544 EVERSON GOSHEN RD
EVERSON WA 102-B1
WHATCOM CO WA 102-B1
Rt#-544 KALE ST
EVERSON WA 102-B1
Rt#-544 MAIN ST
NOOKSACK WA 102-B1
Rt#-544 E POLE RD
EVERSON WA 102-B1
WHATCOM CO WA 102-B1
WHATCOM CO WA 158-D5
Rt#-546 E BADGER RD
WHATCOM CO WA 102-B1
WHATCOM CO WA 158-D3
Rt#-547 E BADGER RD
WHATCOM CO WA 102-B1
Rt#-547 FRONT ST
SUMAS WA 102-B1
WHATCOM CO WA 102-B1
Rt#-547 GARRISON RD
WHATCOM CO WA 102-B1
Rt#-547 HALVERSTICK RD
SUMAS WA 102-B1
WHATCOM CO WA 102-B1
Rt#-547 KENDALL RD
WHATCOM CO WA 102-B1
Rt#-547 REESE HILL RD
WHATCOM CO WA 102-B1
Rt#-547 ROCK RD
WHATCOM CO WA 102-B1
Rt#-547 SUMAS RD
WHATCOM CO WA 102-B1
Rt#-548 BLAINE RD
Birch Bay WA 158-B4
BLAINE WA 158-B3
WHATCOM CO WA 158-B3
Rt#-548 D ST
BLAINE WA 158-B3
Rt#-548 GRANDVIEW RD
Birch Bay WA 158-B5
WHATCOM CO WA 158-B5
Rt#-599 FRWY
TUKWILA WA 286-D7
TUKWILA WA 287-E7
TUKWILA WA 289-E1
Rt#-702 MCKENNA TANWAX
PIERCE CO WA 118-A1
Rt#-706 HIGHWAY
PIERCE CO WA 185-A5
Rt#-706 MOUNTAIN HWY E
PIERCE CO WA 118-B1
PIERCE CO WA 185-A5
Rt#-730 COLUMBIA RIVER HWY
UMATILLA CO OR 121-A3
WALLA WALLA CO WA 121-A3
Rt#-730 HIGHWAY
WALLA WALLA CO WA 121-B3
Rt#-821 HIGHWAY
KITTITAS CO WA 241-B7
KITTITAS CO WA 243-B1
YAKIMA CO WA 243-C4
Rt#-821 THRALL RD
KITTITAS CO WA 241-B7
Rt#-823 E NACHES AV
SELAH WA 243-B5
Rt#-823 HARRISON RD
YAKIMA CO WA 243-B5
Rt#-823 HIGHWAY
YAKIMA CO WA 243-B6
Rt#-823 S 1ST ST
SELAH WA 243-B5
YAKIMA CO WA 243-B5
Rt#-823 SELAH RD
YAKIMA CO WA 243-B6
Rt#-823 WENAS AV
SELAH WA 243-B5
YAKIMA CO WA 243-B5
Rt#-900 S 2ND ST
RENTON WA 175-C5
Rt#-900 S 3RD ST
RENTON WA 175-C5
Rt#-900 17TH AV NW
ISSAQUAH WA 175-D3
Rt#-900 BRONSON WY N
RENTON WA 175-C5
Rt#-900 HOUSER WY S
RENTON WA 175-C5
Rt#-900 MARTIN L KING JR WY
KING CO WA 175-C5
KING CO WA 287-E6
KING CO WA 289-G1
RENTON WA 175-C5
RENTON WA 289-G1
SEATTLE WA 287-E6
TUKWILA WA 287-E6
TUKWILA WA 289-G1
Rt#-900 MILL AV S
RENTON WA 175-C5
Rt#-900 N PARK DR
RENTON WA 175-C4
Rt#-900 NE PARK DR
RENTON WA 175-C4
Rt#-900 NE SUNSET BLVD
RENTON WA 175-C4
Rt#-900 RENTON ISSAQUAH RD SE
ISSAQUAH WA 175-D4
KING CO WA 175-D4
Rt#-900 SE RENTON ISSAQUAH RD
KING CO WA 175-D4
RENTON WA 175-D4
Rt#-900 SUNSET BLVD N
RENTON WA 175-C5
Rt#-900 SW SUNSET BLVD
RENTON WA 175-C5
Rt#-902 W HALLETT RD
SPOKANE CO WA 246-A5
Rt#-902 HIGHWAY
MEDICAL LAKE WA 114-B2
SPOKANE CO WA 114-B2
SPOKANE CO WA 246-A5
Rt#-902 LEFEVRE ST
MEDICAL LAKE WA 114-B2
Rt#-902 MEDICAL LAKE RD
MEDICAL LAKE WA 114-B2
SPOKANE CO WA 114-B2
Rt#-902 S MEDICAL LK TYLER RD
MEDICAL LAKE WA 114-B2
Rt#-902 W SALNAVE RD
MEDICAL LAKE WA 114-B2
SPOKANE CO WA 114-B2
Rt#-903 2ND AV
KITTITAS CO WA 240-A1
Rt#-903 E FIRST ST
CLE ELUM WA 240-B2
Rt#-903 N FIRST ST
ROSLYN WA 240-A1
Rt#-903 S FIRST ST
ROSLYN WA 240-A1
Rt#-903 W FIRST ST
CLE ELUM WA 240-B2
Rt#-903 HIGHWAY
CLE ELUM WA 240-B2
KITTITAS CO WA 240-A1
ROSLYN WA 240-A1
Rt#-903 W NEVADA AV
ROSLYN WA 240-A1
Rt#-903 SALMON LA SAC RD
KITTITAS CO WA 111-B3
KITTITAS CO WA 240-A1
Rt#-903 SECOND ST W
CLE ELUM WA 240-B2
Rt#-903 W SECOND ST
CLE ELUM WA 240-B2
Rt#-903 N SEVENTH ST
ROSLYN WA 240-A1
Rt#-903 STAFFORD AV
CLE ELUM WA 240-B2
Rt#-904 COLUMBIA BASIN HWY
CHENEY WA 246-A7
SPOKANE CO WA 246-A7
Rt#-904 FIRST ST
CHENEY WA 246-A7
Rt#-904 W FIRST ST
CHENEY WA 246-A7
Rt#-904 HIGHWAY
CHENEY WA 246-A7
SPOKANE CO WA 114-B2
SPOKANE CO WA 246-A6
Rt#-906 HIGHWAY
KING CO WA 111-A2
KITTITAS CO WA 111-A2
Rt#-908 NE 85TH ST
KIRKLAND WA 175-C1
Rt#-908 NE REDMOND WY
REDMOND WA 175-C1
Rt#-970 HIGHWAY
KITTITAS CO WA 240-D1
Rt#-970 SUNSET HWY
KITTITAS CO WA 240-B2
Rt#-971 S LAKESHORE RD
CHELAN CO WA 236-B3
Rt#-971 NAVARRE COULEE RD
CHELAN CO WA 236-B3
U.S.-2 1 RD SE
DOUGLAS CO WA 112-C2
U.S.-2 2 1/2 RD NW
DOUGLAS CO WA 236-C7
WATERVILLE WA 236-C7
U.S.-2 6TH ST
NEWPORT WA 106-C3
U.S.-2 12 RD NE
DOUGLAS CO WA 112-C2
U.S.-2 W 14TH AV
AIRWAY HEIGHTS WA 246-A4
SPOKANE CO WA 246-A4
U.S.-2 15TH ST NW
East Wenatchee Bench WA 239-A4
U.S.-2 ALBANY RD
BONNER CO ID 107-A3
PRIEST RIVER ID 107-A3
U.S.-2 E BROADWAY ST
REARDAN WA 114-A2
U.S.-2 W BROADWAY ST
REARDAN WA 114-A2
U.S.-2 N BROWNE ST
SPOKANE WA 349-A9
U.S.-2 S BROWNE ST
SPOKANE WA 349-A10
U.S.-2 S CENTRAL AV
WATERVILLE WA 236-C7
U.S.-2 N CHELAN AV
WATERVILLE WA 236-C7
U.S.-2 CROFT AV
GOLD BAR WA 110-C1
SNOHOMISH CO WA 110-C1
U.S.-2 E COZZA DR
SPOKANE WA 347-A14
U.S.-2 N DIVISION ST
SPOKANE WA 346-J12
SPOKANE WA 347-A14
SPOKANE WA 349-A3
Town and Country WA 346-J12
Town and Country WA 347-A14
Town and Country WA 349-A3
U.S.-2 S DIVISION ST
SPOKANE WA 349-A9
U.S.-2 FRWY
EVERETT WA 265-G3
SNOHOMISH CO WA 171-D2
SNOHOMISH CO WA 265-G3
SPOKANE CO WA 348-A11
U.S.-2 HIGHWAY
ALMIRA WA 237-D7
BONNER CO ID 106-C3
BONNER CO ID 107-A3
BONNER CO ID 244-A2
BOUNDARY CO ID 107-B1
CASHMERE WA 238-C2
CHELAN CO WA 111-C1
CHELAN CO WA 238-A1
COULEE CITY WA 113-A2
Country Homes WA 347-A10
CRESTON WA 113-C1
DAVENPORT WA 114-A2
DOUGLAS CO WA 112-C2
DOUGLAS CO WA 113-A2
DOUGLAS CO WA 236-B6
DOUGLAS CO WA 239-A1
DOVER ID 107-A3
DOVER ID 244-A2
East Wenatchee Bench WA 238-D3
East Wenatchee Bench WA 239-A3
Fairchild Air Force Base WA 114-B2
Fairwood WA 347-C7
GRANT CO WA 113-A2
LEAVENWORTH WA 238-A1
LINCOLN CO MT 107-C2
LINCOLN CO WA 113-C1
LINCOLN CO WA 114-A2
LINCOLN CO WA 237-D7
MOYIE SPRINGS ID 107-B1
NEWPORT ID 106-C3
NEWPORT WA 106-C3
PEND OREILLE CO WA 106-C3
SANDPOINT ID 244-A2
SPOKANE WA 346-J12
SPOKANE WA 347-A11
SPOKANE CO WA 106-C3
SPOKANE CO WA 114-C1
SPOKANE CO WA 246-A4
SPOKANE CO WA 347-F1
SPOKANE CO WA 348-D13
Sunnyslope WA 238-D3
TROY MT 107-C2
WATERVILLE WA 236-C7
WILBUR WA 113-B1
U.S.-2 E MAIN AV
LINCOLN CO WA 113-B1
WILBUR WA 113-B1
U.S.-2 W MAIN AV
WILBUR WA 113-B1
U.S.-2 MISSOULA AV
LINCOLN CO MT 107-C2
TROY MT 107-C2
U.S.-2 E MISSOULA AV
TROY MT 107-C2
U.S.-2 MORGAN ST
DAVENPORT WA 114-A2
LINCOLN CO WA 114-A2
U.S.-2 N NEWPORT HWY
Country Homes WA 347-B9
Fairwood WA 347-B9
SPOKANE CO WA 347-E5
U.S.-2 PINE ST
SANDPOINT ID 244-A2
U.S.-2 E POPLAR ST
DOUGLAS CO WA 236-C7
WATERVILLE WA 236-C7
U.S.-2 N RUBY ST
SPOKANE WA 349-A6
U.S.-2 SAND HILL RD
BOUNDARY CO ID 107-B1
U.S.-2 W SPOKANE FALLS BLVD
SPOKANE WA 349-A9
U.S.-2 STEVENS PASS HWY
GOLD BAR WA 110-C1
KING CO WA 111-B1
MONROE WA 110-C1
SNOHOMISH WA 171-D3
SNOHOMISH CO WA 110-C1
SNOHOMISH CO WA 111-A1
SNOHOMISH CO WA 171-D3
SULTAN WA 110-C1
U.S.-2 STEVENS PASS RD
SNOHOMISH CO WA 171-D2
U.S.-2 NE STEVENS PASS HWY
KING CO WA 111-A1
SKYKOMISH WA 111-A1
SNOHOMISH CO WA 111-A1
U.S.-2 SUNSET FRWY
DOUGLAS CO WA 238-D3
East Wenatchee Bench WA 238-D3
Sunnyslope WA 238-D3
U.S.-2 W SUNSET HWY
AIRWAY HEIGHTS WA 246-A4
SPOKANE CO WA 246-A4
SPOKANE CO WA 348-A12
U.S.-2 WALNUT ST
NEWPORT ID 106-C3
NEWPORT WA 106-C3
U.S.-2 N WASHINGTON AV
NEWPORT WA 106-C3

INDEX

INDEX

STREET	City State	Page-Grid

U.S.-97 HIGHWAY
RIVERSIDE WA ... 104-C2
SHERMAN CO OR ... 127-C1
SISKIYOU CO CA ... 150-C3
Sunnyslope WA ... 238-D3
TONASKET WA ... 104-C2
TOPPENISH WA ... 120-A2
WAPATO WA ... 120-A2
YAKIMA WA ... 119-C3
YAKIMA CO WA ... 120-A2

U.S.-97 MAIN ST
DORRIS CA ... 150-B3
MORO OR ... 127-C2
OKANOGAN CO WA ... 104-C1
OROVILLE WA ... 104-C1

U.S.-97 SANDERS ST
CHELAN WA ... 236-D3

U.S.-97 SHERMAN HWY
GRASS VALLEY OR ... 127-C2
MORO OR ... 127-C2
SHANIKO OR ... 127-C2
SHERMAN CO OR ... 127-C1
WASCO CO OR ... 127-B3

U.S.-97 THE DALLES-CALIF HWY
BEND OR ... 217-C1
BEND OR ... 332-F1
CHILOQUIN OR ... 231-D3
DESCHUTES CO OR ... 143-A1
DESCHUTES CO OR ... 212-C7
DESCHUTES CO OR ... 217-C1
DESCHUTES CO OR ... 332-D14
Deschutes River Woods OR ... 217-C1
Deschutes River Woods OR ... 332-D14
JEFFERSON CO OR ... 135-B1
JEFFERSON CO OR ... 208-C4
JEFFERSON CO OR ... 212-D3
KLAMATH CO OR ... 142-C2
KLAMATH CO OR ... 143-A1
KLAMATH CO OR ... 150-C1
KLAMATH CO OR ... 231-D3
KLAMATH CO OR ... 235-C1
KLAMATH CO OR ... 338-A1
KLAMATH FALLS OR ... 338-A1
MADRAS OR ... 208-C4
REDMOND OR ... 212-D3
Terrebonne OR ... 212-D3
WASCO CO OR ... 127-B3
WASCO CO OR ... 135-B1

U.S.-97 Bus THE DLS-CALIF HWY
BEND OR ... 332-D13

U.S.-97 WEBSTER AV
CHELAN WA ... 236-D3

U.S.-97 WHITCOMB AV
OKANOGAN CO WA ... 104-C2
TONASKET WA ... 104-C2

U.S.-97 WOODIN AV
CHELAN WA ... 236-C3
CHELAN CO WA ... 236-C3

U.S.-101 1ST AV N
ILWACO WA ... 186-A6
PACIFIC CO WA ... 186-A6

U.S.-101 E 1ST ST
PORT ANGELES WA ... 261-F4

U.S.-101 2ND ST SE
BANDON OR ... 220-B6

U.S.-101 7TH ST
NEHALEM OR ... 191-B4

U.S.-101 SW 100TH ST
NEWPORT OR ... 206-A5

U.S.-101 N ALDER ST
ABERDEEN WA ... 178-B7

U.S.-101 S ALDER ST
ABERDEEN WA ... 178-B7

U.S.-101 N BROADWAY ST
COOS BAY OR ... 333-H9

U.S.-101 S BROADWAY ST
COOS BAY OR ... 333-H11

U.S.-101 CHETCO AV
BROOKINGS OR ... 232-C6

U.S.-101 W CURTIS ST
ABERDEEN WA ... 178-B7

U.S.-101 EVANS BLVD
COOS BAY OR ... 333-H11

U.S.-101 FIRST ST
COSMOPOLIS WA ... 178-B7

U.S.-101 E FIRST ST
COSMOPOLIS WA ... 117-A1

U.S.-101 FORKS AV N
FORKS WA ... 169-D1

U.S.-101 FORKS AV S
FORKS WA ... 169-D1

U.S.-101 FRWY
OLYMPIA WA ... 296-D6
THURSTON CO WA ... 180-B5
THURSTON CO WA ... 296-B5
TUMWATER WA ... 296-G7

U.S.-101 E FRONT ST
PORT ANGELES WA ... 261-G5

U.S.-101 S G ST
ABERDEEN WA ... 178-B7

U.S.-101 GARIBALDI AV
TILLAMOOK CO OR ... 191-B7
GARIBALDI OR ... 191-B7

U.S.-101 N GOLF COURSE RD
PORT ANGELES WA ... 261-H6

U.S.-101 H ST
NEHALEM OR ... 191-B4

U.S.-101 S H ST
ABERDEEN WA ... 178-B7

U.S.-101 E HERON ST
ABERDEEN WA ... 178-B7

U.S.-101 W HERON ST
ABERDEEN WA ... 178-B7

U.S.-101 HIGHWAY
CLALLAM CO WA ... 109-C1
CLALLAM CO WA ... 162-D7
CLALLAM CO WA ... 163-B6
CLALLAM CO WA ... 164-A6
CLALLAM CO WA ... 165-A6
CLALLAM CO WA ... 166-A7
CLALLAM CO WA ... 169-C1
CLALLAM CO WA ... 262-A12
COSMOPOLIS WA ... 117-A1
FORKS WA ... 169-C1
GRAYS HARBOR CO WA ... 108-C2
GRAYS HARBOR CO WA ... 109-A2
GRAYS HARBOR CO WA ... 117-A1
GRAYS HARBOR CO WA ... 172-B3
GRAYS HARBOR CO WA ... 177-D2
GRAYS HARBOR CO WA ... 178-A1
HOQUIAM WA ... 178-A6
ILWACO WA ... 186-A6
JEFFERSON CO WA ... 108-C1
JEFFERSON CO WA ... 109-C1
JEFFERSON CO WA ... 169-D3
JEFFERSON CO WA ... 172-A1

U.S.-101 HIGHWAY
JEFFERSON CO WA ... 173-D1
MASON CO WA ... 173-C2
MASON CO WA ... 180-A1
PACIFIC CO WA ... 117-A1
PACIFIC CO WA ... 183-C6
PACIFIC CO WA ... 186-B1
PACIFIC CO WA ... 188-C7
RAYMOND WA ... 117-A1
SEQUIM WA ... 166-B7
SEQUIM WA ... 262-E12
SHELTON WA ... 180-A2
SOUTH BEND WA ... 117-A1
THURSTON CO WA ... 180-B5

U.S.-101 L ST
CRESCENT CITY CA ... 148-B3

U.S.-101 LEVEE ST
HOQUIAM WA ... 178-A7

U.S.-101 LINCOLN ST
HOQUIAM WA ... 178-A7

U.S.-101 N LINCOLN ST
PORT ANGELES WA ... 261-F4

U.S.-101 S LINCOLN ST
PORT ANGELES WA ... 261-E5

U.S.-101 M ST
CRESCENT CITY CA ... 148-B3

U.S.-101 MAIN AV
TILLAMOOK OR ... 197-B2
TILLAMOOK CO OR ... 197-B2

U.S.-101 W MARINE DR
ASTORIA OR ... 300-A5

U.S.-101 NEWPORT AV
COOS BAY OR ... 333-H12
COOS CO OR ... 333-H12

U.S.-101 OCEAN AV
RAYMOND WA ... 117-A1

U.S.-101 OLYMPIC HWY
CLALLAM CO WA ... 164-C6
CLALLAM CO WA ... 165-B6
CLALLAM CO WA ... 166-C7
CLALLAM CO WA ... 261-A6
JEFFERSON CO WA ... 109-C1
JEFFERSON CO WA ... 166-C7
PORT ANGELES WA ... 261-A6

U.S.-101 OREGON COAST HWY
ASTORIA OR ... 188-C1
ASTORIA OR ... 300-A1
BANDON OR ... 220-C4
BAY CITY OR ... 191-B5
BAY CITY OR ... 197-B1
BROOKINGS OR ... 232-C5
CANNON BEACH OR ... 188-B7
CANNON BEACH OR ... 191-A2
CLATSOP CO OR ... 188-C1
CLATSOP CO OR ... 191-A2
CLATSOP CO OR ... 300-A1
CLATSOP CO OR ... 301-F14
COOS CO OR ... 218-B5
COOS CO OR ... 220-C4
COOS CO OR ... 224-B4
COOS CO OR ... 333-J13
CURRY CO OR ... 224-B4
CURRY CO OR ... 228-A1
CURRY CO OR ... 232-B2
DEPOE BAY OR ... 203-A7
DEPOE BAY OR ... 206-B3
DOUGLAS CO OR ... 214-A7
DOUGLAS CO OR ... 218-B2
DUNES CITY OR ... 214-B4
FLORENCE OR ... 214-B4
GARIBALDI OR ... 191-B5
GEARHART OR ... 301-H4
GOLD BEACH OR ... 228-A6
Harbor OR ... 232-D6
LAKESIDE OR ... 218-B2
LANE CO OR ... 132-B2
LANE CO OR ... 209-A6
LANE CO OR ... 214-B4
Lincoln Beach OR ... 203-A7
LINCOLN CITY OR ... 203-B3
LINCOLN CO OR ... 203-B3
LINCOLN CO OR ... 206-B3
LINCOLN CO OR ... 209-A3
LINCOLN CO OR ... 328-D2
MANZANITA OR ... 191-B5
NEWPORT OR ... 206-B3
NORTH BEND OR ... 333-G2
PORT ORFORD OR ... 224-B6
REEDSPORT OR ... 218-B2
ROCKAWAY BEACH OR ... 191-B5
SEASIDE OR ... 188-B7
SEASIDE OR ... 301-H4
TILLAMOOK CO OR ... 191-B5
TILLAMOOK CO OR ... 197-C4
TILLAMOOK CO OR ... 203-B3
WALDPORT OR ... 328-D2
WARRENTON OR ... 188-B2
WHEELER OR ... 191-B5
YACHATS OR ... 209-A3

U.S.-101 OREGON ST
PORT ORFORD OR ... 224-A6

U.S.-101 PACIFIC AV
TILLAMOOK CO OR ... 197-B2
TILLAMOOK CO OR ... 197-B2

U.S.-101 PARK DR
GEARHART OR ... 301-H4

U.S.-101 N PARK ST
ABERDEEN WA ... 178-B7

U.S.-101 S PARK ST
ABERDEEN WA ... 178-B7

U.S.-101 PERRY AV
HOQUIAM WA ... 178-A7

U.S.-101 REDWOOD HWY
CRESCENT CITY CA ... 148-B3
DEL NORTE CO CA ... 148-B3
DEL NORTE CO CA ... 232-D7

U.S.-101 RIVERSIDE AV
HOQUIAM WA ... 178-A7

U.S.-101 RIVERSIDE DR
NEHALEM OR ... 191-B4

U.S.-101 ROBERT BUSH DR
PACIFIC CO WA ... 183-D6
SOUTH BEND WA ... 117-A1
SOUTH BEND WA ... 183-D6

U.S.-101 ROOSEVELT DR
SEASIDE OR ... 301-G6

U.S.-101 S ROOSEVELT DR
CLATSOP CO OR ... 301-F10
SEASIDE OR ... 301-G8

U.S.-101 SEVENTH ST
HOQUIAM WA ... 178-A7

U.S.-101 SHERIDAN AV
NORTH BEND OR ... 333-G5

U.S.-101 SHERMAN AV
NORTH BEND OR ... 333-G5

U.S.-101 SIMPSON AV
ABERDEEN WA ... 178-B7
HOQUIAM WA ... 178-A7

U.S.-101 SIXTH ST
RAYMOND WA ... 117-A1

U.S.-101 SUMNER ST
ABERDEEN WA ... 178-A7
HOQUIAM WA ... 178-A7

U.S.-101 TREMONT ST
COOS BAY OR ... 333-G7
NORTH BEND OR ... 333-G7

U.S.-101 W WISHKAH ST
ABERDEEN WA ... 178-B7

U.S.-101 WARRNTN-ASTORIA HWY
ASTORIA OR ... 300-C9
CLATSOP CO OR ... 188-B2
CLATSOP CO OR ... 300-C9
WARRENTON OR ... 188-B2

U.S.-101 W WASHINGTON ST
CLALLAM CO WA ... 165-D6
CLALLAM CO WA ... 166-A6

U.S.-101 N WEST BLVD
ABERDEEN WA ... 178-B7
COSMOPOLIS WA ... 178-B7

U.S.-101 N WINCHESTER AV
REEDSPORT OR ... 218-C1

U.S.-101 WISHKAH ST
ABERDEEN WA ... 178-B7

U.S.-101 E WISHKAH ST
ABERDEEN WA ... 178-B7

U.S.-195 BROADWAY ST
COLTON WA ... 250-A1

U.S.-195 HIGHWAY
COLFAX WA ... 122-C1
COLFAX WA ... 250-A1
NEZ PERCE CO ID ... 250-B3
SPOKANE WA ... 348-F11
SPOKANE CO WA ... 114-C2
SPOKANE CO WA ... 246-C6
UNIONTOWN WA ... 250-B1
WHITMAN CO WA ... 114-C3
WHITMAN CO WA ... 122-C1
WHITMAN CO WA ... 249-A4
WHITMAN CO WA ... 250-A1

U.S.-195 INLAND ST
WHITMAN CO WA ... 114-C3

U.S.-195 S INLAND EMPIRE HWY
SPOKANE CO WA ... 246-C5
SPOKANE CO WA ... 246-C5

U.S.-195 E JAMES ST
COLFAX WA ... 122-C1

U.S.-195 N MAIN ST
COLFAX WA ... 122-C1

U.S.-195 S MAIN ST
COLFAX WA ... 122-C1

U.S.-197 DESCHUTES AV
MAUPIN OR ... 127-B3

U.S.-197 HIGHWAY
KLICKITAT CO WA ... 196-C6

U.S.-197 THE DALLES-CALIF HWY
DUFUR OR ... 127-B2
MAUPIN OR ... 127-B3
THE DALLES OR ... 196-D7
WASCO CO OR ... 127-B3
WASCO CO OR ... 196-D7

U.S.-199 E F ST
GRANTS PASS OR ... 335-G9

U.S.-199 F ST
GRANTS PASS OR ... 335-H9
JOSEPHINE CO OR ... 335-H9

U.S.-199 REDWOOD HWY
CAVE JUNCTION OR ... 233-B3
DEL NORTE CO CA ... 148-C3
DEL NORTE CO CA ... 233-A6
GRANTS PASS OR ... 335-F9
JOSEPHINE CO OR ... 149-A1
JOSEPHINE CO OR ... 229-A7
JOSEPHINE CO OR ... 233-B3
JOSEPHINE CO OR ... 335-A12

U.S.-395 N 1ST ST
HERMISTON OR ... 129-A1

U.S.-395 W 5TH AV
COLVILLE WA ... 106-A2

U.S.-395 BARNES AV
SENECA OR ... 137-B3

U.S.-395 S CANYON BLVD
JOHN DAY OR ... 137-B2

U.S.-395 N DIVISION ST
Country Homes WA ... 346-J11
Country Homes WA ... 347-A8
Fairwood WA ... 347-A8
SPOKANE WA ... 346-J11
Town and Country WA ... 346-J11

U.S.-395 N ELY ST
KENNEWICK WA ... 342-J10

U.S.-395 S ELY ST
KENNEWICK WA ... 342-J11

U.S.-395 F ST N
LAKEVIEW OR ... 152-A2

U.S.-395 F ST S
LAKE CO OR ... 152-A2
LAKEVIEW OR ... 152-A2

U.S.-395 FREMONT HWY
LAKE CO OR ... 152-A2
LAKEVIEW OR ... 152-A2
MODOC CO CA ... 152-A2

U.S.-395 FRWY
ADAMS CO WA ... 113-C3
ADAMS CO WA ... 121-C1
BENTON CO WA ... 121-A3
Finley WA ... 121-A3
FRANKLIN CO WA ... 121-B1
FRANKLIN CO WA ... 343-F1
KENNEWICK WA ... 343-B9
LEWISTON OR ... 121-A3
MESA WA ... 121-B2
PASCO WA ... 121-A2
PASCO WA ... 343-G1
UMATILLA CO OR ... 121-A3

U.S.-395 G ST N
LAKEVIEW OR ... 152-A2

U.S.-395 HIGHWAY
ADAMS CO WA ... 121-B1
BENTON CO WA ... 121-A3
COLVILLE WA ... 106-A2
CONNELL WA ... 121-B1
DEER PARK WA ... 114-B1
Fairwood WA ... 347-A6
FERRY CO WA ... 105-C1
FERRY CO WA ... 106-A1
Finley WA ... 121-A3
FRANKLIN CO WA ... 121-B1
KENNEWICK WA ... 121-A3
KENNEWICK WA ... 342-J10
KENNEWICK WA ... 343-B10
KETTLE FALLS WA ... 106-A2
MODOC CO CA ... 152-A3
PASCO WA ... 121-A2

U.S.-395 HIGHWAY
SPOKANE CO WA ... 114-B1
SPOKANE CO WA ... 346-J1
SPOKANE CO WA ... 347-A2
STEVENS CO WA ... 106-A2
STEVENS CO WA ... 114-B1

U.S.-395 JOHN DAY HWY
GRANT CO OR ... 137-A2
JOHN DAY OR ... 137-A2
MOUNT VERNON OR ... 137-A2

U.S.-395 JOHN DAY-BURNS HWY
CANYON CITY OR ... 137-B2
GRANT CO OR ... 137-B2
HARNEY CO OR ... 137-B3
HARNEY CO OR ... 145-B1
JOHN DAY OR ... 137-B2
SENECA OR ... 137-B3

U.S.-395 LAKEVIEW-BURNS HWY
HARNEY CO OR ... 144-C2
LAKE CO OR ... 144-B3
LAKE CO OR ... 152-A1

U.S.-395 E MAIN ST
MOUNT VERNON OR ... 137-A2

U.S.-395 N MAIN ST
COLVILLE WA ... 106-A2

U.S.-395 S MAIN ST
COLVILLE WA ... 106-A2

U.S.-395 W MAIN ST
GRANT CO OR ... 137-B2
JOHN DAY OR ... 137-B2

U.S.-395 MCNARY HWY
UMATILLA OR ... 129-A1
UMATILLA CO OR ... 129-A1

U.S.-395 MOUNTAIN BLVD
MOUNT VERNON OR ... 137-A2

U.S.-395 N PARK ST
CHEWELAH WA ... 106-B3
STEVENS CO WA ... 106-B3

U.S.-395 S PARK ST
CHEWELAH WA ... 106-B3
STEVENS CO WA ... 106-B3

U.S.-395 PENDLTN-JOHN DAY HWY
GRANT CO OR ... 129-B3
GRANT CO OR ... 137-A1
LONG CREEK OR ... 137-A1
MOUNT VERNON OR ... 137-A1
PENDLETON OR ... 129-B2
PILOT ROCK OR ... 129-B2
UMATILLA CO OR ... 129-B2

U.S.-395 PIONEER MEM BRDG
KENNEWICK WA ... 343-B8
PASCO WA ... 343-B8

U.S.-395 UMATILLA-STANFLD HWY
HERMISTON OR ... 129-A1
STANFIELD OR ... 129-A1
UMATILLA OR ... 129-A1
UMATILLA CO OR ... 129-A1

U.S.-730 6TH ST
UMATILLA OR ... 129-A1
UMATILLA CO OR ... 129-A1

U.S.-730 COLUMBIA RIVER HWY
IRRIGON OR ... 128-C1
MORROW CO OR ... 128-C1
UMATILLA OR ... 129-A1
UMATILLA CO OR ... 128-C1
UMATILLA CO OR ... 129-A1

U.S.-730 MAIN AV E
IRRIGON OR ... 128-C1

INDEX

424 ENTERTAINMENT & SPORTS POINTS OF INTEREST HOSPITALS

FEATURE NAME City State	Page-Grid
WALLA WALLA COUNTY FAIRGROUNDS W TIETAN ST, WALLA WALLA CO WA	345 - A9
WALLOWA COUNTY FAIRGROUNDS ENTERPRISE-LEWISTON HWY, ENTERPRISE OR	130 - C2
WASHINGTON COUNTY FAIRGROUNDS 873 NE 34TH AV, HILLSBORO OR	198 - D1
WASHINGTON STATE CONV & TRADE CTR 800 CONVENTION PL, SEATTLE WA	278 - A5
WENATCHEE SPEEDWAY WENATCHEE, DOUGLAS CO WA	239 - A4
WESTERN IDAHO FAIRGROUND OFF GLENWOOD ST, ADA CO ID	253 - C2
WEST FENWICK SKATEPARK REITH RD & 42ND AVE S, KENT WA	175 - B7
WEST LINN SKATEPARK 3456 PARKER RD, WEST LINN OR	199 - C4
WHEELER COUNTY FAIRGROUNDS JOHN DAY HWY, WHEELER CO OR	128 - A3
WILSONVILLE MEM SKATEPARK WILSONVILLE RD, WILSONVILLE OR	199 - B6
YAMHILL COUNTY FAIRGROUNDS 2070 NE LAFAYETTE AV, MCMINNVILLE OR	198 - B7

GOLF COURSES

FEATURE NAME City State	Page-Grid
ALLENMORE GC 2125 S CEDAR ST, TACOMA WA	292 - D7
ASPENS LAKES GC 16900 ASPENS LAKES DR, DESCHUTES CO OR	212 - A5
AUBURN CTR GC CENTER ST NE, MARION CO OR	323 - G13
AVALON GC 19345 KELLEHER RD, SKAGIT CO WA	161 - B5
AWBREY GLEN GC NW MT WASHINGTON & NW COLLEGE, BEND OR	332 - A4
BATTLE CREEK CC COMMERCIAL ST SE & MADRAS ST, SALEM OR	325 - A9
BELLINGHAM GOLF & CC 3729 MERIDIAN ST, BELLINGHAM WA	258 - C2
BEND GC COUNTRY CLUB DR & HIGHLAND RD, BEND OR	332 - E13
BLENKINSOP VALLEY GC BLENKINSOP RD, DISTRICT OF SAANICH BC	256 - J1
BOISE RANCH GC E LAKE HAZEL RD, ADA CO ID	253 - B4
BRANDON DUNES GC ROUND LAKE DR, COOS CO OR	220 - B4
BROADMOOR GC 2340 BROADMOOR DR E, SEATTLE WA	278 - E2
BROADMOOR GC 3509 NE COLUMBIA BLVD, PORTLAND OR	310 - B4
BROKEN TOP GC CENTURY DR HWY & CAMPBELL DR, BEND OR	332 - A8
CAPILANO GC STEVENS DR, DISTRICT OF W VANCOUVER BC	254 - F1
CAPITOL CITY GC 5225 YELM HWY SE, THURSTON CO WA	297 - G13
CEDAR HILL GC 1400 DERBY RD, DISTRICT OF SAANICH BC	256 - J4
CEDAR LINKS GC FOOTHILL RD & CEDAR LINKS RD, MEDFORD OR	336 - H8
CENTRALIA PUB GC 1012 DUFFY ST, CENTRALIA WA	299 - H4
COEUR D ALENE PUBLIC GC E FAIRWAY DR, COEUR D'ALENE ID	355 - A7
COEUR D ALENE RESORT GC 115 S 2ND ST, COEUR D'ALENE ID	355 - H12
COLUMBIA EDGEWATER CC 2220 NE MARINE DR, PORTLAND OR	309 - J2
COLUMBIA PARK GC 2701 COLUMBIA DR SE, KENNEWICK WA	342 - J9
COLUMBIA POINT GC 225 COLUMBIA POINT DR, RICHLAND WA	341 - H3
COLWOOD NATL GC 7313 NE COLUMBIA BLVD, PORTLAND OR	311 - F5
CORVALLIS CC COUNTRY CLUB DR, CORVALLIS OR	327 - D12
CRESTVIEW HILLS GC GREEN DR, WALDPORT OR	328 - D7
DOWNRIVER MUNICIPAL GC 3225 COLUMBIA CIR, SPOKANE WA	348 - D6
DUNGENESS GOLF & CC 1965 WOODCOCK RD, CLALLAM CO WA	166 - A6
EAGLE CREST GC CLINE FALLS HWY, DESCHUTES CO OR	212 - C5
EASTMORELAND GC 2425 SE BYBEE BLVD, PORTLAND OR	317 - J5
EMERALD VALLEY RESORT GC 83301 DALE KUNI RD, LANE CO OR	215 - C4
ESMERALDA MUNICIPAL GC 3933 E COURTLAND AV, SPOKANE WA	349 - F4
EUGENE CC 255 COUNTRY CLUB RD, EUGENE OR	330 - A4
EVERETT GOLF & CC 1500 52ND ST SE, EVERETT WA	268 - D1
FOSTER GOLF LINKS 13500 INTERURBAN AV S, TUKWILA WA	289 - G2
GEARHART GOLF LINKS 1300 N MARION AV, CLATSOP CO OR	301 - G2
GLEN ACRES GOLF & CC 1000 S 112TH ST, KING CO WA	286 - B5
GOLD MOUNTAIN GC 7263 W BELFAIR VALLEY RD, BREMERTON WA	174 - A4
GOLF CLUB OF OREGON 905 NW SPRING HILL DR, BENTON CO OR	326 - C7
GORGE VALE GC 1005 CRAIGFLOWER RD, TOWN OF ESQUIMALT BC	256 - C6
GREEN LAKE GC 5701 W GREEN LAKE WY N, SEATTLE WA	273 - J4
HALL, WALTER E REC AREA & GC 1226 W CASINO RD, EVERETT WA	267 - J5
HANGMAN VALLEY GC 2210 S HANGMAN VALLEY RD, SPOKANE CO WA	246 - C6
HARBOR LINKS GC 601 HARBOR ISLE BLVD, KLAMATH CO OR	338 - A3
HERON LAKES GC 3500 N VICTORY BLVD, PORTLAND OR	308 - C1
HIGHLANDS GOLF & CC, THE 5500 E MULLAN AV, POST FALLS ID	354 - F6
HOOD RIVER GC COUNTRY CLUB RD, HOOD RIVER CO OR	195 - C6
ILLINOIS VALLEY GC REDWWOD HIGHWAY 199, JOSEPHINE CO OR	233 - B3
INDIAN CANYON MUNICIPAL GC 4304 W WEST DR, SPOKANE WA	348 - D10
INDIAN LAKES GC OFF S COLE RD, ADA CO ID	253 - C4
INDIAN SUMMER GC 5900 TROON LN SE, THURSTON CO WA	297 - E13
INTERBAY FAMILY GC 2501 15TH AV W, SEATTLE WA	277 - F1
JEFFERSON PARK GC 4101 BEACON AV S, SEATTLE WA	282 - C4
JUNIPER GC 139 SE SISTERS AV, REDMOND OR	212 - D5
KENTUCK GC 675 GOLF COURSE LN, COOS CO OR	218 - B7
LAKE PADDEN GC 4882 SAMISH WY, BELLINGHAM WA	258 - G13
LAKESIDE GC 3245 NE 50TH ST, LINCOLN CITY OR	203 - B4
LAURELWOOD GC E 30TH AV, EUGENE OR	330 - C10
LONGVIEW GOLF AND CC 41 COUNTRY CLUB DR, LONGVIEW WA	302 - H5
MARYSVILLE GC ALLEN ST, BENTON CO OR	327 - F12
MCCALL GC DAVIS ST & LICK CREEK RD, MCCALL ID	251 - D5
MCCORNICK WOODS GC 5155 MCCORNICK WOODS DR SW, KITSAP CO WA	174 - A4
MEADOW PARK GC 7108 LAKEWOOD DR W, TACOMA WA	294 - A6
MEADWOOD GC 24501 E VALLEYWAY AV, LIBERTY LAKE WA	352 - E14
MINT VALLEY GC 4002 PENNSYLVANIA ST, LONGVIEW WA	302 - F4
MOUNT DOUGLAS GC BLENKINSOP RD, DISTRICT OF SAANICH BC	256 - J1
MYLORA GC CITY OF RICHMOND BC	156 - B7
MYRTLE CREEK GC FAIRWAY DR, DOUGLAS CO OR	225 - C1
NEWAUKUM VALLEY GC 153 NEWAUKUM GOLF DR, LEWIS CO WA	187 - C1
NORTH BELLINGHAM GC 205 W SMITH RD, WHATCOM CO WA	158 - D6
OAK KNOLL GC GREEN SPRINGS HWY & OAK KNOLL, ASHLAND OR	337 - J10
OAK KNOLL GC WILLAMINA-SALEM HWY, POLK CO OR	204 - B5
OAKWAY GC 2000 CAL YOUNG, EUGENE OR	330 - B3
OCEAN SHORES GC 500 CANAL DR NE, OCEAN SHORES WA	177 - B6
OSWEGO LAKE CC 20 IRON MOUNTAIN BLVD, LAKE OSWEGO OR	320 - D5
PAINTED HILLS GC S DISHMAN-MICA RD, SPOKANE VALLEY WA	350 - H14
PENINSULA GC GOLF COURSE RD, PORT ANGELES WA	261 - H6
PORTLAND MEADOWS GC 901 N SCHMEER RD, PORTLAND OR	309 - F3
PORT TOWNSEND GC 1948 BLANE ST, PORT TOWNSEND WA	263 - F4
PRAIRIE FALLS GC 3200 N SPOKANE ST, POST FALLS ID	353 - H3
RAINIER GC & CC 11133 DES MOINES MEM DR S, KING CO WA	286 - B6
REAMES CC 4201 HWY 97 SOUTH, KLAMATH CO OR	338 - B13
RIVERIDGE GC 3800 DELTA PKWY, LANE CO OR	215 - B1
RIVERS EDGE GC NW MT WASHINGTON DR & HWY 97, BEND OR	332 - D4
RIVERSIDE CC 1451 AIRPORT RD, CHEHALIS WA	299 - B9
RIVERSIDE GOLF & CC 8105 NE 33RD DR, PORTLAND OR	310 - A4
ROGUE VALLEY CC BLACK OAK DR & COUNTRY CLUB DR, MEDFORD OR	336 - H12
ROSEBURG MUNICIPAL GC NW GARDEN VALLEY & NW DOGWOOD, ROSEBURG OR	334 - D5
ROSE CITY GC 2200 NE 71ST AV, PORTLAND OR	315 - E3
ROYAL OAKS CC 8917 NE FOURTH PLAIN RD, VANCOUVER WA	307 - G2
RUNNING Y RANCH GC 5500 RUNNING Y RD, KLAMATH CO OR	235 - A2
SALEM GC RIVER RD S, SALEM OR	324 - E2
SALISHAN GOLF LINKS OREGON COAST HWY, LINCOLN CO OR	203 - A6
SALMON RUN GC 99040 SOUTH BANK CETCO RIVER R, CURRY CO OR	232 - D6
SAND POINT CC 8333 55TH AV NE, SEATTLE WA	275 - G2
SEMIAHMOO GOLF & CC 8720 SEMIAHMOO PKWY, BLAINE WA	158 - A3
SHAUGHNESSY GC UNIVERSITY ENDOWMENT LAND BC	156 - A5
SHIELD CREST GC 3151 N DELTA HWY, KLAMATH CO OR	339 - G11
SPOKANE CC N COUNTRY CLUB DR, FAIRWOOD WA	346 - F8
SPRING HILL CC 155 COUNTRY CLUB LN, BENTON CO OR	326 - C3
SUNSHINE HILLS GC DISTRICT OF DELTA BC	156 - D7
SUN WILLOWS GC 2535 N 20TH AV, PASCO WA	343 - E4
THREE RIVERS GC 2222 S RIVER RD, KELSO WA	303 - C11
TRI CITY CC GC 314 N UNDERWOOD ST, KENNEWICK WA	343 - B10
TROPHY LAKE GC 3900 SW LAKE FLORA RD, KITSAP CO WA	174 - A5
TUMWATER VALLEY MUNICIPAL GC 4611 TUMWATER VALLEY DR, TUMWATER WA	296 - H10
TYEE VALLEY GC 2401 S 192ND ST, SEATAC WA	290 - C2
UPLANDS GC 3300 CADBORO BAY RD, DISTRICT OF OAK BAY BC	257 - D5
VETERANS MEMORIAL GC 201 REES AV, WALLA WALLA WA	345 - A5
VICTORIA GC 1110 BEACH DR, DISTRICT OF OAK BAY BC	257 - D10
WALLA WALLA CC 1390 COUNTRY CLUB RD, WALLA WALLA WA	344 - J11
WANDERMERE LAKE GC 13700 N DIVISION RD, SPOKANE CO WA	347 - A5
WAVERLEY CC 1100 SE WAVERLY DR, CLACKAMAS CO OR	321 - H1
WEST RICHLAND GC 4000 FALLON DR, WEST RICHLAND WA	340 - A11
WEST SEATTLE GC & REC AREA 4470 35TH AV SW, SEATTLE WA	281 - F5
WILDWOOD GC 21881 NW SAINT HELENS RD, MULTNOMAH CO OR	192 - A5

HOSPITALS

FEATURE NAME City State	Page-Grid
ADVENTIST MED CTR 10123 SE MARKET ST, PORTLAND OR	315 - H7
ALLENMORE HOSP 1901 S UNION AV, TACOMA WA	292 - D7
ASHLAND COMM HOSP 280 MAPLE, ASHLAND OR	337 - B6
AUBURN REGL MED CTR 202 N DIVISION ST, AUBURN WA	182 - C1
BAY AREA HOSP 1775 THOMPSON RD, COOS BAY OR	333 - F8
BONNER GENERAL HOSP 502 N 3RD AV, SANDPOINT ID	244 - A2
BOUNDARY COMM HOSP 6640 KANIKSU ST, BOUNDARY CO ID	107 - B1
BRIDGE, MARY CHILDRENS HOSP 317 MARTIN LUTHER KING JR WY, TACOMA WA	293 - G4
BURNABY GENERAL HOSP SMITH AV, DISTRICT OF BURNABY BC	156 - C5
CAMPBELL RIVER HOSP HWY 19, CAMPBELL RIVER BC	92 - A1
CAPITAL MED CTR 3900 CAPITAL MALL DR SW, OLYMPIA WA	296 - C5
CASCADE COMM HOSP BUSH ST & 2ND ST, CENTRAL POINT OR	230 - C7
CASCADE VALLEY HOSP 330 S STILLAGUAMISH AV, ARLINGTON WA	168 - D5
CENTRAL OREGON COMM HOSP 1253 N CANAL BLVD, REDMOND OR	212 - D5
CENTRAL WASHINGTON HOSP 1201 S MILLER ST, WENATCHEE WA	238 - D4
CHILDRENS HOSP & REGL MED CTR 4800 SAND POINT WY NE, SEATTLE WA	275 - F5
CHILLIWACK GENERAL HOSP 45600 MENHOLM, CITY OF CHILLIWACK BC	94 - C3
CLATSOP COUNTY HOME NEHALEM HWY, CLATSOP CO OR	300 - G10
COLUMBIA BASIN HOSP 200 SOUTHEAST BLVD, EPHRATA WA	112 - C3
COLUMBIA DIST HOSP 500 COLUMBIA RIVER HWY, SAINT HELENS OR	192 - B1
COLUMBIA MEMORIAL 2111 EXCHANGE ST, ASTORIA OR	300 - E5
COQUILLE VALLEY HOSP 940 5TH ST, COQUILLE OR	220 - D5
CURRY GENERAL HOSP 94220 E 4TH ST, GOLD BEACH OR	228 - A6
DAYTON GENERAL HOSP 1012 S 3RD ST, COLUMBIA CO WA	122 - A2
DEACONESS HOSP CHERRY ST & S OKANOGAN AV, WENATCHEE WA	238 - D4
DEACONESS MED CTR 800 W 5TH AV, SPOKANE WA	348 - J10
DEER PARK HOSP 1015 E D ST, DEER PARK WA	114 - B1
DELTA HOSP 5800 MOUNTAIN VIEW BLVD, DISTRICT OF DELTA BC	101 - C1
DOERNBECHER CHILDRENS HOSP 3181 SW SAM JACKSON PARK RD, PORTLAND OR	316 - E2
EAGLE RIDGE HOSP IOCO RD & GUILDFORD WY, PORT MOODY BC	157 - A4
EAST ADAMS RURALHOSP 903 S ADAMS ST, RITZVILLE WA	113 - C3
EASTERN STATE HOSP MAPLE ST, MEDICAL LAKE WA	114 - B2
EASTMORELAND HOSP 2900 SE STEELE ST, PORTLAND OR	318 - A4
ENUMCLAW COMM HOSP 1450 BATTERSBY AV, ENUMCLAW WA	110 - C3
EVERGREEN HEALTHCARE 12040 NE 128TH ST, KIRKLAND WA	171 - C7
FAIRVIEW HOSP PRINGLE RD SE, SALEM OR	325 - A5
FORKS COMM HOSP 530 BOGACHIEL WY, FORKS WA	169 - C2
GEORGE DERBY HOSP CARIBOO RD, DISTRICT OF BURNABY BC	156 - D5
GOOD SAMARITAN HOSP 407 14TH AV SE, PUYALLUP WA	182 - B4
GOOD SAMARITAN HOSP CORVALLIS 3600 NW SAMARITAN DR, CORVALLIS OR	327 - J4
GOOD SHEPHERD MED CTR 610 NW 11TH ST, HERMISTON OR	129 - A1
GORGE ROAD HOSP 62 GORGE RD E, CITY OF VICTORIA BC	256 - E6
GRACE HOSP OAK ST, VANCOUVER BC	156 - B5
GRANDE RONDE HOSP 900 SUNSET DR, UNION CO OR	130 - A2
GRAYS HARBOR COMM HOSP 915 ANDERSON DR, ABERDEEN WA	178 - A7
GRITMAN MED CTR 700 S MAIN ST, MOSCOW ID	249 - C5
GROUP HEALTH CO-OP CENTRAL HOSP 201 16TH AV E, SEATTLE WA	278 - C4
GROUP HEALTH EASTSIDE HOSP 2700 152ND AV NE, REDMOND WA	175 - D2
HAPPY ACRES MEMORIAL HOSP HWY 99W, YAMHILL CO OR	204 - B1
HARBORVIEW MED CTR 325 9TH AV, SEATTLE WA	278 - B6
HARRISON MEMORIAL HOSP 2520 CHERRY AV, BREMERTON WA	270 - J8
HIGHLINE COMM HOSP 16251 SYLVESTER RD SW, BURIEN WA	175 - A5
HIGHLINE SPECIALTY CTR 12844 MILITARY RD S, TUKWILA WA	288 - D1
HOLY FAMILY HOSP 5633 N LIDGERWOOD AV, SPOKANE WA	349 - A2
HOLY FAMILY HOSP VICTORIA DR, VANCOUVER BC	156 - C5
HOLY ROSARY MED CTR 351 SW 9TH ST, ONTARIO OR	139 - A3
IDAHO ELKS REHABILITATION HOSP 600 N ROBBINS RD, BOISE ID	253 - D2
IDAHO STATE HOSP 3100 11TH AV N, NAMPA ID	147 - C1
INTERMTN HOSP 303 N ALLUMBAUGH ST, BOISE ID	253 - C3
JEFFERSON GENERAL HOSP 834 SHERIDAN ST, PORT TOWNSEND WA	263 - E6
KADLEC MED CTR 888 SWIFT BLVD, RICHLAND WA	341 - F1
KAISER SUNNYSIDE MED CTR 10180 SE SUNNYSIDE RD, CLACKAMAS CO OR	199 - D3
KEIZER MEMORIAL HOSP CAPE ARAGO HWY & UNION AV, NORTH BEND OR	333 - G4

INDEX

INDEX

PARKS & RECREATION POINTS OF INTEREST PARKS & RECREATION 431

FEATURE NAME City State	Page-Grid
COEUR D'ALENE NATL FOREST, KOOTENAI CO - ID	355 - J2
COEUR D ALENE PK, SPOKANE WA	348 - G10
COLLIER MEM STATE PK, KLAMATH CO OR	231 - D2
COLMAN PK, SEATTLE WA	282 - E2
COLUMBIA LANCASTER PK, VANCOUVER WA	306 - D5
COLUMBIA PK, PORTLAND OR	308 - C4
COLUMBIA PK, SEATTLE WA	282 - E5
COLUMBIA PK WEST, RICHLAND WA	342 - C6
COLUMBIA PLAYFIELD, RICHLAND WA	341 - F1
COLVILLE NATL FOREST, FERRY CO WA	105 - B1
COMMENCEMENT PK, TACOMA WA	293 - E2
COMMODORE PK, SEATTLE WA	272 - D4
COMMONAGE RESERVE, BRITISH COLUMBIA BC	95 - C1
COMSTOCK PK, SPOKANE WA	348 - J13
CONE ISLANDS STATE PK, SKAGIT CO WA	160 - B4
CONFEDERATION PK, DISTRICT OF BURNABY BC	255 - H9
CONGER PK, KLAMATH FALLS OR	338 - B6
CONNAUGHT PK, VANCOUVER BC	254 - C13
COOS COUNTY FOREST, COOS CO OR	220 - C3
COPELAND ISLANDS MARINE PK, BRITISH-COLUMBIA BC	92 - B1
COPLEY MEM PK, DISTRICT OF SAANICH BC	256 - E1
COQUITLAM RIVER PK, COQUITLAM BC	157 - B4
CORBETT, ELLIOTT R II MEM STATE PK, - JEFFERSON CO OR	211 - A2
CORBIN PK, SPOKANE WA	348 - J5
CORNWALL PK, BELLINGHAM WA	258 - D3
COUCH PK, PORTLAND OR	312 - D5
COUGAR MTN REGL WILDLAND PK, KING CO WA	175 - D4
COULEE DAM NATL REC AREA, STEVENS CO WA	114 - A1
COUNCIL CREST PK, PORTLAND OR	316 - B1
COUNTY PK, SPOKANE CO WA	350 - H3
COVE PALISADES STATE PARK, THE, - JEFFERSON CO OR	208 - A6
COWEN PK, SEATTLE WA	274 - C4
CRAIGHILL PLGD, RICHLAND WA	341 - G3
CRANBERRY LAKE PK, ANACORTES WA	259 - E3
CRATER LAKE NATL PK, KLAMATH CO OR	227 - B1
CREST HEIGHTS PK, EUGENE OR	329 - H11
CRESTON PK, PORTLAND OR	318 - B2
CRESTVIEW PK, TUKWILA WA	289 - E5
CRYSTAL GARDEN, CITY OF VICTORIA BC	256 - G9
CRYSTAL SPRINGS PK, TUKWILA WA	289 - F5
CULLABY LAKE COUNTY PK, CLATSOP CO OR	188 - B3
CUSTER PK, PORTLAND OR	316 - C6
CYPRESS FALLS PK, DISTRICT OF WEST-VANCOUVR BC	156 - A2
CYPRESS PROVINCIAL PK, DISTRICT OF WEST-VANCOUVR BC	156 - A1
DABNEY STATE PK, MULTNOMAH CO OR	200 - C2
DAHL, WALDO J PLAYFIELD, SEATTLE WA	274 - D2
DARCY ISLAND MARINE PK, BRITISH COLUMBIA-BC	159 - D4
DAVID SPENCER PK, CITY OF VICTORIA BC	257 - A7
DAVIS LAKE PROVINCIAL PK, BRITISH-COLUMBIA BC	94 - B3
DAWSON PK, PORTLAND OR	313 - G2
DEADMAN LAKE PROVINCIAL PK, BRITISH-COLUMBIA BC	104 - C1
DEARBORN PK, SEATTLE WA	282 - D6
DEAS ISLAND REGL PK, DISTRICT OF DELTA - BC	156 - C7
DECEPTION PASS STATE PK, SKAGIT CO WA	259 - E13
DEER CREEK PK, ROSEBURG OR	334 - G7
DEERFIELD PK, ALBANY OR	326 - F12
DEER LAKE PK, DISTRICT OF BURNABY BC	156 - D5
DELBROOK PK, DIST OF N VANCOUVER BC	255 - A2
DEL NORTE COAST REDWOODS STATE PK, DEL-NORTE CO CA	148 - B3
DELONG PLGD, TACOMA WA	292 - B6
DELRIDGE PLAYFIELD, SEATTLE WA	281 - G5
DELTA PONDS PK, EUGENE OR	329 - H3
DELTA WATERS PK, MEDFORD OR	336 - G6
DENNY PK, SEATTLE WA	277 - J4
DERBY REACH REGL PK, TOWNSHIP OF LANGLEY-BC	157 - C6
DESCHUTES NATL FOREST, DESCHUTES CO OR	332 - J2
DES MOINES BEACH PK, DES MOINES WA	290 - A5
DES MOINES CREEK PK, DES MOINES WA	290 - A5
DES MOINES CREEK PK, SEATAC WA	290 - B4
DES MOINES MEM PK, DES MOINES WA	290 - A5
DESOLATION SOUND PROVNCL MARINE PK, - BRITISH COLUMBIA BC	92 - B1
DETROIT LAKE STATE PK, MARION CO OR	134 - B1
DEVILS ELBOW PK, LANE CO OR	209 - A7
DEVILS PUNCH BOWL STATE PK, LINCOLN CO - OR	206 - A2
DEWITT PK, PORTLAND OR	316 - D4
DIONISIO POINT PROV PK, BRITISH COLUMBIA-BC	101 - B1
DISCOVERY ISLAND MARINE PK, BRITISH-COLUMBIA BC	257 - J10
DISCOVERY PK, SEATTLE WA	272 - B4
DOE ISLAND STATE MARINE PK, SAN JUAN CO - WA	160 - A3
DOGWOOD PK, MILWAUKIE OR	321 - J3
DORAN PK, DIST OF N VANCOUVER BC	255 - F1
DOUGLAS, DAVID PK, VANCOUVER WA	306 - E5
DOUGLAS GARDENS PK, SPRINGFIELD OR	331 - C9
DOUGLAS PK, VANCOUVER BC	254 - F14
DOWNRIVER PK, SPOKANE WA	348 - D5
DRAKE PK, BEND OR	332 - D7
DRAPER PK, ALBANY OR	326 - D11
DRAYCOTT PK, DIST OF N VANCOUVER BC	255 - F2
DRUMHELLER SPRINGS, SPOKANE WA	348 - G5
DUBOIS PK, VANCOUVER WA	306 - B6
DUNDARAVE PK, DISTRICT OF WEST VANCOUVR - BC	254 - A3
DUNIWAY PK, PORTLAND OR	317 - E1
DUNN, PAUL ST FOREST, BENTON CO OR	207 - A3
DUWAMISH PK, TUKWILA WA	287 - E7
DUWAMISH RIVER PK, SEATTLE WA	286 - A2
EADES PK, ALBANY OR	326 - F6
EAGLE FERN PK, CLACKAMAS CO OR	200 - C5
EAGLE ISLAND STATE PK, PIERCE CO WA	181 - B3
EAGLE ISLAND STATE PK, ADA CO ID	253 - A1
EAGLES PK, ROSEBURG OR	334 - F8
EASTBANK RIVERFRONT PK, PORTLAND OR	313 - G6
EAST DELTA PK, PORTLAND OR	309 - F2
EASTGATE BASIN PK, SALEM OR	323 - D9
EASTGATE LIONS PK, WALLA WALLA WA	345 - E6
EASTGATE WOODLANDS PK, SPRINGFIELD OR	330 - E7
EAST MAGNOLIA PLAYFIELD, SEATTLE WA	276 - D1
EAST MONTLAKE PK, SEATTLE WA	278 - D1
EAST SOOKE REGL PK, BRITISH COLUMBIA BC	164 - D1
EASTVIEW PK, CITY OF NORTH VANCOUVER BC	255 - E4
EASTWOOD PK, ROSEBURG OR	334 - J8
ECOLA STATE PK, CLATSOP CO OR	301 - B12
EDGECLIFF PK, SPOKANE VALLEY WA	350 - B10
EDGEWATER PK, SKAGIT CO WA	260 - A13
EDGEWOOD PK, VANCOUVER WA	306 - A5
EDGEWOOD PK, EUGENE OR	330 - A12
EDWARDS, MYRTLE PK, SEATTLE WA	277 - G4
EIDON PK, DIST OF N VANCOUVER BC	254 - H1
ELEANOR PK, ALBANY OR	326 - E8
ELIZABETH PK, BELLINGHAM WA	258 - C5
ELK-BEAVER LAKE REGL PK, DISTRICT OF-SAANICH BC	159 - C5
ELK FALLS PK, BRITISH COLUMBIA BC	92 - A1
ELLIOT POINTE PK, MUKILTEO WA	267 - E2
ELLIOTT BAY PK, SEATTLE WA	277 - G3
ELLIOTT ST FOREST, COOS CO OR	218 - D3
ELLSWORTH PK, VANCOUVER WA	307 - H7
EMIGRANT LAKE COUNTY REC AREA, JACKSON-CO OR	234 - D4
ENDOLYNE PK, SEATTLE WA	284 - D4
E QUEEN ANNE PLGD, SEATTLE WA	277 - H2
ERROL HEIGHTS PK, PORTLAND OR	318 - C7
ESSEX PK, PORTLAND OR	319 - F3
EVERGREEN PK, VANCOUVER WA	306 - A4
EXHIBITION PK, VANCOUVER BC	255 - E10
FAIRFIELD HILL PK, CITY OF VICTORIA BC	256 - J11
FAIRHAVEN PK, BELLINGHAM WA	258 - B11
FAIRMONT PK, SALEM OR	324 - G1
FAIRMONT PK, SEATTLE WA	281 - E2
FAIRMOUNT PLGD, SEATTLE WA	281 - E6
FAIRVIEW PK, SEATTLE WA	274 - B7
FAIRWOOD CAMELOT PK, FAIRWOOD WA	347 - A8
FALAISE PK, VANCOUVER BC	255 - E13
FALLS PK, POST FALLS ID	353 - G7
FARRAGUT PK, PORTLAND OR	309 - F4
FARRAGUT STATE PK, KOOTENAI CO ID	245 - C1
FATHER BLANCHET PK, VANCOUVER WA	306 - E6
FAUNTLEROY PK, SEATTLE WA	284 - D4
FERNHILL PK, PORTLAND OR	310 - B6
FERRY PK, TACOMA WA	293 - F6
FERRY ROAD PK, NORTH BEND OR	333 - H3
FICHTNER MAINWARING PK, MEDFORD OR	336 - D14
FIELD HOUSE PK, DES MOINES WA	290 - A5
FINCH ARBORETUM, SPOKANE WA	348 - E12
FIRCREST PK, FIRCREST WA	294 - A1
FIRCREST PK, SALEM OR	324 - F4
FIREHOUSE PK, SEATTLE WA	278 - C6
FIREMANS PK, TACOMA WA	293 - H5
FIRLAND PARKWAY, PORTLAND OR	319 - E3
FIRST HILL PK, MERCER ISLAND WA	283 - J2
FIRST HILL PK, SEATTLE WA	278 - B5
FISH CREEK REC AREA, IDAHO CO ID	131 - C1
FISHERMANS WHARF PK, CITY OF VICTORIA BC	256 - F9
FISH HATCHERY PK, JOSEPHINE CO OR	229 - A7
FLAVEL PK, PORTLAND OR	319 - E6
FLEETWOOD PK, CITY OF SURREY BC	157 - B7
FLO WARE PK, SEATTLE WA	278 - D7
FOGARTY CREEK STATE PK, LINCOLN CO OR	203 - A7
FOOTHILLS PK, LAKE OSWEGO OR	321 - G6
FOREST & CEDAR PK, BELLINGHAM WA	258 - C8
FOREST PK, PORTLAND OR	312 - A2
FOREST PK, EVERETT WA	264 - C6
FOREST RIDGE PK, VANCOUVER WA	307 - G4
FORT BORST PK, CENTRALIA WA	299 - C3
FORT CANBY STATE PK, PACIFIC CO WA	186 - A7
FORT CASEY STATE PK, ISLAND CO WA	167 - B5
FORT COLUMBIA STATE PK, PACIFIC CO WA	186 - B7
FORT DENT PK, TUKWILA WA	289 - H3
FORT FLAGLER STATE PK, JEFFERSON CO WA	167 - B6
FORT PK, SPRINGFIELD OR	331 - H7
FORT SIMCOE HIST STATE PK, YAKIMA CO WA	119 - C2
FORT STEVENS STATE PK, CLATSOP CO OR	188 - B1
FORT WALLA WALLA CITY PK, WALLA WALLA WA	344 - H10
FORT WORDEN STATE PK, PORT TOWNSEND WA	263 - G1
FOSTER, JOSEPH MEM PK, TUKWILA WA	289 - F2
FOUR CORNERS COUNTY PK, FOUR CORNERS OR	325 - E1
FRANCIS, THOMAS PK, DISTRICT OF SAANICH - BC	256 - A1
FRANKFORT PLGD, RICHLAND WA	341 - E2
FRANK KINNEY PK, EUGENE OR	330 - B14
FRANKLIN PK, SPOKANE WA	348 - J2
FRANKLIN PK, TACOMA WA	292 - D6
FRASER RIVER PK, DISTRICT OF BURNABY BC	156 - C6
FRAZER PK, PORTLAND OR	314 - C4
FRAZIER, PRENTIS I PK, SEATTLE WA	278 - D4
FREEPONS PK, LAKE OSWEGO OR	321 - F7
FREEWAY LAKES COUNTY PK, LINN CO OR	326 - H14
FREEWAY PK, SEATTLE WA	278 - A5
FREEWAY PK 3, SEATTLE WA	274 - B4
FREMONT CANAL PK, SEATTLE WA	273 - H6
FREMONT NATL FOREST, LAKE CO OR	143 - A2
FRIENDSHIP PK, SPOKANE WA	347 - B14
FRINK PK, SEATTLE WA	278 - E7
FROST, LARRY PK, TACOMA WA	293 - H5
FROULA PLGD, SEATTLE WA	274 - C3
FRUIT VALLEY PK, VANCOUVER WA	304 - E2
FULTON PK, PORTLAND OR	317 - E6
GABRIEL PK, PORTLAND OR	316 - A5
GADDIS PK, ROSEBURG OR	334 - E6
GAME BIRD PK, SPRINGFIELD OR	330 - F3
GAMMANS PK, PORTLAND OR	308 - D5
GARFIELD NATURE TRAIL, OLYMPIA WA	296 - G4
GARFIELD PK, TACOMA WA	293 - F3
GARFIELD PK, CORVALLIS OR	327 - G7
GARFIELD PLAYFIELD, SEATTLE WA	278 - D6
GARFIELD PLGD, EVERETT WA	265 - F2
GARIBALDI PROVINCIAL PK, BRITISH-COLUMBIA BC	93 - C1
GAS WORKS PK, SEATTLE WA	274 - A7
GEARHART MTN WILDERNESS, LAKE CO OR	151 - B1
GEN ANDERSON PK, VANCOUVER WA	306 - D6
GENESEE PARK & PLAYFIELD, SEATTLE WA	283 - F4
GERLINGER, GEORGE T STATE EXP FRST, POLK-CO OR	125 - A3
GIFFORD PINCHOT NATL FOREST, LEWIS CO WA	185 - A6
GILBERT CREEK PK, GRANTS PASS OR	335 - E6
GILMAN PLGD, SEATTLE WA	273 - F4
GINKO PETRIFIED FOREST STATE PK, - KITTITAS CO WA	120 - B1
GLANFORD PK, DISTRICT OF SAANICH BC	256 - F3
GLENHAVEN PK, PORTLAND OR	315 - F3
GLENWOOD PK, PORTLAND OR	319 - G5
GOAT TRAIL PK, MUKILTEO WA	266 - D2
GOETHALS PLGD, RICHLAND WA	341 - F3
GOLDEN & SILVER FALLS STATE PK, COOS CO - OR	140 - C1
GOLDEN EARS PROVINCIAL PK, BRITISH-COLUMBIA BC	94 - A2
GOLDEN GARDENS PK, SEATTLE WA	272 - C1
GOLDSTREAM PROVINCIAL PK, DISTRICT OF-LANGFORD BC	159 - A6
GOODLOW MTN NATURAL AREA, KLAMATH CO OR	151 - A2
GOOSE LAKE REC AREA, LAKE CO OR	152 - A3
GORDON BAY PROVINCIAL PK, BRITISH-COLUMBIA BC	100 - C1
GORGE PK, DISTRICT OF SAANICH BC	256 - E6
GOVERNMENT HOUSE GARDENS, CITY OF-VICTORIA BC	257 - A10
GOVERNOR PATTERSON MEM PK, LINCOLN CO OR	328 - B6
GOVERNOR TOM MCCALL WATERFRONT PK, - PORTLAND OR	317 - F1
GOVERNORS PK, PORTLAND OR	316 - D1
GOWLLAND-TOD PROVINCIAL PK, BRITISH-COLUMBIA BC	159 - B4
GRAND AV PK, EVERETT WA	264 - D1
GRAND PRAIRIE PK, ALBANY OR	326 - F10
GRANDVIEW PK, SEATAC WA	290 - D6
GRANT PK, PORTLAND OR	314 - A3
GRASS LAKE PK, OLYMPIA WA	296 - D3
GREENE, NANCY REC AREA, BRITISH COLUMBIA-BC	106 - A1
GREEN LAKE PK, SEATTLE WA	274 - A2
GREEN PK PLGD, WALLA WALLA WA	345 - C6
GREEN TIMBERS URBAN FOREST, CITY OF-SURREY BC	157 - A6
GREENWOOD PK, SEATTLE WA	273 - H1
GREENWOOD PK, CITY OF NORTH VANCOUVER BC	255 - C3
GRIFFIN PK, JOSEPHINE CO OR	229 - A5
GRIFFIN, WILLIAM PK, DIST OF N VANCOUVER-BC	254 - J3
GRIFFITHS-PRIDAY OCEAN STATE PK, GRAYS-HARBOR CO WA	177 - B4
GROSE, WILLIAM PK, SEATTLE WA	278 - E4
GROTTO, THE, PORTLAND OR	315 - G2
GROVELAND PK, MERCER ISLAND WA	283 - J6
GROVES, LESLIE PK, RICHLAND WA	340 - H10
GUSTAFSON, CARL PK, VANCOUVER WA	306 - E6
GUY LEE PK, SPRINGFIELD OR	330 - F4
HAINS STREET DIKE PK, RICHLAND WA	340 - G13
HAMBLEN PK, SPOKANE WA	349 - D14
HAMILTON PK, TACOMA WA	292 - E2
HAMILTON PK, PORTLAND OR	316 - A3
HAMILTON VIEW PK, SEATTLE WA	276 - E7
HAMPTON PK, DISTRICT OF SAANICH BC	256 - E5
HANCOCK PK, PORTLAND OR	315 - G4
HARBORVIEW PK, SEATTLE WA	278 - B6
HARBORVIEW PK, EVERETT WA	264 - A7
HARMON FIELD, SPOKANE WA	349 - E1
HARNEY PK, PORTLAND OR	318 - E7
HARPER PK, COQUITLAM BC	157 - B4
HARRIS BEACH STATE PK, BROOKINGS OR	232 - C6
HARRISON PK, PORTLAND OR	319 - F1
HARWOOD PK, DISTRICT OF BURNABY BC	255 - J14
HASTINGS MILL PK, UNIVERSITY ENDOWMENT-LAND BC	254 - A11
HAWTHORNE PK, CITY OF SURREY BC	157 - A6
HAWTHORNE PK, MEDFORD OR	336 - D11
HAYS PK, SPOKANE WA	349 - C4
HAZELNUT PK, TUKWILA WA	289 - G3
HAZELWOOD PK, ALBANY OR	326 - A9
HEALS RIFLE RANGE, DISTRICT OF SAANICH - BC	159 - B4
HEALY HTS PK, PORTLAND OR	316 - D2
HEIDELBERG ATHLETIC FIELD, TACOMA WA	292 - B7
HEIRMAN, BOB WILDLIFE PK, SNOHOMISH CO - WA	171 - D4
HELLS CANYON NATL REC AREA, NEZ PERCE CO-ID	131 - B1
HELLS GATE STATE PK, NEZ PERCE CO ID	250 - B5
HELMCKEN PK, TOWN OF VIEW ROYAL BC	256 - B4
HENDERSON PK, ALBANY OR	326 - C8
HENDERSON PK, DISTRICT OF OAK BAY BC	257 - C5
HENDRICKS PK, EUGENE OR	330 - D8
HENDRY, JOHN PK, VANCOUVER BC	255 - C13
HEYBURN STATE PK, CHATCOLET ID	248 - B7
HIAWATHA PLGD, SEATTLE WA	280 - E2
HIDDEN PK, VANCOUVER WA	305 - F2
HIDEAWAY PK, LAKE OSWEGO OR	321 - E4
HIGH BRIDGE PK, SPOKANE WA	348 - F9
HIGH DRIVE PARKWAY, SPOKANE WA	348 - H13
HIGHLAND PK, KELSO WA	303 - E7
HIGH POINT PLGD, SEATTLE WA	281 - F7
HIGHROCK PK, TOWN OF ESQUIMALT BC	256 - D8
HILLCREST PK, MOUNT VERNON WA	260 - D14
HILL, JJ PK, EVERETT WA	265 - E3
HILL, JOSEPH WOOD PK, PORTLAND OR	315 - H2
HILLSDALE PK, PORTLAND OR	316 - C4
HILLSIDE CTR PK, PORTLAND OR	312 - B5
HILLSIDE PK, BEND OR	332 - C5
HILLTOP PK, KING CO WA	288 - C1
HIMES, GEORGE PK, PORTLAND OR	316 - E4
HING HAY PK, SEATTLE WA	278 - A7
HOLLADAY WEST PK, PORTLAND OR	313 - H4
HOLLAND YOUTH PK, MARION CO OR	323 - G14
HOLLYWOOD PK, CITY OF VICTORIA BC	257 - A11
HOLMAN PK, PORTLAND OR	312 - A3
HOLMES PK, MEDFORD OR	336 - G12
HONEYMAN, JESSIE M MEM STATE PK, LANE CO-OR	214 - B4
HONEYMOON BAY NATURE PK, BRITISH-COLUMBIA BC	100 - C1
HORNER PK, DISTRICT OF SAANICH BC	257 - B4
HORSETHIEF LAKE STATE PK, KLICKITAT CO - WA	196 - D6
HOWARD TIETAN PK, WALLA WALLA WA	345 - C10
HOWARTH PK, EVERETT WA	264 - A6
HOWELL PK, SEATTLE WA	279 - F4
HOWELL TERRITORIAL PK, MULTNOMAH CO OR	192 - B6
HUGHES PLGD, SEATTLE WA	285 - F2
HUGO RAY PK, DISTRICT OF WEST VANCOUVR - BC	254 - G3
HUG POINT STATE PK, CLATSOP CO OR	191 - A2
HUMBOLDT NATL FOREST, HUMBOLDT CO NV	154 - C3
HUMBUG MTN STATE PK, CURRY CO OR	224 - B7
HYACINTH PK, DISTRICT OF SAANICH BC	256 - D2
IKAWA PK, TUKWILA WA	289 - H5
ILLAHEE STATE PK, KITSAP CO WA	271 - C6
ILLINOIS RIVER STATE PK, JOSEPHINE CO OR	233 - A4
INDIAN CANYON PK, SPOKANE CO WA	348 - C10
INTERBAY ATHLETIC FIELD, SEATTLE WA	273 - F7
INTERLAKEN PK, SEATTLE WA	278 - C1
INTL CHILDRENS PK, SEATTLE WA	278 - B7
INVERGARRY PK, CITY OF SURREY BC	157 - A6
INVERNESS RAVINE PK, SEATTLE WA	275 - F1
IRON MOUNTAIN PK, LAKE OSWEGO OR	320 - B6
IRVING PK, CITY OF VICTORIA BC	256 - G10
IRVING PK, PORTLAND OR	313 - H2
IRVING PLGD, TACOMA WA	293 - E7
IRWIN PK, EUGENE OR	329 - A1
ISLAND PK, SPRINGFIELD OR	330 - G7
JACKSON COUNTY EXPO PK, JACKSON CO OR	336 - A4
JACKSON, HENRY M PK, EVERETT WA	265 - G1
JACKSON, MARIA C STATE PK, COOS CO OR	140 - C2

INDEX

PERFORMING ARTS

POINTS OF INTEREST

POINTS OF INTEREST - HISTORIC

SHOPPING - REGIONAL

INDEX

INDEX

INDEX

Note Page

The *Thomas Guide*®

Thomas Guide Title: Pacific Northwest   ISBN# 0-528-85869-6   Edition: 7th   MKT: PNW

Today's Date: _____   Gender: ☐M ☐F   Age Group: ☐18-24 ☐25-31 ☐32-40 ☐41-50 ☐51-64 ☐65+

1. What type of industry do you work in?

    ☐Real Estate   ☐Trucking   ☐Delivery   ☐Construction   ☐Utilities   ☐Government
    ☐Retail   ☐Sales   ☐Transportation   ☐Landscape   ☐Service & Repair
    ☐Courier   ☐Automotive   ☐Insurance   ☐Medical   ☐Police/Fire/First Response
    ☐Other, please specify: _____

2. What type of job do you have in this industry? _____

3. Where did you purchase this Thomas Guide? (store name & city) _____

4. Why did you purchase this Thomas Guide? _____

5. How often do you purchase an updated Thomas Guide? ☐Annually ☐2 yrs. ☐3-5 yrs. ☐Other: _____

6. Where do you use it? ☐Primarily in the car ☐Primarily in the office ☐Primarily at home ☐Other: _____

7. How do you use it? ☐Exclusively for business ☐Primarily for business but also for personal or leisure use
    ☐Both work and personal evenly ☐Primarily for personal use ☐Exclusively for personal use

8. What do you use your Thomas Guide for?
    ☐Find Addresses ☐In-route navigation ☐Planning routes ☐Other: _____
    Find points of interest: ☐Schools ☐Parks ☐Buildings ☐Shopping Centers ☐Other: _____

9. How often do you use it? ☐Daily ☐Weekly ☐Monthly ☐Other: _____

10. Do you use the internet for maps and/or directions? ☐Yes ☐No

11. How often do you use the internet for directions? ☐Daily ☐Weekly ☐Monthly ☐Other: _____

12. Do you use any of the following mapping products in addition to your Thomas Guide?
    ☐Folded paper maps ☐Folded laminated maps ☐Wall maps ☐GPS ☐PDA ☐In-car navigation ☐Phone maps

13. What features, if any, would you like to see added to your Thomas Guide? _____
    _____

14. What features or information do you find most useful in your Rand McNally Thomas Guide? (please specify)
    _____
    _____

15. Please provide any additional comments or suggestions you have. _____
    _____
    _____

We strive to provide you with the most current updated information available if you know of a map correction, please notify us here.

Where is the correction?   Map Page #:_____   Grid #:_____   Index Page #:_____

Nature of the correction: ☐Street name missing ☐Street name misspelled ☐Street information incorrect
☐Incorrect location for point of interest ☐Index error ☐Other: _____

Detail: _____

I would like to receive information about updated editions and special offers from Rand McNally

☐via e-mail   E-mail address: _____
☐via postal mail
Your Name: _____   Company (if used for work): _____
Address: _____   City/State/ZIP: _____

CUT ALONG DOTTED LINE

CUT ALONG DOTTED LINE

TG-noCD.06

RAND McNALLY

The most trusted name on the map.

You'll never need to ask for directions again with these Rand McNally products!

- EasyFinder® Laminated Maps
- Folded Maps
- Street Guides
- Wall Maps
- CustomView Wall Maps
- Road Atlases
- Motor Carriers' Road Atlases